Just **Remember** *This*

Frank + Donna —

Hope you like the

Book —

CW

2015

Just **Remember** *This*

Colin Bratkovich

Library of Congress Control Number: 2013911134

ISBN:	Hardcover	978-1-4836-4518-6
	Softcover	978-1-4836-4517-9
	eBook	978-1-4836-4519-3

This book was printed in the United States of America.

Rev. date: 09/30/2014

To order additional copies of this book, contact:
Xlibris LLC
1-888-795-4274
www. Xlibris. com
Orders@Xlibris. com
553441

Contents

American Pop Singers

1900-1950 +

Just Remember This

The Popular Recorded Vocalists before 1950 +

on Records, Radio, and Films

for the Baby Boomer Rock Generation and Beyond

Colin Bratkovich

ABOUT THE AUTHOR

- Colin Bratkovich is a record collector and freelance author. He more so contributed to the latter 1970s biweekly publication *Record Digest*.

Synopsis

I have completed this manuscript *Just Remember This*, or as *American Pop Singers 1900-1950+*, about music before the 1950s in America. It perhaps offers knowledge and insights not previously found in other musical reference books. I have moreover been working on this book very meticulously over the past twelve-plus years. It started as a bit of fun and gradually became serious as I began to listen along with the vocalists of popular music, of the era before 1950, essentially just before the dawn of rock and roll. If you can call it that! Indeed "genre" and labeling of American music started here, and then from everywhere. While the old adage of "always starting from somewhere" could be noted in every century, the 1900s had produced the technology. Understanding the necessity, more so, finds a curiosity on the part of a general public hungry for entertainment, despite six day work weeks, World War I, the Great Depression, and World War II.

Most people then, and in later decades with later changes, had no interest in the mechanics of how a record player spins or how a motion picture or a radio tube works. That's for the scientists! This book sheds light on many of the vocalists, many of them forgotten, many of them buried by the passage of time, more so due to still more technology to come. As a baby boomer, my prospective is *later*, as most all, but not all, of the performers researched were past their prime. More so, many of our elders had it wrong! Big bands? Blackface? Please listen. Just listen! Modern ears just *could* find some rock and roll? Soul? Country and Western? Read and listen. Compare.

INDUSTRY STATISTICS, EVENTS, AND RELATED POPULAR CULTURE (1900-50)

Besides creativity and technology, the idea of making money was, and remained, the ultimate goal. While it is interesting that the ushering in of the year 2000 found the music industry somewhat emerging and merging the likes of recorded music, the conflicting presence of the "music video" or DVD may be considered the same. As the demand of the public for entertainment widens, the techniques are mind-boggling. Since this book is more interested in the earlier aspects of all this mess, some essential facts should be noted. This list is, more so, focused upon popular vocalists, narrowing in upon some of the gossip and unwanted publicity they generated into popular culture. Also included are events and selective spoken word recordings by contemporary politicians and world leaders. They essentially are chronological.

- The pre-1900 concepts of music cylinders (Thomas Edison) and gramophones (Emile Berliner) were nothing more than a novelty, except for those who attempted to produce machines to play them and to the sheet music publishers, who made most of the money. Soon the Columbia Phonograph Company also became a competitor. Another entity was the bulkier piano roll, which, in true retrospective, played instrumental music perfectly. While largely pushed aside by preferable discs and players in 1920, the piano roll, in hindsight, was a modern computer.
- The emergence of the Victor Talking Machine Company in 1901, using the flat disc, made it all more clear and profitable. Eldridge Johnson's talking machines and subsequent recording had merged with (the German) Emil Berliner and became a huge competitor for Columbia.
- Somehow, both Victor and Columbia were able to share a patent for the product, effectively shutting out other would-be competitors until 1917. Edison, meanwhile, continued to produce cylinders, along with a diamond disc flat record, which got around the patent. Was Edison influential within the government?
- Italian opera entity Enrico Caruso is signed by Victor. He would subsequently become the first recording artist to sell over a million recordings collectively. His actual first million-seller would be his version of "I Pagliacci" on Victor 81032 and Victor 88061. Sadly, Caruso would not live to record "electronically," as he would continue to produce recording until his death in 1921.

- A title by Len Spencer "Arkansas Traveler" is released on Victor 1101, Columbia 21, and Edison 8202 and perhaps sells a million?
- A title by recording artist Arthur Collins "The Preacher And The Bear," as recorded on Edison 9000, Columbia 3146 and Columbia 32720, Zon-o-Phone 120, US Everlasting 1092, and Indestructible 2087, claims over a million sales in 1905.
- Sheet music sales reach two million. They indeed dwarf a combined recording industry sale of about twenty million, but do contribute to the popularity of song ditties.
- The popularity of the disc over the cylinder finds Edison along in producing them. They would remain a specialty item only.
- "Why Trusts and Bosses Oppose the Progressive Party," Theodore Roosevelt, Victor 35250, Presidential election, 1912.
- "Labor and Its Rights," President W. H. Taft, Victor 5553, Presidential election of 1912.
- "Discovery of the North Pole," Commander Robert E. Peary, Victor 70012 (1912?).
- Al Jolson's 1913 Broadway success in "Honeymoon Express", who's cast included Fannie Brice (not yet a recorded entity) and (dancer) Jenny Dolly (twin of Rosie-of the contemporary "Dolly Sisters"), providing recorded hits "Asleep In The Deep" and "You Made Me Love You" and found Jolson 'stealing' the show with vocal style. As a result, all subsequent (Jolson) Broadway entities would highlight around (Jolson) introducing song ditties written for him as identified as (recorded) titles of an 'original recording artist', and the 'show' becoming a sideline to see and hear Jolson.
- Because of increased record sales, however primitive, the music publishing industry, looking for more profit, finds itself faced with songwriting entities who also demand more. The subsequent American Society of Composers, Authors, and Publishers (ASCAP) is formed in 1914.
- By 1917, all patents expired. The emergence of independent labels such as Brunswick, Emerson, Okeh, Vocalion, and Pathé soon emerge to compete with Victor, Columbia, and Edison.
- "From the Battlefields of France," General John J. Pershing, WWI, Nation's Forum-69333 (1917?).
- Volstead Act (1919). The Eighteenth Amendment to the US constitution led to the prohibition of intoxicating liquor. It would also accelerate unprecedented social change in the next decade. The unpopular law, for the most part, led to a total disregard to established civil law, from all aspects of American society, rich or poor. Illegal drinking establishments (speakeasies) more so sprang up all over the country, which more than ever before created jobs for musicians and singers, as well as expanded scope for criminal elements. The prohibition of liquor was repealed, for the most part, by the ratification of the Twenty-first Amendment, which came into effect by the end of 1933.
- The real unionization of Broadway and other theaters began with a strike in 1919 by actors. Many, as independent contractors, had become recording artists, as a nonserious sideline.
- A faddish culture of racism finds the 1920 release of Afro-American Mamie Smith's "Crazy Blues," as released on Okeh-4169, amazed at the good sales generated. As one of the newer independent labels, this disc sells its way into to the mainstream of creative marketing. Until this time, few black vocalists, like vaudevillian Bert Williams, had been allowed to record.

- The production of records in the USA exceeds 100, 000 in 1921.

- More independent labels followed, including a black-owned enterprise (Black Swan), in 1921. While it would fail by 1923, the idea of an African American business would not, nor would the careers of its original recording entities, who included Afro-Americans Ethel Waters, Alberta Hunter, and Eva Taylor.
- The emergence of commercial radio in 1920 finds recording artist Vaughn De Leath as the first radio vocalist. (The first Afro-American vocalist on radio, Ethel Waters, would follow in 1921).
- A drop in record sales at Columbia, due to the competitive inclusion of hundreds of contemporary 1920s' independent labels, and the success of commercial radio is somewhat saved by the signing and recordings of blues woman Bessie Smith in 1923.

- The emergence of "electric" recordings in 1925, soon to expand with the use of microphones, creates a recording revolution. By 1927, the inclusion of newer and electric phonograph record players creates a new record-listening public. Previous acoustic recordings are generally discarded, with many recording artists re-rerecording previous material and producing a finer, more listenable product. Record sales that had been previously been in a slump, recover and reach sales figures of over 107, 000, 000 discs.
- The seminude success of American and black Josephine Baker had shock value. Within a few years, Josephine would become French and conquer all of its media of recordings, stage, nightclubs, radio, and films—equal to any white-skinned performer. American jazz exported hot and live! Viva La Josephine!
- The National Broadcasting Company (NBC) becomes the first national network in 1926. Within a year, another, the Columbia Broadcasting Corporation (CBS) would follow.
- President Calvin Coolidge Welcomes Colonel Lindberg on June 11, 1927. "Colonel Lindberg Replies, June 11, 1927," Victor 35836. (Lindberg's solo airplane flight across the Atlantic truly staggered the American idiom in 1927).
- *The Jazz Singer*, the first full-length "talking picture," featuring Al Jolson's vocals, caused a sensation in 1927. Within a few years, most "silent" films are considered passé.
- Music hit animation with the actual voice of Walt Disney (alias Mickey & Minnie Mouse) in "Steamboat Willie", as introduced on 11/18/1928. Using older (acoustic) ditties "Steamboat Bill" (the Arthur Collins recording penned by 'Shields & Leighton Brothers') and "Turkey In The Straw"—dropping the racism from the old 'folk' entity claimed by many, Including Dan Bryant and Bob Farrell), (and, amoung others, the early cylinder recording by Billy Golden), the new and better than acoustic sound, along with personable caractures, became considered more than novel Americana, and more so-big business!
- The rise of Rudy Vallee, fueled by his radio broadcasts (1929) revolutionized the concept of popular singing and marketing.
- The smaller record labels, the sensation of the early 1920s, were not all ready for the newer electric recording process. Many sell out to Brunswick, Columbia, or Victor.
- The stock market crash of October 24, 1929, soon ends the ready money of consumers.
- Scandal. The media was confused about the antics of "rhythm boy" Bing Crosby, as he was reported absent on the film set of *King of Jazz* in November 1929. While arrest reports were somehow lacking, rumors of an unidentified woman passenger, a car accident, and illegal liquor lingered. Bing subsequently got demoted (in the film) with actor John Boles singing "Song of the Dawn." Indeed, without anyone seeking litigation, in true retrospective, Bing would see it through and survive very well.

- The period between 1930 through 1932 finds all independent recording entities bought out or sold. The larger companies Victor, Brunswick (now the American Record Corporation), and Columbia are in receivership or bankrupt state. By the end of 1932, actual record sales are at 6, 000, 000, down from the 1927 high of 104, 000, 000. Electronic phonographs also fell from 987, 000 in 1927, to only 40, 000 in 1932.
- Another new entertainment enterprise Television, is launched in New York City as W2XBS in 1930 as a commercial enterprise by NBC. A year later, as on W2X2AB (CBS) followed. Like the production of phonograph records and films, and unlike commercial radio, the Great Depression severely depressed interest and sales.
- The film industry, eagerly assisting theaters for sound conversions in 1929, was also seeing box office receipts fall. So did admission prices to theaters. By 1933, in order to attract people into theaters, popular radio programs, the only (still) expanding entertainment business, were featured before the featured film.
- The emergence of Bing Crosby as a solo recording entity in 1931 eclipsed that of Rudy Vallee's. Crosby's success and would so dominate the entertainment industry in record sales radio, films, and personal appearances.
- Scandal. The new marijuana restrictions of 1931 found Louis Armstrong arrested in Los Angeles, in February. Louis's days in jail put other musicians and vocalists on alert, including the likes of Bing Crosby.
- Scandal. The newly married and pregnant torch singer Libby Holman is suspected of murdering her very rich husband, who died of a bullet wound on July 6, 1932. As a huge media event, she is later acquitted, with a baby and a huge estate.
- "Oath of Office and Inaugural Address," Franklin D. Roosevelt is sworn in after defeating Republican Herbert Hoover, March 4, 1933, Columbia 50348-D.
- Despite objections from most of the cast, black singer Ethel Waters shares headlines in Broadways' 1933 production of *As Thousands Cheer*. As an Irving Berlin entity, his powerful influence prevailed, as did Water's subsequent performance. It was more so the first appearance of a headlined black entity in an all-white cast, since Bert Williams, as well as the first of its kind for a (black) woman in the segregated America theater.
- The radio industry was the only medium of entertainment to not only sustain, but also to grow during the Great Depression. As it was dominated by "live" music as well as every other conceivable programming, sponsorship soared. Indeed, the lack of capital in consumers' pockets made radio-listening an easy choice. Purchase a recording or hear it on the radio? By 1934, the Mutual Broadcasting System, or MBS, a group of independent stations, not owned by CBS or NBC, was formed. It gave consumers more (free) choices. Go to a film or "live" show or tune on in on radio for nothing? The sales of radios in 1930 were at some 3, 789, 000 units. They would increase every subsequent year, reaching some 13, 000, 000 in 1941. While a decline did show up during the war years between 1942 through 1945, a sales boom again began after the war, with some 16, 000, 000 radios sold in 1947.
- The concept of coin-operated nickelodeons from the early century was perhaps best realized in the advent of the similar coin-operated jukebox. With a weak economy, the advantage of the "juke" was to be fully realized with the repeal of prohibition. The sudden 1934 reopenings and subsequent newer aspects of legal nightclubs (replacing the prohibition era speakeasy) provided music for many. Moreover, it provided opportunities to dance without hiring a more expensive live band. By 1939, the jukebox could be found, nationwide, almost anywhere, including at non-serving entities such as drugstores, grocery stores, and fast-food (rib and hamburger) joints.

They would have been sold into at least 225, 000 places of business, with a need of current record replenishments of some thirteen million discs. While the marketing aspects of radio play was not to be realized in the 1930s, the obvious promotion or non-promotion of jukebox players and listeners was indeed relevant.

- Rudy Vallee's divorce from his then current wife was filled (April 4, 1933) with conflicting tales of adultery, with Rudy even able to crudely wire-tap his spouse's telephone. Would this later become an illegal wire tap? Or trap?
- Jimmie Rodgers dies of TB on May 26, 1933. The popular singer's death becomes a major media event, as well a cultural one, especially in the (rural) southern states.
- The success of Max and Dave Fleischer's cartoon entity Betty Boop found singer Helen Kane suing in April of 1934. It seemed to her and to many that her popular singing style of the latter 1920s was being copied. The court case fascinated the public until May 5, when the court found that a contemporary black vocalist, Baby Esther, had also used the style around the time Helen had become popular. Others using the Betty Boop voice (including Mae Questal and Bonnie Poe) also appeared in court, but oddly, they did not testify. Did Baby Ester ever get any compensation? Is this case still relevant? Luckily, they had less problems with Billy Costello's vocal—the contemporary voice of Popeye!

    - The already noted recording (record) industry received a 1934 jolt and a bolt from a savory (former) Brunswick producer Jack Kapp. When passed over for promotion within Brunswick, Kapp, with investments from British E. R Lewis and others, formed the (American) Decca Record label. Jack also lowered the price of 10-inch 78 rpm records to 35 cents from 75 cents each, declaring Decca as a premium label. Other labels had to follow his lead. Moreover, he convinced many Brunswick (and other AMC) recording artists to jump ship and join him. They included many, such as popular vocalists the Mills Brothers, Lee Wiley, Ethel Waters, and, especially, Bing Crosby. Within about a year the likes of the Boswell Sisters, Ruth Etting, and the Chick Webb Orchestra (with "swing" vocalist Ella Fitzgerald), were to be signed up.

- The death of crooner Russ Columbo becomes a major contemporary 1934 event! Due to an accident with an antique pistol, the young rival to Bing Crosby is pronounced dead on September 2, 1934.
- King's Farewell Speech. King Edward VIII gives up the British throne to marry Walace Simpson, 1936.
- The latter part of 1930s found the entertainment industry somewhat out of the doldrums of the Depression. By 1937, the entire film industry became profitable for the first time since 1930.
- The success of radio programming was to be challenged by the emergence of the powerful musicians' union, the American Federation of Musicians. They demanded a fee for performing, as well as for those radio stations that would play popular recordings on the air.
- The playing of discs on the air was nothing special, nor was it recognized for its marketing aspects before 1933. As the noted aspects of the Depression had dwarfed the recording industry, as per court orders, the words "Not For Radio Broadcasts" were added to most all record labels before the end of 1933. While this did not exist in other countries, the continued use of live music and the need for musicians emerged as an expensive enterprise by the end of the decade.

- ❖ Scandal. In 1937, Ruth Etting divorced her reputed gangster-manager-husband Martin "the gimp" Snyder. By the next year, according to Ruth, both she and her new mate-to-be had received death threats that led to a shooting on October 17, 1938, of Myrl Alderman, also her current piano player. He survived, although Ruth's career soon faded quickly. As a major media contemporary event, despite the rise of Hitler, is it possible that "Don't shoot me, I'm only the piano player!" had relevance here?
- ❖ The 1939 operatic utterances of the black opera entity Marion Anderson at the Lincoln Memorial, due to the likes of Eleanor Roosevelt, became a heated and bold political topic for the Roosevelt administration.

- ♦ "Broadcast from Buckingham Palace," September 3, 1939, HMV-RB 8969. King George the VI, the British monarch, announces war with Hitler's Germany.
- ♦ The "swing" era, led by Ivie Anderson's vocal of "If It Ain't Got That Swing" with the Duke Ellington Orchestra, is more so fueled by the 1930s' success of bandleaders Count Basie, Cab Calloway, Benny Goodman, Artie Shaw, Chick Webb, and many others. While the success of sweet band sounds were also integrated into the new idiom, the outstanding voices of Helen Ward, Ella Fitzgerald, Billie Holiday, Helen Humes, and Maxine Sullivan perhaps best represented "swing."
- ♦ The (again) growing recording industry and the thriving radio industry also found the already established ASCAP group of songwriters wanting a piece of the action, as well as wanting to shut out many younger would-be songwriters. By 1940, a newer group, to rival ASCAP, Broadcast Music Incorporated (BMI) was formed. While obviously more encouraged by the radio industry, the field of songwriters more than doubled, along with the likes of many newer vocalists. BMI more so encouraged radio air time, facing many lawsuits from ASCAP and AFM (musicians union). By 1941, the likes of 127, 000 records were sold, which effectively put the recording business back to the pre-Depression era.
- ♦ "This Was Their Finest Hour," June 18, 1940, British Prime Minister Winston Churchill braces his country for the coming German bombings, HMV 3200. Later, in 1941, Britisher Al Bowlly would be killed during a blitz in London.
- ♦ On November 16, 1941, the Oklahoma town of Berwyn legally changed its name to Gene Autry, Oklahoma. A whole town? Was Gene so popular? Yup!
- ♦ The bombing of Pearl Harbor on December 7, 1941, led to WWII and rationing. The use of shellac to produce records was to be cut off for a few years.
- ♦ An AFM strike in August 1942 found the musicians union taking on the recording industry and the radio industry. In true retrospective, while they won most concessions, their subsequent use on radio and recordings were to become drastically cut. Indeed, the recording industry found it cheaper to use background vocals without instruments and feature vocalists, not bandleaders, to front popular recordings. Moreover, the real and legal use of playing records, flamed and fueled by the networked 1941 program *Make Believe Ballroom* became widely imitated. The official "disc jockey" was born!
- ♦ The musicians strike created less of a need for a band (cutting costs) at the same time it created a new interest from record companies in solo artists and group vocals (they found many that musicians were not needed or required to produce a recording). The rise of the song stylist was found in former band singers and radio entities with less interest in stuffy and loud Broadway entities. The likes of Frank Sinatra, Dick Haymes, Dinah Shore, Jo Stafford, Lena Horne, Anita O'Day, Ella Mae Morse, and other, during WWII became recognized disc sellers, with the likes of Perry Como,

Nat Cole, Doris Day, Billy Eckstine, Andy Russell, Peggy Lee, Sarah Vaughan, Margaret Whiting, and others following soon after the war. The split definitions of "hillbilly" became "country and western," and those defined as "race" as for Afro-Americans in "rhythm and blues." While Latin sound and ethnic sounds were always to be relevant, the likes of Roy Acuff, Red Foley, Roy Rogers, and especially Ernest Tubb would drift into "pop." So would the likes of "bebop" and the "rhythm and blues" dance music of Louis Jordan. While "swing" was abandon, so would pop be—as it was known. In true retrospective, as fueled by post-WWII small record labels in a huge degree, it seems that the public was tired and wanted something different!

- ♦ "War Message to Congress and the Nation," Columbia 36516, Franklin D. Roosevelt, president of America, announces war on Japan in response to the December seventh bombing of Pearl Harbor. Message from December 8, 1941.
- ♦ The NBC radio network splits from its NBC BLUE network. It is renamed the American Broadcasting Corporation, or ABC.
- ♦ The rise in the popularity of Frank Sinatra, more so than his other contemporaries, as a solo entity in 1942 came to rival Bing Crosby's in record sales and radio and films.
- ♦ While on a USO tour, singer and radio entity Jane Froman's plane crashes in Spain on June 22, 1942. Jane survives with crippling injuries; fellow passengers, including vocalist Tamara (Drasin) and comic Ron Rognan do not. (Non-singers, including actor Leslie Howard, actress Carol Lombard and bandleader Glenn Miller, on similar missions during the war, did not survive. In retrospective, Bob Hope was indeed as good as he was—very lucky!)
- ♦ The year 1945, the very end year of WWII, found the concept of television, dwarfed first by the Depression in the early 1930s and in 1941 by the US entry into WWII, something easily exploited. Along with the previously established NBC and CBS, ABC joined in. Mutual and others would follow. In 1946, RCA marketed the television in a huge way with 10-inch round and square screens.
- ♦ The postwar use of taped radio shows was pioneered in 1946 by Bing Crosby. While perhaps it was his own means to escape to the golf course, along with the emergence of the playing of records and the "disc jockey," Bing revolutionized the radio industry.

> Another musicians union strike in 1948 looking for fees from the film industry, as well as the recording industry, failed. Moreover, so did the "big band" era as business was found to function far cheaper by hiring even fewer musicians—as had been discovered during the 1942 strike.

- ❖ Scandals. Drug busts and drug-related problems of musicians and singers seemingly became routine in the latter 1940s, especially noting the continuing problems of Judy Garland, Billie Holiday, and Anita O'Day.
- ❖ A booming postwar recording industry was further defined by emergence of small labels. Moreover, the small labels, to the dismay of the major labels (Victor, Columbia (CBS), and Decca) were hipper and introduced a better variety of musical styles and taste. Even so, the technology advanced. This was more so furthered by the introduction of Columbia Record's 1948 introduction of the 331/3 rpm disc and Victor's subsequent 45 rpm disc. Along with record players which played the standard 78 rpm and the capability of the newer speeds, a new standard was set for the future of popular music.

- ♦ While only a toy in the late 1930s, the emergence of commercial network television by 1950 effectively changed radio programming forever. Newer styles, singers, and musicians, not unlike what radio had exploited in 1929, emerged as like nothing had before on television. Older entities were exposed to a younger crowd as indeed something "old." Radio, more so, became a major tool of the recording industry as the elimination of the talking radio program became transferred into television. Those programs which successfully made it included entities like Jack Benny, Red Skelton, and Ozzie and Harriet.
- ♦ To tune in your radio to a hip DJ who would spin some unknown hick "country and western" or hipper "rhythm and blues" records—what a choice! Indeed, more of a choice than your parents ever had.

Is Americana still concerned by crime, drugs, immigration, racism, religion, poverty, sex, war, and the marketing of recordings and films? Have the politicians responded to the needs of the people? Has entertainment developed into a culture within itself? Does entertainment identify with aspirations of the general public? Did our modern age start in the 1920s?

- ➢ *Note*

  Sources for this section, while covered in the Book List, include

  - *Billboard,* December 27, 1969, "The Disc Survives," Roland Gelatt.
  - *Billboard,* December 27, 1969, "Disk Jockey: Origin of the Species," Dave Dexter Jr.
  - *Billboard,* December 27, 1969, "All Singing, All Dancing, All on Record," Miles Kreuger.

- ➢ See also the Radio and Label sections of this book.

THE ACOUSTIC AGE (1900-24 +)

♦ Cultural Influences

- While this book is mainly concerned with actual recordings, a brief look into the culture of the early century (also pointed out throughout various reviews of recording artists within the reading of this book) should be noted. The "acoustic age," as noted here, chiefly refers the limited technology of recording techniques, which existed from 1900 through the mid-1920s. The early century also defined its "recording" artists in cultural terms, which latter-century recording artists (while still influenced by culture), do not have to contend with, or, within their wildest imaginations, ever dreamed of.

  ➢ They include

Anglo-Saxons. The British and Irish folk songs, including "Yankee Doodle" of the latter 1700s, integrated with musical instruments (such as the bagpipe), in much of rural Americana, especially Appalachian, along with traditional Christian "hymns" ranging from Swedish, Dutch, and other settlers (observed by the British by the mid-1700s), the backbone of the latter genre called "hillbilly" or "country" or "western" was founded.

- Spanish French. The accent on word pronunciation, folk songs, instruments (like guitars) was to evolve with huge influences.

Italian. The "classic" musical stage product was founded in Italian opera, while also noting some use of German, French, and English embellishments.

- German-Slavic (Russian, Polish, Slovenian, and others). Folk songs, accordions. Also note, ethnic Jews from Germany, Austria-Hungary, and (Czarist) Russia.
- Miscellaneous. Greek, Asians.
- Native Americans (American Indians).
- Latino. These include Mexicans and South Americans.

Caribbean. The mix of Native Americans, Spaniards, and black slaves produced a unique culture. Note especially Cuba and British Jamaica and Afro-American. The slave population from Africa brought over a distinctive sound of despair and may be considered the most single contributor to the new culture of Americana. Moreover, the black Moslem culture, while shared, is also to be noted with the likes of (string) Spanish guitars, banjos, and (Cuban) congas, and rumba dance. The practice of African voodoo, with the Christians of Europeans also would contribute, musically, to a huge melting pop.

- The cultural influences would be centered with

- Cities and urban areas, especially New Orleans, Chicago, New York, and Kansas City
- Rural areas, especially the Mississippi delta

- Recorded Vocalists before 1920

  - Notable popular vocalists were a diverse group of performers. They included the likes of Enrico Caruso, Billy Murray, Henry Burr, Harry MacDonough Ada Jones, Byran G. Harlan, Arthur Collins, Al Jolson, Len Spencer, Frank Stanley, Marion Harris, Cal Stewart, Walter Van Brunt, Nora Bayes, Dan Quinn, George J. Gaskin, Charles Harrison, J. W. Myers, Lewis James, Vess Ossman, George M. Cohan, Alma Gluck, Billy Golden, Sophie Tucker, and Bert Williams.

- Printed Word—Sheet Music, Musical Themes

- While sheet music is still with us, the business of selling words and music is no longer just for home entertainment. While there are still pianos and musical instruments to be found and played at home, the technology of radio, television, and recorded music on CDs has replaced the musical instrument and the need for sheet music and piano rolls.
- The early century also found the sales of sheet music as something of less importance for the numerous vocalists performing them, and more important for the (credited) composers of popular ditties. Moreover, the principal avenue of the song trade existed in New York City, as specifically what was known as Tin Pan Alley. It was here at the Brill Building, at 1619 Broadway, that the basis for the eventual writing, swapping, stealing, adapting, and exploitation of the American songbook was to be originated. Moreover, the sheet music would feature the following:

  - a Broadway show tune or entity,
  - a live act, chiefly from vaudeville,
  - and ethnic music and performers.

A popular recording artist featured on the cover actually sold sheet music if identified with a popular tune. Thus, the creative activity in and around Tin Pan Alley was only to be affected by changing times and technology. The "song plugger," a vocalist hired or a vocalist who could also sing could be found on every corner. The need to feed the likes of the piano roll, cylinder or phonograph record, and the commercial penny arcade was to largely precede the likes of (later) radio singers and (jingle) marketing promotions of product. Most vocalists considered recordings as a lesser means to become know to the general public. The sheet music noted artwork and a picture, promoting their acts on Broadway or vaudeville, as well as generating revenue. In true retrospective, while the sale of sheet music ruled the day, the latter century defines the forgotten as, in most cases, those who left behind little or no commercial recording fodder.

- A bit of European music—"classical music." While traditional European music (termed "classical" by the twentieth century's end), is still with us, it is but only a fraction of what it was in the earlier part of the century. The European influences and tastes were much more prevalent in the early part of the century due not only to the mechanical limits of the age, but also to the lesser developments of Americana. The author of this book also finds the classical music of the latter century still enjoying huge sales as the genre and European traditions are indeed carried on. (See Opera—A Bit of It section of this book for

- ♦ Sports themes
  - "Uncle Josh Playing Golf," Victor 16226, Cal Stewart.
  - "Take Me Out to the Ball Game," Victor 5570, Billy Murray and the Hayden Quartet.
- ♦ Ethnic, cultural events, and myths, and/or religious themes (see also below, black American themes)

- "If They'd Only Move Ireland Over Here," Victor 17576, Ada Jones (Irish).
- "My Wild Irish Rose," Columbia A-3615, J. W. Myers (Irish).
- "Yosel," Emerson-13238, Nellie Casman (Jewish humor).
- "Cohen on His Honeymoon," Victor 18501, Monroe Silver (Jewish humor).
- "Silent Night," Victor 17164, Elsie Baker (religious).
- "Stand up for Jesus," Victor 723, Trinity Choir (religious).
- "Casey Jones," Victor 16483, American Quartet (regional, southern American folklore).
- "Mother (A Word that Means the World to Me)," Victor 17913, Henry Burr (a universal theme).

- ♦ The early marketing of cars, airplanes, and beer included the following:
  - "In My Merry Oldsmobile," Victor 4467, Billy Murray.
  - "Budweiser's a Friend of Mine," Victor 16049, Billy Murray and the Hayden Quartet.
  - "Come Josephine in My Flying Machine," Victor 16844, Ada Jones, Billy Murray, and the American Quartet.

- ♦ Political and social justice, including antiwar (World War I), Prohibition, women's rights, work songs, and the late (1919) passage of the prohibition
  - "The Battle Cry of Freedom," Victor 16165, Harlan and Stanley.
  - "It's a Long, Long Way to Tipperary," Victor 17639, American Quartet.
  - "Sister Susie's Sewing Shirts for Soldiers," Columbia A-1671, Al Jolson.
  - "I Didn't Raise My Son to Be a Soldier," Victor 17716, Morton Harvey; Columbia A-1697, the Peerless Quartet. (Woodrow Wilson ran for reelection as president, using this theme in 1916. The United States entered WWI the following year, 1917.)
  - "America I Love You," Victor 17902, American Quartet.
  - "Good-bye Alexander (Good-bye Honey Boy)," Victor 18492, Marion Harris.
  - "I'm Glad My Daddy's in a Uniform," Aeolian-Vocalion 12090, Sophie Tucker.
  - "Over There," Victor 17639, Nora Bayes.
  - "Keep Your Head Down, Fritzie Boy," Columbia A-2600, Arthur Fields and the Peerless Quartet.

- "Tell That to the Marines," Columbia A-2657, Al Jolson.
- "Good-bye France," Columbia A-2678, Nora Bayes.
- "I've Got My Captain Working for Me Now," Columbia A-2794, Al Jolson.
- "Prohibition Blues," Columbia 2823, Nora Bayes.
- "Everybody Wants a Key to My Cellar," Columbia A-2750, Bert Williams.

♦ Fads—usually dance, include fox-trots, Latino rumbas, etc. Other categories under "fads" could be a musician's original work actually published, which would include ragtime on piano rolls (as an instrumental), cylinders, and later, on discs. (This sample reference covers contemporary dance fads, with actual defining vocals.)

- "Cubanola Glide," Columbia A-800, Arthur Collins and Byron Harlan 1910.
- "That Loving Rag," Edsison 10360, Sophie Tucker; Victor 60023, Nora Bayes, 1910.
- "The Ragtime Dream," Victor 17535, the American Quartet, 1914.
- "Ragtime Cowboy Joe," Victor 17090, Bob Roberts, 1912 (also "a top 25 pick," below).
- "Ragging the Baby to Sleep," Victor 17037, Al Jolson, 1912.
- "Ev'rybody Body Shimmies Now," Aeolian-Vocalion 12099, Sophie Tucker and Her Five Kings of Syncopation, 1918.

♦ Black American themes included religious, mammy, and derogatory coon songs. The following coon songs are examples of the prevalent racism of Americana. Unlike the self-explanatory themes of religious and mammy themes, the popular coon song was a direct result of American attitudes and myths about the uneducated former slave population. They were more so a direct consequence of the "separate but equal" rulings of the US Supreme Court in the 1890s. In true retrospective, the flames of racial prejudice were fanned by the revitalized white mimic "minstrel" and the horrid put-down "coon" song, neatly part of the new and expanding wonders of recorded voice and song on disc and cylinders. While the likes of ragtime had indeed originated in black cakewalks, the "hipness" of the Afro-American was hardly realized by most. The coon song more so embedded deep seeds of racial intolerance upon Americana. Attitudes of most white great-grandfathers and grandmothers were to be founded upon the coon song, whether implied or not. The phonograph was indeed a child's toy, with the influence of radio and television when there were none! Want to poke fun at a black person? Comic relief did include the likes of (British and black) Bert Williams, and the likes of others, including Native Americans Asians, Irish, Italians, Jews, and Germans (during WWI), but skin color is most obvious! Just find a coon song and find out! For the purposes of this book, they would include the following:

- "The Preacher and the Bear," Victor 4431. As also recorded on Edison 9000, Columbia 3146, U S Everlasting, Indestructible 1087, and Zone-0—Phone-120 by Arthur Collins, this bit of novelty targets a black preacher being chased by a bear. Penned by Joe Arzonia, actually the publisher, and A. Longbrake, the song was sung by Arthur Collins (1905), a popular minstrel entertainer of his time, and the record is reputed to have sold over a million copies of the narrative tale. The later rock-era entity, as "Running Bear," on Mercury 71474, by Johnny Preston, penned by J. P. Richardson the "big bopper," perhaps based his ditty upon this crude original.

- "If the Man in the Moon Were a Coon," Edison 9372, as recorded by Ada Jones, 1907.
- "All Coons Look Alike to Me," Edison 7317, as recorded by Arthur Collins and Vess Ossman in 1902. (This ditty had more black origins, as penned by Afro-American Ernest Hogan.)

"Con Clancy's Christening," Columbia A31634, as recorded by Len Spencer, 1901, an odd pun of forbidden race mixing and (Irish) baiting as well. Funny?

"Nigger Blues," penned by (white) Leroy "Lasses" White in 1913. This early usage of "blues" could have been something better without the first word of the title. It would later be recorded by George O' Connor on Columbia A-2064 in 1916. Was the ugly 'N' word term of the later century then acceptable?-Sadly-it was!

> *While racism and indignities were rampant against the Irish, Italian, eastern European, Chinese, and especially the American Indians, it was the Afro-American population, by far, that bore the greatest discriminations.

- The (positive) end of the pre-1920 bigotry was found (for Afro-Americans) in the development of the spiritual. The following published song ditties, many to be later developed into something more, and more so included within the scope of this book, would include the likes of popular music itself as blues—the opposite of the religious, jazz, folk, and (later) rock music itself.

- Especially: "There's a Great Camp Meeting," "Sometimes I Feel Like a Motherless Child," "Swing Low Sweet Chariot," "God Is God," "You Shall Reap," "Bye and Bye," "I'm Workin' on the Buildin'," This Ol'-Time Religion," "He Never Said a Mumblin' Word"(also known as "The Crucifixion"), and "I Must Walk My Lonesome Valley."

Specific Release

- "Swing Low, Sweet Chariot," Victor 16453, Fisk Jubilee Singers. Led by J. W. Meyers, a (white) person, this group found its name from an earlier black group that had toured the world before 1900. Indeed, this "spiritual" has remained part of Americana, through slavery into the twenty-first century.
- "Poor Mourner," Victor 1715, Dinwiddie Colored Quartet.
- "Nobody Knows the Trouble I've Seen," Tuskegee Institute Singers, Victor 18237.

THE ACOUSTIC AGE—TOP 25 PICKS (1900-25 +)

- The following are the top 25 acoustic recordings, as heard, by the author of this book. Moreover, historical references are also taken into consideration as the (poor) sounds that were generated were self-limiting in fact. (Please also note that some of the following also find themselves reviewed in the artist section of this book).

1. "The St. Louis Blues," Columbia 14064-D. Blues woman Bessie Smith owns this (W. C. Handy-penned) title, and for an added pleasure, a young and identified Louis Armstrong trumpet adds depth and drama—the very best of the lot by far in 1925. Before this time, the title had already been played as an instrumental and vocal as by many, sadly restricted to only white performers as recording before 1920s. They included likes of Prince's Orchestra on Columbia 5772, and Al Bernard (1919) on Emerson 9163, and a fine vocal as by Marion Harris on Columbia A-2944. (More so, Bessie's own future (1929) film of the same name featured an outstanding filmed vocal, often bootlegged as a recording. Still later films would use this title in 1938 and 1958. Electric-rendered vocals would include a Bing Crosby release on Brunswick 20105, with Duke Ellington's backing, as well as renderings by Louis Armstrong on Okeh 41`350, Emmet Miller on Okeh 41095, and by Milton Brown and his Brownies, a classy white hillbilly band, on Decca 5070. Subsequent versions through the mid-century by Ethel Waters, Maxine Sullivan (also associated with the 1938 film), Lena Horne, and Nat King Cole (also in the 1958 film) should likewise be heard.

   (This tune, in 1935, also had significant political significance, when used as a battle rally song of the African country of Ethiopia defending themselves against the invading (fascist) Italian government led by dictator Benito Mussolini).

2. "Dinah," Columbia 487-D. Ethel Waters, as a new Columbia recording artist, fooled a lot of white buyers as her light and jazzy vocal style sounded "white." Were black people capable of sounding like this? Moreover, just how did this "soft" sound become heard, considering poor acoustics? Somehow, it all sounds quite well and is, more amazingly, an acoustic release capturing Ethel's somewhat personable softer vocal tone.

(Indeed, Ethel's (1925) contemporary understudy Josephine Baker, took her act, and "Dinah," to France, which also produced her own Waters' inspired version on Odeon 49172, released on the continent).

Ethel would rerecord her claimed classic many times, noting the later electric releases on Decca 234 and on Continental 1007. While good enough, her original wins out. A more challenging (1932) version was to be found on a version of "Dinah," as by a fast scatting rendering as by Bing Crosby and the Mills Brothers, on Brunswick 6240. Indeed this version is far from Ethel's lighter original best-selling entity; it's still hard not to claim this ditty as a Waters' standard.

3. "Shine on Harvest Moon," Victor 16259, Harry MacDonough. The early century seemed to find a lot of lyric using "moon." While small groups harmonized simple phrasing, including "barber shop" quartets, this title from Broadway's Ziegfeld Follies of 1908, became a popular (1909) best seller. Other contemporary versions included those by Ada Jones and Billy Murray (Edison 10134), a Frank Stanley and Henry Burr version (Zon-0-Phone 5509), and a Bob Roberts's version (Columbia 668). A later (1931) revival, by Ruth Etting in Ziegfeld Follies of 1931 (Perfect 12737) also found a further stretch of implied creative efforts by Ethel Waters (Columbia 2511-D). In true retrospective, both the new and electric versions were somewhat popular, but considering the age and schmaltz involved in this title, just what did Ruth and Ethel hope to achieve? Yet—the question could be asked of the later (1944) film release of *Shine On Harvest Moon*, which starred Dennis Morgan (as Jack Norworth), and Ann Sheridan (as Nora Bayes): Who did contribute to the somewhat contrived origins of this title? Did they? Yet another contemporary title, known as "By The Light of the Silv'ry Moon" was more so another Ziegfeld-associated entity. When combined with "Shine on Harvest Moon," as credited to Gus Edwards and Ed Madden as "Shine on Harvest Moon" the ditty became recording fodder for the likes of many, including those by Billy Murray and the Hayden Quartet (Victor 16460), Ada Jones (Edison 10362), and the Peerless Quartet (Columbia 799).
4. "Lazy," Brunswick 2595. While Irving Berlin always knew how to write a lyric, it's Al Jolson's (1924) fast-paced version that "sold" this tune! A contemporary group rendering as by the Brox Sisters, Victor 1928, is something different from Jolson! (A later, and differing, softer electric (1942) version by Bing Crosby (on Decca 18427) is also excellent, but Jolson, in this comparison, is hipper! Too bad it's acoustic? Compare.
5. "Crazy Blues," Okeh 4169. This famous recording by blues woman Mamie Smith, penned by Afro-American entity Perry Bradford, also opened many doors, and this Okeh recording release was a transitory step into blues and jazz as never before in 1920. While sexual pleasure is implied, it's obvious that this black woman could compete with the likes of any white-faced contemporary. It's also interesting to compare a contemporary Noble Sissle version with Eubie Blake on piano, recorded a bit later in 1920 on Emerson 10326, which is slightly tamer as well as Afro-American in origin.
6. "Trouble in Mind," Okeh 8312. As recorded by Bertha "Chippie" Hill, this mid-tempo vocal is more so a fabulous 1925 performance, backed by Louis Armstrong's trumpet. Based upon Trixie Smith's "Railroad Blues" (Paramount 12262), penned by Jones, this ditty would later become a standard blues classic for many, especially noting fine and challenging electric versions as from a hillbilly string band with a vocal from Leon Chappelear on Decca 5340, and by Dinah Washington on Mercury 8267.

7. "My Man," Victor 45263. Many baby boomers are familiar with the Barbara Streisand film *Funny Girl*, which was a bio of comedian-vocalist Fannie Brice. This ditty had been first introduced by the contemporary French cabaret entity Mistinguett. As penned by Maurice Yvain, with English lyrics by Channing Pollack, this version of "Mon Homme," perhaps about a woman who enjoys being beaten by her man, is a true "torch," and caused an American sensation. This original rendition from Broadway's Ziegfeld Follies of 1921, ain't bad, although perhaps it is overshadowed by Brice's later electric version on Victor 21168. Moreover, it's this (1927) version, often mistaken for the Brice original that indeed beat out the committed contemporary Ruth Etting version on Columbia 995-D, a challenging 1938 Billie Holiday version on Brunswick 8008, and the (light-years) later (1965) Streisand version on Columbia 43323.
8. "Beale Street Blues," Okeh 8058. As one of the first W. C. Handy-penned ditties, it had to wait to be first defined as a well-sung vocal until a Marion Harris (1921) acoustic version on Columbia A-3474, closely followed by an Esther Bigeou version on Okeh 8058. The subsequent 1927 electric version by Alberta Hunter, on Victor 20771, is also done well, as well as a (much) later 1941 version by Lena Horne on Victor 27543.
9. "Some of These Days," Edison Amb 691. Sophie Tucker's specialty was a novelty, and this cylinder (1911) version of an Afro-American penned ditty, by Shelton Brooks, had her, for a time, an interesting' hip' emulation of black culture and a jazz standard. A later (1927) electric version, on Columbia 826-D, with the very able and jazzy backing by Ted Lewis is also done well, but it was more nostalgic and very much challenged by other contemporary 1920s' versions, especially noting one by Bessie Smith (Columbia 14197-D). A still later 1932 electric rendering by a scatting Bing Crosby, on Brunswick 6351, moreover, proves original Sophie's original premise to sound black and hip, although Crosby, more so, succeeds.
10. "Cake Walking Babies from Home," Okeh 40321. Recorded by Clarence Williams Blue Five, which included Sidney Becket, Louis Armstrong, and Clarence himself, it's (still) vocalist Eva Taylor, who makes it into something memorable (1925). (A slightly earlier (1924) version as by the Red Onion Jazz Babies, essentially the same backing group, with a vocal by Josephine Beatty (aka Alberta Hunter) and Clarence Todd also reeks of jazz (Gennett 5617). It is, moreover, almost as fine as the Taylor vocal.
11. "See See Rider Blues," Paramount 12252. It's recorded by blues woman Ma Rainey, backed by Fletcher Henderson and Louis Armstrong, who defined this ditty as a rocking vocal! (1925). A later (electric) version (by Bea Booze on Decca 8633), with guitar and vocal also wins out. Baby boomers would be later moved by differences in style, noting the Chuck Willis's version on Atlantic 1130, Mitch Ryder and The Detroit Wheels on New Voice 817, and Elvis Presley on numerous live renderings, including on RCA LP (LSP-4362). Even so, It's all "Ma" for us.
12. "Joe Turner Blues," Okeh 8058. Blues queen Sarah Martin scores with this (W. C Handy) entity in 1923.
13. "Steppin' Out," Brunswick 2567. This credited (Howard and Conrad) composition actually is a bit hip and is toughly rendered out by the credited Comedian with Orchestra, who was Al Jolson. Moreover, with the jazzy (1924) Isham Jones Orchestra, it all worked out and sounded quite well—as contrived and planned.
14. "Nobody," Columbia 3423. This 1906 version by Bert Williams was perhaps his best-known version, noting a later (1913) revival on Columbia 1289. As penned by Alex Rogers and Bert himself, this title became identifiable to Bert Williams as his

own theme. As black entities, both Bert and his vaudeville partner George Walker overcame much racism, with Bert (luckily) being noticed by Flo Ziegfeld, who put him in his all-white and very popular Broadway shows.

15. "It Ain't Gonna Rain No More," Victor 19171. Wendell Hall's hillbilly novelty took off in sales and became popular in early local New York City radio in 1924. (This ditty was also recorded on Gennett 5271 and Edison 51261. Indeed, a good marking ploy ahead of its time, it's perhaps among the first popular, selling ditties that became a huge seller due to a radio program broadcast, more so in Hall's own live radio shows.
16. "Someday Sweetheart," Black Swan 2019. Alberta Hunter's fine and raspy (1921) vocal found and defined this sentimental classic and was penned by the Afro-American brothers Reb and John Spikes. Like many original Black Swan label recordings, this ditty was subsequently released on Paramount. Alberta's later electric (1939) Decca rendering contains the obvious enhanced listening experience, although this later version was less known. Subsequent Gene Austin, Bing Crosby, and Dick Todd versions also compete, if not with Alberta, at least with each other.
17. "There'll Be Some Changes Made," Black Swan 2021. This 1921 Ethel Waters release, penned by Higgins and Overstreet, perhaps defined jazz singing for the era. The skillful and articulately voiced Ethel is, moreover, showing off her command of the language, a notable asset of her own vocal style and something too often taken for granted. Ethel was, moreover, ahead of all her contemporaries with this fine bit of jazz, which also rises above a very poor (Black Swan) recording master, later rereleased on Paramount. Subsequent acoustic Eva Taylor, Marion Harris, and Edith Wilson (duet with Doc Strain) versions do indeed offer good vocal comparisons, and were indeed recorded better. (A later electric Sophie Tucker's version on Okeh 40921 attempted to claim it, and a still later Boswell Sisters' group rendering on Brunswick 6291 is, at least, challenging.)
18. "Alexander's Ragtime Band," Victor 16908, Columbia 1032, Edison Amberol 20, and other labels. It was recorded by Arthur Collins and Byron Harlan, already top recording artists by 1911. This title gave Irving Berlin his first huge seller. While the term "ragtime" was an already dated Scott Joplin term for some fifteen years, the infectious and rhythmic timing of this ditty was considered something different and new. While oddly termed as a coon song by some, this Berlin tale of a black bandleader is not mean, not stupid, but one of admiration. Or did Joplin contribute more than influence? (The diverse later electric renderings of this ditty include one by Bessie Smith (Columbia 14219-D), which perhaps finds Alexander not as spunky as Colllins and Harlan had described him. Still other subsequent versions did, including a version by Bing Crosby and Connie Boswell on Decca 1887. Still later, in the 1950s, Billy Eckstine and Sarah Vaughan, on Mercury LP 203161, perhaps did put to rest any confusion about Alexander.)
19. "Ragging the Baby to Sleep," Victor 17081. The term "ragtime" was perhaps far from hip in 1912. Penned by L. W. Gilbert and L. F. Muir, this energetic Al Jolson release luckily saved it and, more so, sold it!
20. "The Prisoner's Song," Victor 19427. Also on Columbia A-257, Edison 51459, Gennett 5588, and Pathé 032085, among others, the serious tenor Vernon Dalhart's (1925) social comments, penned by Guy Massey, were appreciated as well as popularized the song!
21. "Over There," Victor 45130. This stirring World War I theme of patriotism, as penned by Broadway's own George M. Cohan, was perhaps best heard as a recording by this Nora Bayes 1917 rendition.

22. "Ragtime Cowboy Joe," Victor 17090. As recorded by Bob Roberts in 1912 (another Bob Roberts version exists on Edison Amberol 837), this novelty title found itself a rock-era delight, in 1959. While "novelty" has survived in popular music throughout the century, the Chipmunks version, on Liberty 55200, a David Seville enterprise, owes a lot to the pre-rock past. But what about a 1930s' best seller by Pinky Tomlin (Decca 2014)? This also found this title penned by G. Clark and M. Abrahams good recording fodder?
23. "Take Me Out to the Ball Game," Victor 5570. As recorded by Billy Murray and the Hayden Quartet, this title remains relevant in Americana, each summer since 1908.
24. "After You've Gone," Victor 18509. As recorded by Marion Harris (1919), this ditty finally had some standard, after a bland vocal attempt for Henry Burr and Albert Campbell (Pathé 20439) is far bettered by Marion's vocal prowess. Penned by the black team of Henry Creamer and Turner Layton, this ditty would remain relevant with electric versions by Sophie Tucker (Okeh 40837) and especially by Bessie Smith (Columbia 14197-D), and a still later (1930) Paul Whiteman release with a Bing Crosby vocal (Columbia 2098-D). As, given a full-scale arrangement the challenge of a somewhat jazz sound is evident, and the committed Crosby does it well. A contemporary (1930) film short also found the Broadway-voiced Ethel Merman, oddly pulling off a fine blues performance.
25. "My Man Rocks Me (With One Steady Roll)," Black Swan 14127. This (1922) rendering is more than just an adult bedtime story. Blues queen Trixie Smith really does rock out on this J. Berni Barbour penned ditty. While it's a stretch for rock music, the link is real enough. This ditty had most likely been around a while with Trixie clinching it as a recording (Trixie's Black Swan master was subsequently rereleased on Paramount). A later Frankie "Half Pint" Jaxon version with Tampa Red and his Hokum band) is also done well. (Later, Wynonie Harris would revive it, as well as Chuck Berry, as perhaps his own "Reeling And Rocking" (Chess 1683)?). Moreover, the Berry version became a rock classic.

OPERA—A BIT OF IT

The European influences of the opera had origins in musical theater, which essentially had highbrow appeal. The monarchy of each European state had had their share, and in most cases, voices shared with the romance language of Italian. While the harsher Germans had it, as did the lighter French and Spanish, the softer Italian tone had it made, even in England and Russia. While the live concert did draw crowds in the 1800s, Americana, the concept of recorded sound, had more to offer. Even the newer American musical was full of it before jazz or ragtime. Moreover, many later popular song ditties were actually embellishments of master classical composers and are (sometimes) noted elsewhere within this book.

The business of classical music has remained, although not in the masses, as it had existed, at least before the advent of electric recording in the mid-1920s. Nevertheless, the author of this book, in order not to ignore them, has chosen to note the following and very selective operatic entities, including recordings, films, or events (1900-50).

1. After hundred years have passed, the great Caruso is still recognized as the world's first international superstar recording artist. Caruso was, moreover, the first recording artist to sell more than a million records collectively, noting an early American release of "I Pagliacci," on Victor 81032, leading the way in 1904. His native Italian vocals were enough for most, considering that *all* of these recordings were destined to be acoustic. In *his* case, he is not hard to hear!
2. **"O Sole Mio,"** Victor 97243. This (1916) Caruso rendering had eyes for the future, as "There's No Tomorrow," Tony Martin's 1949 rendering, on Victor 78-3582 was a stiff update. More significant is the rock era (1960) rendering by Elvis Presley, as "It's Now or Never" on Victor 47-7777.
3. **"Carry Me Back to Old Virginny,"** Victor 88481. This truly American composition by (Afro-American) James Blaine had already been recorded by the Hayden Quartette. As recorded by soprano Alma Gluck in 1915 the ditty was considered classier. Victor would, moreover, claim it sold over a million, before American involvement in WWI. Alma later married violinist Efrem Zimbalist. They became the parents of TV actor Efrem Zimbalist Jr. and grandparents to the (later) television entity Stephanie Zimbalist (a lot of Zs)!
4. "**The Spaniard That Blighted My Life**," Victor 17318. Somehow, Al Jolson's acoustic and dated ditty from the contemporary (1913) Broadway operetta *The Honeymoon Express*, as by Billy Merson works! Are Jolson's "show off" attempt at rolling *r*'s and comic effect very good? Or is it all so bad, it's good?

5. **"Silent Night, Holy Night"** (1818). As a prayer, "Stille Nacht" by Austrian priest Joseph Mohr, added church music as by music by Franz Gruber founded a true Christmas classic. It was soon translated into many languages, as well as into Italian operatic bliss. The advent of recorded music found prominently Christian Americana eager to purchase for the holiday. While the acoustic efforts of many, including Else Baker, were done well enough, the advent of electric recording, especially noting Bing Crosby's excellent 1935 release on Decca 621, defined the song as "pop," without disrupting its serious message. This would more so continue through the rest of the century, with the likes of many, including Frank Sinatra, Ella Fitzgerald, Nat King Cole, and even Elvis and Barbara Streisand.
6. "**Nobody Knows the Trouble I've Seen**," Victor 19560. The (1925) traditional lament is turned operatic by Afro-American Marion Anderson. More so, and somehow, it became a best seller. A contemporary Afro-American of Marion, who was also operatic, Paul Robeson, would also produce some popular secular spirituals, using European vocal training techniques.

Early Radio. The likes of many symphonic orchestras and musical composers, already on recordings, were also be to be found on numerous radio broadcasts. Maestros, including the likes of Ernest Ansermet, Leonard Bernstein, Samuel Chotzinoff, Vladimir Horowitz Leopold Stokowski, and Arturo Toscanini did indeed find huge audiences. Moreover, the likes of the most popular bandleaders and musicians had found their own musical instructions within the realm of the classic traditions of European masters. Notable entities such as Paul Whiteman, Ted Lewis, Fletcher Henderson, Duke Ellington, and Artie Shaw were indeed much influenced, and perhaps their eventual adaptation of American jazz, or assimilation, were well rooted in classic. Most importantly, for the purposes of this book, the classically trained vocalists, or those who emulated operatic overtones of early commercial radio such as Marion Anderson, Kenny Baker, Rose Bampton, Jules Bledsoe, Maurice Chevalier, Dennis Day, Deanna Durbin, Jessica Dragonette, Morton Downy, Nelson Eddy, Harry Frankel ("Singin'" Sam), Susanna Foster, Charlotte Henry, Allan Jones (later the father of 60s' pop singer Jack Jones), Felix Knight, Frances Langford, James Melton, Jeanette Mac Donald, Grace Moore, Robert Merrill, Frank Munn, Jan Peerce, Ezio Pinza, Dick Powell, Lanny Ross, Beverly Sills, Gladys Swarthout Lawrence Tibbett, Arthur Tracy (the Street singer), and even the likes of the already (old) disc seller, the Irish tenor John McCormack, all found huge audiences despite the popular music dominated by baritone singers over radio waves.

7. From Hungary in 1933 came classic composer Rezso Seress's **"Gloomy Sunday."** As with serious lyrics about attempted suicide, this ditty was actually blamed for a number of them in (contemporary) Hungary and Eastern Europe. By the mid-1930s, this tragic tale also found its way to America with many recorded versions, including an excellent high brow recording by Hildegrande in Britain. As popular culture seemingly mirrors its own life, the exceptional 1941 version by (nonoperatic) Billie Holiday on Okeh 6451, endures.

Popular and featured vocalists within this book who would, or could, also adapt well on some material with operatic influences, some more than others, include many. They are as follows: Al Jolson (rolling *r*'s), Ethel Waters (rolling *r*'s), Adelaide Hall (high-strung vocal), Libby Holman (also a high-strung vocal) and crooners Bing

Crosby, Russ Columbo, Connie Boswell, Tony Martin, Ethel Merman (loud, fit for the stage), Ginny Simms, Dinah Shore, Jo Stafford, Sarah Vaughan, and Elisabeth Welch among others. Moreover, The Likes of Helen Morgan, Paul Robeson, and Jane Froman (somehow) found themselves influencing popular music, and are featured within this book, despite their overly operatic tendencies.

Films. Filmed operatic voices have also confirmed most of this author's disdain for tenors and sopranos, finding most radio entities even more badly off when seen and heard on film. Exceptions are noted below. The popular films of Deanna Durbin and Bobby Breen just do not hold up well, nor do any of Arthur Tracy, who almost ruined 1932's *The Big Broadcast*. Paul Robeson is mostly just tolerated. More so, the team of Jeanette MacDonald and Nelson Eddie appear clumsy and are mostly forgettable. On the other hand, as noted below, the voice of Adriana Caselotti as Snow White remains a classic, as does the performance of Grace Moore, Lily Pons, Dick Powell, and Mario Lanza in other film appearances.

8. ***Show Boat.*** The original 1928 Broadway entity, as penned by Jerome Kern, Oscar Hammerstein II, and P. G. Wodehouse, found these European-born entities—steeped up into operatic impulses—founding an "American" original. While stuck in American racism as well, this entity, also filmed more than twice, is known for its great songs. Moreover, more than a few of them ("Can't Help Loving Dat Man," "Bill," and "Old Man River") were popularized by a few operatic voices who *did* find themselves as featured artists within this book—Helen Morgan and Paul Robeson. It's more so the second (1936) filmed version that finds some interest.

   As the operatic efforts of Allan Jones are a bore (especially singing "Make Believe") the attempt at soprano status had found Irene Dunne prepared. Her spirited black-faced performance of "Gallivanting Around" (from the original production) is truly an embarrassment for audiences of future generations as are her duets with Allan Jones. She is, moreover, good at her attempts at "Can't Help Loving Dat Man" and "After the Ball," which may be considered stiff yet well-done vocals. ("After the Ball" as penned by Charles K. Harris before 1900, had been a sad tale about a guy who saw his girlfriend with another, only later to discover that the man had been her brother. Sad indeed!) Among others, a cylinder (1892) recording by Irish tenor George Gaskin became very popular, with its sheet music selling in the millions. Since the story in the film depicted the Victorian era, this song ditty had actual identification with a contemporary (1893) Broadway entity "A Trip to China Town." As seen in the film, after a disastrous start, Dunn indeed pulls out a fine stage performance despite her highbrow stab at opera!

   Helen Morgan, at thirty-six years of age, recreates her previous stage and film renditions of "Can't Help Loving Dat Man"(with Robeson and Hattie McDaniel) and "Bill" very well. Robeson's filmed "Old Man River" is far better than his recording of the ditty, while his duet with Hattie McDaniel "Ah Still Suits Me" (another added ditty to the film soundtrack), while good enough, fails to match his contemporary recording with Elisabeth Welch, who was sadly not in the American-made film. A later (1952) filmed version found the beautiful but dubbed actress Ava Gardner taking Morgan's mulatto part. Speculation has it that Lena Horne wanted the part, but the studio (MGM) caved in to racism, even at this later time, after WWII. It is more than safe to note that Lena, who had filmed in short sequences doing "Can't Help Loving Dat Man" or "Can't Help Loving That Man" in previous films before Ava got the new film—as well as produced a fine recording—would have been exceptionally good as well as more true to the part than Ava or even Helen Morgan?

9. ***Threepenny Opera***. The (Brit) John Gay's (1728) *The Beggar's Opera* was overhauled by Germans two hundred years later! The (1928) German stage product, founded by Kurt Weill, Bertolt Brecht, and Marc Blitzstein was pre-Hitler, and found its way to France, England, and finally America. As a theme, its influence was socially significant—as this is tale of dockworkers in a murderous fight—and was indeed brilliant. This ditty may just be the best thing that came out of Germany, before WWII, along with the likes of Marlene Dietrich's sultry vocals and presence in the 1930 film, *Blue Angel.* (Both are, more so, pre-Hitler. Indeed, the rise of the Third Reich found many creative Germans, Jews, and non-Jews eventually fleeing Germany, including Weil and Dietrich.) Somehow, this ditty again became more significant in the (later) 1950s as the popular vocal release "Mack the Knife." Like the versions by Louis Armstrong, Bing Crosby, and especially the (younger) Bobby Darin, this ditty finally got the recognition it deserved in America.
10. "**Stein Song**." The University Of Maine's drinking song found origins in Brahm's Hungarian dances. It was to be further adapted by Rudy Vallee as a novel popular song on Victor 22321 in 1930. More so, this ditty was to be adapted by Rudy Vallee as a popular song entity on Victor 22321, as penned by E. A. Fenstad, A. W. Spague, and L. Colcord in 1930.
11. **"Where the Blue of the Night**." This significant 1931 crooning effort for Bing Crosby was claimed by Roy Turk and Fred Ahlert, as well as by Crosby (Brunswick 6226) and Russ Columbo (Victor 22867). Its melody was actually that of "Tit Willow" from the old Gilbert and Sullivan opera *The Mikado.*
12. "**Prisoner Of Love**." The Leo Robin and Russ Columbo 1931 entity on Victor 22867 just may have been influenced by Frederic Chopin's Nocturne no. 7 from 1832. This popular song ditty, introduced by Russ—who was a classically trained violinist before he became a popular vocalist—was to be later claimed by Perry Como, as well as light-years later by James Brown "the Godfather of Soul"
13. ***Charlie Chan at the Opera*****,** 1936. The string of Charlie Chan films of the 1930s found this Fox production featuring Warner Oland (who had played Al Jolson's father in 1927's *Jazz Singer*) as detective Chan and an operatic villain, as played by Boris Karloff. Whether Karloff did sing or was dubbed is unclear, but the fine production, as seen on-screen, remains a gem. Indeed, the famous screen monster is very good and is provided first-rate material known as "Carnival Marche," with ditties "King and Country" and "Ah Romantic Dream." As the music was put together by William Kernell and Oscar Levant, it's also interesting to note that that Levant, like his contemporary (and friend) George Gershwin, became a jazz pianist after first being schooled at home by the classics.
14. "**Smoke Gets in Your Eyes**." Jerome Kern, Oscar Hammerstein II, and Otto Harbach's Broadway entity, as introduced on Broadway by Tamara (who was really born in Russia), took the likes of Irene Dunne (faking the Russian dialect), as seen and heard in the 1934 film *Roberta*, to somehow produce a memorable screen performance. While Dunn's vocal just may be overtly emotional, her trained operatic vocal indeed hits the heart. It is, moreover, worth it to note that Fred Astaire, also in the film, luckily did not attempt it! Contemporary records as by Ruth Etting and

Chick Bullock offer interesting comparisons, as well as the (later)(1958) recording by the Platters.

15. ***Porgy and Bess***. This original (1935) Broadway entity, while perhaps lacking in real substance, with added racism, is nevertheless full of great song ditties. Penned by the Gershwin Brothers and Du Bose Heyward, this operetta, also made into a film several times (and noted elsewhere within this book), found better response and results within pop music. While the original likes of the operatic original cast members (Afro-Americans Todd Duncan, Edward Matthews, and Ann Brown) remain secular, the popular ditties introduced—especially "It Ain't Necessarily So," and "Summertime"—quickly became notable popular song ditties, especially as recording fodder as by Bing Crosby, Billie Holiday, Lena Horne, Mabel Mercer, Maxine Sullivan, and Ethel Waters. (They are noted elsewhere within this book, along with other related titles) They have, more so, despite the rock era, remained relevantly so.
16. ***San Francisco,*** MGM film, 1936. Despite at least half a dozen films with Nelson Eddie, as well as some with Frenchman Maurice Chevalier, operatic Jeanette MacDonald's role in this film (with Clark Gable) and her introduction of the title song ditty "San Francisco" (written by Kaper, Jurmann, and Kahn) within the film is endearing as well as impressive.

    (A soft crooning job by Bing Crosby, "Would You," is heard but not seen in this film—but it's not opera, but a sideline.)

17. ***Song Of Freedom***, Hammer Productions, 1936. This 1936 British film, which far from being great, does boast an interesting story line about black slavery and a search for cultural identity. ("Roots"—before the 1970s!)

    It is, more so, interesting as a Paul Robeson film with Elisabeth Welch, who uplifts the film, sharing with Robeson on the contrived but good "Sleepy River." While the other song ditties within the film by Robeson tend to bore, the young image of Welch is well anticipated and makes it all bearable.

18. **Snow White and the Seven Dwarfs,** RKO Film, 1937. This timeless classic's cartoon value is also found in the soprano voice of Adriana Caselotti. While unknown by most, this Disney feature, for the very young, remains a relevant classic! Adriana's contemporary "Someday My Prince Will Come" recording is somewhat misplaced, but her cartoon vocal, in true retrospective, remains a huge part of the culture. Ditty for the un-accredited Seven Dwarfs on "Whistle While You Work" and "Heigh Ho" are far less operatic!
19. **"The Glow-Worm."** The (1902) German operetta *Lysistrata* found its way to America and Broadway on early century Broadway. Subsequently credited as penned by Paul Lincke and Lilla Cayley Robinson, it became a huge acoustic best-selling ditty in 1908, as sung by soprano Lucy Isabelle Marsh (Columbia 781). Light-years later, in 1946, it was revived as a novelty as by Spike Jones and His City Slickers, featuring a vocal as by Red Ingle and Aileen Carlisle, released on Victor 20-1893. Still later, in 1953, with some added lyrics from Johnny Mercer, it became a best-selling entity as by the Mills Brothers, released on Decca 28384.
20. **"On the Isle of May,"** Decca 3004. This (1940) best-selling ditty, popularized by Connie Boswell, found its melody based upon Tchaikovsky's String Quartet in D Major.

21. ***The Phantom of the Opera,*** Universal Film, 1943. The operatic utterances of Nelson Eddie and Susanna Foster, as well as some classic instrumental stuff ain't bad—even for novices! More so, Susanna's vocal of "Amore et Gloire" remains just as pleasing to modern ears as it did for Claude Rains, who played the masked phantom in this fine horror flick.
22. **"Till the End of Time**." This popular (1945) Perry Como release on Victor 20-1709 was based upon Chopin's Polonaise in A-flat Major in melody.
23. **"Big Stuff."** Billie Holiday's nonoperatic vocal of Leonard Bernstein's classical 1945 composition (Decca 23463) is indeed big stuff!
24. ***Cinderella,*** RKO. The original 1949 film entity, like most all Walt Disney cartoons, was creatively done. It, more so, boasts the operatic vocals of Ilene Woods. While her contemporary recordings of such ditties as "So Here Is Love" and "A Dream Is a Wish Your Heart Makes" are mostly forgotten, seeing and hearing the cartoon classic with the very young remains something perhaps special! The lame voice of "Prince Charming" was Mike Douglas, the future and familiar TV talk show host. In any case, baby boomers win out as the first of many generations to declare a cartoon classic!
25. **Mario Lanza**. After a half century, another Caruso-like personage, this time in the electric age—arrives. Somehow, the American-born tenor is not too boring ("Be My Love," Victor 78-1561)!

Honorable mention

- ***Micro-Phonies*** (Screen Gems), Columbia film, short, 1945. Curly, of the three Stooges, is always funny. As "Senorita Cucaracha," along with Senor Mucho (Larry) and Senor Gusto (Moe), they successfully mimic opera. While the author of this book has yet to find the real recorded voice behind "Voices of Spring," Curly remains utterly amusing, no matter how many times he is seen and heard. Or was it a war time parody of the Third Reich's popular operatic 'German nightingale, Erna Sack-who really did record "Voices Of Spring?(Three tenors? Or two tenors and a suspicious fat lady)?
- ***Babes In Toyland,*** film, 1934. Victor Herbert's early century operetta comes alive with Charlotte Henry, Felix Knight, and especially Stan Laurel and Oliver Hardy.
- ***That Girl from Paris,*** film, 1937. Opera entity Lily Pons somehow pulls a performance for everyone! Even her rendition of "Una Voce Poco F," taken from Rossini's *Barber Of Seville*, while not understood by most watching and listening, is pleasant enough.
- (Any Terry Toon) cartoon featuring with the (bearable) operatic tendencies of Mighty Mouse.

Many other song ditties were based upon operatic melodies, but, for the purposes of this book, we will stop here! (More information is to be found, and noted subsequently, in text.)

BROADWAY'S BEST TWENTY-FIVE SONGS (1900-50)

- The following picks are original Broadway stage entities. Since it is impossible to see the originals, only the original reviews and recordings remain. These subsequent picks are subjective and are listed in alpha sequence, with some comments. Moreover, all titles are also to be found in the text with more recording detail.

  - "Anything Goes," penned by Cole Porter, from *Anything Goes,* 1934. Ethel Merman introduced it, and her subsequent contemporary recording is also a winner. So was a contemporary vocal as by Cole Porter himself. Light-years later, in 1956, Frank Sinatra would redefine it.
  - "As Time Goes By". Broadway entity Herman Hupfeld perhaps achieved greatness as a songwriter owing more to Hollywood than anyone. As introduced by sexy Frances Williams in the 1931 production of "Everybody's Welcome", this author cannot find a contemporary recording from her. The song ditty was however recorded by the contemporariy (singing)) bandleaders Jacques Renard and Rudy Vallee who had also made it a popular crooning item over the air waves on 'live' radio. (Oddly, Bing Crosby, who also made very good (radio) claims on the ditty did not produce a contemporary recording).

    A little more than a decade later, the Warner Brothers 1943 film "Casablanca" found a piano playing character "Sam" (played by singer Dooley Wilson), serenading (actress) Ingrid Bergman at the bequest of (actor) Humphrey Bogart. As a war time release, the film became a huge box office entity, with the song ditty (now becoming related to the war) becoming very much in demand. It was also a time that contemporary vocalists and bandleaders could only play 'live', due to the musicians strike that had already caused a lot of problems, as well as obviously halting careers of many would be recording artists. This was especially evident for Dooley Wilson, who's subsequent recording had to wait a while until the strike was settled.

    As fate would have it, many record companies, due to the strike had began to re-issue old product. When (RCA VICTOR) dug up Rudy Vallee's original (1931) version, it did more than cash in ! While Rudy's original release had been a moderate depression era seller, it's (1943) re-isssue was to become the best selling recording of that year, as well as the best selling recording of Vallee's (long) career.

At the same time, (DECCA) records, who had bought out the original Jacques Renard (BRUNSWICK) master, produed a special green labeled re-issue using the old 'Brunswick' logo. This release, only rivaled by Vallee's, also produced huge (1943) sales, and finding the lesser known Renard becoming popular again. (The somewhat later recordings of Dooley Wilson, (British recording) ofAdelaide Hall and Billie Holiday's (Commadore) were all well done subsequent recordings, each offering a differing vocal style. Did Billie Holiday re-define it? Listen & learn?

- "Black and Blue" or "What Could I Do to Be So Black and Blue," penned by Andy Razaf, Fats Waller, and Harry Brooks, from *Hot Chocolates,* 1928. This bold piece of lyric and music about skin color and the discriminations within the black community had been introduced by Louis Armstrong and Edith Wilson. Both, moreover, produced excellent contemporary recordings with perhaps the Armstrong version a bit more dramatic. A subsequent Ethel Waters version was more poignant and defining. Among numerous other versions, the later Frankie Laine (Mercury) release is an odd and interesting rendering for a white vocalist, considering the subject matter.
- "Body and Soul," penned by Green, Heyman, Sour, and Eyton, from *Three's A Crowd,* 1930. This bit of torch was introduced by Libby Holman. Libby's own and subsequent excellent record was to be challenged by her 1930 contemporaries who included the likes of Helen Morgan, Ruth Etting, Annette Hanshaw, Jack Fulton (on a Paul Whiteman release), and Louis Armstrong. Later, the likes of Sarah Vaughan and Lee Wiley would challenge the older versions, and light-years later, they would be challenged by Tony Bennett.
- "Brother, Can You Spare a Dime?" penned by Jay Gorney and E. Y. Yip Harburg, from *New Americana,* 1932. Rudy Vallee effectively introduced this ditty about the hard-pressed days of the Great Depression, but perhaps Bing Crosby's recording is a bit more poignant. Bing or Rudy?
- "Can't Help Lovin' Dat Man," penned by Jerome Kern and Oscar Hammerstein II, from *Show Boat,* 1927. Helen Morgan introduced this semi-operatic ditty on stage, and her subsequent Victor recording defined it well. Helen would later introduce this classic in film, and also do it well. Numerous other versions followed, especially noting effective Ethel Waters and Lena Horne renderings.
- "Dancing in the Dark," penned by Howard Dietz and Arthur Schwartz, from *The Band Wagon*, 1931. Introduced by Fred Astaire and his sister Adele on stage, this ditty also became a subsequent contemporary Fred Astaire recording. A contemporary recording by Bing Crosby would, moreover, define it.
- "Easter Parade," penned by Irving Berlin, from *As Thousands Cheer*, 1933. Clifton Webb introduced it, and Gene Austin's contemporary recording somehow failed to exploit it. A later filmed version, used in the 1942 film *Holiday Inn*, by Bing Crosby, defined it. A subsequent film, *Easter Parade*, found a Judy Garland vocal done very well. Bing or Judy? A hard choice!
- "Heat Wave," penned by Irving Berlin, from *As Thousands Cheer*, 1933. Ethel Waters introduced it, and her subsequent contemporary recording was a winner and defined it. A later 1954 filmed version by Marilyn Monroe in *There's No Business Like Show Business* is more so sultry and well remembered. (Was Marilyn dubbed?)
- "I Can't Give You Anything but Love," penned by Jimmy McHugh and Dorothy Fields, from *Blackbirds of 1928*, 1927. This ditty had originally been slated into

another previous review *"Delmar's Revels"* but was cut. As part of an all-black review, it had been reserved for Afro-American star Florence Mills, who had just died. In any case, this ditty was introduced by Adelaide Hall, who did not, for some odd reason, produce a contemporary 1927 recording. Moreover, this ditty became a hot item and was to become much recorded with a contemporary 1927 recording by Cliff Edwards—perhaps outselling all others? A later Louis Armstrong version reintroduced it, with a subsequent Ethel Waters version mimicking the Louis Armstrong version for about a third of the recording. Later, in 1938, Adelaide Hall finally recorded it, with Fats Waller's backing and humorous comments. (Is it more than a myth that Waller claimed that he had originally written this ditty and had sold it?)

- "I Get a Kick out of You," penned by Cole Porter, from *Anything Goes*, 1934. Ethel Merman introduced it and subsequently made a contemporary recording. Light-years later in 1955, Frank Sinatra would redefine it.
- "I Got Rhythm," penned by George and Ira Gershwin, from *Girl Crazy*, 1930. Ethel Merman's electrifying introduction on stage was not met by a contemporary recording by her. (Merman would record it some sixteen years later. A filmed clip of Ethel Merman performing this ditty, not in its entirety, perhaps as an early 1930s' radio broadcast, does exist). Moreover, this ditty did receive contemporary 1930s' recording efforts, the most notable, and more so electrifying, as by Ethel Waters. It is also interesting to speculate, if Waters had had the chance to be on Broadway (in an all-white cast), would she have pulled it off better than Merman? Sorry, Ethel! Which Ethel?
- "I Must Have That Man," penned by McHugh and Fields, from *Blackbirds of 1928*, 1927. This bit of torch was introduced by cast member Adelaide Hall. Her subsequent recording was, more so, excellent, as was a competing contemporary recording by Annette Hanshaw, as Gay Ellis. Hall's later second recording of this ditty in 1932 also hit the mark, as well as a still later version by Valaida Snow.
- "I'll Be Seeing You," penned by Sammy Fain and Irving Kahal, from *Right This Way*, 1938. Introduced by Broadway entity Tamara (Tamara Drasin), this Broadway entity was initially considered a failure with its companion song ditty from the same show "I Can Dream, Can't I?" at least becoming a contemporary 1938 popular recording as a Tommy Dorsey release, with a stiff Jack Leonard vocal. (This somewhat bit of schmaltz would later be revived by a best-selling Andrews Sisters version in 1950.

"I'll Be Seeing You" was considered the dog by contemporaries as its lyrics were found to be perhaps full of overly sentimental bliss and bull, and its initial 1938 introduction had impressed no one. Luckily, a few years later in 1940, Tommy Dorsey, looking for some material for his new and nasal new band singer Frank Sinatra decided to record the failed ditty. The resulting vocal, more so, became identified with Frank Sinatra with his smooth rendering defining it well, at least for the first time. Dick Todd also produced a fine crooning version at this time.

As the war clouds of Europe had already erupted in 1939, it would become a matter of time when America would enter the war. As time progressed, the very title of this ditty indeed become important, and all its initial sentiment and mushy lyrics (hardly the intention of the original Broadway show) became a standard as well as one of the great songs of the (WWII) era. While many versions where then recorded, an early 1944 rendering by Bing Crosby became very popular.

In subsequent months, the initial 1940 Tommy Dorsey release with Sinatra's fine vocal was rereleased. By now a solo entity, Frank had become a major rival to the older Crosby, but Bing, who most likely had heard Sinatra's original, perhaps felt challenged and his own recording indeed produced more than an alternative. While on a small label, the Billie Holiday version, cut later in 1944 on Commadore is, in true retrospective, an impressive and committed performance. Billie's attempt at soft tones finds her intimate vocal perhaps defining this ditty! While it's still a good debate, as all the versions noted are excellent, this ditty just may be the best of many song ditties identified with those hard-pressed years of war.

- "I'm Just Wild about Harry," penned by Eubie Blake and Noble Sissle, from *Shuffle Along*, 1922. This bland but rhythmic ditty was introduced on stage by Afro-American Lottie Gee in this very influential all-black review, which also included the likes of Josephine Baker, Adelaide Hall, and Elisabeth Welch in the chorus. While A recording by Lottie Gee just can't be found, subsequent popular contemporary (white) artists Marion Harris and Vaughn De Leath's recording made this ditty a popular item and so did later (1930s) filmed versions by Alice Faye and Pricilla Lane. (Later, in 1948, President Harry S. Truman used this ditty as his presidential campaign theme.). A still later (1953) Broadway revival of *Shuffle Along,* with Eubie Blake (back again) directing an orchestra, found Thelma Carpenter's excellent vocal redefining it as a recording.
- "It Ain't Necessarily So," penned by George and Ira Gershwin and Du Bois Heywood, from *Porgy and Bess,* 1935. The stiff and operatic original cast, who included (Afro-Americans) Todd Duncan and Anne Brown, was easily dismissed in 1935. So was a contemporary recording by Duncan and John Bubbles of the original cast. In true retrospective, *Porgy And Bess* became known as a great asset to the American theater, but largely because of its great songs, with less than operatic vocal tones. As a recording, the fine contemporary crooning job by Bing Crosby is impressive along with a subsequent Maxine Sullivan version that perhaps defined this ditty? (Light-years later in 1959, Lena Horne updated it well.)
- "The Lady Is a Tramp," penned by Lorenz Hart and Richard Rodgers, from *Babes in Arms*, 1937. Despite the likes of Dan Daily and Mitzi Green, subsequent contemporary recordings were better, especially noting those by Midge Williams and Adelaide Hall. A later 1948 filmed version, *Words And Music,* found Lena Horne's sparkling and far less stiff reintroduction and her own subsequent recording actually defining it. A later 1957 Frank Sinatra film *Pal Joey* reintroduced it well in film, and his subsequent recording may be considered a challenge to Lena's previous rendering.
- "Memories of You," penned by Eubie Blake and Andy Razaf, from *Blackbirds Of* 1930. This all-black musical starred Ethel Waters with Buck and Bubbles, Flournory Miller, and, among others, Minto Cato. Cato introduced this ditty on stage, while the contemporary 1930 Ethel Waters recording, full of torch sentimentally—with rolling *r*'s—oddly work! A contemporary and differing Louis Armstrong version followed, with good results.
- "Moaning Low," penned by Ralph Rainger and Howard Dietz, from *The Little Show,* 1929. Libby Holman introduced this ditty with sultry energy and was shockingly successful. Her two subsequent 1929 recordings were also a success

and perhaps captured her original performance. Contemporary releases by Lee Morse and especially by Eva Taylor, on a Charleston Chasers release, are also done well. A still later Lena Horne version (from 1940s) was also done well.

- "Oh Lady, Be Good," penned by George and Ira Gershwin, from *Lady Be Good*, 1924. This original production included Fred Astaire, Adele Astaire, and Cliff Edwards. A contemporary Cliff Edwards recording was moreover very good, as well as a fine 1926 recording by Fred and Adele themselves. Moreover, a later and completely different approach by Ella Fitzgerald's superb scatting may be considered, if not definitive, a vocal wonder.
- "Someone to Watch over Me," penned by George and Ira Gershwin, from *Oh, Kay!* 1926. This fabulous bit of torch was introduced by Gertrude Lawrence of the original cast. Her subsequent contemporary recording is, more so, done well. Years later in 1939, an edgy Lee Wiley version defined it.
- "Summertime," penned by Ira Gershwin, George Gershwin, and Du Bose Heyward, from *Porgy and Bess*, 1935. This operatic and original cast of Afro-Americans, who included the likes of Todd Duncan, Ruby Elzy, Ann Brown, and, among others, Ford Buck, found this whole production a bit odd, as well as its original audiences. What is lasting is, however, its fine music with this title "Summertime" perhaps its very best. Moreover, less operatic contemporary recordings by Bing Crosby and Billie Holiday were excellent. So were numerous later renderings, especially noting those of Mabel Mercer and Ethel Waters in the 1940s and Lena Horne in the 1950s.
- "Supper Time," penned by Irving Berlin, from *As Thousands Cheer*, 1933. Ethel Waters introduced this somber ditty about a lynching, but did not record her heart-wrenching and definitive recording until some fourteen years later. While the oddity of Ethel's later recording remains, it should be noted that a contemporary (Victor)1933 recording WAS rendered by Gertrude Niesen. Indeed Gertrude's 'torch' singing was done well, Ethel's racial identity and (subsequent) original statement on stage is entirely missing, as Gertrude's own 'white' identity is used just only promote another (Irving Berlin) popular standard.
- "There's a Small Hotel," penned by Rodgers and Hart, from *On Your Toes*, 1936. This original cast of Ray Bolger, Doris Carson, and Tamara Geva, among others, contributed far less to this great song ditty may be considered. Among others, a contemporary Paul Whiteman recording, on Victor 25270, featured a good enough vocal by Durelle Alexander, Hildegarde and also a Benny Goodman release that very much hid an excellent vocal by Helen Ward. Moreover, when Bing Crosby recorded it later during WWII, it was sadly a noncommercial V-Disc release on V 700. Luckily, a later definitive rendering by Frank Sinatra (Capital LP W 912) captured it well, and in true retrospective, well into the rock era.
- "You Can't Stop Me from Loving You," penned by Mann Holiner and Alberta Nichols, from *Rhapsody in Black*, 1931. This all-black review starred Ethel Waters, Eloise Uggams, and, among others, Valaida Snow. Ethel Waters, more so, introduced this jazzy ditty on stage, and if her contemporary 1931 recording mirrors her stage performance, this ditty may be perhaps her greatest achievement as a vocalist of much deserved stature.

MUSICAL FILM PICKS (1927-55)

The following films reflect only the opinions of the author of this book. Many of these films are already noted within this book, and many indeed contained a "film" soundtrack. Many films of this era, except for their musical content, are very boring, and many others contain, perhaps, just one ditty for any interest for comment in retrospective. For the purposes of this book, the vocalists, featured in film, seemed to reflect upon contemporary pubic tastes, good, bad, and indifferent. The following film listings are those of full-length films and film shorts. While the interest in recording artists is important, it is more often the case to note that in most cases there is a huge gap between filmed musical sequences and subsequent contemporary recordings. Indeed, the visual image is clear for some and distorted for many.

- ❖ *Full-length* Films. While films may be enjoyable, they all have moments to be quickly forgotten. The following twenty-five picks are noted pieces of musical expressions found in and on films from 1927 through 1955. They especially merit a considerable review. These picks also include what were considered "B" movies, or full-length films made with budget limits.

1. *The Wizard of Oz*, MGM, 1939. As already noted within this book, this childhood dream, with the likes of Judy Garland, among others, cannot be beat. As filmed for the most part in color, Tin-man (Jack Haley), Scarecrow (Roy Bolger), and Lion (Bert Lahr) find munchkins and witches (Margaret Hamilton and Billie Burke). This film is a true feast for the eyes, in black and white and in color, as the myth of Oz as based on L. Frank Baum's novel, is real enough? Did wizard (Frank Morgan) have it so good?

The film score boasts the likes of Harold Arlen and E. Y. Harburg whose song (a) "Over the Rainbow" was introduced by Judy in the film and also translated as a contemporary recording on Decca 2672. Other ditties, like (b) "Ding Dong, the Witch Is Dead," in reality a morbid song ditty, is pure camp-for adults? Another, as the scarecrow's theme (c) "If I Only Had a Brain," is perhaps, a good spoof upon the likes of many, as well as another question for the adults who patronized this film without their kids. (d) "If I Were King of the Forest" found Bert Lahr brave? Yes, he was brave enough to sing this—a song that is so bad, that it's good! (e) "We're Off to See the Wizard" remains a walk! So is (f) "We're Off to See the Wizard." (g) "Come Out. Come Out Wherever You Are," found the "good" witch, Billie Burke being dubbed? Do flying houses kill?

In true retrospective, the likes of the future, in baby boomer television, indeed made this film and, especially, Judy Garland an American icon. Moreover, the later rock era found "Ding Dong the Witch Is Dead" as by the Fifth Estate on Jubilee 5573 in 1967 something to further exploit. Moreover, the title of rocker Elton John's LP *Good-bye Yellow Brick Road* should be followed!

2. *Holiday Inn*, Paramount, 1942. Like *The Wizard of Oz*, this film's (later) exposure on TV finds Bing Crosby and Fred Astaire familiar entities among baby boomers. As a WWII entity, this Irving Berlin score finds the "Song of Freedom" sequence, with Crosby's introduction of Franklin Roosevelt's image and war production, a cheering proposition. By the end of the film, however (finding Bing crooning out "White Christmas" for the second time in the film), it's all the musical sequences which truly make this film a great one. As dubbed by Martha Mear, actress Marjorie Reynolds found "White Christmas" with Bing Crosby as something special in the first filmed sequence. Indeed, this sequence is perhaps the most recognized by later generations of the pre-rock era (with the possible exception of "Somewhere over the Rainbow" with Judy Garland).

As a schmaltzy plot about enterprising entertainers who open a nightclub for various holidays, it all works. New Year's Eve features (a) "Let's Start the New Year Right," with Bing. Lincoln's Birthday features (b) "Abraham" with Bing (in blackface), with no disrespect intended. (Perhaps a group of Afro-American dancers could have been used? In hindsight?) Valentine's Day finds Bing crooning out (c) "Be Careful, It's My Heart." Washington's Birthday features Fred Astaire and Marjorie Reynolds in a dance sequence. Easter finds Bing crooning out (d) "Easter Parade." Independence Day finds Fred in a dance sequence and Bing's already mentioned (e) "Song Of Freedom." (f) "I'll Capture Your Heart" with Bing, Fred Marjorie, and Virginia Dale, could be anytime, all year. So could Crosby's fine renditions of (g) "Lazy," (h) "Happy Holiday," and (i) "Plenty to Be Thankful For."

3. *The Big Broadcast,* Paramount, 1932. As the first of the *Big Broadcast* films, the attempt to gather together the top radio stars of the time (1932) worked. Despite a stupid plot, which is saved by antics of George Burns and (especially) Gracie Allen, the youthful image of Bing Crosby (in his first major film), indeed proved his popularity, especially among women. While his renditions of (a) "Please," (b) "Here Lies Love," and (c) "Dinah" also translated into some fine Brunswick recordings, his radio theme song (d) "Where the Blue of the Night," may also be found to be a major film entity as well. (An earlier film short also found Crosby crooning this popular ditty out). As filmed at the height of the Depression years, this film also captured some of the principal recording and radio entities of the era (1932). While this author does not appreciate "street singer" Arthur Tracy, the others compensate.

They include the following: (e) "When the Moon Comes over the Mountain" and (f) "It Was So Beautiful" by Kate Smith, (g) "Minnie The Moocher" and (h) "Kicking the Gong Around" by Cab Calloway, (i) "Tiger Rag" and (j) "Good-bye Blues" by the Mills Brothers, (k) "Shout Sister, Shout" and (l) "Crazy People" by the Boswell Sisters, and (m) "Trees" by Donald Novis, among others.

It is also interesting to point out that because of the Depression, film revenues had decreased. For those who could afford entertainment, the purchasing of a radio indeed provided more. This film, perhaps, found success in presenting some fine visual images of these radio entities live on film.

4. *Top Hat,* RKO, 1935. Picking the best of the Fred Astaire and Ginger Rogers musicals is not an easy task. As noted elsewhere in the text, Fred and Ginger became popular largely through visual images, and not largely as recording artists. (In true retrospective, Fred's somewhat effeminate vocals were poor attempts compared to the crooners of the early 1930s. Moreover, the contemporary crooners of the time, including Rudy Vallee and Bing himself, did not initially like the term, originally a meaning for vulgarity.) The classy (ballroom) dancer Astaire indeed had an edge. (In the 1920s, his musical stage legacy, with his sister Adele, mingled with British royalty). In any case, his earlier film association with the young and great-looking film talent Ginger Rogers created "real" film chemistry and excitement. This film, with an Irving Berlin score to boot, finds Fred actually pulling of a good vocal with (a) "Cheek To Cheek." Others include (b) "Top Hat, White Tie and Tails," (c) "No Strings," (d) "Isn't This a Lovely Day?," and the fabulous dance and vocal sequence of (e) "The Piccolino" with Ginger.
5. *Gold Diggers of 1933,* Warner Brothers, 1933. As a visual delight, this Busby Berkeley staple of excellence is perhaps, the best of the series of sound Gold Diggers films. (Others included *Gold Diggers of Broadway*, *Gold Diggers of 1935,* and *Gold Diggers of 1937*—all from Warner Brothers studio.) While indeed some scenes included fab visions of seminude showgirls, this film "pick," on the surface, only fits in for the featured recording artists of this book. Penned by Al Dubin and Harry Warren, the song selections to be found in this film did nothing for the featured performers as recording artists. Dick Powell's filmed introductions of (a) "The Shadow Waltz" and (b) "I've Got to Sing a Torch Song" indeed found in Bing Crosby's (Brunswick) recordings, better renditions. Other ditties included Ginger Rogers singing out (c) "We're in the Money" and (d) "My Forgotten Man," as fine vocals as by Etta Moten and Joan Blondell (Joan may be dubbed by Moten as well?), are best remembered as "filmed."
6. *Cabin in the Sky*, MGM, 1943. This tall tale actually is about all sorts of abuse from the more militant Afro-American generation of the later 1960s through the 1970s. In true retrospective, this bit of Americana, adapted from the Broadway play of 1940, as penned by John Latouche, Vernon Duke, Harold Arlen, and E. Y. Harburg, is more than superb. Moreover, as one of the very few all-black, full-length films from a major studio of a racist society, the film should have been applauded. Stereotypes in all communities, indeed, find this film very much a child's dream—as like in the *Wizard of Oz*. (If one looks close, a scene from MGM's *Wizard of Oz* is actually cut in!). This film features Ethel Waters (although old) as well as the likes of many fab Afro-American performers such as the very young and beautiful Lena Horne. Ethel croons out (a) "Cabin in the Sky" with Eddie "Rochester" Anderson, as well as (b) "Taking A Chance on Love," and (c) Happiness Is a Thing Called Joe."(The latter title is not in the original Broadway production.) Lena Horne is given (d) "Life's Full of Consequences" with Eddie "Rochester" Anderson, as well as a reprise of (e) "Honey in the Honeycomb." Other musical sequences featured Ethel with the Hall Johnson Choir on (f) "Li'l Black Sheep," John C. Bublett on (g) "Shine" (with a fab dance routine) and some excellent Duke Ellington music (with Duke himself, to boot). (Louis Armstrong is also in it—but he may be missed—so look hard! Indeed, this waste of Louis is perhaps the only real drawback of this superb film!)

7. *Broadway Through a Keyhole,* United Artists, 1933. As a "gangster," character actor Paul Kelly never did find the fame that James Cagney (also a musical performer), Edward G. Robinson, Humphrey Bogart, or John Garfield had. Nevertheless, this "gangster" flick (as penned by contemporary gossip-newspaper entity Walter Winchell—an important name in 1933) is more than fun. (Winchell, is also "heard" within the film. Some years later, his voice commentary in the latter 1950s television series *The Untouchables* became familiar to many baby boomers). In addition to Kelly and other contemporary big names of the era (including the likes of a real speakeasy proprietor) such as Texas Guinan, Eddy Foy Jr., and Blossom Seeley, this film boasted great-looking Constance Cummings and crooner Russ Columbo. (A very young Lucille Ball may also be spotted in a very minor role).

In any case, this oldie sparks with the familiar tale of greed, betrayal, and (even) decency. More so, the contemporary images of the Depression era, via Hollywood, pursues the likes of the all-too-real types of criminals, whom the cast members, especially Texas Guinan (who may have had real run-ins with New York's reputed mobsters "Irish" Costello and "Dutch" Schultz. All are neatly exploited, with some fine musical sequences that fit perfectly into the story.

Russ croons out (a) "You're My Past, Present, and Future," as well as a well-done duet with Constance (b) "I Love You, Prince Pizzicato," both fine ditties penned by Gordon and Revel. While Eddie Foy Jr. 's (c) "When You Were a Girl on a Scooter and I Was a Boy on a Bike" starts to gets a bit boring, the energy in the film picks it all up. To top it all off, there is a mild but effective try at a Busby Berkley clone, consisting of showgirls led by (platinum blonde) Frances Williams in (d) "Doing the Uptown Lowdown," who cannot help but tease the eyes, however briefly!

8. *Stage Door Canteen*, United Artists, 1943. As one of the (many) WWII films with music, made to directly contribute to the war effort, this film especially stands out. It is certainly not to be considered the usual lighthearted entity made to relieve the war-weary world of that noble struggle against the Axis powers. As a real drama, without actual fighting scenes, this well-written story about servicemen taking a break in a New York canteen (still) rings true. (In fact, canteens were run at low cost or no cost for American service personnel, usually returning from war or waiting to be shipped off to war). The interest in servicemen and servicewomen also includes mention of British, Russian, and Chinese nationalities also attending the canteens and contributing to the reality of the situation—many would not come back. Many would not come back. The reality of such stage and film entities, found in the film, devoting "free" time was indeed true. Moreover, the talents of contemporary (1943) Americana were evident, and they include William Terry, Cheryl Walker, Alfred Lunt, Katherine Cornell, Judith Anderson, Hugh Herbert, Paul Muni, William Demarest, Lynn Fontanne, Helen Hayes, Sam Jaffe, George Jessel, and (among) others—Katherine Hepburn. Indeed, this film merited some serious attention. And more so, it delivered!

The musical sequences are featured as a relief between the interactions of the various war stories. A real and smoky nightclub atmosphere is truly captured. One (still) gets a feeling of sitting back and "being" there. They include the following picks:

1. "Quicksands," by Ethel Waters with the Count Basie Orchestra,
2. "Why Don't You Do Right?," by Peggy Lee with the Benny Goodman Orchestra,
3. "Marching Through Berlin," by Ethel Merman,
4. "The Machine Gun Song," by (Britisher) Gracie Fields, and
5. "She's a Bombshell from Brooklyn," by (hot!) Lina Romay and the Xavior Cugat Orchestra.

Other antics include the likes of Kay Kyser and Orchestra, along with Sully Mason, Harry Babbit, along with others such as Edgar Bergan and Charlie McCarthy, as well as a Gypsy Rose Lee striptease, which is just a tease!

9. *Flying Down to Rio*, RKO, 1933. This film introduced Fred Astaire and Ginger Rogers as a screen duo, below the starring contemporaries (Latino) Dolores Del Rio and Gene Raymond. The magnetism of Fred and Ginger is a solid reason for the highly visual dance and song sequence of (a) "The Carioca." But so is its introduction as by (Afro-American) Etta Moten and Dolores Del Rio herself. As perhaps the longest dance sequence ever filmed, featuring many performers, the artistic results are still astounding. Also found in the film are (b) "Music Makes Me" (as by Ginger), and a weak vocal as by Fred on (c.) "Flying Down To Rio," which is compensated by the well-staged visual of a bunch of showgirls standing on airplanes, high in the air! See it! Believe it!
10. *Stormy Weather*, Twentieth Century Fox, 1943. For the most part, stupid film plots find musical sequences saving films. Unlike most other films of the era (1943), this major production featuring Afro-Americans is exceptional. As a pinup girl, Lena Horne (like Betty Grable), found an eager WWII audience. As the exception to the rule, this film is not stopped by racism and also centers on Lena's (considerable) musical talents. She is also assisted by the likes of some other fine Afro-American entities (as she was in *Cabin in the Sky*). Unlike *Cabin*, this film is less than the Broadway entity. Like other musicals of its era, the film also had its old standards, new renditions. Luckily, the resulting film works as Lena is, moreover, supported by the likes of dancers Katherine Dunham, the Nicholas Brothers, Ada Brown Fats Waller, and, among others, her other star—Bill "Bojangles" Robinson himself.

Musical sequences include

1. "There's No Two Ways about Love" with Lena, Robinson, and Calloway,
2. "Diga Diga Do" with Lena,
3. "Honeysuckle Rose," with Fats Waller reintroducing his own 1928 Broadway entity, in a very long and exhausting dance sequence "Jumping Jive"(with the Nicholas Brothers and Cab Calloway),
4. "That Ain't Right" with Ada Brown with Fats Waller, and
5. the film's own title and clincher, Lena's fabulous visual singing of "Stormy Weather."

11. *Meet Danny Wilson*, Universal International, 1952. Frank Sinatra, Shelly Winters, Raymond Burr, and Alex Nicol starred in this "gangster" yarn. When released, this film did not gel (as expected) as a box office entity. Frank's personal (divorce) problems may have influenced a negative reaction from the public. This film, in true retrospective,

had an eye for future generations. It is certainly better than his previous films. While his recording career at Capital was yet to be defined, the Sinatra film career and his visual appeal is defined in this flick. Sinatra had matured. Indeed, by 1952, and while shedding his "skinny" image, Frank's attention to his craft is impeccable. More so, as an actor involved in a somewhat shoddy film plot, he somehow lifts the story effectively. To be fair, so does the fine acting of Shelly Winters and Raymond Burr. (Raymond Burr—before he was television's "Perry Mason"). Frank's fine singing included the following standards: (a) "All Of Me," (b) "You're a Sweetheart," (c) "I've Got a Crush on You," (d) "Lonesome Man Blues," (e) "She's Funny That Way," (f) "How Deep Is the Ocean," and (g) a fine duet with Shelly in "A Good Man Is Hard to Find" (indeed the very old Marion Harris acoustic entity).

12. *The Road to Rio*, Paramount, 1948. Bing Crosby, Bob Hope, and Dorothy Lamour are in top form. Highlights include Bing Crooning out (a) "But Beautiful" (also a fine Decca recording), and (b) "You Don't Have to Know the Language" (with Bing and the Andrews Sisters), which is also seen and done well.
13. *Applause*, Paramount, 1929. This film is initially for the eyes, with creative camera work by director Rouben Mamoulian. Shots of older beefy-legged chorus girls, as well as some younger ladies exposing lots of fleshy skin are hard to miss. So are close-up visuals of sweaty, often rough and seedy male patrons, many with ugly, distorted faces as well as minds. Also hard to miss are overhead visual shots of burlesque chorus lines, a propeller airplane, and the sights of 1929 New York City. This film, more so, exposes the more realistic aspects of burlesque and vaudeville circuits, thriving in the era between 1910 and 1929. This film is far from "happy." Anyone looking for a smile will be looking a long while.

At this time, Helen Morgan, about twenty-nine years old, fresh from her triumphant vocals in *Show Boat*, was at the high point of her career. Just why she chose to play on older, middle-aged, and fading burlesque entity for this film is hard to figure. Her successful art of singing, upon a white piano, is missing in this film. Indeed, her current 1929 song ditty (a) "What Wouldn't I Do for That Man," while featured in this film, finds her singing it without backup and it sounds fragmented. As a matter of fact, the whole film lacks any dynamic musical scenes, although there is plenty of music, risqué dancing, and music. There is also a jazzy dance band featured, but it is unidentified and sadly without a vocal. The excellent acting from everyone concerned, including Joan Peers—who played her young mostly convent-raised daughter—did not include competing vocal talents. Another song ditty (as by D. Morse and J. Burke), (b) "Give Your Baby Lots Of Love" is featured in fragments throughout the film, and again, despite the lack of emphasis, Helen's melodious vocal shines through. (Sadly, Helen never recorded this ditty) Indeed, this hard-bitten musical perhaps could have concocted at least one better crafted musical sequence for Helen, although, as it is—it's still a brilliant film. Helen's odd choice of a film is moreover an exposure of her own fine acting abilities. She indeed pulls this one off! (A better, contemporary rendition of "What Wouldn't I Do for That Man," with the classy Helen Morgan seen and heard on a white piano may be found in another 1929 film *Glorifying the American Girl.*

14. *Easter Parade*, MGM, 1948. Judy Garland never needed anyone to carry a film. Teamed with Fred Astaire, moreover, this film does not dump it all upon her. Highlights of this Irving Berlin-penned score include (a) "Better Luck Next Time"(as by Judy), (b) "A Couple of Swells," (as by Judy and Fred), (c) "A Fella with an Umbrella" (with Judy

and Peter Lawford), (d) "When the Midnight Choo Choo Leaves for Alabam'"(as by Judy and Fred), (e) "Beautiful Faces Need Beautiful Clothes" (as with Judy and Fred), and, among others, (f) "Easter Parade," (as by Judy and Fred). Indeed, this old song from Irving Berlin and schmaltz never looked or sounded so well in a film! It's all because of Judy?

15. *Going Hollywood*, MGM, 1933. This flaky film plot with Marion Davies is for the most part made up by Bing Crosby's crooning (a) "Our Big Love Scene," (b) "Temptation," (c) "Beautiful Girl," (d) "After Sundown," (e) "We'll Make Hay While the Sun shines," and the title ditty (f) "Going Hollywood." All were penned for the film as by Arthur Freed and Nacio Herb Brown. All were also huge successes as Brunswick recordings, except for "Going Hollywood," which, for some odd reason, was not recorded or released. It was, however, to be bootlegged off the film soundtrack in the 1930s!
16. *Hallelujah*, MGM, 1929. As an Afro-American entity, this film is among the very rare featured films. As a siren of casual living, Nina Mae McKinney brings down the religious Daniel L. Hayes in almighty and biblical fashion. To be sure, (a) "Swanee Shuffle" (as by Nina Mae) is a fine bit of the "jazz age" simmering with outrage. While stereotypes are found galore, the grim aspects of rural southern life are somewhat truthful. Another Irving Berlin-penned ditty, (b) "Waiting at the End of the Road," is found in the film as by the Dixie Jubilee Singers. (A contemporary Ethel Waters Columbia recording of this ditty was a best seller. So was a Columbia Paul Whiteman release with a Bing Crosby vocal.) Another ditty, identified by the author of this book as (c) "E. I. O." as wailed out as by blues entity Victoria Spivey also ain't bad.
17. *Follow the Fleet*, RKO, 1936. With this likes of Fred Astaire and Ginger Rogers, it's hard not to pick this one. Nor are the added weight of Irving Berlin' s writing abilities for film songs. Nor are the acting abilities of Everett Horton (a familiar voice found in Bullwinkle cartoon flicks in 1960s television). Harriet Hillard (later Mrs. Ozzie Nelson, mother of Ricky and David, later TV icons) sang (a)" Get Thee Behind Me Satan" and (b) "But Where Are You?" Others in this (1936) film included Randolph Scott (later to be best known for his Western films), Betty Grable (late a major film entity), Tony Martin (later a major recording entity with some film work, and Lucille Ball (the later TV icon). Like many stupid film plots of the era (or any era), the fine character actors found between musical sequences, gel. (c) "Let's Face the Music and Dance" finds Fred's vocal, with Ginger's dancing, a winner. The same may be found with (d) "I'm Putting All My Eggs in One Basket." Another ditty, (e) "Let Yourself Go," finds Ginger's vocal, along with a dance sequence with Fred, yet another example of screen perfection. (No sweat?)
18. *Pennies from Heaven*, Columbia, 1936. It is a fine Crosby Depression-era film with Decca recordings that were even better. Bing even gets a little serious, for a while. While this thin plot does indeed wear thin by its end, this story about an ex-convict's surviving family ain't bad. It also includes Louis Armstrong belting out (a) "Skeleton in the Closet," more so a big deal in 1936. Bing also croons out (b) "One, Two Button Your Shoe," (c) "So Do I," and the title itself (d) "Pennies from Heaven."
19. *The Blue Angel*, Ufa, 1930. While this film breaks a rule (not being made in the United States, it must be considered the best exception to the rule.) This pre-Hitler (German) production found a version made for English-speaking audiences, and, as luck would have it, it introduced Marlene Dietrich to the rest of the world. The cool fire of her personality, as an actress and vocalist, indeed finds her rendition of (a) "Naughty Lola" creating much excitement. This ditty, as well as (b) "Falling in Love Again," work themselves very well into the seductive and serious story line of the film. (Marlene's

contemporary Victor recordings of these ditties are also very good). The music heard in this film also note, in true retrospective, the huge European influences upon the popular music found in the United States.

20. *Bright Eyes*, Fox Studios, 1934. For most of the 1930s, a little actress, considered a midget by some, somehow sang and danced her way into the American idiom, with the full merits of the tough Depression-era box office. This film, moreover, featured "On the Good Ship Lollipop," as penned by Sidney Clare and Richard Whiting, with Shirley Temple teaching all the adults around her just what charisma is.
21. *365 Nights in Hollywood*, Fox Studio, 1934. As an aspiring Hollywood starlet, Alice Faye is a beautiful young woman who needs a break. While actor James Dunn provides her one, Alice convincingly croons out the effective and original ditties penned by Richard Whiting and Sidney Clare (a) "Yes to You" and (b) "My Future Star." Moreover, the likes of Hollywood are to be seen and heard and, more so, become a pleasant bit of glitz, with her early platinum blonde image, perhaps patterned by Jean Harlow? (Alice's own 1934 contemporary recording of "Yes to You" on Romeo 2407 is done very well).
22. *Roaring Twenties*, Warner Brothers, 1939. This gangster flick from 1939, as penned by Mark Hollinger, was possibly based upon the real life of New York City's reputed mobster Larry Fay. While the musical sequences are found to be limited, they are most effective. While the likes of James Cagney, Humphrey Bogart, and Paul Kelly do not sing, actress Pricilla Lane, formerly part of a vocal sister act with contemporary bandleader Fred Waring (who had been in the business back in the 1920s), does sing—and very well! Her vocals on "I'm Just Wild about Harry," "Melancholy Baby," and "It Had to Be You," all 1920s' standards, sparkle. She, more so, looks and sounds much like the young Ruth Etting did in the 1920s. Gladys George, another actress in the film, also performs a very good version of "In a Shanty in Old Shanty Town." Perhaps the term "Roaring Twenties" started with this well-done Warner Brothers flick? While this 1939 retrospective film was not far off in years, a later Warner Brothers television series, of the same name, was. As launched in 1960, that it was essentially the same product of the earlier film became evident to those who had seen it. This well-produced TV series found great success with many baby boomers and their elders. So did the vocals of twenty-three-year-old contract actress Dorothy Provine, singing many of the old standards very well. (Dorothy also found recording success, generating two best-selling 12-inch albums, consisting of the old standards she presented in the series. In the age of rock and roll? Yes.)
23. *The Phantom Empire*, Mascot Pictures, 1934. This Gene Autry serial flick was pre-Flash Gordon. While Buster Crabb and the latter-century antics of Harrison Ford and others were dazzling, this guitar-playing Hollywood cowboy somehow got lost in inner space—for twelve episodes! The obvious quirkiness is awful but remains oddly interesting. Gene battles crooks with ray guns and helps destroy an atom-smashing machine. Was this all far-fetched in 1934? What about television? He also crooned out some junk (a) "Uncle Noah's Ark" (so bad, it's good) along with his fine classic (b) "That Silver Haired Daddy Of Mine." Was this a cultural event?
24. *College Humor*, Paramount, 1933. This flaky story line had at least some good comic relief (George Burns and Gracie Allen). It also featured some fine song ditties, which figured huge in Bing Crosby's recording career. It is for sure that Bing's Brunswick recordings of (a) "Down the Old Ox Road," (b) "Moonstruck," and (c) "Learn to Croon" are matched in this contemporary film (1933). So is an added rendition of his earlier Victor release (d) "I Surrender, Dear." While "image" is everything in

Hollywood, it is interesting to note Bing's own parody of himself so early in his career. It somehow all works!

25. *Princess Tam Tam* (made in France), 1935. This French feature film had nothing to do with the American Hollywood film industry except for perhaps some borrowed techniques of camera work and most likely from the influential Bushy Berkley? It is a simple tale about a dispute between a married French couple separating and both of them liking elsewhere, which includes an African trip and a hookup with a young and very beautiful black woman, who was also a bit of a thief. She is, moreover, transformed into something more, as she is brought back to France, as bait. As far as this author can find out, this film did not have an English language version, and the copy which was inspected had subtitles in English, which may or may not have been originally used.

What does make this film look a bit smarter than it is, is the beautiful image of American-born Josephine Baker. Though this film does not exploit the wildness of Josephine's nude dancing and singing in Paris some ten years earlier in *Revue Nègre*, this film does exploit her (still) great looks and body. In addition to her skimpy outfits, her caricature is used and seen—as it is artfully injected into the film—as many white women were. Moreover, and unlike all contemporary American (Hollywood) films, this film banked on Josephine's (black) appeal for mostly (French) white audiences, who couldn't get enough of seeing her. Apart from some exotic dance sequences by Baker, she manages to croon out (in French) "Neath the Tropical Blue Skies" and "Dream Ship." Who needs to know French?

Film Shorts. Perhaps the "short" films, in true retrospective, ellipses must full-length films. Much of the creativity discovered in many of these cheaply produced films was due more so to budget restraints. Subsequently, numerous high-powered musical performances resulted, providing much delight for the ear and the eye. Included as "shorts" are selected cartoon features, featuring very legit musical numbers.

1. *Boogie-Woogie Dream,* a Leslie Winik Production (1944). This "dream" is so real that it makes one wonder if this film were full-length, would it be as good. It is, more so, an independent production! While the talents of Teddy Wilson's Orchestra, Albert Ammons, and Pete Johnson are enough for a great musical, the electric vocals of a young and glamorous-looking Lena Horne are explosive! Indeed, her seemingly spontaneous rendition of (a) "Unlucky Woman" more so remains as hot and sultry as when first seen and heard! Lena's (b) "Out of Nowhere," is also good. Moreover, this well-crafted screen plot about an aspiring would-be band singer is truly creditable and creative. Probably filmed in New York City in 1941 and released in 1944?
2. *Rufus Jones for President*, Vitaphone (1933). This "dream" is pure camp. Its use of stereotypes is easy to point out, but its limitations are unrealized. The huge unlikely aspect of an Afro-American becoming president in 1933 was, indeed, a dream, as well as a fact. Moreover, this film finds Ethel Waters at the height of her career. Her rendition of (a) "Am I Blue?" (which she had introduced on film in the earlier 1929 film *On with the Show*) is almost wasted, but interesting. Her subsequent belting out of (b) "Underneath the Harlem Moon" is superb, even without smoking weed! Sammy Davis Jr. (about seven years old) in his film debut seems to take it all in—and indeed does a fine job. His dancing and vocals, especially on (c) "You Rascal You" and (d) "I Do, I Do" are pure camp and not to be overlooked!

3. *St. Louis Blues*, Alfred Sack Amusement Enterprises (1929). Bessie Smith's visual (despite poor camera work) creates a stir, as the theme of *St. Louis Blues* is exploited to the fullest. Her tough image is especially noted in realistic bar scenes and remains a sight and sound to see and hear! The original credits also note the participation of both W. C. Handy (author of this already famous song ditty), along with Rosamond Johnson, two of the most important and contemporary Afro-Americans of their time.
4. *I Surrender Dear*, Educational Films (1931). This stupid plot, as part of Hollywood slapstick master Mack Sennett's production somehow survives. Its early images of Bing Crosby capture his youth and brilliance as a musical entity. Song ditties include those that would define him as a solo artist. They include (a) "I Surrender Dear"(also a Victor recording), (b) "Out of Nowhere," and (c) "At Your Command." These were also to become excellent contemporary recordings for Brunswick.
5. *The House I Live In*, MGM (1945). This well-crafted script finds Frank Sinatra explaining to a group of kids what it meant to be an American—obviously filmed during WWII. Moreover, his meaningful vocal of "The House I Live In" is (still) very much felt, in true retrospective.
6. *Sympathy in Black,* Paramount (1935). As written by Duke Ellington himself, this serious focus upon Afro-American culture remains a masterpiece of social and musical comment. For certain, the talents of Freddie Washington are appreciated. Much more should be appreciated in "A Hymn of Sorrow," which finds an (unaccredited) Billie Holiday effectively wailing out some soulful lyrics.
7. *The Black Network*, Vitaphone (1936). While this contrived plot is just OK, the musical sequences are very good. The Nicholas Brothers sing "Lucky Number" as well as dance. Among others, the true highlight of this film finds Nina Mae McKinney dressed to kill. Indeed, she smokes up the screen with her rendition of "Half of Me."
8. *Bundle of Blues*, Vitaphone (1933). In 1933, Duke Ellington and his Orchestra found themselves backing Ethel Waters in New York's Cotton Club. It was at this Cotton Club gig that Ethel introduced Harold Arlen's ditty "Stormy Weather." Ethel's hit contemporary recording, however, had been backed by the (unaccredited) Dorsey Brothers. (A later Ethel Waters radio appearance with Duke Ellington on this ditty, however, does exist). As understudy to Ethel, and band singer for Duke Ellington, Ivie Anderson found much applause for her rendition as well. This film finds a creative attempt by Ivie and Duke. It is also interesting to compare this low-budget attempt with Lena Horne's later (1943) full-length film rendition in *Stormy Weather*.
9. *Be Like Me*, Vitaphone (1931). This very early look at Ethel Merman is tough as a bar entity; she effectively belts out the title "Be Like Me" and "After You've Gone" as well as any blues singer. The quirky plot, however thin, is lifted and works.
10. *Pie, Pie Blackbird*, Vitaphone (1932). This fantasy, which originally was meant for Nina Mae McKinney as a small Broadway entity somehow found its way to the screen. Musical genius Eubie Blake is seen and heard leading his band and crooning out "You Rascal You." Moreover a fabulous-looking Nina Mae McKinney finds herself blurting out "Everything I've Got Belongs to You." The Nicholas Brothers are also found dancing very fast—so fast that they burn up the pie!
11. *Star Night at the Coconut Grove*, Paramount (1934). As one of two of these reviewed film shorts filmed in color, this glitzy tour of the Hollywood of the mid-1930s finds film stars galore. As master of ceremonies, Leo Carrillo (known to millions of baby boomers later as "Pancho" in the *Cisco Kid* television series indeed finds a mouthful of stars and starlets to introduce. When he got to Mary Pickford (already old and a screen legend), she in turn introduced Bing Crosby. Bing's crooning job on "With Every Breath I Take" is superb. It also makes the rest of this nonsense worth the wait.

12. *Record Making With Duke Ellington*, Paramount (1936). A serious look at the actual record-making process in 1936, using the "Variety" record label. Ivie Anderson's vocal on "Oh Babe, Maybe Someday" is both seen and heard.
13. *The Singing Brakeman*, Columbia (1929). This early look at Jimmie Rodgers decked out in a (train) brakeman's uniform is interesting enough. It is, moreover, more than a coffee break at a rural train stop that Jimmie may be seen and heard strumming out upon a guitar and crooning a yodel out upon the likes of the blues for (a) "Waiting for a Train," (b) "Daddy and Home," and (c) "Blue Yodel-T for Texas."
14. *La Fiesta of Santa Barbara*, MGM (1935). This odd bit of contrived Hollywood spin of Mexican and Spanish culture somehow works. In addition to the likes of Leo Carillio, Buster Keaton, Gary Cooper, and Gilbert Rolland, among others, this color film also exploits the likes of "singing cowboy" Joe Morrison (whose recording for the George Olson Orchestra "The Last Round Up" on Columbia-2791-D is redone.) After patiently hearing and seeing his very famous Western ditty, written by Bostonian Billy Hill and also recorded as by Bing Crosby and Gene Autry, the wait is well worth it. While the author of this book has not kept up on Spanish, a fine ditty about cockroaches is soon to be seen and heard. As indeed sung in Spanish "La Cucaracha," the song of the cockroach, is found to be good rhythmic harmony as by the Gumm Sisters or Garland Sisters (Judy and her sisters).
15. *I'm Glad You're Dead You Rascal You*, Dave Fleischer Cartoon, Paramount (1932). Fleischer's creativity in early animation survives very well. Louis Armstrong and his band (at the height of his recording career), are seen and heard in actual film as well as in an animated segment. Unlike a contemporary (all) film short, this cartoon very much succeeds in presenting Louis's fine vocal on "I'm Glad You're Dead You Rascal You," also a contemporary Louis Armstrong Okeh recording.
16. *Snow White*, Dave Fleischer Cartoon, Paramount (1933). This should not be confused with the excellent and operatic (1938) Walt Disney film. Fleischer's cartoon entity Betty Boop found much popular interest in the early 1930s. A dispute about her vocal (between Helen Kane and Mae Questre) was at one time news, but that's another story. In any case, this cartoon also featured Cab Calloway's vocal of his contemporary Brunswick recording "St. James Infirmary" in animation, as well as a fine (filmed) look at his actual band.
17. *When It's Sleepy Time Down South*, Dave Fleischer Cartoon, Paramount (1932). The Boswell Sisters are featured in animation as well as in film crooning out this title.
18. *Radio Rhythm*, Paramount (1929). This Rudy Vallee farce succeeds in capitalizing on his huge radio audiences. While stiff, Rudy's flare for comic timing serves him well. Apart from crooning out a bit of one of his recordings "A Little Kiss Each Morning," he gets together with Mae Questre on "Don't Take Her Pooh Pooh Poo Doo Away" in an attempt at humor that works. For sure, it's a "live" Betty Boop" that moreover livens things up for Rudy!
19. *A Rhapsody in Black And Blue*, Paramount (1932). This Louis Armstrong version of "I'm Glad You're Dead, You Rascal, You" is better found in the Fleischer cartoon short of the same name. As yet another "dream" sequence however, his vocal of "Shine," also a contemporary Okeh recording, does stir some excitement.
20. *That Goes Double*, Vitaphone (1933). As a rare Russ Columbo entity, this slow-moving feature also contained a bit of old-time vaudeville. As Russ is called to "double" for himself, the split screen is evidence that Russ just may be a parody of himself. While the "real" Russ is identified in a tuxedo, he croons out a few of his standards "My Love" and "Prisoner of Love" very effectively. It is, moreover, an iffy ending that clinches it that turns out to (even) be a bit humorous.

- Ten more fine musical moments featured in any films (1927-50) which are lifted by these vocal performances in otherwise fair musical productions or nonmusical productions are as follows:

21. *The Jazz Singer* (1927) finds Al Jolson belting out (most) of "Blue Skies" in the first talkie.
22. *On With The Show* (1929) finds slick Ethel Waters introducing "Am I Blue?"
23. *The Big Pond* (1930) finds Maurice Chevalier (more that once) introducing "You Brought a New Kind of Love to Me."
24. *Reaching for the Moon* (1930) finds Bing Crosby jazzing up "When the Folks High-UP Do The Mean Low Down."
25. *Blue of the Night* (1932) finds Bing Crosby crooning out "Auf Wiedersehen, My Dear."
26. *Marie Galante* (1934) finds Helen Morgan introducing "Song of a Dreamer."
27. *Swing While You're Able* (1937). Pinky Tomlin introduces "I'm Gonna Swing While I'm Able."
28. *Buck Privates* (1941). The Andrews Sisters introduce "Boogie-Woogie Bugle Boy."
29. *Reveille With Beverly* (1943), Betty Roche's vocal with Duke Ellington in "Take the 'A' Train."
30. *Hollywood Canteen* (1944) finds Roy Rogers introducing "Don't Fence Me In."

- Five notable musical performances as by unlikely performers with very good results are as follows:

31. "Thanks for the Memory," by Bob Hope and Shirley Ross in *The Big Broadcast of 1938*. (A contemporary recording, also by Hope and Ross, on Decca 2219, is gem, and more amazingly in true retrospective, an original "B" side.)
32. "Lydia the Tattooed Lady," by Groucho Marx in the 1939 movie *At the Circus*. As a contemporary recording, a version by Rudy Vallee, on Decca 2708, is done well, noting Vallee's own usual attraction to novelty. In comparison, moreover, Groucho's vocal performance remains a curious triumph, and, more so, a huge lift to an otherwise dumb film.
33. "Old-Time Religion," by Walter Brennan in *Sergeant York*, 1941. This traditional spiritual had been around for many years. Perhaps, an already old acoustic version by the Tuskegee Institute Singers, on Victor 18075, an indeed rare Afro-American vocal release for its pre-1920 time had prompted Warner Brothers to add this ditty to the screenplay, considering its traditional folk entity and its adaptable release during the actual WWI era, where the real Alvin C. York from rural Tennessee lived. (Gary Cooper played the title role.) The catchy tune was perfect. More so was quirky actor Brennan, totally committed in his "preacher" role! Indeed, his enthusiastic vocal, seen and heard in the film, is believable and special! Seeing is believing!
34. "They're Either Too Young or Too Old," by Bette Davis in *Thank Your Lucky Stars*, 1943. A somewhat contemporary Jimmy Dorsey release, with a fine Kitty Kallen vocal, on Decca 18571, is also good, although the (nonvocalist) actress Bette Davis still scores with a somber, poignant vocal (even above the Kallen vocal).
35. "As Time Goes By," by Dooley Wilson in *Casablanca*, 1942. Actor and Afro-American Dooley Wilson had scored on Broadway, but this truly pleasant surprise of his vocal truly contributed to the film's subsequent success and, moreover, became its theme. (More information about this ditty is found in the 'Broadway' section of this text).

- ♦ Five most overrated musical films are given below. (Some of these films did win contemporary approval, in critical notices of their time, or of box office success. In true retrospective, however, in competition with other contemporary reviewed films of this book, for various reasons, they are given a more critical eye.)

36. *Singing in the Rain*, MGM (1952). Gene Kelly's own singing and dancing in *Singing in the Rain*, adapted from the older (1929) hit is done well, but so what?
37. *Here Come the Waves*, Paramount (1944). Bing Crosby and Betty Hutton had star power, but this film mostly fails. Moreover, despite the fine contemporary song ditty "Accent on the Positive," the usual production value of such a major release simply sucks. (The contemporary Crosby and missing Andrews Sisters recording, more so, succeeds! So does a contemporary Johnny Mercer version, which was just half as good as the Crosby-Andrews Sisters recording!)
38. *The Great Ziegfeld*, MGM (1936). Despite some great visual shots and good acting from William Powell, Luise Rainer, Myrna Loy, and, among others, Frank Morgan, the musical talents of Fanny Brice (performing some of "My Man"), Ray Bolger, and either Dennis Morgan or Allen Jones (in a possible dubbing) are more than a bit hard to follow, as this film is at least four hours long. Indeed, this film does induce sleep! This story of Florenz Ziegfeld, while ably acted by William Powell, was actually more interesting than this. He indeed expanded the American theater, successfully using the talents of many, as well as provided, perhaps, the first use of (acceptable) soft-core porn, with a creative touch of nudity on stage. The Hugh Hefner of his day? Or was it rival Broadway producer George White?
39. Perhaps a look at a previous (Paramount) 1929 film *Glorifying the American Girl*, which actually involved the real Florenz Ziegfeld, before he died, merits a close look. As an ambitious project, this early talkie about the ambitions of a young flapper, Mary Eaton, is real enough. Her fair vocals are OK, noting a short and peppy version of (a) "Baby Face," as penned by Harry Akst and Benny Davis, is her best. She is, more so, a dancer, who overcomes her grabby dancing partner, and her exploitive and almost evil money-minded sellout mother. She also loses out in her real love life to fame, which is perhaps fair. What was wrong with all this are poor production values that distract the viewer from Eaton's beautiful body! The (1929) use of lighting, dialog, and even a few color shots are primitive and hard to follow. While the later *The Great Ziegfeld* solved all the technical problems (after Flo died), it is suspect that such great visuals had really existed? Yet, perhaps this earlier 1929 film is a bit more accurate, and honest? Did real audiences in theaters put up with a lot of heat or cold? Bad lighting and hard listening (before microphones) sometimes made it "live" and well?

What at least saves much of this earlier film, besides the antics of Eddie Cantor, is the inclusion of Rudy Vallee, stiffly crooning out (b) "I'm Just a Vagabond Lover," and Helen Morgan's torch rendering of (c) "What Wouldn't I Do for That Man?" Indeed, both Rudy and Helen are captured at the height of their fame in 1929. More so, remembering its limitations, viewing this flick may find contemporizes such as the (real) Flo and his real (last) wife Billie Burke (later of *Wizard of Oz* fame), as Jimmy Walker and wife (mayor of New York City), Irving Berlin (songwriter), Texas Guinan (entertainer and speakeasy owner) and others, including film honcho Adolph Zukor.

40. *The King of Jazz*, Universal, 1930. This early and color film finds Paul Whiteman in good form along with his Rhythm Boys Bing Crosby, Al Rinker, and Harry Barris; band members Joe Venuti, Eddie Lang, and the Brox Sisters; and actor John Boles. New song ditties introduced in the film include the following: (a) "A Bench in the Park," penned by Yellen and Ager and performed by the Brox Sisters, the sisters G (another girl group chorus), and the Rhythm Boys, is vocally clever enough, with a risqué setting. (b) "Happy Feet," also penned by Yellen and Ager is a typical peppy Whiteman jazz number with the Rhythm Boys and a lot dancing feet as seen and heard in the film. (c) The upbeat "I Like to Do Things for you," yet another ditty penned by Yellen and Ager, works well in the film for the Rhythm Boys. (d) "It Happened in Monterey," as penned by Billy Rose and Mabel Wayne, featured a fair vocal by actor John Boles. (e) "Song of the Dawn," another ditty penned by Yellen and Ager was also performed in the film by John Boles. It was, more so, decided to add some previous Whiteman material (with the Rhythm Boys) to the soundtrack, performing (f) the silly "So the Blackbirds and the Bluebirds Got Together" and the very good (g) "Mississippi Mud," indeed finding Crosby, Rinker, and Barris in top form! Also performed and resurrected was Whiteman's instrumental of Gershwin's *Rhapsody in Blue*, which Whiteman had introduced in the (already) gone acoustic age and more so in the silent era of film. As seen in the film, Whiteman is seen on a huge piano, with changing screen sequences dazzling in rare (early) color process along with added cartoons brilliantly added, as pioneered by Walter Lantz.

While all this produced some very creative moments and camera angles, it also noted its own obvious (dated) flaws in production. Mostly boring? Sleep-inducing? Or maybe the inclusion of "Oswald The Lucky Rabbit" (originally with Walt Disney and Ub Iwerks, then currently with Walter Lantz) was too short? Yet this film's appeal, in true retrospective, is its historical moments with great performers. (Off the set, mythology has it that the alcoholic antics of Bing Crosby put him in jail, with actor John Boles bumped up into introducing the awful "The Song of The Dawn" in the film. Indeed, a more interesting yarn than the film!)

- ♦ The ten worst. Do they really suck? While many who read this may consider some of the picks noted above belonging to this list, it is also hard to judge the very worst, noting there were so many! Nevertheless, the following films, full-length and film shorts included, are found to have limited, or flawed, misdirected use of musical talents. They, more so, produced nothing, in true retrospective, for musical entities who appeared within them.

41. *Rio Rita*, Radio Recorders (1929). This major Broadway success of Flo Ziegfeld starred Babe Daniels, John Boles, Dorothy Lee, and, among others, the antics of Bert Wheeler and Robert Woolsey. In reality, not even the risqué humor of Wheeler and Woolsey can save this garbage! (Later, in 1942, Abbot and Costello, with Kathryn Grayson, John Carroll, Tom Conway, and others remade this film at RKO. While it's better than the first, so what?) Abbot—not on first!
42. *Free and Easy*, MGM (1930). While Buster Keaton was indeed a comic genius, this so-called major musical of its time, with Anita Page and Robert Montgomery, is far from humorous.

43. *Meet the Boyfriend*, Paramount (1931)? Lillian Roth's vocal abilities are noticed, as well as her own good-looking frame of a body. After this, the whole film, along with its dumb title are apparent. Apart from an unidentified male quartet, this college setting finds Roth's lament about her boyfriend Jimmy more than juvenile! While her fairly good vocal on "I'm So Unhappy Without You" (a guess) should have saved it, her forced and unfunny antics, seen and heard with her very stupid-looking boyfriend, Jimmy, on "Me and My Boyfriend Jimmy" is truly nauseating.
44. *San Antonio Rose*, Universal (1941). The talents of Jane Frazee, Eve Arden, Shemp Howard (of *The Three Stooges*), and others fail to make the Bob Will's-penned hit a filmed memory.
45. *Singapore Sue*, Paramount (1931)? This short subject had possibilities, with contemporary (Chinese American) Anna Chang along with Joe Wong and Pickard's Chinese Syncopators. Set in a bar in Singapore, Anna is cast as a bar maid who can tease sailors, who include among them British actor (Cary Grant) in perhaps his first film role. While Anna's own crooning job on "How Can a Gal Say No?" is OK, Jo Wong's horrid vocal on "Open up Those Eyes" (?) and subsequent duet with Anna, ruins everything. Moreover, Anna's vocal fails to lift anything in the film that includes a surprisingly bad acting job by Grant! Junk or junk? It's all "Wong," or all wrong?
46. *Puddin' Head*, Republic (1941). Led by Judy Canova, this film's title should have been a problem! While American censors did not pick upon it, British folks did and changed its title as *Judy Goes to Town*. While Judy Canova was no slouch, it's more than unfortunate that this film lives up to its own title! Is this, more so, a pun on Mark Twain? Get it?
47. *Yolanda and the Thief*, MGM (1945). This highbrow attempt at creativity with Fred Astaire was perhaps an embarrassment. The great Astaire perhaps never sweat, except when this lavish attempt at creative expression became more of a sleeping pill.
48. *Good News*, MGM (1947). The news is all bad. June Allison and Pete Lawford make it all not happen!
49. *The Kissing Bandit*, MGM (1948). This title, in itself, is a warning! The good cast, including Frank Sinatra, Katherine Grayson, Ann Miller, Cyd Charisse, and Ricardo Montalban, among others, fail to liven things up!
50. *Minstrel Man*, PCR (1944). Benny Fields, Gladys George, Molly Lamont, and others find "blackface" performances fun! In true retrospective, while racism was still very much rampant in 1944, so were poor musical performances.

ASSORTED FILMED GOODIES (1927-55)

➢ Filmed song ditties noted above are listed by year. Additional titles *not* noted above are mentioned within other parts of the text of this book.

- "Blue Skies," Al Jolson in *The Jazz Singer*, 1927.
- "My Man," Fannie Brice in *My Man*, 1928.
- "If You Want the Rainbow," Fannie Brice in *My Man*, 1928.
- "Singing in the Rain," Cliff Edwards in *Hollywood Revue of 1929*.
- "Am I Blue?," Ethel Waters in *On with the Show*, 1929.
- "Birmingham Bertha," Ethel Waters in *On with the Show*, 1929.
- "Waiting at the End of the Road," Dixie Jubilee Singers in *Hallelujah*, 1929.
- "Swanee Shuffle," Nina Mae McKinney in *Hallelujah*, 1929.
- "E I U," Victoria Spivey in *Hallelujah*, 1929.
- "Waiting for a Train," Jimmie Rodgers in *The Singing Brakesman*, 1929
- "Daddy and Home," Jimmie Rodgers in *The Singing Brakesman*, 1929.
- "Blue Yodel-T For Texas," Jimmie Rodgers. in *The Singing Brakesman*, 1929.
- "How Am I to Know?" Russ Columbo (unaccredited) in *Dynamite*, 1929.
- "Tiptoe Through the Tulips," Nick Lucas in *Gold Diggers of Broadway*, 1929.
- "Painting the Clouds with Sunshine," Nick Lucas in *Gold Diggers of Broadway*, 1929.
- "St. Louis Blues," Bessie Smith in *St. Louis Blues*, 1929.
- "Sunny Side Up," Janet Gaynor in *Sunny Side Up*, 1929.
- "Turn on the Heat," Sharon Lynn in *Sunny Side Up*, 1929.
- "Baby Face," Mary Eaton in *Glorifying the American Girl*, 1929.
- "I'm Just a Vagabond Lover," Rudy Vallee in Glorifying the American Girl, 1929.
- "What Wouldn't I Do for That Man," Helen Morgan in *Glorifying the American Girl*, 1929.
- "What Wouldn't I Do for That Man," Helen Morgan in *Applause*, 1929.
- "Give Your Little Baby Lots of Lovin'," Helen Morgan in *Applause*, 1929.
- "A Little Kiss Each Morning," Rudy Vallee in *Radio Rhythm*, 1929.
- "You Brought a New Kind of Love to Me," Maurice Chevalier in *The Big Pond*, 1930.
- "You Got Love," Rhythm Boys in *Confessions of a Co-Ed*, 1930.
- "Dancing with Tears in My Eyes," Ruth Etting in *Roseland*, 1930.
- "Let Me Sing and I'm Happy," Ruth Etting in *Roseland*, 1930.
- "Falling in Love Again," Marlene Dietrich in *The Blue Angel*, 1930.
- "Naughty Lola," Marlene Dietrich in *The Blue Angel*, 1930.

- "Does My Baby Love," Van & Schenck in 'They Learned About Women', 1930
- "This Must Be Illegal," Lillian Roth and Jack Oakie in *Sea Legs*, 1930
- "Stetson Hat," Ethel Shutta in *Whoopee*, 1930.
- "My Baby Just Cares for Me," Eddie Cantor in *Whoopee*, 1930.
- "I'll Adore You," Lee Morse in *Song Service*, 1930.
- "Just Another Dream Gone Wrong," Lee Morse in *Song Service*, 1930.
- "A Bench in the Park," The Brox Sisters and Rhythm Boys in *The King of Jazz*, 1930.
- "It Happened in Monterey," John Boles in *The King of Jazz*, 1930.
- "I Like to Do Things for You," Rhythm Boys in *The King of Jazz*, 1930.
- "So the Blackbirds and the Bluebirds Got Together," Rhythm Boys in *The King of Jazz*, 1930.
- "Great Day," The Rhythm Boys in *The King of Jazz*, 1930.
- "Happy Feet," The Sisters G, Rhythm Boys in *The King of Jazz*, 1930.
- "Mississippi Mud," Rhythm Boys in *The King of Jazz*, 1930.
- "I Can't Go on Like This," Helen Morgan in *Roadhouse Nights*, 1930.
- "Sing, You Sinners," Lillian Roth in *Honey*, 1930.
- "When the Folks High Up Do the Mean Low Down," Bing Crosby in *Reaching for the Moon*, 1930.
- "I Surrender Dear," Bing Crosby in *I Surrender Dear*, 1931.
- "Out of Nowhere," Bing Crosby in *I Surrender Dear*, 1931.
- "At Your Command," Bing Crosby in *I Surrender Dear*, 1931.
- "Be Like Me," Ethel Merman in *Be Like Me*, 1931
- "After You're Gone." Ethel Merman in *Be Like Me*, 1931.
- "I Got Rhythm," Ethel Merman singing in a newsreel? 1931?
- "Auf Wiedersehen, My Dear," Bing Crosby in *Blue of the Night*, 1932.
- "I'm Glad You're Dead, You Rascal, You," Louis Armstrong in *I'm Glad You're Dead You Rascal You*, 1932.
- "You Rascal You," Eubie Blake in *Pie Pie Blackbird*, 1932.
- "Everything I've Got Belongs to You," Nina Mae McKinney in *Pie Pie Blackbird*, 1932.
- "Shine," Louis Armstrong in *A Rhapsody in Black and Blue*, 1932.
- "Here Lies Love," Bing Crosby in *The Big Broadcast*, 1932.
- "Where the Blue of the Night," Bing Crosby in *The Big Broadcast*, 1932.
- "Please," Bing Crosby in *The Big Broadcast*, 1932.
- "When the Moon Comes over the Mountain," Kate Smith in *The Big Broadcast*, 1932.
- "It Was So Beautiful," Kate Smith in *The Big Broadcast*, 1932.
- "Shout Sister Shout," Boswell Sisters in *The Big Broadcast*, 1932.
- "Crazy People," Boswell Sisters in *The Big Broadcast*, 1932.
- "Minnie the Moocher," Cab Calloway in *The Big Broadcast*, 1932.
- "Kicking the Gong Around," Cab Calloway in *The Big Broadcast*, 1932.
- "Good-bye Blues," Mills Brothers in *The Big Broadcast*, 1932.
- "Tiger Rag," Mills Brothers in *The Big Broadcast*, 1932.
- "Trees," Donald Novis in *The Big Broadcast*, 1932.
- "When it's Sleepy Time Down South," Boswell Sisters in *When It's Sleepy Time Down South*, 1932.
- "My Love," Russ Columbo in *That Goes Double*, 1933
- "Prisoner of Love," Russ Columbo in *That Goes Double*, 1933.

- "Did You Ever See a Dream Walking" Ginger Rogers & Art Jarrett in "Sitting Pretty". 1933
- "We Just Couldn't Say Good-bye," Annette Hanshaw in *Here Comes the Show Boat*, 1933.
- "We're in the Money," Ginger Rogers in *Gold Diggers of 1933.*
- "Shadow Waltz," Dick Powell in *Gold Diggers of 1933.*
- "I've Got to Sing a Torch Song," Dick Powell in *Gold Diggers of 1933.*
- "My Forgotten Man," Etta Moten and Joan Blondell (dubbed?) in *Gold Diggers of 1933.*
- "Doing the Uptown Lowdown," Frances Williams in *Broadway Through a Keyhole*, 1933.
- "You're My Past, Present, and Future," Russ Columbo in *Broadway Through a Keyhole*, 1933.
- "I Love You, Prince Pizzicato," Russ Columbo and Constance Cummings in *Broadway Through a Keyhole*, 1933.
- "The Carioca," Etta Moten, Dolores Del Rio in *Flying Down to Rio*, 1933.
- "Come up and See Me Sometime," Lillian Roth in *Take a Chance* 1933.
- "Music Makes Me," Ginger Rogers in *Flying Down to Rio*, 1933.
- "Flying Down to Rio" Fred Astaire and chorus in *Flying Down to Rio*, 1933.
- "Stormy Weather," Ivie Anderson in *Bundle of Blues*, 1933.
- "St. James Infirmary Blues," Cab Calloway in *Snow White*, 1933.
- "Going Hollywood," Bing Crosby in *Going Hollywood*, 1933.
- "We'll Make Hay While the Sun Shines," Bing Crosby and Marion Davies in *Going Hollywood*, 1933.
- "Our Big Love Scene," Bing Crosby in *Going Hollywood*, 1933.
- "After Sundown," Bing Crosby in *Going Hollywood*, 1933.
- "Beautiful Girl," Bing Crosby in *Going Hollywood*, 1933.
- "Temptation," Bing Crosby in *Going Hollywood*, 1933.
- "Learn to Croon," Bing Crosby in *College Humor*, 1933.
- "Down the Old Ox Road," Bing Crosby in *College Humor*, 1933.
- "Moonstruck," Bing Crosby in *College Humor*, 1933.
- "I Surrender Dear," Bing Crosby in *College Humor*, 1933.
- "Lovable," Bing Crosby in *Sing Bing Sing*,1933
- "Am I Blue?" Ethel Waters in *Rufus Jones for President*, 1933.
- "Underneath the Harlem Moon," Ethel Waters in *Rufus Jones for President*, 1933.
- "You Rascal You," Sammy Davis Jr. in *Rufus Jones for President*, 1933.
- "I Do, I Do," Sammy Davis Jr. in *Rufus Jones for President*, 1933.
- "I Found a New Way to Go to Town," Mae West in *I'm No Angel*, 1933.
- "The Lady with a Fan," Cab Calloway in *Hi De Ho*, 1933.
- "Za Zuh Zaz," Cab Calloway in *Hi De Ho*, 1933.
- "Build a Little Home," Eddie Cantor in *Roman Scandals*, 1933.
- "No More Love," Ruth Etting in *Roman Scandals*, 1933.
- "Everything I Have Is Yours," Joan Crawford in *Dancing Lady*, 1933.
- "By A Waterfall". Dick Powell and Ruby Keeler in "Footlight Parade". 1933
- "Shanghai Lil". James Cagney in "Footlight Parade". 1933.
- "Nasty Man". Alice Faye in George White's Scandals Of 1934. 1933.
- "Inka Dinka Doo," Jimmy Durante in *Palooka*, 1934. (Somehow, naked women's breasts are actually shown for a few seconds! Enjoy this silly song ditty and watch this flick!)

- "Blue Sky Avenue," Gene Austin in *Gift of Gab*, 1934.
- "Song of a Dreamer," Helen Morgan in *Marie Galante*, 1934.
- "Talking to Myself." Ruth Etting in *Gift of Gab*, 1934.
- "I Ain't Gonna Sin No More," Ethel Waters in *Gift of Gab*, 1934.
- "On the Good Ship Lollipop," Shirley Temple in *Bright Eyes*, 1934.
- "Blue Mood," Alberta Hunter in *Radio Parade of 1935*, 1934.
- "My Old Flame," Mae West in *Belle of the Nineties*, 1934.
- "Troubled Waters," Mae West in *Belle of the Nineties*, 1934.
- "Future Star," Alice Faye in *365 Nights in Hollywood*, 1934.
- "Yes to You," Alice Faye in 365 *Nights in Hollywood*, 1934.
- "That Silver Haired Daddy of Mine," Gene Autry in *The Phantom Empire*, 1934.
- "Uncle Noah's Ark," Gene Autry in *The Phantom Empire*, 1934.
- "Rock and Roll," the Boswell Sisters in *Transatlantic Merry-Go-Round*, 1934.
- "When You're in Love," Russ Columbo in *Wake up and Dream*, 1934.
- "Too Beautiful for Words," Russ Columbo in *Wake up and Dream*, 1934.
- "Coffee in the Morning (Kisses in the Night)," Russ Columbo, Constance Bennett, and the Boswell Sisters in *Moulin Rouge*, 1934.
- "How I'm Doing," the Mills Brothers in *Twenty Million Sweethearts*, 1934.
- "Out for No Good," Dick Powell and the Mills Brothers in *Twenty Million Sweethearts*, 1934.
- "I'll String along with You," Ginger Rogers in *Twenty Million Sweethearts*, 1934.
- "With Every Breath I Take," *Bing Crosby in Star Night at the Coconut Grove*, 1934.
- "Dancing on the Ceiling," Jessie Mathews in *Evergreen*, 1934
- "When You've Got a Little Springtime in Your Heart," Jessie Mathews in *Evergreen*, 1934.
- "Daddy Won't Buy Me a Bow Wow," Jessie Mathews in *Evergreen*, 1934.
- "Tinkle, Tinkle," Sonnie Hale in *Evergreen*, 1934.
- "Needle in a Haystack," Fred Astaire in *The Gay Divorcee*, 1934.
- "Midnight, the Stars and You," Helen Ward in *Midnight, the Stars and You*, 1934.
- "To Love You Again," Adelaide Hall in *An All-Colored Vaudeville Show*, 1935.
- "Hymn of Sorrow," Billie Holiday (unaccredited) in *Sympathy in Black*, 1935.
- "The Last Round-Up," Joe Morrison in *La Fiesta de Santa Barbara*, 1935.
- "La Cucaracha," Garland Sisters (featuring Judy Garland) in *La Fiesta de Santa Barbara*, 1935.
- "Top Hat, White Tails And Hat," Fred Astaire in *Top Hat*, 1935.
- "No Strings," Fred Astaire in *Top Hat*, 1935.
- "Isn't it a Lovely Day," Fred Astaire and Ginger Rogers in *Top Hat*, 1935.
- "The Piccolino," Fred Astaire and Ginger Rogers in *Top Hat*, 1935.
- "Dream Ship," Josephine Baker in *Princess Tam Tam*, 1935.
- "Neath the Tropical Blue Skies," Josephine Baker in *Princess Tam Tam*, 1935.
- "I'm Shooting High," Alice Faye in *King of Burlesque*, 1935.
- "Smoke Gets in Your Eyes," Irene Dunne in *Roberta*, 1935.
- "Yesterdays," Irene Dunn in *Roberta*, 1935.
- "Give Me a Heart to Sing to," Helen Morgan in *Frankie and Johnny*, 1936.
- "Since Black Minnie's Got the Blues," Mabel Mercer and Harry Roy in *Everything Is Rhythm*, 1936.
- "Can't Help Lovin' Dat Man," Helen Morgan, Paul Robeson, and Hattie McDaniel in "*Show Boat*," 1936.

- "Bill," Helen Morgan in *Show Boat*, 1936.
- "There's Something In The Air". Tony Martin in "Banjo On My Knee" 1936
- "Where The Lazy River Goes By" Tony Martin & Barbara Stanwyck (dubbed?) in "Banjo On My Knee". 1936
- "The Little Things You Used to Do," Helen Morgan in "Go Into Your Dance," 1936.
- "After the Ball," Irene Dunne in *Show Boat*, 1936.
- "Pennies from Heaven," Bing Crosby in *Pennies from Heaven*, 1936.
- "One, Two, Buckle Your Shoe," Bing Crosby in *Pennies from Heaven*, 1936.
- "So Do I," Bing Crosby in *Pennies from Heaven*, 1936.
- "Skeleton in the Closet," Louis Armstrong in *Pennies from Heaven*, 1936.
- "Lucky Number," the Nicholas Brothers in *The Black Network*, 1936
- "Half of Me," Nina Mae McKinney in *The Black Network*, 1936.
- "I've Got You under My Skin," Virginia Bruce in *Born to Dance*, 1936.
- "Let's Face the Music and Dance," Fred Astaire in *Follow the Fleet*, 1936.
- "I'm Putting All My Eggs in one Basket," Fred Astaire in *Follow the Fleet*, 1936.
- "Let Yourself Go," Ginger Rogers in *Follow the Fleet*, 1936.
- "Get Thee Behind Me Satan," Harriet Hilliard in *Follow the Fleet*, 1936.
- "But Where Are You," Harriet Hilliard in *Follow The Fleet*, 1936.
- "Pick Yourself Up," Fred Astaire and Ginger Rogers in *Swing Time*, 1936.
- "The Way You Look Tonight," Fred Astaire and Ginger Rogers in *Swing Time*, 1936.
- "A Fine Romance," Fred Astaire and Ginger Rogers in *Swing Time*, 1936.
- "Sleepy River," Paul Robeson and Elisabeth Welch in *Song of Freedom*, 1936.
- "Rockin The Town" Gertrude Niesen is *Start Cheering*, 1937
- "Oh Babe, Maybe Some Day," Ivie Anderson in *Record Making with Duke Ellington*, 1937.
- "Una Voce Poco Fa," Lily Pons in *That Girl from Paris*, 1937.
- "I'm Gonna Swing While I'm Able," Pinky Tomlin in *Swing While You're Able*, 1937.
- "All God's Chillun Got Rhythm," Ivie Anderson in *Day at the Races*, 1937.
- "They All Laughed," Ginger Rogers in *Shall We Dance*, 1937.
- "They Can't Take That Away from Me," Fred Astaire in *Shall We Dance*, 1937
- "Slap That Bass," Fred Astaire in *Shall We Dance*, 1937.
- "You're a Sweetheart," Alice Faye in *You're a Sweetheart*, 1937
- "Mutiny in the Nursery," Maxine Sullivan in *Going Places*, 1938.
- "Jeepers Creepers," Louis Armstrong in *Going Places*, 1938.
- "The Yam," Ginger Rogers in *Carefree*, 1938.
- "Some Day My Prince Will Come," Adriana Caselotti in *Snow White and the Seven Dwarfs*, 1938.
- "Thanks for the Memory," Bob Hope and Shirley Ross in *The Big Broadcast of 1938*.
- "Two Sleepy People," Bob Hope and Shirley Ross in *Thanks for the Memory*, 1938.

(Not to be confused with the song ditty "Thanks for the Memory," which had been Introduced by Hope and Ross in *The Big Broadcast of 1938*.)

- "The Man in the Flying Trapeze" Alfalfa (Switzer) – in *Our Gang – Clown Prince*, 1939
- "Bo Weevil Song," Tex Ritter and Mantan Moreland in *Riders of the Frontier*, 1939.

- "Over the Rainbow," Judy Garland in *The Wizard of Oz*, 1939.
- "Ding-Dong! The Witch Is Dead," Judy Garland and others in *The Wizard of Oz*, 1939.
- "Come Out, Come Out, Wherever You Are," Billie Burke (dubbed) in *The Wizard of Oz*, 1939.
- "If I Only Had a Brain, Heart, Nerve," Ray Bolger, Bert Lahr, and Jack Haley in *The Wizard of Oz*, 1939.
- "Follow the Yellow Brick Road," Judy Garland and others in *The Wizard of Oz*, 1939.
- "If I Were King of the Forest," Bert Lahr in *The Wizard of Oz*, 1939.
- "We're Off to See the Wizard," Judy Garland, Ray Bolger, Bert Lahr, and Jack Haley in *The Wizard of Oz*, 1939.
- I'm Just Wild about Harry," Alice Faye in *Rose of Washington Square*, 1939.
- "I'm Just Wild about Harry," Priscilla Lane in *Roaring Twenties*, 1939.
- "Melancholy Baby," Priscilla Lane in *Roaring Twenties*, 1939.
- "In a Shanty in Shanty Town," Gladys George in *Roaring Twenties*, 1939.
- "My Sweet Heart". Valaida Snow in *Pieges* 1939.
- "Lydia, The Tattooed Lady," Groucho Marx in *At the Circus*, 1939.
- "You Are My Sunshine," Tex Ritter in *Take Me Back to Oklahoma*, 1940.
- "I'm Nobody's Baby," Judy Garland in *Andy Hardy Meets a Debutant*, 1940.
- "I've Got a One-Track Mind," Ginny Simms and the Kay Kyser Orch. in *You'll Find Out*, 1940.
- "You Ought to Be in Pictures," Porgy Pig and Daffy Duck (both Mel Blanc) in *You Ought to Be in Pictures*, Looney Tunes (cartoon), 1940.
- "The Last Time I Saw Paris". Ann Southern in "Lady Be Good". 1940
- "Stop Dancing Up There". Kay Starr in "Stop Dancing Up There" in a Panoram" 1941?
- "You Stepped Out Of A Dream" Tony Martin in Ziegfeld Girl". 1941
- "Old-Time Religion," Walter Brennan in *Sergeant York*, 1941.
- "Boogie-Woogie Bugle Boy," Andrews Sisters in *Buck Privates*, 1941.
- "Bounce Me Brother with a Solid Four," Andrews Sisters in *Buck Privates*, 1941.
- "Beat Me Daddy, Eight to the Bar," Andrews Sisters in *Buck Privates*, 1941.
- "Blues in the Night," William Gillespie (unaccredited) in *Blues in the Night*, 1941.
- "Just One of Those Things," Lena Horne in *Panama Hattie*, 1942.
- "Happy Holiday," Bing Crosby, Marjorie Reynolds (dubbed) in *Holiday Inn*, 1942.
- "White Christmas," Bing Crosby, Marjorie Reynolds (dubbed) in *Holiday Inn*, 1942.
- "Abraham," Bing Crosby in *Holiday Inn*, 942.
- "I'll Capture Your Heart," Bing Crosby, Fred Astaire, Virginia Dale in *Holiday Inn*, 1942.
- "Lazy," Bing Crosby in *Holiday Inn*, 1942.
- "Let's Start the New Year Right," Bing Crosby in *Holiday Inn*, 1942.
- "Easter Parade," Bing Crosby in *Holiday Inn*, 1942.
- "Song of Freedom," Bing Crosby in *Holiday Inn*, 1942.
- "Plenty to Be Thankful For," Bing Crosby in *Holiday Inn*, 1942.
- "Be Careful it's my heart", Bing Crosby in *Holiday In*, 1942
- "A-Tisket, A-Tasket," Ella Fitzgerald in *Ride 'Em Cowboy*, 1942.
- "Can't Get Out of This Mood," Ginny Simms in *Seven Days' Leave*, 1942.

- "Cuddle Up a Little Closer," Betty Grable in *Coney Island*, 1942.
- "Blues in the Night," Bugs Bunny (Mel Blanc) in cartoon *Bugs Bunny Gets the Boid*, 1942.
- "Blues in the Night," Daffy Duck and Porgy Pig (both Mel Blanc) in cartoon *My Favorite Duck*, 1942.
- "As Time Goes By". Dooley Wilson in Casablanca. 1942.
- "Knock On Wood". Dooley Wilson in Casablanca 1942.
- "I Had the Craziest Dream," Helen Forrest with the Harry James Orchestra in *Springtime in the Rockies*, 1942.
- "DerFurher's Face", Carl Grayson vocal in "Donald Duck In Nutzi Land" 1942.
- "Every Little Movement Has a Meaning of Its Own," Judy Garland in *Presenting Lily Mars*, 1943.
- "Three O'Clock in the Morning," Judy Garland in *Presenting Lily Mars*, 1943.
- "Broadway Melody," Judy Garland in *Presenting Lily Mars*, 1943.
- "You'll Never Know," Alice Faye in *Hello, Frisco, Hello*, 1943.
- "Quicksands," Ethel Waters and the Count Basie Orchestra in *Stage Door Canteen*, 1943.
- "She's a Bombshell from Brooklyn," Lina Romay and the Xavier Cugat Orchestra in *Stage Door Canteen*, 1943.
- "Why Don't You Do Right?" Peggy Lee and the Benny Goodman Orchestra, in *Stage Door Canteen*, 1943.
- "Cabin in the Sky," Ethel Waters and Eddie Rochester Anderson in *Cabin in the Sky*, 1943.
- "Happiness is a Thing Called Joe," Ethel Waters in *Cabin in the Sky*, 1943.
- "Taking a Chance on Love," Ethel Waters and Lena Horne in *Cabin in the Sky*, 1942.
- "Honey in the Honeycomb," Ethel Waters and Lena Horne in *Cabin in the Sky*, 1943.
- "Life is Full of Consequences," Eddie Rochester Anderson and Lena Horne in *Cabin in the Sky*, 1943.
- "Li'l Black Sheep," Hall Johnson Choir and Ethel Waters in *Cabin in the Sky*, 1943.
- "Shine," John W. Burlett in *Cabin in the Sky*, 1943.
- "Stormy Weather," Lena Horne in *Stormy Weather*, 1943.
- "Diga Diga Do," Lena Horne in *Stormy Weather*, 1943.
- "Honeysuckle Rose," Fats Waller in *Stormy Weather*, 1943.
- "That Ain't Right," Ada Brown and Fats Waller in *Stormy Weather*, 1943.
- "There's No Two Ways about Love," Lena Horne, Eddie Rochester Anderson, and Cab Calloway in *Stormy Weather*, 1943.
- "They're either Too Young or Too Old," Bettie Davis in *Thank Your Lucky Stars*, 1943.
- "Thank Your Lucky Stars," Dinah Shore in *Thank Your Lucky Stars*, 1943.
- "Like a Fish out of Water," Ginny Simms in *Hit the Ice*, 1943.
- "Night and Day," Frank Sinatra in *Reveille with Beverly*, 1943.
- "Take the 'A' Train." Betty Roche (unaccredited) and Duke Ellington's Orchestra in *Reveille with Beverly*, 1943.
- "Cow Cow Boogie," Ella Mae Morse and Freddie Slack's Orchestra in *Reveille With Beverly*, 1943.
- "Don't Fence Me In," Roy Rogers in *Hollywood Canteen*, 1944.

- "San Fernando Valley," Roy Rogers in *San Fernando Valley*, 1944.
- "Say It with Love," Martha Tilton in *Swing Hostess*, 1944.
- "Unlucky Woman," Lena Horne in *Boogie-Woogie Dream*, released in 1944.
- "Out of Nowhere," Lena Horne in *Boogie-Woogie Dream*, released in 1944.
- "I Couldn't Sleep a Wink Last Night," Frank Sinatra in *Higher and Higher*, 1944.
- "Mairzy Doats," Bing Crosby and Bob Hope in a *Newsreel*, 1944.
- "Saga Of Jenny" Ginger Rogers in "Lady In The Dark", 1944
- "Have Yourself a Merry Little Christmas," Judy Garland to Margaret O'Brien in *Meet Me in St. Louis*, 1944.
- "Meet Me in St. Louis," Judy Garland, Lucille Bremer, Joan Carroll, Harry Davenport, and others in *Meet Me in St. Louis*, 1944.
- "The Boy Next Door," Judy Garland In *Meet Me in St. Louis*, 1944.
- "The Trolley Song," Judy Garland and others in *Meet Me in St. Louis*, 1944.
- "A Kiss Goodnight," Dale Evans in *Don't Fence Me In*, 1945.
- "There's Only One of You," Dale Evans in *The Big Show-Off*, 1945.
- "I Can't Begin to Tell You," Betty Grable in *The Dolly Sisters*, 1945.
- "The House I Live In," Frank Sinatra in *The House I Live In*, 1945.
- "It Might As Well Be Spring," Jeanne Crain (dubbed?) in *State Fair*, 1945.
- "That's for Me," Vivian Blaine, Dick Haymes, and Jeanne Crain in *State Fair*, 1945
- "Can't Help Lovin' That Man," Lena Horne in *Till the Clouds Roll By*, 1946.
- "Ain't It the Truth," Lena Horne in *Studio Visit*, released in 1946.
- "Dig You Later (A-Hubba Hubba Hubba)," Perry Como in *Doll Face*, 1946.
- "And Her Tears Flowed Like Wine" Lauren Bacall in the *Big Sleep*, 1946.
- "You're the Top," Ginny Simms and Cary Grant in *Night and Day*, 1946.
- "The Blues are Brewing," Billie Holiday in *New Orleans*, 1946.
- "West End Blues," Louis Armstrong in *New Orleans*, 1946.
- "It's Better to Be by Yourself," Nat Cole Trio in *Breakfast in Hollywood*, 1946.
- "If I Had a Wishing Ring," Andy Russell in *Breakfast in Hollywood*, 1946.
- "Look for the Silver Lining," Judy Garland in *Till the Clouds Roll By*, 1946.
- "Who?" Judy Garland in *Till The Clouds Roll By*, 1946
- "On the Atchison Topeka and the Santa Fe," Judy Garland in *The Harvey Girls*, 1946.
- "Personality," Dorothy Lamour in *Road to Utopia*, 1946 (the original sheet music more so features Crosby, Hope, and Lamour—an astoundingly popular film combination! Moreover, it is Dorothy's vocal that is heard in the film and not Crosby's, noting his popular contemporary Decca recording of the ditty).
- "Buttons and Bows," Bob Hope and Jane Russell in *The Paleface*, 1948.
- "But Beautiful," Bing Crosby in *Road to Rio*, 1948.
- "You Don't Have to Know the Language," Bing Crosby and the Andrews Sisters in *Road to Rio*, 1948.
- "It's Magic," Doris Day in *Romance on the High Seas*, 1948.
- "Woody Woodpecker Song", Gloria Wood vocal in *"Wet Blanket Policy"* 1948
- "Easter Parade," Fred Astaire in *Easter Parade*, 1948.
- "A Couple of Swells," Judy Garland and Fred Astaire, "Easter Parade ". 1948.
- "Better Luck Next Time," Judy Garland in *Easter Parade*, 1948.
- "When the Midnight Choo-Choo Leaves For Alabam," Judy Garland and Fred Astaire in *Easter Parade*, 1948.
- "Beautiful Faces Need Beautiful Clothes," Fred Astaire and Judy Garland in *Easter Parade*, 1948.

- "A Fellow with an Umbrella," Judy Garland and Peter Lawford in *Easter Parade*, 1948.
- "Blue Shadows on the Trail," Roy Rogers and Sons of the Pioneers in *Melody Time*, 1948.
- "The Lady Is a Tramp," Lena Horne in *Words and Music*, 1949.
- "Blue Room". Perry Como in Words And Music 1949
- "They Can't Take That Away from Me," Fred Astaire and Ginger Rogers in *The Barkleys of Broadway*, 1949.
- "Silver Bells," Bob Hope and Marilyn Maxwell in *The Lemon Drop Kid*, 1949.
- "Blue Gardenia," Nat King Cole in *Blue Gardinia*, 1952.
- "Santa Baby," Eartha Kitt in *New Faces of 1952*, 1952.
- "His Eye Is on the Sparrow," Ethel Waters in *Member of the Wedding*, 1952.
- "All of Me," Frank Sinatra in *Meet Danny Wilson*, 1952.
- "She's Funny That Way," Frank Sinatra in *Meet Danny Wilson*, 1952.
- "I've Got a Crush on You," Frank Sinatra in *Meet Danny Wilson*, 1952.
- "You're a Sweetheart," Frank Sinatra in *Meet Danny Wilson*, 1952.
- "Lonesome Man Blues," Frank Sinatra in *Meet Danny Wilson*, 1952.
- "How Deep Is the Ocean," Frank Sinatra in *Meet Danny Wilson*, 1952.
- "A Good Man Is Hard to Find," Frank Sinatra and Shelly Winters in *Meet Danny Wilson*, 1952.
- "Singing in the Rain," Gene Kelly in *Singing in the Rain*, 1952.
- "Diamonds Are a Girl's Best Friend," Marilyn Monroe in *Gentlemen Prefer Blondes*, 1953. (Dubbed?)
- "Love, You Didn't Do Right by Me," Rosemary Clooney in *White Christmas*, 1954.
- "Heat Wave," Marilyn Monroe's sultry filmed version of the Ethel Water's original (1933) Broadway entity is given new life in *There's No Business Like Show Business*, 1954. (Dubbed?)
- "The Man That Got Away," Judy Garland in *A Star Is Born*, 1954.
- "Gotta Have You Go with Me," Judy Garland in *A Star Is Born*, 1954.
- "It's a New World," Judy Garland in *A Star Is Born*, 1954.
- "That's Amore," Dean Martin in *The Caddy*, 1954.
- "I'll Never Stop Loving You". Doris Day in "Love Me or Leave Me". 1955
- "I Was A Little Too Lonely" Nat King Cole in "Istanbul". 1956.
- "When I Fall In Love". Nat King Cole in "Istanbul". 1956
- "Now You Has Jazz," Bing Crosby and Louis Armstrong in *High Society*, 1956.
- "Well, Did You Evah!" Bing Crosby and Frank Sinatra in *High Society*, 1956.
- "Who Wants to Be a Millionaire?" Frank Sinatra and Celeste Holm in *High Society*, 1956.
- "You're Sensational," Frank Sinatra in *High Society*, 1956.
- "Mind If I Make Love to You?" Frank Sinatra in *High Society*, 1956.
- "Whatever Will Be, Will Be," Doris Day in *The Man Who Knew Too Much*, 1956.
- "There's a Small Hotel," Frank Sinatra in *Pal Joey*, 1957.
- "I Didn't Know What Time It Was," Frank Sinatra in *Pal Joey*, 1957.
- "The Lady Is a Tramp," Frank Sinatra in *Pal Joey*, 1957.
- "Bewitched, Bothered and Bewildered," Frank Sinatra and Rita Hayworth (dubbed?) in *Pal Joey*, 1957.
- "I Could Write a Book," Frank Sinatra and Kim Novak (dubbed?) in *Pal Joey*, 1957.

- "All the Way," Frank Sinatra in *The Joker Is Wild*, 1957.
- "Chicago," Frank Sinatra in *The Joker Is Wild*, 1957.
- "High Hopes," Frank Sinatra in *A Hole In the Head*, 1959.
- "Ain't That a Kick in the Head?" Dean Martin in *Oceans 11*, 1960
- "My Kind of Town," Frank Sinatra in *Robin and the 7 Hoods*, 1964
- "I Like to Lead When I Dance," Frank Sinatra in *Robin and the 7 Hoods*, 1964.
- "Don't Be a Do-Badder," Bing Crosby in *Robin And the 7 Hoods*, 1964.
- "Bang Bang," Sammy Davis Jr. in *Robin and the 7 Hoods*, 1964.
- "Seems Like Old Times," Diane Keaton in *Annie Hall*, 1977.
- "Minnie the Moocher," Cab Calloway in *The Blues Brothers*, 1980.

Oddball Film Song Ditties

a. "Ramona." This 1927 silent film song of the same name, which starred Dolores Del Rio, was used to promote the film as by radio broadcasts and actual recordings. Subsequent contemporary recordings by Del Rio herself and Gene Austin made this a hot-selling contemporary song ditty! (Notes: (a) Delores, more so, should not to be confused by the actual contemporary vocalist known as Ramona. (b) This film should not be confused with a late (all-talking) film of the same name starring Loretta Young.)
b. "Blues in the Night." Sometime around 1941, Johnny Mercer and Harold Arlen penned this title song for the contemporary film release of the same name. As seen in the film, its introduction (in prison) was subsequently sung by an (unaccredited) and black film actor, identified as "William Gillespie." It's more than likely that no one knew the song would become a classic popular song, perhaps the best of many as produced by either Mercer or Arlen.

This author, was most likely influenced by a few Merrie Melodies (Warner Brothers) cartoon shorts when shown on TV in the 1950s. Investigation into many contemporary WWII era versions found many differing vocal renderings, including recorded picks by Cab Calloway, a Benny Goodman release featuring Peggy Lee and Dinah Shore, a Jimmie Lunceford release featuring (unaccredited) Willie Smith, an Artie Shaw version featuring "Hot Lips" Page as well as a Johnny Mercer, Jo Stafford, and Pied Pipers release. (The voices of Bugs Bunny, Daffy Duck, and Porgy Pig in cartoon shorts have been identified as Mel Blanc's.) In true retrospective, Did Gillespie produce a record? Why didn't anyone (especially Lunceford, who was also in the film) hire him? (This ditty is sometimes known as "My Mama Done Told Me.")

c. "How Am I To Know?" Russ Columbo (unaccredited) in *Dynamite*. This 1929 film found Russ in prison singing this ditty, with some annoying background. While his performance is still good in the film, he never did record it. Subsequent recordings did appear including releases as by Gene Austin and an Arden-Ohman Orchestra release with a vocal by Scrappy Lambert. It would, more so, be revived by many, including a (1937) Teddy Wilson release, with a fine Helen Ward vocal and a lesser known yet defining Billie Holiday release in 1944 on Commadore Records.
d. "Paradise." Contemporary 1932 film entity, Pola Negri, who had made silent films, found this ditty in *A Woman Commands*. An aging but still sultry film actress, she was born in Russian-controlled Poland before WWI. She had subsequently become a well known film and cabaret star, whose fans (even) included Adolph Hitler—soon

to become contemporary leader of Germany. Just how Adolph decided to change his race theory about non-Germans is unclear, but Polo, in her prime, was indeed a beautiful woman! Like so many early film stars, Pola's (English) film version have been largely forgotten, although contemporary crooning recordings by Bing Crosby and Russ Columbo, provided this song ditty, penned by Gordon Clifford and Nacio Herb Brown, a lot more recognition than the film ever did. (Pola did later record the ditty-in French).

e. "Would You?" 1936. This contemporary Jeanette Mac Donald song ditty, penned by Arthur Freed and Nacio Herb Brown, from the contemporary MGM film *San Francisco*, along with Clark Gable, also featured the identified voice (but not the person) of Bing Crosby. More so, Crosby's vocal is indeed welcome in the fine film, as was his own contemporary recording!

f. "I've Got You Under My Skin," 1936. The beautiful legs of Eleanor Powell had nothing to do with actress and (assigned) singer Virginia Bruce's introduction this ditty in *Born to Dance*. Subsequent contemporary recordings by Al Bowlly (on a Ray Noble release) and Lee Wiley produced some recognition for this Cole Porter-penned classic, although Josephine Baker's (1937) recording defined it, sadly outside of the United States. Fortunately, after some horrid attempts at reviving it, Frank Sinatra recorded it in 1956. It has since become recognized as a Frank Sinatra classic. Thank you, Frank!

- Note: More films are to be noted within this book and are not necessarily bad.
- *Viewing vintage film is better in retrospective.*
  The video and later development of DVD formats provide viewers a better and easier view of filmed musicals or vocals in film. While purists insist original big screen viewing is best, the ability to re-play enables newer audiences to 'find' and observe a bit more that was initially intended.

MEDIA, NEWSPRINT, AND LOCATIONS (1900-50)

The "live" aspect of entertainment is the obvious start for any would-be performance or performer. While the front porch or the den is most appealing, the tent show, along with a traveling carnival is, perhaps, a step up. Besides traditional opera, it may be safe to put pre-Civil War plantations as a gathering place for soulful laments. Even prisons are noted. So is the music of the religious. This include's the music heard in Christian churches, synagogues, or laments heard in mosques. While word of mouth was more original, the subsequent use of written media exploited the situation. So did the use of posters along with the added use of artistic drawings and pictures. The use of films was another advance. (After 1927, the use of "talkies" in films just about buried vaudeville). The use of newsprint, moreover, in newspapers, periodicals, and newsletters, even after the huge steps of technology was and still remains important. The following include important (selective) media newsprints and centers of American entertainment (1900-50).

a. Selective newsprint include all the obvious major newspapers of urban dwellers. For certain, top dollar was always found in the big city. Nevertheless, smaller publications were important. Smaller cities and rural areas were always considered good tryouts, practices, promotions, and beginnings for most entertainers. Smaller publications also found ethnic, cultural, and racial audiences, usually not found in major newsprint. Entertainment for most (considering the forty-eight-hour work week) was not as usual as the in the latter century. As a matter of fact, the simple idea of sitting back and reading newsprint, with a (small) entertainment section, was enough for most.

   ➢ Noted print entities covering the contemporary time period from 1900 to 1950 include the following:

* *Albuquerque Tribune,* NM.
* *Atlanta Constitution,* Atlanta, GA. / *Atlanta Journal,* Atlanta, GA.
* *Atlantic City Press,* NJ.
* *Arizona Republic,* Phoenix, AZ.
* *Asheville Times, Asheville,* NC.
* *Ballyhoo Magazine, NYC, NY (1930s)*
* *Baltimore Afro-American,* MD. (Perhaps the term "Afro-American" originated here?)
* *Baltimore Evening Sun,* MD.
* *Best Songs,* Charlton Publishing Corp., Derby, CN. (September 1948, Frank Sinatra on cover.)
* *Billboard, The,* NY. (Perhaps the most influential of all entertainment trade publications?)
* *Billboard, The,* April 20, 1946, issue—cover features the King Cole Trio on cover (Nat on piano, Oscar Moore on guitar, and Johnny Miller on bass).
* *Boston Globe,* MA / *Boston Evening Transcript,* MA / *Boston Herald,* MA. / *Boston Post,* MA.
* *Bristol News Bulletin,* Bristol, TN.
* *Broadcast Songs,* NY, NY (October 1946, Dinah Shore on cover).

* *Buffalo Courier-Express,* NY, / *Call Bulletin,* San Francisco, CA.
* *Cash Box, The,* NY, founded in 1941, this influential trade magazine grew to rival *Billboard.*
* *California Eagle,* Los Angeles, CA, / *Camden News,* AK.
* *Chicago* (Magazine), IL, / *Chicago Bee,* Chicago, IL, / *Chicago Daily Times,* IL / *Chicago Daily News,* Chicago, IL.
* *Chicago Defender,* IL. (Perhaps the very best source about Afro-American entertainment?)
* *Chicago Evening Post,* Chicago, IL, / *Chicago Herald* and *Examiner*, Chicago, IL.
* *Chicago Sun*, Chicago, IL (1941-48), / *Chicago Sun-Times,* Chicago, IL (1948+)
* *Chicago Tribune,* IL, / *Chicago Stage Bill* (legitimate Theatre Publication), IL.
* *Cincinnati Post,* OH, / *Cincinnati Times-Star,* Cincinnati, OH.
* *Cleveland Gazette,* OH, / *Cleveland Plain-Dealer*, OH.
* *Columbia Daily Tribune,* Columbia, MO.
* *Commercial Appeal,* Memphis, TN, / *Cosmopolitan,* NY.
* Cosmopolitan 'Blue Melody' about Bessie Smith-editor J.D. Salinger Sept. 1948
* *Crisis, The,* Harlem, New York City, NY. As controlled by W. E. B. Du Bois, this (black) 1920s monthly publication perhaps recorded the Harlem Renaissance better than any others.
* *Daily Oklahoman,* Oklahoma City, OK.
* *Daily Princetonian,* University, NJ.
* *Daily Variety,*
* *Dallas Morning News,* TX.
* *Denver Post,* CO, / *Denver Star,* CO.
* *Detroit Free Press,* MI.
* *Detroit News,* MI.
* *Downbeat,* New York, NY. (October 20, 1948—Lena Horne on cover).
* *Evening Bulletin,* Providence, RI.
* *Esquire,* New York, NY.
* *Fortune Magazine, NYC, NY(Miguel Covarrubias Radio Supplement, May, 1938)*
* *Gene Autry Comics,* Dell, 1949. Gene started this market in 1941. Other contemporaries, including Tex Ritter and Roy Rogers, were soon to follow his lead.
* *Harvard Crimson*, University, MA.
* *Hit Parader.*, New York, NY. (1946—Perry Como on cover.)
* *Houston Press,* TX.
* *Hollywood Citizens News,* Hollywood, CA. / *Hollywood Reporter,* Hollywood, CA.
* *Indiana Daily Student,* Indiana University, IN.
* *Jersey Journal,* NJ.
* *Kansas City American,* Kansas City, MO, / *Kansas City Journal-Post,* Kansas City, MO.
* *Kansas City Star,* Kansas City, MO, / *Kansas City Post,* MO.
* *Knoxville News Sentinel,* Knoxville, TN.
* *Life Magazine, NY,* / *Look Magazine,* NY.
* *Life Magazine-Jane Froman on cover* March 14 1938
* *Life Magazine-Hildegarde on cover 04/17/1939.*
* *Look Magazine, Des Moines,* IA
* *Los Angeles Daily News,* CA, / *Los Angeles Evening Express,* CA.
* *Los Angeles Evening Herald,* CA, / *Los Angeles Examiner,* CA.
* *Los Angeles Express,* CA, / *Los Angeles Herald Express,* CA.
* *Los Angeles Illustrated News,* CA, / *Los Angeles Sentinel,* CA, / *Los Angeles Times,* CA.
* *Metronome,* NY. (The "Rolling Stone" of its day?)
* *Memphis Commercial Appeal,* TN, / *Memphis Press Seminar,* Memphis, TN.

* *Memphis World Newspaper,* Memphis, TN.
* *Miami Daily News,* FL, / *Miami Herald,* Miami, FL.
* *Miami Times,* FL.
* *Minneapolis Journal,* MN, / *Minneapolis Star Journal,* MN.
* *Milwaukee Post,* WI, / *Milwaukee Sentinel,* WI.
* *Montgomery Examiner,* Montgomery, AL.
* *Nashville Banner,* Nashville, TN, / *Nashville Tennessean,* Nashville, TN.
* *Newark News,* NJ.
* *Newark Star Ledger,* Newark, NJ.
* *New Orleans Age,* LA, / *New Orleans Daily Picayune,* LA.
* *New Orleans Morning Tribune,* LA, / *New Orleans Item,* LA.
* *New Yorker, Magazine,* NY, / *New York American,* NY.
* *New York Amsterdam News,* NY, / *New York Daily Citizen,* NY.
* *New York Daily News,* NY, / *New York Daily Mirror,* NY.
* *New York Enquirer,* NY.
* *New York Evening Graphic,* NY. (In 1930, staff writer Walter Winchell began to broadcast his column on radio. Local "Broadway" gossip, more so, would become national news? Yes!)
* *New York Herald-Tribune,* NY, / *New York Journal,* NY.
* *New York Sun,* NY, / *New York Times,* NY.
* *New York World,* NY, / *New York World-Telegram,* NY, / *Newsweek,* NY.
* *Norfolk Journal and Guide,* VA.
* *Oakland Tribune, Oakland,* CA.
* *Oklahoma City Advisor,* OK, / *Omaha Bee News,* Omaha, NE
* *Ohio State News Columbus, OH*
* *Omaha World Herald,* Omaha, NE
* *Opry House Matinee* (Songbooks assoc. with the Grand Ole Opry radio program), Nashville, TN.
* *Pasadena Evening Post,* CA.
* *Philadelphia Daily News,* PA, / *Philadelphia Evening Bulletin,* PA.
* *Philadelphia Inquirer,* PA, / *Philadelphia Record,* PA, / *Philadelphia Tribune,* PA.
* *Pittsburgh Courier,* PA.
* *Playbill, the Martin Beck Theatre,* New York City, NY.
* *Playgoer Magazine on Theatre,* Los Angeles, CA.
* *Popular Songs,* April 1936, Dell Publishing Company, Dunellen, NJ. (Jane Froman on cover.)
* *Popular Song Hits,* an Engel-van Wiseman Publication, executive offices New York, NY. (July 1935—Bing Crosby and Ethel Merman on cover.)
* *Portland Oregonian,* OR, / *Portland Herald Express,* Portland, OR.
* *Portland Evening News,* Portland, ME.
* *Portsmouth Times,* OH.
* *Public Ledger,* Philadelphia, PA.
* *Radio Broadcast,* Garden City, NY.
* *Radio Mirror,* NY. (October 1938—Ozzie, Harriet, and David Nelson on cover.)
* *Rochester Times Union,* NY.
* *Roy Rogers* (*Dell Comics* no 11), 1948, Dell, NY. (For many young boomers, after viewing a Rogers film—and later in the 1950s, a Rogers TV program—a comic and a record was a neat thing! Yup.)
* *Roxy Theatre Weekly Review,* New York City, NY, 1929+.
* *Raleigh Times,* Raleigh, NC.

* *Reader's Digest,* NY, 1922+.
* *San Antonio Express,* San Antonio, TX.
* *San Diego Union,* CA.
* *San Francisco Chronicle,* CA / *San Francisco Examiner,* CA.
* *Saturday Evening Post, The.*
* *Salt Lake City Telegram,* UT, / *Salt Lake Tribune,* UT.
* *Savannah Tribune,* GA.
* *Seattle Post Intelligencer,* WA.
* *Shreveport Times,* LA.
* *St. Joseph Gazette,* MO.
* *St. Louis Star-Times,* MO, / *St. Louis Post-Dispatch,* MO, / *St. Louis Times,* MO.
* *Spokane Chronicle,* Spokane, WA.
* *Tacoma Daily Ledger,* WA, / *Tacoma Daily News,* WA.
* *Tampa Tribune,* FL.
* *Targum, The,* Rutgers College, NY, / *Terre Haute Star,* IN.
* *This Week in Chicago Nightclubs,* Chicago, IL, 1930s+.
* *Time,* NY. (The cover issue of February 21, 1949, featuring Louis Armstrong, was entertaining and historic, as well as a bold move! Musical influence and history? Social justice? Yes. That's Louis!)
* *Toledo News Bee,* Toledo, OH.
* *Tulsa Tribune,* Tulsa, OK.
* *University of Kansas Newspaper,* KS.
* *Vanity Fair,* NY, / *Variety,* NY, / *Vogue,* NY.
* *Vanity Fair*-'Negro Blues Singers'-Carl Van Vechten, March 1926
* *Wall Street Journal,* New York City, NY, 1889+.
* *Washington Bee,* DC, / *Washington Post,* Washington, DC.
* *Washington Herald,* Washington, DC.
* *Winston-Salem Journal,* Winston-Salem, NC.

b. The Musical Theaters—Broadway (on or near Broadway, New York, NY). The musical theater had found its origins in Europe (especially in the London (musical) stage). Its most original imitation,

(for high-brows) became New York's "Broadway." Moreover, most all of American popular songs found their origins on Broadway, at least until the advent of talking films and music written for films themselves. The likes of Al Jolson, Eddie Cantor, as well as the Ziegfeld showgirls such as Fannie Brice, Helen Morgan, and Ruth Etting, among others, gained much public recognition. (The original "talkie" film, *The Jazz Singer* (1927), was originally a Broadway entity). Until 1933, Bert Williams was the only person of color to be allowed to be a headliner in an integrated Broadway production. Within the middle of racism, many song ditties nevertheless emerged as composed by Afro-American composers. They included the likes of Eubie Blake, Shelton Brooks, Henry Creamer Roger Graham, J. Turner Layton, Nobel Sissle, the Spikes brothers, Spencer Williams, and Bert Williams himself. It was surely a white man's world, which made the few all-black reviews more important. As the Roaring Twenties progressed, there was a gradual integration of both personalities and music. Again, noting Bert Williams as the only black entity of consequence in stage and subsequent acoustic recording before the emergence of Mamie Smith's in 1920, like most others, black as well as white, the restrictions of acoustic recordings almost always ruined real musical appreciation of recorded show tunes. The advancement of electric recording in the mid-1920s more so improved listening abilities, and appreciation of Broadway entities as well as rival forms of entertainment (radio and motion pictures) would not require Broadway.

♦ The following are major Broadway entities. Few were really on Broadway, circa 1930. This group of theaters are all in Downtown New York City, roughly from

* Eighth Street on the west,
* Sixth Street on the east,
* and from Fifty-Third Street through Fifth Streets. "Uptown" follows.

 ✓ Additional comments are also selective.

- Alvin Theatre, Fifty-Second Street, west of Broadway.
- Ambassador Theatre, Forty-Ninth Street, west of Broadway.
- Apollo Theatre (Downtown) Forty-Second Street, W. of Broadway.
- Bayes Theatre, Forty-Fourth Street, west of Broadway (named for actress and vocalist Nora Bayes).
- Belasco Theatre, Forty-Fourth Street, east of Broadway.
- Bijon Theatre, Forty-Fifth Street, west of Broadway.
- Biltmore Theatre, Forty-Seventh Street, west of Broadway.
- Belmont Theatre, Forty-Eighth Street, east of Broadway.
- Booth Theatre, (named for Edwin Booth, actor & brother of John Wilkes Booth, assain of Abraham Lincoln in 1865), Fourty-Fifth Street, west of Broadway.
- Broadhurst Theatre, Forty-Fourth Street, west of Broadway.
- Capital Theater, Fifty-First Street, west of Broadway.
- Casino Theatre, Thirty-Ninth Street, east of Broadway.
- Chanin's Forty-Sixth Street Theatre, Forty-Sixth Street, west of Broadway.
- Charles Hopkins Theatre, Forty-Ninth Street, east of Broadway.
- Cort Theatre, Forty-Eighth Street, east of Broadway.
- Craig Theatre, Fifty-Forth Street, east of Broadway.
- Earl Carrol, Fiftieth Street, east of Broadway. (After closing in New York City, in the early 1930s, Earl opened a later site, with restaurant in Hollywood in 1938.)
- Edyth Totten Theatre, Forty-Eighth Street, west of Broadway.
- Eltinge Theatre, Forty-Second Street, west of Broadway.
- Empire Theatre, Fortieth Street, east of Broadway.
- Erlanger's Theatre, Forty-Fourth Street, west of Broadway
- Ethel Barrymore Theater, Forty-Seventh Street, west Of Broadway.
- Forrest Theater, Forty-Ninth Street west of Broadway.
- Forty-Fourth Street Theatre, Forty-Fourth Street, west of Broadway.
- Forty-Ninth Street Theatre, west of Broadway.
- Frolic Theatre, Forty-Second Street, west of Broadway.
- Fulton Theatre, Forty-Sixth Street, west of Broadway.
- Gaiety Theatre, Forty-Sixth Street, west of Broadway.
- Gallo Theatre, Fifty-Fourth Street, west of Broadway.
- Garrick Theatre, Thirty-fifth Street, east of Broadway.
- George M. Cohan Theatre, Forty-Third Street, east of Broadway.
- Globe Theatre, Forty-Sixth Street, west of Broadway.
- Guild Theatre, Fifty-Second Street, west of Broadway.

- Hammerstein's Theatre, Fifty-third Street, west of Broadway. (After many name changes, this site became known as the Ed Sullivan Theatre by the end of the century.)(Oscar Hammerstein I),
- Henry Miller's Theatre, Forty-Third Street, east of Broadway.
- Imperial Theatre, Forty-Sixth Street, west of Broadway.
- Klaw Theatre, Forty-Fifth Street, west of Broadway.
- Liberty Theatre, Forty-Second Street, west of Broadway.
- Little Theatre, Forty-Fourth Street, west of Broadway.
- Longacre Theatre, Forty-Eighth Street, west of Broadway.
- Masque Theatre, Forty-Fifth Street, west of Broadway.
- Lyceum Theatre, Forty-Fifth Street, east of Broadway.
- Lyric Theatre, Forty-Third Street, west of Broadway.
- Majestic Theatre, Forty-Fourth Street, west of Broadway.
- Mansfield Theatre, Forty-Seventh Street, west of Broadway.
- Martin Beck Theatre, 302 West Forty-Fifth Street, west of Broadway.
- Maxine Elliott's Theatre, Thirty-Ninth Street, east of Broadway.
- Morosco Theatre, Forty-Fifth Street, west of Broadway.
- Music Box Theater, Forty-Fifth Street, west of Broadway (owned by Irving Berlin).
- National Theatre, Forty-First Street, west of Broadway.
- New Amsterdam Theater, Forty-First Street, west Of Broadway (associated with Flo Ziegfeld productions).
- New York Theatre (Jardin de Paris), Forty-Fifth and Broadway.
- Playhouse Theatre, Forty-Eighth Street, east of Broadway.
- Plymouth Theatre, Forty-Fifth Street, west of Broadway.
- Princess Theatre, Thirty-Ninth Street, east of Broadway.
- Ritz Theatre, Forty-Eighth Street, west of Broadway.
- Royale Theatre, Forty-fifth Street, west of Broadway.
- Sam H. Harris Theatre, Forty-First Street, west of Broadway.
- Selwyn Theatre, Forty-Third Street, west of Broadway.
- Shubert Theatre, Forty-Fourth Street, west of Broadway
- Sixty-Third Street Theatre, Sixty-Third and Broadway.
- Times Square Theatre, Forty-Third Street, west of Broadway.
- Vanderbilt Theatre, Forty-Third Street, east of Broadway.
- Waldorf Theatre, Fiftieth Street, east of Broadway.
- Wallack's Theatre, Forty-Second Street, west of Broadway.
- Winter Gardens, Fifty-First Street, east of Broadway (associated with Al Jolson since 1911).

c. The vaudeville show, which contained other acts besides music, began to fail even before the Great Depression of 1929. Besides films (before 1927 silent), phonograph records and radio made vaudeville look pale. Many vaudevillians, in fact, found that many theaters built originally for live vaudeville shows, converted over to films. Many theaters, while still used for live personal appearances, looked for specific headliners—usually a band, orchestra, or vocalists—whose marketing appeal was the result of film, radio, or phonograph sales. By the mid-1920s, due to technical advances, the media of radio had invaded the places of entertainment. To a large degree, the appealing marketing aspects of live broadcast, even dwarfed the radio studio broadcast.
d. Burlesque. The very pit of the musical theater (and very near to the brothel itself), was the strip joint. As with the likes of live vaudeville shows, the emergence of film,

radio, and the Great Depression—for the most part—sunk this business. For many, this business was also a start, with a quick finish. (A notable exception was the success of Gypsy Rose Lee, who became a legit film entity in the 1940s.) For many others, the surviving strip shows did employ some great musicians, especially for drummers!

e. The emergence of live radio in the 1920s, moreover, provided entertainment for the masses as never before. While the marketing of music was a huge aspect, so was the location of the "hooked-up" broadcast, as well as the question of even spinning actual records, as a substitute. While this question of record-spinning remained unsettled until the early 1940s, the marketing of personalities was fully realized. In fact, the rise of Rudy Vallee in 1928 as a major vocalist was principally fueled by his live radio broadcasts, originating from New York's High-Ho Club. Previously, while emerging radio entities had found audiences as live entities and recording artists, the appeal of the singing bandleader (Vallee), found the programmers of WABC (New York) truly exploiting things further. What Al Jolson had achieved in vaudeville, Broadway, as a recording artist and as a very "new" film entity, Rudy, who would also use them all, achieved more recognition, and in far less time. This instant success would indeed become the cornerstone for all who would follow, and the entertainment industry moreover followed suit. For the purposes of this book, the rise of many, especially considering those of Bing Crosby and Frank Sinatra, owed much to Rudy Vallee, also noting his youth, which was chiefly marketable to young women.

The following (selective) auditoriums, ballrooms, bars, carnivals, clubs, country clubs, expositions, honky-tonks, hotels, lounges, lodgers, opera houses, parks, roadhouses, restaurants, roofs, speakeasies (illegal establishments that served alcoholic beverages during prohibition 1919-34), supper clubs, taverns, theaters, and other places of entertainment may be considered the principal avenues of live entertainment. Some were parts of circuits, many even owned by entertainers themselves. Some are so designated by region and culture. Some other avenues were dives or, in reality, tent shows, cruise liners, and even radio broadcast studios Some would include houses of prostitution, gambling establishments, and prisons. Others would include barns or even Mississippi River steamboats. Hopefully, most of the hot spots, whether large auditoriums or small bars or cabaret, are noted.

They, more so, should provide a good tally of just where most popular vocalist entertainers, found within this book, were to be seen and heard between 1900 and 1950, besides listening to a phonograph record. Also note

- ♦ As already indicated, the media of radio, "hooked" into many of these nightspots. This practice began in the mid-1920s. As a marketing tool, it had changed entertainment, noting the huge success of Rudy Vallee in 1928. A separate list of radio program broadcasts within this book is, more so, linked with many of these sites.

♦ Selective college campuses (especially important for the development of musicals of the 1920s and 1930s) include the following:

➢ Gonzala University (associated with Bing Crosby), Harvard University, Murray College (Kentucky), Louisiana State University, Mississippi State University, Northwestern University, Rutgers University, Tulane University, `University of Akron, University of Alabama, University of Arkansas, University of Illinois, University of

Maine, University Of Missouri, University of North Carolina, University of Nebraska, University of Pennsylvania, University of Pittsburg, University of Southern California, University of Virginia, Washington and Lee University, Wellesley College, and Yale University (associated with Rudy Vallee).

- ➢ Also note, moreover, a few college publications in the section above.

Numerous military bases were indeed an honor to visit, noting the great struggles of WWII. While not all are noted, they were indeed part of the entertainment agenda, which spread worldwide. A few key locations are noted below, including Stage Door Canteens, along with (AFRS), or the Armed Forces Radio Service radio programs and V-Discs, for the colossal war effort that kept America united and safe. After the attack on Pearl Harbor, domestic nightclubs became very real ways to raise funds for the war effort. On any given day, a serviceperson could walk into a service club or military base and dance with Hollywood stars like Bette Davis, Betty Grable, or Ginger Rogers, or perhaps see and hear (for free) the voices of Gene Autry (in uniform), Judy Garland, Lena Horne, Ethel Merman, Ginny Simms, Frank Sinatra, Sophie Tucker (who had done the same during WWI), Rudy Vallee (also in the Coast Guard), or Ethel Waters. By 1942, the effort followed servicemen to distant war fronts around the world, including hospitals. This included every continent, including, along with many islands in the Pacific, the Caribbean and even the Artic. Apart from the talents of Hollywood film entities and comics like Bob Hope and Jack Benny, vocalists who made it "over there" included the likes of many, including the Andrews Sisters, Bing Crosby, Marlene Dietrich, Morton Downey, Tamara ((Drasin)—killed in a plane crash), Jane Froman (almost killed in a plane crash), Al Jolson, Frances Langford, Ella Logan, Ann Moray, Martha Raye, Lily Pons, Dinah Shore, and Martha Tilton. In true retrospective, the only sad part of American unity was that most Afro-Americans were restricted in where they could appear within their own country and officially they were not allowed to tour overseas. This included the likes of established black entities like Hattie McDaniel and Ethel Waters, as well as the younger likes of Lena Horne, who was also a GI pinup, and Billy Eckstine. A few notable exceptions included a group of electrifying appearances by Josephine Baker in North Africa (who was already there, essentially an established French entertainer) and Alberta Hunter, and very much unreported in the U.S. (except by Afro-American newsprint), Alberta Hunter's USO travels through China, Burma, India, Russia and Europe-at the request of General Eisenhower in Frankfort, Germany, 1945. (Like Baker, Americans Adelaide Hall and Elisabeth Welch had fewer racial problems in their adapted resident country, performing for British and American servicemen throughout the war.)

- ♦ The numerous American legions, scattered all over the United States, before and after both world wars, sponsored many gigs as well as radio remotes.
- ♦ The names of churches and synagogues, fertile ground for the development of music and numerous entertainers, are sometimes linked to the listing below.

- ▪ Traveling Circuits

a. Steamboats, ocean liners, and other maritime avenues of entertainment were another originating source of entertainment.

b. Sites such as Fox, Keith's, and Orpheum, later merged as RKO, were also vaudeville (live entertainment) circuits. Others included Pantages, Columbia, Mutual Burlesque, Balaban and Katz, which also would merge. Noted personages that appeared on marquees or made them function and or extend from theatre vaudville, radio, to talking films included the likes of Fred L. Ames, E.F. Albee, Balaban Brothers-A.J. & Barney, Martin Beck, David Belasco, Timothy Blackstone, Irwin Chanin, Chrninsky Brothers-Eprhraim & Simon, John Cort, Robert W. Dowling, S.H. Dudley, Abe Erlanger, Edwin Forrest, Sam Goldwyn, Niles T. Granlund (N.T.G.), Oscar Hammerstein (1), Bernard Jacobs, Katz Brothers-Morris & Sam, Benjamin F. Keith (B.F.K), Mark Klaw, Jesse Lasky, George Lederer, Marcus Lowe, Ed Lowry, David Merrick, Louis B, Meyer, Morris Meyerfeld, Oliver Moroso, David T. Nederlander, Tony Pastor (not the latter-bandleader), Alexander Pantages, Frederick Proctor, Selwyn Brothers-Arch & Edgar, Shubert Brothers-Abe, Jacob & Lee, Skouras Brothers-Charles, George & Spyros, Gustov Walker, Warner Brothers-Albert, Harry, Jack, Sam, Percy C. Williams & Adolph Zukor, amoung others-including some noted in text.

c. Opera. Many a show, for many a town.
d. Church groups.
e. Circus. The clowns, the wild animals—the European tradition had indeed found Americana profitable, noting B. T. Barnum and the eventual Barnum and Bailey merge. The American influence became most obvious when "cowboy" and (American) Indian tales acts were added, indeed much fodder for the likes of the following:
f. Bill Cody's "Wild West" Circus—the traditional circus, perhaps best Americanized by Buffalo Bill, and attractions such as Annie Oakley and Will Rogers, indeed real chunks for the otherwise mythical "wild West." He, more so, toured Europe, exporting Americana and its romantic legions and myths (1882-1912?)! (Kit Carson did the same!)
g. Medicine show. It was a crude mix of entertainment, with quack remedies for the sick or the ailing. (Indeed, these rural road shows featured both black as well as white circuits. The early success of Ma Rainey and her protégé Bessie Smith, well before 1920, may be noted.)
h. Minstrel show. The blackface era that thrived before 1920 was also part of vaudeville. White minstrel entities who emerged as major recording artists were Al Jolson and Sophie Tucker.
i. Carnival (almost a circus). Rides, live shows, and all sorts of featured acts finds this business, however limited, still surviving the centuries.
j. Florence Ziegfeld, inspired by both B. T. Barnum and Bill Cody and naked women made the live aspects of vaudeville a huge enterprise, eventually as a Broadway production.
k. Chautauqua. While hardly a carnival, the traveling expanded "medicine" show, before 1925, was more rural and profitable (many associated with the Methodist Church).
l. Rodeo. Catch that cow before selling it?
m. A segregated circuit for Afro-Americans, TOBA (Theater Owner's Booking Association), was to be later absorbed by others, with black entertainers gaining many white patron in the 1920s.

- By the mid-1930s, most vaudeville houses were regulated to film showings, with only some live Gigs and (radio) hookups. In subsequent years, many became flop houses, featuring burlesque.

Gangland control. While the criminal element had traditionally been part of the entertainment industry before 1919, the passage of the Volstead Act, which prohibited the sale of alcohol, did, in fact, provide racketeers a great means to get rich, and indeed with public demand and support. It would thus be for the whole decade of the Roaring Twenties that such notable and colorful public servants such as Lucky Luciano (New York), Frank Costello (New York), Owney Madden and Dutch Schultz (New York), Meyer Lansky (New York and Los Angeles), Abe Bernstein (Detroit), John Lazia (Kansas City), Nig Rosen (Philadelphia), Chuck Polizzi (Cleveland), and Longy Zwillman (Newark) emerged. Moreover, while this list is far from complete for the rest of the country, the aspects of the Chicago mobs would truly capture the attention of the public, indeed, and the later myths.

The likes of Al "Scarface" Capone would, more so, become public knowledge. While the later 1920s and the Great Depression made money tight and the bank robbery business also found such would-be Robin Hoods such Baby Face Nelson, Bonnie and Clyde, and John Dillinger, the Capone mob would capture the heart of the public, as well as the irk of Eliot Ness and the FBI. Moreover, the likes of Capone's Frank "the Enforcer" Nitti, Jack "Greasy Thumb" Guzik, and Frank "Machine Gun" McGurn battling Ness and his gangland rivals George "Bugs" Moran, Hymie Weiss, and a gentle-looking florist Dion O'Banion's own long funeral procession would become folklore generated into film and regrettable forgotten facts of unspeakable and glorified crime. Moreover, the flow of liquor and the lure of the high life found most musicians, bandleaders, and vocalists all part of the underworld. The speakeasy would become a norm and a novelty for entertainment and pleasure as well as for the viability of (illegal) alcohol. If not mob-owned, they were, to be sure, under mob control and influences. In fact, any number of entertainers were subject to any kinds of police raids, at anytime that the payoff was not met. In fact, the politics of three large cities in the United States of the era included Jimmy Walker (New York City), Big Bill Thompson (Chicago), and Thomas Pendergast (Kansas City), who were frequent visitors and participants. Notable vocalists such as Rudy Vallee, Helen Morgan, and Russ Columbo, who had gotten deeply involved in owning their own nightclubs, subsequently gave themselves the headache of breaking the law, managing payoffs, as well as the friendships of the notable hoods who supplied the booze. It should also be noted that many sites, originally illegal speakeasy establishments, became legal and legit when Prohibition ended (1933). More so, in addition to associations, many entertainers were tied to managers with alleged mob connections. They included Joe Glaser, who at times managed both Louis Armstrong and Billie Holiday, and "Moe the Gimp" Snyder, the longtime manager and husband to Ruth Etting.

Change of ownerships, name change, and location changes are not always noted, as well as relevant perceptions, perhaps lost in the fog of time. Nevertheless, this list should provide at least some creditability to the numerous performers who performed in them.

The numerous sites in New York City just cannot be overlooked. While all other cities are relevant, the entertainment industry was by far, between 1900 and 1950, tied to New York media influence, attitude, and monies in all (commercial) means and ways. (Legit Broadway already noted.)

> ➢ Any additional comments are also selective.

- Abadie's Café, Marais and Bienville, New Orleans, LA (before 192**0).**
- Academy of Music, Broad and Locust Streets, Philadelphia, PA.
- Academy of Music, Norfolk, VA.
- Academy of Music, Wilmington, NC (1920s).
- Academy of Music, Fourteenth Street, New York City, NY.

- Academy of Music, Selma, AL.
- Academy, Charleston, SC.
- Ace of Clubs (Ritz Building), Chicago, IL (1920s).
- Adams Theatre, Newark, NJ.
- Addison Hotel (Ballroom), Detroit, MI.
- Adelphi Theater, Clark Street, near Harrison, Chicago, IL (one of at least two Chicago sites).
- Adelphi Theatre, Philadelphia, PA.
- Adelphia Theatre, Chestnut at 13th, Philadelphia, PA
- Adolphus Hotel (Ballroom), Dallas, TX.
- Adrian's Tap Room (President Hotel), 234 W. Forty-Eighth Street, New York City, NY (musician Adrian Rollini).
- Aeolian Hall, Forty-Second Street, New York, NY. (In 1924, George Gershwin, associated with bandleader Paul Whiteman's Orchestra, introduced his fab piano instrumental *Rhapsody in Blue* here.
- Aimee Semple McPherson Temple, Los Angeles, CA.
- Al Levy's Grill (Supper Club), 1750 Spring Street, Los Angeles, CA. (Al Levy started as a pushcart vendor in the early 1900s.)
- Al Levy's Tavern, 1623 North Vine Street, Hollywood, CA
- Al Malaikah Temple, 665 W. Jefferson Boulevard, Los Angeles, CA (1906-20).
- Alabama Theatre, Birmingham, AL (1927+).
- Alamo Café, 125th Street, NYC, NY (before 1920+).
- Alamo Hotel (Alamo Café), 837 W. Wilson, Chicago, IL.
- Albany Hotel, Albany, NY.
- Albee Theatre, Cincinnati, OH.
- Albee Theatre (Albee Square), Brooklyn, NYC, NY.
- Albert Theatre Lancaster, NY
- Alcazar Theatre, 2600 Farrell Street, San Francisco, CA (1911+).
- Alexander Theatre, or "Alex,"216 N. Brand Blvd. Glendale, CA (1925+).
- Alexandria Hotel, Fifth Street and Main (Indian Grill Room), Los Angeles, CA (1920s).
- Alf Bonner's Place, Gill, AR (before 1920).
- Alfred's Resturant, 886 Broadway, San Francisco, CA (1929+).
- Alhambra Theatre, 2110 Seventh Avene, Harlem, NYC, NY.
- Alhambra Theatre, 334 W. Wisconsin Avenue, Milwaukee, WI.
- Alhambra Theatre, Cleveland, OH.
- Allerton Hotel (Tip Tap Lounge) 701 N. Michigan, Chicago, IL.
- Allen Theatre, Cleveland, OH (1921+).
- Alpine Hotel, McKeesport, PA.
- Alvarado Hotel, Central Avenue at First, Albuquerque, NM.
- Ambassador East Hotel (Pump Room), 1201 N. State Parkway, Chicago, IL (1938+).
- Ambassador Hotel, (Ballroom), Atlantic City, NJ. (Reputed mobster Michael (Mickey) Duffy gunned down, 1931).
- Ambassador Theatre, Locust Street and Seventh, St. Louis, MO (1926+).
- Ambassador West Hotel (Buttery Room), 1300 N. State Street, Chicago, IL (1924+).
- Ambassador's Club, Fifty-Seventh Street, NYC, NY.
- American Theatre, Market Street and Seventh, St. Louis, MO.
- Angola Penitentiary, near Highway 66, LA. (Alan Lomax "found" singing inmate Huddie Leadbetter here, recording for the Library of Congress (1933). One of the three prisons noted in this section.)

- Animule Hall, New Orleans, LA. (Bandleader Jelly Roll Morton led the house band before 1917.)
- Annex Café (Tom Anderson's), Basin and Iberville, New Orleans, LA (before 1920).
- Annex Theater, Perry, OK.
- Ansonia Café, 1654 W. Madison Street, Chicago, IL (associated with Cliff Edwards gigs before 1920).
- Antoine Restaurant, New Orleans, LA.
- Antlers Hotel (Fun Room), Colorado Springs, CO (1940s+).
- Apex Club, 330 E. Thirty-Fifth Street (Jimmie Noone's *Apex Blues*) Chicago, IL (1928-30).
- Apex Club, Los Angeles, CA (1928+).
- Apollo Theatre, 125th Street, between Seventh and Eighth Avenues, Uptown, Harlem, NYC, NY. (1934+). After 1934, this site perked up with new talent. Perhaps the most original early (vocal) discoveries included Ella Fitzgerald (from Chick Webb's Orchestra), Billie Holiday, the Ink Spots, Thelma Carpenter (1930s), Billy Eckstine (already a musician), and Sarah Vaughan (1940s).
- Apollo Theatre, Clark at Randolph, Chicago, IL (one of many Chicago sites).
- Apollo Theatre, Forty-Second Street, NYC, NY (not to be confused with another NYC site, in Harlem).
- Arabian Tent Club, Baltimore, MD (1920s).
- Aragon Ballroom, Santa Monica, CA.
- Aragon Ballroom, 1106 W. Lawrence Avenue, Chicago, IL (1926+).
- Aragon Ballroom, Ocean Park, CA (1940s).
- Arbor Dance Hall, Seventh Avenue and Fifty-Second Street, NYC, NY (before 1920).
- Arcade Theatre, Lake Charles, LA.
- Arcadia Ballroom, Detroit, MI.
- Arcadia Ballroom, NYC, NY.
- Arcadia Ballroom, St. Louis, MO.
- Arcadia Ballroom, 4444 N. Broadway and Wilson, Chicago, IL (1920s).
- Arcadia Ballroom, Providence, RI.
- Arcadia Café, Philadelphia, PA (1930s).
- Arcadia Hall, Halsey Street and Broadway, Brooklyn, NYC, NY (1920s+).
- Arena, Philadelphia, PA.
- Argonot Hotel (Ballroom), East Colfax Avenue, Denver, CO (1913+)
- Arkota Ballroom, Sioux Falls, SD.
- Arlington Square Theatre, Boston, MA (1920s).
- Armando's (Supper Club), NYC, NY (1930s+)
- Armor Ballroom, Marion, IA.
- Armory, Bridgeport, CN.
- Armory, Fairmont, WV.
- Armory, Jacksonville, FL.
- Armory, Louisville, KY.
- Armory, Mankato, MN.
- Armory, Newark NJ.
- Armory, Syracuse, NY.
- Armory, Wilkes-Barre, PA.
- Arrowhead Inn, Burnham, IL (1920s).
- Art's Café, Philadelphia, PA (1930s).
- Arthur Hotel, Lakewood, NJ (1940s).

- Ash-Trumbull Club, Detroit, MI (1940s)
- Astor Hotel (Roof Garden), 1514 Broadway, NYC, NY.
- Athens Club, Oakland, CA.
- Athletic Park Pavilion, Richmond, VA.
- Atlantic City Casino, Absecon & Beach Thoroughfare Atlantic City, NJ.
- Atlanta Women's Club, Atlanta GA.
- Atlantic City Convention Hall, Atlantic City, NJ.
- Atlas Hall, Milwaukee, WI (1940s).
- Attucks Theater, Norfolk, VA.
- Auburn State Prison, Auburn, NY (especially a 1934 gig by Cab Calloway).
- Auby's Lagoon, Miami, FL (1930s).
- Auditorium, Evansville, IN
- Auditorium, Louisville, KY
- Auditorium Theatre, Houston, TX.
- Auditorium Theatre, Ventura, CA.
- Auditorium, the, Hot Springs, AK.
- Auditorium, Long Beach, CA.
- Auditorium Theatre, Atlanta, GA (1920s).
- Auditorium Theatre, Charlotte, NC.
- Auditorium Theatre, Oakland, CA.
- Auditorium Theatre, San Bernardino, CA.
- Auditorium Theatre, Spokane, WA.
- Auditorium Theatre, Roanoke, VA.
- Auditorium Theatre, 50 East Congress Street, near Michigan Blvd., Chicago, IL.
- Audubon Theatre, Bronx, NYC, NY.
- Augie's Minneapolis, MN (1940s).
- Avadon Ballroom, Los Angeles, CA (1940s).
- Avenue Theatre, Thirty-First Street and Indiana, Chicago, IL (1920s).
- Avery Hotel, Boston, MA.
- Avon Ballroom, Catalina Island, CA.
- Babette's Club, (former vaudvilian Blanche Babette), Pacific Avenue, Atlantic City, NJ. (1930s)
- Backstage Club, W. Fifty-Sixth Street, NYC, NY (1922). Billy Rose, who was for a time married to Fanny Brice, was a Broadway entity who produced many shows and a songwriter. He, more so, found the NYC nightclub business worth tackling. Among his other clubs, those noted are the Casa Manana, Casino de Paree, and the Diamond Horseshoe. This Backstage Club was perhaps his first shot at clubs and, perhaps, founded his association with reputed mobster, Arnold Rothstein. It is, moreover, alleged that Helen Morgan, who had previously worked in speakeasy clubs in Chicago, sat on a piano while performing here at the cramped "backstage." For Helen, the image stuck.
- Bacons Casino, Forty-Ninth and Wabash Avenue, Chicago, IL (1920s).
- Bahamian Club, Los Angeles, CA (1920s).
- Bailey Club, Baltimore, MD (1920s).
- Bailey's 81, Atlanta, GA (1920s).
- Baker Hotel, Commercial Street (Peacock Terrace Ballroom, Crystal Ballroom), Dallas, TX (1926+).
- Baker's Lounge, Detroit, MI (1934+).
- Bal Tabarin, Wilshire Boulevard, Los Angeles, CA.

- Bal Tabarin, Columbus Avenue and Chestnut Street, San Francisco, CA. (Myth has it that both Ginny Simms & Tony Martin shared early gigs here in 1932?)
- Bal Tabarin, 225 W. Forty-Sixth Street, NYC, NY.
- Balboa Club, San Diego, CA (1920s).
- Ballyhoo Club, Los Angeles, CA (1930s) (associated with singer-dancer Carmen Miranda's gigs, 1932).
- Baltimore Coliseum, Baltimore, MD.
- Bamba Club, Los Angeles, CA.
- Bamboo Gardens, 103rd and Euclid, Cleveland, OH.
- Bambu Hut, Ontario, CA (1940s).
- Bamville Club, 65 West 129th Street, Harlem, NYC, NY (1920s).
- Band Box (nightclub), 36 W. Randolph, Chicago, IL (1940s).
- Band Box Club, 161 W. 131st Street, Harlem, NYC, NY (1920s).
- Band Box (Lucille's Band Box), Eighteenth Street, Kansas City, MO (1920s).
- Band Box, Cleveland, OH (1920s).
- Bandit's Cave (Greenwich village), NYC, NY (1920s).
- Banker's Inn Club, near Huntertown, IN (1930s).
- Banks Club, 133rd, Uptown, Harlem, NYC, NY (before 1920).
- Bar of Music (lounge), Howard Street, Chicago, IL (1940s).
- Bar of Music (lounge), Hollywood, CA. (1948+)
- Barassos Theater, Memphis, TN (1920s).
- Bardavon Theatre, Poughkeepsie, NY (1920s).
- Barn (nightclub), San Antonio, TX (1940s).
- Barney Gallant's (nightclub), 85 W. Third Street, NYC, NY.
- Barney Gordon's Saloon, Kater and Thirteenth Streets, Philadelphia, PA (before 1920).
- Barritz Restaurant, 57 Boradstreet, Philadelphia, PA
- Barron Long's, Roadhouse, Los Angeles, CA (1920s).
- Barron's Exclusive Club, 2259 Seventh Avenue at 134th Street, Harlem, NYC, NY. (Afro-American reputed mobster-owner Barron Wilkins was killed in front of this site in 1926.)
- Barron's Lounge, 439 Lenox Avenue, Harlem, NYC, NY (another Barron Wilkins site).
- Basin Street, New Orleans, LA. A section of this street included Storyville, a high-crime area, full of brothels and gambling houses, before 1917. The emerging "Dixieland jazz" music of such musicians as Jelly Roll Morton, Buddy Bolden, Joe "King" Oliver, Sidney Bechet, and Louis Armstrong, among others, perhaps found its origins here?
- Bath Club, W. Fifty-Third Street, NYC, NY (1920s).
- Beachcomber Hotel (club), Miami Beach, FL (1940s+).
- Beachcomber, Omaha, NE (1940s).
- Beale Street in Memphis, Tennessee, frequented many (black) musical trends in the early century, including the likes of cornet musician W. C. Handy. More so, Handy's own published "Memphis Blues" (1912) and "Beale Street Blues" (1916) compositions defined both this city and street light-years before B. B. King, as well as Elvis and Graceland.
- Beaumont Auditorium, Beaumont, TX.
- Beaux Arts Café, Philadelphia, PA.
- Bee Hive, 1503 E. Fifty-Fifth Street, Chicago, IL (1948+).
- Belasco Theatre, 337 Main Street, Los Angeles, CA (1920s).
- Belasco Theatre, 17 Madison Place, Washington, DC.
- Bellerive Hotel, Kansas City, MO.

- Bellevue Hotel, San Francisco, CA.
- Bellevue-Stratford Hotel, Philadelphia, PA.
- Belvedere Hotel (Palm Grill), Santa Barbara, CA (1920s).
- Bemus Point Casino, Bemus Point, NY.
- Benedict Club, Matamoras Street, San Antonio, TX.
- Benjamin Franklin Hotel (Kite and Key Room), Philadelphia, PA.
- Benjamin Harrison Literary Club (speakeasy), Pittsburgh, PA (early gigs for Maxine Sullivan, 1930s).
- Berchel Theatre, Des Moines, IA.
- Berghoff, Ft. Wayne, IN (1940s).
- Berkshire Hotel (Barbarry Room), NYC, NY.
- Berkshire Playhouse, Stockbridge, MA.
- Berthana Ogden, UT.
- Beverly Gardens, Ninety-First and Western, Chicago, IL.
- Beverly Hills Country Club, Newport, KY (1940s+).
- Beverly Wilshire Hotel (Florentine Ballroom), 9500 Wilshire Blvd., Beverly Hills, CA (1928+).
- Big Apple Nightclub, Columbia, SC (1936+). (Perhaps the contemporary 1930s dance started here?)
- Big Apple, 135th and Seventh Avenue, Uptown, Harlem, NYC, NY. As associated with Adelaide Hall gigs in 1924, this site became a term later became associated with the whole of NYC. Later, in 1938, Adelaide Hall would open a similar club, of the same name, in Paris, France. This term would also to become a popular "dance" entity recording by many, including a popular, Tommy Dorsey Orchestra release, with a fine vocal by Edythe Wright, on Victor 25652.
- Big Gaiety Theater, Milwaukee, WI.
- Big Johns, 2234 Seventh Avenue, Uptown, Harlem, NYC, NY (1920s+).
- Bijou Dream Theatre, 310 West Second Street, Ashland, WI.
- Bijou Theatre, Knoxville, TN.
- Bijou Theatre, Mobile, AL (1922+).
- Bijou Theatre, Nashville, TN.
- Bijou Theatre, 112 E. Broughton, Savannah, GA.
- Bill LaHiff's Tavern, Forty-Eighth Street, NYC, NY.
- Billy Berg's Nightclub, Vine Street, Los Angeles, CA (especially Frankie Laine solo gigs in 1946).
- Billy King's Restaurant, Lake Street and Oak, Chicago, IL.
- Billy Rose's Music Hall, 1697-99 Broadway, NYC, NY (1930s).
- Billy Sunday's Tabernacle, Norfolk, VA (1920s).
- Biloxi Community Center Biloxi, MS.
- Biltmore Gardens, Fifth Street and Grand Avenue, Los Angles, CA.
- Biltmore Hotel (Starlight Ballroom, Biltmore Bowl), Fifth Street and Olive, Los Angeles, CA.
- Biltmore Hotel, Providence, RI.
- Biltmore Hotel (Baccante Room), Providence, RI.
- Biltmore Hotel, Atlanta, GA.
- Biltmore Hotel, Coral Gables, FL.
- Biltmore Hotel, Palm Springs, CA.
- Biltmore Theater, Los Angeles, CA.

- Biograph Theatre, Chicago, IL. Bank robber John Dillinger was shot in front of this site (1934).
- Birdland, 1678 Broadway, NYC, NY (the musical term) (1949+).
- Birdland, 2200 Park Avenue, Miami Beach, FL (the musical term).
- Biscayne Plaza Theatre, 206 Biscayne Street, Miami Beach, FL (1926+).
- Bismarck Hotel (Walnut Room), 171 W. Randolph, Chicago, IL (briefly known as the "Randolph"). During WWI, as the name 'Bismarck, a former German chancellor, became unpopular.
- Black Cat Ballroom, Delaware, NJ.
- Black Cat Café (Greenwich Village), NYC, NY (1930s).
- Black Cat Club, San Francisco, CA.
- Black Curtain, Tulsa, OK (1927+)
- Blackhawk Restaurant, 139 N. Wabash Avenue, Chicago, IL (1920s+). Many bands, including the Coon-Sanders Orchestra (with vocals, in 1924) and the Kay Kyser Kollege of Musical Knowledge Orchestra (with featured vocalists Ginny Simms and Harry Babbitt as radio broadcasts in 1937) performed here.
- Black Orchid, Fifty-Second Street, NYC, NY (1940s).
- Blackstone Hotel and Theatre, 60 E. Hubbard (Balinese Room, Mayfair Room), Chicago, IL (1911+).
- Blatz Palm Garden, City Hall Square, Milwaukee, WI.
- Blossom Inn, Detroit, MI (1930s).
- Blue And Gold, 136 Turk Street, San Francisco, CA.
- Blue Angel (nightclub), NYC, NY (1943+).
- Blue Boar Cafeteria, Atlanta, GA (1930s).
- Blue Bonnet Hotel, San Antonio, TX (1930s).
- Blue Grotta, Wabash, and Van Buren, Chicago, IL (1930s).
- Blue Heaven, Willoughby, and Vine, Hollywood, CA. (This Gene Austin-owned club was named after his 1927 vocal hit ditty "My Blue Heaven"—perhaps the best known of Austin-owned clubs? (1930s))
- Blue Mirror Club, Newark, NJ.
- Blue Moon Club, 1211 U Street, Washington, DC (managed by musician Jelly Roll Morton, 1930s).
- Blue Note, Boston, MA.
- Blue Note, 56 W. Madison, Chicago, IL (1940s, first site).
- Blue Note, Philadelphia, PA.
- Blue Room, Wichita, KS.
- Blue Room Club, Los Angeles, CA (associated with blues and Joe Turner gigs in 1945).
- Blue Room, Balboa, CA (1940s).
- Blue Spruce, Colorado Springs, CO (1940s).
- Bluebird, Youngstown, OH (1940s).
- Boardner's Cocktail Lounge (Steve Boardner), Cherokee Ave & Hollywood Blvd., Los Angeles, CA. (1944+)
- Boat House, Atlantic City, NJ.
- Bob Lo Pavilion, Detroit, MI.
- Bohemian Caverns, Eleventh and U Streets, Washington, DC (1920s).
- Bon Air Country Club, Evanston, IL.
- Bonnie's, Bristol, CN (1940s).
- Bonstelle Playhouse, Woodward Avenue, Detroit, MI.

- Boogie-Woogie, Cleveland, OH (the musical and dance term—indeed a good name for a club)!
- Book-Cadillac Hotel, (Grand Ballroom), Washington Blvd. Detroit, MI. (1924-51)
- Booker T. Washington Theatre, Twenty-Third and Market, St. Louis, MO.
- Bossert Hotel (Grill, Marine Roof), 98 Montague St., Brooklyn, NYC, NY (1920s+).
- Boston Madison Square Garden (later known as Boston Gardens), Boston, MA (1928+).
- Bottle Inn, the, St. Louis, MO.
- Boulevard Theater, Los Angeles, CA.
- Bournehurst Ballroom, Buzzards Bay, MA.
- Bowl, the, Springfield, IL (1940s).
- Bowman's, Aurora, IL (1940s).
- Bracker's Inn, City Island, NYC, NY. (Ozzie Nelson had an early gig here, 1929.)
- Brandeis Theatre, Omaha, NE (1920s).
- Brandt's Audubon Theater, Queens, NYC, NY.
- Brass Rail (nightclub) 52 W. Randolph, Chicago, IL (1940s).
- Brenan Auditorium, Gainesville, GA (1920s).
- Brewery (this speakeasy was near 1933 Chicago World's Fair site), Chicago, IL.
- Brick House, Gretna, LA.
- Broadstreet Theatre, NYC, NY.
- Broadway Theatre, Gary IN.
- Broadway Theatre, San Diego, CA.
- Broadway Theatre, Washington, DC.
- Broadwood Hotel, Philadelphia, PA.
- Bronx Opera House, Bronx, NYC, NY.
- Brookline Country Club, Mill Road, Brookline, PA (1930s).
- Brookside Club, Kansas City, MO.
- Brown Derby Café, 1628 N. Vine Street and Hollywood Blvd., Hollywood, CA.
- Brown Derby Café, 3427 Wilshire Blvd., Los Angeles, CA (first site, others existed in LA area).
- Brown Hotel (Crystal Ballroom), Louisville, KY (1923+).
- Brown's Opera House, 2961 Sixteenth Street, San Francisco, CA.
- Buck Lake Ranch, Angola, IN (1940s+).
- Bucktown Tavern in Jefferson Parish, New Orleans, LA (1920s).
- Buffalo Ball Park, Buffalo, NY.
- Buffalo Country Club, Buffalo, NY.
- Bug Twenty-Five (25), Franklin Street, New Orleans, LA (before 1920).
- Burnham Inn, Burnham, IL (before 1920).
- Burns Theatre, Colorado Springs, CO (1920s).
- Bushwick Theatre, Brooklyn NYC, NY (1920s).
- Bustanoby's Cabaret, Thirty-Ninth Street, NYC, NY (before 1920).
- Butler's Standard Theatre, St. Louis, MO.
- Cabin Club, Cleveland, OH.
- Cabin Inn, 3520 S. State Street, Chicago, IL (1930s).
- Cabin in the Sky, Sixty-Fourth and Cottage Grove Chicago, IL (briefly owned by Ethel Waters 1944-45)
- Cabin Inn, St Louis, MO.
- Cadle Tabernacle (church organization ownership) Indianapolis, IN.
- Café de Paree, Los Angeles, CA.

- Cafe de Paris, 459 E. 31st Street, Chicago, IL. (Adelaide Hall's 1927 gig here came to an abrupt end, along with the club, due to a gang inspired Al Capone era bombing, after hours).
- Café de Paris, Fifty-Fourth Street near Broadway, NYC, NY (1920s).
- Café des Beaux Arts (Rose Room) 80 W. Fortieth Street, NYC, NY.
- Café Esquire, Hollywood, CA (1930s).
- Café Gala, Sunset Blvd., Los Angeles, CA.
- Café James, E. Fiftieth Street, NYC, NY (1940s).
- Café International, Los Angeles, CA.
- Café La Boheme, Los Angeles, CA.
- Café La Maze, Sunset Blvd. Los Angeles, CA.
- Café Lafayette, Los Angeles, CA (1920s).
- Café Roxy, Sunset Blvd., Hollywood, CA (1935+).
- Café Royal (Touraine Cocktail Bar), Boston, MA.
- Café Society, West Fourth and Washington Place, Greenwich Village, NYC, NY (1938-49). (This Barney Josephson-owned spot had featured Billie Holiday, Lena Horne, Helen Humes, Josh White, Leadbelly, Woody Guthrie, and others.)
- Café Society, 128th East 58th Street, Uptown, Harlem, NYC, NY (1940-49). (The second Barney Josephson-owned spot, associated with many, including Mildred Bailey, Burl Ives, Joe Turner, Rosetta Tharpe & Kay Starr.)
- Cafe Tia Juana, Cleveland, OH
- Café Society (ownership associated with actor-comic Jerry Colonna), Los Angeles, CA (1941).
- Café Society (Joe Tenner's) Fillmore, San Francisco, CA (1940s).
- Café Zanzibar, between Fiftieth and Fifty-First Streets (on top of Winter Garden Theatre), NYC, NY (1940s).
- Cain's Dancing Academy, Tulsa, OK.
- California Ballroom, Modesto, CA.
- California Cabana Club (Beach Club), Santa Monica, CA (1946+).
- California Theatre, Sacramento, CA.
- California Theatre, San Francisco, CA.
- California Theatre, San Diego, CA.
- Cal Mar Club, Market Street, Stockton, CA.
- Cal-Neva Club, Lake Tahoe, NV and CA (built on the border line—I guess?) (1940s).
- Cameo Restaurant, Tenth and Peach, Erie, PA.
- Cameo Theatre, 528 S. Broadway, Los Angeles, CA (1910+).
- Campbell Gardens, Campbell and Madison, Chicago, IL (1920s).
- Canadarago Park, Richfield Springs, NY.
- Congress Hall (Glass Hat), Michigan and Congress, Chicago, IL.
- Canobie Lake Park Dance Hall, Salem, NH.
- Canton's Grand Opera House, Canton, OH.
- Cap Fear Hotel, Wilmington, NC.
- Cape Playhouse, Dennis, MA.
- Capital Cocktail Lounge, Duluth, MN (1940s).
- Capital Lounge, N. State Street, Chicago, IL (1940s).
- Capital Palace Club, 575 Lenox Avenue, Uptown, Harlem, NYC, NY.
- Capital Theatre, Fifty-Second and Broadway, Uptown, Harlem, NYC, NY.
- Capital Theatre, Albany, NY.
- Capital Theater, 1521 Elm Street, Dallas, TX (Especially a Roy Rogers gig in 1938)

- Capital Theatre, San Francisco, CA.
- Capital Theatre, Wheeling, WV.
- Capri Club, La Cienega, Los Angeles, CA.
- Capital Theatre, Esplanade Avenue and N. Claiborne, New Orleans, LA.
- Carey Walsh's Saloon (Coney Island), NYC, NY (before 1920).
- Carlton Theater, Jamaica, Long Island, NYC, NY.
- Carman Theatre, Philadelphia, PA.
- Carnegie Hall, Fifty-Seventh and Seventh Avenue, Downtown, NYC, NY (1890+). This very highbrow center of European classical music somehow introduced the likes of "yeas" or "jazz," when, as early as 1914, a black orchestra (Clef Club) led by James Reese Europe played there. This form of crude jazz may often be pitted with the better-known| Dixieland jazz from New Orleans. It would be some years later, into the mid-1930s, that this site again would accommodate contemporary popular music, due chiefly to the jazzy gigs of Benny Goodman and Duke Ellington. Moreover, Ivie Anderson sang there, as well as Ethel Waters.
- Carlton Theatre, Tren Red Bank, NJ.
- Carmel Gardens by the Sea, Second and Broadway, Santa Monica, CA.
- Carnival (Nicky Blair's), NYC, NY. (1940s)
- Carnival (Club), Minneapolis, MN. (1940s).
- Carolina Theater, Durham, NC.
- Carpenter Hotel (Ballroom) Sioux Falls, SD.
- Carter Hotel (Ballroom) Philadelphia, PA.
- Casa Blanca, W. Fifty-Sixth Street, NYC, NY. Alleged mobster Larry Fay was killed at this site in 1932.
- Casa D' Amore (nite club) Cahuenga Blvd., Hollywood, CA.
- Casa Madrid, Club Louisville, KY (1930s).
- Casa Madrid, Club Hyannis, MA (1940s).
- Casa Manana Seventh Avenue, near Broadway, NYC, NY (1938+).
- Casa Manana Ballroom Café, Culver City, CA.
- Casa Manana, Fort Worth, TX (1936+).
- Casablanca (nightclub), Chicago, IL (1940s).
- Casanova Club (speakeasy), 151 W. Fifty-Fourth Street, NYC, NY (including Ruth Etting's and Helen Kane's gigs (1928-29)).
- Casanova Club, Hollywood, CA.
- Cascades Gardens, Sheridan Road and Argyle, Chicago, IL (1920s+).
- Casino Cabaret (formerly Casino Gardens), Clark and Kinzie, Chicago, IL.
- Casino Café (Casino Theatre), San Diego, CA.
- Casino de Paree, NYC, NY (1935+).
- Casino Gardens Ballroom, Ocean Park, CA.
- Casino Gardens Ballroom, Santa Monica, CA.
- Casino in the Park (Essex House), NYC, NY.
- Casino Theatre (Ballroom), Newport, RI.
- Casmir Theatre, 4750 Milwaukee Avenue, Chicago IL.
- Cass Theatre, Detroit, MI.
- Castilian Gardens, Valley Stream, Long Island, NYC, NY (1920s).
- Castle Ballroom, St. Louis, MO.
- Castle Farm (Hall) l, near Cincinnati, OH.
- Castle Gardens, State and Quincy, Chicago, IL (1920s).

- Castle House, Forty-Sixth Street, NYC, NY (1913+) (the dance team of Vernon and Irene Castle).
- Castle Royal, 215 Wabasha Street (Wabasha Cave), St. Paul, MN (1930s-41).
- Castle Square Theatre, Boston, MA.
- Castro Theatre, San Francisco, CA. (1922+).
- Catagonia Club (Pod and Jerry's), 166 W. 139th Street, NYC, NY (1930s).
- Catalina Casino, Avalon, Catalina Island, CA (1929+).
- Catalina John's Restauranr, Los Angeles, CA (1940s)
- Cathay Circle Theatre (Fox), Wilshire Blvd. Los Angeles, CA (1926+).
- Cathedral Hall, Houston, TX.
- Cat's Meow Club, Hoboken, NJ (esp. Frank Sinatra) (1930s).
- Cavalier Beach Club (Cavalier Hotel), Virginia Beach, VA.
- Cave of Winds, Chicago, IL (1940s).
- Cedar Point Ballroom, Sandusky, OH.
- Central Park Casino, NYC, NY.
- Central Theatre, Dallas, TX.
- Central Theatre, Jersey City, NJ.
- Central Theatre, Passaic, NJ.
- Central, Alden, NY (1940s).
- Century Club, Los Angeles, CA.
- Century Theatre, Buffalo, NY.
- Century Theatre, Century Grove Roof, NYC, NY (1920s).
- Century Theatre, Baltimore, MD. (1920s+).
- Chagrin Valley Hunt Club, Gages Mill, OH.
- Chanin Auditorium, Forty-Second Street and Lexington (fifteenth floor), NYC, NY.
- Chapeau Rouge, Forty-Ninth Street, NYC, NY (1930s).
- Chapel Theatre, Great Neck, NY.
- Chapman Park Hotel (Zephyr Room) 3401 Wilshire Blvd., Los Angeles, CA.
- Charles Hurst Ballroom, Salem, MA.
- Charlie Dale Club, Spokane, WA (1920s).
- Charlie Foy's Supper Club, 15463 Ventura Blvd., San Fernando Valley, Sherman Oaks, CA. Owner Charlie Foy was a former vaudevillian and a brother of Eddie Foy Jr. (1940s).
- Charlie Turpin's House, St. Louis, MO (1920s).
- Charlotte Hotel, Charlotte, NC.
- Charm Club, Manhattan, NYC, NY (1920s).
- Chase Hotel (Chase Club) (Zodiak Room) Lindell St. Louis, MO (1922+) (as Park Plaza in 1931).
- Chasen's Restaurant (vaudevillian Dave Chasen), 9039 Beverly Blvd., Beverly Hills, CA (1936+).
- Chateau Theatre (Chateau Ballroom), 3810 N. Broadway, Chicago, IL.
- Chateau La Mar Café, Chicago, IL.
- Chateau Madrid, 231 W., Fifty-Fourth Street, NYC, NY (1920s).
- Chatham Club, Doyers Street (Chinatown), NYC, NY (ethnic site, featuring jazz (1920s)).
- Chelsea (Club), Atlantic City, NY (1940s).
- Chermot (Ballroom),Omaha,NE.
- Cherry Blossom, 1822 Vine Street, Kansas City, MO.
- Cherry Springs Dance Hall, Cherry Springs, TX.
- Chester Theater, Bronx, NYC, NY.

- Chesterfield Club, Des Moines, IA (1940s).
- Chesterfield Club, Kansas City, MO (1930s). This exclusive men's club featured seminude women waitresses and the likes of jazz music, as club mythology has it, including vocals by Julia Lee.
- Chez Ami, Buffalo, NY.
- Chez Paree, 610 N. Fairbanks Ct., Chicago, IL (1932+).
- Chez Pierre, 247 E. Ontario, Chicago, IL (1920s).
- Chi Chi Club, 217 N. Palm Canyon Drive, Palm Springs, CA.
- Chi Chi Club, Hollywood, CA (1930s+).
- Chi Chi Club, Salt Lake City, UT (1940s).
- Chicago Stadium, 1800 W. Madison, Chicago IL (1929+).
- Chicago Theatre, 175 N. State Street (and Lake Street), Chicago, IL (1921+).
- Chicken Coop (ownership associated with actor Canada Lee), Harlem, NYC, NY (1940s).
- Chicken Shack, Chicago, IL.
- Chief Theatre, Pocatello, ID.
- Child's Gingham Club, Pittsburg, PA (1930s).
- Chin Chow, 4709 S. Parkway, Chicago, IL (1930s). (This famous ethnic Restaurant featured jazz.)
- Chinese Skyroom, San Francisco, CA.
- Chris Convention Hall, Flores and Houston Streets, San Antonio, TX.
- Chubby's Café, Camden, NJ (1940s).
- Church's Park, Fourth and Beale, Memphis, TN.
- Chutes (Cabaret), Fulton Street, San Francisco, CA (one of three sites, before 1920).
- Cinderella Ballroom, Broadway and Forty-Eighth Street, NYC, NY (1920s).
- Cinderella Ballroom, Fifth and Hill Streets, Los Angeles, CA.
- Cinderella Café, Cottage Grove and Sixty-Fourth Street, Chicago, IL (1920s+).
- Cinderella Club, Denver, CO.
- Circle Club, Indianapolis, IN (1940s).
- Circle Playhouse, Annapolis, MD (1920s).
- Circle Theater, Indianapolis, IN.
- Circle Theatre, Euclid at 102nd, Cleveland, OH
- Circus Café, 1857 W. North Avenue, Chicago, IL (1920s).
- Ciro's, Philadelphia, PA.
- Ciro's (nightclub), 8433 Sunset Blvd., Hollywood, CA.
- Ciro's (nightclub), Miami Beach, FL (1940s).
- City Auditorium, Houston, TX.
- City Auditorium, Montgomery, AL.
- City Auditorium, Omaha, NE.
- City Auditorium, Raleigh, NC.
- City Auditorium, Richmond, VA.
- City Auditorium, Macon, GA.
- City Auditorium, Chattanooga, TN.
- City Theatre, Fourteenth Street, NYC, NY.
- Civic Auditorium, San Francisco, CA.
- Civic Center, Corinth, MS.
- Civic Center, Detroit, MI.
- Civic Opera House, 20 N. Wacker Drive, Chicago, IL (1929+).
- Clam House Room, 146 W. 133rd Street, Harlem, NYC, NY (1920s+).
- Claremont Hotel, Cleveland, OH.

- Claremont Inn, Riverside Drive NYC, NY.
- Claridge Hotel (Ballroom), Memphis, TN.
- Clark Gables, Dunellen, NJ (1940s).
- Clemmer Theatre, Spokane, WA (1914+). During (silent) film intermissions, this site featured live entertainment. In 1925, before leaving for Los Angeles, artists included Bing Crosby and Al Rinker. Myth?
- Click Restaurant Club (Frank Palumbo's), Philadelphia, PA.
- Clift Hotel, 495 Geary Street San Francisco, CA.
- Clinton Theatre, Clinton, IA.
- Clique (Club), NYC, NY (1940s).
- Clover Club, Amarillo, TX.
- Clover Club, Biscayne Blvd., Miami, FL.
- Clover Club, 8433 Sunset Blvd., Hollywood, Los Angeles, CA (1930s+).
- Club Abby, 203 W. Fifty-Fourth Street, NYC, NY. (Reputed mobster Dutch Schultz survived gunplay here in 1931. Did the jazz band keep playing?)
- Club Alabam, 747 N. Rush Street, Chicago, IL (1930s+).
- Club Alabam, Adams Street, Detroit, MI (1920s).
- Club Alabam, 216 W. Forty-Fourth Street, Manhattan, NYC, NY (1924+).
- Club Alabam, 4215 S. Central Avenue, Los Angeles, CA.
- Club Alabam, Oakland, CA (1940s).
- Club Alabam, 1820 A Post Street, San Francisco, CA.
- Club Alvaradere, E. Thirty-Fifth Street and S. Calumet, Chicago, IL (1920s+).
- Club Argonaut, W. Fiftieth and Seventh Avenue, Manhattan, NYC, NY. One of many clubs associated with actress Texas Guinan and reputed mobster Owney Madden. Reputed mobster "Frenchy" DeMange somehow got lost in front of this site in 1931. He was later "found" alive. Early in 1932, reputed mobster Vincent Coll, suspected by some as the perpetrator, was found murdered in a drugstore.
- Club Bali, Washington, DC (1940s).
- Club Belvedere, Hot Springs, AR.
- Club Brazil, NYC, NY (1940s).
- Club Cabaret, Uptown, Harlem, NYC, NY.
- Club Cadix, Chestnut Street, Philadelphia, PA. Reputed mobsters Michael Duffy and John Bricker were involved in gunplay at this site in 1927; Duffy survived, Bricker did not.
- Club Caprice, Coronado Hotel, St. Louis, MO.
- Club Cassano (nightclub), Cincinnati, OH (1930s).
- Club Caverns, Seventeenth and U Street at Eleventh, Washington, DC.
- Club Chantee, NYC, NY (1920s). Associated with reputed mobster Richard Reese Whitemore, this nightspot burned down in 1926.
- Club Charles, Baltimore, MD (1940s).
- Club Charming, Chicago, IL (1940s).
- Club Congo, Washington, DC.
- Club Congo, Detroit, MI (1940s).
- Club Congo, Salem, OR (1940s).
- Club Deauville, Miami Beach, FL (1930s).
- Club Deauville, Fifty-Ninth Street and Park Avenue, NYC, NY (1920s).
- Club Delmonico, Park Avenue and Fifty-Ninth Street, NYC, NY (1930s).
- Club De Lisa, Fifty-Fifth and State Streets, Chicago, IL (1933+). Associated with the reputed mobster interests and ownership of the brothers Mike, Louie, and Jim, this center for Afro-American entertainment outlasted a fire (1941) and a reopening.

- Club Deluxe, 142 Street and Lenox Avenue, Uptown, Harlem, NYC, NY. Owned by (black) ex-boxing champ Jack Johnson (1920-23), later became the Cotton Club, with change of ownership.
- Club de Montmartre Theatre-Restaurant, Palm Beach, FL. (1926-29)
- Club Durante, Fifty-Seventh Street, NYC, NY (1920s). This famous speakeasy was fronted by jazz pianist Jimmy Durante, who also sang, later to become the same beloved entertainer of baby boomer TV. Frequent patrons included the likes of reputed mobsters Owney Madden and Lucky Luciano.
- Club Eighteen (18), Fifty-Second Street, NYC, NY.
- Club Eighty Six (86), Geneva, NY (1940s).
- Club Eleven (11), Waukegan, IL (1940s).
- Club Equity, 45 Eddy Street, San Francisco, CA (1930s).
- Club Final, First Street, Los Angeles, CA.
- Club Forest (Jefferson Parish), New Orleans, LA (1930s).
- Club Forty (40), Salina, KS (1930s).
- Club Fifty Two 52, Cherokee Ave. & Hollywood Blvd., Los Angeles, CA (1940s)
- Club Gallant, 40 Washington Square, South, Greenwich Village, NYC. NY. (1921-24)
- Club Harlem, Fifteenth and Paseo, Kansas City, MO.
- Club Harlem, 32 N. Kentucky Avenue, Atlantic City, NJ.
- Club Harlem, Lenox Avenue, Harlem, NYC, NY (1927+).
- Club Hollywood, Madison, WI (1948+).
- Club Hot-Cha, Uptown Harlem, NYC, NY (1930s).
- Club Intime, (in Harding Hotel), 203 W. 54th Street, NYC, NY. (1929).
- Club Kentucky 203 W. Forty-Ninth Street, NYC, NY. (Duke Ellington led the house band, 1920s).
- Club Madrid, Louisville, KY.
- Club Madrid, Philadelphia, PA (1920s).
- Club Marion, Columbia MS. (1940s).
- Club Max, 11 East Pearson, Chicago, IL (1920s).
- Club Mirador, NYC, NY. (1925)
- Club Moderne, Long Beach, CA (1940s).
- Club Napoleon, W. Fifty-Fourth Street, NYC, NY (1920s+).
- Club New Yorker, 38 East Fifty-First Street, NYC, NY (1930s).
- Club Ninety Nine (99), Joliet, IL.
- Club on Time, NYC, NY (1920s).
- Club Paradise, Atlantic City, NJ.
- Club Paramount, 162 E. Huron, Chicago, IL (1930s).
- Club Park Mor, Kalamazoo, MI
- Club Plantation, 108th and S. Central, Los Angeles, CA.
- Club Plantation, 3617 Delmar Blvd., St. Louis, MO (1940s).
- Club Regal, (Melody Room), Columbus, OH (1940s)
- Club Rhapsody, Niagara Falls, NY.
- Club Richmond, 157 West Fifty-Sixth Street, NYC, NY (associated with bandleader Harry Richmond in 1925).
- Club Ritz, 3947 S. Parkway, Chicago, IL.
- Club Royale, 416 S. Wabash, Chicago, IL (1920s).
- Club Royale, Macon, GA.
- Club Seventeen (17), Los Angeles, CA (1930s).
- Club Seville, 8433 Sunset Blvd., Hollywood, Los Angeles, CA.

- Club Silhouette, 1555 Howard Street, Chicago, IL.
- Club Sixty Seven (67), Muncie, IN (1940s).
- Club Vasques, 74 Newfield, Middleton, CN.
- Club Whiteman (Broadway at Forty-Eighth, Manhattan), NYC, NY (1927-30). Bandleader Paul Whiteman briefly owned the club; it was associated with the Rhythm Boys—Bing Crosby, Al Rinker, and Harry Barris. More so, the (1927) grand opening included vocals by Ruth Etting.
- Club Zanzibar, Forty-Ninth and Broadway (Brill Building, Second floor) NYC, NY (1944-49),
- Cobblestone the, Storm Lake, IA.
- Cocoanut Grove (Melody Lounge), 17 Piedmont, Boston, MA (tragically burned down in 1942).
- Coconut Grove, Bakersfield, CA (1920s+).
- Cocoanut Grove, 913 E. Sixty-Third Street, Chicago, IL (1920s+).
- Coconut Grove (Hotel Ambassador), 3400 Wilshire Blvd., Los Angeles, CA (1921+). Bing Crosby and Russ Columbo both found solo recognition in 1930, greatly aided by remote radio broadcasts. This famous nightclub, frequently attended by many film entities, also found itself fine fodder for (contemporary) films—notably, the (full-length) 1937 feature (B and W) *Coconut Grove*, with Harriet Hilliard (a featured vocalist), as well as fine (color) 1935 film short *Star Night at the Coconut Grove*, especially noting (featured vocalist) Bing Crosby.
- Cocoanut Palms Club, Detroit, MI (1930s).
- Coconut Grove, Reading, PA.
- Coconut Grove Ballroom, Salt Lake City, UT.
- Coliseum (Ballroom), York, PA.
- Coliseum (Ballroom), Davenport, IA.
- Coliseum (Ballroom), Greensburg, PA.
- Coliseum (Ballroom), Harrisburg, PA.
- Coliseum (Ballroom), St. Paul, MN.
- Coliseum (Ballroom), St. Louis, MO.
- Coliseum Theater, 1513 S. Wabash, Chicago IL.
- Coliseum Theater, NYC, NY.
- College Auditorium, Hanover, NH.
- College Auditorium, Lansing, MI.
- College Inn, Coney Island, Brooklyn, NYC, NY (before 1920+).
- College Inn, Dayton, OH (1940s).
- Collier Theatre, Philadelphia,
- Colonial Gardens, Rochester, IN.
- Colonial Hotel, Bogalusa, LA.
- Colonial Inn, Miami Beach, FL.
- Colonial Theatre, Boston, MA.
- Colonial Theatre, Cleveland, OH
- Colonial Theatre, 20 W. Randolph, Chicago, IL (1905-26, later known as the Oriental).
- Colonial Theatre, Dayton, OH.
- Colonial Theatre, Utica, NY.
- Colonial Theatre, Sixty-Second and Broadway, NYC, NY. In 1922, a contemporary all-black revue *Runnin' Wild*, found young Elisabeth Welch introducing the faddish 1920s' dance,—as composed by James P. Johnson—the "Charleston." Too bad, a contemporary recording, with vocals, was not produced!

- Colonial Theatre, Fort Wayne, IN.
- Colonial Theatre, Pittsfield, ME (1920s).
- Colonnades Ballroom, Ocean Park, CA (1944+).
- Colony Club, 744 N. Rush St., Chicago, IL (1930s).
- Colony Club, Sunset Blvd., Los Angeles, CA.
- Colony Club Restaurant, 564 Park Avenue, NYC, NY.
- Colosimo's Café, 2126 S. Wabash, Chicago, IL (1910-20s). This entity had actually been named for reputed mobster, Jim Colosimo. Moreover, Jim himself was found to have been shot and killed here in 1920. More so, after his death, other reputed mobsters, including Al Capone, who may have had something to do with "Big Jim's" "bullet-ridded demise, continued to operate this site. (Incl. gigs by Sophie Tucker, Al Jolson, Ruth Etting)
- Columbia Hall, Jersey City, NJ.
- Columbia Park, Nanticoke, PA.
- Columbia Theater, Columbia, SC.
- Columbia Theatre, Davenport, IO.
- Columbia Theater, Sharon, PA (1920s).
- Columbia Theatre, San Francisco, CA.
- Columbia Square Playhouse, 6121 Sunset Blvd., Hollywood, Los Angeles, CA (CBS radio).
- Columbus Auditorium, Green Bay, WI.
- Coon-Chicken Inn, Salt Lake City, UT. (A blaintly racist meaning? Sadly yes-one of a chain of western American supper clubs). (1920s+).
- Condon's Club (Eddie), 47 West Third Street, Manhattan, NYC, NY (1945+, the address of the club owned by bandleader Eddie Condon was most influential, as were vocal gigs by Lee Wiley).
- Commander Perry, Toledo, OH. (1930s-340s)
- Commercial Hotel, Elko, CO (1940s).
- Commodore Ballroom, Lowell, MA.
- Coney Island, Cincinnati, OH.
- Congress Hotel (Casino Room, Joseph Urban Room), 520 S. Michigan Avenue, Chicago, IL.
- Congress Hotel and Annex, (Pompeian Room), Chicago, IL
- Congress Restaurant, NYC, NY (1930s).
- Connie's Inn, 2221 7th Avenue, and 131st Uptown, Harlem, NYC, NY (1920s-30s). Established by bootlegging brothers Connie and George Immerman, this hot spot of jazz also became associated with reputed mobster, Dutch Schultz and, especially, Louis Armstrong, Harlan Lattimore, and Edith Wilson).
- Connie's Inn, Forty-Eighth Street, near Broadway and Seventh Street (second site of this famous club), NYC, NY (1930s).
- Connor's Cafe, 135th Street, Uptown, Harlem, NYC, NY (before 1920+).
- Consistory Auditorium, Buffalo, NY.
- Constitution Hall, Washington, DC.
- Continental, Kansas City, MO (1940s).
- Convention Hall, Asbury Hall, Asbury Park, NJ.
- Convention Hall, Cleveland, OH.
- Convention Hall, Philadelphia, PA.
- Convention Hall, Hutchinson, KS.
- Convention Hall, Kansas City, MO.

- Convention Hall, St. Louis, MO.
- Copacabana (nightclub), 1940+, E. Sixteenth Street near Fifth, Manhattan, NYC, NY (especially associated with Frank Sinatra, Lena Horne, Perry Como, Sarah Vaughan, and also with reputed mobster Frank Costello)?
- Copacabana (nightclub), Miami, FL (1940s).
- Copacabana (nightclub, owner Mexican American Joaquin Garay) 2215 Powell Street at Bay, San Francisco, CA (1941+).
- Copley Square Hotel (old Bar and Grill), 47 Huntington Avenue, Boston, MA.
- Copley Plaza (Oval Room), Boston, MA.
- Coral Gable Golf and Country Club, Coral Gables, FL (1920s).
- Cordray Theatre, Portland, OR.
- Corn Palace, Mitchell, SD.
- Coronado Theatre, Rockford, IL.
- Coronet Club, Philadelphia, PA.
- Cort Theatre, Dearborn near Randolph Street, Chicago, Il.
- Cort Theatre, San Francisco, CA (Especially Al Jolson gig here in 1915).
- Cort's Jamaica Theater, Philadelphia, PA. (1920s).
- Cosmopolitan Hotel, Denver, CO.
- Costello's Grill, 118 N. Dearborn Street Chicago, IL. (1940s).
- Country Center, White Plains, NY.
- Country Club House, Evanston, IL.
- Cotton Club, Tremont Street, Boston, MA. Reputed mobster Charles 'King' Solomon killed here, 1933.
- Cotton Club, 5342 West Twenty-Second Street, Cicero, IL. This Cotton Club, not related to the more famous New York City entity, was perhaps the most famous of the many clubs controlled by the reputed Chicago mobster Ralph Capone, Al's brother, in the (1920s). To be fair to Al, there was no discrimination, as in the NYC Cotton Club, as any white or black patrons could attend.
- Cotton Club, 644 Lenox Avenue (Harlem) Uptown, NYC, NY. This original location was associated with (ex-boxer-champ) Jack Johnson and especially (reputed mobster) Owney Madden. This club would feature Afro-American entertainment at its best from 1923 through to 1935. Alternation house bands were led by Duke Ellington, Cab Calloway, Mills Blues Band, and Jimmie Lunceford, among others. Vocalists included Edith Wilson, Ethel Waters, Adelaide Hall, Ivie Anderson, Aida Ward, Nina Mae McKinney, the Dandridge Sisters—including Dorothy Dandridge—and the (very young) Lena Horne, in 1934. (A latter-century (1984) film, by the same name, may be very familiar with baby boomers).
- Cotton Club, Broadway, at Forty-Eighth Street, NYC, NY (1936-40), the second NYC site.
- Cotton Club, Dayton, OH.
- Cotton Club, 2226 East Fifty-Fifth Street, Cleveland, OH.
- Cotton Club, 1305 Caroline, Houston, TX.
- Cotton Club, San Francisco, CA (1940
- Cove Club, Philadelphia, PA.
- Cow Palace, 2600 Geneva, Daily City, CA (1941+).
- Cox Theatre (Shubert) Seventh Street, Cincinnati, OH (1921).
- Crandall's Theatre, Ninth and East Streets, NW, Washington, DC.
- Crawford Theatre, St Louis, MO.

- Crazy Cat, Forty-Eighth Street and Broadway NYC, NY (1920-30s), especially Cab Calloway's gigs.
- Creole Café, Oakland CA (1920s).
- Creole Palace, 206 Market Street, San Diego, CA.
- Crescent Temple, Trenton, NJ (1920s).
- Cressmoor, Hobart, IN (1940s).
- Cricket Club, Washington Blvd., Los Angeles, CA.
- Crillon, Forty-Eighth Street, NYC, NY.
- Criterion Theatre Club, on Times Square, NYC, NY (1920s).
- Crosby Inn, 3002 S. State Street, Chicago, IL (1920s).
- Crown Theatre, Dodge City, KS.
- Crystal Ballroom, Fargo, ND.
- Crystal Café, Brooklyn, NYC, NY (1930s).
- Crystal Cavern, Washington, DC. For a time, Blanche Calloway managed this site (1940s).
- Crystal City Amusement Park, Tulsa, OK.
- Crystal Inn, Bakersfield, CA (1940s).
- Crystal Park, Cumberland, MD.
- Crystal Slipper (Ballroom), Cleveland, OH. (A young 21 year old crooning barber Perry Como had an early gig here in 1933? Myth?)
- Crystal Springs Dance Pavilion Ballroom, Fort Worth, TX (1930s).
- Crystal Theatre, Albuquerque, NM.
- Crystal Theatre, Atchison, KS.
- Crystal Theatre, Okemah, OK.
- Curly's Theatre Café, Minneapolis-St. Paul, MN (1940s+).
- Curran Theater, 445 Geary Street, San Francisco, CA (1922+).
- Czar Club, Cleveland, OH.
- Daffydill Club, Greenwich Village, NYC, NY.
- Dago Frank's Café, Chicago, IL (especially, Alberta Hunter gigs before 1920).
- Dago Tony's, New Orleans, LA (before 1920).
- Dailey's Meadowbrook, Cedar Grove, NJ.
- Daly's 63rd Street Theater, NYC, NY.
- Dallas Sportatorium, Dallas, TX (featured wrestling, radio, and live C & W music).
- Dandy Restaurant, Gay and Baltimore Streets, Baltimore, MD.
- Danny's Hideaway, Los Angeles, CA.
- Dave Ming's Ninety-Seventh Street Corral, Los Angeles, CA (1940s).
- Dave's Café, Fifty-First and Michigan, later at 343 East Garfield, Chicago, IL (1920s-30).
- Davenport Hotel (Italian Gardens), Spokane, WA.
- Davidson Theatre, Milwaukee, WI.
- Davis Theatre, 532-34 Smithfield Street, Pittsburg, PA.
- Dawn Club, Annie Street, San Francisco, CA (1940s).
- De Give's Opera House, Atlanta, GA.
- De Luxe Café and Gardens, 3503 S. State, Thirty-Fifth and State, Chicago, IL.
- Deauville Café, 68 W. Randolph, Chicago, IL (1920s).
- Deauville Club, Santa Monica, CA (1930s-40s).
- Deep Ellum—a red-light section of South Dallas, TX, on or near Elm Street (especially influenced "Blind" Lemon Jefferson, Robert Johnson, and Leadbelly (1920s+)).
- Deertrees Theatre, Harrison, ME.

- Del Fey Club, NYC, NY (1920s).
- Dells (The), Roadhouse, Dempster Road, Morton Grove, IL (1920s+).
- Delmonico's Restaurant, Fifth and Forty-Fourth Streets, NYC, NY. (This famous site closed in 1923).
- Dempsey-Vanderbilt Hotel (Pago-Pago Room) Miami, FL (associated with ex-boxer-champ Jack Dempsey and the wealthy Vanderbilt family, 1930s)
- Denham Theatre, Denver, CO.
- Denver Municipal Auditorium, Denver, CO.
- Derby Club, Calumet City, IN.
- Deshler-Wallick Hotel, (Le Veque Tower Ballroom), Columbus, OH (1916-60s)
- Dewey Theatre, Fourteenth Street, NYC, NY.
- Diamond Horseshoe (basement of Paramount Theatre), NYC, NY (1938+).
- Diamond Mirror, Lawrence, MA (1940s).
- Diane Ballroom, Los Angeles, CA (1930s+).
- Diana Dancing Academy, Fourteenth Street and Third Avenue, NYC, NY (1930s).
- Dick's Place (Bar), St. Louis, MO (C & W).
- Dickie Wells Club, 133rd Street and Seventh Avenue, Harlem, NYC, NY (1930s, associated with contemporary (jazz) trombone musician Dickie Wells).
- Dixie Drug Store, Helena, AK (1920s). Owner Jack Greenfield perhaps founded his own speakeasy during Prohibition times? (Bluesman Floyd Campbell gigs here as early as 1922.)
- Diemer Theatre, Springfield, MO. Dixie Tabernacle, Nashville, TN.
- Dixie Theatre, Atlanta, GA (before 1920).
- Dixie Theatre, Washington, DC.
- Doll House, Hollywood, CA (1930s+).
- Doll's House (Lounge), Palm Springs, CA. (Peggy Lee in 1938?)
- Don the Beachcomber, Los Angeles, CA (1934+).
- Don's, Danville, IL (1940s).
- Doric Theatre, Elkhart, TX.
- Dorywalski's Hall, Grant Street, Buffalo, NY (1930s).
- Douglas Theater, 142nd and Lenox Avenue, Uptown, Harlem, NYC, NY. (Just upstairs were numerous nightclubs, differing with name changes, including the first site of the NYC Cotton Club.)
- Douglass Theatre, Macon, GA.
- Douglass Theatre, 1300 Block, Pennsylvania Avenue, Baltimore, MD
- Dove's Capital Ballroom, Alexandra, VA.
- Dover Club, NYC, NY (1920s).
- Downbeat Club, Central Avenue, Hollywood, CA.
- Downbeat Club, 66 W. Fifty-Second Street, NYC, NY (especially Sarah Vaughan's gigs, 1940s).
- Downbeat Club, Philadelphia, PA.
- Drake Hotel, 140 E. Walton Street (Camellia House, Gold Coast Room), Chicago, IL.
- Dream Theatre, Columbus, GA (1920s).
- Dreamland Ballroom, Paulina and 1761 W. Van Buren, Chicago, IL (1920s).
- Dreamland Dancing Academy, 120 W. 125th Street, NYC, NY (1930s).
- Dubuque Opera House, Eighth and Iowa Streets, Dubuque, IA.
- Dreamland Café, 3520 S. State Street, Chicago, IL (1920s+), featured Louis Armstrong, Cab Calloway, Adelaide Hall, Alberta Hunter, billed as "Dreamland's Queen," Edith Wilson, and others.

- Dreamland, 125th and Seventh Avenue, NYC, NY.
- Dreamland, Fourth Street, Los Angeles, CA (1920s).
- Dreamland Ballroom, Omaha, NE.
- Dreamland Theatre, Tulsa, OK.
- Drive-in Radio, Mesa, AZ (late 1940s). See a film and live radio program (KTYL)?
- Drool Inn, Uptown, Harlem, NYC, NY (1920s).
- Du Drop Inn, Chicago, IL.
- Du Pont, Wilmington, DE.
- Du Sable, Chicago, IL.
- Duffy's, Nantucket Beach, MA (1940s).
- Duffy's Tavern, W. Forty-Fourth Street, NYC, NY (1920s?), possibly the source for a later 1945 film *Duffy's Tavern*, based upon the popular, contemporary 1940s' radio program.
- Dunbar Hotel (Showboat Café), 4225 S. Central Avenue, Los Angeles, CA.
- Dunbar Palace, 2389 Seventh Avenue, Uptown, Harlem, NYC, NY.
- Dunbar Theatre, Broad and Lombard Streets, Philadelphia, PA (1920s).
- Duquesne Gardens, Pittsburgh, PA.
- Dusty Bottom (Tenet Dance Hall), Thirty-Third and Wabash, Chicago, IL.
- Duval Armory, Jacksonville, FL.
- E & E Tavern, San Angelo, TX (1940, owned by Ernest Tubb).
- Eagles Ballroom, Milwaukee, WI.
- Eagles Hall, Fort Worth, TX.
- Earl Carroll Theatre, Sunset Blvd., Hollywood, CA (1938+). In the 1920s, Carroll's Broadway *Vanities* revues found more nudity than those of rival Flo Ziegfeld. More so, his move to the West Coast was a lavish success—an inspiration for the (later) 1950s' *Playboy* success of Hugh Heffner?
- Earle Theater, Washington, DC.
- Earle Theater, Eleventh and Market Streets, Philadelphia, PA.
- East Market Gardens, Akron, OH.
- East Side Show Spot (Byline Room), 137 E. Fifty-Second Street, NYC, NY (especially Mabel Mercer's gigs).
- Eastern Star Café, Detroit, MI (1930s).
- Eastman Theatre, Rochester, NY.
- Eastwood Gardens, Detroit, MI.
- Eblon Theatre, Kansas City, MO.
- Ebony Club, 1678 Broadway, NYC, NY (1940s).
- Ebony Lounge, Chicago, IL.
- Economy Hall (Cheapskate Hall), 1422 Ursuline Street, New Orleans, LA (before 1920).
- Eddie Klein's Villa (nightclub), Pittsburgh, PA (1930s).
- Eddie Peyton's Club, Crafton, PA (1930s)
- Eddie Spivak's (nightclub), Hollywood, CA (1940s).
- Edelweiss Gardens, 4816 S. State, Chicago, IL (especially Bandleader-vocalist Ted Lewis's gigs, 1920).
- Edgewater Ballroom, San Francisco, CA.
- Edgewater Beach Hotel (Marine Room), 5349 N. Sheridan Road near Foster Avenue, Chicago, IL.
- Edison Hotel (Grand Ballroom, Green Room), NYC, NY.
- Edmond's Cellar "Bucket of Blood,"132nd Street and Fifth Avenue, Harlem, NYC, NY (associated with Ethel Waters's gigs before 1920).

- Eighty One Theater, 81, Decatur Street, Atlanta, GA (associated with Bessie Smith's gigs, others).
- Egg Harbor, Atlantic City, NJ (before 1920).
- Eighteen (18 Club), NYC, NY (1930s).
- Eighth Street Theater, Chicago, IL.
- Eighty One Club (81), Austin, TX (1940s).
- Eighty-Sixth Street Theater, NYC, NY.
- El Adobe, Bakersfield, CA (1940s+).
- El Capitan Theatre, 6838 Hollywood Blvd., Hollywood, CA (1926+).
- El Capitan Theatre, 2353 Mission, San Francisco, CA (1928+).
- El Dorado Ballroom, Houston, TX.
- El Dorado Café, NYC, NY.
- El Dorado Club, Playhouse Square, Cleveland, OH (1920s)
- El Garron, NYC, NY (1920s).
- El Gaucho Club, Salt Lake City, UT (1940s).
- Elbow Room, Milwaukee, WI (1940s).
- Electric Park, Waterloo, IA.
- Elephant Café, Atlantic City, NJ (1920s).
- El Grotto Supper Club (Pershing Hotel), 6412 Cottage Grove Avenue, Chicago, IL (1940s).
- El Fey Club, West Fifty-Fourth Street, NYC, NY (1924-29). Associated with film entity and entertainer Texas Guinan, as well as having mob-controlled connections, this famous speakeasy, perhaps featured professional dancer, George Raft? Raft, the (later) film entity, perhaps also worked for reputed mobsters Owney Madden and Larry Fay, perhaps delivering illegal beer?
- El Miramar Hotel, Santa Monica, CA.
- El Mocambo (nightclub), Chicago, IL (1940s).
- El Morocco Nightclub (Marrakech Room, Champagne Room), 154 at Fifty-Fourth Street, NYC, NY (1931+). It famously out lasted Prohibition and became legit.
- El Patio Ballroom, Lakeside Park, Denver, CO.
- El Patio Ballroom, Vermont Avenue, Los Angeles, CA.
- El Patio Ballroom, San Francisco, CA.
- El Rado Café, Fifty-Fifth Street and Prairie, Chicago, IL (1929+).
- El Rancho Vegas Hotel, Reno, NV.
- El Rancho Vegas, Las Vegas, NV. (1940s)
- El Rancho Vegas, NV. The official start of what the city of Las Vegas would (later) claim as the center of American entertainment, after (1950), was to be founded here in 1941.
- El Rey Theatre, Los Angeles, CA (1936+).
- El Torro (nightclub), Miami, FL (1940s).
- Elmer's Cocktail Lounge, State near Randolph Street, Chicago, IL (1940s).
- El Torreon Ballroom, Thirty-First Street, Kansas City, MO (1927-36). The Coon-Sanders Orchestra opened this site in 1927.
- Eleventh Street Opera House, Philadelphia, PA.
- Elis Auditorium, Knoxville, TN.
- Elitch's Gardens (Trocadero Ballroom), Denver, CO.
- Elite Café no. 1, 3030 S. State Street, Chicago, IL.
- Elite Café no. 2, 3445 S. State Street, Chicago, IL.
- Elite Theatre, Meridian, MS.
- Elk's Hotel, Broad Street above Vine, Philadelphia, PA.

- Elk's Rest, Fairmont, WV.
- Elk's Temple Hotel, Parkview and Sixth, Los Angeles, CA.
- Elks Club, Miami, FL.
- Elks Club, Spokane, WA.
- Elks Club, (No. 44),32 South Fifth Street, Minneapolis, MN.
- Elks Hall, Central Avenue, Los Angeles, CA.
- Elks Rendezvous, Lenox Avenue, Harlem, NYC, NY (especially Louis Jordan's gigs in 1938).
- Elks Theatre, Albuquerque, NM.
- Elks Theatre, Tuscaloosa, AL.
- Elms Ballroom, Youngstown, OH (1930s).
- Elms Club, Excelsior Springs, MO (1940s).
- Elmore Theatre, Pittsburgh, PA.
- Embassy Club, Fifty-Seventh Street, NYC, NY.
- Embassy Hotel (Jungle Room), Ninth Street, Los Angeles, CA.
- Empire Hotel, Hollywood, CA.
- Embers (nightclub), NYC, NY (1940s).
- Emery Hall, Cincinnati, OH (1920s).
- Emporium (White's), Chicago, IL (1940s).
- Empire Ballroom, Allentown, PA.
- Empire Ballroom, Forty-Eighth Street and Broadway, NYC, NY (1930s).
- Empire Theater, Montgomery, AL. (Hank Williams's first live appearance here, 1938?)
- Empress Theatre, Sacramento, CA.
- English Theater, Indianapolis, IN.
- Enna Jettick Park, Auburn, NY.
- Entertainers Café (with a glass bottom floor!), 209 E. Thirty-Fifth Street, Chicago, IL (1920s).
- Erie Café, Erie and Clark, Chicago, IL.
- Erie Centennial Country Club, Pittsburg, PA.
- Erlanger Theater, 127 N. Clark, Chicago, IL (1926+).
- Erlanger Theatre, Buffalo, NY.
- Erlanger Theatre, Philadelphia, PA.
- Ernest Tubb Record Shop, Nashville, TN (Ernest hosted live radio from this site, 1940s+).
- Essex House, Manhattan, NYC, NY.
- Essex Theatre, Boston, MA.
- European Club, 26 W. Fifty-Third Street, NYC, NY (1920s+).
- Everglades Club, Forty-Eighth Street, Times Square, NYC, NY (1920s+).
- Everleigh Club, Chicago, IL (1920s).
- Exclusive Club 133rd Street, Harlem, NYC, NY. (1933)
- Fairyland Park Ballroom, Seventy-Fifth and Parkway, Kansas City, MO.
- Famous Door, Diversey and Clark Streets, Chicago, IL (1930s).
- Famous Door, Bourbon and Conti Streets, New Orleans, LA (1940s).
- Famous Door, Willoughby Street and Vine, Hollywood, CA (1936+).
- Famous Door, 35 W. Fifty-Second Street, NYC, NY (1934-36). This first site of addresses of five, all on Fifty-Second Street, featured many, including Louis Prima, Billie Holliday, and Bessie Smith.
- Fairgrounds Park, Tulsa, OK.
- Fairmont Hotel (Venetian Room), 950 Mason Street, San Francisco, CA.
- Fairview Theatre, Atlanta, GA

- Farm House Country Club, Robbins, IL (1920s).
- Farmers' Warehouse, Petersburg, VA.
- Fay's Follies Club, NYC, NY (1920s). It was associated with reputed mobster Larry Fay.
- Fay's Theatre, Philadelphia, PA.
- Ferguson Hotel (Cotton Club), Cincinnati, OH.
- Fernbrook Club, Wilkes-Barre, PA.
- Fernbrook Park, Dallas, PA.
- Fiesta Danceteria Ballroom, NYC, NY.
- Fifth (5th) Avenue Club, NYC, NY (1926+).
- Fifty Fourth (54th) Street Club, NYC, NY (1920s).
- Fifty-One Hundred Club (51 Nightclub), 5100 N. Broadway, Chicago, IL (1930s+). Comic and vocalist Danny Thomas—and later, a TV icon and also founder of St. Jude Hospital—found 1940s' success here.
- Finnochio's (nightclub), 506 Broadway, San Francisco, CA (1936+).
- Firth Avenue Theatre, Seattle, WA.
- First A. M. E. Church, Eighth Street and Towne Avenue, Los Angeles, CA.
- Fiums Café, 3440 S. State, Chicago, IL (1920s).
- Five Hundred Club (500), Atlantic City, NJ.
- Five Points Theatre, Denver, CO (1920s).
- Five Spot (nightclub), Manhattan, NYC, NY (1940s).
- Flame Club, Chicago, IL (1940s).
- Flamingo Hotel, Las Vegas, NV (1945+). (Reputed mobster Bugsy Siegel's interests in this enterprise perhaps helped to define the "Las Vegas strip," for future generations.)
- Flatbush Theater, Brooklyn, NYC NY.
- Flint Athletic Club, Flint, MI. (1940s)
- Florentine Gardens (Zanzibar Room), 5955 Hollywood Blvd., Hollywood, CA.
- Florida Theatre, Jacksonville, FL. (1927+)
- Flying Trapeze Cafe, Fifty-Seventh and Broadway, NYC, NY (1930s).
- Fontenelle Hotel (Ballroom) Omaha, NE.
- Four-Forty Club 440 (Mona's), 440 Broadway, San Francisco, CA (1940s)
- Four Hundred Club, on the Board Walk, Atlantic City, NJ.
- Florida Theatre, Jacksonville, FL.
- Foley Ballroom, Bangor, ME (1920s)
- Follies Theatre, Main Street, Los Angeles, CA. (Ivie Anderson's gig here, early 1920s).
- Folies-Bergere, Atlantic City, NJ.
- Folly Beach Pier, Charleston, SC.
- Foot National Guard Armory, Hartford, CN.
- Forbid den City (nightclub), 363 Sutter San Francisco, CA (1938+), featured Larry Chang as Frank Sinatra, Chinese style! Eat Chinese, and hear Frank in Chinese, as nightclub mythology has it?
- Fordham Theater, NYC, NY.
- Fords Theater, Baltimore, MD.
- Forestville Tavern, Chicago, IL (1920s).
- Forrest Club, New Orleans, LA.
- Forrest Theatre, Walnut between Eleventh and Twelfth Streets, Philadelphia, PA.
- Forum Theatre, Los Angeles CA.
- Forum (club), Wichita, KS.
- Four Duces, 2222 S. Wabash, Chicago, IL (1920s).
- Fox Criterion Theatre, Seventh and Grand, Los Angeles, CA.

- Fox Terminal Theatre, Newark, NJ.
- Fox Theater, San Francisco, CA.
- Fox Theater, Detroit, MI.
- Fox Theatre, 710 B Street, San Diego, CA.
- Fox Theatre, Atlanta, GA.
- Fox Theatre, Brooklyn NYC, NY.
- Fox Theatre, Oakland, CA.
- Fox Theatre, Philadelphia, PA.
- Fox Theatre, Riverside, CA.
- Fox Theatre, San Bernardino, CA.
- Fox Theatre, St. Louis, MO.
- Fox Theatre, Tucson, AZ.
- Fox Theatre, 1328 E Street NW, Washington, DC (1927+, later known as Loew's Fox Capital Theatre).
- Fox-Dodge City Theatre, Dodge City, KS.
- Franks Place (Roadhouse), near San Francisco, CA (1920s).
- Frank Dailey's Terrace Room, Newark, NJ (especially Frank Sinatra's gig in 1943).
- Franklin Gardens, Evansville, IN.
- Franklin Theater, Birmingham, AL (1920s).
- Frederick Douglas High School, Columbia, MO.
- French Casino, 4812 N. Clark, Chicago, IL (1930s).
- French Casino, Miami, FL (1930s).
- French Casino, Seventh Avenue and Fiftieth Street, NYC, NY (1930s).
- French Grotto, 1309 Walnut Street, Philadelphia, PA
- French Tavern, Walnut at Sixteenth Streets, Philadelphia, PA
- Frenchy's, Ohatchee, WI. (1940s)
- Friar's Inn, 343 S. Wabash, Chicago, IL (1920s-30s).
- Friars Club, 57 East Fifty-Fifth Street, NYC, NY.
- Frivolity Club, Broadway at Fifty-Third Street, NYC, NY (1920s).
- Frog Hop Ballroom, St. Joseph, MO.
- Frolic Theater, Bessemer, AL (1920s).
- Frolic Show Bar, Detroit, MI (1940s).
- Frolic Theater, Birmingham, AL.
- Frolics Theatre Restaurant, E. Fifty-Fifth Street Chicago, IL (1940s).
- Frolics Café (mid-nite) 18 E. Twenty-Second Street, Chicago, IL. (1920s+).
- Frolics Club, Miami, FL.
- Frolics Club, Virginia Beach, VA. (1940s)
- Funky Butt Hall (Kinney's Hall), 1319 Perdido Street, New Orleans, LA (before 1920).
- Furnace (club), Manhattan, NYC, NY. (1920s)
- Gables (club), Deerfield, MA.
- Gabyle Theatre, North Judson, IN (1930s+).
- Gairty, the, Baltimore, MD (1920s).
- Galloway Saloon, Hunter, TX (before 1920).
- Galvez Hotel, Galveston, TX.
- Garde Theatre, New London, CT
- Garden (Ballroom), Fiftieth Street and Broadway NYC, NY (1930s).
- Garden Court Hotel (Ballroom), Los Angeles, CA (1920s).
- Garden Of Allah, Coast Highway, Seal Beach, CA.
- Garden Of Allah, Arlington Hotel), Seattle, WA. (1946+).

- Garden Pier, Atlantic City, NJ.
- Garden Theatre, Bennettsville, GA (1920s).
- Gardener Park Auditorium, Dallas, TX.
- Garrick Stage Barr Lounge, 100 W. Randolph, Chicago, IL. (Mythology has it that Dinah Washington, before playing gig, had worked as a custodian at this site. (1940s))
- Garrick Theatre, Michigan and Griswold, Detroit, MI.
- Garrick Theater, 507 Fifty-Eighth Street, Philadelphia, PA.
- Gateway Casino, Atlantic City, NJ.
- Gay White Way (George White's) NYC, NY (1940s).
- Gayety Village, Chicago, IL (1940s).
- Geary Theatre, 415 Geary Street, San Francisco, CA.
- George Washington Hotel, Washington, PA.
- George's Playhouse, Waterloo Rd., Stockton, CA. Rose Maddox's rhythmic 1949 "George's Playhouse Boogie" is reputed to be inspired by her own gigs at this honky-tonk site. Myth?
- German Ball, Rocky Mountain, NC.
- German Village Restaurant, West Fortieth Street, NYC, NY. Featured Sophie Tucker as a singing waitress around 1907? She must have been heard as annoyingly loud? Myth?
- Germania Dreamland Hall, Rose Street, Pittsburgh, PA.
- Gibby's Resturant, 192 N. Clark, Chicago, IL.
- Gibson's Standard Theatre, 1124-28 South Street, Philadelphia, PA.
- Gibson Hotel (Fountain Room, Ballroom, Roof Garden) Fountain Square, Cincinnati, OH.
- Girard's Grill, 154 Union Square, San Francisco, CA (Before 1920)
- Gladys Ballroom, Montevideo, MN.
- Glady's Clam House. (Afro-American blues entity, Gladys Bentley) Seventh Avenue, Harlem, NYC, NY (1933)
- Glass Hat, Boston, MA (1940s).
- Glass Hat (Belmont Plaza Hotel), Lexington and Forty-Ninth Streets, NYC, NY (1940s).
- Glen Island Casino, Long Island Sound near New Rochelle, NY.
- Glen Park Casino, Williamsville, Buffalo, NY.
- Globe Theater, Boardwalk and St. Charles, Atlantic City, NJ.
- Globe Theater, Superior Avenue, Cleveland, OH.
- Golden Dragon Theater, New Orleans, LA
- Golden Gate Hall (Million Dollar Ballroom), 142nd and Lenox Ave, Harlem, NYC, NY.
- Golden Gate Theater, 1 Taylor Street, San Francisco, CA (1922+).
- Golden Inn, Pacific Avenue, Atlantic City, NJ. (1920s)
- Golden Pheasant Restaurant, Cleveland, OH.
- Golden Pumpkin Café, Madison and Hamlin, Chicago, IL (1920s).
- Golden Slipper, Baton Rouge, LA.
- Goodman's Dance Hall, 162 E. Eighty-Sixth Street, NYC, NY (1930s).
- Goodlow's Club, Baltimore, MD.
- Goodyear Theatre, Akron, OH.
- Gotham Club-Bar, Mt. Vernon Avenue, Columbus, OH. (1940s)
- Gotham Theater, Fulton Street, Brooklyn, NYC, NY.
- Grace Hayes Lodge, 11345 Ventura Blvd., Studio City, CA (associated with singer-actress Grace Hayes).
- Granada and Marbro Theater, 6427 N. Sheridan (near Devon), Chicago, IL (1926+).
- Granada Café, 6800 S. Cottage Grove, Chicago, IL (1920s).

- Granada Theater, San Francisco, CA.
- Granada Theatre, Santa Barbara, CA (1924+).
- Granada Theatre, Sault Lake City, UT.
- Grand Central Hotel, St. Louis, MO.
- Grand Opera House, Meridian, MS. (1920s).
- Grand Opera House, 119 N. Clark, Chicago, IL (later known as the RKO Grand in 1942).
- Grand Terrace Ballroom (*a*) 3955 S. Parkway (Grand Blvd.), and (*b*) later moved to Thirty-Fifth and Calumet, Chicago, site address (1920s-30s). Associated with reputed mobster, Ed Fox.
- Grand Theater, 3110 S. State Street, Chicago, IL (1911+).
- Grand Theatre, West Paul Beach, FL (1920s+).
- Grand Theater Renton, WA.
- Grand Theater, Long Beach, CA (1930s+).
- Grand Theater, Macon, GA.
- Grand Theatre, Greenville, SC (1920s).
- Grand Theatre, Hartford, CN.
- Grant Hotel, 6 N. Dearborn, Chicago, IL.
- Grand Union Hotel, (Ballroom), Saratogo Springs, NY
- Grauman's Chinese Theatre, Hollywood Blvd., Hollywood, CA (1927+).
- Grauman's Egyptian Theatre, 6712 Hollywood Blvd., Hollywood, CA (1922+).
- Grauman's Million Dollar Theater, 2075 Broadway, Los Angeles, CA (1918+). It was the first of many lavish theaters pioneered by Sid Grauman.
- Gray Dawn, Jamaica Avenue, Queens, NYC, NY (1930s).
- Graystone Ballroom, 4237 Woodward Avenue, Detroit, MI (1920s+).
- Graystone Hotel, Cincinnati, OH.
- Great Northern Hotel, NYC, NY.
- Great Northern Theatre, 21 W. Quincy Chicago, IL (also known as the Lyric and Hippodrome).
- Greater Majestic, San Antonio, TX.
- Green Mill Gardens 4802-06 N. Broadway, Chicago, IL (1907+). This club survived Prohibition, and beyond! Al Jolson,. Ruth Etting, Helen Morgan as well as reputed mobster Jack McGurn were as associated with this entity as a speakeasy. After Prohibition, it featured others including Billie Holiday and Anita O'Day.
- Green Mil (club), Culver City, CA.
- Green Parrot Dance Hall, Dallas, TX.
- Green Street Music Hall, 629 Green Street, San Francisco, CA.
- Green Tree Inn, Witchita, KS (1940s)
- Greenwich Village Inn, Greenwich Village, NYC, NY (1920s).
- Greenwich Village Vanguard, NYC, NY. (1940s).
- Grenada Café, Chicago, IL (1930s).
- Greyhound (nightclub), Jeffersonville, IN (1930s).
- Greyhound Inn, Cicero, IL (1920s).
- Grossinger's Hotel, Catskill Mountains, NY. This ethnic (Jewish) center of entertainment, part of the "borscht belt," had been established in 1913. While entertainment was not always kosher, it's a good bet that the food was!
- Grove Theater, NYC, NY.
- Grove (club), Houston, TX.
- Gruewald Hotel (Cave Room) New Orleans, LA (until 1923).

- Guessie's Kentucky Lounge, S. Ashland Avenue, Chicago, IL.
- Gus's Palm Gardens, San Antonio, TX (1930s).
- Ha-Ha Club, 39 W. Fifty-Second Street, NYC, NY (1920s).
- Half Moon Nite Club, Steubenville, OH (1930s).
- Half Way Inn, Mishawaka, IN (1930s).
- Halfway House, City Park Avenue, near New Orleans, LA (before 1920).
- Hambone Kelly's, San Francisco, CA.
- Hamid's Steel Pier, Atlantic City, NJ.
- Hamilton Park, Waterbury, CN.
- Hamilton, Hagerstown, MD (1940s).
- Hampton Beach Casino, Hampton Beach, NH.
- Handcock Opera House, Austin, TX (1920s).
- Hangover Club, Los Angeles, CA (1940s).
- Hanna Theatre, Euclid Avenue and East Fourteenth Street, Cleveland, OH (1921+).
- Harding Theatre, 2741 N. Milwaukee Avenue, Chicago, IL (1925+).
- Harding Theatre, San Francisco, CA (1926+).
- Harlem Club, 32 N. Kentucky Avenue, Atlantic City, NJ.
- Harlem Opera House, 207 W. 125th Street NYC, NY (especially Ella Fitzgerald, 1934).
- Harlem Uproar House, Fifty-Second Street near Broadway (Harlem?), NYC, NY (1930s).
- Harlem (nightclub) Deep Ellum, Dallas, TX (1920s+).
- Harmony Club, NYC, NY (1920s).
- Harold's Club, Virginia Street, Reno, NV.
- Harris-Alvin Theatre, Pittsburgh, PA (1930s).
- Harris Theatre, Chicago, IL
- Harrisburg Hotel, Harrisburg, PA.
- Harvard Club, Cleveland, OH.
- Hartman Theatre, Columbus, OH.
- Havana-Madrid Club, 1650 Broadway, NYC, NY (1940s). This ethnic (Cuban-Latino) entity also featured others, especially noting a hugely successful Dean Martin and Jerry Lewis gig in 1946.
- Harvard Inn, the Bowery, NYC, NY (associated with reputed mobster Frankie Yale before 1920).
- Hawaiian Gardens, S. Halstead Street, Chicago, IL (1920s).
- Hawaiian Gardens, Kansas City, MO. (As nightclub myth has it, club bartender Joe Turner was first recognized for his singing here, 1930s.)
- Hawthorn Cabaret Inn, Cicero, IL. (Reputed mobster Al Capone survived gunplay here in 1926.)
- Hedgerow Theatre, Moylan-Rose Valley, PA.
- Heigh-Ho Club, 35 East Fifty-Third Street, NYC, NY. Rudy Vallee's 1929 recording "Heigh Ho Everybody, Heigh Ho," on Victor 22029, directly related to his successful (1928) gigs here.
- Helen Morgan's Fifty-Fourth Street Club (Chez Morgan?) NYC, NY (Helen Morgan in the 1920s).
- Helen Morgan's Open Air Night Club, 134 W. Fifty-Second Street, NYC, NY. On June 28, 1928, federal Prohibition Agents, without much cooperation from local NYC law enforcement, famously closed down this speakeasy site, along with ten others. Were (Democrats) NYC Mayor Jimmy Walker and NY (state) Governor Al Smith, who was accepting his party's presidential nomination, away in Houston, Texas, embarrassed

by the (Republican) Calvin Coolidge administration? Al would lose to (Republican) Herbert Hoover. Helen, later a winner, won an acquittal for peddling booze. Politics!

- Henry's Cafe, near Hollywood and Vine, Los Angeles, CA (1920s)
- Henry's European Restaurant, 10 E. Walton (Arcadia Room), Chicago, IL (1940s+).
- Herbsy Theatre, San Francisco, CA (1932+).
- Hershey Park Ballroom, Hershey Park, PA.
- Hey Hay Club, Fourth and Cherry, Kansas City, MO.
- Hi Hat Club, Chicago, IL (1930s).
- Hialeah, Atlantic City, NJ (1940s).
- Hickory Hotel, Hickory, NC.
- Hickory House, 144 W. Fifty-Second Street, NYC, NY (1930s).
- High Hat Club, Fifty-Second Street, NYC, NY (especially with Helen Kane's gigs in 1926).
- Highlands Ballroom, St. Louis, MO.
- Hi-Note Club, 450 N. Clark Chicago, IL (1940s+).
- Hill Hotel, (Ron-D-Voo Club), Omaha, NE.
- Hill Street Theatre, Los Angeles, CA
- Hillsboro Theater, Nashville, TN.
- Hilton Hotel, EL Paso, TX (1939+), perhaps the first large hotel pioneered by Barron Hilton? Hilton became better known in the 1950s, acquiring many other hotels as an excellent chain of them.
- Himmelreich's Grove, Reading, PA.
- Hinz Theatre, Walnut, MI.
- Hippodrome Theater, Sixth Avenue, between Forty-Third and Forty-Fourth Streets, NYC, NY (1905-39)
- Hippodrome Theatre, Eutaw Street Baltimore, MD.
- Hippodrome Theatre, Nashville, TN.
- Hippodrome Theatre, 21 W. Quincy, Chicago, IL.
- Hippodrome Theatre, Cleveland, OH.
- Hippodrome Theatre, Youngstown, OH.
- Holiday Ballroom, 7724 S. Kedzie, Chicago, IL.
- Holland Hotel, Forty-Second Street, NYC, NY.
- Hollander Hotel (Vogue Room), Cleveland, OH. (In 1936, reputed mobster William Swartz was gunned down in front of this site). In 1940, a young singer, as identified as Dean Martin, (before Jerry Lewis), began a gig here that lasted about 3 years.
- Holiday Inn. Special note: The popular 1950s chain of supper club inns started as a fictional nightclub inspired by the successful 1942 Bing Crosby film of the same name.
- Holyoke Theatre, Holyoke, MA.
- Hollywood Bowl, Highland Avenue, Los Angeles, CA (1922+).
- Hollywood Café, 203 W. Fifty-Ninth Street and Broadway, NYC, NY.
- Hollywood Casino, 6000 Sunset Blvd., Hollywood, Los Angeles, CA.
- Hollywood Club, Kalamazoo, MI (1940s).
- Hollywood Canteen, 1451 Cahuenga Boulevard, off Sunset, Hollywood, CA (1942+). As part of the American war effort and one of many canteens for service people, this West Coast entity included many contemporary film (movie) stars donating their time for free. It was originated by film entities Bette Davis and John Garfield, inspired by the (East Coast) efforts of the (NYC) "Stage Door Canteen." It was likewise to be produced as a contemporary (1944) film of the same name. Other contemporary films

of the same patriotic war era include *Star Spangled Rhythm* (1942), *Thank Your Lucky Stars* (1943), and *Follow the Boys* (1944).

- Hollywood Swing Club, Hollywood, CA (1940s).
- Hollywood Corner Tavern, Moore, OK.
- Hollywood Dinner Club, Galveston, TX (1920s).
- Hollywood Gardens, Pelham Parkway, near Long Island, NYC, NY (1930s).
- Hollywood Lounge, 87 W. Randolph, Chicago, IL (1940s).
- Hollywood Palladium, 6215 Sunset Strip, Hollywood, CA (1940+).
- Hollywood Restaurant, Forty-Eighth Street and Broadway, Manhattan, NYC, NY (1920s+).
- Hollywood Theatre, Detroit, MI.
- Hollywood Theatre, San Diego, CA.
- Hollywood Theatre, (Warner Brothers), 51st Street, NYC, NY.
- Hollywood Theatre, (Warner Brothers), Hollywood Blvd. at Wilcox, Los Angeles, CA.
- Home Theatre, C Street and 12th Place, Washington, DC.
- Homer Theater Homer, LA.
- Hoofer's Club, Uptown, Harlem, NYC, NY (1920s).
- Hopkins's Theatre, 526 S. State Street, Chicago, IL.
- Horan's Madhouse Club, Philadelphia, PA (1920s).
- Horn Palace, San Antonio, TX.
- Horticultural Hall, Boston, MA.
- Hot Spot Café (Gladys's Hot Spot), Washington Blvd., Culver City, CA.
- Hot-Cha Bar and Grill, 134th Street and Seventh Avenue, NYC, NY. (1930s)
- Hotel Astor, Seventh Avenue and Forty-Fourth Street (Astor Roof), NYC, NY.
- Hotel Astoria (Red Room, Ballroom), New Orleans, LA.
- Hotel Belvedere (Cabana Club), Long Beach, CA (1940s).
- Hotel Benson (Ballroom), Portland, OR.
- Hotel Biltmore (Ballroom), Dayton, OH.
- Hotel Biltmore (Biltmore Cascades, Bowman Room) Forty-Third Street and Vanderbilt Avenue, NYC, NY (1920s+).
- Hotel Blackstone, (Lounge) Omaha, NE
- Hotel Bradford (Roof), Boston, MA.
- Hotel Brunswick (Egyptian Room), Boston, MA.
- Hotel Butler (Ballroom), Seattle, WA.
- Hotel Cleveland (Bronze Room), Cleveland, OH.
- Hotel Commadore (Century Room, Palm Room), right at Grand Central, NYC, NY.
- Hotel Delano (Bar and Grill, Ballroom), 108 W. Forty-Third Street, NYC NY.
- Hotel Detroit-Leland (Ballroom), Cass and Bagley Avenues, Detroit, MI.
- Hotel Dixie (Plantation Bar and Lounge), 250 W Forty-Third Street, NYC, NY.
- Hotel Eastgate (Bar and Grill), 162 E. Ontario, Chicago, IL.
- Hotel Governor Clinton (Grill, Balloon Room), Seventh Avenue, and Thirty-First Street, NYC, NY.
- Hotel Great Northern (Bar and Grill, Ballroom), 118 W. Fifty-Ninth Street, NYC, NY.
- Hotel Hershey (Castilian Ballroom), Hershey, PA (1933+).
- Hotel Kentucky (Ballroom), Louisville, KY.
- Hotel Lowry (Ballroom), St. Paul, MN.
- Hotel McAlpin (Marine Grill, Roof), Thirty-Fourth Street and Broadway, NYC, NY (1920s+).
- Hotel Minerva, (Cafe Minerva), 208 Huntington Avenue, Boston, MA

- Hotel Montclair (Ballroom), NYC, NY.
- Hotel Morrison (Cameo Room, Terrace Gardens), 79 W. Madison, Chicago, IL (1920s+).
- Hotel Muehlbach (Plantation Grill), Kansas City, MO (1920s+, associated with Coon-Sanders's gigs).
- Hotel New Yorker (Terrace Room), Eighth and Thirty-Fourth, NYC, NY (1920s+).
- Hotel Nicollet (Minnesota Terrace), Minneapolis, MN.
- Hotel Pennsylvania, (Ballroom), 39th & Chestnut Streets, Philadelphia, PA
- Hotel Pennsylvania (Café Rouge Ballroom's phone number noted in house bandleader Glenn Miller's 1940's popular recording "Pennsylvania 6-5000," as penned by Jerry Gray, on Bluebird-B-10754. This contemporary "sweet band" number is instrumental, except when the whole band shouts out the phone code. Perhaps the best known phone number in Americana? Other Pennsylvania hotel entities included a Grill, the Madhattan Room, and Roof located at Seventh Avenue and Thirty-First to Thirty-Third Streets, near Penn Station, Manhattan, NYC, NY.
- Hotel Piccadilly (Grill Room, Georgia Room), Forty-Fifth Street, west of Broadway, NYC, NY.
- Hotel Pierre (Neptune Grill, Cotillion Room), Fifth Avenue and Sixtieth Street, NYC, NY (1920s+).
- Hotel Richmond (Ballroom), Richmond, VA.
- Hotel Roanoke (Ballroom), Roanoke VA.
- Hotel Roosevelt (Blossom Ballroom), 7000 Hollywood Blvd., Hollywood, CA (1927+). As well as its elegant hosting of early Academy Awards, the reported gunplay in the lobby by reputed gangster Mickey Cohen, in 1947, did scare some people. More so, no one was reported hurt! Myth?
- Hotel Roosevelt (Victory Room), Washington, DC.
- Hotel Schenley (Ballroom), Pittsburgh, PA.
- Hotel Sherman (College Inn, Sherman House, Panther Room), 112 W. Randolph, Chicago, IL. As a well-known popular nightspot, this site also originated the *Barn Dance* radio program in 1924.
- Hotel Sinton (Ballroom), Cincinnati, OH. (Especially Jane Froman gigs in 1930)
- Hotel Somerset (Balinese Room), Boston, MA.
- Hotel St. Paul (Ballroom), St. Paul, MN.
- Hotel St. Francis (Rose Room, Mural Room), Union Square, San Francisco, CA.
- Hotel St. George (Grill), Brooklyn, NYC, NY.
- Hotel Statler (Grill, Ballroom), Boston, MA.
- Hotel Taft (Taft Grill), Seventh Avenue and Fiftieth Street, NYC, NY (1920s+).
- Hotel Taft (Ballroom), New Haven, CN.
- Hotel Utah (Ballroom), Salt Lake City, UT.
- Hotel Utica (Ballroom), Utica, NY.
- Hotel Vincennes (Plantation Lounge), 601 E. Thirty-Sixth Street, Chicago, IL (1920+).
- Hotel Washington (Ballroom), Indianapolis, IN.
- Hotel Winton (Rainbow Room), Cleveland, OH.
- Hotfeet Club, W. Houston Street, NYC, NY (1930s).
- Hotsy Totsy Club, 1721 Broadway near Fifty-Fourth Street, NYC, NY (1920s+). (As associated with reputed mobster Jack "Legs" Diamond, this site was, more so, the scene of vicious gunplay, which involved Diamond, who survived famously this bit of mayhem in 1929.)

- Hough Hoskins Club, Thirty-Second and State, Chicago, IL (associated with Alberta Hunter's gigs before 1920).
- Hour Glass (Supper Club), NYC, NY.
- House of Lords, NYC, NY (1930s).
- House of Morgan, NYC, NY (briefly associated with Helen Morgan as owner, 1936).
- House That Jack Built, N. Milwaukee Avenue, north of Chicago, IL (1920s).
- Houston Auditorium, Houston, TX.
- Houston Country Club, Houston, TX.
- Howard Theatre, 1615-21 Howard Street, Chicago, IL (1918+).
- Howard Theater, Seventh and T Streets, Washington, DC (1910+).
- Hub Theatre, Boston, MA.
- Hudson Theatre, Union Hill, NJ.
- Hudson Theatre, Forty-Sixth Street near Broadway, NYC, NY.
- Hurricane Club, Forty-Ninth and Broadway (Brill Building, second floor) NYC, NY (1940-44).
- Hyperion Theatre, New Haven, CN.
- Ideal Beach, Monticello, IN.
- IMA Auditorium, Flint, MI.
- Imperial Theatre, Pocahontas, AR.
- Imperial Theatre, San Francisco, CA.
- Indian Creek Club, Miami Beach, FL.
- Indiana Theatre (Indiana Roof), Indianapolis, IN.
- Inferno Club, Harlem, NYC, NY.
- Ingleterra Ballroom, Peoria, IL.
- Illinois Theatre, Chicago, IL
- Italian Village, Chicago, IL.
- International Ampatheater, Forty-Second and Halstead, Chicago, IL (1934+).
- International Casino Supper Club, Times Square, NYC, NY (1930s).
- International Theatre, Niagara Falls, NY.
- Iris Theatre, Velva, ND.
- Iroquois Club, Newark, NJ (before 1920).
- Iroquois Gardens, Louisville, KY (1940s)
- Iroquois Theatre, 20-32 W. Randolph, Chicago, IL (destroyed by a tragic fire in 1903). witnessed by vaudvillin Eddie Foy Sr.
- Irving Place Theatre, E. Fifteenth Street, NYC, NY.
- It Club, 5450 S. Michigan Avenue, Chicago, IL (1930s).
- It Club, El Cerrito, CA (1940s).
- It Club, Vine Street, Hollywood, CA, owned by actress Clara Bow, Hollywood's "It Girl"(1920s).
- Ivanhoe Auditorium, Kansas City, MO.
- Ivie's Chicken Shack (Supper Club), 1105 and 1/2 East Vernon Avenue, Los Angeles, CA (owned by and associated with Ivie Anderson in the mid-1940s).
- Ivory Theater, Chattanooga, TN (before 1920).
- Jack Dempsey's Resturant, Eighth Avenue, NYC, NY (associated with the ex-professional boxing champion).
- Jack's Basket, Thirty-Second and South Central Avenue, Los Angeles, CA.
- Jack Olsen's Cafe, (Jack Olsen), 919 Fifteenth Street, Denver, CO. (1920s)
- Jack's Resturant, 615 Sacramento, San Francisco, CA.

- Jack's Rathskeller, Juniper and South Streets., Philadelphia, PA (included Ethel Waters's gigs before 1920).
- Jade (Chineese Supper Club), Hollywood Blvd., Los Angeles, CA. (Night club mythology-Peggy Lee in 1938)?
- Jade Club, Hollywood, CA.
- Jaffa Mosque Shrine, Altoona, PA.
- Jai-Lai, Columbus, OH (1940s).
- Jam Room Ballroom, Milwaukee, WI.
- Jantzen Beach Ballroom, Portland, OR.
- Jefferson Davis Hotel, Montgomery, AL,
- Jefferson Hotel (Banquet Hall, Junior Ballroom), Dallas, TX.
- Jefferson Hotel, Columbia, SC.
- Jefferson Hotel, Peoria, IL.
- Jefferson Hotel, Jefferson Blvd. and Washington Streets, St. Louis, MO.
- Jefferson Hotel (Roof Garden, Ballroom), Richmond, VA (actually had a live alligator in a pool)!
- Jefferson Theater, Fourteenth Street, NYC, NY.
- Jefferson Theatre, Birmingham, AL (1920s).
- Jerusalem Temple, New Orleans, LA.
- Jimmy Lake's Night Club, Ninth Street, Washington, DC.
- Jimmy Ryan's (Club), 53 W. Fifty-Second Street, NYC, NY (especially Billie Holiday gigs, 1930s).
- Jimmy's Glass Bar, Wilkes-Barre, PA (1940s).
- Jinx Club, Brooklyn, NYC, NY (1940s).
- Jockey Club, Kansas City, MO (1940s)
- John's Grill, 57 Ellis Street, San Francisco, CA (before 1920)
- John's Rendezvous Restaurant, 50 Osgood Place, San Francisco, CA.
- Joie Theatre, Fort Smith, AR.
- Jolson's Fifty-Ninth Street Theatre, Seventh Avenue and Fifty-Ninth Street, NYC, NY (owned by Al Jolson, 1921+).
- Jones Night Spot, Indianola, MS.
- Journal Square Theater, Jersey City, NJ.
- Journey's Inn, Camden, AL.
- Joyland Casino, Lexington, KY.
- Jungle Club, Manhattan, NTC, NY (1920s).
- Jungle Inn, Cleveland, OH.
- Jungle Inn, Washington, DC.
- Kaawatha Theater, Chicago, IL (1920s). The singer-dancer Carol Chilton, of whom the author of this book cannot find any contemporary recordings, found gigs and recognition here.
- Kalurah Temple, Binghamton, NY (1920s).
- Kantor's Hall, Passaic, NJ.
- Kedzie Theatre, 3202 W. Madison, Chicago, IL (1910+).
- Keeneys (Frank) Theatre, Brooklyn, NYC, NY. (Fannie Brice 1st gig here in 1906?)
- Keith Theater, Syracuse, NY.
- Keith Theater, Dayton, OH.
- Keith's Theatre, 614 Washington, Boston, MA (also known as Keith Albee Boston).
- Keith's Theatre, Chester, NY.
- Keith's Theatre, 1116 Chestnut Street, Philadelphia, PA.

- Keith's Theatre, Cincinnati, OH.
- Keith's Theatre, Grand Rapids, MI.
- Keith's Theatre, Louisville, KY.
- Keith's Theatre, Madison, NY.
- Keith's Theatre, Omaha, NE.
- Keith's Theatre, Portland, ME.
- Keith's Theatre, Syracuse, NY.
- Keith's Theatre, Union City, NY.
- Keith's Theatre, Yonkers, NY.
- Keith's Theatre (Colonial), Sixty-Second to Sixty-Third Street and Broadway, NYC, NY.
- Keith's Eighty-First Street Theatre, NYC, NY.
- Kelly's Café, Atlantic City, NJ (1920s).
- Kelly's Stables (Bert Kelly), 431 N. Rush, Chicago, IL.
- Kelly's Stables (the Stables), 141 W. Fifty-First Street (first site address), NYC, NY (1930s-40s).
- Kenmore Hotel, Albany, NY.
- Kenmore Theater, Brooklyn, NYC, NY.
- Kentucky Theater, Louisville, KY.
- Keyshore Rooms, Lake Villa, IL.
- Kiel Auditorium, St. Louis, MO.
- Kimo Theatre, Albuquerque, NM (1920s+).
- Kinema Theatre, Seventh and Grand Streets, Los Angeles, CA.
- King Phillip Ballroom, Wrentham, MA
- King Tut Café, 606 W. Sixth Street, Los Angeles, CA
- King's Court, Summer Avenue, Memphis, TN.
- King's Tropical Inn, Culver City, CA.
- Kings Ballroom, Lincoln, NE.
- King's Terrace, 240 W. 52nd Street, NYC, NY. (1930s)
- Kirnan Theatre, Baltimore, MD.
- Kit Cat Club, Fifty-Third Street near Fifth Avenue, NYC, NY (1930s).
- Kit Kat Club, Broad and Spruce Streets, Philadelphia, PA.
- Kitty Davis's Airline Night Club, 1610 Alton Road, Miami, FL (1940s). This Kitty, a real female pilot, could fly around and entertain? An original nightclub concept for sure!
- Knickerbocker Hotel, Board Walk, Atlantic City, NJ (1920s).
- Knickerbocker Hotel, Ivar Street and Hollywood Blvd., Hollywood, CA.
- Knickerbocker Theatre, Holland, MI.
- Knickerbocker Theatre, 1396 Broadway, NYC, NY.
- Knickerbockers Yacht Club, Port Washington, NY.
- Knights of Columbus Hall, Glens Falls, NY.
- Knotty Klub, Munising, MI (1940s).
- Koppin Theater, Detroit, MI.
- Kraft Music Hall, Sunset and Vine, NBC Studios, Hollywood, CA. The association with second radio host Bing Crosby (1935-46) defined "live" contemporary radio entertainment.
- Kyle Theatre, Beaumont, TX.
- La Golondrina Nightclub, Olvera Street, Los Angeles, CA.
- La Grande Ballroom, Copland, TX.
- La Monica Ballroom, Santa Monica, CA (1920s+).

- La Martinique (nightclub), Fifty-Seventh Street, NYC, NY (especially Dick Haymes's solo gigs, 1940s+).
- La Paradise Café, Washington, DC.
- La Rue Nightclub and Restaurant, Los Angeles CA (1939+).
- La Salle Hotel, Battle Creek, MI.
- La Salle Hotel (Lotus Room, Blue Fountain Room), 10 N. La Salle Street, Chicago, IL.
- La Vie, Forty-Seventh Street and Broadway, NYC, NY (1920s).
- La Vie Parisienna, 3 East Fifty-Second Street, NYC, NY.
- Labor Temple, Fourteenth Street and Woodlawn, Kansas City, MO.
- Lafayette Hotel, Asbury Park, NJ.
- Lafayette Theatre, Detroit, MI.
- Lafayette Theatre, 2227 Seventh Avenue, Harlem, NYC, NY (Fats Waller house pianist in 1920s).
- Lafayette Theatre, Los Angeles, CA.
- Lake Breeze Pier, Buckeye Lake, OH.
- Lake Club, Springfield, IL
- Lake Compounce, Bristol, CN.
- Lake Placid Club, Lake Placid, NY.
- Lake Whalom Playhouse, Fitchburg, MA.
- Lakewood Theatre, Portland, OR
- Lakeside Park, Dayton, OH.
- Lakeside Park Ballroom, Denver, CO.
- Lakeview Ballroom, Foxboro, MA.
- Lakewood Park., Mahanoy City, PA.
- Lamb's Café, Clark and Randolph Streets, Chicago, IL. (In 1915, a white Louisiana musician Tom Brown and his Dixieland band traveled this far north, as part of a vaudeville act.)
- Land O' Dance Club, Canton, OH (1920s).
- Laankershim Hotel (Tavern Bar), 55 Fifth Street, San Francisco, CA.
- Lareida's Dance Pavilion, Dishman, WA.
- Larry Potter's Supper Club, Hollywood, CA (1948+).
- Last Frontier Hotel (Ramona Room), Las Vegas, NV (1940s).
- Last Stop, 2372 Seventh Avenue, Harlem, NYC, NY (1930s).
- Last Word (nightclub), Los Angeles, CA.
- Latin Casino, Cherry Hill, NJ.
- Latin Casino, Philadelphia, PA (1940s).
- Latin Quarter, 23 W. Randolph, Chicago, IL.
- Latin Quarter, Boston, MA (1937+). (These "Latin Quarter" nightspots were pioneered by Lu Walters, father of newsperson Barbara Walters, very much a (later) TV icon for baby boomers.)
- Latin Quarter (Mademoiselle's Room), Broadway at Forty-Eighth Street, NYC, NY (1937+).
- Latin Quarter, Miami Beach, FL (1940+).
- Le Ruban Bleu (nightclub), 4 E. Fifty-Sixth Street, NYC, NY (1930s+).
- Lee Avenue Theater, NYC, NY.
- Legion Stadium El Monte, CA (1940s+).
- Leland Baptist Church, Detroit, MI.
- Leland Hotel (Sky Club), Aurora, IL. (Gene Autry's live radio broadcast gigs (1930-31))
- Lennox Rathskeller Hotel, St. Louis, MO.

- Lenox Club, 143rd Street and Lenox, Harlem, NYC, NY (1920s+). It featured breakfast dances! (1920s+))
- Lenox Theater, Augusta, GA.
- Lensic Theater, W. San Francisco Street, Santa Fe, NM.
- Leon and Eddie's Night Club, Oakland, CA (1940s).
- Leon and Eddie's (Leon Enken and Eddie Davis) 18 W. Fifty-Second St. (later at 33 W. Fifty-Second Street), NYC, NY (1928+).
- Lerner Theatre, Elkhart, IN.
- Leroy's Lounge, 135th and Fifth Avenue, Uptown, Harlem, NYC NY (1910+).
- Les Ambassedurs, Fifty-Seventh Street, NYC, NY (1920s).
- Les Ambassadeurs, Miami Beach, FL.
- Lester Mapp's Salon, San Francisco, CA.
- Levaggi's Nightery (Flamingo Room), Boston, MA.
- Leveggis Hotel, Boston, MA.
- Levita Taxi Dance Hall, New Orleans, LA.
- Lewisohn Stadium, City College of New York, NYC, NY (Especially Frank Sinatra gig in 1943)
- Lexington Hall, Downtown, NYC, NY.
- Lexington Hotel (Silver Grill, Hawaiian Room), Forty-Eighth and Lexington Avenue, NYC, NY.
- Liberty Theater, Chattanooga, TN.
- Liberty Theater, Spokane, WA (associated with Bing Crosby's and Al Rinker's gigs in the mid-1920s).
- Liberty Ballroom, S. River, NJ.
- Liberty Hall, El Paso, TX.
- Liberty Inn, 661 N. Clark and Erie Streets, Chicago, IL (1920s).
- Liberty Theater, Chattanooga, TN (1920s).
- Liberty Theater, Stanton Island, NY.
- Library of Congress (Coolidge Auditorium), Washington, DC. It featured Folk, Jazz, and Blues.
- Liberty Theatre, Pittsburgh, PA
- Liberty Theatre, 1 South Mission Street, Wenatchee, WA
- Lido (Ambassador), Los Angeles, CA. This famous open-air spot was open daily and featured a house orchestra with vocalists for dancing, with a swimming pool graced by Hollywood starlets to boot. A fine, early color (1935) film short *Starlit Days at the Lido*, more so, capitalized upon this location.
- Lido Cabaret, San Francisco, CA.
- Lido (club) South Bend, IN. (1940s).
- Lido Venice (club), Boston, MA.
- Lido Venice (club) Palm Beach, FL.
- Lido Venice (club) 35, E. Fifty-Third Street, NYC, NY (especially Libby Holman's gigs in 1929).
- Lighthouse Cafe, 30 Pier Avenue, Hermosa Beach, CA (1949+).
- Lincoln Auditorium, Syracuse, NY.
- Lincoln Café, Harlem, NYC, NY (before 1920).
- Lincoln Gardens Café, 459 E. Thirty-First Street and Cottage Grove, Chicago, IL (1922-24). It was associated with many transplanted New Orleans musicians, and house bands included Joe "King" Oliver and Louis Armstrong.
- Lincoln Hotel (Blue Room), Forty-Fourth Street at Eighth Avenue, NYC, NY.

- Lincoln Hotel (Indiana Roof), Indianapolis, IN.
- Lincoln Park (near South Carrollton Avenue), New Orleans, LA (before 1920).
- Lincoln Park, Savannah, GA.
- Lincoln Tavern, 1858 W. Wabansia, Chicago, IL. (The advent of Prohibition found this site, like many, converted into a speakeasy. For some, this (front) site was then an ice cream parlor. Tasty flavors?)
- Lincoln Theater, Baltimore, MD.
- Lincoln Theater, Louisville, KY (1920s).
- Lincoln Theater, Kansas City, MO.
- Lincoln Theater (Blue Room) 58 W. 135th Street, Harlem, NYC, NY.
- Lincoln Theater, Broad and Lombard Streets, Philadelphia, PA.
- Lincoln Theater, Cleveland, OH.
- Lincoln Theater, New Orleans, LA (1930s).
- Lincoln Theatre, Central Avenue, Los Angeles, CA.
- Lincoln Theatre, Pittsburgh, PA.
- Lincoln Theatre, Trenton, NJ.
- Lindy's (nightclub), NYC, NY (1920s).
- Lindy's Resturant, 3656 Wilshire Blvd., Los Angeles, CA.
- Litchford Hotel, (Lounge) Columbus, OH
- Litonia Nightclub, Camden, NJ.
- Little Club, Forty-Fourth Street, near Broadway and Eighth Avenue (speakeasy) NYC, NY (1920s).
- Little Club, 70 E. Fifty-Fifth Street, NYC, NY. (Grand opening featured Doris Day, 1947.)
- Little Theatre, Albuquerque, NM (1930s+).
- Little Troc (Felix Young's), Los Angeles, CA. (Grand opening featured Lena Horne, 1942.)
- Loberto Theatre, Santa Barbara, CA.
- Lobster House (Schneider's), Brooklyn, NYC, NY (1930s).
- Locerne Theatre, Orlando, FL. (1920s)
- Locust Street Theatre, Philadelphia, PA.
- Loew's Grand Theatre, Peachtree Street Atlanta, GA.
- Loew's Journal Square Theatre, Jersey City, NJ.
- Loew's Penn Theatre, Pittsburg, PA.
- Loew's State Theater, Broadway, Manhattan, NYC, NY.
- Loew's State Theatre, Los Angeles, CA.
- Loew's State Theatre, New Orleans, LA.
- Loew's State Theatre, St. Louis, MO.
- Loew's State Theatre, Syracuse, NY.
- Log Cabin (nightclub), Euclid Avenue, Cleveland, OH.
- Log Cabin Club, 168 W. 133rd Street, Harlem, NYC, NY (1930-40s).
- Log Cabin Farms, Armonk, NY.
- Log Cabin Pavilion, Fort Wayne, IN.
- Log Cabin (Fred Thigpen's), Georgiana, AL (1930s+).
- London Chop House, Detroit, MI (1940s).
- Lone Star Club, Kansas City, MO.
- Long Bar, San Francisco, CA.
- Longhorn Ranch, Dallas, TX.
- Lookout House (Club), Cincinatti, OH (1938-39)

- Loring Theatre, 1405 Nichollet Avenue, Minneapolis, MN. (1920-58)
- Lorraine Gardens, 3501 S. Prairie, Chicago, IL (1920s).
- Los Angeles Country Club (LACC), Los Angeles, CA.
- Los Angeles Memorial Coliseum, 3911 S. Figueroa, Los Angeles, CA (1923+).
- Lotus Gardens Café, Cleveland, OH.
- Louisiana Restaurant, New Orleans, LA.
- Lovejoy's Night Club, Los Angeles, CA (1930s).
- Lowry Hotel, St. Paul, MN.
- Lowry Hotel, Albany, NY.
- Lucca Restaurant, 501 S. Western, Los Angeles CA.
- Lucca Restaurant, San Francisco, CA.
- Luigi's Cafe, Detroit. MI. (1920s) (Reputed mobster Sam Trombanick, of the bootlegging 'purple gang', may have had business, as well as a musical 'jazz' interest, in this site?
- Luna Pier, Toledo, OH.
- Lyceum Theater, Chicago, IL (before 1920).
- Lyceum Theatre, New London, CN.
- Lyceum Theatre, Memphis, TN.
- Lyceum Theatre, San Diego, CA.
- Lyceum Theatre, Stamford, CN.
- Lynbrook Night Club, Long Island, NYC, NY.
- Lynn Theatre, O'Donnell, TX.
- Lyonhurst Ballroom, Marlborough, MA.
- Lyric Theater, Bridgeport, CN.
- Lyric Theater, Burgundy and Iberville Streets, New Orleans, LA.
- Lyric Theatre, Baltimore, MD.
- Lyric Theatre, Austin, TX
- Lyric Theatre, Baltimore, MD.
- Lyric Theatre, Indianapolis, IN.
- Lyric Theatre, Big Spring, TX.
- Lyric Theatre, North Hampton, PA.
- Lyric Theatre, Shenandoah, PA.
- Lyric Theatre, Louisville, KY.
- Lyric Theatre, 213 W. Forty-Second Street, NYC, NY.
- Macauley Theatre, Louisville, KY (1920s).
- Macon Hotel, (Cocktail Lounge), Columbus, OH
- Madison Gardens, Toledo, OH.
- Madison Square Garden, Twenty-Sixth and Madison Streets, Downtown, NYC, NY (1890-1925), first site.
- Madison Square Garden, Fiftieth Street and Eighth Avenue, Downtown, NYC, NY (1925-60s), the second site of this New York City center of entertainment. (A third site was undertaken in 1968.)
- Majestic Theatre, Brooklyn, NYC, NY.
- Majestic Theatre, Dallas, TX.
- Million Dollar Pier, Atlantic City, NJ.
- Mardi-Gras Club, W. Madison Avenue, Chicago, IL.
- Madison Theater, NYC, NY.
- Madrid Ballroom, Louisville, KY.
- Madrid Club, Harrisburg, PA.
- Madrillon Restaurant, Washington, DC (especially Helen Forrest's gigs, mid-1930s).

- Madura's Danceland, 114th and Indianapolis, Hammond, IN.
- Maher's Hall, Shenandoah, PA.
- Mahjong Club, NYC, NY (1920s).
- Mahogany Hall (Madame Lulu White's) 235 Basin Street, New Orleans, LA (before 1920).
- Main street Theatre, Kansas City, MO.
- Majestic Theatre, Milwaukee, WI.
- Majestic Theatre, Boston, MA.
- Majestic Theatre, Brooklyn, NYC, NY.
- Majestic Theatre, Cedar Rapids, IA
- Majestic Theatre, 18 W. Monroe, Chicago, IL (1906+). Late in 1945, it was known as the Shubert.
- Majestic Theatre, Fort Worth, TX.
- Majestic Theatre, Los Angeles, CA (1920s).
- Majestic Theatre, Nocona, TX.
- Majesty (nightclub) Chicago, IL (1940s.)
- Mammy's Chicken Koop, 60 W. Fifty-Second Street, NYC, NY (1930s).
- Manhattan (nightclub), Newport, KY (1940s).
- Manhattan Casino, St. Petersburg, FL.
- Manhattan Center, Thirty-Fourth and Eighth Avenue, NYC, NY.
- Manhattan Club, 11739 Parmiee, Watts, CA.
- Manhattan Theatre, Broadway and Fifty-Third to Fifty-Fourth, NYC, NY (1930s).
- Manley Club, Chicago, IL (1920s).
- Mansfield Theatre, Forty-Seventh Street east of Broadway, NYC, NY. (1940s).
- Maple Leaf Club, Denver, CO (1920s).
- Maple Leaf Club, Sedalia, MO (before 1920). Afro-American composer Scott Joplin's composition "Maple Leaf Rag" originated at this site, 1899.
- Marbro Theatre, 4110 W. Madison (and Roosevelt) Chicago, IL (1927+).
- Marigold Ballroom, Minneapolis, MN.
- Marigold Gardens, 817 W. Grace, Chicago, IL (Ruth Etting's first solo singing gig here, 1921).
- Mark Hopkins Hotel (Peacock Court) 850 Mason Street, 1 Nob Hill, San Francisco, CA. White Bandleader Anson Weeks was a house bandleader at this site in the latter 1920s. Moreover, his choice of a (black) featured vocalist, Ivie Anderson (before she joined Duke Ellington), was risky and rare.
- Market Street Theatre Newark, NJ.
- Marlborough House, NYC, NY (1930s).
- Marlowe Theatre, Jackson, TN (1920s).
- Martinique Inn, Indiana Harbor, Indiana (1920s).
- Marvin Theatre, Findlay, OH (1920s).
- Maryland Hotel Ballroom, Pasadena, CA (1920s).
- Maryland Theatre, Baltimore, MD
- Mason Theatre, (Erlanger's), Los Angeles, CA (1920s)
- Masonic Auditorium, Temple at Second Streets, Detroit, MI
- Masonic Opera House, Rocky Mount, NC (1920s).
- Masonic Temple, Davenport, IA
- Masonic Temple, Lansing, MI.
- Mastbaum Theater, Market and Twenty-Second Street, Philadelphia, PA.
- Mayan Theatre, 1633 Los Angeles Street, Los Angeles, CA.

- Mayfair Casino, Cleveland, OH (1930s).
- Mayfair Club, Yates Ville, PA (1940s).
- Mayfair Gardens, North Avenue and Charles, Baltimore, MD.
- Mayfair Hotel (Georgian Room), 1256 W. Seventh Street, Los Angeles, CA.
- Mayflower Hotel, Akron, OH.
- Mayfair Supper Club, 54 B Way, Boston, MA (1940s).
- Mayfair Theatre, Asbury Park, NJ. (1927-70s)
- Mayfair Yacht Club, NYC, NY (1920s).
- Mayflower Hotel Washington, DC.
- Mayflower, Houma, LA (1940s).
- May's Opera House. Pigua, OH. (Mills Brothers gigs,1920s).
- McElroy's Spanish Ballroom, SW Fifth and Main Streets, Portland, OR.
- McFaddins School, Murfreesboro, TN (associated with Roy Acuff's gig here in the 1930s).
- McVickers Theater, 23 W. Madison Street, Chicago, IL (fourth building site rebuilt in 1922).
- Meadow Brook Country Club, St. Louis, Mo.
- Meadowbrook Ballroom (Frank Dailey) Cedar Grove, NJ.
- Meadowbrook Gardens, Culver City, CA.
- Meads Acres, Topeka, KS.
- Mealy's Ballroom, Allentown, PA.
- Mecca Temple, NYC, NY (1940s).
- Mechanic's Hall, Boston, MA.
- Medinah Temple, 600 N. Wabash, Chicago, IL (1912+).
- Melba Theatre, Dallas, TX.
- Melody Club, Union City, NJ (1940s).
- Melody Mill Ballroom, North Riverside, IL.
- Melody Lane (Starlite Room), Wilshire Blvd. and Western Avenue, Los Angeles, CA (1930s+).
- Memorial Auditorium San Luis Obispo, CA.
- Memorial Auditorium, Athens, OH.
- Memorial Auditorium, Atlanta, GA.
- Memorial Auditorium, Canton, OH. (While a scheduled show did proceed on New Year's Day, 1953, the star attraction, Hank Williams, had died on route to the gig, in a car.)
- Memorial Hall, Independence, KS.
- Memorial Hall, Coffeyville, KS.
- Memorial Hall, Columbus, OH.
- Mercantile Hall, Philadelphia, PA (1940s).
- Mermaid (nightclub), Los Angeles, CA (1940s).
- Merry Garden Ball Room, Belmont and Sheffield Avenue, Chicago, IL (1920s+).
- Merry-Go-Round, Youngstown, OH (1940s).
- Metropole Café, Seventh Avenue and Forty-Eighth Street, NYC, NY.
- Metropolitan Opera House, Philadelphia, PA.
- Metropolitan Opera House (MET), NYC, NY.
- Metropolitan Theater, Providence, RI.
- Metropolitan Theatre, Boston, MA.
- Mezzanine Cocktail Lounge, 245 South Wabash, Chicago, IL (1930s)
- Metropolitan Theatre (Met), 4644 S. Parkway, Chicago, IL (1917+).
- Metropolitan Theatre, 5012 Euclid, Cleveland, OH.
- Metropolitan Theatre, Los Angeles, CA.

- Miami Club, Toledo, OH (1940s).
- Michelson's (club), Cincinnati, OH (1920s).
- Michigan Theatre, Fifty-Fifth and Michigan, Chicago, IL.
- Michigan Theatre, Ann Arbor, MI.
- Michigan Theatre, Detroit, MI.
- Michigan Theatre, Jackson, MI
- Michel's, 38 E. Fifty-Third Street, NYC, NY.
- Midelburg Auditorium, Charlestown, WV
- Midland Theatre, Kansas City, MO (1927+).
- Mike Todd's Theatre Café, 4812 N. Clark, Chicago, IL (1939+).
- Midnight Frolic Cabaret (New Amsterdam Theatre's Roof Garden), NYC, NY.
- Midnight Sun (nightclub), NYC, NY (1938+).
- Midway (Cabaret), 591 Pacific Street, San Francisco, CA (before 1920).
- Midway Dancing Gardens, Sixtieth and Cottage Grove, Chicago, IL (1924+).
- Midway Gardens, Fort Wayne, IN.
- Miller's Theater, Pine Bluff, AK (1920s).
- Million Dollar Theatre, Los Angeles, CA.
- Milton Point Casino, Rye, NY.
- Milton's Tap Room, Troost Avenue, Kansas City, MO (associated with Julia Lee gigs (1930s-40s).
- Mimic Club, Manhattan, NYC, NY.
- Mimo Club, Harlem, NYC, NY (1940s).
- Mineral Springs Club, South Bend, IN (1930s).
- Minnesota Theater, Minneapolis, MN.
- Minton's Playhouse, 210 West 118th Street, Harlem, NYC, NY (1938+).
- Mirador Club, Fifty-First Street and Seventh Avenue, NYC, NY (1920s).
- Mishler Theatre, Altoona, PA (1920s).
- Mission Beach Ballroom, San Diego, CA.
- Mission Theatre, Salt Lake City, UT.
- Missouri Cafe, 12th Street, Kansas City, MO. (1920s)
- Missouri Hotel (Kit Cat Club), St. Louis, MO.
- Mobile Auditorium, Mobile, AL.
- Mobilian Theater, 261 Dauphin Street Mobile, AL.
- Mocambo (nightclub), Miami, FL (1940s).
- Mocambo Nightclub and Restaurant, 8588 Sunset Blvd., Hollywood, CA (1939+).
- Mon Paree, NYC, NY (1930s).
- Mona Lisa Restaurant, Wilshire Blvd., Los Angeles, CA.
- Monaco's Restaurant And Lidio Annex, (Frank Monaco), Euclid Avenue, Cleveland, OH.
- Monaco Theatre Restaurant, San Francisco, CA (1940s).
- Monogram Theater, 3440-53 S. State Street, Chicago, IL (1913-30).
- Montclair Theatre, Montclair, NY (1920s).
- Mount Pocono Casino, Mount Pocono, PA.
- Mount Zion Baptist Church, Newark, NJ (especially Sarah Vaughn as a child).
- Monte Carlo Club (Fefe's), 40 E 54th Street, NYC. NY (Especially Lee Wiley). 1930s-40s)
- Monte Carlo Club, Fifty-First Street and Broadway, NYC, NY (1920s).
- Montecito Country Club, Montecito, CA.
- Monette's Supper Club, 133rd Street, Uptown, Harlem, NYC, NY. Contemporary (Afro-American) blues and jazz vocalist Monette Moore (not a featured vocalist in

this book) owned interest in this club in the early 1930s. Moreover, Billie Holiday got one of her first gigs here, in 1933.

- Montmarte Café (next to the Green Mill), 4806 Broadway and Lawrence, Chicago IL (1920s+).
- Montmarte Café, NYC, NY (1920s+).
- Montmarte Cafe, Hollywood Blvd., Hollywood, CA (especially associated with Paul Whiteman's Rhythm Boys—Bing Crosby, Al Rinker, and Harry Barris in 1929).
- Monsignor Club, W. Forty-Seventh Street and Ninth Avenue, NYC, NY (1920s).
- Monte Christo (Club), Erie Street & St. Clair, Chicago, Il (1930s)
- Moonlight Ballroom, Canton, OH (1930s).
- Moonlight Gardens, Myers Lake Park, Canton, OH.
- Moonlite Gardens, Cincinnati, OH.
- Moore Theater, Seattle, WA.
- Morressey's Hair Salon, (Speakeasy), Cherokee Ave.&Hollywood Blvd., Los Angeles, CA. (1930s).
- Moose Hall, 1748 Welton Street, Denver, CO.
- Mosaic Theater, Little Rock, AK (1920s).
- Mosque Auditorium, Richmond, VA.
- Mosque Theatre (Terrace Room), Newark, NJ.
- Moulin Rouge (Club, Elmo Badon's), heart of Vieux Carre, Bourbon Street, New Orleans, LA.
- Moulin Rouge (Club), Brooklyn, NYC, NY (1930s).
- Moulin Rouge Café, 416 S. Wabash, Chicago, IL (1920s).
- Moulin Rouge Night Club, Hollywood, CA (1948+).
- Mound Club, St. Louis, MO (1920s).
- Mounds Club, Chardon Road, Willoughby Hills, OH.(1930-50) A young 22 year old singer Dino Crocetti, (later known as Dino Martini, & later as Dean Martin), had an important gig here, 1939. Later in 1947, this site that was perhaps associated with reputed mobster Tommy McGinty, a (still) unsolved incident involving a robbery of over 300 patrons, attracted international attention.
- Municipal Auditorium, Birmingham, AL.
- Municipal Auditorium, Eau Claire, WI.
- Municipal Auditorium, Jackson, MS
- Municipal Auditorium, Memphis, TN.
- Municipal Auditorium, Oklahoma City, OK.
- Municipal Auditorium, Atlanta, GA.
- Municipal Auditorium, Denver, CO.
- Municipal Auditorium, Kansas City, MO.
- Municipal Auditorium, Savannah, GA. (1920s)
- Municipal Auditorium, Shreveport, LA. This site hosted radio broadcasts of *Louisiana Hayride*, in 1948. Hank Williams's early electrifying live appearances here gained national recognition.
- Municipal Auditorium, St. Louis, MO (1936+).
- Municipal Auditorium, New Orleans, LA.
- Murat Temple, Indianapolis, IN (1920+).
- Murrain's Cabaret, Seventh Avenue, Harlem, NYC, NY (1940s).
- Murray's (Club), Central Avenue, Los Angeles, CA.
- Murray's Gardens, Forty-Second Street, near Seventh Avenue, NYC, NY (1920s).
- Music Box Restaurant, Cleveland, OH.

- Music Box, (Blue Room), O'Farrell Street, San Francisco, CA (1930s+)
- Music Hall, Cincinnati, OH.
- Musselman's Grove, Claysburg, PA.
- Mustin Beach Club, Pensacola, FL.
- Naking Inn, Eight and Washington, St. Louis, MO. (1920s-30s)
- Nameless Café, Chicago, IL (1940s).
- Natatorium Park, Spokane, WA.
- National Hall, Mission at Sixteenth Street, San Francisco, CA.
- National Press Club, Washington, DC.
- National Theater, Louisville, KY.
- National Theater, Washington, DC.
- National Theatre, Greensboro, NC.
- National Theatre, Boston, MA.
- Navajo Ballroom, Big Bear Lake, CA.
- Neal House, Columbus, OH.
- Nebraska Theater, Sulphur Springs, FL (1930s).
- Nemo Theatre, 322 Opelousas Avenue, New Orleans, LA.
- Nest Club (Ye Olde Nest) 169 W. 133rd Street, Harlem, NYC, NY (1920s+).
- Nest Club, E. Thirty-Fifth and S. Calumet, Chicago, IL (1920s).
- Netherlands Plaza (Ballroom) l, Cincinnati, OH.
- Nettings on the Charles, near Waltham, MA.
- New Albert Auditorium, 1224 Pennsylvania Avenue, Baltimore, MD.
- New Broadway Theatre, Cape Girardeau, MS. (1920s).
- New Douglas Theatre, Lenox Avenue and 142nd Street, NYC, NY.
- New England Mutual Hall, Boston MA.
- New Grant Theatre, Evansville, IN.
- New Green Mill, Washington Blvd., Los Angeles, CA (1920s).
- New Haven Lawn Club, New Haven, CN.
- New Hicks Hotel, Rocky Mount, NC.
- New Holland Park, New Holland, PA.
- New Kenmore Hotel (Rainbow Room), Albany, NY (1940s).
- New Montauk Theatre, Passaic, NJ
- New Orleans Club, Cleveland, OH (1930s).
- New Orleans Swing Club, San Francisco, CA (1940s+).
- New Orpheum Theater, Seattle, WA.
- New Park Theatre, Boston, MA.
- New Tempo Club, 168 W 132nd Street, Uptown, Harlem, NYC, NY.
- New Secord, Toledo, OH.
- New World Café, Atlantic City, NJ (associated with Frankie "Half Pint" Jaxton gigs, before 1920).
- New Yorker (Harry's), 400 N. Wabash, Chicago, IL (1940s).
- Newark Theater, Newark, OH.
- Nick's Café, Los Angeles, CA (1946+).
- Nightingale Ballroom, Kaukauna, WI.
- Ninety One (91) Theater, 91 Decatur Street, Atlanta, GA.
- Nim's Cafe, Spokane, WA (1920s)
- Nixon Grand Theater, Broad and Montgomery Streets, Philadelphia, PA.
- Nixon's Theater, Pittsburgh, PA.

- Nixon's Apollo Theatre, (Samuel F. Nixon), Boardwalk at New York Avenue, Atlantic City, NJ.
- Nora Bay's Roof (Wunder Bar) Manhattan, NYC, NY (associated with Nora Bayes, Al Jolson, 1930s).
- Noon Club, San Francisco, CA (1931+).
- Norman Auditorium, La Crosse, WI.
- Normandie Ballroom, Boston, MA (1930s).
- Normandie, French Ocean Liner. In the years from 1932 to 1942, it featured the real (Austrian) Von Trapp Family in 1938, among others. (Not Julie Andrews!). It was mysteriously sunk in NYC harbor during WWII.,
- North Fork Resort, North Fork, NC. (Jimmie Rodgers led a small string band gig here, 1927.)
- North Hempstead Country Club, Long Island, NYC, NY (1930s).
- North Memphis Cafe, Memphis, TN.
- North Park Theatre (Shea's), Buffalo, NY. (1920+)
- Northside Coliseum, Dallas, TX.
- Nut Club, Alton Rd. and Dade Blvd., Miami Beach, FL.
- Nuttings-on-the-Charles, Waltham, MA. FFF
- Nuova Villa Tommaro Restaurant, Coney Island, NYC, NY. (In 1931, reputed mobster Joe "the Boss" Masserina was gunned down at this ethnic site, possibly by reputed mobster Bugsy Siegel?)
- O'Henry Hotel, Greensboro, NC.
- O'Leary's Barn, 137 W. Fifty-Second Street, NYC, NY (later, second site of NYC's Kelly's Stables).
- Oaks (nightclub), Minnesota City, MN (1940s).
- Ocean Pier, Wildwood, NJ.
- Oasis (nightclub), Detroit, MI (1930s).
- Oasis (nightclub), New Orleans, LA (1940s).
- Oasis (nightclub), Seattle, WA.
- Oasis Bar, Los Angeles, CA.
- Ocean Pier, Wildwood, NJ.
- Odeon Dance Hall, Glenwood Springs, CO (1927+).
- Odeon Theater, St Louis, MO.
- Oh Henry Ballroom, 8900 Archer Avenue, Willow Springs, IL (named for the popular "O Henry" candy bar, rebuilt several times, later called the Willow Brook Ballroom (1921+)).
- Ohio Theatre, Euclid Avenue, Cleveland, OH.
- Oklahoma Freestate Fairgrounds, Muskogee, OK (1920s+).
- Old Absinthe House, 238 Bourbon Street, New Orleans, LA (1920s).
- Old Faithful Inn, San Francisco, CA (before 1920).
- Old Garrick Theater, NYC, NY.
- Old Globe Theatre, Balboa Park, San Diego, CA (1935+).
- Old Howard Theatre, Boston, MA (before 1920).
- Old Orchard Pier, Old Orchard Beach, ME.
- Old Pueblo Club, Tucson, AZ.
- Olmos Club, San Antonio, TX.
- Olympia Theatre, Detroit, MI.
- Olympia Theatre, E. Flagler Street and Second Avenue, Miami, FL (opened in 1926).
- Olympic Auditorium, Eighteenth Street and Grand, Los Angeles, CA (1924+).

- Olympic Hotel (Georgian Room, Spanish Ballroom) Seattle, WA.
- Olympus Hotel (Café), Ninth and Pacific, Tacoma, WA.
- One Hundred and Fifth Street Theater (105th), NYC, NY.
- Onyx Club, 35 West Fifty-Second Street, NYC, NY (1933-35, 1937-39). This site and another at 72 West Fifty-Second Street found Maxine Sullivan in early gigs with musician John Kirby.
- Onyx Club, 57 West Fifty-Second Street, NYC, NY (1942-49), third site included Billie Holiday and Sarah Vaughan.
- Opera House, San Francisco, CA.
- Orange Grove Theater, Hope Square, Los Angeles, CA (1920s).
- Orange Theatre, Orange, CA.
- Orchestra Gardens, Detroit, MI (1930s).
- Orchestra Hall, 220 S. Michigan Avenue, Chicago, IL (1904+).
- Orchid Club, 33 West 5nds Street, NYC, NY (1949+).
- Orchid, Springfield, IL (1940s).
- Oriental Café, 3532 S. State Street, Chicago, IL.
- Oriental Cafe, near Book-Cadillac Hotel, Detroit, MI (1920s)
- Oriental Gardens, Ninth and R Streets, Washington, DC.
- Oriental Theater (Oriental Ballroom, upstairs), 20-32 W. Randolph, Chicago, IL (1926+).
- Oriole Gardens, Chicago, IL.
- Oriole Terrace Club, Detroit, MI.
- Orpheum Ballroom, 1425 Welton Street, Denver, CO
- Orpheum Theater, Des Moines, IA.
- Orpheum Theater, Newark, NJ.
- Orpheum Theater, Davenport, IA.
- Orpheum Theatre (Hennepin), Minneapolis, MN.
- Orpheum Theatre, 203 Main and Beale Streets, Memphis, TN.
- Orpheum Theatre, Sioux City, IA.
- Orpheum Theatre, Springfield, IL.
- Orpheum Theatre, Ninth and St. Charles, St. Louis, MO (1917+).
- Orpheum Theatre, Lima, OH.
- Orpheum Theatre, 1 Hamilton Place, Boston, MA.
- Orpheum Theatre, Cleveland, OH.
- Orpheum Theatre, Fresno, CA
- Orpheum Theatre, Gary, IN.
- Orpheum Theatre, Kansas City, MO.
- Orpheum Theatre, Lincoln, NB.
- Orpheum Theatre, Madison, WI.
- Orpheum Theatre, Muskogee, OK.
- Orpheum Theatre, Nashville, TN.
- Orpheum Theatre, New Orleans, LA.
- Orpheum Theatre, Oakland, CA.
- Orpheum Theatre, Omaha, NE.
- Orpheum Theatre, Phoenix, AZ.
- Orpheum Theatre, Portland, OR.
- Orpheum Theatre, Sacramento, CA.
- Orpheum Theatre, Fifth and B Streets, San Diego, CA.
- Orpheum Theatre, Seattle, WA.

- Orpheum Theatre, St. Paul, MN.
- Orpheum Theatre, Stockton, CA.
- Orpheum Theatre, Webster City, IA.
- Orpheum Theatre, Wichita, KS.
- Orpheum Theatre, 110 S. State Street, Chicago, IL (1907+).
- Orpheum Theatre, 1192 Market Street, San Francisco, CA (1926+).
- Orpheum Theatre, 842 S. Broadway, Los Angeles, CA. (1926+)
- Orpheum Theatre, Eighty-Sixth Street and Third Avenue, Yorkville, NYC, NY.
- Osters Ballroom, Cleveland, OH.
- Over the Rainbow (nightclub), 9015 Sunset Strip, Los Angeles, CA. (Ownership was associated with Vincent Minnelli and Judy Garland in the mid-1940s. One floor below was the Rainbow Bar and Grill.) Get it?
- Owen Brennan's Old Absinthe House, Bourbon Street, New Orleans, LA (1940s).
- Owl Café, Helena, AR.
- Owl Club, Austin, TX.
- Owl Theater, 4653 S. State, Chicago, IL (1916+).
- P. Wee's, Beale Street, Memphis, TN.
- Pabst Theater, Milwaukee, WI.
- Pacific Square Ballroom, San Diego, CA.
- Pair O'Dice Club, Las Vegas, NV (an early Vegas entity, before 1933, a speakeasy).
- Painted Post, Ventura Blvd., San Fernando Valley, CA (ownership by Western film actor Hoot Gibson, featured C & W acts, 1940s).
- Palace Hotel (Rose Room), Market and New Montgomery Streets, San Francisco, CA.
- Palace Gardens, near 600 N. Clark Street, Chicago, IL (1920s).
- Palace Theater, Youngstown, OH.
- Palace Theater, Peoria, IL.
- Palace Theatre, Akron, OH.
- Palace Theatre, Ballinger, TX.
- Palace Theatre, Fort Wayne, IN.
- Palace Theatre (Keith's) 1564 Broadway, NYC, NY (vaudeville's center, 1913+).
- Palace Theatre, Rochester, NY.
- Palace Theatre (Million Dollar Theatre), Dallas, TX.
- Palace Theatre (Proctor's), Newark, NJ.
- Palace Theatre, 159 W. Randolph, Chicago, IL (1926+).
- Palace Theatre, 324 Beale Street, Memphis, TN.
- Palace Theatre, Canton, OH.
- Palace Theatre, Cleveland, OH.
- Palace Theatre, Milwaukee, WI.
- Palace Theatre, White Plains, New York.
- Palais D'OR, Boston, MA. (1930s)
- Palais D'OR, Broadway at 48th, NYC, NY (1930s)
- Palais Royal (Ben Marden's) Club, Broadway and W. Fifty-Eighth Street, NYC, NY.
- Palais Royale Café, W. Madison St, Chicago, IL. (1920s)
- Palais Royale, Nyack, NY.
- Palladium Ballroom Café, Sunset near Vine, Hollywood, CA.
- Palm Garden (Blatz Hotel), Milwaukee, WI.
- Palomar Ballroom, Norfolk, VA
- Paradise Gardens, Twelfth Street and Central, Los Angeles, CA (1920s).
- Paradise Theater, Detroit, MI.

- Palm Gardens, Wilmington, DE (1940s).
- Palm Tavern, 446 Forty-Seventh Street, Chicago, IL (1933+).
- Palmer House (Empire Room, Gas Light Club), 17 E. Monroe, Chicago, IL (1933+).
- Palomar Ballroom, Vermont at Third, Los Angeles, CA (1930s).
- Palomar Theater, Seattle, WA.
- Palumbo's Lounge, Philadelphia, PA.
- Pan Pacific Auditorium, 7600 Beverly Road, Los Angeles, CA (1940-72)
- Panama Café, 3501 S. State, Chicago, IL (1920s+). (Especially Alberta Hunter gigs before 1920).
- Panama Club, Eighteenth and Forest, Kansas City, MO (1930s+).
- Panama Inn, Forty-Sixth and State Street, Chicago, IL.
- Pandora Club, Broad Street, Philadelphia, PA (1920s).
- Pansy Club, 204 W. Forty-Eighth Street, NYC, NY.
- Pantages Club Theater, 6233 Hollywood Blvd., Hollywood, CA.
- Pantages Theatre, San Francisco, CA.
- Pantages Theatre, Fifth and B Street, San Diego, CA (1924-29).
- Pantages Theatre, Seattle, WA.
- Pantages Theatre, Spokane, WA.
- Pappy Daily's Record Shop, Eleventh Street, Houston, TX (1947+, especially Hank Williams).
- Paradise Cabaret Restaurant (N. T. G's), Broadway at Forty-Ninth Street, NYC, NY (1930s). This nightclub was actually on the second floor of the Brill building, the center of the music publishing industry.
- Paradise Ballroom, 128 N. Crawford Avenue, Chicago, IL.
- Paradise Gardens Cafe, Atlantic City, NJ (Frankie "Half Pint" Jaxon, Bessie Smith, and others, 1920s).
- Paradise Gardens, Thirty-Fifth Street near Calumet, Chicago, IL (1920s).
- Paradise Theatre, Detroit, MI.
- Paradise Theatre, Bronx NYC, NY.
- Paramount Grill, 235 W. Forty-Sixth Street, NYC, NY (1930s).
- Paramount Inn, Buffalo, NY.
- Paramount Theatre, Broadway and Forty-Third Streets, NYC, NY (especially the sensational (solo) gigs of Bing Crosby in 1931 and Frank Sinatra in 1942).
- Paramount Theatre, Brooklyn, NYC, NY.
- Paramount Theatre, Centralia, IL.
- Paramount Theatre, Des Moines, IA.
- Paramount Theatre, Sixth and Hill Street, Los Angeles, CA (1929+).
- Paramount Theatre, Middletown, NY.
- Paramount Theatre, Nashville, TN.
- Paramount Theatre, New Haven, CN.
- Paramount Theatre, Newark, NJ.
- Paramount Theatre, Oakland, CA
- Paris Inn, 210 E. Market Street, Los Angeles, CA (1920s).
- Park Avenue Club, West Hampton, Long Island, NYC, NY (1920s).
- Park Central Hotel (Coconut Grove Room, Grille, and Roof), Fifty-Sixth Street and Seventh Avenue, NYC, NY (1920s+).
- Park Theatre, Erie, PA (1920s).
- Park Theater, Louisville, KY.
- Parkway Ballroom, South Parkway At Forty-Fifth Street, Chicago, IL.

- Parody Club, Forty-Seventh Street and Broadway, NYC, NY (1920s).
- Pasadena Civic Center, Pasadena, CA.
- Pasadena Playhouse, Pasadena, CA.
- Paseo Hall Ballroom, Kansas City, MO.
- Pastime Theatre, Muskogee, OK.
- Pastor's Theater, Fourteenth Street, NYC, NY (1881-1908). Founded by Tony Pastor (also a name of a later bandleader), this theater concept of variety acts, perhaps founded the concept of touring "vaudeville," at least in America. Among the many contemporary acts that played here were George M. Cohan, Lillian Russell, May Irwin, Eva Tanguay, and a young blackfaced Sophie Tucker.
- Patagonia (Pod's and Jerry's Club), 168 W. 133rd Street, Harlem, NYC, NY (1930s).
- Patio (nightclub), Cincinnati OH (1940s).
- Pavilion Ballroom, Myrtle Beach, SC.
- Pavilion Ballroom, Santa Monica, CA.
- Pavilion Royal Restaurant, Merrick Road, Long Island, NYC, NY.
- Paxtang Park Pavilion, Harrisburg, PA.
- Paxton Hotel (Ballroom) Omaha, NE.
- Peabody Hotel, Main and Monroe Streets, Memphis, TN (1800s-1923), first site.
- Peabody Hotel (Roof), 149 Union Street, Memphis, TN (1925+). This second site found its own posh roof a perfect site for ballroom orchestra sounds and voices. While segregated, as most hotels were, North or South, some of its other rooms served as recording studios for many Afro-American blues entities, as well as much of traveling contemporary "big band" entertainment. (Ducks walking to roof)?
- Pearl Theater, Twenty-First Ridge Avenue, Philadelphia, PA.
- Pebble Beach Lodge, Pebble Beach, CA.
- Peery's Egyptian Theatre, Ogden, UT (1924+).
- Pekin Café, Philadelphia, PA.
- Pekin Café, Forty-Sixth Street, NYC, NY.
- Pekin Café, Spokane, WA.
- Pekin Theatre and Café (Beaux Arts Cabaret club, upstairs), 2700 S. State Street, Chicago, IL. As a center for ragtime and jazz before 1920, this site oddly became a victim of Prohibition—closing in 1920 after some gunplay and becoming a Chicago police station.
- Pelham Health Inn, NYC, NY.
- Penn Athletic Club, Philadelphia, PA.
- Penn Theatre, Pittsburgh, PA.
- Penthouse (nightclub), Detroit, MI (1930s).
- Peony Park, Omaha, NE.
- Perino's Restaurant (Sky Room) 3927 Wilshire Blvd., Los Angeles, CA.
- Perry Theatre, Erie, PA.
- Perseverance Hall, 907 St. Claude Avenue, New Orleans, LA (before 1920).
- Pershine Theatre, Philadelphia, PA (1920s).
- Pershing Hotel (El Grotto Room, Palace Café), Cottage Grove and Sixty-Fourth Streets, Chicago, IL.
- Pete Lala's 25 Club, Conti Street, New Orleans, LA (associated with Louis Armstrong before 1920).
- Petrelli's Steakhouse, Culver City, CA (1931+).
- Pettibone Club, Cleveland, OH.

- Pheasant Tavern, Astoria, Queens, New York City, NY. (Myth has it that Joe Bari, later known as Tony Bennett, was a singing waiter here, in 1946)?
- Philadelphia House, Atlantic City, NJ (before 1920).
- Philharmonic Auditorium, Los Angeles, CA (1940s). This European-classical music center became a center of jazz due to the efforts of Norman Granz, also a record producer. Later, known live shows were known as *Jazz at The Philharmonic* (especially noting gigs by the Nat Cole Trio).
- Philmont Country Club, Philadelphia, PA.
- Philpitt's Store, 810 Franklin Street, Tampa, FL.
- Phoenix Theatre, 3104 S. State Street, Chicago, IL (1906-28).
- Piccadilly Cafe, Broad Street, Philadelphia, PA (1920s)
- Piccadilly Circus Lounge, NYC, NY (1940s).
- Piccadilly Hotel (Grill Room), NYC, NY (1930s).
- Piccadilly (club), Providence, RI (1940s).
- Pickwick Club, Bench Street Boston, MA (1920s). A (1925) floor collapse was blamed on the contemporary dance fad the Charleston, with singer Teddy Williams escaping injury.
- Pied Pipe (club), Greenwich Village, NYC, NY (1940s).
- Pier Casino, Old Orchard Beach, ME.
- Pilgrim Baptist Church, 3301 S. Indiana Avenue, Chicago, IL. When (converted) bluesman Tomas Dorsey arrived here in the early 1930s, he also composed some music, now known as "gospel music."
- Pirate's Cave, 972 Market Street, San Francisco, CA (before 1920).
- Pirate's Den (Don Dickerman's), 8 Christopher Street, Greenwich Village, NYC, NY.
- Pirates Den, Hollywood, CA (1940-41); 335 N. La Brea Avenue, Hollywood, CA (ownership associated with the interests of Rudy Vallee, Bing Crosby, Bob Hope, Fred Mac Murray, Errol Flynn, and others).
- Pla-Mor Café, 3825 W. Madison, Chicago, IL (1928+).
- Pla-Mor Ballroom, Lincoln, NE.
- Pla-Mor Ballroom, Linwood and Main, Kansas City, MO (1927-50s).
- Planet Mars (Club), Chicago, IL (1931+).
- Plantation Café, 338 East Thirty-Fifth Street, Chicago, IL (1920s, associated with reputed mobster Al Capone).
- Plantation Café, Fiftieth and Broadway, NYC, NY (1920s). It was perhaps the first highbrow restaurant to offer an all-black revue in New York's Manhattan, actually above the Winter Gardens Theatre. It was at this site, in 1925, that Ethel Waters introduced "Dinah," which became a contemporary best-selling Columbia Records release, also noting the club's own "Plantation Orchestra," on its label.
- Plantation Café, Culver City, CA (1928-30, owned by actor Fatty Arbuckle).
- Plantation Club, 126th, near Lenox Avenue, Harlem, NYC, NY. Harry Block (reputed mobster) opened this site and somehow recruited Cab Calloway as a headliner to rival the interests of (reputed mobster) Owney Madden's Cotton Club. Block was subsequently found dead and the club closed, in 1930.
- Plantation Club, Dallas, TX.
- Playdium (two sites) 3825 W. Madison Street and 1702 W. Van Buren Chicago, IL (1920s+).
- Playground Club (managed by Tommy Guinan, Texas's brother), NYC, NY (1920s).
- Playhouse, Rutland, VT.
- Playhouse, Weston, VT.

- Playhouse, Worchester, MA.
- Play-Land Casino, Rye, NY.
- Plaza Hotel, (Persian Room), 5th Avenue, Manhattan, NYC, NY
- Plaza Restaurant, Pittsburgh, PA.
- Plaza Theater, El Paso, TX (1930+).
- Pleasure Beach, Bridge Port, CN.
- Pleasure Club, Lake Charles, LA (1940s).
- Pleasure Point Plunge (roadhouse), East Cliff Drive, Santa Cruz, CA (1920s+).
- Plymouth Theatre, Boston, MA.
- Plymouth Theatre, Eliot Street, Boston, MA
- Poli Theatre, Scranton, PA.
- Poli Theatre, Wilkes-Barre, PA.
- Poli's Theatre, Washington, DC.
- Poli's Theatre, Hartford, CN.
- Polk Theatre, Lakeland, FL (1928+).
- -Poodle Dog Café, Liberty Street, New Orleans, LA (before 1920). Myth?
- Pop Grey's Dance Hall, South Street, Chester, PA.
- Portola Louvre Cafe, Market Street and Powell, San Francisco, CA.
- Post Lodge, Larchmont, NY (1940s).
- Power's Hotel Coffee Shop, Fargo, ND.
- Power's Hotel, (Thomas F. Powers),400 Broadway, Fargo, ND. (1914-80s)
- Powers Theatre, Grand Rapids, MI.
- Premier Club, 3130-32 Troost, Kansas City, MO.
- President Follies Theatre, San Francisco, CA.
- President Hotel, Atlantic City, NJ.
- President Hotel, Swan Lake, NY (1930s+).
- Preview Cocktail Lounge, Chicago, IL (1940s).
- Prima's Club, Los Angeles, CA (owned by and associated with Louis Prima in the 1940s).
- Primrose Dance Palace, 322 West 125th Street, NYC, NY (1930s).
- Primrose Country Club, Newport, KY.
- Princess Theatre, Chicago, IL (1920s).
- Princess Theatre, Nashville, TN.
- Princess Theatre, Waynesboro, MS.
- Proctor's Theater, Albany, NY.
- Proctor's Theatre, Schenectady, NY.
- Proctor's Theatre, Yonkers, NY.
- Proctor's Theatre, Eighty-Sixth Street, NYC, NY.
- Proctor's 125th Street Theatre, NYC, NY.
- Prom Ballroom, St. Paul, MN (1930s).
- Prudden Auditorium, Lansing, MI.
- Public Music Hall, Cleveland, OH.
- Public Theatre, Manhattan, NYC, NY.
- Punchbowl, Broadway and Forty-Ninth Streets, NYC, NY. (This 1930s' bar was owned by ex-boxer-champ Jack Dempsey. Moreover, its title is an obvious pun. Take a swing at Dempsey?)
- Pueblo Auditorium, Pueblo, CO.
- Purcell's Cabaret, 520 Pacific, San Francisco, CA (before 1920).
- Purple Cat, Chicago, IL.
- Purple Grackle (roadhouse) Route 20, east of Elgin, near Elgin, IL (1920s).

- Putnam Theatre, Brooklyn, NYC, NY.
- Pyramid Club, 5610 Hollywood, Blvd., Los Angeles, CA (briefly owned by Russ Columbo in 1931).
- Pythian Castle Hall, Pennsylvania Avenue, Baltimore, MD.
- Pythian Hall, St. Louis, MO.
- Pythian Temple, Dallas, TX.
- Pythian Temple, Wheeling, WV.
- Pythian Temple, 2013 Centre Avenue, Pittsburg, PA.
- Pythian Theater, Columbus, OH.
- Quaker Outing Club, Market Street, near Philadelphia, PA.
- *Queen Mary*, British Ocean Liner (1936+), featured entertainment, transported troops during WWII.
- R. J. Reynolds Memorial Auditorium, Winston-Salem, NC.
- Radio City Music Hall, 50th-51st and Sixth, Seventh Avenue (Rockefeller Plaza) NYC, NY, combined as with Radio City Theatre and RKO's Roxy Theatre in 1932+.
- Radio Franks. 70 E. Fifty-Fifth Street, NYC, NY. Owned by radio personalities Frank Bessinger and Frank Wright, later Jerry White replaced Frank Wright. (1929-1949?)
- Radisson Hotel (Flame Room), Minneapolis, MI (1930s+).
- Radisson Hotel, St. Louis, MO.
- Radium Club, Uptown Harlem, Lenox Avenue, NY, NY (1935).
- Rafe's Paradise, Atlantic City, NJ (before 1920).
- Rainbow Gardens, 4812 N. Clark (and Lawrence), Chicago, IL (1920s).
- Rainbow Gardens, Denver, CO.
- Rainbow Café, W. Madison Street, Chicago, IL (1920s).
- Rainbow Rendezvous Ballroom, 47 E. Fifth Avenue South, Salt Lake City, UT.
- Rainbow Room, sixty-fifth floor of RCA building, Rockefeller Center Roof, NYC, NY (1934+).
- Rajah Theater, Reading, PA.
- Ranch Inn, Elko, NV (1940s).
- Rathskeller Club, Pittsburgh, PA (1920s).
- Ravine Park, Blairsville, PA (1940s).
- Raymond Theatre, Pasadena, CA.
- Raymoor Ballroom, 253 Huntington Street, Boston, MA.
- Rayo Theater, Richmond, VA.
- Reb's Café (ownership of black songwriter Reb or Benjamin Spikes), Los Angeles, CA (1920s).
- Rector's Supper Club, Broadway and Times Square, NYC, NY (closed in the early 1920s).
- Red Barn (dance club), Sacramento, CA (1940s+).
- Red Feather, Los Angeles, CA (1948+).
- Red Head (the), Greenwich Village, NYC, NY (1920s).
- Red Mill Cabaret, San Francisco, CA (before 1920).
- Red Mill Cafe, Forty-Third and State, Chicago, IL.
- Red Rooster, 2800 Fremont, Las Vegas, NV.
- Redondo Beach Ballroom, San Diego, CA (1930s+).
- Regal Theater, 4719 S. Parkway and Forty-Seventh Street, Chicago, IL (1920s+). Bandleader-vocalist Blanche Calloway headlined the grand opening of the huge Chicago entity in 1928.

- Regent Theater, Baltimore, MD.
- Regent Theatre, 116th Street, NYC, NY. (Before 1920, Eddie Cantor was an usher here. Myth?)
- Regent Theatre, Paterson, NJ.
- Reisenweber's Café, Eighth Avenue and Fifty-Eighth Street, NYC, NY (1900+). Sophie Tucker found early success here in the Jazz Room. More so, The original Dixieland Jazz Band, after some success in Chicago, found a gig in the Four Hundred Room in 1917—more so of a reason to be heard and sign a recording contract with Victor Records. While these white boys from New Orleans, led by Nick LaRocca (cornet)—who sometimes contributed intermittent vocals—owed much to their hidden Afro-American (New Orleans) influences, there's no doubt that in a racist society they were needed.
- Renaissance Casino, 144 W. 138th Street, Harlem, NYC, NY (1920s+).
- Reno Club, Twelfth and Cherry, Kansas City, MO (1930s). Bandleader Count Basie was part of the house band in 1935. Featured the vocals of Jimmy Rushing.
- Rendezvous Ballroom, Palm and Washington, Balboa, CA (1928+).
- Rendezvous Café, Clark and Diversey, Chicago IL (1927). As associated with reputed mobster Bugs Moran, this speakeasy became the source of a problem for contemporary singer-comic Joe E. Lewis. After leaving the Green Mill—that had associations with a rival gang, led by AL Capone and his subordinate, Jack "Machine Gun" McGurn—Lewis found his throat slashed, barley escaping with his life. (A later 1957 Frank Sinatra film, *The Joker Is Wild*, somewhat fictionalized this caper.)
- Rendezvous Club (Lucky Roberts), St. Nicholas Avenue, Harlem, NYC, NY (1920s).
- Rendezvous Restaurant, Miami, FL.
- Republic Theater (burlesque), Forty-Second Street, NYC, NY (1931+, owned by Billy Minsky).
- Rex Hotel (Rex Café), 2138 S. State Street, Chicago, IL (1920s-30s). Ownership was associated with reputed mobster Dennis Cooney.
- Rhodes Dance Hall, Providence, RI.
- Rhum-Boogie Club, 732 Highland Street, Los Angeles, CA (1940s)
- Rhumba Casino, 222 N. Clark, Chicago, IL (1941+).
- Rhumbboogie Night Club (Ritz Building), 343 Garfield Blvd., Chicago, IL (1947). Boxing champ Joe Louis's club included such entities as Floyd Campbell, Sarah Vaughan, and the Ink Spots.
- Rhythm Club, Natchez, MS. (1930s-1942). A tragic (1942) fire at this site took the lives of many, including bandleader Walter Barnes and his vocalist Juanita Avery.
- Rhythm Club, Chicago, IL (1930s).
- Rhythm Club, 168 West 132nd Street, Harlem. NYC, NY (1920s).
- Rhythm Club, 3000 Jackson Avenue, New Orleans, LA (1940s).
- Rialto Music House, 330 S. State Street, Chicago, IL (1920s).
- Rialto Theatre, Elyria, OH.
- Rialto Theatre S. Pasadena CA (1924+).
- Rialto Theatre, Lewistown, PA.
- Rialto Theatre, St. Louis, MO.
- Rialto Theatre, Tucson, AZ.
- Rialto Theatre, 810 Broadway, Los Angeles, CA (1917+).
- Rialto Theatre, Omaha, NE.
- Rialto Theatre, Ninth and S Streets, Washington, DC.
- Rice Hotel (Empire Room), Houston, TX.

- Richard's Restaurant, Berwyn, IL (1940s).
- Rio Cabana Night Club, Chicago, IL (1940s).
- Ringside Café, Fiftieth Street and Seventh Avenue, NYC, NY (1920s).
- Riobamba Club, Fifty-Seventh Street, near Third, NYC, NY (associated with Frank Sinatra's gig here, in 1943).
- Riptide (nightclub), Miami, FL (1940s).
- Rittenhouse Hall, Fifty-Third and Haverford Avenue, Philadelphia, PA.
- Ritz Ballroom, Bridgeport, CN.
- Ritz Ballroom, Garfield Blvd., Chicago, IL.
- Ritz Ballroom, Oklahoma City, OK.
- Ritz Ballroom, Pottsville, PA
- Ritz Bar, Wilmington, DE (1940s).
- Ritz Theatre, Wilshire Blvd. and La Brea, Los Angeles, CA.
- Ritz Theatre, Newburgh, NY.
- Ritz Theatre, Tooele, UT.
- Ritz Tower Grill, Park Avenue and Fifty-Seventh Street, NYC, NY (1920s+).
- Ritz Café, Oklahoma City, OK (1930s+).
- Ritz-Carlton Hotel, Boston, MA.
- Ritz-Carlton Hotel (Mayfair Club, Crystal Room), E. Forty-Sixth Street and Madison Avenue, NYC, NY (1920s+). This plush hotel found its way into popular contemporary slang and song in Irving Berlin-penned ditty "Puttin' on the Ritz" (1929). The term "Ritz" may, more so, be a term noting or dressing like highbrows or the limited crowd who could afford the Ritz. A year later, popular bandleader-singer Harry Richmond, aping Al Jolson, found himself in a 1930 film of the same name.
- Ritz Carlton Hotel, (Trellis Room), Grill),(Restaurant), Atlantic City, NJ. (Associated with alledged mobster, 'Nucky' Johnson 1921-41).
- Ritz Theater, Elizabeth, NJ.
- Ritz Theatre, Woodbridge, NY.
- Ritz Theatre, Tulsa, OK.
- Riverside Club, Andalusia, AL.
- Riverside Rancho, Feliz Blvd. and Riverside Drive, Los Angeles, CA (associated with gigs by Tex Ritter, the Maddox Brothers And Rose, and C & W contemporaries, 1940s).
- Riverside Theater, Milwaukee, WI.
- Riviera Club, St. Louis, MO.
- Riviera Club (Ben Marden's Club), Fort Lee, NJ.
- Riviera Club, Corpus Christi, TX (1940s).
- Rivoli Theater, Toledo, OH. While on tour here in 1932, Adelaide Hall heard pianist Art Tatum. She, more so, hired the blind musician, providing him his first gigs, as mythology has it.
- Rivoli Theater, Broadway, NYC, NY.
- Rivoli Theater, Elyria, OH.
- RKO Theater, Dayton, OH.
- RKO Theater, Denver, CO.
- RKO Theater, Minneapolis, MN.
- RKO Theater, Portland, OR.
- RKO Theater, Spokane, WA.
- RKO Theater, St Paul, MN.
- RKO Theater, Trenton, NJ.
- RKO Theater, Los Angeles, CA.

- RKO Theater, Salt Lake City, UT.
- RKO Theater, Seattle, WA.
- RKO Theater, Tacoma, WA.
- RKO Theater, Toledo, OH.
- RKO Theatre, San Diego, CA.
- Roadside Home (speakeasy), near Joliet, IL. Myth has it that Ann Brown, alias Mrs. Al Capone, sang jazzy entities here in the 1920s.
- Robin Hood Dell, Philadelphia, PA.
- Rockford Theatre, Rockford, IL,
- Rockland Palace, Uptown Harlem, NYC, NY.
- Rockland Palace, Miami, FL.
- Roc-Mar, Schenectady, NY (1940s).
- Roman Pools Casino, Miami, FL (1930s).
- Romanoff's Restaurant, 326 N. Rodeo Dr. Hollywood, Los Angeles, CA. (This owner's royal claim?)
- Rook Theatre, Watonga, OK.
- Rooney Plaza Hotel Miami Beach, FL.
- Roosevelt Grill (Ballroom), Madison Avenue and Forty-Fifth Street, NYC, NY (1920s+).
- Roosevelt Hotel (Blue Room, Fountain Grill), New Orleans, LA (1923+).
- Roosevelt Theater, Cincinnati, OH.
- Roosevelt Theater, 1862 Center Avenue, Pittsburgh, PA.
- Rosebud Bar, St. Louis, MO (1900-06). Piano player Tom Turpin was a (rare) black owner of this site. As a friend of Scott Joplin, Turpin promoted many contemporary Joplin-penned ragtime entities. Joplin's "Rosebud-March" was published in tribute to Turpin.
- Rosedale Theater Detroit, MI (1930s).
- Roseland Ballroom, Fulton and Flatbush Avenue, Brooklyn, NYC, NY (another NYC site, same name).
- Roseland Ballroom, 1658 Broadway, NYC, NY (1919+, an early house band was led by Fletcher Henderson from 1922-24).
- Roseland Dance Palace, Lawrence, MA.
- Roseland State Ballroom, Boston, MA.
- Roseland State Theatre, Chicago, IL (1930s).
- Roseland Theater, Mace Spring, VA (especially a Carter Family in gig here in 1929).
- Rosemont (dance hall), Fulton Street, Brooklyn, NYC, NY (1920s+).
- Ross Ballroom, 6130 Pacific Blvd., Huntington Park, CA.
- Ross, Fenton Farm, Asbury Park, NJ (1930s).
- Roxy Theatre, Glendale, CA.
- Roxy Theatre, 5185 Broadway, Los Angeles, CA (1932+).
- Roxy Theatre, (Sam Ruthafel's) NYC, NY (later combined with Radio City Music Hall in 1932).
- Roxy Theatre, Huntington, WV.
- Royal Chinese Grill (in Hotel Alamac), Seventy-First Street and Broadway, NYC, NY (1930s).
- Royal Frolics, 416 S. Wabash, Chicago, IL (1930s).
- Royal Gardens, 459 E. Thirty-First Street, Chicago, IL (1918+). Bill Johnson, Joe "King" Oliver, Jimmie Noone, and Freddie Keppard, all transplanted New Orleans musicians, were part of the house band. (This site was later named Lincoln Gardens, among others.)

- Royal Palais, Galena, IL.
- Royal Palm, Miami, FL.
- Royal Room, Hollywood, CA (1940s).
- Royal Roost (near Forty-Seventh and Broadway), NYC, NY (1940s).
- Royal Theater, Baltimore, MD.
- Royal Theatre, South Street, Philadelphia, PA.
- Royal Theatre, Washington, DC.
- Ruby Gatewood's Tavern, Artesian and Lake, Chicago, IL (Memphis Minnie, Bill Broonzy gigs, 1940s).
- Rue de La Daix, 247 W. Fifty-Fourth Street, NYC, NY (1920s).
- Russell's Danceland, Sylvan Park, NY.
- Russo's, St. Louis, MO.
- Rustic Cabin, Englewood Cliffs, Teaneck, NJ (especially Hoboken Four-Frank Sinatra gigs, 1935-38). More so, mythology has it that Frank was a singing waiter at this club, for a time?
- Ryman Auditorium, Nashville, TN (1891+). The *Grand Ole Opry* radio program was centered here in 1943. Hillbilly, or C & W performers such as Roy Acuff, Eddy Arnold, Ernest Tubb, Red Foley, Bill Monroe, and Hank Williams, among many others, made this location key.
- Saenger Theater, New Orleans, LA (1927+).
- Saints Revival School of the Holiness Church, Lexington, MS. (Ethel Waters's gig here, 1930s).
- Salem Baptist Church, Chicago, IL (associated with Mahalia Jackson).
- Salon Royal, Manhattan, NYC, NY (1920s).
- Saltair (Ballroom) Salt Lake City, UT.
- Sam Baker's Hotel, Little Rock, AS.
- Sam Houston Hall, Houston, TX.
- Sam's Place (Restaurant & Bar), Sunset Beach, CA (featured C & W, Roy Rogers, others, 1930s).
- Sandy's Bar, Paterson, NY. (1940s)
- San Francisco Canteen (Stage Door), San Francisco, CA (1942-45).
- San Jacinto Club, 1422 Dumaine Street, New Orleans, LA.
- Sands Point Bath Club, Long Island Sound, NYC, NY.
- Sandy Beach Park, Russell's Point, OH.
- Sans Souci, Restaurant 6000 Cottage Grove, Chicago, IL.
- Sans Souci, Fifth Avenue, Times Square, NYC, NY (1914). This short-lived entity was owned and operated by the contemporary dance team of Vernon and Irene Castle. Besides the obvious social impact of introducing short hair for women by Irene, the hidden aspects of their dance act were formidable. While justifiability credited as popularizing the fox-trot, the influences of Vernon's (black) backed band was less known, unless one had a chance to see them perform. It was, more so, due to their insistence that they would use (Afro-American) Jim Europe's Orchestra to play their music, which indeed ushered out waltz music and invited in the remnants of ragtime and the new "yea" or later, "jazz." This nightclub was perhaps the first of its kind to provide integrated music and, perhaps, also the reason that reasons were found to have it closed by the city of New York. (It should also be noted that while on tour, Vernon and Irene would also use other (black) musicians, including Fred Danby, something that was considered very unusual for the times.)
- Salon Royal, NYC, NY.

- Santa Fee Railroad (flat-railroad car), Gene Autry, OK. (a Gene Autry radio remote gig in 1941).
- Santa Monica Pier (Swing Shift), Santa Monica, CA.
- Santa Rita Hotel, Tucson, Arizona.
- Saratoga Club, 575 Lenox Avenue, Harlem, NYC, NY (1930s).
- Sardi's Resturant, 234 W. Forty-Fourth Street, NYC, NY (1921+).
- Sardi's Restaurant, near Hollywood and Vine, Los Angeles, CA
- Sarong Room, E. Huron Street, Chicago, IL (1940s).
- Savannah Auditorium, Savannah, GA.
- Savoy Ballroom, Forty-Seventh Street and S. Parkway, Chicago, IL (1926+).
- Savoy Ballroom, 596 Lenox Avenue, Harlem, NYC, NY (1927+). This nightspot perhaps founded the Lindy Hop, named for the transatlantic air flight contemporary hero and aviator, Charles Lindberg, in 1927. The mid-1930s found this a hot spot for many jitterbug dancers, fueled by the likes of many, including Ella Fitzgerald's fast-paced vocals with Chick Webb's "swing" Orchestra.
- Savoy Ballroom, Center Avenue, Pittsburgh, PA.
- Savoy Plaza (Cafe Lounge), Fifth Avenue and Fifty-Eighth Street, NYC, NY (1920s+).
- Savoy Theater, Atlantic City, NJ.
- Savoy Theatre, San Francisco, CA.
- Saxon Auditorium, Toledo, OH.
- Savannah Clu (Greenwich Village), NYC, NY (1940s).
- Saxony Club, Miami, FL.
- Say When Club, San Francisco, CA (1940s).
- Scenic Temple, South Boston, MA.
- Schindler's Theatre, 1005-09 W. Huron, Chicago IL (1909+).
- Scollay Square Theatre, Boston, MA.
- Schiller's Café, 318 E. Thirty-First Street, Chicago, IL (before 1920). A transplanted New Orleans (white) band, known as the Stein's Dixie Jass Band, led by (white) bandleader Nick La Rocca, gained much recognition at this site. The band would subsequently change its name to the Original Dixieland Jass Band in 1917 and set off numerous (white) imitation of the (mostly) black-based brothel music of New Orleans. (La Rocca also contributes with some incidental vocals, although his music is, for the most part, instrumental.) Subsequent (black) composed ditties, "Darktown Strutter's Ball" (Shelton Brooks) and "St. Louis Blues" (Handy), did note both debt and depth to his "jazz," at least until some real Afro-American entities, forbidden to record before 1920—including Jelly Roll Morton, King Oliver, Sidney Bechet, and Louis Armstrong—made it all sound more completive.
- S. H. Dudley Theatre, Washington, DC.
- Schroeder Hotel (Ballroom), Fifth and Wisconsin, Milwaukee, WI (1928).
- Schroeder Dance Hall, Schroeder, TX. (Ernest Tubb gigs, others).
- Scottish Rite Hall, San Francisco, CA.
- Sea Breeze Swim Club, Daytona Beach, FL (1930s).
- Sebastian's Cubanola, Hollywood, CA.
- Sebastian's Cotton Club, Washington Blvd., Culver City, Los Angeles. CA. Reputed mobster Frank Sebastian's (1930-31) booking of Louis Armstrong gigs created a national sensation, along with Louis's marijuana drug bust when caught smoking outside the club.
- Second Avenue Theatre, Second Avenue, NYC, NY.

- Selwyn Theater, Boston, MA.
- Selwyn Theatre, 133 N. Jefferson, Chicago, IL (1930s+).
- Selwyn Theatre, W. Forty-Second Street, NYC, NY.
- Seneca Hotel, Chicago, IL.
- Seven Gables Inn, Boston, MA (1930s).
- Sewanee Inn, N. La Brea, Los Angeles, CA. Around 1938, a young pianist, Nat Cole, was asked to perform vocals, earning a paper crown for his showmanship from club owner, Bob Lewis. Nat subsequently disregarded the headwear and became Nat "King" Cole, as nightclub legend has it?
- Shadowland (nightclub), San Antonio, TX (1930s).
- Shady Rest Country Club, Westfield, NJ.
- Shamrock Hotel, Houston, TX (1949+).
- Shea's Buffalo Theatre, Main Street, Buffalo, NY.
- Shea's Hippodrome, Buffalo, NY.
- Sheraton Hotel (Tally Ho Room), 505 N. Michigan, Chicago, IL.
- Sherman Theatre, Goodland, KS.
- Sherman's (club), Caroga Lake, NY.
- Sherry's Restaurant, 9039 Sunset Blvd., West Hollywood, CA; Los Ageless, CA (1940s). Associated with reputed mobster Nathan Sherry, gunplay almost cost reputed gangster Mickey Cohen his life (1941).
- Sh O'Bar,228 Bourbon Street, New Orleans, LA. (1930s)
- Shore Acres<Sioux City,IA.
- Shoreham Hotel, Washington, DC.
- Showboat (club), 205 N. Lake (and Dearborn Streets), Chicago, IL (1920s).
- Showboat (club), Wylie Avenue, Pittsburgh, PA.
- Showplace Night Club, 62 E. Columbia, Detroit, MI (1930s).
- Shrine Auditorium, 665 W. Jefferson Blvd., Los Angeles, CA (1926+).
- Shrine Temple, Cedar Rapids, IA.
- Shrine Temple, Rockford, IL.
- Shubert Theater, Newark, NJ.
- Shubert-Majestic Theatre, 263-65 Tremont St. Boston, MA (1910+).
- Shubert Theatre, Cincinnati, OH.
- Shubert Theatre, New Haven, CT.
- Shubert Theatre, Philadelphia, PA.
- Shuffle Inn, 2221 Seventh Avenue, Harlem, NYC, NY (later Connie's Inn, 1920s).
- *Sidney*, the (this Mississippi River steamboat employed Louis Armstrong, 1920).
- Sign of the Drum, 4430 Reading Road, Cincinnati, OH (especially Doris Day's gig, 1939).
- Silver Club, Chicago, IL (1940s).
- Silver Dollar (casino), 64 Eddy Street, San Francisco, CA.
- Silver Slipper, 110 Market Street, Los Angeles, CA.
- Silver Slipper, 201 W. Forty-Eighth Street, Manhattan, NYC, NY (1920s+).
- Silver Slipper, Atlantic City, NJ (1920s).
- Silver Slipper, 184 W. Randolph, Chicago, IL (1920s+).
- Silver Slipper, Cleveland, OH.
- Silver Slipper, San Diego, CA (1940s).
- Silver Theatre, Silver Springs, MD (1938+).
- Silver Tip (Club), 1430 Pyramid Place, Hollywood, CA (1940s)
- Simplon Club, 26 W. Fifty-Third Street, NYC, NY (1930s).

- Sing Sing (prison), Ossining, NY (especially a Ruth Etting gig here in 1932).
- Sir Francis Drake Hotel,(Persian Room), (Starlight Roof), Union Square, San Francisco, CA
- Six O Six Club (606), 606 S. Wabash, Chicago IL.
- Sky Club, Battle Creek, MI (1940s).
- Skyline Club, N. Lamar, Austin, TX (1940s+, especially Hank Williams's gigs).
- Skyline Club, Pittsburgh, PA.
- Skylon Ballroom, Sioux City, IA.
- Slapsy Maxie's Night Club, 5665 Wilshire Blvd., Hollywood, CA (1940s). It was operated by Maxie Rosenbloom, the contemporary (retired) boxer. ("Slapsy" was his nickname. Slap him?)
- Slapsy Maxie's Night Club, San Francisco, CA (1940s), S. F. Site.
- Sleepy Hollow Ranch, Quakertown, PA.
- Slim Jenkins Supper Club, 7th Ave, Oakland, CA (1933-60s)
- Sloppy Joes, 133 W. Fifty-Fourth Street, NYC, NY (1930s).
- Small's Paradise Club, 2294 Seventh Avenue, Uptown Harlem, NYC, NY (1925+).
- Smoke Shack, 169 W. 133rd Street, Harlem, NYC, NY (1930s).
- So Different (SD) Club, 520 Pacific Street, San Francisco, CA.
- Southern Club, Montgomery, AL.
- Southern Club (Grill), Hot Springs, AK.
- Southern Hills Country Club, Tulsa, OK.
- Southern Pacific (roadhouse), San Francisco, CA (1920s+).
- Southland Cafe, 76 Warrenton Street, Boston, MA.
- Spa Theatre, Saratoga, NY.
- Spaw Club, Nokomis, IL (1940s).
- Spider Web, 2112 Seventh Avenue, Harlem, NYC, NY (1929-30s).
- Spikes Brothers Music Store, 1703 Central Avenue, Los Angeles, CA (ownership as by Afro-American songwriters (Reb) Benjamin and John, 1920s.)
- Spinning Wheel, Twelfth and Troost, Kansas City, MO (1939-1940s).
- Spot (The Spot Nite Club), Gary, IN.
- Spotlite Club, 56 West Fifty-Second Street, NYC, NY (1940s).
- Spreckels Pavilion, San Diego, CA.
- Springer Opera House, Columbia, GA (1920s).
- Springer Opera House, Springer, GA.
- St Regis Hotel (Bar and Grill), Chicago, IL.
- St. James Theatre, NYC, NY.
- St. Joseph Auditorium, St. Joseph, MO.
- St. Charles Theatre, New Orleans, LA.
- St. Claire Hall, Christian College, Columbia, MO.
- St. George Hotel (roof) Fifty-First Clark Street, Brooklyn, NYC, NY (1920s+).
- St. Louis Theater, St. Louis, MO.
- St. Moritz Grill, 50n Central Park South Street, NYC, NY (1920s+).
- St. Moritz Hotel, Miami Beach, FL.
- St. Regis Hotel (Lounge, Seaglades Room, Viennese Roof), Fifth Avenue and Fifty-Sixth Street NYC, NY.
- Stadium Theatre, Woonsocket, RI.
- Stage Door Canteen, W. Forty-Fourth Street, near Schubert Alley, NYC, NY (1942+). As part of the American war effort, and one of many canteens for service people, this entity was, more so, sponsored by the American Theatre Wing. For

free, any serviceperson could enjoy contemporary entertainment. Opening night in 1942 found the likes of Selena Royle, Jane Cowl, Billy De Wolfe and vocals by the Broadway entities Brits Gertrude Lawrence and Ella Logan. (This popular nightspot was to be, moreover, produced as a popular (1943) film of the same name. It also inspired the West Coast "Hollywood Canteen" and many local canteens all over the country.)

- Stanley Theatre, Journal Square, Jersey City, NJ.
- Stanley Theatre, 719 Liberty Avenue, Pittsburgh, PA. (1928+).
- Stanley Theatre, Nineteenth and Market Street, Philadelphia, PA.
- Star Light Ballroom, Sacramento, CA (1940s+).
- State and Lake Theatre, 190 N. State (and Lake Street) Chicago, IL (1919+).
- State Arsenal, Springfield, IL.
- State Fair Park (Modernistic Ballroom), near S. Eighty-Fourth Street, Milwaukee, WI.
- State Line Club, West Bottoms, Kansas City, MO (1930s+).
- States Restaurant, State & Adams Streets, Chicago, IL (before 1920)
- State Theatre (Loew's), Boston, MA.
- State Theatre, Akron, OH.
- State Theatre, Hartford, CN.
- State Theatre, Detroit, MI.
- State Theatre, Lexington, VA.
- State Theatre, State Street, Milwaukee, WI. (Hildegarde- resident pianist 1920s)
- State Theatre, New Brunswick, NJ (1921+).
- State Theatre, Newark, NJ.
- State Theatre, 702 S. Broadway, Los Angeles, CA (1921+).
- States Theatre, 3507 S. State, Chicago, IL (1914+).
- Statler Hotel, Cleveland, OH.
- Statler Hotel, Washington, DC (1940s+).
- Statler, St. Louis, MO (1940s).
- Steel Pier Amusement Park (Marine Ballroom), Atlantic City, NJ.
- Step Inn, Columbus, OH.
- Stevens Hotel, 720 S. Michigan Blvd. (Boulevard Room, Oak Room), Chicago, IL.
- Stillwell's Ballroom, Big Bear Lake, CA.
- Stockton Club, near Hamilton, OH.
- Stork Club (speakeasy) W. Fifty-Eighth Street, NYC, NY (1929-1931), first NYC site.
- Stork Club (Cub Room), 2 E. Fifty-Third Street, Manhattan, NYC, NY (1930s-50s). This second site perhaps became even better known throughout America when a contemporary (1945) film, of the same name, with Betty Hutton and Andy Russell (also a featured vocalist within this book), was produced.
- Strand Ballroom, Broad and Bainbridge Streets, Philadelphia, PA.
- Strand Theatre, Altoon, PA.
- Strand Theater (Boston), 543 Columbia Road, Dorchester, MA (1918+).
- Strand Theatre, 510 W. Wisconsin Avenue, Milwaukee, WI.
- Strand Theater, Modesto, CA.
- Strand Theatre (also on roof location, Strand Roof Danceland), 1579 Broadway, NYC, NY.
- Strand Theatre, Brooklyn, NYC, NY.
- Strand Theatre, 14 Main East, Battle Creek, MI.
- Strata, Martin, TN (1940s).
- Stratford Theatre, 715 W. Sixty-Third Street, Chicago, IL.

- Street's Blue Room, Kansas City, MO.
- Streets of Paris Club, Hollywood, CA (1940s).
- Stroll (the)—this term referred to the nightspots along (South) State Street in Chicago, IL.
- Stroll (the)—this term referred to the nightspots along Seventh Avenue in NYC Harlem. This stroll, more so, found a landmark fronting Connie's Inn (Tree of Hope), for wishes, as mythology has it!
- Strollers Club, NYC, NY (1930s).
- Studebaker Theatre, 410 S. Michigan, Chicago, IL.
- Stuyvesant Casino, NYC, NY.
- Suburban Gardens, New Orleans, LA.
- Suburban Inn (Sam Pick's), Milwaukee, WI.
- Subway Club, Eighteenth and Vine, Kansas City, MO (1930s+).
- Sugar Land Prison, Sugar Land, TX. As a singing and entertaining inmate, Huddie Leadbetter was credited to composing his "Midnight Special" here before parole in 1925. Myth?
- Summit Beach, Akron, OH.
- Sundown Club, Phoenix, AZ (1940s).
- Sunnybrook Ballroom, near Pottstown, PA.
- Sunset Inn, Santa Monica, CA.
- Superb Theatre, Roxbury, MA.
- Surf Ballroom, Clear Lake, IO (1933-47). The second site (1948+) became tragically associated with the rock era in 1959 (Buddy Holly, Ritchie Valens, and the Big Bopper's last gig)!
- Surf Beach Club, Virginia Beach, VA.
- Sunset Ballroom, near Carrolltown, PA.
- Sunset Cafe, 315 E. Thirty-Fifth and Calumet, Chicago, IL (1921-37). As managed by (reputed mobster) Joe Glaser in the 1920s, it just could be that trumpeter-musician Louis Armstrong became well known as a scatting vocalist here. So were many others, including Blanche and Cab Calloway, Adelaide Hall, Alberta Hunter, Frankie "Half Pint" Jaxon, Edith Wilson. (Joe Glaser, moreover, later became Louis's manager.) In 1926, Louis Armstrong introduced his sensational vocal scat recording "Heebie Jeebies"(as penned by Boyd Atkins) to live audiences at this site. His contemporary Okeh recording, with his "hot five," more so, became a major influence upon Americana, along with a self-penned recording of "Sunset Café Stomp," vocal as by Mae Alix, on Okeh 8423.
- Sunset Cabaret, Twelfth and Highland, Kansas City, MO (1930s+).
- Sunset Inn, Los Angeles, CA (1920s).
- Sunset Park, Oxford, PA.
- Sunset Blvd., "the Strip" area, Los Angeles, CA (live entertainment in many clubs on this venue)!
- Southern Tavern, Cleveland, OH.
- Sutton Club, NYC, NY.
- Swede's (speakeasy), Hollywood, CA (Hollywood folklore and Mildred Bailey's gigs in 1925)?
- Sweets Ballroom, Oakland, CA.
- Swiss Gardens Nightclub, Cincinnati, OH.
- Sylvania Hotel, Philadelphia, PA.
- Sylvio's Club, Chicago, IL.

- Syracuse Hotel, Syracuse, NY.
- Syria Mosque, Pittsburg, PA.
- T & D Theater, Oakland, CA.
- Tabernacle, Salt Lake City, UT.
- Tahoe Village Casino, South Shore, Lake Tahoe, NV (1940s+).
- Taft Auditorium, Cincinnati, OH.
- Ta it's Café, San Francisco CA.
- Tampa Theatre, Tampa, FL.
- Tango Palace, Forty-Eighth Street and Broadway, NYC, NY (1930s).
- Tavern on the Green, Central Park, NYC, NY (1930s).
- Teck Theatre (Shubert's), Buffalo, NY.
- Temple Theatre, Rochester, NY.
- Temple Theatre, Lewistown, PA (1920s).
- Tent Café, Los Angeles, CA (1920s, Bing Crosby's and Al Rinker's gig here in 1925).
- Terminal Theatre, Newark, NJ.
- Terrace Club, Hermosa Beach, CA (1940s)
- Terrace Gardens, 145 E. Fifty-Eighth Street, NYC, NY.
- Terrace Theatre, Danville, IL.
- Texas Centennial, Dallas, TX.
- Texas Guianan Century Club, (in Century Theatre), NYC, NY (1927)
- Texas Guinan Club, Valley Stream, Long Island, NYC, NY. (The contemporary 1925 entertainer Texas Guinan, who also was a silent-film entity of early Westerns, owned part of this speakeasy and others, including the interests of reputed mobster, Larry Fay. (More so associated with Guinan were young dancers Ruby Keeler and Barbara Stanwyck—then known as Ruby Stevens.)
- Texas Theatre, Crawford Street, Palestine, TX (1921+).
- Textile Hall, Greenville, SC.
- Theater Club, Oakland, CA (1940s).
- Theater-in-the Dale, New Milford CN
- Theatrical Club, Boston, MA.
- Thirty One Club (31), Montgomery, AL.
- Thomas' Club, Washington, DC.
- Three Deuces (Off Beat Club, upstairs, in 1930s), 222 N. State Street, Chicago, IL (1920s+, especially noting early gigs for Anita O'Day in the 1930s).
- Three Deuces, 72 W. Fifty-Second Street (also on 70 W. Fifty-Second Street), NYC, NY.
- Three Hundred (300) Club, 151 W. Fifty-Fourth Street, NYC, NY. (Entertainer Texas Guinan and reputed mobsters Owney Madden and Larry Fay had ownership in this speakeasy establishment in 1927?)
- Three Steps Down (Greenwich Village, NYC, NY (1920s).
- Three Thirty One Club (331), Los Angeles, CA (especially Nat Cole Trio's gigs in the 1940s).
- Three Rivers Inn, Syracuse, NY.
- Three Sixes, Detroit, MI (1940s).
- Three Sixty Five (365) Club (Bimbo's), 365 Market Street, San Francisco, CA (1931+). Entertainment included a nude woman swimming in a fishbowl (tank)! Myth?
- Thelma Todd's Sidewalk Café, Pacific Palisades, Los Angeles, CA (1930s). Contemporary film entity Thelma Todd founded this site with the possible financial

help of her (later divorced) husband Pat DiCirro and Lucky Luciano, both reputed mobsters. Speculation exists that DiCirro also had something to do with her early death at age thirty years (1935).

- Thunderbird Hotel, Las Vegas, NV (1948, an early addition to the Las Vegas Strip).
- Tia Juana Club, Pittsburgh, PA (1940s).
- Tic Toc Lounge, 245 Tremont Street, Boston, MA.
- Tiddly Winks (nightclub), San Francisco, CA (1934+).
- Tillie's Chicken Shack, Fifty-Second Street, NYC, NY (1930s).
- Tillie's Inn, 148 W. 139th Street, Harlem, NYC, NY (1930s).
- Tin Roof Café, Washington and Claiborne Avenue, New Orleans, LA (before 1920).
- Tip Top Club, Union City, NJ (1940s).
- Tip Top Dance Hall, Dallas, TX (1920s).
- *Titanic*, British Ocean Liner featured entertainment, sunk in 1912, one of three ocean liners noted.
- Tivoli Café, 574 Pacific, San Francisco, CA.
- Tivoli Theater, Main Street, Danville IL.
- Tivoli Theatre, Sixty-Third and Cottage Grove, Chicago, IL (1921+).
- Tivoli Theatre, Los Angeles, CA.
- Tobacco Planters Warehouse, Rocky Point, NC.
- Tom Anderson's Cabaret & Restaurant, Rampart Street, New Orleans, LA.
- Tom Archer's Ballroom, Des Moines, IA.
- Tom Breneman's Restaurant, 1539 N. Vine Street, Hollywood, CA. (Tom Breneman hosted his popular radio program *Breakfast in Hollywood* (mid-1940s). Featured vocalists early AM!)
- Tomba Ballroom, Sioux City, IA.
- Tomlinson Hall, Indianapolis, IN.
- Tondelayo's (nightclub), Fifty-Second Street, NYC, NY (1940s).
- Tony Pastor's (nightclub), Broadway, NYC, NY (1940s).
- Tony's (Tony Soma), W. Fifty-Second Street, NYC, NY (especially Mabel Mercer's gigs, 1942-49)
- Toots Shor's Restaurant, Fifty-Second Street, Manhattan, NYC, NY (1940s+).
- Top Hat (Club), Madison, WI (1940s)
- Topper Terp Tavern, Cincinnati, OH.
- Torch Club Cafe, Columbus, OH (1940s)
- Totem Pole Ballroom, Auburndale, MA.
- Totem Pole, Norumbego, MA.
- Tower Ballroom, Pittsburg, KS.
- Tower Theatre, 802 S. Broadway, Los Angeles, CA (1927+).
- Town Casino Restaurant, Buffalo, NY.
- Town Club, Chicago, IL (1920s).
- Town Hall, 113 Forty-Third Street, NYC, NY.
- Town House Apt. & Hotel (Zebra Room, Lafayette Park), Wilshire Blvd., Los Angeles, CA.
- Town House, Reno, NV (1940s).
- Towne Room, Milwaukee, WI (1940s).
- Trader Vic's, Hollywood, CA.
- Tradesman's Club, Chicago, IL (1940s).
- Tranchina's Restaurant, New Orleans, LA.
- Trans Lux Theatre, Fifty-Eighth and Madison, NYC, NY.

- Treagle's Dreamland, New Orleans, LA (1940s).
- Treasure Island (nightclub) San Francisco Bay, CA.
- Tremar Ballroom, Des Moines, IA.
- Tremont Theatre, Boston, MA.
- Triangle Club, Chicago, IL (1920s).
- Trianon Ballroom, Cleveland, OH.
- Trianon Ballroom, Los Angeles, CA.
- Trianon Ballroom, Oklahoma City, OK.
- Trianon Ballroom, 6201 S. Cottage Grove and Sixty-Second, Chicago, IL (1922+).
- Trianon Ballroom, Seattle, WA.
- Trianon Ballroom, Toledo, OH.
- Trianon Club, Forty-Eighth Street and Broadway, NYC, NY (1920s).
- Trianon Club, Alliance, OH (1930s).
- Trocadero Cafe (Billy Wilkerson's) 8610 Sunset Blvd., Hollywood, CA (1930s+). This famous nightspot became the title of a 1940s (contemporary) film. Daytime featured a sidewalk café.
- Trocadero (nightclub), NYC, NY (featured Fred and Adele Astaire, 1920s).
- Troika Restaurant (supper club), 1011 Connecticut Avenue, Washington, DC.
- Tromar Ballroom, Des Moines, IA.
- Tropical Club, 389 Twelfth Street, Oakland, CA.
- Trouville Club (Billy Berg's) West Hollywood, CA (1940s).
- Tune Town Ballroom, St. Louis, MO.
- Turner Inn, 634 W. Fifteenth Street, Los Angeles, CA.
- Turner's Arena, Washington, DC.
- Turnpike Casino, Lincoln, NE.
- Turnpike, Hempstead, LI (1940s).
- Turpin Theater, St. Louis, MO.
- Twelfth Street Theater (Twelfth Street), Kansas City, MO.
- Twenty Five Gambling Joint (25), New Orleans, LA (before 1917).
- Twenty One (Jack & Charlie's 21 Club), 21 W. Fifty-Second Street, NYC, NY. (1929+).
- Twenty Two (22 Club), Miami Beach, FL (1940s).
- Twenty-One Club (21 Nightclub), Baltimore, MD (1940s).
- Twin-City Club, Winston-Salem, NC.
- Two Mile House (2 Mile), St. Louis, MO (C & W).
- Two Two (22) Club, Detroit, MI (1930s).
- Ubangi Club, Harlem, NYC, NY.
- Uline Area, Washington, DC.
- Union Building, Iowa City, IA.
- Union Club, Hudson Street, Hoboken, NJ. (Frank Sinatra found solo recognition in 1937.)
- Union Masonic Hall, 2956 S. State, Chicago, IL.
- Union Sons Hall (Funky Butt Hall), 1319 Perdido Street, New Orleans, LA (before 1917).
- Unique, Milwaukee, WI (1940s).
- Unique Theatre, Second Avenue and Fifth Street, Staples, MN.
- United Artists Theatre, 45 W Randolph, Chicago, IL (an Apollo Theatre site before 1927).
- University Gymnasium, Laramie, WY.
- University Auditorium, Rock Hill, SC.
- University Club, New York City, NY (1920s).

- Uptown (Tony Pastor Nightclub), NYC, NY (1940s).
- Uptown Ballroom, Modesto, CA.
- Uptown Ballroom, Portland, OR.
- Uptown House, 7th Avenue and 134th Street, Harlem, NYC, NY (1930s).
- Uptown Theater, 4814 N. Broadway (and Lawrence Avenue), Chicago, IL (1925+).
- Uptown Theatre Detroit, MI.
- Val Air Park Ballroom, Des Moines, IA.
- Valencia Ballroom, York, PA.
- Valencia Theatre, Brooklyn, NYC, NY.
- Valentino Inn, Chicago, IL (1920s).
- Valley Area, Holyoke, MA.
- Vanderbilt Biltmore Country Club, Ashville, NC (1930s).
- Vanderbilt Hotel, Park Avenue and Thirty-Fourth Street, NYC, NY.
- Vanity Fair, Huntington, WV.
- Vendome Hotel, Buffalo, NY.
- Vendome Theater, 3143 S. State Street Chicago, IL (1919-33).
- Venetian Theatre, Milwaukee, WI.
- Venice Ballroom, Los Angeles, CA.
- Venice Pier, Nashville, TN.
- Verdi Theatre, 2035 W. Thirty-Fifth Street, Chicago, IL.
- Verdome Hotel, Evansville, IN.
- Verdome Night Club, Los Angeles, CA.
- Vernon Country Club, Vernon, CA (1912-29).
- Versailles Club, 14 E. Sixtieth Street, NYC, NY (speakeasy site, 1920s).
- Versailles Club, 151 E. Fiftieth Street, NYC, NY (1940s+, especially Perry Como's solo gigs in 1943).
- Victor Hugo's Restaurant, Beverly Drive at Wilshire, Beverly Hills, CA. (This is the second site, 1937.)
- Victoria Theater (Hammerstein I), 1481 Broadway, NYC, NY (1899-1916). Vaudeville!
- Victoria Theatre, 10936 S. Michigan Avenue, Chicago, IL.
- Victoria Theatre, 2961 Sixteenth Street, San Francisco, CA.
- Victoria Theatre, Steubenville, OH.
- Victory Club, Clark near Chicago Ave, Chicago, IL.
- Victory Theatre, Bayonne, NJ.
- Vieux Carre (Shim Sham Club), New Orleans, LA.
- Villa Madrid, Pittsburgh, PA (1940s).
- Villa Mateo, Daly City, CA.
- Villa Nova, Sunset Strip, Los Angeles, CA (1933+).
- Villa Olivia (Ballroom) Route 20, east of Elgin, IL. (1920s+)
- Villa Vallee, 14 E. Sixtieth Street, NYC, NY (associated with Rudy Vallee's gigs, 1929-30).
- Villa Venice Theatre Restaurant, Milwaukee Avenue and Des Plaines River, north of Chicago, IL (1920s+).
- Villa Venice, 10 E. Sixtieth Street, NYC, NY (associated with Will Osborne's gigs in 1929).
- Village Barn, 52 W. Eighth Street, NYC, NY (1930s).
- Village Barn, Augusta, GA (1940s).
- Village Grove Nut Club, 15 Barrow Street (Greenwich Village) NYC, NY (1920s+).
- Village Vanguard (Greenwich Village), NYC, NY.

- Vincent's Club, E.9th Street, Cleveland, OH. In 1937, a young 24 year old Chicagoan Frank LoVecchio, later known as Frankie Laine, journeyed to Cleveland for his first major singing gig. Myth?
- Virginia Theatre, Wheeling, WV.
- Vogue Ballroom, Grand Street, Los Angeles, CA.
- Vogue Terrace Club, Pittsburgh, PA (1940s).
- Vogue Terrace Club, McKeesport, PA.
- Vogue Club, Fifty-Seventh Street, NYC, NY (1930s). In 1933, this site featured the jazz vocals of many, including those of Dolores Reade, of whom the author of this book cannot find any contemporary recordings. Moreover, it was at this time that a young and struggling vaudevillian Bob Hope caught her act. They would be married the following year and would remain so for the rest of the century.
- Volunteer Theater, Chattanooga, TN (1930s).
- Waldorf-Astoria Hotel (Starlight Roof, Empire Room, Wedgewood Room), Park Avenue and Fiftieth Street, NYC, NY (1930s+). A contemporary (1945) film *Weekend at the Waldorf*, with Ginger Rogers, Lana Turner, and the then leader of the house band, Xavier Cugat, identified this very plush hotel even more so.
- Wallace Theater, Indianapolis, IN (1920s).
- Wallick Hotel,(Poppy Room), Broadway at 43rd Street, NYC, NY (before 1920)
- Walnut Street Theatre, Vicksburg MS. (1920s).
- Walt Whitman Hotel, (Ballroom), Camden, NJ.
- Walter Theatre, Indianapolis, IN.
- Walton Roof (Walton Hotel), Philadelphia, PA.
- Wander Inn, Philadelphia, PA (1930s).
- War Memorial Auditorium, Nashville, TN.
- Wardon Park Hotel, Washington, DC (1930s+).
- Warehouse, the, Dyersburg, TN.
- Warfield Theatre (Loew's) 982 Market, San Francisco, CA.
- Warner's Theatre, 401 W. 7th Avenue, Los Angeles, CA.
- Warner's Theatre, Broadway and Fifty-First Street, NYC, NY. (Al Jolson's talkie film, *The Jazz Singer*, debuted here in October 1927.)
- Warwick Hall, 543 E. Forty-Seventh Street, Chicago, IL (brief ownership by Louis Armstrong in 1927).
- Warwick Hotel (Raleigh Room), NYC, NY.
- Washington Auditorium, Washington, DC.
- Washington Restaurant, Newark, NJ. (Before 1920)
- Washington Theater, Indianapolis, IN.
- Washington Theater, St. Louis, MO.
- Watts Country Club, Watts, near Los Angeles, CA.
- Wayside Park Café, Los Angeles, CA (1920s).
- Webster Hall, Detroit MI (1930s).
- Westchester County Civic Center, White Plains, NY.
- Westchester Theatre, Mount Vernon, NY.
- Western Palisades Ballroom, Santa Monica, CA.
- Westwood Supper Club, Richmond, VA.
- Westwood Gardens, near Dearborn, MI.
- Weylin Hotel (Caprice Room), Fifty-Fourth Street and Madison Avenue, NYC, NY.
- Whitby Grill (Whitby Hotel), W. Forty-Fifth Street, NYC, NY (1930s).

- White City Ballroom (White City Amusement Park), Forty-Seventh and South Parkway, Chicago, IL.
- White City Ballroom, Ogden, UT.
- White Elephant Café, 1338 E. Sixth Street, Los Angeles, CA.
- White Elephant Club, Chicago, IL (1940s).
- White Elephant Hotel, Nantucket, MA.
- White Rose Bar, Sixthth Avenue near Fifty-Second Street, NYC, NY (1943+).
- Whitehall Hotel, NYC, NY.
- Wigwam Theatre, San Francisco, CA.
- Wilbur Theatre, Boston, MA.
- Wilburs-on-the-Taunton, Taunton, MA.
- Wilby Theater, Selma, AL.
- Will Oakland's Terrace, Fifty-First and Broadway NYC, NY (1920s+).
- Willard Hotel. Washington, DC.
- William Penn Hotel (Chatterbox, Terrace Room) Pittsburgh, PA.
- Willows Ballroom, Pittsburgh, PA (1930s).
- Wills Point, Sacramento, CA (owned by country-swing bandleader Bob Wills in the 1940s).
- Willon's Warehouse, Fayetteville, NC.
- Wilshire Bowl Café, 5655 Wilshire Blvd., Los Angeles, CA (1930s-40s).
- Wilson Theater, Detroit, MI.
- Wiltern LG Theater, Wilshire Blvd. and Western, Los Angeles, CA (1930+).
- Windmill, Natchez, MS. (1940s).
- Windsor Theatre, Bronx, NYC, NY.
- Winter Gardens Café, Chicago, IL (1930s).
- Winthrop College Auditorium, Rock hill, SC.
- Winthrop Hall, Boston, MA (before 1920).
- Winter Garden (National), Houston Street, East Side, NYC, NY (1920s+). The striptease was considered the bottom of the entertainment world, although it indeed saw a lot of nudity, noting its use by such highbrows such as Flo Ziegfeld, Earl Carroll, and George White. As an original burlesque house, pioneered by the brothers Minsky—Abe, Billy, Herbert, and Morton—taking off more, along with body movements, was considered more than risqué. Billy Minsky eventually moved his shows among the highbrow elite on Forty-Second Street, with perhaps a bit tamer show. Mob influenced? Later, in the 1930s, a major entity, Gypsy Rose Lee, emerged from burlesque. After 1950, the burlesque act would take over many of the former elite clubs, which would begin to close with changing times and rock and roll. A fine (later) 1968 film *The Night They Raided Minsky's* may be familiar to baby boomers. So might a 1963 film *Gypsy*, which starred Natalie Wood as Gypsy Rose Lee. A sadder view is found in the realistic 1929 film *Applause*, with Helen Morgan as an aging burlesque queen, and also a film pick within this book. Moreover, there was a lighter and later 1946 film drama *Doll Face*, which included Perry Como as a singer in a burlesque show (with some film-writing credit to Lee herself). This film is noted elsewhere within this book—see Perry Como.
- Wisconsin Roof Garden (Ballroom), 536 Wisconsin Ave, Milwaukee, WI.
- World's Fair, ST. Louis, MO (1904). While the excuse was the hundredth anniversary of the Louisiana Purchase, this fair perhaps promoted such American commodities as hamburgers, hot dogs, iced-tea, ice cream cones, and puffed wheat. Musically, it successfully promoted Scott Joplin's sheet music sales of ragtime, attended by Joplin

himself. His contemporary composition "Cascades" was, more so, written to document the event. Later, in 1944, a film entity, *Meet Me In St. Louis*, found Judy Garland nostalgically recalling the fair—and perhaps not fairly?

- World's Fair, Century of Progress, Chicago, IL (1933-34), between Twelfth and Thirty-Ninth Streets, lakefront of Lake Michigan. Entertainment included Sally Rand's seminude "fan dancing" in the Streets of Paris exhibition, a key attraction. (A fine, novel contemporary Cab Calloway ditty, "The Lady with a Fan," is a noted pick for Cab.) It was also noted that the young vaudeville "Gumm Sisters" act of Frances Etehl, Mary Jane and Dorothy Virginia became known as the "Garland Sisters, with Frances Ethel (later) becoming known as "Judy".
- World's Fair, World of Tomorrow, Queens, NYC, NY (1939-40), Flushing Meadows. As well as the first occasion for using the new concept of television in the United States for a presidential address (Franklin Roosevelt), the (black) likes of Ethel Waters were also televised. Other significant entertainment also included Billy Rose's *Aquacade*, which included seminude (swimming) girl hostesses—a nightclub atmosphere in the water? All televised? Guess you had to be there!
- Woodmansten Inn, Pelham Parkway, Bronx, Brooklyn, NYC, NY (1920s).
- Woodmansten Inn, 1572 Williamsbridge Road, Westchester, NY.
- Woody's, Cleveland, OH (1940s).
- Wonder Bar, East 17th & Euclid, Cleveland, OH. (1930s)
- Wonderland Cave Nightclub, Bella Vista, AK (initially a speakeasy in a real cave, 1930+).
- Whyte's, Forty-Third Street and Fifth Avenue, NYC, NY (1930s).
- Yacht Club Café, Los Angeles, CA.
- Yacht Club, 38 W. Fifty-Second Street (one of many addresses on Fifty-Second Street), NYC, NY.
- Yeah Man Club, Uptown Harlem, Seventh Avenue, NYC, NY (1935).
- York Hotel, Plush Room, San Francisco, CA.
- Yes Yes Club, State Street, Chicago, IL (1940s, especially Anita O'Day's gigs).
- Young's Million Dollar Pier, Atlantic City, NJ.
- Zamboanga Club, Los Angeles, CA (1940s).
- Zeppelin Inn, Thirty-First and S. Indiana Avenue, Chicago, IL.
- Ziegfeld Theater, Fifty-Fourth Street and Sixth Avenue, NYC, NY.
- Zion Temple Church, Los Angeles, CA.
- Zucca's Terrace Ballroom, Hollywood, CA.

e. Foreign media. While this book centers on American vocalists and music, the influences from abroad are obvious. Specific references within this book note Maurice Chevalier, Marlene Dietrich, Evelyn Dove, Gracie Fields, Greta Keller, Lilian Harvey, Arturo Machin, Mabel Mercer, Carmen Miranda, and Edith Piaf.

While these entities had impact, the process of importing American culture found the likes of Fred and Adele Astaire's dance steps mingling with the highbrows brilliantly. The more profound influences of American spirituals, jazz, and blues would be received suspiciously at first, as something less familiar. Even so, the critics, using phonograph recordings alone, became familiar very fast. In true retrospective, they sometimes provided greater insight and success for many, especially for (unidentified) Afro-Americans. Indeed, the racism of the times suddenly found color-blind recording a major foe. While style sometimes betrayed much in playing and vocals, so did emulations. The natural hipness of the black entertainer was the other side of the "black face," despite their own mythology. Even the advent of (later) 1950s rock and roll continued much more of these attitudes, although the scorn and stigma, also part of it, was turned to pride and power.

f. Personalities and recording artists. Bob Hope (England), Al Jolson (Russia?), and Sophie Tucker (Russia) were born elsewhere, but were essentially raised American. Other entertainers influenced by American pop, jazz, and blues recordings include the likes of Al Bowlly (a Brit with Greek heritage born in (Portuguese) controlled Mozambique,Africa), Dick Haymes (Argentinean), Carmen Lombardo (Canadian), Bob Nolan (Canadian), Will Osborne (Canadian), Helen Morgan (Canadian?), Dick Todd (Canadian), Ella Logan (Scotland), and Mabel Mercer (black and British). Of special note—many Afro-Americans such as Josephine Baker, Adelaide Hall, Lizzie Miles, Paul Robeson, Valaida Snow, Elisabeth Welch, and Midge Williams became more popular outside of the United States. (Josephine Baker became identified as a symbol of French entertainment, while Hall and Welch became essentially British entities. Paul Robeson's films, recordings, radio work produced in Britain were very popular, more so in Britain. While his political beliefs got him in deep trouble in America (as a communist), his recordings and personal appearances in Europe, Asia, and especially in the USSR (Russia) provided him with huge recognition, dwarfing anywhere in the United States.)

* Note: Print (selective)
* *BBC Empire Broadcasting* (BBC Radio Program guide), /*Calgary Daily Herald*, Calgary, Canada.
* *Evening Telegram Toronto*, Canada.

- *Good Noise, The*, British, / *Gramophone*, the (British, 1923-50).
- *Gramophone Record Review* (monthly), British, 1933+, Discography, London, England, 1940s.
- *Hot News*, London, England, / *Jazz Hot* (Hot Club of Paris, 1935-39), in French and English.
- *Jazz Journal*, British, / *Jazz Music*, London, England, / *Bulletin du Hot Club de France*,
- *Jazz Hot*, France, / *Jazz Tango French*, / *Jazz* Belgium (1940s).
- *London Evening News*, London, England, / *London Evening Standard*, London, England.
- *La Figaro*, France, / *Lustige Blatter*, Berlin, Germany (1920s).
- *Manchester Guardian*, Manchester, England.
- *Melody Maker*, as perhaps the British equal to America's *Billboard* (1926+)!
- *Metronome*, London, England (not to be confused with the American publication).
- *Ottawa Journal*, Ottowa, Canada
- *Paris Herald*, Paris, France, / *Swing Music*, London, England (1930s+).
- *Radio Pictorial* (Radio Program Guide of Radio Luxemburg), / *Tempo*, Sydney, Australia.
- *Theatre World Magazine*, London, England (1930s), / *Toronto Daily Star*, Toronto, Canada.
- *Vancouver Sun*, Vancouver, Canada.

♦ Note: Selective Sites

- Abby Theatre, Dublin, Ireland.
- Alhambra Theater, Paris, France.

- Adelphi Theatre, London, England. (Ruth Etting's only London gig found the diva walking out after one show, due to lack of funds, or poor management? (1937)
- Admiralspalast Theater, Berlin, Germany (1920s).
- Alexander Young Hotel, Honolulu, Hawaii (not yet a state).
- Alhambra Theatre, London, England. (Eddie Cantor gig in 1914?)
- Alhambra Theatre, Paris, France
- Ambassadeurs Resturant, Casino, Cannes (1920s)
- Argyle, London, England (1920s).
- Agua Caliente, Tijuana, Mexico.
- Atlantico, Buenos Aires, Argentina.
- Bellmanspo Resturant, Stockholm, Sweden
- Belfast Hospital, Belfast, N. Ireland (Especially a Gene Autry gig in 1939).
- Benneweis Cirkus, Copenhagen, Denmark.
- Beumont State Theatre, London, England.
- Big Apple Nightclub (La Grosse Pomme), 73 Rue Pigalle Paris, France (owned and associated with Adelaide Hall. Guests included vocalist Mabel Mercer and bandleader Django Reinhardt (1937-38).
- Blue Bird Cafe, Montreal, Canada. (1920s)
- Bolshoi Theater, Moscow. Soviet Union. This famous theater know for opera, had origins in the 1700s. (Paul Robeson gig in 1949)
- Boudon's Café, Paris, France.
- Bowman's Cabaret, Vancouver, Canada (1920s).
- Bricktop's, Mexico City, Mexico (associated with Ada "Bricktop" Smith in the 1940s).
- Bricktop's Café, Via Veneto, Rome, Italy (associated with Ada "Bricktop Smith, 1949).
- Bricktop's Le Grand Duc, Paris, France. (1924-26) As mythology has it, the first of (transplanted black vaudvillian) Ada 'Bricktop' Smith's managed night spots (followed by her (1926)-'Music Box' & (1929)-'Monico or as Chez Bricktop' found her singing (without producing any contemporary recordings), employees such as the (Brit & black) vocalist & pianist Leslie 'Hutch' Henderson, American jazz house bands, a waiter of considerable writing talent-Langston Hughes, as well as patrons such as T.S. Eliot, 'jazz age' friends F. Scott Fitzgerald & wife Zelda, Cole Porter, Ernest Hemingway, Pablo Picasso, Evelyn Waugh, a bit of European royalty as well as visiting cabaret guests, including Adelaide Hall, Edith Wilson, Josephine Baker, Valaida Snow and Ethel Waters.
- Bricktop's Monico, 66 Rue Pigalle, Paris France. (1929-38). (Also called 'Chez Bricktop') Perhaps Bricktop's most successful nightspot, featuring Mabel Mercer vocals, (starting in 1931),-until the eve of WWII-that scared most patrons away.
- Brick top's Music Box, Paris France. (1926-29)
- Baltabaris Club, The Hague, Holland.
- Buckingham Palace (Command Performance), London, England.
- Cabin Club, Soho, London, England.
- Café Anglais, London, England.
- Cafe Bismark, Hamburg, Germany. (Illegal jazz by un-nazi German 'swing kids' found here (1938-39), until found & shut down.
- Cafe de Ambassadeurs, Paris, France. Myths have it that this restaurant had been around since before the French Revolution? Good speculation that American likes of Helen Morgan (1927?), Adelaide Hall and Valaida Snow had (pre-WWII) gigs at this site?

- Café de Paris, 3 Coventry Street, Piccadilly, London, England. (Pre-WWII American gigs include Nick Lucas, Sophie Tucker, Adelaide Hall, Ethel Waters, Marion Harris, Hildegarde).
- Cafe de Paris, 41 Avenue dei Opera, Paris, France
- Café du Dome, Paris, France (1920s).
- Canidrome Gardens (Ballroom), Shanghi, China. (Pre-WWII gigs by Alberta Hunter, Midge Williams and Valaida Snow is good speculation? So are visits from Madame Chiang Kai-Shek, W. Somerset Maughan, Pan Yuliang, Charlie Chaplin & Pauletta Goddard).
- Calcutta Gardens, Calcutta, India. (1920s).
- Capital Theatre, Swanston Street, Melbourne, Australia.
- Capital Theatre, 890 Rue Sainte Catherine D., Montreal, Canada.
- Carlton Cafe Ballroom, Shanghai, China (Valaida Snow in 1928)?
- Carlton Hotel, Amsterdam, Holland
- Carlton Hotel, Belgrave Road, Victoria, London, England. (Especially a Hildegarde gig-invited by royal invitation in 1934).
- Casa Loma Hotel, Toronto, Canada. As nightclub folklore has it, musician-sax player Glen Gray, played a gig at this site in 1928 as part of the Orange Blossom Band. Shortly after, he formed another group as the Casa Loma Orchestra in 1929. Recognition would follow for two decades.
- Casanova Club, Paris, France. (Especially a Hildegarde gig in mid-1930s).
- Casssino de Vrca, Rio de Janiro, Brazil (1920s-30s)
- Casablanca Club, Acapulco, Mexico.
- Casani Club, London, England.
- Casino Copacabana, Rio de Janeiro, Brazil.
- Casino da Urca, Rio de Janeiro, Brazil.
- Casino de Paris, 16 Rue de Clichy, Paris France (especially Josephine Baker's gigs, 1930-32).
- Casino Muncipale, San Remo, Italy. (Attracted illegal American jazz, and Italian tastes, despite Benito Mussolini's fascism before WWII). Incl. Pre-WWII Adelaide Hall, Valaida Snow gigs.
- Cathay Hotel, Shanghai, China (pre-WWII).
- Chalet Hotel, Montreal, Canada.
- Champs-Elysees Music Hall, Paris, France (especially Josephine Baker's gigs, 1925-26).
- Chez Florence, France. Managed by Florence Jones Ebery, who like Bricktop, Invested in her own club. (As myth would have it, house-band musician Sidney Bechet was involved in gun-play here, in1928? Was he backing a Alberta Hunter gig at this time)? Or was it Edith Wilson?
- Chez Josephine, Rue Fontaine, Paris, France (Josephine Baker's own club, 1926-28).
- Chez Maurice, Montreal, Canada.
- Chez Mitchell, 61 Rue Blanche, Paris, France. (Especially Lizzie Miles gigs in 1924-26)
- Circus Schumann, Copenhagen, Denmark.
- Cirkus Theater, Stockholm, Sweden.
- Ciro's, London, England. (Especially (pre-WWII) American gigs of Helen Morgan and Rudy Vallee in 1937.
- Ciro's (Hotel Reforma), Mexico City, Mexico (1940s).
- Ciro's Restaurant, Biarritz. (1930s)
- Claridge's (Cabaret) Paris, France (1920s).
- Club Alabam, Madrid, Spain. (Before the 1936-39 Spanish Civil War).
- Club Gabiorenden, Montreal, Canada.

- Club Kursaal, Havana, Cuba.
- Club O Rio, Cannes, France (1930s).
- Club Ramonaga, London, England (1930s).
- Coliseum Theatre, London, England. (Especially Pre-WWII Edith Wilson, Valaida Snow gigs).
- Columbus Ballroom, Toronto, Canada.
- Colon Opera House, Buenos Aires, Argentina. (Argentine President Kipolito Trigoyen publicly censers Josephine Baker's gig, 1929)
- Colston Hall, Bristol, England.
- Consul Theatre, Basel, Switzerland.
- Continental, Cairo, Egypt (1930s).
- Copacabana the, Rio de Janeiro, Brazil. This site most likely inspired the 1940 NYC site.
- Cotton Club, Paris, France. (Alberta Hunter gig in 1929).
- Criterion Restaurant (Rose Garden), London, England.
- Crystal Beach, Ontario, Canada.
- Danceland, Montreal, Quebec, Canada.
- Den-La Femina Club, Athens, Greece (1930s).
- Denmark, 1940. While on tour, American Valaida Snow was detained by invading Germans, despite the fact that the United States was still neutral. She was subsequently returned, literally a POW, in 1942.
- Devonshire Restaurant, Piccadilly, London, England.
- Diable Ameureux, Brussells, Belgium
- Dolphin Nightclub, Cannes, France (1930s).
- Dorchester Hotel, London, England. Many BBC radio broadcasts originated here in the 1930s. Moreover, Jack Jackson's house band orchestra featured and recorded Alberta Hunter in 1934.
- Drury Lane Theatre, London, England. (Especially Pre-WWII gigs of Paul Robeson, Alberta Hunter, Elisabeth Welch. Adelaide Hall).
- Eden Bar Club, Vienna, Austria. (Welcomed American jazz, including a Valaida Snow gig-before nazi's took over in 1937.)
- El Dorado Café, Berlin, Germany (1920s). This pre-Hitler German nightclub featured American jazz. Speculation exists that there was possibly entertainment from Marlene Dietrich, Greta Keller and Leni Riefensyahl (later Hitler's favorite film producer), and visitors, who included the (black) faces of Evelyn Dove, Josephine Baker, and Adelaide Hall, performed at this site. More so, this site was also the possible inspiration for the (later) John Kander and Fed Ebb Broadway and film productions of *Cabaret*?
- Elephant Theatre, London, England.
- Elmwood Casino (Ambassador Room, Tudor Lounge) Windsor, Ontario, Canada.
- Embassy Club, London, England.
- Empire Theatre, Leicester Square, London, England. (Especially Fred & Adele Astaire, 1925-26).
- English Channel, 1944. American bandleader Glenn Miller's touring plane was shot down, subsequently never found.
- Excelsior Club, Alexander, Egypt (1930s).
- Excelsior Lido, Venice, Italy (1920s).
- Fairfield Hotel, Croyden, England.
- Finsbury Park Empire, London, England.
- Floral Frascat Restaurant, London, England.

- Florida Club, South Bruton Meus, London, England. The popular jazz club had featured Al berta Hunter in 1928. Briefly owned by Adelaide Hall as 'Old Florida Club' (1938-40) until German blitz destroyed it.
- Florida Dance Hall, Tokyo, Japan (before WWII).
- Folies-Bergere Music Hall, Paris, France.
- French Trocadero, Montreal, Canada.
- Frisco's (nightclub), London, England (1930s).
- Gaiety Theatre, Dublin, Ireland.
- Gaiety Theatre, London, England.
- Gran Casino de la Playa, Havana, Cuba (1920s+).
- Grande Carte, Paris, France (1920s).
- Green Park Hotel, London, England (1920s).
- Grosses Schauspielhaus, Berlin, Germany (1920s).
- Haus Vaterland, Berlin, Germany.
- Harbour Bar, Bombay, India (1930s).
- Hippodrome Theatre, London, England. (Especially Fannie Brice, Sophie Tucker gigs before 1920)
- Holborn Empire Theatre, London, England.
- Holborn Empire Theatre, Glascow, Scotland. (Especially a Adelaide Hall & Fats Waller gig, 1938.)
- Holborn Empire Theatre, London, England. (Especially Louis Armstrong, Fats Waller, Rudy Vallee; (pre-WWII) gigs.)
- Holland-1937. Touring Valaida Snow is presented a gold plated trumpet from Queen Wilhelmia.
- Hot Club, Vienna, Austria (post-WWII).
- Hotel Los Galmingos, Acapulco, Mexico
- Imperial Hotel, Tokyo, Japan (especially Midge Williams's gigs here before WWII).
- Imperial Theatre, Toronto, Ontario, Canada.
- Jardins des Petite Champs, Istanbul, Turkey (1930s).
- Jig's Club, London, England.
- Johann Strauss Theatre, Vienna, Austria (featured American jazz in the 1920s).
- Kabaray De Komika, Berlin, Germany.
- Kansas City Bar, Tia Juana, Mexico.
- Kingsway, Toronto, Canada.
- Kit Kat Club (Haymarket) London, England. This old club, founded before George Washington was born, at least found the likes of (pre-WWII) Americans such as Nick Lucas, Sophie Tucker, Ethel Waters, Cab Calloway and Fats Waller welcomed.
- Knickerbocker Hotel, Monte Carlo, Monaco (1920s+).
- Knokke Casino, Belgium.
- -L'Ange Bleu Club, Paris, France.
- L'Enfer, Paris, France.
- La Coupole, Café, Paris, France (1920s).
- La Femina Club, Athens, Greece.
- Latino Americano, Juarez, Mexico (1920s).
- Le Bal Nègre, Paris, France (1920s).
- Le Bateau Ivre, Paris, France (1920s).
- Le Chat Noir, Paris, France (1920s).
- La Gaite, Amsterdam, Holland (1930s).

- Le Grand Hermitage Muscovite, 24 Rue Coumartime, Paris, France (1920s), Russian-owned club that featured American jazz.
- Le Boeuf sur le Toit (The Cow on the Roof) Paris, France (1920s+). (Especially Elisabeth Welch in 1930).
- La Scala Theatre, Berlin, Germany (1920s).
- Le Jardin de Ma Soeur, Paris, France (1920s).
- Le Hot Club De Rennes, Paris, France.
- Les Ambassadeurs, Paris, France (1920s).
- Lido, Paris, France.
- Leicester Square Theatre, London, England.
- London Casino, London, England.
- Lyceum Theatre, London, England.
- Lyric Park, Copenhagen, Denmark.
- Manila Hotel, (Ballroom) Manila, Phillipines.
- Maxim's Restaurant, Paris, France
- Melrose Theatre, Perth, Australia.
- Meridian Club, Montreal, Canada.
- Merry Sol, Biarritz, France.
- Metropole Restaurant, Dublin, Ireland. (Especially a Gene Autry gig in 1939).
- Metropol (nightclub), Berlin, Germany (1920s)
- Massey Hall, Toronto, Canada.
- Mitchell's (cabaret), Paris, France (1920s).
- Moscow Conservatory, Moscow, Soviet Union. (Paul Robeson in 1937).
- Moulin Rouge Music Hall, Paris, France. (As known in literature and film—perhaps (Pre-WWII) American gigs include those of Adelaide Hall, Elisabeth Welch, and Louis Armstrong.
- Mount Royal Hotel, Montreal, Canada.
- Montmartre Music Hall, Paris, France.
- Monsignor Restaurant, London, England (especially Al Bowlly).
- Municipal Theatre, Oran, Algeria, N. Africa. Josephine Baker's WWII efforts to intergrate American forces are based less upon myth but fact, especially at this gig in 1943!
- Murray's Club, Soho, London, England (featured American ragtime before 1920).
- Mutual Street Arena, Toronto, Ontario, Canada.
- National Scala, Copenhagen, Denmark.
- National Scala Theatre, Stockholm, Sweden.
- National Theatre, Sydney, Australia.
- Nest Club, London, England.
- New Mayfair Hotel, London, England.
- Nut-House, London, England.
- Odeon Theatre, Paris, France.
- Olympia Theatre, Paris, France.
- Olympic Games, Berlin, Germany (August 1936). The stunning success of being black was obvious with the on-field merits of Jessie Owens and Ralph Metcalf in Hitler's Germany. The forgotten contemporary success of Adelaide Hall's jazzy vocal gig at Berlin's Rex Theatre should also be noted, considering that jazz music, and being black, was otherwise banned—except for these Olympics. Perhaps the last time jazz was played legally in Germany by foreigners until 1945?
- Opera House, Manchester, England. (Especially a Ruth Etting gig in 1937)

- Orpheum Theatre, Calgary, Canada.
- Orpheum Theatre, Edmonton, Canada.
- Orpheum Theatre, Regina, Canada.
- Orpheum Theatre, Vancouver, Canada.
- Orpheum Theatre, Winnipeg, Canada.
- Pavilion, The, London, England.
- Palace Hotel, Nice, France (1920s).
- Palace Theatre, Manchester, England.
- Palladium, Oxford Circus W., London, England. Europe's most prestigious music hall? Pre-WWII American gigs include Nick Lucas, Sophie Tucker, Helen Morgan, Alberta Hunter, Josephine Baker, Ethel Waters, Adelaide Hall, Paul Robeson, Louis Armstrong, Mills Brothers, Cab Calloway, Fats Waller.
- Palaisdes Beaux Arts, Brusse ls, Belgium. (1930s)
- Paradise Club, London, England.
- Paramount Dance Hall, Shanghi, China. (Pre-WWII)
- Paramount Theatre, London, England. (Especially a Gene Autry gig in 1939).
- Peninsula Hotel or the Penn (Ballroom) Hong Kong, China (1928+). WWII British forces surrendered to the Japanese here in 1941 and later accepted surrender by the Japanese in 1945.
- Phoenix Theatre, London, England.
- Piccadilly Hotel, London, England.
- Plaza Hotel, Shanghai, China.
- Plantation Club, Paris, France (1920s).
- Portugal, 1943. While on a USO tour, American vocalist Jane Froman's plane crashed near Lisbon. Jane survived with injuries that lasted the rest of her life. Others, including comic Ron Rognman and the Russian-born Broadway entity, Tamara (Drasin), lost their lives.
- Pré Catelan, Paris, France.
- Presidente Hotel, Acapulco, Mexico.
- Prince Edward Theatre, London, England. (Especially Josephine Baker gig in 1933)
- Princess Club, London, England. (Especially a Gene Austin gig in 1925).
- Princess Theatre, Honolulu Hawaii. (Hawaii was not a state until 1959.)
- Raffles Hotel, Singapore. (1920s)
- Rectors, Paris, France.
- Regent Theatre, Brisbaine, Australia (Especially a Nick Lucus gig in 1939).
- Rex Theatre, Berlin, Germany.
- Ritz Hotel, London, England. (named by original Swiss owner Cesar Ritz), Picadilly, London, England. (Hildegarde gigs in 1930s).
- RKO Theatre, Leicester Square, London, England (1931+).
- Royal Albert Hall. London, England. (Especially Paul Robeson gigs in 1930s).
- Royal Alexandra, Toronto, Canada.
- Royal Theatre, Nairobi
- Salle Pleyel, Paris, France. (Especially pre-WWII gigs from Louis Armstrong, Cab Calloway).
- Salle Rameau, Paris, France.
- Savoy Plaza Hotel, London, England. (Mythology has it that Rudy Vallee, before he started crooning, was a visiting (stand in) clarinet or sax member of the Savoy Havana (house) band, around 1924-25? He would later return to croon here, more famously, in a 1937 gig).

- Scala Theater, Copenhagen, Denmark.
- Scheveningen Casino, Holland.
- Selbourne Hall, Johannesburg, South Africa.
- Shea's Hippodrome, Toronto, Ontario, Canada (1914+).
- Shea's Theatre, Victoria Street, Toronto, Ontario, Canada.
- Silver Slipper, Nassau, Bahamas.
- Silver Slipper, Toronto, Ontario, Canada.
- Smetana Hall, Prague, Czechoslovakia. (Paul Robeson gig in 1949).
- Stall Theatre, London, England.
- St. Denis Theatre, Montreal, Canada.
- St. Kilda Palais Ballroom, Melbourne, Australia.
- St. Moritz, Switzerland.
- State Theatre, Vancouver, Canada
- Stork Club, London, England.
- Stray Theatre, London, England.
- Tchaikovsky Hall, Moscow, Soviet Union. (A 1949 Paul Robeson gig, including his pro-Stalinist views, more so reflected post WWII 'cold war' heat.
- Teatro 18 de Julio, Monteuideo, Uruguay (1920s-30s?)
- Teatro Nuevo, Barcelona, Spain. (Before the 1936-39 Spanish Civil War).
- Teatro Roma, Madrid, Spain. (Before the 1936-39 Spanish Civil War).
- Thaila Theater, Hamburg, Germany.
- Theatre Royal, Drury Lane, London, England.
- Theatre Royal, Edinburgh, Scotland.
- Tivoli Theatre, London, England.
- Top Hat Club, Toronto, Canada.
- Top Hatters Cabaret, Kings Cross, Sydney, Australia. (1930s)
- Trivoli Theatre, Melbourne, Australia.
- Trocadero Club, Sydney, Australia (1936+).
- Trocadero, Montreal, Canada.
- Tropicana, Havana, Cuba (1939+).
- Tushinski Theatre, Amsterdam, Holland.
- UTA Theater, Berlin, Germany (one of many pre-Hitler German sites featuring American jazz).
- Villa Venice, Havana, Cuba (1939+).
- White Mouse Cabaret, Berlin, Germany (1920s).
- Winter Garden, Berlin, Germany (1920s).
- Vancouver Hotel, Vancouver, British Columbia, Canada.
- Ventouris Supper Club, Paris, France.
- Zelli's (nightclub), (Joe Zelli's Royal Box), Paris, France (1920s).
- Zentral Theater, Magdeburg, Germany.

RADIO'S POPULAR VOCALISTS AND PROGRAMS (1921-50 +)

❖ The Use of Radio, 1921-50

- The advent of commercial radio in the early 1920s opened up huge marketing opportunities never before realized. At first, popular local vocalists, including the likes of various ethnic entities, depending where you lived, sprouted up overnight. Many would-be Carusos also found an audience. Early radio also found recording artists pitching their art (with bandleaders) upon the airwaves.
- It may generally be assumed that Vaughn De Leath, in 1920, was the first recording vocalist found on radio. Despite the racism of the times, it may also be assumed that Ethel Waters, touring for Black Swan Records, was the first Afro-American recording artist heard on the radio as a vocalist, in 1922 in New Orleans, LA, on WVG radio.

As it turned out however, the radio listener actually found that many products indeed—including entities such as soap, soup, cheese, milk, nuts, coffee, tea, and beer, among others—were ideal snack items to devour while listening to the radio. Other high-end entities, such as cars, trucks, and boats (along with oil) also found themselves in a huge showroom, more so, "living rooms" of Americana. Indeed, many entertainers became identified with their radio sponsors! (Many are noted below.)

So indeed were many magazines and books something to devour after listening to the radio. So were magazines and books devoted to radio stars overlapping the existing market of film stars and developing into a larger enterprise. Within time, radio itself introduced and promoted many newer vocalists and film entities.

When the smoke cleared (cigarettes and cigars were also fine listener tools), it was radio, more than films—noting that films were also advertised on the radio—that indeed introduced more products to Americana than any other media, before 1950. Gotta headache? Stomach problem? Liver? Constipated from perhaps munching too many peanuts? Want relief? Perhaps some of these commercials make one sick listening to them! Need a laxative? A car? Gas for it? Before commercial radio, publishers of song ditties had produced even more revenue than the musical entities (including vocalists and musicians). The American Society of Composers, Authors, and Publishers (ASCAP), formed in (1914), made sure of it. Based in New York City (within the Tin Pan Alley section), the power of ASCAP, originally formed to prevent fraud and the use of uncredited recording material, found its agents (or song-pluggers) in every aspect of the music industry. It, more so, forced theaters and other places of entertainment to pay fees to credited composers, authors, publishers, and composers, as ASCAP. The new radio commercial, as well as the exploitation of recording artists on radio, became an easy mark for song-pluggers. Radio also opened up the field for more songwriters, indeed far from the Broadway idiom. For many in ASCAP, this heresy was unacceptable, which would gradually lead to another organization, in later decades, which sought to include everyone (BMI).

- The rise of Rudy Vallee in 1928, as a disc seller and commodity due to live radio broadcasts in New York City, was spectacular. So was a newer musical trend of "crooning."
- The rise of Bing Crosby and Russ Columbo in 1931, as radio crooners, despite the Depression would (even) overtake Vallee's popularity. More so, a more intimate style of crooning and style would emerge.
- A fine early 1930s Boswell Sisters recording "Sing a Little Jingle," on Brunswick 6128, is a perfect example of the new art form and the marketing of product over the air.
- Ethel Waters became the first Afro-American on *American Review* (1933-34) to headline a network program.
- The rise of radio, more so, found many "common" folk and the language and usage of slang. Many would-be song composers indeed found themselves unable to publish new songs or to even join ASCAP. Within the time before 1940, many ASCAP entitles would not allow their songs to be thus performed with (the few) non-ASCAP ones. (This attitude found its way into films as well.)
- By 1940, a rival organization, Broadcast Music Incorporated (BMI), largely supported by the growing radio industry itself, was formed. Its original organization had been founded by many of same songwriters and performers who, more so, included many black and country song entities.
- Radio revenues indeed ruled the roost. The spinning of discs, even those with less scratchy grooves, was generally risky and illegal in the United States before 1942. It was generally believed that recordings purchased had already found their own audiences. Any live radio promotions were fine—actually promoted recordings and recording artists. Any recording played on the "air," however, was strictly limited to radio transcriptions, noting that during the Great Depression years from 1929 through 1934, sales for recordings slipped over 75 percent while the sales of radios increased.
- The loss of record sales hurt all recording entities concerned, although no one would realize, except in some countries like England, that the spinning of records was indeed good marketing and the Depression had been a fluke. Moreover, at the time, most consumers had more important things to purchase than recordings and, for that matter, purchasing theater and film tickets. While the record industry did pick up by the mid-1930s, when hard times started to ease up a bit, live remote hookups best promoted newer musical trends.
- The latter 1930s also found another marketing tool to popularize and sell records—the "jukebox." Instant revenue was created as owners of small shops in cafés, stands, carnivals, and bars, with the repeal of Prohibition in 1934 by most states, gave consumers more to hear, and cheaply. This also applied to small bars that could not afford live gigs. Record companies, in turn, also found the jukebox a cheap and excellent marketing tool.

- "On the air" radio, perhaps a risky compromise, was a proposed idea of making radio pay for each playing of a recorded entity. This theory, in a media dominated by comics, soap opera and live hooked-up musical performances also found great opposition and, as it turned out, was a justified fear. Until the early 1940s, the "disc jockey" was a rare entity.
- A powerful musicians union, whose ranks swelled with the popularity of the big bands since the mid-1930s, were equally dead set against the playing of discs. Who would bother to listen to "studio" work on the radio? Who would get paid?
- The efforts of James Petrillo, the boss of the American Federation of Musicians Union, led to a major strike against the major recording companies in 1942. The quest to get more revenue for his union (subsequently leaving most Afro-Americans without a voice), indeed fueled rage and concerns upon publishers, jukeboxes, over-the-air-disc-playing, and record companies. It also led to the use of more singing groups with less musicians. Recording companies, moreover, found it far easier to record without paying for all those musicians.
- As it turned out, thanks largely to the newer (BMI) publishers and radio stations realizing a cheaper enterprise, the "disc jockey" playing (BMI) recordings emerged.
- This, more so, led to the demise of live radio and, indeed, ushered out the comics, comedians, soap operas, and, more importantly, the expensive live musical programs that the musicians union had demanded payments for. Indeed, the whole music industry changed by the end of the strike in 1944. ASCAP recordings were, in a large degree, also getting "air time" and were being played. More so, sales soared.

  - The success of the Martin Block program *Make Believe Ballroom*, finally made legal by 1941, made the "disc jockey" an accepted and cheaper form of a radio program.
  - The record companies, in a large way, found smaller groups of musicians to pay. Vocal groups, as well as single vocal entities, were also on the rise, detaching themselves from the big band hogs.
  - The single vocalist, no longer needing the bandleader, was, more so, a profitable commodity. So were vocal groups. A later 1948 musicians' strike would also fail. The newer trends of "rhythm and blues" and "country" were, moreover, less complicated and less expensive to produce.
  - The rise of small labels, which had died during the Depression, so was resurrected, largely after WWII. Again, it was easy and cheap to produce music, especially that of R & B and country, and leaving out the more expensive (union) musician.
  - The continued rise of the DJ, found the more expensive live radio program at odds within the radio industry. The split became more apparent in the *Billboard* issue of August 2, 1947, when it conducted its own First Annual DISK Jockey Poll. Selective results are as under:

    - "All Around Popular Male" included Bing Crosby, Frank Sinatra, Perry Como Dick Haymes, Art Lund Buddy Clark,. Frankie Laine, Mel Torme, Tony Martin, and Andy Russell.
    - "All Around Popular Female" included Dinah Shore, Jo Stafford, Peggy Lee, Margaret Whiting, Maratha Tilton, Doris Day, Monica Lewis, Billie Holliday, Sarah Vaughan, and Anita O'Day.
    - "Male Band Vocalist" included Stuart Foster, Eddie Howard, Harry Babbitt, Art Lund, Jack Hunter, Vaughan Monroe, Buddy De Vito, Jimmy Saunders, Frankie Lester, and Bill Lockwood.

- "Female Band Vocalist" included June Christy, Marjorie Hughes, Fran Warren, Doris Day, Rosalind Patton, Carolyn Grey, Anita O'Day, Marion Morgan, Peggy Lee, and Jane Russell.
- "Most Promising Newer Names-Male Vocalists" included Frankie Laine, Art Lund, Mel Torme, Vic Damone, Buddy Clark, Joe Alexander, Gordon Mac Rae, Bill Lockwood, Clark Dennis, Johnny Desmond, and Ray Dorey.
- "Most Promising New Names-Female Vocalists" included Fran Warren, Rosalind Patton, Jane Russell, Doris Day, June Christy, Monica Lewis, Sarah Vaughan, Betty Rhodes, Peggy Lee, and Marjorie Hughes.
- "Singing Groups" included Pied Pipers, Modernaires, Mills Brothers, Ink Spots, Dinning Sisters, Andrews Sisters, King Cole Trio, Charioteers, Starlighters, and Mel-Tones.

- It is more significant that the DJ was officially given a huge voice within the magazine as its own influence within the music industry (unwittingly) signaled "air time" and payola. As the first of many such polls, the DJ literally created sales by playing records, indeed fueling the industry like never before. In true retrospective, while many old-timers blamed it on the rock and roll of the 1950s, it had started in the "pop" idiom of the 1940s. Was it the corruptible DJ who created the "rock" revolution? Or was it just a group of young and populous teenagers searching for newer sounds and hipper recording entities?

- The newer format of the 33 and a 1/3rd rpm on LP and the 45 rpm single was easier than the bulky 78-rpm format. (The attempt had been made by Victor in the early 1930s to use 331/3 speed, but economic times had crushed it). The newer technology contributed to the decline of pop music and the rise of rhythm and blues and country music in the 1950s. So did a growing youth market of teenagers who had money and were observing newer sounds. More so, the growing number of smaller, independent record labels provided DJs with more of a choice for listeners.
- Despite the use of tape, pioneered by Bing Crosby in 1946, the radio program was basically one of spinning records by 1950. In true retrospective, the DJ was king.
- The spinning of records also founded competition for live radio artist programs themselves. The mid-1940s found many DJs offering "tribute" programs made up of original recordings, something that was against the law in the 1920s and 1930s. Many older records that had never been heard over the radio, became better known and recognized. (Bing Crosby, radio's most successful vocalist, found that his already huge catalog of records was being broadcast in "tribute" programs from KOL in Seattle, WA; WREC in Memphis, TN; and on WEAU in Eau Claire, WI.)
- By the latter 1940s, the emergence of television put most live radio entities to rest. Indeed, much of the radio business was shifting to television. Many of these programs, including the likes of *Jack Benny, Burns and Allen, Ozzie and Harriet, and Red Skelton*, became well known to many baby boomers. Did they survive in the newer TV media? Most did not.

❖ Radio Programs Featuring Vocalists

- The following (selected) radio programs and entities have some relevance to the text and/or purposes of this book, and were popular from 1920 through 1950. Indeed, many recording artists were "discovered" in radio itself. While network broadcasts are important (as well as big time), local stations are also noted. Many broadcasts indeed started as locals and were picked up by the networks later on. Others (1925) had existed before network broadcasts. The huge radio audiences of the 1930s had found the practice of network broadcasting an exciting prospect as well as an increasingly regular fixture.

- Radio (National) Networks included the following:

- Columbia Broadcasting Company (CBS), 1928. This network was founded by a group of many interests, who included the likes of William Paley and Arthur Judson absorbing the previous United Independent broadcasters (UIB).
- National Broadcasting Company (NBC), 1926. This network was set up by the interests of Radio Corporation of America (RCA), Westinghouse, interests from AT & T, and General Electric. As originally broadcast from NYC on WEAF, the "Red" East Coast interests would coordinate with others, which included a chain of West Coast stations, to be known as "Blue."
- Mutual Broadcasting System (MBS), 1934. A group of independent radio stations, not owned by CBS or CBS, found the effects of the Great Depression something oddly advantageous. The likes of WOR in New York, WGN in Chicago, WXYZ in Detroit, and WLW in Cincinnati combined into a huge enterprise, also attracting other smaller independent stations as a means to survive.

- American Broadcasting Company (ABC) was a later entity that split from NBC Blue or the Blue network in 1944 and became an entity of its own.

- Jan. 1942. Gen. Douglas MacArthur specifically requested a short wave radio broadcast of Bing Crosby, for the morale of his (then) trapped troops in the Philippines. This resulted in the Armed Forces Radio Service (AFRS). These programs, such as *Command Performance*, *Jubilee*, *Mail Call*, and *One Night Stand* consisted of live airchecks from various locations as well as Victory Discs (V-Discs) which were legal transcription recordings by a variety of performers, free of charge, broadcast to servicemen and servicewomen throughout the world. A few were broadcast in the United States as well and sometimes were carried by the major networks, free of charge.
- The problem of live airchecks became an exercise of switching time zones and (sometimes) switching from different locations from around the country.

A program originating from New York at 10:30 p. m. for example, found earlier listeners in Chicago (9:30 p. m.), and earlier in Denver (8:30 p. m.). Indeed, it would be a post-dinner delight in Los Angeles, at 7:30 p. m. The same program could be broadcast from Chicago the next week, changing broadcast time, or not allowing the program to be heard whole. The reality of *taped* broadcasts did not become a factor until 1946, although the use of prerecorded transcription discs, generally used for commercials (also a "find" for collectors), was principally limited due to poor quality and opposition by musicians union.

- Selective programs (1921-50). Complete identification is noted, if found (from various sources). When identification is not complete, the name of the vocalist, or vocalists is used.

A.

* *Abbot and Costello*, NBC, ABC (1942-49). The comic duo in action! On first? Featured vocalist, Connie Haines.
* *Adventures of Ozzie and Harriet*, CBS, NBC (1944+). The popular bandleader and wife founded this family program. Early vocals, other than their own, featured the King Sisters. Later, when the show moved to TV, they would include sons David and Ricky Nelson. More so, Ricky made it into the early middle-class baby boomers' hearts, featuring the new idiom of rock and roll.
* *American Family Album of Familiar Music*, NBC (1933-34), with Haenschen's Orchestra, Frank Munn, and Virginia Rae.
* *American Review*, NBC (1933-34). This short-lived variety program, sponsored by American Oil Company (AMOCO) is also sadly neglected in true retrospective. It starred Afro-American Ethel Waters, with fine backup by the Dorsey Brothers Orchestra. It may be considered the first attempt at "network" at prime time radio, by a black entity.
* *Amos "n" Andy*, WGN, WMAQ, WJZ, and NBC (1926+). Whitefaced vaudevillians Freeman F. Gosden and Charles J. Correll turned comic talents into accepted black dialect to become one of radio's best-known programs, starting in Chicago as *Sam "n" Henry* and moving to NYC. In true retrospective, the stereotyping is real enough, as Gosden and Correll just may have founded their act upon the real Afro-American team of F. E. Miller and Aubrey Lyles, who were comics as well as Broadway producers. Gosden and Correll were seen in real blackface in the (1930) film *Check and Double Check*, indeed based upon their popular radio program which sometimes featured vocals, long-sponsored by Pepsodent, among others. Moreover, some real black voices participated in many broadcasts, including the likes of Edith Wilson. (Young baby boomers may be more familiar with the (later) popular 1950s' TV program with real Afro-Americans including Tim Moore, Ernestine Wade, and the aged songwriter, Spencer Williams, minus Gosden and Correll)
* *Andrews Sisters*, CBS, KNX (1944+); many guests.
* *Armour Program* with Phil Baker, NBC (1933-34); featured Phil's own vocals.
* *Arthur Godfrey's Talent Scouts*, CBS (1938+). Like Major Bowes before him, Godfrey looked to "discover" singers. (He would later do a similar program on television (1950s). PerhapsGodfrey's major 1940s' finds were Vic Damone, Tony Bennett, and Al Martino.

B.

* *Baby Rose Marie*, NBC (1926-34). As a three-year-old, this child act did the same for radio that Shirley Temple would do for (talking) films of the early 1930s. (Rose Marie could not be recognized (light-years away) by many baby boomers in the TV entity *Dick Van Dyke Show.)*
* *Back Where I Came From*, CBS (1941). Featured Woody Guthrie, Burl Ives, Leadbelly, and Josh White.
* *Baker's Broadcasting* with Joe Penner and Ozzie Nelson and also Harriet Hilliard, NBC (1933-34).
* *Baker's Chocolate Program* (1932); featured the Boswell Sisters.
* *Barn Dance*, WBAP (1922), Fort Worth, TX. The loose use of the term "barn dance" could also be applied to early WLS Chicago program *Barn Dance* and WSM Nashville program *Grand Ole Opery.*

* *Beale Street Boys,* WMCA (1930) NYC, and NY; vocal group.
* *Beale Street Palace Theater,* WMC (1923+), Memphis, TN; featured Bessie Smith, others.
* *Beat the Band,* NBC. (1940-43), Featured Ted Weems orchestra and band singers Perry Como, Parker Gibbs, and Marvel Maxwell—later known as Marilyn Maxwell.
* Ben Bernie, the Old Maestro, WJZ (1930), CBS, NBC. This early bandleader had been on the air as early as 1923. Through the years till 1943, he featured the vocals of Dick Stabile, Buddy Clark, Dinah Shore, and Ethel Waters. Among his sponsors were Pabst Blue Ribbon Beer, Bromo Seltzer, and US Rubber.
* Benny Goodman's *Swing School,* NBC (1937-39). In addition to others (including *Let's Dance*), the popular bandleader's radio audience promoted "swing" better than anyone else. He also featured vocals by Mildred Bailey, Martha Tilton, and Louise Tobin.
* *Beverly Hill Billies,* KMPC (1930+) Los Angeles, CA. This early West Coast hillbilly group, formed by Zeke Manners, indeed predated the likes of the popular baby boomer TV sitcom! It is, more so, interesting to note that Buddy Ebsen, the future member of the popular 1960s' TV program, was a popular dance entity with his sister—similar to Fred Astaire in the mid-1930s! (Other members of the original Beverly Hill Billies included the future single entities of Elton Britt and Stuart Hamblen.)
* *Big D Jamboree,* CBS, KRLD (1947+) Dallas, TX; C & W.
* *Blackstone Plantation* with Sanderson and Crumit, NBC (1920s+). This program was hosted by Julia Sanderson and Frank Crumit.
* *Blue Monday Jamboree* (1935), Berkeley, CA; featured the Williams Four Quartet—siblings John, Charles, Robert, and Midge. (Later, Midge emerged as a solo vocalist.)
* *Bond Bread Program* with Sanderson and Crumit, CBS (1933-34); Frank Crumit.
* *Boone County Jamboree,* WLW (1930s+), Cincinnati, OH; Merle Travis, Grandpa Jones.
* *Breakfast Club,* WMAQ, NBC (1933+), Chicago, IL. Don McNeil hosted this program on TV, well into the 1960s. Vocalists included Nancy Martin, Marion Mann, June Allison, and the Vagabonds.
* *Breakfast in Hollywood* (1941-48), Hollywood, CA; Tom Breneman, host, included Andy Russell.
* *Buddy Clark Program,* WABC, NBC (1930s+); Vocalist Buddy Clark, sponsored by Carnation.

C.

* *California Melodies,* CBS, KHJ (1932+), Los Angeles, CA; Jo Stafford, guests included Bing Crosby.
* *California Melodies,* Mutual, KHJ (1940-42), Los Angeles, CA; vocals by Maxine Gray.
* *Campbell Room,* CBS Network (1946-47); sponsor Campbell's Soup and Hildegarde's vocals!
* *Camel Caravan, The,* CBS (1930s); Annette Hanshaw, Deane Jan, and Irene Taylor.
* *Camel Caravan, The,* CBS (1936-39). This second program included Benny Goodman's orchestra, opening it up for the swing era. He also established radio

hookups to include broadcasts from various locations around the country. Guest vocalists included Louis Armstrong, Mildred Bailey, Ella Fitzgerald, Billie Holiday, Martha Tilton, Maxine Sullivan and Helen Ward.

* *Cavalcade of America*, WABC (1940), NYC, NY. Sponsored by Du Pont, this program attempted to represent American music from its roots. Its folk singing "guests" included the truly integrated likes of Woody Guthrie, Burl Ives, Leadbelly, and Josh White.
* *Caravan,* CBS (1934); included Connie Boswell, Ruth Etting, sponsored by Oldsmobile.
* *Carson Robinson's Crazy Buckaroo's Hillbilly and Cowboy Music*, CBS (1933-34). Carson's acoustic recordings in the '20s preceded the likes of Jimmie Rodgers and Gene Autry!
* *Chamber Music Society of Lower Basin Street*, NBC (1940-44), NYC, NY; featured Cab Calloway, Dinah Shore, Lena Horne, Dick Todd, and orchestra conducted by Paul Lavalle.
* *Chase and Sandborn Hour*, NBC (1931+). Eddie Cantor—Eddie's variety act did very well on the airwave, following Frenchman Maurice Chevalier on this program. Indeed better (in true retrospective), than his successful (in blackface) contemporary films. Eddie introduced many artists, including the operatic Deanna Durbin, a 1930s success in (later) films. Moreover (for the focus of this book), on subsequent radio programs, he later introduced or featured the likes of vocalists Dinah Shore, Thelma Carpenter, and Eddie Fisher.
* *Chase and Sandborn Coffee Hour*, NBC (1933); featured Ruth Etting and Jimmy Durante.
* *Chase and Sandborn with Edgar Bergan and McCarthy* (1937+); vocalists included Dale Evans.
* *Chesterfield Supper Club*, NBC (1946+). Perry Como would emerge a major entity on this program, backed by the Mitchell Ayers Orchestra. So would Jo Stafford, the King Cole Trio, Peggy Lee, Kay Starr, and Frankie Laine.
* *Chicago's Sweetheart of the Air*, KYW, later WLS (1924-26), Chicago, IL; featured Ruth Etting.
* *Chick Webb's Orchestra*, WJZ (1935+), NYC, NY; vocalists included Ella Fitzgerald.
* *Cities Service with (operatic) Jessica Dragonette and Frank Parker* (1933-34).
* *Clarence Williams and Pals Show*, WOV (1929), NY; featured Clarence Williams, the brilliant composer and piano player (for many, including (wife) Eva Taylor, publisher and bandleader, also pioneered his own Afro-America local radio program, including Eva).
* Cleo Brown, WABC (1935+), NYC, NY; vocal and piano.
* *Club 15*, CBS (1940s) Hollywood, CA; featured Margaret Whiting, the Andrews Sisters, Jerry Gray Orchestra, Dick Haymes, and Evelyn Knight.
* *Clicquot Club Eskimos*, WEAF, later on network NBC (1920s+), NYC, NY. This radio program was sponsored by Clicquot Club ginger ale soda. Its musical orchestra thus became so named after its sponsor. Vocals were usually provided by band member Tom Stacks. Guest vocalists included Annette Hanshaw. After the show left the air, the dance band group retained its name.
* *Coconut Grove Program from the Ambassador Hotel*, KNX (1930-31). This very famous hotel-nightclub of Los Angeles, California, found Gus Arnheim and his Orchestra

playing for the most elite of contemporary Hollywood film stars. It was around this time that Paul Whiteman and the Rhythm Boys had parted company and they found themselves at this gig with Arnheim. Within a few months, the Rhythm Boys broke up, with Bing Crosby as a solo vocal act truly electrifying the place. His crooning style indeed impressed a huge audience, who felt he was singing only for them. Another young baritone, a violinist in Arnheim's Orchestra—by the name of Russ Columbo—sounding much like the crooning Crosby, filled in to sing for Bing when he failed to show up. Many in the hooked-up radio audience, upon hearing these broadcasts, would not find any difference, vocally, between them.

- *Command Performance* (1942+). It was produced by both CBS and NBC for the war effort and broadcast by Armed Forces Radio Service (AFR N). Perhaps the best-known WWII for service personnel, this program perhaps generated the most diverse of all or any entertainments. Guest vocalists included Roy Acuff, Andrews Sisters, Fannie Brice, the Nat Cole Trio, Bing Crosby, Jimmie Davis, Delta Rhythm Boys, Dale Evans, Alice Faye, Helen Forrest, Judy Garland, Lena Horne, Johnny Mercer, Ginger Rogers, Roy Rogers, Tex Ritter, Dinah Shore, Ginny Simms, Frank Sinatra, and Ethel Waters.
- *Conqueror Record Time*, WLS (1931), Chicago, IL. This early Gene Autry entity found Gene's own sponsor—the ARC record label, Conqueror. This label was, more so, marketed by Sears Roebuck, which had initially owned World's Largest Store (WLS).
- Connie Boswell, Ray Noble Orchestra, WAAB (1935+).
- *Consolidated Chemical Radio Hour*, XERA (1938-41), Del Rio, Texas. For some reason, the original Carter Family had been more concerned with recordings and live shows up to this time. In any case, this appliciation entity of folk music, a major force in the development of hillbilly (later termed "country" music), seemingly did not bother with the likes of *National Barn Dance* and *Grand Ole Opery* at this time. When originating in Del Rio, XERA's other transmitter, across the border in Rosarita Beach, Mexico, powered the group's voices throughout the Southwest, upto Canada, as well as in Mexico. Great marketing!
- *Continental Shoes*, Continental Broadcasting (1930), Hollywood, CA; the Boswell Sisters.
- Coon-Sanders Nighthawks Club WDAF (1920s), Kansas City, MO; live from the Hotel Muehlbach, featuring, Carleton Coon and Joe Sanders. Later from Chicago's Blackhawk Restaurant, broadcasts of WGN (1920s-30s).
- *Corn Products Program with Will Osborn*, CBS (1933-34); the bandleader and vocalist.
- *Cotton Club*, CBS, NBC (1930s); live remote broadcasts from the popular NYC nightclub.
- *Cowboy Church*, KEHE (1938), Los Angeles, CA; featured Stuart Hamlin.
- *Cowboy Joe*, KFI (1929), Los Angeles, CA; featured Stuart Hamblen.
- *Crazy Barn Dance* WBT (1930s) (Crazy Water Crystals Co.), Charlotte, NC, and Atlanta, GA; featured Monroe Brothers.
- *Crockett Family of Kentucky* (1924-30s), KMJ, Fresno, CA. ; KNX, LA; WABC, NYC, NY; moved from West Coast to East and featured the Crockett Family. Guests included Riley Puckett, Buell Kazee, and Jo Stafford.

D.

* Dale Evans, WBBM, CBS (1939+), Chicago, IL; featured Dale Evans; slick pop vocals before Roy Rogers!
* *Dance Parade*, WNEW (1930s), NJ; Frank Sinatra.
* Dinah Shore, CBS (1944+). Before TV and Chevrolet, Dinah was sponsored by Bird's Eye Foods.
* *Dick Haymes Show*, CBS (1940s); Dick Haymes and guests.
* Dick Todd, NBC (1930s+).
* *Dinner Bell Roundup*, KXLA (1940s), Pasadena, CA.
* *Dixie Jamboree*, WBT (1944), CBS, Charlotte, NC.
* *Dixie Nightingale*, WOR (1920s), NYC, NY; featured Afro-American Eva Taylor, a fixture on radio since the early 1920s, on this indeed early radio entity.
* *Dodge Victory Hour*, NBC (1928). Perhaps the first attempt at "network" hookup? Dodge's contemporary Victory V-6 model sponsored vaudevillian Fred Stone from Chicago, comic Will Rogers in Hollywood, Al Jolson in New Orleans, and bandleader Paul Whiteman in New York City.
* *Duffy's Tavern*, CBS (1941-42), NBC-Blue (1942+). This popular radio entity depended on its guest stars. Vocalist guests included Bing Crosby and Tony Martin. This program, originally known as *Duffy's Variety*, became so popular during WWII that it was made into a film, of the same name, by 1945. A subsequent early 1950s TV show came later, with less success. While many "Duffy's Taverns" existed, it's a good bet that this program was inspired by a 1920s New York nightspot, of the same name. Its ethnic (Irish) appeal is obvious. Was the later *Jackie Gleason* television program, featuring singer Frank Fontaine perhaps a hint for Gleason? Or, even the likes of the opening of the later (1971) TV sitcom *All in the Family*, with the vocals of Carrol O'Connor and Jean Stapelton? A subsequent TV sequel, *Archie Bunker's Place*, is, more so, familiar with the older radio entity or an older generation of radio listeners.

E., F.

* Ed Sullivan, NYC, NY. Gossip columnist Ed Sullivan started as an interviewer on WABC in 1932. One of his finds was former vaudevillian Jack Benny. By 1936, Ed had his own program, *Ed Sullivan Entertains*, which ran until the early 1950s. As most baby boomers know, his greatest fame came later in television, with his own *Toast of the Town*, with a succession of early "rock" acts. In true retrospective, they dwarfed his own personal and more familiar preferences of older vaudeville acts and personalities. He, moreover, ended up promoting Elvis Presley, about whom he had great misgivings, considering Elvis's gyrating hips. Ed's subsequent introduction of the Beatles, the Rolling Stones, the Supremes and others, made Sullivan an icon in his own right of the latter century, anthem to his own generation and, in comparison with the older, bland acts, obviously un-hip.
* Edna Fisher, KFRC (1920s+), San Francisco, CA. Edna, also a contemporary vocalist, pioneered local San Francisco radio. She also introduced many, including (black) singer-musician Henry Starr.
* *Ethel Merman Time*, WHN (1923+), NYC, NY.
* *Ethel Waters Jazz Masters*, WVG (1922) New Orleans, LA. This early (1922) broadcast featuring Ethel Waters also notes the first appearance of an Afro-American vocalist over the airwaves.

* *Eva Taylor's Crooner Show*, WJZ (1932-33), NYC, NY. Afro-American Eva Taylor, a fixture on radio since the early 1920s, even pulled off her own (local) program.
* *Eveready Hour* (1923-1925). This very early hillbilly entity, Wendell Hall, whose song ditty, "It Ain't Gonna Rain No Mo, '" released on many labels including one on Victor 19171, could also be termed "folk." Wendell also got married "on the air" in 1924! As sponsored by the National Carbon Company, Hall would, more so, remain a radio NYC entity for another decade.
* *Ex-Lax Big Show* with Gertrude Nielson or as Gertrude Niesen,, Lulu McConnell, and Isham Jones, CBS (1933-34).
* *Fats Waller's Rhythm Club*, WWL (1932), Cincinnati, OH. This local show featured Fats Waller, imported from Harlem, to host, play, and sing. Waller, more so, also promoted a fine (black) vocalist, Una Mae Carlisle, on this program.
* Fats Waller show, this similar Waller program also featured him playing and singing.
* *Fifteen Minutes of Bing Crosby*, CBS (1931-32). This first solo (network) Crosby program eventually found a sponsor with Cremo Cigars. As a result, Bing became known as the "Cremo singer."
* *Fitch Bandwagon*, NBC (1937+). It featured bandleader hosts, sponsored by Fitch Soap, perhaps best remembered in the mid-1940s, featuring bandleader Phil Harris and (then) wife, Alice Faye.
* *Fleishmann Hour with Rudy Vallee*, WEAF, NBC (1930+), NYC, NY. Rudy introduced to national network radio the likes of many new voices such as Alice Faye, Dorothy Lamour, Francis Langford, the Mills Brothers, Midge Williams, Goebel Reeves, Kate Smith, and Lee Wiley.
* *Florsheim Frolics*, NBC (1931?); an early Jane Froman program (Florsheim Shoe Co.).
* *Flow Gently, Sweet Rhythm*, CBS. (1939-41). Hosted by black actor Canada Lee, this rare Afro-American prime-time entity featured Maxine Sullivan, as backed by John Kirby's Orchestra.
* *Follies of the Air*, CBS (1932+). This radio show aired before Broadway legend Florence Ziegfeld passed away. Among many Broadway entities, Fanny Brice, dropping vocals, introduced her radio character "Baby Snooks," subsequently a huge radio entity. Later known as *Ziegfeld Follies of the Air*. Guests included Ruth Etting, Helen Morgan, and (vaudevillian) Benny Fields.
* *Freddy Rich Entertains* CBS (1933-34). with Mildred Bailey, Jack White, Do Re Mi Trio, and The Eton Boys,
* *Freddie Rose's Song Shop*, WSM, Nashville, TN. Somehow, vaudevillian and songwriter Fred Rose found his way to Nashville, hosting this popular (1933) radio program featuring "Tin Pan Alley" show tunes. Later, Rose would collaborate with Gene Autry, Roy Acuff—founding Acuff-Rose music publishing in 1942—and the likes of Hank Williams.

G.

* *Gene Autry and the International Buckle Busters*, WJJD (1931-32), Chicago, IL; mornings
* *Gene Autry's Melody Ranch*, CBS (1940+). It was Gene's own national program, sponsored by Wrigley's Spearmint Gum. Apart from sidekick Smiley Burnette, Gene's many (vocalist) guests included the Jimmy Wakely Trio, and Johnny Bond (also the title of a contemporary 1940 Autry film).
* George Burns and Gracie Allen; both former vaudevillians started on radio with popular bandleader Guy Lombardo, featuring vocals by his brother Carman. It was

aired as the *Robert Burns Panatella Program* from 1932 to 1933 on CBS. They also made films. Like others, they featured vocalists often, with a major "find" of Tony Martin, a featured vocalist found in this book. Among many sponsors were White Owl Cigars, noting George's use of cigars, something he would retain for later (visual) television. Subsequent moves between networks (CBS) and (NBC), found George and Gracie cultural icons before they moved to the more familiar eyes and ears of baby boomers on early 1950s' television. (The radio theme, also used on TV, originally a 1920 Broadway entity ditty "The Love Nest," as penned by Otto Harbach and Louis Hirsch, is also a Frank Crumit vocal pick, noted within this book.) After Gracie died in (1964), comic George Burns, who lived to be a hundred, became a huge film entity in 1975 (The Sunshine Boys) and a (1979) novelty recording entity, recording Sonny Throckmorton's "I Wish I Was Eighteen Again". Or was this a parody of the more pogient acoustic "I Wish I Was Single Again", by George's older (1925) contemporary (whom George probably never met), the blind-vocalist, guitarist, songwriter & Georgia radio entity, Riley Puckett?

* George Jessel, CBS (1933-34). Jessel was a comic and a Broadway entity who could also sing. He also featured contemporary vocalists, including Vera Van.
* George Olson and Ethel Shutta, WEAF (1936); after their divorce, for the money?
* *GI Jive*, AFRN. Johnny Mercer's penned contemporary recording was also a popular WWII entity. Featured a sexy record-spinning DJ "GI Jill,"(Martha Wilkerson).
* *GI Journal*, AFRN (1942+); another popular contribution to WWII entertainment.
* *Ginny Simms Show*. Ginny had appeared on radio as early as 1932, before becoming a band singer. After leaving Kay Kyser, she went on network NBC (1942+), then on CBS. Ginny featured many, as well as introduced nationally, the vocals of Mike Douglas, the future baby boomer TV show icon.
* *Golden State Blue Monday Jamboree*, KFRC (1931) San Francisco, CA. Jane Green's vocals.
* *Grand Ole Opery, The*, WSM (1925+), Nashville, TN. By 1940, this program became a network pickup on NBC. Like many others, this radio program had evolved into something bigger, over time. It had starred as a clone of Chicago's WLS' *Barn Dance*, also using that name in 1925, using Nashville's WSM station. As sponsored by National Life Insurance, and Purina, the program's first broadcasts were made in a studio of the National Life Insurance building, in Nashville. The program was then moved to newer and larger locations over time, with radio hookup, including that of the Hillsboro Theater, the Dixie Tabernacle, the War Memorial Auditorium, and finally the Ryman Auditorium in 1943. By this time, the name of the program had evolved into *Grand Ole Opery* and had dwarfed all its rivals, including the Chicago *National Barn Dance*. Over the years, this "love" broadcast included many, including the likes of Roy Acuff, Eddy Arnold, Judy Canova, Red Foley, Bill Monroe, Goebel Reeves, Tex Ritter, Kay Starr, Ernest Tubb, and Hank Williams. Of special note—(Canadian) radio entity Hank Snow promoted his folk songs, still American, if North American.
* *Guest Star*; Treasury Department sponsored program, which noted the selling of "war bonds" to win WWII, and after. While not an official AFRN entity, its broadcasts to service people around the world had the same uplifting effect. Contemporary vocalists included the Andrews Sisters, Louis Armstrong, Gene Autry, Fannie Brice, the King Cole Trio, Buddy Clark, Bing Crosby, Vic Damone, Doris Day, Johnny Desmond, Dick Haymes, Hildegarde, Lena Horne, Al Jolson, Peggy Lee, Tony Martin, Ozzie and Harriet Nelson, Andy Russell, Frank Sinatra, Ginny Simms, Jo Stafford, Kay Starr, Maxine Sullivan, and Ethel Waters.

* *Gus Arnheim's Orchestra*, KNX (1930-31), Los Angeles, CA. Broadcast from LA's Coconut Grove, it featured the Rhythm Boys, plus solo efforts by Bing Crosby and Loyce Whiteman. Bing Crosby, after slowly emerging as a solo artist, found great recognition and also created a sensation.

H.

* *Hal Kemp Program*, CBS (1935-36); vocals by Skinnay Ennis and Maxine Gray; sponsored by Eno Salts.
* *Happy Baker's*, CBS (1933-34); Phil Ducy, Frank Luther, and Jack Parker—male trio—with Harriet Lee, noted as a contemporary "deep-voiced blues singer."
* *Happiness Boys*, WEAF (1923-33). New York, NY. The antics of vaudeville performers Billy Jones and Ernie Hare were the first marketed radio commodity. Sponsored by the Happiness Candy Company, the popular act was to also exploit themselves, as many of their acoustic recordings were to be featured. It is also a sure bet that many recordings, including the contemporary (comic strip) caricature Barney Google, on Edison 51155, also a plug, sounded better on radio. So did the same record's flip side "Don't Bring Lulu," which was not a plug but a novel pun about contemporary flappers and social behavior. Moreover, it's a sure bet that the surviving recording, "How Do You Do," on Edison 51500, opened the program. Another novelty, which may be considered a plug, "Does the Spearmint Lose its Flavor on the Bedpost Overnight," on (Cameo-504), is also contemporary (1920s) commentary. More so, this novelty, had eyes for the future! Indeed, as later (1961) ditty, as "Does Your Chewing Gun Loose Its Flavor," on Dot 15911, by Britisher Lonnie Donegan, found favor and sales as a rock-era entity.
* *Harlem*, NBC (1937). A short-lived network prime-time program, it was hosted by Louis Armstrong. Guests included vocalists Cleo Brown and Mills Brothers, sponsored by Fleishmann's Yeast.
* *Harlem Serenade with Hall Johnson Singers*, CBS (1934-35).
* *He's in the Jailhouse Now*, WSB (1922), Atlanta, GA; a folk program featuring one Ernest Rogers, moreover it was years earlier before Jimmy Rogers had started to record.
* *Health and Happiness Show*, WSM (1949), Nashville, TN; Hank Williams and wife Audrey.
* *Heigh Ho, Everybody, Heigh Ho*, WABC, NYC, NY. Rudy Vallee's successful (1928) gig here was greatly enhanced by live radio remote. Like never before, NYC's "Heigh Ho" Club became the best-known club in NYC, with Rudy Vallee becoming even more popular, like no other solo act before him, eventually outlasting his gig at the club and the club itself. (Rudy eventually recorded his radio greeting as "Heigh Ho, Everybody, Heigh Ho" in 1929.
* Henry Starr, KPO (1930s), San Francisco, CA; featured (black) singer-musician Henry Starr.
* *Hi Hat Hattie and Her Boys*, KNX (1930s), Los Angeles, CA; featured actress and singer Hattie McDaniel. (Hattie had been a Bessie Smith-inspired blues entity in the 1920s.)
* *Hildegarde's Raleigh Room*. NBC (1944-46) Sponsored by Raleigh Cigarettes).
* *Hollywood Barn Dance*, KHJ, CBS (1932+), Hollywood, CA, West Coast (C & W); featured the Songs of Pioneers, Stafford Sisters, Eddie Dean, and others.
* *Hollywood Hotel*, CBS (1938-39); Frances Langford.
* *Hollywood on the Air*, KECA-NBC (1933-34). This program also previewed upcoming films with special promotional material from contemporary musical entities.

Guests included Bing Crosby, Ruth Etting, Jane Froman, Ginger Rogers, and Gene Austin.

* *Home Town Boys,* Skillet Lickers, Riley Puckett, Roba Stanley, Moonshine Kate (1922+) (WSB), Atlanta, Ga.
* *Hootenanny*, CBS (1947); featured the likes of Woody Guthrie, Pete Seeger, Brownie McGee, and Cisco Houston. (Later revived as a TV entity in the early 1960s).

I., J.

* Ink Spots, WJZ (1935+), NYC, NY.
* *Iowa Barn Dance Frolic*, WHO (1932+); Des Moines Iowa.
* *Jamboree*, WWVA (1933+), Wheeling, WV.
* *Jane Froman and her Orchestra*, NBC, WJZ (1931+); sometimes spelled "Frohman."
* *Jack Benny's Canada Dry Ginger Ale Show*, NBC (1932-33). Vaudevillian comic Jack Benny launched his first radio program in 1932. His bandleader, George Olsen, featured vocals by Ethel Shutta, who was married to Olsen at this time. Shutta's rendering of "Rock-a-Bye Moon" became Benny's radio theme, which caused confusion when they left the popular show. After a few years, Benny used the Bing Crosby hit "Love in Bloom." In true retrospective, it was a major loss for Shutta. Benny's success in radio lasted well into the 1950s with various sponsors (including Jell-0, Chevy Automobiles, Grape Nuts, and Lucky Strike cigarettes); he also moved between networks NBC and CBS. His later jump to TV is, moreover, well known to baby boomers, finding the likes of the later radio regulars who included announcer Don Wilson, Mary Livingston (his wife); comics Mel Blanc and Eddie "Rochester" Anderson; and novelty vocalist Phil Harris and (Irish tenor) Dennis Day.
* *Jack Oakie's College*, CBS (1936-38). The actor and comic Jack Oakie's Los Angeles program found vocals provided by a young teenager, Judy Garland. It was sponsored by Camel cigarettes.
* *Jack Webb Program*, KFRC, ABC (1946), San Francisco, CA; included Midge Williams.
* *Jimmie Davis*, KWKH (1932+), Shreveport, LA. Jimmie Davis, another would-be Jimmie Rodgers, found this local, deep south station a fine way to exploit his talent. Indeed, his popularity would become so exploited that he would (later) become governor of Louisiana. More so, the power of the airwaves is very much proven here, in a rural and local setting, without networks. Other hillbilly entities able to promote themselves on this station included Leon Chappelear and the Shelton Brothers.
* *Jimmy Durante Program*, NBC (1943+); Jimmy Durante. Vocalists featured included Peggy Lee and Georgia Gibbs. Among his sponsors were Camel cigarettes and Rexall Drugs.
* *Jimmie Rodgers Program*, KMAC (1932), San Antonio, Texas. This local station perhaps featured Jimmie Rodgers on the air before he died (in 1933). It was also possible, when Jimmie couldn't fulfill his commitments that his records could be played on the air! Indeed an odd event before 1942!
* *Jimmie Rodgers Entertainers*, WWNC (1927), Ashville, NC; Jimmie Rodgers.
* John McCormack, tenor, NBC (1933-34); the old Irish tenor entity of the acoustic age.
* *Johnny Presents Ginny Simms*, CBS (1940s); Ginny Simms solo!
* Johnny Marvin, tenor, WEAF, NBC (1932-35), NYC, NY.

* Judy Canova, CBS, NBC (1943+). While heavily stereotyped, Judy's hillbilly accent, found her vocals limited. Nevertheless, its influence continued for almost a decade.
* *Jubilee* NBC, AFRS (1940s), Hollywood, CA. This (mostly Afro-American) WWII program featured a black DJ host, Ernie "Bubbles" Whiteman. Contemporary guest vocalists included Cab Calloway, the Charioteers, Nat Cole Trio, Bing Crosby, the Delta Rhythm Boys, Ella Fitzgerald, Lena Horne, Helen Humes, the Ink Spots, Louis Jordan, Peggy Lee, Ella Mae Morse, Martha Tilton, Valaida Snow (with trumpet), Maxine Sullivan, Ethel Waters, and Josh White.

K., L.

* *Kate Smith Sings* (1931+). Kate Smith was indeed a huge woman, but among all the mean jokes about her frame, her crooning job heard on radio was indeed a huge success. While Kate worked for the likes of NBC and CBS, this early program was perhaps her best? Kate would subsequently promote the likes of General Foods, Calumet Baking Soda, A & P Food Stores, Sanka Coffee, Terriplane Cars, and Grape Nut Flakes—later, on TV, surviving radio.
* Kay Starr, ABC (1948); Kay Starr and guests.
* *Kay Kyser's Kollege of Musical Knowledge*, NBC, others (1938-40s). Bandleader Kay Kyser was at least a good musician and showcased the likes of such vocalist as Ginny Simms, Harry Babbitt, Sully Mason, Ish Kabibble, Mike Douglas (the later TV host—known to many baby boomers), and, among others, the King Sisters, as well as a few films. (Inspired by the radio program he, more so, sold, through the years, Lucky Strike cigarettes and Pillsbury products.)
* *Kellogg's College Prom Pep on the Air Program*, NBC Blue Network (1933-34); featured Ruth Etting, bandleader Red Nichols, and guests.
* *Kraft Music Hall*, NBC Red (1935-40s), Hollywood, CA. While hosted by others, this program found its greatest success with the likes of Bing Crosby. Within the eventual ten-year time frame of this program, Crosby would sell much cheese, as well as feature just about everybody else in contemporary show business. More so, after a few years, Bing became identified as a very witty host, on par with contemporary radio comics Jack Benny and Fred Allen.
* *La Palina Club Smoker*, CBS (1920s); guests included vocals from Johnny Marvin.
* *Let's Dance*, NBC, WEAF, NBC (1934-35), NYC, NY. This early network program brought bandleaders Benny Goodman and Fletcher Henderson's "swing" into the national spotlight. Sponsors included National Biscuit Co-Ritz Crackers. Vocalists included Buddy Clark and Helen Ward.
* *Let's Listen to Phil Harris*, NBC (1933-34); Bandleader Harris and Leah Ray's blues songs.
* *Light Crust Doughboys*, KFJZ, WBAP (1931+), Fort Worth, TX. Sponsored by Light Crust Flour & Elevator Co., this group, originally known as the "Fort Worth Doughboys," was originally managed by Pat "Pappy" O'Daniel, until 1935. ("Pappy" would later sponsor his son's own "swing band" and radio program as well as successfully become a future Texas governor and senator). Rotating members of the Light Crust Doughboys at one time or another would include the likes of swing band specialists Milton Brown, Bob Wills, and Tommy Duncan.
* *Lombardo Land Program*, WEAF, NBC (1930s); popular (Canadian) bandleader Guy Lombardo and His Royal Canadians; featured vocals by (brother) Carmen.

* *Lone Star Rangers*, WOR (1932) NYC, NY; Tex Ritter vocals.
* Louis Armstrong Orchestra, WABC (1936).
* *Louisiana Hayride*, KWKH (1948+), Shreveport, LA. This relatively late entity, not related to the earlier Boswell Sisters' single release of 1933, defined Hank William before the *Grand Ole Opery*. It would also introduce to C & W radio audiences the likes of Kitty Wells, who was to become a major entity in the next decade of C & W. Later, in the mid-1950s, among others, the program featured George Jones, Johnny Horton, Elvis Presley, and Johnny Cash.

M.

* *Major Bowes Capital Family*, NBC (1933-34). Edward Bowes perhaps started his "amateur" format here. Bowes moved to CBS in the latter 1930s. In any case, Major Bowes may be credited as to later discovering "the Hoboken Four." (They included the likes of Frank Tamburro, Jimmy Petro, Patty Prince, and Frank Sinatra). Other voices included the operatic Beverly Stills and Robert Merrill, as well as Teresa Brewer.
* Maddox Brothers and Rose, KTRB (1937), Modesto, CA; early Maddox family on radio.
* *Magic Key of RCA*, NBC Blue, WJZ (1935-39), Los Angeles, CA. The mid-1930s found RCA Victor promoting new record players—Magic Brain—which stacked more than one record for continuous play. Victor and Bluebird Record sleeves for this period note these portable turntables. Amazing? A diverse guest format for this program included Gene Austin, Ruth Etting, Jane Froman, Paul Robeson. Dick Todd, Rudy Vallee, Bea Wain, and Midge Williams.
* *Mail Call*, AFRN (1942+); another armed forces radio program.
* *Majestic Theatre of the Air*, CBS, WNBC (1929); featured Ruth Etting, Eddie Cantor.
* *Make Believe Ballroom*, WNEW (1935+), NYC, NY. Hosted by Martin Block, this very controversial program perhaps did the most to change over the whole radio industry. In essence, after 1941, Block found a cheaper format to host a radio program—play records on the air! Probably when he could not find a live guest star to appear? Apposed by publishers (ASCAP), the program was upheld in court, with rival publisher BMI, who had allowed use of its recorded interests to be played. This major program's use of recordings generally banned from radio play since 1933 in the United States indeed changed history. Why pay a band when recordings are available?

* *Marion Hutton*, Mutual (1948); Marion Hutton, Clark Dennis, and the Ray Sinatra Orchestra.
* *Martin and Lewis Show*, NBC (1948-49); the popular Dean Martin and Jerry Lewis act on radio!
* *Maxwell House-Martha Tilton Time*, NBC (1941+); Martha Tilton.
* *Maxwell Hour Show Boat*, NBC (1933-34); Lanny Ross, tenor; Annette Hanshaw was somehow described as a blues singer; Conrad Thibault, baritone; Murial Wilson, soprano; Molasses "n" January; and Don Voorhee's Show Boat band.
* *Maxwell House Coffee Time*, NBC (1940s); King Sisters, Tony Martin, and Frances Langford.
* McClatchy Broadcast Network, KFBK (1939+), Sacramento, CA, also included KFWB in Hollywood, CA, and other West Coast stations; sponsored by Anacin aspirin. Pioneered West Coast and western C & W, especially the Maddox Brothers and Rose.

* *Merv Griffin Show*, KFRC, Mutual (1946-48), San Francisco, CA; featured vocals by Merv Griffin, the (later) band singer with Freddie Martin and the still later TV entity and icon.
* *Midday Merry-Go-Round*, WNOX (1934), Knoxville, TN; featured Roy Acuff.
* *Midnight Jamboree*, WSM (1940s+); Ernest Tubb's program from his Nashville Record Shop!
* *Midwestern Hayride*, WLW, Cincinnati, OH; programmed live hillbilly, and C & W.
* *Mildred Bailey Program*, CBS (1944); Mildred Bailey.
* Mills Brothers, WLW (1931), Cincinnati, OH. The *original* Mills Brothers (John, Herbert, Harry, and Donald) considered the ultimate "radio" entity? As performers in and around Cincinnati, Ohio, radio myth has it that the siblings had forgotten their instruments (except for a guitar) when arriving at the radio station. They then improvised vocals on the air for instruments, and indeed solidified their unique act. The popularity of "four boys and a guitar" indeed became novel!
* *Moon River*, WLW (1930s+), Cincinnati, OH; featured Doris Day and Rosemary Clooney.
* *Music from Hollywood*, CBS Network (1937), Hollywood, CA. Hosted by the fine singing Alice Faye, this program was sponsored by Chesterfield Cigarettes.
* *Music That Satisfies*, CBS (1932-33). Program hosts included the Boswell Sisters, Bing Crosby, Ruth Etting., Jane Froman and was sponsored by Chesterfield cigarettes.

N., O.

* *National Barn Dance*, WLS (1924+), NBC, Chicago, IL. Yup. While Chicago was the heir to transplanted New Orleans Jazz in the early 1920s, it also became a magnet for folk and hillbilly acts. Originally *Barn Dance*, this local program became "National" with NBC, in 1933. Indeed, the very origins of country music was found here, before Nashville's *Grand Ole Opery* by a year. Performers included Gene Autry, Roy Acuff, Rex Allen, Eddie Dean, George Gobel, Riley Puckett, Goebel Reeves, the Hoosier Hot Shots, Red Foley, Patsy Montana, Lulu Belle, and Scotty—all found huge recognition here—among others.
* *Negro Achievement Hour*, WABC (1930); various contributors, including Alberta Hunter.
* *Nestlé's Chocolateers*, CBS (1933-34); Ethel Shutta, and Don Bestor's Orchestra. Chocolate!
* Nick Lucas, WEBH (1924), Chicago, IL.
* Nick Lucas, NBC (1931-32); sponsored by Campbell's Soup.
* *Ninety-Nine Men and a Girl*, CBS (1939). The "girl" was one Hildegarde Loretta Sell, whose name on the show was Hildegarde. The ninety-nine men were members of an orchestra. Popular girl!
* *Noonday Variety Show*, WDAY (1930s), Fargo, SD; featured Peggy Lee.
* *Oke and Woody Show*, KFVD (1937), Hollywood, CA; featured (hillbilly) Jack Guthrie and (cousin) Woody Guthrie.
* *Oklahoma's Yodeling Cowboy*, KVOO (1928-29), Tulsa, OK. Gene Autry started here.
* *Old Dominion Barn Dance*, WRVA (1940s+), Richmond, VA. The Carter family, which by 1941 dropped Sarah and A. P., played here later, in 1946. This newer group consisted of (original) member Maybelle with her daughters Anita and June, who became known to baby boomers.
* *Old-Fashioned Barn Dance*, KMOX (1930), St Louis, MO.

* *Old Gold Hour*, WABC, CBS (1928-30), NYC, NY. The popular bandleader Paul Whiteman's spotlight never dimmed in the 1920s. This broadcast, as sponsored by the tobacco company, provided the Rhythm Boys (Al Rinker, Harry Barris, and Bing Crosby himself) some valuable airtime and, more so, for Jack Fulton, Charles Gaylord, Austin Young, the Ponce Sisters and Mildred Bailey, within a few years.
* *One-Half Hour*, NBC (1940s), Los Angeles, CA; Johnny Mercer.
* *One-Night Stand,* AFRS (1940s).

P.

* *Parade of Stars*, CBS, NBC (1931+). Both networks contributed to this National Unemployment Relief program, well before the emergence of Franklin Roosevelt's 1932 election and his government relief measures for the Great Depression in 1933. Contemporary vocalists who contributed for free on this remote fed program included Eddie Cantor, Morton Downey, and Bing Crosby.
* *Paramount on Parade*, CBS (1930), NYC, NY. Fats Waller started singing, while playing, on this program. (This title also became a title of an unrelated Paramount film short).
* *Penthouse Serenade*, WEAF, NBC (1935), NYC, NY; Don Mario, tenor.
* *Perfectly Frank* (1950s). This (very) later radio program breaks the rules of this book. As its own time after 1950 was perhaps dated by contemporary airtime, the timeless and flawless creativity of Sinatra is not. Moreover, Frank's early Capital records are exploited, but Frank goes even further. While the time for the exploitation of rhythm and blues and rock and roll had already evolved, so had Frank! This program, when found and heard, puts Frank in a category by himself. (It is also much better than any other previous Sinatra outing and, ironically, less known and heard!)
* *Pete Kelly's Blues*, NBC (1951). Actor and musician Jack Webb's crime drama about a fictional bandleader in the 1920s also featured a lot of jazz. (Later, a huge 1955. TV entity).
* *Pepsodent Radio Show* starring Bob Hope (1938+). There was a lot of tooth as well as nose in the career of Bob Hope before 1938, yet this program, after a few others, which included W*oodbury Soap,* put the former vaudevillian and budding film entity in the ears of many! The films and subsequent USO shows (beginning through WW II through Vietnam), TV and familiarized profile, even without friends like Bing Crosby, made the British-born Hope part of Americana itself. Hope provided a boost for many careers, including, for the purposes of this book, the vocal talents of Tony Bennett, in 1950. While not a featured vocalist within this book, it is, more so, a fact that Hope could carry a tune, noting his adapted radio theme, later used for television and personal appearances. Indeed, "Thanks for the Memory" remains an original classic introduced by him (and Shirley Rose, originally as a B-side recording. See text elsewhere in this book—Musical Film Picks).
* Phil Baker and Hal Kemps Orchestra, CBS (1930s); vocals by Skinnay Ennis.
* *Philco Radio Time—Bing Crosby's Show*, ABC (1946-48). This upstart program found Bing Crosby, backed by a Skitch Henderson-led orchestra, using the new *tape* process, that had originally been pioneered in Nazi Germany before the war. Sponsored by Philco, this (then) revolutionary change from live programs (or faulty transcription records) inspired many others. This process also helped the recording industry at large, ptting recorded masteres on tape instead of metal discs. (Within this post-WWII

period, the playing of recordings as a (cheaper) broadcasting tool became the norm. This competition, as well as the contemporary advent of TV, would upstage Crosby, and more so the whole commercial radio culture that had sprung up since 1920.)

* *Piano Sitting Sob Sister of Song*, CBS (1933-34); Helen Morgan, Albert Bartlett, and Tango King.
* Pickens Sisters, Jane, Grace, Patti, Helen WEAF (1930s), NYC, NY; the vocal group.
* *Pinex Program*, CBS, Little Jack Little Orch. (1930s). Little Jack Little, the already known vocalist and songwriter of the 1920s, had by the early 1930s, become a singing bandleader.
* *Program of Songs by Lee Wiley*, CBS (1936). This radio program found Lee adapting Donald Heywood-penned ditty "I'm Coming Virginia," the already old Ethel Waters hit of 1926, with great skill. The creativity of this program (when found) indeed put it ahead of all its contemporary musical competitors. (It's a pity that Lee became very ill for a while, in the late 1930s. It indeed lost her much exposure.)
* *Pursuit of Happiness, The*, CBS (1939); Norman Corvin was the host and it featured Paul Robeson.

Q., R.

* *Radio Franks*, WMCA (1926+), NYC, NY; featured vocals of Frank Bessinger and Frank Wright, who subsequently operated a popular restaurant. Later, Jerry White replaced Frank Wright.
* *Radio Hall of Fame*, CBS (1943+). Sponsored by Philco, this program ran about three years. Among its (guest) vocalists were the Andrews Sisters, Bing Crosby, and Martha Tilton.
* *Renfro Valley Barn Dance*, WHAS (1937-50s), Louisville, KY, C & W. Also carried by NBC Blue, CBS and MBS (Mutual), this program drifted from WLW in Cincinnati to Dayton, Ohio. Featured vocals included the Coon Creek Girls, Red Foley, Molly O'Day, and Homer and Jethro.
* *Reveille with Beverly*, AFRS (1940s); featured a hot record-spinner Beverly Jean Hay. (Also a contemporary film of the same name, with Ann Miller as Beverly. Great exposure from Ann!)
* *Rita Rio*, NBC (1940s). This vocalist-bandleader also led her own all-girl band.
* *Roemer's Homers Radio Hour*, WMCA, CBS (1930+), NYC, NY; featured Ozzie Nelson and Orchestra and Harriet Hilliard, sponsored by Roemer Furniture.
* Romeo of Song, Russ Columbo, NBC (1931-32). Russ's baritone vocals rivaled those of Bing Crosby's.
* *Roy Rogers Show*, Mutual (1944+). This cowboy entity of film had also been a member of the Sons of the Pioneers vocal group. Along with Dale Evans—a former band singer, Roy's radio, film, and (later) TV products founded a huge marketing entity. (In true retrospective, very much more than contemporaries Gene Autry and Tex Ritter (who had both preceded him) ever dreamed. Perhaps it was Dale, who also found more than a few very young female baby boomers admirers?) In any case, these radio broadcasts, in true retrospective, seem to stand up better than Roy's many films and early television, as well as his numerous recordings.
* *Rhythm at Eight*, WABC, CBS (1935); Ethel Merman; sponsored by Lysol.
* *Rhythm Club*, WABC, CBS (1934), NYC, NY. This local NYC program should not be confused with Fats Wallers's previously named Cincinatti radio gig.

* Rudy Vallee, WABC (1928), NYC, NY. Vallee created a live sensation over the air with his remote radio pick up from NYC's Heigh Ho Club. Within a year, in 1929, he switched to other clubs, including his own, as well as broadcast for both WJZ and WNCA.
* *Ry-Krisp Program*, NBC (1934-35), NYC, NY; featured Eva Taylor.

S.

* *Saddle Mountain Roundup*, KVOO (1938), Tulsa, OK.
* *Saturday Night Jubilee*, WREC (1930s), Memphis, TN; Kay Starr.
* *Saturday Night Serenade*, CBS (1947-48); Vic Damone, sponsored by Pet Milk.
* *Saturday Night Swing Show*, CBS (1938+); featured various swing bands, including live remote broadcasts from Europe. Time changes? Tired?
* *Sealtest Show Presents Rudy Vallee*, NBC (1940-43).
* *Seven Star Revue*, CBS (1933-34); featured the likes of Nino Martini, Jane Froman, Julious Tannen, and Ted Husing.
* *Shell Chateau*, NBC (1935+). Broadcast from NYC and Los Angeles, it featured Al Jolson; sponsored by Shell Oil Co.
* *Singing Brakeman, The*, WTFF (1928), Washington, DC. Jimmie Rodgers, the pivotal entity of what was to become country music, put in some good air licks here. This railroad theme also followed him throughout his career, as well as in the 1929 film short by the same name.
* *Singing Sam* (1930-34). This entity also made phonograph records. He also sold Barbasol and Coke.
* *Songs by Sinatra*, CBS (1945-47). Frank at his best, sponsored by Old Gold cigarettes.
* *Songs to Delight Your Ears and Heart*, NBC (1934), Los Angeles, CA. The importance of Russ Columbo cannot be discarded. Along with Bing Crosby, his crooning on radio, ushered in a new era in popular music. (Like Crosby, many of these early radio programs survive. In true retrospective, even as bits and pieces, they are well worth the time and energy to seek out.)
* *Songs of the Pioneers*, KFWB (1934+), Los Angeles, CA; included Len Sly, later known as Roy Rogers.
* *Spotlight Review*, CBS (1948); vocalist Dorothy Shay, and the Spike Jones Orchestra; sponsored by Coca-Cola.
* Stafford Sisters, KHJ (early 1930s), Los Angeles, CA. This sister-act of siblings consisting of Pauline, Christine, and Jo would be an early exposure to fame for Jo Stafford.
* *Stage Door Canteen* (1942+). Live guests for service people, just like the contemporary film!
* *Stagebrush Western Theatre*, KHL (1940s), Los Angeles, CA; C & W.
* *Starr Time*, WREC (1930s), Memphis, TN; Kay Starr.
* *Stars in the Making*, KPO, NBC (1930s), San Francisco, CA; featured Edna Fisher's vocals.
* *Summer Session*, Mutual (1938); vocals by Nan Wynn.
* *Sunkist Musical Cocktails*, KHT, CBS (1930), Los Angeles, CA; featured Bing Crosby, locally.
* *Suppertime Frolics*, WJJD (mid-1940s), Chicago, IL; C & W.
* *Swingtime*. A popular AFRN program during WWII.

T., U, V.

* *Texaco Town Radio Show* (1937); Eddie Cantor, including Pinky Tomlin.
* *Time to Smile*, NBC (1940-46); Eddie Cantor, including Dinah Shore and Thelma Carpenter.
* Tito Guizar romantic Mexican tenor sings as six hands pluck three harps, CBS (1933-34); sponsored by Brillo.
* *Tom Glazer's Ballad Box* (1945-47); the Almanac Singers.
* *Town Hall Party*, KFDV (1940s+), Los Angeles, CA.
* *Town Hall Tonight*, WEAF (1930s+); hosted by Broadway entity and comic Fred Allen, Portland Hoffa, and many vocalists, especially noting Bob Eberly.
* *Treasury Star Parade*. This program, sponsored by the US Treasury Department, was one of many that promoted the sales of war bonds during WWII. A drama show, it featured contemporary vocalists, including the likes of Jane Froman and Rudy Vallee.
* *Van Heusen Program*, WOR—actually originating signal in Newark, NJ; CBS, NYC, NY (1929). It featured Annette Hanshaw.
* *Vanity Fair Pond's Program* with Victor Young and Lee Wiley, NBC (1933-34).
* *Vaughn De Leath's Musical Program Show*, WEAF (1922) NYC, NY. While starting on WJZ, a year earlier, the program name is not known, nor are any transcriptions found. This program also invited Afro-Americans (such as Eva Taylor), a rare and radical move in those times of deep-rooted segregation. Vaughn was also previously involved with Lee De Forest (the noted inventor of the radio) in a trial broadcast in 1920. Her radio presence assured her the position as the "first lady" of radio.
* *Vaughan de Leath Program*, NBC Blue (1938-39); Vaughan still going strong in the 1930s.
* *Viva American*, CBS (1940s); Mexican-flavored music, featured vocals by Elsa Miranda.

W.

* *Waltz Time with Abe Lyman and Frank Munn*, NBC (1933-34).
* *Wayfaring Stranger, The*, CBS (1940-42); folk vocals by Burl Ives.
* *Wendell Hall, the Red Headed Music Maker*, WEAF, NBC (1930s); sponsored by F. W. Fitch.
* *Wheeling Jamboree*, WWVA (1940s+), Wheeling, WV; C & W.
* *Whispering Baritone*, WMCA (1925+), NYC, NY. While a throat injury during WWI slowed him down, Jack Smith, or "Whispering" Jack Smith, became a radio entity, as well as recording artist directly due to the new electric process, which picked up novel utterances, including whispers.
* *Whispering Pianist*, WSB (1924), Atlanta, GA. Pianist Art Gillham, after some success in Chicago, became known for his novel whisper vocals here. A year later, on NYC's WJZ, Art became involved with radio rival "Whispering" Jack Smith, who produced a similar vocal.
* *Woodbury Program with Bing Crosby and Lennie Hayton*, KHJ, CBS (1933-34), Los Angeles, CA. It was another early Crosby program with the contemporary bandleader. While selling the soap, guest group vocalists included the Boswell Sisters, the Mills Brothers, and the three Williams Sisters—Alice, Ethelyn and Laura. Single entities included Kay Thompson and Irene Taylor.

* *Woody and Lefty Lou*, KFDV (1938), Los Angeles, CA; Woody Guthrie and Lou Crissman.
* World's first drive-in radio station, KTYL (late 1940s), Mesa, AZ. This creative idea used the fairly new drive-in world's original movie concept for C & W music. Just drive in, turn on your car radio, and watch singers and musicians perform, within a plated glass window!

X., Y., Z.

* *Your All-Time Hit Parade*, CBS (1943-44). This offshoot of *Your Hit Parade* found the likes of Frances Langford, Frank Sinatra, and Sophie Tucker. Since this program consisted of older and standard tunes, the addition of the novel Sophie Tucker seemingly made it entertaining.
* *Your Hit Parade*, CBS (1935-40s). As an important tracking device, this long-running gimmick of a program attempted to calculate the popularity of contemporary song titles by record and sheet music sales, number of performances heard on radio and jukeboxes, and as seen in various personal appearances. While the playing of records was largely prohibited, a song ditty did not have to earn anything necessarily, for a recording artist, or artist. In reality, this was a good thing because its sponsor (Lucky Strike tobacco) would have gone broke looking for the public's favorite version of any given song. Moreover, the country's largest disc seller of popular music between 1935 and 1945 was Bing Crosby, and he already had a radio program sponsored by Kraft cheese at this time. As an added moment of flair, the firm of Price, Waterhouse, and Co. would deliver its results, in order, during the show. No cheating was allowed, which made it something to think about during a whole week. It became almost like "hearing" trade magazines like *Billboard* or *Variety*. Radio folklore has it that President Franklin Roosevelt was a listener. With this format of regular vocalists, the show proceeded over the years to even develop entities of its own. Some of the vocalists who would appear on this program included Bell Baker, Buddy Clark, Doris Day, Dick Haymes, Hildegarde, Frances Langford, Lanny Ross, Andy Russell, Dinah Shore, Ginny Simms, Frank Sinatra, Conrad Thibault, Martha Tilton, Margaret Whiting, Bea Wain, and Lee Wiley, among others.

Note: There is a huge number of radio programs which the author of this book cannot identify as of original programs. Among them are programs which featured vocalists as guest stars, or local airchecks which found release sometimes as bootleg) items. It was as "guest" vocalists on various shows that most Afro-Americans found exposure, as racism within networks generally shut them out. The same case can be made for Latino and hillbilly country acts, which were to be heard in (limited) more local programs

❖ Foreign Broadcasts, Selective (Relative to Americana)

✓ The innovative Carter Family broadcasts from Mexico, as noted in text (Carter Family).
✓ Canadian broadcasting (CBC) was also important, especially noting the rise of "Canadian Crosby" or crooner Dick Todd—noted in text.
✓ The use of the British (BBC) was more so influential, especially in remote broadcasts from the United States, especially those from New York's Cotton Club in the 1930s—with local NYC radio (WABC).

- ✓ The BBC produced many popular and diverse radio entities from America and the continent. They included (transplanted American-French) Josephine Baker, (transplanted Americans) Adelaide Hall, Alberta Hunter, Marion Harris—most of her latter career), Hildegarde, (operetic) Paul Robeson, Elisabeth Welch and Valaida Snow, (Brit and black cabaret divas) Evelyn Dove and Mabel Mercer, (French cabaret diva) Mistinguett, (Polish diva in French cabaret), Pola Negri, and especially noting (Austrian diva) Greta Keller, (French cabaret) Leo Marjane, (Chilean diva) Rosita Serrano, and (Brit) Lilian Harvey, being (more) popular continental favorites in Hitler's Germany—at least for a while. The BBC's popular program 'Soft Lights And Sweet Music' probabily provided the transplanted (black) American diva Elisabeth Welch her best shot at becoming a major entertainment entity, lacking the extreme racism found in the U.S. The same held for Adelaide Hall, although her first residence was in France, subsequently to England. In true retrospective, based upon their excellent (British) recordings, Marion Harris, Alberta Hunter and Valaida Snow should have stayed, although Valaida's stay in a Nazi prison camp (while on tour on the continent) was perhaps unnerving? More ever, Paul Robeson's successful (British) recordings (something this author cannot fully understand), along with radio and (good) films dwarf anything he attempted in America. By contrast, young Hildegarde recieved her best notices on the BBC than she had previously in America. By the time she did return, she was (much) better known, just before war hit in 1939. The innovative BBC also featured the playing of commercial records over the air in the (1930s), long before it was legal in the U.S.
- ✓ Radio Cité Broadcasts, Paris, France. It featured American jazz (1930s). French broadcasts, linked with CBS's *Saturday Night Swing Show*, found Django Reinhardt's jazz and Adelaide Hall's vocals, from her 1938 Paris "Big Apple" Club special late-night entertainment—considering numerous time zones and war threats.
- ✓ Radio Luxemburg. It featured English language popular vocals, including American entities.
- ✓ Radio Moscow—Heavy propaganda & the singing of (visiting) Paul Robeson).
- ✓ Radio Tokoyo. Sadly, WWII and the propaganda of 'Tokoyo Rose', whiped out the previous Japanese generation who followed American jazz, incuding the interests of (Japanese Americans) Alice Fumiko and Betty Inada, international (Japanese) film entity Dick Mine, and (Americans) who sang (in Japanese) Burton Crane and (especially) Midge Williams.
- ✓ *Good Morning*—a 1939 radio program from Melbourne, Australia, found (traveling) Nick Lucas, well past his prime, signing up for morning broadcasts and finding great success. If not for Australia's entry into WWII at the time, Nick may have stayed.
- ✓ Radio El Mundo from Buenos Aires, Argentina, featured its own jazz, as well as the likes of Bing Crosby—who made a live broadcast appearance there in 1941. Was Eva Peron listening?
- ✓ The BBC also initiated radio for WWII Allied service personnel. In addition to the transplanted American acts of Adelaide Hall and Elisabeth Welch, the vocal likes of Brits Al Bowlly (until killed in a London blitz in 1941), Ann Shelton, Dorothy Squires, and especially the young Vera Lynn—on her own BBC radio program, *Sincerely Yours*—promoted believable propaganda for any listener.

- ✓ German Radio.—Nazi war propaganda, efforts, along with Erma Sack (also a favorite in fascist Italy), and boring opera, at least produced Lale Anderson, with her well done vocals, especially featuring "Lili Marlene". Another (Nazi Germany) oddity, was the (Cliliean) cabaret star—Rosita Serrano, who dropped her natural (Spanish), and sang in (German). Her success, even after the war started was considerable, especially noting her well done renditionion of the Mexican folk entity "La Paloma", as released on (Telefunken-A-2563). Telefunken, was also to release the recording in (Axis) partner Japan, who (somehow) liked to listen to (German), at least until (Rosita) was found to be contributing to charity work for Jewish refugees and working for the Allies. Speculation has it, that both Lale and Rosita were more so backed (on Radio) by 'Charlie and His Orchestra, a band aping American jazz, led by Karl Scwedler, who's crooned (injected) Nazi propaganda, was not only sad, but silly.
- ✓ After the United States entered the war, German Marlene Dietrich (transplanted) in addition to her home front AFRN work, broadcast her own version in German, for the US Office of Strategic Services (OSS), along with other ditties. This propaganda effort found many listening Germans, along with Allies.
- ✓ As part of live Allied propaganda broadcasts from England (1944) to Nazi-occupied Europe, the USO touring Bing Crosby, heard easily by Germans, listened and dubbed him "Der Bingle."

- o More—selective LPs which featured original Radio Master airchecks. Also note that *any* 331/3 LP record issue was not contemporary. As issued commercially, long-playing albums contained original noncommercial material, some of it from rude personal wire recordings, radio disc transcription, and from tape. (Tapings started commercially after WWII.) After the advent of the LP, a huge market for this material emerged. Confusion about the differences between commercial recording or recordings produced for radio also followed. Recordings that merit review may be noted as Radio Masters throughout this book. Specific LP and CD products are also noted in the LP and CD sections of this book.

RECORD LABELS (1900-50)

- In 1877, Thomas Edison invented the metal cylinder—and not the phonograph record, as most generally assume. The true inventor of the phonograph record was a German, Emil Berliner. While his invention (1887) of flat zinc discs, called the "Gramophone" was to be greatly enhanced, Berliner's invention grew into the concept of the "standard" 78 rpm speed, noting some players could spin well over 100 rpm.
- The battle over the Edison cylinder and the Berliner disc, and others, between 1887 through to about 1912, was a bit like the later century's change from 78 rpm speed to the emergence of 331/3 rpm speed and 45 rpm speed in the latter 1940s, but a bit more drastic. Indeed, by the early 1900s, Edison himself began to produce a disc similar to the 78 rpm, as well as his cylinders. Berliner, in the meantime, also produced the first of the crude microphones, which led to slightly better recorded sounds, upto 5, 000 Hz. By 1901, Berliner and a competitor, Eldridge Johnson, formed the Victor Talking Machine Company.
- The hunt for playable machines led to the formation of the Columbia Phonograph Company in 1892, as well as hundreds of others. While experimenting with wax masters and commercial flat discs, using metal needles, the "standard" was set, by 1905, to the degree of 76 rpm to 78 rpm. By the war year of 1917, the major record labels would be Brunswick, Columbia, Edison (still producing some cylinders), Emerson, Okeh, Victor, Vocalion, and a European-owned entity, Pathé.
- The success of (Italian) Enrico Caruso in America on Victor causes a sensation, with his release of "I Pagliacci" on Victor 81032. Moreover, Caruso would become the world's first superstar recording artist, becoming the first single-recording artist to sell over a million records, collectively. Caruso would, more so, remain an important recording entity for the next twenty years, recording a substantial number of Victor Red Seal-labeled (operatic) acoustic recordings, including the 1916 release of "O Sole Mio" (m Victor 87243). He also attempted popular standards, in his operatic style, such as the (1917) release of "Over There," on Victor 87394.
- Early twentieth century acoustic recording found "group" vocal recordings transferred onto discs and cylinders. The likes of many, including the American Quartet, Hayden Quartet, and Peerless Quartet were popular, if, more so, schmaltzy.
- Folk, spiritual, and ethnic recordings also sell.

- Recordings of Broadway ditties also do well. Irving Berlin (1911+), Victor Herbert (1903+), George M. Cohan (1903+)—also a performer and recording artist—Irving Caesar (1920+), Jose Collins (1913), George Gershwin (1919+), Otto Harbach (1911+), Louis Hirsch (1912), Gus Kahn (1908+), Jerome Kern (1912+), Sigmund Romberg (1916+), Paul Rubens (1902+), George White (1920+), and Florenz Ziegfeld (first major production in 1909), among others, produce opera-influenced productions, gradually mixed with newer "popular" song ditties. Besides Cohan, vocals were provided by Nora Bayes (1910+), Fannie Brice (1920+), Eddie Cantor (1919+), Maurice Chevalier (at least 1918+), Frank Crumit (1920+), Raymond Hitchcock (1904+), Elsie Janis and Al Jolson (1911), Gertrude Lawrence (1918+), Beatrice Lillie (1919+), Harry MacDonough (1904+), Marilyn Miller (1920), Stella Mayhew (1905+), Jack Norworth (1910+), Chauncey Olcott (1913+), Blanche Ring (1909+), Lillian Russell (1912), Aileen Stanley (1920+), John Steel (1920+), Anne Wheaton (1917+), Frances White (1916+), and Bert Williams (1902+)—Bert being the only black entity allowed in the white world of entertainment. Finding original records by these acoustic artists, with the possible exception of some Al Jolson releases, is a limited field. Cylinders are also less desirable in sound quality and playability.
- Popular "dance" music is, more so, initiated with the release of sheet music and subsequent recordings. Musical trends develop faster, as the traditions of the European waltz, as superseded by the likes of (mostly) Afro-American-penned idioms, such as ragtime and the later rhythmic jazz music. Other trends beginning in 1912, are rhythmic fox-trot dance steps of Latin origins, perhaps best popularized by the team of Vernon and Irene Castle. They were, more so, backed by Harlem Afro-American-led bands, notably by James Europe, on their (instrumental) recordings. It is likely speculation that the term "yeas" or "jazz" started with them, although the sounds of Chicago-led bands at the Pekin Inn from transported New Orleans musicians is equal to that!
- With the notable exception of the black vaudevillian Bert Williams and a few scattered religious hymn singers, people of color were forbidden to record before 1920. While it's interesting to note that the musical trends of the pre-1920 era largely had black origins, the obvious racism of Americana prevented many black entities from competing. Separate black shows did exist before as well as after 1920, although those after 1920 were, more so, fueled by recordings of actual Afro-American entities, as well as another "new" 1920s' advancement, commercial radio. Pre-1920, black vaudeville and black revues included the likes of Bert Williams (1902) and George Walker (Bert's partner in 1902+), and after 1910, they included the likes of Ma Rainey, Bessie Smith, Alberta Hunter, Mamie Smith, Lucille Hegamin, Ethel Waters, and Edith Wilson. All would later become recording artists in the 1920s. (Original acoustic records by these artists are usually worth pursuing, despite their obvious and limited sound quality.)
- The white-led Original Dixieland Jazz Band's (1917) instrumental recordings of "Livery Stable Blues," on Victor 18255, and "Darktown Strutter's Ball," on Victor-2297, officially put jazz into mainstream circulation. Led by Nick La Rocca (heavily influenced by the black music of Joe "King" Oliver and Jelly Roll Morton), the trend was set for the rest of the century. The jazzy appeal of Marion Harris's vocals was trendsetting, at least until 1920. By the early 1920s, when the racism of the early century was overcome by the commercial appeal of original

Afro-American musicians, the differences between the black entities became more apparent. While the likes of the East Coast Fletcher Henderson were overtly different from the New Orleans style of Oliver and Morton, and the later emergence of Sidney Bechet and Louis Armstrong, so was the effect upon others, who included Paul Whiteman, Ted Lewis, Bix Beiderbecke, George Gershwin, and Duke Ellington.

- White racism was to be much trumped by the commercial concerns of a struggling new record label, Okeh. It was, moreover, the (1920) sales success of Afro-American vaudevillian Mamie Smith's "Crazy Blues" on Okeh 4169 that was to inform the rest of America that the culture of black America, a huge and hidden chunk of American idiom, had existed. While some limited acknowledgments of such notable entitles as Scott Joplin, Shelton Brooks, James Blaine, James Reed Europe, and W. C Handy, among others, were known, the ridicule of the popular coon song had, more so, defined the Afro-American in popular culture. The mystery and novelty of a black American who could sing was, moreover, to be found out through many of Mamie Smith's (black) contemporaries, who were to be eagerly signed up by the other recording companies—indeed awakened by the new discoveries and, perhaps, more irked by Okeh's sales success.
- The term "blues," noting a mood, came to be used as a term to identify black idiom. It was, as well, used by white vocalists attempting to emulate or perceive new 1920s' styles. While obvious Broadway entities such as Libby Holman attempted a "black" idiom, the perceptions of Sophie Tucker and Marion Harris, in previous decades were wrong, at least in true retrospective. Other white singers had more success at blues, noting those releases of Emmett Miller, and (even), in some cases, Al Jolson. Ultimately, the opposite of the religious, in the secular South prevailed, curiously within the segregated yet shared culture of most Southerners. The later 1920s would, more so, produce the likes of the Carter Family and Jimmie Rodgers, whose rural "blues," while shared, may be considered far less contrived.
- The term "hillbilly," not always but usually designated for white and Southern folk music products, was perhaps derived from a popular 1925 string group called Al Hopkins and the Hill Billies. From it came the later 1940s' term "country" music, as well as yet others, including "bluegrass" for the state of Kentucky and yet another product of merge, "country-swing."
- The 1920s also brought into existence many new record companies, brought on by better economic times. Indeed, hundreds of new labels sprang up, with many signing up the black artists, as well as those who were to be heard on a (yet) newer invention—commercial radio, in 1920. Many were to be called "hillbilly," and, more so, ethnic, classical (operatic), and religious. While jazz and blues reigned, the whole range of America was to be exploited.
- The mid-1920s brought along the discovery of "electronic" recordings, which boosted hearing to almost 10, 000 Hz, and with the emergence of the microphone in 1929 (an embellishment of Berliner's earlier invention), the true modern era of recorded (listenable) sound began. Another medium, of "talking" motion pictures, also began with the 1927 commercial success of *The Jazz Singer*, which was ably put over by Al Jolson, the former acoustic singer (full of vocal tricks), who had already made the successful transition to electric recording and to a filmed recording. Many original record releases from 1925 through 1929 are

desirable, whether acoustic or not, although most of those by popular vocalists did sell well, and are usually easier to find than those issued after 1929 through 1935.

- The 1929 stock market crash in October largely put an end to good times, as well as to the sale of phonograph records, phonographs, sheet music, and the popularity of (talking) films. Moreover, the hundreds of record labels that had sprung up went out of business or were bought out by others. Radio, on the other hand, became more than novel, as well as a cheap way to become entertained. It was, more so, the forbidden playing of phonograph records on "the air," that caused most of the Depression-plagued public to become more aware and hip to radio. Depression-era original record releases are, more so, usually very desirable, as fewer were made, or sold, after the Depression kicked in.
- The emergence of "swing," starting with the 1932 Ivie Anderson vocal for the Duke Ellington release of "It Don't Mean a Thing if It Ain't Got That Swing" became a musical style and term by 1935.
- After 1935, records, in general, began to sell again. With some exceptions, most records are less rare. Small labels are the exception. Moreover, as always, watch out for most reissued products.
- The event of World War II and later musical trends of the postwar boom are reflected in the many new record labels issued. Musical trends became stale much faster as the music industry, and the population of the country became larger, and younger.

➢ The following record labels are used within this book. They, moreover, indicate an original recording, which is a very important ingredient of this book. It is, more so, important to note that while many original recordings were to be rerecorded by major artists, the record label indicated as a pick *must* apply only to that recording. It was, and still is, a challenge to find out if a recording was *also* released on another commercial label and was an authentic *reissue*. Moreover,

  - Always look for a release number. It will tell its purchaser the time of original release. While difficulties may exist in the changing of number series, as well in competing and differing popular, race, hillbilly classical-operatic 78 rpm album release and special release and product, it is not very hard to figure how things were issued.
  - Always look for the matrix number. While regular issues—including reissues—differ, the integrity of the matrix number designates the actual recorded date and, moreover, the "take" of number of versions that were originally recorded. For those who wish to enjoy *original* musical performances, the understanding of matrix numbers is key! It is, more so, fairly simple for a *single*-release product, noting each number to be found on each record label.
  - Always consider label color and design. While some records match up as original issue numbers and matrix, they may still be second pressings, or more. Records and their sleeves constantly changed with time.

- The following is a general guide for the record labels found within this book, as released between 1900 and through 1950. Those labels noted but not used within the text of this book may be, more so, used for other references, including those ditties released commercially on subsidiary labels.

- (All selective record labels noted are noted song picks found within this book.)

- ♦ Abbott. A small label of the 1950s.
- ♦ Aeolian-Vocalian. Originally needed its own player, discs records produced vertically, changed over to standard discs using 78 rpm, or close to it in 1919.
- ♦ Ajax. A record label owned by the Canadian company Compo Company of Lachine, Quebec, issued in US.

- ♦ Alladin. A small Los Angeles label founded in 1945 by Eddie and Leo Mesner.
- ♦ Apollo. A small NYC label founded by Ike and Bess Berman in 1942.
- ♦ ARC or The American Record Company. From 1929 until it was bought out in 1939, the company issued perhaps the most amount of record labels. Many of these labels had been independent labels that had been wiped out due to the Great Depression and had been simply bought out, along with their *original masters*. Founded as ARC in 1929, the company was bought out in 1930 by Consolidated Film Industries, or CFI. The subsequent CFI management would pick up the mighty "Brunswick" label in 1931, along with "Vocalion," and "Melotone," in receivership from Warner Brothers, the film company, due to expire in 1939. Moreover, for a time, between 1934 and 1938, ARC issued Columbia and Okeh products, after its controlling interest, owned by Grimsby-Grunow failed in 1934. More so, the last real ARC releases would be issued into 1939, until it had subsequently been purchased by William Paley, the new owner of Columbia, as part of CBS or Columbia Broadcasting Corp.

  - As part of a marketing strategy during a time of great economic need and the inability of the general public to consider purchasing a recording, many of these labels found their way into dime stores, drug stores, and even retail catalog stores, as well as the remaining (premium) record store. Thus, a regular Brunswick release could sell for seventy-five cents to a dollar in a record store, and an issue of the *same* song ditty could be sold for considerably less at Sears Roebuck and Co. on the Conqueror label.

- A specific example would be as follows:

  - The Bing Crosby 1934 78 rpm pick "Love in Bloom" is indicated by its original Brunswick release number, Brunswick 6936. This original label, more so, indicates a matrix number, LA-182-A. This *original Brunswick* release, in *gold*, not *silver*, lettering was to be subsequently released on other labels. They would include the 78rpm issues of Banner 33198, Oriole 2993, Melotone 13165, Perfect 13050, and Okeh 2878), along with purple labeled Vocalion 2878 (Conqueror 8412, and (Romeo 2367). All have the *same* original *matrix number* on them, and may be treated as such. If the matrix number should differ, such as LA-182-B instead of LA-182-A, which is very doubtful, you have found something very odd, which would be an alternate take, or an original performance, as well as a probable winner to hear and compare. Any subsequent *radio* renditions by Bing Crosby are *not* originals, nor is a *rerecording on Decca.*

- The American Record Company labels, from time to time, would thus include the following:

    - Actuelle (purchased from the Pathé Phonograph and Radio Corp. in 1929).
    - ARC (its own label—the American Record Company).
    - Banner (purchased from the Plaza Music Company in 1929).
    - Brunswick (in receivership from Warner Brothers in 1931).
    - Cameo (purchased from the Cameo Record Corp. in 1929).
    - Columbia (issued some of this product between 1934 and 1938).
    - Domino (purchased from the Plaza Music Company in 1929).
    - Jewel (purchased from the Plaza Music Company in 1929).
    - Melotone (in receivership from Warner Brothers in 1931).
    - Okeh (issued this product between 1934 and 1938).
    - Oriole (purchased from the Plaza Music Company in 1929).
    - Pathé (purchased from the Pathé Phonograph and Radio Corp. in 1929).
    - Perfect (purchased from the Pathé Phonograph and Radio Corp. in 1929).
    - Regal (purchased from the Plaza Music Company in 1929).
    - Romeo (purchased from the Cameo Record Corp. in 1929).
    - Variety (purchased from the Cameo Record Corp. In 1929).
    - Vocalion (in receivership from Warner Brothers in 1931).

        - Additional comments on the post-1939 (CBS) Columbia products are as under:

- Any *green*-labeled Columbia 78 rpm issues of Bing Crosby are real Brunswick reissues, but not original Columbia Masters. More so, many Okeh releases, which also found reissued product, including masters of Bing Crosby and Gene Autry, are now owned by (post-1939) Columbia.
- Any Bessie Smith and other artist releases that had been recorded before 1939 are not *red*-labeled Columbia originals, although matrix numbers do indicate an original recorded performance. (They are still old and are excellent recordings, yet *not* originals.)

    - ARA. A small 1940s label.
    - ARTO. A small label of the 1920s.
    - ASH. A small label owned by Sam and Moe Ash in the 1940s.
    - ATCO. A small record label associated with Atlantic in the 1950s).
    - Atlantic. A small label founded by Ahmet Ertegun and Jerry Wexler in 1949 that grew into a major label).
    - Atlas. A small label of the 1940s.
    - Banner. A small label in the 1920s, later associated with ARC.

        - ✓ Banner Record Sleeve

    - Bell. A small label of the 1920s.
    - Beltone. A small post-WWII label of the 1940s.
    - Biltmore. A 1940s label that reissued out-of-circulation recordings.
    - Black Patti. A small Chicago label of the 1920s.

- Black Swan. A small black-owned label founded by the early (black) pioneer Henry Pace. It was founded on the (1921) success of Ethel Waters that would lead to financial rewards until marketing problems led to a subsequent merge with Paramount in 1923. Paramount, more so, reissued Black Swan its original masters.
- Black & White. A small 1940s label.
- Bluebird. This label was a budget label owned by Victor. It contained reissues as well as a series of *original* recordings for the budget market. In some cases, a Bluebird original would sell so well that it would be reissued as a regular Victor release. (The popular hillbilly and blues series were discontinued and subsequently put on the Victor label after WWII.)
- Broadway. A label issue of 1920s associated with Paramount.
- Brunswick. The Brunswick-Balke-Collender Co. became a huge entity in the 1920s. It was, moreover, associated with the famous bowling entity, as well as perhaps by Al Jolson, also a mid-1920s investor. It would later be principally bought out by the Warner Brothers film studio, and later become part of American Record Company. By 1939, ARC was bought out by CBS; the original masters of Brunswick were, more so, divided up between the newer CBS Columbia label and by Decca. It is, moreover, a confused issue since then (1939), as many *original* masters were to be subsequently claimed by Columbia as well as Decca. Thank God for matrix numbers!
- Brunswick (English). Somehow, American Decca masters continued to be released on this label after 1934.

    - ✓ Bullet. A small post-WWII issue label of the 1940s.
    - ✓ Cameo. A small label issue of the 1920s.
    - ✓ Cardinal Records. A small label of the 1920s.
    - ✓ Capital. This label issue was founded by Johnny Mercer, Glenn E. Wallichs, and Buddy De Sylva in Los Angeles in 1942.
    - ✓ Champion. A small label issue of the 1920s, originally controlled by Gennett. Later, after 1934, many masters were bought and reissued on Decca.
    - ✓ Challenge. A small record company.
    - ✓ Chess. A small Chicago label founded by Leonard and Phil Chess in 1949.
    - ✓ Clef. A small l label of the early 1950s.
    - ✓ Clarion. A small label issue of the 1920s and 1930s.
    - ✓ Coast. A small label of the 1940s.

- Columbia (1). This pre-1900, Columbia Phonograph Company was a premium label issue. Like Victor, its policy of segregation, excepting a very few led by (British) vaudevillian Bert Williams, would become changed due to the success of rival Okeh Record Company's release of Mamie Smith's (1920) "race" recordings. After signing up (black) vaudevillian Edith Wilson in 1921 and, among others, vaudevillian Eddie Cantor and the yet-to-be recorded (black) belter Bessie Smith (both in 1923), the label avoided failure when its (then) best-known (established) recording artist, Al Jolson, left Columbia to buy a stake in Brunswick Records in 1924. It, moreover, merged with the Okeh label in 1926. Due to the Great Depression, it went bankrupt in 1934 and was subsequently issued by American Record Company until 1939.
- Columbia (2). The company, as owned by William Pauly's Columbia Broadcasting Company, started in 1939 after buying out the American Record Company, which had released many older Columbia Phonograph Company masters as well as most

previous Brunswick masters. Subsequent "Columbia" or "CBS" releases would be best known as *red*-labeled releases, although some variations including *green*-colored labels were sometimes used.

- Commadore. A small label started by recording pioneer Milt Gabler in NYC, issue from the 1930s to 1940s.
- Conqueror. A small label issue of the 1930s. (Issued by mail house and department store Sears Roebuck and Co.
- Continental. A small label issue of the post-WWII, 1940s.
- Coral. A small label founded in 1949 (later acquired by Decca).
- Cosmo. A small record company of the post-WWII era, 1940s.
- Crown. A small label issue of the 1930s/Anther in the 1940s.
- Cub. A small label issue of the 1940s.
- Damon. A small post-WWII label issue of the 1940s.
- Decca. This label issue was started as part of the English Decca Company in 1934, led in American operations by former Brunswick producer, Jack Kapp. Subsequent success for Kapp followed when he acquired (from Brunswick) such popular entities as Ethel Waters, the Boswell Sisters, and (especially) Brunswick's (then) most successful recording entity, Bing Crosby. From 1934 through about 1938, it was issued on a blue label, with a design that most collectors refer to as "sunburst." In 1942, the label started to issue a black label. Special-issue album releases, and purple-colored labels and reddish labels also appeared. Moreover, a sepia race and hillbilly series had briefly appeared in the later 1930s.
- De Lux. A small label issue of the 1940s.
- Derby. A small label issue of the 1940s.
- Disc. A small label issue of the 1940s.
- Disque Gramophone (French)
- Diva. A small label issue of the 1920s and 1930s.
- Domino. A small label of the 1920s.
- Durium. A small label issue of the early 1930s. Also associated with "Hit of the Week" records.
- Edison Ambero or Edison Diamond Disc or Edison. The company founded originally by Thomas Edison as a cylinder product. Later, Edison would issue discs as well.
- Electradisk. A small record company.
- Elite. A small label issue of the 1940s; ownership associated with Dolly Dawn
- EmArcy. A small label of the early 1950s.
- Emerson. A small NYC label founded by Victor Emerson in 1916.
- Enterprise. A small post war label.
- Essex. A small Philadelphia label of the early 1950s.
- Exclusive. A small Los Angeles label issue of the 1940s.
- Excello. A small Nashville label founded by Ernie Young in 1953.
- Federal. A small label issue of the 1920s. Not to be confused with the later 1950s entity.
- Four Star or 4 Star. A small Pasadena, California-based label started by Dick Nelson in 1945.
- Gala. A small label issue of the 1930s+.
- General Records. A small NYC label (early 1940s)

- ➢ Gennett. As owned by the Starr Piano Company of Richmond, Indiana, this label recorded much diverse material from popular, blues, jazz, hillbilly, and spoken word. It was the first to issue the "Champion" label. The company went out of business in 1930 due to the Great Depression, with a slight resurrection in the 1940s by a different owner, Joe Davis.

  - ▪ The Starr Piano Company would be involved with the following other labels:

    - Bell (leased some material).
    - Black Pattti (leased some material).
    - Buddy (leased some material).
    - Challenge (leased some material).
    - Champion (Starr Piano's own budget label).
    - Conqueror (leased some material).
    - Herschel (leased some material).
    - Gold Seal (leased some material).
    - Savoy (leased some material).
    - Superior (leased some material).
    - Supreme (leased some material).
    - Supertone (leased some material).

- ➢ Gotham. A small label issue of the 1940s.
- ➢ Grey Gull. A small label issue of the 1920s.
- ➢ Guild. A small label issued in the 1940s.
- ➢ Harmograph. A small label issue of the 1920s.
- ➢ Harmony. A small label issue of the 1920s and 1930s.
- ➢ Hit. A small NYC label of the early 1940s.
- ➢ Hit of the Week. Also noted in text as HOW. A small label issue of paper-thin quality of 1930s (1931-33).

  - ✓ Note: The author of this book, on hearing many record issues, including some featured with this text, has, more so, concluded that original masters were cut from original contemporary radio broadcasts.

- ➢ Holiday. A small label of the 1950s.
- ➢ HMV. As His Masters Voice label issued Victor masters in Britain, S. Africa, and Australia.
- ➢ H. R. S. A small label issued in the 1940s.
- ➢ Jewell. A small label issue of the 1940s.
- ➢ Jubilee. A small NYC label founded in 1948 by Jerry Blaine.
- ➢ Juke Box. A small label issue of the 1930s.
- ➢ Kapp. A small record label named for David Kapp, the 1950s.
- ➢ Keen. A small record label of the 1950s.
- ➢ Keynote. A small NYC label issue of the 1940s.
- ➢ King. A small Cincinnati, Ohio, label founded by Syd Nathan in 1945.
- ➢ Lincoln. A small label issue of the 1920s.
- ➢ Liberty Music Shops (LMS). A small label issue of the 1930s and 1940s. Library of Congress. These issues were not commercial records and are not used for the purposes of this book. Moreover, when found, these noncommercial recordings should not be

confused with contemporary (commercial) recordings. It is, moreover, notable that many of these recordings, after a passage of time, have subsequently been issued as commercial recordings as (later) LP and CD commercial products.

- Majestic. A small label issue of the 1940s. Ownership included the noted former mayor of (Prohibition era) New York City, Jimmy Walker.

    - ✓ Majestic Record Sleeve (1940s).

- Mary Howard Records. A small label of the 1940s. Oddly used matrix numbers to identify record releases.
- Master. A small label issue of the 1930s—an ARC product.
- Melotone. A small label issue of the 1930s.
- Mercury. A small label founded in Chicago in 1945, later a major entity.
- Meritt. A small record label of the 1920s.
- MGM. A label issue effort of the 1940s, owned by the huge interests of the film company Metro Golden Meyer.
- Modern. A small Los Angeles record label founded by Jules and Saul Bihari in 1945.
- Montgomery Ward. The well-known mail house-department store, more so, issued Victor masters on its own so-named label (1930s+).
- Musicraft. A small label issue of the 1940s.

    - ✓ Musicraft Record Sleeve issue (1940s).

- National. A small label issue of the 1920s.
- National. A small label issue of the 1940s.
- Nordskog Records. A small label (1921-23).
-
- Odeon. As a major label before 1900, this German-owned label, more so, converted over from cylinder to record by 1920.
- Okeh. A small label founded in 1918, with its name taken from principal owners' initials—Otto K. E. Heinemann. Okeh's independence, more so, broke the color line of "race" after issuing a vocal by (black) vaudevillian Mamie Smith in 1920. It later merged with Columbia in 1926. Later, an ARC label, and subsequent post-1939 label.
- Oriole. A small label issue of the 1920s, later an ARC label.
- ORP. A small (English) label of the 1930s.
- Paramount. This label had started before 1920, as owned by the New York Recording Laboratories of Port Washington and as controlled by the Wisconsin Chair Company of New York and Port Washington, in Wisconsin. While many of its masters were acquired from other labels, notably the major purchase of the New York-based Black Swan, it was known as a "Chicago" label, as many of its masters were recorded there. Among many, perhaps it was the find of the previously unrecorded Ma Rainey that founded Paramount's own "race" entities, which would become considerable. In 1929, a newer recording studio in Grafton, Wisconsin, was initiated, closing a few years later due to the Great Depression. Paramount, moreover, issued many other labels to exploit its product. They included the following:

    - Broadway.
    - Federal (not the post-WWII entity).
    - Harmograph (St. Louis-based).

- Herwin (St. Louis-based).
- Hudson.
- National (not the post-WWII entity).
- Puritan.

- Paraphone. A British issue entity associated with the Columbia Gramophone Co.
- Pathé. As the French Pathé Phonograph & Radio Corp., this label had been a major player in the 1920s. They also issued Pathé-Actuelle and Perfect labels. It merged with the Plaza Music Company and the Cameo Record Corp. in 1929, which originally formed ARC or the American Record Company.
- Perfect. A small label issued in the 1920s, originally associated with Pathé. Later issued and associated with ARC.
- Philco. A small label issued in the 1940s.
- Premier. A small label of the 1930s.
- Puritone. A small label of the 1920s, associated with the Columbia label.
- Q. R. S. This label issue appeared in the late 1920s and 1930s.
- RCA Victor. The Radio Corp. of America was the same issue product as the Victor label.
- Regal. A small label issued in the 1920s.
- Regal. A small label issued in the 1940s and 1950s.
- Rex was a major British label from the 1930s.
- Romeo. A small label issued in the 1920s. Later issued by ARC.
- Savoy. A small Newark, New Jersey, label founded by Herman Lubinsky in 1942.
- Schrimer. A small label issued in the 1940s.
- Signature. A small label issued in the 1940s.
- Special edition. A special issue and reissue label of AMC.
- Specialty. A small label founded in Hollywood by Art Rupe in 1945.
- Sterling. A small NYC label founded in 1945.
- Stinson. A small NYC label founded in NYC in 1945.
- Sun. A small label from the 1920s to 1930s. (Not to be confused with the Memphis, Tennessee, label of the 1950s founded by Sam Phillips.)
- Sunshine Records. A small label from 1921 to 1923.
- -Supertone. A small label of the 1920s.
- Telefunken (German)
- Timely Tunes. A small label issue of the 1930s.
- Tono Radio Records. A small (Danish) label issue of the 1930s.
- Trumpet. A small label issued in the 1940s.
- Ultraphone. A (European) French label of the 1930s.

V-Disc. As a WWII entity, these noncommercial recordings were specially recorded (for free) by contemporary recording artist of the era. They would include: the Andrews Sisters. Nate King Cole Trio, Perry Como, Bing Crosby, Billie Holiday, Lena Horne, Louis Jordan, Tony Martin, Peggy Lee, Ginny Sims and Frank Sinatra. While not a huge factor for the purposes of this book, many of these may be found and should not be confused with contemporary (commercial) recordings. Many are, more so, radio transcriptions, although in a special noncommercial category. Moreover, as times changed, many original V-Disc recording transcriptions have been issued commercially.

- Variety. A small label issued in the 1930s by ARC.
- Velvet Tone. A small label issued in the 1920s and 1930s. Associated with the Columbia Phonograph Company.
- Verve. A small record company of the mid-1950s.
- Victor. The Victor Talking Machine Company was founded by a 1901 merge of Emil Berliner's gramophone interests and a rival, Eldridge Johnson's, Consolidated Talking Machine Company, which pioneered the famous hound dog listening to music from a playing gramophone—an early phonograph player. Moreover, the famous term "His Masters Voice," was put into the minds and hearts of all future generations of Victor record buyers. The label may be credited as marketing the recording industry's first "superstar" seller of discs—Italian-born Emile Caruso. While it did sign up the black and British vaudevillian Bert Williams, the company, more so, embraced a segregated policy against most people of color until 1923, when it signed up Lizzie Miles. A subsequent release of Lizzie Miles's product on its British label His Masters Voice or HMV, moreover, founded "race" releases in Britain, as previous race releases on smaller American labels could not produce the needed distribution as Victor possessed. In 1929, the Radio Corporation of America, or RCA, acquired the company. Victor also acquired and used the "Bluebird" label in the later 1920s. More so, releases would be known as "Victor" until 1942, when "RCA Victor" would become predominant—as issued on the record label.
- Vocalion. A Brunswick-owned label issued from the 1920s till 1930s. Later owned and issued by the new Columbia Broadcasting Corporation (after 1939).
- Zone-O-Phone. A major label issued before 1910.
- Zonophone. This English label merged with Regal in 1932. Issued many American Victor recording artists.

♦ More

Radio masters include radio broadcasts, not commercial recordings—the rarest are of pre-1935 vintage. It is, more so, very difficult to find early program broadcasts as only wire recorders and better-sounding yet seldom-used radio disc transcriptions were used to record anything. This was also the time of the Depression, when entertainment, except for those who were involved within the industry, could actually enjoy (see also the Radio section of this book).

- "Boot or Bootleg" is material of questionable origins.
- "Masters" are studio master takes, indicated by matrix numbers.
- "Film Masters" are notable musical performances preserved in films. Many film masters have been subsequently marketed as "radio masters" but are actually filmed performances by numerous radio performers. See also the Film section of this book.

- New labels noted within this book, issued after 1950, would include the following: A & M, ABC Paramount, Abbot, Alladin, Argo, Atlantic, Checker, Chess, Delmark, Dot, Evergreen, Epic, Era, Essex, Excello, Grand Award, Imperial, Jubilee, Kapp, Laurie, London, Modern, Momoment, Olympic, Quest, Reprise, Sandy Hook, Sun (the Memphis label), Take Two, Vee-Jay, Verve, Warner Brothers, and Word.

- Alias. Many recording artists used, or were given, other names from their recording companies as marketing ploys or they were just plain label mistakes on the product. In other cases, many originals state “vocal refrain,” as the identity of a famous entity was not yet to be known or was just forgotten. Still other reasons concerned the rights of exclusive recording contracts and possible violations of them. Within this book, look out for the likes of (some) recordings by the following:

- Ivie Anderson “vocal chorus.”
- Connie Boswell or “Connee” Boswell.
- Gene Austin as “George Hobson,” “Bill Collins.”
- Gene Autry as “Sam Hill,” “John Hardy,” “Tom Long,” “Overton Hatfield.”
- Bing Crosby, Al Rinker, and Harry Barris—the Rhythm Boys, as “vocal refrain.”
- Big Bill Broonzy as “Big Bill,” “Sammy Sampson,” or “Big Bill Johnson,” “Hokum Boys,” “Big Bill” Broomsley.
- Sammy Davis Jr. as “Shorty Muggins.”
- Vaughan De Leath as “Gloria Geer” or “Betty Brown.”
- Annette Hanshaw as “Gay Ellis” or “Dot Dare.”
- Harriet Hilliard became “Harriet Nelson.”
- Billie Holiday as “Lady Day,” “vocal refrain.”
- Alberta Hunter as “Alberta Prime, “May Alix,” or “Josephine Beatty”(a Mae Alix did exist as well.)
- Frankie Jaxon is also Frankie “Half Pint” Jaxon.
- Leadbelly or “Huddie Leadbelly,” “Huddie Leadbetter.”
- Dinah Shore as “Dinah Shaw.”
- Roy Rogers as “Leonard Slye” or “Dick Weston.”
- Eva Taylor as “Irene Gibbons” or “Irene Williams.”
- Rudy Vallee as “Frank Mater.”
- Fats Waller as “Thomas Waller” or “Maurice.”
- Ethel Waters as “Mamie Jones”(another vocalist, Aileen Stanley, also used this name, as well as a real Mamie Jones).
- Josh White as “Pinewood Tom” or “Singing Christian.
- Sarah Vaughan as “Sarah Vaughn.”

Four more aliases-record labels: Grey Gull (Betty Brown); Harmony (Gay Ellis); Columbia (Irene Gibbons); and Capital (Lady Day). All picks that can be found!

More III. Look into Original Album Concepts and Radio’s Most Popular Vocalists and Programs.

FEATURED VOCALISTS

a. The following essential vocalists are listed *A* through *Z*.
b. Song title 'picks' are totally determined by the author.
c. Comparisons of songs, choices of record releases and vocal style differences noted by the author are specificially chosen by the author.
d. Opinions of the author, as well as omissions by the author are not meant to offend, but to only inform.

Roy Acuff

The likes of this mid-1930s hillbilly singer Roy Acuff just may define "simple" and "bland." While a creature of his time (whose influences would include Jimmie Rodgers and Gene Autry), the average listener of his radio shows and personal appearances could even be considered square. When compared to the likes of contemporary Bill Monroe, the music produced may be considered far less complicated. Like most hidden jewels, however, he left behind some very good recordings, which speak for themselves, as well as the times. More so, the legality of bars, or local honky-tonks—places of drink and entertainment—noting the repeal of Prohibition in 1934, were to become common, replacing the old 'saloon" of pre-prohibition days, that had usually restricted women. As a meeting place providing drinks and music (along with the newer placement of juke boxes), the legit re-established business of selling achohol easily became part of Americana itself. Indeed, the likes of Roy Acuff and the Crazy Tennesseans, who became perhaps the most popular act of radio's *Grand Ole Opry* (WSM, Nashville, TN) by 1940 were to be relevant, and Roy himself was to become dubbed by many as "the King of Country Music" providing a valid musical contribution for both men and women patrons of establishments playing jukeboxes. The following are Roy Acuff picks:

5. "New Greenback Dollar," Vocalion 03255. The "country" fiddle and its follow-up vocals, featuring Roy and his cross-talking "crazy Tennesseans" is almost a blues effort.
6. "Steamboat Whistle Blues," Vocalion 03255. This *is* a blues effort, and this tale of a prisoner yearning to become free (when he hears a steamboat whistle) is indeed very effective.
7. "Great Speckled Bird," Vocalion 04252. Yup. While this bit of corn remains (very) dated and is still not for everyone, at least this penned bit of religious preaching (found in the Bible) became Roy's signature tune.

8. "Steel Guitar Blues," Conqueror 9086. This (far) more interesting recording than "Great Speckled Bird" is a fine example a simple voice with some very fine dobro pickin'.
9. "Just to Ease My Worried Mind," Okeh 5820. With fiddles and the sound effects of a train whistle, this very simple (self-penned) country blues ditty is very effective.
10. "The Precious Jewel," Okeh 5956. Like "The Great Speckled Bird," this bit of "corn" (also greatly influenced by the earlier recordings of the Carter Family) is very digestible.
11. "Worried Mind," Okeh 6229. This (1940) classic, as penned by Jimmie Davis and Ted Daffan is far from simple in content, as these "country" boys indeed had serious thoughts as well as plans for the future. Roy's version, in comparison with the best-selling contemporary Bob Wills's version, with a softer vocal by Tommy Duncan on Okeh-6101, is cruder, but perhaps that's the gist of it all? Or what about a Ted Daffan release, with a vocal by Chuck Keeshan on, Conqueror 9699, or the well-done contemporary pop version by Dick Todd on Bluebird B-1114? (The non-singing songwriter Ted Daffan would later (1943) produce another classic "bar" song release "Born to Lose" (Okeh 6706), which would become well known to many baby boomers as resurrected as a Ray Charles best seller in 1962.
12. "Wreck on the Highway," Okeh 6685. Yup. There's plenty of whiskey and blood on the highway. The cultural and social aspects of the ditty (as penned by Dorsey M. Dixon), in true retrospective, remain awesome. Some things never change. (Perhaps a few honky-tonk owners, however, did not want to find this ditty on their jukeboxes? Would any bar owner? Perhaps a designated driver would help?)
13. "Night Train to Memphis," Okeh 6693. This ain't all there is, but it's an effective "ride" to Memphis. Penned by Beasley Smith, Marvin Hughes, and Owen Bradley, this (1942) entity just may be Roy's best.
14. "I'll Forgive You but I Can't Forget," Okeh 6723. Released in 1944, this weepy tale, penned by J. L. Frank and Pee WeeKing, perhaps best heard on a honky-tonk jukebox, still rings true. Forget what? Just listen, with a beer in hand!
15. "Blues on My Mind," Okeh 6735. With fiddles flashing, Roy's effective (rural) blues vocal, while not hard-bitten, is crudely relevant. Penned by Fred Rose, this somewhat contrived title is turned into something more as it remains a good earful of country blues. Just listen!
16. "Wabash Cannonball," Columbia 20034. This very well-known ditty, by Roy Acuff, had actually been a vocal entity by Roy Acuff and his Crazy Tennesseans, but it did not feature Roy's vocal. This 1947 rerelease on Columbia replaced an earlier confused release, on Columbia 37008, which featured a reissued vocal by "Dynamite" Hatcher, as well as another vocal by Roy. This rambling "train" entity, had previously been a Carter Family entity, on Victor 23731, as well as a Hugh Cross release, on Columbia 15339-D. In true retrospective, it's also interesting to speculate upon a (later) rock-era Chuck Berry entity "Promised Land" (Chess-1916). While Chuck's own inspiration for this tune is indeed found in "Wabash Cannonball," just which earlier version (as by these white, hillbilly entities) had found favor in Chuck's urban ears?
17. "Freight Train Blues," Columbia 20034. Like its flip side "Wabash Cannonball," this ditty had been an Acuff entity, using Sam "Dynamite" Hatcher's vocal on Conqueror 9121, along with other releases in 1938. In any case, Roy's new (1947) release, using his own vocal, again based upon Red Foley's original (1934) recording "I Got the Freight Train Blues" moves on well enough!

18. "New Jon Blond," Columbia 20106. Also known as "New Pretty Blond," this ditty penned by Moon Mullican and Lou Wayne perhaps had its Louisiana Cajun origins defined by Moon's (1946) vocal, on (King-578) although Roy's approach is noteworthy and worth it. (Moon Mullican, perhaps known best by future generations for his hot piano antics (especially by 1950s' rocker Jerry Lee Lewis), had been a country-swing pianist and vocalist for Cliff Bruner's Texans, especially noting a 1939 release, penned by Ted Daffan, "Truck Driving Blues" on Decca 5725.)
19. "Blue Eyes Crying in the Rain," Columbia 37822. This sad ditty (penned by Fred Rose) may indeed be a candidate, in true retrospective, for the best country music record? (Later renditions from Willie Nelson (similar in vocal style to Acuff) and Elvis in the (mid-1970s), more so, offer interesting latter-day comparisons, noting Roy's original just had to be played on 78-rpm-equipped jukeboxes).

Ivie Anderson

While usually always in Duke Ellington's shadow, the hidden contributions of Ivie Anderson are indeed huge. The tight and controlling Ellington would never get loose in laying down rhythm tracks, and it, more so, needed a clever and disciplined vocalist to cope. Luckily, Duke found Ivie Anderson, a West Coast entity (Los Angeles), whose vocals were capable of anything. Moreover, by 1932, Ellington's self-penned composition "It Don't Mean a Thing (if it Ain't Got That Swing)," which was to signal the new "swing era," owes more to Ivie's vocal, as she proclaimed it! Without Ivie's cool vocal, it is more than a good bet that the swing era would not have been so labeled. Moreover, it's obvious that Ivie's clear, cool, and rhythmic vocals, prone to scatting, also had a cheerleading aspect that was much overlooked in its time. More so, her own health concerns and subsequent death in 1948, somewhat clouded her contemporary, and subsequent, importance.

➢ Picks

1. "It Don't Mean a Thing (if it Ain't Got That Swing)," Brunswick 6265. Ivie's on track, as she attacks the Irving Mills and Duke Ellington-penned lyrics. With fine rhythmic skill, Ivie also defined the "swing" era, a trendy musical term that would last well past the US entry into WWII. In fact, despite the emergence of Ella, Billie, Maxine, Dolly, or whomever, no one would better Ivie, and only hope to match her!
2. "Happy as the Day Is Long," Brunswick 6571. Ivie's a master of rhythm singing—again. It's a long guess if Harold Arlen and Ted Koehler had any idea of how this ditty would be sung (like many others), when they took ownership on penning this ditty (for *Cotton Club Parade*).
3. "Raising the Rent," Brunswick 6571. Again, Ivie still demonstrates that she's good and fast in this ditty penned (again) by Harold Arlen and Ted Koehler for the *Cotton Club Parade.*
4. "My Old Flame," Victor 24651. This slow ballad is dated, but good. This ditty, penned by Arthur Johnston and Sam Coslow, had been featured by the (very) risqué Mae West in her film *Belle of the Nineties*, in (1934). Mae, in fact, recorded this tune with Duke himself and may be seen in the film as well. Released on the Biltmore label (Biltmore 1014), Mae indeed proves she was no slouch. Ivie, however, is softer-voiced. While not warm, her coolness is effective.

5. "Troubled Waters," Victor 24651. This slow ballad, penned by Arthur Johnston and Sam Coslow, again finds Ivie very involved in a cool and dry ballad. Also interesting is yet another sultry and hot Mae West version, on Biltmore 1014, the flip side of "My Old Flame."
6. "Get Yourself a New Broom," Brunswick 6607. This rhythm singing is infectious on yet another ditty penned for the 'Cotton Club' from Harold Arlen and Ted Koehler.
7. "Truckin'," Brunswick 7514. Ivie again plays the rhythm game—and wins. As this bit of slang, penned by Ted Koehler and Rube Bloom for New York City's Cotton Club, this ditty (1935) found other contemporary and hip versions by Fats Waller (Victor 25116) and the Mills Blue Rhythm Band—vocal by Red Allen on Columbia D-3078. As much as slang, this ditty may be a pun? As a best seller, the contemporary Fats Waller version won over both Allen's fine vocal and Ivie's (better), cool release. Yet another version—a seldom-heard one by Adelaide Hall, recorded in Europe, complete with her high vocal that works, with some tap dancing—however, does indeed compete with Ivie's version.
8. "Cotton," Brunswick 7514. This very dated ditty, penned byTed Koehler and Rube Bloom for the Cotton Club, full of racial stereotypes, is, nevertheless, sung to perfection.
9. "Love Is Like a Cigarette," Brunswick 7627. A true saying, even for the latter century, this ditty is penned by Richard Byron, Jermoe Jerome and Walter Kent. Ivie's jazzy speech is indeed a fine art form. In true retrospective, latter-century listeners may find the message of this ditty politically incorrect.
10. "Kissin' My Baby Goodnight," Brunswick 7627. This "Fox-Trot Vocal Chorus Ivie Anderson" description on the original label release ain't really a fox-trot. Its message, however, penned by George W. Meyer, Mack David and Pete Wendling, remains relevant.
11. "Isn't Love the Strangest Thing?" Brunswick 7625. A real (Duke Ellington) question, ballad style.
12. "It Was a Sad Night in Harlem," Brunswick 7710. As the best of her slower titles thus far, this ditty, penned by Al Lewis and Helmy Kresa is more than good. Perhaps its use of the word "Harlem" also helps? In any case, it indeed seems that Ivie knows what she is singing about.
13. "I've Got to Be a Rug Cutter," Brunswick 7989. Don't let this novelty fool you. Ivie's vocal is pure rhythm, with Ellington's lyrics delivered in machine-gunning speed.
14. "There's a Lull in My Life," Master 117. Another slow title penned by Gordon and Revel.
15. "Oh Babe! Maybe Someday," Brunswick 7667. Not a badly sung Ellington-penned title except for the schmaltzy title itself.
16. "All God's Chillun Got Rhythm," Variety 591. Penned by Gus Kahn, Bronislaw Kaper, and Walter Jurmann for the 1937 Marx Brothers film *A Day at the Races*, this somewhat contrived title is given enough rhythmic interpretation, as by Ivie Anderson and Her Boys from Dixie, to succeed. While chiefly an Ellington band singer, this release became Ivie's break as becoming a solo entity, with the Ellington band actually "Her Boys from Dixie," i. (Ivie also appears in the contemporary film, in a fine visual glimpse of her talent, performing this ditty.)
17. "Swingtime in Honolulu," Brunswick 8131. This contrived title, penned by Henry Nemo, Irving Mills, and Duke Ellington himself is "swing" in its 1938 heyday. While just another excuse to dance, it was as likely to become popular in Honolulu as well.

18. "When My Sugar Walks Down the Street," Brunswick 8168. A fine jazzy vocal perhaps gives Ivie a chance to re-define this old Gene Austin ditty as a classic!
19. "You Gave Me the Gate," Brunswick 8169. Like most swing entities, this excuse for a dance (as penned by Irving Gordon, J. B. McNeely, Jimmy Farmer, and Duke Ellington himself), scores.
20. "I'm Checking Out, Goo' Bye," Columbia 35208. Ellington's fast rhythms, as penned by Duke Ellington and Billy Strayhorn, are again expressed well from the jazzy voiced Ivie.
21. "A Lonely Co-ed," Columbia 35240. Penned by Duke Ellington himself, Ivie takes on another contrived theme and succeeds.
22. "Mood Indigo," Columbia 35427. This classic never sounded better.
23. "Solitude," Columbia 35427. Another jazzy vocal. (Did Billie Holiday's version match Ivie's)?
24. "Killing Myself," Columbia 35640. Again, Ivie cuts through rhythm. She is joined (for a few words) vocally by Billy Strayhorn (one of Ellington's brilliant arrangers). Penned by Duke Ellington himself.
25. "Me and You," Victor 26598. Good enough!
26. "At a Dixie Roadside Diner," Victor 26719. This ditty penned by JoeBurke and Edgar Leslie ain't bad.
27. "Five O'Clock Whistle," Victor 26748. This swing ditty, penned by Kim Gannon, Josef Myrow, and William C. K. Irwin, also hit the contemporary dance floors and jukeboxes as by Glenn Miller's Orchestra—with a fine vocal by Marion Hutton, on Bluebird 10900, as well as by Ella herself, on Decca 3420. More so, it's Ivie's win in vocal comparisons—but by a nod!
28. "Chocolate Shake," Victor 27531. Ivie sounds like she is also shaking, which also describes this fine, fun, danceable ditty, penned by Paul Webster and Duke Ellington.
29. "I Got it Bad, and That Ain't Good," Victor 27531. As the most contemporary of all her ballads, this title, penned byDuke Ellington and Paul Webster, features Ivie just singing her heart out. As usual, while lacking sweetness of voice, her cool depth hits lower registers in all the right places. More so, this ditty is perhaps the most memorable of all the originals she had introduced, and this classic rendering ain't bad—and that's good!
30. "Rocks in My Bed," Victor 27639. Ivie is again effective and very cool and full of sexual expression, both in vocal prowess—(as usual) as well as in lyrics (as credited to Duke Ellington). Perhaps this style also had some impact on the up and coming diva Peggy Lee? It's for certain jazzy, and perhaps leaning toward "urban blues." Just listen!
31. "I Don't Mind," Victor 20-1598. This may be Ivie's last recording with Duke. In any case, this gem, as penned by Billy Strayhorn and Duke Ellington, again defined jazz singing, more so, at its best.

- Note: The end of WWII found Ivie making an attempt to live in California (where she was born, in about 1904), thus ending her fabulous relationship with Duke Ellington.
- Later recordings (as a single entity), sometimes as "Ivy," include the following:

32. "Play Me the Blues," Excelsior 3114. Ivie sings up a storm, and as cool as ever! Penned by Leon Rene, this ditty competes with any other postwar attempt at contemporary jazz.

33. "Mexico Joe," Excelsior 3113. The cool Ivie (again) proves she was a master of swing, and without Duke, in this ditty penned by Rene and Lane.
34. "The Voot Is Here to Stay," Black & White 772. What? This ain't swing (although it just could be a stab at postwar R & B. Penned by Baranco, Harper, and Anderson, this cool knockout performance is noted by its lyrics. Perhaps the WWII "swing shift" term and musical expression coexisted very well together? Very hip indeed! Just listen!
35. "He's Tall, Dark and Handsome," Black & White 823. This ditty, penned by Tobias and Sherman, had been a flapper-era hit title by Jane Gray, on Harmony 548-H. Ivie, who had been around then, defines this ditty as R & B, which more so notes Ivie's maturity as a vocalist.

Ivie Anderson's superior vocal style remains with us. Her poor health (died in 1949) and the great shadow of Duke Ellington seemingly limits her exposure to the public at large. As a visual performer, she also excelled in the following:

36. "All God's Chillun Got Rhythm" (1937) from the film *A Day at the Races.*
37. "Stormy Weather" (1930s). The Duke Ellington film short *A Bundle of Blues* features Ivie singing her heart out in a very tasteful setting. Ivie had been the understudy for Ethel Waters (who introduced the Harold Arlen-penned ditty, with Duke backing her up at the Cotton Club in 1933). This filmed sequence by Ivie, preceded the (better-known) full-length film *Stormy Weather*, which featured Lena Horne's fab rendition in that film. Call it a tie?
38. "Oh Babe, Maybe Someday" (1937) from the film short *Record Making with Duke Ellington.*

The Andrews Sisters

In 1937, three sisters named Andrews—from Minneapolis, Minnesota—Patty, Maxine, and La Verne (all still in their teens except La Verne, who was about twenty-two years old in 1937) produced some recordings. Emulating their idols, the Boswell Sisters, this sister act became the most commercially successful group of the pre-rock era. While many of their band arrangements were (and still are) considered schmaltzy (in retrospective), their fast-paced vocals (usually led by Patty) became hugely popular and, indeed, very imitated. The success achieved by the Andrews Sisters, greatly assisted by the likes of radio, film, personal appearances, and WWII itself was unprecedented. A middle-class Americana emerging out of the ashes of the Great Depression indeed found in this sister act a mirror of itself.

Specific mention may be made of the following:

The impact on young teenage girls. While not a "women's lib" generation, the seeds of that latter group of women are found (especially) in the success of this sister act.

- The later impact on the young GIs of WWII. The USO shows and radio appearances made deep and lasting impressions on the armed services. So was a filmed visual image, in many "B" films. They were not forgotten.
- The musicians strike of mid-1942 had little effect. As a group, however schmaltzy, they were considered a safe version of hip.

- The recordings with Bing Crosby provided them with some star power. In turn, along with some fine rhythmic vocals, they gave the aging crooner youth.

Picks

1. "Jammin," Brunswick 7863. Are Sam Coslow's penned lyrics greeted with a smoking hot vocal harmony?
2. "Bei Mir Bist du Schon," Decca 1562. This reworking of an already old German-Yiddish show, *I Would if I Could* (1933), was credited as penned by Sammy Cahn, Shalon Secunda, Saul Chapin and Jacob Jacobs. Backed by Vic Schoen and his Orchestra, in early 1938, this wordy bit of fluff, as pursued by some fine rhythmic phrasing, became a huge best-selling entity. Its very danceable and novel lyric indeed found its place on many a dance floor, as well as having some schmaltzy swing. More to come!
3. "Joseph! Joseph!" Decca 1691. Another bit of nonsence, as penned by (Sammy Cahn, Nellie Casman, Saul Chapman and Samuel Steinberg) somehow turns out well.
4. "Shortenin' Bread," Decca 1744. If Afro-Americanisms (or Southern emulations of speech) are heard, there is no disrespect intended to Connie Boswell. Perhaps even Fats Waller, who also had a contemporary version, would have agreed?
5. "Hold Tight, Hold Tight (What Some Seafood Mama)," Decca 2214. This fast-tempo ditty, penned by Kent, Brandow, Robinson, Ware, and Spotswood, may just sound like an early attempt at rock and roll. Fats Waller's contemporary version also ain't bad.
6. "Well All Right," Decca 2462. The sisters (again) sound like they are rockin', as this ditty, penned by Frances Faye, Don Raye, and Dan Howell, scores.
7. "Beer Barrel Polka (Roll out the Barrel)," Decca 2462. While in true retrospective this title itself just may be the ultimate in schmatlz, this old eastern-European beer-drinking ditty, as credited to Lew Brown, Wladimir Timm and Jaromir Vejvoda, also remains a good excuse to drink. While just making it as a pick, it's also possible that good taste may indeed become somewhat compromised with age—as this (1939) release indicates. Moreover, for some, after a few beers, this ditty may seem relevant!
8. "Ciribiribin," Decca 2800. A modest beginning (1939), with Bing Crosby, it is done well! (This old while the Italian waltz had been popular before 1900. This 1939 update by Jack Lawrence is hipper.)
9. "Rhumboogie," Decca 3097. This stupid title, penned by Raye and Price, ain't bad.
10. "Beat Me Daddy, Eight to the Bar," Decca 3375. This attempt at rhythmic phrasing is again successful.
11. "Scrub Me Mama with a Boogie Beat," Decca 3553. This Don Raye-penned ditty, like most of his penned ditties, is novel and fun.
12. "Boogie-Woogie Bugle Boy," Decca 3598. Penned by Don Raye and Hughie Prince, this (1941) recording (full of typical Andrews Sisters rhythmic jive) is perhaps their best-known recorded title. Rendered in the Abbot and Costello film *Buck Privates*, its commercial value increased. In true retrospective, this recording also had eyes for the future. As released by Bette Midler, on Atlantic 2964, in 1973, this ditty again became a best seller. Moreover, Bette's fine version stuck pretty close to the Andrews Sisters' original. More so, as a rock-era hit, its own rhythmic sound indeed gives the Andrews Sisters some claims to rock and roll itself. Just listen!
13. "Bounce Me Brother with a Solid Four," Decca 3598. This flip side of "Boogie-Woogie Bugle Boy" is another rhythmic ditty, as penned by Raye and Prince, and is also very good.
14. "Daddy," Decca 3821. This novel ditty, penned by Bob Troup, is about a woman who likes diamond rings, and more!

15. “Gimme Some Skin, My Friend,” Decca 3871. More (black) slang! Credited as penned by Raye, DePaul, and Mack, its schmaltzy and campy sound somehow works!
16. “Don’t Sit Under the Apple Tree,” Decca 18312. This original Broadway entity had been changed in title as by Sam Stept, Lew Brown, and Charles Tobias. As a subsequent (1942) best seller, it’s a good bet that perhaps no one really knew or cared about it?
17. "Mister Five by Five," Decca 18470. This black label Decca release (1942), penned by Gene De Paul and Don Raye, is for short people. It also described Jimmy Rushing, a fine contemporary bluesman, with the Count Basie Orchestra.
18. “Shoo-Shoo Baby,” Decca 18572. The sisters are complimented by better material and writing. Penned by Phil Moore, this curious combination of rhythm, blues, and pop-singing almost in itself rocks. This very relevant ditty was performed in numerous USO live shows and did not fail to please its war-weary audiences, as well as to bring down the house!
19. “Massachusetts,” Decca 18497. Penned by Lucky Roberts and Andy Razaf, this bit of fluff works well, and most likely sold very well in Massachusetts. (A contemporary Anita O’Day vocal cuts the schmaltz and, more so, defined this ditty?)
20. “Rum and Coca-Cola,” Decca 18636. This contrived bit of calypso, credited as a ditty penned by Morey Amsterdam, is, in reality, an enlightening tale about American GIs and local prostitutes, somewhere in the Caribbean. Amsterdam’s campy lyrics, which were hidden from censorships, as perhaps leaning upon local Caribbean themes did the trick? Moreover, Lionel Belasco’s (1907) “L Annee Passe”), a published piece of music penned in Trinidad, Jamaica, perhaps gave Amsterdam some, but not all, inspiration. It’s also interesting to speculate the effects of the American soft drinks’ own contribution to the war effort. It’s also more than a good bet that the sisters (Andrews) had (just) considered their (best-selling) rendering as just another “happy” song?
21. “One Meatball,” Decca 18636. It’s dumb, but it’s dumb done well! Did Josh White’s meatball also roll off the table?
22. “Pistol Packin’ Mama,” Decca 23277. Bing and the Andrews Sisters bounce this country ditty, as penned by Al Dexter and originally released by him on Okeh 7608, out into pop territory and rhythmic singing
23. “Jingle Bells,” Decca 23281. Bing and the Andrews Sisters have always had a best seller with this original WWII release up until the CD age, into the next century.
24. “Santa Claus Is Coming to Town,” Decca 23281. Bing and the Andrews Sisters again have some Yule-time fun.
25. “A Hot Time in the Town of Berlin,” Decca 23350. Yeh, this says a lot about WWII, as this best seller was taken very seriously by many service men, including the father of this author. The original 78 rpm release of this bit of WWII history credits two fine musicians (turned servicemen) writing honors (Sgt. Joe Buskin and Pvt. John De Vries). This dated vocal (1944) finds Bing and the Andrews Sister in fine form, along with some novel inspiration and slang about the coming destruction of Hitler’s Reich.
26. “Is You Is or Is You Ain’t My Baby,” Decca 23281. Penned by rhythm and blues pioneer Louis Jordan and Billy Austin, Jordan’s original on Decca 8659 was more than good. Nevertheless, as masters of lyric-bending, as well as with some fine authentic urban Afro-American slang, Bing and the Andrews Sisters indeed add some explosive vocal harmony.
27. “Don’t Fence Me In,” Decca 23364. Is this a “cowboy” title, penned by Cole Porter? Yes it is! Moreover, and despite a fine contemporary Roy Rogers version on Victor

20-3073, a very hip Bing Crosby, in perfect lyrical interplay with the rhythmic Andrews, makes it all happen.

28. "The Three Caballeros," Decca 23364. Bing and the Andrews Sisters again excel as they take on a Latin beat. Penned by Manual Esperon, Ray Gilbert, and Ernesto Cortazar, this novel and contrived ditty was featured in the contemporary (1945) Disney cartoon feature by the same name. Moreover, despite the schmaltz, it all works!
29. "Ac-Cent-Tchu-Ate-the Positive," Decca 23379. Don't bother with this Johnny Mercer-penned ditty as featured in the Crosby film *Here Come the Waves*, minus the Andrews Sisters! Instead, get this recording, featuring a lively Bing and the Andrews Sisters' vocal performance and enjoy good listening.
30. "South America, Take It Away," Decca 23569. Bing and the Andrews Sisters again hit a Latin beat in this ditty, penned by Harold Rome, from the musical revue, *Call Me Mister*. While dated and schmaltzy, Bing and the Andrews Sisters (again) demonstrate and generate some interesting rhythmic harmony.
31. "Them That Has, Gets," Decca 23656. Gene De Paul and Don Raye (again) penned another winner, however wordy. The sisters are, moreover, backed by Eddie Heywood and His Orchestra.
32. "Christmas Island", Decca—23722. As backed by Guy Lombardo and his Royal Canadians, this seasonal ditty may claim exemption from being labeled schmaltz.
33. "Tallahasse," Decca 23885. This Frank Loesser-penned title is just OK for Bing and the Sisters. Moreover, the capital city of the state of Florida just may have found this ditty an excellent effort.
34. "Anything You Can Do, I Can Do Better," Decca 40039. Bing and the Andrews Sisters are joined by the very popular crooner of the 1940s, Dick Haymes. Bing had traditionally been at his best on Irving Berlin-penned titles, and this fast-paced ditty is, indeed, no exception. Perhaps Haymes, in fact, had something to prove, and as it turns out, he survives. Moreover, all the vocals jell, with the girls winning out, especially in lyric. Perhaps the ultimate women's lib song? As written by a male?
35. "Near You," Decca 24171. Somehow, this bit of sentimental fluff became one of the best-selling entities of the whole decade. While a contemporary version by Bob Lamm—for the Francis Craig Orchestra on an independent label (Bullet 1001)—and penned by J. Bulleit and K. Goell did indeed sell a few more copies, the sisters do well enough. Or call it sentimental mush?
36. "You Don't Have to Know the Language," Decca 24282. Bing and the Andrews Sisters pronounce and strive at interpretation of lyric. While it's all a bit schmalz, as penned by (Burke & Van Heusen), it is (still) something that works!
37. "I'm Bitin' My Fingernails and Thinking of You," Decca 24592. By the latter '40s, the harmony and energy of the Andrews Sisters had become familiar and they were recognized recording artists. This ditty pairs them with (fellow Decca) recording artist Ernest Tubb. His "ruff" and rural vocal somehow works well with the smoother sound of the sisters, following Patty's (usual) vocal lead.
38. "I Can Dream, Can't I?" Decca 24709. A 1930s' Broadway entity, this ditty had been introduced by "Tamara," although the Harry James release, featuring Helen Humes, made it more of a familiar popular tune. This Andrews Sisters revival, some ten years later, while not as good as the Helen Humes vocal, is still good enough and, more so, a best seller.
39. "Quicksilver," Decca 24827. This somewhat contrived, country-western entity, as penned by I. Taylor, G. Wyle, and E. Pola, somehow all works. Bing and the ladies again score, although by this time (1950), they are all sounding a bit aged.

40. "I Wanna Be Loved," Decca 27007. This ain't bad, although a Dinah Washington version (with less schmaltz) got it done better.
41. "Mele Kalikimaka," Decca 27228. Bing and the ladies somehow make this schmaltzy Hawaiian Christmas, without snow, somehow work.

➢ Visual Image

In the (1941) Abbot and Costello film *Buck Privates*, the sisters introduced the following:

42. "Boogie-Woogie Bugle Boy."
43. "Bounce Me Brother Eight to the Bar."
44. "You Don't Have To Know The Language". Andrews Sisters & Bing!

Louis Armstrong

- The appreciation of Louis Armstrong, as a twentieth-century musician—even into the next century—is still indeed greatly acknowledged. His gritty vocal talents with huge amounts of Afro-Americanisms of language, while certainly full of novelty, became the very fundamental aspects of what developed into "jazz," defining it. While this New Orleans' trumpet player (born about 1900 in that great city) did not invent it, his many mentors, including the likes of Joe "King" Oliver, schooled him deeply. Along with many contemporaries, including the likes of Kid Ory and Sidney Bechet, he rushed into the 1920s with a musical impetus not before exploited. While many would argue about just who could or would be better, it would all never have been the same without Louis.
- His attempt at jazz vocals, including his "scatting," along with his playing, perhaps clinched it?

Perhaps the Afro-American communities of Chicago had heard him first? Perhaps even pianist Fletcher Henderson, the "Colored King of Jazz," just didn't understand it? Even Bix Beiderbecke, a young and early (white) disciple, perhaps tried a bit too hard to emulate him? Perhaps it could never be explained just how things meshed so well for him in the 1920s. As a backup musician, his legacy could have been enough. The purposes of the book, moreover, highlight his jazz and pop vocals. His stylistic approach to rhythmic ditties (scatting) popularized a basic Afro-American style. His attempt at ballads led to some fine crooning, despite his gritty vocals. Unlike any other vocalist, black or white before him, he was, for a time, an unexplained and inexplicable success. By the early 1930s, his vocals became identifiable as "jazz" itself. His influence upon the likes of blues, pop and hillbilly were indeed considerable. His dabbling and his interest in Latino rhythm would also win for him great musical and best-selling notice. So indeed was his interest in white pop and early (1930s) Bing Crosby's crooning efforts. His own (vocal) emulation is easier. The Ethel Waters (1933) Brunswick release of "I Can't Give You Anything but Love" found her knee deep in flattery, for about a third of the song. Paying more serious attention to detail would find the likes of Fats Waller, Cab Calloway, Valaida Snow, Chick Bullock, Bing Crosby, Louis Prima, and especially Billie Holiday finding Louis's own vocal and trumpet as something more. So would indeed the drift of all popular music for the rest of the century. Moreover, this heavy, little black man also became a stereotype in himself. Whatever image he had, he was to most a living and breathing musical idiom, far beyond the racism and restrictions of the century. His achievements, in true retrospective, were due to his own interest in anything he liked. The results were thus to become worldwide!

❖ Picks

1. "Gut Bucket Blues," Okeh 8261. In late 1925, he formed a band called Louis Armstrong and His Hot Five, consisting of Kid Ory (on trombone), Johnny Dodds (on clarinet), Lil Hardin (on piano), Johnny St. Cyr (on banjo), and Louis himself (on cornet, with his oen gritty vocal style. As shared a bit with Kid Ory, its novel approach left no doubt that this vocal, or whatever it was, was distinctly Afro-American.
2. "Heebie Jeebies," Okeh 8300. Perhaps the inspiration of for this ditty was a "rag" entitled "Heliotrope Bouguet," as penned by Scott Joplin and Louis Chauvin. In any case, as credited to Boyd Atkins (also Afro-American), the spirited scatting vocal by Louis found on this fast-paced dance ditty was to become an historic event. Whether Louis forgot the lyrics or perhaps he dropped them is hard to determine. The excitement of his slurring of words, his improvisation, his scatting is, more so, without doubt. Louis was not the first to scat. Indeed, many of the "blues queens" of the era had done it before him. No one, however, sounded as Louis did. No one had his voice, his vocal. His style. His jazz, from New Orleans via Chicago, indeed found great notice on this recording. (A contemporary Ethel Waters version is also good but not as powerful as Louis's version. A (later) group rendering by the Boswell Sisters may be considered a bit better than the Waters's version, and at least a challenge to Armstrong.)
3. "Big Butter and Egg Man," Okeh 8423. This 1926 recording (with his Hot Five) also includes a shared "hot" vocal with Mae Alex. (Alberta Hunter?)
4. "West End Blues," Okeh 8597. This Chicago recording of 1928 credits Louis with his Hot Five. While Louis is at a loss with a limit of words, his mood is a breathtaking experience. There was perhaps some speculation that this was a written effort by Joe "King" Oliver and Clarence Williams. It's obvious that Louis's scatting delivered no real lyric, or needed to. (Louis would recreate his effort year later in the 1946 film *New Orleans*. A contemporary Ethel Waters version, with moody drama, more so delivers a bold and poignant performance with lyrics that indeed take a swipe at a serious accounting of the real urban "west end.")
5. "A Monday Date," Okeh 8597. This side is more of a pop vocal, with some great Dixieland playing.
6. "Basin Street Blues," Okeh 8690. This Spencer Williams-penned ditty found Louis very familiar with its title. As part of New Orleans, Basin Street was originally part of a drainage mark until drainage pipes were installed underneath the so-named street, by the end of the 1800s. As myth would have it, he was associated with Madame Lulu White and Mahogany Hall at 235 N. Basin Street (before 1917), as well as Jelly Roll Morton's instrumental "Mahogany Hall Stomp." Spencer William's (1928) lyrics more so add leaps and bounds to the mythology of New Orleans about an implied brothel featuring jazz music and perfectly fits into Louis's mumbling of words in his moody vocal. (A later 1937 version featuring another New Orleans-associated entity vocalist Connie Boswell, also with Bing Crosby, would perhaps redefine this ditty)? Listen and compare!

7. "St. James Infirmary," Okeh 8657. The novel approach wears thin, as this chilling tale of the dead is defined. Louis's own gritty vocal is put to good use here, and along with a truly haunting horn section, including Louis's own horn, this classic recording becomes a serious item. Gambling Blues? A fine but subdued Gene Austin version also exists! Is Louis purposely stereotyping of Afro-Americans? Yet another rendering, with a more novel approach, is to be found on a (later) Cab Calloway version.
8. "Tight Like This," Okeh 8649. Another bit of Afro-Americanisms is cleverly exploited. Accompanied by Don Redman, another fine musician who would also lead his own band, this hot novelty (penned by L. Curl) just could be kin to Georgia Tom Dorsey's "Its Tight Like That," as released by Tampa Red and Georgia Tom on Vocalion 1216. Perhaps Frankie "Half Pint" Jaxon got it done better (Vocalion 1228), also in association with Tampa Red. In comparison, it's Louis's urban sounds that further develop his ditty, knee deep in (black) culture.
9. "I Can't Give You Anything but Love," Okeh 8669. This 1929 recording, a Blackbird entity, ain't bad. (A later (1933) Ethel Waters release, on Brunswick 6517, would even produce a parody of Louis, for at least a third of her vocal.)
10. "Black and Blue," Okeh 8714. While just as serious as "St. James Infirmary," this race-baiting ditty, as penned by Fats Waller, Harry Brooks, and Andy Razaf, had even more significance. As a real Broadway entity from the all-black revue "Hot Chocolates" as well, Louis was involved in introducing it (along with Edith Wilson). If Edith's version (Brunswick 4685) is skeptical about the aspects of skin color within the (black) community, Louis (with his blazing trumpet) is more dramatic about It. (A contemporary Ethel Waters version, on Columbia 2184-D, is even more poignant, with added drams.)
11. "Ain't Misbehavin, '" Okeh 8714. Penned by Fats Waller and Andy Razaf, this Broadway classic from "Hot Chocolates" is fully exploited by the novel Louis. Other versions would follow, including a fine and jazzy vocal by Eva Taylor (on a Charleston Chasers release), by a white bandleader Seger Ellis (perhaps trying to emulate Louis), and a slower and torch version by Ruth Etting, among others.
12. "When You're Smiling," Okeh 8729. This dumb novelty song ditty, as penned by Larry Shay, Mark Fisher and Joe Goodwin needed a fresh rhythmic approach. Luckily, Louis provided all it needed!
13. "Rockin' Chair," Okeh 8756. The combined talents of writer Hoagy Carmichael and Louis are heard loud and clear, as Hoagy's attempt at a an interracial vocal succeeds. This novel recording is, moreover, defined, noting a later version by Mildred Bailey oddly overshadowed it.
14. "Dallas Blues," Okeh 8774. This ditty had been around since 1912 as a title using the word "blues" and a penned instrumental by a white guy, Hart Wand. By the early 1920s, it was credited to Wand-Garrett. An acoustic die-hard "blues" version by (white singer) Lee Morse in 1925 had perhaps defined it? Louis, as usual, tears into these lyrics. Or does he? A contemporary version by Fats Waller and bandleader Ted Lewis, on Columbia 2527-D, also ain't bad.
15. "St. Louis Blues," Okeh 41350. By 1929, this Handy-penned ditty had already become part of the American idiom. Moreover, Louis again excels and does not disappoint his listeners. (Louis had backed, not vocally, the fine acoustic and defining (1925) Bessie Smith vocal on Columbia 14064-D).
16. "My Sweet," Okeh 41415. By 1930, Louis Armstrong and His Orchestra (with musicians changing on practically every recording or "live" date) had already become

an American institution. More so, this gritty vocal. penned by Hoagy Carmichael and S. Gorrell, found its expected public acceptance in sales, despite the Great Depression.

- The following eleven recordings were recorded in Los Angeles and released as part of a highly publicized gig at (Frank) Sebastian's New Cotton Club between 1930 and 1931. While toward the end of the gig in early 1931 there just may have been some trouble between Louis and his reputed mobster-employer, it was the excitement generated at this nightspot, more so than his previous ones (including Chicago's Dreamland Café and New York's Savoy Ballroom) that provided Louis with national recognition as a "live" entity, in addition to an influential recording artist. (These original recordings find Louis and his Orchestra noted as Louis Armstrong And His Sebastian New Cotton Club Orchestra on the Okeh Record label).

17. "Confessin' That I Love You," Okeh 41448. Louis's own (crude) crooning job contributes much to this otherwise sad and weeping tale, penned by Dougherty, and Neiburg. Confessing?
18. "If I Could Be with You One Hour Tonight," Okeh 41448. Indeed a relevant shot at this much-recorded ditty, as penned by (black) composers Henry Creamer and James P. Johnson, finds Louis committed!
19. "Memories of You," Okeh 41463. The original contemporary Ethel Waters release (and its original flip side (noted below)) finds Louis's own vocal versions laying some legitimate claims.
20. You're Lucky to Me," Okeh 41463. The Ethel Waters version is challenged!
21. "Body and Soul," Okeh 41468. This Los Angeles, California, recording featured a fine crooning vocal, much indeed like his previous "I'm Confessin'." Moreover, this attempt at this popular contemporary torch entity was indeed a contrast to the likes of the highbrow versions of Libby Holman and Helen Morgan. Another contemporary version, by Jack Fulton for the Paul Whiteman Orchestra, when compared to Louis's version, if jazzy, is very lightweight. Yet another pop version by Ruth Etting, while containing no grit, is at least as stylistic as Louis's vocal.
22. "Sweethearts on Parade," Columbia 2688-D. Penned by Carmen Lombardo, brother of the famous Guy Lombardo, this ditty had been a (1928) Lombardo best seller on Columbia 1628-D. While noting that Lombardo's sound just could have been the ultimate "sweet band," it's also obvious that Carmen, who also sang for his brother, had a stiff voice. Louis's differing vocal with it's obvious grit, finds it all more interesting listening!
23. "You're Driving Me Crazy," Okeh 41478. This Broadway entity from *Smiles* had received a quirky crooning job from contemporary, Nick Lucas. With a little dialog from a young Lionel Hampton, this fast-paced ditty could almost rock and roll! Louis again demonstrates his effective vocal abilities, as perhaps referring to himself, or his trumpet, as a "satchel mouth." The name, more so, stuck as "Satchmo"—something that credited composer (Walter Donaldson), in vocal slang, could never have imagined?
24. "The Peanut Vendor," Okeh 41478. This Latino-flavored title, based upon "El Manisero," credited to M. Simons, had already become a contemporary hit as performed by Don Azpiazu and his Havana Casino Orchestra. The vocal by Cuban-styled vocalist Arto Machin, on Victor 22483, had somehow dominated sales of a Depression-weary record-buying public, not usually impressed by a truly ethnic enterprise. The ever-creative Louis, armed with his own trumpet solo and his usual vocal grittiness, along with his (then) Los Angeles-based Sebastian New Cotton Club

Orchestra, attacks both lyrics and structure, and in the process, somehow produces a superior recording. Louis is, moreover, to be he heard, vocally and instrumentally, at his absolute zenith here, noting a truly dramatic vocal, with a somber and poignant mood.

25. "Just a Gigolo," Okeh 41486. From out of the Ted Lewis band (the singing bandleader himself), Ted Lewis, on Columbia 2378-D, scored well vocally. An import from (pre-Hitler) Germany, this ditty had been known as "Schoner Gigolo" (penned by Julious Brammer). Its English lyrics, by Irving Caesar and Leonello Casucci, contain a sad tale about a returned WWI war vet and is, moreover, a poignant and powerful story, full of clichés. A contemporary (1931) crooning job by Bing Crosby, on Victor 22701, more so defined it with a really creative and interesting vocal. Louis's approach is also effective, if slightly more rhythmic, and full of his usual grit. Indeed something of substance to listen to and compare!
26. "Shine," Okeh 41486. This already old title from 1909 had been penned by Cecil Mack and Ford Dabney (titled "That's Why They Call Me Shine"). As both authors were Afro-Americans, this ditty's racial references were originally novel, but hardly a coon song. After surviving ragtime, the early 1920s found a worthy instrumental by a jazzy (white) group, the California Ramblers, recorded on Columbia 127-D. Louis had been more than likely been aware of this ditty while starting out as a musician in New Orleans, and this subsequent (1931) recording with vocal and trumpet, more so, would define it. While this ditty would remain a standard, a contemporary (1932) Bing Crosby and the Mills Brothers version, perhaps most inspired by Louis, on Brunswick 6276, furthered the advancement of defining jazz vocals. Indeed, Bing's remarkable crooning and scatting in harmony with the (original) Mills Brothers is nothing short of a spectacular vocal performance!
27. "Walking My Baby Back Home," Okeh 41497. Contemporaries Nick Lucas, Annette Hanshaw, and Lee Morse also got it right, noting a huge difference in styles. (Josephine Baker in Paris?)
28. "I Surrender, Dear," Okeh 41497. The crooning Bing Crosby mega hit (1931) still found Louis interested, as well as a bit influenced. As usual, he does not disappoint.
29. "When Its Sleepy Time Down South," Okeh 41504. This curious pick of a theme song, by Louis himself, is OK. Penned by Leon Rene, Otis Rene and Clarence Muse, this black-penned ditty seems in itself to designate old stereotypes. Moreover, if it pleased Louis, it must have been OK.
30. "I'll Be Glad when You're Dead, You Rascal You," Okeh 41504. This (1931) ditty was rivaled by the contemporary recordings of Cab Calloway (Brunswick 6196), the (original) Mills Brothers (Brunswick 6225), and also by Fats Waller and Jack Teagarden (Columbia 2558-D).
31. "Blue Again," Okeh 41498. This title was penned by Dorothy Fields and Jimmy McHugh for the *The Vanderbilt Revue*. This light and rhythmic ditty became a typical sweet band entity for a Hotel Pennsylvania Trio release, with a (group) vocal refrain sounding like chipmunks (Crown 3042). Among other versions, a contemporary Marion Harris version, on Brunswick 6016, confirmed its identity, until Louis got a hold of it! Indeed, the creative and rhythmic Louis had other concerns, both vocally and instrumentally, as this ditty is turned into something (almost) rocking, and very special!
32. "When Your Lover Has Gone," Okeh 41498. Louis attempts a fine torch song, perhaps influenced by a contemporary Ethel Waters version, on Columbia 2409-D; more so, he succeeds.

33. "Little Joe," Okeh 41501. This nifty novelty was penned by N. Miller and J. Styne, and perhaps finds Louis at his wildest vocal. The backing rhythm section sounds a bit out of control, but so what!
34. "Them There Eyes," Okeh 41501. While penned by familiar (black) team of William Tracey, Doris Tauber, and Maeco Pinkard, this ditty, as a vocal, took off as a Gus Arnheim hit (Victor 22561) with a sparkling and rhythmic vocal by Bing Crosby (as a Rhythm Boy). While Louis may have indeed been inspired by the (Rhythm Boys) vocals, his subsequent and playful vocal obviously differs. (A later Billie Holiday version of this ditty, moreover, emulated Louis, not Bing!)
35. "Stardust," Okeh 41530. As already noted, Louis recorded a lot of material that Bing Crosby also recorded. This ditty, above the others, defines a jazz vocal, as much as Bing defined this as a pop entity. (Louis recorded two versions, with the "B" take being the best.)
36. "You Can Depend on Me," Okeh 41538.
37. "The Lonesome Road," Okeh 41538. While led by Gene Austin's earlier version, Louis's own vocal is obviously a major change, which sounds like an interesting comparison. While still other versions are good, perhaps a (later) rendering, as by Sister Rosetta Tharpe, is better?
38. "Lazy River," Okeh 41541. Louis truly does put you on a (Carmichael) "river."
39. "Georgia on My Mind," Okeh 41541. Was a later rock-era version by Ray Charles influenced by this 1931 version? A later (1938) Ethel Waters version was not. Good comparisons? Yes!
40. "All of Me," Okeh 41552. While contemporaries such as Russ Columbo and Mildred Bailey (on a Paul Whiteman release) crooned out this ditty as soft as possible, it's more than obvious that Louis's cruder and rhythmic crooning also scores.
41. "Lawd, You Made the Night Too Long," Okeh 41560. It's interesting to compare the contemporary Bing Crosby's and Boswell Sisters' vocals on Brunswick 20109, which also featured Don Redman's Orchestra. Moreover, while the slang use of "lawd" is no problem for Bing, the real and Southern accents of the Boswell Sisters are indeed kin to Louis. Moreover, a most interesting comparison!

Note: The above Okeh-labeled records were, in many cases, reissued on the Columbia label (which had bought out Okeh, as an independent label, as far back as 1929) in the early 1930s. In 1932, Louis proceeded to record for quite a few recording labels, including Victor, Decca (red label—Columbia), Capital, and Kapp. While Louis continues to interest us as a vocalist, his influence as a personality became more of a selling point for most of the rest of his great career (spanning into the '70s). The following recordings, moreover, have merit:

42. "Hobo, You Can't Ride on This Train," Victor 24200. This early hit of 1933 proved that Louis still had "it," and this ditty's title itself indicates a fine tale can be told. Hop aboard!
43. "I Gotta Right to Sing the Blues," Victor 24245. Yes he did!
44. "There's a Cabin in the Pines," Victor 24335. Louis (again) achieves excellence and (somehow) croons out this ditty just as effectively as a contemporary Bing Crosby version, on Brunswick 6610, as well as many others.
45. "Old Man Mose," Decca 622. Another well-done novelty, aspenned by Zilner Randolph and Louis himself.

46. "Public Melody Number One," Decca 1347. This contrived ditty penned by Ted Koehler and Harold Arlen was fortunate enough to have Louis do it.
47. "Pennies from Heaven," Decca 15027. This somewhat odd 12-inch 78rpm (1936) release, found Bing Crosby and the (very) highbrow female contemporary pop vocalist, Frances Langford, subsequently Crooning out this ditty with Louis. While it's also a bit of a mystery that Frances Langford, who was not in the film by the same name as both Louis and Bing were, it's also odd that Louis's own orchestra, was not used for backing. In any case, this ditty, penned by Johnston and Burke, is pleasant enough and, more so, proves that Louis's own (crude) crooning could retain a soft touch. Moreover, the Jimmy Dorsey Orchestra does indeed contribute a fine "sweet" band backing for all three fine voices.
48. "Pennies from Heaven Medley," Decca 15027. This side, penned by Arthur Johnston and Johnny Burke, features

* Frances Langford singing "Let's Call a Heart, a Heart,"
* Frances Langford and Bing singing "So Do I," and
* Louis Armstrong singing "Skelton in the Closet." (Louis had introduced this ditty in the film itself.)

49. "The Flat Foot Floogie," Decca 1876. The Mills Brothers (with John Mills Sr. replacing his son in 1936), produce some harmony with Louis on this excellent and folksy novelty, claimed bu Bud Green, Slim Galliard and Slam Stewart
50. "My Walking Stick," Decca 1892. Despite the contemporary (1938) film *Alexander's Ragtime Band* and a subsequent and stiff Tony Martin release, on Brunswick 8153, this Irving Berlin-penned ditty is best defined in this release, along with the equally rhythmic Mills Brothers.
51. "WhenThe Saints Go Marching In". Decca-2230. In his youth, Louis witnessed many New Orleans funerals. As the mixed culture found the Bible especially handy for those who have passed on, this adapted 1939 jazzed up funeral march was indeed historical, as well as relivant.
52. "Jeepers Creepers," Decca 2267. This ditty, penned by Harry Warren and JohnnyMercer, was introduced by Louis in the film *Going Places*. While perhaps this (horse) name is dumb, this excellent recording survives the film. (Both Louis and Maxine Sullivan were also featured in the film.)
53. "W. P. A.," Decca 3151. Along with the Mills Brothers, Louis provides some political satire, as penned by J. Jones, upon unflattered contemporary about a contemporary 1940 Franklin D. Roosevelt *New Deal* program.
54. "Marie," Decca 3151. Louis and the Mills Brothers produce rhythmic impulse and a fine prototype for "rock and roll." Moreover, the latter 1930s had seen a revival of the already old Rudy Vallee hit, by Jack Leonard as a Tommy Dorsey release. More so, this rhythmic rendering is far better and perhaps the real inspiration for the later 1953 R & B vocal by the Four Tunes on Jubilee 5128. Just listen!
55. "Where the Blues Were Born in New Orleans," RCA Victor 20-2088. This (contrived) ditty was penned by Cliff Dixon and Bob Carleton for the low-budget (1945) film *New Orleans*. Somehow, it all works, as Louis's narrative vocal of a highly fictionalized film drama about Louis's hometown benefits hugely because of Louis himself. His ditty also introduces to the screen, and to this recording, some (true) backing jazz entities. They include Barney Bigard (on clarinet), Red Callender (on

bass), Charlie Beal (on piano), Bud Scott (on guitar), Kid Ory (on trombone), Minor Hall (on drums), and Louis himself (on trumpet). Good old Dixieland alive?

56. "Blues for Yesterday," RCA Victor 20-2456. This (1946) recording, penned by Lester Carr is another contrived ditty, especially fit for Louis. It succeeds.
57. "Blues in the South," RCA Victor 20-2456. It is the flip side of "Blues for Yesterday." This contrived ditty, penned by Lester Carr and William Johnstone, also works.
58. "You Won't Be Satisfied Until You Break My Heart," Decca 23496. It is a duet with Ella Fitzgerald.
59. "The Frim Fram Sauce," Decca 23496. Another duet with Ella Fitzgerald.
60. "My Sweet Hunk O' Trash," Decca 24785. This latter-1940s' release, as penned by James P. Johnson and Flournoy E. Miller, is no fluke. The original record label itself credits Billie Holiday and Louis Armstrong and demonstrates a surprising lack of ego on Louis's part. Moreover, both Louis and Billie deliver a smoking and fine novelty with both artists at their playful and skillful best. (Louis, at one point of this recording, suspiciously turns a word into a suspected four-letter word! In reality, he does not! Listen for it!)
61. "La Vie En Rose," Decca 27113. Louis, already popular in France, contributes his gritty vocal style to Edith Piaf's most popular song ditty!
62. "A Kiss to Build a Dream On," Decca 27720.
63. "That's My Desire," Decca 28372. This duet with Velma Middleton (1950) features a live campy exchange of the (then) current Frankie Lane best seller on Mercury 5007.
64. "Blueberry Hill," Decca 30091. The (1940) Gene Autry entity, also recorded by Connie Boswell, is, moreover, revived by Louis in 1956. Later in the same year, Fats Domino, on Imperial 5407, would claim it and produce a best-selling entity.
65. "A Theme from the Three Penny Opera," Columbia 40587. This 1956 release, penned by Kurt Weill and Marc Blitzstein (who wrote the English lyrics from this German opera), is better known as "Mack the Knife." This tale perhaps took place in a German port city in the early 1930s. Perhaps the crime could also have taken place in an American port city? Indeed, Louis did it well. So (later) did Bing Crosby, Bobby Darin, and Ella Fitzgerald.

➢ *High Society*, Capital LP W 750. As featured in the excellent 1956 LP, Louis, along with his band and Bing Crosby, amazingly creates musical heat with

66. "Now You Has Jazz."

- Apart from an electrified filmed performance, this recording is also excellent and captures the spirited rendering. While it's true that Bing Crosby hogs up most of this vocal duet, Louis still scores heavily, along with his contemporary (1956) (racially mixed) band. The two old men (then both in their middle fifties) somehow gel, and this contrived lesson of jazz, as penned by Cole Porter, somehow works!

67. "Hello Dolly," Kapp 573. This early 1964 recording, penned by Jerry Herman, has Louis competing with the arrival of the Beatles! While this piece of pop is considered just OK, Louis's vocal and trumpet (again) demonstrate timeless innovation.
68. "What a Wonderful World," ABC 10982. This lightweight bit of schmaltz, penned by George Douglas, George D. Weiss, and Bob Thiele, is, nevertheless, an effective 1968 pop vocal. While the signs of rock and roll and "modern" jazz perhaps distracted from Louis a bit, the sheer oddity of Louis's vocal style (again) trumpts. Moreover, a (1988)

reissue on A & M 3010, released some seventeen years after his death (1971), again found some best-selling popularity.

♦ Visual Image

- Louis Armstrong became very much a "world" entity by the end of his (1933) European tour. While noting the many racial barriers he encountered, Louis was featured in quite few films, usually playing "current" hits. Ditties like "Pennies from Heaven"(1936), "Going Places" (1937), and even "The Five Pennies" (1959), with comic Danny Kaye as jazz entity Red Nichols, ain't bad. The best however are in

➢ *High Society.* Already noted as a recording, this (1956) film found

69. "Now You Has Jazz." It finds the old men, both Bing and Louis, with a fine band, creating a fine visual performance.
70. "I'll Be Glad When You're Dead, You Rascal You." Already noted as a pick, this fine ditty also found its way as a title for a black-and-white Fleischer cartoon. The creative *Betty Boop* series of the early 1930s featured, at times, both animation and live filmed performances of contemporary popular entertainers. This one featured Louis and his band in "jungle" gear.
71. "West End Blues." Louis is seen playing and scatting in the 1946 film *New Orleans.*

❖ Special Louis Armstrong Section

• The vocalists who influenced Louis Armstrong's own (progressive) vocal style are usually overlooked. Louis had originally been a member of various New Orleans bands and orchestras before emigrating to Chicago in the early 1920s. As a studio musician, he backed up the many "blues queens" of the era, as well as some fine early bluesmen. The following are (selective) recordings, featuring vocals (not including Louis). More so, many of them are featured vocalists noted within this book. As most listed are of acoustic sound quality, his distinct trumpet idiom may be noted on these recordings also noted as backed-up by Louis. (Most of this information was found in the *Esquire Jazz Book* (1944).

* "Cake Walking Babies," Gennett 5617 (the Red Onion Jazz Babies with Josephine Beatty, alias Alberta Hunter, doing the vocal).
* "Nobody Knows the Way I Feel Dis Morning," Gennett 5626 (same as above).
* "Early Every Morn'," Gennett 5626 (same as above). Flip side.
* "Texas Moaner Blues," Okeh 8171 (the Clarence Williams Blue Five; Eva Taylor, vocal).
* "Everybody Loves My Baby," Okeh 8181 (same as above).
* "Mandy Make Up Your Mind," Okeh 40260 (same as above).
* "Cake Walking' Babies," Okay 5627 (same as above).
* "See See Rider Blues," Paramount 12252 (Ma Rainey).
* "Jelly Bean Blues," Paramount 12238 (same as above).
* "Courtin' the Blues," Paramount 12238 (same as above). Flip side.
* "What Kind of Man is You," Okeh 8313 (Baby Mack).
* "He Likes It Slow," Okeh 8355 (Butterbeans and Susie).

* "Lazy Woman's Blues," Okeh 8279 (Blanche Calloway).
* "Lonesome Lovesick Blues," Okeh 8279 (same as above).
* "Mistreatin' Daddy Blues," Paramount 12298 (Ida Cox).
* "Trouble in Mind," Okeh 8312 (Bertha Chippie Hill).
* "Georgia Man," Okeh 8312 (same as above). Flip Side.
* "Pleading the Blues," Okeh 8429 (same as above).
* "Mama's All Alone Blues," Okeh 8185 (Margret Johnson).
* "Thunderstorm Blues," Columbia 14050-D (Maggie Jones).
* "Early in the Morning," Okay 8187 (Virginia Liston).
* "(Blue Yodel No. 9) Standing on the Corner," Victor 23580 (Jimmie Rodgers).
* "St. Louis Blues," Columbia 14064-D (Bessie Smith).
* "Ain't Gonna Play Second Fiddle," Columbia 14090-D (same as above).
* "Nobody Knows the Way I Feel," Columbia 14058-D (Clara Smith).
* "Broken Busted Blues," Columbia 14062-D (same as above).
* "How Do They Do It," Okeh 8713 (Victoria Spivey).
* "Adam and Eve Had the Blues," Okeh 8258 (Hociel Thomas).
* "Jack of Diamond Blues," Okeh 8328 (Sippie Wallace).
* "Special Delivery Blues," Okeh 8328 (same as above). Flip side.
* "Dead Drunk Blues," Okeh 8449 (same as above).
* "Lazy Man Blues," Okeh 8470 (same as above).
* "Find Me at the Greasy Spoon," Paramount 12337 (Coot Grant).
* "You've Got to Beat Me," Paramount 12256 (Trixie Smith).
* "Mining Camp Blues," Paramount 12256 (same as above).
* "Railroad Blues," Paramount 12262 (same as above).
* "The World's Gone Jazz Crazy," Paramount 12262 (same as above). Flip side.

➢ The Legacy of Louis Armstrong

- Perhaps the best way to appreciate Louis is to listen to any latter-century band trumpeter. Louis, by combining scatting vocals with his trumpet, led the a musical style into mainstream Americana. Without him, the music would not have become the influence it became. Louis did not invent Dixieland or jazz, but did define it, and more so than any of his contemporaries. The brothel music of (1800s) New Orleans indeed progressed. So indeed did a quirky and gravel-voiced native, who inexplicabaly gave it class.

Eddy Arnold

- The 1930s had brought along much emulation of the likes of Bing Crosby and his recordings. While the success of Dick Todd and Perry Como (with the Ted Weems Orchestra) indeed provides proof of such enterprise, the latter 1930s found Bing himself rapidly aging, and changing, as a vocalist. Soon after Perry Como left the Ted Weems organization in the early 1940s (due to the musicians strike and WWII), RCA Victor signed the radio-singing Perry Como to a recording contract. Perry's vocals, in fact, had seemed to even follow Crosby's changes—vocally. At around the same time, the emerging "country and western" market (still called "hillbilly," as coined in the 1920s), reeling from the success of post-Prohibition honky-tonk (small bar) songs became very popular. Fed by a developing jukebox industry), many a rural bar and grill seemed hungry for one of its own. As well as the examples of the recordings of Roy Acuff and Bill Monroe (found elsewhere in this book), the cultural and regional borders of this music became more apparent. Such entities as "Walking the Floor over You"(by Ernest Tubb on Decca 5958) and "Pistol Packin' Mama" (by Al Dexter on Okeh 6708) provide any listener a good earful what defined "country." Bing's own contemporary emulation of these ditties (on Decca 18371 and Decca 23277) provided some added energy for him, as well as recording fodder.

While Bing's stylistic differences are very much evident (as well as the big band backups) the still potent appeal of Bing, as a film, radio, and recording entity, still required "country treatment." The search for a smooth-edged crooner by Victor also led to the signing of one Eddy Arnold, a radio entity from Franklin, Tennessee. Although he was indeed a real farm boy (known as the Tennessee Plowboy," his simple vocals amounted to a low-keyed crooning sound. The fiddles and steel guitar backgrounds heard on most early recordings, moreover, identify "country." While a similar Decca Records discovery, Red Foley, would provide Eddie a stylistic country rival, the fodder that resulted indeed gave country music its own crooners, in addition to Bing Crosby.

- Selective Picks

1. "Mommy, Please Stay Home with Me," Bluebird 33-0520. This odd tale of tragic consequences is perhaps real. Penned byWally Fowler, J, Graydon Hall, and Arnold himself, this tale finds a bar-hopping mother discovering her neglected child near death when she finally gets home.
2. "Cattle Call," Bluebird 33-0527. Penned by Tex Owens, this contrived tale of a yodeling cowboy is not for everyone. While a marginal pick, this ditty did have much contemporary (1944) appeal.
3. "I Walk Alone," Bluebird 33-0535. This Herbert Wilson-penned ditty by Eddie actually displays some blues.
4. "You Must Walk the Line," Bluebird 33-0540. Penned by WallyFowler, J. Graydon Hall, and Arnold himself, this follow-up to "I Walk Alone" ain't bad. Moreover, perhaps a very young Johnny Cash was listening?
5. "That's How Much I Love You," Victor 20-1948. Penned by Arnold, Wally Fowler, and J. GraydonHall, this ditty defines the effective vocal prowess of the soft understatement, without becoming mellow. As a matter of fact, the likes of contemporary versions, as by Frank Sinatra on Columbia 37231, while not country, is interesting enough. (A later (1950s) rerecording, unlike most other Arnold reissues, is more rhythmic, and better. It would be released on the RCA Camden LP label, on CAL 471, in 1959.)
6. "It's a Sin," Victor 20-2241. This mushy but effective bit of schmaltz, penned by Fred Rose and Zeb Turner, is crooned out well enough. (Much later in 1961, Elvis would also croon it out, and oddly, in even softer vocal tones.)
7. "I'll Hold You in My Heart Till I Can Hold You in My Arms," Victor 20-2332. Penned by Hal Horton, Tommy Dilbeck, and Eddie himself, this schmaltzy tale is at least honest. (Much later, in 1969, Elvis would turn it this ditty into one of his own blues entities.)
8. "Easy Rockin' Chair," Victor 20-2481. This Fred Rose-penned ditty is a fast-paced effort, with Eddie's smooth and slick vocal rockin' in between some lively fiddling and steel guitar-picking. While Eddie was hardly as crude and rhythmic as contemporaries

Hank Williams and Rose Maddox (of the Maddox Brothers and Rose), Eddie could, and did, demonstrate some rhythmic abilities. Indeed, this ditty, more so, proves it! Just listen.

9. "Rockin' Alone in an Old Rockin' Chair," Victor 20-2488. As another lightweight rhythm number, this Bob Miller-penned ditty is pleasant enough.
10. "Anytime, "Victor—20-2700. This ditty ain't bad, although it just ain't the Emmett Miller version, on Okeh 41095. While it just may be that the rough edges of Emmett's vocal are more appreciated, it's more than an oddity that his ditty, as penned by Herbert "Happy" Lawson, could still be relevant in 1947. Moreover, the drift to schmaltz did not end with Arnold! Yet another version, by another Eddie, and also on the Victor label (as by Eddie Fisher on Victor 20-4359), would follow Arnold's lead.
11. "Bouquet of Roses," Victor 20-2806. Did Eddie define "schmaltz" for C & W? While his crooning vocals did indicate that there was smoothness in the crude country, this marginal pick, penned by Steve Nelson and BobHilliard, was, nevertheless, a huge seller in 1947.
12. "Texarkana Baby," Victor 20-2806. As the buried flip side of "Bouquet of Roses," this ditty, penned by Clark and Rose, had a bit more punch as well as some (very) dry Arnold novelty.
13. "Cuddle Buggin' Baby," Victor 21-0342. This fine attempt at blues, with shades of fiddles, keyboard, and steel guitar (as penned by Red Rowe), finds Eddy at his very best. While crooning out this harmless ditty, Eddy is seemingly enjoying himself, which perhaps makes the pre-rock rhythmic ditty retain its pleasant (enough) message.
14. "I Wanna Play House with You," Victor" 21-0476. This (very) schmaltzy lyric, penned by Cy Coben, at least finds the crooning Arnold sounding more hillbilly and oddly effective. (While the same title "I Wanna Play House with You" was later to be used in the Buddy Holly LP release *Holy in the Hills*, on Coral 57463, the Holly rendering is really the Arthur Gunther-penned ditty "Baby Let's Play House." While it's true that in some worded lyric, Gunther could have been inspired by Arnold's "I Wanna Play House," the use of this somewhat common contemporary (1950s) slang term ends with Gunther. Moreover, the original Gunther (1954) release on Excello 2047 was to be overshadowed by a wilder Elvis Presley version, on Sun 217. It was thus, the Elvis version that was to inspire Buddy Holly. Sorry, Eddy!
15. "Anything That's Part of You," Victor 20-4569. This crooned-out ballad, penned by Don Robertson, had eyes for the future. Moreover, a later (1962) embellishment, in ballad style, would be lifted by a committed and somewhat sophisticated Elvis Presley version (Victor 45-7992).
16. "I Really Don't Want to Know," Victor 20-5525. This fine ditty, penned by Don Robertson and Howard Barnes and released in 1954, finds itself surfacing, and bettered, throughout the rock era. As a Billy Ward and His Dominos recording (King 1368), a light group sound is attempted. A better, soulful attempt was later made, as by Solomon Burke (Atlantic 2157) and Little Esther Phillips (Lenox-5560), in the early 1960s. A later Elvis Presley version, somehow labeling it C & W, was also attempted, as this ditty made the rounds.
17. "You Don't Know Me," Victor 20-6502. While a bit late in the game, this (1955) recording, as penned by Cindy Walker and Eddy himself is crooned out very well. Moreover, this could also be the best ditty that Arnold's name, as a songwriter, was to be associated with. Moreover, this sappy number perhaps defines a "soft" vocal style for C & W performers, and perhaps the "Nashville" idiom of the 1950s through the 1960s. While the rock era had already taken off, a contemporary (1956) pop takeoff

as by Jerry Vale, in true Italian American style (Columbia-40710), became a best seller—despite Elvis and rock and roll. A later (1962) Ray Charles rendering, on ABC Paramount 10345, perhaps added a bit more soul. Still a later, soft (1967) version by Elvis, on Victor 47-9341, should also be noted.

18-19-20. Eddie's 1966 LP (LSP-3715) is hardly hip, although the excellent "Nashville Sound' exploites his boring croon to generate some interest. The following are picks: a. "Somebody Like Me". This contemporary single release on (Victor-47-8965), penned by Wayne Thompson, had been a huge (C&W) best selling entity. b. "Tip Of My Fingers". Country musicians Bill Anderson (who also penned and sang this ditty) and Roy Clark (previously a guitarist with Wanda Jackson and later known as a TV baby boomer entity on "Hee-Haw") had both been influenced by Eddie's croon while growing up. They had also recorded previous versions Eddie's subsequent version, then considered a 'soft' alternative to "pop" gone "rock", aint bad if sleep inducing! c. "Lay Some Happiness On Me". This (Jean Chapel and Bob Jennings) penned ditty is a bit of mid tempo fluff that Eddie did extremely well even at this end of the game!

- ➢ The later career of Eddy Arnold found his appeal to pop a bit stiff. While he did indeed croon out a lot of pleasant enough fodder, the highbrows of the music business generally wrote him off. While numerous television appearances had indeed kept Eddy busy into the 1970s, perhaps the untold but real disdain against him, as an original C & W vocalist, more so, hindered him. While he was no Frank Sinatra, he was still Eddy Arnold!

Fred Astaire

- ▪ The purposes of a creative (would-be) recording artist, did not seemingly fit the fragile, weak-voice, baritone dancer, Fred Astaire. Nevertheless, he did indeed produce a huge amount of recordings, which was fortunately fueled by his filmed movie star image. Moreover, his real talents, as seen in any of his films, are to be seen on any studio dance floor. Indeed, by the end of the 1930s, his visual image in films, especially those with Ginger Rogers, were a huge success and were considered a huge part of Americana itself. In true retrospective, while the case just has to be made for his successful recordings, his screen image introducing them must be included into any serious review of his singing abilities.

  - ➢ The principal reasons for Fred Astaire's success should be noted as follows:

- * His earlier success in personal appearances, on Broadway (as a dancing partner who also sang), with his sister, Adele, in the 1920s.
- * His early association with the Gershwin Brothers on Broadway, and in later films, gave him great material. So did his association with the likes of Irving Berlin and Rodgers and Hart, who all contributed to many of his film soundtracks.
- * His very beautiful costar, Ginger Rogers. In addition to his great dancing, it was also the "star" quality of Ginger (who could also croon out a song better than he could) that matched both of these talented entities, making them into something

special to watch and hear. Moreover, while Ginger was no slouch on the dance floor, it was Fred's lead that led to final clinches. (Oddly, Ginger's own attempts at recordings were limited, although she clearly had the better voice. Moreover, the visuals of Ginger's vocals in film, also remain, if limited, fun to watch and hear.)

* His harmless projection of his own image, which was essentially of a man who had a great talent on a dance floor as well as a person who could project humor and wit.
* Fred was never challenged directly. While others, who included the likes of Buddy Ebsen, Gene Kelly, George Murphy, and Donald O'Connor, did compete, the likes of Bill "Bojangles" Robinson, the Nicholas Brothers, and the Will Mastin Trio, among others, were to be limited by racism. (To be fair to Fred, who was to be greatly impressed by Robinson, the prevalent racism of the times was not his fault.)

  - In any case, Fred Astaire, like Judy Garland, survives best in film and should be regarded as a surviving and relevant musical (film) entity.

Picks

1. "Oh, Lady, Be Good Medley (Parts 1 and 2)," Columbia E-3970. This British release, recorded in the 20s (with his sister Adele), this ditty also picks up the sound of dancing feet. Considered a Gershwin classic, it has got more. This melody also includes "Fascinating Rhythm" and "I'd Rather Charleston," with sister Adele possessing the better vocal.
2. "Night and Day," Victor 24193. A Broadway entity, the production of *The Gay Divorce* found Fred successfully recording this soon-to-be Cole Porter classic. Backed by the Leo Reisman Orchestra, Fred's weak baritone works, although other versions of this ditty, which would include those by Maxine Sullivan and Frank Sinatra, would, more so, define this ditty as a recording.

   - *Flying Down to Rio*, RKO, 1933. This film provided film audiences some great visual talent for the first time. (Other vocals are noted in review.)

3. "Carioca" found Ginger's and Etta Moten's vocals and dance the principal highlight.

   - "Music Makes Me" features Ginger's vocal.

   - *The Gay Divorcee*, RKO, 1934. This second Astaire-Rogers film release (based on the Broadway production *The Gay Divorce*) does not translate into what could be a choice.

     - "The Continental," the impressive dance sequence found in the film would later be defined as a recording by a (much later) Frank Sinatra recording in 1950.

4. "Needle in a Haystack." Penned by Con Conrad and Herb Magidson, while a bit clumsy, it succeeds in the film for Fred. A contemporary Ruth Etting recording perhaps defined it best as a recording.

- *Roberta*, RKO, 1935. Another converted Broadway musical, this Astaire-Rogers effort again works. Actress-singer Irene Dunne also added vocals to the film.

    - "Smoke Gets in Your Eyes." Introduced by Irene Dunne, it is a sure classic, if highbrow in presentation. (A fine, later version by Platters, on Mercury 71383—much later, in 1958—would also define this ditty as a rock-era best seller.)
    - "I'll Be Hard to Handle." Penned by B. Dougall, it ain't bad.
    - "Yesterdays." A stiff and highbrow filmed introduction, by Irene Dunne, still succeeds in the film. (A later Billie Holiday recording, on Commadore 527, defined this ditty, penned by Jerome Kern and Otto Harbach and T. B. Harms.)
    - "Lovely to Look At." This ditty, penned by Dorothy Fields and Jerome Kern, also finds its first recognition as a standard, as sung by Irene. The dance sequence by Fred and Ginger is better. (A contemporary Eddie Duchin recording (with stiff vocal by Lew Sherwood, on Victor 24871), may be considered less than the film effort—in true retrospective.)

- *Top Hat*, RKO, 1935. In addition to Edward Everett Horton and Lucille Ball, brilliant dancing and a sparkling Irving Berlin-penned film score found Fred and Ginger at their zenith.

    - "The Piccolino" is a long dance sequence that works. So does Ginger's contemporary recording on Decca F-5747.

5. "Cheek to Cheek." Fred even pulls off a winning vocal!
6. "Top Hat, White Tie and Tails." Fred somehow (again) pulls off a good vocal in the middle of a dance sequence. (A contemporary Boswell Sisters rendering, as a recording, further defined it.)
7. "Cheek to Cheek," Brunswick 7486. Yes—even this weak vocal entertains the ear. Fred, moreover, pulls off as a rare (for him) defining vocal recording of an Irving Berlin classic that is almost as good as seeing and hearing in the filmed version. (So is a recording by Ginger, on Decca F-5747).
8. "No Strings." Fred's film intro is OK. Ginger's own subsequent recording, on Decca F-5746, is better. Better than both of them, as a recording, is a contemporary George Hall release, with a Dolly Down vocal on Bluebird B-6098.
9. "Isn't It a Lovely Day?" Ginger's subsequent recording, on Decca F-5746, is also good.

- *Follow the Fleet*, RKO, 1936. This (Irving Berlin) film score also featured a few vocals by Harriet Hilliard (later Harriet Nelson).

    - "Let Yourself Go." Just What did Irving Berlin have to do with contemporary (1936) "swing"? Actually, as introduced by Ginger Rogers in the film,—a bit! Ginger's vocal is, moreover, hot—and it's a wonder that a contemporary recording by her could not be a hit! A subsequent dance sequence with Fred is also to be seen, as well as a (on purpose) flubbed vocal by Ginger. (Ginger's own contemporary recording—oddly, a British release (only)—on Decca F-5963, is done well.)

- "Get Thee Behind Me Satan." Harriet Hilliard's vocal of this fine ballad, as seen and heard, is done well. (Harriet also recorded a version, on Bluebird B-7607, with Ozzie Nelson.)
- "But Where Are You?" While a bit clumsy in the film, Harriet manages to carry off this slow bit of ditty of highbrow appeal. (Harriet also recorded a version, better than the one in the film, on Brunswick B-7607. So also did Jane Froman, a very highbrow one, to be found on Decca-710.)

10. "I'm Putting All My Eggs in One Basket." Fred introduced this clumsy ditty in the film. Ginger's contemporary (British release, on Decca F-5963) is better.
11. "Let's Face the Music and Dance." Another vocal with Fred and a subsequent dance sequence with Ginger.
12. "Let Yourself Go," Brunswick 7608. Fred's subsequent (1936) OK vocal recording actually became a contemporary best-selling entity! Moreover, he did not introduce this ditty (vocally), and Ginger's filmed version is far better!

➢ "Swing Time," RKO, 1936. Jerome Kern and Dorothy Fields are responsible for this film's classic ditties. Vocal highlights are

13. "Pick Yourself Up." Fred and Ginger both dance and do subsequent vocals.
14. "A Fine Romance." Another excellent ditty by both Fred and Ginger, which truly benefits on-screen. (A contemporary recording with Bing Crosby and Dixie Lee, finds that Dixie Lee seemingly successfully mimics Ginger as seen in the film? A differing and more jazzier contemporary Billie Holiday version, more so, defines this ditty? Listen and decide.)
15. "The Way You Look Tonight." Another fine ditty, written for this excellent film for Fred and Ginger, also reeks of sophistication and elegance when seen and heard on the screen. A contemporary (Bing Crosby and Dixie Lee) recording is, more so, just as elegant as it is stiff, without the benefit of being filmed. It is interesting to speculate if Bing could have put on a tux and Dixie Lee a ballroom gown, in their attempted emulation of Fred and Ginger? While they do indeed produce a winning vocal, is it more than interesting to hear a contemporary Billie Holiday version, whose (differing), mid-tempo jazz vocal just could have defined this classic? Listen and learn.

➢ *Shall We Dance*, 1937. The Gershwin Brothers are responsible for penning this film score, including the title.

- "They All Laughed." Ginger's own vocal film introduction is done well, if too short. (Later, Bing Crosby would do it better, although not as a (1937) contemporary recording. Oddly, Bing's (1956) recording is late but surprisingly effective, on LP Verve V-2020).

16. "They Can't Take That Away from Me." As usual, Fred's filmed version is good enough. A contemporary (1937) Connie Boswell recording is far better. Later, Frank Sinatra would, more so, define it. (Much later in the century, Tony Bennett and (rocker!) Elvis Costello, would do it justice.)
17. "Let's Call the Whole Thing Off." The clever visual of Fred and Ginger (dancing on skates!) while duetting remains something indeed fun to watch and hear.

18. "Slap That Bass." Fred is seen dancing around a cruise ship with a black crew singing. While Fred's vocal is good enough, perhaps, in true retrospective, he should have let the black crew keep singing and he should have (just) danced.

   - *Carefree*, RKO, 1938. Irving Berlin again adds substance to ditties such as the following:

      - "The Yam." Ginger's vocal in the film is fine. (So was her contemporary (1938) recording, on Bluebird B-7891.)
      - "Change Partners."

19. "Since They Turned Loch Lomond into Swing."

   Perhaps the best of the Astaire's and Roger's films are reviewed above, although all are good musicals. After the (1939) film *The Story of Vernon and Irene Castle*, Fred and Ginger split. Some ten years later, they would again appear in *The Barkleys of Broadway*. While Fred had been involved in some fine musical films without Ginger before 1939—noting, with Joan Crawford in *Dancing Lady* (1933) and with Joan Fontaine in *A Damsel in Distress* (1938)—the screen chemistry was obviously missing (more so in *Damsel in Distress*). After 1939, Fred went on to dance in films with some great dancers, including the likes of Eleanor Powell, Rita Hayworth, and Cyd Charisse, who, although perhaps better dancers, lacked Ginger Roger's warmth. The following are noteworthy Astaire films and recordings after 1940:

   - *Holiday Inn*, Paramount, 1942. This film may be regarded as one of Bing Crosby's better efforts, and is most likely the best known of all Crosby's films. It was in this film that Bing introduced many classics, including "White Christmas." Apart from being a showcase for Irving Berlin-penned ditties, this film also features Fred's superior talents on the dance floor.

20. "I'll Capture Your Heart," Decca 18427. This vocal duet with Bing Crosby (and Margaret Lenhart) is a fine recording, even without *Holiday Inn. Are Fred's dancing feet heard?*

   - *Easter Parade*, MGM, 1948. While viewing this film in true retrospective, it is clear that despite a fine performance from Fred, Judy Garland steals the show. Highlights from this Irving Berlin-penned soundtrack include

      - "It Only Happens When I Dance With You."

21. "Happy Easter."
22. "A Couple of Swells," Fred and Judy.
23. "Easter Parade." Crosby had introduced this ditty to film in *Holiday Inn*.

   - *The Barkleys of Broadway*, MGM, 1949. As it turned out, this film would become the last time that Ginger Rogers (a much older actress in 1949), would star in a film with Fred. Unlike the previous films of the 1930s, the film was dominated by Fred, despite the good efforts of Ginger Rogers. Highlights include Fred's shoes moving on

> a. "Shoes Have Wings,"
> b. "You'd Be Hard to Replace," and,
> c. "Manhattan Downbeat."
>
> Fred and Ginger also reintroduce

24. "They Can't Take That Away from Me." (This ditty had been introduced by Fred in the previous (1937) film *Shall We Dance*.

Gene Austin

- The attempts to stamp out tenors from popular music was ignited with the new technology of electric recording in the mid-1920s. Even so, the popularity of Gene Austin cannot be overlooked. While himself a weak tenor, his eventual attempt to croon, captured for himself an audience, a very diverse following. In true retrospective, his recorded legacy would include some fine acoustic and electric standards that would be considered both pop and hillbilly.

Gene Austin Picks

> Before becoming known as "Gene Austin," Gene found a lot of work as a backup vocalist for many, including the folk acts of the Blue Ridge Duo, the Ambassadors, and the blind country musician and vocalist George Reneau. The following two, released as George Reneau entities, merit review:

1. "Lonesome Road Blues," Vocalion 14809. It's mostly 1 Reneau, the noted "blind musician of the Smokey Mountains" along with Gene at work on this interesting title.
2. "Softly and Tenderly," Vocalion 14809.

> The following two Victor titles found the established recording artist and vaudevillian Aileen Stanley and folk entity Carson Robinson sharing their fame with the very much unknown, young (about twenty-five years old) vaudevillian and songwriter Gene Austin.

3. "When My Sugar Walks Down the Street," Victor 19585 (vocal with Aileen Stanley). As an acoustic enterprise, this quirky ditty, as penned byJimmy McHugh, Irving Mills, and Austin himself, even includes some quirky bird noises. This much-recorded standard would later find Ivie Anderson, on a Duke Ellington release (Brunswick 8168), as an electric recording, defining it.
4. "Way Down Home," Victor 19637. This vocal duet with Carson Robinson (a contemporary hillbilly entity with a cowboy theme—and pre-dates the likes of Jimmie Rodgers and Gene Autry) just ain't bad.
5. "Flapper Wife," Victor 19638 (1925). A person with a wife who has a good time? Penned by Beatrice Burton and Carl Rupp, it is hardly sexist, in modern terms?
6. "Yes Sir, That's My Baby," Victor 19656. A huge entity of the 1920s and penned by Gus Kahn and Walter Donaldson, this title ain't bad. Other contemporary versions include a fine vocal heard on the dance band Coon-Sanders Orchestra release (Victor 19745), the Blossom Seeley release (Columbia 386-D), a rare and differing rendering

at popular recording fodder from blues entity Sarah Martin (Okeh 8262), and the especially quirky Lee Morse version (Perfect 11580).

7. "Everything Is Hotsy Totsy Now," Victor 19656. This type of 1920s' slang sold its way into the hands and hearts of the time—more so, claiming the times?
8. "Save Your Sorrow for Tomorrow," Victor 19857. This weeper of a song ditty, penned by B, G. DeSylva and Al Sherman, would light-years later be updated into sophistication by Peggy Lee. (Years later, does a Bobby Darin recording "Sorrow Tomorrow," as credited to Pomus and Shuman, sound similar?) Listen and learn.
9. "Five Foot Two, Eyes of Blue," Victor 19899. This somewhat peppy (Sam M. Lewis, Joe Young, and Ray Henderson) novelty works well enough to describe a flapper, at least by Gene's own point of view!
10. "Sleepy Time Gal," Victor 19899. Also a fine, contemporary best seller for Nick Lucas. Listen to both!
11. "Sweet Child," Victor 19928. Another bit of slang, penned by Richard Whiting, Al Lewis, and Howard Simon, is sweet!
12. "Bye, Bye, Blackbird," Victor 20044. Penned by Mort Dixon and Ray Henderson, this curious vocal style, also heard on contemporary recording of Cliff Edwards, Nick Lucas, and Billy Jones, may indeed be a wake-up call for the era. As noted on the original 78 rpm release, "Tenor with violin, cello, and piano," Gene's vocal should have been ignored. When heard however, its own jazz-inspired piano and hillbilly violin (or fiddle) somehow do not negate the cello. Somehow, Gene's quirky vocal makes it all work.
13. "Ya Gotta Know How to Love," Victor 20044. This flip side of "Bye, Bye, Blackbird," penned by Bud Green and Harry Warren, ain't bad.
14. "To-Night You Belong To Me," Victor-20371. This ditty, penned by Billy Rose and Lee David, became yet another huge vocal hit for Gene's not-always-on-the-mark vocal abilities. (A rock era version by Patience And Prudence owes nothing to Gene's weak croon, but perhaps to the contemporary flapper 'girl' harmony group, the Ponce Sisters-Ethel and Dorothea).
15. "I've Got the Girl," Victor 20397. This Walter Donaldson-penned ditty ain't bad. A poor-sounding contemporary (1926) version (as credited to the Don Clark Biltmore Hotel Orchestra) on Columbia 824-D, with an unaccredited vocal refrain, was, in true retrospective, more important. As released at more than 78 rpm, its own horrid sound was no rival to Gene's competent vocal, although a contemporary Nick Lucas version, on Brunswick 3370, was. (Nevertheless, this ditty had significant (future) revue, without Gene or Nick. The Don Clark release with a chipmunk-sounding vocal chorus was later credited to Al Rinker and Bing Crosby. It seems that before joining Paul Whiteman's organization, the future "Rhythm Boys" found the gig with Don Clark. Light-years later, in the 1970s, his ditty and this recording was to be resurrected by some dedicated Crosby collectors and, through modern technology, released at the correct 78 rpm speed, on a bootleg release. Both Al and Bing sound better—sadly, too late. Better late than never?)
16. "Thinking of You," Victor 20411. Also known as "I'm So Lonesome Thinking of You," this ditty, as penned by Walter Donaldson and Paul Ash, ain't bad.
17. "Someday Sweetheart," Victor 20561. This attempt at Afro-American-penned material, as penned by Reb and John Spikes, was trendy and, more so, succeeds. (While many versions exist, perhaps Alberta Hunter's early acoustic 1921 version is better?)
18. "Ain't She Sweet," Victor 20568. Annette Hanshaw's contemporaryof the Milton Ager and Jack Yellen penned version, as "Ain't He" is sung better and is, more so, perky and more energetic. (Years later, the Beatles even tried to rock it.)

19. "Muddy Water," Victor 20569. A Paul Whiteman release, Bing Crosby's peppy vocal is better! So is Bessie Smith's contemporary rendering, more so sung "low" and moody. In true retrospective, it's a good bet that Gene even knew about most of his rival recording artists at the time, as if he needed to care about it at the time (1927).
20. "One Sweet Letter from You," Victor 20730. It's good enough vocally, although a contemporary Charlestown Chaser version of this Sidney Clare, Lew Brown and Richard Whiting penned ditty, featuring a jazzy, better sung Kate Smith vocal, has more energy.
21. "My Blue Heaven," Victor 20964. In 1927, this recording, penned by George Whiting and Walter Donaldson, became a huge, best-selling entity. Sung with a fast-paced simplicity and combined with light crooning, Gene Austin infuses some rhythmic flavor as well. (Light-years later, the rock era would claim it as a Fats Domino release, on Imperial 5386).
22. "Cindy Cindy," Victor 20873. Oddly, this ditty was not credited as an official "Gene Austin," but as by "Bill Collins." Other contemporary versions included a rendering from Vernon Dalhart (Challenge 405) and perhaps a better performance from Riley Puckett (Columbia 15232-D)? (As an already an older folk entity, perhaps founded in the secular religious "Come on Board Little Children" this ditty was claimed by Nat Shilkret and Bill Collins-alias Gene himself.
23. "My Melancholy Baby," Victor 20977. Penned by Ernie Burnett and George A. Norton, this ditty had already been a (1915) acoustic entity as by tenor Walter Van Brunt, on Edison 50923. Gene's updated crooning job is, more so, electric, and hardly as stiff. (While still reeking of sentiment and schmaltz, a later (1935) Ella Fitzgerald rendering, with a more interesting backing by Teddy Wilson (Brunswick 7729), is at least worth comparing?)
24. "Nothin'," Victor 21080. Annette Hanshaw's perky contemporary version of this Roy Turk and Lou Handman penned ditty is even better?
25. "The Lonesome Road," Victor 21098. This so-so vocal was penned by Nat Shilkret and Gene himself. This ditty had eyes for the future and, in true retrospective, provides a better appreciation of Gene's credited songwriting abilities. (As a blues entity, a future Lonnie Johnson version, on Bluebird 34-0714, is superb. So is a fine Louis Armstrong version on Okeh 41538 and a mid-1930s Bing Crosby version. Moreover, this classic ditty about a soulful journey also found the likes of a Sister Rosetta Tharpe version on Decca 2243—who perhaps defined it best!
26. "Ramona," Victor 21334. This best-selling entity of 1928 is a curious film entity. Penned by L. Wolfe Gilbert and Mabel Wayne for the silent film of the same name, this contrived marketing scheme worked. As a radio event, contemporary and (hot) film starlet Dolores del Rio, who was also in the film, perhaps sang it on radio hookup (in California) while the Paul Whiteman Orchestra (from New York City) provided backing orchestration. This historic (NBC) transcontinental broadcast was indeed a "first," and, in true retrospective, considering the primitive nature of the technology of the times, it was a notable achievement. A contemporary Paul Whiteman recording was released on Columbia 21214-D, with an Austin Young vocal. Dolores, moreover, did produce a recording in Spanish, on Victor 4054. While the silent film is more easily forgotten, the easily found recording by Austin, when found, lingers.

In any case, it was Gene's version that seemed to catch on. Victor Records reported that his recording was reputed to have sold over a million copies.

27. "She's Funny That Way," Victor 21779. Perhaps a contemporary Emmett Miller version is similar? In any case, Gene's rendering was the better-known, better-selling contemporary recording. In true retrospective, this ditty, penned by Richard Whiting and Neil Moret, would become much recorded in the future and even became a popular film entity, as sung, in parts, by actor Cecil Kellaway in the (1944) crime drama *The Postman Rings Twice*. Better and later vocals included those by Connie Haines, Thelma Carpenter, and Billie Holiday as "He's Funny That Way."
28. "Wedding Bells," Victor 21893. Penned by Irving Kahal, William Raskin, and Sammy Fain, this ditty should not be confused with a later (1949) song ditty of the same name, as released by Hank Williams and penned by Claude Boone.
29. "How Am I to Know," Victor 22128. Another fine ditty, penned by Jack King and Dorothy Parker, that had been introduced by Russ Columbo in the contemporary film *Dynamite*. Russ, however, was not yet a major vocal recording entity and, subsequently, did not record it. Luckily, Gene did. (This ditty would later be recorded by many and was defined by a later (1940s) Billie Holiday version.)
30. "Carolina Moon," Victor 21833. This contrived "moon" song, penned by Benny Davis and Joe Burke is crooned out well enough.
31. "Weary River," Victor 21856. This fine ditty, penned by Grant Clark and Louis Silver had been introduced in the early (part-sound) 1928 film of the same name as by actor Richard Barthelmess. Considering that Richard was likely dubbed, it's a good break for this ditty that, among others, both Gene and contemporary Rudy Vallee made decent best-selling recordings of it.
32. "A Garden In The Rain". Victor-21815.
33. "I've Got a Feeling I'm Falling," Victor 22033. Another best seller by Gene, a fine standard, penned by Harry Link, Billy Rose, and Fats Waller himself).
34. "Ain't Misbehavin'," Victor 22068. Perhaps Fats penned this ditty for Louis Armstrong for his *Hot Chocolates* Broadway revue? A contemporary Charleston Chaser version with an Eva Taylor vocal is better, among much competition. Indeed, such company included the likes of Vaughn De Leath (as Gloria Geer), Ruth Etting, and Seger Ellis. Decades later, many others, including the likes of Kay Starr and Sarah Vaughan would lay claims as well.
35. "My Fate Is in Your Hands," Victor 22223. As mythology has it, despite objections from Victor's all-white (1929) studio orchestra, Fats Waller, who also penned this ditty with Andy Razof, is rumored to be found backing Gene's studio vocal on piano. (A contemporary, lesser-known version by Marion Harris is better.)
36. "St. James Infirmary," Victor 22299. Don't let this weak crooner fool the ear! This classic ditty, penned by Joe Primrose—and, more so, claimed by a contemporary Louis Armstrong version (Okeh 8657)—is superb. Also known as "Gambler's Blues," this spooky tale about death, while lacking the intensity of the Armstrong vocal, still manages to hold its listeners. It is, more so, something to hold Joe Primrose up to ransom for, as this ditty had Anglo-Saxon origins. Indeed, a "St. James Infirmary" had existed in London, England, before the time of Henry VIII, providing the crude medical knowledge of the era. As a transplanted folk entity, this ditty had somehow remained relevant, and on hearing, it still is! (Yet another version, by Cab Calloway, is also good, noting a frantic and more novel approach.
37. "Maybe It's the Moon," Banner 32256.
38. "Blue Kentucky Moon," Banner 32285. Another soft croon, with some lively jazz, that was perhaps penned by Walter Donaldson for the likes of Gene himself? Moon'd again?

39. "Guilty," Banner 32285. This kind of early 1930s' material found Gene's attempt s at crooning a bit late, as his (still) good enough vocal was no match when competing with the likes of Bing Crosby and Russ Columbo. Was Gene fully aware of his competitors in 1933? In true retrospective, unlike the 1920s, it is a good bet that he was indeed! Listen and compare.
40. "Rollin' Down the River," Victor 22451. This Fats Waller and Stanley Adams penned ditty more ever found Gene producing a (surprisingly) better vocal, that had more to do with style.
41. "Nobody Cares If I'm Blue," Victor 22518. If and when Gene put his quirky tenor voice into a song title, he produced a very fine recording. It's, more so, interesting to seek out, hear, and compare contemporary (1930) renderings by Marion Harris, Annette Hanshaw, and Lee Morse.
42. "Love Letters in the Sand," Victor 22806. While Ruth Etting's contemporary version is better, this ditty failed to catch on until, light-years away in 1957, Pat Boone made it a rock-era best seller.
43. "When Your Lover Has Gone". Victor-22635. Gene's weak vocal is no match for Ethel Waters contemporary version, nor as interesting as Louis Armstrong's attempt at it!
44. "Please Don't Talk About Me When I'm Gone". Victor-22635. (Another weak croon bettered by a current Ethel Waters version! Listen & compare!
45. "Easter Parade," Romeo 2189. Somehow this classic ditty from the (1933) Irving Berlin Broadway entity *As Thousands Cheer*, did not become associated with Gene, whose rendering is better than the contemporary (1933) vocal by actor Clifton Webb, as featured on a Leo Reisman release (Victor 24418). (Later, in the 1940s, both Bing Crosby and Judy Garland put more defining claims upon it!)
46. "Just a Little Home for the Old Folks," Banner 32614.
47. "A Little Street Where Old Folks Meet," Banner 23614.
48. "Ridin' Around in the Rain," Victor 24663. Gene's original became a contemporary Bing Crosby Brunswick best seller!
49. "Blue Sky Avenue," Victor 24725.

Visual Image

Gene Austin may be seen (in a tux), backed by the Gus Arnheim Orchestra while crooning out both.

50. "Blue Sky Avenue" in the (1934) film *The Gift of Gab* (with musicians Candy and Coco).

Gene Autry

The popularity of country music, as it developed, was perhaps less contrived than what became of "western" music. As greatly aided by the Hollywood film images of cowboys of the silent era, the early sound films added even more to the myth. The latter 1920s found one Gene Autry, a rather weak-voiced tenor, trying to croon, perhaps like Gene Austin or Jimmie Rodgers. Yet Gene was more than all that. He was, in fact, a real Texan, who was raised in rural Oklahoma. Perhaps the early recordings of Carl T. Sprague and Carson Robinson, both with cowboy images, found the young and real cowboy's attention. Indeed, Sprangue's "When the Works All Done This Fall," on Victor 19747, and Carson's "My Carolina Home," on Victor 20795, found themes of working-class value and home much in common with Gene's real and truly Western dreams of Americana. While in reality, earlier pre-twentieth-century novels and comic strips had largely created this myth, history could not have found a better person to fuel the myth than Gene himself. Gene was indeed the ultimate good guy; he wore a white hat and, more so, was filmed singing somewhere out on the range! A great job!

- By late 1930s, his career, in films and on radio became so huge that (like Bing Crosby), his image, to be found in B-grade Hollywood films, personal appearances and radio, had created for him a huge audience. This all would, more so, export itself worldwide. Much of Gene's recording output would contain the negative factor of yodeling, and others are somewhat flawed by marketing considerations. Like contemporary rival Jimmie Davis, Gene originally found song ditties whose hillbilly appeal was simple. They also related directly to the easy myth of solving problems of men and women, horses, dogs, lawyers, mothers, saloons, and jail and sometimes the social problems and hardships of making a living. Singing "cowboy" rivals, including the likes of Rex Allen, Eddie Dean, Afro-American Herb Jeffries, Tex Ritter, and (later) Roy Rogers, among others, would all find success directly founded in Gene.

➢ The following are Gene Autry picks:

1. "My Alabama Home," Victor 40400. This Jimmy Long-penned ditty, however crude, is a simple but effective beginning to a prolific recording career.
2. "My Dreaming of You," Victor 40400. While Gene was born in Texas, he was raised in the rural state of Oklahoma, yes—somewhat of a "real" cowboy. It was perhaps Gene's fate to somehow befriend the brother of the 20s recording artist Frankie Marvin, whose name was Johnny Marvin (whose recording of "Deed I Do" on Victor 20397 ain't bad). Marvin indeed helped Gene gain an actual recording date in a trip to New York City (1929). This ditty, written by Johnny Marvin, was the result of that session.
3. "Dust Pan Blues," Diva 6030. This matter-of-fact tale about a country boy cleaning floors contains elements of truth, as well as dust. It is a plea to his girlfriend—this boy's walking out—and he wants her to follow. Simple? Penned by the Marvin Brothers, this old entity still rings true.
4. "Slu-Foot Lou," Diva 6031. The humorous tale about a very tall and thin girl, penned by Frankie Marvin, ain't all that bad.
5. "Stay Away from My Chicken House," Diva 6032. This very unlikely named ditty, penned by the Marvin Brothers, ain't just about chickens. It's indeed, so bad—it's good. Apart from the (usual) embellishment of Jimmie Rodgers, Gene is also assisted by various animals, including a hog, horse, cow, and rooster—featuring Frankie Marvin's animal imitations. While still very primitive and simple, the clumsy attempt at creativity is obvious.
6. "Blue Days," Banner 32123. Yes. Gene really did have the blues, Just like Jimmie Rodgers!
7. "The Death of Mother Jones,"-Banner 32133. This sad tale of Mother Jones just may be based upon an actual pioneer who had just passed away in 1930. Mary Jones—not necessarily of the Old West—but an early union leader who crusaded upon of the

dangers experienced by coal miners. As a matter of fact, this ditty has all the earmarks of social change—something not usually associated with the pre-rock era and Gene Autry himself.

8. "High Steppin' Mama Blues," Banner 32473. This self-penned ditty by Gene himself is a simple but effective bit of 1929 nostalgia. While his emulation of Jimmie Rodgers vocals are flawless, his observations of the "shimmy" and "hula," as by his cheating, dancing companion are novel. It's also interesting to compare the Jimmie Rodgers entity "High Powered Mama" on Victor 22523, which also mentions a similar dancing and cheating situation, recorded in 1930. While it's a long stretch for Gene to have had any influence on Jimmie Rodgers, it's more likely that the "self-penned" claims may be open to some debate.
9. "Mississippi Valley Blues," Conqueror 7908. As a "Vocal Duet, Guitar Acc.," this ditty features Gene and Jimmy Long with very dated bit of yodeling and a definite rural blues theme. This ditty seems to have gotten much inspiration from Jimmie Rodgers's "Mississippi River Blues" (Victor 23535), which makes it all perhaps true grit.
10. "That Silver Haired Daddy of Mine," Conqueror 7908. This flip side of "Mississippi Valley Blues" is less of a blues entity and more of what would (later) become a hillbilly or a country entity. As another duet with Jimmy Long, this simple tale of Daddy, penned by Jimmy Long and Gene himself, was a radio favorite as well. Was the earlier (1928) Jimmie Rodgers's ditty "Daddy and Home" Gene's inspiration for this classic?
11. "The Yellow Rose of Texas," Perfect 12912. In 1933, Gene and Jimmy Long pioneered this standard; it was (already) a public domain entity and perhaps a real ditty of the Old West. Much later, in 1955, Mitch Miller (known by young baby boomers for his sing-along's on television), reworked this recording with great success, on Columbia 40540.
12. "That's How I Got My Start," Romeo 5093.
13. "The Death of Jimmie Rodgers," Perfect 12922. It's no secret that Gene was inspired by Jimmie Rodgers and may indeed be considered a commercial rip-off that worked
14. "The Last Round Up," Melotone 12832. This ditty, penned by Billy Hill, became a huge hit in the Broadway entity *Ziegfeld Follies of 1934*. While the George Olson Orchestra (with a vocal as by Joe Morrison, on Columbia 279-D, and the Bing Crosby version, on *Brunswick 6663 were contemporary best-selling entities, it's Gene's recording that got that real true-grit sound. Indeed, the opening Jimmie Rodgers's yodel, just about ruins it, at least in comparisons with the Crosby version.
15. "Tumbling Tumbleweeds," Romeo 5434. This very fine and dated ditty, penned by Bob Nolan, is western all the way. Gene is backed by what sounds like a mandolin, as well as vocally by Jimmy Long and Smiley Burnette. (The contemporary Bob Nolan version was that as by the Sons of the Pioneers, which included vocals by Nolan, Tim Spencer, and one Leonard Slye. (Leonard would change his name to Roy Rogers, who would become a major competitor to Gene in films, radio, and recordings). This ditty was also to be used as an Autry film title.
16. "Ole Faithful," Melotone 13354. Gene again excels in this tale of a horse, penned by Michael Carr and Jimmy Kennedy. It would be interesting to speculate that perhaps Gene's horse, Champion, seen in most of his films, just might have felt a little jealous? Other versions, including a Riley Puckett release, on Bluebird B-6313, also ain't bad.
17. "You're the Only Star in My Blue Heaven," Conqueror 9098. This ditty reeks of sentimental mush that could be described as a weeper, with Gene getting into some raw crooning and songwriting.

18. "Nobody's Darling but Mine," Perfect 6-04-52. The contemporary Jimmie Davis version is indeed challenged? Gene or Jimmy?
19. "Rhythm of the Range," Melotone 7-12-60. This well-done ditty, penned by Johnny Marvin and Gene himself, may be contrived, yet is convincing. Its use of the words "rock" and "rhythm," while very simplistic, may be considered a clash of fiddles, fickle, and (futuristic) mid-1950s "rockabilly."
20. "Take Me Back to My Boots and Saddle," Vocalion 04172. While in true retrospective this contrived ditty is indeed very dated (penned by Lenard Whitcup, Teddy Powell, and Walter G. Samuels), like (most) other Gene Autry recordings, this one at least speaks volumes in title alone.
21. "Back in the Saddle Again," Vocalion 05080. This ditty, penned by Ray Whitley and Gene himself, was recorded in 1939. It also became his theme song—unfortunately, in true retrospective, reeking of formula.
22. "South of the Border," Vocalion 05122. This bit of country "corn" works well as Gene croons up a tale of Mexico, penned by Kennedy and Carr, which became a standard of its time.
23. "Be Honest with Me," Okeh 5980. This simple ditty, penned by Fred Rose and Gene himself, is truly "honest," (1941).
24. "Good-bye Little Darlin, '" Okeh 05463. This ditty, penned by J. Marvin and Gene himself, found itself also recorded by Bing Crosby, on Decca 3856. It's interesting to speculate (in true retrospective), the interest that Bing (and his recording producer Jack Kapp) had for this type of western fodder. In any case, Gene's radio and film work by this time (1940) had already become a staple in American entertainment—in fact, much like Bing himself.
25. "Blueberry Hill," Okeh 05779. Yep, this ditty is yet another standard that ranged from the likes of Connie Boswell (Decca 3366) and, among others, through to the rock era and that of the very fine version by Fats Domino (Imperial 5407).
26. "You Are My Sunshine," Okeh 06274. This very raw-sounding folk ballad is so clumsy that it's somehow worth it. Cedited as penned by Charles Mitchell and Jimmie Davis, this folk song was also a Jimmie Davis release, on Decca 6813. Oddly, this slower-paced Autry version is a bit more effective as this sad tale, about losing, produces a winning vocal.
27. "Deep in the Heart of Texas," Okeh 06643. This rhythmic burst of energy (sounding very dated) is a contrived bit of work, penned by June Hershey and Don Swander, with guitar strings, accordion keys, and clapping hands. What limits!
28. "Have I Told You Lately That I Love You," Columbia 37070. This post-WWII release, penned by Scotty Weisman, found Gene, while always less than slick, still able to produce a sincere vocal approach that works. Contemporary rival Tex Ritter's version on, Capital 296, is also good, and similar. (This much-recorded ditty would later find the likes of Elvis Presley and Ricky Nelson 1950s recording fodder).

- ➢ Note: The following picks are seasonal recordings which, in true retrospective, do not represent the best tastes of marketing recordings—but did (and still do) represent a solid "kiddie" market.

29. "Rudolph the Red-Nosed Reindeer," Columbia 38610. This ditty is perhaps the best-known entity of the entire pre-rock era (with the possible exception of Bing Crosby's White Christmas, on Decca 18429). It's origins had been found in a Chicago department store Christmas time give away as a story by Robert L. May. As penned

into a light hearted song by Johnny Marks, this ditty may not be considered the best vocal of this ditty either, but it was the first, and it is (still) identified with Gene.

30. "Here Comes Santa Claus Down Santa Claus Lane," Columbia 20377. This ditty, penned by Oakley Haldeman and Gene himself, was a good 1950 (seasonal) follow-up to "Rudolph," of the year before. (Elvis Presley's hipper version of this classic Christmas entity was released in 1957, on RCA Victors LP LOC 1035—part of a package that found itself banned from most radio airplay of that later time. The authors of this book can only speculate how Gene felt about all this.)
31. "Frosty The Snowman". Columbia-38750 Another baby boomer entity introduced by Gene, as penned by Jack Rollins and Steve Nelson, later to be associated with classic Christmas cartoons, noting (UPA studio & still later with (Rankin- Bass) - with the voice of comic Jackie Vernon. insert subsequent Gene Autry.
32. "Peter Cottentail," Columbia 38750. This Easter-season ditty, penned by Steve Nelson and Jack Rollins, while not as popular as Gene's Christmas entities, still brought the kiddies some music in many an Easter basket.

Visual Image

- The "singing cowboy" image of Hollywood, in true retrospective, was an expletive visual kiddie show which—in truth-existed in the myths of Hollywood. The likes of such entities as Ken Maynard, Tex Ritter, Roy Rogers, Dale Evans, Herb Jefferies (an Afro-American singer and "cowboy," in segregated exploitation films), Duncan Runordo (a real Mexican entity), among others, all produced recordings and hardly relevant (low-budget) films, much like Gene did. These (mostly) pathetic time-waster films, featuring the ten gallon hat, white or black hats, six shooters, horses, saddles, Indians, ranchers, planters, gunslingers, sheriffs, saloon dancers, blue jeans and ex-rebels, were very popular. Americana indeed!
- Other contemporary actors, hardly singers, had better budgets and perhaps did better. The likes of such contemporaries as John Wayne (who had started in low-budget), Randolph Scott, Henry Fonda, Gary Cooper, George Montgomery, and (British) Errol Flynn perhaps produced far better screen classics. Nevertheless, Gene's own success at the box office was huge, and indeed, in recognition alone, dwarfs over all his contemporaries.

  - The following Gene Autry film is interesting enough:

    - *The Phantom Empire*, Mascot Pictures. This very odd (1934) serial-film is science fiction in stone-age form. As a film, this even pre-dates the Buster Crabb *Flash Gordon* action entities—it just may well be the first of the kind. Along with his (usual) sidekick, Smiley Burnette, singing cowboy Gene and a group of juvenile horse riders look for a murderer, find a lost underground city (inner space), strange people with ray guns, atom smashers, and something called "television!" Futuristic in 1934? You bet! Indeed, this quirky film is so bad, it's good! Moreover, a final yodel is (even) welcomed. How did he do it? Somehow it all works! Look and listen.
    - Among all this mayhem, and adding to the campyness of it all, Gene even finds the time to effectively croon out such dumb ditties like the following:

33. "I'm Getting a Moon's Eye View of the World" (from an airplane!),
34. "I Call on Oscar, I Call on Pete,"
35. "Uncle Noah's Ark," and a filmed version of his previously recorded classic
36. "That Silver Haired Daddy of Mine" (indeed, something Buster Crabbe could never do)!

Mildred Bailey

As one of the first female band vocalists to emerge as a popular entity before swing (with Paul Whiteman), Mildred Bailey's dry, rather high, moody uttering provided a "white" alternative for popular and jazz vocals. Indeed, the voice of Al Rinker's sister (Al Rinker of the Rhythm Boys), would later became known as a definite entity of jazz singing. Identified as part of the Paul Whiteman organization, Mildred's little voice, carried with her huge frame, found brilliant elocution and exploitation—a true vocal prowess. Not unlike softer tones heard on the recordings of Ethel Waters and Eva Taylor (both vocal influences), Mildred delivered rhythmic lyric as a true jazz entity.

The following picks are with noted orchestra backing, as well as solo efforts.

1. "Can't You See," Victor 22828. Paul Whiteman's orchestra is mellow and so is his band's vocalist, Mildred herself. As penned by Roy Turk and Fred Ahlert, this bit of mushy lyric is greated well by Mildred's soft tone, but only if the listener has the patience to wait for the vocal, since Whiteman's long introduction hogs up about half of recording!
2. "When it's Sleepy Time Down South," Victor 22828. A good enough crooning job on a popular contemporary 1931 entity. Was Louis Armstrong, on Okeh 22828, allowed more leverage with these lyrics?
3. "My Good-bye To You," Victor 22876. As penned by Gus Kahn and Matty Malneck this bit of stiffness actually becomes mellow, featuring Whiteman's well done orchestra and Mildred's vocal.
4. "Too Late," Victor 22874. Whiteman and Mildred compliment the Bing Crosby version (Brunswick 6203). Another crooning attempt is found on a contemporary Buddy Lane version, emulating on Crown 3231). Penned by Sam Lewis and Victor Young, this sad tale was perhaps overdone by all, but this act of crooning really did, Indeed, define it.
5. "All of Me," Victor 22879. By the time of this first best seller (1931), Mildred's easy vocal is pleasant enough, with a little emotion cleverly phrased in Paul Whiteman's arrangement. Moreover, this Seymour Simons, and Gerald Marks) ditty became a classic, with many contemporary versions, especially noting a superb crooning job as by Russ Columbo and a gusty Louis Armstrong's attempt at crooning. (A later Frank Sinatra version, would revive and perhaps claim it).
6. "Concentratin, '" Victor 22880. Whiteman and Mildred get a little fast-paced on this hip ditty (penned by Andy Razaf and Fats Waller). A contemporary Blanche Calloway version, on Victor 22862, had been a somewhat rhythmic, dance band release. Whiteman, however, had other ideas. Moreover, his violin section provides a "country" fiddle, with Mildred's especially novel and sweet-voiced vocal. A fine and contemporary Connie Boswell version would follow.
7. "I'll Never Be the Same," Victor 24088. Paul Whiteman again assists Mildred with beautiful backing. Mildred sings her heart out without novel gimmicks. Penned by Gus Kahn, Matt Malneck, and Frank Signorelli, this version competes with Ruth

Etting's differing but excellent version. Listen and compare! Later, in the 1950s, Frank Sinatra defined it?

8. "We Just Couldn't Say Good-bye," Victor 24088. Perhaps contemporary Annette Hanshaw's version of the Harry Woods penned ditty is better? Or a contemporary and rhythmic group vocal by the Boswell Sisters?
9. "Love Me Tonight," Victor 24117. While Maurice Chevalier's film introduced this ditty, penned by Richard Rodgers and Lorenz Hart, of the same name, Mildred's version, holding back tears, is more effective. (A contemporary Bing Crosby crooning job, using the same title, on Brunswick 6351, is a different song, penned by Ned Washington, Victor Young, and Bing himself.)
10. "Rockin' Chair," Victor 24117. While Hoagy Carmichael had already been interpreted better by Louis Armstrong (Okeh 8756) with Hoagy himself duetting, Mildred somehow succeeds well enough and, more so, claims this ditty as her own signature song. Mildred indeed croons up a storm, as this rhythmic fat lady's high-toned tonsils also amuse her listeners. A later recording on Vocalion 3553, also ain't bad.
11. "Dear Old Mother Dixie," Victor 24137. Penned by Gus Kahn and Matt Malneck, Mildred seeks to convince her listeners that she's really a Southerner. (In reality, as native of Seattle, Washington, she claimed (some) American Indian heritage. In this aspect, she shared honors with vocalists Lee Wiley, Edith Wilson, Kay Starr, and her brother Al Rinker (of the Rhythm Boys).
12. "Is That Religion," Brunswick 6558. This (1933) recording, penned by Mitchell Parish and Maceo Pinkard, with the excellent Dorsey Brothers backing her, is somewhat dated by Mildred's attempt to "sound" black. While her (white) contemporary Connie Boswell, who was raised in New Orleans, could pull it off, Mildred barely does.
13. "Harlem Lullaby," Brunswick 6558. It is the flip side of the "Is That Religion," and Mildred again attempts a Southern accent. Penned by Margod Millhane and Williard Robinson, Mildred's persistence perhaps pays off, despite her clumsiness.
14. "There's a Cabin in the Pines," Brunswick 6587. While the classic Bing Crosby version, on Brunswick 6610, remains the best crooning job, other contemporary versions are not bad, including by the likes of Chick Bullock, Johnny Mercer, and Mildred!
15. "Lazy Bones," Brunswick 6587. Mildred scores, despite yet another attempt at "sounding" Southern or black. This very fine ditty, penned by Hoagy Carmichael and Johnny Mercer, is also very novel, and perhaps this excuse alone is enough for Mildred's vocal to become effective.
16. "Snowball," Brunswick 6655. The lyrics by Hoagy Carmichael seemingly imply racial stereotypes. Mildred's easy vocal, moreover, also seems to smooth things out. Just listen.
17. "Shouting in That Amen Corner," Brunswick 6655. Penned by Andy Razaf and Smalls, there should have been no problem with Mildred's versions of (real) Afro-American material. While all this at least provides interesting listening, the clumsy-voiced Mildred would (later) find a way to do it better.
18. "Doing the Uptown Lowdown," Brunswick 6680. This title, penned by Mack Gordon and Harry Revel, isa contrived black-oriented and fast-paced piece of work. Mildred, moreover, is rhythmic enough!
19. "Give Me Liberty or Give Me Love," Brunswick 6680. This stupid title, penned by Leo Robin and Ralph Rainger, had been written for the screen in the Claudette Colbert (1933) film *Torch Singer*. Mildred's fine rendering, moreover, turns this ditty into something listenable at home, if you could afford purchasing this fine Depression-era disc?

Note: The mid-1930s found the swing era in bloom—as a term and reality in Ivie Anderson's vocal, in a Duke Ellington 1932 release "It Don't Mean a Thing if It Ain't Got That Swing," on Brunswick 6265. The following recordings, more so, find Mildred in the good company of many great musical entities, including the likes of Benny Goodman, Teddy Wilson, and Red Norvo, noting that she would regulate herself as a band singer on some but not all releases.

20. "Junk Man," Columbia 2892-D. This is Benny Goodman's own rhythmic lead on this George W. Meyer and Frank Loesser swing entity. Moreover, Mildred's playful vocal is more than capable, as she indeed "swings"!
21. "Ol' Pappy," Columbia 2892-D. It is the flip side of "Junk Man." This Benny Goodman entity, penned by Al J. Neilburg, Symes, and Jerry Levinson, is again given further credibility as by Mildred's excellent vocal.

- Note: The following find Mildred with her own band, husband Red Novero, and others.

22. "It's Love I'm After," Vocalion 3367. This very fine ditty, penned by Sidney Mitchell and Lew Pollack, was perhaps meant to highlight some clever crooning. It succeeds.
23. "Long About Midnight," Vocalion 3378. This (1936) recording, penned by Alex Hill and Irving Mills, proclaims Mildred Bailey and Her Orchestra, on its original record release. It can also be proclaimed as a fine swing band, which just might have claimed the likes of Artie Shaw, John Kirby, Cozy Cole, Dave Barbour, and Teddy Wilson, among others. (A contemporary group rendering by the Mills Brothers is a fine and interesting comparison.)
24. "Trust in Me," Vocalion 3449. This ditty, penned by Milton Ager, Ned Wever and Jean Schwartz, ain't bad. (In true retrospective, this ditty found itself challenged by a (later) Etta James version, on Argo 5385, a rock-era entity. Moreover, Mildred's cool jazz style, as compared with Etta's gospel-influenced vocal, is something to listen for, in comparisons.

(On another recording (Argo 5380) in 1961, Etta James would also find a 1942 entity, "At Last," good recording fodder. She indeed blows away a stiff Ray Eberle vocal, as a Glenn Miller release, released on Victor 27934.)

25. "Smoke Dreams," Brunswick 7815. Mildred, as a band singer (with Red Norvo (her then husband) and Orchestra) excels here, as the term "jazz vocalist" truly applies to her. This moody vocal was penned by Arthur Freed and Nacio Herb Brown. It also benefits by Red on xylophone, which somehow works very well.
26. "Lover, Come Back to Me," Vocalion 3902. This somewhat stiff Hammerstein and Romberg penned ditty had been recorded by many, especially noting the previous Rudy Vallee and Annette Hanshaw versions. Mildred is clearly more rhythmic, and less inclined to croon, as had Vallee or Hanshaw. A still later version by Mildred-joined by the Delta Rhythm Boys—on Decca 3953 is (even) better!
27. "From the Land of Sky Blue Water," Vocalion 3982. This ditty, penned by Nelle Richmond Eberhart and Charles Wakefield Cadman, found initial investigation as a theme of (later) baby boomer-era beer commercial. Moreover, even without beer, it's a well-done vocal!

28. "I Was Doing All Right," Brunswick 8068. This very fine Gershwin Brothers-penned ditty still owes much to fine interpretation from Mildred.
29. "The Weekend of a Private Secretary," Brunswick 8088. This bit of novelty, penned by Johnny Mercer and Bernie Hanighen, describes in detail a tale about a young woman's trip to pre-Castro Cuba. Its Latin rhythm is for sure catchy. Some stereotypes noted could perhaps find this campy ditty politically incorrect by the end of the century?
30. "You and Your Love," Vocalion 5006. This ditty, penned by Johnny Mercer and Johnny Green, is sung to perfection by Mildred. This smooth, low-keyed vocal performance is also a fine example of what a medium-tempo vocal is about. Moreover, this vocal indicates a more polished and jazzy style, to be heard a bit later on many subsequent (1940s) Billie Holiday recordings. Did Billie attempt to emulate Mildred? Or did they both influence each other's styles at the end of the 1930s?
31. "Arkansas Blues," Vocalion 4801. Credited on Mildred's record to Lada-Williams, or Anton Lada and Spencer Williams, this electric rendering of the earlier (1921) acoustic ditty that had been perhaps best recorded by Lucille Hegamin and (especially) Mamie Smith provided Mildred with the type of recording fodder that also provided a challenge. Led by Afro-American pianist Mary Lou Williams, this tale of a black person riding back down to Arkansas to see mammy found Mildred (without her previous clumsiness) full of an ambition and attitude that drops an identity of race, as her Arkansas-bound train ride slickly rambles down the track to a successful conclusion.
32. "Barrelhouse Music," Vocalion 4802. This contrived bit of blues, penned by Willard Robison, also finds Mildred's slick yet soft vocal effective.
33. "I'm Forever Blowing Bubbles," Vocalion 5086. This (already) old standard, penned byJean Kenbrovin and John Kellette, had been a "standard." A best-selling entity in 1919 for Helen Clark and George Wilton Ballard (Edison 50534), its novel approach from the already forgotten acoustic era indeed required an update. Luckily, Mildred's electric recording further revived it.
34. "Blue Rain," Vocalion 5277. This ditty, penned by Johnny Mercer and James Van Heusen, sounds much like a contemporary (1939) Billie Holiday release. Moreover, pianist Teddy Wilson makes himself heard. Was the older Mildred also influenced by Billie?
35. "I Thought about You," Columbia 35313. The ditty penned by Johnny Mercer and James Van Heusen was realized before a contemporary Dinah Shore version. (A later, defining Frank Sinatra version would have to wait until the advent of LPs and the 1950s).
36. "Darn That Dream," Columbia 35331. This time, Mildred is (again) known as a band singer, a "canary," for Benny Goodman. In any case, Mildred's vocal of this ditty (penned by Eddie de Lange and Jimmy Van Heusen) indeed "swings."
37. "Wham (Re-Bop-Boom-Bam)," Columbia 35370. There is nothing phony about Mildred's lyrical hipness. Penned by Taps Miller and Eddie Durham, this whole bit of urban slang indeed works. While the vocal help of Afro-American Roy Eldridge is a huge asset, it's a shared triumphant! Mildred's own vocal prowess is, indeed, no fluke!
38. "Lover, Come Back to Me," Decca 3953. Vocally backed by the Delta Rhythm Boys, Mildred remains "hip" (second recording).

Note: Like many other pre-WWII vocalists, Mildred found it hard after the war. The rise of rhythm and blues was a big part of it, as well as Mildred's health. She did cut a few interesting sides before her death in 1951.

39. "That Ain't Right," Victor 20-2457. Was it right to attempt a Nat Cole Trio recording? This version of the ditty, penned by Cole and Irving Mills, seems to indicate that Mildred was led into the right direction. Ain't that right? Just listen!
40. "I Don't Want to Miss Mississippi," Victor 20-2457. Penned by Seger Ellis, this ditty finds Mildred reverting back to her crooning vocal style of the early 1930s. It's also all right!
41. "When We're Alone (Penthouse Serenade)," Majestic 1040. The already old Ruth Etting entity is successfully updated by Mildred's committed soft-spoken vocal.

Josephine Baker

As a young and black vaudevillian in 1922, Josephine, at around fifteen years of age, found herself involved in early (black) Broadway entities like *Shuffle Along* and *Chocolate Dandies*, which included the likes of Sissle and Blake. She, more so, found her way to become Ethel Waters' understudy at New York's Plantation Café that unusually found the real blackfaced Waters, with her *Plantation Revue* in all-white Manhattan, away from Harlem. It was here that Ethel introduced "Dinah" in 1924, with her subsequent best-selling recording, noting "Plantation Revue" on its Columbia Record label. Shortly after the success of the recording, Josephine Baker accepted an offer that Waters had refused—to appear in Paris, France. Josephine, more so, took along Waters's entire act, including "Dinah." With added nudity, she then proceeded to conquer France, with huge success in stage, nightclubs, radio, and (French) films. Within five years, she became more French than American, finding much less segregation, along with roles in film that freely exploited her beauty and art, indeed far from the likes of playing plantation era nannies and wisecracking maids that American contemporaries Ethel Waters, Nina Mae McKinney, and others were to be offered in major film studios back in the States. Even later, when Lena Horne got a little more, she could not attain the equality Josephine attained in France. She was, more so, welcome in the rest of Europe, Africa, and South America. Indeed, the poor girl from St. Louis (named for a French King) in Missouri, more so, did it so well, coming off very sophisticated, while also creating controversy as becoming too highbrow. French?

➢ The following (picks) were recorded in Paris, France.

1. "That Certain Feeling," Odeon 49170. This Gershwin Brothers-ditty found the shrill-voiced Josephine somehow winning over a shocked French audience. Did Josephine wear her famous (1926) seminude banana skirt when she sang this ditty (and others) on stage? Why not speculate?
2. "Who?" Odeon 49070. A Brox Sisters version had made this Jerome Kern-penned Broadway entity a best seller in 1925. Josephine's lack of vocal control is made up by enthusiasm!
3. "Dinah," Odeon 49172. The Waters vocal style hit France long before she would tour there. Young Josephine's vocals had a soft touch, indeed very much like Ethel's (except for occasional vocal crackling). This dry style, for the most part, would follow her all through her recording career. Other song ditties, many noted here, also find Josephine picking up on contemporary (1926) vocal techniques heard on recordings, especially noting the high voices of Gene Austin and Nick Lucas.
4. "Sleepy Time Gal," Odeon 49173. The Gene Austin and Nick Lucas versions are challenged!

5. "I Wonder Where My Baby Is Tonight," Odeon 49174. The Walter Donaldson-penned hit had found much recognition, especially as by a Henry Burr and Billy Murray novel release and a differing Lee Morse version. More so, the jazzy high voice of Josephine improves upon it.
6. "I Love My Baby," Odeon 49226. The earlier 1925 contemporary Aileen Stanley version had found a spirited vocal with a skatting male behind her, which may have been 'Ukule Ike' Cliff Edwards or Billy 'Uke' Carpenter? A differing low-keyed Lee Morse vocal version also followed, providing much recognition of this ditty, penned by Harry Warren and Bud Green, in the States. While the lighter-voiced Josephine is somewhat clumsy, she's (still) hot, steamy, and jazzy!
7. "I've Found a New Baby," Odeon 49227. More than American contemporaries Ethel Waters's and Eva Taylor's recordings of this classic, another hot jazz standard is exported to France!
8. "Skeedleum," Odeon 49227. This Spencer Williams-penned ditty finds Josephine!
9. "Where'd You Get Those Eyes," Odeon 19931. A Ted Lewis dance band release was best known, while Vaughn De Leath's version, on Gennett 3347, was better. Is Baker better? Just listen!
10. "Pretty Little Baby," Odeon 166031. This hot 1926 ditty, had been a contemporary Bene Bernie release with a so-so vocal from Arthur Fields. that almost spoiled the record. Josephine's vocal is more, living up to her wild image that could be only imagined by most, in her contemporary semi-nude stage act. (A later 1930 rerecording, on Columbia DF-230, finds more vocal control. Compare?)
11. "After I Say I'm Sorry," Odeon 166032. The Walter Donaldson-penned hit somewhat finds Josephine able to use her weak, yet freewheeling vocal to an advantage over better-known contemporary versions such as those by Frank Harris,—the really stiff-voiced Irving Kaufman, and Betty Morgan?
12. "Then I'll Be Happy," Odeon 166032. Josephine scats up this ditty, penned by friend—Sidney Claire, Cliff Friend and Lew Brown, differing greatly from the slower, fine Whispering Jack Smith version on, Victor 19856.
13. "Breezing Along with the Breeze," Odeon 166041. This ditty, penned by Haven Gillespie, Seymor Simons, and Richard Whiting was fine recording fodder for many, including Johnny Marvin's 1926 best seller (Columbia 699-D) and a group effort by the Singing Sophomores on Columbia 4235-D.
14. "Hello Bluebird," Odeon 16641. The Nick Lucas version is at least challenged.
15. "Blue Skies," Odeon 166042. Josephine brought (Irving Berlin's) "Blue Skies" to France! While still clumsy and hardly the product of the contemporary Vaughn De Leath's version, Josephine's uninhibited (1927) jazzy vocal still provides listeners with interesting comparisons.
16. "He's the Last Word," Odeon 166042. The popular Ben Bernie dance number hit penned by Walter Donaldson and Gus Kahn eventually found its better version by Annette Hanshaw's perky vocal. Even so, no one figured this ditty would eventually become another jazzy vocal import to France.
17. "Bye, Bye, Blackbird," Odeon 166033. This (1927) recording perhaps found many Frenchmen familiar with previous recordings by Gene Austin, Vaughn De Leath, Cliff Edwards, Nick Lucas, or the (then) legendary recording entity Billy Murray?
18. "J'ai Deux Amours," Columbia DF-229. This ditty, penned by Geo. Kuger and H. Varna, breaks one the this rules of this book, as it is French and *sung* in French. Up to about his time (1930), Josephine had largely exported to France contemporary American popular music and jazz, as a performer and as a recording artist. This ditty,

translated as "Two Loves," finds Josephine explaining to her French audiences that her "Two Loves" are both America and (Paris) France. Noting that she would still render more American popular tunes in the future, this ditty signals that she was becoming *more* French and far less influenced by what was going on in the United States, especially noting her success in France, along with the rest of Europe and South America, which were being virtually ignored by a prejudiced American media. Whle amoung others, a well done yet little known(American) vocal from Morton Downey was produced, this ditty would become better known a decade and a half later in the United States, with the fine Frankie Laine release as "Two Loves I Have.")

19. "Suppose," Columbia—DF-230. This dated emotional ditty, penned by Demon and Dixon, somehow lingers.
20. "King for a Day," Columbia DF-407. This boring ditty, that had been a hammed up vocal release by contemporary Ted Lewis, the novel singing bandleader. penned by Sam Lewis, Joe Young, and Ted Fiorito, is some what improved by young Josephine.
21. "You're Driving Me Crazy," Columbia DF-709. Another American classic is imported to France!
22. "You're the One I Care For," Columbia DF-709. Better than Ruth Etting or Belle Baker versions?
23. "I've Got Young Under My Skin (Vous faites partie de moi)," Columbia DF-2130. Is this (1937) recording Josephine's best recording? The lighthearted, 1920s, flapper-era voice is gone! Sung (in French and English) with more authority and maturity, Josephine, puts some claims on this classic penned by Cole Porter, Henneve, and Palez.

- The following are film masters, more so, exploiting Baker's beautiful presence:

24. "Dream Ship," film master, 1935.
25. 4. "Neath the Tropical Blue Skies," film master, 1935.

More: As age found Josephine an unwilling target, she remained a musical entity, although America would largely ignore her. WWII found her a member of the French Resistance, as well as entertaining troops. The postwar period (and old age) found her still popular around the world, with a few trips back to the States being better received.

Tony Bennett

Tony Bennett was among the post-WWII group of pop male vocalists who became best-selling entities. After much failure (before 1950) he finally began to receive notice—largely due to the likes of baby boomer television. Moreover, Tony did have a good knowledge of what he could sing. Besides his obvious (ethnic) Italian identity, his own appreciation of pop-singers, which included the likes of Bing Crosby, Louis Armstrong, Ethel Waters, Ella Fitzgerald, Billie Holiday, and Frank Sinatra, among many others, provided him with enough material and personality to emulate with his (very) good voice. While not sounding as Crosby or Sinatra, his intimate touch and projected vocals somehow indicate a softness, as if he had cold in his throat. His voice seems, at times, high-pitched, and somehow Bennett's rich elocution, while not as fascinating as by contemporary Sarah Vaughan, puts him in a class by himself. While a later cusp entity, Bennett was inserted, nevertheless, into this book. While not the survivor that Lena Horne became, his musical longevity in the newer century labels him an icon. While it's debatable if he was or is better than Bing, Perry, Frank, Nat, or Dean, the music he emulates is the same. As a matter of fact, his classy songbook consists of lyrics made up by Berlin, Arlen, and the Gershwins. Moreover, his insertion within this book just may have much to do with his (later) success, as many of his latter-century CD releases somehow indicate a connection with a younger, post-rock-era crowd.

- The following selections are Tony Bennett picks:

1. "Because of You," Columbia 39362. Tony (real name—Anthony Benedetto) dusted off this already dated ditty, penned by Arthur Hammerstein and Dudley Wilkinson, as a 1941 Larry Clinton release (with a fine vocal by Peggy Mann) and made it a 1951 best seller, due to his own soft and throaty vocal.
2. "Cold, Cold Heart," Columbia 39449. While the Hank Williams original (MGM 10904) is more than great, the practice of providing a pop alternative for R & B and C & W was, and still is, relevant. As a matter of fact, Tony does well as a completely different arrangement, and as well as a vocal is to be found and heard. As a matter of fact, from another prospective, Dinah Washington also recorded a fine and different contemporary version.
3. "Blue Velvet," Columbia 39555. This 1951 pop ditty, penned by Bernie Wayne and Lee Morris, is not bad, although within a few years, the group vocals and sounds of the (R & B.) Clovers was better. Moreover, the later rock era found Bobby Vinton's 1963 version a bit more polished.
4. "Rags To Riches," Columbia 40048. A major hit of 1953, this gem, penned by Richard Adler and Jerry Ross, could have been a good fit for Al Jolson, but he had passed away. Tony, in part sings it, and in part, he sounds somewhat like Jolson, although Tony's vocal tone is softer, when needed.
5. "Stranger In Paradise". Columbia-40121. As penned for the contemporary Broadway entity "Kismet" by Robert Wright and George Forrest, Tony's (bad) habit of showing off his vocal prowness is somehow saved by his edgy croon on this very stiff production. Tenor or baratone? Or both?
6. "In the Middle of an Island," Columbia 40965. A 1957 best seller, this ditty was an easy alternative to the contemporary rock and roll explosion. Penned by Nick Acquaviva and Ted Varnick, Tony's interpretation of this ditty fully explained his dilemma. In true retrospective, it could have been titled "In the Middle of Rock and Roll, a Music I Don' Know Much About."
7. "Love Song From Beauty And The Beast". Columbia-41086. When Shirley Temple grew up and left the movies, and before she got into politics, she hosted her own "Storybrook" TV program. As penned by Mack David and Jerry Livingston, this self explaining 1958 ditty perhaps gave Tony his best song title ever? While not as well known as others, amoungst lush strings, Tony's mellow vocal, without show boating (too much), is simply supurb. Lovely? Listen and find out!
8. "Firefly". Columbia-41237. This Carolyn Leigh and Cy Coleman penned ditty found Tony perhaps getting a bit impatient with lyrics that needed a lift? Somehow, he succeeds.
9. "I Left My Heart In San Francisco," Columbia 42332. Sadly by the early 1960s, Tony Bennett's "adult" appeal found him at odds with a younger generation of would-be rockers. This ditty, forgetting all this, is sung to perfection. Penned by Douglass Cross and George Cory some years earlier and generally ignored, it was indeed Tony's

good fortune to somehow find it and record it. In true retrospective, after listening to others, no one has yet been able to sing it as well or as convincingly as Tony. As a rock-era best-selling entity, perhaps its time betrays time itself. So, indeed, does Tony's intimate vocal about a city that should have adopted him.

10. "I Wanna Be Around," Columbia 42634. Bennett definitely will always *be* around, as this fine ditty, penned by Sadie Vimmeastedt and Johnny Mercer, attests! In direct contrast, a contemporary (Smash Records) James Brown version (MGS 27058) also finds a fully committed effort, if, more so, differing in style. While R & B entities had been interested in pop ditties since the mid-1940s, it's interesting enough that the "King of Soul" was still interested enough in 1964, to bother? In true retrospective, *both* versions are excellent. Listen and compare? Is it worth it?
11. "The Good Life," Columbia 42779. Also known as "La Belle Vie" in France, penned by Sacha Alexander and Jack Reardon, Bennett delivered another winner, despite rock and roll.
12. "If I Ruled the World," Columbia 43220. While not from the Beatles, this English ditty, penned by Leslie Bricusse and Cyril Omadel, finds Bennett's vocal committed as ever!
13. "Fly Me to the Moon," Columbia 43331. The Bart Howard-penned cabaret ditty finds Tony's vocal style differing with a contemporary Nat King Cole version. Still later, Frank Sinatra claimed this ditty!
14. "Love Story". Columbia-45316. The contemporary 1970 film theme became excellent recording fodder for many. As penned by Carl Sigman and Frances Lai, this bit of mush, despite the dominance of rock, managed to become very popular. In retrospective, which the slightly younger yet considered obsolete crooner Andy Williams nailed the song as a contemporary 1971best seller. Tony's lesser known vocal more so, when heard-is just as good! It's also interesting to note that Andy's Columbia single number had one digit more than Tony's. Listen to both excellent vocals, owing nothing to the contemporary rock era and compare.

- Note: Despite numerous LP releases, Tony Bennett's image just didn't generate the interest that Sinatra, Como, and Dean Martin were to experience. His music, not yet influenced by rock and roll, also found him pretty much alienated from the younger generation. While he could still pack concert halls, most of the seats were of an older crowd. As time rolled, Bennett learned. While his devotion and dedication to the song ditties of the pre-rock era never waned, he began to incorporate a few into his act. By the 1990s, he began to use the media of television (again), which had greatly helped him since early 1950s, more to his advantage. Moreover, his personal appearances, noting his age, actually provided him an asset, and he indeed became an event, bettering his own game as "guest star."

15-22. *MTV Unplugged*, Columbia CK-66214. As a cable project, HMO somehow realized that this pre-rock 1950s' musical icon had something to offer. While the likes of Sinatra and Dean Martin were somewhat put off by age, the energetic Bennett was not. His gray hair even added to his appeal. So did his still fine vocal that somehow even sounded better? Or perhaps, his old songs found their better emulation in Tony performing them. Nostalgia? Perhaps in some way. ? In many others, moreover, this CD and its HMO video offer a proven master vocalist of old songs performing them live. Once more, the audience found many young faces. Perhaps the olden, pre-rock days weren't so dull? The following standards are highlights:

a. "That Old Devil Moon."
b. "Speak Low."
c. "It Had to Be You"
d. "Steppin' Out with My Baby."
e. "Moon Glow." This duet with K. D. Lang, a fine latter-century contemporary recording artist, is on par with a fine update to the (1934) Ethel Waters recording.
f. "They Can't Take That Away from Me." George and Ira Gershwin get a twist and a turn as Tony is joined by British rocker Elvis Costello in a duet. While Tony had been singing and performing this classic ditty for years, the added ingredient of Costello makes it all the more tasteful for a younger audience. It also demonstrates, as he had with K. D. Lang, an acknowledgment of musical diversity.
g. "Body and Soul."
h. "Autumn Leaves / Indian Summer."

"Blind" Blake

- As yet another curious twist to the music of the twentieth century, one "Blind" Blake (aka. "Arthur Phelps," "Blind Arthur," and "Blind George Martin") may be considered even more hidden from the light of recognition than (fellow Paramount blind guy), "Blind" Lemon Jefferson. What little we know about Blind Lemon's recorded life (cut short in a Chicago snowstorm in 1929) is indeed more than enough! The following Blind Blake recordings, however, do leave us a good trail to follow, even with a bit of *rock*, while strumming some primitive blues, with plenty of (similar) guitar pickers to follow *him.*
- Picks are as follows:

1. "Early Morning Blues," Paramount 12387.
2. "West Coast Blues," Paramount 12387. This (1927) release, also the flip side of "Early Morning Blues," finds Blake using the term "Old Country Rock." More so, within a year, his fellow Paramount singer and bluesman William Moore produced a recording "Old Country Rock," released on Paramount 12761. In true retrospective, a bit of rock for future generations?
3. "One Time Blues," Paramount 12479. While it's a long shot to the (1980) film *The Blues Brothers*, the trail to the likes of Kokomo Arnold and Robert Johnson are indeed hot.
4. "Bad Feeling Blues," Paramount 12497.
5. "Doggin' Me Mama Blues," Paramount 12673.
6. "Ramblin' Mama Blues," Paramount 12767.
7. "Hastings Street Blues," Paramount 12863. While the name of this street may be just anywhere, it's on good authority (from numerous record collectors at record shows) that this Hastings Street was in a high-vice crime area of Detroit, Michigan. While such speculation just may indeed be true, it's a fact that the spoken word heard on this ditty had much influence on the (later, postwar) John Lee Hooker entity "Boogie Chillen," on Regal 3295.
8. "Diddie Wa Diddie," Paramount 12888. While this bit of recorded slang is novel, the rhythmic tempo (with guitar) is superb. This ditty was also released on Broadway 5105 as a "Blind George Martin" entity. While in this case the differences found between "Blind Blake" and "Blind George" cannot be heard or found, it was still a trip

to listen for some. While mistakes may be made, it's no mistake that this type of talk would (later) define blues entity Bo Diddley himself (1955).

9. "Hometown Skiffle," Paramount 21453. Blake is found somewhere in this (1930) promotional record for Paramount. In any case, Blake is joined by the likes of "Blind" Lemon Jefferson, Will Ezell, Charlie Spand, the Hokem Boys, and Papa Charlie Jackson.

The Boswell Sisters—Connie, Martha, and Helvetia

It seems that Martha (on piano), Helvetia or "Vet"(on violin), and Connie (on cello), while practicing classical music in middle-class white neighborhoods of New Orleans, also got hooked on the jazz music that had been produced on Bourbon Street. The sisters eventually would add the playing of guitar (by Vet) and saxophone and trombone (by Connie) and would harmonize vocally on the type of singing heard on new recordings by previously unknown female recording artists of the early 1920s—those of Mamie Smith and Ethel Waters—and perhaps as previous (vocal) sister acts like the Brox, Williams, and Pickens Sisters, much to the dismay of their parents. By March 1925, the rebelling little group of sisters, dabbling in local radio, had cut a few recordings.

- Note: Group recordings and solo recordings refer to vocal lead. Connie is credited for all as a vocalist, although split.

♦ The following are included as a group effort:

1. "I'm Gonna Cry"(Crying Blues), Victor 19639. This first side, recorded in the primitive acoustic recording mode, sounds much like a race recording, as the husky lead vocal of Connie betrays her not. Her Southern accent indeed raises questions about "sounding" black. It's also a good bet, however, that this talented sister act really dug the music and is not a rip-off.
2. "Nights When I'm Lonely," Victor 19639. It is the first official side crediting this great sister act. While far from projecting a blues idiom, the primitive tone cannot be overlooked in the raw flip side of "I'm Gonna Cry."
3. "We're on the Highway to Heaven," Victor 22500. This (1930) release had (probably) been the result of radio work on the West Coast. Indeed, as heard, this typical sweet band effort sounded nothing like the two previous and acoustic gritty sides cut some five years before. While bandleader Jackie Taylor was at least kind enough to note "Vocal refrain by The Boswell Sisters," this B side, found the sisters very much limited to about one minute of sweet harmony of credited lyrics by Al Dubin and Joe Burke, which had, more so, been from a contemporary film entity *Oh Sailor Beware.*
4. "Heebie Jeebies," Okeh 41444. This Okeh release, featuring the huge Louis Armstrong entity, challenges Louis, as well as any other previous version. The unique harmony of the sisters, a staple of all their recordings, perhaps changes things. Another fling at this ditty, on Brunswick 6193, finds Connie a bit raunchy. Indeed, much like Elvis Presley in the (later) rock era, hip Afro-American-penned material, with some embellishment, generates much interest
5. "Don't Tell Him What Happened to Me," Okeh 41470. This ditty is very interesting to compare with a contemporary Nick Lucas version as "Her" and an excellent torch

approach as by Ruth Etting version. So indeed is the fine "group" sound that the Boswell Sisters, which is at least an interesting approach, although not as intimate.

6. "When I Take My Sugar to Tea," Brunswick 6083. This (1931) recording sold better than previous efforts. The Dorsey Brothers are suspected as the backup orchestra, and provide enough jazz backup. Penned by Sammy Fain, Irving Kahal, and Pierre Norman, this fast-paced vocal is more than pleasant. A change of tempo, with unique harmony is done creatively enough—a staple for the Boswell Sisters "sound."
7. "What'd Do To Me," Brunswick 6083. Penned by Milton Ager, this bit of fast "group" slang is done well, noting that the lyrics are sped by so rapidly that it's a bit hard to be hip. More so, this rendering should be played more than once anyway! Indeed, listen and enjoy!
8. "Shout Sister, Shout," Brunswick 6109. This clever arrangement (even) beats out the Clarence Williams Washboard Band release (which featured an Eva Taylor vocal) on Okeh 8821.
9. "Roll on, Mississippi, Roll On," Brunswick 6109. The Boswells find easy claim to the Mississippi, as this fast-paced and jazzy vocal penned by Ed West, McCaffrey, and Dave Ringle remains a winner.
10. "I Found a Million Dollar Baby," Brunswick 6128. This ditty, penned by Harry Warren, Mort Dixon, and David Rose, as a group effort, more than betters the earlier (male) "group" sound of the *Radio Franks* on Champion 15178. (The *Radio Franks* had originally been conceived as a local (1920s) NYC radio program featuring vocals from Frank Bessinger and Frank Wright.) In any case, this Boswell update competed with the contemporary Bing Crosby crooning effort, which noted a vocal that comes off a bit too loud. Perhaps Crosby had a cold? Listen and compare!
11. "Sing a Little Jingle," Brunswick 6128. This ditty indeed defines a typical radio commercial of the 1931 era. Penned by Mort Dixon and Harry Warren, this very pleasing group harmony vocal, while dated, lingers.
12. "It's The Girl," Brunswick 6151. The sisters and (perhaps) the Dorsey Brothers, score again, as this schmaltzy lyric, penned by David Oppenheimer and Abel Baer, is merited by some fine hip harmony.
13. "Heebie Jeebies," Brunswick 6173. The second recording is noted for its high energy and is sung at a faster pace!
14. "An Evening in Carolina," Brunswick 6218. This Walter Donaldson-penned ditty is more than good, even as an acoustic entity by Marion Harris. In fact, it's better than a fine and contemporary Nick Lucas release. Listen and compare!
15. "Was That the Human Thing To Do," Brunswick 6257. This ditty, penned by Joe Young and Sammy Fain excels despite (good) competition from another contemporary sister act. More so, the Pickens Sisters, on Victor 22929, were no slouches. Call it a tie!

- The Depression-era year of 1932 had seen record sales (still) falling short, as radio, even more than films, found many staying at home, listening to popular music for free. Nevertheless, Brunswick Records boldly released a series of 12-inch 78 rpm records, which included the Brunswick stable of orchestras led by Red Nichols, Don Redman, and Brunswick house band-orchestra leader—Victor Young. Also included were vocalists who were very popular on contemporary radio, including Bing Crosby, the Mills Brothers, and the Boswell Sisters. The following releases, minus the limited (on vocal) Red Nichols releases, are noted:

16. "Stardust," Brunswick 20100. Victor Young let the "group" sound in (for just a bit) as the girls, led by Connie, got into "Stardust," the then popular ditty that Bing Crosby had resurrected as a Brunswick artist.

17-19. "Gems from George White's Scandals, PT 1 and 2," Brunswick 20102. George White was a Broadway entity and producer, who had became well known for production of songs and nudity on stage—indeed a rival to his principal competition, Flo Ziegfeld. This attempt at producing a credible and creative (1932) 12-inch 78 rpm recording, to squeeze songs as melodies, in true retrospective, worked (almost)! Led by Victor Young's Orchestra, featured vocalists included the Boswell Sisters as well as the likes of Bing Crosby, the Mills Brothers, and (unfortunately) the stiff-voiced Frank Munn—who ruined it all! Nevertheless, the Boswells do a fine vocal on (a) "This is the Missus," (b) That's Love," and (c) Life Is Just a Bowl of Cherries," as part of a melody with the Mills Brothers and Bing Crosby.

20. "Lawd, You Made the Night Too Long," Brunswick 20109. As yet another 12-inch 78 rpm release, this ditty credits "Bing Crosby, Boswell Sisters, with Don Redman & His Orchestra." Even as it may be claimed that Crosby, at this time, was at the height of his vocal abilities, the claimed Boswell Sisters are excellent in singing low, with Connie's (usual) lead. Moreover, the middle of the song is meshed in with Bing, who exploits his vocal, with (black) bandleader Redman's backing, perfectly! (This 12-inch record would later be booted on 78 rpm, cutting off the vocals between the Boswells and Bing.)

21-22. "OK America PT 1 and PT 2," Brunswick 20112. Victor Young at least finds some quality time for the Boswells on (a) "Strange As It Seems", penned by Fats Waller and Andy Razaf and (b) "Old Man of the Mountain," penned by Billy Hill and Joe Young which finds the Boswells starting and the Mills Brothers finishing the vocals—indeed, much like in a contemporary radio program!

23. "There'll Be Some Changes Made," Brunswick 6291. This complete reworking of the already dated acoustic Ethel Waters classic (Black Swan 2021) reeks of creativity. Indeed, Connie's lead vocal, projecting her thick, husky, and bold Southern drawl is superb.

24. "Between the Devil and the Deep Blue Sea," Brunswick 6291. This ditty, penned by Ted Koehler and Harold Arlen finds some kinetic energy heard as brilliant vocal harmony.

25. "If It Ain't Love," Brunswick 6302. There's no watering down of rhythmic potent content heard on this ditty. Penned by Andy Razaf, Don Redman, and Fats Waller, this classic recording just ain't bad at all.

26. "Doggone I've Done It," Brunswick 6335. As penned by Dave Franklin, this bit of slang is complimented by Connie's crude and interesting 'southern' tounge.

27. "Hand Me Down My Walking Cane," Brunswick 6335. Or walking stick?

28. "We Just Couldn't Say Good-bye," Brunswick 6360. The group harmony as compared to contemporary releases by Annette Hanshaw and Mildred Bailey is a pleasant debate.

29. "Old Yazoo," Brunswick 6360. The Fats Waller-penned ditty finds (real) Southern, Louisiana-style vocals perfectly fitting the mood and the mode. Just listen!

- In true retrospective, it seems that the more hip material from black origins meshes quite well both vocally and instrumentally. Is this jazz? Is this blues? Is it hillbilly? Moreover, the Southern accents of the Boswells are indeed real and credible. So is the (not always accredited) backing by the Dorsey Brothers, whose adaptability, already demonstrated while backing the likes of Emmett Miller in the 1920s, provide the vocals of the Boswells (principally that of Connie) merited rhythmic direction.

30. "Down on the Delta," Brunswick 6395. While recorded with the Dorsey Brothers in 1932, this fast-paced ditty, as penned by Fats Waller and Andy Razaf, just ain't the rural blues entity that had already been pioneered as "folk."
31. "Charlie Two-Step," Brunswick 6418. A rural dance hall and the rhythmic vocals of these Boswell girls indeed makes this somewhat crude ditty, as credited to Hoagy Carmichael, another winner.
32. "Down among the Sheltering Palms," Brunswick 6418. Perhaps this already old classic ditty would later be challenged by a later (shared) Al Jolson and Mills Brothers release. Listen and compare.
33. "Louisana Hayride," Brunswick 6470. This (1932) recording should not be confused with the later (1948) radio entity of the south, KWKH, of Shreveport, Louisiana. From the Max Gordon revue of *Flying Colors* and penned by the sophisticated Arthur Schwartz and Howard Dietz, this ditty maintains a Southern flavor. More so, this slick Connie Boswell lead vocal really rocks, as it is a crude and bold effort that indeed works. Novel vocal participation by assorted unidentified band members is also noted as a creative punch, adding even more interest.
34. "Mood Indigo," Brunswick 6470. It is interesting to speculate if the sophisticated Duke Ellington, who penned this ditty with Irving Mills and Barney Bigard, had heard this creative version. In any case, this Boswell Sisters rendering, as matched by all others—including a fine, differing Ivie Anderson vocal backed by Duke, on Columbia 35427—is indeed in a class of its own. Listen and compare.
35. "Minnie the Moocher's Wedding Day," Brunswick 6442. Don't let this stupid title, penned by Ted Koehler and Harold Arlen, discourage listening! While Cab Calloway, in true retrospective, will always lay claim to "Minnie the Moocher," this follow-up by the Boswells is typically novel, rhythmic, and fun.
36. "Forty-Second Street," Brunswick 6545. While the sisters did not appear in this great film of 1933, this fast-paced version works as a recording. (Another contemporary version of the Harry Warren and Al Dubin, released on Victor 24253, by the Don Bestor Orchestra, featuring a vocal Dudley Mecum, is far less hip in comparisons!)
37. "Shuffle Off to Buffalo," Brunswick 6545. This version of another "Forty-Second Street" film entity, penned by Al Dubin and Harry Warren, also beats out the filmed version. A contemporary Harlan Lattimore version, however, is stiff competition? Listen and compare.
38. "In a Little Second Hand Store," Brunswick 6552.
39. "Puttin' It On," Brunswick 6625. Rock! Rock! Rock! Pre-rockabilly?
40. "Swanee Mammy," Brunswick 6625. As also known as "Swanee Woman," penned by Neil Moret and Jo Trent, this obscure ditty scores!
41. "The Gold Diggers' Song-We're in the Money," Brunswick 6595. Beautiful Ginger Rogers introduced this Harry Warren and Al Dubin ditty in the contemporary film *Gold Diggers of 1933*. While Ginger's great body is missing, this novel recording still works!
42. "That's How Rhythm Was Born," Brunswick 6650. This just (could) be more pre-rockabilly? Penned by the (very) contemporary (1933) team of Richard Whiting, Arthur Swartz, and Howard Johnson, this rhythmic and uninhibited vocal by the Boswells is a creative expression clearly ahead of its time!

43. "Coffee in the Morning (Kisses in the Night)," Brunswick 6733. This pleasant ditty penned by Al Dubin and Harry Warren, had been introduced by Russ Columbo and Constance Bennett and subsequently by the Boswells themselves, in the contemporary (1934) film *Moulin Rouge*. Luckily, this contemporary recording was made!
44. "Everybody Loves My Baby," Brunswick 6783. The earlier acoustic Eva Taylor version is updated!
45. "You Ought to Be in Pictures," Brunswick 6798. Want to be a movie star? A picture is not needed, as this excellent mix of schmaltz and sentiment, penned by Edward Heyman and Dana Suesse, is more than lifted into a fine vocal performance. Contemporary (1934) renderings by (bandleader-singers) Rudy Vallee and Little Jack Little find interesting vocals in comparisons. (Still later, in 1940, the cartoon voices of Daffy Duck and Porgy Pig, identified as Mel Blanc, offer (baby boomer) recognition?)
46. "Crazy People," Brunswick 6847. This rhythmic ditty, penned by Edgar Leslie and James Monaco, had been introduced by the sisters in the (1932) Crosby film *The Big Broadcast*. Luckily, this recording retains all of its energy!
47. "Why Don't You Practice What You Preach," Brunswick 6929. Good advice? Penned by Ralph Freed, Al Goodhart, Maurice Siegler, and Al Hoffman, this jazzy group vocal remains hip, as well true.
48. "Rock And Roll," Brunswick 7302. The sisters can be seen and heard performing this ditty penned by Sidney Clare and Richard Whiting from the contemporary (1934) film *Transatlantic Merry-Go-Round*. While the term "rock and roll" applies to a boat rocking on a contrived sea voyage (with the Boswells appearing as a much toned-down act in the film), in true retrospective, this recording retains its own rhythmic performance and appeal!
49. "The Object of My Affection," Brunswick 7348. Penned by Harry Tobias, H. Coy Poe, Jimmy Grier, and Pinky Tomlin, this ditty had already been crooned out by Pinky Tomlin and backed by the popular contemporary bandleader Jimmy Grier, released on Brunswick 7308. This version, retaining Grier, who also added a few spoken words, became a better-selling (1935) entity.
50. "Alexander's Ragtime Band," Brunswick 7412. This (1935) recording of the already old Irving Berlin-penned classic was to be reissued on Vocalion 4239 due to the popularity of the (1938) film of the same name. In true retrospective, this fine recording was to be yet subsequently bettered with a then contemporary recording, featuring Connie and Bing Crosby (noted below in the text).
51. "Every Little Moment," Brunswick 7454. This ditty penned by Dorothy Fields and Jimmy McHugh is a nifty bit of lyrics, with the Boswells vocals sounding so well—indeed for every little moment!
52. "Way Back Home," Brunswick 7454. Back home in the south? Who cares? This listener of this fine ditty, penned by Al Lewis and Tom Waring, wants to be get there? Is it the fastest? Or is this ditty the "best-est" ever?
53. "Cheek to Cheek," Decca 574. The film version of this Irving Berlin classic, by Fred Astaire from *Top Hat*, 1935, is fab to watch and hear. The contemporary single release, by Fred Astaire himself (Brunswick 7486), ain't bad—especially for Fred. This even better Boswell Sisters version, however, beats all other recorded versions. Listen and Learn?
54. "Top Hat, White Tie and Tails," Decca 574. In this the flip side for "Cheek to Cheek," the Boswells again attempt to beat out Fred Astaire and again succeed. The (always) creative attempt is still in place, with a simulated "tap dance" sound effect inserted (from an unidentified orchestra), which indeed succeeds. This more than pleasant rendition of yet another Irving Berlin classic from *Top Hat* is indeed tops.

55. "I'm Gonna Sit Right Down and Write Myself a Letter," Decca 671. The better-known contemporary Fats Waller version, on Victor 25039 found this ditty, penned by Joe E. Young and Fred E. Ahlert, excellent recording fodder, producing, in true retrospective, a jazz classic. Moreover, this lesser-known group rendering is done better!
56. "The Music Goes Round and Round," Decca 671. Among many others (including the excellent Edythe Wright version, as a Tommy Dorsey entity on Victor), this mid-30s novelty, that was originally introduced and penned by Mike Reilly, Eddie Farley, and Red Hodgson on Decca, clearly defines what rhythmic harmony is all about. In any case, this is clearly just more fun, with Connie's interested vocal bettering all her contemporaries—another masterpiece!

- The following title was oddly and *only* issued in Australia!

57. "The Darktown Strutter's Ball," Columbia DO-1255. The very fine already old Shelton Brooks-penned classic is given new life, as well as an understood vocal. Oddly, it was to be only issued in Australia, and, in true retrospective, needs to be appreciated! Get it!

Note: Basically, by the mid-30s, the Boswell Sisters had broken up after achieving great recognition and fame as recording artists, and in radio and films. Connie, however, despite the swing era, would remain a recording, film, and radio entity. The Following credited solo-artist picks retreat back to 1931, while she was still with her sisters. In addition to duets with Bing Crosby, Connie would also later become known and credited as "Connee."

- The following solo-credited picks were issued as solo and credited vocals by Connie, noting that the early stuff was originally issued, and sometimes even "flip-sided" with regular Boswell Sisters releases They are as follows:

58. "I'm All Dressed up with a Broken Heart," Brunswick-6162. This Fred Fisher, Harold Stern and Stella Unger is a classy bit of mush, that Connie does very well.
59. "What Is It," Brunswick 6162. As penned by former Rhythm Boy Harry Barris. this ditty was more famously associated with Bing Crosby and Loyce Whiteman on contemporary radio broadcasts. Connie however, had other ideas, as her strong but soft vocal puts good claims upon it.
60. "Time On My Hands," Brunswick 6210. Perhaps the up-and-coming female vocalist Lee Wiley (as a band singer with Leo Reisman, on Victor 22839) did it better? But this version remains a winner.
61. "Concentratin' On You," Brunswick 6210. This ditty penned by A. Razaf and Fats Waller emanates pure energy. Is it hard to compare contemporary versions by Blanche Calloway and Mildred Bailey?

- As noted previously in the text above, the 1932 (Brunswick) series of releasing (more expensive) 12-inch 78 rpm recording are noted (below) as separate "Connie Boswell" efforts (mostly) but not always released as Boswell Sisters-credited releases. Get it? If not, a (possible) listener should find the recording (probably also reissued on CD) and find out? Just listen?

62. "Washboard Blues," Brunswick 20108. The 12-inch release found Connie being ably backed by the Casa Loma Orchestra! Does Connie's husky Southern tongue better

the original (1928) vocal by Hoagy Carmichael, who also penned this ditty, on the fine previous Paul Whiteman release on Victor 35877? Definitely!

63-65. "New Orleans Pt 1 and 2," Brunswick 20110. Another 12-inch release, among some jazzy efforts from Red Nichols and his Orchestra, in which Connie can be found (in melody) on bits of (a) "Dear Old Southland," (b) "Rampart Street Blues," and (c) "River Stay 'Way from My Door."

66. "My Lips Want Kisses," Brunswick 6297. As penned by Abel Baer, Dave Oppenheimer and Fisher this stupid title is saved by Connie ! Should Connie be believed? Yes!

67. "The Night When Love Was Born," Brunswick 6332. It's interesting to compare a contemporary Ruth Etting contemporary version of this Dave Oppenheimer, Joe Young and Abel Bauer ditty, as Connie's vocal tougher prowess wins out! Sorry Ruth!

68. "Humming to Myself," Brunswick 6332. Connie comes close to rocking, as her (always) clever vocal changes tempo a few times, in this ditty penned by Sammy Fain, Monty Siegel, and Herbert Magidson.

69. "Say It Isn't So." Brunswick 6393. The lush strings of this best seller are on par with Connie's clear, crisp, floating vocal.

70. "Me Minus You," Brunswick 6405. A thick (Southern) accent is punched through this ditty penned by Webster and Loeb.

71. "Underneath the Arches," Brunswick 6483. Better than contemporary Ethel Shutta's version as a George Olsen release? Yes!

72. "I Cover the Waterfront," Brunswick 6592. Connie's got it covered—until at least the (later) challenge of a Billie Holiday version, on Columbia 37493. As a note of interest, this well-sung ditty was originally the title of a film entity not used in that (1934) film.

73. "Under a Blanket of Blue," Brunswick 6603. It's all a dream, as tenderly suggested by a soft-crooning Connie, in this ditty penned by Symes, Neiburg, and Livingston.

74. "It's the Talk of the Town," Brunswick 6632. Yeah. Connie has good claim on this classic, penned by Symes, Neiburg, Livingston.

75. "This Time It's Love," Brunswick 6632. Penned by Lewis and Coots, this ditty had also found a contemporary Adelaide Hall version sung somewhat off-key, in a stiff soprano voice. Connie's vocal on this ditty is somewhat slicker and indeed better. Just listen?

76. "Dinner at Eight," Brunswick 6640. Set the table for dinner and add flowers, with perhaps gardenias? Connie indeed serves out another classic vocal, penned by Fields and McHugh.

77. "Carioca," Brunswick 6871. Featured in the film *Flying Down to Rio* and penned by Vincent Youmans, Edward Eliscu, and Gus Kahn, this Latin sound worked well in the film. The fine film version, introduced by Etta Moton, seems to claim no recorded version? Connie however, fills the gap. While she had been "soft" before, this ditty perhaps notes an ability to substitute a hard, edgy vocal style, for a truly soft, polished, and pleasant vocal style, at will (another similarity to the vocal abilities of Elvis Presley, light-years later).

78. "The Boulevard of Broken Dreams," Brunswick 6871. This ditty, penned by Al Dubin and Harry Warren, has added drama with special thanks indeed to Connie. Introduced in the contemporary 1934 film *Moulin Rouge*, with Russ Columbo, this recording just may have been a crooning event, if recorded with Russ. In any case, Connie's powerful vocal is still a very sensitive and a very pristine performance, if overly sentimental. Just listen?

79. "Emperor Jones," Brunswick 6640. Paul Robeson, the famous contemporary Afro-American vocalist and actor was to be found in a contemporary film (1933) of the same name. This title, not found in that film, apparently sparked Connie's creative interest. Penned by Allie Wrbell, Connie interprets a full-blown drama and holds her listeners ears with great skill.
80. "Lost in a Fog," Brunswick 7303. Connie excels and never gets lost in this superbly recorded and defined rendition of this classic penned by Dorothy Fields and Jimmy McHugh.
81. "Isn't It a Shame," Brunswick 7303. Connie does it all, and it's not a shame, as this ditty, penned by Abner Silver, Al Sherman, and Al Lewis, is matched.
82. "With Every Breath That I Take," Brunswick 7354. The (contemporary) Bing Crosby original was subsequently recorded by Buddy Clark and (this) fine effort softly crooned out by Connie.
83. "Blue Moon," Brunswick 7363. Why listen to contemporary vocals by Al Bowlly or others, including a Bob Crosby version? Is Connie better? Just listen!
84. "All I Do Is Dream of You," Brunswick 6921. The very sappy ditty, penned by Nacio Herb Brown and Arthur Freed, was recorded by many contemporaries who, more so, lacked Connie's winning mid-tempo vocal.

- A move to Decca Records in (1935) found the sisters producing some recordings and subsequently retiring, except for Connie.

85. "In Other Words-We're Through"-Brunswick-6754. Connie again defines a classic, as penned by A.J. Neiburg, Marty Symms and Jerry Livingston. (Not the later Bart Howard song ditty)
86. "Moon Over Miami," Decca 657. Connie sounds very convincing, and this ditty, penned by Joe Burke and Edgar Leslie, ain't nothing but mellow.
87. "On the Beach at Bali-Bali," Decca 829. Bob Crosby's orchestra accompanied Connie's slick-lipped vocal with pleasant ease, as she (again) excels in this ditty penned by Jack Maskill, Al Sherman, and Abner Silver.
88. "I Met My Waterloo," Decca 829. With this ditty penned by Nat Schwartz and Connie herself, Connie scores (again) as a sweet band singer, but with required full-name credit, as backed by up as by Bob Crosby's orchestra.
89. "Whispers in the Dark," Decca 1420. Connie (with Ben Pollack and His Orchestra), contributes her stylistic abilities to this film title, penned by Frederick Hollander and Leo Robin.
90. "That Old Feeling," Decca 1420. This flip side of "Whispers in the Dark" also hides another classic. Penned by Lew Brown and Sammy Fain, this ditty joins yet another winner for Connie's reputation as a popular recording entity. (A contemporary and novel Adelaide Hall and Fats Waller version recorded in Europe and released on HMV B-8849, is, moreover, novel and competing.)
91. "Bob White," Decca 1483. This block-busting burst of energy, chiefly provided by Connie, inspires Bing also to provide a fine vocal performance. While perhaps a contrived ditty that embraces swing, this fast-paced and danceable ditty works!
92. "Basin Street Blues," Decca 1483. As the flip of "Bob White," this interpretation of this classic indeed puts Connie, with her husky Southern accent, back onto already familiar (with her) street in New Orleans. Bing, more so, cleverly assists!
93. "Gypsy Love Song," Decca 1678. The (contemporary) semi-operatic vocal duet with Bing Crosby and Frances Langford, on Decca 2316, truly sucks. Connie, moreover,

with some fine backing by Bob's Orchestra—Bing's bother—livens things up! Penned by Hubert and Henry Bache Smith, this contrived (1937) effort was in fact, not a duet, but a solo effort by Connie. Too bad, Bob Crosby's arrangement was not used by Bing and Frances? Or possibly by Bing and Connie?

94. "Alexander's Ragtime Band," Decca 1887. As noted above in the text, this already old acoustic ditty had, more so, been revived and recorded as a contemporary (1935) Boswell Sisters rendering. This later (1938) recording was subsequently recorded to resurrect the popular Irving Berlin-penned classic again as it had been used and featured the contemporary film of the same name, with film entities Alice Faye (also a featured vocalist in this book) and Tyrone Power.

This classy vocal duet featuring both Bing and Connie, moreover, had more to listen for. As introduced by the still very popular Eddie Cantor, his plea for the "march of dimes," on the recording itself, became an anthem as well for fighting the polio disease. (In fact, Connie herself was a courageous victim of the disease.)

95. "I Let a Song Go Out of My Heart," Decca 1896. The Duke Ellington influence on contemporary (1938) music was huge. So, indeed, was this ditty penned by Henry Nemo, Irving Mills, John Redmond and Duke himself. More so was Connie's fine vocal.
96. "Heart and Soul," Decca 2038. Connie indeed had a lot of "heart and soul" in her softer vocals. This ditty, penned by Hoagy Carmichael and Frank Loesser, adds further proof! (A fine contemporary version, by the Larry Clinton Orchestra, with a Bea Wain vocal, on Victor 26046, is also interesting but not as good as Connie's. A later rock-era version, by the Cleftones on Gee 1064, featured a creative group sound for this classic).
97. "Deep in a Dream," Decca 2259. Connie is deep in a dream and sings her heart out. (A later Frank Sinatra version in the mid-1950s, on the Capital LP W 581, is, for sure, a wetter dream, penned by Jimmy Van Heusen and Eddie DeLange, but Connie's still serious. Connie or Frank?
98. "Sunrise Serenade," Decca 2450. A fine vocal (again), penned by Frankie Carle and Jack Lawrence.
99. "An Apple for the Teacher," Decca 2640. Another great duet recording with Bing that became a huge best seller.
100. "Ho-Die-Ay Start the Day Right," Decca 2640. Another hit for Connie and Bing. This time, Bing even gets a bit feisty as he attempts to match Connie.
101. "They Can't Take That Away from Me," Decca 2879. This Gershwin-penned ditty is best heard on this fine rendition. Who are they? Who cares? Just listen to Connie's bold vocal, which explains everything as well as who "they" are. Ask Fred Astaire and Ginger Rogers?
102. "Between 18th and 19th on Chestnut Street," Decca 2948. Penned by Will Osborne, Dale Jones, and Dick Rogers, this (1940) ditty was an attempt by the old bandleader Will Osborne (also a radio entity) at a newer rhythmic style. While the (former) sweet bandleader succeeds with this fine ditty, this version by Connie and Bing defines it. While Connie always sounds huskier and hipper than Bing, he still contributes heavily! Connie and Bing always sound as if they are enjoying themselves anyway, but the lyrics on this ditty find both of them in some friendly competition. Bing sounds truly inspired, as he seems to enjoy this wordy tale along with Connie. (The street may be in St. Louis, MO?)

103. "On the Isle of May," Decca 3004. Connie's gifted voice could produce perhaps a thick soprano, and this classic highbrow performance indeed works. Credited to Tchaikovsky and adapted by Andre Kostelanetz and David Mack, this ditty met no boundaries.
104. "Blueberry Hill," Decca 3366. It's only fitting that another New Orleans entity, Fats Domino in 1956 (on Imperial 5407), would revive this ditty penned by Al Lewis, Larry Stock, and Vincent Rose. Connie, however, did it better, and with less grit than (1940) contemporary, Gene Autry. Listen and learn?
105. "The Nearness of You," Decca 3366. Connie succeeds (as usual) with this ditty penned by Hoagy Carmichael and Ned Washington. (A later Sarah Vaughn version offers interesting vocal comparisons.)
106. "Yes Indeed," Decca 3689. Connie and Bing do it—again.
107. "Tea for Two," Decca 3689. In this flip of "Yes Indeed," Connie and Bing revert to a fine update to the acoustical Marion Harris best seller. Connie indeed becomes a "show-off," as her fine vocal indicates. Bing, as usual, shyly hides his voice, but both succeed in their rendition of this ditty penned by Irving Caesar and Vincent Youmans.
108. "The Clock Song," Decca 3858. Somehow, this ditty, penned by Jerry Bresler, Hal Salzman, and Larry Wynn, ticks away with a (slight) bit of drama.
109. "Sand in My Shoes," Decca 3893. Connie sounds more than good! Penned by Frank Loesser and Victor Schertzinger, as a film entity for the forgettable *Kiss the Boys Good-bye*, this ditty indeed features Connie at her mellowest. When heard, this very pleasing vocal is "easy listening" itself.
110. "Mighty Lak' a Rose," Decca 18423. This (already) old ditty, also known as "Mighty Like a Rose," was perhaps Scottish in tradition and folklore. It was indeed an oddity, penned by Ethelbert Nevin and Frank L. Stanton, and a huge acoustical success. As a recording, it became an entity for George Alexander on Columbia 1585, in (1903), and it linger on for a Marguerite Dunlap release on Victor 5837. in 1911 and for the operatic Geraldine Farrar on Victor 88537 in 1916. Connie's better sounding electric recording, moreover, is competent. More so, another rendering, by George Whiting, Nat Schwartz and J. C. Johnson, called "Little Black Boy," turns this ditty into less than a mammy song and much of a plea for racial tolerance. This song was to become part of Ethel Waters stage act in the early 1930s, although she would not get around to recording it until 1947, on Mary Howard Records.

- Following are post-WWII Connie, or "Connee" picks:

111. "Let It Snow, Let It Snow," Decca 18741. While later in the game, Connie recorded this Christmas entity, as penned by Jule Styne and Sammy Cahn in 1946, and made it a classic!
112. "Old Buttermilk Sky," Decca 18913. Connie's strong vocal on this ditty penned by Haogy Carmichael and Jack Brooks became a best-selling entity this late in the game (1946).

113-114. *Connie Boswell and the Original Memphis Five in Hi-Fi*, RCA Victor LP 1426. By the 1950s, Connie was basically out of the game with a lesser yet still a good voice. This LP release, featuring a fine jazz group of the 1920s, provided Connie With some fine backing. Highlights for Connie included

a. "When My Sugar Walks Down the Street."
b. "Make Love to Me."

➢ Radio

The effect of (latter) 1920s commercial radio was perhaps best centered upon the rise of Rudy Vallee in 1929. While the aspects of the medium were huge, so were the problems of playing commercial recordings. The Boswell Sisters were to be perhaps better documented than most of the era, as most all major recording entities did not seek out to rock the boat and encourage their recordings to be aired. The idea of transcription recording, generally frowned upon, was perhaps a perfect solution—and perhaps cheaper, in 1930. The emerging Boswell Sisters, in true retrospective, were, more so, documented at that time by the "Continental Shows," during some appearances in Hollywood, California. The following eight picks are notable and good-sounding radio entities:

115. "I'm in Training for You." This ditty, penned by L. Wolf Gilbert and Abel Baer for the contemporary 1930 film "Paramont On Parade, sounds as if it may be a bit risqué. Connie's lead, more so, clinches it!
116. "Does My Baby Love." A good question? Indeed, this title penned by Milton Ager and Jack Yellen is a good one, that had been performed by the likes of Gus Van and Joe Schenck, the well known vaudevillian team who had more ever performed the ditty in the contemporary 1930 film "They Learned About Women". A better question posed by a group of girls? Yes! The fresh harmony of the Boswells is more than novel!
117. "Song of the Dawn." This ditty by Ager and Jack Yellen was penned for the contemporary (1930) film *King of Jazz*. Performed in the film by actor John Boles, perhaps replacing Bing Crosby because of bad behavior, this ditty was performed somewhat stiffly. Luckily, this group effort livens things up!
118. "Rarin' to Go." This peppy title, penned by L. Wolf Gilbert and Abel Baer for the contemporary 1930 Clara Bow film "Love Amoung The Millionaires" is matched by some energetic group singing.
119. "There's a Wah-Wah Gal in Agua Calliente." This dumb Walter Donaldson-penned title, while dated, is another rhythmic rave-up job by the girls!
120. "I'm on a Diet of Love." This somewhat risqué title, penned by L. Wolf Gilbert and Abel Baer for the 1929 film "Happy Days", benefits from another peppy vocal performance.
121. "When the Little Red Roses Get the Blues For You." This dumb title was nevertheless a creditable Al Jolson commercial release. It is, more so, bettered by Connie's raved-up lead vocal!

- The following three are not of transcription quality but well worth hearing:

122. "Minnie the Moocher's Wedding Day." The single release is exploited with a Bing Crosby introduction on a *Woodbury* program (1933).
123. "Heebie Jeebies." The single release, with Connie's almost wild vocal lead, is featured in a *Woodbury* (1934) Bing Crosby program.
124. "I'll Never Say Never Again." This Harry Woods-penned ditty was featured in a 1935 *Dodge Show*.

➢ Visual Image

- The Boswell Sisters were seen in many films, as well as in a creative Fleisher screen cartoon.

125. "When It's Sleepy Time Down South." Cartoon and Visual (1932).
126. "Shout Sister Shout." The girls are seen jamming it out in the 1932 film *The Big Broadcast*.
127. "Crazy People." The girls do it again in the 1932 *The Big Broadcast*.
128. "Rock and Roll." The girls are on a cruise ship in the *1934 film Transatlantic Merry-Go-Round*. While the film is innocent enough, the vocal harmony is good to see and hear.

➢ As a polio victim, Connie is usually to be seen sitting, hiding her disabilities. Later, as a solo radio entity, which provided her a more comfortable setting, she became the huge success she had already achieved as a Boswell Sister. As a sideline to her radio work, Connie appeared in many films, again with deserving artistic merit and success.

Al Bowlly

While the scope of this book (rarely) extends overseas, there are a few exceptions. As a British entity, Al Bowlly achieved, by the end of the 1930s, fame and recognition that was comparable to that of Bing Crosby. As an American entity, his success was limited, yet to be noted. As a would-be crooner of the latter 1920s, he was influenced by Americans Rudy Vallee and especially Bing Crosby. Al was known by many as a crooning Vallee or Crosby emulation from Britain. More so, his sweet and pleasant vocals with the likes of British dance bandleaders Lee Stone and Ray Noble made him very well known, with some of that success finding its way across to the United States. Some recordings were thus released and, after a while, found emulation, even by the likes of Rudy or Bing.

▪ Some of the following Al Bowlly picks note American (Victor) Ray Noble releases, which were originally released and recorded in Britain on the HMV label until 1934.

1. "Lady of Spain," Victor 22774. A fine lady? Indeed! This is, more so, a fine crooning job, penned by Robert Hargreaves, Tolchard Evans, Stanley J. Damerell and Henry Tilsley.
2. "Goodnight Sweetheart," Victor 25016. One of the most popularized recordings of the early 1930s, this bit of fluff, on its original (American) Victor release is credited to Ray Noble, Jimmy Campbell, and Reg Connelly. As a fine, soft crooning effort, both Russ Columbo and Bing Crosby would record it, with similar results. While it's still a debate on just who the vocal clone is, both credit Noble, Campbell, and Vallee as writers. (A contemporary Rudy Vallee recording, oddly, just cannot be found.)
3. "All of Me," Durium EN-8. It ain't Russ Columbo, but it's still good crooning!
4. "Save the Last Dance for Me," Durium EN-8. Just like its flip side "All of Me," it's a crooning match with Russ Columbo.
5. "Goodnight Vienna," Durium EN-9. Another classic European touch, penned by Eric Maschwitz and George Postford, who were popular British radio entities of the eary 1930s, subsequently landed Ray and Al in the middle of Europe!(This ditty should

noy be confused with the later rock era likes of the Ringo Starr release of a John Lennon penned song ditty of the same name).

6. "By the Fireside," Durium EN-11. This time, a contemporary Rudy Vallee version is also an interesting comparison in crooning.
7. "Was That the Human Thing to Do?" Durium EN-11. This crooning vocal was also recorded by the Boswell Sisters and the Pickens Sisters.
8. "You Can't Stop Me from Loving You." Decca F-2487. American bandleader Roy Fox made out better in England than at home. This (Roy Fox) release identifies Al indeed providing a fine and smooth vocal on the original Ethel Waters Broadway entity from *Rhapsody In Black.*
9. "Weep No More My Baby," Decca F-3783. This ditty penned by John Green and Edward Heyman works well for Lee Stone and Al.
10. "Close Your Eyes," Decca F-3783. The contemporary Ruth Etting rendering invites comparisons!
11. "You're My Thrill," Decca F-3980. Another crooning job (with Lee Stone) that works! (Other versions include renderings by Lena Horne and Ozzie Nelson as penned by Sidney Clare and Jay Gorney.)
12. "Love Is the Sweetest Thing," Victor 24333. This Ray Noble-penned ditty and Al's vocal match up!
13. "Midnight, The Stars And You," Victor 24700. While this American 1934 (Victor) release did merit some recognition, it was hardly the (1932) best seller as released in Britain on HMV B-6461. Penned by Reginal Connely, Jimmy Campbell, and Harry Woods, this classy crooning job allowed by Ray Noble's excellent backing perhaps defined (British) excellence? (Light-years later, in 1980, this ditty did find itself into more American ears (mostly baby boomers) when used effectively in the soundtrack of the Jack Nicholson film *The Shining.)*
14. "When You've Got a Little Springtime in Your Heart," Victor 24720. This excellent ditty from the Richard Rodgers and Lorenz Hart stage production of *Evergreen* had found (British) entity Jessie Mathews introducing it on the London stage, and in a subsequent British film. While not unlike the highbrow singing of Mathews (in which she sang the song at least twice), this "sweet band" dance band effort arranged by Ray Noble becomes a compliment due to Al's mellow vocal.
15. "The Very Thought of You," Victor 24657. This original recording, released and publicized in America and penned by Roy Noble, became a best seller. More so, Bing Crosby, on Decca 179, would emulate it and define it as his own. A later version, by Billie Holiday, perhaps defined it.
16. "Isle of Capri," Victor 24777. Al's initial visit to this song ditty, penned by Jimmy Kennedy and Hugh Williams is indeed very pleasant!
17. "It's Bad for Me," Victor 24872. The contemporary Cole Porter-penned ditty is well defined!

By the end of 1934, Al Bowlly, along with Ray Noble, arrived in the United States on extended tours, which also produced some recordings made in (below) America (below), along with some reissued British recordings (above) and numerous radio appearances. While Bowlly went back and forth across the Atlantic and recorded with other bands, Ray Noble and His Orchestra stayed on in the United States and became essentially known as an American organization. Bowlly, however, stayed on in England as a recording and radio entity, despite some success in America.

18. "Blue Moon," Victor 24849. This original recording, a cast off film ditty penned by Richard Rodgers and Lorenz Hart, perhaps led the pack of subsequent renderings. While over the years this ditty would be crooned out again by the likes of Connie Boswell, Bob Crosby, Mel Torme, and Billy Eckstine, the (later) rock era made it a bit more interesting. Indeed, the "group" doo-wop sound of the Marcels on Colipix 186 is indeed creative enough. More so is, perhaps, a crude and earthy version by Elvis Presley, released on his first Victor LP, as well as on 45 EP, on 45 rpm, and (still) on 78 rpm.
19. "Red Sails in the Sunset," Victor 25142. This fine crooning job (later) found Bing's version, on Decca 616, a good contemporary comparison. As penned by Hugh Williams and Jimmy Kennedy this wistful song ditty perhaps best defined sentimentally and 'mush'. Listen and compare Al and Bing's crooning!
20. "Dinner for one, Please, James," Victor 25187. Nat King Cole's (later) version of the Michael Carr penned ditty provides pleasing comparisons! Order both versions for (listening) consumption!
21. "If You Love Me," Victor 25240. Ray Noble's self-penned ditty found Al perfectly able to croon it out. Overly sentimental? Mushy enough?
22. "When I'm With You," Victor 25336. A film entity in the series of very popular Shirley Temple films of the 1930s, this ditty, penned by Mack Gordon and Harry Revel, was featured in the film *Poor Little Rich Girl* (1936). This Bowlly recording, moreover, is also a huge winner.
23. "I've Got You My Skin," Victor 25422. This Cole Porter-penned ditty was introduced in the contemporary (1936) film *Born to Dance* by a fine actress who could sing (Virginia Bruce). It was only given, as recording fodder, slightly more recognition as a Roy Noble release, with its flip side "Easy to Love" (also from the film). A Lee Wiley version followed, perhaps influenced by Al's stiff vocal? Subsequently, a Josephine Baker version followed, sadly to become best known as a "standard," outside of the United States. (Frank Sinatra would later redefine it as his own in the 1950s.)
24. "Easy to Love," Victor 25422. While this (1936) Cole Porter-penned ditty is introduced well, Al is a bit stiff when compared to a brighter Maxine Sullivan version, on Vocalion 3848. Later versions by Lee Wiley and Dick Haymes are also interesting comparisons.
25. "Goodnight Angel". HMV-BD-565. This (British) release of the (Allie Wrubel and Herb Magidson) penned ditty is crooned soft and mushy, and hardly the contemporary (American) 1937 Artie Shaw rhythmic 'swing' entity, featuring a well done vocal by Nita Bradley, who seems to be very much influenced (vocally) by contemporary diva Billie Holiday?
26. "When That Man Dead And Gone" HMV-BD.-922. This war-time British release As 'The Radio Stars with Two Guitars", Al and Jimmy Mesene's duet found this contemporary (Irving Berlin) penned ditty about Adolph Hitler playful enough. It was destined to become more than sobering propaganda! Soon after being recorded, Al was killed in a 1941 German blitz.

Fanny Brice

- For most baby boomers, the career of Barbara Streisand (in the midst of the rock era) is one of amazing success, as the Streisand legacy is one which directly originates on the musical stages of Broadway. Except for a few rock entities (including "Stoney End"), the style and charisma of Barbara Streisand is reminiscent of the pre-rock era (if one bothers to find out), which, in some ways, doesn't matter to her huge audience.

- The career of Fanny Brice, a Broadway performer and (acoustic) recording entity and a later film and radio personality as well (radio's *Baby Snooks*), was prolific. Indeed the subject of Streisand's latter '60s film *Funny Girl*, and its sequel, *Funny Lady*, left some fine recordings behind her. Despite acoustic limits, later-1920s electric recordings find Brice's voice and elocution superb. It's also a pity that Fanny showed little interest in pursuing a recording career as her clear and crisp vocals are much appreciated icons. Perhaps it was all considered novel by her? Or perhaps her radio success, with some film work, was all that she wanted? Picks are as follows:

1. "My Man," Victor 45263. The original acoustical version (based on the French title "Mon Homme," with English translation by Channing Pollock, from Maurice Yvain's original French lyrics), was introduced by Brice herself. Featured in the sensational *Ziegfeld Follies of 1921*, the thirty-year-old Broadway entity also scored heavily as a recording artist. This recording, despite its acoustic flaws, indeed finds her in a fine vocal exercise of quality.
2. "Second Hand Rose," Victor 45263. This flip of "My Man," penned by Grant Clark and James Hanley, also reeks of quality.
3. "My Man," Victor 21168. This (1927) is an electric rerecording. Indeed, Fanny's strong vocal comes through, unlike the previous acoustic effort. A fine contemporary version, by yet another Ziegfeld girl, Ruth Etting, is also excellent, more so emulating a bit upon Brice's original style.
4. "I'd Rather Be Blue over You," Victor 21815. Another good piece of 1920s nostalgia, penned by Billy Rose and Fred Fisher, again features a clear and crisp vocal style.
5. "If You Want the Rainbow," Victor 21815. This clear vocal on the flip of "I'd Rather Be Blue Over You," penned by Billy Rose and Mort Dixon, cannot fail to please.
6. "Cooking Breakfast for the One I Love," Victor 22310. While novel, Fanny turns this bit of fluff, penned by Billy Rose and Henry Tobias, into a solid and bouncy vocal, pleasant enough to be heard before or after breakfast. A contemporary Libby Holman vocal, in comparison, is a bit clumsy. Or perhaps, Brice had had a better breakfast?
7. "When a Woman Loves a Man," Victor 22310. Brice originated this fine classic, penned by Ralph Rainger and William A. Rose! More so, her fine bright vocal, dropping much of her usual novelty act, indeed reveals a strong-voiced diva of considerable quality. Contemporary Libby Holman also attempted this ditty with a fine and jazzy backing by Rodger Wolf Kahn. For the most part, the Holman vocal lacks Brice's warmth as well as fails to follow the jazzy Kahn lead.
8. "Sheik of Avenue B," Victor 45323. Another Brice (electric) rendering, penned by Bert Kalmar, Harry Ruby, S. J. Downing, and A. Friend that (again) proves her worth as a fine vocalist.

- ➢ Visual Image Fannie Brice appeared in many films, yet, as a vocalist her (1928) film *My Man* (Warner Brothers-Vitaphone), recapturing her earlier 1921 stage success with Ziegfeld is best. The highlights include

9. "My Man."
10. "If You Want the Rainbow"

Big Bill Broonzy

- The blues of the 1920s were properly defined by the words of the songs which contained the elements of social behavior as well as race—black or white. The various recordings of William Lee Conley (Big Bill Broonzy), from the late 1920s through to the 1950s, are the defining link that were labeled "the blues," "rural blues," "urban blues," and "folk." More than "Blind" Lemon Jefferson, Papa Charlie Jackson, Ma Rainey, Bessie Smith, Charlie Patton, Robert Johnson, Memphis Minnie, Arthur Crudup, or crooning bluesman Lonnie Johnson, Big Bill defined the blues for the later rock generation. While anyone can argue regional merits, as well as anyone else not mentioned, the popularity of "Big Bill," among others, was unmatched. While not as original as some others, he, nevertheless, defined what would be labeled as "Mississippi delta blues." For sure, many transplanted contemporaries and rivals took that train ride through nearby Memphis or the train rides from the cotton belts of the south to go north to Chicago. Indeed, many other Mississippi transients found Chicago an escape from racism as well as a hard life. Indeed "Big Bill" was one of them. He also sang for them. His vocals found rural and gradual urban audiences well pleased. His signature "Whoo" vocal tells the tale, the tale of "Chicago blues." As mentor to many, including the likes of Muddy Waters, the vastness of his recorded legacy indeed says it all. Just listen!

  - The following are picks:

1. "House Rent Stomp," Paramount 122656. This bit of rhythmic guitar lick is actually a dance number, however rural. Perhaps Big Bill first heard this ditty on a front porch somewhere deep down in the delta? In any case, a lot of myth can be created on listening to this entity, which is what good music is all about. (A contemporary (1929) ditty, "House Rent Shuffle" on Vocalion 1410, by Lil Johnson, more than "answers" this concept.)
2. "Hometown Skiffle," Paramount 21453. This ditty features less outstanding blues than actual content. Bill may be identified as part of the Hokum Boys, with such notable blues entities as Blind Lemon Jefferson, Blind Blake, Will Ezell, Charlie Spand, and Papa Charlie Jackson—which, in all fairness, creates a very listenable folk entity.
3. "I Can't Be Satisfied," Perfect 157. This bit of rural "gut bucket" guitar-strumming is a very effective piece of work (released as "Sammy Sampson").

   - Note: The following two entities were released as "Big Bill Johnson."

4. "Big Bill Blues," Champion 16400. Like most of his best recordings, this simple, but effective self-penned ditty (about a dream of his), becomes a recorded fact in this fine recording about (Bill) not being able to get "something." Another version, as a "Big Bill" release on Paramount 12656 is also effective, if not the same.
5. "Mr. Conductor Man," Champion 16426. This tale of getting up in the morning, hearing a train whistle, and packing up a suitcase to get on a train is familiar—and (still) effective.
6. "Brown Skin Shuffle," Champion 40074. Although not strictly a "Big Bill" release, this ditty's cross talkin' (with someone known as "Smith"—with his banjo), is "rural" and fun. Perhaps "getting dirty" and "going to town" are not for everyone—but they

seem to land on the ears of the many as anthem. This ditty was self-penned and released as "Johnson and Smith."

- Note: The following entities are "Big Bill" releases.

7. "Let's Reel and Rock," Melotone 7-06-64. Chuck Berry would (almost) do it later, in the 1950s!
8. "Big Bill's Milk Cow No. 2," Romeo 6-07-57. The problem here is that this theme is generally assumed as an original entity of contemporary bluesman Kokomo Arnold, on Decca 7026. While originality is always found to be suspect on these blues entities, it is safe to assume that these rural American folk,

(both black and white) did indeed have a lot of cows around. While it's not a stretch that Kokomo's cow belonged to Bill, Robert Johnson's calf (on Vocalion 03655), and, among others, Josh White's cow (on Banner 33361), are perhaps, members of the same herd. The barnyards, and tales of them, are in fact found in many of the ditties found within this book. While questions are raised about roosters, however, it is also a fact that there were more of them. Indeed, the effort of producing an interesting sound needs to be also seen as well as heard. The need to watch where we step is also knee deep. Perhaps, contemporary bluesman Charley Patton was also a neighbor? The flip side of Bill's version is "Big Bill's Milkcow No 3," but, in true retrospective, this era far preceded latter-century cloning. (Yet another piece to this barnyard tale is an earlier (1925) Dora Carr entity, "Cow Cow Blues," on Okeh 8250. Backed by piano wizard "Cow Cow" Davenport, whose signature piano style on her recording contributes to its title, Dora's vocal and lyric contents lack much barnyard odor. On the other hand, her vocal introduction sounds at least like a fragment of what "Milk Cow Blues" would develop into. Links? Murky? You bet! Let a good listener's ear be the judge.)

9. "The Mill Man Blues," Vocalion 04280. Bill's own self-penned tale about some good meat, cows, and butter is full of the (usual) quips and puns about "the blues." This theme had already been exploited back in the '20s as in "Organ Grinder Blues" (by Ethel Waters, on Columbia 14365-D; Victoria Spivey, as a vocal for a "Clarence Williams Blue 5" release on Okeh 8620; and "Kitchen Mechanic Blues," by Clara Smith, on Columbia 14097-D; among others). Bill's sexual exploitation of his own lyric are more rural and (more) crude—more Mississippi Delta?
10. "Friendless Blues," Bluebird B-5535. The start of this is just awesome as Bill's guitar licks are matched with his own mournful voice of despair—standard for the (future) likes of Big Boy Crudup and Muddy Waters. This time, the story relates his (own) mother's death, and his powerful story (1934)—in true retrospective—still works.
11. "I'll Be Back Home," Bluebird B-5998. This tale of a freight train ride (from his woman) from the sleet and snow of Chicago winter (?), through Memphis, on toward New Orleans—maybe? In any case, this ride is fun to travel, and the price of a ticket is to only listen to this fine experience.
12. "Serve It to Me Right," Bluebird B-5674. This ditty is full of risqué contradictions as well as some bold directness. Moreover, it seems like Bill found an excuse to leave his (current) mate. His pallet is not served to his satisfaction—but who knew (in true retrospective)—what women's lib was in 1934?

13. "Southern Blues," Bluebird B-5998. This train journey through southern states is not just an observation. A contrived train whistle does not sound as if it's contrived, and this tale, for sure, keeps its passengers entertained.
14. "Unemployment Stomp," Vocalion 4378. This (Chicago) recorded entity, leads off with a Louis Armstrong-styled cornet, followed by a boogie-woogie piano and a faster-paced "Big Bill" vocal. While the serious Depression times were indeed a fact of life, this ditty (recorded in 1937) is more of a farce and novel as it seems that one of Bill's instruments is broken and his wife is leaving him! In any case, dancing to this ditty and hearing Mr. Roosevelt's name at the same time may still be a contrived contemporary bit of bunk that somehow all (still) works.
15. "Living on Easy Street," Vocalion 4429. A simple blues entity? For sure! This very urban tale of Chicago-living is fair enough, as this slang term is bent into reality.
16. "Baby, I Done Got Wise," Vocalion 4429. This flip side of "Living on Easy Street" is the opening entity—on piano, as opposed to guitar or vocal. It is a true story, however contrived, about a man (perhaps Big Bill himself?) who finds out about "tricks." What a guy!
17. "Key to the Highway," Okeh 6242 A 12-bar blues, this (1941) recording—credited to Chas Segar and Big Bill himself—just may be, in true retrospective, the most celebrated recording Bill ever produced. Nevertheless, it should also be noted that the claimed coauthor, Charles "Chas" Segar (also a fellow bluesman), had recorded this ditty—possibly included with Bill's own guitar backing—the previous year (1940), as released on Vocalion 5441. A shared culture indeed!
18. "All by Myself," Okeh 6427. This upbeat rhythmic ditty (with a fine "urban" piano) trading licks with Bill's guitar is a danceable "boogie-woogie."
19. I'm Gonna Move to the Outskirts of Town," Okeh 6651. "Big Bill" and his "Chicago Five" are indeed on the move. This very influential ditty jut may be Bill's very best, or at least his most recognized. For certain, a Josh White version reeks of admiration as well as emulation.
20. "I'm Woke Now," Okeh 6724. The instrumental introduction on this ditty is winded—yes, it's got horns! Perhaps there are some that will not like Big Bill using big city urban backings, but it only really proves his versatility. Indeed, the slang used in his vocal had made it all urban!
21. "Roll Theme Bones," Columbia 36879. This ditty is (really) rhythm and blues—Chicago style (1945).
22. "I Love My Whisky," Mercury 8122.
23. "I Stay Blue All the Time," Mercury 8160.

Cleo Brown

- This vocalist-pianist lounge singer found her recording as early as 1935. As one of many transplanted Mississippi to Chicago entities, Cleo's success was steeped in the culture of (black) church music. Her vocal style features very soft tones, with some edgy and distinct Afro-American slang thrown in. Her own piano playing, moreover, finds her leading herself into some interesting recordings. Cleo's vocals, while not as distinctive as her 1935 contemporary Billie Holiday's, find Billie's principal jazzy pianist Teddy Wilson playing in much the same occupying keyboard style as Cleo. Picks are as under:

1. "Here Comes Cookie," Decca 409. No, the piano lead is not Teddy Wilson, nor is the soft-toned vocal that of Billie Holiday. Cleo so scores, as this Mack Gordon novelty is cleverly sung out.
2. "You're a Heavenly Thing," Decca 410. This soft touch of a vocal, penned by Joe Young and Little Jack Little, is pleasantly crooned out, a moving mid-tempo backing.
3. "The Stuff Is Here and It's Mellow," Decca 410. Stuff? This rhythmic ditty, penned by Willie 'the Lion' Smith, Walter Bishop Sr., and Clarance Williams, is more about drinking alcohol than other hard drugs. Recorded after the end of Prohibition, it was more than a fact that the purchasing of spirits was cheap, and it indeed livened up reasons for having a party.
4. "Boogie-Woogie," Decca 477. The soft and almost sweet vocal tones of Cleo's vocal does not distract from Cleo's own piano-playing, as she scores with the already old Pinetop Smith's original "Boogie-Woogie." Did this ditty define a musical dance or trend or both? It did!
5. "Me and My Wonderful One," Decca 486. The mellowness and softness of Cleo's lead vocal and piano lead clear interprets this wordy ditty, penned by Dick Smith, Harry Stride, and Bernard Maltin.
6. "Never Too Tired for Love," Decca 512. Cleo hands these lyrics skillfully, as this ditty penned by Michael H. Cleary and Dave Oppenheim is rhythmically performed.
7. "Mama Don't Want No Peas an' Rice an' Coconut Oil," Decca 512. This obvious novelty, penned by L. Wolf Gilbert and Charles Lofthouse has its share of Afro-American references, and it finds Cleo bending lyrics at a fast pace, without betraying her soft, cool sound.
8. "When Hollywood Goes Black and Tan," Decca 632. Yeah Man. This Leon and Otis Rene-penned ditty is full of contemporary (1935) references. An excuse for rhythmic jazz? Louis Armstrong? Truckin? Stepin Fetchit? Who taught Fred Astaire? The current Braddock-Joe Louis prizefight?
9. "When?" Decca 632. This crooning job, penned by Leon Rene is good, and, more so, much like the contemporary vocals of Valaida Snow.
10. "You're My Fever," Decca 718. The rapid vocal is good, as this ditty penned by Green and Brown again finds Cleo up to the challenge.
11. Breaking in a New Pair of Shoes," Decca 718. This obvious dance number, penned by Sam H. Stept, Ned Washington, and David Franklin, is far from loud but is effective.
12. "Latch On," Decca 795. The reference to swing makes it official as another cool and effective dance number, penned by Leon and Otis Rene, is made into another winner!
13. "Slow Poke," Decca 795. This Rene-penned ditty is perhaps much like the contemporary "Lazy Bones." It is, moreover, full of more Afro-American slang, which is something easy for Leon and Otis Rene.

- The following are 1936 "Hotshots" 78 rpm masters that were acquired by the author. This (perhaps) bootlegged label was considered risqué.

14. "Who'll Chop Your Suey." This ditty penned by Sidney Bechet and Rousseau Simmons is just as much about food as it is about sex. Ordering out?
15. "Tramp." Yes. This self penned ditty is about explicit sex.

Chick Bullock

This vocalist produced so many recordings that one cannot fail to run into his name when record-hunting. He was also a bit of a mystery in his time, as rumors of a deformed face found him in dim light when performing, starting around 1930s as a crooner influenced by Bing Crosby. While quantity is not usually quality, there are many Chick Bullock's early crooning efforts that just should not be ignored. Picks include

1. "I'm One of God's Children," Victor 22632. Also known as "I'm One of God's Children Who Hasn't Got Wings," this Broadway entity from the contemporary Ballyhoo production—penned by Oscar Hammerstein, Harry Ruskin, and Louis Alter—found its way to be better popularized by torch singer Libby Holman. Indeed, Libby's uninhibited style did make a statement, as she gets a lot of her vocal on her rendering. As heard on a contemporary Nat Shilkret release, Chick is (typically) given less time to be heard, although, like most band singers, he makes the most of it. While, in true retrospective, Libby's vocal style still sounds more radical than Chick's (Crosby-like) croon, it must be noted that "crooning," was still considered vulgar in 1931. Indeed, this interesting crooning job should not be ignored!
2. "Green Eyes". Victor-22729. As backed by Don Azpiazu and His Havana Casino Orchestra, Chick's quirky crooning perhaps better defined this ditty?
3. "Singing the Blues," Victor 22806. As a "High Hatter" release, this confused vocal, backed by Lenard Joy, is at least interesting! Penned for a contemporary (1931) Broadway entity of the same name by Dorothy Fields and Jimmy McHugh, this ditty should not be confused with an earlier title "Singing the Blues Till My Daddy Comes Home" penned by Joe Young, Sam M. Lewis and Con Conrad.
4. "Lazy Lou'siana Moon". Banner 0671. This Walter Dolaldson penned ditty ain, 't lazy, but Annette Hanshaw's contemporary version is better. Listen & compare!
5. "Let's Have Another Cup of Coffee," Victor 22936. Assisted by the "Three Waring Girls," Chick perhaps (vocally) defined this contemporary (Irving Berlin) classic, as a band singer with Fred Waring's Pennsylvanians" (1932).
6. "It's The Girl". Banner-32236. It's not as good as the contemporary Boswell Sisters version, yet it's still interesting ! Listen and compare.
7. "In a Shanty in Old Shanty Town," Victor 24050. A (1932) film found the likes of a good contemporary film *Crooner* turning into something not right, as its actor star David Manners is dubbed. Just *why* such a great part would be given to a nonvocalist was beyond even contemporary reasoning, as Bing Crosby, Russ Columbo, or even Chick Bullock himself, in the era of the *Crooner* could have made the film a more creditable entity. In any case, this song ditty from the film, penned by Little Jack Little, Joe Young, and John Siras, is at least creditable. (In addition to this best-selling entity featuring Chick with Ted Black's Orchestra, this 1931 ditty also found recognition with a version by Ted Lewis, on Columbia 2652-D). More so, a filmed 1939 version, by Gladys George in *Roaring Twenties*, is done very well.
8. "Stardust," Perfect 11326. While the classic Crosby vocal (Brunswick 6169) is not matched, this version indeed has a sound of its own. A Roy Smeck release, a strumming Hawaiian guitar provides Chick some fine backing to croon this tune out. Whether Chick is strumming is another question, like contemporary Nick Lucas, although he does seem to emulate Nick (vocally) a bit.

9. "There Ought To Be Moonlight Savings Time". Perfect-12718. As a typical 'moon' song, this Irving Kahal and Harry Richmon d penned ditty is crooned out harmlessly enough.
10. "Git Along," Perfect 12843. This ditty, penned by lightweight tenor-turned-crooner Gene Austin finds Chick in a very differing vocal style than that of Austin. Chick is, moreover, joined by Cab Calloway, whose uninhibited vocal style, directed by Cab's own orchestra arrangement, along with (white) bandleader Roy Smeck on strings, provides for Bullock some truly great inspiration. This rare interracial recording, more so, delivers a fine rhythmic entity, with Chick actually keeping pace with Calloway! Git it?
11. "I Want You For Myself". Conqueror-7779. The Irving Berlin penned ditty, backed by Andy Sanella And His Pennzoil Orchestra, at least produced a steel guitar leading the vocal?
12. "Are You Making Any Money" Conqueror 8217. Herman Hupfeld's other depression era 'question' song ditty "Brother Can You Spare A Dime" was stirring and poigient. This ditty is silly, as well as a proposition? A contemporary Paul Whiteman release featuring his female band singer Ramona (Davies), not to be confused with the famed song title 'Ramona", perhaps found that prostitution for some was as clever as it was necessary? Chick's (male) version is more comical, as perhaps a pimp checking up on things? While all this is silly enough, it' all remains good listening. Still interested? Spin it again!
13. "Annie Doesent Live Here Anymore". Conqueror-8279. This girl Annie had waited for any word, or letters until she got fed up and met a rich guy, as identified by Harold Spina, Joe Young and Johnny Burke, who wore a top hat?
14. "Alchoholic Ward Blues". Oriole 1903. The struggles of the Prohibition era are noted?
16. "Stars Fell On Alabama". Perfect-13078. Amoung many contemporary versions, perhaps Alberta Hunter's odd crooning job, recorded in England, at least matches Chick as something interesting to compare with?
16. "Winter Wonderland". Perfect-13103. Chick was one of the first to introduce this holiday classic! As a post Ziegfeld Broadway production, penned by Smith and Bernard, this ditty had first been recorded by Parker Gibb on (Columbia), who was a vocalist with the contemporary Ted Weems Orchestra, who sounded much like Cliff Edwards. Within a year or two, Weems would hired a young singer Perry Como as his bandsinger. Years later in 1946 as a solo artist, in 1946, Perry would revive it, and more so establish this song ditty as a 'standard'. for the rest of the century.
17. "Smoke Gets in Your Eyes," Perfect 15860. This highbrow entity had been introduced in the contemporary (1934) Fred Astaire and Ginger Rogers's film *Roberta* by (operatic) Irene Dunne. A fine contemporary Ruth Etting version on Brunswick 6769 probably defined it, yet Bullock's somewhat cruder crooning job, if not better, is more interesting. (Later, this ditty became familiar again in the rock era, as recorded by the Platters on Mercury 71383.)
18. "Underneath the Harlem Moon," Perfect 15678. Like another contemporary crooner Harlan Lattimore, on Brunswick 6401, the racial lyrics by Mack Gordon and Harry Revel skip by. This upbeat ditty, nevertheless, works, although (Afro-American) Lattimore perhaps had more claim upon credibility?
19. "Mighty River," Perfect 15678. This flip side of the above, penned by B. Baskette, is at least crooned out at mid-tempo, much like its flip side.
20. "There's a Cabin in the Pines," Perfect 15775. Another attempt at Crosby (found on Crosby's own recording on Brunswick 6610) finds Bullock's crooning cruder and less

soft, if effective enough, and more like another contemporary version from another attempted croon from Johnny Mercer!

21. "Sugar Blues," Vocalion 2805. An official Clarence Williams release, Chick's somewhat clumsy vocal somehow works. Perhaps Chick's attempt at crooning met no restrictions with Williams's (black) band, which was considered an oddity for its time (1934).
22. "Wagon Wheels". Perfect 15894. Forget about the popular contemporary 1934 Paul Whiteman best seller, which featured a stiff vocal by Bob Lawrence on Victor-24517. Chick at least makes this stupid Billy Hill and Peter De Rose penned ditty more interesting? Listen and compare!
23. "The House Is Haunted". Perfect-15922. Welll done croons by Bing Crosby and Russ Columbo had only rendered over the radio had found a stiff Kenny Sargert vocal on a Glen Gray release, on Brunswick-6858 and Chick's (better) croon as contemporary recordings of this Billy Rose and Basil Adlam penned ditty.
24. "When the New Moon Shines on the New Mown Hay," Banner 33139. It's not that Chick's voice is something special, although his clumsy attempts at vocals with good and jazzy backings are. This ditty penned by Harry Woods, Jimmy Campbell, and Reg Connelly, is clumsy anyway, and perhaps that's why the whole silly concept is a bit interesting? Just Listen!
25. "My Gal Sal". Melotone 6 06 10 The boring old Paul Dresser penned ditty is somehow turned into a pleasant croon.
26. "You've Got To Get High To Sing". Melotone 6 06 13 A stupid song with an interesting title?
27. "Dixie Lee," Melotone M-12879. Again, Chick and his Levee Loungers do it fast and jazzy!
28. I Can't Dance, I Got Ants in My Pants," Melotone M-12680.

29, 30. a. "In A Little Red Barn In Indiana". Melotone-M-13052. Just how Paul Dresser's penned ditty about his own home state in Indiana, noted in pre-1900 sheet music and as a recording as "On The Banks Of The Wabash", which was to be recorded by George J. Gaskin, (amoung many) later became known as "Back Home In Indiana", as penned by Ballard Mac Donald and James Hanley seems strange, but did happen. By the time Chick renderer the pleasant tune in 1934 with a jazzy mid-tempo backing, the song title, as penned by Joe Young, Jean Swartz and Joe Ager, became known as "In A Little Red Barn In Indiana".

b. Still later in 1940, Chick would render the same tune as "Back Home In Indiana", crediting the already noted Hanley and Mac Donald, releasing it on Okeh-6261. While both renderings demonstrate good crooning and are pleasant enough, Chick's first attempt is a bit better?

As a further note: In 1913, the state of Indiana proclaimed Dresser's original "On The Banks Of The Wabash" the official state song. When later in the decade the song was sold and the re-done Ballard Mac Donald and James Hanley claims upon the tune as "Back Home In Indiana" became better known, the state of Indiana itself became confused. It was to become even later confused by the also noted (later) "In A Little Red Barn", as by Joe Young, Jean Swartz and Joe Ager. This was to become rectified only by a 1997 Indiana general assemble vote to officially restore Paul Dresser's "On The Banks Of The Wabash".

31. "I'm Livin' in a Great Big Way," Melotone M-13389. This ditty, penned by Jimmy McHugh and Dorothy Fields, had become a best-selling entity for contemporary Louis Prima (Brunswick 7419).
32. "About a Quarter to Nine," Melotone M-13389. While the contemporary (1935) Al Jolson film *Go into Your Dance*" claimed this ditty first, a contemporary Jolson recording was somehow not attempted. Luckily, Chick's crude crooning job is done well enough—as well as a softer crooning effort as by contemporary Ozzie Nelson, on Brunswick 7425. (Jolson would record this ditty some ten years later.)

Cab Calloway

Many baby boomers know "Cab" Calloway (real name Cabell) from the (1980) film *The Blues Brothers*. As a musical entity of the film, as well as a living icon, the seventy-three-year-old projected a fresh combination of energy and musicianship that rivaled or overwhelmed both Dan Aykrod and Jim Belushi. Other musical entities in this fine film, including Aretha Franklin and Ray Charles, must have been also taken aback by his vitality. None of these other musical entities had, in fact, even been born when Cab first became prominent.

Cab first became famous with the help of his sister Blanche—a musical entity herself. As a bandleader, of the early 1930s, he was perhaps greatly aided with an appearance in the Bing Crosby film *The Big Broadcast* (1932). Along with Bing, Cab is found to compete well with his other contemporaries, who would include the Mills Brothers, Kate Smith, the Boswell Sisters, and the awful Arthur Tracy. As in the "Blues Brothers," almost fifty years later, Cab's rendition of "Minnie the Moocher" was an awesome performance to watch and hear. So indeed were his contemporary radio appearances, Cotton Club shows, and, more importantly for the purposes of this book, his original Brunswick recordings. There is nothing special about Cab's voice. He may be described as a tenor (or part-tenor), who knew how to project his scatting vocals over his hard playing band. His use of novelty titles was mixed by his uninhibited physical efforts as well. Perhaps he could have been influenced most (vocally) by scatting contemporaries Frankie "Half Pint" Jaxon, Louis Armstrong, and his own sister (Blanche). More so, his presence found applause from diverse audiences of both black patrons and white patrons, as his movements on stage were wild and electrifying. As a dance bandleader, his musical legacy, documented in numerous films of the 1930s, competes even with a later rock generation, including that of a (later) hip-shaking Elvis Presley. His influence upon comic Danny Kaye should also be noted, as seen in various Kaye films and concert performances. More importantly, Cab's own his charismatic vocal personality indeed translated itself well on to many recordings.

➢ Vocal picks include the following:

1. "St. Louis Blues," Brunswick 4936. Cab creates a little drama here, along with his Jungle Band.
2. "Happy Feet," Banner 0835. Cab usually raves up his orchestra and jumps in—both vocally and physically. This is no explanation; on hearing this ditty, one can somehow visualize. Perhaps this ditty is just a good danceable entity, but it should still be applauded?

3. "Git Along," Perfect 12843. The wildness of Cab's vocals are actually led by his (own) well-led orchestra, with an added bonus on this ditty, with the contemporary bandleader Roy Smeck (Wizard of the Strings). Cab is joined vocally by (white) crooner Chick Bullock, whose vocal is obviously inspired by Cab's uninhibited vocal style! It's indeed a fine record as well as a rare interracial jam that remains something fun to play and hear. Get it!
4. "The Vipers Drag" Perfect 15412. An early drug song?
5. "Is That Religion?" Brunswick 6020. (Much better than the contemporary Mildred Bailey version! Listen and compare!
6. "St. James Infirmary," Brunswick 6105. While this version is not the dramatic Louis Armstrong one (Okeh 8657), Cab's novel approach is still very good—very good indeed! Listen and compare the stylistic differences between Louis, and Gene Austin's original as well!
7. "Minnie the Moocher," Brunswick 6074. This may be considered as Cab's ultimate statement. This definitive release is rowdy and novel enough, as well as inspiring. While the serious and social commentary about drug use remained relevant throughout the century, so indeed did Cab. Penned by Irving Mills, Clarence Gaskill, and Cab himself, this bit of "hot" 1931 jazz deserved much emulation. It did! It Does!
8. "Black Rhythm," Brunswick 6141. As penned by Irving Mills and Donald Heywood for the "Cotton Club' this ditty obviously had more to do with (Afro-Americans) Donald Heywood and Cab. This ditty home ever became the basis for a Broadway entity.
9. "You Rascal You," Brunswick 6196. Louis Armstrong did it. So did the Mills Brothers. Cab's interpretation is also awesome!
10. "Kickin' the Gong Around," Brunswick 6209. Mmm. This bit of drug slang is a powerful statement, penned by Harold Arlen and Ted Koehler, for Cab's contemporary 'Cotton Club' appearances, which can also become very entertaining as a recording. Cab is again energetic, and perhaps his previous search for Minnie the Moocher just didn't help?
11. "You Dog (Aw You Dog)," Banner 332323. This slang term just could be "rap" (1931)!
12. "Eadie Was a Lady." Melotone M-12583. This interesting tale of a lady who likes to drink is sung out in much the same idiom as Cab's original "Minnie." While Minnie's problems were with drugs, Eadie's novel tale is well worth it! (The contemporary original by Ethel Merman is also done well, with obvious stylistic differences and interesting comparisons.)
3. "Cabin in the Cotton," Brunswick 6272. Somehow, this slow-tempo ditty works for Cab and perhaps band member Bennie Payne? It's a good fit for a "Cotton Club' review, although this title was actually af a contemporary film of the same name (not used as a vocal in the film). It would also become better known as well crooned out contemporary Bing Crosby recording, amoung many. Listen and compare!
14. "Strictly Cullud Affair," Brunswick 6292. This ditty can also provide something novel for white listeners as well?
15. "Minnie the Moochers Wedding Day," Brunswick 6321. This stupid title finally found Minnie. This Harold Arlen and Ted Koehler penned ditty, who had been hired by the management of the "Cotton Club', had picked up upon Cab's 'Minnie the Moocher', harmlessly enough. A contemporary Boswell Sisters version, on Brunswick 6442, using vocal harmony, may just be better?
16. "I've Got the World a String," Brunswick 6424. This (later) standard, penned by Harold Arlen and Ted Koehler is done well enough for Cab's introduction to Cotton

Club audiences, noting the contemporary Bing Crosby version is indeed more poignant. (Lee Wiley put claims upon this ditty a bit later, although Frank Sinatra, light-years later, would redefine it.)

17. "I've Gotta Right to Sing the Blues," Brunswick 6460. The ditty also known as "I Gotta Right to Sing the Blues" (another Cotton Club favorite) found Cab's version seriously challenged by contemporary Louis Armstrong as well as the (later) definitive rendering by Lena Horne. In any case, this ditty is serious stuff, and Cab's vocal is no slouch! Listen and compare. (Lee Wiley also recorded it, but it was not released as a contemporary 1933 recording.)
18. "Doing the New Low Down," Brunswick 6513. As part of the Brunswick recording project to reproduce the *Blackbirds* revues, covering the years from 1928 to 1930, this ditty found Cab, the bandleader who also did his own vocals as a vocalist, backed by the Don Redman Band. He is also assisted by the Mills Brothers, who win out, vocally.
19. "Reefer Man," Banner 32944. Yeah—another campy drug song that perhaps was ahead of its time.
20. "The Man from Harlem," Banner 32866. This jiving tune perhaps asks just what this man is smoking?
21. "Harlem Camp Meeting," Victor 24494. Pure camp!
22. "The Lady With A Fan," Victor 24451. The 1933 Chicago World's Fair did inspire one Sally Rand to dance in the seminude—or perhaps on some occasions in the nude? Cab's own contemporary commentary is novel enough, as many "fan" dancers were to be seen at New York's Cotton Club along with Cab. Nevertheless, Cab's timely recording forever dates this ditty, along with Chicago's more famous entities.
23. "Zaz Zuh Zaz," Victor 24557. Nonsense? Gibberish? In any case, it works! "Zaz" to all listeners!
24. "Jitter Bug," Victor 24592. This title became a dance fad. Thanks to Cab at the Cotton Club!
25. "Chinese Rhythm," Brunswick 6992.
26. "Copper Colored Gal". Brunswick-7748.
27. "Utt Da Zay," Vocalion 5062. This bit of gibberish, also known as "The Taylor Song" (penned by Ram Mills), remains pure camp and fun.
28. "Blues in the Night," Okeh 6422. Perhaps the most relevant of many versions of this (Johnny Mercer and Harold Arlen) ditty, penned for the contemporary (1941) film title?
29. "Virginia, Georgia, and North Carolina," Okeh 6717. This (1941) release, penned by Little Shay and Cab himself, found Cab dropping much of his personality and attempting to compete with the contemporary swing sounds found in recordings fit for train travel—much like those of Duke Ellington and Glenn Miller. Along with a vocal chorus featuring The Cabaliers, his effective vocal and orchestra, he indeed proves that his recorded product is as good as anyone else's. All aboard! Or perhaps just another great excuse for a dance record?

- Visual Image

As already noted above, the visual image of Cab Calloway, more so than many other contemporaries, was personable and defined his success. He, moreover, appeared in many films, mostly in film shorts, throughout the 1930s and 1940s. The best are

30, 31. "Minnie the Moocher," 1932. While many survive, the visual vitality found in the Bing Crosby film *The Big Broadcast*, is hard to beat. Light-years later, in 1980, the filmed sequence in *The Blues Brothers* is also fabulous.

32. "Kickin' the Gong Around." Also featured in the (1932) film *The Big Broadcast*, the young Cab, in the follow-up for story of a drug-habit-plagued "Minnie," again finds Cab electrifying!

33. "St. James Infirmary," 1932. This Fleischer cartoon is a creative bit of work!

The following two ditties, already reviewed as recordings above, come to life on the screen, in the (1933) film short *Hi-De Ho*. (After much time tracking it down, this film short differs greatly from a similarly titled full-length 1940s film release.)

34. "Zaz Zuh Zaz."
35. "The Lady with the Fan."

> More: Cab's use of Afro-American slang also brought him notice in official language. As the author of *The New Cab Calloway's Hepsters Dictionary*, the aspects of "jive" street language were to be made official. (*The Cab Calloway's Hepster's Dictionary*: *Language of Jive*, Copyright 1944, by Cab Calloway, Inc., was indeed an enlightened publication.) The forerunner of "rap?"

Blanche Calloway

- Blanche Calloway's legacy as a black and female bandleader had been well known within the Afro-American community before the likes of her brother, Cab Calloway. Moreover, Blanche did her own vocals, with some good results, linking jazz and blues with her pleasant (high) voice. While less highbrow than contemporary Adelaide Hall, her vocals are, nevertheless, jazzy, even without Ethel Waters.

  - The following are two Blanche Calloway solo picks from 1925.
    While good enough, it's obvious she's emulating Bessie Smith. Moreover, an accompanying trumpet sounds much like Louis Armstrong, a certain favorite of many contemporary blues women, indeed (again) like Bessie.

1. "Lazy Woman's Blues," Okeh 8279. This blues, penned by R. J. Jones, is full of typical grit and despair.
2. "Lonesome Lovesick," Okeh 8279. While being "lonesome" is indeed part of having the blues, this ditty, penned by R. J. Jones, is effectively depressing.

  - The following release find Blanche leading a dance band, and, moreover, leading her Joy Boys, usually with her own vocals. Moreover, unlike her previous blues recordings, her voice is sweetened and far more rhythmic, as well as jazzy.

3, "I Need Lovin'," Victor 22641. While given a rousing and rhythmic start, Blanche's fast-paced and bright vocal seemingly challenges her Joy Boys, as this solid ditty, penned by Henry Creamer and James P. Johnson, scores.

4. "Just a Crazy Song," Victor 22661. There's a lot of scatting and slurring with the Joy Boys, as this attempt at novelty, penned by Bessie Smith and Clarence Williams, is a relevant one, as well as, perhaps, an amusing pun.
5. "I'm Getting Myself Ready For You," Victor 22659. Blanche's lyrics are red hot, as her spin upon Cole Porter's penned ditty from for the 1930 Broadway entity 'The New Yorkers" succeeds! Is she ready? Yes.
6. "Loveless Love," Victor 22659. This (Handy) classic, also known as "Careless Love," perhaps receives its best vocal treatment?
7. "It's Right Here for You," Victor 22717. This blues ditty, penned by Perry Bradford, becomes a bit more rhythmic and more jazzy.
8. "Without That Gal," Victor 22733. Contemporary (1931) Ethel Waters and Ruth Etting versions are somewhat challenged. While not as dramatic as the Waters version, its rhythmic content is still jazzy and explosive! (Also note the substitution in lyric from "Gal" to "Man" for these gender versions.)
9. "When I Can't Be with You," Victor-Timely Tunes C-1578. This medium-tempo bit of jazz singing, penned by Redman and Palmer, finds Blanche in somewhat of a high-shrill vocal. Somehow, it all works!
10. "Make Me Know it," Victor 22736. This fine dance record, while a bit subdued, is cleverly sung, with some risqué lyric snuck in by Fess Williams, who penned it.
11. "I Got What It Takes," Victor 22866. Perhaps the difference between "blues" vocals and "jazz" vocals, is clearly defined? As this rhythmic ditty, penned by Clarence Williams and H. Jenkins, is light and jazzy. Its contrived lyrics also find the exciting Blanche committed! Will she give it away?
12. "Concentrating on You," Victor 22862. This ditty, penned by Andy Razaf Razaf and Fats Waller, is sung fast and (perhaps) a bit too furious? Both contemporaries, Mildred Bailey (on a Paul Whiteman release) and Connie Boswell also recorded it and, more so, took a bit more time. Listen and compare!
13. "Last Dollar," Victor 28862. Blanche's somewhat fast-paced shrill vocal is at least rhythmic enoughfrom the contemporary (white) musician Red Nichols, who penned this ditty. Moreover, Blanche is indeed driving her rhythmic band hard!
14. "Growling Dan," Victor 22866. This obvious companion—and perhaps companion to her brother's contemporary and better-known "Minnie The Moocher"—is, moreover, just as novel. It is penned by Blanche herself and Clyde Hart with some fine scatting thrown in!
15. "Blue Memories," Victor 22896. After a setup for about a third of the song, instrumentally—penned by Calloway and Mosley—Blanche's rather crude vocal, while soft, perhaps depends more upon her slower-paced band to mesh. Moreover, they succeed!
16. "Catch On," Perfect 16054. This jazzy and rhythmic ditty, penned by Farrell and Calloway, finds Blanche capable of handling it all.
17. "What's a Poor Girl Gonna Do," Melotone M-13191. This very contrived ditty, penned by Calloway and Cameron, seemingly and foolishly notes the chase between men—both Democrats and Republicans! Luckily, it's danceable!
18. "Louisiana Liza," Vocalion 3112. This obvious swing entity, penned by Stein and Calloway and developed since and after the start of Blanche's band, while contrived, is yet another strong and rhythmic statement.

- Moreover, could it have been that Blanche's rhythmic dance band vocals had been an influence on contemporaries Ivie Anderson and Valaida Snow?

Eddie Cantor

When Eddie Cantor passed away in 1964, he left behind a huge legacy of recordings, as well as Broadway, radio, and films. Like (his idol) Al Jolson, his contemporary blackface routine did not hold up well. As a recording artist, his acoustic renderings, capturing his loud, personable voice, showcase him best. Indeed, Jolson was better able to make the transition to electric recordings, as he was the better singer. Nevertheless, it's Eddie's natural wit and charisma, founded on stage, that later translated well onto novelty recordings, and subsequently onto successful radio programs and films. Cantor was, more so, the more successful film and radio entity, a founder of comic expression whose antics that would find many emulators, including the likes of Milton Berle, Danny Kaye, and Jerry Lewis. The following are Eddie Cantor picks:

1, 2. "That's the Kind of Baby for Me," Victor 18342. Penned by Jack Egan and Alfred Harriman for the *Ziegfeld Follies of 1917*, this ditty found Cantor introducing this wordy and fast-paced ditty (in an Al Jolson-inspired vocal), along with his own special antics and mannerisms.) For the most part, the mood and style as heard on this recording would be duplicated on every recording than followed it, especially noting *another* contemporary (1917) version as released on Aceolion-Vocalion 1220.
3. "You Don't Need the Wine to Have a Wonderful Time," Pathé 22163.
4. "When It Comes to Lovin' the Girls, I'm Way Ahead of the Times," Emerson 10105.
5. "You Ain't Heard Nothin' Yet," Emerson 10134. Penned by Gus Kahn, B. G. De Sylva, and Al Jolson himself), a contemporary Jolson recording on Columbia A-2836, in comparison, proves Jolson to be the better vocalist. Even so, Cantor's quirky voice remains full of pure, if dated, entertainment! Is it still worth it to listen and compare both acoustic renderings? Or did it matter that (Jolson) was Cantor's idol anyway?
6. "The Argentines, Portuguese, and the Greeks," Emerson 10200. For many later-century ears, this ditty penned by Edgar Meeker reeks with bias. While its acoustic limitations find it hard enough, Cantor's own easy speech (his principal asset as a recording entity) also puts down the Irish. Yet he also notes a successful participation of the American dream for all. While hardly a great vocal or song title, this (1920) recording is interesting enough as a "pick" for daring to be insensitive and rude. Like his (blackface) image, the good-natured Cantor perhaps had no insight for how the (American) melting-pot culture would change.
7. "Dixie Made Us Jazz Band Mad," Ererson 10263. While as contrived as a jazz song, it's actually a well-done excuse for a recording.
8. "Margie," Emerson 10301. Perhaps Cantor's articulate abilities were meant for the stage? In any case, this acoustic entity, penned by Benny Davis, Con Conrad, and J. Russell Robinson, however schmaltzy, cans for retrospective a fine, quirky (acoustical), musical performance. As myth has it, perhaps this ditty was penned with Cantor's own daughter Marjorie in mind? Or was it a flapper? (A contemporary Frank Crumit version is an interesting comparison.)

9. “He Loves It,” Columbia A3754. This (1923) release, penned by Grant Clarke and Edgar Leslie, is a silly contemporary commentary about a married man whose wife abuses him. (Contemporary Elsie Clark’s version, on Okeh 4725, also makes fun of the guy! Dated? Later-century thinking has men being the bastards? Or is it all just too novel?
10. “I’ve Got the Yes We Have No Bananas Blues,” Columbia A-3964. Another fine and popular novelty penned by Frank Silver and Irving Cohen, from Broadway’s 1922 *Make It Snappy*. It is perhaps best identified with Cantor’s articulate voice—with usual antics thrown in!
11. “No, No, Nora,” Columbia A3964. Another novelty penned by Gus Kahn, Ted Fiorito, and Ernie Erdman about a flapper! A (1923) contemporary sheet music had a picture of Ruth Etting on it, although the (then) Chicago radio vocalist did not produce contemporary recording.
12. “If You Knew Susie,” Columbia 364-D. From the 1925 Broadway entity *Big Boy*, Cantor’s personality trumps, as this novelty (by Buddy De Silva and Joseph Meyer), perhaps defining “schmaltzy,” still works?

Note: The advent of electric recordings found Cantor’s loud vocals and style very obsolete for phonograph recording, although his articulate voice was still perfect for the Broadway stage, radio, and talking films. This author’s own dislike of Cantor’s hugely successful electric recording release of “Making Whoopee” (Victor 21831) may be found in the “Rubbish” section of this book. Subsequent rerecordings of his earlier acoustic recordings, more so, do not better his previous efforts. The following five electric recordings, however, do merit a good hearing:

13. “I Faw Down and Go Boom,” Victor 21862. This title penned by James Brockman and Leonard Stevens is perhaps the most inept excuse of a (1929) title than for a fall into songwriter’s hell. Cantor, moreover, found it as simple recording fodder. Somehow, like so many of previously recorded ditties of his choice, his silly antics do put his (personal) claims on it. Did Cantor, more so, hope to make “faw” into a word? In cartoons later?
14. “Ballyhoo Theme-Cheer Up,” Hit of the Week-K-6. This (1931) release found Cantor’s natural wit and cynicism directed at the dismal (contemporary) state of Americana. As the era Depression deepened, the failure of banks, bread lines, and the suspicions of the public was substantial. More so, Eddie’s distain for the likes of the contemporary and optimistic song ditty “Happy Days are Here Again” is far from comical, and his commentary is poignant and biting—a huge chunk of Cantor revealed!? More so, this author’s own research has found that this ditty had been penned by Misha and Wesley Portnoff and the contemporary editor of the satirical magazine *Ballyhoo*, Norman Anthony. About a year later, a contemporary Broadway entity *Ballyhoo* (perhaps also inspired by *Ballyhoo* magazine), along with song ditties (other than “Cheer Up”), would find a limited stay under Broadway lights. Perhaps this production needed Eddie Cantor?
15. “There’s Nothing Too Good for My Baby,” Victor 22851. Penned by Benny Davis, Harry Akst, and Cantor himself for his contemporary film *Palmy Days*, this (1931) recording as a Gus Arnheim release tries to reestablish Cantor as a relevant recording artist. Yet it’s more than obvious that Cantor’s acoustic attributes are obsolete, and it’s the Arnheim Orchestra that gives this recording a lift. (A more interesting

contemporary version, as an Eddie Kirkeby release on Oriole 2348 found Elmer Feldkamp's softer croon defining (Cantor's) original as a recording.)

16. "The Man on the Flying Tapeze," Melotone 13001. This simple (1934) ditty, penned by Walter O'Keefe, finds Cantor's pleasing personality breezing along—indeed just like his earlier and successful acoustic renderings! Wisely limiting his efforts to radio and popular film, it's a good bet that with money rolling in, he was not much concerned to add to his recording legacy, which he most likely had not taken seriously, at least since the mid-1920s. (A subsequently 1939 *Our Gang* film short *Clown Prince* found Alfalfa sillier, but interesting.)
17. "Alexander's Ragtime Band," Decca 1887. Introduced by Cantor himself (in charity work for the (1938) March of Dimes), the sincere spoken words of Eddie Cantor also introduce a fine vocal of the already classic Irving Berlin ditty by Bing Crosby and Connie Boswell (s*poken word by Eddie Cantor only*).

- Radio. Eddie Cantor was indeed a radio pioneer since at least 1922. More so, starting in 1929 until the advent of TV in the latter 1940s, his radio programs became a known American institution.
- Film. The following films merit review:

- *Roman Scandals* (MGM) 1933. The zany antics of Cantor are placed within ancient Rome, with his singing of forgettable songs. Costars included the beautiful Gloria Stuart, as well as a cast of thinly clad young chorus girls with Busby Berkley perhaps taking advantage of seminude statues of that contrived era and story line. Ruth Etting, who was also in it and contributed the ditty "No More Love," was disappointedly short and with sadly less to do later in the film. Indeed, Cantor is the center of the film-it was all about him! Is it bad? His vocal on (18). "Build a Little Home," while pleasant enough, is no great epic. As entertainment, this film works, although as a musical, featuring (more) of contemporary singer Ruth Etting (who had previously starred with Cantor on Broadway) would have made it far more interesting, in hindsight! A blackface segment that, in true retrospective, may offend later generations who might view it, was, more so, a product of its time despite its attempt at humor. Interested enough?
- *Whoopee!* While the title of this Broadway entity which became a popular (1930) film sucks, Cantor's introduction of the jazz standard (penned by Donaldson and Kahn) (19). "My Baby Just Cares for Me" is worth it. (Cantor introduced it as in blackface and *not* in blackface.

The *not*-in-blackface rendering (in true retrospective) is better as well as more palatable! (This ditty, more so, became a popular contemporary (1930) recording for Ted Weems (featuring an Art Jarrett vocal, as well as a Ted Fio Rito Orchestra) release featuring a vocal by Frank Luther. More so, this ditty has been much confused with the earlier jazz classic "When My Baby Smiles at Me" that had been recorded by popular bandleader Ted Lewis, who also provided his own vocal initially as an acoustic entity in (1920), released on Columbia A2908.

- *Thank Your Lucky Stars* (Warner Brothers) 1943. The contributing antics of Eddie Cantor (in a double role as a parody of himself) are still funny. Perhaps the younger Jerry Lewis had been very much interested in this film?

- Special note: The charity work on behalf of the March of Dimes is a legacy that Cantor, in true retrospective, has benefited many generations since.

Thelma Carpenter

As part of a second generation of singers who grew up on (mostly) electric recordings, Thelma, perhaps, found the voices of Ethel Waters, Helen Humes, and Billie Holiday most essential? Her clear-cut vocals indeed find a lot of Waters (as many others did). More so, the ear of bandleader Count Basie found her a perfect follow-up for the slightly older Helen Humes, whom Thelma replaced for a while. Her success in mid-1940s later produced some fine solo releases, with added recognition with Eddie Cantor on radio. The following releases find the excellent voice of Thelma Carpenter:

1. "Love Grown on the White Oak Tree," Brunswick 8455. This long-worded title, penned by Todd, is fortunately paced up into a contemporary (1939) excuse for swing, as a Teddy Wilson release, featuring a slick vocal from Thelma.
2. "This Is the Moment," Brunswick 8455. A typical Teddy Wilson introduction finds this slower (urban) type of jazz, penned by Jimmy Mundy, Teddy Wilson, and Carpenter, perhaps best fitting the images of smoky rooms and lots of alcohol, indeed much in the same mood as (earlier) Teddy Wilson recordings with Billie Holiday? Listen and learn.
3. "She's Funny That Way," Bluebird B 10477. This (1939) Colman Hawkins release finds Thelma taking on the (older) ditty that had been (most) associated with Gene Austin. It is, more so, a differing vocal as compared with Austin's style and sung in the same "urban" style as her previous ditty "This Is the Moment." Sung as "He's Funny That Way," it's interesting to note the (later) 1944 rendering by Billie Holiday, indeed sounding much like Thelma's version, although both vocals heard (on this song ditty) are as similar in voice as they are in creativity. Listen and compare.

More so, a (1944) release by Connie Haines was likely issued as the result of the popular 1944 film *The Postman Always Rings Twice* and not in response to the (contemporary) Billie Holiday release on the small (Commadore) label.

4. "I Didn't Know about You," Columbia 36766. The contemporary Lena Horne release finds interesting comparisons, as this Count Basie release finds Thelma's vocal edgier than Lena's rendering. Just listen!
5. "All of My Life," Musicraft 320. The fine and jazzy backing of the Herman Chittison Trio work well in a lead for Thelma to define an Irving Berlin-penned classic as her own!
6. "These Foolish Things Remind Me of You," Majestic 1017. The earlier vocals of Helen Ward, and especially a Billie Holiday version (which may have been the earlier recording Thelma had been most influenced by), challenged by Thelma's softer approach? (A contemporary version by Herb Jeffries is, more so, a bit stiffer, like an earlier Buddy Clark version?). Who's better? Just listen!
7. "My Guys Come Back," Majestic 1017. The obvious post-WWII title, penned by Mel Powell and Ray McKinley, is, more so, a celebration in mid-tempo.
8. "Just A-Sittin' and A-Rockin'," Majestic 1023. This group concept version of the contemporary Delta Rhythm Boy's version is challenged.

9. "Hurry Home," Majestic 1023. A familiar phone message? While far from great, this attempt at good singing works well enough for this schmaltzy title penned by Joseph Meyer, Buddy Benier, and Bob Emmerich.
10. "Seems Like Old Times," Majestic 1030. Penned by Carmen Lombardo and Jacob Loeb, this ditty became a best-selling (1946) entity for Guy Lombardo's Orchestra, featuring a schmaltzy vocal by Don Rodney and the Lombardo Trio. It was subsequently recorded by contemporaries Vaughn Monroe, Kate Smith, and (luckily) by Thelma's low and jazzy vocal. Moreover, the ditty would become a "theme" used by the contemporary radio and (later) TV personality Arthur Godfrey. (Light-years later in (1977), actress Diana Keaton would render it well in a (Woody Allen) film *Annie Hall.).* Who did it best-it's Thelma!
11. "A Jug of Wine," Majestic 1030. Another old bit of a parody penned by Frederick Loewe and Allan J. Lerner for the contemporary Broadway entity 'The Day Before Spring', more so, finds the needs for bread, wine, and "thou" perfectly good for the likes of Thelma's crafty vocal.
12. "Harlem on My Mind," Majestic 1104. The Ethel Waters standard is updated and challenged.
13. "I'm a Fool about Someone," Columbia 30141. It's no surprise to find Thelma slow, articulate, and moody as this Jeanne Burns-penned ditty seeks to explain. Get it?
14. "Just You, Just Me," Columbia 30141. This dry (1947) rendering (a totally differing vocal and arrangement found on the earlier Cliff Edwards recording, originally from the (1929) film "Marianne") finds Thelma in good mid-tempo form, with a good low and light jazz vocal penned by Raymond Klages and Jesse Greer.
15. "Pie in a Basket," Columbia 30212. Perhaps this (1950) recording was recorded by Thelma as an attempt as a contemporary folk entity? Or perhaps Columbia Records wanted her to show off her versatility as a vocalist? In any case, this bit of a (British?) tale from perhaps medieval times was somehow found deemed as unfit for radio play and was subsequently banned. In true retrospective, this simple ditty just *must* be heard!

Is It really immoral or just stupid? Or dumb? Listen and decide! What did Thelma think about it? (A previous (1931) Bo Carter recording, on Columbia 14661-D, sounding nothing at all (vocally) with the sophisticated Carpenter, known as "Banana in Your Fruit Basket," is somewhat based upon the same "folk" parody—all the way from Britain?)

16. "Bali Ha'I," Victor LK-1008. This stupid song from Broadway's South Pacific indeed benefits from Thelma's soft vocal abilities.

Note: The following two ditties are all that remains of a contemporary (1952) revival of the (1921-22) revue *Shuffle Along*, produced by Henry Le Tang and featuring Thelma Carpenter and Avon Long. While this latter-day entity failed, the excellent recordings rendered by Thelma contribute to her recorded legacy, and more so, in true retrospective, toward a list of great Broadway originals. (These subsequent (1953) recordings were part of a contemporary RCA Victor 10-inch 331/3 album LPM 3154.)

17. "I'm Just Wild about Harry." This (1953) update of the ditty penned by Noble Sissle and Eubie Blake for their historic (1921) Broadway entity *Shuffle Along* had found most of its contemporary recognition as an instrumental; a popular acoustic rendering by Marion Harris, more so, produced a memorable vocal. (If Lottie Gee, who had

introduced it in the original production, had rendered a contemporary vocal recording, this author has yet to find it.) A subsequent (vocal) rendering in the (1939) film *Rose of Washington Square,* seen and heard by Alice Faye (backed by a fine and jazzy Louis Prima backing), did much to revive it. So did a (likewise) vocal performance from Pricilla Lane in *Roaring Twenties* in the same year. More so was the (1948) reelection of Harry Truman, who successfully used it as his campaign theme. This subsequent recorded update finds Thelma's vocal in a bright and cheerful "Broadway" mode, with the problem of an added (male) voice (Avon Long?) almost ruining the good listening.

18. "Gypsy Blues." As another early (1953) 331/3 album release, Thelma takes on a lesser-known yet still relevant ditty from Sissle and Blake, originally seen and heard in (1921) *Shuffle Along*. Speculation in 1921 had it that Eubie Blake's interest in the previous Victor Herbert classic "Little Gypsy Sweetheart" had led him to pen his "Gypsy Blues." While this ditty did enjoy good success in sheet music sales, as a recording it would become best known as a popular instrumental fox-trot dance record. Released by the very popular (white) bandleaders Paul Whiteman (Victor 18839) and Ray Miller (Columbia A3640), along with others including a more obscure release by pianist Fletcher Henderson (instrumental, on Black Swan 2025), the vocal was largely dropped from popular song. While both contemporary performers Gertrude Saunders and Florence Mills did indeed introduce this ditty as a vocal in the original production, a contemporary recording cannot be found. Fortunately, this revival from Thelma finds her in excellent voice, although spoken words from a male voice (possibly Avon Long) may be considered this recording's only flaw. Listen and learn.
19. "Yes, I'm Lonesome Tonight," Coral 62241. The (1960) recording as by Elvis Presley of the (old) piece of sentiment (also a release as by Vaughn De Leath in the 1920s) found Thelma recording an "answer" record, providing her with a contemporary (1961) best seller.

The (Original) Carter Family

The earlier recorded acoustic entities of Southern folk ballads—many dating back to the British isles—may be considered the first recorded attempt at documenting the culture itself. Like most acoustic recordings, the principal interest was to record not hard-to-hear vocals but instruments like fiddles and guitars. The recorded "country," however, found its place in the (new) electric recordings of the mid-1920s and in, especially, the Carter family (A. P. Carter, Sara Carter, his wife, and their sister-in-law Maybelle). Contemporaries such as the East Texas Serenades ("Shannon Waltz," Brunswick 282), Darby and Tarleton ("Birmingham Jail," Columbia 1512-D), and Ernest Stoneman (of the Stoneman family, "The Titanic," Okeh 40288), among others, while competitive, never reached the recognition of personage of the Carter unit. It should also be noted that all of these recorded entities find much drifting into a (shared) Afro-American culture. Labels such as "hillbilly," "blues," "ethnic Mexican" and "Native American" indeed find their influences into Carter-covered recording material. In August 1927, the trio of Sara (whose slick vocals would lead), A. P. Carter, and Maybelle (with her guitar) found themselves in a Victor recording session in (rural) Bristol, Tennessee.

The Carter Family would become a huge (founding) cornerstone in "hillbilly," the earlier term for "country" music. They would also become huge radio entities, whose groundbreaking exploitation of radio broadcasts would carry their music south to Mexico, the Southwest, and north to Canada. The appeal of this music oddly found these rural and transplanted Appalachian Mountain folk very well-known and appreciated. The music, moreover, found listeners everywhere. As the 1930s progressed, steady record sales began to become keepsakes as radio appearances, and radio transcriptions as well, promoted the recordings themselves. (Radio-spinning was not yet legal. In true retrospective, regional appeal, as defined, was to be expanded into a worldwide audience.)

- The following are Carter Family picks:

1. "Keep on the Sunny Side," Victor 21434. This bit of uneven harmony is saved by Maybelle's guitar—like so many other Carter family entities and (again) like so many other titles recorded by the Carter family, based upon (already) old folk poems and ballads.
2. "Wildwood Flower," Victor V40000. This (already) old ballad, perhaps from colonial days, found daylight with Sara's usual vocal coolness and Maybelle's fine guitar work. This (1928) ditty, penned by Maud Irving and J. P. Webster, may also be considered folk music at its very rural best.
3. My Clintch Mountain Home Victor V40058. Sarah's vocal tone, in mid tempo pace is seemingly spiels nothing from (Afro-American) games Blaine's earlier claims to (Carry me Back to Old Virginny)—without (Mammy) but mother.
4. "Wabash Cannonball," Victor 23731. AP was known to find song titles from many rural sources, and this "train" theme (as usual) works.

- Note: The expressions "blues" or "blues singer" are usually reserved for Afro-American entities. In true retrospective, neither Sarah nor Maybelle were ever as raunchy as Ma Rainey. There were, however, a few who were, including a rough Columbia (white) female, Aunt Molly Jackson. Her version of "Kentucky Miner's Wife—Ragged Hungry Blues," on Columbia 15731, competes with any black entity.

5. "Worried Man Blues," Victor 40317. This blues tale is a hard-bitten story of the Depression era (which had started in October 1929, when the stock market crashed). There's more here as well. Consider train rails and on the "other" side of the tracks, perhaps contemporary "Blind" Lemon Jefferson's "Right of Way Blues," on Paramount 12510. Was a "mystery train" already on the track before the futuristic rock era? Within the next ten years, wasn't indeed Bill Monroe's "Six White Horses"—which featured a vocal as by the obscure Clyde Moody, on Bluebird B-8568—better than a coach ride? A bit later, within fifteen more years, an independent postwar owner Sam Phillips, more so, livened things up with "Mystery Train." Credited to Sam himself and Little Junior Parker, this bit of R & B (on Sun 192) was launched again as a vocal release by claimed coauthor, Little Junior Parker. Within a year, and with some further embellishment by Elvis Presley (on Sun 223), this ditty reached its peak in its wildness and recognition. Indeed, the journey of its written language is a long ride in cultural aspects. Perhaps another question may even be less than a stretch? Just where did Blind Lemon Jefferson and A. P. Carter begin their journey? This "folk" tale is, for sure, a "ride." A ride between cultures?
6. "Lonesome Valley," Victor 23541. AP found this old spiritual and claimed it (as a writer). This ditty, however, scores high. Its simple message even found its way into the college crowd of the early '60s (in true retrospective).

Note: The Following recordings were recorded in Louisville, Kentucky, with the (already) legendary Jimmie Rodgers. The speculation here is that since Ralph Peer was manager to both Jimmie himself and the Carters, it would be profitable to record them together (1931). Indeed, the Great Depression worsened, and record sales, even for the popular Carter Family and Jimmie Rodgers, had fallen

7-9. "Jimmie Rodgers Visits the Carter Family," Victor 23574. A contrived script has Jimmie talking it up with the Carters. This record included parts of the following folksy entities:

   a. "My Clinch Mountain," vocals by Sara and Maybelle.
   b. "Little Darling Pal of Mine," vocals by Sara and Maybelle.
   c. "There'll Be a Hot Time in the Old Town Tonight," vocals by Sara, Maybelle, AP, and Jimmie.

This ditty had been a popular turn of the century entity, especially noting numerous versions by the popular Irish American tenor, Dan Quinn. As well as comparable renderings on cylinders and records, his pre-1900, (1897) version of the credited Theodore Metz penned ditty on Berliner-527, aint' bad.

10. "The Carter Family and Jimmie Rodgers in Texas," Bluebird B-6762. Another contrived script had the Carters visiting Jimmie. (Note: This recording was released in 1937, as Jimmie had passed away in 1933. This record included an interesting version of Jimmie's blue yodel "T for Texas," featuring vocals by Sara and Jimmie.
11. "I Never Will Marry," Bluebird B-8350. This sad tale of a young maiden's suicide is done well. For the most part, Sara's vocal prowess was very limited, which is somehow why this ditty is effective. Perhaps Sara's vocal limitations are hidden by Maybelle's own guitar-picking?
12. "Can the Circle Be Unbroken," Banner 3465. This ditty (more than any other) may be considered the very best Carter Family entity. It is, for sure, in true retrospective, their best-known song ditty. While for sure this ditty had been around a bit before the Carters recorded it, it would as well be much recorded by the Carters as by future "Carter Family" units. This version finds Sara in (rare) top form vocally. The backing vocals by Maybelle and AP are also done very well. AP should also be credited for its structure, as this effective bit of religious folk music is best defined as by this excellent recording.
13. "I'm Thinking Tonight of My Blue Eyes," Perfect 35-09-23. Later (1941) versions by Jimmie Davis (Decca 6006) and Bing Crosby (Decca 18316) of this A. P. Carter-credited ditty are far less crude. Better?
14. "Cannon Ball Blues" Conqueror 8816.
15. "Jealous Hearted Me," Decca 5241. This effective slow folk entity, based upon Ma Rainey's (1924) recorded entity "Jealous Hearted Blues," on Paramount 12252, may just ask where indeed did Ma find it? Did perhaps an Afro-American friend of Maybelle, Lesley Riddle, who helped her with some guitar licks also provide a bit of assistance to AP for this ditty? Or was it just a bit of integrated folk?
16. "No Depression," Decca 5242. The Great Depression indeed provided effective (1936) contemporary commentary, with vocal harmony. Did A. P. Carter, who was credited with penning this ditty, really "live" it? You bet!

17. "Hello, Stranger," Decca 5479. On many Carter Family ditties, Sara's vocals do not give way to the masculine gender found in lyrics. Sang as written, Sara also finds Maybelle an effective duetting partner. The whole arrangement is soothing to the ear as well as for the soul.

Note: The original Carter Family broke up in 1941. This book will not further note the emergence of Maybelle and daughters June and Anita as the "Carter Family." (June later married Johnny Cash and, along with the newer Carter Family unit, remained country music icon well into the rock era.)

June Christy

This vocalist was stuck between the end of the big band era and the advent of rock. As a cusp artist, this artist was originally suspect for the purposes of this book. She, nevertheless, made it, as she perhaps was most influenced by the likes of Ella Fitzgerald and Anita O'Day and later by her own contemporary, Sarah Vaughan. Her clever vocals are, moreover, cool and jazzy and perhaps the foundation for the few jazz singers who came after her—those not influenced by the rush of rhythm and blues and rock. June's backing orchestra, consisting of the likes of Stan Kenton and later Pete Rugolo, are tight, which provide her with a good lead as well as a challenge. The following are the picks:

1. "Nat Meets June," Columbia 37293. Noted as "Fox-Trot-Mergentroid," on its original and red Columbia label, this *very* unusual title finds June attempting to sing some jazz with Nat Cole. Backed by an all-star band, known as the Metronome All Stars, the young June and established Nat Cole deliver excellent vocals, however brief. A white girl singing great jazz? Yes!
2. "Tampico," Capital 202. The Stan Kenton control indeed fits June. It's not Anita O'Day!
3. "Just A-Sittin' and A-Rockin'," Capital 229. This ditty penned by Duke Ellington, Billy Strayhorn, and Leo Gaines, had originally been an instrumental for Duke in 1941. Stan Kenton's (1946) arrangement, more so, had it easy for a crisp vocal for June. (Contemporary vocals found the differing styles of Thelma Carpenter and a group rendering from the Delta Rhythm Boys offering good listening. Choose?)
3. "Shoo-Fly Pie and Apple Pan Dowdy," Capital 235. A jazzy vocal alternative to the contemporary Dinah Shore release, on Columbia 36943, is evident.
4. "Soothe Me," Capital 15031. Soothe who? This obvious attempt at a sophisticated concept, penned by Joe Green, finds June's vocal slick and smoking cool, oozing sex appeal.
5. "How High the Moon," Capital 15117. This fast and jazzy vocal finds June scatting a bit, as this title, penned by Morgan Lewis and Nancy Hamilton, is successfully turned into a rousing and awakening production. (A differing contemporary version, by Les Paul and Mary Ford, was also a Capital recording, issued on Capital 1451.)
6. "Willow Weep for Me," Capital 15179. A bit of moody and jazzy singing again pays off, as this old Ann Ronell-penned ditty that had been interestingly recorded in 1933 by Irene Taylor (a Paul Whiteman release) and by the continental cabaret entity, Greta Keller. Listen to all!

- Away from Stan Kenton

7-14. *Something Cool*, Capital LP H 516. June Christy with Pete Rugolo and His Orchestra. The early 1950s were a creative period for Capital records, and this LP concept, especially for the new 10-inch release does not disappoint its listeners—then and now! The cool—and sexy-voiced June Christy is, more so, found to be well backed by Pete Rugolo and His Orchestra, providing an exceptional jazzy experience for all ears. This LP, more so, is a tale about a woman's trip to a bar on a hot day. Indeed interesting? The titles are as under:

a. "Something Cool." June is indeed "cool," as this title, penned by Bill Barnes, provides the title of this concept LP. In any case, June is a woman who finds the town she is in too "hot." Her subsequent acceptance of a bar patron's "cool" drink, leads into more of a tale. A "cool" tale? Listen and learn!
b. "It Could Happen to You." This excellent ditty penned by Johnny Burke and Jimmy Van Heusen, already a film entity as well as a fine release by Bing Crosby and contemporary Jo Stafford, is livened up with some fast-paced jazzy singing. Could it happen to you? Just anyone?
c. "Lonely House." The moody instrumental leads June into an almost creepy story about living alone. More so, this gem penned by Kurt Weill and Langston Hughes is more than a tall tale—with June's very able bending of lyrics. Just listen!
d. "Midnight Sun." Another sensuous vocal and cool tale, penned by Sonny Burke, Lionial Hampton, and Johnny Mercer, obviously finds June explaining her midnight adventures. A good soap opera to keep following?
e. "I'll Take Romance." The sophisticated team of Oscar Hammerstein II and Ben Oakland penned this ditty, perhaps never imaging that it could be made into a mid-tempo and jazzy entity? More so, June is seemingly still excited about the whole thing, which continues to find this whole album something indeed interesting.
f. "A Stranger Called the Blues." June's involvement with a stranger, in this ditty penned by Mel Torme and Robert Wells, continues to linger, as perhaps a few regrets are now more than evident. The "blues"? Or conscience?
g. "I Should Care." By now, the whole thing is over, and, as this tale indicates—in this ditty penned by Paul Weston, Axel Stordahl, and Sammy Cahn—it just may have been all worth it!

Buddy Clark

The emergence of Bing Crosby, as noted throughout this book, had a definite effect upon American popular music, especially during the early years of the Depression era. As mythology has it, a young would-be singer (Samuel Goldberg) wanted to be Bing Crosby so badly that he changed his name to "Buddy Clark" to boast initials B. C. (It's interesting to also note that "Bing Crosby" was partly an assumed name, as used by Harry Lillis Crosby). In any case, Buddy Clark worked hard in mid-1930s radio and produced many recordings, finding limited success. Ironically, when Buddy finally did begin to produce best sellers in the latter 1940s, he became a victim of a plane crash at around thirty-seven years of age. For the most part, Buddy would project a mostly bland baritone style, with some interesting recordings. Picks include

1. “With Every Breath I Take,” Banner 33298. The contemporary (1934) Crosby version is challenged.
2. “The Rhythm of the Rhumba,” Columbia 3013-D. This Ralph Rainger-penned ditty features Buddy and fellow vocalist Joe Host in a rhythmic ditty on a Lud Gluskin and His Continental Orchestra release.
3. “On Your Toes,” Brunswick 7633. Buddy is identified as “vocal refrain” as a (1936) Ruby Newman release on this nifty ditty penned by Rodger and Hart, a contemporary Broadway entity of same name.
4. “These Foolish Things Remind Me of You,” Brunswick 7676. This very stiff song ditty, as a Nat Brandywynne and His Stork Club Orchestra release, features Buddy as a band singer, holding on well.
5. “A Sail Boat in the Moonlight,” Variety 586. As a Johnny Hodges Band singer, most found Johnny Hodges to really’ be’ Duke Ellington’s outfit. More so, Buddy’s vocal is truly good, as all his usual blandness is missing! Does this “swing” as much as the contemporary Teddy Wilson release featuring Billie Holiday? Listen and compare two fine vocals!
6. “Spring Is Here,” Vocalion 4191. This uppity ditty penned by Rodgers and Hart, from their contemporary Broadway entity *I Married an Angel,* somehow survives? Call is schmaltz mixed with mush?
7. “On a Little Street in Singapore,” Varsity 8101. The contemporary Harry James release, featuring his (nasal) vocalist Frank Sinatra, offers interesting vocal comparisons!
8. “Let’s Be Buddies,” Okeh 5912. The Cole Porter-penned ditty from the contemporary Broadway entity *Panama Hattie* is perfect for Buddy?
9. “We Could Make Such Beautiful Music Together,” Victor 27358. This long (boring) title, penned by Robert Sour and Henry Manners and backed by (usually bland) Wayne King, finds a (saving) and solid vocal from Buddy!
9. “I’ve Told Every Little Star,” Decca 23662 A duet with Hildegarde!
10. “Chiquita Banana,” Columbia 37051. This ditty began as a radio ad jingle for the ‘Chiquita Banana Company’ in 1944 and has been part of the Americana ever since. Penned by Len Mackenzie, Garth Montgomery, and William Wires, this Xavier Cugat release, featuring Buddy’s articulate vocal, became one of many who first recorded it. Wheres Carmen Miranda? Very familiar?
11. “Linda,” Columbia 37215. As a lead vocalist backed by Ray Noble’s Orchestra, Buddy found the recognition that had previously eluded him. As mythology has it, this ditty had been penned by Jack Lawrence, while serving in WWII, about a daughter of his friend, Lee Eastman. Moreover, in true retrospective, this “Linda” grew up to become Mrs. Paul McCartney, the wife of the Beatle himself!
12. “Peg of My Heart,” Columbia 37392. This bland old ditty, penned by Alfred Bryan and Fred Fisher, had been a Broadway entity as *Ziegfeld Follies of 1913*. An acoustic entity for many, the Henry Burr best seller on Columbia 1404 from 1913 was oddly and successfully updated.
13. “I Love You So Much It Hurts,” Columbia 38406.
14. “Baby, It’s Cold Outside,” Columbia 38463. Duet with Dinah Shore.

Rosemary Clooney

As a young, popular band singer (with 1940s bandleader Tony Pastor), Rosemary and younger sister Betty found success. Both Clooney sisters may be considered good vocalists, competing with the likes of the very established Jo Stafford and Dinah Shore. By 1950, Rosemary struck out mostly as a solo act, within the same style, and became a best-selling entity despite the emergence of "rock and roll." Her associations with the (then) aging Bing Crosby, to be fair, helped. More so, her appearance in the (1954) film *White Christmas* won her much recognition. As an added note, it's also fair, at this late in the game, that Bing also benefited. Vocally, it's Rosemary's sparkling and soft vocals in the film and on duetting recordings that gave Bing (in 1958) a lift! The following are Rosemary Clooney picks:

1. "Sooner or Later," Cosmo Records 721. This (1946) rendering of the ditty penned by Charles Wolcott and Ray Gilbert from the contemporary Disney film *Song of the South* was a little-known but great recording fodder for the relatively unknown and mellow voice of Rosemary.
2. "Zip Ah Dee Doo Dah," Cosmo 723. Another *Song of the South* ditty found Rosemary's vocal (if heard) bettering the better-selling (contemporary) Johnny Mercer version.
3. "Who Killed 'Er," Columbia 38142. As a Tony Pastor and His Orchestra release, this novelty, penned by Janice Torre, Fred Spielman, and Hoagy Carmichael, in true retrospective, belongs to the trash bins of Doctor Demento? For the most part, the vocal efforts of Tony Pastor are limited, although his excellent swing band is not. This ditty, indeed, finds itself tangled up in (futuristic) politically incorrect lyric, and its simple message becomes so bad that it's good. Among other things, the vocals by Rosemary, Betty and Tony are sure that a butler with a bloody knife is campy enough! The sisters are indeed very glad that someone is dead! What a fine item for a contemporary dance floor?
4. "At a Sidewalk Penny Arcade," Columbia 38142. A nonnovelty ditty, the flip side of "Who Killed 'Er is a soft ballad. Penned by Martin Kalmanoff, Aaron Schroeder, Edward White, and Jimmy McDonald, it is for slow dancing!
5. "You Started Something," Columbia 38297. Rosemary (again) scores, on another Tony Pastor release. Credited as Vocal Chorus by Rosemary Clooney, this ditty was penned by Al Rinker and Floyd Huddleson.
6. "Grieving for You," Columbia 38383. Rosemary is (again) very convincing, as her softness can even be considered cool on this Tony Pastor release, penned by Joe Gibson, Joe Ribaud, and Joe Gold.
7. "Saturday Night Mood," Columbia 38383. Great mood! Get up and dance?
8. "'A'—You're Adorable," Columbia 38449. Another Tony Pastor release, as the "Clooney Sisters," it could be the contemporary "King Sisters"—Alyce, Donna, Louise, and Yvonne Driggs, minus two. It wasn't!
9. "Don't Cry Joe, Let Her Go, Let Her Go," Harmony 1071. The contemporary Frank Sinatra best seller is challenged and well done!
10. "There's a Broken Heart for Every Light on Broadway," Harmony 1074. While hardly contemporary for 1949, this interesting ditty, penned by Fred Fisher and Howard Johnson, had been an acoustic release by Elsie Baker on Victor 17943. Although an obvious clumsy title, Rosemary's differing (soft) vocal, is more than a fine update, although not defining.

11. "Me and My Teddy Bear," Columbia 38766. This "kiddie" ditty penned by J. Fred Coots and Jack Winters found many baby boomers (like this author) appreciative!
12. "Beautiful Brown Eyes," Columbia 39212. A softer version of the contemporary (1951) ditty released by Jimmy Wakely on Capital 1393, penned by Dick Smith and Alton Delmore.
13. "Mixed Emotions," Columbia 39333. A contemporary Dinah Washington version finds more than interesting comparisons.
14. "Come on-a My House," Columbia 39467. This (1951) bit of novelty penned by Ross Bagdasarian and William Saroyan was a bit contrived, but worked.
15. "Be My Life's Companion," Columbia 39631. Mushy stuff, penned by BobHilliard andMilton DeLugg, that indeed proved successful for Rosemary!
16. "Tenderly," Columbia 39648. This bit of fluff indeed highlights Rosemary's clear (soft) vocal style. The ditty was penned by Jack Lawrence and Walter Gross.
17. "Half As Much," Columbia 39710. Rosemary "does" Hank Williams well enough.
18. "Hey There," Columbia 40266. From the Broadway entity *The Pajama Game*, penned by Richard Adler and Jerry Ross.
19. "This Ole House," Columbia 40266. This bit of silly contrived mystery, penned by Stuart Hamblen, was recorded by him and released on Victor 20-5739. Rosemary's version, with creaks, was a huge best-selling entity.

Note: As a Columbia recording artist, Rosemary was either not allowed or was not invited by Decca to produce the soundtrack to the (1954) film *White Christmas*. The fabulous soundtrack actually produced featured (then) Decca artists Peggy Lee, and Trudy Stevens, who were not in the film! Perhaps Peggy Lee was originally to appear in the film? Among many Irving Berlin ditties found in the film, "Love, You Didn't Do Right by Me" emerged as Rosemary's best. While also well done on the soundtrack by Peggy Lee (released on a contemporary Decca single as well), Rosemary's own Columbia recording was more memorable than Peggy Lee's bright yet cooler original. So indeed as Rosemary's "Count Your Blessings Instead of Sheep," and a duet with sister Betty (Vera Ellen was featured in the film) "Sisters." As a further note, this film (1954) was successful rip-off the earlier (1942) *Holiday Inn*." In true retrospective, it's more than a wonder that a real film soundtrack was not made! While a smart move by contemporary bootleggers who copped the film itself—in fact this was an end result—this all made Decca Records and perhaps a lazy Crosby look more than foolish. Or does anyone really care anymore?

20. "Sisters," Columbia 40305. While Rosemary and Vera Ellen shared this film delight in *White Christmas*, this version, with Rosemary and her sister Betty ain't bad.
21. "Count Your Blessings Instead of Sheep," Columbia 40370. Another entity of *White Christmas*, and very good!
22. "Suzy Snowflake," Columbia 46255 (or MJV 123-2). This bit of a "kiddie" record found its way into many baby boomers' homes. Rosemary does well, and this ditty, penned by Sid Pepper and Roy Brodsky, in true retrospective, had eyes (as well as ears) for the future.

23-35. *Fancy Meeting You Here*, RCA Victor LSP-1854. By 1958, rock and roll was already "here" to stay, although nobody knew for sure. By this time, both Crosby and Clooney had parted ways with Decca and Columbia. As an early LP concept, this duetting combination finds its traveling journey about the world well worth the trip. Indeed, Clooney's superb vocals are the true highlights of this LP, with excellent backing by Billy May and His Orchestra. Bing, for his part, is competent, with some of his occasional good humor added. The following all find an inspiring vocal performance:

a. "Fancy Meeting You Here." Penned by Sammy Cahn and James Van Heusen, this sparking duet, 1950s' style, for sure pleased the many "adults," on first hearing.
b. "On a Slow Boat to China." Penned by Frank Loesser, this update of an earlier Benny Goodman entity with a vocal by Al Hendrickson on Capital 1508 is done very well
c. "I Can't Get Started." Penned by Ira Gershwin and Vernon Duke, this classic version found mention of RCA Victor's hottest contemporary recording artist, Elvis Presley. Faddish (1958) film entity Bridget Bardot and Greek tycoon Aristotle Onassis are also mentioned.
d. "Hindustan." Another sparkling vocal performance, penned by Oliver G. Wallace and Harold Weeks.
e. "It Happened in Monterey." Crosby had been originally involved with ditty when he was with the Paul Whiteman organization in 1930. This fine update of this ditty penned by Mabel Wayne and Billy Rose ain't bad.
f. "You Came a Long Way from St. Louis." Penned by J. B. Brooks and Bob Russell, this classic duet finds Bing again successfully hamming it up.
g. "Love Won't Let You Get Away." Penned by Sammy Cahn and James Van Heusen, this ditty is perhaps the best in the bunch.
h. "How about You." This classic ditty had been perhaps best heard by an earlier Frank Sinatra recording with Tommy Dorsey in 1940, and Frank's more recent update of his own on Capital. Bing and Rosemary ham it up and update this original ditty (penned by Ralph Freed and Burton Lane) with Rosemary's mention of Frank Sinatra himself.
i. "Brazil." A fine bit of clever vocal on this ditty penned by Bob Russell and Ary Barroso make this ditty a winner.
j. "Isle of Capri." Again Bing and Rosemary sparkle in this ditty penned by Jimmy Kennedy and Will Grosz. (The older Al Bowlly hit is revived)!
k. "Say Si Si Para vigo me voy." Another lesson in popular singing. Penned by Ernesto Lecuono, A. Stillman, and F. Luban, it works well enough.
l. "Calcutta." Bing and Rosemary indeed found this city of interest in this ditty penned by Jay Livingston and Ray Evans.

Visual Image. Rosemary's own family TV show became a staple in the mid-1950s. Her best sighting is, however, found in the 1954 film *White Christmas*. Rosemary was (then) at the peak of her popularity and her (early '50s') long dress and her tasteful vocals including the filmed (36). "Love, You Didn't Do Right By Me" perhaps captured the essence *of what popular* music was supposed to be. Indeed no one at that time, figured that the emerging "rock and roll" fad, would drastically change everything.

Nat King Cole

The late 1930s found the likes of a small combo, including Oscar Moore, Wesley Prince, and a pianist who did his own vocals—Nathaniel Cole. After a series of small-label releases, the Nat Cole Trio was signed by Johnny Mercer for his new Capital label. Jazz releases followed as well as a noted, crisp vocal style from Nat. To the disapproval of many contemporary jazz entities, Nat began to release "pop" songs and, moreover, to sell them. While originally a challenge to rival MGM's Afro-American baritone Billy Eckstine, Nat would achieve more. Nat's greatest gift was his use of his intimate speaking voice. Unlike the booming baritone of Eckstine, his softer vocals did not become outdated, and Nat would, as Sinatra and Dean Martin, compete well with the new wave of rock and roll. Moreover—and like no other black-skinned performer before him—in his subsequent recordings, using the newer technologies of 33 1/3 rpm, 45 rpm, 45 EP rpm, as well as in original 78 rpm issue, he would pioneer his popular vocal style into a major force upon all of Americana, both black and white.

The Nat "King" Cole legacy can be divided into the recordings recorded as a vocalist for a hot jazz Trio, and as a solo male vocalist performer. The following are picks as the Nat Cole Trio:

1. "Sweet Lorraine," Decca 8520. Sweet Lorraine? Why not?
2. "Slow Down," Decca 8556.
3. "Scotchin' with the Soda," Decca 8556.
4. "Hit That Jive, Jack," Decca 8630.
5. "That Ain't Right," Decca 8630. This and the above flip represent the "hip" jazz chatter of 1942 and the Trio at its best.
6. "Straighten up and Fly Right," Capital 154. This Capital recording became a best seller as well as a combination of fine jazzy slang and vocal style. Perhaps this ditty is the best of the Trio recordings?
7. "Gee Baby, Ain't I Good to You," Capital 169. Another "great."
8. "Come to Baby Do," Capital 224. Here is a hint of later pop, the (later) vocalist. Was Nat influenced at all by the contemporary soft and mellow Doris Day vocal with Les Brown? Or was it a similar yet slightly cooler vocal also heard on a contemporary Duke Ellington release featuring Joya Sherrill? In any case, it all sounds jazzy! Listen and compare all vocal styles.
9. "The Frim Fram Sauce," Capital 224. The flip of the above, this creative piece of "modern" jazz history also contains a great slick and cool vocal.
10. "It Is Better to Be by Yourself," Capital 239.
11. "(Get Your Kicks on) Route 66," Capital 256. This Bobby Troup-penned ditty remains a good ride on the connecting highway of Americana, as well as some excellent jazz. In true retrospective, this post-WWII-era ditty came to represent a newer America on the move. (The later-1960s' TV program *Route 66* used this song ditty as its theme.) While the latter century largely replaced this famous "highway," its own legacy and legend may be traced directly to Nat and the Trio's classic recording!
12. "You Call It Madness, but I Call It Love," Capital 274. This classic had already found the likes of a dated Russ Columbo crooning job in 1931. A contemporary (1946) Billy Eckstine version, on National 9019, found Nat in heavy competition.
13. "I Love You For Sentimental Reasons." Capital-304. Nat's sincere rendering of this (W. Pat West and Deek Watson) penned ditty is still full of mushy sentiment! (Note: Not the previous Ginny Simm's recording)
14. "The Best Man," Capital 304. This novelty works well.
15. "The Christmas Song," Capital 311. Penned by Robert Wells and Mel Torme himself, this original recording of this Christmas classic originally noted "The King Cole Trio With String Choir, Vocal By King Cole." It is interesting to compare this 1946 release with Nat's subsequent recordings. While far from raw, this version, by far, features a

jazzy backing, which perhaps finds Nat's vocal a bit brighter? Associated with Nat like no other popular song ditty (besides "Get Your Kicks on Route 66"), it's still an odd bit of trivia to find out just which version! Indeed, the same can be noted for Bing Crosby's "White Christmas," also a Christmas classic and recorded by Bing a number of times.

16. "My Baby Likes to Be-Bop," Capital 15026. This Walter Bishop-penned title is sung as a duet. It is noted on its original label as "Johnny Mercer And The King Cole Trio, Vocal Duet By Johnny Mercer And King Cole." The talented Mercer and contemporary owner of Capital Records indeed had no problem with this integrated novelty, which successfully cashed in on the (current) "bebop" fad
17. "Orange Colored Sky," Capital 1184. This unusual bit of modern (1950) jazz also became a bit of television trivia as well. Engineered by jazzman Stan Kenton, also a contemporary Capital recording artist, Nat's truly great vocal bettered the television project itself. (It failed). Kenton was assisted by the likes of Shorty Rogers, Art Pepper, and Maynard Ferguson—an interesting bit of "modern" jazz, more so, effective and sounding fine and not interfering with Nat's classic vocal.
18. "Nat Meets June"(Mergentroid), Columbia 37293. This Metronome All Stars release features some short and hot jazzy vocals by Nat and newcomer June Christy.

Note: The 1939 Trio had already been broken up in the early '40s, as Wesley Prince had been replaced by Johnny Miller. By the later '40s, both Oscar Moore and Johnny Moore had been subsequently replaced by Irving Ashley and Joe Comfort. With guitar, bass, and piano as backing, Nat's "Trio" sound behind his vocals sounded a little more brassy. As his popularity grew, strings were added, with a lush sound and matching vocal vocal style. Pioneered by the likes of Nelson Riddle and Billy May, the Capital Records' sound of the 1940s' jazzy sounds disappeared, with most orchestrations sounding almost classically operatic. Capital Records would, more so, acquire Frank Sinatra by 1953 and successfully use Riddle and May for his coming of age as a vocalist. It is, more so, interesting to note that Nat's earlier sound, with his Trio, had some influence upon the up-and-coming, more to do with the emergence of rock and roll—a trend that Nat was capable of performing, but perhaps just didn't dig?

- As a solo artist on Capital Records, following are the picks:

19. "Can I Come in for a Second," Capital 847. This Sammy Cahn-penned title, a vocal duet with the jazzy Nellie Lutcher (also a Capital recording artist), is a fine vocal with a novel approach that works.
20. "For You My Love," Capital 847. The flip of "Can I Come In for a Second" also involves Nat in another fine duet with Nellie Luther.
21. "Nature Boy," Capital 15054. This surprise vocal hit of 1948 features Nat with a pop background orchestration by Frank De Vol. Penned by Eden Ahbez, this material signaled a complete change for Nat with a clever vocal style that became a huge best-selling entity as well.
22. "Don't Blame Me," Capital 15110. This title is perfect for Nat and a fine update to the (1933) Ethel Waters classic.
23. "Little Girl," Capital 15165. A return to "roots" and jazz—and a reminder of Nat's versatility as well. Penned by Madeline Hyde. and Frances Henry, Nat's breezy 1948 vocal remains a classic bit of jazz. Earlier versions included an unusual Harold Arlen

vocal with jazzy violinist Joe Venuti on, Columbia 2488 D, as well as a vocal by one Tommy Taylor, with Mitchell Ayres and his Fashions In Music on Bluebird B-10627.

24. "Mona Lisa," Capital 1010. This release, backed by Les Baxter and Orchestra, is perhaps Nat's most popular song. The mellow lyrics are perfectly vocalized by Nat's tender and effective commitment. Penned by Jay Livingston and Ray Evans, the song was a film entity as featured in the obscure film *Captain Carey*. Originally a best-selling ditty for Art Lund (on MGM 10689), it's indeed Nat's classic that lingers. Later versions included a rock-era version by Conway Twitty, on MGM 12804, which attempts to stir things up a bit.
25. "Little Christmas Tree," Capital 1203. This pop ditty, with Pete Rugolo and Orchestra, is superb and is penned by film entity Mickey Rooney.
26. "Jet," Capital 1365. This vocal, accompanied by Joe Lipman and Orchestra and The Ray Charles Singers, finds soft lyrics, penned by Harry Revel, Bennie Benjamin, and George Davis Weiss especially appealing to Afro-Americans?

Note: The Ray Charles Singers are not related the popular musical entity, Ray Charles.

27. "Always You," Capital 1365. This reworking of Tchaikovsky's "Romance", by Michael Boarke and James P. Dunne with Les Baxter and Orchestra is a vocal masterpiece by Nat.
28. "Too Young," Capital 1449. Again with Les Baxter and Orchestra, this ditty, penned by Sylvia Dee and Sidney Lippman, became another best seller in 1951. Too young? This mellow vocal tells it all.
29. "Red Sails in the Sunset," Capital 1468. This classic ditty had been recorded by many, including a best-selling Decca recording by Bing Crosby. Given new life by Nat, a fine Pete Rugolo and Orchestra backing helps the ditty reek in mellowness. (Another contemporary group version by the Five Keys was perhaps still better? Maybe?)
30. "Because of Rain," Capital 1501. Another mushy vocal, penned by Ruth Pole and William Harrington, accompanied by Pete Rugolo, does well-despite rain.
31. "Calypso Blues," Capital 1627. The versatility of Nat is clearly heard as it is clearly sung with great skill, penned by Don George and Nat himself.
32. "Lush Life," Capital 1672. "Lush" is the word, as penned by Billy Strayhorn, and Nat's fine vocal may be his best ever, as his listeners are made believers in this type of living or dreaming.
33. "Unforgettable," Capital-1808. This original vocal, penned by Irving Gordon and with backup provided by Nelson Riddle and Orchestra, was a great pop hit of 1951. This ditty, in true retrospective, became a huge poplar entity, light-years away, in the 1990s. With a little cheating, and creativity, Nat's daughter Natalie, who had become a popular vocalist, produced a modern 'duet; with her (late) dad. It's interesting to note that this bit of trivia made huge inroads into a music industry that had forgotten Nat as well as most pre-rock music. This ditty also provided something that was missing. The age of "rap" also found some interest in the lush Nelson Riddle backing, or at least something seldom heard. Perhaps the fact that this music, common in the early 1950s, with some beautiful, soft vocals was unlike anything selling? Perhaps Nat *had* to be rediscovered?
34. "Because You're Mine," Capital 2212. Sammy Cahn and Nicholas Brodszky's penned ditty found Nat's soft vocal mellow enough?
35. "Pretend," Capital 2346. Another Nelson Riddle Orchestrated backing which compliments Nat's mellow vocal, as it does not attempt to play instruments too loud

and the vocal can be concentrated on for the listener. This 1952 release, penned by Lou Douglas and Cliff Parman, more so solidified Nat's hold on contemporary music as much as Sinatra had a decade before.

36. "Blue Gardenia," Capital 2389. The filmed murder mystery which killed Raymond Burr also provided Nat some valuable (filmed) notice. It must also rank as, perhaps, his best ever, penned by Lester Lee and Bob Russell.
37. "Mrs. Santa Claus," Capital-2616. This ditty penned by Jack Fulton, Lois Steele, and Hazil Houle is more than fine Christmas product, as backed by Nelson Riddle. It's just another seasonal classic!
38. "The Little Boy That Santa Claus Forgot," Capital 2616. With social commentary as well (about a boy without a father), this seasonal ditty's heart-wrenching message (penned by Michael Carr, Tom Connor, and Jimmy Leach) remains, in true retrospective, a fact of life over fifty years later.
39. "Answer Me My Love," Capital 2687. Yes—Answer yes! This plea, as penned by Carl Sigman and Gerhard Winkler, just has to be 'yes' ?

40-48. *Nat "King" Cole Sings for Two in Love*, Capital H 420. This chosen 10-inch LP was an attempt at a concept. Its original cover artwork with a (white) couple in a painted café reflected perhaps a separation of race as well. While perhaps one can only guess how Nat felt about being marketed in this way, there is no doubt that his tender vocals indeed fit the mood for any couple's religion or race! Assisted by Nelson Riddle's lush strings, this LP included the following:

a. "Love Is Here to Stay." This Gershwin Brothers-penned ditty had been a fine hit for Bea Wain as part of the Larry Clinton orchestra, on Victor 25761. While less than the bombastic approach as heard on the later Frank Sinatra update, this ditty is best heard as by Nat.
b. "A Handful of Stars." The message of "stars" is easily understood as Nat's vocal of this gem penned by Jack Lawrence and Ted Shapiro indeed works.
c. "This Cant Be Love". As previously defined as a recording in the 'swing era' by Martha Tilton, and stiffly yet well done on the lesser known (British) release by Adelaide Hall, Nat's straight vocal style is very pleasing. Perhaps re-defining?
d. "A Little Street Where Old Friends Meet." Perhaps even Harry Woods and Gus Kahn, in the early 1930s, never heard black crooner Harlan Lattimore's contemporary crooning job on this classic. Nat attempts to do better. It's also interesting to wonder if Nat had heard of Harlan, although (rival) Billy Eckstine did.
e. "There Goes My Heart." This bit of pop, penned by Abner Silver and Benny Davis, fits well into this LP concept. So indeed does Nat's commitment.
f. "Dinner for One Please, James." This Michael Carr-penned ditty perhaps indicates that the couple painted on the original LP cover had not ordered. Perhaps they broke up? Was Al Bowlly's earlier croon better?
g. "Almost Like Being in Love." The theme of this LP continues, as this ditty penned by Frederick Loewe and Alan. Jay Lerner rolls with the flow, and works.
h. "Tenderly." This ditty, penned by Walter Gross and Jack Lawrence, identifies Nat's smooth vocal style. As good as Rosemary Clooney's contemporary recording? Listen and compare!

49. "The Christmas Song," Capital 2955. The second version of this Christmas classic is backed by Nelson Riddle's Orchestra.

50. "Long, Long Ago," Capital 2985. This modest duet with Dean Martin, penned by Alfred Fisher, is not what it could have been, yet it still ain't bad. (Its flip side, "Open up the Doghouse," *is* bad. Sorry, guys.)
51. "If I May," Capital 3095. As the 1950s progressed, the rise of rock and roll started to change the music business. As this new music failed to attract most adults, the record industry, for the most part, decided to hang on to its pre-rock audiences with music designated for adults. Nat, already considered "adult," was thus joined by the likes of Bing Crosby, Frank Sinatra, Perry Como, and, among others, Tony Bennett. While his attempt at network television failed, due only to racism, his groundbreaking style influenced many. So indeed did this fluffy attempt at rock and roll. Penned by Charles Singleton and Rose Marie M. McCoy, Nat is also backed vocally by Capital's own Four Knights, perhaps to supplant "doo-wop"? Listen and decide.
52. "A Blossom Fell," Capital 3095. This flip side of "If I May," penned by Howard Barnes, Dominic John, and Harold Cornelious, is perhaps the "adult" side. It indeed works, and better!
53. "Send for Me," Capital 3737. A contrived, upbeat, and mid-tempo bit of rock and roll, penned by Ollie Jones—that works!

54-58. *St. Louis Blues*, W 993. Nat was dubbed with a film entity, which, despite its lack of focus on W. C. Handy's bio, remains interesting. It is also interesting to speculate on just why Afro-American entities, including the likes of like Duke Ellington, Cab Calloway, or Count Basie, could not have backed Nat's soundtrack? While the competitive Riddle was no slouch, truer retrospective should have demanded a black entity. (Handy, still alive at the time of the film in 1958, nevertheless, indicated his approval of this LP on its original liner notes.) The following are at least interesting picks, despite the fact that these blues do indeed sound a bit bleached. Or did Nat have to answer to anyone about it anyway? Or does he come off with a stylistic bit of personable singing?

a. "Harlem Blues."
b. "Friendless Blues."
c. "Memphis Blues."
d. "Yellow Dog Blues."
e. "St. Louis Blues."

Further note: This film *St. Louis Blues* also found the likes of Pearl Bailey, Eartha Kitt (maintaining her sexy early 1950s' image), and, among others, Ruby Dee. With a bit more money invested, this talented cast could have been better, perhaps?

59-74. *The Magic of Christmas* or *The Christmas Song*, Capital SW-1444, later as Capital SW-1967. This LP, more than any other Nat King Cole product, remained fully visible to music buyers into the end of the century. Backed by Ralph Carmichael's arrangement, not one song ditty is spoiled, as was in the 1950s by the likes of the hideous "Singing Pussy Cats," and other stupid novelty. However, the original issued (1960) "The Magic of Christmas," turned out to be a botched marketing effort, which was quickly corrected with a fine third rerecording of Nat's most familiar Christmas song ditty, "The Christmas Song." As the lead song, the reissued LP (on SW 1967) in 1962, more so, found good liner notes that also finds Nat (on its cover), in front of a fireplace, in a seasonal setting—with much public recognition, along with huge sales into the latter century! (A still later CD issue further clinched it.)

➢ This excellent LP, released in two forms includes the following:

a. “The Christmas Song.” Nat’s third recording of this classic is, by far, the most recognized and, more so, stands up very well with his earlier versions (on SW-1967 only).
b. “Deck the Halls.”
c. “Adeste Fideles.”
d. “Oh Tannenbaum (Oh Christmas Tree).”
e. “O, Little Town of Bethlehem.”
f. “I Saw Three Ships.”
g. “O Holy Night.”
h. “Hark, the Herald Angle Sing.”
i. “A Cradle in Bethlehem.”
j. “Away in a Manger.”
k. “Joy to the World.”
l. “The First Noel.”
m. “Caroling, Caroling.”
n. “God Rest Ye Merry Gentlemen.”
o. “Silent Night.”

➢ Note: This review of Nat’s vocals does not include his musicianship and his brilliant piano work. His “Penthouse Serenade” release of the early 1950s excels in piano work, as noted on Capital T-332, as well as his “group” appearances with the mid-1940s’ Metronome All-Stars. In true retrospective, did Nat do the right thing when he basically abandoned jazz?

75. “(In Other Words) Fly Me To The Moon,” from the Capital LP Nat King Cole with George Shearing, SW-1675. The Bart Howard-penned cabaret ditty found Nat and blind pianist Shearing finally defining it as a classic. A later Tony Bennett version was also done well, although a mid-1960s Frank Sinatra version further redefined it. Listen to all versions and decide.
76. “Ramblin’ Rose,” Capital 4804. This best seller, a harmless ditty penned by Joe and Noel Sherman, finds Nat in a sing-along with an unidentified chorus. (Not to be confused with an earlier Perry Como title of the same name.)

Radio. As a fixture on live radio in the 1940s, perhaps Nat’s vocal duet with Frank Sinatra on *Songs by Sinatra* (and with Trio backing) found Frank with a fine contemporary rival vocalist in more interesting (musical) territory?

77. “Exactly Like You.”

♦ Visual Image

The vastness of the images of the Nat Cole Trio and Nat’s own solo performances are noted in many films and filmed personal appearances. With a bigger budget, his 1958 film *St. Louis Blues* would have been indeed better. Moreover, despite racism, Nat, for a short time, had the first network television musical program that starred an Afro-American. While much fodder remains, perhaps the best are to be found earlier. They are as follows:

78. "It Is Better to Be by Yourself." Also a single release with the Trio (noted above), this ditty, penned by Bob Levinson, Howard Leeds, and Nat Cole himself, was featured in the 1946 film *Breakfast In Hollywood*. Nat and company are seen and heard jamming in a small, local Hollywood nightclub. They, more so, put on an impressive, rhythmic show, despite its brief appearance. Catch it!
79. "Blue Gardenia." From the already mentioned film of the same name, the soft-toned (solo) Nat's vocal, as seen and heard in a nightclub setting, remains a teary-eyed experience.
80., 81. "I Was A Little Too Lonely". This (Jay Livingston & Ray Evans) penned ditty found Nat introducing it in the 1956 film "Istanbul". The early 1950s had found both Doris Day and pianist-night club entity Jeri Southern softly introducing "When I Fall In Love", as penned by (Victory Young & Ray Evans) as a recorded this bit of mush as recordings. Later, as (also) found in the film "Istanbul", Nat perhaps defined it, with Errol Flynn and (actress Cornell Borchers), looking on.

Russ Columbo

As a musician (a violinist), and part-time freelancing vocalist, the young Russ Columbo, about twenty-two years old in 1930, seemingly had more going for him than his contemporary (and friend), Bing Crosby. As part of the Gus Arnheim organization, in 1930, it was not uncommon to hear Crosby, perhaps attempting to be Rudy Vallee, wail out a good crooning title with Russ backing him up with strings. Indeed, Russ, also affected by Vallee, had already made a few electric vocal recordings before 1930 (including "Back in Your Own Backyard" on Okeh 41037). It would, however, be the huge success that greeted Bing that convinced Russ to put his violin aside. It was also a certainty that Victor Records, after losing Crosby to Brunswick, had found in Russ a contemporary rival for Crosby.

There were other reasons that prompted Victor Records to record Russ. It should be noted that Russ had attraction more for the female audience who were younger by about eight years, and available. (Bing had married the rising film star Dixie Lee in 1930.) Russ's contemporary crooning style is indeed almost identical to Crosby's. These baritone qualities, slightly effeminate, with a pleasant tone, as much defined the era! Tenors beware!

- ➢ The following are Russ Columbo picks:

1. "Back in Your Own Backyard," Okeh 41037. This contemporary (1928) ditty had become an Al Jolson entity and had also been recorded (better) by Ruth Etting. Russ seems to have been influenced by neither, as perhaps this vocal seems to have been influenced by contemporary Rudy Vallee. (Around ten years later, a (differing) Billie Holiday version perhaps defined it as a jazz entity? Listen and learn vocal styles.)
2. "I Don't Know Why?" Victor 22801. This plea for the affections of a woman is a sure winner. Penned by Fred E. Ahlert and Roy Turk, this very effective crooning job, influenced by Bing Crosby, finds its mark. A later (1945) Frank Sinatra version, on Columbia 36918, is less throaty, while more nasal. What a style!
3. "Guilty," Victor 22801. This very effective crooning effort compliments the fine contemporary best-known Ruth Etting version, on Columbia 2529-D, along with a Gene Austin version on Banner 23385, among other labels.

4. "You Call It Madness but I Call It Love," Victor 22802. While this ditty sounds extremely dated, this crooning job, as penned by Con Conrad, Gladys Du Bois, Paul Gregory, and Russ himself, was good enough to become known as his radio show theme. Later versions of this ditty included the likes of post-WWII crooner Billy Eckstine.
5. "Sweet and Lovely," Victor 22802. This title became a popular Columbo entity in 1931. In a true battle of crooners, this ditty was also a popular recording for Bing Crosby, on Brunswick 6179. This ditty may also seek to fool many keen ears, as this ditty—penned by Gus Arnheim, Harry Tobias, and Jules Lemare—indeed defines both vocal styles as identical in voice.
6. "Goodnight, Sweetheart," Victor 22826. The Bing Crosby version, on Brunswick 6203, of this title, credited as penned by Ray Noble, Jimmy Campbell, Reg Connelly, and Rudy Vallee, is just like the Columbo version—but, does Russ whistle? Or perhaps, did (British) Al Bowlly have something to contribute?
7. "Where the Blue of the Night," Victor 22867. As the most recognized ditties of the Bing Crosby legacy (excluding "White Christmas), this title was heard at the beginning of almost every Crosby radio show (as his theme song). In 1931, moreover—credited to the likes of Roy Turk, Fred Ahlert, and Bing himself—many contemporary radio listeners were not convinced. Indeed, when Russ's own contemporary recording was issued, the identical vocal style, even more so than as heard on the radio, confirmed for many that Bing's version, on Brunswick 6226, was essentially the same thing! (Russ did record it first, yet Bing had already rendered it in his film short *Blue of the Night.)*
8. "Prisoner of Love," Victor 22867. Penned by Leo Robin, Clarence Gaskill, and Russ himself, this flip side of "Where the Blue of the Night" has remained a classic crooning job. By the mid-1940s, both Perry Como and Billy Eckstine also attempted to croon out this ditty, and there was also a group effort by the Ink Spots. (Light-years later, a hipper, smoking vocal, by James Brown on King 5739, is all R & B. It is, moreover, interesting to speculate just how Russ would have reacted to the (ultimate) "Godfather of Soul" (1963) version).
9. "All of Me," Victor 22903. Russ croons out this title well. Contemporary versions had included the likes of Mildred Bailey (with Paul Whiteman), Nick Lucas, and Louis Armstrong. Later, in the mid-1940s, Frank Sinatra (Columbia 38163) would redefine this ditty as well as become associated with it.
10. "Save the Last Dance for Me," Victor 22903. While this entity, penned by Walter Hirsch and Frank Magine, just ain't the same song as the later rock-era hit by the Drifters (on Atlantic 2071), it's not a bad crooning job.
11. "Time on My Hands," Victor 22826. Penned by Harold Adamson, Mack Gordon, and Vincent Youmans, this title became another huge Russ Columbo classic, along with a masterful contemporary Leo Reisman 1931 release (on Victor 22839) featuring the (then) up-and-coming female vocalist Lee Wiley, defining this ditty.
12. "You Try Somebody Else," Victor 22861. Russ speeds up this ditty penned by Roy Turk and Fred Ahlert a bit and succeeds! So did contemporaries Kate Smith and Rudy Vallee. Listen and compare!
13. "Just Friends," Victor 22903. Mmm. Russ wants to be only friends, but how can it be? This dated crooning job still works, or perhaps its message, penned by John Klenner and Sam M. Lewis, was never out of date?
14. "Living in Dreams," Victor 22976. While dated, this John W. Green-penned ditty finds Russ successfully dealing with an up-tempo arrangement that works.

15. "Paradise," Victor 22976. Bing Crosby also recorded this ditty penned by Gordon Clifford and Nacio Herb Brown. Moreover, it led to more speculation about which one is better. Or perhaps Russ comes off a bit softer on his version? More Speculation had it that Russ had been seeing the contemporary film entity, slightly older than Russ but still 'hot', Pola Negri; who had introduced this ditty in the contemporary 1932 film *"A Womam's Command"*. Did he record it as a favor for her? Listen and decide!
16. "Auf Wiedersehen, My Dear," Victor 22976. The early 1930s found this ethnic-linked ditty, penned by (Al Hoffman, Ed Nelson, Al Goodhart, and Milton Ager, at odds with the still popular but tenor style of Morton Downey (Melotone 13197). While the Irish tenor was indeed good enough for this (German) entity, Russ's contemporary crooning job was (even) considered hip! Get it? (Bing did a masterful version in the film 1931 short *Blue of the Night*. Too bad he did not produce a contemporary recording!)
17. "As You Desire Me," Victor 24076. This title itself was considered hot stuff. While in reality its crooned-out message is a bit stiff—as penned by Allie Wrubel and perhaps sharing the title of "Como Me Queres"—the mushy lyrics (still) work.
18. "The Lady I Love," Victor 24076. Also noted as "La Mujer Qu'e Yo Amo," this ditty credited to Joe Young and Bernice Pethere finds Russ's crooning job very capable of showboating. Luckily, he pulls it off very well.
19. "Lonesome Me," Victor 24077. Most of the time, the slow tempos found on most Russ Columbo recordings found little more than a "waltz" response, intended for contemporary dance floors and ballrooms. This ditty, penned by Razaf, Waller, and Con Conrad, finds an instrumental bridge in the middle of the vocal. A "Russ Columbo and His Orchestra recording," as noted on its original release, Russ's vocal is noted as "vocal refrain," perhaps noting that Russ was also a fine musician. As a violinist for Gus Arnheim, he had learned his trade as a bandleader. Indeed, this sweet band effort, along with his fine vocal, is no fluke.
20. "My Love," Victor 24077. This short self-penned ditty, by Russ himself, is stiffly and effectively crooned out.
21. "Street of Dreams," Victor 24194. The contemporary Bing Crosby version, found on Brunswick 6464, is a more serious and poignant statement. It is, nevertheless, worth it to listen and, more so, compare.
22. "Make Love the King," Victor 24195. Yes! Do it, as Joe Young, Bill Gaston and Con Conrad are credited as writers.
23. "When You're in Love," Brunswick 6972. Penned by Bernie Grossman Jack Stern and Russ himself, this lively ditty, introduced in his contemporary 1934 film *Wake up and Dream*, couldn't have sounded better than it did. As a matter of fact, the fine contemporary Jimmy Grier Orchestra provided Russ some fine lively backing, which he had had also provided for Bing, that same year.
24. "Let's Pretend There's a Moon," Brunswick 6872. Another lively crooning job, introduced in the 1934 film *Wake up and Dream* (penned by Bernie Grossman, Jack Stern, and Grace Hamilton), is even better as a recording!
25. "I See Two Lovers," Special Edition 5001. This ditty penned by Allie Wrubel and Mort Dixon and recorded in 1934 was somehow lost on this Special Edition label. In any case, this sensitive version is crooned out well and could, more so, match the fine 1934 contemporary Helen Morgan version, on Brunswick 7391.
26. "Too Beautiful for Words," Special Edition 5001. This ditty was meant to be the main theme for the (1934) film *Wake up and Dream*. Russ, more so, is indeed committed, as

this crooning job is a bit upbeat (for him)! Penned by Bernie Grossman, Jack Stern, and Russ himself, this ditty was to be much exploited within the film, as Russ does it at least three times and does it indeed well. Sadly, his early death put an end to all these plans, as well as a *sure* best seller, contemporary 1934 Brunswick release. This tardy, but appreciated Special Edition release was perhaps ten years late—but worth it!

➢ Radio

- The legacy of Columbo's crooning—the noted "Romeo of Song"—was indeed a battle with Crosby in the early 1930s. Russ, moreover, had a few programs, including the popular *Songs to Delight Your Ears and Heart*. The following radio renderings are, more so, a huge chunk of his legacy:

27. "You Call It Madness," 1933. Russ's radio theme, also a commercial recording, is crooned out well.
28. "More Than You Know," 1933.
29. "Time on My Hands," 1933.
30. "You're My Past, My Present, My Future," 1933. Russ is found to be promoting a song ditty from his then current film *Broadway Through a Key Hole.*
31. "Kisses in the Dark," 1934
32. "Lover."
33. "The House Is Haunted," 1934. Amazing! Bing Crosby also produced an existing radio aircheck in the same year. It is no more a coincidence that both crooners did not render a contemporary recording. Do they both sound identical? Is the house boring as well as haunted? Just listen!
34. "Easy Come, Easy Go," 1934. The contemporary Lee Wiley and Ruth Etting recordings are indeed challenged.
35. "With My Eyes Wide Open I'm Dreaming," 1934. Another "crooning" comparison with Bing finds both airchecks similar. Also, both entities did not produce a contemporary recording.
36. "Stardust," 1934. The contemporary Crosby recording is at least challenged!
37. "True," 1934.
38. "Rolling in Love," 1934.
39. "I've Had My Moments," 1934.
40. "I'm Not Lazy, I'm Dreaming," 1934.

➢ Visual Image.

The early (as well as unpredicted) death of the young crooner left little to find in visual entities but, in true retrospective, serve all future generations of researchers a good image of his youth and vitality. In fact, the many years of Bing Crosby's visual image (that hides his early youth and charm), earn for Bing, mixed visual vitality. Russ, however (when found), does not have this problem. Russ produced musical shorts and (limited) full-length film work, ranging from run-of-the-mill to very good. Although limited for him, his best film was *Broadway Through a Keyhole*, a 1933 gangster yarn. The following two song ditties, featuring Russ, contributed to this fine film:

41. "You're My Past, Present, and Future." After not even seeing or hearing Russ in about at least the first half hour of the melodrama musical *Broadway Through a Keyhole*,

Russ is found with his violin in hand, crooning out this very fine ballad in a Miami nightclub. While dated, this performance remains a good (1933) fit.

42. "Pizzicato." Russ and costar Constance Cummings (a costar from *Broadway Through a Keyhole*) provide the viewers with a gem of a duet in the nightlife of 1933.
43. "Prisoner of Love." Despite some interruptions, Russ may be both seen and heard introducing his radio-promoted song ditty in the film short *That Goes Double*. He, moreover, comes off a bit less stiff, and, perhaps, within this film, defines his (short) crooning legacy for later generations.
44. "My Love." Russ also introduced this ditty in his film short *That Goes Double*. Good enough.
45. "Coffee in the Morning, Kisses at Night." Russ may be seen and heard as part of a duet with Constance Bennett in a musical sequence for the 1933 film, *Moulin Rouge*. While Bennett's surprisingly perky vocal performance indeed lifts Russ, the subsequent Boswell Sisters' performance is far better.
45. "When You're in Love," from *Wake up and Dream*. Russ may be seen and heard in a duet with June Knight.
46. "Too Beautiful for Words," from *Wake up and Dream*.

- Earlier, in Hollywood, Russ did produce vocal dubbing for some obscure films. Moreover, in an unaccredited performance in the 1929 film *Dynamite*, he is seen (crudely) strumming a guitar in a prison cell.

47. "How Am I to Know." Penned by Dorothy Parker and Jack King, the unknown and unnamed Russ does a fairly good crooning job on Gene Austin's contemporary (1929) hit on Victor 22128. For those who may be interested, this performance is somewhat flawed, as too many distractions from cast members are both seen and heard. It is, moreover, more than too bad that when Russ did achieve fame as a violinist and solo vocalist, he did not get around to officially record this ditty. As a pick, the author of this book does find exceptions and excuses for some—and this is one of them!

Note: While it is not known for sure that the fatal accident that befell Russ Columbo in August 1934 (a gun accident at twenty-six years of age) changed the course of popular music, Russ must be credited as an important entity of the early 1930s' Depression era, who was (almost) as popular as (his friend) Bing Crosby.

Perry Como

The influence of Bing Crosby on the onetime band singer of the mid-1930s—of the Ted Weems Orchestra—is very evident to all listeners of any Perry Como recordings. Like so many other contemporary vocalists, the emulation of Crosby indeed merited notice, and with a bit of luck, to be duplicated. The success achieved with Ted Weems, moreover, turned out to be just the beginning for Perry. Indeed by the early 1940s, the medium of radio had brought him much attention and, moreover, the attention of RCA Victor, who had found a popular Crosby clone. After leaving Ted Weems, perhaps due to the striking musicians' ban (1942), the clean-cut Perry Como's RCA Victor recordings were promoted heavily. By 1945, about thirty-two years old, Perry usually found himself on the best-seller lists. While his film career would turn out to become regarded less than memorable, radio and the new media of television would provide him notable recognition. The mid-1950s found his easygoing appeal genuine, as well as a popular "adult" alternative to rock and roll. His smooth, relaxed vocal style, easier than that of Bing Crosby, indeed earned him a group of best-selling entities that (even) rivaled many of the new rock entities.

- The following are Perry Como picks as a vocalist with the Ted Weems orchestra:

1. "Lazy Weather," Decca 822. If one found this old blue label (Decca) 78 and put it on an old Victrola or turntable, a smooth vocal is easily identified as a contemporary Bing Crosby entity. While Perry was certain not to be Crosby or possibly another (Italian) entity like Russ Columbo, this recording is good, and indeed a good emulation. This ditty was not recorded by Bing or Russ, but comparisons with contemporary (black) crooner Harlan Lattimore's version, with the Don Redman Orchestra, merit fine listening and comparisons. (As a further note, the incidental whistling heard on this ditty is that of one Elmo Tanner, not Perry's).
2. "Fooled by the Moon," Decca 921. The "sweet band" arrangement by Ted Weems for this ditty penned bySammy Cahn and Saul Chaplin must have found favor on many contemporary ballroom floors.
3. "A Gypsy Told Me," Decca 1695. Perry again excels on this 1938 recording, penned by Jack Yellen and Sam Pokrass penned ditty from taken from the contemporary Sonja Henie and Don Ameche film *"Happy Landing"* that had been introduced by Leah Ray and Don Ameche. Is Perry better? Yes!
4. "In My Little Red Book," Decca 1695. This light vocal, penned by Ray Bloch, Nat Simon, and Al Stillman, finds a bragging Perry, wisely looking up some 'good' numbers.
5. "Goodnight Sweet Dreams, Goodnight," Decca 1704. While not 'Goodnight Sweetheart", this Teddy Powell and Leonard Whitcup play on words does not confuse Perry's excellent vocal.
6. "Goody Good-bye," Decca 2794. It's not "Goody Goody", yet Perry's expected soft vocal on this James Cavanough and Nat Simon penned ditty delivers a pleasant good-bye.
7. "I Wonder Who's Kissing Her Now," Decca 2919. This ditty became a best seller in a most unusual way. Although its initial (1939) release sold in moderation, a (1947) reissue, due to a contemporary film title released on Decca 25078, found more buyers and listeners. Indeed, the solo act of Perry Como had made him a hot property in the latter 1940s. Just how and why Ted Weems had recorded it as a sweet band entity should, perhaps, merit a previous (1937) Jimmie Davis release on Decca 5363.

(The acoustic era of 1909 and 1910 had already claimed this ditty—penned by Frank Adams, Will Hough, Harold Orlob and Joe Howard—as a Broadway showtune. Numerous and awful renderings by Henry Burr (Columbia 707), Billy Murray (Victor 16426), and the Latin sensation of that era, Manual Romain (Edison 10287) had been best-seller versions.)

8. "It All Comes Back to Me Now," Decca 3627. It's a good tune, and this 1941 rendering, penned by Joan Whitney, Alex Kramer and Hy Zaret is more than good enough.
9. "May I Never Love Again," Decca 3627. Marco Sano and Jack Erickson's plesant lyrics find Perry in his usually good mid-tempo Bing Crosby mood, which wasn't bad in 1941.

10. "Ollie Ollie Outs in Free," Decca 4138. Is it a game of harmless tag? This harmless ditty, penned by Helen White and Clarence Freed, find Perry playful enough with silly lyrics !

- RCA Victor solo picks are as follows:

11. "Long Ago and Far Away," Victor 20-1569. While still aping Bing, Perry's vocal became a bit more polished, smooth, and even careful. It is also interesting to compare this ditty, penned by Jerome Kern and Ira Gershwin, with the contemporary Bing Crosby version, on Decca 18608). Bing's vocal is still adequate, although his pioneering crooning style of the early 1930s is obviously missing.
12. "Temptation," Victor 20-1658. The already classic Bing Crosby Brunswick hit of 1933, penned by. Freed and N. H. Brown, is revived. While it's a stretch, in true retrospective, to match Crosby's excellent performance, Perry does well.
13. "Till the end of Time," Victor 20-1709. Credited to Buddy Kaye and Ted Mossman, this best seller for Perry was based upon Chopin's classic Polonaise in A-flat Major.
14. "A Hubba-Hubba-Hubba, Dig You Later" Victor 20-1750. This ditty, penned by Harold Adamson and Jimmy McHugh, also dates itself with WWII and the homecoming for soldiers from the winning war effort against Japan. This bit of slang was also showcased (by Perry) in the (1945) film *Doll Face.*
15. "Prisoner of Love," Victor 20-1814. As well as Bing Crosby, the similar crooned-out efforts of Russ Columbo did indeed influence Perry. While this light rendering of a Columbo original is a bit lacking in comparison, it's still interesting. So is a (1946) contemporary version, crooned out with a bit more depth, by Billy Eckstine. (Much later, James Brown would define it in a radically different style.)
16. "Winter wonderland," Victor 20- 1968.
17. "When You Were Sweet Sixteen," Victor 20-2259. This overly sentimental ballad penned by Thornton had been popular in the acoustic age. Best-selling acoustic renderings included those by George J. Gaskin, on Columbia 4281; Jer Mahoney, on Edison 7410; Harry MacDonough, on Victor 769; and John W. Meyers, on Victor 3135. The tenor traditions are negated by Perry's very fine and smooth vocal style.
18. "Rambling Rose," Victor 20-2947. This ditty, penned by Joe Burke and Joe McCarthy, should not be confused with the later Nate "King" Cole recording of the same name.
19. "Missouri Waltz", Victor-20-3316. Perry's 1949 smooth croon landed upon an old song ditty that had also found the state of Missouri proclaiming it as it's official state song that same year. As credited to J. R. Shannon and F. K. Logan, also known as "Hush A Bye Ma Baby", Perry's defining vocal is sung as a lullabye, and can indeed be used to put a child, as well as some adult, to induce sleep.

The murky origins of this ditty had possible origins in old English folklore and in slave plantations days when black maids took care of small children. Becoming published in 1912 as "Missouri Waltz, credited to John V. Eppel and Frederick Knight Logan. In 1914 the song title, according to J. R. Shannon became known as "Hush A Bye Ma Baby", followed by numerous recorded versions, including a stiff 1916 acoustic vocal as "Hush A Bye Ma Baby:, as by Edna Brown on Victor-1814. Since then, the song had been taken up by the University of Missouri, although the song's revival had a lot to do with the presidential election of 1948, providing (Missourian) Harry Truman a winning campaign theme song for his Democratic convention. (He also used another song ditty, "I'm Just Wild About Harry").

Because of all this, along with the passage of time, some lyrics referring to implied pickaninnies, found in Edna Brown's best selling 1918-17 earlier version, caring for white infants were dropped. Amoung these other word changes, it's interesting to note that Perry's version uses the term 'old folks', instead of 'darkies'. Perry more so still retains 'manny', as the song thus remains a defined "mammy' song. While in retrospective this designation became identified by many as a derogatory "coon" song, it is not. Sadly, because of all this controversity, Perry's lifting of this folk entity has been largly forgotten, and hardly, found in re-issued Como recorded product.

20. "Blue Room," Victor 20-3329. While Perry Como never became a huge film entity, this classic penned by Rodgers and Hart is given a fine update. (Perry also may be seen introducing this ditty in the contemporary (1948) film entity.) Originally, this ditty had been popular in the 1920s. As part of the Broadway entity *The Girl Friend* and a group recording by the Revelers on Victor 20082, this ditty had already been a best-selling entity.
21. "Some Enchanted Evening," Victor 20-3402. The likes of (1949) found Richard Rodgers and Oscar Hammerstein II busy in the Broadway entity *South Pacific* and the operatic renderings of a real Italian, Ezio Pinza. This was all good for the stage as well as a later 1958 film. However, as the best song of this production, Perry's (sometimes) vocal abilities to approach becoming a tenor are not needed for his own superb recording. While no one questions Perry's own (Italian American) roots, his own soft-voiced style defined this ditty better than Pinza as a popular song. Among many other contemporary versions perhaps Perry's only challenge was from a rendering from Jo Stafford.
22. "Bali Ha'i" Victor 20-3402. Another ditty byRichard Rodgers and Oscar Hammerstein II from *South Pacific* finds many questions about this seemingly stupid title, not evident in "Some Enchanted Evening," on its original flip side. While much recorded, perhaps contemporary Thelma Carpenter's version is better than Perry's?
23. "Hoop-Dee-Doo," Victor 20-3747. Popular slang found a ditty penned by Milton De Lugg and Frank Loesser just right for Perry (and the Fontaine Sisters) in 1950. Was a contemporary version by Kay Starr better? Who still cares? Hoop-Dee-Doo?
24. "Youre Just In Love" With the Fontaine Sisters as a backing vocal group (Bea, Geri & Marge), Perry's smooth vocal found upon this Irving Berlin-penned ditty is pleasant enough?
25. "The Christmas Symphony," Victor 20-3933. This seasonal entity, penned by Phil Perry, Joe Canduilo, and Charles F. Reade, was a contrived bit of fodder that had (always) worked for Crosby, now for Como.
26. "There is No Christmas Like a Home Christmas," Victor 20-3933. This ditty by Carl Sigman and Mickey J. Addy, like its flip side "The Christmas Symphony," is a fine effort to also produce the huge success that Crosby had in seasonal releases.
27. "Don't Let the Stars Get in Your Eyes," Victor 20-5064. This 1952-53 best seller, penned by Slim Willet, is a fine bit of fluffy pop that works.
28. "Pa-Paya Mama," Victor 5447. A fast-paced clever novelty penned by George Sandler, Norman Gimble and Larry Coleman ain't rock and roll, but is is for kids-at least in 1954!
29 "Papa Loves Mambo," Victor 20-5857. This 1954 novelty, penned by Al Hoffman, Dick Manning, and Bix Reichner, is a contrived cash in ride into the contemporary 'mambo' dance of the mid-1950s.

30. "Home for the Holidays," Victor 20-5950. While Perry had already been in the seasonal mood since 1946, this (1954) ditty, penned by Robert Allen and Al Stillman, became his most popular rendering of a seasonal entity. Introduced by Perry himself, this ditty had become a Christmas classic and, indeed, remained so each season past the dawn of a new century.
31. "Hot Diggity (Dog Ziggity Boom)," Victor 20-6427. This attempt at rhythmic singing, competing with the up-and-coming rock and roll fad, somehow works. Indeed, much like "Pa-Paya Mama" and "Papa Loves Mambo," this contrived bit of contemporary slang, penned by Al Hoffman and Dick Manning, still demonstrates a willingness by Perry to compete. On the other hand, he just ain't no Clyde McPhatter!
32. "Round and Round," Victor 20-6815. Perry again limps into a bit of rhythm. Perry's soft approach, popularized by his contemporary television program, also found this ditty (penned by Lou Stallman and Joe Shaperio) yet another "adult" response to rock and roll.
33. "Catch a Falling Star," Victor 20-7128. This 1958 title, penned by Paul Vance and Lee Pockriss, is a fine bit of popular singing, which also features Perry's best vocal.
34. "Magic Moments". Victor-20-7128. This Hal David and Burt Bacharach penned ditty features a silly sing a long from the Ray Charles Singers (not releated to THE Ray Charles). In retrospective, it's Perry's well done soft vocal style overcoming all the extra noise!
35. "Love Makes The World Go Round". Victor-47-7353. This time, a nerdy sing a long provided by the Ray Charles Singers, penned by Ollie Jones, does not get in the way of Perry's well done vocal.
36. "It's Impossible," Victor 74-0387. Jumping forward past Elvis, Motown sounds, and the Beatles, this (1970) entity still made it to best-seller lists. Penned by Sid Wayne and Canache Armondo Manzanero, this lush pop sound, succeeds beyond expetations.

- Visual Image.

The familiar success of Perry Como in baby boomer television land made Perry part of the household, specially noting his Christmas specials. Yet were they just bland and full of Hoop-Dee-Do? Perhaps earlier film efforts may shed a bit more light on his earlier appeal and success?

- The (1945) film *Doll Face*, found Perry doing a singing act in a striptease show. (Yup, it's Perry!) While the ladies leave more on their bodies than many who paid for their original movie tickets would wish to see, Perry effectively croons out

37. "A Hubba-Hubba, Dig You Later." (The contemporary recording is reviewed above.)
38. "Blue Room". Perry is seen and heard in the 1949 film *"Words And Music"*. (The contemporary recording is reviewed above)

Carleton Coon and Joe Sanders Orchestra

- The (1920s) rhythmic "dance bands" had been created largely upon the hidden sounds of Afro-Americans, the success of (white) jazz leader recordings Nick La Rocca in the late teens cought the attentions of the general public, as well as in the music of popular novelty acts of Sophie Tucker, and the likes of popular music, especially found in recordings of Marion Haris.

While it's a far shot away from what was really jazz, the symphonic orchestra of Paul Whiteman, much influenced by the newer rhythmic sounds, began to incorporate what was heard into his arrangements. To be fair, so did the more conservative emerging (black) bandleaders of the early 1920s, influenced by contemporary "white" entertainment, who would include the likes of Blake and Sissle, Fletcher Henderson, William Grant Still, and, by 1924, Edward (Duke) Ellington. With the color line finally broken, the subsequent (black) recordings issued influenced many would-be musicians, both black and white. The likes of such (white) bandleaders and musicians as Bix Beiderbecke, Isham Jones, Ted Lewis, Phil Napoleon, Red Nichols, Jack Teagarden, and even a few local (white) Kansas City white musicians, Joe Sanders and Carleton Coon played jazz as they heard it, much of it from phonograph records, without discriminating from "white" or "black" musical sources. The popularity of Carleton Coon and Joe Sanders (orchestra), called the Nighthawks was, more so, fueled by the media of radio and subsequent recordings. For the purposes of this book, moreover, their dry-mouth-sounding vocals, heard among some "hot jazz" licks, are much appreciated. Moreover, the successful efforts of the Coon-Sanders Orchestra pioneered the way for many to follow. Most bandleaders did not produce their own vocals. For the most part, small units of bandleaders were less interested in vocals and were more into musical improvisation. Indeed, these local Kansas City hicks competed well with those of the big cities, especially competing with the contemporary high, and more novel-sounding (mousey or chipmunk) vocals from established acts like Van and Schenck and Paul Whiteman's newer Rhythm Boys. Moreover, Carleton Coon and Joe Sanders were indeed to leave behind them some competing and interesting best-selling jazz—with simple vocals.

Picks are as follows:

(Note: Vocals are by either Carleton Coon or Joe Sanders or both.)

13. "Night Hawk Blues," Victor 19316. This original written for their radio programs, penned by Joe L. Sanders, finds an attempt to "jazz" things up with vocals by both Carleton and Joe. It, more so, delivers!
14. "Red Hot Mama," Victor 19316. This ditty, penned by Gilbert Wells, Bud Cooper, and Fred Rose, finds both Carleton and Joe attempting to improvise vocal freedom, or scat.
15. "Alone at Last," Victor 19728. This ditty penned by Gus Kahn and Ted Fiorito finds Joe's vocal more than adequate!
16. "Yes, Sir, That's My Baby," Victor 19745. This vocal owes nothing to Gene Austin!
17. "Flaming Mamie," Victor 19922. Another hot flapper, penned by Fred Rose and Paul Whiteman, that had found a sweltering previously recorded Aileen Stanley version (Victor 19283) as well done as a subsequent Eva Taylor version. In any case, after a long, fast-paced jazzy introduction, Joe Sanders's own vocal, while far from great led by the band, still manages to raves things up even more!

18. "Everything's Gonna Be All Right," Victor 20003. This jazzy novelty, penned by Benny Davis and Harry Akst, features Joe on, perhaps, his best vocal.
19. "My Baby Knows How," Victor 20390. Joe's vocal is up a notch as this hot (1926) ditty, penned by Benny Davis, Harry Akst, and Harry Richmond, reveals.
20. "I Need Loving," Victor 20408. The ditty penned by Johnston and Creamer was claimed as a recording a bit later by Blanche Calloway.
21. "Stay out of the South," Victor 21258. Both Carleton and Joe find their vocals on this Harold Dixon-penned ditty.
22. "Is She My Girl Friend?" Victor 21148. Jack Yellen and Milton Ager's penned ditty perhaps defines the era of the 'roaring twenties' in a carefree spirit, is greeted by Joe's breezy vocal with some well done jazz backing that more than covers up Joe's limits as a vocalist.
23. "Here Come My Ball and Chain," Victor 21812. Another fine novelty, penned by Lou Davis and J. Fred Coots, with a vocal by Joe.
24. "Little Orphan Annie," Victor 21895. The comic strip was popular in 1928. With a bit of flair, Joe not only penned this ditty with Gus Kahn, but he also did the so-so vocal for this still interesting ditty.
25. "I Got a Great Big Date with a Little Bitta Girl," Victor 22123. A good excuse for a long song title? Joe sang it as well as penned it in 1929.
26. "Kansas City Kitty," Victor 21939. This novelty penned by Donaldson and Leslie found Joe's vocal more than willing to explain himself about Kitty on a dance floor. Or perhaps a contemporary vocal by flapper Edith Evans, on Brunswick 4291, is more interesting?
27. "The Darktown Stutters' Ball," Victor 22342. As the earlier century entities, Arthur Collins and Byron Harlan had successfully recorded much novelty, which included "coon songs." Their acoustic vocal, as released on Columbia A 2478, certainly implies racial relations, at least for the listeners in 1918. In true retrospective, it's own credited (black) writer (Shelton Brooks) perhaps got away with something? This later (1931) version, with a (usual) enthusiastic vocal by Carleton is, more so, a dance record.

Bing Crosby

There is an image problem here, in the person of Harry Lillis Crosby—real name. The name "Bing," taken from an early comic strip of the early part of the century, stuck with him his whole life. To most of the people alive in the latter century, the image of Bing identified with Christmas and, for that matter, old age. The following picks find a recording artist who eventually, and sadly (in true retrospective), could not focus upon an idiom. The fact of the matter is that this prolific list of picks, which originally was intended to focus upon a small group of recordings, found history and success far too huge to ignore. While it is still very true that the recordings chosen here are not for everyone, it should be noted that these picks represent a small part of the recorded output of this (very) popular vocalist and entertainer. Unfortunately, all the junk he left behind (which indeed *sold* anyway) hides his brilliance, his art. Popular culture indeed seeks out its own hipness. While age is always a factor, commercial success may also destroy creativity, destroy incentive. By the end of the century, this fact remains in the careers of many show business personalities who were to follow. While indeed (later) entities would continue to struggle to achieve the success that Crosby would find, few possessed his talents. Crosby had literally conquered all that the then show business world had thrown at him, except perhaps, as a Broadway entity, yet noting many song ditties he subsequently recorded had origins there.

It's interesting to notice that Crosby's early vocal influences were all heard on phonograph records and (mostly) all of them were "acoustic." The diverse qualities of style ranged from (Catholic) church choirs, Irish tenor John McCormack, the comic qualities of Van and Schenck, as well as the contemporary jazz and race recordings of the early 1920s, especially noting the likes of Ethel Waters (jazzy phrasing) and Louis Armstrong (scatting). His timely 1926 first "electric" recordings for the (very) popular Paul Whiteman found Bing ready for Americana—an America that would eventually consider him as a huge part of the culture itself.

The introduction of electric recording and the further development of the microphone had made it all possible for small voices and the "small" talk to be recorded, thus producing something totally new. The "whisper," "sweet talk," and the art of "parlor game" of an earlier age all could be effectively picked up electronically. More importantly, the vulgar act of "soft" intimate speech, or the art of the "crooner," was transformed into a recording technique. Casual conversations about life and (especially) sex were to become softly heard on recordings! Morals threatened! While there would be others, it would be Bing Crosby's intimate style that led the recording industry into its "modern" age. An "age" in fact, and in true retrospective, that indeed remains.

According to myth and some facts, after starting off on his own with Al Rinker in 1926, they somehow joined up with the Paul Whiteman Orchestra (a band as popular as the Beatles, in a later decade). With the help of Al Rinker's sister (Mildred Bailey), a local speakeasy vocalist, who later (also) became associated with Whiteman as a recording artist, Bing and Al found sudden recognition. Vocally, they sounded much like Van and Schenck. While on tour with Whiteman, a Whiteman regular, Harry Barris was added. This trio became known as Paul Whiteman's Rhythm Boys or the Rhythm Boys. Featured solo recordings by Bing would find him very able to sing with a jazzy beat and, on slower material, having an uncanny ability to croon. As more of a complex personality than was known about him in the 1920s, his lazy attitude would not hinder him for very long. They subsequently became associated with many of the best jazz musicians of the era, sharing the plagues of (illegal) alcohol and (legal until 1931) weed. Among others, they would include the likes of (Tommy and Jimmy) Dorsey, Bix Beiderbecke, Joe Venuti, Frankie Trumbauer, Jack Teagarden, Victor Young, and (especially) guitarist Eddie Lang. While not getting too far ahead of the "story," this vocalist, who would learn to sing "for" the listener, easily eclipsed the likes of Al Jolson and the sensation of 1929, Rudy Vallee. His later, somewhat superficial, autobiography, *Call Me Lucky*, is very misleading—or perhaps not!

Following are Bing Crosby Picks (1926-30) usually part of a duet, trio, or chorus.

1. "Wistful and Blue," Victor 20418. This Crosby and Rinker vocal had first become a known entity as a Columbia release by Ruth Etting. As the first of many Paul Whiteman credited recordings, both Bing and Al were designated as "vocal refrain" in this successful attempt at rhythmic or jazz singing.
2. "Muddy Water," Victor 20508. A fine instrumental start, it provides Bing with his first real solo shot as a recording artist. He, in fact, sounds full of pep, as his excellent

vocal seems to bounce its way through rhythmic backings. Penned by Jo Trent, Pete De Rose, and Harry Richmond, this ditty's infectious lyrics and its descriptions of the Mississippi Delta perhaps were influenced by the national concerns and building of dams, following the great floods that had occurred there in the mid-1920s. It is also interesting to compare Crosby's jazzy vocal with the likes of a contemporary Bessie Smith version on Columbia. Her blues rendering is powerful and sad, with added drama. Bessie, for sure, found no emulation of Crosby's bubbly attitude and may be considered a totally different entity. Listen and compare!

3. "Side by Side," Victor 20627. Did contemporary Nick Lucas do it better? Listen and compare.
4. "Magnolia," Victor 20679. The Rhythm Boys, alias "vocal refrain" were novel themselves. Penned by Buddy De Sylva, Lew Brown, and Ray Henderson, this clever mid-tempo vocal succeeds. (A contemporary solo vocal version by vaudevillian and singer Dolly Kay also offers interesting comparisons.)
5. "I'm Coming, Virginia," Victor 20751. Bing and Al again demonstrate some fine rhythmic singing. In comparison, a contemporary Columbia Ethel Waters version, with backing by Will Marion Cook, reeks of tradition. While Ethel's emotional plea is crooned out articulately enough, Crosby's version is indeed more danceable as well as hip.
6. "Mississippi Mud-I Left My Sugar Standing in the Rain," Victor 20783. It's a fine and novel version by Paul Whiteman's Rhythm Boys Vocal Trio with piano. Penned by Harry Barris, Sammy Fain, and Irving Kahal, this ditty (again) refers to the Mississippi Delta, with a lighthearted and whimsical attitude.
7. "Mary, What Are You Waiting For?" Victor 21103. Walter Donaldson's breezy penned ditty luckily found Bing's carefree baritone to define this silly 'flatter' era title.
8. "Old Man River," Victor 21218. As penned by Oscar Hammerstein II and Jerome Kern for the contemporary Broadway entity 'The Showboat', this ditty, despite it's racism, was to become an American classic. More fortunately, Bing's jazzy and loose vocal, as well as dropping the racism, indeed defined it, especially in comparison with the contemporary and stiff Paul Robeson version, which was also backed by Paul Whiteman.
9. "Sunshine," Victor 21240. Was this Irving Berlin-penned ditty, with the Rhythm Boys and others, inspired by contemporary crooner Nick Lucas? If so, it's still very well done!
10. "Mississippi Mud," Victor 21274. Another version of this Harry Barris-penned ditty betters the first release. Its play on rhythm is indeed infectious, and these Rhythm Boys had it!
11. "From Monday On," Victor 21274. This flip side of "Mississippi Mud" is again a bouncy enough ditty. Penned by Harry Barris and Bing himself, it's a credit to Paul Whiteman for not taking liberties with this fine lyric unknown to anyone else.
12. "Mississippi Mud," Okeh 40979. Moonlighting with the Frank Trumbauer Orchestra produced this classic version, bettering the two previous Paul Whiteman versions. (A contemporary Lee Morse version, on Columbia 1584-D, is also jazzy as well as competitive. Listen and compare!)
13. "High Water," Victor 35992. This 12-inch release, penned by J. Keirn Brennan and McCardy, finds a slightly high baritone vocal performing well enough, although odd.
14. "I'm Winging Home," Victor 21365. With vocal chorus, this title, penned by Russell and Tobias, with Whiteman indeed succeeds with contemporary 1928 slang as well.

15. "You Took Advantage of Me," Victor 21398. The (1928) contemporary ditty penned by Richard Rodgers and Lorenz Hart found Bing's loose and jazzy vocal perhaps very much in the spirit of the times just before the Great Depression. (A differing and perhaps defining version can be heard in the later 1940) Lee Wiley version on Gala-3. Listen and compare?
16. "There Ain't No Sweet Man That's Worth the Salt of My Tears," Victor 21464. This long-winded ditty, penned by Fred Fisher, finds Bing's fine lead vocal a good experiment in jazz. A contemporary Libby Holman rendering on Brunswick, for sure, got the designated gender right, with Bing's (differing) vocal possibly winning out? Listen and compare!
17. "Louisiana," Victor 21438. Led by Bing himself, this fine and danceable rhythmic ditty, penned by Andy Razaf, Bob Schafer, and J. C. Johnson, clearly owes much to its (black) origins. Moreover, Crosby's 1928 vocal and Whiteman's backing do it justice, as hip and jazzy.
18. "Get out and Get under the Moon," Columbia 1402-D. The contemporary Helen Kane version is challenged in a differing style! Listen and compare.
19., 20. "That's Grandma," Columbia 1455-D. (a.) This ditty, claimed by James Cavanaugh, Harry Burris, and Bing himself, turned out to become yet another excuse to scat. In between, moreover, this somewhat of a bit fast-paced silly storytelling about a very unconventional "grandma" is a very faddish tale per 1927/1928 Americana. While hardly a cultural event, the likes of contemporary radio entities, Ernest Hare and Billy Jones, vaudevillians Moran and Mack (or George Moran and Charles Mack), vaudevillian and Broadway entity Eddie Cantor, and the beautiful Ziegfeld star Peggy Joyce (who became very wealthy), as well as everyone's current hero, Charles Lindberg are noted. As this 1928 (Columbia) version was released first, it should be noted that although recorded first on (Victor) in 1927, it was not to be released (b.) on Victor 27688 until 1941.
21. "I'll Get By," Columbia 1694-D. This (1928) rendering found Bing moonlighting away from Paul Whiteman, unaccredited as a vocalist for the Ipana Troubadors, a jazzy group led by Sam Lanin who had led the contemporary (radio) house band for the 1920s sponsor (of toothpaste). While his high baritone vocal is perhaps a bit weak, it's still worth it? In any case, the more popular and contemporary Ruth Etting would, more so, define this ditty as a recording.
22. "Let's Do It," Columbia 1701-D. This Cole Porter-penned ditty is very interesting (with Whiteman).
23. "Coquette," Columbia 1775-D. A somewhat weak or (weaker) baritone perhaps betrays Bing as emulating Rudy Vallee's contemporary rendering. Listen and compare.
24., 25. "Louise," Columbia 1819-D The rush to always find recording fodder found a Paul Whiteman attempt at a popular novelty from the contemporary (1929) film *Innocents of Paris*. While this contrived ditty was set in Paris, a (real) French entity, Maurice Chevalier, introduced this entity in the film, using his classy French accent, as a clever novelty. Chevalier's own subsequent recording, found on Victor 21918, had then produced (surprisingly) a best seller. Whiteman's following contemporary (and best-selling) rendering of this ditty (penned by Leo Robin and Richard Whiting), released on Columbia 1771-D, was perhaps just considered another (and successful) excuse for a popular fox-trot dance release, and a bland and (maybe) bored Crosby vocal? In any case, it was decided to produce yet another contemporary second recording. This attempt found Bing himself dropping his (solo) vocal shot and getting together with Barris and Rinker. With a (still) slightly improved Whiteman backing,

Bing, Al and Harry, as the Rhythm Boys, seemingly had ideas on just how to "make a record," with their (usual) wit, along with contemporary slang along with fine scatting. Listen and learn? Was Louise still on the phone? Find the second version and find out?

26. "So the Blackbirds and the Bluebirds Got Together," Columbia 1819-D This ditty penned by Harry Burris and Billy Moll finds silly and clumsy lyrics with a good excuse for scatting. The ditty would later be added to the (1930) soundtrack of Whiteman's *King of Jazz.*
27. "I'm Crazy over You," Okeh 41228. Moonlighting with the popular contemporary bandleader Sam Lanin again—but this time as with Sam Lanin and His Famous Players—Bing (again) was in luck, with a good vocal, although still unaccredited. Penned by Al Sherman and Al Lewis, this attempt at a jazzy vocal indeed finds a vocal influence of contemporary Rudy Vallee.
28. "The Spell of the Blues," Okeh 41181. Moonlighting with probably the first Dorsey Brothers Orchestra found Bing's rendition of this ditty penned by Harry Ruby, Dave Dreyer, and Arthur Johnston more than good listening!
29. "Let's Do It," Okeh 41181. Cole Porter's ditty is still interesting with the Dorsey's Orchestra; indeed, it is better as Dorsey's independent band inspires Crosby's vocal to be brighter and hipper than Rudy Vallee's contemporary recording? Listen and compare!
30. "My Kinda Love," Okeh 41188. Penned by Jo Trent and Louis Alter, this contemporary 1920s' ditty—perhaps considered liberating (as well as moonlighting away from Whiteman)—produces something better. Listen and learn.
31. "Baby, Oh Where Can You Be," Columbia 1851-D. As another effort (away) from Whiteman, this (1929) solo rendering, penned by Ted Koehler and Frank Magine, finds Bing crooning in fine mid-tempo in the same style of his (later) Brunswick recordings.
32. "I Kiss Your Hand, Madame," Columbia 1851-D. This original flip side of "Baby, Oh Where Can You Be," penned by Ralph Erwin, Sam M. Lewis, Fritz Rotter and Joe Young, also finds Bing in his (later) acclaimed crooning form.
33. "Waiting at the End of the Road," Columbia 1974-D. The contemporary Ethel Waters crooning job is emotional and (almost) religious. This Paul Whiteman arrangement features, in contrast, a very hip and jazzy Crosby vocal. (Speculation has it that this ditty featured Bix Beiderbecke's backing for the last time? Or does anyone still care?)
34. "Can't We Be Friends?" Columbia 2001-D. This solo freelancing effort found Crosby perhaps finding an even more creative way to vocalize upon Libby Holman's original (sultry and sexy) rendering from her contemporary Broadway entity *The Little Show.* In any case, Crosby succeeds as his emotional vocal, full of pathos and regret, produces a fine recording.
35. "Gay Love," Columbia 2001-D. This title, also known as "Amor Alegre," penned by Levant and Clare, finds Bing—in another freelancing attempt—in good crooning form and, indeed, more relevant than (most) contemporary (1929) recordings with Whiteman. (In true retrospective, this entity was rendered at a time when "Gay Love" was hardly considered as it would be by the end of the century.)
36. "If I Had a Talking Picture of You," Columbia 2010-D. Was (perky) Annette Hanshaw's recording better? Listen and compare.
37. "Great Day," Columbia 2023-D. With Whiteman and Chorus, Bing's leading vocal perhaps gets a bit lost, although it's effective enough. Penned by Vincent Youmans,

Billy Rose, and Edward Eliscu, this (1929) ditty had been the title of a so-so Broadway show of the same name. Luckily, this recording, in true retrospective, recalls the show.

38. "After You're Gone," Columbia 2098-D. The already classic ditty, penned by (Afro-Americans) Creamer and Layton, is done well.

39., 40. "A Bench in the Park," Columbia 2164-D. This ditty found the Brox Sisters leading in vocals, with the Rhythm Boys only slightly heard as a production number in *The King of Jazz*. Another subsequent (1930) version of this Milton Ager and Jack Yellen penned ditty, found on Columbia 2223-D, identifies this ditty as a Rhythm Boys group vocal.

41. "Happy Feet," Columbia 2164-D. Another loose bit of writing from Milton Ager and Jack Yellen, a Rhythm Boys release, from the film *King of Jazz* indeed works well enough.

42. "You Brought a New Kind of Love to Me," Columbia 2171-D. The classic Maurice Chevaliers release (on Victor 22405), penned by Irving Kahal, Sammy Fain, and Pierre Connor, had been introduced by the perky Frenchman in a typical French accent as found in the contemporary (1930) film *The Big Pound*. In true retrospective, Bing does it better—as does a contemporary Ethel Waters version on Columbia 2222-D—and, more so, defines this ditty.

43. "Living in the Sunlight, Loving in the Moonlight," Columbia 2171-D. This flip of "You Brought a New Kind of Love to Me" (also introduced by Maurice Chevalier in *The Big Pound*) finds Bing a bit more mid-tempo and bouncy. (As the last of the Paul Whiteman recordings found for review, this ditty. penned by Al Lewis and Al Sherman also found Bing yet to define himself as a solo entity. In fact, Crosby's vocal on this ditty, perhaps due to Whiteman's backing, still finds Bing's vocals very much influenced by that of Rudy Vallee.

44. "Three Little Words," Victor 22528. This recording with the Rhythm Boys was an historic event. The ditty penned by Bert Kalmar and Harry Ruby was used in the film *Check and Double Check* with interesting results. While truly racially stereotyped, this "Amos and Andy" attempt to jump from contemporary 1930 radio to actual blackface makeup in film did employ many black entities. More relevant were Duke Ellington and His Orchestra, and just when the Rhythm Boys made an appearance in the film for (perhaps) as much as two seconds, their fine medium-tempo (group) vocal is heard a bit more. More importantly, the subsequent Duke Ellington release, with the Rhythm Boys and noted under the Ellington Orchestra, was also issued. As a matter of history, this original issued recording indeed finds a (black) entity headlined over that of a (white) vocal performance. As a matter of true retrospective, this contemporary issue noted a huge change in the music business. (A contemporary Columbia recording, in true retrospective, with an unaccredited "white" Columbia house band, as an Ethel Waters release, contains a better vocal, but its release was less significant in 1930.)

45. "Them There Eyes," Victor 22580. This last official recording of the Rhythm Boys was penned by the likes of Maceo Pinkard, William Tracey, and Doris Tauber. This fine bit of rhythmic vocals would, more so, be matched by a contemporary and differing Louis Armstrong version. (Much later, Billie Holiday would redefine it.)

46. "Fool Me Some More," Victor 22561. A very committed artist is evident here, as well as a definite vocal prowess. Indeed, this rapid-paced lyric, penned by Haven Gillespie and Peter De Rose, finds Bing's vocal inspired as well as generating some jazzy excitement.

47. "It Must Be True," Victor 22561. This flip of "Fool Me Some More," is a bit slower, as well as a very effective crooning job. Bing sounds far different from what he sounded

with Whiteman's Orchestra. Penned by Harry Barris, Gordon Clifford, and Gus Arnheim—the bandleader himself, this ditty remains a sure winner.

48. "The Little Things in Life," Victor 22580. This Irving Berlin-penned classic is crooned out effectively and perfectly.
49. "I Surrender Dear," Victor 22618. The Gus Arnheim arrangement as heard is a bit of a challenge and, more so, a creative attempt at a new sound. Indeed, the band seems at a loss at just what tempo this ditty would end up to become. After what sounds as spontaneous shifting around a while, this ditty (penned by Harry Barris—a former Rhythm Boy—and Gordon Clifford) indeed introduces for Bing a vocal challenge. In true retrospective, the subsequent vocal became a powerful statement as well as perhaps the ultimate crooning job! In fact, when Crosby hits some high vocal notes, he maintains an intimate plea and is pleasantly over the top. While it may be noted that Bing had already demonstrated this new style on his previous recordings with Gus Arnheim, this innovative ditty became better known. Indeed, this recording would also become the title of a contemporary film short vehicle, starring Bing. It would also be used, for a while, as Bing's radio theme.
50. "Thanks to You," Victor 22700. This ditty, penned by Grant Clarke and Pete Wendling was originally a sweet band entity and meant for ballroom dancing. Bing's effective vocal, moreover, gave this ditty such an effective crooning job that perhaps the dancing audience stops, just to hear Bing. Or did this really happen? Thank you Bing!
51. "One More Time," Victor 22700. This ditty penned by B. G. De Sylva, Lew Brown, and Ray Henderson, is a fast-paced ditty that reeks with a vocal expression full of jazzy excitement. While Gus Arnheim indeed must be recognized for his energetic arrangement, it's Bing's own vocal that generates all the heat. Did Crosby rock? Just listen!
52. "Just a Gigolo," Victor 22701. This original release notes "Bing Crosby Baritone with Orchestra." Penned by Julious Brammer, Irving Caesar, and Leonello Casucci, this dated tale of a WWI veteran was meant to be somewhat of a novelty, which it was. Bing's masterful rendering of lyric, moreover, famously gives this tale more substance. Indeed, this crooning job is full of emotion and cannot fail to leave its listeners a bit of sadness, along with a smirk. Louis Armstrong's differing contemporary version also works, but his gritty style leaves it as more of a novelty. Listen and compare.
53. "Wrap Your Troubles in Dreams," Victor 22701. This (1931) release of a sad tale, penned by Ted Koehler, Billy Moll, and Harry Barris, is very effectively crooned out, yet perhaps it finds Bing with a cold in his usually softer crooning! Later versions by Bing are OK, with an interesting (1939) bootleg version featuring Bing (perhaps mimicking his earlier recording with a cold?) at his sarcastic and witty best (noted later in text).
54. "Out of Nowhere" Brunswick 6090. This ditty began Crosby's association with Brunswick. Penned by Johnny Green and Ed Heyman, this fine crooning job again set standards for the world of popular music (1931). Indeed, a fine contemporary Ruth Etting version on Columbia seems to have even influenced the diva! In true retrospective, this Brunswick recording was considered a gamble. It seems that Bing was still recording for Victor at this time but perhaps was looking for a better contract. After this release along with its flip side, "If You Should Ever Need Me," this Depression-era decision proved to be the correct one.
55. "If You Should Ever Need Me," Brunswick 6090. This is another fab crooning job by Crosby, penned by Joe Burke and Al Dubin, which scores.

56. "Ho Hum," Victor 22691. This vocal duet with Arnheim band singer Loyce Whiteman is a fine mid-tempo and novel entity. Penned by Edward Heyman and Dana Suesse, this ditty also demonstrates just how witty and comical Bing indeed could become. Loyce's bubbly vocal is also excellent, and it's to her credit that Bing's antics (as heard on the recording) do not detract her. While it's unknown just how many "takes" were made, it is more than obvious that Bing does his best to more than loosen and break her up!
57. "I'm Gonna Get You," Victor 22691. The fast-paced Gus Arnheim introduction is matched by Bing's hot vocal. Penned by Gus Arnheim, Harry Tobias, and Jules Lemare, this ditty was to be the last release with Gus Arnheim's excellent backing.
58. "Just One More Chance," Brunswick 6120. A husky and powerful baritone is heard on this ditty penned by Sam Coslow and Arthur Johnston. While the dated whistling also heard on this vocal is a bit much, the crooning vocal heard still provides its listeners with a winner. It is also interesting to compare this Brunswick recording with a later (1939) vocal on Decca 2999. By that time, success and laziness had indeed sunk in. Like many rerecordings, it indeed sucks. Listeners beware! Stay with Brunswick originals!
59. "Were You Sincere," Brunswick 6120. This kind of mushy crooning was new, and meant a lot in 1931. Penned by Jack Meskill and Vince Rose, this croon job remains effective and sincere and, more so, is just as mushy as the contemporary Ruth Etting version?
60. "I Found a Million Dollar Baby," Brunswick 6140. Bing's froggy throat still manages to croon out a fine classic, penned by Harry Warren, Billy Rose, and Mort Dixon. Perhaps in this case, a contemporary Boswell Sisters version, with a Connie Boswell lead, is crooned out a bit better?
61. "I'm Through with Love," Brunswick 6140. Bing again excels, as this crooning job again surprises its listeners with a vocal prowess full of quirky tricks. Penned by Matty Malneck, Fud Livingston, and Gus Kahn, this dated vocal remains effective.
62. "Many Happy Returns of the Day," Brunswick 6145. Torch! Ever run into a married girlfriend after a year? This Joe Burk, L Dubin and Alfred Bryan update of an old (British) birthday and anniversary greeting found Bing in a harsh emotional croon.
63. At Your Command," Brunswick 6145. Credited as penned by Harry Barris, Harry Tobias, and Bing himself, this vocal performance almost succeeds in labeling Crosby a tenor. Luckily, the label never stuck. Indeed, the Crosby crooning vocal style, once considered vulgar, had, for the most part, put most tenors of popular music out of work.

64., 65. "Stardust," Brunswick 6169. This ditty penned by Mitchell Parish, and Hoagy Carmichael became one of the most recorded of the era and, in fact, the century. (a) Bing's original crooning vocal (1931) indeed defined it. Following Bing's superb crooning job, notable recordings by Louis Armstrong (whose differing vocal style nevertheless stresses to produce a Crosby croon), Chick Bullock (who emulated Crosby with class), Boswell Sisters (release featuring Connie Boswell's crooning), and Louis Prima (who usefully tries to be both Crosby and Armstrong) made it all sound very interesting! (b) Later, in 1939, Bing's own rerecording on Decca 2374 offered a more polished style, which may be heard as good, but not nearly as good as in his original (Brunswick) crooning style. More so, the subsequent and fine (1941) Tommy Dorsey release (on Victor 27233), featured an effective vocal by Frank Sinatra, who seemingly based his vocal on Bing's later (Decca) recording, with added nasal tone. Listen and compare! (Also known as Star Dust).

66. "Dancing in the Dark," Brunswick 6169. This 1931 classic, penned by Howard Dietz and Arthur Schwartz, was indeed a boost for the many fledging ballrooms of those hard Depression times. Despite film and the nice Fred Astaire original rendering, Bing gives this (already classy) ditty a vocal depth which Astaire's weak baritone could never have achieved. Listen and compare.
67. "Sweet and Lovely," Brunswick 6179. Penned by Gus Arnheim, Harry Tobias, and Jules Le Mare, this ditty is a crooning effort that is so soft and dated that, in true retrospective, it just about disappeared from popular music within a few years. It is interesting that one of its credited writers, bandleader Gus Arnheim, found that two of his contract band members produced contemporary (1931) recordings of this ditty. Noted as a "battle of crooners," the Russ Columbo version, on Victor 22802, sounds almost identical to that of Crosby's. Or perhaps, Bing sounds much like Columbo? In any case, the stakes were high, as both crooners indeed would compete for contemporary audiences on film, radio, and records.
68. "I Apologize," Brunswick 6179. This overdone and sentimental vocal (penned by Al Hoffman and Al Goodheart), nevertheless, hits its mark for 1931.
69. "Now That You've Gone," Brunswick 6200. This ditty, penned by Gus Kahn and Ted Fiorito, finds some fine (1931) "boo-boo-booing."
70. "A Faded Summer Love," Brunswick 6200. The conventional lyrics, penned by Phil Baxter, find Crosby's vocal full of humming and a backing, as well as sounding mushy and overly full of sentiment. Perfect for 1931? (A contemporary Rudy Vallee version found Rudy himself crooning out better and softer vocal tones than earlier in his career, perhaps realizing that Bing, his onetime follower, had a better voice?)
71. "Goodnight Sweetheart," Brunswick 6203. Russ Colombo's vocals are just a tad higher than Bing's. A low-voiced baritone comparison? And what about the (British) Al Bowlly's crooning job?
72. "Too Late," Brunswick 6203. This ditty penned by Sam Lewis and Victor Young is slow and full of sentimental mush that somehow works. This ditty was also the first theme song for the contemporary 1931 Crosby program *Fifteen Minutes with Bing Crosby,* eventually to become sponsored by Cremo Cigars. (Other contemporary versions found renderings as by Mildred Bailey and Buddy Lane.)

Note: Between the time Bing left Gus Arnheim and The Cocoanut Grove, in a dispute over money, missing shows, etc., Bing was offered to make some film shorts with the legendary Mack Sennet. The visual image of the young crooner, despite stupid story lines, had much impact on the Depression-weary public, and he was more successful than Rudy Vallee had been earlier. Most record companies had also crashed since the stock market crash of 1929, and record sales dwindled from over a hundred million sold in 1929 to six million by 1932. Bing was unaffected. His new crooning style shocked critics of the era and replaced most "tenor" types. (Indeed, tenor Dick Powell would enjoy success in film musicals and radio, yet his contemporary recordings were pale in sales to those of Crosby). The solo recording entities who did hang on to success included the likes of Louis Armstrong, Connie Boswell, Ruth Etting, Ethel Waters, and Kate Smith. These artists also used the "crooner" style, to their advantage. Indeed, these crooners, or those who adapted crooning, became masters at the (newly) invented microphone, the great boost to electric recording. The vocalist whose original description was one of vulgar and improper language became the rage (and hope) of the fledging recording and film industry, and resulted in huge earnings from the live radio broadcasts! While the Depression cut into the ability of Americana to purchase records and see films, they had the ability to hear crooners over the airwaves for free. It should be noted that while Bing did find some new and stiff competition in the likes of Russ Columbo, Ozzie Nelson and (Afro-American) Harlan Lattimore, his record sales still put him far ahead of *all* his crooning rivals.

73. "Where the Blue of the Night Meets the gold of the day," Brunswick 6226. This ditty replaced "I Surrender, Dear" as Bing's theme song, probably because of the fact that it was not recorded for Brunswick. The writer credits include Roy Turk, Fred Ahlert, and Bing himself. This was all very odd. Moreover, Russ Columbo, a major rival (and a soundalike, in many noted recordings, also recorded this ditty, possibly even before Crosby, on Victor 22867). Both versions sound almost identical, and it's not a stretch to question even Crosby's name as a credited writer. In any case, this sappy and sentimental classic would remain a Crosby classic despite Columbo's excellent effort. In future years, in addition to radio and even later television appearances, Bing would use this ditty effectively. (Later Decca rerecordings of this ditty (perhaps) distract for many the key elements of Crosby's brilliant rise.)
74. "I'm Sorry, Dear," Brunswick 6226. The flip of "Where the Blue of the Night," penned by Anson Weeks and Harry Tobias, is crooned out well. Should it, nevertheless, be confused with the previous "I Apologize"?
75. "Dinah," Brunswick 6226. This recording *shares* credit with the Mills Brothers, who were the first popular black group. This recording of the original Ethel Waters classic is a very different update. Indeed, the very hip Mills Brothers rave it up in tempo and vocal style. After throwing slang Afro-Americanisms like dice, Bing joins in the fun, with an excellent scat vocal of his own. This truly exciting and innovative recording, indeed, proves Crosby's debt to black culture, as well as a successful, fresh adaptation for his own vocal style. Bing may also be credited with some contemporary 1932 musical integration, as he indeed holds his own with a dynamite vocal performance of the Mills Brothers. This very segregated era had demanded that (white) folk were not supposed to sound or act like this. It is, in true retrospective, also a bit ironic that the same ditty that had found people questioning Ethel Waters's color—on her original version of "Dinah" (Columbia) in 1925—could honestly question Bing's own racial identity, found in this drastically raved-up version.
76. "Can't We Talk It Over," Brunswick 6240. This dreary song ditty's (original flip side of "Dinah") only redeeming quality is that Bing was able to keep his spirits up while brilliantly embellishing lyrics, despite Helen Crawford's organ backing, as penned by Ned Washington and Victor Young.
77. "I Found You," Brunswick 6248. Penned by J. Campbell, R. Connelly, and R. Noble, this ditty was also recorded (with only a pipe organ backing) along with "Can't We Talk It Over." Sadly, Bing's good vocal is (almost) wasted on a song that is perhaps best to be heard as a guy finding hardly any sun and many clouds until he finally finds her. Does the dreary organ backing indicate a funeral parlor meeting?
78. "Snuggled on Your Shoulders," Brunswick 6248. Bing's soft baritone on this ditty, penned by J. Young and C. Lombardo, remains effective.

79, 80. "St. Louis Blues," Brunswick 20105. This classic Handy recording had already been recorded by many, which included an early Marion Harris best seller. It had, more so, already been defined by Bessie Smith's acoustic rendering in 1925. Fortunately, Bing (who was already familiar with Duke at least since "Three Little Words") was able to run into Duke (also a fellow Brunswick recording artist in 1932) andput his own claims upon it. Indeed, the mood created by the Duke's arrangement is superb. Marking time, Bing produces a surprisingly strong vocal in response. In true retrospective, despite many other fine Brunswick recordings, with fine backing orchestrations, this recording is a recording event in itself. Released as a rare 12-inch entity, there were at least two takes issued, differing only slightly. Both indeed reflect high dramatic quality, with a Crosby vocal loaded with prowess and pain. Indeed, this (perhaps unplanned) release, another racial oddity for its era, remains a classic recording in any era! (Take A or B?)

81. "Starlight," Brunswick 6259. It ain't "Stardust," but it is indeed a well-done vocal, penned by Joe Young and Bernice Petkere.
82. "How Long Will It Last," Brunswick 6259. Bing's question is a common one. His commitment to this sad tale of woe, penned by Max Lief and Joseph Meyer, despite its sappy lyrics, improves upon it.
83. "Love, You Funny Thing," Brunswick 6268. Bing's medium-tempo vocal skills are very evident, as he explains it all, in this ditty penned by Roy Turk and Fred E. Ahlert.
84. "My Woman," Brunswick 6268. Crosby must have taken himself very seriously here, as this plea for his "woman," is almost a blues entity. Penned by Max Wortell, Irving Wallman, and Bing himself, this sad tale finds a sensuous and cool vocal and reveals an attitude that is indeed personal. Yup. Bing actually had many sexual overtones in 1932.
85. "Shadows on the Window," Brunswick 6276. This classic, penned by Ned Washington and Victor Young, about consenting adults still remains true. This ditty should also be noted for a mature subject, like a few others, hidden among novelties and run-of-the-mill love songs. While torch songs are generally a given for contemporary female vocalists, this one should have been given a nod of approval.
86. "Shine," Brunswick 6276. Another fine vocal with the Mills Brothers again results in something unique. Is this somewhat a stereotype, or is this ditty (penned by Ford Dabney, Cecil Mack, and Lew Brown) more than novel? While a contemporary Louis Armstrong version also "shines," this recording has more firepower. Indeed, the highly rhythmic Mills Brothers' vocals find Bing matching them in a fantastic vocal scat exchange.
87. "Paradise," Brunswick 6285. This title penned by Gordon Clifford and Naio Herb Brown is a perfect fit for Bing. Does Russ Columbo's crooning version also fit? What a battle!
88. "You're Still in My Heart," Brunswick 6285. The backup musicians seem to indicate the guitar of Eddie Lang and the violin of Joe Venuti. This dated vocal, penned by Jack Yellen and Dan Dougherty, seems to be all about hearts and flowers, which covers the subject matter well enough. As a further note, this ditty indeed sounds like a (lost) later-1950s' television show theme. Or at least familiar?

89., 90. "Gems from George White's Scandals," Brunswick 2001. It was a 12-inch, 78 rpm release of a contemporary Broadway entity, penned by Lew Brown and Ray Henderson. Bing was part of a contemporary 1932 (Brunswick) recording artist stable, ready to claim songs from George White's original production which starred Rudy Vallee—indeed still a (recording) rival and onetime vocal "crooning" influence. After putting the Boswell Sisters, the Mills Brothers, and the (horrid) Frank Munn aside, Bing does a fine, if limited, crooning job on (a.). "Life Is Just a Bowl of Cherries," and (b.) "The Thrill Is Gone."

91. "Face the Music Medley," Brunswick 20106. This highly unusual recording, penned by Irving Berlin, features Broadway entities in a collective shot at creativity. The orchestra is that of Victor Young, one of Brunswick's house bands, and also one that would subsequently follow Bing and his Brunswick producer Jack Kapp to Decca,

a bit later. Included as "Soft Lights and Sweet Music," this classic found Bing very much interested and committed to the eventual 12-inch Brunswick release.

92. "Lawd, You Made the Night Too Long," Brunswick 20109. This ditty penned by Sam. M. Lewis and Victor Young somehow did not feature Victor Young's backing, but it featured the diverse and (black) bandleader, Don Redman. With some fine vocal harmony, the added vocals of the Boswell Sisters require this 12-inch recording to be heard on both sides. Indeed, this somewhat haunting arrangement and subject matter created an interesting sound. So did Bing's own vocal, which again demonstrates his total vocal commitment to contribute to something different and unusual. Indeed, this ditty scores! Was the differing-in-style contemporary Louis Armstrong version better? Listen and compare!
93. "Lazy Day," Brunswick 6306. This ditty, penned by Grace Kahn, Gus. Kahn, Eric Maschwitz and George Posford, should not be confused with the likes of the Irving Berlin classic "Lazy." This somewhat folk ballad, which speeds up in tempo, should, in turn, not be negated. Indeed, a fine backup orchestra, led by Isham Jones, is capable of keeping good time for some fine crooning. (A contemporary Ruth Etting rendering, more so, finds good vocal comparisons.)
94. "Happy-Go-Lucky-You," Brunswick 6306. Bing's intimate interpretation of lyrics, penned by Jack Murray, Al Goodhart, and Al Hoffman, saves this otherwise stupid title.
95. "Let's Try Again," Brunswick 6320. Again Bing's personal and intimate attitude bends this "adult" entity, penned by bandleader Isham Jones and Charles Newman, into something special.
96. "Sweet Georgia Brown," Brunswick 6320. The original vocal of this Ethel Waters classic (1925), had indeed been fast and uninhibited. This fine "electric" update, with the (very) respected Isham Jones Orchestra, provided a bigger backing sound. Indeed, this fast-paced ditty also found Crosby more than willing to jump into some fine rhythmic tempos. Some fine scatting should also be noted, and this jazzy vocal is no fluke. (Note: At least a few Brunswick takes were issued.)
97. "Cabin in the Cotton," Brunswick 6329. This simple ditty is crooned out to perfection. Penned by Mitchell Parish and Frank S. Perkins, it was not used in the contemporary film of the same name.
98. "With Summer Coming On," Brunswick 6329. This overly sentimental ditty, penned by Roy Turk and Fred Ahlert, indeed defines "overly sentimental." Indeed, a contemporary version by (black) crooner Harlan Lattimore, on Columbia 2671-D, at least matches Crosby in commitment and vocal style. Listen and compare!
99. "Love Me Tonight," Brunswick 6351. While this title is dated, this pleading for love, including sex, is not overblown. Penned by Ned Washington, Victor Young, and Bing himself, another "adult" message is indeed effective. So indeed is some fine jazzy backup by bandleader Lennie Hayton. (This 1932's ditty is not to be confused with a contemporary 1930's ditty penned by Rodgers and Hart, which was also a film title.)
100. "Some of These Days," Brunswick 6351. While this classic found origins in Sophie Tucker's acoustic rendering in 1911, this ditty, penned by (Afro-American) Shelton Brooks, finds, in Bing's own high-powered (1932) scatting, a redefined classic!
101. "Waltzing in a Dream," Brunswick 6394. While waltz music is not covered much in this book, this schmaltzy title, penned by Ned Washington, Victor Young, and Bing himself and backed by the fine bandleader Isham Jones, is crooned out well enough.
102. "Please," Brunswick 6394. This ditty title, penned by Leo Robin and Ralph Rainger, was used in Bing's first full-length feature film *The Big Broadcast*, as well as in a film

short of the same name. Indeed, Bing's crooning is fine, and this plea just had to "please" much of his contemporary 1932 female audience!

103. "Here Lies Love," Brunswick 6406. This ditty, again penned by Leo Robin and Ralph Rainger, was also featured in *The Big Broadcast*. While indeed a fine and deep crooning job, its own implications about suicide, found in the film, is stupidly understood.
104. "How Deep Is the Ocean," Brunswick 6406. This Irving Berlin-penned ditty remains a classic as well as a huge winner for a very involved Crosby crooning effort. Indeed all subsequent renderings, including a contemporary Rudy Vallee rendering, lack Bing's sensitive vocal commitment. Listen and compare.
105. "Brother, Can You Spare a Dime," Brunswick 6414. This Broadway entity from *New Americana* deals with the hard times of the Depression. Penned by the likes of E. Y. Harburg and Jay Gorney, its comment on the social impact upon Americana was indeed more than true. In fact, this ditty perhaps described, with bare and vital lyric, without sugarcoating, much reality. Recorded by contemporary Rudy Vallee, on Columbia 2725, with stirring opening commentary, this ditty also became a much-appreciated, best-selling entity. While Vallee's version was indeed no slouch, Crosby's approach and attitude is also a most sensitive and believable rendering. In true retrospective, this ditty became a Crosby classic, forever describing the hard times of Great Depression, as they really were.
106. "Let's Put out the Lights and Go to Sleep," Brunswick 6414. The flip side of Bing's "Brother, Can You Spare a Dime" was penned by the likes of Herman Hupfeld. This return to myth and novelty, remains a lighthearted crooning job. So indeed is a novel contemporary Rudy Vallee version on Columbia 2715-D. Rudy's bolder lyrics say "bed," instead of Bing's "sleep." Interested?
107. "I'll Follow You," Brunswick 6427. Bing's boring plea is at least heard very well, as penned by Fred Turk and Fred E. Ahlert.
108. "Someday We'll Meet Again," Brunswick 6427. Like most Brunswick masters above, Bing is truly committed to become overly sentimental and, indeed, hits the heart on this ditty penned by Al Goodhart and Milton Ager. It is also worth it, perhaps, to speculate that this vocal performance is an emulation or an exact match for contemporary (black) crooner Harlan Lattimore. Moreover, the Lattimore version, as found on an Ed Lloyd release (Conqueror 8029), is just as committed. Just listen and compare!
109. "Just an Echo in the Valley," Brunswick 6454. This ditty penned by Reg Connelly, Jimmy Campbell, and Harry Woods was later included in the Crosby film *Going Hollywood*. While this stupid title also included equally dumb lyrics, Bing's crooning vocal (again) saves a song!
110. "A Ghost of a Chance," Brunswick 6454. While the word "tender" is perhaps another word for a sissy's relations regarding the male gender, contemporaries of Croby's also knew that he could box. As yet another example of crooning, this classic ditty (penned by Ned. Washington, Victor Young, and Bing Crosby) is sung tenderly and with commitment. (A contemporary Will Osborne release, with Will performing his own vocal, is also crooned out well.) Listen and compare.
111. "It's Within Your Power," Brunswick 6454. While these lyrics are indeed a bore, this soft crooning job is good. Penned by Mack Gordon and Harry Revel, this ditty may at least hold the attention of its listeners until sleep is induced.
112. "Street of Dreams," Brunswick 6464. Crosby returned to reality and life when he took on this ditty by Sam. M. Lewis and Victor Young. Indeed, the Great Depression had

had its own dreams, as well as some implied drug addiction, perhaps. Just listen to this very sensitive crooning effort!

113. "You're Getting to Be a Habit with Me," Brunswick 6472. This ditty penned by Al Dubin and Harry Warren had been a film entity for tenor Dick Powell and subsequently for Bing. Backed by the hugely popular and contemporary (1932) Guy Lombardo Orchestra, this nifty crooning job casually notes the use of cocaine. While a bit over the top for later-century listeners, in true retrospective, except for perhaps musicians, Crosby's own message, unlike "Street of Dreams," cannot be in dispute. (A later Frank Sinatra version would redefine this ditty.)
114. "Young and Healthy," Brunswick 6472. Crosby again excels, as this mid-tempo vocal performance (penned by Dubin and Warren) full of youth and pep hits its mark of quality.
115. "You're Beautiful Tonight, My Dear," Brunswick 6477. The low-baritone vocal, penned by Joe Young and Carmen Lombardo, reeks of sentimentality and a solid bit of crooning.
116. "I'm Playing with Fire," Brunswick 6480. This Irving Berlin-penned ditty is actually below par for him. While this was indeed an oddity for Berlin, Bing's fine crooning job is not.
117. "Try a Little Tenderness," Brunswick 6480. Crosby's very tender and sensitive crooning job perhaps made something out of this mushy classic. Penned by Jimmy Campbell, Reg Connally, and Harry Woods, this much-emulated ditty also found a gender flip by a fine and contemporary Ruth Etting version. (This standard was to be recorded by many artists, including Otis Redding (Volt-141, light-years away in 1966) who gave a noted and radically funkier rock-era performance.)
118. "Linger a Little Longer in the Twilight," Brunswick 6491. While this ditty did not "linger" along as did "Try a Little Tenderness," alow penned by Jimmy Campbell, Reg Connally, and Harry Woods, Bing's masterful crooning truly lingers, along with a contemporary Ruth Etting version.
119. "I've Got the World on a String," Brunswick 6491. This classic, penned by Ted Koehler and Harold Arlen and originally written for New York City's Cotton Club would be the most emulated for the rest of the century. Cab Calloway's introduction of this ditty at the Cotton Club, more so, resulted in his recording, as released on Brunswick 6424. While Cab's vocal was done well enough, Bing's 1933 crooning version remains the most sensitive piece of work, as would a (much) later Frank Sinatra version. Indeed, Frank redefined this ditty so effectively that it would become closely associated with him and his art. In any case, while sounding much more dated, Crosby's vocal remains as a consistent reminder of what popular music became, largely because of his recordings.
120. "You've Got Me Crying Again," Brunswick 6515. This ditty penned by Charles Newman Isham Jones is full of sexual innuendo and frustration. (Many other contemporary versions exist; Connie Boswell and Ruth Etting sing it warmly, and less like Bing. A Lee Wiley version is cooler!)
121. "What Do I Care, It's Home," Brunswick 6515. If a listener of this ditty, penned by Roy Turk and Harry Smolin, can ignore the stupidity of this title, Bing's vocal becomes relevant.
122. "My Honey's Lovin' Arms," Brunswick 6525. Another frantic jazz performance, with the equally credited Mills Brothers, is creative enough. Penned by Harry Ruby and Joseph Meyer, this bit of jazzy slang may easily be defined as the "rap" of its era. While all this scatting remains something special, this Crosby and Mills Brothers

collaboration, in true retrospective, became indeed expected. As always, its listeners are not to be disappointed. Just listen!

123. "Someone Stole Gabriel's Horn," Brunswick 6533. This classic, penned by Ned Washington, Edgar J. Hayes, and Irving Mills, indeed finds Bing and the Dorsey Bothers Orchestra in fine, jazzy company. While dated, Crosby's vocal takes on a fast-paced challenge and even improves upon it.
124. "Stay on the Right Side of the Road," Brunswick 6533. As the original flip of "Someone Stole Gabriel's Horn," this ditty (penned by Rube Bloom and Ted Koehler) again offers some fine jazz by Crosby and the Dorsey Brothers. Indeed, at an even faster pace provided by the Dorseys, Bing's vocal answers the rhythmic challenge. Did Bing "rock"?
125. "Learn To Croon," Brunswick 6594. Backed by the fine contemporary Jimmy Grier Orchestra, this ditty (penned by Sam Coslow and Arthur Johnston) literally defined "crooning" itself. While it was indeed a contrived film title, Crosby's light and determined baritone does the song justice, as his croon delivers! In true retrospective due largely to a visual image from the contemporary (1933) film, *College Humor* this ditty may be seen and heard as a true representation of an era!
126. "Moonstruck," Brunswick 6594. Another "moon" song penned by Sam Coslow and Arthur Johnston that is more than its title indicates due to Bing's clever phrasing! Check it out? Using moonlight?
127. "Shadow Waltz," Brunswick 6599. This ditty, penned by Al Dubin and Harry Warren—despite its schmaltzy and dated title—is a slow and effective crooning effort, bettering any other contemporaries.
128. "I've Got to Sing a Torch Song," Brunswick 6599. Like "Shadow Waltz," this ditty (penned by Al Dubin and Harry Warren) was featured in the Dick Powell film *Gold Diggers of 1933*. Like any Dick Powell screen effort, what was found to be pleasant enough on-screen was to be even better recording fodder for Crosby's sensitive crooning. (It is also interesting to note one of male genders indeed using the term "torch song." While sharing recorded titles, before this time, female vocals by such entities as Ruth Etting, Libby Holman, Helen Morgan, and Ethel Waters had been somewhat associated with the term.)
129. "Down the Old Ox Road," Brunswick 6601. Penned by Sam Coslow and Arthur Johnston, this film entity could be found in Crosby's own 1933 *College Humor*. As a recording, moreover, this piece of excellent crooning remains a true classic and has to be noted as among Bing's best efforts. (Other versions would follow, including a fine update by Maxine Sullivan.)
130. "Blue Prelude," Brunswick 6601. This blues song is indeed poignant enough. Penned by Joe Bishop and Gordon Jenkins, this sad tale about a possible suicide again proves that this era had its serious moments. More so, a masterful Crosby vocal is not to be lost, nor are other subsequent versions, including a later excellent effort by Lena Horne.
131. "There's a Cabin in the Pines," Brunswick 6610. Not to be confused with the previous "Cabin in the Cotton," this bit of inspirational and dated crooning penned by Billy Hill remains a fine example of just what the term "crooning" was in 1933.
132. "I've Got to Pass Your House," Brunswick 6610. This ditty may indeed be a long "soap opera," as its adult theme, penned by Lew Brown, is effectively narrated by Crosby's fine vocal. (Note: Two Brunswick takes exist and both are done well.)

133. "I Would If I Could, but I Can't," Brunswick 6623. In this yet another wordy title, penned by Alan Grey, Mitchell Parish, and Bing himself, a sensitive Crosby vocal puts things together enough to link together a fine recording.
134. "My Love," Brunswick 6623. Bing's attempt at sensitivity and intimacy perhaps finds his vocal of this ditty (by Ned Washington and Victor Young) sounding a bit effeminate. While committed, it's also to his credit that he stumbles not over some stupid lyrics.

- The next three titles were all penned by Sam Coslow and Arthur Johnston for the Crosby film *Too Much Harmony.*

135. "Black Moonlight," Brunswick 6643. This ditty was introduced in the film by Kitty Kelly, noting racial differences. With what may be considered confused, this rendering explains little. Bing's recording transcends the film and remains an artful Crosby effort, revealing a strong baritone.
136. "Thanks," Brunswick 6643. Perhaps this crooning job was a direct response to the previous recording, also a film entity, "Please?" In any case, this ditty also scores.
137. "The Day You Came Along," Brunswick 6644. Crosby gets a bit husky but remains focused. (Judith Allen rendered this ditty in the film).
138. "I Guess It Had to Be That Way," Brunswick 6644. A strong effort that works well.
139. "The Last Round-Up," Brunswick 6663. Crosby croons out a creditable "cowboy" classic, oddly a contemporary Broadway entity (penned by Billy Hill), however dated. (Other current and notable (1933) releases found a George Olsen release with a Joe Morrison vocal as well as a Gene Autry release, which invite many ears to a very much gone idiom.)
140. "Home on the Range," Brunswick 6663. While this (traditional) ditty is far from hip and had more to do with Americana in the 1800s, it nevertheless did have something to do with contemporary (1933) culture. While it's obvious that Crosby's own (Brunswick) recording (credited as "Arr. David W. Guion") sparked new interest, the contrived "singing cowboy" found in rodeo, Broadway, and (especially) in (1930s) Western films found (for Crosby and others) even more recording fodder to record and sell. It could also be a fact that the newly elected President Franklin D. Roosevelt, naming his favorite song ditty, chose "Home on the Range."

More so, this ditty was not a contrived song ditty, as most were, including Broadway's "The Last Round-Up." As myth and fact collide, the song did indeed find its way for early settlers of America in the Old West. As "My Western Home," perhaps this ditty may have been written down as a poem by a Dr. Brewster M. Higley, and the music may have been penned by a Daniel E. Kelly in the 1870s? And who was Crosby's record-noted David W. Guion (already) mentioned above? There are also tales of this ditty—as "A Home on the Range"—being sung by an (unaccredited) Afro-American saloon keeper of the early century. In any case, Bing's own 1933 (Brunswick) release of "Home on the Range," backed with "The Last Round-Up," put him in league with the likes of Gene Autry. He would subsequently rerecord this same ditty for Decca (which is *not* as good), along with many subsequent contrived western songs penned especially for folks in (films) seen wearing hats and guns, achieving great success, and adding to the myth.

- The next five titles are film entities all penned by the team of Arthur Freed and Nacio Herb Brown for *Going Hollywood.* Backing orchestration is provided by Lennie Hayden.

141. "Beautiful Girl," Brunswick 6694. While a bit fluff, this crooned-out ditty also defines fine singing.
142. "After Sundown," Brunswick 6694. Perhaps this contrived ditty just could be influenced by a Spanish or Mexican ballad? Crosby's crooning, a bit stretched, indeed much like "The Last Round-Up," fails not.
143. "We'll Make Hay While the Sun Shines," Brunswick 6695. Bing's mid-tempo vocal still shines.
144. "Temptation," Brunswick 6695. This tenor-type rendering was perhaps Al Jolson type material, or was Bing also sounding loud? Bing does pull it off! (Later, others, including the likes of Perry Como, would attempt to emulate Crosby's fine original.)
145. "Our Big Love Scene," Brunswick 6696. Yes. This "big love scene" is a bit much. Crosby, moreover, a "show-off," hits all the right notes, as this crooning job is for real.
146. "We're a Couple of Soldiers," Brunswick 6696. This Harry Woods-penned ditty is OK despite some stupid lyrics. A bootlegged outtake, however, is far better and reviewed later in the text.
147. "Let's Spend an Evening at Home," Brunswick 6724. The somewhat quirky ditty, penned by the likes of Harry Barris and Ralph Freed, is betrayed not by Bing's bright vocal.
148. "Did You Ever See a Dream Walking?" Brunswick 6724. Bing "answers" his own question? Penned by Mack Gordon and Harry Revel, this ditty, despite a possible pun, finds Bing at his (fluffy) best at this type of material.
149. "Shadows of Love," Brunswick 6794. Bing's mood indeed projects "shadows." Penned by the likes of Alvin S. Kaufman., Mildred Kaufman, and Mickey Kippel, this dated vocal expression, while a bit over the top in lyric content, still scores.
150. "Little Dutch Mill," Brunswick 6794. This ditty penned by Ralph Freed and Harris Barris is a very simple example of a contrived ethnic location. Somehow, it all works.
151. "Love Thy Neighbor," Brunswick 6852. This bit of mush (penned by Gordon and Revel) was introduced in the Crosby film entity *We're Not Dressing*. While this may also be noted as mushy crooning, it is all done well.
152. "Riding Around in the Rain," Brunswick-6852. In a husky baritone vocal, Bing's "ride" in medium-tempo timing, penned by Gene Austin and Carmen Lombardo, is worth taking despite the weather. (It is also worth noting Gene Austin's own (original) contemporary recording, in comparison with Bing's version.)
153. "She Reminds Me of You," Brunswick 6853. Yes, Bing's vocal performance lifts this ditty, penned by Mack Gordon and Harry Revel, despite its mushy lyrics.
154. "May I," Brunswick 6853. One just may like this ditty (penned by Mack Gordon and Harry Revel) that is full of the kind of sentimental fluff, at mid-tempo, that Bing was just so good at!
155. "Goodnight, Lovely Little Lady," Brunswick 6854. This ditty penned by Mack Gordon and Harry Revel was featured in the film *We're Not Dressing*. While this recording does not refer to it, the actual film demanded of Bing to sing it to a bear. (Who says that light-years later Elvis made stupider flicks?)
156. "Once in a Blue Moon," Brunswick 6854. This ditty, penned by Mack Gordon and Harry Revel, finds Bing's vocal a bit overdone.

157. "Straight from the Shoulder," Brunswick 6936. At last! A ditty penned by Mack Gordon and Harry Revel that's a cut above the rest! This is, indeed, a medium-tempo Crosby classic, again defining popular music of 1934.
158. "Love in Bloom," Brunswick 6936. This ditty, penned by Leo Robin and Ralph Rainger, was to be adapted by comic Jack Benny for his popular contemporary (1934) radio program. Benny would, more so, keep it as a "theme" in 1950s' television, becoming very much known to many baby boomers. Crosby's original vocal, moreover, remains a true crooner classic that got sidelined (by Benny). So, indeed, did a fine backing by Irving Aaronson (1934).
159. "Give Me a Heart to Sing to," Brunswick 6953. This ditty, penned by Ned Washington, Victor Victor Young, and Maxon F. Judell, had originally been introduced by the likes of contemporary diva Helen Morgan. Bing's crooning job is strong. So indeed is another crooning effort from yet another contemporary diva, Ethel Waters.
160. "I'm Hummin', I'm Whistling, I'm Singing," Brunswick 6953. This (very) stupid title, penned by Gordon and Revel, is at least done well.

Note: The above title, no. 160, signals the end of Bing's association with Brunswick in mid-1934. Many of these original titles had been and would be continued to be issued on Brunswick and the subsidiary Banner, Conqueror, Harmony, Melotone, Okeh, Oriole, Perfect, Silvertone, and Vocalion (American record company labels). While all titles are original, many hard-core collectors listened for differing "A" takes or "B" takes. When Brunswick's producer Jack Kapp switched to join the new label from England, called "Decca," he took Bing, Ethel Waters, the Mills Brothers, the Boswell Sisters, and others with him. Most hard-core Bing Crosby collectors will always point to the Brunswick period (1931-34) as Crosby's zenith. While this is indeed the case for jazz and vocal influence, the early Decca "sunburst" label releases did provide Bing with some interesting releases.

➢ Decca-Sunburst Label Picks

161. "Just a Wearing for You," Decca 100. Recorded on side One of the first Decca release, this already old acoustical age ditty, penned by Carrie Jacobs Bond and Framk L. Stanton, is crooned out reasonably enough.
162. "I Love You Truly," Decca 100. This flip side of Bing's first Decca 78 finds him committed to a truly dull song ditty from earlier in the century, penned by Carrie Jacobs Bond. (For those baby boomers of the latter century and for those after, this ditty may be familiar as heard in the later (1946) Jimmy Stewart Christmas film classic *It's a Wonderful Life,* sung by Ward Bond and Frank Faylon, as seen on television more than once a year.)
163. "Someday Sweetheart," Decca 101. Bing projects a crooning job on this classic, penned by Reb and John Spikes, from the 1920s. Among others, perhaps the acoustic Alberta Hunter version gives Bing a run for his money? Or perhaps a Gene Austin version ain't bad? In any case, in comparisons, Crosby was, indeed, no slouch. Just listen!
164. The Moon Was Yellow," Decca 179. This ditty penned by Fred E. Arlert and Edgar Leslie is very good recording fodder, and Bing, in an almost operatic crooning job, cleverly demonstrates how good he can be! (Frank Sinatra would also, much later, record it very well.) Bing or Frank?
165. "The Very Thought of You," Decca 179. Mmm. Is this better than Al Bowlly's original vocal? It's obvious that the (British) Al Bowlly successfully sought to emulate

Bing, although Bing is fully committed in his version. Perhaps Bing was impressed with Bowlly's recording? Or was a contemporary Billie Holiday version, in a jazzy mood (not sounding like Bing) better? Listen and learn.

166. "Two Cigarettes in the Dark," Decca 245. From the film *Kill the Story*, which Bing did not appear in, this ditty (penned by Paul Frances Webster and Lew Pollack) seems to define actual cigarette sex? Surprisingly, Bing did record this stupid song ditty and, more so, improved upon it. Or is his excellent vocal a form of mockery? Or perhaps a rare soft crooning job from Alberta Hunter, as found on a contemporary (British) release from Jack Jackson?
167. "With Every Breath I Take," Decca 309. This crooner classic, penned by Leo Robin and Ralph Ranger, finds Bing very committed. More so, a subsequent Buddy Clark release was founded upon this recording. (Much later, Frank Sinatra would record an excellent version). Bing, Buddy, or Frank?
168. "Maybe I'm Wrong Again," Decca 309. It's a good bet that Bing's radio crooning on the contemporary (1934) *Woodberry* program led him to record this ditty penned by Jack Bennett and Jo Trent.
169. "June in January," Decca 310. This crooning job became yet another crooner classic (penned by Leo Robin and Ralph Rainger), which Bing would also introduce as an original in his film entity *Here Is My Heart*. While much emulated, despite its age, the hearing of this flawless Crosby vocal may be considered vintage.
170. Love Is Just Around the Corner," Decca 310. This fast-paced novelty, penned by the likes of Leo Robin and Lewis Gensler for the Crosby film entity *Here Is My Heart*, again betrays Bing's own masterful knowledge of lyrics and just how to use it properly.
171. "It's Easy to Remember," Decca 391. Both Richard Rodgers and Lorenzo Hart penned this ditty for the Crosby film *Mississippi.* Crosby, more so, finds it an effective crooning job that is sensitive and "easy."
172. "Down by the River," Decca 392. Perhaps crying and sentiment is a bit too much? If so, this crooning job of this ditty (penned by Rodgers and Hart) indeed defines that sort of stuff! Just listen.
173. "Soon," Decca 392. Bing's emotions are a bit slow-paced as he effectively croons out this emotional ringer penned by Rodgers and Hart.
174. "I Wished on the Moon," Decca 543. This ditty, penned by Ralph Ranger and Dorothy Parker, is a refined crooning job. (A bootleg version is even better.)
175. "Two for Tonight," Decca 543. It's Bing's crooning that made this otherwise silly song ditty that was also his contemporary (1934) film title (penned by Harry Revel and Mack Gordon), worth it.

The following four song ditties were also part of the soundtrack penned by Gordon and Revel.

176. "I Wish I Were Alladin," Decca 547. This mid-tempo novelty is the best song from *Two for Tonight*!
177. "From the Top of Your Head," Decca 547.
178. "Without a Word of Warning," Decca 548.
179. "Takes Two to Make a Bargain," Decca 548.
180. "Red Sails in the Sunset," Decca 616. Crosby's fine journey, penned by Jimmy Kennedy and Hugh Williams, is weirdly and effectively crooned out.
181. "Moonburn," Decca 617. Yet another "moon" song? Penned by Hoagy Carmichael and Edward Heyman, Bing's bright vocal (in mid-tempo) does not disappoint or fail!

182. "On Treasure Island," Decca 617. This ditty penned by Joe Burke and Edgar Leslie had also become a huge best seller as a (1935) Tommy Dorsey release, featuring a bright vocal by Edythe Wright, on Victor 25144. In comparison with Bing's croon, it's all good listening!
183. "Silent Night," Decca 621. Seasonal and secular.
184. "Adeste Fideles," Decca 621. This and the above are fully credited to Bing as vocalist. It is interesting to compare these recordings to Bing's re-recordings of the same titles in the 1940s, as Bing is in better voice in 1935 (seasonal and secular).

Note: The earlier (1928) 12-inch 78 rpm Paul Whiteman release on Columbia 50098-D as "Christmas Melodies" perhaps found Bing in chorus with band members (including Harry Barris, Jack Fulton, Charles Gaylord, and Austin Young) singing "Noel" and "Silent Night? It *had* been considered his vocal by many discographers and collectors for years! Still, it's a hard call! Is it? This author is (still) not sure!

185. "My Heart and I," Decca 631. A fine ditty penned byLeo Robin and Frederick Hollander that had been crooned out in the contemporary (1936) film *Anything Goes*.
186. "Would You," Decca 756. Oddly, this crooned-out ballad, penned by Arthur Freed and Nacio Herb Brown, was found to be heard in the contemporary (1936) Clark Gable and Jeanette MacDonald film *San Francisco.* Moreover, Bing may be heard, but not seen, in the film! Get it?
187. "Robins and Roses," Decca 791. This ditty penned by Edgar Leslie and Joe Burke is OK. (The outtake, later reviewed, is better.)
188. "It Ain't Necessarily So," Decca 806. Bing finds Broadway's "Porgy and Bee" more than great recording fodder, as his (vocal) attention attempts to define this ditty!
189. "I Got Plenty of Nothin, '" Decca 806. Another *Porgy and Bess* entity that Bing's vocal abilities do not fail!
190. "I'm an Old Cowhand," Decca 871. This Johnny Mercer-penned novelty gets a good ride from Bing's vocal with Jimmy Dorsey and Orchestra (as Jimmy had split with his brother Tommy). This best-selling ditty, also a somewhat contrived excuse to "swing," somehow works, in spite of its silly lyrics, defineds it. More so, this ditty had been introduced in the 1936 contemporary Crosby film *Rhythm on the Range*. As luck would have it, Bing's own exploitation of the Hollywood myth, was a success, becoming a profitable enterprise in "Gene Autry" territory!
191. "I Can't Escape from You," Decca 871. This crooning job, penned by Leo Robin and Richard A. Whiting, is superb recording fodder that Bing was (obviously) prepared for.
192. "The House Jack Built for Jill," Decca 905. A classy ditty penned by Leo Robin and Frederick Hollander also found Bing at his usual best

The following two ditties were originally penned by Jerome Kern and Dorothy Fields for the Fred Astaire and Ginger Rogers film *Swing Time*. More importantly, they feature a duet with Dixie Lee, Bing's wife. While *perhaps co*nsidered a bit highbrow, both Bing and Dixie (perhaps even mimicking Ginger as she was heard in the film) exhibit attitude and a fine novel approach. Indeed Dixie, not known as a vocalist, holds her own, as well as reveals herself as clever and witty.

193. "The Way You Look Tonight," Decca 907.
194. "A Fine Romance," Decca 907.

195. "Beyond Compare," Decca 912. This is another soft arrangement that succeeds. It was penned by Mort Green and former Rhythm Boy, Harry Barris.
196. "Me and the Moon," Decca 912. Another 'moon' song, penned by Walter Hirsch and and Lou Handman is a pleasant bit of mush.
197., 198. "Pennies from Heaven," Decca 947. This ditty was penned by Arthur Johnston and Johnny Burke, for the popular (1936) Crosby film of the same name. This original release (a.) was backed by the Georgie Stoll Orchestra and the best-known contemporary version of this classic crooning job. Indeed, this title itself found a Depression-weary public very much in tune with its initial message. Within a bit of contemporary time, this 1936 release was to find much emulation by others. No less impressive was a second Crosby version (b.). Released on Decca 15027, this rare 12-inch 78 rpm recording also featured the likes of Louis Armstrong and contemporary highbrow diva, Francis Langford, sharing vocals. Oddly, while Louis was also featured in the film, Francis Langford was not. Another oddity concerns the fact that while the Jimmy Dorsey Orchestra replaces the Georgie Stoll backing well enough, why indeed wasn't Louis Armstrong's Orchestra used? In any case, for all concerned, Bing, Louis, and Francis all do justice for yet another definitive classic of the Depression era.
199., 200. "Pennies from Heaven Medley," Decca 15027. Bing and Frances Langford do a duet of "So Do I," as well as a vocal by Frances on "Let's Call a Heart a Heart" and by Louis, on another ditty (penned by Johnson and Burke) in the film, "Skelton In The Closet". Not bad for a flip side of the 12-inch "Pennies from Heaven."
201. "Let's Call a Heart a Heart," Decca 947.
202. "One Two, Button Your Shoe," Decca 948. This light and novel ditty—also from *Pennies from Heaven*—with the Georgie Stoll Orchestra, is effective enough.
203. "So Do I," Decca 948, backed by the Georgie Stoll Orchestra.
204. "Blue Hawaii," Decca 1175. This is the same title that Elvis Presley recorded and starred in, in the film *Blue Hawaii*, light-years away (in 1961). This ditty was penned originally for the Crosby film *Waikiki Wedding* in 1937 by the already familiar Leo Robin and Ralph Rainger, and Bing provides a masterful crooning job on (this) contrived bit of Hawaii. It is, more so, interesting to speculate if Presley's equally impressive vocal (on the RCA Victor album LSP 2426) was influenced by Bing's older recording?

(It is also of interest to note that "Blue Hawaii" had been only a flip side to a Harry Owens-penned ditty "Sweet Leilani," also to be found in the Crosby film. While a huge contemporary best-selling success, in true retrospective, this mushy vocal, is *not* a noted pick in this review!

205. "What Will I Tell My Heart," Decca 1185. This is another classic soft croon penned by Peter Tinturin and Jack Lawrence.
206. "Too Marvelous for Words," Decca 1185. Excellent!
207. "I Never Realized," Decca 1186. It does not take much time to realize how fine this Cole Porter-penned ditty is crooned?
208. "Moonlight and Shadows," Decca 1186. Perhaps this ditty, penned by Leo Robin and FrederickHollander, had been written for Bing yet ended up in a Dorothy Lamour film *The Jungle Princess*. Dorothy's own contemporary (1937) vocal, on Brunswick 7829, is also done well.
209. "Never in a Million Years," Decca 1210. Crosby croons out yet another ditty with class (penned by Gordon and Revel).

210. "Peckin'," Decca 1301. Bing, with the help of Jimmy Dorsey's arrangement, gets involved in a fine and contemporary jazz vocal. While Crosby is not given a lot, he accepts a limited role, which was as much as most contemporary up-and-coming band singers were given in 1937. Penned by the likes of Ben Pollack and Harry James, the original recording, on Variety 556—featuring some hard-playing and a vocal by Ben Pollack and the guys from the band—indeed provided Jimmy Dorsey an artistic challenge from a current rival bandleader. Along with Bing's vocal, Jimmy produced a fine recording, even better than others, including Pollack's.

- The following two ditties make the first association with the John Scott Trotter Orchestra, a house band for Decca and Crosby's radio work.

211. "The Moon Got in My Eyes," Decca 1375. Featured in the Crosby film *Double or Nothing*, the usual crooning job was becoming an expected product, as this ditty, penned by Johnny Burke and Arthur Johnston, indicates.
212. "Smarty," Decca 1375. This mid-tempo novelty, penned by Ralph Freed and Burton Lane, is, more so, almost smart enough for the witty Crosby.
213. "It's the Natural Thing to Do," Decca 1376. The emergence of "swing" in the mid-1930s, produced for Crosby—in this ditty penned by Johnny Burke and Arthur Johnston—a competitive and competent light "swing" dance-floor vehicle. More so, it succeeds!
214. "All You Want to Do Is Dance," Decca 1376. This flip side of "It's the Natural Thing to Do," also penned by Arthur Johnston andJohnny Burke, was featured in the Crosby film *Double or Nothing*. This ditty also scores, as an obvious appeal for contemporary (1937) dance floors and jukebox play, along with the (usual) film promotion. Does this Crosby-led vocal actually shake things up a bit?
215. "Remember Me," Decca 1451. While contemporary (1937) radio (rival) Kenny Baker pleasantly introduced it in the current film entity *Mr. Dodd Takes the Air*," this ditty (penned by Harry Warren and Al Dubin) should have been originally written for Bing. In true retrospective, did Bing's own crooning recording define it? Or a contemporary version by Dolly Dawn? Listen and forget?
216. "Bob White," Decca 1483. This is a dynamic duet between Bing and Connie Boswell, penned by Johnny Mercer and Bernie Hanighen. Its contemporary swing value, more so, also found huge assets, indeed, upon many dance floors.
217. "Basin Street Blues," Decca 1483. This original flip side of "Bob White" was, perhaps, intended to be a B-side for the more-played swing number. While this may be so, this less commercial side features excellent vocals for the already old Spencer Williams-penned classic. It is also more than obvious that Bing is clever enough to concede (on the recording) most of its gutsy rendering to Connie's (real) thick Southern accent!

Note: The following two ditties were penned by James Monaco and Johnny Burke for the (Crosby) film *Doctor Rhythm*, released in 1938.

218. "On the Sentimental Side," Decca 1648. Another original crooning job for Bing had (again) produced the usual recording fodder, noting a perhaps more interesting soft vocal from Billie Holiday, on Vocalion 3947, with a (jazz) guitar lead identified as by Freddie Green? Was the loss of Crosby's old buddy, Eddie Lang, affecting his choice

of recording fodder? Or did Lang, like Green, make it all sound better? Listen and learn!

219. "My Heart is Taking Lessons," Decca 1648. (Do la, la, la's almost ruined it?)
220. "The Moon of Manakoora," Decca 1649. This ditty, penned by Frank Loesser and Alfred Newman had originally been associated with actress Dorothy Lamour, as was "Moonlight and Shadows."

Note: The above noted Decca releases are blue "sunburst" releases found relevant enough to be noted within this book. By this time (1937), Bing had already become an American institution, and not directly affected by the newer musical trends such as "swing." Earlier followers found a bonanza of Crosby radio shows, musical films, and recordings flooding the market. A closer investigation indeed finds a new Crosby recording released weekly. This saturation of the market, which would continue into the early '50s, would keep Bing in the face of his public, but which public? The film ditties would find some fine recordings fully explored upon within this book. They would also include literally hundreds of other ditties which were not even to be used as trash can bottoms. In true retrospective, most of the films produced junk. While it must be acknowledged that the exploitation of ethnic (Irish), cowboy, Hawaiian, Broadway, and religious entities were best sellers, only the seasonal (Christmas) remain, if at all, relevant. (The exceptions will be noted as picks.)

Within time, the husky, clear baritone of Crosby's vocals would also be abandoned. While searching for a new style, it's obvious that Bing generally got lazy enough to enjoy a golf game rather than commit himself for recording anymore To be fair, there was just too much material, and Bing was committed to business first, and creativity, second. Perhaps his image, graced even upon milk cartons, as well as age got the best of him? Luckily, the duets with Connie Boswell and Louis Jordan and the shared and somewhat schmaltzy work with the Andrews Sisters, along with some (occasional) commitment, was enough. He had indeed dropped the drinking and drugs of his youth. He did have a family—what a guy!

- ➢ The following are plain blue label Decca releases.

221. "Don't Be That Way," Decca 1794. This huge Benny Goodman instrumental hit of the mid-1930s is bettered by Crosby's committed fast-paced vocal. While house bandleader John Scott Trotter is no match for Goodman, his arrangement for Bing's vocal results in a gem of a recording. Penned by Edgar Sampson, Mitchell Parish, and Benny Goodman himself, this ditty should have had some effect upon the very creative Goodman, when heard.
222. "Swing Low Sweet Chariot," Decca 1819. Bing croons out a (traditional) spiritual.
223. "I've Got a Pocketful of Dreams," Decca 1933. Penned by James V. Monaco and Johnny Burke, this fast-paced excuse for (1938) swing, however contrived, reflects more competitive dance floor fodder.
224. "A Blues Seranade," Decca 1933. The crooning job of this ditty (penned by Mitchell Parish and Frank Signorelli) ain't bad. (The bootlegged outtake is better.)
225. "Alexander's Ragtime Band," Decca 1887. This very fine duet with Connie Boswell also had a contemporary introduction by Eddie Cantor for the March of Dimes. In true retrospective, while times have changed since 1938, the worthy cause as well as the worth of this fine Irving Berlin-penned classic recording has not.
226. "Small Fry," Decca 1960. This novelty duet with Johnny Mercer was penned by Frank Loesser and Hoagy Carmichael. While all children must be safe, this clever lyric,

penned for the contemporary (1938) (Crosby) film *Sing You Sinners* is better heard on this recording. Hardly bad, the standards of the era found Crosby into lyrics of child abuse or more. Or perhaps, Bing's usual wit made it all sound so good? Indeed, a masterful and musical explanation by Crosby and Mercer. Just listen!

227. "You Must Have Been a Beautiful Baby," Decca 2147. Penned by Harry Warren and Johnny Mercer, for the contemporary Dick Powell film entity *Hard to Get*, this ditty was somewhat lost. Crosby's (defining) somewhat machine-gunned vocal is a pure delight, with another excellent crooning job that is indeed inspired. (This ditty also found Bing's own brother, Bob, providing him fine backing).
228. "Summertime," Decca 2147. George Gershwin and Du Bose Heyward should have been most glad indeed to hear this sober vocal with an equally creative Matty Malneck string backing for their brilliant Broadway production *Porgy and Bess*
229. "Sing a Song of Sunbeams," Decca 2359. Another silly film entity, penned by Johnny Burke and James Monaco for *East Side of Heaven,* somehow works well enough.
230. "Deep Purple," Decca 2374. Another interesting Matty Malneck string backup, indeed, adds to this version of this ditty penned by Mitchell Parish and Peter De Rose. Moreover, Bing must have again been interested, as his vocal, as in "Summertime," scores.
231. "Start the Day Right," Decca 2626. Another duet with Connie Boswell again provides Bing with more than creditable competition. More so, this clever lyric, penned by Al Lewis, Charles Tobias, and Maurice Spitalny is masterfully sorted out by both. Bing or Connie?
232. "An Apple for the Teacher," Decca 2640. This ditty, penned by James. V. Monaco and Johnny Burke, is a fast-paced bit of novelty, crooned out to perfection by Bing and Connie.
233. "Go Fly a Kite," Decca 2641. Or take a hike? This ditty, penned by James Monaco and Johnny Burke just had to "fit" in the contemporary (1939) film *The Star Maker*. Luckily, Bing was interested enough to provide a lighthearted vocal. Is it possible that Bing's kite gets lost in the wind? Just listen.
234. "What's New," Decca 2671. This ditty was revived in the later '70s by Linda Ronstead. While familiar to some baby boomers, it's interesting to note this 1938 Crosby version. Penned by Bob Haggart and Johnny Burke, Bing's very cool vocal style marks a definite break in style from the earlier (Brunswick) and (Decca) recordings. While his crooning efforts up to this point had demonstrated a more polished style, this newer vocal was a softer, dry approach, with less emphasis on emotion and more on mood. This one, for a start, scores. (A contemporary Nan Wynn version is also done well).
235. "In My Merry Oldsmobile," Decca 2700. This relic of a recording from the acoustic era had been resurrected for the contemporary (1939) Crosby film bio of songwriter (Gus Edwards) in *The Star Maker*. Oldsmobile must have been very pleased, noting that (about) ten years previously, Bing (as a Rhythm Boy), had been featured for ads for Chevrolet. Or who cares anymore?
236. "Ciribiribin," Decca 2800. This title was originally penned by bandleader Harry James, Jack Lawrence, and A. Pestalozza and was used by Harry James as his theme. A fine contemporary Harry James release found his vocalist, Frank Sinatra, on Columbia 35316, scoring well. This Crosby vocal, noting a good Joe Venuti arraignment, also finds Bing in good (vocal) spirits. Better, moreover, are Pattie, Maxine, and Laverne—the Andrews Sisters. Indeed this sister act, in true retrospective, found in the (already) old

Crosby, a fine mentor. For Bing, the sisters provided some much-needed youth. Indeed a fine beginning to a successful collaboration that also helped define the next decade!

237. "Between 18th and 19th on Chestnut Street," Decca 2948. This fast-paced novelty is almost rocking, with the added husky voice of Connie Boswell, on this ditty penned by Will Osborne and Dick Rogers.
238. "Too Romantic," Decca 2998. Penned for the film entity *The Road to Singapore* by Johnny Burke and James Monaco, this ditty is a mushy bit of crooning that scored. More importantly, it scored with Dorothy Lamour, as the first of the "road" films, along with Bing and comic, Bob Hope. What a team?

Another contemporary version found a young upstart vocalist who had left Harry James for the Tommy Dorsey Orchestra. Dorsey's subsequent release, on Victor 26500, featuring a Frank Sinatra vocal indicated for many contemporaries some (serious) and direct competition for Crosby. Were Frank's (1940) nasal vocal qualities an alternate for Bing?

239. "Sierra Sue," Decca 3133. This pristine bit of singing, already an old standard from before WWI, penned by Joseph B. Carey, at least found Crosby interested enough in his "newer," softer croon to produce a good recording. Nevertheless, it's still a good bet that sleep will be induced before it's done playing!
240. "Trade Winds," Decca 3299. Penned by Cliff Friend and Charles Tobias, another contrived Hawaiian entity works for Bing, although a subsequent and contemporary Tommy Dorsey release, featuring a Frank Sinatra vocal, is better.
241. "Rhythm on the River," Decca 3309. Penned by James Monaco and Johnny Burke, this contrived rhythmic ditty, reeking of formula for the title of the contemporary (Crosby) 1940 film, is done well enough.
242. "That's for Me," Decca 3309. As the original flip side of "Rhythm on the River," this (very) pleasant sounding ditty, penned by James Monaco and Johnny Burke, is also good enough for its listeners. (This title is not to be confused with the later ditty penned by Rodgers and Hammerstein from *State Fair*.)
243. "It Makes No Difference Now," Decca 3590. This (1940) contemporary attempt at Jimmie 'svis's original "country swing" classic, penned by Jimmie Davis and Floyd Tillman, finds Bing in good spirits, driven by a jazzy arrangement provided by Bob Crosby and His Orchestra.
244. "It's Always You," Decca 3636. As another ditty penned by Jimmy Van Heusen and Johnny Burke for another "road" film, *The Road to Zanzibar*," this ditty reeks less of "formula."(As already noted above, the younger contemporary band singer for Tommy Dorsey, Frank Sinatra, would subsequently record another version, indeed challenging Bing's excellent original! Listen to both!)
245. "Yes, Indeed," Decca 3689. This jazzy ditty, penned by Sy Oliver, is given a boost by Connie and Bing as well fine backing provided by Bob Crosby's Bob Cats. (A later decade would find Bill Haley and His Comets very much interested in this ditty.)
246. "Tea for Two," Decca 3689. The flip of "Yes Indeed" finds this ditty (penned by Vincent Youmans and Irving Caesar), an acoustic (1924) classic of Marion Harris, finally becoming redefined as performed by Bing and Connie.
247. "Good-bye, Little Darlin', Good-bye," Decca 3856. The ditty (penned by Gene Autry and Johnny Marvin) is well done.
248. "Be Honest with Me," Decca 3856. This classic, penned by Gene Autry and Fred Rose finds Bing's vocal honest enough.

249. "You Are My Sunshine," Decca 3952. Bing's vocal on this folk entity is perhaps just as good as previous claims upon it by Jimmie Davis and Gene Autry?
250. "Birth of the Blues," Decca 3970. Yet another excuse for a film title, using the word "Darkies" penned by Ray Henderson, Buddy G. De Sylva, and Lew Brown, from the 1920s, at least had some creditable Broadway history from *George White's Scandals of 1926*. Indeed, Harry Richmond's 1926 release, on Vocalion 15412, had been Jolson-inspired vocally, and a group rendering by the (then) contemporary Revelers, on Victor 20111, had differed. This fine (1940) update is backed by Jack Teagarden's Orchestra, which indeed provided Crosby some contemporary relevance. While Bing's vocal is far from flawed, his easy approach, aided greatly by Teagarden's backing, simply seeks to explain the contemporary (black) idiom with good intentions. Fair enough?
251. "The Waiter and the Porter and the Upstairs Maid," Decca 3970. This contrived novelty was penned by Johnny Mercer for the (Crosby) film *Birth of the Blues*. Vocal assistance from the likes of cast members Mary Martin and sometimes musician-vocalist Jack Teagarden, at least allow this wordy tale to become a bit humorous. Ever wonder how Eddie Rochester Anderson, the one Afro-American lead in the film, felt?
252. "The Whistler's Mother-In-Law," Decca 3971. This novelty is a campy, big band contrived delight, with Woody Herman, his Woodchoppers, and his vocalist, Murial Lane. Penned by Bert Stevens and Larry Wagner, this attempt at contemporary 1941 relevance, greatly aided by Woody, demonstrates Crosby's skills as a jazzy entity, considered by many as his best (unused) vocal asset.
253. "Let's All Meet at My House," Decca 4162. Another novelty, penned by Jimmy Van Heusen and Johnny Burke, is again further given creditability by Bing and fine backing by Woody Herman's Orchestra (a big deal in 1941)!
254. "Moonlight Cocktail," Decca 4184. This ditty, penned by Lucky Roberts, and Kim Gannon, later became for bandleader "Spike Jones" his theme song. Spike, in fact, was, like Woody Herman, a big deal in the 1940s. More so, as a Crosby vocal, this very much overlooked rendering by Crosby remains creditable!
255. "Conchita, Marquita, Lolita, Pepita, Rosita, Juanita Lopez," Decca-4343. Yes, this contrived novelty, penned by Jule Styne and Herbert Magidson, proves Crosby's (interested) flare for novelty as well as excellent elocution.

- The following are original black label Decca releases:

256. "I'm Thinking Tonight of My Blue Eyes," Decca 18316. It seems the Carter Family and, more recently, a contemporary Jimmie Davis rendering could provide Crosby some good recording fodder.
257. "I Want My Mama," Decca 18316. This traditional Mexican folk entity, also known as "Mama yo quir," finds Bing and Woody Hermann's backing in fine spirits.
258. "Got the Moon in My Pocket," Decca 18354. While this mid-tempo range is perfect for Bing, by this time (1942) it reeks of formula. Penned by Jimmy Van Heusen and Johnny Burke for the contemporary Bob Hope film *My Favorite Spy*, it's (still) pleasant enough 'moon' song.
259. "Walking the Floor over You," Decca 18371. This contemporary Ernest Tubb-penned classic is, more so, turned into something more! Along with Bob Crosby's Bearcats, Bing's clever phrasing of this novel honky-tonk tale ain't bad!

260. "When My Dreamboat Comes Home," Decca 18371. As the original flip of "Walking the Floor over You," this ditty, penned by C. Friend and D. Franklin, was even overlooked at the time of its release. More so, backed by Bob Crosby's Bearcats, Bing's vocal mode is in a fine, jazzy, and interested mood. (Years later, rocker Fats Domino would revive it.)
261. "Nobody's Darlin' but Mine," Decca 18391.

The following ten ditties, all penned by Irving Berlin, were featured in the 1942 Crosby film *Holiday Inn*. Contrived for a film plot about American holidays during WWII, this film, as well as these recordings, should note a musical that works. Indeed, Crosby is found to be at his best, despite some heavy competition from the artful Fred Astaire on the dance floor.

262. "Be Careful, It's My Heart," Decca 18424. This slow-crooning job remains effective.
263. "Happy Holiday," Decca 18424. The theme of this film strongly indicates the season between Christmas and New Year. As a recording, this ditty remains a Christmas classic.
264. "Easter Parade," Decca 18425. Mmm. This ditty had been around since (1933) when Clifton Webb had introduced it in Berlin's Broadway entity *As Thousands Cheer*. Webb's subsequent (stiff) recording did nothing for the song, neither did a better vocal by Gene Austin. While it's odd that Crosby had not recorded this ditty in (1933) in better voice, this (1942) rendering proves that if prepared, Bing could still produce an excellent recording, with a slightly different crooning style. The subsequent Judy Garland recording in 1948 would later challenge Bing's defining version! Bing or Judy?
265. "Abraham," Decca 18425. The weaker and the most contrived ditty of this soundtrack had found Crosby (in the film) in blackface. Luckily, this recording, about Abe Lincoln, betrays no such (modern) negative implications as Bing improves upon slightly weaker recording fodder.
266. "I've Got Plenty to Be Thankful For," Decca 18426. This mid-tempo crooning job is thankfully much less contrived than "Abraham," as Bing defines yet another (Irving Berlin) entity.
267. "Song of Freedom," Decca 18426. As a contrived ditty for the film and contemporary times, this WWII-era ditty was a patriotic salute to the armed forces. While (very) dated, its message was not.
268. "Lazy," Decca 18427. This update of the (1925) Al Jolson acoustic recording finds Crosby defining another classic by crooning.
269. "I'll Capture Your Heart," Decca 18427. A pedestrian duet with Fred Astaire and Decca studio vocalist Margaret Lenhart (dubbing for actress Marjorie Reynolds) somehow works.
270. "Let's Start the New Year Right," Decca 18429. Yes. Start the New Year with another defined (Berlin) classic, and everything will be OK.

271, 272, 273, 274. "White Christmas," Decca 18429. This ditty (a.), released originally in 1942, became an instant best seller. Indeed, more than the contemporary film *Holiday Inn*, this classic crooning job, since WWII, has become a huge part of Americana. Crosby's sensitive recording of this ditty would, in true retrospective, outsell all others, and subsequently, it would become identified with him more than any other song title he ever rendered. In fact, despite a fine contemporary version by Frank Sinatra, as well as perhaps a few unconventional versions through the years, including one by Elvis Presley, this ditty has always been designated as by "Bing Crosby" himself.

As a most curious sideline, Crosby tampered with his own success. Originally backed by the Ken Darby Singers and John Scott Trotter's Orchestra, his original success seemed to even question this original 1942 rendering. By 1947, using the same Ken Darby Singers and the John Scott Trotter Orchestra, Crosby again recorded his own classic and released it on (b.) Decca 23778. While he no longer had Russ Columbo to rival him, nor any other (1940s) versions to even challenge him, including those of Sinatra, Perry Como, and Rosetta Tharpe, it is truly amazing that his attempt to duplicate himself indeed lessens his own art. In fact, this newer version would also sell a million and was not even noted, by most, as a rerecording. A still later (1954) studio recording (c.), for the film (named after the song) *White Christmas,* at least betrays a rerecording. (d.) A slightly flawed original 1942 "A" take, once booted, is not bad at all.

275. "God Rest Ye Merry Gentlemen," Decca 18511. This Christmas entity, however traditional, would remain, in true retrospective, associated with Bing from 1942 and for the rest of the century.
276. "Moonlight Becomes You," Decca 18513. This contrived "moon song," penned by Van Heusen and Burke, was crooned very well out toward Dorothy Lamour in his film *Road to Morocco.*
277. "The Road to Morocco," Decca 18514. The simple duet, penned by Johnny Burke and James Van Heusen with Bob Hope is pleasant enough.
278. "Sunday, Monday or Always," Decca 18561. Penned by the already familiar Van Heusen and Burke for the film entity *Dixie*, this bit of mushy crooning at least defines "mushy" crooning?
279. "People Will Say We're in Love," Decca 18564. A fine duet, penned by Rodgers and Hammerstein, found Bing and the excellent Trudy Erwin, perhaps defining Broadway's *Oklahoma!* Frank Sinatra, and WWII very much interested in this fine recording.
280. "I'll Be Home for Christmas," Decca 18570. Was this ditty first known as "I'll Be Home for Christmas—Tho Just a Memory," as penned by Buck Ram in 1942? In any case, this subsequent (1943) ditty known as "I'll Be Home for Christmas—If Only in My Dreams" was found to be claimed by Buck Ram, Kim Gannon, and Walter Kent. More so, it was crooned out very carefully by Bing in the same year. With its obvious contemporary WWII-era implications, this ditty, in true retrospective, became a true classic—a popular entity (still) identified with Crosby.
281. "It Could Happen to You," Decca 18580. This ditty, penned byJames Van Heusen and Johnny Burke, was introduced by Dorothy Lamour in her (1944) contemporary film *And the Angels Sing.* Somehow, Bing got a hold of it and defined it.
282. "San Fernando Valley," Decca 18586. This simple ditty, penned by Gordon Jenkins, is a bit of mid-tempo country that Crosby seemed to be interested in. While Roy Rogers later had contemporary claims upon this Western farce, perhaps the "King of the Cowboys" had also found Bing's version something to start with?
283. "I'll Be Seeing You," Decca 18595. While Dick Todd had already given this prewar Broadway entity a Crosby croon, perhaps it was Frank Sinatra's contemporary (1940) rendering for Tommy Dorsey that had more depth as a recording? Bing's subsequent wartime (1944) version perhaps captured the moment? As very fine example of Bing's later crooning style that succeeds, his interested (defining) vocal is obvious.

(A contemporary (1944) reissue of Sinatra's recording (with Tommy Dorsey) would challenge Bing's recording, along with a version by Billie Holiday on the small Commadore label, which would subsequently challenge both Bing and Frank. Just listen.)

284. "Evelina," Decca 18635. Bing finds a way to produce a classic rendering of the ditty penned by Harold Arlen and E. Y. Harburg.
285. "There's a Small Hotel," V-Disc 700. As a general rule, this book does not deal with special noncommercial issues such as V-Disc (Victory Disc recordings) transcriptions broadcast for service personnel around the world. However, this rendering finds Crosby's crooning job of this classic ditty, penned by Rodgers and Hart (previously defined by Helen Ward on a 1936 Benny Goodman release on Victor 25363), perhaps the supreme exception?

Indeed, Bing is found to be extremely sensitive and emotional, and this performance at the USO benefit show is just too good to pass up. After an introduction by Bob Hope and Eddie Duchin at piano lead, Bing croons his heart out, with an audience response stunned by such inspired artistry! In true retrospective, this performance remains flawless. Sadly, it was not to be duplicated on regular commercial release. (Frank Sinatra would redefine it as a commercial recording in the 1950s.)

286. "Swinging on a Star," Decca 18597. Penned by Van Heusen and Burke, this very popular novelty became an instant classic. Introduced in the film *Going My Way*, it is yet another example of schmaltzy pop that succeeds! Crosby, more so, won a contemporary (1944) Academy Award for best actor as a singing priest, introducing this ditty to an (even) wider audience. While relevance is beyond even the brightest among us, this recording's appeal to the kiddies, as well as ethnic (Catholics), had a huge impact. (Did this recording also find supporting vocals by the Williams Brothers, which included the (later) popular vocalist Andy Williams as a child?)
287. "On the Aitcheson, Topeka and the Santa Fe," Decca 18690. A pop best seller in mid-tempo that works? Yup. This train ride was also taken by contemporaries Judy Garland and Johnny Mercer. It is, indeed, interesting enough to take this ride, along with them, as well.
288. "I'd Rather Be Me," Decca 18690. Contemporary comic Eddie Bracken found his voice on this ditty penned by Harold Arlen and Johnny Mercer and dubbed Eddie Bracken with Bing's (real) voice in the film, *Out of this World*? Rather be who?
289. "It's Been a Long, Long Time," Decca 18708. This ditty, penned by Jule Styne and Sammy Cahn, finds Crosby's vocal aided greatly by the supporting vocals of the Les Paul Trio and also Paul's guitar.
290. "Whose Dream Are You," Decca 18708. Les Paul and his Trio also do well for Bing for this Meredith Wilson-penned ditty.
291. "Aren't You Glad You're You," Decca 18720. Another ditty, penned by Burke and Van Heusen, and used in the contemporary film *Bells of St. Mary*. That nice? Or pleasant enough?
292. "Personality," Decca 18790. With Eddie Condon as backup, Bing's vocal is provided enough lift. This somewhat novel ditty, more so a bit jazzy, was penned by Van Heusen and Burke for the (Crosby, Hope, and Lamour) film entity *Road to Utopia*. (The able and sultry-voiced Dorothy Lamour actually introduced this ditty in the film.)
293. "Day by Day," Decca 18887. Vocal backup by Mel Torme and the Mel-Tones.

294. "Prove It by the Things You Do," Decca 18887. Also with Mel Torme and the Mel-tones.
295. "Pistol Packin' Mama," Decca 23277. This (1942) "country" ditty, penned and first released by Al Dexter, is given even more peppy energy by Crosby and the Andrews Sisters. (No gun control here!)
296. "Santa Claus Is Coming to Town," Decca 23281. This ditty had been penned by J. Fred Coots and Haven Gillespie in 1934. Contemporary (1934) recordings from a Harry Reser Orchestra release, with a vocal by Tom Stacks, and by the George Hall Hotel Taft Orchestra, with a vocal by Sonny Schuyler (Bluebird B 5711) may be considered as novel, noting only fair vocal performances. As the emergence of swing in the following year (1935) expanded, also released on a contemporary Tommy Dorsey release on (Victor 25145). As the vocal of (band singer) Cliff Weston is weak, he is lifted by Dorsey's well-done (contrived) "swing" arrangement and also by the added bright and spirited vocal of Edythe Wright. In comparison, it's a good bet that bandleader Vic Schoen's (1943) arrangement for Bing and the Andrews Sisters had been founded on Tommy Dorsey's previous rendering. Vocally, however, Bing and the Andrews Sisters indeed speed things up considerably and, more so, define an energetic (if schmaltzy) Christmas classic. Latter-century listeners of this ditty in reissue generally dismiss all this as seasonal, yet, somehow, it all remains relevant for many, at least until year's end.
297. "Jingle Bells," Decca 23281. This flip of "Santa Claus Is Coming to Town" also finds Bing and the Andrews Sisters engaging in a seasonal vocal farce that also works. (A bootlegged outtake, differing greatly from James Lord Pierpont's original credited words, noted later in the text, is better)!
298. "Is You Is, or Is You Ain't, Ma Baby," Decca-23350. This ditty was originally recorded by R &B entity Louis Jordan, who penned it with Bill Austin. Crosby and the Andrews Sisters swing and sway with it. As noted within its title, its play upon contemporary slang is more than novel!
299. "There'll Be a Hot Time in the Town of Berlin," Decca 23350. This bit of contemporary (WWII) propaganda, penned by musicians-turned-servicemen Joe Buskin and John De Vries became a welcomed novelty for a war-weary public. Bing and the Andrews Sisters had performed this ditty in many USO shows with much enthusiasm and energy. Indeed, a real and patriotic statement, this schmaltzy joke was truly upon the likes of Hitler's Germany. So was this excellent recording, which finds it dated, by the conflict itself (1944).
300. "Don't Fence Me In," Decca 23364. This Cole Porter-penned ditty became identified as a fine "country" entity. Despite the fact that Roy Rogers had first introduced this classic on film, it was indeed Bing's rendering (with the Andrews Sisters) that had been recorded before Roy got around to producing his own recording. Listen and compare!
301. "The Three Caballeros," Decca 23364. This contrived bit of Mexican folklore, penned by Manuel Esperon, Ray Gilbert, and Ernesto Cortazar, is rhythmic enough for a fine vocal performance by Crosby and the Andrews Sisters, originally from the contemporary 1944 Walt Disney cartoon feature of the same name.
302. "Ac-Cent-Tchu-Ate-the Positive," Decca 23379. Another film ditty (from Crosby's *Here Comes the Waves*) which failed on film but was famously a popular contemporary novelty. Penned by Harold Arlen and Johnny Mercer, this clever bit of lyrics is also rhythmic enough. More so, the popular contemporary Johnny Mercer recording gave Bing a fine challenge. Luckily, this subsequent Crosby vocal with the Andrews Sisters is an infectious performance of rhythmic singing and energy. While the backup

orchestra by Vic Schoen may be suspect, this recording just may be the very best of the Crosby and Andrews Sisters releases. Sorry, Johnny!

303. "There's a Fellow Waiting in Poughkeepsie," Decca 23379. Penned by Johnny Mercer and Harold Arlen, this dated WWII entity finds Crosby and the Andrews Sisters (again) at their rhythmic best. While clever and novel lyrics are always a plus, so are the inspired vocals found on this ditty! Are they rocking?
304. "You've Got Me Where You Want Me," Decca 23410. This duet with Judy Garland is a winner.
305. "You Belong to My Heart," Decca 23413. An attempt at Spanish idiom, penned by Agustin Lara and Ray Gilbert and assisted by the truly authentic contemporary Xavier Cugat, is interesting and done very well.
306. "My Baby Said Yes," Decca 23417. This duet with fellow Decca recording artist Louis Jordan and his Tympany Five is a bit of low-keyed novelty (penned by Teddy Walters and Sid Robin) that indeed wins!
307. "Your Socks Don't Match," Decca 23417. This flip of "My Baby Said Yes," penned by Leon Carr and Leo Corday, again found both Crosby and Jordan coolly exchanging some contemporary slang. In true retrospective, there should have been more.
308. "Connecticut," Decca 23804. Another excellent duet with Judy Garland found Crosby at least interested and ready for the likes of Judy.
309. "Tallahassee," Decca 23885. This Frank Loesser penned ditty did well for Bing and the Andrews Sisters along with the city in the state of Florida.
310. "Sioux City Sue," Decca 23508. This novelty (penned by Dick Thomas and Ray Freedman) found contemporary Bob Haggart and the Jesters in vocal support. While a bit testy, it works. (The contemporary Hoosier Hot Shots release, on Decca 18745, is almost as good.)
311. "You Sang My Love Songs to Somebody Else," Decca 23508. As the flip side of "Sioux City Sue," this bit of nonsense, penned by Allan Roberts and Doris Fisher, also found Bob Haggart and the Jesters in competent and novel vocal support.
312. "I Can't Begin to Tell You," Decca 23457. Penned by James Monaco andMack Gordon, this ditty had been introduced in the contemporary film *The Dolly Sisters* by Betty Grable. It would, more so, find a contemporary recording by her as well as another by Andy Russell. Somehow, Crosby's own soft vocal commitment stands out, well, perhaps due to the collaboration with his contemporary (guest) concert pianist, Carmen Cavallaro.
313. "South America, Take It Away," Decca 23569. While a bit contrived, this ditty, penned by Harold Rome for the contemporary Broadway entity *Call Me Mister*, is indeed lifted by Bing's own (interested) and playful (Spanish accented) vocal performance and the rhythmic Andrews Sisters!
314. "Blue Skies," Decca 23646. The Irving Berlin classic from the 1920s is redefined by this classic recording by Crosby. As part of a (1946) revival, a Crosby film of the same name, the (interested) Crosby found this ditty great recording fodder. In true retrospective, if the film fails for many later viewers, this excellent (Decca) recording fails not!
315. "I'll See You in Cuba," Decca 23646. Earlier acoustic endeavors such as a (1920) version by The Three Kaufields, on Emerson 10158, were playful enough. Also featured in the 1946 film *Blue Skies*, this Irving Berlin-penned ditty rendered in the film missed its mark. This Decca recording, however, a fine duet with Trudy Erwin, found Bing at his comfortable best and, more so, defined another Berlin song as a classic!

316. "Pinetop's Boogie-Woogie," Decca 23843. This "Pinetop" Smith standard from the '20s is revived well enough, with some fine contemporary backing by Lionel Hampton and His Orchestra. What's surprising about his ditty is Crosby's own attempts to take a few chances with his rusty "jazz" vocal abilities, inspired by the exciting Hampton arrangement. While the faults in Bing's (sometimes uncontrolled) voice are sadly evident, it's still a fine effort.
317. "What Am I Gonna Do About You," Decca 23850. Backed both vocally and instrumentally, this attempt at a cool vocal style, penned by Sammy Cahn and Jule Styne, is indeed effective.
318. "Feuding and Fightin, '" Decca 23975. This obvious novelty, penned by Burton Lane and Al Dubin, finds a loose and novel approach by Bing, with Bob Haggart and the Jesters, at least acceptable.
319. "Good-bye, My Lover, Good-bye," Decca 23975. This sure novelty in title found a Bob Haggart's arrangement good recording fodder for Bing and the Jesters.
320. "Alexander's Ragtime Band," Decca 4008. Released on a red label, this Decca release found Al Jolson—in a good enough voice—in a fine duet with Bing. (Speculation has it that this recording was taken from a contemporary (1947) radio program.) Is this duet as good as the previous (1938) recording with Connie Boswell? No!
321. "Anything You Can Do, I Can Do Better," Decca 40039. Another (special) original (Decca) red label release, this ditty, penned by Irving Berlin for *Annie Get Your Gun*—contemporary (1947) Broadway entity—somehow lives up to its "special" release designation by Decca Records. Joined by (then) vocal threat to Frank Sinatra, Dick Haymes proves just what a very good vocalist he was. So were the (more) familiar Andrews Sisters in great voices, who found Berlin's ditty full of what was (unknown) woman's lib? It is more interesting to speculate that for Bing, with great material and a (vocal) challenge provided by Haymes, it would get him out of his doldrums. This resulting recording indicates that he had!
322. "Kokomo Indiana," Decca 24100. This ditty, penned by Josef Myrow and Mack Gordon, indeed found Crosby somewhat interested. (It's original flip side, a vocal with Lee Wiley, "I Still Suits Me," amazingly fails! What a bummer!)
323. "The Christmas Song," Decca 24144. While it is certain that the (original) Nat Cole Trio recording of this Mel Torme-penned classic was the best, Crosby ain't bad. As a matter of fact, this rendering sounds much like an earlier 1930s crooning effort. For those who were tired of this newer crooning style or those who still, perhaps purchased his newer (1940s) contemporary recordings to help induce sleep, this rendering indeed retains interest. It is also a fine seasonal crooning job. Was Bing holding back all this time?

324, 325. "Happy Birthday; Auld Lang Syne," Decca 24273. These traditional titles are essentially British, with "Auld Lang Syne," fit for a Scot. (Both song titles were, more so, titled as one for this release). As a medley, all this harmony, with The Ken Darby Singers, also found an excellent, if traditional, orchestra led by Victor Young. While the title "Happy Birthday" is perhaps a wasted pun, this seasonal classic is, at least, done well. (As an instrumental, perhaps Guy Lombardo's instrumental rendering was to be best recalled, at least until a latter-century rock influenced (yearly) television broadcast, as presented by host Dick Clark, changed things).

326. "Now Is the Hour," Decca 24279. While this vocal reeks of sentimental mush, this best-selling entity, also known as "Maori Farwell Song," penned by Maewu Kaihau, Clement Scott, and Dorothy Stewart, at least provided its listeners with something anticipated.

327. "You Don't Have to Know the Language," Decca 24282. The film *Road to Rio,* found the Andrews Sisters vocally jamming with Bing, in a fine visual image. (This recording, like that found in the film, does not disappoint.)
328. "But Beautiful," Decca 24283. As another film entity, this ditty penned by Johnny Burke and Jimmy Van Heusen, was featured in *Road to Rio*. While this recording drags a bit, this slow crooning job should, nevertheless, be appreciated.
329. "Galway Bay," Decca 24295. This song about Ireland remains a true classic. Penned by Dr. Arthur Colahan, this somewhat traditional ditty indeed seems real, if contrived. However, it is sincere enough to convince anybody (especially Bing, who was interested) to find something green to wear.
330. "Blue Shadows on the Trail," Decca 24433. Another contrived Western theme? Indeed, this title is a clear indication! Penned for the contemporary Disney cartoon *Melody Time*, this ditty, penned by Eliot Daniel and Johnny Lange, had found the Roy Rogers' version (Victor 20-2780) good enough. Crosby, more so, with a fine vocal arrangement with the Ken Darby Choir, gave this fodder a superb rendering, and with backing orchestration provided by Victor Young, he indeed produced a classic recording. Roy or Bing?
331. "A Fellow with an Umbrella," Decca 24433. Yet another Irving Berlin-penned ditty defined!
332. Far Away Places," Decca 24532. Yes, those places far away were something to croon about. Penned by Joan Whitney and Alex Kramer, this ditty indeed found attention from just about everywhere.
333. "If You Stub Your Toe on the Moon," Decca 24524. Featured in the contemporary (Crosby) film *A Connecticut Yankee in King Arthur's Court*, this novelty, penned by Burke and Van Heusen, stumbles not.
334.-339. "Christmas Carols Pt 1 and 2," Decca 24670. These vocals are very traditional, and it's this type of idiom that defines this music and its yearly commercial success since released. Titles are as follows: (a.) "Deck the Halls," (b.) "Away in a Manger," (c.) "I Saw Three Ships," (d.) "Good King Wenceslas," (e.) "We Three Kings of the Orient Are," and (f.) "Angels We Have Heard on High."
340. "Ichabod," Decca 24703. Yup. The voice in this ditty (penned by Don Raye and Gene De Paul), in the Disney short, betrays Cosby's voice ditto for this Decca release.
341. "Dear Hearts and Gentle People," Decca 24798. Crosby's medium-tempo style is still a pleasant experience (sometimes). Penned by Bob Hill and Sammy Fain, this ditty became a popular best seller, with a somewhat folksy appeal.
342. "Mule Train," Decca 24798. While not as good as the contemporary Frankie Lane version, this vocal betrays a strong-voiced vocalist, seldom used or found this late in the game (1949).
343. "Way Back Home," Decca 24800. It's not as good as the earlier Boswell Sisters rendering of the same title. Yet, assisted by the Glee Club and Fred Waring's Orchestra, it's, oddly, still a winner.
344. "Quicksilver," Decca 24827. This very contrived ditty, penned by Irving Taylor, George Wyle, and Eddie Pola, is, nevertheless, shared well with the Andrews Sisters.
345. "Sunshine Cake," Decca 24875. This novelty, penned by Van Heusen and Burke, is a kiddie show that somewhat worked in the Crosby film *Ridin' High*. This recording, moreover, at least finds Carol Richards and the Jeff Alexander Chorus exploring this novelty for the better. Somehow, Bing and company pull off a good rendering for a mediocre song ditty.

346. "The Horse Told Me," Decca 24875. Yup. Both Van Heusen and Burke penned yet another stupid title for the Crosby film *Ridin' High*. While dumb and juvenile enough, this recording, indeed like "Sunshine Cake," minus Carol Richards, somehow works.
347. "Harbor Lights," Decca 27219. While this could not be Hawaii, this crooned-out tale, penned by Jimmy Kennedy and Hugh Williams, finds Crosby, with orchestra and chorus direction by Lynn Murray, producing a winner. Was Rudy Vallee's previous rendering on, Bluebird B-7067, crooned out any better? Listen to both and compare.
348. "Beyond the Reef," Decca 27219. Penned by Jack Pitman, this original flip side of "Harbor Lights" also found Crosby and Lynn Murray's arrangement of another song of the sea yet another (boring) winner. (It is interesting to note that light-years later, Elvis Presley would also record both "Beyond the Reef" and "Harbor Lights.")
349. "Mele Kilikimka," Decca 27228. This nonsense sounded good at Yule time. Only at Yule time! As the Andrews Sisters help out, this very (contrived) "Hawaiian Christmas" song, penned by Robert Alex Anderson, still fills its holiday obligations. Get a present for listening? From whom?
350. "Silver Bells," Decca 27229. This ditty, penned by Jay Livingston and Ray Evans, was originally introduced on screen by Bob Hope and former band singer (sexy) film entity Marilyn Maxwell in the (1949) film *Lemon Drop Kid*. This rendering, made a few years later, found Bing and Carol Richards defining another Christmas classic.
351. "A Marshmallow World," Decca 27230. This seasonal stuff, penned by Peter De Rose and Carl Sigman, indeed provided grown-ups and small kids attention. Crosby, assisted by the Lee Gordon Singers and by the Sonny Burke Orchestra, produced a fine and easy seasonal farce that worked. (Later versions included an emulating Dean Martin version, as well as a fine vocal as by Brenda Lee.)
352. "Autumn Leaves," Decca 27231. The early 1950s found much musical change, but this excellent crooning job, penned by Joseph Kosma, Johnny Mercer, and Jacques Prevert, found Crosby comfortable enough. Indeed, backed up by Axel Stordahl, usually associated with the likes of Frank Sinatra, this traditional backing was all Crosby had needed.
353. "In the Cool, Cool, Cool of the Evening," Decca 27678. This schmaltzy and filmy ditty, penned by Haogy Carmichael and Johnny Mercer, became a duet with actress Jane Wyman, subsequently nominated for a "best song' academy award.
354. "Zing a Little Song," Decca 28255. What? Another schmaltzy and filmy duet with Jane Wyman? While, in true retrospective, this bit of formula, penned by Harry Warren and Leo Robin, while ain't great, it still rates for a mild nod.
355. "Little Jack Frost Get Lost," Decca 28463. This seasonal duet with Peggy Lee, penned by Al Stillman, Seger Ellis, and Lew Pollack, is a bit less schmaltzy, if contrived.
356. "Sleigh Ride," Decca 28463. A masterful ride that indeed sounds less contrived than most others. Penned by Leroy Anderson and Mitchell Parish, this ditty is indeed a sure seasonal winner. (Somehow, Crosby got himself in trouble mentioning a brand name in this ditty. Just listen!)

The following picks include a mix of (some) worthwhile recordings starting from the mid-1950s. By this time, the prolific Crosby empire was running out of creativity, as noting the Andrews Sisters had aged greatly. In hindsight, the rise of small, independent record labels that had accelerated greatly after WWII indeed gave rise to creativity and rock and roll. Crosby, seemingly wanted no part of the new wave, and the aged crooner indeed found himself as Bing Crosby—an icon of the past. As a further note, the latter 1940s had found much Crosby product released on 45 rpm and albums at 331/3 rpm as well as 78 rpm. This would continue into the next couple of decades, with reissued classic recordings mixed with a few notable attempts at contemporary music.

357-60. "The Country Girl," Decca ED-2186. This 45 EP release was a surprisingly strong film soundtrack from the Crosby film by the same name. Indeed, Bing and Grace Kelley made this vehicle a serious acting challenge for both, something very much unusual for Crosby. The following ditties were all penned by Harold Arlen and Ira Gershwin and must be considered lost and neglected recordings. The somewhat poignant titles are as follows:

a. "It's Mine, It's Yours."
b. "The Land Around Us."
c. "The Search Is Through."
d. "Dissertation on the State of Bliss." This one finds only Patty, of the Andrews Sisters, in vocal harmony with Bing.

361. "Count Your Blessings Instead of Sheep," Decca 29251. A botched-up *White Christmas* LP, at least finds this single release of a fine Irving Berlin-penned ditty crooned out well enough. (A contemporary Rosemary Clooney version better defined it.)

362. "Mississippi Mud," Decca 38031. This green-labeled Decca single was a promo for the (1954) Decca LP album (DX 151) set *Bing*. In true retrospective, while this reissued product included some Decca originals, all original Columbia, Victor, and Brunswick masters are sadly missing, with many original Decca masters as well. Just *why* Crosby rerecorded most of this stuff (with some commentary) for this album is unclear. Luckily, this version of "Mississippi Mud" is the fine exception for a botched product. Indeed, this "modern" approach to his classic "Mississippi Mud," backed by Buddy Cole, betrays a sparkling (interested) vocal! (As luck would have it, this single negates the reason to purchase this somewhat awful LP.)

363-365. *High Society*, Capital W-750. This LP features a film soundtrack that features Bing, Louis Armstrong—an idol of Bing's, and Frank Sinatra—who idolized both men. The highlights of this Cole Porter score included following duets:

(a). "Now You Has Jazz." The aged Crosby and Armstrong indeed performed a vocal delight with Louis's own contemporary 1956 Orchestra in fine backing. Somehow Bing comes to life! (Also released on a single (Capital-3506).)
(b.). True Love." This duet with Grace Kelly is slow, but effective crooning.
(c.) "Well, Did You, Evah." Crosby and Sinatra get it right. (This ditty and "True Love" were issued on single release (Capital-3507).)

366-370. *Bing Sings Whilst Bregman Swings*, Verve V-2020. This attempt at modern pop, found as by the contemporary LP releases pioneered by Nat King Cole and Frank Sinatra, almost succeeds. Buddy Bregman's Orchestra is indeed good enough, despite Bing, as he literally runs out of gas. Perhaps if he had been more committed, a better vocal would have emerged? In any case, the fine exceptions are

a. "I've Got Five Dollars." The Rodgers and Hart classic is indeed updated.
b. "Have You Met Ms. Jones." This ditty penned by Rodgers and Hart finds Bing committed!

c. "Mountain Greenery." This has got to be the ultimate redefined version of this ditty penned by Rodgers and Hart.
d. "Blue Room." Perry Como had redefined this ditty by Rodgers and Hart a decade earlier. This newer version at least challenges Como.
e. "They All Laughed." This Gershwin Brothers-penned ditty found Crosby ready to finally define it. Indeed he does!

371. "I Heard the Bells on Christmas Day," Decca 30126. This adaptation of a piece of literature became credited as by Johnny Marks and the works of Henry Wadsworth Longfellow. The committed Crosby vocal, more so, found this seasonal entity a bit more serious. (A later Frank Sinatra version is also done well). Bing or Frank?
372. "Seven Nights a Week," Capital 3695. With some fine backing by Nelson Riddle, Crosby almost "rocks and rolls" with a fast backing, vamping, and bouncing back beat. Penned by the familiar Jimmy Van Heusen and Sammy Cahn, this interesting alternative to the real thing also found Bing somewhat interested. Or perhaps the title alone was enough of an inspiration for the aged man?
373. "Man on Fire," Capital 3695. The flip of the "Seven Nights a Week," penned by Sammy Fain and Paul Francis Webster, is a serious bit of crooning, with a fine Nelson Riddle backing. Could Crosby compete with Sinatra's contemporary 1957 Capital releases? Indeed, this film title recording does!
374. "Around the World," Decca 30262. This Victor Young-penned ditty was used for a film of the same name. By this time (1957), the "crooner" had a hard time to find his voice, and this ditty defiantly notes an effective vocal "groan" that somehow works. Earlier times had found Bing dubbed "the groaner," although earlier vocals produced a far better vocal product.
375-376. *Songs I Wish I Had Sung*, Decca DL-8352. This LP started as a somewhat creative project on Bing's part to group together classic popular vocals he himself had not attempted. Indeed, he even supplied notes for this album project on its original issue. More so, this just had to be a serious attempt to compete with contemporary LP success as by his much-matured onetime rival, Frank Sinatra. While recording fodder may have not always been chosen by the likes of Capital's Billy May, Nelson Riddle, or Gordon Jenkins, Crosby's own notes included ditties made famous by the likes of Al Jolson, Ted Lewis, Rudy Vallee, Russ Columbo, Fats Waller, the Mills Brothers, Nat King Cole, Bob Hope, Sinatra himself, and a fairly new entity, Dean Martin. While not using May, Riddle, or Jenkins, the choice of Jack Pleis, a lesser name was still a good one, with excellent vocal backing by Jud Conlon's Rhythmaires. In addition, a fine Decca cover was found exhibiting a stylish-looking entity. What resulted, however, was a very wasted effort or perhaps a recording artist interested neither in time restrains nor vocal preparedness. This lax attitude had, indeed, been noted on recordings since the latter 1930s, with a gradual vocal deterioration over the years. There were two notable exceptions.

(a). "Memories Are Made of This." Crosby comes alive, as his interest in this somewhat contemporary Dean Martin hit is exemplary. As much as Dean had emulated him, Bing's own vocal is found to be sensitive enough, with a lush backing (differing from Martin's guitars) provided by Jack Pleis. While in comparison, perhaps Dean still wins out, Bing's product is extremely good and just as classy as Dean's original.

(b.). "Thanks for the Memory." Unlike the contemporary 1956 Dean Martin hit "Memories Are Made of This," this dated (1938) Bob Hope and Shirley Ross hit, which had become Bob Hope's radio and television theme song, was due for an update. Indeed, Bing must have relished the day to record this ditty and do it as well as Dick Todd's (1938) version, which had mimicked Bing himself. Vocally, Bing indeed takes a bit more time for this recording, knowing that time diminished his great croon, as heard on the previous Todd rendering. Luckily, his interest won out, as Bing's vocal control produced a gem of a recording!

377-388. *Bing with a Beat*, RCA Victor LPM-1473. This LP concept, with a fine contemporary (white) jazz group (Bob Scobey and his Frisco Jazz Band), was also a serious challenge for Bing. For the most part, except for his recent duet with Louis Armstrong on "Now You Has Jazz," Crosby's jazz chips had been considered cashed-in years before, noting a demising vocal style that was dated. Even so, Crosby seemed interested, and despite mixed results with Bregman and Pleis, a creative approach, aided by his old friend Matty Matlock, no stranger to producing successful recordings, was a good choice. Crosby, while not in his best vocal form, still manages to pull off a fine performance and at last could claim a fine contemporary and complete LP release. Song titles included old standards not previously associated with Bing. The following reviewed picks are notable and are listed by title, only because they are at least part of an LP release with relevance.

(a.) "Let a Smile Be Your Umbrella." A 1928 Roger Wolf Kahn release, penned by Irving Kahal, Francis Wheeler, and Sammy Fain, with a vocal by Franklyn Baur, finds a needed update. Moreover, Bing's loud vocals are matched and hidden by Scobey's horny orchestration.

(b.) "I'm Gonna Sit Right Down and Write Myself a Letter." This Fats Waller original had already been updated by contemporary Billy Williams on Coral 61830 in 1957. This version, even with Crosby's loud and husky vocal, at least matches Williams's version.

(c.) "Along the Way to Waikiki." This (1917) ditty penned by Gus Kahn and Richard Whiting had been around as an acoustic vocal rendering by the Peerless Quartet, on Victor 18326. Crosby's update, despite the fact that he had lost his middle-tempo voice, is in fine harmony with Scobey's brassy, Dixieland backing.

(d.) "Exactly Like You." Bing revives this classic (penned by Jimmy McHugh and Dorothy Fields), long identified with Ruth Etting and Libby Holman and as a jazzier entity by Jimmy Rushing.

(e.) "Dream a Little Dream of Me." The (1931) Ozzie Nelson crooning classic, penned by Gus Kahn, Wilbur Schwandt, and Fabian Andre, is not bettered, although it is somewhat revived well enough!

(f.) "Last Night on the Back Porch." This novelty, penned by Carl Schraubstader and Lew Brown, had been an acoustic Paul Whiteman entity, with vocals by the American Quartet—a collection of pre-1920s voices—on Victor 19139. It had also been more famously revived on early radio by Ernest Hare and Billy Jones with a novelty (mid-1920s) acoustic recording released on Okeh 4948. Along with some fine Scobey instrumental lead, Crosby indeed finds some voice in an interesting revival.

(g.) "Some Sunny Day." The Irving Berlin-penned ditty that Marion Harris's (1922) acoustic rendering had defined is challenged by Crosby and some fine Dixieland company.
(h.) "Whispering." The (1920) acoustic John Steel release, on Victor 18695 (penned by John Schonberger, Richard Coburn, and Vincent Rose), is far bettered.
(i.). "Tell Me." Penned by J. Will Callahan and Max Kortlander, this update of the acoustic Al Jolson release finds an aged Crosby vocal somewhat better.
(j.). "Mack the Knife." The classic penned by Kurt Weill and Marc Blitzstein, from the early '30s, had been remade famously by Louis Armstrong in 1956. Crosby, likewise, does well, although he just might be heard, out of breath, near the end of his own brassy vocal. Indeed, keeping pace with Scobey's band required much skill. A later Bobby Darin version in 1959, moreover, defined this classic.
(k.) "Down Among the Sheltering Palms." This ditty, penned by James Brockman and Abe Olman, had been identified with the Lyric Quartet as an acoustic venture in 1915. Later, the Boswell Sisters, in the early '30s defined it as an electric recording. Still later, in the later 1940s, Al Jolson (older) and the Mills Brothers improved upon it. Bing's dragging vocal is far from great, although his Dixieland backing is.
(l.) "Mama Loves Papa." The 1924 acoustic Isham Jones instrumental on Columbia 2506, penned by Cliff Friend and Abel Baer, is updated well, along with a committed Crosby vocal—obviously a little late to cover a better (identified) Jane Green vocal on a Virginians 1923 acoustic release (Victor 19215).

389-400. *Fancy Meeting You Here*, RCA Victor LPM-1854. This return to mushy pop actually had assets. Indeed, Rosemary Clooney's duet vocal is better, yet Crosby's timing, greatly aided by the likes of the Billy May Orchestra, is more than a plus. While the "travel" theme is a bit contrived, the following vocals, on this original LP, are not. They are

(a). "Fancy Meeting You Here."
(b.). "On a Slow Boat to China."
(c.) "I Can't Get Started."
(d.) "Hindustan."
(e.) "It Happened in Monterey." The excellent song ditty that got away from Crosby in the (1930) film *King of Jazz* is finally attempted and done well, if vamped a bit by May's pleasing arrangement and Clooney's (better) voice uplifting Crosby's vocal.
(f.) "You Came a Long Way from St. Louis."
(g.) "Love Won't Let You get Away" (in reprise, twice).
(h.). "How About You."
(i.) "Brazil."
(j.) "Isle of Capri."
(k.) "Say Si Si Para vigo me voy."
(l.) "Calcutta."

401. "How Lovely Is Christmas," Kapp-196X. As a seasonal entity, Crosby had already become a true marketing icon. This slow ditty penned by Arnold Sundgaard and Alec Wilder, while a murky attempt at crooning, it still manages to work.

402. "The Second Time Around," MGM 12946. Yes, Crosby is very effective (this late) on this single 45 rpm release, penned by Sammy Cahn and James Van Heusen, for the film entity *High Time.* Crosby's vocal sparkles in this ditty, and this recording (somehow) rises to the indeed rare occasion.

403-416. *I Wish You a Merry Christmas*, Warner Brothers, W 1484. The familiar Crosby product of Irish, Hawaiian, cowboy, religious, and seasonal Christmas recordings had indeed stayed mainstream despite rock and roll. Indeed, much reissue of 78 rpm origin found newer 45 rpm singles, 45 rpm extended play, and 331/3 rpm—a fine seasonal gift of vintage and sentiment. Indeed, much Decca products, constantly reissued over the years, consistently remained best-selling entities. A 1957 12-inch LP *Merry Christmas*, with back cover notes dating from the 1940s, was an especially popular-selling (reissue) LP on DL 8128). In 1962, Warner Brothers provided an old theme and a new concept for Crosby—an original Christmas LP, in mono or "stereo." While noting arrangers Bob Thompson, Peter Matz, and Jack Halloran, this original concept warranted attention. Luckily, Crosby is in good spirits and takes his time. While his vocals crack in some instances, his very commitment to this project produced a fine seasonal album.

a. "Winter Wonderland."
b. "Have Yourself a Merry Little Christmas."
c. "What Child Is This."
d. "The Holly and the Ivy."
e. "The Little Drummer Boy."
f. "O Holy Night."
g. "The Littlest Angel."
h. "Let It Snow, Let It Snow."
i. "Hark, the Herald Angel Sing."
j. "It Came upon the Midnight Clear."
k. "Frost, the Snowman."
l. "Pat-A-Pan."
m. "While Shepherds Watched Their Flocks."
n. "I Wish You a Merry Christmas."

417. "Do You Hear What I Hear," Capital 5088. This seasonal release is a bit of excellent marketing. Penned byNoel Regney and Gloria Shayne, it is fortunately combined with a fine committed vocal by Bing. As a single release, this ditty enjoyed modest sales and may be considered Crosby's last successful jab at contemporary music in the new age of rock and roll.

418-420. *12 Songs of Christmas*, Reprise (LP) F 2022. This project involved Bing, Frank Sinatra, and the very popular 1930s bandleader, Fred Waring. While it's a pity it's not all Bing, this LP set limits on all three entities. The following are fine Crosby crooning jobs, with excellent backing from Fred Waring's Orchestra:

a. "Christmas Candles." Penned by Kay O'Dea this contrived ditty found much relevance with Crosby's fine vocal, loaded with a full blown chorus that works.
b. "It's Christmas Time Again." Yes it is, Crosby, chorus, and Fred Waring's backing again do well on this gem penned by Elliott, Burke, and Harwood.
c. "The Secret of Christmas." This ditty penned by Cahn and Van Heusen is no secret; its seasonal message is indeed a winner.

Note: The following two Brunswick masters turned up on reissue product LP in the later 1960s. To the delight of many (old) ears, they, more so, found Bing Crosby at the height of his "crooner" vocal abilities. (Subsequent reissues for these and other original (Brunswick) material by Sony restored the original mono sound brilliantly.

421. "Sweet Sue," Brunswick Master, 1932. Bing got down with some fast-paced jazz (backed by Lennie Hayton), perhaps greatly inspired by a (contemporary) Mills Brothers release (LP *Bing Crosby Story*, Epic E2E 201).
422. "Here Is My Heart", Brunswick Master. 1933. This well crooned film title, penned by Leo Robin and Ralph Rainger) was not to be released for about 25 years, (on LP the BoyFriends-Harmony HL-7174). Or did Jack Kapp and Bing decide to stiff Brunswick, and give the title to (Bing's) brother Bob, who indeed provided fine recording fodder on (Decca), as a contemporary Dorsey Brothers release?

➢ Radio

Despite all one might hear about the media of radio before 1950, it was Bing himself who had dominated the forgotten era. There are tons of old radio programs out on the market, and many feature Crosby. Considering all, the better programs, like his recordings, are crooned out best in the early 1930s. They include Cremo (cigars), Woodbury (soap), guest airchecks, and radio promo transcriptions. Many booted and regularly issued records of those early broadcasts have, moreover, found the light of day through many differing record labels. The following (known) picks should be found, whatever label.

423, 424 Crosby's first (solo) radio broadcast from 1931 included (a) "Just One More Chance" and (b) "I'm Through with Love." (Both better his commercial Brunswick recordings.)
425. "Out of Nowhere." An early aircheck (1930?) with Gus Arnheim is done very well and leads into
426. "What Is It." Another aircheck with Gus Arnheim, also featuring a bright vocal of Loyce Whiteman (at the same broadcast) and providing Bing with an opportunity to offer a few surprises as their spontaneous vocal duet and injecting much humor in an otherwise stiff occasion.
427. "As Time Goes By," from the *Cremo Show* (1931). Crosby's crooning beats out Rudy Vallee's very good contemporary recording. (Too bad Bing never commercially recorded this ditty back then.)
428. "I Surrender Dear," from the *Cremo Show* (1931). This ditty was used as Bing's first radio theme.
429. "Where the Blue of the Night." From *Woodbury Program* (1934), this ditty replaced "I Surrender Dear" as his theme and would remain so for the rest of his long radio and subsequent (television) career.
430. "Please." Radio promo for the contemporary 1932 film *The Big Broadcast* transcription.
431. "Here Lies Love." Radio promo for the contemporary 1932 film *The Big Broadcast*, transcription. Bing himself, as well as actor Stuart Erwin, introduces this ditty.
432. "Thanks." Radio promo for the contemporary 1933 film *Too Much Harmony* with bandleader Jimmy Grier.
433. "I Knew You When," *Woodbury Program*, 1934. Not a Crosby commercial recording.
434. "Riding Around in the Rain," *Woodbury Program*, 1934.

435. "The House Is Haunted," *Woodbury Program*, 1934. Neither Crosby or Russ Columbo produced a contemporary recording of this ditty, but a competitive Columbo radio aircheck does. On hearing, the idea of cloning may be more relevant! Listen and compare.
436. "A Thousand Goodnights," *Woodbury Program*, 1934. Not a Crosby commercial recording.
437. "With My Eyes Wide Open I'm Dreaming," *Woodbury Program*, 1934. Another "crooner" battle with an existing Columbo aircheck from the same year is well worth it! (A contemporary recording by Russ or Bing does not exist.)
438. "Love in Bloom," *Woodbury Program*, 1934.
439. "I'm Humming, I'm Whistling, I'm Singing," *Woodbury Program*, 1934.
440. "Old Faithful," *Woodbury Program*, 1934. Not a Crosby commercial recording.
441. "It's Easy to Remember," *Woodbury Program*, 1934.
442. "Lullaby of Broadway," *Woodbury Program*, 1934. Not a Crosby commercial recording.
443. "Time on My Hands," *Kraft Music Hall* program, 1937. Bing challenges the already old Russ Columbo recording, at least as an aircheck, noting an existing Columbo radio version. Check them out? (Crosby did not produce a contemporary recording.)
444. "South of the Border," *Kraft Music Hall* program, 1939. Crosby beats out Gene Autry's contemporary recording. (Not a Crosby commercial recording.)
445. "Iowa," *Kraft Music Hall* program, 1944? Bandleader Meredith Wilson and Bing make a few mistakes and, moreover, ham it up for the live radio audience!
446. "Shoo Shoo Baby." This may be a *Kraft Music Hall* Program (1944?), but whatever it is, along with backing vocals by the contemporary Merry Macs, it's a raved-up performance that somehow succeeds.

(Yes—even this late, Bing could get inspired! Not a Crosby commercial recording.)

- Bootleg and unknown labeled recordings and noncommercial radio

Both Sides of Bing Crosby, Curtain Calls 100/2. There is a great bootleg trade of Bing Crosby recordings all over the world. Bing's natural wit creates a lot of fun, as well as shatters many myths. His usage of unprintable words is also found to be interesting and certainly not appropriate for the likes of a film image of a singing priest. Perhaps his role in *The Country Girl* was a bit truer to life? Highlights from this LP include studio and radio outtakes that had previously been booted, mostly on 78 rpm. Included are

447. "Wrap Your Troubles in Dreams." This ditty from a later 1939 Decca rerecording session (not the original Victor recording of 1931) finds Crosby crooning out obscenities and enjoying it.
448. "Jingle Bells." Performed with the Andrews Sisters and got great cooperation from them as well. As an outtake from the Decca recording, this is far more interesting!
449. "Blues Serenade." This outtake from the Decca recording can produce nonstop laughing and is certainly better than the issued commercial recording.
450. "Argument with Jack Kapp." This is actually a great 1936 outtake of "I Wished on the Moon."
451. "Rollicking Rockaway Raoul." Somehow this ditty got itself recorded on the set of Crosby's 1933 film *Going Hollywood*. Raoul Walsh, the fine director of the film, seemingly found Bing's full attention and, indeed, sarcasm. While noted for partying and drinking, an intoxicated Crosby still manages to be very articulate, as he spills out some campy humor. (This may or may not be considered a Brunswick master.)

452. "Robins and Roses." The Decca recording is improved upon as Crosby's wit finds itself expressed upon itself with lyric.
453. "Seventh Air Force." A gusty WWII-era performance, not of commercial standards, finds the empire of Japan at the butt end of truly witty and wicked sarcasm.
454. "Jimmy Valentine." This ditty is an outtake of the (otherwise) boring and insipid 1939 release "Melody of Gus Edwards Song Hits," on Decca 2700, directly related to his contemporary film *The Star Maker,* of already 'old' standards. It is, more so, a good guess that Bing himself perhaps knew that what he was rendering stank up the studio, so he produced his own offbeat bit of lyric to make things interesting. In fact, he does!

- Visual Images.

The early 1930s found Bing Crosby at his most creative peak as a vocalist and a serious jazz entity. Film shorts such as *Blue of the Night*, *I Surrender Dear*, *Dream House*, and *Star Night at the Coconut Grove* while trivial in content, find the young crooner in his best vocal form. So indeed did bit parts in *Reaching for the Moon*, and *Confessions of a Co-Ed.* Full-length films, starting in 1932 with *The Big Broadcast,* led to such entities as *College Humor*, *Going Hollywood*, *We're Not Dressing*, *She Loves Me Not,* and *Here Is My Heart* firmly established Crosby as a profitable and marketable commodity who exceeded all expectations.

While a familiar audience was growing, many of the ditties written for films were becoming predictable and reeked of formula, with many fine titles becoming film titles, including, *Two for Tonight*, *Pennies from Heaven*, *Rhythm on the Range*, *Holiday Inn*, and *Going My Way*. Other films, including those with "road" themes (with Bob Hope and Dorothy Lamour), defined Crosby as a huge part of Americana itself. Indeed, his vocal style adapted much, and his film work, for the good and bad, left behind an uneven legacy of film ditties, with some nevertheless classic recordings that had originated from them. Marketed by weekly radio and recordings, familiarity did not fail.

By the latter 1940s, the aging process found roles suited for him as well as an aging audience. Films such as *A Connecticut Yankee in King Arthur's Court*, *White Christmas*, *High Society*, *High Time*, and *Robin and the Seven Hoods* at least found him in fine yet old and identifiable crooning form. Moreover, one film, *The Country Girl* (1954), tapped into a more serious performance, certainly different from his firmly established clean and wholesome image.

Other oddities included his voice only in *San Francisco*, the popular Clark Gable, Jeanette MacDonald, and Spencer Tracy film, as well as the Eddie Bracken film *Out of This World.* Still another film of quality and interest would include a Walt Disney cartoon *The Adventures of Ichabod and Mr. Toad*, finding a (huge) familiar audience identifying him only by ear.

- The (most) familiar images of Bing at the piano are in:

455. "White Christmas" (1942). The image of Bing singing this ditty (from *Holiday Inn)* is, by far, the most identifiable visual image of Bing Crosby.
456. "Now You Has Jazz" (1956). This ditty features an old Bing and an old Louis Armstrong (from *High Society*), and Bing somehow sounds and looks good.

457. "When the Folks High Up Do the Mean Low-Down." In the film *Reaching for the Moon* (which starred Douglas Fairbanks Jr. and Bebe Daniels), Bing is seen (as a very young man), as well as heard, attempting to shake things up in a party scene. He succeeds, as his rhythmic style is demonstrated as sensational, even for 1930. (This ditty was actually *bootlegged* on 78 rpm in the '30s.)
458. "You Got Love." In the film *Confessions of a Co-Ed* (which starred Sylvia Sidney and Phillip Holmes), Bing sings "Out of Nowhere," as a solo artist, and (for about only thirty seconds) is seen actually scatting some fine jazz licks as a Rhythm Boy with Harry Barris and Al Rinker on "You Got Love."
459. "Auf Wiedersehen My Dear." In the Mack Sennett short, *Blue of the Night* (1931), Bing belts out a ditty (not commercially released) with vocal quality and conviction (*bootlegged* on 78 rpm in the 1930s)
460. "I Surrender, Dear." In the Mack Sennett film short, by the same name (1931), Bing is shown in front of a band, fully dressed in early 1930s' style It is here that one can see clearly the then up-and-coming crooner, who would change popular music—as if you were in the audience (*bootlegged* on 78 rpm in the 1930s).
461. "Lovable." This is from the Mack Sennett film short *Sing Bing Sing*, filmed in 1931 and released in 1933. This is another pleasant crooning job, penned by Kahn and Woods, oddly not officially recorded, although indeed *bootlegged* in the 1930s. Among others, a fine commercial release of this ditty was released in 1932 by Rudy Vallee on *Hit of the Week*-D-2-3.
462. "Learn to Croon," from *College Humor*, 1933.
463. "Down the Old Ox Road," from *College Humor,* 1933.
464. "Moonstruck," from *College Humor,* 1933.
465. "Our Big Love Scene," from *Going Hollywood*, 1933.
466. "Temptation," from *Going Hollywood*, 1933.
467. "We'll Make Hay While the Sun Shines," with Marion Davies, from *Going Hollywood,* 1933.
468. "Going Hollywood." This (1933) film title was also filmed with a Crosby vocal. It was, oddly, not recorded as a commercial release. (It was, however, bootlegged off the film itself in the 1930s. By the latter 1960s, this fine film version was to be released legally.)
469. "Please," from *The Big Broadcast*, 1932.
470. "Here Lies Love," from *The Big Broadcast*, 1932.
471-472. "Where the Blue of the Night," from (a.) the film short *Blue of the Night* and from (b.) *The Big Broadcast,* 1932.
473. "Lazy," from *Holiday Inn,* 1942.
474. "Easter Parade," from *Holiday Inn*, 1942.
475. "Be Careful, It's My Heart," from *Holiday Inn*, 1942.
476. "You Don't Have to Know the Language," jamming with the Andrews Sisters in *The Road to Rio,* 1946.
477. "I'll Capture Your Heart," with Fred Astaire, Marjorie Reynolds, and Virginia Dale in *Holiday Inn,* 1942.
478. "Mairsey Doats." A rare "live" newsreel (1944) caught Bing (without his toupee!) and Bob Hope taking off on the contemporary novelty recording, penned by Milton Drake, Al Hoffman, and Jerry Livingston, (as popularized by the Merry Macs and the King Sisters on records.). Indeed, the real roar of approval from a crowd of USO service people is, more so, captured!
479. "Peace on Earth" - "Little Drummer Boy". (1977). Duet with (rocker) David Bowie.

➢ *Stop Here*! This monster of entertainment has gotten enough!

❖ The original crooner, in his youth, was indeed hard to top before age caught up with him.

➢ Legacy. The Bing Crosby legacy of junk remains relevant. His marketing image that included milk cartons and board games, in addition to radio sponsors is overwhelming! Even so, his place in popular culture also remains. Perhaps his age hurts. Unlike Russ Columbo, his early brilliance as a "pop" icon gets lost. Later, in the 1960s, he attempted LPs with Louis Armstrong and (another) with Rosemary Clooney. He also attempted a Beatles ditty "Hey Jude" along with a TV sitcom and was a "host" for a televised *Kraft Music Hall*, which may only be noted as feeble and frail. A later 1970s' Crosby found more attempts at recording with the likes of Fred Astaire and Johnny Mercer, which also lack, for the most part, energy. In true retrospective, this artist is unfairly rated as an old icon, stuck in the era before rock. In reality, Bing Crosby was, or remains, a huge part of just what "popular music" really is. Indeed, even considering the junk, hopefully omitted in this review, the marketing of Crosby remains an international phenomenon.

Arthur Crudup

Like many blues entities, Arthur Crudup had more of an influence upon a later idiom of music, "rock and roll." He was, more so, part of a second wave of recorded blues singers, borrowing from the likes of many, especially from the likes of Big Bill Broonzy and Blind Lemon Jefferson. Or, did he? The culture was embedded deep, especially in the Mississippi Delta. Signed by Victor for its stable of blues artists in 1941, Arthur, whose nickname was "Big Boy," because of his huge size, was already in his mid-thirties.

The following picks are well-done blues, which were, in true retrospective, destined to become better known well after he recorded them. Arthur's subsequent recordings would affect many after him, including B. B. King. Just why a young, white, transplanted Mississippi teenager, living in Memphis, Tennessee, memorized his recordings will always be a mystery. Discounting the strict segregation of the era, it's more than obvious that Crudup's bold sound deeply embedded itself into heart of Elvis Presley. It would, more so, affect the world! The following are Arthur Crudup picks:

1. "If I Get Lucky," Bluebird B-8858. Getting lucky is perhaps not a rare thing for a bluesman, at least in the slang term! It's likewise a means to lose the blues!
2. "Kind Lover Blues," Bluebird B-8896.
3. "Mean Old Frisco Blues," Bluebird 34-0704. The common "train" theme finds his woman gone! Will she ever come back?
4. "Gonna Follow My Baby Blues," Bluebird 34-0704.
5. "Rock Me Mama," Bluebird 34-0725. The sexual term "rock" is well defined! The music? Or is the (later) musical term also in mind? In any case, Arthur claims this (1944) ditty on a personal level. Just listen.
6. "Cool Disposition," Bluebird 34-0738. Is this a wet dream about a great woman? It seems WWII is the reason Arthur is away, but this 1944 recording could apply to a select number of women at any other time!

7. "So Glad You're Mine," Victor 20-1949. The sexual innuendo of Arthur is obvious, as a statement of happiness is realized. (Elvis, on Victor (LP) LPM 1392), more so raves it up a bit, with the same conclusion as Arthur.)
8. "That's All Right," Victor 20-2205. The folk origins of this bit of slang finds Arthur's claim to this title finds Blind Jefferson's "Black Snake Moan," on Paramount 12487, a bit suspect? So is a subsequent release by Son House on, Paramount 13042, as "My Black Mama." Did Arthur hear these recordings? Or did he already know them? He had already used it often, as found on his very first recording in 1941, on "If I Get Lucky." Or did he use the same lines in the same tent show with Jefferson and House? In any case, Crudup's tight sound and vocal is also danceable. The differing and later Elvis version, on Sun 209, is notably looser. Call it a hillbilly sound with back beat?
9. "Crudup's After Hours," Victor 20-2205. Another personal statement!
10. "My Baby Left Me," Victor 22-0109. Another fine ditty that Elvis liked and later recorded.

Frank Crumit

- The acoustic age (in general) produced vocals using novelty titles that, in general, made the playing of a phonograph recordings a most pleasant way to spend an evening. Frank Crumit may be considered a true 1920s' entity, with a fairly quirky vocal style, in fact, perfect for acoustic recordings. Rivaled by Nick Lucas and Cliff Edwards, his novel style indeed helped the 1920s roar. Picks include

1. "Margie," Columbia A 3332. (Also associated with Eddie Cantor.)
2. "The Love Nest," Columbia A 2973. On first hearing, this hard-to-hear acoustic recording indeed reeked of familiarity. This tight vocal style, with rolling *r*'s is somewhat operatic, and has much in common and emulation of contemporary Al Jolson. While the record itself notes that it was penned by Louis A. Hirsh (as "Hirsch"), perhaps Frank Mandel and Otto Harbach contributed, as noted on original sheet music from the Braodwat entity "Mary". This tune may be familiar with many baby boomers used in the TV sitcom *The George Burns and Gracie Allen Show*, from the early 1950s.
3. "My Little Bimbo down on the Bimbo Isle," Columbia A-2981. Yeah!
4. "My Honey's Lovin' Arms," Columbia A-3699. This 1922 acoustic rendering, penned by Joseph Meyer and Herman Ruby, may also be considered somewhat crude. A later 1933 electric version by Bing Crosby and the Mills Brothers, on Brunswick 6525, would define it.
5. "Old Fashioned Love," Columbia A-3933. Thanks to Frank, this ditty became better known despite Alberta Hunter's and Eva Taylor's fine contemporary recordings!
6. "Ukelele Lady," Victor 19701. This ditty penned by Gus Kahn and Richard Whiting, ain't bad, although contemporary Vaughn De Leath, on Columbia 361-D, is better.
7. "The Girl Friend," Victor 20124. This Broadway entity of 1926 of the same name, by Richard Rodgers and Lorenz Hart, earned Crumit a contemporary thumbs-up!
8. "Mountain Greenery," Victor 20124. The quirky Crumit style (again) works—somehow! Another fine rendering of a 1925 contemporary s Rodgers and Hart penned classic for the Broadway entity *'Garrick Gaities'* found Frank more than able to produce another interesting recording. Light-years away in 1956, found an aged Crosby vocal somehow defining it.

9. "Abdul Abulbul Amir," Victor 20715. This old and novel tale has dubious origins from the Crimean War in 1854. (!) Crumit's easy storytelling-vocal reaches a zenith, as his message still soothes and tickles the ear.
10. "The Song of the Prune," Victor 21430. Yup. The effectiveness of prunes is well known. Moreover, is this novelty.
11. "I Learned About Women From Her," Victor 21735.
12. "A Gay Caballero," Victor 21735. This title's meaning, as penned by Lou Klein and Frank himself, has indeed changed by the end of the century.
13. "The Return of Abdul Abulbul Amir," Victor 22482. This retelling of a tall tale still works.
14. "Little Brown Jug," Victor 24092. The implications of "hillbilly" and "western" and "folk "find this electric recording a fine adaptation by the still quirky Crumit. Indeed, traditional English music halls vibrated with this type of stuff, although Frank's accent does not. Perhaps the jug could be passed out to others, but this offbeat recording still ain't bad.

Vic Damone

- Vic Damone was a popular vocalist who started in the latter 1940s. Like Frankie Laine, he had been an offshoot of the popular music as defined by Bing Crosby and (especially) Frank Sinatra. Moreover, and also like Laine (although Laine did not sound like Sinatra), he had become part of the newer wave of small (record label) companies, who competed with the likes of Victor, Columbia, and Decca. This following picks are well-done pop ditties, which fit into his fine and strong baritone vocals.

1. "I Have but One Heart," Mercury 5053. Penned by Marty Symes and Johnny Farrow, this ditty was seemingly based on "O'Marinariello." The young (would-be) Sinatra finds a few lyrics in Italian! Luckily, all this (usually) boring stuff works (for him). Listen and be surprised!
2. I Love You So Much It Hurts," Mercury, 5261. The contemporary (1948) country entity, found Jimmy Wakely's version, on Capital 15243, effective. More so were subsequent differing versions by the likes of a Buddy Clark release on Columbia 38406 and a Mills Brothers version on Decca 24550. As an upcoming pop vocal wonder, Vic's vocal delivered good contemporary competition for this Floyd Tillman-penned ditty.
3. "You're Breaking My Heart," Mercury 5271. Another Italian song ditty "Mattinata", penned by Pat Genaro and Sunny Skylar in 1946, is put into mainstream American popular music.
4. "Why Was I Born," Mercury 5326. Vic's vocal sounds uppity, yet it ain't Helen Morgan! Nevertheless, Vic's interest in this old ditty does indeed make it all work. Just listen!
5. "In the Still of the Night," Mercury 5350. This Cole Porter-penned ditty had been a stiff ditty, penned for the operatic (1937) film *Rosalie*. A subsequent and (still) stiff contemporary vocal by Jack Leonard, on a Tommy Dorsey release (Victor 25663), became a sweet band success. A Joan Whitney vocal for Will Osborne, on Decca 1467, is better. (Vic's later (1950) rendering is, moreover, a bombastic, if crooning, effort. While always emulating Sinatra's early style, Vic's own show-off vocal is (more)

Sinatra, and effective. (A later rock-era (1956) version by the Five Satins (Ember 1005), as "In the Still of the Nite," is a fine-sounding vocal doo-wop.)

6. "My Heart Cries for You," Mercury 5563. This fine (1951) best seller, penned by Percy Faith and Carl Sigman, was adapted from the classical European "Chanson de Marie Antoinette." Perhaps Vic's own vocal is inspirational in itself and was, likewise, rivaled by a contemporary Guy Mitchell pop version on Columbia 39067. A C& W version by Jimmy Wakely, on Capital 1328, is also oddly smoother than both Damone's or Mitchell's version.
7. "April in Paris," Mercury 70020. As a revival of a 1932 Broadway entity 'Walk A Little Faster' that was hardly known, the Jerome Kern and E. Y. Harburg penned ditty penned by fit perfectly into Vic's classy style. Or what about a (contemporary) Frank Sinatra version?
8. I'm Walking Behind You," Mercury 70128. This ditty became a huge best seller for contemporary Eddie Fisher. As Both Fisher and Damone made it within the cusp to become featured artists within this book, it's interesting to note that both of these young, Sinatra-inspired vocalists (who had started commercially in the latter 1940s), with good looks to boot, produced recordings that could be directly compared to Frank's own contemporary rendering. In true retrospective, while (1953) sales gave the nod to Eddie Fisher, the better version belongs to Frank. Or Vic? Indeed, this ditty offers interesting speculation?
9. "On the Street Where You Live," Columbia 40654. This well-done popular title, penned by Alan J. Lerner and Frederick Loewe, indeed sold its share in 1956 despite rock and roll and Elvis.

Jimmie Davis

The Jimmie Davis story is one of early "country blues," noting the crude and rural ditties he performed. From the small community of Beech Springs, Louisiana, he had turned at least twenty-one years of age by the start of the 1920s. The son of sharecroppers, he had graduated high school and later attended college. While a country boy, and perhaps not very hip, he was very slick and was keenly interested in the newer sounds of popular music, which included the pop sounds of Gene Austin. He would also become interested in radio and the broadcasting of (local) radio, at station KWKH in Shreveport, Louisiana It may have been in Shreveport that he made a crude recording of the popular 1928 standard "Ramona," also a contemporary Gene Austin release, on Victor 21334. As more of an oddity, he sold it (privately) by mail or in person, on his self-promoted "Doggone" label. By this time, the rural sounds of Jimmie Rodgers became popular, and like others, Jimmie Davis sought to follow him and his rural and yodeling country blues. The following selections seek to explore some fine efforts, however crude, which became part of Americana itself. Picks include

1. "The Barroom Message," Victor V-40154. This girl named "Sweet" Nellie sent a message to her male companion that really hurt! It seems she was dying, and Jimmie does some yodeling about it all in an (illegal) Prohibition-era contemporary (1929) bar. Or perhaps this ditty is a bit older and adapted?
2. "Out of Town," Victor V-40215. Who says Jimmie Rodgers had caught the only train in town? Moreover, while the yodeling is sometimes hard to take, its rural blues message, considering yellow dogs and tomcats, is interesting. So is the train, some nineteen coaches long!

3. "Doggone That Train," Victor V-40286. It seems that Corrine, his gal, is put on a train north? By the time Corrine says good-bye, it's obvious that she wants to leave, and while noting some fine and crude guitar work, perhaps it's Jimmie's weird yodeling that made her want to get away from him fast?
4. "My Louisiana Girl," Victor V-40302. The magnolia's bloom, and the sugarcane, cotton, and corn of the deep South's Mississippi Delta is where this Louisiana girl was to be found. While a bit contrived, the guitar work is fair enough. Better yet, there's no yodeling!
5. "She's a Hum-Dum Dinger," Victor 23587. This blues ditty about a gal who could strut her stuff is a fine tale. Why, even the local preacher can't control himself! As a bonus, besides the fact that there's no yodeling, a faster-paced guitar is strummed to end this crude rendering of some real rural slang.
6. "Arabella Blues," Victor 23517. Arabella, when is she coming home? While it all gets a bit redundant, this crude blues lament is indeed genuine. While Jimmie may have found a new "mama" in New Orleans, it is, moreover, a bit of conjecture.
7. "Bear Cat Mama from Horner's Corners," Victor 23517. She's a lot of things, and her name is Sal. She's from New Orleans, and among many other amazing things, besides "keen" she's sweet and tall, and other things. Moreover, if she's a daughter of a Jelly Roll King, might she also be black? In any case, no matter what she is, she's an interesting example of rural blues.
8. "In Arkansas," Victor 23525. This one is definitely for the hicks as the crude yodeling and the Southern myth that Arkansas was the most hillbilly state is exposed. Moreover, it's all part of the culture!
9. "A Woman's Blues," Victor 23544. What makes a woman hang her head and cry? More so, this tale about women seems to favor the women from Alabama. What happens when a woman gets "blue?"
10. "Lonely Hobo," Victor 23648. This "poor boy" tale is contrived, but since it's about trains and keeping out of jail, this 1930 rendering is at least honest. More so, the reason this guy is a hobo is also due to having been deceived. Familiar?
11. "Davis' Salty Dog," Victor 23674. While the Allen Brothers (Austin and Lee) had founded their own "Salty Dog," on Columbia 15175-D, it was obvious that Papa Charlie Jackson's "Salty Dog Blues," on Paramount 12064, had been a bit earlier. While blues and country seem to be a bit mixed, it's also highly probable that, for all concerned, many others, including the likes of Charlie Jackson, had discovered as much about shared folk entities and had written about what had been heard. Moreover, it's the legacy of most blues entities, and that's sad enough.
12. "Organ Grinder Blues," Victor 23763. This gritty blues ditty had been an obvious pun. Among other versions, it's the poignant 1928 Ethel Waters version, on Columbia 14365-D, of this (Clarence Williams claimed) classic that had indeed defined "grinder." Even so, Jimmie's skin color, as heard in some previous blues renderings, does nothing to prevent him from becoming a fine blues singer. Moreover, it sounds as if Jimmie's blues are also wicked enough. Just listen!
13. "Tom Cat and Pussy Blues," Victor 23763. This ditty is so risqué that the pun is useless. While the yodeling is a bit annoying, these rural blues are wickedly full of dirt. While it's for sure that censors were more ridged, it's more than a guess that this X-rated ditty is more than conjecture and more than a smirk, perhaps?
14. "It's All Coming Home to You," Bluebird B-5156. Credited to Jimmy himself and Leon Chappelear, this (1933) recording found Jimmie a good case to croon out this simple yet affective folk yarn. (This ditty also notes (co-credited writer)

Leon Chappelear, a fine guitarist and vocalist, who had been very much interested and influenced (vocally) by Jimmie Rodgers and Jimmie Davis, and musically by the (local) jazzy aspirations of Milton Brown and His Brownies, whose fame had originated on radio broadcasts from Texas—eventually known as "western swing." Leon's own vocals would prove to become a looser style with a swagger (much like Elvis Presley, later in 1954), especially noting his own recordings such as "I'm a Do Right Papa" (a self-penned ditty with Jimmie Davis as cowriter and the older Bertha Hill blues ditty "Trouble in Mind," among others as Leon's Lone Star Cowboys.) More so, backing Jimmie Davis on this recording are the Shelton Brothers (Joe and Bob Attlesey), whose band members were matched and sometimes collaborated with the Lone Star Rangers. Indeed, both bands would eventually become a major influence on the later likes of Bob Wills and His Texas Playboys.

15. "Alimony Blues," Bluebird B-5635. Pay up!
16. "Nobody's Darlin' but Mine," Decca 5090. While by this time (1934) it was a good bet despite the hard times of the Great Depression that Jimmie was not going to go away, Jimmie's own simple song writing is best defined with this ballad. Sung with a lot of heart, Jimmie was, perhaps, aiming at a contemporary crooner, "country" style? He, more so, succeeds, as his sincerity, with a crude vocal attempting to become soft, is very effective.
17. "Come On Over To My House," Decca 5249. Are his intentions honorable?
18. "Mama's Getting Hot and Papa's Getting Cold," Decca 5249.
19. "I Wonder Who's Kissing Her Now," Decca 5363. This (1937) rendering would be well noted as by the sweet band of Ted Weems, with a smoother crooning vocalist, Perry Como, on Decca 2919.
20. "Honky-Tonk Blues," Decca 5400. Jimmie's previous "Barroom Message," had been released in Prohibition times (1930). This ditty, released in 1937, refers to post-Prohibition times, as well as an honest reason to get the blues at a local (Southern) place of refreshment. (Backing provided by "Brownies Musical Brownies," the remnants of Milton Brown's (previous) Orchestra.)
21. "Jimmie's Traveling Blues," Decca 5435.
22. "Good-bye Old Booze," Decca 5505. This good ole boy drinking song, penned by Johnny Roberts and Davis himself, is as crude as it is appealing.
23. "It Makes No Difference Now," Decca 5620. While credited to the likes of Floyd Tillman and Jimmie Davis, this excuse for country swing was as likable as was considerable. More so, a later Bing Crosby version, on Decca 3590, was also well done.
24. "My Blue Heaven," Decca 5779. So Jimmie wanted to become a crooner like Gene Austin? It's all interesting enough to ponder about Jimmie's stronger (than Austin) vocal.
25. "You Are My Sunshine," Decca 5813. Like many song ditties of rural Americana, "You Are My Sunshine" had been around for some years before Jimmie Davis claimed it in 1940. Was it just a coincidence that it had been released and claimed by (Paul) Rice as a contemporary Rice Brothers Gang (Decca 5763) that had preceded Jimmie's later (Decca) label hillbilly series number? Or what about another (1939) hillbilly release by the Pine Ridge Boys on Bluebird B-8263? Or perhaps Jimmie's claim as noted on his release (as by Charles Mitchell and Jimmie Davis) had had more to do with shared culture than theft? If so, the likes of many claimed song ditties as rendered and or claimed such as by "Big Bill" Broonzy, Arthur Crudup, Leadbelly, Jimmy Rogers, Merle Travis, or Clarence Williams, among many others, indeed make Davis look less like a suspect of foul play. In any case, Jimmie's own rendering is more

of a "country weeper," and while it has always been known that some of these slick, country hicks could croon out a good ballad, the familiar up-tempo (Davis) vocal wins out! (Subsequent contemporary versions as by a best-selling Gene Autry effort, on Okeh 06274); Bing Crosby, on Decca 3952; and a filmed version by Tex Ritter indicated that the ditty became part of the culture. By 1943, it was widely reported that the British Prime Minister Winston Churchill, at the Casablanca Conference with President Roosevelt, had become very much aware of the song ditty. By the next year (1944), Jimmie Davis had become elected as governor of his home state of Louisiana. Light-years later in 1962, a Ray Charles recording on ABC Paramount 10375 produced a huge best seller as in contemporary pop and in rhythm and blues.

26. "I'm Waiting for Ships That Never Come In," Decca 5867. The previous Nick Lucas best seller is (vocally) brought down to earth, as Jimmie's vocals had become less crude.
27. "Sweethearts or Strangers," Decca 5902. As penned with Lou Wayne, Jimmy again produced another tear producing classic.
28. "I'm Thinking Tonight of My Blue Eyes," Decca 6006. The Carter family or Bing Crosby?
29. "Live and Let Live," Decca 6053. A fine ditty penned by Wiley Walker and Gene Sullivan, perfect for (1942) honky-tonk jukeboxes.
30. "Walkin' My Blues Away," Decca 6083. Is this just an effective self-penned ditty that reeks of jazz influence?
31. "Columbus Stockade Blues," Decca 6083. A strong, folksy, blues entity, penned by Eva Sargent and Jimmie himself, again gains relevance. It is more so interesting that Darby and Tarlton's previous 1927 (Columbia) recording, penned by Tom Darby and Jimmy Tarlton, about serving time in a Columbia, Georgia jail had a cell mate a decade earlier? Check 'em out!
32. "There's a New Moon Over My Shoulder," Decca 6105. Somehow this published song ditty, crediting Ekko Whelan, Lee Blastie, and Jimmie himself, had found its way into a successful and contemporary (1944) Tex Ritter recording, as released on Capital 194. While perhaps full of contrived country and a bit jazzy, the simple and rural appeal of this ditty, for whoever attempted to render it, was for real. More so was Jimmie's own subsequent recording, which became a huge best seller in 1945. Tex or Jimmie?
33. "Grieving My Heart out for You," Decca 18756. Did this postwar (1946) bar song, penned by Logan Snodgrass and Jimmie himself, have some effect upon the later "rockabilly" style of the 1950s?
34. "Tired of Crying over You," Decca 18832. Tired? Or does this Lawrence Welk-backing induce sleep?
35. "I Just Dropped in to Say Good-bye," Decca 46066.
36. "Bang Bang," Decca 46016. A self-written ditty, an influence on (future) rockabilly?

Sammy Davis Jr.

As one of the most recognized icons of the century, Sammy Davis Jr. owes his success mainly to television, the new medium of the 1950s, as well as the latter century and the rock era. As far as recordings are concerned, moreover, despite enormous sales of 1972s' "The Candy Man"—released on MGM 14320—the material recorded is mostly of a pre-rock product and performance. As a man of multiple talents, Sammy Davis Jr. perhaps was a paradox between (changing) musical tastes, redefining (his) Afro-American aspirations and identity with huge success. For the most part, this performer was claimed by a part of entertainment that had begun to disappear at the start of the rock era, yet, for him, did not matter. As part of the Will Masters Trio, his legacy in (black) entertainment was legendary by the time he was Ten. As seen and heard in the 1933 film short *Rufus Jones for President* with Ethel Waters, his childhood talents upon the dance floor were obvious. As a grown-up, his later 1940s interest in contemporary baritone Billy Eckstine led to some recording activity. His 1950s/1960s identification with the likes of Frank Sinatra, Dean Martin, Broadway, and film entertainment led to wider notice beyond race and, more so, despite rock and roll. As a popular icon, the oddity of his limits and preference to mostly pre-rock material as a recording artist perhaps found an attitude that recordings were only a lesser part of his (whole) bag of talents, which were indeed considerable. Like (fellow Rat Pack member) Dean Martin, also on the cusp of 1950, he also made it into this book. Picks include

1. "I Don't Care Who Knows," Capital 15390. This 1949 recording, penned by Buddy Johnson, indeed sounds much like the style of (contemporary) Billy Eckstine.
2. "Be-Bop the Beguine," Capital 70022. Sammy tries hard to find a vocal style and almost finds it. This ditty penned by Richard Hazard and B. Jordan also features a creative Dave Cavanaugh Orchestra backing. Sammy indeed sounds hip and be-bop-ish.
3. "We're Gonna Roll," Capital 70052. This Bobby Black-penned ditty is not strictly a Sammy Davis Jr. entity, as Sammy recorded it under the name of "Shorty Muggins." Sammy does his best to emulate contemporary bluesman Joe Turner, performing some good rhythm and blues. In true retrospective, it's more than a pity that Sammy did not pursue more of this type of material and vocal style.
4. "Hey There," Decca 29199. The pop aspirations from the Broadway entity *The Pajama Game*, penned by Richard Adler and Jerry Ross, are OK.

5-6. *Boy Meets Girl*, Decca LP DL 8490. Carmen McRae (a fairly new pop diva whose good vocals would compliment anyone) found Sammy good company. Highlights are, (a.) "Happy to Make Your Acquaintance"(penned by Frank Loesser) and (b.) "They Didn't Believe Me"(penned by Jerome Kern and Herbert Reynolds).

7. "That Old Black Magic," Decca 29541. Perhaps Sammy had decided to record this (old) Johnny Mercer-penned ditty as a pun? In any case, this (1955) articulate-voiced vocal does indeed make its claim.
8. "Too Close for Comfort," Decca 29861. Sammy introduced this ditty, penned by Jerry Block and David Weiss in his own 1956 (Broadway) entity *Mr. Wonderful.*
9. "What Kind of Fool Am I," Reprise 20048. The bombastic Broadway entity had arrived, and among much junk, this alternative to rock, as a contemporary Broadway entity penned by Anthony Newley and Leslie Bricusse ain't bad.

10-11. *Robin and the Seven Hoods*, LP Reprise 2021. This 1964 film entity also has a good soundtrack. As a Rat Pack entity to boot, the chemistry between Sinatra, Martin, Sammy, and added attraction, Bing Crosby, ain't bad. Sammy scores heavily in the film, as well as in the following ditties: (a.) "Bang Bang" and (b.) "Mr. Booze"—with Crosby.

12. "I've Gotta Be Me," Reprise 20779. The Walter Marks penned ditty also found Sammy defining himself in a song ditty title?
13. "The Candy Man," MGM 14320. This ditty from the pen of stuffy Anthony Newley and Leslie Bricusse had been produeced for the 1971 film 'Willy Wonka And The

Chocolate Factory'. Somehow, despite rock and roll, Sammy's recording became a huge best-selling entity; with much appeal for the kiddies and grown-ups.

Visual Image.

14, 15. Visual Image at seven years old—Little Sammy may be found with Ethel Waters as the first black president in 1933's *Rufus Jones for President,* singing and dancing in "You Rascal You" and "I Do, I Do."

16. Sammy's 1964 visual in *Robin and the Seven Hoods* in "Bang Bang" is sensational!
17. Sammy's 1974 visual and identical live recording on TV with Johnny Carson on the *Tonight Show* of. "Singing in the Rain," the old 1929 song ditty, is updated into something new. Check it out!

Dolly Dawn

- As a member of the George Hall Orchestra, Dolly Dawn found recognition and fame in the mid-1930s. As a sweet band, the Hall band had already found some notice with vocals by Scrappy Lambert, Sonny Schuyler, and Loretta Lee. (Lee's vocal on the Crosby contemporary (1934) ditty "Young and Healthy," on Bluebird B-5022 perhaps gave Dolly something to emulate.)

  Dolly's own attempt at "sweet" vocals for George Hall were, more so, a mixed and more interesting bag with the emergence of swing. For the most part, vocals on rhythmic ditties also echoed Mildred Bailey, with some fine results. Slower, sweet numbers would find Dolly somewhat lost, without much style, and sounding much like (rival) band singer Harriet Hillard (Nelson). In any case, Dolly would indeed "swing" as well as the rest of them, as both orchestra and vocalist tackled swing. Later, Dolly Dawn and her Dawn Patrol releases (still using Hall), prove Hall much less of the "hog," than his contemporaries.

Picks are as follows:

1. "I Never Saw a Better Night," Bluebird B-6016. This duet with Sonny Schulyer, penned by Johnny Mercer and Lewis Gensler, is pleasant enough. While a very straight Schulyer vocal limits humor, Dolly's easy and loose vocal (with what could be somewhat risqué lyrics), contributes to a winner despite its obvious vintage (1935).
2. "Weatherman," Bluebird-B-6017. This very fine mid-tempo ditty, penned by Irving Caesar and Newell Chase, finds the influence of Mildred Bailey's contemporary recordings very much in evidence—which indeed sounds very good.
3. "No Strings," Bluebird B-6098. While Fred Astaire's version of the Irving Berlin classic in the film *Top Hat* ain't bad, Fred's recording (Brunswick 7486), in true retrospective, is easy to overlook. This unconventional swing version features Dolly scatting, which most likely found patrons of contemporary dance floors (1935) much more than pleased. Sorry, Fred.
4. "Shine," Bluebird B-6170. Just why Dolly attempted to emulate Louis Armstrong's recording (Okeh 41486) is not known. It is for certain on par with the Bing Crosby and the Mills Brothers version (Brunswic 6276), although it's all (vocally) Armstrong's influence for Dolly. Penned by Cecil Mack, Lew Brown, and Ford Dabney, this

obvious attempt to emulate Afro-Americans works, and this white female's attempt at scatting is indeed no fluke.

5. "It's a Sin to Tell a Lie," Bluebird B-6378. This slow ballad (penned by Billy Mayhew) finds itself lost in 1936. Vocally, Dolly's ballad sound somewhat emulates Ruth Etting, with George Hall perhaps doing Guy Lombardo's orchestrations. Oddly, it's hard to figure that Dolly had heard Ruth's contemporary version, recorded and released in England. In any case, this sweet band entity somehow works, although it's a little less in comparison with the contemporary Fats Waller version (Victor 25342).
6. "Robins and Roses," Bluebird B-6381. While the mid-tempo (contemporary) Bing Crosby version, on Decca 791, ain't bad, Dolly's more-spirited swing style works better for this ditty penned by Edgar Leslie and Joe Burke.
7. "You Can't Pull the Wool over My Eyes," Bluebird B-6382. Penned by Milton Ager, Charles Newman, and Murray Mencher, this bit of rhythmic and danceable fluff works very well.
8. "Sing a Song of Nonsense, Pocket Full of Love," Bluebird B-6576. While nonsense for the excuse to "swing" is contrived, this ditty, penned by Stanley Adams and Hoagy Carmichael, ain't bad. While other contemporary rhymes did better, like Ella Fitzgerald's "A-Tisket, A-Tasket" on Decca 1840 and Maxine Sullivan's "Loch Lomond" on Vocalion 3654, it's all good and novel, especially on a dance floor.
9. "How Could You," Bluebird B-6797. This ditty "swings" lightly, with Dolly effectively taking over (penned by Al Dubin and Harry Warren). A contemporary Miff Mole release, with a Midge Williams vocal, on Brunswick 7842, also excels.
10. "The Mood That I'm In," Bluebird B-6861. The foreign-recorded version by Valaida Snow was most likely never heard by Dolly, although the contemporary Billie Holiday version just could have been. Which version or this of this Jimmy McHugh and Dorothy Fields is better? Listen and compare.
11. "Have You Got Any Castles Baby," Variety 621. This Richard Whiting and Johnny Mercer penned ditty was perhaps an idea about using contemporary slang? If so, it's a good term that Dolly's capable vocal makes for some interesting listening!
12. "Remember Me," Variety 623. This pleasant ditty, penned by Al Dubin and Hary Warren, had been introduced well enough by contemporary tenor Kenny Baker in the (1937) film *Mr. Dodd Takes the Air*. As a recording, it was Bing Crosby's contemporary version on, Decca 1451, that made this recording best known. In true retrospective, however, Dolly's vocal at lower key works well, as part of this George Hall Orchestra release—rivaling Crosby's crooning effort. Remember? No.
13. "You Can't Stop Me from Dreaming," Variety 652. This ditty, penned by Cliff Friend and Dave Franklin, finds Dolly's vocal in perfect swing mode, along with her "Dawn Patrol."
14. "You're a Sweetheart," Vocalion 3874. As a film entity of the same title (1938) for Alice Faye, this ditty found stiff competition from the likes of many contemporaries, including Ethel Waters on Decca 1613.
15. "How'd Ja Like to Love Me," Vocalion 4018. This swing fest, was originally penned by Frank Loesser and Burton Lane for the contemporary film entity *College Swing. While* the energetic Martha Raye introduced it, it's Dolly's (even) better recording that lingers. Watch Martha & listen to Dolly!
16. "Says My Heart," Vocalion 4098. The (very) pleasant contemporary Harriet Hilliard vocal, on the Ozzie Nelson release (Bluebird B-7520), is challenged and in much the same vocal style.

17. "There Won't Be a Shortage of Love," Elite 5018. This Elite release also indicates "Hits by Dolly Dawn." Indeed, this swing-era special, penned by CarmenLombardo and John Jacob Loeb, was for sure a hit, for many-with Dolly, if heard, leading the vote for best vocal!

Doris Day

While baby boomers knew her from "grown-up" films and as an "older" woman who sometimes sang in films, the product Doris Day (real name Doris Kappelhoff) and "image" were one. In 1945, as a band vocalist (between marriage, a child, and divorce) with Les Browns Orchestra, she had finally scored with "Sentimental Journey." Along with much radio exposure at home and the millions of servicemen overseas (who greatly identified with it), as well as a lot of P. A. touring (with Les Brown), Doris Day became instantly identified by an entire generation. This clear-voiced, young band singer, perhaps most influenced (vocally) by the likes of Ella Fitzgerald, would, moreover, become a huge single-recording entity and a major film star despite rock and roll.

Picks are as follows:

1. "Let's Be Buddies," Okeh 5937. Buddy Clark's earlier version of this Cole Porter-penned classic is also very danceable, as Doris, with Les Brown's Orchestra, kicks off the dance floor!
2. "If It Ain't Hep That Step but I'll Dig It," Okeh 5964. This bit of (then current) language, penned by Johnny Mercer and Hal Borne, like all Les Brown releases, is very danceable and done well by Doris.
3. "Broomstreet," Okeh 6049. Harmless novelty, danceable, and subject to swing—indeed ruled the era (1941). Penned by D. Vance, Josef Myrow, and Buck Ram, this ditty set no standards, but is a much-recorded proof of just how good Doris's lead vocal could be.
4. "Beau Night in Hotchkiss Corners," Okeh 6098. This novelty, penned by Herb Magidson and Ben. Oakland, also attempts to "swing" and, indeed, succeeds.
5. "Keep Cool Fool," Okeh 6167. This fine bit of swing still works (penned by James Price Johnson and Josef Myrow). An interesting comparison to the group concept of the contemporary Ink Spots, perhaps?
6. "Tain't Me," Columbia 34267. This ditty penned by Jack Palmer and Lanier Davis just could be jazz, or even an attempt at the pre-rock style of (contemporary) Ella Mae Morse. In any case, it all sounds very well.
7. "Sentimental Journey," Columbia 36769. While this record is a Les Brown release, it's Doris Day herself (finally), sounding less like Ella (and her contemporaries) as well as a "canary" for a band vocalist, with an identifiable (vocal) style. Indeed, this fine best-selling WWII entity (penned by Bud Green, Ben Homer, and Les Brown himself) became an anthem for the celebration of victory itself (1945).
8. "My Dreams Are Getting Better All the Time," Columbia 36779. This ditty, penned by Manny Curtis and Vic Mizzy was the follow-up release number of "Sentimental Journey" and again scores due to Doris's mellow rendering.
9. "Till the End of Time," Columbia 36828. While the contemporary Perry Como release (Victor 20-1709) sold more, this fine vocal by Doris is somewhat highlighted by Les Brown's backup orchestration. Indeed, this backing beats out the semiclassical

approach provided by Russ Case and Orchestra on the Como version. Does anyone care?

10. "Day by Day," Columbia 36945. This ditty, penned by Sammy Cahn, Axel Stordahl, and Paul Weston, should have been written for Doris, as it works very well in sound and meaning-for her. Indeed, the contemporary Bing Crosby version (Decca 18746), with Mel Torme and his Mel-Tones, is at least matched.
11. "Aren't You Glad You're You," Columbia 36875. Despite Bing Crosby's hit, on Decca 18720, this rendering of the ditty (penned by Burke and Van Heusen) is far hipper. Indeed, Doris's vocal is better, and so is Brown's backing much better that John Scott Trotter's arrangement. Sorry, Bing!
12. "We'll Be Together Again," Columbia 36875. This ditty features Doris satisfying the ears and bettering the contemporary hit by Frankie Lane (Mercury 5091).
13. "Come to Baby Do," Columbia 36884. The mellow success of Doris and Les Brown is more than realized in this ditty penned by Inez James and Sidney Miller. A Contemporary (1945) version from Joya Sherrill (as a Duke Ellington release on Victor 20-1748) is perhaps lighter in voice, yet cooler than Doris's vocal. A (more) differing group sound as heard on a contemporary King Cole Trio version, with a jazzy vocal by Nat King Cole, is just as interesting as Joya or Doris.
14. "There's Good Blues Tonight," Columbia 36972. Ah, Yes! This ditty, penned by Edna Osser and Abe Osser, is better than the best-selling Tommy Dorsey entity (with a vocal by Sy Oliver, on Victor 20-1842).
15. "I've Got the Sun in the Morning," Columbia 36977. This Irving Berlin-penned ditty (from *Annie Get Your Gun*) is best heard on this fine vocal by Doris.
16. "It's Magic," Columbia 38188. As an entity, this Doris Day record scores. Indeed, the 1948 film *Romance on the High Seas* found Doris herself introducing this pleasant ditty penned by Sammy Cahn and Jule Styne. Another contemporary version, moreover, by Sarah Vaughan (Musicraft 557) just may, however, have topped Doris's original?
17. "It's a Great Feeling," Columbia 38676. As the title of a film entity, penned by Jule Styne and Sammy Cahn, this ditty pleases the ear, perhaps better than the film, which also featured Doris introducing it. (1949).
18. "At the Café Rendezvous," Columbia 38676. This flip side of "It's A Great Feeling," also penned by Jule Styne and Sammy Cahn, doubles the pleasure of its "other side," as well as being (another) ditty from the film itself.
19. "Bewitched," Columbia 38698. The Rogers and Hart never sounded better? Or did Frank Sinatra later define it?
20. "When I Fall In Love:. Columbia 39786.
21. "April in Paris," Columbia 39881. Doris's own contemporary (1952) film of the same title revived this already old ditty penned by Vernon Duke and E. Y. Harburg.
22. "Domino," Columbia 39596. Yet another mellow-voiced recording, penned by Jacques Plante, Louis Ferrari and Don Raye, which will produce sleep pleasantly!
23. "Secret Love," Columbia 40108. This film entity was introduced by Doris, who also starred in the film. This ditty, penned by Sammy Fain and Paul Francis Webster for the film *Calamity Jane*, was perhaps the best thing about the film? Indeed, this ditty even got itself nominated for an Academy Award for best song in 1953. It won!
24. "If I Give My Heart to You," Columbia 40300. Backed by the Mellomen, Doris is pleasant enough in this ditty penned by Jimmy Crane, Al Jacobs, and Jimmy Brewster, in 1954.

25-29. *Love Me or Leave Me*, Columbia LP CL 710. This best-selling 1955 film soundtrack LP, as a film "soundtrack" features Doris singing Ruth Etting standards like

a. "Love Me or Leave Me."
b. "Mean to Me."
c. "Ten Cents a Dance."

It's interesting to point out that Doris (featured in this film "biography" of Ruth Etting), sounds nothing like Ruth Etting at all, as Ruth's style of singing (covered in another chapter of this book) can be considered bolder, if more quirky, than Doris's, although Ruth's enunciation of words (like other singers) is (at) least captured by Doris. Doris performs better on the following new ditties penned for this 1955 soundtrack:

d. "I'll Never Stop Loving You," penned by Nicholas Brodsky and Sammy Cahn.
e. "Never Look Back," penned by Chilton Price.

30. "Whatever Will Be, Will Be (Que Sera, Sera)" Columbia 40704. Doris played fine film role, married to James Stewart, in the 1956 Alfred Hitchcock film *The Man Who Knew Too Much*. While dramatic enough, her superb vocal of this ditty (penned by Jay Livingston and Ray Evans), greatly added more to this excellent film plot.
31. "Everybody Loves a Lover," Columbia 41195. This snappy 1958 best-selling entity, penned by Richard Adler and Robert Allen, is loaded with echo and even features Doris duetting with herself. Despite all these 1950s' gimmicks, the pleasant sound works in spite of the success of rock and roll. (The Shirelles would later produce a fine 'girl group'recording of this ditty in 1963).
32. "Song is You," Columbia - LP - CL - 942. This update of the Hammerstein and Kern penned ditty differs greatly from a weak 1932 Paul Small crooning job, inspired by Rudy Vallee. Doris more so gets a bit moody, indeed interested.

➢ Visual Image.

As a major film entity, the image of Doris Day remains huge. While her earlier and wilder days as a band singer are seemingly hard to find, her subsequent musical films are anthems. As a pick, perhaps her acting abilities, combined in a tense moment in the 1956 Alfred Hitchcock film *The Man Who Knew Too Much*, find her ably rendering out

33. "Whatever Will Be, Will Be." This is indeed a classic film, with music cleverly included. It is, more so, due to Doris's own creditability that it all works! Hear and see it! (Also, find the subsequent recording (a pick above), and listen to it again! High marks!
34. "It's Magic". From "Romance In The High Seas". 1948
35. "I'll Never Stop Loving You". From "Love Me Or Leave Me". 1955.

Vaughn De Leath

Vaughn De Leath was a promising would-be popular vocalist of the early 1920s. She is generally credited to be the first woman to sing popular music on the new media of commercial radio, in 1920. While speculation about radio programs and broadcasts are indeed sketchy for this early period, the clear vocals of Vaughan De Leath, about twenty-four years old in 1921, no doubt found an audience. Indeed, her radio broadcasts also created for her an interest in recording, although her acoustic recordings were most likely less in sound quality than her "radio" vocals. While novel, her live broadcasts found her to be labeled a bit crude, much like contemporary black blues singer recordings and much indeed a "crooner," perhaps the first to be so labeled. Her subsequent and successful commercial electric recordings, moreover, proved that her pioneering crooning efforts were indeed part of popular music itself. The following are Vaughn De Leath picks:

1. "All by Myself," Okeh 4355. The Irving Berlin penned ditty aint bad.
2. "All by My Lonesome Blues," Okeh 4492-B. This ditty, credited to D. Mac Boyle and Sam Coslow, sounds like an emulation of a contemporary Ethel Waters release, "Down Home Blues," as penned by Tom Delaney (Black Swan 2110). Indeed, both performers were, at this time (circa 1920), in search of a style—not an easy task, especially in the acoustic age.
3. Lovin San The Shiek Of Alabam Bell-P-182 subsequent numbers after 3 added one number
4. "I'm Just Wild about Harry," Gennett 4905. Penned by the Afro-American team of Noble Sissle and Eubie Blake from their creative 1922 *Shuffle Along*, this fine recording by Vaughn, indeed, pushed this ditty into wider (white) circulation, along with a contemporary version by Marion Harris. (In true retrospective, this ditty had eyes and sound for the future. Indeed, the 1948 presidential election of Harry Truman found this title more than a political inspiration.)
5. "Ukelele Lady," Columbia 361-D. This quirky acoustic ditty scores. So indeed does Vaughn, as this novelty, penned by Gus Kahn, Richard Whiting, and Eagen, is successfully embellished by her own unique vocal tricks, backed by some very loose Hawaiian strings. (A contemporary 1925 Margaret Young version on Brunswick 2861 is also done well.)
6. "Where'd You Get Those Eyes," Gennett 3347. This Walter Donaldson-penned ditty most likely sounded better on radio, something hard indeed to pirate in the early 1920s. Nevertheless, this quirky crooning job, considering its poor acoustics, ain't bad and is worth the attempt to sit down and hear! A later electric version recorded by Josephine Baker in Paris, France, perhaps defined this ditty? Listen and compare!
7. "Bye, Bye, Blackbird," Cameo 963. This Gloria Geer release was also released on Romeo 240. As a staple of the era, this ditty, penned by Mort Dixon and Ray Henderson is (alias) Vaughn herself, and this flapper entity, compared to the contemporary Gene Austin version on Victor 20044, is a fine improvement despite acoustic limits.
8. "Blue Skies," Okeh 40750. The contemporary (1927) Irving Berlin classic finds the very able Vaughn very able to deliver a classic! While Al Jolson introduced this ditty on film in *The Jazz Singer*, he did not record! Among other contemporary versions included an uninhibited jazzy version by Josephine Baker, which was not well known in the States. A later, spunky version in the 1930s by Maxine Sullivan perhaps defines it. More so, a slower, mellower version by Bing Crosby, in the 1940s, became the best-known version. Listen and compare.
9. "The Whisper Song," Okeh 40814. A great novelty, perhaps, hidden in this song title? Penned by Cliff Friend, this ditty was also known as "When the Pussy Willow Whispers to the Catnip." While this (female) version of Vaughn's may be better, a contemporary (1927) version by Cliff Edwards is equally interesting and fun. Listen
10. "Are You Lonesome Tonight," Edison 52044. While this ditty, in true retrospective, had something to do with rock music and Elvis in 1960, this sentimental classic,

penned by Roy Turk and Lou Handman, was also another original 1920s' classic. (Al Jolson would record it (later) in the 1940s.)

11. "Here Comes Fatima," Champion 15178. While Rudy Vallee would later find college appeal and juvenile novelty a fine marketing ploy, this contrived "name" entity, penned byLou Brown and Cliff Friend, while not as popular as "Georgia Brown," "Dinah," or "Lulu," was still a good name for a contemporary 1920s' flapper.
12. "Baby Your Mother," Victor 20873. Sentimental and schmaltzy, it was penned by Andrew Donnelly, Dolly Morse, and Joe Burke (play on Mother's Day?).
13. "Like An Angel You Flew Into Everyone's Heart". Victor-20674. This 1927 penned ditty, by (Harry E. Stone, John McLaughlin, Jimmy McHugh & Irving Mills), in true retrospective, gets a bit lost. As it's subject matter was founded upon the successfully heroic solo air flight of Charles Lindbergh from New York to Paris, the most celebrated contemporary event of the 'Roaring Twenties"! Sadly the passage of time leaves Vaughn's well sung lift of this sappy title less obvious than the likes of numerous other 'tribute songs'. This would especially note the best selling (Howard Johnson & Al Sherman) penned "Lindbergh The Eagle Of The USA", recorded by many and on many labels, perhaps best known on (Columbia-1000-D) and it's flip (penned by Abel Baer & L.W. Gilbert) "Lucky Lindy", as by stiff (tenor) Vernon Dalhart.
14. "The Toymaker's Dream," Victor 21975. The creativity put into this otherwise novelty, penned by Ernie Golden, is easy enough to remain likable.
15. "Honolulu Moon," Columbia 1026-D. A *Clicquot Club Eskimos* release, this dull ditty, penned by Lawrence, finds Vaughn ably assisted by Tom Stacks, the usual and able vocal lead of a group not named for a nightclub, but a soda! Mixed with bootleg . . .
16. "Aloha Oe Blues," Columbia 1251-D. As a contrived "Hawaiian" entity (by Noble and Luckens), this dance band release, by the faceless Moana Orchestra, luckily featured a vocal chorus by Vaughn De Leath. More so, Vaughn's softer crooning is a bit up-tempo, between some Hawaiian guitar strings. Blues? Not really!
17. "I Wanna Be Loved by You," Columbia 1604-D. As a band singer for the popular Ben Selvin Orchestra, Vaughn returns to a quirky and novel flapper approach, and with an obvious improvement in sound—as this electric recording indicates.

Note: The two following recordings were made with the popular Whiteman organization. While strictly "Paul Whiteman" entities, Vaughn's sparkling vocals reveal a good voice, as well as well as a "hip" one.

18. "The Man I Love," Columbia 50058-D. As an early Gershwin classic, Vaughn's sparkling vocal works well. Indeed, this version competes with the likes of others, including the likes of fellow contemporary diva's Marion Harris and Ruth Etting.
19. "Button up Your Overcoat," Columbia 1736-D. The peppy Ruth Etting version is challenged.
20. "Sometimes I'm Happy," Brunswick 3608. Another "standard, as penned by Vincent Youmans and Irving Caesar that indeed had original 1927 claims put upon it by Vaughan. Later versions by Anita O'Day and Lee Wiley invite interesting comparisons!
21. "Ain't Misbehavin,'" Grey Gull 2501. This Betty Brown (aka Vaughan) version of this 1920s' classic is somewhat jazzy. While the vocal somewhat gives up at the end of this rendering, this ditty, not in the same league as other contemporaries, ain't bad.
22. Crazy Words Crazy Tune. Brunswick-3443. "Vo do de O"-Yes! This (Jack Yellen & Milton Ager) penned ditty is full of that 1920s 'flapper' slang, and Vaughn's vocal is fresh and peppy enough !

Delta Rhythm Boys

The idiom of "group" singers and sounds is perhaps as old as time itself. The success of the Mills Brothers moreover changed many existing perceptions of what could be achieved. The late 1890s and the early 1900s had found the acoustic age full of "barber shop" vocal quartets, but the rhythmic Mills Brothers, also capable of the more conservative "barber shop" vocals, indeed pioneered "rhythm and blues," just as much as Louis Jordan. The Delta Rhythm Boys (previously the New Orleans Quintet) had originally sought to emulate the Mills Brothers and, like the contemporary (mid-1930s) Ink Spots, indeed found themselves on some very good recordings from 1935 through the 1940s. Unlike the Mills Brothers and the Ink Spots, however, the change of personnel did not reflect enough public interest, and the various members of the group (including Traverse Crawford, Lee Gaines, Ruben Bleu, Rene De Knight, Kelsey Pharr, and Karl Jones—all within various periods of time) became nameless. The following picks are noted:

1. "Lover Come Back to Me," Decca 3953. This duet with Mildred Bailey indeed improved with time using her emulation of black speech.
2. "Dry Bones," Decca 4406. Perhaps James Weldon Johnson's own Bible influenced this inspired song ditty?
3. "Praise the Lord and Pass the Ammunition," Decca 4406. Along with the Kay Kyser version, on Columbia 36640, the WWII relic remains relevant. As myth has it, Frank Loesser had found the words for this ditty when he heard the phrase used by servicemen used when Pearl Harbor was attacked by the Japaneese on December 7th, 1941? In any case, this ditty was to indeed become part of Americana itself.
4. "Gee Baby Ain't I Good to You," Decca 18650. This ditty (penned by Don Redman and Andy Razaf) "sounds" much like the (rival) Ink Spots? Added confusion for this ditty was another (similar-sounding) group version, recorded by the Gulf Coast Five. A contemporary Nat Cole Trio version, on Capital 169, may have been more hip, yet in style, this Delta Rhythm Boys rendering finds a bit of a doo-wop vocal—clearly ahead of its time. Could this be the first? Just listen.
5. "Just A-Sittin' and A-Rockin," Decca 18739. Post-WWII vocals of June Christy (a Stan Kenton release) and a Thelma Carpenter release—all fine, good listening despite differing styles.
6. "It's a Pity to Say Goodnight," Decca 23670. Ella Fitzgerald leads the vocal team in a fine ballad!
7. "September Song," Victor 20-2460. This sophisticated ditty, penned by Maxwell Anderson and Kurt Weill, is found to be improved upon. Just listen.
8. "Take the 'A' Train," Victor 20-2461. The brilliant original 1941 Duke Ellington instrumental, on Victor 27380, penned by Billy Strayhorn, was to be subsequently recorded with added lyrics for a vocal from Ellington's new band singer Joya Sherrill, oddly not included in the contemporary film *Reveille with Beverly*. In true retrospective, it's more than a shame that in spite of Betty Roche's smoking-hot performance (on a train), as seen and heard in the film among Duke's blaring orchestra, she does not produce a contemporary recording until 1952. Nevertheless, this group rendering is no slouch, perhaps adding more smoke for the Ellington train!
9. "One O' Clock Jump," Victor 20-2463. Count Basie's instrumental hit of 1937, on Decca 1363, penned by Lee Gaines and Count Basie himself, is still (very) danceable. The added group vocals also add more pep and excitement.

Billy Eckstine

While this book is chiefly concerned with vocal influences, the efforts of musicians such as Earl Hines (with whom Billy started as a vocalist in the late 1930s), Charlie Parker, Fats Navarro, Miles Davis, Howard McGhee, Gene Ammons, Dexter Gorden, Art Blakey, and especially Dizzy Gillespie must be noted. As a "movement" within the (then) current drifts of playing of the instruments, these sounds, a creative advancement of jazz, marked in the initial success of the vocal styles of both Billy Eckstine and Sarah Vaughan. Indeed, the end result of the "double playing" of a musical instrument, while no mean feat for a musician, was of equal challenge for a would-be vocalist. The resulting musical trend "bebop," became largely an urban sound with limited, but creative appeal. It is also interesting to note that the already traditional Louis Armstrong had a hard time accepting all this, while Earl Hines, his onetime pianist on many of his Okeh recordings, helped usher in the new style. More importantly, Hines also hired Billy Eckstine, an urban jazz vocalist influenced hugely by Harlan Lattimore, with huge "crooning pop" aspirations as well. Eckstine picks are as follows:

1-2. "Jelly, Jelly Blues," Bluebird B-11065. There's a "Hawaiian" sound heard in this classic. Penned by Earl Hines and Billy Eckstein (later changed to "Billy Eckstine"), this unusual bit of urban blues indeed found Billy's very deep baritone vocal as something very special. Indeed, light-years away, rock's own Allman Brothers Blues Band, found it more than inspiring. (Re -recorded with own band on National - 9021).
3. "Water Boy," Bluebird B-11329. While this bit of dated tradition (as a contemporary update of Paul Robeson's version from the 1920s by Avery Robinson), is still somewhat sluggish, Billy's baritone qualities are more recognizable.
4. "Somehow," Bluebird B-11432. Credited to Earl Hines and His Orchestra, with vocal refrain by Billy Eckstein, this rather traditional vocal, penned by Mort Maser, still scores.
5. "Skylark," Bluebird B-11512. This much-recorded entity (early 1940s) is given much-appreciated mood and depth by Billy's vocal and Hines's urban backing. This (Johnny Mercer and Hoagy Carmichael) ditty originally had pop aspirations, but, in true retrospective, is best defined in this "urban blues" rendering.
6. "The Jitny Man," Bluebird B-11535. Another Earl Hines release, this ditty, full of urban slang, penned by Gerald Valentine and Hines, indeed finds Billy in an edgy rather than novel mood.
7. "Stormy Monday Blues," B-11567. This interesting ditty, penned by Bob Crowder, Hines, and Billy himself, indeed finds Billy's sad, moody vocal in perfect harmony with a creative Hines orchestration.
8. "My Heart Beats for You," RCA Victor 20-2636. The Earl Hines release is a more traditional ballad (penned by Allen and Kendricks). While Billy's vocal is a bit over the top, perhaps Hines saves the day as his lead does not let his vocalist get too dramatic.
9. "Good Jelly Blues," Deluxe 2000. Released as a Billy Eckstein Orchestra, this obvious attempt at a follow-up to his "Jelly, Jelly Blues," while contrived, ain't dramatically bad.
10. "I Want to Talk about You," Deluxe 2003. Another release by Billy Eckstine and His Orchestra, this (dated) attempt at pop is at least somber and moody, indeed a staple of the emerging Eckstine vocal style. (Its flip side—a Sarah Vaughn vocal, with Eckstine's Orchestra—introduces "I'll Wait and Pray." Sarah, while attempting to emulate Eckstine's moody idiom, actually improves upon it.)

The postwar 1940s found the likes of new recording companies growing like weeds all over America. The "National" label was one of many, and it would indeed pioneer newer sounds of rhythm and blues, with very hip groups such as the Ravens. Eckstine's signing was an obvious attempt at the popular market, aiming Billy at the likes of Bing Crosby and Frank Sinatra, both on major labels, and both white. Like for another emerging label, Capital, who had Nat King Cole, racial stereotyping meant nothing. In true retrospective, Eckstine's deep baritone vocals did achieve huge success (with both black and white audiences), indeed, more so, than his than his onetime idol, Harlan Lattimore.

11. "A Cottage for Sale," National 9014. A somber ballad style finds this crooning effort a winner, although the earlier Ruth Etting version is better. Ruth or Billy?
12. "Prisoner of Love," National 9017. It's a trip from the Russ Columbo crooning job through a group effort of the Ink Spots and a contemporary (1946) softly crooned job by Perry Como. It's, moreover, Eckstine's deep baritone quality that at least makes it interesting enough. (Perhaps the (later) interest in this ditty from James Brown had been Billy's rendering, nevertheless figuring a (huge) differing vocal approach in Brown's style. Listen to all!
13. "You Call It Madness," National 9019. The Russ Columbo light baritone original finds Eckstine's deeper baritone a fine comparison. Russ or Billy?
14. "I Do, Do You?" National 9086. This ditty, penned by Gerald Valentine and Eckstine himself, among Billy's hogging and booming baritone vocal also found, in support, a bit of rhythm guitar.
15. "Blue Moon," MGM 10311. While already a classic since the mid-1930s, this classic (penned by Rodgers and Hart) had been best defined by the husky-voiced Connie Boswell. Eckstine's brassy baritone, more so, redefined it. Subsequent renderings from such entities as Sammy Davis Jr., Mel Torme, Elvis Presley, and the Marcels, would, more so, provide differing voices for this ditty.
16. "I Left My Hat in Haiti," MGM 10916. This stab at creativity largely fails despite the (already) old bandleader Woody Herman and Orchestra. Billy and Woody stumble along this (Burton Lane and Alan Jay Lerner) film entity from the Fred Astaire film *Royal Wedding*, although Eckstine's vocal does emerge well enough.
17. "Here Come the Blues," MGM 10916. Billy and Woody Herman (almost) get it right, as this contrived stab at the blues, penned by Don Raye and Gene De Paul, at least finds a booming vocal—a fine exercise in vocal expression.
18. "I Love You," MGM 11144. Billy and Sarah Vaughan vocalize the hell out of this Cole Porter classic.
19. "Passing Strangers," Mercury 71120. This 1957 release, penned by Stanley Applebaum and Mel Mitchell, found another vocal duet with Sarah Vaughan more than good.

20-31. *The Best of Irving Berlin*, Mercury 203161. By the late 1950s, a lot had changed (due to rock and roll). Bill Eckstine, while still a huge entity in popular music, had become what was a "pop" star, brass-baritone style. Indeed, many contemporary popular vocalists had been influenced by his vocal style, including Sammy Davis Jr., Johnny Mathis, and even the original rock superstar, Elvis Presley. The 1950s had also found room—for the many left-behind pre-rock artists—for a marketing ploy at "adult" entertainment, found on LP (Long Play) 12-inch albums. Who could have ignored the (non-rock) success of contemporary pairings such as Bing Crosby and Rosemary Clooney, or the (younger) likes of Steve Lawrence and Edie Gorme? While many would have found an Eckstine and Vaughn a better LP pairing with the likes of old beboppers more to their liking, this meeting of two fine vocalists, as a "songbook" concept does indeed score. More so, this pairing of the familiar Billy Eckstine and Sarah Vaughan perhaps found the 12-inch concept at its zenith.

As well as not crediting the fine orchestra of Hal Mooney, which is as enjoyable as any contemporary effort of Billy May, Gordon Jenkins, or Nelson Riddle, this LP's (original) liner notes use more than three-quarters of its space in the praise of songwriter Irving Berlin, along with his photograph! Luckily, the fine original color cover, portraying both Billy and Sarah, smartly delivers the goods as a recording!

Titles include the following:

a. "Alexander's Ragtime Band."
b. "Isn't it a Lovely Day."
c. "I've Got My Love to Keep (Me Warm)."
d. "All of my Life."
e. "Cheek to Cheek."
f. "You're Just in Love."
g. "Remember."
h. "Always."
i. "Easter Parade."
j. "The Girl I Marry"
k. "Now It Can Be Told."

Legacy

The success of Billy Eckstine, while saturated "pop," may be considered a major breakthrough. Similar in style were the likes of Herb Jeffries, whose vocal on "Flamingo," on Victor 27326 as a Duke Ellington release, had indeed found notice. So did other neglected Ellington vocalists, such as a Johnny Hodges vocal on "I Let a Song Go Out of My Heart," on Brunswick 8093, and a novel WWII Ray Nance vocal, on "A Slip of the Lip," on Victor 20-1528, who had preceded Eckstine. So did Jimmy Rushing, a Count Basie vocalist. (A later Basie band singer, who did not record until after (1950), Joe Williams, was perhaps a better baritone, although he never achieved the success that Eckstine had achieved.

Cliff Edwards

Most baby boomers were very familiar with Cliff's distinctive voice. By the time most baby boomers were five years old, most were enchanted with the "new" media of television and a cartoon character by the name of "Jiminy Cricket." While the Walt Disney studio had already introduced the character to prewar audiences in the feature cartoon film *Pinocchio* (1940), few could have predicted that latter-century television would exploit the cartoon (and all the other Disney characters) to untold popularity and familiarity. Moreover, the end of the century found more in the likes of video and DVD. What next?

The high-pitched vocals of Cliff Edwards, also known as "Ukulele Ike," with an added attraction of his own ukulele-playing, found this vaudevillian a perfect candidate for acoustic recording. With a quirky vocal perfectly mimicking his (own) strumming, he may have been accused by his early contemporaries as jazz improvisation, or scatting. Moreover, his slightly effeminate refrains of popular novelties found him in good competitive (acoustic) company. So were the similar crooning efforts of a few others who would survive the acoustic age, who would include both Frank Crumit and Nick Lucas. The following are Cliff Edwards picks:

1. "Virginia Blues," Gennett 4843. Later speculation has it that this (1922) contemporary and jazzy Ladd's Black Aces release, penned by Fred Meinken, did not include any (real) "blackfaces." What can be heard is a quirky vocal, identified as the veteran vaudevillian (around twenty-six years old) Cliff Edwards.
2. "Where the Lazy Daisies Grow," Regal 9620.
3. "She's My Sheba, I'm Her Sheik," Pathé 10882. This (Spencer Williams and Jack Palmer) bit of fun defined some of the contemporary slang.
4. "Insufficient Sweetie," Pathé 025121. Yeah, is this "white jazz"? Penned by Gilbert Wells and Edwards himself, this bit of (1924) nonsense remains jazzy and playful, and hardly insufficient.
5. "Charlie, My Boy," Pathé 025122. Another novel ditty, penned by Kahn and Fiorito, which somehow works.
6. "I Wonder What's Become of Sally." Pathé 025122. This ditty penned by Milton Ager and Jack Yellen is about a "flapper" named Sally. Find her!
7. "He's the Hottest Man in Town," Pathé 025123. Indeed, Cliff's own hot vocal on this novel ditty penned by Jay Gorney and Owen Murphy had many (1924) flappers laughing.
8. "Heart Breaking Creole Rose," Pathé 025153. This ditty, penned by Chuck Endor and Edward Ward, oddly (for its time) breezily skips "race" as an attitude.
9. "It Had to Be You," Pathé 032047. Both Gus Kahn and Isham Jones indeed knew how to compose good pop. Moreover, Cliff knew how to croon them out. This effective bit of schmaltz is, more so, proof, noting that the contemporary Marion Harris version is less full of it (schmaltz)! Compare!
10. "Hard Hearted Hannah," Pathé 03254. This Jack Yellen-penned ditty is campy enough in title. So were indeed the newfound rights of (1924) flappers, whose liberation Cliff's quirky vocal seemingly enjoys singing about. Sultry flapper Frances Williams had introduced this ditty in the (1924) broadway entity "Innocent Eyes", lacking a recording. (Other contemporary recordings of this ditty found more than a few female entities perhaps finding some kinship with the hard-hearted flapper? They would include the likes of Belle Baker version (Victor 19436) and Dolly Kay (Columbia 151-D) as well as the (black) entities of Lucille Hegamin (Cameo 624) and Rosa Henderson (Ajax 17060).
11. "Somebody Loves Me," Pathé 032073. This effective Broadway entity, penned by Ballard MacDonald, B. G. De Sylva, and George Gershwin (1924), is effectively crooned out, despite poor acoustics, by Cliff. (The contemporary Marion Harris version is a bit better.)
12. "I Want to Walk Again Blues," Pathé 032041. Along with Gilbert Wells, Cliff produced a contrived yet well done, self penned 'blues' ditty.
13. "Alabamy Bound," Pathé 025127. Penned by Bud De Sylva, Bud Green, and Ray Henderson, this novelty perhaps needed Cliff more than it did Al Jolson. Contemporary vaudevillian Blossom Seeley also scored a fine version of this ditty on Columbia 304-D.

- Cliff starred in the 1924 Gershwin (Broadway) production of *Lady Be Good.* Other entities within the show were the acts of younger (singing and dancing) Fred and Adele Astaire.

14. "Oh Lady Be Good," Pathé 025130. The quirkiness of Cliff perhaps defines this classic penned by Gershwin Brothers better than Fred Astaire ever did? (A few decades later, Ella Fitzgerald would *totally* revamp this title into a differing style.)
15. "I'll Buy the Ring," Pathé 025131. Also known as "I'll Buy the Ring and Change Your Name," this ditty, penned by Jack Miller, William Raskin, and Ed Rose, perhaps describes more than a proposition.
16. "Facinating Rhythm," Pathé 025126. Another "Oh Lady Be Good" Gershwin classic, which had been introduced by Fred Astaire and his sister Adele, was, more so, defined as an excellent recording by Cliff.
17. "Paddlin' Madeline Home," Pathé 025149. This Harry Woods-penned novelty finds Cliff out on a boat with a (flapper) date. Just why Cliff should throw away his paddles merits listening.
18. "Remember," Pathé 025163. A fine Irving Berlin-penned ditty is remembered.
19. "Clap Hands, Here Comes Charley," Pathé 025167. Another bit of free-spirited nonsense, penned by Billy Rose, Ballard McDonald, and Joseph Meyer, that works!
20. "My Best Girl," Pathé 032088. Cliff, as found in the lyrics of this ditty penned by Walter Donaldson, acknowledges his favorite, although contemporary Nick Lucas had similar aspirations.
21. "You're So Cute," Perfect 11553.
22. "I Can't Get the One That I Want," Perfect 11553. An interesting statement as this ditty penned by Fred Rose, Herman Ruby, and Lou Handman, finds no sympathy for Cliff.
23. "Say Who Is That Baby Doll," Perfect 11593. Another hot (1920s) number, penned by Roy Turk and Maeco Pinkard, asked a good question!
24. "The Lonesomest Girl in Town," Perfect 11594. This title penned by Al Dubin and Jimmy McHugh finds a flapper lonesome.
25. "Keep on Croonin' a Tune," Perfect 11598. Croon it in the park? Anywhere? This ditty bySammy Fain, Irving Weill, and Jimmy McHugh perhaps exploited the likes of the popular singing style as vulgar as well as (very) hip.
26. "Meadlark," Perfect 11633. Were the flappers as numerous as some real birds? This silly tale, penned by Hal Keidel and Ted Fiorito, still serves Cliff well enough.
27. "I'm Tellin' the Birds, I'm Tellin' the Bees How I Love You," Perfect 11634. Lew Brown and Cliff Friend's penned ditty finds a surprisingly low-keyed vocal approach that somehow sounds very well!
28. "I Can't Believe You're in Love with Me," Perfect 11638. Perhaps Cliff is grateful enough, finding this (1927) ditty penned by Clarence Gaskill and Jimmy McHugh—sounds pretty good!
29. "Me and My Shadow," Perfect 11643.
30. "Bring Home the Bacon," Perfect 14282. Released in 1928, this ditty was found to be Cliff Edwards's, noting that he was unaccredited on a contemporary Fred Ozark's Jug Blowers release. While it's simple to figure any new or young recording artists struggling to become known and famous, this release perhaps found an unselfish performer. Indeed, Cliff had (by this time) became a very well-known and respected entertainer of vaudeville and as a recording artist who had survived the transition from acoustic to electric recording. More so (within a year despite his aged image), he would

start to appear in the new film media—"talkies." Penned by Frank Bannister, Lew Cowell, and the vaudeville team of Gus Van and Joseph Schenck, this ditty breezes along to become a revitalized jazz classic, more so updating the previous (1924) acoustic version best seller by Blossom Seeley, on Columbia 136-D.

31. "The Whisper Song," Perfect 25206. This silly novelty, penned by Cliff Friend, is also known as "When the Pussy Willow Whispers to the Catnip." Somehow it works, as it also did for contemporary Vaughn De Leath. Listen and compare!
32. "Together," Columbia 1295-D. Together, both Cliff and Nick Lucas shared this title, in addition to vocal style, in this contemporary recording penned by Buddy De Sylvia, Lew Brown and Ray Henderson.
33. "Mary Ann," Columbia 1295-D. The team of Abner Silver and Benny Davis, more so, provide yet another flapper for Cliff to croon about. Check it out!
34. "That's My Weakness Now," Columbia 1471-D. Did flapper Helen Kane sing it better?
35. "I Can't Give You Anything but Love," Columbia 1471-D. Cliff's 1928 electric recordings were also good, as this vocal reveals a good croon. Indeed, this classic (Fields and McHugh) recording from the contemporary revue *Blackbirds of 1928* was to be subsequently recorded by many better singers, but this crooned-out version still ranks as very good, more than competent.
36. "Come Back Chiquita," Columbia 1254-D. A novelty penned by L. Wolf Gilbert and Mabel Wayne, it's more than reasonable to find Cliff's request for Chiquita reasonable!
37. "After My Laughter Came Tears," Columbia 1254-D.
38. "Halfway to Heaven," Columbia 1523-D. J. Russell Robinson and Al Dubin's great lyric are put into a ringer as Cliff's crooning vocal start is transformed into an interesting quirky, scatting croon!
39. "Anita," Columbia 1609-D. Was Anita as much fun as Hannah? This ditty, penned by Sidney Clare and Lew Pollack, seems to indicate she was!
40. Me and the Man in the Moon," Columbia 1705-D. Edgar Leslie and James Monaco's flimlt 'moon' song is at made into something interesting by Cliff!
41. "Just You, Just Me," Columbia 1907-D. (Later, Thelma Carpenter would define this ditty)?
42. "Singing in the Rain," Columbia 1869-D. Forget about the overrated Gene Kelly film title of the same name made light-years away, in 1952. Penned originally for Cliff's (1929) film entity *Hollywood Review* by Arthur Freed and Nacio Herb Brown, this pioneering musical number is pleasant enough, reveling, moreover, a middle-aged man. Indeed, in true retrospective, this original rendering lacks no harm and needs not the forgotten film image to remain a true icon of the Roaring 1920s.
43. "Orange Blossom Time," Columbia 1869-D. Sometimes a schmaltzy, waltz type of dittypenned by Joe Goodwin, for the contemporary film 1929 *Hollywood Review,* can succeed!
44. "I'll See You in My Dreams," Columbia 2169-D. The already dated ditty penned by Gus Kahn and Isham Jones updates the previous (1924) Marion Harris acoustic version. As an electric recording (1930), this ditty was far less influenced by other "electric"-voiced contemporaries of the time. Overly sentimental? Schmaltz? May be so, but Cliff makes it all work—some ten years before you can say "Jiminy Cricket!"
45. "A Great Big Bunch of You," Brunswick 6319. Harry Warren and Mort Dixon's novelty perhaps found better contemporary success as in a "Merrie Melodies' 1932 feature? Evem so, this vocal, and Annette Hanshaw's (better) contemporary recordings remain interesting!

46. “It’s Only a Paper Moon,” Vocalion 2587. This 1933 electric recording, penned by Harold Arlen, E. Y. Harburg, and Billy Rose, retains the likes of acoustic recordings. Indeed, this vocal is full of gimmicks, including Cliff’s ukulele strumming, the staple of his art and of “Ukulele Ike” of the 1920s. Even so, this electric rendering benefits from a clear-sounding, if unusual, vocal, which ain’t bad. (This much-recorded ditty would later be defined as a jazz classic by the Nat Cole Trio.)
47. “I Want to Call You Sweet Mama,” Vocalion 2578. This self penned ditty’s crudeness is refreshing!
48. “Love Is Just Around the Corner,” Romeo 2428. While Bing Crosby’s original, on Decca 310, is better, this very competitive version of the novelty still scores.
49. “The Night Is Young and You’re So Beautiful,” Decca 1106. Penned by Billy Rose, Irving Kahn, and Dana Suesse, this ditty at least found Cliff, in his later days, more than capable to record new recording fodder in an old style successfully.
50. “When You Wish Upon a Star,” Victor 26477. While the year 1940 is “late” for Cliff, this classic recording from Disney’s animated film *Pinocchio,* penned by Leigh Harline and Ned Washington, is crooned out to perfection. Indeed, while tears flowed from many young ones in many theaters in 1940, they were bound to be repeated on each rerelease through the years. Moreover, this ditty remained popular on television and video, and the tears, from some sentimental adults, are not contrived but are, indeed, real. Jiminy Cricket! Yes!

➢ Radio

Cliff had been a radio entity in the mid-1920s before it’s national hookup aspiration became apparent. He subsequently became a guest star, along with more than a few gigs throughout the 1930s and 1940s. Identified as a radio entity, his (1934) rendering of an old standard merits more than interest:

51. “When You and I Were Young Maggie Jones.” As a folk entity of the 1800s, this ditty seemingly had roots as a published entity by a (Canadian) teacher and his pupil Maggie, and was subsequently credited to George Washington Johnson and James Butterworth. Earlier-century recordings were numerous, especially including the bland tenor recordings of Will Oakland and Henry Burr. A copywriter change was seemingly made in 1922 with credit as “When You And I Were Young Maggie Jones Blues,” noted by Jack Frost and Jimmy McHugh. A later (1923) version (Van and Schenck), while still acoustic, perhaps is heard a bit better. While Cliff’s (1934?) captured radio rendering is obviously electric, it’s more to his credit that he betrays a good solid vocal, not needing to become very novel because his natural voice already is. The latter century would, more so, find this ditty (still) excellent recording fodder, with perhaps the better recording identified as a Riley Puckett version, released in 1935 on Columbia 15005-D.

➢ Visual Image.

52. Singing in The Rain.” Cliff introduced this ditty as the highlight of the 1929 film *Hollywood Review.*

➢ More: Bootlegs

53. "I'm Gonna Give It to Mary with Love," ARC-Master. The obvious lyrics are dirty, although Cliff is fast and rhythmic!
54. "I'm a Bear in a Lady's Boudoir," ARC-Master. Cliff is out for fun with this risqué lyric.

Ruth Etting

The vocal style of Ruth Etting made her a major recording entity of the latter '20s and '30s. While the older styles of Nora Bayes and (especially) Marion Harris, among others, indeed had influences, this Ziegfeld girl (of the *Ziegfeld Follies of 1927*) found she had more of a voice as her earlier radio work and recordings (1926) indicated. Earlier work in Chicago nightclubs had, more so, helped. As a "torch singer," this vocalist would promote drama and emotion into song titles with heart-wrenching lyrics about male-female relationships, as well as a term that had applied to "blues" or a singer of sad songs. The break between Afro-American "blues" sometimes led examples of just what emulation is. Ruth would not attempt to emulate Afro-American vocalists or idiom. Within a decade, most aspiring white entertainers would, or would indeed be influenced by them. Ruth was subject to much novelty as almost a mimic of a little girl, as contemporaries such as Helen Kane and Annette Hanshaw were also to experience. When not engaging in these a "little girl" antics, her vocal dryness indicates a popular crooning style as well.

Putting aside some of her earlier acoustic renderings, her electric recordings are clearly understood. Ruth's personal life also made headlines as her association with real-life mobsters, became public. While it is important to stick with musical influences and actual recordings of the recording artist, the Ruth Etting career also became one of scandal and was closely followed by the American public. Most importantly, the likes of radio, live Broadway, and the film work that also followed her found her (personal) soap opera destroying her otherwise well-groomed (public) image in 1937. A later (1955) film entity, *Love Me or Leave Me*, with recording and film star Doris Day (as Ruth), revived the tale of the famed singer of "torch," as perhaps the origin of the term "don't shoot me, I'm only the piano player." Any further explanation of this story should be found in the film! In any case, the following recordings are Ruth Etting picks:

1. "Nothing Else To Do," Columbia 580-D. Accompanied by piano, this earliest vocal, penned by Joe Goodwin, Larry Shay, and Roy Bergere, already finds Ruth defining a vocal style of stretching lyrics. In addition, her sweet vocal betrays a bit of jazz and is indeed controlled. While not developed, or sidelined, Ruth's got it!
2. "Could I? I Certainly Could," Columbia 633-D. In typical "flapper" voice, a bit contrived, this novelty, penned by Jack Yellen and Milton Ager, benefits from Ruth's peppy attitude. Would others, including the likes of Annette Hanshaw and Helen Kane be influenced by this style?
3. "Lonesome and Sorry," Columbia 644-D. Another 1926 ditty, penned by Davis and Con Conrad, again finds Ruth's bubbly approach refreshing.
4. "Hello Baby," Columbia 716-D. This ditty, penned by Seymor Simons and Richard Whiting, indeed notes social changes in its very title. As a typical dance band entity led by Art Kahn, Ruth has little to contribute, but her freestyle vocal when heard, as a liberated "flapper," ain't bad.
5. "Deed I Do," Columbia 865-D. This best seller of 1927, penned by Walter Hirsch and Fred Rose, ain't bad (and better than contemporary Johnny Marvin's versions,

on Edison 51928 and Victor 20357), noting that Johnny Marvin himself was a huge 1920s' recording entity.

6. "It All Depends on You," Columbia 908-D. Penned by Buddy De Sylva, Lew Brown, and Ray Henderson, this ditty scores on an OK vocal and in title alone.
7. "Sam, the Old Accordion Man," Columbia 908-D. This (very) dated bit of schmaltz penned by Walter Donaldson, is still full of (1927) nostalgia, as this mid-tempo vocal with actual accordion backup is indeed sung perkily enough. (An interesting contemporary version by the Williams Sisters, on Victor 20452, is also full of nostalgia, although a group rendering with a huge difference in style. Moreover, while it's obvious that Ruth had not been influenced by the Williams Sisters, others, including the Pickens Sisters and the up-and-coming Boswell Sisters, just could have been. Just listen and compare.)
8. "Wistful and Blue," Columbia 924-D. This mid-1920s entity ain't bad (penned by Julian Davidson and Ruth Etting herself). This best seller of 1927 would also be recorded later in the same year by Paul Whiteman and His Orchestra with vocal chorus on Victor 20418. Within a few years, the "vocal chorus" would be identified as the young contemporaries Al Rinker and Bing Crosby. Another contemporary recording by Annette Hanshaw, on Pathé 36623, perhaps did it well. Ruth's jazzy word-stretching did define this ditty better than any others. Just listen.
9. "My Man," Columbia 995-D. Perhaps the original acoustic Fannie Brice version inspired Ruth to record this ditty? Or maybe it was the newer, brighter, and contemporary electric Brice rerecording, on Victor 45263? Or perhaps even the fact that both ladies were associated with Flo Ziegfeld? In any case, Ruth does justice to Brice's classic, and without the usual (Etting) mid-tempo inclusion and without her usual vocal workout. Indeed, Ruth sings it straight, and very well.
10. "I'm Nobody's Baby," Columbia 1104-D. This "jazz-age baby" just defines it. With a little-girlish vocal, typical of the time, this ditty (by Milton Ager, and Lester Santly) finds some hints of Al Jolson. Even so, it's still Ruth's version that others would associate with the ditty, noting a previous acoustic Marion Harris recording.
11. "Shaking the Blues Away," Columbia 1113-D. The score by Irving Berlin and Franklyn Baur for Broadway's *Ziegfeld Follies of 1927* also scored for Ruth, as her live gig in the show itself also became associated with her. This rhythmic ditty also offers some insight on Berlin himself, as his description of Afro-Americans found in lyrics is, by modern terms, perhaps, at least insensitive. While Ruth's spunky vocal is perhaps carefree enough, she does not choose to emulate black dialect, which is most likely what Berlin intended.
12. "It All Belongs to Me," Columbia 1113-D. This ditty by Irving Berlin, also from Ruth's own *Ziegfeld Follies of 1927* introduction, is another winner.
13. "The Song Is Ended," Columbia 1196-D. Contemporary Annette Hanshaw's version of the Irving Berlin penned ditty also offers a well-done and competing alternative. Listen and compare!
14. "The Varsity Drag," Columbia 1237-D. This contrived ditty by B. G. De Sylva, and Ray Henderson was meant for a jazz-hungry college audience, and indeed, Ruth's novel flapper vocal scores.
15. "Keep Sweeping Cobwebs off the Moon," Columbia 1242-D. Ruth is officially backed-up by Ted Lewis and His Orchestra, a fine contemporary entity and also jazzy. While Ted's music is good, his singing, however incidental, is novelty at best. Luckily, Ruth's fine vocal of the Joe Young, Sam M. Smith and Oscar Levant 'moon' song is exploited well enough and makes this novelty work.

16. "When You're with Somebody Else," Columbia 1288-D. This ditty was penned by L. Wolfe Gilbert, Abel Baer, and Ruth herself. While very much dated, this attempt at torch is indeed defined by its own title. How true!
17. "Back in Your Own Backyard," Columbia 1288-D. Ruth's upbeat style borrows from Al Jolson but greatly improves upon Jolson's own ditty, as Ruth simply sings it better. Sorry, Al! A lesser-known contemporary version by Russ Columbo adds more serious comparisons, as does a later (totally) differing) approach by Billie Holiday. Listen to all for interesting vocal comparisons!
18. "Because My Baby Don't Mean Maybe Now," Columbia 1420-D. This typical 'flapper' hit of the Roaring Twenties (1928), penned by Walter Donaldson, is indeed peppy enough.
19. "Happy Days and Lonely Nights" Columbia 1454-D. This ditty penned by Fred Fisher and Billy Rose features Ruth's spirited vocal with some added "bounce" and some added guitar licks which sound "Hawaiian." It's also interesting that Ruth's forced "girlish" vocal (adapted into commercial recordings by contemporary rivals Annette Hanshaw and Helen Kane) is to be best highlighted here.
20. "Love Me or Leave Me," Columbia 1680-D. This ditty penned byWalter Donaldson and Gus Kahn was originally from the brilliant Eddie Cantor Broadway entity *Whoopee*. Among other versions subsequently recorded, the latter-1940s' version by Sarah Vaughn is also done well and is competently different! (This ditty, more so, became the title of the film based on Ruth's career, which starred Doris Day (a diva herself, by the time of the release of the 1955 film bio). In this fine and emotional torch song, Ruth is convincing enough, as oddly, this ditty became best associated to Ruth by the latter-day film (by Doris Day).
21. "You're the Cream of My Coffee," Columbia 1707-D. As yet another standard of the era, this bit of lighthearted fluff, penned by Buddy De Sylva, Lew Brown, and Ray Henderson, should be noted as a flapper novelty, in mid-tempo, that is sung quite well.
22. "I'll Get by, as Long as I Have You," Columbia 1733-D. Ruth again defines another Fred Ahlert penned classic, and this time with a true and jazzy backing. (A later (1940s) generation of vocalists, including recordings by Billie Holiday and Dick Haymes, also find very good and competing versions to listen and compare!)
23. "Glad Rag Doll," Columbia 1733-D. This sentimental ditty, penned by Dan Dougherty, Milton Ager, and Jack Yellen, using a metaphor for a doll, while contrived, is indeed effective.
24. "Mean to Me," Columbia 1762-D. This title penned by Roy Turk and Fred Ahlert became a standard. Perhaps Ruth's contemporaries Helen Morgan and Annette Hanshaw did better, or perhaps not? Later and differing stylistic versions found in subsequent decades as by Billie Holiday, Sarah Vaughn, and Doris Day perhaps offer more? In any case, it's very interesting to compare all the excellent renderings.
25. "Button Up Your Overcoat," Columbia 1762-D. This ditty penned by B. G. De Sylva, Lew Brown, and Ray Henderson, typifies the Roaring Twenties. Ruth's carefree attitude is novel enough, and so indeed are contemporary Helen Kane and Vaughn De Leath versions.
26. "Deep Night," Columbia 1801-D. This title was crooned well by Rudy Vallee, on Victor 21868, as well. Ruth's typical sweet and dry vocal, in contrast with one of Rudy's few attempts at becoming serious, is interesting to compare.
27. "Maybe Who Knows," Columbia 1801-D. Penned by Johnny Tucker, Joe Schuster, and Ruth herself, this tale of hearts, while dated, still scores.

28. "I'm Walkin' Around in a Dream," Columbia 1830-D. She is walking around in a dream, but that just could mean that this medium-tempo ditty, penned by Ted Lewis, Larry Yoell, and Robert E. Spencer, is good listening.
29. "Ain't Misbehavin'," Columbia 1958-D. This ditty (by Fats Waller, Harry Brooks, and Andy Razaf) was truly an Afro-American entity, introduced by Louis Armstrong in *Hot Chocolates*, an all-black revue The obvious Louis Armstrong version on Okeh was a winner. So was a very hot and contemporary Charleston Chasers version, with a fast-paced jazzy vocal by Eva Taylor. A contemporary Gene Austin version is sung well enough. Ruth's version, however, is altogether different. Indeed, her vocal is sung sweetly and smugly, which also may be found to be schmaltzy. Despite all this, Ruth's vocal, perhaps defining "schmaltz," is worth more than one play.
30. "At Twilight," Columbia 1958-D. Another fine vocal that hits the heart (penned by Harry Pinkard and William Tracey) finds Ruth's usual sweet and dry vocal drifting along well and without her usual lyric-stretching.
31. "What Wouldn't I Do for That Man," Columbia 1998-D. This ditty penned by Jay Gorney and E. Y. Harburg just may be the perfect torch song. While this un-liberating lyric would find much disapproval among 1970s' "women's lib," perhaps its intimate appeal, found it the title itself, deserves attention. In addition to Ruth's fine version, a contemporary Helen Morgan version could be a bit softer, with Ruth a bit stronger and slightly faster. Is it a hard choice between them? Or is the (unaccredited) vocal of Eva Taylor on a contemporary version by Charlestown Chasers better?
32. "More Than You Know," Columbia 2038-D. While dated, Ruth's vocal prowess is again found on yet another torch song. Penned by Vinceny Youmans, Billy Rose, and Edward Eliscu, this ditty had been introduced on Broadway in *Great Day* by Mayo Mehot, noting that a contemporary (1929) recording of Mayo cannot be found. (Mayo was later married to actor Humphrey Bogart). Ruth, more so finds contemporary competition from Helen Morgan's recording, whose patented soft-vocal approach never did vary. (Much later, a cooler Lee Wiley version would define it.)
33. "Crying for the Carolines," Columbia 2073-D. This ditty, penned by Harry Warren, Sam H. Lewis, and Joe Young, is another serious and familiar tale about a young flapper stuck in the big city In fact, this tale remains relevant, except for the obvious dated Etting vocal style.
34. "Ten Cents a Dance," Columbia 2146-D. Penned by Richard Rodgers and Lorenz Hart, this clever commentary on the art of dancing (1930) is also of social significance. Ruth's own vocal attack upon some very tough Depression-era lyrics, along with her typical and slow to mid-tempo style, is to be perfectly exploited here. Moreover, this ditty may be her best effort, as her tale about a very hard-bitten ballroom dancer remains, in true retrospective, a very relevant part of Americana. (A later (1935) rerecording on Columbia 3085-D is OK, but it confuses the issue.)
35. "Funny, Dear, What Love Can Do," Columbia 2146-D. While it's a good bet that Ruth was unaware of the Marion Harris version of this contemporary ditty (penned by Joe Bennett, George Little, and Charles Straight), it is fair to note that since both versions are electric recordings, the vocal styleis similar.
36. "Let Me Sing When I'm Happy," Columbia 2172-D. Penned by Irving Berlin, this obvious Al Jolson-style ditty indeed found Al's own release, on Brunswick 6500, an expected winner. Ruth, who emulated Jolson in certain instances on some recording, moreover, directs her vocal version for her listeners, not at them!

37. "A Cottage for Sale," Columbia 2172-D. As a true torch song, this ditty, penned by Larry Conley and Willard Robison, finds this cottage a sad place and, more so, explains some good reasons why this place had, some time before, been a better place to visit! (A later (1940s) version by Billy Eckstine offers interesting comparisons!)
38. "It Happened in Monterey," Columbia 2199-D. While this ditty penned by Mabel Wayne and Billy Rose is probably best heard some twenty-five years later (recorded by Frank Sinatra on his LP *Songs for Swinging Lovers*, Capital W 653), this rendition still beats out the contemporary original Paul Whiteman release from his film *The King of Jazz*, with Jack Fulton as vocalist, on Columbia 2098-D. Indeed, Ruth's added use of "torch" singing is more effective and also interlopes with another ditty, penned by Sam Lewis, Joe Young, and Mabel Wayne, called "In a Little Spanish Town." More so, this ditty was also a previous Paul Whiteman release, also using Jack Fulton (Victor 20266), and it is also improved by Ruth's vocal.
39. "Exactly Like You," Columbia 2199-D. This ditty penned by Jimmy McHugh and Dorothy Fields is another winner, at least for 1930s. Perhaps a torch song should not be sung in mid-tempo, but Ruth's typical attempt at wordy lyric finds her sweet vocal, more so, definitive, or owned?

40, 41. "Dancing with Tears in My Eyes," Columbia 2206-D. (a.) This sad tale is pure torch, at least until Ruth guides her listeners into mid-tempo. Penned by Joe Burke and Al Dubin in 1930, this ditty also became a Ben Selvin Orchestra release; (b.) as on Columbia 2216-D, it was also tied to a contemporary Ruth Etting film short *Roseland.*

42. "Don't Tell Him What Happened to Me," Columbia 2280-D. This fascinating tale of woe, penned by B. G. De Sylva, Lew Brown, and Ray Henderson, just may be true. Indeed, this torch song speaks for itself, and Ruth's vocal warmth indeed rings true. (A contemporary Nick Lucas version as "Don't Tell *Her*," rather than "Him" is also done well, and is also an interesting comparison.)
43. "Body and Soul," Columbia 2300-D. Yeah. Ruth's version competes with anyone. Indeed, many of her contemporaries recorded this ditty, who included the likes of fellow divas Libby Holman—who introduced it on Broadway—Helen Morgan, and Annette Hanshaw.
44. "Just A Little Closer". Columbia-2307-D. A flapper's question? Close enough to what?
45. "I'll Be Blue Just Thinking Of You". *Columbia-2707-D.*
46. "If I Could Be with You One Hour Tonight," Columbia 2300-D. This much-recorded ditty also found a contemporary version by an earlier vocal influence, Marion Harris. While others, including a Louis Armstrong version, differ, an Eva Taylor version still remains a fine entity to compare and compete with as well.
47. "I'm Yours," Columbia 2318-D. The original and superb version of this ditty, penned by John W. Green and E. Y. Harburg, indeed finds Ruth's version in heavy competition with contemporaries Nick Lucas and Johnny Marvin. (A later Billie Holiday version would redefine this ditty.) Listen and compare both fine vocal styles.
48. "Laughing at Life," Columbia 2318-D. This title alone (penned by Charles Kenny, Nick Kenny, Cornell Todd, and Bob Todd) is a "soap opera" enough in typical torch style. More so, does a competing contemporary version from the likes of an older vaudevillian-turned-crooner, Belle Baker, on Brunswick 4962 hand out handkerchiefs?
49. "Reaching for the Moon," Columbia 2398-D. While oddly unused as recording fodder by Bing Crosby in the contemporary (1931) film of the same name, this Irving Berlin-penned title at least found Ruth ready to render it.

50. "You're the One I Care For," Columbia 2398-D. This boring ditty (penned by Harry Link, Bert Lown, and Chauncey Gray) from 1931 found Ruth at work to make it into something better than the contemporary Belle Baker version, on Brunswick 6051. As part of her already perfected vocal "formula," or treatment, she starts off crooning a torch song, while later picking up the pace for a jazzy ending. (More so, a contemporary version by Josephine Baker released in France, while hardly known in America, provided this ditty more recognition. While the shrill voice of Baker is exposed, the end of Josephine's version does liven up this ditty better than Ruth's version Does Ruth herself get a little bored? Who can blame her? Listen and compare!
51. "Were You Sincere," Columbia 2445-D. While the contemporary Bing Crosby version is indeed the best (Brunswick 6120), Ruth may still claim a winner in her crooning effort of this ditty penned by Rose and Meskill.
52. "Falling in Love Again," Columbia 2445-D. This is an English version of a talkie hit from UFA Pictures *The Blue Angel;* a stunning contemporary (1930) version on screen by Marlene Dietrich is tops. So indeed is a Dietrich original recording, recorded in Europe in English language (with a thick German accent, on Victor 22593. Penned by Fredeick Hollander, this ditty also benefits from Ruth's own vocal approach, if subdued. A male version by crooner Nick Lucas also provides good comparisons in vocal style.
53. "Out of Nowhere," Columbia 2454-D. The contemporary Bing Crosby version on Brunswick 6090, is crooned out much like this.
54. "I'm Good for Nothing but Love," Columbia 2505-D. She's good, as she is bad, as this title, penned by Lew Pollack and Mort Green, indicates Ruth could generate some sweet heat. Moreover, the lyrics are serious enough, as the subjects of molestation and low self esteem find this ditty far less than fluffy and, more so, relevant. Moreover, this is not a novelty and is far from risqué, a very real and perhaps scary bit of social commentary.
55. "Guilty," Columbia 2529-D. Ruth is indeed very "guilty" introducing this ditty by Harry Akst, Richard Whiting, and Gus Kahn, to the Depression-era list of "best sellers." Her excellence in vocal expression is a typical torch song and, compared with a contemporary Russ Columbo crooning job, easy. Moreover, while Russ is good, his tonsils, unlike Ruth's, sound like a ball of socks got swallowed and got caught in them. Another version, by Gene Austin, is a bit slicker, but mushy.
56. "Cuban Love Song," Columbia 2580-D. Long before Castro, the city of Havana, Cuba, had been a hot-bed for pleasure seekers and Hispanic music. With the exception of Edmondo Ros; the likes of Dorothy Fields, Jimmy McHugh, and Herbert Stothart were far from Latin, the contrived use of "Cuban," originally used as a contemporary 1931 film title of the same name, succeeds.
57. "I'll Never Be the Same," Banner 32499. Is a contemporary version by Mildred Bailey any better? Or was a contemporary version (recorded in Britain) by Elisabeth Welch as "Little Buttercup" more poignant? as Or did Frank Sinatra finally define this ditty in the (1950s)? Listen and decide!
58. "Take Me in Your Arms," Banner 32634. This torch is lit as Ruth's delivery of this ditty penned by Mitchell Parish and Fred Markush is indeed heart-wrenching enough.
59. "Linger a Little Longer in the Twilight," Banner 32714. Another (contemporary) Bing Crosby version, on Brunswick 6491, penned by Harry Woods, Jimmy Campbell, and Reg Connelly, finds Ruth's version, in vocal comparison, a drier performance.

60. "Nevertheless," Oriole 2291. Ruth is very sincere and direct, and this ditty, penned by Harry Ruby and Bert Kalmar, is, nevertheless, an emotional ploy on lyric that works. Nevertheless?
61. "Cigarettes, Cigars," Perfect 12737. Ruth, as a sexy vendor of smokes, introduced this ditty (penned by Rodgers and Hart) in *Ziegfeld's Follies of 1931*.
62. "Shine on Harvest Moon," Perfect 12737. Nora Bayes had helped introduce this ditty for Ziegfeld in 1908. Reintroduced by Ruth in *Ziegfeld's Follies of 1931,* she at least overcomes its blandness on (this) her contemporary recording. Is a contemporary Ethel Waters version better? Listen and compare!
63. "Without That Gal," Oriole 2291. This side, penned by Walter Donaldson, is somewhat of a gender designation and is cleverly vocalized. Moreover, another contemporary version by Ethel Waters (Columbia 2481-D) overshadows Ruth's version with added drama.
64. "Love Letters in the Sand," Conqueror 7823. This familiar title of the (early) rock era, as a huge Pat Boone best seller (Dot 15570), finds more applause in Ruth's vocal. Indeed, Ruth, after a slow start, finds her stylistic mid-tempo moments, which greatly aids this ditty penned by Nick Kenny, Charles Kenny, and J. Fred Coots. (Contemporary 1931 renderings by Ted Black (Victor 22799) and Gene Austin (Victor 22806) are a bit stiff and perhaps more like the (later) Boone version.)
65. "When We're Along—Penthouse Serenade," Columbia 2630-D. Ruth is in a dream, as this sappy lyric (penned by Will Jason and Val Burton) finds her home in a penthouse with her mate, a perfect spot to come together. While softly vocalized, Ruth's medium tempo is used for a bit and closes down just in time to make this a classic—something more indeed to listen for.
66. "The Night When Love Was Born," Columbia 2681-D. Perhaps a contemporary (1932) Connie Boswell version is just as good? Better? Listen to both excellent vocals and decide!
67. "Lazy Day," Banner 32448. The contemporary Bing Crosby version is perhaps a bit more involved in crooning, but this version is no slouch.
68. "Hold Me," Banner 32739. Torch! Another sappy song ditty, penned by David Oppenheim, Ira Schuster, and Little Jack Little that somehow Ruth manages to speed up a bit in the middle of her rendition and somewhat save!
69. "You've Got Me Crying Again," Conqueror 8154. Mmm. Try contemporary versions by Bing Crosby, Connie Boswell, and Lee Wiley! Dated? Just listen.
70. "Try a Little Tenderness," Melotone 12625. The (contemporary) Bing Crosby version, on Brunswick 6480, while not changing gender, indeed finds Ruth speaking for her own gender. While Crosby could be accused of chauvinism, in latter-century terms, there remains no doubt that both versions were softly vocalized and were indeed a turn-on for contemporary 1933 listeners.
71. "Talking to Myself," Columbia 2954-D. Ruth's medium-tempo abilities dominate this ditty penned by Herb Magidson and Con Conrad. (Ruth may be seen introducing this ditty in the 1934 film, *The Gift of Gab*.)
72. "Stay as Sweet as You Are," Columbia 2979-D. This ditty, penned by Mack Gordon and Harry Revel, may indeed describe Ruth's fine vocal prowess, also swinging to medium tempo.
73. "Close Your Eyes," Brunswick 6657. Ruth even gets a bit mushy-voiced, as the ditty, penned by Bernice Petkere, remains effective. (A contemporary Al Bowlly version recorded in England, and most likely not known by Ruth, offers good comparisons.)

74. "Build a Little Home," Brunswick 6697. Sentimental? This ditty, penned by Al Dubin and Harry Warren, penned ditty is fully of fluff and schmaltz. As part of the 1933 *Roman Scandals* film, it had been introduced by Eddie Cantor, instead of Ruth, who was also in the film. Indeed, Cantor wasted it, but perhaps in hindsight, Ruth at least saved it on this recording. Moreover, it's sung well enough.
75. "No More Love," Brunswick 6697. Ruth introduced this Al Dubib and Harry Warren penned ditty in the film *Roman Scandals*, and this recording is far better. Or perhaps a contemporary Irene Taylor version, on Vocalion 2597, provides an interesting (vocal) comparison? Listen to both vocals of a dull song lifted by well-done singing.
76. "Everything I Have Is Yours," Brunswick 6719. Yeah! Believe her! This very soft vocal, penned by Harold Adamson and Burton Lane, is a sure winner, and it was originally introduced by Joan Crawford in the contemporary film *Dancing Lady*. While Joan is no slouch (in the film), Ruth defined it as a recording despite (another) contemporary rendering released by Rudy Vallee, on Victor 24458. In no disrespect for Joan's well-done vocal, it's too bad that Ruth did not do it in the film. Anyone still care?
77. "Smoke Gets in Your Eyes," Brunswick 6769. Following Irene Dunn's rendering in the contemporary film *Roberta*, Ruth defined this ditty, penned by Jerome Kern and Otto Harbach, as a recording. Yet another contemporary (1934) Chick Bullock release differs, which, if better, is less known. (Light-years later (1958), the Platters would resurrect this ditty in the rock and roll era.)
78. "Easy Come Easy Go," Brunswick 6892. A contemporary 1934 Lee Wiley version of this Edward Heyman and John W. Green penned ditty, in faster tempo, is a cooler and more effective style, as released on Brunswick 6855. Nevertheless, Ruth's warmer vocal is a welcome comparison. Indeed, a very interesting comparison between two very interesting female vocalists.
79. "Were Your Ears Burning, Baby," Brunswick 6914. This ditty penned by Mack Gordon and Harry Revel is snappy enough and even borders upon some jazzy croon
80. "With My Eyes Wide Open I'm Dreaming," Brunswick 6914. The very sentimental bit of mush, as penned by Mack Gordon and Harry Revel, still finds Ruth at her best.
81. "Out in the Cold Again," Columbia 2955-D. How can Ruth's warm vocal get cold? Or does this ditty penned by Ted Koehler and Rube Bloom thaw?
82. "A Needle in a Haystack," Columbia 2979-D. Introduced in the contemporary (1934) Fred Astaire and Ginger Rogers film, 'The Gay Divorcee": this ditty penned by Con Conrad and Herb Magidson worked well enough. As a recording, Ruth's delivery is typical and, moreover, produces a definitive recording of this fine but schmaltzy ditty.
83. "I've Got an Invitation to Dance," Columbia 2985-D. While dated and schmaltzy and penned by Marty Symes and Levinson Neiburg, Ruth's usual elocution of this somewhat cumbersome ditty remains well worth it to hear.
84. "March Winds and April Showers," Columbia 3014-D. Penned by Teddy Powell, Walter G. Samuels, and Leonard Whitcup, this very fluffy and pleasant (1935) mid-tempo and personable ditty remains a winner.
85. "Things Might Have Been So Different," Columbia 3014-D. Sam M. Lewis and J. Fred Coots penned this bit of mush that somehow works-at least for Ruth!

- Ruth's trip to England in 1936: Along with some personal appearances, she also recorded some material on the British label Rex. The following two are Rex picks:

86. "It's a Sin to Tell a Lie," Rex 8853. (A contemporary Dolly Dawn vocal sounds like Ruth a bit, although it's a good bet that this British release never made it over to Dolly's ear.)
87. "Holiday Sweethearts," Rex 8881. Ruth's American accent pleasantly defines some good English lyrics, claimed as penned by Caesar, Carter, and Charles Henderson.
88. "In the Chapel in the Moonlight," Decca 1084. This bit of schmaltz, penned by Billy Hill, is smooth, and despite its blandness, Ruth again produces a very pleasant vocal.
89. "Goodnight My Love," Decca 1107. This Decca release, penned by Mack Gordon and Harry Revel, was indeed sweetly vocalized for contemporary ballroom dancing. Introduced in a contemporary (1936) Alice Faye and Shirley Temple film entity *Stowaway*, it's odd that the Faye version, recorded on Brunswick 7821, was to be overshadowed by Ruth's (still) fine version. Moreover, a totally different approach by Benny Goodman, with a bright Ella Fitzgerald vocal, on Victor 25461—also good recording fodder—is perhaps better?
90. "It's Swell of You," Decca 1212. This ditty penned by Gordon and Revel perhaps labeled the word "swell," a part of a generation that used better ones. Even so, this wordy crooning job is catchy enough, as well as Ruth, as usual, injects her own personable word-stretching style.

Note: While Ruth Etting's recordings were a principal source of her fame, the media of radio should not be overlooked. The farm girl from Nebraska had actually been an early pioneer in Chicago radio—KYW, WLS—in the mid-1920s. By the early 1930s, her "network" radio appearances and programs became hugely popular. The following include some surviving gems:

- *Ruth Etting, America's Radio Sweetheart*, Totem 1018 (LP) picks include:

91. "Dancing with Tears in My Eyes," a transcribed commercial for Columbia's Tele-Focal Radios, with excellent backup by Ben Selvin's Orchestra (1930).
92. "Whose Honey Are You" (1935).
93. "Zing Went the Strings of My Heart" (1935).
94. "Tormented"(alias "Stormy Weather") (1936).

- Visual Image.

Ruth, never a major film entity, nevertheless did find herself in some interesting musical shorts, including (1930) *Roseland*. Just *why* Ruth never succeeded in a major film role, considering the major factor of racism did not apply to her, is hard to figure. She was, by 1930, a consistently successful recording artist with Broadway credits as well. The right vehicle? Or perhaps was it her poor husband (manager)? In any case, the following are worth seeing and hearing:

95. "Let Me Sing and I'm Happy." While in a limo, Ruth croons out this ditty in *Roseland*.
96. "Dancing with Tears in My Eyes." Ruth is both seen and heard, in a dance hall setting, in a truly creditable performance in *Roseland*.
97. "Talkin' to Myself." Ruth is even rhythmic, as seen and heard in the 1934 film *Gift of Gab*.

98. "No More Love." This ditty, penned by Dubin and Warren, was featured in the 1933 film *Roman Scandals*. In it, Ruth is seen introducing this ditty, rather meekly, with an interruption of a Busby Berkeley segment, which—in all honesty—improves upon it. Like all of her (full-length) films, Ruth is much short-changed as she could have contributed much to this Eddie Cantor vehicle. (The noted recording of this ditty is better!)

> ➢ Ruth formally "retired" around 1938, at around forty years of age, except for a brief fling at radio and nightclub work after WWII. Why? Tired of it all? Divorce?

Alice Faye

- Alice Faye was essentially a young and hot-looking chorus girl, who was handpicked by Rudy Vallee in a George White revue (*Scandals of 1931*) for what was perhaps a talent search for his popular contemporary radio program. While there is much-deserved conjecture for this yarn, there is no doubt that the very beautiful Alice Faye (perhaps about seventeen years old in 1933), as well as a formidable dancer, had a good, strong set of pipes. Her flat vocal style perhaps owed much to that of the already established singing style of Ruth Etting, who had coincidentally risen from the chorus as well—some ten or twelve years earlier.
- After a bit of time with Rudy Vallee, Alice was signed up for Hollywood, which totally and successfully exploited her image and youth. As a musical entity, her own durable vocals carried over through much material, which eventually led her to become starred in some of the most successful, money-making contemporary films of the 1930s and early 1940s. The following are Alice Faye picks:

1. Honeymoon Hotel,". Bluebird-B-5171. This Al Dubin & Harry Warren penned ditty is a lot of fun, and this 'hotel' for married folks perhaps had "Cupid" as it's desk clerk? Or are all these guests really married?
2. "Shame On You," Bluebird-B-5175. Like "Honeymoon Hotel", this Rudy Vallee release using Alice Faye as his band singer, found some 'hot' lyric, penned by Edward Heyman and Harold Arlen, not really full of shame?
3. Nasty Man," Brunswick B-099. This risqué bit of lyrics, penned by Jack Yellen, Irving Caesar, and Ray Henderson, found Alice—already a known radio entity with Rudy Vallee's *Fleishmann* program—delivering the needed rhythmic vocal punch that wins win over the ears as a recording. Its odd number indicates a British release. Does Alice know what's on this nasty man's mind?
4. Here's the Key to My Heart," Brunswick B-099. This fine 1934 ditty, penned by Sidney Clare and Richard Whiting, was introduced in her contemporary 1934 film *She Learned About Sailors*. This rhythmic recording finds the background of Freddy Martin's Orchestra and perhaps Rudy Vallee's talking voice attempting to embellish another somewhat risqué and novel product. This succeeds, as the "key," indicated within the lyrics, indeed works! (It is the original British flip side of Nasty Man.)
5. "Yes to You," Romeo 2407. This bright vocal, penned by Sidney Clare and Richard Whiting, is a fine crooning job and was, more so, introduced in the film *365 Nights in Hollywood.* Yes!

6. "According to the Moonlight," Romeo 2483. Another fine, pleasant vocal, penned by Jack Yellen, Herb Magidson, and Joseph Meyer, especially noting Alice's own debt to Ruth Etting.
7. "I've Got My Fingers Crossed," Melotone M-6 03 09. Another film entity, from *King of Burlesque*, finds Alice very capable of handling yet another rhythmic ditty (penned by Ted Koehler and Jimmy McHugh).
8. "Spreadin' Rhythm Around," Melotone M-6 03 08. Another film entity from *King of Burlesque*, penned by Ted Koehler and Jimmy McHugh, finds Alice again doing well with a wordy, rhythmic vocal, using the somewhat new term "swing." No one could have suspected it at the time (1936) that another, slicker, wilder, and defining vocal was also produced as a jazzy Teddy Wilson release with a vocal by the up-and-coming Billie Holiday, on Brunswick 7581.
9. "I'm Shooting High," Melotone M-6 03 08. Another ditty penned by Ted Koehler and Jimmy McHugh, with an easy vocal refrain, finds Alice again producing another rhythmic winner.
10. "Goodnight My Love," Brunswick 7821. This ditty had been introduced by Alice in a contemporary 1936 film *Stowaway*, with Shirley Temple. Penned by Mack Gordon and Harry Revel, this schmaltzy ballad, while not bad, finds Alice a bit less committed, as a contemporary rendering from a vocal influence, Ruth Etting (Decca 1107), is far better. Yet, in stylistic comparisons, a contemporary Benny Goodman release, with a committed young vocalist named Ella Fitzgerald, presents a newer, slicker, yet articulate version.

- The following three ditties were all penned by Irving Berlin for the (1937) film *On the Avenue.*

11. "This Year's Kisses," Brunswick 7825. This is a schmaltzy ballad that is crooned out OK. (A contemporary Teddy Wilson release, featuring a Billie Holiday vocal, would, more so, define this ditty as "jazz.")
12. "Slumming on Park Avenue," Brunswick 7825. A wordy, rhythmic ditty that works! Want to go slumming? Smelling the garbage?
13. "I've Got My Love to Keep Me Warm," Brunswick 7821. Another good song entity that found more identity as a contemporary jazz item when recorded by Billie Holiday. (A later revival by Billy Eckstine and Sarah Vaughan in the 1950s, as an Irving Berlin tribute, also contributes to good listening.

- The following three ditties were all penned by Mack Gordon and Harry Revel for the 1937 film *Wake Up and Live.*

14. "Never in a Million Years," Brunswick 7860. While this ain't bad, a contemporary Bing Crosby version, on Decca 1210, with a fine Jimmy Dorsey backing, is defining.
15. "It's Swell of You," Brunswick 7860. This term "swell" is a bit much, but it, more so, represents a time and era (1937). (A contemporary Ruth Etting recording, perhaps got it right?)
16. "There's a Lull in My Life," Brunswick 7876. A stylistic, contemporary Duke Ellington release, with a cool Ivie Anderson vocal, perhaps best defines this ditty. Listen and compare!

"Wake up and Live," Brunswick 7876. This film title song ditty is rhythmic and, more so, the best sung (by Alice) as original recording fodder.

- Alice married singer Tony Martin and later bandleader-radio personality Phil Harris. She continued to make films until the mid-1940s, although her commitments to a family found her musical films becoming less. She, more so, paved the way for others, including Betty Grable, whose vocals, while done well, are a bit less than Alice's range, as well as her trail of recordings.

    - Visual Image.

The numerous films of Alice Faye perhaps overshadow her importance as a recorded entity, a problem for many good-looking women who could also sing. Considering much of the filmed fodder that is out there, perhaps Alice Faye the vocalist is best found in the lesser-known 1934 film *365 Nights in Hollywood*." In it, this hot, platinum blond brightly croons out

18. "Yes to You"

and

19. "My Future Star."

- The oddity of the limits of Alice Faye's recording output did not stop her from introducing many popular entities in (just) films. Unlike contemporaries Fred Astaire and Ginger Rodgers, her films, in true retrospective, do not stand up well, although her singing vocals are better! Indeed, the clips of Alice singing in films are still good, usually without the stupid film plots, with a few noted exceptions. The added fact that Alice retired from films (for the most part) at about thirty years of age, is also an oddity The following are noted ditties filmed by Alice, which became good recording fodder by others.

20. "You're A Sweetheart" (from the 1937 film of the same name). Ethel Waters and Dolly Dawn, both produced excellent contemporary 1938 recordings. Later, Frank Sinatra would reintroduce this ditty is his 1951 film *Meet Danny Wilson*.
21. "I'm Just Wild about Harry" (from the (1939) film *Rose of Washington Square*). The earlier (1922) recording of Marion Harris (who had found it good recording fodder in the contemporary Broadway entity *Shuffle Along*) is revived smartly by Alice's clear vocal, with jazzy backing from Louis Prima. Indeed worth hearing and seeing!
22. "You'll Never Know" (from the 1943 film *Hello Frisco, Hello*). Both Dick Haymes and Frank Sinatra produced excellent contemporary recordings of this huge Academy Award-winning song ditty.
23. "Nasty Man". The filmed version of the George White "Scandals" in 1933 found a very hot and sexy showgirl (Alice Faye) introducing this ditty on screen! Oddly, while Rudy Vallee in backing her on screen, the Alice Faye recording, was backed by Freddie Martin's orchestra. How come? Or does Rudy really matter?

Eddie Fisher

Eddie Fisher may be considered the most popular of the "new" vocalists to follow Crosby and, especially, Sinatra in the late 1940s. Indeed, in 1950, Fisher was considered a stronger vocalist than the (then) fledging Sinatra. Perhaps if the rise of rock and roll had not occurred, who knows? In any case, the future did produce Carrie Fisher, aka "Princess Leia" of *Star Wars*, as well as the following picks:

1. "Thinking of You," Victor 20-3901. This (1927) Broadway ditty from *Five O'Clock Girl*, penned by Harry Ruby and Burt Kalmar, had already been recorded often, including a (stiff) vocal by Franklyn Baur, an a (1928) Harry Archer release. In 1950, it was revived in the schmaltzy film *Three Little Words* with Fred Astaire and Red Skelton. Luckily, Eddie recorded it and produced a best seller, although, in true retrospective, contemporary Sarah Vaughan produced a more interesting recording!
2. "I'm Yours," Victor 20-4574. Not to be confused with the classic by Johnny Green and E. Y. Harburg, this Robert Mellin-penned ditty was crooned out well enough. (The original contemporary Don Cornell version, on Coral 60690, also ain't too bad a bag of mush).
3. "Lady of Spain," Victor 20-4953. The old (1931) Ray Noble Orchestra ditty, penned by E. Reaves, S. J. Damerell, and Tolchard Evans and with a vocal by Britisher Al Bowlly (Victor 22774) is pleasantly revived.
4. "Wish You Were Here," Victor 20-4830. This contemporary title of (writer) Harold Rome's current Broadway entity took a turn to became associated with the Korean War conflict, then red hot in 1952.
5. "I'm Walking Behind You," Victor 20-5293. This original British (Billy Reid Orchestra) release, featured a fine vocal by Dorothy Squires on Polygon 1068. Fisher took this ditty and defined it as an American pop standard, and oddly, this ditty outsold Sinatra's fine contemporary version on Capital 2450, as well as a Vic Damone version on Mercury 70128. All similar in style?
6. "I Need You Now," Victor 20-5830. This is probably Eddie's best pop vocal, penned by Jimmy Crane and Al Jacobs.
7. "With These Hands". Victor 20-5365. This 1953 emotion and slick 'pop' ditty, as penned by (Abner Silver & Benny Davis) would later be exploited and claimed as by a more simmering vocal style-unlike Eddie, as by British (rock) era (1964) performer Tom Jones, with American release on (Parrot-9787).
8. "Cindy, Oh, Cindy," Victor 20-6677. Despite fellow Victor recording artist, Elvis Presley, this 1956 ditty, penned by Burt D'Lugoff and Robert Nemiroff, became a best seller.

Ella Fitzgerald

The swing era got its start with Ivie Anderson's defining vocal on the 1932 Ellington release "It Don't Mean a Thing, If It Ain't Got That Swing," on (Brunswick 6265), and lasted roughly until the 1942 musicians union strike. While Ivie Anderson was indeed the catalyst, as it would all turn out, it would be young Ella Fitzgerald, influenced by Connie Boswell, Ethel Waters, and Ivie herself, who would be best identified with swing and jazz vocals, noting contemporary (mid-1930s) competition from the likes of Helen Ward, Billie Holiday, Bea Wain, Maxine Sullivan, Dolly Dawn, and Midge Williams, among others, among others, in true retrospective.

In 1935, the young Ella (whose birthday is somewhere between 1915 and 1918), orphaned, was taken under the wings of the brilliant drumming bandleader Chick Webb and his wife. Within a few years, Webb's inspiring drumming inspired some fine swing numbers, with a somewhat girlish Fitzgerald vocal, filled with vocal clarity and excitement. Indeed, Harlem and Chick Webb and Ella were the perfect place to "swing," with some jitterbugging dance steps that bordered on wild and uninhibited.

- The following picks, with some noted exceptions, are all for the Chick Webb Orchestra:

1. "Love and Kisses," Decca 494. Not bad, even with a lot of Webb, as Ella took on a contemporary 'pop' ditty penned by Rudolph Frimi and Paul Frances Webster, she wins!
2. "I'll Chase the Blues Away," Decca 494. The flip of the "Love And Kisses" is, more so, about rhythm in mid-tempo.
3. "Rhythm and Romance," Decca 588. George Whiting, Nat Schwartz and James C. Johnson's penned ditty is as slick and smooth as Ella's a good voice.
4. "Sing Me a Swing Song and Let Me Dance," Decca 830. This infectious dance title, penned by Hoagy Carmichael and Stanley Adams, while contrived, indeed works. (A contemporary Benny Goodman release, featuring Helen Ward's vocal, also "swings.") Listen and compare!
5. "All My Life," Brunswick 7640. This Teddy Wilson and His Orchestra release (by Sidney D. Mitchell and Sammy Stept) provided a surprising Ella vocal truly emulating contemporary Billie Holiday. (It would not happen again!)
6. "My Melancholy Baby," Brunswick 7729. This standard ballad, found Ella in an early effort at a ballad style, differing greatly from the earlier version and (weaker vocal) of Gene Austin's.
7. "Goodnight My Love," Victor 25461. This Benny Goodman record got Ella better known and was also an attempt on Goodman's part to perhaps steal away Ella from Webb. More so, both Alice Faye and Ruth Etting also found this ditty (penned by Gordon and Revel), as introduced in the contemporary Shirley Temple film *Stowaway*, good recording fodder. Moreover, as well as from Webb, the Goodman arrangement provides the bright-voiced Ella with a stylistic clash, as compared to the likes of both Ruth and Alice. Just listen!
8. "Take Another Guess, Oh Yes," Victor 25461. Another Goodman side, this contrived ditty, penned by Murray Menchler, Charles Newman, and Al Sherman, indeed "swings." An even better version, with another sparkling Fitzgerald vocal, was also released by Webb on Decca 1123. Take your pick, or guess?
9. "A Little Bit Late On," Decca 831. Another fine dance record, penned by Jerry Livinson and AlNieburg, indeed "swings." Wanna jitterbug?
10. "Big Boy Blue," Decca 1148. This time, Ella Fitzgerald and the Mills Brothers, team up for a 1937 fast-paced experiment. Indeed, this bouncy and rhythmic ditty succeeds, although somewhat less than a contemporary swing number, penned by Jack Lawrence, Dan Howell and Peter Tinturin. In fact, it just may be rock, as Ella' little voice meshes well with the Mills clan.
11. "Vote for Mr. Rhythm," Decca 1032. Chick Webb for president? This ditty (credited to Leo Robin, Ralph Rainger, and Al Siegal) is yet another dance number that indeed could have elected just about anybody. Yes!

12. "You'll Have to Swing It, Mr. Paganini," Decca 1032. This Sam Coslow-penned novelty pokes fun at classical European music. Or perhaps, it's just another excuse to get up and dance!
13. "Rock It for Me," Decca 1586. This swing dance number just could be rock and roll or at least a contemporary excuse to pound and jitterbug the dance floor. Indeed, Ella's rhythmic vocal, penned by Kay Werner and Sue Werner, more ever driven by Webb, sounds less than contrived! Or could it just be something spontaneously produced that retained energy? Just listen! It is not contrived! It's indeed the real thing!
14. "A-Tisket A-Tasket," Decca 1840. This novelty, a play on the old nursery rhyme penned by Al Feldman and Ella, for the most part, put Ella and Webb into more circulation. Indeed, this best-selling entity "swings," and features Ella's flawless and articulate vocal prowess at its novel best. In true retrospective, this novelty easily identifies as a good excuse to dance—the swing era itself, with only "It Don't Mean a Thing If It Ain't Got That Swing," as its major rival.
15. "I'm Just a Jitterbug," Deccaa 1899. This ditty penned by Mack David and Jerry Livingstone, an obvious contrived and contemporary dance number, at least lives up to its "swinging" title. Ella's vocal and Webb again excel.
16. "I Want To Be Happy," Decca 15039. This original 12-inch 78 rpm side found the old (Vincent Youmans) standard (from 1925's Broadway entity *No, No, Nanette* much improved upon as a vocal, especially noting the earlier Shannon Four release on Columbia 222-D. While Ella does not get much vocal, Chick Webb's fab swing arrangement, in direct competition with the (then) current (1937) Benny Goodman instrumental of this same ditty was perhaps intended to show Goodman who's boss!
17. "Hallelujah," Decca 15039. Another Broadway entity from the 1920s, penned by Vincent Youmans, Leo Robins, and Clifford Grey, originally from 1927's *Hit the Deck* had, more so, found many contemporary recordings, noting a (boring) vocal from Franklyn Baur as a Nat Shilkret release on Victor 20599. While originally released as a 12-inch 78 rpm flip side, featuring a limited vocal from Ella, it's (still) more than obvious that Ella's bright vocal style was what was needed to (finally) lift and define this ditty!
18. "Everybody Step," Decca 1894. Ella and Chick Webb, up to this point (mid-1938), had already taught the world how to swing, both instrumentally and vocally. This contrived reworking of an already dated (Irving Berlin) ditty, which had, in an older style, been a fine entity for bandleader Ted Lewis (Columbia 3499 D), indeed find some challenges. Moreover, both Webb and, more importantly, Ella do produce a fine rhythmic rendering, and much unlike the previous Lewis rendition.
19. "Wacky Dust," Decca 2021. Is this novelty drug culture? Perhaps both Stanley Adams and Oscar Levant, who penned this ditty, knew it for sure. In any case, Ella's performance of this novelty was indeed a sure bet.
20. "Undecided," Decca 2323. This wordy, rhythmic ditty, penned by Sydney Robin and Charles Shavers, again swings. (For a later rock-and-roll generation, Ella's rendering was at least an inspiration for the Johnny Burnette Trio.)
21. "'T ain't What You Do," Decca 2310. Ella tears into some fine lyrics, penned by George Young and Sy Oliver. Again, Ella's sparkling rhythmic vocal makes it all work. (A fine contemporary Adelaide Hall version, recorded in Europe, is also done very well and interesting to compare.)
22. "Chew Chew Chew Your Bubble Gum," Decca 2389. Penned by Buck Ram, Chick Webb, and Ella herself, this contrived bit of novelty perhaps found many contemporary jitterbugging couples swallowing their gum.

23. "If You Ever Change Your Mind," Decca 2481. This very well-done change of pace, penned by Grady Watts, Bud Green, and Maurice Sigler, is slower and smoother. Indeed, near the end of her rendering, a fine vocal expression indeed stamps this ditty as her own. To compliment things a bit, a fine contemporary Ethel Waters version on Bluebird, should also be noted and heard. Indeed, comparisons should be heard and made!
24. "If Anything Happened to You," Decca 2481. This very fine ditty penned by Jimmy Van Heusen also proves that Ella hit "it" vocally, even in her earlier years.
25. "Stairway to the Stars," Decca 2598. This (1939) entity had been recorded by many others as contemporary recordings, including Kay Kyser's Orchestra with a stiff vocal by Harry Babbit on Brunswick 8381, and a Harry James Orchestra release with a fine vocal by Frank Sinatra. Ella, moreover, is more inspired. Penned by Frank Signorelli, Matty Malneck, and Mitchell Parish, this attempt at medium-tempo swing indeed finds Ella defining this ditty.
26. "I Want the Waiter with the Water," Decca 2628. Why not? Swing away with this cleaver novelty penned by Kay and Sue Werner! (To be fair, a contemporary Ozzie Nelson version, ain't bad.)

Note: When Chick Webb passed away in 1939, Ella kept the band together. The advent of WWII as well as the musicians' strike of 1942 founded more change, especially among Afro-American orchestras and bands always needing funds. Indeed, the emergence of small groups, replacing numerous bands and their numerous members, was also an economic fact for the recording industry and for the record companies themselves. While the hog bandleaders would still do well, a rise of independent vocalists put most bands behind their vocalists. Like the 1920s, vocalists were again hot. The success achieved by the likes of former band singers Frank Sinatra, Dick Haymes, Perry Como, Dinah Shore, Jo Stafford, Billie Holiday, Doris Day, Billie Eckstine, and Ella herself, indeed, found the decade of 1940s (WWII and the postwar period) fertile ground. While these singers had adjustments to make, including the likes of more vocal backgrounds, the focus of name recognition would find bandleaders leading less people.

27. "Little White Lies," Decca 2556. Along with Her Savoy Eight, Ella excels vocally, sounding nothing like the earlier styles of Marion Harris, Annette Hanshaw, or Lee Morse in 1930 and, more so, provides good competition for the likes of contemporary Dick Haymes.
28. "Five O'Clock Whistle," Decca 3420. A contemporary Duke Ellington release, with an Ivie Anderson vocal, indeed challenges Ella.
29. "Taking a Chance on Love," Decca 3490. The contemporary Ethel Waters classic is somewhat challenged.
30. "I'm Getting Mighty Lonesome," Decca 4315. Along with Her Four Keys, Ella sings her heart out (penned by Buck Ram).
31. "My Heart and I Decided," Decca 18530. With Ella again in the lead of a mellow group sound, the Four Keys indeed sound soft and effective enough on this old Walter Donaldson penned ditty.
32. "I Put a Four Leaf Clover in Your Pocket" Decca 18472. Again, with Her Four Keys, Ella's own vocal lead finds this ditty, penned by John Jacob Loeb and Benny Davis, a bit of a pun as this title indeed insinuates a bit of novel mischief.
33. "He's My Guy," Decca 18472. A low-budget film 1943 musical *Hi Ya Chum*, which starred Jane Frazee, found this ditty (penned by Don Raye and Gene De Paul)

introduced to the film. Like most instances, recorded versions by a professional recording artist who was not in the actual film indeed produced a better result. As well as a fine contemporary version às by Dinah Shore on Victor, Ella's version also demonstrates an ability to match or better her contemporaries, as this ditty demonstrates. As a further note, this ditty, perhaps, sounds suspiciously like the classic by Kern and Hammerstein "Can't Help Lovin' Dat Man," which had been introduced by Helen Morgan in 1927. Or does it? Just listen and compare, if you even care.

34. "Cow Cow Boogie," Decca 18587. Ella and the Ink Spots make it all sound very interesting, as this very hip novelty's very title indicates. Indeed, despite this excellent rendering, a fine contemporary Freddie Slack version on Capital with a hot Ella Mae Morse vocal gave Ella and the Ink Spots some stiff competition.
35. "Benny's Comin' Home on Saturday" Decca 18713. Backed by the Randy Brooks Orchestra, this ditty, as penned by Akkan Roberts and Doris Fisher, is a return to a big band style. Indeed, Ella is in top form here, as the vocal about a returning service person indeed "swings."
36. "A Kiss Goodnight," Decca 18713. While this ditty penned by Freddie Slack, Floyd Victor, and Woody Hermann had been originally well done by the likes of a (1945) contemporary Freddy Slack release (Capital 203) with a fine vocal by Liza Morrow, as well as a Woody Hermann release (Columbia 36815) with a good vocal from Frances Wayne, it was obvious for the premier voice of Ella to define it as a recording. (As a visual image, the likes and sexy legs of Dale Evans, in a pop-sounding vocal found in the contemporary film *Don't Fence Me In*, also proved that Dale was equipped with a great voice as well!)
37. "Into Each Life Some Rain Must Fall," Decca 23356. This dated 1944 ballad, a best-selling entity with the Ink Spots, found Ella's contribution a bit less than what should have been.
38. "I'm Beginning to See the Light," Decca 23399. Ella and the Ink Spots, again create some fine vocals to stretch or digest. Just don't fall asleep.
39. "That's the Way It Is," Decca 23399. The Ink Spots (again) provide Ella some vocal challenges and harmony that succeeds!
40. "It's Only a Paper Moon," Decca 23425. Along with the Delta Rhythm Boys, this already dated classic (introduced by Cliff Edwards in 1930) is given new life with a completely differing vocal style and contemporary (1940s) arrangements. On hearing, it is, more so, a fine example of the popular music of the era and just how vocal groups could contribute to Ella's fine lead.
41. "You Won't Be Satisfied Until You Break My Heart," Decca 23496. Ella and Louis Armstrong provide a fine match, as this ditty (by Freddy James and Larry Stock) is pleasant enough.
42. "The Frim Fram Sauce," Decca 23496. Ella and Louis Armstrong provide a little "extra" for their contemporary version of the King Cole Trio hit on Capital 224.
43. "Stone Cold Dead in the Market" Decca 23546. By the time of this recording, Louis Jordan, a former alto sax man of Chick Webb's Orchestra, had founded a band of his own. More so, he pioneered "rhythm and blues" and was, for the era, the biggest exponent of the style that led to rock and roll a decade later. This novelty, penned by Wilmouth Houdini, finds both Ella and Louis hamming it up with Jamaican chatter, and, indeed, sparks fly with some interesting lyrics.
44. "Petootie Pie," Decca 23546. Penned by L. Pack, F. Paparelli, and R. Lev, this is more R & B in style, and along with Louis Jordan and his Tympany Five, Ella performs an excellent and jazzy scatting vocal.

45. "I'm Just a Lucky So and So," Decca 18814. Perhaps Ella indeed found this Duke Ellington and Mack David penned entity, released on Victor 20-1799 with an Al Hibbler vocal, an inspiration. In any case, this fine ditty scores and perhaps a bit better than Hibbler did on this fine mid-tempo ballad.
46. "I Didn't Mean a Word I Said," Decca 18814. This soft and cool vocal, penned by McHugh and Adamson, defines a matured Fitzgerald vocal style, backed ably by bandleader Billy Kyle.
47. "It's a Pity to Say Good-bye," Decca 23670. If the listener of this ditty drifts asleep, it's OK. Moreover, this Billy Reid-penned ditty also finds the Delta Rhythm Boys supplying Ella with fine vocal assistance.
48. "Guilty," Decca 23844. This breezy, low-key vocal of the mature Ella is a fine update to the (much) earlier Ruth Etting and Russ Columbo versions.
49. "A Sunday Kind of Love," Decca 23866. Best heard by Ella's version, this classic penned by Barbara Belle, Anita Leonard, Stan Rhodes, and Louis Prima again highlights fine vocal gifts. As backup, Ella finds the Sandy Love Quintet more than adequate.
50. "Oh Lady Be Good," Decca 23956. If anyone wants to hear the ultimate "scat" vocal, this has got to be it! Indeed, this drastic reworking of the classic (by Gershwin Brothers) becomes perhaps a totally different entity, indeed differing from the likes of all previous recordings, including the well-known version of Cliff Edwards in the 1920s. Backed by Bob Haggart and His Orchestra, it is a wonder and a challenge that Ella's machine-gunned vocal attack could gel with orchestration, but it somehow all works out.
51. "Flying Home," Decca 23956. This original (swing) piece was meant to be instrumental. Penned by Benny Goodman and Lionel Hampton, Lionel had already created a classic some years earlier, in 1940. Ella, moreover, had other ideas and does more with it vocally. This scatting vocal is perhaps just as tough as any, including her recent update of "Oh Lady Be Good." Indeed, this exercise of tonsils found worded slang classical improvisation at its best. While Louis Armstrong's (1920's) scatting remains relevant, Ella has huge claims upon the style. Another surprise found in this recording is a fine backing orchestra, led by Vic Schoen. While usually associated with sweet band sounds and schmaltzy backups, Schoen surprisingly demonstrates great skill, especially for keeping up with Ella's remarkable no word-words.
52. "My Baby Likes to Bebop," Decca 24332. The contemporary Johnny Mercer and Nat King Cole version is challenged.
53. "It's Too Soon to Know," Decca 24497. The sentimental background gets a little sappy, but Ella's mellow (big-voiced) vocal saves it all (penned by Deborah Chessler).
54. "Baby, It's Cold Outside," Decca 24644. Ella and Louis Jordan again unite and score in novel fun.
55. "I Gotta Have My Baby Back," Decca 24813. The combination of Ella and the Mills Brothers on "Big Boy Blue" had helped the younger Ella become better known. This later example of vocal abilities, while no longer needed, builds upon versatility. As a country entity, this Floyd Tillman-penned ditty, while slower, finds Ells smoothly blending on with a fine and typical Mills Brothers' effort.
56. "My Happiness," Decca 24446. With a group sound, along with the Song Spinners, Ella's vocal abilities are seemingly versatile enough. Other contemporary 1948 versions of this ditty (penned by Betty Peterson Blasco, and Borney Bergantine) include Jon and Sandra Steele's (Damon 11133), the Marlin Sisters' (Columbia 38217), and John Laurenz's (Mercury 5144), which all fall short of Ella's version.

Note: The 1950s, even before rock and roll, found Ella and her surviving contemporaries at odds with a newer wave of music. Ella's versatility had already demonstrated an adaptation to rhythm and blues, which may be claimed as something she had pioneered with her rhythmic vocals with Chick Webb in the 1930s. As noted in some of the picks above, a further interest, with the likes of Louis Jordan and others, found Ella always ready to record anything with great professionalism.

Later 1940s' and early 1950s' efforts found Ella touring and recording much live material. As well as some efforts with the Charlie Parker "Bird land" types, she managed to claim deserved recognition from the likes of *Down Beat, Metronome*, *Esquire*, *Playboy*, and other jazz-oriented publications. While considering contemporaries such as Thelma Carpenter, the "new" Sarah Vaughn, June Christy, Pearl Bailey, Rosemary Clooney, Dakota Stanton, and Dinah Washington, the idiom of "jazz" put Ella into a category of fewer challenges. While never a shouter, the lead of rock material found in the likes of Ruth Brown, Lavern Baker, and Etta James, among others, was not followed. Unlike Dinah Washington and Valaida Snow, and like her 1930s' rival Billie Holiday, she would remain essentially a "jazz vocalist" and, within time, establish herself as the ultimate diva of the idiom itself.

57-58. *Pete Kelly's Blues*, Decca LP-8166. This LP is meant to be a film soundtrack. It's just too bad that Ella is not pictured on the LP cover as Peggy Lee is. While it's true Peggy Lee's vocals are flawless, Ella's vocals are above a challenge from Peggy and offer Peggy more of an example. There is also a huge possibility that Ella faces racism here. Through no fault of Peggy's, Ella is faceless on the original LP cover! In any case, the highlights of this LP finds Ella, when not humming, scatting along well on (a.) "Pete Kelly's Blues," penned by Sammy Cahn and Ray Heindorf, and the (1920s) standard (b.) "Hard Hearted Hannah."

The following LP issues (recorded between 1956 to the early 1960s) are standout popular and jazz performances marketed to "adult" record buyers, who essentially dreaded rock and roll.

59-60. *Compact Jazz Count Basie and Joe Williams*, Verve 835 329-2. The Count Basie Orchestra found great voices throughout its existence since the mid-1930s. This CD features vocalist Joe Williams, not to be confused with the "blues" singer of the same name. As a latecomer to recording, this Joe Williams, like many, was side-railed by the emergence of rock, and unlike many, a fine jazz and pop vocalist, heavily influenced by the likes of Ethel Waters and Ella herself.

This CD issue also includes a few duets with Ella, which (also) makes this release of '50s material notable. The picks are as under:

- "Too Close for Comfort." This ditty, as penned by Jerry Bock, Larry Holofcener and GeorgeWeiss, is essentially good "modern" 1950s jazz singing.
- "Party Blues." Penned by Basie, Joe Williams, and Ella, this obvious collaboration deserved a good rendition, and indeed it does. There is a lot of scatting found here, and Joe gets in some good licks, perfectly matching Ella and gelling with Basie's excellent backing.

- As a further note, Ella, in her usual good voice on later recordings is somewhat durative from her newly established 1950s' (Verve) style,—which also defined excellence.

61. "Mack the Knife, Ella in Berlin," Verve 4041. This gig has Ella taking Berlin—almost thirty years after Hitler. (The Nazi had banned American (imported) jazz records in the 1930s, including those of Ella, despite some actual record smuggling). This recording finds Ella, in fact, putting to rest lyrics, and scats the hell out it. While live entertainment may also breed complacency, this return to Ella's scatting roots destroys the myths of age. Indeed, this hot vocal of "Mack the Knife" remains remarkable! Who needs lyrics?

62-68. *Ella Wishes You a Swinging Christmas*, Verve 4042. The artistic (unicorn) original cover for this LP does not fail expectations of this superb vocal effort and concept. Backed by the Frank De Vol Orchestra and (sometimes) by an unidentified vocal group, Ella "swings" out on

a. "Jingle Bells." An (unidentified) vocal group behind Ella sound like a 1950s TV commercial, but Ella finds a way to make it all sound very hip.
b. "Santa Claus Is Comin' to Town."
c. "Have Yourself a Merry Little Christmas."
d. "What Are You Doing New Year's Eve." Ella scores high on this Loesser-penned ditty.
e. "Sleigh Ride."
f. "Good Morning Blues." This ditty (out of the Count Basie Orchestra and vocalist Jimmy Rushing), is updated well by Ella.
g. "Rudolph, the Red Nosed Reindeer." Ella successfully injects a little folk phrase into this (already) old Gene Autry classic, with a reference to "Tom Dooley" a contemporary recording by the Kingston Trio, on Capital 4049.

69-71. "Ella Fitzgerald's Christmas," Capital ST 2805. This late (1967) effort is all pop and traditional. While not half as good as her previous Verve Christmas effort, this conventional release, backed by Ralph Carmichael's Orchestra (like the latter Christmas product of Nat King Cole), still finds Ella delivering the goods, as these seasonal titles should! Picks are as follows:

a. "Away in a Manger."
b. "Sleep My Little Jesus."
c. "We Three Kings."

72-74. *Ella Swings, Chuck Swings*, Olympic Records 7119. This LP is founded upon an early remote radio broadcast featuring Chick Webb's Orchestra with Ella from Harlem's Savoy Ballroom in 1939. In many ways, this concert defines the swing era and luckily captures Chick Webb's pulsating drumming.

(Chick Webb would pass away the same year!) The following are the Ella Fitzgerald vocals, all driven by Webb and all superbly met by Ella's rhythmic vocal abilities:

a. "Oh, Johnny." The contemporary swing version of this old novel standard, penned by Abe Oline and Ed Rose, became a best seller by Orrin Tucker, with his fine rhythmic vocalist Bonnie Baker (Columbia 35228). It is challenged by Webb and Ella! Ella is joined in the vocal with a band member, who just may be Louis Jordan?

b. "I Want the Waiter with the Water." Ella betters her own contemporary recording (reviewed above).

c. "'T ain't What You Do." Ella swings out, with the band members joining in on the vocals! (She, more so, matches her contemporary recording.) Get up and swing!

- Visual Image and Legacy.

The already noted "Pete Kelly's Blues" remains a fine showcase. So do numerous guest appearances on TV, notably with Frank Sinatra. Ella just may be most familiar in commercials for audio tape as well as concerts into the '80s. There is an earlier entity, however.

75. "A-Tisket, A-Tasket a Red and Yellow Basket." Ella's 1938 recording is somewhat updated in the 1942 Abbot and Costello film *Ride 'Em Cowboy*.

Ella's subsequent television appearances throughout the 1950s, 1960s, and beyond are anthem to good taste. So was her vocal influence upon all other pre-rock singers. In true retrospective, perhaps her own earned title of "The First Lady of Pop" is more appropriate than (even) "swing."

Red Foley

The Kentucky-born Red Foley, like many other would-be recording artists, first found notice on radio—Chicago's WLS *National Barn Dance*. He would later become a fixture in Nashville's WSM *Grand Ole Opery* and KWTO *Ozark Jubilee* from Springfield, Missouri. As a minor recording entity for Vocalion in 1934, the struggle as a radio entity to finally gain recognition and best-selling success, by 1941, found Foley, like contemporary Ernest Tubb, dropping Jimmie Rodgers's style of yodeling and settling upon emulating Crosby. Indeed, Bing had already made successful inroads on "country" material, some indeed fueled by his a film "cowboy" image in *Rhythm on the Range*. Unlike contemporary Ernest Tubb, also a Jimmie Rodgers follower in the beginning, Foley's vocals were less edgy as his throat was used less. Like Tubb, success followed due to less emulation of Rodgers and more of a crooning job, indeed like Crosby. Picks are as follows:

1. "Old Shep," Melotone 6-03-53. This is the first rendering of Red's self-penned folk classic.
2. "I Got the Freight Train Blues," Conqueror 8285. Penned by John Lair, this 1934 release should not be confused with an earlier "Freight Train Blues" (penned by bluesmen Tommy Dorsey and Everett Murphy, a noted 1924 acoustic Clara Smith release). Red's ride is interesting enough, however, and contains as much (Southern) slang, as Clara's. Indeed, like much of the culture, this hillbilly recording shares a lot of language with Afro-American idiom. Or are they just words, as accented by region? (Later, Roy Acuff would record Red's original ditty as "Freight Train Blues.")

3. "The 1936 Flood," Vocalion 8676. A sad tale, it is clumsily told with feeling (penned by Bob Miller) and, in true retrospective, is documented.
4. "Old Shep," Decca 5944. This second and best-known recording about a young boy and his dog had much rural appeal, however clumsy. Mythology has it that Elvis Presley, then a young, rural youth himself, sang this ditty at the Mississippi and Alabama Fair in 1945. (Eleven years later, it would appear on Elvis's second album, Victor LPM-1382.)
5. "Smoke on the Water," Decca 6102. This (dated) entity contains historical data to back it up. Penned by Zeke Clement and Earl Nunn, its implied message of the defeat of the Axis powers, noting the defeat of the Japanese fleet in the Pacific, reeks of the kind of patriotism that was universal in 1944. (Perhaps the unity of America was never as exact as at the time of the attack of Japan upon the U. S. Navy at Pearl Harbor on December 7, 1941). While Red's "Smoke on the Water" is not alone as a WWII entity, its contemporary best-seller status more than proves its worth. Other very fine efforts of that era of world crisis include Elton Britt's "There's a Star Spangled Banner Waving Somewhere" on Bluebird B-9000, a previous country effort that signaled unity.
6. "Hang Your Head in Shame," Decca 16698. A confession? Played in a honky-tonk jukebox, this ditty (as penned by Fred Rose, Edward Nelson and Steve Nelson) perhaps provided anger as well as shame. Still does? Listen!
7. "Shame on You," Decca 18698. This country weeper is just good enough for this list. It is strangely backed by Lawrence Welk's Orchestra (very well know by the baby boomers of (later) 1950s television). (Originally a Spade Cooley release (a contemporary country swing bandleader), Cooley's own penned tale of "shame" featured a vocal by Tex Williams on Okeh 6731.)
8. "Sunday Down in Tennessee," Decca 36197.
9. "Atomic Power," Decca 46014. This ditty, penned by Fred Kirby, soon after the events of the a bombings of Hiroshima and Nagasaki in Japan, ignited a debate within the United States and the world, indeed still with us! It was estimated that over a million more Allied lives would have been lost without this very serious and heart-wrenching decision by President Truman in August 1945. As recording fodder, this ditty goes over far more than a propaganda "war" entity. It is, more so, far from a good song, as it tries to (dangerously) incorporate religion within it. Nevertheless, this ditty, recorded by Red in 1946, is a pick as perhaps the most bizarre of the age. Listen and ponder!
10. "Tennessee Saturday Night," Decca 46136. The infectious beat of this (dated) dance ditty still stirs up some dust, electric guitar, and novel spoken word. This Billy Hughes-penned ditty later found its way as an early Pat Boone effort, on Dot 15377. (As a further note, Boone, who also married Red's daughter Shirley, also produced a granddaughter Debbie Boone, also a popular vocalist, light-years away in the 1970s.)
11. "Freight Train Boogie," Decca 46035. Red incorporated the folk tale of Casey Jones to produce something contemporary in 1947! Let's boogie! Or let's rock? Contemporary ears could not call it "rock," yet, in true retrospective, could it?
12. "Never Trust a Woman," Decca 46074. A woman's tale is evident as both Red and Jenny Lou Carson were credited as writers. A perfect (1947) honky-tonk entity?
13. "Tennessee Border," Decca 46151. This James Work-penned ditty was perhaps just made to be on old "bar" tale? Or is it good comment about a lot of real social life? (Also note a another version with Ernest Tubb as "Tennessee Border No. 2.")

14. "Candy Kisses," Decca 46151. This simple ditty, penned by George Morgan most likely provided, for many bar patrons, some sweetness—for sour-tasting beer?
15. "Tennessee Border No 2," Decca 46200. Red teams up with Ernest Tubb and pokes fun at just what a (25 cent) marriage license meant (later '40s) at the Tennessee border.
16. "Chattanoogie Shoe Shine Boy," Decca 46205. This best-selling entity of 1950, in true retrospective, is more than borderline in racial attitude. Red's free and breezy vocal, moreover (penned by Harry Stone and Jack Strapp), made it a classic. Perhaps this tale is just another sad tale of a shoe shine boy finding his own rhythmic impulse when earning something for himself? Or is it just a crude put-down?
17. "Midnight," Decca 28420. This (1952) weepy tale, penned by Chet Atkins and Boudleaux Bryant, was one of those perfect honky-tonk bar entities? Listen after midnight!
18. "Hot Toddy," Decca 28587. This novelty, penned by R. Flanagan and H. Hendler, has some fine guitar licks with a strong (OK) vocal. Like many other ditties from the early 1950s, it's hard not to get up and rock, just a bit. This drinking song also notes some social dating habits of the times that are indeed still relevant!
19. "Have a Little Talk with Jesus," Decca 29505. By the mid-1950s, Red turned out a lot of gospel material. This ditty, with Sister Rosetta Tharpe—odd for the times—succeeds.
20. "One by One," Decca 29065. While Kitty Wells did not make the cusp to be a featured artist in this book, this (1954) honky-tonk tale, penned by Johnny Wright, Jack, and Jim Anglin, finds both Kitty and Red counting (very) personal transgressions (sins) against each other. Listen!

Helen Forrest

- It is to her credit that while primarily known as a band singer, this much-traveled vocalist (as with Artie Shaw, Benny Goodman, and Harry James) was able to stand up to the hogs (or bandleaders). Helen Forrest's autobiography *I Had the Craziest Dream* (also a recorded entity) also gives a good accounting of the times (1940s). Her controlled vocals may be considered very good and are most often confused with the likes of many other female recording artists, often labeled "birds" or "canaries."

Picks

1. "They Say," Bluebird 10075. This best-selling Artie Shaw entity ain't bad.
2. "Between a Kiss and a Sigh," Bluebird 10055. Another outing with Artie Shaw.
3. "How High the Moon," Columbia 35374. This 1940's ditty found Helen's vocal with that of Benny Goodman's Orchestra. Penned by Nancy Hamilton and Morgan Lewis, this ditty would find better recognition about a decade later, as recorded by Les Paul and Mary Ford on Capital 1451.
4. "Taking a Chance on Love," Columbia 35869. Via Benny Goodman, Helen took on a contemporary Ethel Waters release, on Liberty Music Shop 310, and indeed sang it as a swing classic. Surprisingly, another contemporary version by Ella Fitzgerald, while good enough, some how lacks Helen's commitment! While Waters's version remains the ultimate version, Helen's enthusiasm also remains contagious as well as a very fine vocal.

5. "The Devil Sat Down and Cried," Columbia 36466. Helen is joined by Dick Haymes and (maybe) Harry James himself on this sparkling novelty penned by Walter Bishop.
6. "Skylark," Columbia 36533. Sweet!
7. "Mister Five by Five," Columbia 36650. Helen scores heavily (as a Harry James entity) despite a contemporary Andrews Sisters version on Decca 18470. Did this ditty describe Jimmy Rushing?
8. "I Had the Craziest Dream," Columbia 36644. This film entity (from *Springtime in the Rockies*), as penned by Mack Gordon and Harry Warren, is indeed done well by Helen. (Contemporary film entity Betty Grable, perhaps the ultimate pinup girl of WWII, starred in the film. She later married Harry James. Sorry, Helen, it's in your book.)
9. "I've Heard That Song Before," Columbia 36668. Penned by Sammy Cahn and Jules Styne for the film entity *Youth on Parade*, Helen again produced a winner for many a dance floor.
10. "It's Always You," Columbia 36680. Did Helen sing better with Goodman? This ditty, penned by Burke and Van Heusen, seems to showcase and discipline her mellow and moody vocal.
11. "It Never Entered My Mind," Columbia 39478. Helen sounds more than well on this Benny Goodman release penned by Rodgers and Hart.
12. "Any Old Time," Victor 20-1575. Artie Shaw's self-penned ditty with Billie Holiday, on Bluebird B-7759, somehow found Artie and Helen attempting a remake. Oddly, Helen clearly drops her vocal to emulate Billie, sounding very much like her. Indeed, after playing this record many times, it is Billie—almost! Listen and compare! Note also Helen's vocal ability to mimic or at least try something new—or old?
13. "Time Waits for No One," Decca 18600. This (1944) solo recording, penned by Cliff Friend and Charles Tobias, meant a lot for war-weary GIs, perhaps figuring the time is now?
14. "Baby, What You Do To Me," Decca 18778. Helen and the Les Paul Trio team up with some good-sounding vocals between guitar licks. Penned by Lionel Newman, Don Grainger, and Harry James himself, this ditty works despite the fact Harry James did not participate.
15. "Some Sunday Morning," Decca 23434. A very fine duet with Dick Haymes.
16. "I'll Buy That Dream," Decca 23434. Another fine duet with Dick Haymes.
17. "Come Rain or Shine," Decca 23548. Helen and Dick Haymes team up for a contemporary version of this classic penned by Johnny Mercer and Harold Arlen for the Broadway entity *St. Louis Woman*. (Other versions include a Margaret Whiting version (Capital 247) as well as the original, which was done by Ruby Hill and Harold Nicholas (of the Nicholas Brothers) on Capital 10055.)

Jane Froman

- Jane Froman was a popular radio entity of the early 1930s, who also became a popular recording artist. Her stiff crooning style (perfect for contemporary radio) won her a huge listening audience, and she also appeared in a few films and on Broadway. While always a bit more than highbrow in her vocals, and perhaps most influenced by the likes of Helen Morgan, her subsequent success did produce some good recordings. Later, as part of a USO show during WWII, her plane crashed, which resulted in multiple injuries. (A later 1952 bio film *With a Song in My Heart*, which starred actress Susan Hayward with Jane's vocals, founded more interest in her later career.

➢ The following are Jane Froman picks:

1. "Sharing," Victor 22461.
2. "June Kisses," Victor 22460.
3. "Lost in a Fog," Decca 180. This classic penned by Fields and McHugh is done well enough, although a contemporary Connie Boswell version, on Brunswick 7303, is stronger and better.
4. "I Only Have Eyes for You," Decca 181. Penned by Dubin and Warren, this ditty had been introduced as a filmed entity in the (1934) Dick Powell film *Dames*. Luckily, Jane's crooning effort, captured on this recording, is somewhat better. (A later rock-era version, by the Flamingos on End 1046, is perhaps the ultimate doo-wop!)
5. "But Where Are You," Decca 710. This ditty, penned by Irving Berlin, had been introduced by Harriet Hillard in the contemporary (1936) Fred Astaire and Ginger Rogers film *Follow the Fleet*. Her subsequent recording is better and is an interesting comparison to the (almost) operatic style of Jane's version.
6. "Please Believe Me," Decca 710. This very upper crust rendering, penned by Al Jacobs and Larry Yoell, is, nevertheless, effective.

➢ In 1938, Jane and others attempted a series of recordings on Victor, penned by the Gershwins. Sadly, they are oversung and (mostly) fail to deliver anything special. The following pick, however, does indeed hit it's mark as a sophisticated torch song.

7. "Boy What Love Done to Me, Columbia 36414. Penned by George and Ira Gershwin, this soft lyric perhaps provided a challenge for most singers. Jane's highbrow style, moreover, works well here as her bright voice retains a needed reserve.
8. "Tonight We Love," Columbia 36414. With violin strings blazing, Jane's effective high-pitched vocal somehow delivers an effective bit of schmaltz. Penned by Ray Austin, Freddy Martin, and Bobby Worth, this bit of converted classical music—Tchaikovsky's Piano Concerto in B-flat—had also been an effective enough recording by Tony Martin, on Decca 3988.

➢ The following two ditties were part of the Disney (1941) cartoon film soundtrack *"Dumbo,"* penned by Oliver Wallace, Frank Churchill, and Ned Washington. Moreover, Jane's vocals are very good.

9. "Baby Mine," Columbia 36460.
10. "When I See an Elephant Fly," Columbia 36460.

➢ The following are postwar releases:

11. "I Got Lost in His Arms," Majestic 1049. This Irving Berlin-penned ditty had been a postwar Broadway entity for Ethel Merman in his *Annie, Get Your Gun*. While Merman's onstage vocals were excellent, most of her subsequent recordings are loud and, perhaps, annoying. While Jane's own highbrow vocal style is (also) not for everyone, Jane's controlled and committed vocal on this ditty somehow produces a winner.
12. "For You For Me Evermore" Majestic-1086
13. "A Garden In The Rain". Majestic-1086.
14. "With a Song in My Heart," Capital 2044. This ditty penned by Rodgers and Hart had been a somewhat stiff vocal as rendered by Ran Weeks on a (1929) Leo Reisman

release, on Victor 21923. Moreover, Jane's (1952) vocal approach is much the same as by Hildegarde in (1939). Indeed, this ditty would also become the title of a film bio of her life, with actress Susan Hayward playing her as well as lip-singing Jane's actual semi-operatic voice. Beware of the rest of this soundtrack despite its contemporary "best seller" credentials!

- *Yours Alone*, love songs by Jane Froman, Capital (10-inch) LP H 354. Selections.

  This early '50s LP found Jane recording 1930s' ditties that she may have done only on radio. In any case the following find Jane, while a bit highbrow, much less uppity. The ears of this author, more so, find Jane has improved vocally. Picks are as under:

15. "Be Still My Heart." The ditty penned by Allan Flynn and Jack Egan is, indeed, done well.
16. "More Than You Know." While more like Helen Morgan's version than Lee Wiley's defining version, it's still worth it and well done!
17. "There's a Lull in My Life."
18. "A Little Kiss Each Morning." The Rudy Vallee original is actually challenged and improved!
19. "Hands Across the Table." As good as Helen Ward? Or Lee Wiley?
20. How About You." Done well! Listen for Frank Sinatra? Or Dick Todd?
21. "What Is There to Say." This ditty penned by Vernon Duke and E. Y. Harburg is finally claimed by Jane.
22. "Song From Desiree". Capital-F-2979. An original 1954 film ditty, penned by Alfred Newman and Ken Darby, found a contrived effort to fit into a historical drama of the French-Napoleon era, starring Jean Simmons and Marlon Brando. It is also a perfect fit for Jane's high brow vocal—which comes off very well.

Judy Garland

- A recording artist who becomes popular, after finding his/her own "image," always has to make sure that the "image" remains. The emergence of "talking" films in the late 1920s had provided Americana true visual images of favored recording and radio artists, which, in turn, created problems of "image" in itself. By the early 1930s, "film image" became "star" power for many, which provided a platform for many to win, loose, or regain recognition. The Depression years indeed found musical entities, hardly recording artists, establishing huge audiences. Indeed, the likes of Fred Astaire, Ginger Rodgers, Alice Faye, and Shirley Temple all found success chiefly through the media of film, with recordings and radio, a sideline. While it may be noted that Astaire had been a Broadway success and had indeed produced some successful recordings, his visual image as a dancer, on film, was his principal asset. While noting the racism of the era, there was one "star" would shine above all. More than Fred Astaire, Judy Garland became a huge recording entity, such that she even topped some fine filmed musical sequences. More so, she had a far better voice and transferred far better than Astaire's voice onto recorded disc. As an entertainer, Judy owed much to film exposure, which carefully crafted for her an art form like no other before her. In true retrospective, the same film industry that had popularized her, also contributed to her early demise.

The "visual image" of the fourteen-year-old girl of latter 1936 (born Frances Gumm) was indeed one of a child star, one of vaudevillian "live" stage shows. Her parents were from the show business and perhaps saw early the radio success of Baby Rose Marie, a huge entity of New York Radio, and later of national network hookups. After dropping her singing sister act "Gumm Sisters," ambitious parents and film studio moguls, in an attempt to create preteen images, found the likes of Deanna Durbin (who sang European opera), Mickey Rooney (who sang and did anything he was given), and Judy Garland herself, who could sing popular songs much like an adult.

The following picks include films, which figured so much into the art of this fine recording artist.

1. "Stompin' at the Savoy," Decca 848. While actually an early Bob Crosby release, the young Judy sounds good enough. While obviously influenced by an (equally) young Ella Fitzgerald vocal, this ditty (by Andy Razaf, Chick Webb, Edgar Sampson, and Benny Goodman) indeed "swings," and with some authority.
2. "Swing, Mister Swing," Decca 848. The flip of "Stompin' at the Savoy," this obvious attempt at contemporary swing, penned by J. Russell Robinson, Irving Taylor, and Harry Brooks, while contrived, indeed works. It it more ever a bit of Mendelssohn? Just listen!

- "La Fiesta of Santa Barbara" (1936). The young Judy may be seen and heard singing with her sisters as the "Gumm Sisters" (in color). This musical short features a fine rhythmic ditty:

3. "La Cucaracha." This Mexican folk song was adapted by Stanley Adams and Edward Marks and had already been a full-length (1934) film. Luckily, this spirited rendition is more lasting, however brief.
4. "All God's Chillun Got Rhythm," Decca 1432. While Ivie Anderson owns this title, the rhythmic influences of Ivie indeed merit Judy's efforts.
5. "Dear Mr. Gable," Decca 1463. This film ditty was introduced by Judy herself in *Broadway Medley of 1938*." As a schmaltzy title, about film idol Clark Gable, this nostalgic ditty had already been around since at least 1913. Moreover, this reconstruction of the 1913 hit "You Made Me Love You," penned by James V. Monaco and Joseph McCarthy, obviously found the acoustic Al Jolson version (Columbia 1374) a vocal influence on the young singer. Indeed, the Jolson style, already passé by 1938, would remain with Garland, personified by her, from time to time, for the rest of her career.

- *The Wizard of Oz*, film, MGM (1939). This (mostly) color film, an innovation for its era, had been a gamble to produce. Originally something for the likes of the established Shirley Temple, a better-known film entity with a huge following, veteran actor and dancer Buddy Ebsen, who had previously been associated with previously successful Shirley Temple films, was also considered (Bill Bojangles Robinson, most likely because of race, was not). Eventually, the dropping of Shirley, found Judy, with the able talents of Frank Morgan, Ray Bolger, Jack Haley, Bert Lahr, Billie Burke, The Munchkins (singing midgets), and others—a hell of a cast for this more-than-a-kiddie classic. Moreover is Judy's filmed version of

6. "Over the Rainbow."

The name Dorothy, the character of the L. Frank Baum novel, which had already been a "silent film" but, more importantly, a musical stage production, found Judy (formerly Frances Gumm) identified with it for the rest of her life. Indeed, this film myth never died, despite future personal problems. Americana never forgot her, and the rerun on TV, video, and DVD remained very popular for generations.

7. "Over the Rainbow" Decca 2672. The visual image, as found in the film *The Wizard Oz*, had originally found this ditty penned by Harold Arlen and E. Y. Harburg, as truly priceless. Indeed, Judy's flawless vocal remained an inspiration for its audiences, which were countless for the baby boomer and their own kiddies, generations since 1939. While this recording could not generate its own video, in true retrospective, this original blue Decca release was, for many years, a classic that has remained familiar despite its obsolete 78 rpm speed.
8. "The Jitterbug," Decca 2672. As the flip of "Over the Rainbow," this ditty had also been penned by Arlen and Harburg for the film. In true retrospective, had it remained in the film the timeless appeal of the film's own myth, would have been lost. In any case, Judy's clear and crisp vocal is a spirited vocal and, indeed, danceable.
9. "I'm Nobody's Baby," Decca 3174. This budding film title from the successful Mickey Rooney series of "Andy Hardy" flicks, *Andy Hardy Meets a Debutante*, had Judy stealing the show. This recording, moreover, found Judy turning on many preteens of 1940, providing a fine update to this 1920s classic of Marion Harris (Columbia A 3433), Aileen Stanley (Vocalion 14172) and especially that as by Ruth Etting (Columbia 1104-D).
10. "I'm Nobody's Baby." This "live" filmed stuff from *Andy Hardy Meets a Debutante* is juvenile and full of the stuff adults wished for young adults in the times (1940s). Because of Judy, the myth still works!
11. "Buds Won't Bud," Decca 3174. This ditty, penned by Arlen and Harburg ditty, while dated, found "Judy Garland" in big letters with an orchestra directed by Bobby Sherwood. More importantly, it provided Judy with more fine contemporary material, which she effortlessly performed well. (An edgier vocal by Connie Haines, on a contemporary Tommy Dorsey release (Victor 26609) is also very good and merits comparisons.)
12. "The Birthday of a King," Decca 4050. This 1941 release, penned by H. H. Neidlinger, is true Christmas cheer.
13. "The Star of the East," Decca 4050. Another contrived Christmas entity, this original 1941 ditty penned by Amanda Kennedy and George Cooper, still remains a winner.
14. "Our Love Affair," Decca 3593. Penned by Arthur Freed and Rodger Edens, this ditty found itself in the contemporary Mickey Rooney and Judy Garland film *Strike Up the Band*. Moreover, Judy's vocal is done well and is also good competition for the likes of a Tommy Dorsey release (Victor 26736), which featured a more mature Frank Sinatra vocal.
15. "How About You," Decca 4072. As a film entity (from the Mickey Rooney and Judy Garland box office hit of 1941 *Babes in Arms*), this ditty's initial response was from that of Judy's preteen audiences. Nevertheless, this ditty penned by Ralph Freed and Burton Lane has remained a classic, while also noting a contemporary Tommy Dorsey release, with a fine Frank Sinatra vocal (Victor 27749) as well as by Dick Todd (Bluebird B-11406).

16. "For Me and My Gal," Decca 18480. From the film of the same name, this 1942 best seller was a bit of nostalgia for the most part. As an acoustic entity, versions included those of Van and Schenck (Victor 18258), Henry Burr and Albert Campbell (Pathé 20163), and Billy Murray (Edison 50407). As in the film, a young Gene Kelly, with a so-so vocal, shares a vocal with Judy in this classic (penned by Edgar Leslie, Ray Goetz, and George W. Meyer), which is saved, as in the film, as well as on record, by Judy's fine vocal.
17. "When You Wore a Tulip," Decca 18480. The flip of "For Me and My Gal," this stupid title, penned by Jack Mahoney and Percy Wenrich, had also been an acoustic entity and a best-selling entity by the American Quartet, on Victor 17652. Indeed, this acoustic wonder must have been an inspiration for the likes of bandleader and sing-along master Mitch Miller of baby boomer 1960s television, Columbia records, and other fans of barber shop quartets and vocal groups of 1917. Luckily, Judy and Gene are above all this, and Judy's vocal wins out over all this sort of stuff.

- *Presenting Lily Mars,* film, MGM (1943). This almost-forgotten film boasts of song titles that include

18. "Three O'Clock in the Morning,"
19. "Every Little Movement Has a Meaning of Its Own," and especially
20. "Broadway Melody."

Indeed, both contemporary bandleaders Tommy Dorsey and Bob Crosby provided Judy with relevant backings in this fine 1942 film. (Perhaps the musicians' strike prevented recordings?)

21. "Zing Went the Strings of My Heart," Decca 18543. Judy had rendered this ditty on radio in 1935. This 1943 best seller had been recorded earlier by Judy and perhaps released because of the contemporary musicians strike. Backed by lush strings, this Victor Young backing indeed greeted Judy's fine vocal. Much later (in the '50s rock era), the Coasters (Atco 6116) would record this novelty, penned by James F. Hanley, with more energy, with no disrespect to Judy.
22. "Embraceable You," Decca 23308. In 1930 Ginger Rogers had introduced this ditty on Broadway in "Girl Crazy, without a contemporary recording. This update by Judy is almost ruined by an unidentified "male quintet." Luckily, it's Judy's style that wins one's ears over and, in true retrospective, offers fine comparisons to a contemporary and more-committed Billie Holiday version on Commadore 7520 or a previous highbrow (but) fine Jimmy Dorsey release, featuring Helen O'Connell (Decca 3928).
23. "Could You Use Me," Decca 23308. This flip side of "Embraceable You" also boasts another Gershwin Brothers' score and, despite Mickey Rooney, wins the day on account of Judy.

24, 25. "The Trolley Song," Decca 23361. (a) This film title (from *Meet Me in St Louis*, along with the next three titles) again dabbled into the nostalgic time of the St Louis World's Fair of 1904. Released in the war year of 1944, this title, penned by Ralph Blane and Hugh Martin, indeed promoted the film better than it's flimsy plot. (b.) Judy's moving scene with the Trolly car remains something to see and hear. (Note: In retrospective, it's only some well-done musical sequences, featuring Judy, that save this otherwise stupid film.)

26, 27. "Meet Me in St. Louis, Louis," Decca 23360. (a) The acoustic age had tenors like Billy Murray (Edison 8722) among other labels and versions, as By S. D. Dudley (Victor 2807) and a J. W. Myers (Columbia 1848), each claiming best-selling versions in 1904, as penned by Andrew B. Sterling and Kerry Mills. Judy's film (b), and this recording, moreover, save this ditty as the real classic.

28, 29. "Have Yourself a Merry Little Christmas," Decca 23362. (a) This ditty, more than any of the other filmed entities found in *Meet Me in St. Louis*, retains relevance and remains a classic. Indeed, introduced as something contemporary, this title (by Hugh Martin and Ralph Blane) would remain a film classic for Judy (rendering it to little Margaret O'Brien). Moreover, it is a warm Yule-time Christmas entity, worn down well by original 78 rpm needles, as well as reissues on 45 rpm, LPs, and (later) century CD issues. (b) The original recording is just as lasting and better than the filmed version. Or perhaps Frank Sinatra would come close to redefining it, as his second try, on Capital LP W894, which indeed aspires to the excellence of the Judy Garland original. Listen and compare!

30, 31. "The Boy Next Door," Decca 23362. (a) As the flip of "Have Yourself a Merry Little Christmas," this ditty (by Ralph Blane and Hugh Martin), perhaps defines a "flipping classic." As another Garland winner, this recording retains a soft style with a vocal so personable and reeking with Class, that it is even better than seeing it in the (b) film. (Again, within about ten years, a Frank Sinatra version on Capital LP H 488, as "The Girl Next Door," perhaps redefined this classic, noting the Garland original as something very hard to strive for in style and performance. Luckily for Frank, he does. Judy or Frank?

32. "You've Got Me Where You Want Me," Decca 23410. This ditty penned by Harry Warren and Johnny Mercer is a fine duet with Bing Crosby. Moreover, this pleasant exchange is a winner, with Judy's vocal the real highlight of the recording and with Bing indeed benefiting being paired up with her.

33, 34. "On the Atchison, Topeka, and the Santa Fe," Decca 23436. (a) This film ditty (from *The Harvey Girls*) finds Judy assisted vocally by a contemporary vocal group, the Merry Macs. As a fast-paced ditty, this pleasant tale of a train ride, penned by Harry Warren and Johnny Mercer, indeed finds Judy's vocal coasting along some nifty and novel lyrics with finesse. So indeed did a contemporary Bing Crosby version, on Decca 18690 and a Johnny Mercer release on Capital 195. While it is indeed hard to judge just which train ride is more pleasant, perhaps a ticket for all three provides fine comparisons. Moreover, contemporary 1945 record buyers did, as all three became best sellers! All aboard? (b). The subsequent (1946) film *The Harvey Girls*, more so, features great visuals with Judy's vocal, Ray Bolger, and cast!

35. "Changing My Tune," Decca 23688. This ditty, penned by Gershwin Brothers finds much life on dated but fine Judy Garland tonsils. While Garland's vocal sounds a bit older now, it's all Judy, with her signature voice all over it.

36. "Connecticut," Decca 23804. A welcome duet with Bing produces yet another winner, penned by Hugh Martin and Ralph Blane.

- *Till the Clouds Roll By*, MGM, color (1946). This bio of songwriter Jerome Kern found a contemporary musical cast which included the likes of many, with only Judy and Lena Horne leaving anything behind (still) worth watching and hearing. Judy is cast as Marilyn Miller, a real life Broadway entity who had appeared in Some of Kern's productions in the 1920s. Judy impressively renders

37. "Look for the Silver Lining."
38. "Who."

- *Easter Parade*, film, MGM (1948). As perhaps second to only *The Wizard of Oz*, this Judy Garland film also found the likes of Fred Astaire and indeed produced a fine pairing of talents for the screen. While originally an excuse for already proven Irving Berlin-penned classics, the film benefited as professionalism from all concerned is demonstrated throughout the whole film.

Highlights included

39. "Easter Parade," with Astaire.
40. "Everybody's Doing It."
41. "I Want to Go Back to Michigan."
42. "Better Luck Next Time."
43. "A Fella with an Umbrella," with Peter Lawford.
44. "A Couple of Swells."
45. "Easter Parade," MGM 30185. A departure from Decca records and an MGM record label for Judy was a change for Judy, but this recording retains much of the excellence of any Decca master. This ditty, had had a long history, as introduced on Broadway in *As Thousands Cheer* by actor Clifton Webb. There was also a contemporary 1933 vocal recording by him on a Leo Reisman release on Victor 24418. A Gene Austin release (Romeo 2189) was better, but less known. More recently, a 1942 film introduction by Bing Crosby in *Holiday Inn* had also been a fine contemporary recording by him on Decca 18425. Garland, moreover, does it well, and is a fine match for the Crosby vocal, which is another winner, as well as another comparison to become familiar with, at least for sleeping purposes.
46. "Better Luck Next Time," MGM 30187. Yet another Irving Berlin-penned classic defined!
47. "Get Happy," MGM 30254. Released on 78 rpm, or the newer 45 rpm, this ditty penned by Arlen and Koehler again finds a bit of Al Jolson hamming it up. Fortunately for Judy, it all works.

By 1950, while few knew it at the time, problems with pills and marriage problems caused Judy to Leave film work and recordings. Touring, however, still found her a huge following. Finally, a film *A Star Is Born*, in 1954, indeed well-crafted for her talents as well as age, put her back in Hollywood.

- *A Star Is Born*, film, Warner Brothers (1954). While not the great box office entity it was intended to be, this film, in true retrospective, is a true classic, however botched. The thirty-two-year-old Judy, indeed deemed "old" in the era in fashion and presentation, rises up above all that, as well as perhaps a script not developed enough. Indeed, the principal reason to see and hear this film is Garland herself—a smart entertainer who electrified her audiences anytime when performing.

Visual highlights include Judy performing:

48. "The Man That Got Away."
49. "It's a New World."

50. "Gotta Have Your Go with Me."

- The following three ditties, all classics, penned by Harold Arlen and George Gershwin, are matching recordings from the film *A Star Is Born*.

51. "The Man That Got Away," Columbia 40270. Perhaps the best known of all from the film *A Star Is Born*, this classic found Judy's emotional involvement with lyrics, indeed, real. This ditty would also follow Garland around and may be considered another signature tune.
52. "It's a New World," Columbia 8008. Another winner, sung with class and emotion.
53. "Gotta Have Your Go With Me," Columbia 8005. Yup, Judy again scores!

54-58. *Judy*, LP Capital T-734. This 1956 entity, backed by Nelson Riddle's lush strings, had assets. As an obvious attempt to duplicate contemporary Frank Sinatra LP success, this LP, mostly, succeeds, with Garland's vocals attempting and redefining some already old standards. The following are picks:

a. "I Feel a Song Coming On." This ditty had been a best seller for Francis Langford, on Brunswick 7512. Penned by Jimmy McHugh, Dorothy Fields, and George Oppenheimer, it had been a film entity from *Every Night at Eight* (1935). Judy, moreover, with Riddle's usual excellence, redefines this classic and claims it for her own.
b. "Last Night When We Were Young." Judy had already recorded this ditty on MGM 30432.

This version of the ditty penned by Arlen and Harburg is better.

c. "Life Is Just a Bowl of Cherries." Penned by Ray Henderson and Lew Brown in 1931 for Broadway's *George White's Scandals of 1931,* this ditty had found recognition by Rudy Vallee (Victor 22783) and by Bing Crosby, in a refrain on Brunswick 20102. About ten years later, a pop version by Jayne P. Morgan (Derby 837) had updated this Depression classic, stripped from its original impact. Judy, more like Morgan, does the same.

d. "I Will Come Back" or "Maybe I'll Come Back." Penned by Charles L. Cook and Howard Jeffrey, this ditty is, perhaps, a mystery for the author of this book. Luckily, it doesn't matter much as Judy again scores.
e. "Memories of You." The original Broadway title penned by Eubie Blake and Andy Razaf (1930), already a Ethel Waters classic, is at least challenged.

59-62. *Judy at Carnegie Hall*, Capital 1569. This 1961 live show at Carnegie Hall, in New York, perhaps, best describes the later career of Judy Garland. While she would do a few films before her death in 1969, her career would usually focus on P. A., usually on television and usually taping live appearances. As a double LP, this release won acclaim as a Grammy winner and a best-selling entity despite rock and roll. While the young vocalist was more enduring, this mature-voiced version of Judy Garland, as a live program, indeed endures.

a. "This Can't Be Love." This 1938 ditty penned by Rodgers and Hart is done more than well.

b. "Do It Again." The ditty penned by Buddy De Sylva and George Gershwin from the '20s also becomes a Judy Garland entity.
c. "A Foggy Day." The Gershwin Brothers penned this classic for Fred Astaire in the 1937 film *A Damsel in Distress.* While best seen in the film, Fred's recording, on Brunswick 7982, is typically weak and meek. The older Garland, moreover, has no such problem, even as a live entity.
d. "Chicago." The old Fred Fisher-penned title from the early '20s, recorded by Aileen Stanley on Okeh 4792, was already updated by Frank Sinatra in 1957 on Capital 3793. This version is almost as good.

- Legacy

The best way to define this twentieth-century giant of entertainment, who died at forty-nine in 1969, is perhaps more than one can attempt to describe. While her contrived film image remains, so indeed remains a visual image so firmly implanted upon Americana and the world that oddly clashes with life itself. *The Wizard of Oz* had many heroes and villains, often found in life. Indeed, "Over the Rainbow," remains Judy's own visual and vocal treasure, shared and true in life. Perhaps the Hollywood moguls, this time, got more than they had bargained for? Or perhaps, the exploited teenage star of the 1939 film really did steal the show?

Woody Guthrie

- The pre-rock era was also a time of protest, political instability, and social unrest. While the absence of national television and a smaller news media actually contributed to less coverage of racism, union organization, and war protest, they, nevertheless did exist. The right to organize unions as by the Franklin Roosevelt administration in 1934, did much to reform America, as well as perhaps stop a much more sinister revolt of the masses. So did a government program called Social Security. The civil rights of persons of color was an ongoing struggle, with entertainers generally finding goals distant and wondering just how the entertainment industry got them as far as they did. The pre—rock songs of Woody Guthrie, moreover, addressed these issues and, indeed, may be considered anthem, in true retrospective, for the social changes and music that rocked the later 1960s.
- Woody Guthrie was a Southerner, whose "Western" Oklahoma upbringing led him into the local music of rural and hillbilly music. The folk appeal of the recordings of the Carter Family, Jimmie Rodgers, and (forbidding) sounds of the numerous black "blues" recordings, all influenced Woody.

  So did the Great Depression and the events of the "great dust bowl" storms of the era. Indeed, his own personal observations and sympathies for the suffering masses also led him to champion many left-wing movements, including the Communist Party. Much of Woody's recorded music is thus full of protest, calling upon fellow Americans the perils of the poor, disenfranchised, and those of different ethnic and racial backgrounds.

Picks are as follows:

a. *Dust Bowl Ballads*, Vol. 1, Victor P-27. The late '30s and early '40s (before WWII) found much of the country in fear of the wars raging in Europe and Asia. Many

Americans were not sure of just what Germany, Japan, and Italy were about to do. The contemporary record industry responded with major recording artists, including Paul Robeson, the operatic Lawrence Tibbett, and Bing Crosby, in such patriotic propaganda as "Ballad for Americans." While it should be noted that they indeed become best-selling entities of the era, they are all (in true retrospective) short, spoken word essays, contrived pieces of propaganda. In the meantime, the contemporary John Steinbeck novel *The Grapes of Wrath* and its subsequent film version, which starred Henry Fonda and which noted the social problems of Americans caught up in the great dust bowl of the early 1930s, also received much contemporary notice. It, for certain, struck a chord in Woody Guthrie, already a hillbilly radio personality by 1940. Indeed, Woody identified deeply with the well-done film and especially by actor Henry Fonda's skillful performance as a drifter in Oklahoma and California. The resulting 78 rpm albums produced some very crude, emotional, and personal statements, perhaps defining social protest. In true retrospective (while not huge sellers), the following recordings contributed greatly to Americans speaking up and for those millions, indeed, without a voice.

1. "Talkin' Dust Bowl Blues," Victor 26619. (a.) This first recording of a theme set is so simple, so plain and earthy, that somehow its listeners are actually "there," as Woody actually was! As a rural blues entity, Woody challenges its listeners into exploring a great American tragedy, and it may be considered a guide for this truly focused theme album. In any case, the many yarns about dust also include one chilling tale about a girlfriend actually buried in dust! Get out your shovel, or at least listen?
2. "Blowin' Down This Road," Victor 26619. While most of this set contains a self-played guitar and harmonica, this effective tale about the basic needs of a drifter (and his family) is more than a social problem. (Light-years later, one Bob Dylan, just must have found this ditty an inspiration!)
3. "Do Re Mi," Victor 26620. The plight of the "lost" farmers of the dust bowl is found in John Steinbeck's *The Grapes of Wrath.* Those who could not catch the 1940 film or at least find the "Do" or "dough" to see the flick were indeed out of money. Perhaps Woody's definition is still relevant, as charity for Americans was a difficult subject.
4. "Dust Can't Kill Me," Victor 26620. Yes it can!
5. "Tom Joad," Victor 26621 (Parts 1 and 2) Both sides. The "jungle" camps of the dust bowl immigrants is indeed found in the film *The Grapes of Wrath*. The "rights" of hungry children, the brutal efforts of law enforcement, and social consequences are all explored—just listen.

b. *Dust Bowl Ballads,* Vol. 2. Victor P-28, 78 rpm album:

6. "The Great Dust Storm," Victor 26622. Yes, it's a fact.
7. "Dusty Old Dust," Victor 26622. There's a lot of dust found here—what's new? Perhaps when a preacher can't even continue, there's a problem.
8. "Dust Bowl Refugee," Victor 26623. A survivor—maybe?
9. "Dust Pneumonia Blues," Victor 26623. (Now he's sick!). This ditty, however (minus the dust), is very much influenced by Jimmie Rodgers. Thankfully (as noted by Woody), it's free of yodeling!
10. "I Ain't Got No Home in This World Anymore," Victor 26624. This drifter ain't got no home. His brothers and sisters are on the road because a rich man took the farm away. His wife died and could it all be any worse? (In true retrospective, the

contemporary (1940) populations of Russia, Poland, and China, among others, were involved in a world war. A very troubled world indeed.)

11. "Vigilante Man," Victor 26624. He's on the run. Woody asks the question, is he dangerous?

The following ditties were, for the most part, released in 78 rpm album sets. They will not be reviewed as such.

12. "Pastures of Plenty," Disc 5010. This ditty was originally part of a newer "Dust Bowl" set (on Disc Records, not Victor) in 1947. While not as effective as the earlier Victor recordings as a set, this recording is a key exception. Woody is very much the social commentator here, as he describes the travels or migrant workers. In true retrospective, despite Woody's plea, the shame of America still traveled with the times into the twenty-first century.
13. "Midnight Special," Disc 6043. This recording is basically a Leadbelly entity with Woody and Cisco Houston in vocal and instrumental backup. While the rest of the set is not what it could have been, this rerecording of a previous Leadbelly entity ain't bad. The racial mix, even for the times, is somewhat dismissed, but significant for the times.
14. "Pretty Boy Floyd," Ash 360-1. While Woody's later years were spent as an urban dweller (in New York City), much of his Oklahoma roots are featured in his songs, mostly self-written. This well-told ditty, while simple enough, is a gangster yarn of the early 1930s despite being recorded in 1946. In any case, the sympathy for a gangster who provided food for families of the Depression era is clearly noted and felt by the listener of this recording, however contrived.
15. "Car Song," Cub 3A. This children's set did contain this very fine recording—even for adults.

The very creative Woody imitates a sputtering car—with very good results.

16. "This Land Is Your Land," LP Folkways FP-27. After an extensive search, this ditty just could not be found on 78 rpm. Moreover, this classic is, perhaps, Woody's best-known ditty, and his own love of country, perhaps composed while riding on a train, rambles on. For many, this ditty is a true anthem for Americana, rivaling the converted poem of Francis Scott Key's "The Star Spangled Banner" and Irving Berlin's "God Bless America." (An early '60s folk group, the New Christy Minstrels, perhaps defined Woody's dream best, as found on Columbia 42592.)

- ➢ Woody had some influence upon contemporary 1940s "country" and "western" music. Moreover,

    - A (1944) release by his cousin Jack Guthrie, "Oklahoma Hills," on Capital 201, became a best-selling entity. Penned by both Jack and Woody (who had been singing with him on Los Angeles radio (KFVD) before his recording contract with Victor in 1940, this very "Western" title was indeed effective.
    - A (1949) release by the Maddox Brothers and Rose on Four Star 1289, "Philadelphia Lawyer"—based on Woody's radio performance of "Reno Blues"—is serious tale of divorce as well as violence and passion. More so, the rough-edged Rose Maddox vocal, in honky-tonk style, indeed works.

- More

The following 78 rpm albums are "Almanac Singers" entities. They consist of Woody, Pete Seeger, John Peter Hawes, and Lee Hays. While Woody is not lead vocal on all ditties (thus not deemed a complete Woody Guthrie entity), some are. Woody is thus found, as lead vocal, on the following:

- a. *Deep Sea Chanties and Whaling Ballads*, General Album G-20.

17. "Blow the Man Down," General Album 5016-A.

- b. *Sod Buster Ballads*, General Album G-21.

18. "Hard, Ain't It Hard," General Album 5019-B.
19. "I Ride an Old Paint," General Album 5020-A.
20. "House of the Rising Sun," General Album 5020-B.

Connie Haines

Connie Haines was a slick band singer, who gained fame with Harry James and, especially, Tommy Dorsey. As a Savannah, Georgia-born Southerner, her "Southern accent," like singer-songwriter Johnny Mercer, could easily find itself into a lyric, whenever inclined to do so. As an early radio entity, who subsequently was featured in the *Major Bowes* program, Connie learned how to get along. While the recordings of Ethel Waters and Helen Morgan did indeed have an early influence, the likes of Jo Stafford, and the contemporary late 1930s' voices of Ella Fitzgerald, Helen Ward, and Ginny Simms must have had a huge influence upon her. Even so, the more-than-capable Connie had a voice that could hold up with the best of them, including the likes of contemporary Frank Sinatra, with whom she sang along with the Pied Pipers vocal group—who included Jo Stafford.

- The following eight are Connie Haines picks with Tommy Dorsey's Orchestra :

1. "Buds Won't Bud," Victor 26609. The more-than-competent Connie swings into something a little more adult than the contemporary Judy Garland version. Listen and Compare.
2. "Swing Time up in Harlem," Victor 27249. This contrived title, credited to Tommy Dorsey himself, found Tommy hogging up most of this recording with something borrowed from a Duke Ellington arrangement? More so, when played on a 78 rpm record player, a contemporary (1940) listener just might identify Connie's swift "swing" vocal as Ella Fitzgerald's? Just listen!
3. "Oh, Look at Me Now," Victor 27274. The Frank Sinatra lead finds Connie in good company.
4. "You Might Have Belonged to Another," Victor 27274. Another gem with Sinatra.
5. "Will You Still Be Mine," Victor 27421. This ditty penned by Tom Adair and Matt Dennis was first released in 1941. Some three years later, like other material recorded before the musicians' strike of 1942, this ditty was rereleased on Victor 20-1576, receiving even more recognition, despite being a Tommy Dorsey release, as Connie herself had, by this time (1944), become better known.

6. "Let's Get Away from It All," Victor 27377. Connie's and Frank's vocals, along with the Pied Piepers, produce another bland, yet pleasant recording.
7. "Kiss the Boys Good-bye," Victor 27461. This film entity, penned by Frank Loesser and Victor Schertzinger, found better recognition with a fine rendering by Connie and a version similar in style as by contemporary Bea Wain. More so, the 1941 peace-time draft found this ditty's appeal more relevant as a popular jukebox hit than in the contemporary film. By the end of the year (1941), the Japanese had bombed Pearl Harbor, adding to this title's timely significance.
8. "Snootie Little Cutie," Victor 27875. Connie and Frank trade off some hip contemporary lyric, along with some lighthearted humor that somehow works.

> ➢ During the war years, Connie became a radio entity on the popular *Abbot and Costello* program, and she eventually left Tommy Dorsey. Later postwar recordings included

8. "Do You Love Me," Mercury 2063. This Harry Ruby-penned ditty found Connie's bright 1946 vocal swinging along with an orchestra led by Johnny Warrington.
9. "She's Funny That Way," Mercury 3006.
10. "The Darktown Strutters Ball," Signature 15197. A Fine duet with Alan Dale.

Adelaide Hall

Adelaide Hall, whose birth date ranges within the years 1904 to 1909, sounds very much like a trained soprano on her recordings (starting in 1927) and—as an Afro-American, for latter-century CD buyers, seemingly more like contemporary Afro-American Marion Anderson—a real opera singer. On investigation, Adelaide's high pitch is not for everyone, but it did indeed produce jazz with some excellent results, along with some fine pop ditties as well. More so, her early 1920s' Broadway contemporaries had included the likes of Florence Mills (who died in 1927, leaving no commercial recordings), Valaida Snow, Elisabeth Welch, and Josephine Baker, who were all destined, by the end of that decade, to become well-known entities in Europe, exporting Americana to the world!

1. "Creole Love Call," Victor 21137. This 1927 recording was an early Duke Ellington effort, which featured a sophisticated and high vocal, indeed without real words. While far from scatting, and not actually humming, young and unaccredited Adelaide Hall's vocal utterances indeed contributed greatly to a jazz classic, as an Ellington original, penned by Rudy Jackson as a melody without words.
2. (a). "The Blues I Love to Sing," Victor 21490. This second ditty, from the same 1927 recording session that had produced "Creole Love Call," again only credits Ellington, but Adelaide, is again in a "crooning" vocal, with (at least) some real words, "The Blues I Love To Sing."

   (b). A subsequent take 2, later issued, is also very good.

3. "Chicago Breakdown," Okeh 8675. This later-1927 session finds Adelaide's vocal prowess tested, imitating various Ellington instrumentation. While this vocal is much limited, it's all worth it.
4. "I Must Have That Man," Brunswick 4031. This original 1928 recording, from the Broadway entity *Blackbirds of 1928*, had peen penned by Dorothy Fields and Jimmy

McHugh. Moreover, Adelaide's crooning vocal, accompanied by Lew Leslie's Orchestra, indeed defined this classic.

5. "Baby," Brunswick 4031. As the flip of "I Must Have That Man," this medium-tempo-paced ditty, penned by Dorothy Fields and Jimmy Mc Hugh, also allowed Adelaide to do some fine crooning, with some non-word improvisation, indeed as much as she had done originally with Duke Ellington.
6. "Too Darn Fickle," Oriole P-108. Recorded in London while touring, this ditty, penned by Gordon and Revel, finds Adelaide a bit clumsy but at least interesting.
7. "Strange as It Seems," Brunswick 6375. Penned by Fats Waller and Andy Razaf, this bit of crooning is a bit too loose and high-strung, but it retains for its listeners something to digest.
8. "I Must Have That Man," Brunswick 6518. This (1932) second recording of her 1928 classic is noted here as a separate entity. As part of a Brunswick records album set, this version found Adelaide backed by Duke Ellington, who provided for her a tighter, more controlled sound than did Lew Leslie's original. While it is debatable which version is better, this vocal—as in the first is also, if a bit faster—also excels.
9. "Baby," Brunswick 6518. As the flip side of "I Must Have That Man," this second (1932) attempt, backed by Ellington (instead of Lew Leslie's assembled (1928) crew), also betrays a tighter sound, which Adelaide skillfully adapts and croons out.

Note: While in New York City in 1933, Adelaide recorded the following two titles with the Mills Blue Rhythm Band (not to be confused with the Mills Brothers). While unreleased in the 1930s, they are fine examples of urban jazz and were bootlegged for some time before a legit release.

10. "Drop Me off in Harlem."
11. "Reaching for the Cotton Moon."

- Note: For the most part, Adelaide, after touring England several times, settled down there. Moreover, she became a huge European success and became better known overseas than in America. The following picks, recorded in Europe, do hold some interest. They include

12. "Trucking," Ultraphone AP-1574. This major hit of Fats Waller's also found an Ivie Anderson vocal as a Duke Ellington release competing with it. Moreover, Adelaide's is a bit more personal as she may be heard tap-dancing, as well as crooning out this fine novelty with much pep and energy.
13. "I'm in the Mood for Love," Ultraphone 1574. The contemporary 1935 (Fields and Mc Hugh) penned ditty oddly found Adelaide's high notes into something interesting.
14. "East of the Sun," Ultraphone AP-1575. With the backing of the John Ellsworth Orchestra, the soprano-voiced crooner sings the high notes of thos Brooks Bowman penned ditty and makes it all sound OK. Within ten years, a different approach by a vocalist with a different type of voice, Sarah Vaughan, would define this ditty.
15. "Where or When," Tono Radio Record K-6002. While this Broadway ("Babes in Arms") ditty from the contemporary (1937) musical, *Babes in Arms,* had bypassed Broadway to become a huge best seller for Hal Kemp featuring an OK vocal by Skinnay Ennis on Brunswick 7856, later generations just have to question this kind of bland success. It's more than a stretch to assume that Adelaide's (Danish) recording was hardly heard in America or even known at all. In any case, Adelaide is seemingly

very much interested in this ditty and adds energy to spark some well-done, fast-paced jazz singing. (A later-1940s' generation would find Lena Horne claiming this ditty twice with her effective sultry and crooning vocals.)

16. "That Old Feeling," HMV B-8849. While visiting Europe in 1938, Fats Waller got together with Adelaide. Moreover, their novel approach, with Waller on the pipe organ with his incidental slang voice, indeed inspired Adelaide's vocal. Indeed, both performers produce a fine bit of energy and define this classic 1938 ditty, penned by Lew Brown and Sammy Fain.
17. "I Can't Give You Anything but Love," HMV B-8849. Adelaide and Fats Waller again pull off an interesting novelty, with a successful attempt by Adelaide to (almost) break up Fats. (This ditty, claimed as penned by Fields and McHugh, had been introduced by Adelaide in *Blackbirds of 1928* some ten years before but was not recorded. More so, this much-recorded ditty is a classic, rivaling all previous versions, including those by Louis Armstrong and Ethel Waters.)
18. "Deep Purple," Decca 7083. A fine attempt at 1930s pop.
19. "'T ain't What You Do," Decca 7121. The contemporary Chick Webb release with an Ella Fitzgerald vocal is challenged.
20. "Have You Met Miss. Jones," Decca 7305.
21. "The Lady Is a Tramp," Decca 7345. Later, Lena Horne, would change things a bit, excluding Adelaide's own acquired English accented vocal, which is indeed stiff.
22. "This Can't Be Love," Decca 7501. Adelaide's straightlaced vocal is fine on this classic penned by Rodgers and Hart.
23. "Ain't It a Shame about Mame," Decca 7709. This ditty, about British royalty—penned by James Monaco and Johnny Burke—is highly sophisticated and American in origin. Considering all this, the adapting Hall voice accommodates, wins some approval, yet has limited appeal.
24. "As Time Goes By," Decca 8202. WWII had found the film "Casablanca "reintroduce this 1931 classic by Dooley Wilson in the film. After the musicians strike, Wilson also had a recording, as did contemporary Billie Holiday. Moreover, this British recording is done completely different, and should be heard. Indeed, the Hall voice, in adapted English as in English accent, is just as sensitive as Billie Holiday's version, noting a huge difference in style.

Note: By the 1950s, Adelaide Hall had become almost an institution in Britain, as Josephine Baker had become in France, although Hall indeed kept her clothes on. Adelaide did return, however, to America in 1957, adding weight to a fine contemporary Broadway musical *Jamaica,* which starred Lena Horne.

25, 26. "Jamaica," RCA Victor, LOC 1036. This 1957 Broadway soundtrack is chiefly a Lena Horne vehicle, penned by Arlen and Harburg, with Adelaide's contributing vocals somewhat limited. The following excellent vocals featured Adelaide:

a. "Savannah's Wedding"
b. "For Every Fish."

- Visual Image.

The author of this book looked long and hard to catch a look at the (young) Adelaide. The Vitaphone film short of the early '30s, *An All-Colored Vaudeville Show* (which also featured the fab Nicholas Brothers dancing), finally came our way:

27. "To Love You Again." This may or may not be the title of this filmed ditty. In any case, the elegant Adelaide is dressed in a long gown, and (after vocalizing like a soprano, like many recordings indicate) she raises the tempo and starts to croon and, as heard in the above pick "Truckin," slightly lifts her skirt and dances.

Annette Hanshaw

The flapper age of the latter '20s produced much social change, which the new electric recording process exploited into the "media" of recordings and into the home itself. At last, the listener could actually hear something, without a "canned" effect. This first generation of pop music—including vocalists and instrumentalists—would also offer more creativity than ever before and, indeed, more originality than a later generation.

Annette Hanshaw, about twenty-five years old in 1926 (?), with clear voice projection, bounced off jazz rhythms with a style of her own, usually ending her renditions stating her signature, "That's all." While many had alias recording identities, her "Gay Ellis" name was easily betrayed! More so, Annette's popularity in the late 1920s rivaled even that of vocal influence of Ruth Etting, as well as contemporaries such as Libby Holman, Helen Kane, Helen Morgan, Eva Taylor, and Ethel Waters. Indeed, this young flapper's spunky vocals are a bit jazzy and, moreover, represent a clear break from the Victorian habits and attitudes that had defined the era before WWI. Noting also that many of Annette's first recordings were (still) acoustic, they nevertheless carried a clear message of change and liberation.

Picks are as follows:

1. "Black Bottom," Pathé 32207. The mid-1920s found the New Orleans style of music (of Afro-American origin) drifting deeply into the popular music, especially those of danceable foot-tapping possibilities. Black songwriters such as Jelly Roll Morton, Perry Bradford, and Eddie Heywood had, more so, found white ears listening and playing, even before the (1920) Afro-American breakthrough, led by Mamie Smith, into recorded American Popular music. It's more than a good bet that the (white) Broadway producer George White had both seen and heard Perry Bradford's "Original Black Bottom Dance" in the off-Broadway all-black revue *Dinah* in the early 1920s. Or what about Jelly Roll Morton's "Black Bottom Stomp"? The term also found its way as a (1923) Lizzie Miles release as "Black Bottom Blues," an Eddie Heywood-credited ditty. With "dance" origins perhaps existing into the earlier part of the century, the early 1920s found (black) entities (who also sang) such as Alberta Hunter and Ethel Ridley claiming to have originated the contemporary dance subsequently claimed by (white) entities, especially George White's own Ann Pennington? Indeed, this "Black Bottom" song ditty, featured in *George White's Scandals of 1926*—penned by the white team of Ray Henderson, Buddy De Sylva, and Lew Brown with the lyrics full of black slang and obvious racial references—became a vocal as well, and like the Charleston which had proceeded it, this ditty reeked of a rip-off. Continued success, as a Johnny Hamp instrumental version (Victor 21001),

found many (black as well as white) flappers hitting dance floors with much energy. More so, the *George White's Scandals of 1926* found more emulation. After George White's success, a Ma Rainey (1927) vocal release (Paramount 12590), entitled "Ma Rainey's Black Bottom," seems to indicate the bottom of a river and, perhaps, part of an anatomy? Yet another contemporary release, "Take Your Black Bottom Outside"—penned by Williams and recorded by Ethel Waters (Columbia 14214-D)—directly notes, as a "race" record, an obvious part of a human anatomy, and indeed a black one, as well as the need to leave—and fast!

Annette Hanshaw's version of the title (by Henderson, De Sylva, and Brown) from the George White revue finds a bright, spirited, and peppy vocal performance, with jazzy implications. Led by unaccredited studio orchestra, perhaps led by the (white) backings of Red Nichols, Miff Mole, Jimmy Lytell, and Irving Brodsky, this ditty works well and may be considered the ultimate vocal version of this classic. Or did a contemporary and similar peppy vocal by the Ponce Sisters actually challenge Annette?

2. "Six Feet of Papa," Pathé 32211. Can a very young flapper of the 1920s sing the blues? Or is it jazz? In any case, this ditty, penned by Billy Moll and Arthur Sizemore, was perhaps another excuse to play jazz, but Annette, as in "Black Bottom," while easily led, provides a young, loose, and hot vocal performance.
3. "Don't Take That Black Bottom Away," Pathé 32213. This bit of camp, penned by Sam Coslow, Addy Britt, and Harry Link, refers to the popular dance again. Another contemporary version, by Jessie Shaw, on Romeo 303, is also relevant.
4. "Do Do Do," Pathé 32226. Annette's durable attack on lyrics found no material unchallenged by her vocal abilities. This version of the Gershwin Brothers-penned ditty, from the Broadway entity *Oh Kay*, more so proves her vocal abilities. While the original Gertrude Lawrence version, found in the show as well as on Victor 20331, was indeed done well, so is a similar version by Helen Morgan. Annette's attitude is far better! Listen and compare!
5. "Mine, All Mine," Pathé 32320. This (1927) recording, penned by Herman Ruby, Rudy Cowan, and Sammy Stept, is full of contemporary slang. Noting the likes of popular film entities such as Clara Bow, John Gilbert, and Richard Dix, a few contemporary song ditties (found elsewhere in this manuscript) are noted as "Big" or "Big Bad Bill" and "Lovin' Sam from Alabam." As recording fodder, this ditty could not have been better chosen or rendered for the perky likes of Annette's vocal. (A contemporary version from a slightly older vaudevillian and flapper Jane Green, on Victor 21145, is also full of fun, although, in true retrospective, Jane's vocal betrays a bit of stiffness when compared to Annette's attitude.)
6. "Here or There," Pathé 32235. The spunky Hanshaw vocal is found to bounce all over this ditty penned by Jesse Greer and Benny Davis.
7. "I've Got to Get Myself Somebody to Love," Pathé 32235. Yeah. Penned by Joe Young and Lou Handman, it was true. Still true! Another fine and spunky vocal performance!
8. "He's the Last Word," Pathé 32240. The loose, devil-may-care attitude of Annette is fully captured in this crisp and clear vocal style. (A lesser Josephine Baker version, recorded in France, is jazzy enough to compete with Hanshaw, although Josephine's vocal of this carfree ditty penned by Walter Donaldson and Gus Kahn, is even looser!)

9. "Ain't He Sweet," Pathé 32244. Accompanied by Ivan Brodsky on piano, this loose vocal again demonstrates a vocal style that needed little help or embellishment. It was originally a best seller for the popular Ben Bernie Orchestra as "Ain't She Sweet" on Brunswick 3444—featuring a vocal by Scrappy Lambert and Billy Hillpot—and the defining Gene Austin release as well, on Victor 20568. However, in true retrospective, this title can be considered a '20's classic, best defined by Annette's jazzy performance. (Baby boomers of the rock era also know this title as an early Beatles entity, released on Atco 6308.)
10. "Rosy Cheeks," Pathé 32259. This ditty, penned by Seymore Simons and Richard Whiting, had been a typical and rhythmic contemporary Nick Lucas best seller. Is Annette better? Listen and compare.
11. "Aw Gee! Don't Be That Way Now," Pathé 32267. This bit of slang noted in this title is hip for its times and heard clearly in this ditty penned by Roy Turk and J. Russell Robinson.
12. "Just Like a Butterfly," Pathé 32267. The best contemporary (1927) version of this schmaltzy ditty (penned by Mort Dixon and Harry Woods) somehow works! (A contemporary Peggy English version on, Vocalion 15568, also works much like Annette's, but not as well. An even lesser-known (English) recording by Helen Morgan is a bit uppity, yet interesting enough. Listen and Compare!
13. "Wistful and Blue," Pathé 36623. While this is a Ruth Etting original, Annette's clear and jazzy vocal is a fine challenge for the original Ruth Etting release. In addition, Annette is backed by a fine jazz band, the Original Memphis Five, and her vocals may be considered very "hot." Yet another contemporary release, a Paul Whiteman release, features a bouncy vocal by the up-and-coming Al Rinker and Bing Crosby (Victor 20418), which is also done well and more in the style of the established contemporary vocal act, Van and Schenck. Listen to all!
14. "What Do I Care," Pathé 36623. Fine backing by the Original Memphis Five gives Annette's vocal another defined jazz classic penned by Sidney Clare and Harry Woods!
15. "Nothin, '" Pathé 11471. This ditty penned by Roy Turk and Lou Handman is far from nothing. Annette again leads the way, as her energy even surpasses her excellent backup band (again the Original Memphis Five). A fine contemporary 1927 Gene Austin version on Victor 21080, while better known, pales in comparison. This just could be Annette at her jazzy best. Just listen!
16. "Who's That Knockin' at My Door," Pathé 32293. Annette tackles this bouncy ditty with much energy and creates a jazz classic. A contemporary Libby Holman version, on Brunswick 3667, is a fine comparison, and Annette indeed wins out! That's all!
17. "The Song Is Ended," Pathé 32314. The Ruth Etting best seller of this Irving Berlin-penned ditty is indeed challenged! Listen and compare both versions and perhaps discover Annette's principal vocal influence.
18. "Miss Annabelle Lee," Perfect 12362. Considered a "jazz standard" later, this ditty (by Sidney Clare and Lew Pollack) also finds in, later decades, some questionable (for some) lyrics trying to credit "darkies" as a good term from Stephen Foster, although, not unlike many other contemporary (1927) lyrics. In any case, when compared with all other current versions, including a popular and jazzy "Knickerbocker" release featuring a vocal from Irving Kaufman, it's more than obvious that Annette's perky vocal is more fun to listen for than Kaufman's stiff voice. Sorry, Irving!

19. "We Love It," Perfect 12444. Who are we? This ditty penned by Billy Rose and Mort Dixon luckily finds the ever-perky Annette having some innocent fun. We love it! That's all! We love it!
20. "After My Laughter Came Tears," Perfect 14940. This ditty penned by Charles Tobias and Roy Turk defined a good torch song, although it is far from it. While first defined as a recording by Cliff Edwards, this ditty, released as a contemporary Lou Gold (excuse) for a hot dance record, finds Annette's jazzy skills as a vocalist tops! Better than Cliff? Yes!
21. "Japanese Sandman," Perfect 14977. The earlier (1921) acoustic vocal hit by Nora Bayes, on Columbia A-2997, penned by Richard Whiting and Raymond Egan, is sweetened and, more so, bettered!
22. "You Wouldn't Fool Me, Would You?" Columbia 1769-D. Mmm. This question, penned by Ray Henderson, Buddy De Sylva, and Lew Brown, finds Hanshaw's vocal in a "little girl" mode, something forced upon the likes of contemporaries Helen Kane (most of the time) and (sometimes) even Ruth Etting.
23. "Lover, Come Back to Me," Columbia 1769-D. Annette's vocal again wins out over other versions, including a winning challenge by a contemporary Rudy Vallee release.
24. "For Old Time's Sake," Harmony 666-H. This ditty, penned by Buddy De Sylva, Lew Brown, and Ray Henderson, found a young-voiced vocal controlled well and sentimental enough.
25. "In a Great Big Way," Harmony 832-H. The perky Annette's no slouch in providing a this ditty (by Fields and McHugh) some needed energy!
26. "Big City Blues," Columbia 1812 D. Annette gets a bit mellow, yet is pleasantly fast-paced and jazzy, as her own original (1929) best-selling recording (penned by Sam Mitchell, Con Conrad, and Archie Gottler) put Hanshaw's talents into the limelight as never before.
27. "That's You, Baby," Columbia 1812-D. This flip side of "Big City Blues," also penned by Sam Mitchell, Con Conrad, and Archie Gottler, is almost as good. Annette, as usual, has fun with these lyrics, as this appealing flapper number indeed defines novel fun.
28. "I Must Have That Man," Harmony 706-H. This "Gay Ellis" release ain't bad. In fact, it is an open challenge to the high vocal found on the original contemporary Adelaide Hall version, released with Lew Leslie's Orchestra on Brunswick 6518.
29. "A Precious Little Thing Called Love," Diva 2859-G. Accompanied by the New England Yankees, this ditty is another winner. The simple lyrics, penned by Lou Davis and J. Fred Coots, are sung well and in a dry voice, with some infectious humor implied. (Another contemporary version, by Ethel Shutta, a fine vocalist for the contemporary George Olsen Orchestra on Victor 21832, also ain't bad, but it is without Annette's prowess.)
30. "Mean to Me," Diva 2859-G. This contemporary classic, penned byRoy Turk and Fred E. Ahlert, finds Annette's fast-paced version no slouch. It's also a good question if contemporaries Ruth Etting or Helen Morgan had heard this (original) rival version that was destined to become a jazz classic.
31. "I've Got a Feeling I'm Falling," Diva 2915-G. This Fats Waller-penned ditty found best-selling recognition from Gene Austin. Annette, more so, put her own (jazzy) claims upon it.
32. "Moanin' Low," Okeh 41292. The Libby Holman original classic, on Brunswick 4445, is at least challenged. So is a contemporary Charlestown Chasers release with a fine vocal by Eva Taylor.

33. "Ua Like No A Like," Diva 2945-G. Sometimes a boring piece of work may be lifted! As a Frank Ferrera's Hawaii Trio entity, this ditty (credited as penned by "Sweet Constancy ") is somehow lifted into something likable and, oddly, very listenable. Moreover, its Hawaiian theme featuring a Hawaiian guitar sound, founded as a recorded work, can be credited (in part) to Frank Ferreira himself, as instrumental and acoustic, before 1920. This electric recording, further graced with a straightlaced vocal, actually defines a Hanshaw vocal as un-hip and, indeed, far less than jazzy. Somehow, despite its clumsiness, it all works!
34. "Pagan Love Song," Diva 2945-G. Frank Ferrera's "Hawaiian" treatment of this film entity, penned by Naico Herb Brown and Arthur Freed for the (1929) film *The Pagan*, again provided Annette something new to adapt to. While contrived as "Hawaiian," Hanshaw's vocal may be noted as a creditable attempt at pop as well as creative in vocal and backing.
35. "The Right Kind of Man," Okeh 41327. The (jazzy) Annette (again) pleases the ear in this ditty penned by Abel Baer and L. Wolf Gilbert.
36. "I Have to Have You," Okeh 41351. The vocal styles of Helen Kane and Annette are close, as Helen projects more flirtations and Annette edges in on sensuous vocal overtones. Annette, more so, connects with her rhythmic backings, as this comparison with the contemporary Helen Kane release, on Victor 22192, still declines to declare a clear winner between (similar), if contrived, vocal styles.
37. "I Get the Blues When It Rains," Velvet Tone 1910-V. This can only be described a "excellent, as Annette's pleasing and jazzy vocal, as penned by (Harry Stoddard and Marcy Klauber), maintains listeners.
38. "Am I Blue," Harmony 940-H. The contemporary (original) Ethel Waters classic recording on Columbia 1837-D is indeed challenged by Hanshaw's vocal attitude and abilities. Check it out!
39. "Tiptoe Through the Tulips with Me," Harmony 1012-D. Annette, as "Gay Ellis," tiptoes very well through some stupid lyrics, penned by Joe Burke and Al Dubin. Moreover, this version even beats out the contemporary original by Nick Lucas, on Brunswick 4418.
40. "Ain't Cha," Harmony 1075-H. The contemporary Helen Kane original is turned into a jazzy dance recording, backed by the Frank Auburn Orchestra. Check out both Helen and Annette!
41. "Nobody Cares If I'm Blue," Harmony 1196-H. Annette's bright vocal finds this ditty penned by Harry Akst and Grant Clarke just perfect for her shinning vocal style. So were other contemporary versions by (one of her vocal influences) Marion Harris, Gene Austin (hiding his weak voice with his usual quirky and winning attributes), and a (usual) low-key effort by Lee Morse that works! Is it hard to figure who is better? Just listen!
42. "Daddy, Won't You Please Come Home," Velvet Tone 1940. This "standard" is more than good! As a title, "Baby, Won't You Please Come Home," this acoustic ditty found the likes of both Eva Taylor's jazz and Bessie Smith's blues versions. While noting no disrespect, this (electric) version is better, and Annette's jazzy vocal is as smart and peppy as ever.
43. "If I Had a Talking Picture of You," Diva 3066-G. Hanshaw's usual peppy vocal is more than good as this ditty (penned by B, G, De Sylva, Ray Henderson, and Lew Brown), originally featured in the contemporary 1929 film *Sunny Side Up*, is well claimed by Annette and is better than a released and better-known Paul Whiteman release, featuring a Bing Crosby vocal. (In true retrospective, film entity Janet Gaynor,

who also introduced the film title seemingly, did it with the same perky approach heard in the contemporary style very much heard in the recordings of Ruth Etting, Helen Kane, or Handsaw. Charles Farrell, more so, from the same film, was less than good.)

44. "I'm a Dreamer, Aren't We All," Diva 3066-G. Another ditty from *Sunny Side Up*, penned by B. G. De Sylva, Lew Brown, and Ray Henderson, finds Annette's style not unlike the fine vocal of actress Janet Gaynor.
45. "Happy Days Are Here Again," Diva 3106-G. Mmm. In true retrospective, despite another quality performance, Hanshaw is not identified with this ditty as she should be. Originally, this ditty was penned for a contemporary 1929 film *Chasing Rainbows* by Milton Agar and Jack Yellen. While the film turned out to be less than memorable, the song itself, as rendered by contemporary recording artists, fared better. By a stroke of fate, this film song was released at the start of the Great Depression, although no one knew it at the time! As perhaps a pun, some of them included the likes of a stiff Charles King release on Brunswick 4615, and as a best-selling entity for the Benny Meroff Orchestra with a vocal by Dusty Rhodes on Brunswick 4709, in 1930. This ditty, more so, earned its better vocal performance when Hanshaw recorded it with her usual cheerful and defining vocal style.

    In yet another turn of history, the success of this ditty was yet to be found. By 1932, the Depression had not receded, and had gotten worse. The recording industry, like the rest of the country, was reeling downward. With record sales dropping to about six million, compared with over a hundred million in 1929, most people were concerned about food and, for entertainment preferred free radio. Moreover, the 1932 presidential election found Franklin D. Roosevelt's campaign dusting off this ditty, promoting its lyrics as its theme. As luck would have it, this pun of a song of the Depression era became the anthem for the Democratic Party. For the next fifty years, this somewhat schmaltzy ditty would remain part of the party platform and Americana.

46. "Little White Lies," Diva 3196-G. This Walter Donaldson-penned ditty had been a huge best seller for the contemporary Fred Waring Orchestra, with a vocal as by Clare Hanlon on Victor 22494. Another contemporary version, a late and electric recording by (then) diva Marion Harris (Brunswick 4873) proved that she still could produce a fine vocal! While it's most likely that Annette was not aware of the fine Harris version, Annette's (usual) peppy attitude perhaps adds a bit more to her rendition, when compared. Yet another contemporary (1930) version as Lee Morse finds a differing, cooler vocal is jazzy. Listen and compare!
47. Would You Like to Take a Walk," Velvet Tone 2315-V. Why walk around and miss this fine vocal? Perhaps any listener of this ditty, penned by Harry Warren, Mort Dixon, and Billy Rose, might just like to sit back and enjoy this pleasant bit of nostalgia that had also been recorded by contemporaries Rudy Vallee and Skinnay Ennis.
48. "Body and Soul," Harmony 1224-H. This much-recorded classic had been introduced by Libby Holman in the Broadway entity *Three's a Crowd* and did not escape Annette's attention. Nor did it escape other notable contemporaries such as Helen Morgan, Ruth Etting, or Louis Armstrong. Annette is in good company here as vocal comparisons and style are to be heard!

49. "Ho Hum," Harmony 1324-H. This fab vocal is only matched by a contemporary duet recording as heard on a Gus Arnheim Orchestra recording, penned by Dana Suesse and Edward Heyman, featuring a sparkling vocal performance by Loyce Whiteman and Bing Crosby on Victor 22691.
50. "(That's) The Way I Feel Today," Clarion 5037-C. This odd Andy Razaf, Don Redman and Howard Quicksell penned ditty is very well done ! 'Howdy or Howard Quicksell'? Who cares?
51. "Walking My Baby Back Home," Clarion 5248-C. This jazz classic again found Hanshaw prepared. More so were other differing contemporary (1930) versions as by Lee Morse and Louis Armstrong. Listen to all!
52. "Love Me Tonight," Banner 32541. Annette croons her heart out and (perhaps), by this time, shared a vocal style with Bing Crosby's original.
53. "We Just Couldn't Say Good-bye," Banner 32541. As the flip side "Love Me Tonight," this ditty (again) reminds one of Mildred Bailey (as a Paul Whiteman vocalist on Victor 24088). To be fair, a contemporary Boswell Sisters version, on Brunswick 6360, indeed contains interesting and sparkling vocals.
54. "Fit as a Fiddle," Perfect 12866. Annette's a sure vocal "fit" as she claims this ditty by Arthur Freed, Al Hoffman, and Al Goodheart in 1932.
55. "Let's Fall in Love," Vocalion 2635. This title is so good that while Annette's rendition may be dated, her flawless, light crooning of this ditty penned by Harold Arlen and Ted Koehler is nothing short of superb!
56. "This Little Piggie Went to Market," Vocalion 2635. A stupid title penned by Sam Coslow and Harold Lewis that somehow works! (A contemporary recording by June Vance, a Victor Young release on Brunswick 6747 (more so, a flip side of a Harlan Lattimore vocal), is almost as good! As was a rendering by Ethel Shutta.
57. "Say It Isn't So," Perfect 12843. A less than perky-voiced Hanshaw is still in good voice, but she is joined by other contemporaries, like Morton Downey (stiff tenor), Singing Sam (quirky and poor-voiced), and Will Osborne (crooning). While it's a vocal crap shoot, both Annette and Will luckily lift this recording above the awful vocals of Downey and Singing Sam!

- A *Showboat* radio program led to a (1933) film short. In it, Annette croons out

58. "We Just Couldn't Say Good-bye." Her only filmed appearance? She oddly retired at around thirty-four years of age, except for some radio appearances in the latter 1930s.

- That's All!

Marion Harris

This "jazz baby," was instrumental in ushering in the new "jazz age," just before the start of Prohibition and the 1920s. Like Al Jolson, she attained huge popularity in the acoustic age, although Al was able to find an even larger audience in the (later) media of radio and talking films. The following picks demonstrate a contemporary attempt at popular singing, with the usual limits of poor sound quality and racial bias. While some clumsy attempts at Afro-Americanism and material are evident, so indeed is a fine, soft, and clear vocal. Her later electric recordings demonstrate an even better voice and what the acoustic age had hidden. Later-1920s' contemporaries, especially Ruth Etting, were, for sure, as impressed by the competitive quality found in Marion's output. Picks include as under:

1. "I Ain't Got Nobody Much," Victor 18133. This ditty, penned by Roger Graham and Spencer Williams somehow found conflicting authors (Charles Warefield and David Young). Moreover, there is a difference in lyric content between "I Ain't Got Nobody Now" and "I Ain't Got Nobody." In any case, this Afro-American attempt at popular music worked well for Marion in 1916. While it should be noted that black entities were not allowed to record (with the exception of Bert Williams), it was through no fault of Marion's. (The ditty would also be fine recording fodder far into the century and with better electric recording technique as "I Ain't Got Nobody.")
2. "Paradise Blues," Victor 18152. There are some blues, and this sad song about an old piano man, perhaps, signals the end of the use of "ragtime." Penned by Walter Hirsch and Spencer Williams, this somewhat compromise of authorship betrays much Afro-Americanisms. Marion's vocal is, however, her own. Within a few years, many entities, both white as well as black, would emulate this style. For sure, the likes of Mamie Smith, Eva Taylor, Ethel Waters, Vaughan De Leath, and Libby Holman found these blues well worth exploring.
3. "Don't Leave Me, Daddy," Victor 18185. The vaudevillian aspect of the music finds this ditty, penned by J. M. Verges, identified as a "coon song." To later-century ears, this ditty sounds just "old." At further hearing, however, this attempt at being hip or black is not degrading. For certain, it does not contain the usual and forced emulation found in the likes of (white) contemporary Sophie Tucker. As a further note, this ditty, perhaps, found later emulation for Russell and Herbert and the likes of their own "Oh Daddy." First released on Black Swan 2010 by Ethel Waters in 1921, this very same-sounding vocal and lyric had a lot to do with the rest of that decade.
4. "I Wonder Why," Victor 18270. Marion teams up with Billy Murray (a very popular entity in circa 1917) on this Broadway ditty penned by Harry Bache Smith and Jerome Kern.
5. "When I Hear That Jazz Band Play," Victor 18398. This (1917) recording, penned by the likes of Gene Buck and Dave Stamper, just may be the first vocal using the New Orleans-inspired word. As used by Florence Ziegfeld in *Midnight Frolic*, its popularity was assured.
6. "Everybody's Crazy 'bout the Doggone Blues," Victor 18443. These "blues," penned by Henry Creamer and J. Turner Layton, are only acceptable.
7. "Good-Bye Alexander, Good—Bye Honey Boy," Victor 18492. This parody of Irving Berlin's 1915 "Alexander's Ragtime Band," was penned by the likes of two Afro-Americans Henry Creamer and J. Turner Layton. An attempt at schmaltzy dialog by Marion is found here, but this appeal at patriotism in 1918 was typical for the WWI era.
8. "Mammy's Chocolate Soldier," Victor 18493. This "mammy song," penned by Sidney Mitchell and Archie Gottler, is also a WWI entity. Though it's full of the racism of the times, its content is not of contempt, but of compassion.
9. "After You've Gone," Victor 18509. A fine recording (1918) of this Afro-American penned ditty by the already familiar Creamer and Layton. It would be much emulated in later times.
10. "A Good Man Is Hard to Find," Victor 18535. This very fine recording, penned by Eddie Green, perhaps found some frowns on grown-up Victorians.

11. "Jazz Baby," Victor 18555. This simple (1919) effort penned by Blanche Merrill and M. K. Jerome, nevertheless, helped usher in the new age. Within a year, another ditty, "I'm a Jazz Vampire," would also be claimed by Marion, and much in the same way.
12. "Take Me to the Land of Jazz," Victor 18593. Another wordy ditty (penned by Edgar Leslie, Bert Kalmar, and Pete Wendling) that catches the jazzy theme of its day (1920).
13. I Ain't Got Nobody," Columbia A-2271. This version, essentially the same ditty as "I Ain't Got Nobody Much" as credited to Charles Warfield and David Young, at least notes better recording techniques, although still acoustic.
14. "Everybody but Me," Columbia A-2939. This James Hanley-penned ditty is liked by everyone!
15. "St. Louis Blues," Columbia A-2944. A fine (1920) acoustic recording of the Handy classic.
16. "Sweet Mama, Papa's Getting Mad," Columbia A-3300. Yeah!
17. "I'm a Jazz Vampire," Columbia A-3328. A contrived Carey Morgan-penned ditty that (again) founded contemporary (1920) jazz. Luckily, Marion's cool attempt to explain it all above the neck succeeds!
18. "Look for the Silver Linin'," Columbia A-3367. Marion found this Broadway entity, penned by Jerome Kern and Buddy De Sylva, for the contemporary 1920 hit *Sally*, very good recording fodder. (This ditty subsequently became associated with Broadway entity Marilyn Miller, who also would (later) introduce it in a 1929 film *Sally*. So would Judy Garland—*as* Marilyn Miller—in the 1946 film *As the Clouds Go By*.)
19. "I'm Nobody's Baby," Columbia A-3433. A (not too much) later electric Ruth Etting version perhaps defined the 1921 Milton Ager, Benny Davis and Lester Santly penned ditty better. (Again, the sound of acoustic recordings, when compared to electric, are usually a problem of hearing! Compare it to a subsequent Judy Garland electric version.
20. "The Memphis Blues," Columbia A-3474. As mythology has it, Handy's published blues in 1912 had been attributed to the then contemporary mayor of Memphis, Edward Crump. As an instrumental, the (white) Prince Orchestra recorded it on Columbia 5591. A subsequent (1915) and clumsy vocal version by Arthur Collins and Byron Harlan (Columbia 1721) and credited to George Norton and Handy, became known as the best-selling vocal. While late in the game, Marion's (1921) vocal is far more creditable. Subsequent versions by Esther Bigeou on Okeh 8026 and Monette Moore on Ajax 17093, more so, provided Marion well-done contemporary (and black) competition! (Esther also provided recorded contemporary versions of "St. Louis Blues" and "Beale Street Blues.")
21. "Beale Street Blues," Columbia A-3474. Another (W. C. Handy) winner.
22. "Some Sunny Day," Columbia A-3593. This Irving Berlin-penned ditty is expertly sung!
23. "I'm Just Wild About Harry," Brunswick 2309. This ditty by Noble Sissle and Eubie Blake from their Broadway entity *Shuffle Along*, an all-black revue, nevertheless, found the familiar Marion ably defining yet another original (Afro-American) ditty. By this time (1922), the obvious competition from (real) black voices, silenced before 1920, made the attempt of the likes of Marion at jazz and blues a bit pale in comparison. Nevertheless, this (black) and pop entity perhaps found Marion's version and her (white) contemporary Vaughan De Leath's version less confused as well as godsend of recognition for both Sissle and Blake. (Much later, in 1948, President Harry Truman found it to be a very useful campaign song—no matter who sang it.)

24. "Sweet Indiana Home," Brunswick 2310. Another standard hit penned by Walter Donaldson, released in 1922.
25. "Blue," Brunswick 2310. The mood is "blue," and this well-sung ditty, penned by the (white) team of Grant Clarke, Lou Handman, and Edgar Leslie is creditable.
26. "Carolina in the Morning," Brunswick 2329. This ditty penned byWalter Donaldson and Gus Kahn is yet another pop rendering limited by poor acoustics.
27. "You've Got to See Mama Every Night," Brunswick 2410. Did contemporary versions as by Sophie Tucker and Lizzie Miles compete?
28. "Rose of the Rio Grande," Brunswick 2330. This Harry Warren, Edgar Leslie and Ross Gorman penned ditty was considered classy in 1923. Despite it's acoustic limits, it still is.
29. "Who's Sorry Now," Brunswick 2443. This acoustic ditty found more recognition in the (later) rock and roll era. Perhaps Connie Francis found electric recording of the ditty, penned by Harry Ruby, Bert Kalmar, and Ted Snyder, a bit better? Connie's schmaltzy (1958) recording, on MGM 12588, indeed made it a best-selling entity.
30. "It Had to Be You," Brunswick 2610. Another bit of schmaltz, penned by bandleader Isham Jones and Gus Kahn, which somehow still works!
31. "How Come You Do Me Like You Do," Brunswick 2610. The catchy Gene Austin-penned ditty works! again produced a best-selling entity for Marion. As a best-selling 1924 entity, it was recorded by many, including challenging versions as by "blues" queens Edith Wilson and Trixie Smith, indeed providing Marion with recorded competition that had been unheard-of before 1920! (More than a match? This author cannot find a contemporary recording by Austin.)
32. "There'll Be Some Changes Made," Brunswick 2651. The previous (1921) Ethel Waters classic is at least challenged!
33. "Charlestown Charlie," Brunswick 2735. Gene Austin's own recording of his self-penned ditty about the contemporary dance craze ain't half as good as Marion's vocal!
34. "Tea for Two," Brunswick 2747. The Broadway classic penned by Vincent Youmans and Irving Caesar is defined as a recording!
35. "I'll See You in My Dreams," Brunswick 2784. This ditty by Gus Kahn and Isham Jones found a voice in Marion!

Note: The above song ditties became popular recording fodder for many later vocalists. Like most acoustic efforts, they fall short on most (later) ears in production quality. Indeed, later electric versions are usually thought of as originals, or even as rerecordings. The following thirteen recordings, however, *are* "electric." They, more so, do not betray Marion Harris, as they indeed prove to any listener that she still had a fine voice, without being quirky!

36. "Did You Mean It," Victor 21116. This electric recording (finally) proved that this diva was a true *diva*. Penned by the likes of Phil Baker, Sid Silvers, and bandleader Abe Lyman, this "hearts and flowers" type ditty found Marion's vocal abilities in high gear. By 1927, the use of electric recording had replaced the likes of Marion's acoustic style, and now her vocals could be considered in a different aspect. This ditty truly passed her beyond all doubters, as her "diva" vocal sound is very much appreciated. Like her old contemporary Fannie Brice, she more than holds her own lock on to popular music, although Brice was not as interested in producing recordings. For sure,

the likes of younger singers like Ruth Etting and Libby Holman took note of one of their own early vocal influences.

37. "The Man I Love," Victor. 21116. As the original B side to "Did You Mean It," this Gershwin Brothers-penned ditty gained more recognition than its original A side. Marion indeed sang her heart out and made her version a huge best-selling entity. For certain, this torch song had even greater impact upon the likes many other singers and versions. A true 1920s classic!
38. "Funny, Dear, What Love Can Do," Brunswick 4663. An "electric" rendering that (finally) put Marion in real listening competition with later-1920s contemporaries. More so, Ruth Etting's (1930) version (Columbia 2146-D) offers good listening and comparisons.
39. "My Fate Is in Your Hands," Brunswick 4681. A (far better) vocal than the contemporary Gene Austin best seller, as penned by (Razaf and Waller), for "Connie's Review "Load Of Coal"
40. "You Do Something to Me," Brunswick 4806. Again, the vocal abilities that were hidden on most of Marion's recordings (as being acoustic) are presently found on this sophisticated Cole Porter-penned ditty.
41. "If I Could Be with You One Hour Tonight," Brunswick 4873. Another (black) yet pop entity, penned by the familiar Henry Creamer and James P. Johnson, provides Marion with something she could compete with her contemporaries in electric form! Among other fine contemporary versions, her completion was to be fierce, which included differing vocals and arrangements from the likes of Eva Taylor, Louis Armstrong, the George Lee Orchestra (with a George Lee vocal) and a similar Ruth Etting vocal—noting Ruth's own vocal embellishment.
42. "Little White Lies," Brunswick 4873. This (1930) electric recording more than demonstrated Marion's not-yet-lost voice, more so competing with all contemporaries, including the somewhat similar bright-voiced Annette Hanshaw and a differing cooler vocal version by Lee Morse.
43. "Nobody Cares If I'm Blue," Brunswick 4812. Another fine recording that finds contemporary (1930) recording artists Annette Hanshaw, Lee Morse, and Gene Austin also producing good, contrasting vocal versions. Who performed this ditty (penned by Harry Akst and Grant Clarke) best?
44. "Blue Again," Brunswick 6016. This ditty penned by Fields and McHugh was to become a standard defined by (gritty) Louis Armstrong. Nevertheless, Marion's contemporary (and differing) version is indeed very good and, more so, better than (other) contemporary) (1931) versions as heard on a Duke Ellington release, with a vocal as by Sid Gerry on Victor 22603 and a stiff sounding Dick Robertson on a Red Nichols release on Brunswick 6014.

- The following four are recordings recorded in England in the early 1930s:

45. "My Canary Has Circles Under His Eyes," Columbia DB-453. This dumb song ditty, penned by Jack Gordon, Ted Koehler, and Ed Pola) somehow makes its own case! Is it perhaps due to some good singing by Ruth Etting? No, it's Marion!
46. "Oo-oo-ooh! Honey, What You Do To Me," Decca F-5160. This ditty, penned by N. Moret, C. Friend, and H. Tobias, also combines another ditty called "Ooh That Kiss," by H. Warren, M. Dixon, and J. Young. It's also done well enough! (it's not Annette Hanshaw.)

47. "One Morning in May," Decca F-3954. Later, Dick Todd would re-define this Hoagy Carmichael and Mitchell Parish penned ditty. Marion or Dick?
48. "Singing the Blues Till My Daddy Comes Home," Decca F-5160. Penned by Sam Lewis, Joe Young, J. Russell Robinson, and Con Conrad, this ditty had been an acoustic entity by Aileen Stanley, who had been a (1920) contemporary. This fine electric update, more so, defined it! Or at least until a later (1937) Midge Williams version? Listen and decide!

Dick Haymes

As one of the 1940s' best-known baritone vocalists, the popularity of Dick Haymes, in film, radio, and the recording studio was considered, by many, just as important as the advent of Frank Sinatra. It is also interesting to compare the smoothness of the rich baritone vocals of Dick Haymes, with the likes of both Bing Crosby and Frank Sinatra. Indeed, more so with the newer, contemporary Sinatra vocal, similar in style and directly competing. Sinatra, whose nasal vocals, differed from that of Crosby's, could not emulate, only admire. Moreover, both Haymes and Sinatra sound interestingly similar in style and vocal tone at least during the 1940s. Other contemporaries, seeking to emulate this new style would include the likes of many such as Mel Torme, Vic Damone, and Billy Eckstine. Others, especially noting the likes of band singer Teddy Walters, whose recordings and subsequent recognition with Artie Shaw and Jimmy Dorsey, would remain hidden. Walter's renderings indeed speak for themselves, noting the likes of his vocals on "You Do Something To Me" (Musicraft 391) with Shaw and "There I've Said It Again" (Decca 18670) with J. Dorsey. (Indeed, the latter-cited ditty with Dorsey would later be rediscovered in the rock era by both Sam Cooke (Keen 8-2105) and Bobby Vinton (Epic 9638). Walters was, moreover, one of many whose competition with the likes of Mel, Vic, and Billy would be (commercially) a losing game. While time has rendered all of this contemporary rivalry a bit more than passé, the fortunes of the smooth Dick Haymes were considerable in the 1940s. The following are noted picks of this influential song stylist.

Picks are as follows:

1. "I'll Get By as Long as I Have You," Columbia 36285. Like Frank Sinatra, the Argentine-born vocalist spent some time as a band singer with Harry James. This smooth vocal became a huge best seller during WWII and, also like Sinatra, as a reissue product on Columbia 36698. While identified with Haymes, this classic penned by Roy Turk and Fred Ahlert had already been claimed by many—perhaps first known as an obscure (1929) Ipana Troubadour release with an unaccredited vocalist, who perhaps was trying to sound like Rudy Vallee and, more so, was to be later identified as Bing Crosby. Luckily, the (then) more popular contemporary Ruth Etting also recorded it and, more so, defined it. While identified with Haymes in the 1940s, a somewhat lesser-known contemporary version by Billie Holiday just may be better. Listen and compare!
2. "The Devil Sat Down and Cried," Columbia 36466. Harry James (may) even be assisting on some of vocals, but luckily it's the fresh-voiced Helen Forrest who joins in with Dick for most of this novelty.
3. "Idaho," Columbia 36613. This playful novelty was released as a Benny Goodman entity; penned by Jesse Stone—also known as Charles Calhoun—it became a huge

best seller in 1942. (More so did a contemporary version by Alvino Rey, featuring (King Sister) Yvonne King on Bluebird B-11331).

4. "You'll Never Know," Decca 18556. As a film entity in 1943, penned by Harry Warren and Mack Gordon), this title was introduced by Alice Faye. While the search for a Faye rendering is still on, Haymes's own (solo) contemporary recording is a fine bit of smooth crooning.
5. "It Cant Be Wrong". Decca-18557. Dick's 1943 well done croon (with thc Song Spinners) hits the mark and lifts this (Kim Gannon & Max Steiner) penned ditty!
6. "Put Your Arms Around Me, Honey," Decca 18565. This s already dated ditty from the acoustic age, found Dick, assisted by the vocal group Song Spinners, smooth enough. Acoustic-age versions included those of Arthur Collins and Byron Harlan (Zon o phone 5734). Other versions included recordings by Ada Jones on Edison Amb. 669 and the all-female That Girl Quartet on Victor 5827, as penned by Albert Von Tilzer and Junie McCree (1911). While a bit schmaltzy, stick with Dick's version as it may be (at least) electronically when (really) heard!
7. "The More I See You," Decca 18662. As a forgotten film entity, *Billy Roses Diamond Horseshoe,* Dick may be found introducing this fine ditty penned by Mack Gordon and Harry Warren, and this fine recording, indeed, outlasts the film. Light-years away, and vastly reworked, this ditty again found recognition as authentic rock-era entity, as a 1966 Chris Montez release (A and M 796).
8. "Laura," Decca 18666. The ditty was a fine film title and was penned by Johnny Mercer and David Raskin. Meant to be a bit of a haunting ballad, this ditty was effective and so is Dick's smooth crooning job. Moreover, a contemporary Frank Sinatra version, on Columbia 38472, may just be a fine emulation, although not done consciously, of the Haymes original.
9. "Long Ago and Far Away," Decca 23317. The title was a huge best-selling entity in (1944). Penned by Jerome Kern and Ira Gershwin, this winner features a fine duet between Helen Forrest (also a former band singer with Harry James) and Dick himself. As a film entity from *Cover Girl*, a pairing of Gene Kelly and Rita Hayworth may be dismissed. Other contemporary recordings, including the likes of releases by Bing Crosby (Decca 18608), Perry Como (Victor 20-1569), and Jo Stafford (Capital 153), are, however, relevant. Dick, Bing, Perry or Jo?
10. "Love Letters," Decca 18699. As a film entity (in the 1945 film of the same name), this title (penned by Edward Heyman and Victor Young) had eyes, as well as ears, for the future, in true retrospective. Seemingly, Haymes's smooth crooning job was not enough. As an early rock-era entity in 1962, a fine reworked vocal—by Ketty Lester, on Era 3068—became a best seller. Some five years later, a fine crooning job by Elvis Presley, on RCA Victor 47-8870, also revived it.
11. "It Might as Well Be Spring," Decca 18706. As yet another film entity, this ditty was featured in *State Fair*, starring Jeanne Crain, Dana Andrews, and, among others, Dick Haymes. Penned by Rodgers and Hammerstein, this classic is soft, mellow, and mushy. (Interestingly, speculation exists that this title was introduced in the film by a (dubbed) Jeanne Crain.) Does anyone care?
12. "That's for Me," Decca 18706. While Dick did a little bit of singing in this ditty in the film *State Fair*, it was Vivian Blaine's featured (filmed) performance that took notice. Luckily, this recording makes up for it!
13. "You Make Me Feel So Young," Decca 18914. This ditty had been penned by Josef Myrow and Mack Gordon for the very forgettable film *Three Little Girls in Blue* (1945). Upon listening, it's indeed a mystery that this ditty did not become a

huge best seller. Haymes is very much on target, and with an excellent mid-tempo arrangement by Gordon Jenkins, this very pleasant ditty cannot fail to please. To be fair, a contemporary Martha Tilton version, on Capital 272, is also excellent. (A later Frank Sinatra version (1956), with an even brighter arrangement by Nelson Riddle on LP Capital W 653, improves upon it and redefines it as a recording.)

14. "Some Sunday Morning," Decca 23434. This duet with Helen Forrest, penned by Ray Heindorf, M. K. Jerome, and Ted Koehler, had been introduced by Alexis Smith in the contemporary Errol Flynn film *San Antonio*. While the film version ain't bad, this contrived bit of "western" popular music is best heard as a pleasant duet, with Dick and Helen Forrest.
15. "I'll Buy That Dream," Decca 23434. Another fine duet with Helen Forrest.
16. "Come Rain or Shine," Decca 23548. Duet with Helen Forrest.
17. "Easy to Love," Decca 23780. Dick interprets this Cole Porter-penned title well.
18. "How Are Things in Glocca Morra," Decca 23830. The contemporary (1947) Broadway entity *Finian's Rainbow* had found Ella Logan (on the Columbia Masterworks 78 rpm album on MM 686) pleasantly introducing this ditty penned by E. Y. Harburg and Burton Lane. Dick, more so, claims this silly title for himself.
19. "I Wish I Didn't Love You So Much," Decca 23977. Frank Loesser's penned ditty is perhaps best heard !
20. "Christmas Dreaming," Decca 24169. This Yule-time ditty, penned by Irving Gordon and Lester Lee, is smooth and sincere enough. So is a contemporary Frank Sinatra version, on Columbia 37809, which is, indeed, similar in style.
21. "Little White Lies," Decca 24280. This already old Walter Donaldson-penned ditty ain't bad. Moreover, this "Vocal with 4 Hits and a Miss and Orchestra," is still a typical contemporary attempt by the recording industry to cut down orchestrations and use vocal groups as backing. This Gordon Jenkins arrangement is fresh enough, indeed in a differing mode and style than found in the likes of previous renderings, including (1930) recordings of Marion Harris, Annette Hanshaw and Lee Morse. Indeed, the smooth Haymes vocal scores again, egged on by his vocal backing, which is pleasant enough.
22. "Anything You Can Do, I Can Do Better," Decca 40039. As penned by (Irving Berlin) for the Broadway entity "Annie Get Your Gun," for Ethel Merman, this 1948 entity subsequently found itself a film entity, which starred contemporary Betty Hutton As recorded by Bing Crosby, the Andrews Sisters and Dick Haymes, this attempt by Decca Records to produce an instant best seller featuring its most successful contemporary recording artists, on a special red label issues indeed became something special. Bing, always interested when inspired, seems loose enough to recording with Haymes, considered a major rival. More so, the Andrews Sisters, are also interested in some campy lyrics, as this self proclaimed "woman's lib" statement, while novel, moreover challenges the wit of both Crosby and Haymes.
23. "You're Just in Love," Decca 27317. This duet (1950) with Ethel Merman from Broadway's *Call Me Madam* is pleasant enough. A contemporary Perry Como release with a vocal group (the Satisfiers) is, more so, better?

Hildegarde

- This American entity oddly made her way to England and subsequently became a huge entity as a popular radio vocalist in 1933. Her dry and sweet vocals are, more so, articulate, and, indeed, pleasant. Her choice of highbrow song entities are pleasantly not full of over-sung attempts at grabbing her listeners. Hildegarde's flowing vocals are unassuming on any material, especially noting her success with Cole Porter-penned material. Just *why* she never became a major Broadway or film entity is a good question, or perhaps she was content enough with cabaret, recordings and radio? The following are Hildegarde picks:

1. "I Was in the Mood". Columbia - DB -1247.
2-3. "Darling Je Vous Aime Beaucoup," Columbia 258-M. Penned by Ann Sosenko, this (British) release capitalized upon Hildegarde's great pre-WWII success on BBC radio. Also recorded in France on Pathe - 538.
4. "For You For Me". Columbia - 258 -M. A pleasant vocal with lots of emotions produces a winner, as penned by Leo Towers and Redd Arden!
5. "Honey Coloured Moon". Columbia - FB - 1123. Hildegarde's light, mid tempo vocal easily fit as a Henry Hall BBC dance record. As penned by Osman Carter and Mable Wayne, this ditty was perhaps originally a radio broadcast that was recorded and released?
6. I believe in Miracle Columbia - DO 1381.
7. "Love is a Dancing Thing". Columbia - FB- 1266. The contemporary 1935 broad way entity, has penned by Arthur Schwartz and Howard Deitz had oddly not been defined as a recording - until Hildegarde's light touch!
8. "Gloomy Sunday Columbia" -F-1366. (Somehow, Hildegarde drops her cheerful vocal for this song of dread).
9. "Pennies from Heaven". Columbia - 1598 -D.
10. "Will You Remember" Columbia-FB-1700. Hildegarde's pleasant approach at this boring Sigmund Romberg Aida Johnson Young penned ditty, from the contemporary Nelson Eddie and Jeanette Mac Donald film "Maytime" is less overbearing and better remembered!
11. "Bon Soir". Columbia - FB - 1841. This bit of French, has penned by Geoffrey Gwyther, which is full of smaltz, is at least well done!
12. "Love Walked In". Columbia-FB-1992. (The Gershwin Brothers are defined)

A few Noel Coward songs, defined:

13. "Dance Little Lady, Dance!". Decca - 23099.
14. "A Room with a View". Decca - 23101.

Three Rogers and Hart songs defined:

15. "My Heart Stood Still". Decca - 23133.

16. "Isn't it Romantic?". Decca - 23135.
17. "With a Song in My Heart". Decca - 23135.
18. "All the Things You Are". Decca - 23115. Oscar Hammerstein and Jerome Kern found their contemporary Broadway entity defined.
19. "What is there to Say?". Decca - 23163. Vernon Duke is defined!

> (Later, Jane Froman would claim, in similar vocal style,"With A Song In My Heart" and "What Is There To Say").

20. "My Ship" Decca-23208. This (I. Gershwin & Kurt Weil) Broadway entity from "Lady In The Dark" is well defined!

The 1941 Cole Porter Broadway entity *Let's Face It* found Hildegarde's rendering of the soundtrack a major event in the issued 78 rpm album. While she was not in it, her claims upon this Broadway product were relevant, and remain so.

21. "Ace in the Hole," Decca 23242. The highbrow attitude as implied in Porter's lyrics is brightly sung by Hildegarde as well as (simply) brought down a notch in this fast-paced vocal exercise. Does sex make Hildegarde boring? Or are Cole Porter's lyrics confined to just him? Listen!
22. "Ev'rything I Love," Decca 23242. This slower-paced ditty is done well. At the end of this rendering, Hildegarde attempts to embellish the final set of lyrics, and she succeeds in not overdoing it! Congratulations, or does anyone (still) care?
23. "You Irritate Me So," Decca 23243. The usual Cole Porter lyric, perhaps mimicking his own previous "You're the Top" finds the able Hildegarde doing it well, noting the proof that, as a recording artist, she is better than Ethel Merman.
24. "A Little Rumba Numba," Decca 23243. As the most suspect Porter-penned ditty of the lot of *Let's Face It*, Hildegarde easily succeeds in cashing in on contemporary Latin influences.
25. "I Hate You, Darling," Decca 23244. It just may be that this title, penned by anyone else other than by Cole Porter, would have been labeled "dumb." In any case, this pleasant song ditty is, more so, embellished by Hildegarde's bright and flowing vocal style.
26. "Farming," Decca 23244. Cole Porter is at it again, as he dates his penned ditty by noting many (1941) contemporary (nonwar) people and events. While it's a long shot that buying a farm would attract Greta Garbo or Mae West, or writers like John Steinbeck, Hildegarde's (usual) pleasant vocal is no choir!
27. "A Pink Cocktail for a Blue Lady". Decca - 23245. A fine night club ditty, penned by Herb Madison, Ben Oakland, found Hildegarde in the right place!

The following two ditties, from the 1942 entity *by Jupiter* penned by Rogers and Hart are defined!

28. "Everything I got". Decca - 23254.
29. "Nobody's Heart". Decca - 23254.
30. "Leave us Face it We're in Love". Decca - 23297. Another well done song ditty, as penned by Abe Burrows and Frank Loesser, previously introduced by "Archie", on the contemporary 1944 radio program *Duffy's Tavern.*
31. "All of a Sudden My Heart Sing". Decca - 23348. This mushy ditty, penned by Harold Rome, Laurent Herpin and Jamlan finds Hildergarde vocal ready!
32. "Lili Marlene". Decca - 23348.
33. "Everytime we Say Goodbye". Decca - 23378. This 1944 Cole Porter penned ditty just had to mean a lot to the war weary listeners.
34. "I've Told Every Little Star," Decca 23662. This duet with Buddy Clark somehow works for this ditty penned by Kern and Hammerstein, previously released by crooner Paul Small in 1933. A brighter rock-era version (Canadian American 123) by Linda Scott led this author to these earlier recordings.
35. "I'll Close my Eyes". Decca - 23378. Close your eyes and listen to this poignant ditty, as penned by Billy Reid and Buddy Kay.

Billie Holiday

The fame which Billie Holiday achieved, and deserved, in her lifetime was due to a lot of the usual hard work. Her original recordings of the early 1930s and 1940s, while fully appreciated by the die-hard record collectors of earlier times, were, in true retrospective, to become anthem for the pre-rock era of jazz and posthumously after her death in 1959. Her 1956 book *Lady Sings the Blues*, which sought to describe her career, had been like no other previous bio, with obscenities and truth mirrored into a reality that was perhaps true only for Eleanor Gough (alias Billie Holiday). Moreover, the book and popular 1960s' diva Diana Ross found in the 1972 film of the same name, a winning combination, seemingly connecting with contemporary rock-era culture, noting drug addiction. Despite all previous and then current jazz entities, Billie Holiday's recorded legacy was largely resurrected and found to interest a wider audience, including young rock fans, who would find her vocals and music of great interest.

For the most part, the early 1930s found record producer and jazz fan John Hammond discovering Billie, whose original vocal style was founded in the popular recordings by Ethel Waters, Bessie Smith, and, more so, Louis Armstrong. More credit should go to contemporary (white) bandleader Benny Goodman, who first recorded her and who would produce recordings with her, off and on, for the remainder of the decade. Benny, a dedicated jazz freak since the 1920s, became more so associated with the likes of other musicians just like him, including "studio band" entities Red Nichols, the Dorsey Brothers, Eddie Lang, Jack Teagarden, and Glen Miller, among others. More tellingly, along with his original interests in Ted Lewis, King Oliver, Fletcher Henderson, and Louis Armstrong, he had played behind the likes of contemporary (1920s) divas Ethel Waters and Eva Taylor, producing (studio) recordings. Goodman's continued interest in his craft would later define him as the "King of Swing" and, while not originating the style, fueled great interest and energy into it. With the help of many, including the "Colored King of Jazz" Fletcher Henderson, and Teddy Wilson, Goodman's "swing" indeed became popular as a recorded orchestra and on contemporary live radio. While others, including contemporaries Duke Ellington, Count Basie, Chick Webb, Artie Shaw, and Teddy Wilson, may have been more than his equal, his musical legacy remains very relevant, especially noting his (early) association with Billie Holiday.

Billie's picks are as follows:

The following recordings were made with Benny Goodman's Orchestra, crediting young Billie with a vocal, unaccredited "vocal."

1. "Your Mother's Son-in-Law," Columbia 2856 - D. Speculation has it that critic John Hammond had been friendly with the up-and-coming bandleader Benny Goodman, who had been instrumental in setting up the young eighteen-year-old Billie Holiday for the recording date—also a scheduled Ethel Waters recording date. The vocal laid down by Billie is dry and sweet, sounding much like Ethel Waters herself. Penned by Albberta Nichols and Mann Holiner, this ditty scores, with speculation existing that the likes of musicians Charlie and Jack Teagarden, Art Karle, Buck Washington, Dick McDonough, Artie Bernstein, and Gene Krupa were part of Goodman's Orchestra. In any case, the young Billie skillfully founded her fast-paced vocal behind the band's lead, which would become a jazz classic.

2. "Riffin the Scotch," Columbia 2867-D. The small-voiced Billie again scores and sounds less like Waters, after a bit of a wait featuring a contrived "Scottish" riff in jazzy style in this ditty penned by (young) Johnny Mercer, Dick McDonough and Benny Goodman himself.

Note: The following recordings (American Music Corporation) found Brunswick releases produced as "Teddy Wilson and His Orchestra," with vocal chorus by "Billie Holiday," along with other (AMC) labels such as Vocalion and Okeh, identified as part of Billie Holiday and Her Orchestra, which was only used as a (house band) for recording. It should also be noted that (many) musicians came and went for various sessions, although speculation of most recordings betray Buck Clayton (trumpet), Lester Young (tenor sax), Buster Bailey (clarinet), and Teddy Wilson (piano lead).

3. "I Wished on the Moon," Brunswick 7501. The (black) pianist Teddy Wilson takes most of the credit here (with Benny Goodman still moonlighting as a sideman). More important is Billie's solid vocal, establishing a fine ballad style, influenced much by Louis Armstrong and just as moody as Teddy Wilson's arrangement. A fine contrast to the contemporary Bing Crosby hit (Decca 543), it's a safe bet that no material was to be unchallenged by Billie.
4. "What a Night, What a Moon," Brunswick 7511. This faster-tempo again credits Teddy Wilson, yet it's Billie's hot and jazzy vocal, penned by John Jacob Loeb brazenly about a girl finding a guy, that really scores!
5. "It's Too Hot for Words," Brunswick 7511. The lyrics, penned by Walter Samuels, Leonard Whitcup, and Teddy Powell, are hot, and so is Billie.
6. "Sunbonnet Blue A". Brunswick-7498. This simple (Kahal & Fain) penned ditty simply rocks!
7. "I'm Painting the Town Red," Brunswick 7514. Another vocal attack finds this ditty, penned by Charles Tobias, Sam Stept, and Charles Hewman, sparked with fast rhythm as another winner for Billie!
8. "Twenty-Four Hours a Day," Brunswick 7550. Billie almost rocks and rolls here in this ditty penned by Arthur Swanstrom and Hanly Like and somehow stays in time with her backing.
9. "Yankee Doodle Never Went to Town," Brunswick 7550. Billie's vocal tears into this wordy parody of "Yankee Doodle," a tune, penned by Arthur Freed and Bernie Hanighan, almost like a later-era rock entity!
10. "Spreading Rhythm Around," Brunswick 7581. This ditty by Ted Koehler and Jimmy McHugh, had been penned for the contemporary (1936) Alice Faye entity *King of Burlesque.* Her subsequent and rare (for her) record release, on Melotone 6-03-08, features a fairly good vocal, with a "sweet" band arrangement by Cy Feuer. In comparison, this Teddy Wilson's excuse for contemporary swing is wild and uninhibited and so is Billie's own rhythmic vocal, which is a totally different product than the contemporary Alice Faye rendition. Listen to both!
11. "You Let Me Down," Brunswick 7581. This Harry Warren-penned ditty is much lifted by Teddy Wilson's arrangement and Billie's great vocal! Indeed, this performance lets no one down. (A fine and contemporary and little-known (European) Valaida Snow version is, more so, a challenge for Billie.)
12. "Miss Brown to You," Brunswick 7501. Introduced in the contemporary film *The Big Broadcast of 1936*, as part of a Bill "Bojangles" Robinson's and Nicholas Brothers' performance, this ditty, perhaps, caught the attention of Teddy Wilson. Penned byLeo

Robin, Richard Whiting, and Ralph Rainger, this song became a contemporary swing entity, with Billie's energetic vocal truly defining it.

13. "What a Little Moonlight Can Do," Brunswick 7498. Penned by Harry Woods, Billie again challenges Teddy Wilson's fast-paced arrangement and indeed pulls of more than a bit of "swing!"
14. "Eeny Meeny Miney Mo," Brunswick 7554. This ditty, penned by Johnny Mercer and Matt Malneck, had (already) become a well known sweet band entity for contemporary Bob Crosby and coauthor, Johnny Mercer. This ditty's lyric makes mention of contemporaries Louis Armstrong, Kate Smith, Rudy Vallee, Paul Whiteman, and (Bob's brother) Bing Crosby, forever dating its (1935) contents. Moreover, in comparison with Bob Crosby's and Mercer's versions, Billie's vocal may be described as a successful fast-paced (vocal) attack upon this novelty, as well as defining the ditty.
15. "These Foolish Things Remind Me of You," Brunswick 7699. It ain't Benny Goodman's current "canary" or "girl singer," yet this jazzy vocal does hit the mark! Or what about a stiffer current Buddy Clark rendering? Helen or Billie? Or perhaps a (later) Thelma Carpenter version (influenced by Billie's recording but softer) is better? Listen to all differing vocal styles!
16. "Easy to Love," Brunswick 7762. This Cole Porter-penned ditty had found recorded prominence with a Ray Noble release, featuring (British) crooner, Al Bowlly. While the contemporary and brighter-voiced Maxine Sullivan version may indeed be better, this jazzy effort remains a pleasant and (different) alternative. (A later Lee Wiley version may be closer to Billie's vocal in mood and tone, although Lee's (low) voice contains no grit and is far more smoother.)
17. "The Way You Look Tonight," Brunswick 7762. Despite the excellent likes of Fred Astaire and Ginger Rogers on-screen, this ditty—penned by Fields and Kern and reeking of elegance—had, more so, found an excellent and contemporary recording by Bing Crosby and Dixie Lee to compliment and emulate them. While it's always hard to figure something better, Billie's subsequent (differing) jazzy and mid-tempo vocal is perhaps only lessened by Teddy Wilson's (usual) arrangements sounding a bit too familiar.
18. "I Can't Give You Anything but Love," Brunswick 7781. While hardly defining, Billie's fine vocal of this (already) well-known classic from the previous decade does provide any good listener of the popular culture (before 1936) something to compare the likes of Cliff Edwards, Baby Cox, Grace Hayes, Louis Armstrong, Ethel Waters, and the Mills Brother with Billie's vocal style. Listen and learn.
19. "Pennies from Heaven," Brunswick 7789. Perhaps Billie (and Teddy Wilson) had been influenced by the contemporary (1936) recording "Pennies from Heaven" melody with some excellent vocals provided by Bing Crosby, Louis Armstrong (her idol), and Frances Langford. In any case, while this recording is far from the original recording or from Bing's own (single) release of great crooning, this great excuse for a good and loose jazz vocal is indeed produced very well!
20. "This Year's Kisses," Brunswick 7728. The Alice Faye original is completely challenged in vocal and jazz backing. Listen and compare!
21. "He Ain't Got Rhythm," Brunswick 7824. The contemporary Jimmy Rushing vocal, found as a Benny Goodman release, provided for listeners good jazz comparisons! Check them both out!
22. "The Mood That I'm In," Brunswick 7844. Billie's soft grit finds her vocal perfect for this ditty, penned by Abner Silver and Al Sherman, although a contemporary and brighter version from Dolly Dawn is just as good. Still another contemporary (British)

release by Valaida Snow (that was most likely never heard by either Billie or Dolly) also put good (vocal) claims on this ditty. Billie, Dolly, or Valaida?

23. A "This Is My Last Affair," Brunswick 7840. The poignant lyrics of this ditty, penned by Haven A. Johnson, are put to good use. Sit and listen!
24. "Why Was I Born," Brunswick 7859. The (earlier) and similar torch moods of Libby Holman and Helen Morgan find Billie's medium-tempo vocal producing a (completely) differing result, more so, due to Teddy Wilson's jazzy backing! Listen to all.
25. "Mean to Me," Brunswick 7903. This old (1920s) Ruth Etting standard finds the likes of musicians Teddy Wilson, Johnny Hodges, Lester Young, Buck Clayton, Cozy Cole, Allen Reuss, and Artie Bernstein as part of a contemporary 1937 Teddy Wilson and His Orchestra release, more so, with Billie's differing vocal.

26, 27. "I'll Get By," Brunswick 7903. (a) Another old standard from the 1920s, more so, revived as an excuse for jazz and (some) new singing from Billie (1937) as a Teddy Wilson release. (b) Billie's second recording on Commadore 553, in 1944, finds her more interested in controlling the recording session as her vocal is highly personable and her vocal is far more exploited. Billie version 1 or Billie version 2? Which one is better? Or, perhaps the rich-voiced contemporary (1944) Dick Haymes's vocal as a (Harry James) release? If not slicker, better? Or what about a contemporary release from a new vocalist named Sarah Vaughn?

28, 29. "Easy Living," Brunswick 7911. (a) This pop title, penned by Leo Robin and Ralph Rainger, remains a true (1937) masterpiece as a slow and moving ballad, sung with depth. Indeed, Teddy Wilson contributes much background for Billie to become inspired, as Billie's attempt to sound "soft" almost works. (b). A subsequent (1947) rerecording ain't bad, finding Billie's vocal a bit better, yet not as good, backing, from Wilson,. Listen to both!

30. "No Regrets," Vocalion 3276. After a guitar intro to Billie's interesting vocal, this jazzy material, penned by Charles Tobias and Roy Ingram, speeds up in the middle.
31. "Did I Remember," Vocalion 3276. This ditty, penned by Harold Adamson and Walter Donaldson, had been actually been introduced by Cary Grant in the contemporary (1936) film *Suzy*. Other contemporary recordings are the likes of an (OK) vocal by Charles Chester as a Shep Fields release on Bluebird B-6476, and a Tommy Dorsey release featuring the (good) voice of Edythe Wright on Victor 25341, along with this official Billie Holiday and Her Orchestra recording. While (perhaps) just only providing the current world of popular music (another) excuse for jazz, the contemporary competition noted became better known than Billie's jazzy version, yet remembering all this does indeed demand a hearing on all these differing vocal and instrumental arrangements!
32. "Summertime," Vocalion 3288. This Gershwin title sparkles, and Billie's fine vocal defines it. As part of the 1935 Broadway entity (penned by Du Bose Heyward, and Ira, and George Gershwin), it almost found itself defined as a European operetta attempt about local (black) folk in Charleston, South Carolina. While noting the original and contrived operatic attempts by Afro-Americans Todd Duncan and Anne Brown from the original production, it was obvious that this ditty, along with the other well-penned ditties from this production, had misfired. Luckily, the somewhat contemporary mid-1930s' versions, recorded by Bing Crosby and Billie, were of well-done renderings with Billie's more obvious Afro-American vocal clearly identified with the (images) found in the play, that should have been found in the

contemporary play. Subsequent recordings, including versions by Mabel Mercer, Ethel Waters, and Lena Horne, would, more so, redefine it. Listen to all and decide!

33, 34. "Billie's Blues" (I Love My Man), Vocalion 3288. (a) Credited to Billie herself as a writer, although contrived with (Blind Lemmon Jefferson's "Matchbox"), this powerful urban blues indeed works, with no less a jazz theme. For the most part, Billie was not a blues singer, but this recording breaks all categories and boundaries. Many baby boomers just may call it or consider it as rock, and Billie's rare "belting blues" vocal, influenced much by the likes of Bessie Smith herself, remains a classic, as credited to Billie Holiday and Her Orchestra. (b) Commadore 614. Billie's later (1944) rendering is more subtle, yet it remains a jazz classic and, more so, a jazzier version! Listen to both and decide.

35. "A Fine Romance," Vocalion 3333. Billie's faster-paced jazzy vocal indeed changes the mood of likes of this Fred Astaire and Ginger Rogers filmed entity, as well as a (stiff) contemporary (1936) recording, featuring a Bing Crosby and Dixie Lee duet of this classic penned by Fields and Kern.

36. "I've Got My Love to Keep Me Warm," Vocalion 3431. While first associated with Alice Faye in the contemporary (1937) film *On the Avenue*, this ditty, somehow, became best associated with Billie's own (contemporary) release. After discarding the overcoat among other concerns, Billie's bit of a quirky jazz vocal does indeed define this Irving Berlin-penned classic as her own.

37. "Let's Call the Whole Thing Off," Vocalion 3520. This is another Fred Astaire and Ginger Rogers film entity, penned by Ira and George Gershwin, that found its way to Teddy Wilson's jazz and Billie's vocal.

38. "They Can't Take That Away from Me," Vocalion 3520. A jazzy version of the Gershwin Brothers-penned ditty for the then current Fred Astaire and Ginger Rogers film *Shall We Dance* is given a new spin.

39. "A Sailboat in the Moonlight," Vocalion 3605. Penned by Carmen Lombardo and John Jacob Loeb, this ditty had already been a best-selling entity by the Guy Lombardo Orchestra, with a vocal by Carmen Lombardo, released on Victor 25594, in 1937. It was, more so, a contemporary Johnny Hodges release, featuring a vocal from (white) vocalist Buddy Clark, on Variety 586, who perhaps produced his best ever (less stiff) recording. Billie's version, when compared, has a lot more (predictable) grit, indeed much better than the (stiff) Carmen Lombardo and on more serious conclusions with Buddy's masterful (vocal) performance. Both versions are very good, and both are in differing styles. Buddy or Billie?

40. "Getting Some Fun Out of Life," Vocalion 3701. Billie's vocal is almost breezy, as this ditty penned by Edgar Leslie and Joseph A. Burke in a jazzy, mid-tempo mood becomes much appreciated.

41, 42. "Travelin' All Alone," Vocalion 3748. This faster-paced vamping of the (slower, heart-wrenching) Ethel Waters recording (Columbia 1933-D) is converted and redefined as a mid-tempo jazz classic.

43. "Now They Call It Swing," Vocalion 3947. As credited to the likes of Vaughan De Leath, Walter Hirsh, Lou Handman and Norman Cloutier, it's more than obvious some of the old crowd of the 1920s were still around to cash in on new trends. This contrived 1938 statement of the swing era is, in true retrospective, dated, but the wordy Holiday vocal is slick enough.

44. "On the Sentimental Side." Vocalion 3947. As a Bing Crosby original, penned by Burke and Monaco, a soft crooning job had already been expected. While it has been more than established that Teddy Wilson usually led Billie's house recording band, it's

jazz pianist Freddy Green's guitar lead that perhaps gave her a differing tilt to a vocal directly influenced from the Crosby recording. While (previously noted) recording fodder directly from Crosby had offered a good enough alternative, it's Billie's own vocal that is more defining on this ditty! Listen to both!

45. "Back in Your Own Backyard," Vocalion 4029. Without waiting for an instrumental lead, Billie's jazzy vocal (again) redefines an older (1920s) standard, differing greatly in style from the likes of Al Jolson, Ruth Etting, and Russ Columbo.
46. "When a Woman Loves a Man," Vocalion 4029. While not to be confused with a similar title from the 1920s, this 1938 ditty penned by Bernie Hanighen, Johnny Mercer, and Gordon Jenkins perhaps gave Billie the type of recording fodder she best excels in.
47. "The Very Thought of You," Vocalion 4457. Already a standard by 1938 and a hit for crooner Bing Crosby in 1935, Billie's challenge indeed succeeds. More so, she surpasses her "Easy Living" performance and again redefines a classic.
48. "Any Old Time," Bluebird B-7759. This 1938 Artie Shaw release, with a vocal refrain by Billie Holiday, indeed found a sweet vocal, limited and floating along well, within the framework of Shaw's own soft touch of an arrangement as well as his own self-penned ditty. (Speculation has it that this ditty was quick to be withdrawn from commercial circulation when it was found that Billie had broken her contract with AMC, when recorded as a current Artie Shaw release.)

49, 50. "My Man," Brunswick 8008. (a) Fannie Brice's signature tune of the 1920s is effectively challenged in 1937 in vocal style and arrangement, although, perhaps, Billie's own (b) second recording in 1948, released on Decca 24638, does indeed challenge herself.

51. "Nice Work If You Can Get It," Brunswick 8015. While the brighter yet no less jazzy contemporary Maxine Sullivan recording *is* better, this rendering does remain good listening.
52. "If Dreams Come True," Brunswick 8053. This excuse for jazz, penned by Irving Mills, Edgar Sampson, and Benny Goodman, finally finds a vocal excuse after a long intro.
53. "Everybody's Laughing," Brunswick 8259. This Teddy Wilson release, penned by Sammy Lerner and Ben Oakland, like all his usual (brilliant) arrangements, still benefits most by Billie's vocal.
54. "Here It Is Tomorrow Again," Brunswick 8259. This flip side of the above, penned by Roy Ringward and P. Gibson, again reeks of quality.
55. "April in My Heart," Brunswick 8265. This ditty penned by Helen Meinard and Hoagy Carmichael indeed reaches the heart—in April or any other month.
56. "Say It with a Kiss" Brunswick 8270. It's very interesting to compare contemporary Maxine Sullivan's (very bright) vocal style (Victor 26124) with Billie's softened grit. Maxine or Billie?
57. "They Say," Brunswick 8270. This flip side of "Say It with a Kiss" again sparks some interesting contemporary company for Billie (and Teddy Wilson's arrangements). Indeed, a contemporary Ethel Waters version (Bluebird 10025), with the Eddie Mallory Orchestra, is smoother and more polished, as is (another) contemporary Helen Forrest vocal, as an Artie Show release on Bluebird 10075. While ties are heated and hated about this (1938) song ditty, the excellence and contrasts in styles are found to be too close to call, although the Forrest release became the contemporary best seller. Billie, Ethel, or Helen?

58. "You Go to My Head," Vocalion 4126. This title penned by J. Fred Coots and Haven Gillespie can be termed as "smooth," as well as a forerunner for 1950s' jazz. Moreover, this 1939 recording remains a classic. For Helen Ward? Others?
59. "I'm Gonna Lock My Heart," Vocalion 4238. This somewhat lighthearted ditty, penned by Jimmy Eaton and Terry Shand, somehow works.
60. "Some Other Spring," Vocalion 5021. Billie's haunting vocalizing, penned by Arthur Herzog and Irene Kitchings, is full of despair, and perhaps this torch song, as introduced by Billie's already established vocal style, may be considered defined upon first hearing.
61. "Them There Eyes," Vocalion 5021. Yes! This high energy flip side of "Some Other Spring," when subsequently played, indeed helps to wipe away tears! Moreover, this fine update of the already old vocal by the Rhythm Boys (as a Gus Arnheim entity as well as a Louis Armstrong release) indicates the huge influence that the Louis Armstrong recording had had upon Billie (*beware* of her re-recorded Decca release—in comparison, it's truly garbage). Indeed, Billie had got it right the first time!
62. "Strange Fruit," Commodore 526. The racial message conveyed in this title (credited to Lewis Allan for lyrics, with E. B. Marks) represents a crucial milestone in the short history of American popular music, more so a shocking reminder of racial tensions and white racism. As a recording, as speculation has it, Billie's own interest in this tale about lynching (black) citizens, all too common in the American South in 1939, found current recording companies refusing to let her record it, fearing boycotts and reprisals. Luckily, Milt Gabler, the owner of the small label Commadore, with backing by Frankie Newton, enabled her to record it. In true retrospective, it was Holiday's own experience in racial and social equality that became identified as highlighted protest within a popular recorded song entity. (Ethel Waters's previous (1933) dramatic rendition of Irving Berlin's "Suppertime" (about lynching) on Broadway *had* been effective, yet Waters did not produce a contemporary recording. When she (finally) did record it in 1946, the Holiday recording had long preceded it.)

Billie's (vocal) approach to this highly potent ditty, specifically about a black man hanging from a tree branch in the state of Georgia, is handled professionally and is indeed "soulful," a word defined later in the century but more than relevant for Billie's handling of lyrics. As an artist statement also, this ditty scores. More so, as a political statement, considering the world situation of 1939, it laid bare the lingering problems of Americana itself and, indeed, provided a shameful glimpse of the new world and that of the troubled old world, noting the march of the Axis powers and communism. Heard in the latter century, this chilling tale remains powerful as Billie's commitment is total, indeed a masterful stroke of genius that still strikes a chord when heard or played. As a rule, all recording artists seek to "find" a song ditty to "define," or become associated with. Yet few other recording artists (ever) define the ugly side of the culture.

63. "Fine and Mellow," Commodore 526. As the flip of "Strange Fruit," while obviously not as controversial, this blues entity is, nevertheless, another classic. Penned by E. B. Marks and Billie herself, this is a cool approach to blues (actually rare for the jazzy Billie)! Fine and Mellow? Yes!
64. "Yesterdays," Commadore 527. Another fine vocal, penned by Jerome Kern, Otto Harbach, and T. B. Harms, had been introduced as a film entity by the somewhat operatic actress Irene Dunne in *Roberta*, some years back in 1935. This vocal attempt by Billie, more so, finds a discarding of jazzy backing mood, something new for Billie. Moreover, this careful and poignant vocal scores and, indeed, defines this ditty.

65-66. "Solitude," Okeh 6270. (a) Penned by Duke Ellington, Irving Mills, and Eddie De Lange, this familiar release returns to a predominate rhythm section, featuring a typical Holiday mid-tempo vocal phrasing. It is also interesting to compare this version with the contemporary Duke Ellington release, which featured a fine Ivie Anderson vocal that is tight and controlling due to the common touch of Ellington's and Ivie's cool, jazzy style. For the most part, Billie's version is loose and free, which is something Billie, usually, did not have to deal with. (b) Billie's later version, on Decca 23853, is also done very well, although just why she rerecorded this one is hard to figure. Listen and decide?

67-68. "God Bless the Child," Okeh 6279. (a) In true retrospective, this 1941 ditty remains a true Holiday classic and is even penned by the likes of Arthur Herzog and Billie herself. As a social commentary, this sad tale, finding a small child a bit hungry and (poor), obviously meant a lot to Billie. More so, as product of Baltimore's urban poor, this ditty is not contrived. Moreover, her fine vocal truly is bare and emotional.

(b). Another version, on Decca 249272, was recorded in 1949, yet, unlike most rerecordings, it retains a (still) committed vocal from Billie, although far from a jazzy mode. This second version is, more so, much like a popular Christmas hymn, as arranged elaborately by Gordon Jenkins. In true comparisons, it's also a tribute to Billie's vocal abilities, which were considerable. Jazz or hymn? Or look into the Bible for Mathew 25:29?

69. "Love Me or Leave Me," Okeh 6369. While hardly challenged as a vocal, Billie's dragging low style at least fits the mood for this old torch entity, much identified with Ruth Etting in the 1920s.

70. "Gloomy Sunday," Okeh 6451. Also known as a "Famous Hungarian Suicide Song," penned by Sam M. Lewis, Rezso Seress, and Laszlo Javor, Billie (again) took on recording fodder that was controversial and, perhaps, something of an artistic (vocal) challenge. Moreover, the early and slow vocal style, often projected by Billie on previous occasions, seemingly fits the mood for the very somber and sad lyrics found in this ditty. As it turned out, this recording finds a lush musical backing, and Billie's vocal hits a dramatic mark and may be considered yet another classic ditty defined.

71. "I Can't Believe You're in Love with Me," Columbia 36335. This ditty by Clarence Gaskill and Jimmy McHugh from the 1920s is finally defined as a vocal.

72, 73. "I Cover the Water Front," Columbia 37493. (a) Billie excels on this ditty (penned by Johnny Green and Ed Heyman) differing much with the previous (very well done) Connie Boswell recording. (b). While her (lower) vocal is perhaps dragged a bit with jazz, her second (1944) rendering of this ditty (Commadore 559) finds her with more time to prepare for recording. Or perhaps she wanted to take another crack at the song ditty itself? In any case, this second recording (about a minute longer) betrays a vocal depth not heard on the first version. Does Billie redefine herself? Listen and compare.

74. "Long Gone Blues," Columbia 37586. Yes. This ditty credited to T. Smith and Billie is urban blues.

75. "Travelin' Light," Capital 116. This record credits the legendary Paul Whiteman and His Orchestra, the same bandleader of 1920s' fame, and a vocal as by "Lady Day." Credited to Jimmy Munday and Johnny Mercer, this lush bit of pop indeed found Billie in good spirits, as her mellow voice lifts Whiteman's quiet and somewhat dull arrangements into yet another classic vocal. (Billie's contract problem with the

previous Artie Shaw Bluebird release of "Any Old Time," led her to be identified only as "Lady Day" for this (early) release on the new (Capital) record label.

The following selected Commadore recordings were recorded in March and April 1944. Speculation exists that studio musicians included pianist Eddie Heywood, whose keyboard style was a bit looser than that of the more controlled style of Teddy Wilson. More so, these (Commadore) masters seem to indicate that Billie herself is in control of the recording sessions. These recordings, while moderate sellers, also confirm that Billie was more than a match for her newer "pop" competitors, including the likes of former band singers, like herself, such as Jo Stafford, Peggy Lee, Lena Horne, and Dinah Shore.

76. "I'm Yours," Commadore 585. While the classic Ruth Etting best seller had been challenged by (1920s) contemporaries Nick Lucas and Johnny Marvin, this version is, more so, a huge difference in style. It is challenged, more so, in (vocal) style on this classic by Johnny Green and E. Y, Harburg. More so, Billie's committed vocal finds her much (more) at ease, as her vocal, while always low-keyed, is beautifully rendered in a soft tone, only rarely heard in her previous recordings with Teddy Wilson. Did Billie define this ditty? If not, her claims upon it are valid!
77. "My Old Flame," Commadore 585. The (already) older and cool jazz vocal of Ivie Anderson is at least challenged.
78. "As Time Goes By," Commadore 7520. This wartime hit (featured in the film *Casablanca*) was, more so, featured in the film by actor Dooley Wilson. As the very popular (Wilson) rendering would not become a contemporary for him until the end of the (1942) musicians strike, the popularity of the film, revived interest in two earlier versions from 1931. Indeed, the reissued Rudy Vallee original, as rereleased on Victor 20-1526, replacing Victor 22773, became a huge best-selling wartime entity in 1943. So did a reissued Jacques Renard recording (Brunswick 6205), cleverly using the (old) defunct original with a new green label. Moreover, the song ditty became well known in England (without a musicians' strike despite the war) for an elegant yet stiff recording for the (transplanted) American, Adelaide Hall.

With all this crooning again going on and, indeed, a fortunate turn of public taste during the war and the musicians strike, Dooley Wilson did produce a recording at the end of the strike, as released on Decca 4006. However, the likes of Billie's (1944) version lacks any (vocal) comparisons. While her style had already been firmly established in the last decade, her rendering of "As Time Goes By," more so, defines her as a popular recording artist, very capable of soft crooning and, moreover, with control and class. Billie's poignant and newfound mellow approach, indeed, defined this classic ditty penned by Herman Hupfeld.

79. "Embraceable You," Commadore 7520. While any Gershwin Brothers-penned ditty is classy, this Holiday version—despite some fine contemporary (1940s) competition from Judy Garland and Helen O' Connell vocal, as found on a (1941) Jimmy Dorsey release, and the mellow style of Ginny Simms—with Billie's own commitment to this soft and mushy material just may be better. Listen and compare.
80. "I'll Be Seeing You," Commadore 553. This ditty, penned by Sammy Fain and Irving Kahal, had already been crooned out by Dick Todd and defined by Frank Sinatra (as a band singer in 1940), as well as rendered subsequently by Bing Crosby in (1944). It is also likely that Billie had been influenced by both versions before her (1944) recording was attempted. While this ditty reeks of sentimental schmaltz, it's easy to

dismiss, although it's obvious that Sinatra took it seriously, and (surprisingly) Crosby also took his crooning act seriously enough to produce a very fine contemporary recording. Billie's lesser-known (1944) rendering, more so, lifts this recording fodder as something more, as her soft vocal indeed puts good claims upon this classic. Dick, Frank, Bing, or Billie?

81. "He's Funny That Way," Commadore 569. This popular ditty from the 1920s had been recorded by many, especially noting the best-selling Gene Austin release. In a gender change, it's 'She's or "He's', without a problem for singers to be required to keep with lyrics as written. It was more likely, however, that Billie had heard the (1939) version, by Thelma Carpenter, of this ditty penned by Richard Whiting, Neil Moret, and Anne-Rachel. Or perhaps the contemporary (1944) film that resurrected the song. Billie's popular vocal approach, while a bit lower than Thelma's, is somehow softer spoken. More so, a contemporary Connie Haines version also had relevance. Listen and learn?
82. "How Am I to Know," Commadore 569. Another (old) song ditty, penned by Jack King and Dorothy Parker, found Billie perhaps more interested in the previous (1937) Teddy Wilson release, featuring Helen Ward, than in the earlier popular styles of others, including the likes of Gene Austin. In any case, Billie's own softness effectively and softly, perhaps, defines another popular song ditty.

Note: Billie signed with Decca Records, in the latter half of 1944, with perhaps the hope of further exploiting other pop aspirations as well as a jazz singer.

83. "Lover Man," Decca 23391. This popular ditty was a best seller in early 1945. The lush orchestra, conducted by Toots Camarata, plus the added sounds behind the Holiday vocal, as never before, produced for her a winner. Moreover, Billie's vocal accepts the challenge, as she masterfully blends in with the fast-moving melody, seemingly with ease. Penned by Jimmie Davis, Roger 'Ram" Ramirez, and James Sherman, this ditty also became a contemporary WWII entity, greeting returning service people and, indeed, pleasing them with her mellow phrasing. (Another contemporary version by the up-and-coming Sarah Vaughan (Musicraft 499) is a differing and fresh vocal style, yet after Billie had already defined it.)
84. "That Ole Devil Called Love," Decca 23391. As the flip of "Lover Man" along with Camarata's Orchestra, this ditty, penned by Allen Fisher and Doris Fisher—like its more famous flip—finds Billie's soft vocal hitting the heart, much like the older torch songs of a previous era.

Note: Postwar problems with drugs and a jail sentence diminished Billie's contemporary image and stature, as scandal indeed took its toll. In true retrospective, Billie never sounded better as a popular vocalist as her current (Decca) releases indicated. While some earlier followers were to be indeed turned off by her pop material—as substitute for the jazzy material that had established her in the previous decade—perhaps the need to move on was not considered. Moreover, being a true black diva, more was expected as the postwar period of "rhythm and blues" was emerging. The new wave would, more so, prove unsettling for many, including Billie. In any case, the rest of the Decca picks are of considerable merit and contribute much to the Holiday legacy.

85. "Big Stuff," Decca 23463. How did Leonard Bernstein (the classical maestro himself) get involved with jazz and Billie Holiday? Or was he (Holiday's) follower? In any

case, Bernstein was indeed a Billie Holiday fan, and this contrived ditty, penned by Bernstein himself, remains an oddity that found the skillful Holiday vocal adapting very well to the challenge found in this type of material.

86. "The Blues Are Brewin'," Decca 23463. Introduced in the (1946) film *New Orleans*, this somewhat contrived title, penned by Eddie De Lange and Louis Alter, also found Billie herself introducing this ditty in the film. Moreover, while the film ain't much, the musical performances by Billie and Louis Armstrong are strong and indeed carry the film. Indeed, this recording ain't no slouch, and the Holiday vocal also carries this ditty well.
87. "You Better Go Now," Decca 23483. I believe Billie when she wants me to go, and so will the listener of this polished vocal, penned by Irvin Graham and S. Bickley Reichner—more so, another (Holiday) classic.
88. "No More," Decca 23483. Again, the soft approach works, as the ditty penned by Toots Camarata and Bob Russell is, more so, greeted by Billie's own stylish vocal, backed by Camarata's string section.
89. "Don't Explain," Decca 23565. This sad tale (penned by Andy Razaf and Billie herself) is obviously based upon personal experience, indeed "very" personal. Does Billie's sensitive vocal redefine the meaning of "torch"? Just listen, and "don't" explain it, as all matters taken to heart just don't have any.
90. "Good Morning, Heartache," Decca 23676. This title, penned by Irene Higginbotham, Ervin Drake, and Dan Fisher, notes a sad tale. Moreover, the Holiday vocal, always full of human expression, does not disappoint its listeners' expectations. Good morning, or "bad morning"?
91. "There Is No Greater Love," Decca 23853. Another fine contribution, penned by Isham Jones and Marty Symes, to the fine Holiday "diva" legacy that, indeed, scores.
92. "Weep No More," Decca 24551. This attempt at creativity sadly did not find much contemporary (later-1940s) interest. Penned by Gordon Jenkins and Tom Adair, this contrived attempt at rhythm and blues was, for the most part, ignored by the jazz-based fans of the previous decade, who had become a bit snooty. In true retrospective, Billie's vocal rises to the occasion (bettering this recording fodder) and, along with the Bobby Tucker Trio and the Stardust, finds the current group style good enough for her. It's, more so, too bad that Billie's versatility as a vocalist was unappreciated (at the time) as she's good at it. While far from a jazz classic, it remains a Holiday entity and an example of vocal prowess and ability.
93. "Porgy," Decca 24638. Although Ethel Waters had rendered a classic recording of this ditty twice, her stylistic (early) 1930s' vocal was perhaps the only good lift for a (very) boring song ditty. Using more modern (1948) backing (Bobby Tucker and His Trio and the Stardust vocal), which in itself sounds like a contemporary gimmick, Billie's own stylistic vocal more than challenges the (Waters) version, with a resulting recording differing much in voice as it does in a (slicker) arrangement. While hardly a jazz classic, Billie's softer vocal in mid-tempo provides this ditty a new energy, indeed redefining another (Waters) classic.
94. "Gimmie a Pigfoot," Decca 24947. This attempt at rhythm and blues is indeed inspiring, considering a fair backup studio orchestra, led by Horance Hendereson. While slick enough, noting some lyrics full of crude slang, Billie's vocal is superb. (As compared with the earlier (1933) Bessie Smith release, on Okeh 8949, the Holiday version is very urban, compared to the earthiness of the Smith vocal. Listen and compare. Billie or Bessie? Or both?

95. "You Sweet Hunk O' Trash," Decca 24785. This bit of slang, penned by James P. Johnson and Flournoy E. Miller, features a fabulous duet for both Billie and Louis Armstrong. A major idol of Billie's own youth, as well as a vocal influence, the elder Louis scores heavily on his vocal. While Louis is exciting and perhaps wickedly deceiving is his interpretation of this novelty, Billie's dragging and jazzy vocal is equally hot. Perhaps the orchestration, by Sy Oliver, could have been better, but luckily, the Armstrong and Holiday vocal performances indeed delivers something special.
96. "Ain't Nobody's Business If I Do," Decca 24726. While (again) the case may be made that the backup jazz band is thin, on Decca releases and not up to the scale set in the previous decade under Teddy Wilson, Billie's vocal still sparkles. More so, it's a fine update to this old blues standard that had been best claimed by Bessie Smith's (1923) acoustic (Columbia A 3844) recording that most likely had been Billie's inspiration. This recording, moreover, finds the typical low-down (Holiday) vocal style as a "bright" one, in comparison to the earthy vocal of Bessie. How can Billie be considered a "bright" vocalist? Listen to both Billie and Bessie versions of this ditty and find out.
97. "Crazy He Calls Me," Decca 24796. Billie's pop vocal style was never better, and Gordon Jenkins does a masterful job of handling the backing orchestra, as penned by Carl Sigman and Bob Russell.
98. "Now or Never," Decca 24947. Penned by Curtis R. Lewis and Billie Holiday, it's obvious that this ditty involved Billie from the start. While the interested vocalist had most likely found the new wave of rhythm and blues labeling her passé, this attempt at recording finds Billie willing to take on some chances with her (limited) vocal and produce a contemporary bit of R & B. While this recording failed to catch much attention at its released time, in 1950, in retrospective, it's a bold move that failed. While far from good, it's interesting enough. Listen and decide.

After being dropped by Decca in 1950, Billie moved on to record for many labels before her (untimely) passing away in 1959, at the age of forty-four. The following (post-1950) releases are found to be solid, noting a deeper-voiced vocalist, stripped of most of the vocal abilities she had once had. Nevertheless, these titles do impress:.

99. "Detour Ahead," Alladin 3094. Billie pulls off some serious speech, as penned by Johnny Frigo, Herb Ellis and Lou Carter, provide the right words.
100. "If the Moon Turns Green," Clef 89108. A more serious 'moon' song, as penned by Paul Coates, Bernie Hanighen, become very relivant.
101. "Autumn in New York," Clef 89108. It ain't Margaret Whiting or Frank Sinatra, it's Billie! It's obvious Billie's version was overlooked, and it's also good for vocal comparisons between Margaret, Frank or Frank?

Radio

The following LPs, issued after Billie's passing, find some good radio masters:

102, 103. *The Golden Years*, C3L 21. This safer mono LP release of this reissue of 1930s material contains excellent (1937) live (radio) material, recorded with Count Basie's Orchestra (with whom she had not recorded any commercial recordings) when things were indeed hot.

a. "Swing, Brother, Swing!" Billie gets down and tops the band!
b. "I Can't Get Started." Billie again proves who's boss.

Also: While the (1974) LP release of *Here's Johnny-Magic Moments from the Tonight Show* found a Billie Holiday live performance in 1955, it was Steve Allen, *not* Johnny Carson, who had hosted *The Tonight Show* at that time.

104. Billie's knockout performance of "Them There Eyes" (on par with her first recording—*not* the re-recording on Decca), was something to take notice of for any (1974) baby boomer who had seen the contemporary Diana Ross film about her and *now* found the real thing!

Visual Image.

The narrow path of racism left much that was undocumented for Afro-Americans, which did not exclude Billie. The following filmed images, however, do find the diva at her best:

105. "Hymn of Sorrow." The (1934) Duke Ellington film short *Symphony in Black* features an (unaccredited) Billie Holiday soulful rendering of this ditty. While the viewer can easily miss her (less than a minute) appearance, it's well worth looking for.
106. "The Blues Are Brewing," found in the (1946) film *New Orleans*.
107. "Fine and Mellow" / "Billie's Blues (I Love My Man)" (Live, early TV, 1957), from the CBS *The Story of Jazz* on the TV program *Seven Lively Arts*. Usually, when a live gig is performed, certain expectations are found in the audience. By the mid-1950s, the decline of Billie Holiday musically and physically was a known fact. This performance, however, is somehow, the ultimate Billie. As in a true jazzy setting, the excellent black-and-white footage finds an older, cool performer ready to rumble! Her backing musicians, including the likes of Coleman Hawkins, Lester Young, Ben Webster, Roy Eldridge, and (young) Gerry Mulligan, create a smoky nightclub setting—indeed, perfect for Billie. Given all this, she does not disappoint. Moreover, Billie is fully in charge of the proceedings. Generating cool fire (both in voice and body gestures) she truly electrifies her audience. Time? Rock? Anytime is good, as any new convert will testify, upon viewing this classic, and ultimate jazz performance.

Libby Holman

This (very) highbrow diva just made it into this book. As a vocalist, her (1920s) fame was the result of Broadway shows and entering into the "electric" age of recording at just the right time. Her erratic voice, somewhat of a confused high soprano, is semi-operatic. Tested by the likes of the new jazz, she adapted well enough to rival the likes of contemporaries Ruth Etting and, especially, Helen Morgan. While not completely casting aside the acoustic influences of Ada Jones, Sophie Tucker, Fannie Brice, and Marion Harris, Libby's attempts at jazz vocals are usually clumsy. Nevertheless, some of her dated recordings do indeed contain some interesting vocals, backed up by some fine jazzy arrangements. Moreover, we find Libby searching for a style between some fine jazz licks, perhaps emulating contemporary Ruth Etting. Various influences from classical European opera to jazz (replacing ragtime) crept into the musical theater, with singers like Libby adapting change. The following picks represent much of that change.

1. "Who's That Knockin' at My Door," Brunswick 3667. This spirited ditty ain't bad and is even rhythmic. Penned by Seymour Simons and Gus Kahn, its bouncy and loose lyrics are somehow let loose by Libby's (very) controlled vocal, although a contemporary Annette Hanshaw version, on Pathé 32293, is sung with less restrictions.
2. "Carefree," Brunswick 3667. This flip side of "Who's That Knockin' at My Door," penned by Jo Trent and Peter De Rose, is just as spirited but a tad less novel. This diva is indeed "carefree" as her liberation is for certain to be celebrated. What a flapper!
3. "There Ain't No Sweet Man That's Worth the Salt of My Tears," Brunswick 3798. This ditty finds Libby sounding a little out of her "Broadway" element, perhaps an attempt at emulation of contemporary Ruth Etting. While failing at this, the spirited vocal is done well with a fine backup orchestra conducted by William F. Wirges. Another contemporary (1928) version of this Fred Fisher penned ditty, was recorded by Paul Whiteman's Orchestra, on Victor 25675. This version featured a vocal solo by one of his discoveries, Bing Crosby. It is also sung in the same bouncy manner as Libby's, and much unlike his (later) crooning vocal style.
4. "The Way He Loves Is Just Too Bad," Brunswick 3798. Libby was no blues queen, but ditties like this, penned by Billy Curtis, Jackie Rose, and Andy Robbins—as Libby tells it—are bound to stir things up.

5, 6. "Moaning Low," Brunswick 4445. This vocal attempts to slur words and sing jazz—as more than a music, with unmistakable and obvious sexual overtones. Penned by Howard Dietz and Ralph Rainger for the Broadway musical *The Little Show*, which also starred Libby herself, a few surviving records of this ditty still work. Another version, possibly a take, with more of Libby's sultry vocal, was released as a jazzy Cotton Pickers' entity, (b) on Brunswick 4446. As did a contemporary Charleston Chasers release, with a faster-paced vocal as by Eva Taylor, on Columbia 1891 D.

7. "He's a Good Man to Have Around," Brunswick 4447. Sophie Tucker introduced this ditty, as well as "I'm Doing What I'm Doing For Love," in the contemporary (1929) film *Honky-Tonk*. Both ditties, penned by Jack Yellen and MiltonAger, contain risqué lyrics—Sophie' s specialty. Libby's higher-pitched vocals, however, beat out Sophie's harshness. Other contemporary versions, by Kate Smith on Diva 2970 D) and Lee Morse on Columbia 1866 D, moreover, compete a bit more with the odd but committed style of Libby's vocal.
8. "I'm Doing What I'm Doing for Love," Brunswick 4453. Yes! Libby makes no bones about it, and with these red-hot lyrics, penned by Jack Yellen and Milton Ager, she confirms just how boldly a modern (1929) woman could express herself.
9. "Find Me a Primitive Man," Brunswick 4666. While it would take an additional ten years to finally define this Cole Porter-penned masterpiece with Lee Wiley's version (LMS L 296), this dated version lacks no heat.
10. "Can't We Be Friends," Brunswick 4506. Penned by Kay Swift and Paul Jones, this lover's lament retains its appeal. This tale of being turned down is no tearjerker, however, as its message is more of the moment. Indeed, an obscure contemporary Bing Crosby version, on Columbia 2001 D, attempts the opposite (masculine) point of view, very similar to Libby's mood. Moreover, this ditty finds Libby a bit more focused as a vocalist, and, indeed, she gives an artful performance, bettering her previous torch efforts.

11. "I May Be Wrong, but I Think You're Wonderful," Brunswick 4506. This breezy vocal, penned by Harry Ruskin and Henry Sullivan, is pleasant enough, or even "swell" enough.
12. "My Man Is on the Make," Brunswick 4554. Perhaps this expression is not dated—from 1929! For certain, this ditty penned by Richard Rodgers and Lorenz Hart, is a winner as Libby and the fine Colonial Club Orchestra make this a jazzy winner. So was a Knickerbockers release, with an even jazzier Eva Taylor vocal on Columbia 2067 D. (A quirky and contemporary Helen Kane version (Victor 22475) is almost as good.)
13. "Why Was I Born," Brunswick 4570. This very high-voiced effort initially almost loses its listener but somehow grabs you by the heart. In fact, a contemporary Helen Morgan version (Victor 22199), also works out the same "torch song" way. Perhaps Helen's softer tone, in comparison, may define it, but not by much.
14. "Happy Because I'm in Love," Brunswick 4613. She's happy, and perhaps sappy, but Libby also makes it all sound a bit raspy (voiced) in this ditty penned by Billy Rose, Edward Eliseu, and Vincent Youmans.
15. "When a Woman Loves a Man," Brunswick 4699. While contrived, this very dated effort at singing with a jazzy backing, as a Roger Wolfe Kahn release, is still interesting enough. Penned by Ralph Rainger and Billy Rose, this ditty had been a better-sung contemporary Fannie Brice entity (Victor 22310). (This title should not be confused with a fine Billie Holiday ditty of the same name, penned in 1938 by Mercer, Hanighen, and Jenkins.)
16. Cooking Breakfast for the One I Love," Brunswick 4699. This original side of "When a Woman Loves a Man" was also an original contemporary Fannie Brice entity, penned by Henry Tobias and William Rose, who (again) released the better version. It's interesting to note that Brice's usual attempt at novelty is also a success, while Libby's unsure vocal is clumsy but persistent.
17. "What Is This Thing Called Love," Brunswick 4700. This Cole Porter-penned ditty found its initial rendering by this (1930) version. Libby, for the most part, sings it straight, with a bit of Ruth Etting's "love" at the end of her rendering. Moreover, a contemporary Fanny Brice release, on Victor 22310, is better. A later Lena Horne version, on Victor 27820, would improve and finally define it, noting a totally different vocal approach in 1941.
18. "A Ship without a Sail," Brunswick 4700. The heart strings almost find an opera, and Lee Wiley would (later) do much better with this ditty penned by Rodgers and Hart (Gala 4).
19. "Something to Remember You By," Brunswick 4910. Libby introduced this Broadway entity in 'Three's A Crowd". This operatic outburst penned by Howard Dietz and Arthur Schwartz, nevertheless, lends great support to the term "torch song."
20. "Body and Soul," Brunswick 4910. Libby put original claims upon thisl Broadway entity, penned by Edward Heyman, Robert Sour, Frank Eyton and Johnny Green. introduced by Libby in 'Three's A Crowd". This is perhaps one of the most recorded ditties of its time (1930). Indeed, the contemporary Helen Morgan version, on Victor 22532, is most like Libby's, except for Helen's softer tone. Or are Libby's slower torch songs an attempted emulation of Helen? More ever, Ruth Etting also put her own dry vocal torch edge claims on this dittyLibby, Helen or Ruth?. Get out the handkerchiefs!
21. "Love for Sale," Brunswick 6044. This Cole Porter classic finds Libby's initial recording very highbrow. Is this perhaps the way Cole originally wanted to hear

his very risqué lyrics? This ain't no down and dirty blues ditty. Its polished vocal message is indeed sophisticated. Perhaps it's Libby's own "rolling *r's*" that date this yet interesting vocal.

22. "I'm One of God's Children," Brunswick 6044. This Harry Ruskin, Louis Alter, and Oscar Hammerstein penned ditty, also known as "I'm One Of God's Children Who Hasn't Got Wings', from Broadway's 'Ballyhoo', perfectly fits Libby's high strung vocal tendencies.
23. "You Are the Night and the Music," Victor 24839. Libby herself introduced this (very) highbrow ditty, penned by Arthur Schwartz and Howard Dietz, for the Broadway entity 'Revenge With Music".

By the mid-1930s, scandal and swing music had a lot to do with keeping Libby out of the record business. Curiously, except for newsreels, a visual image of her, in film as a performer, is surprisingly lacking. By 1942, it seems she was ready to tackle recording again and seemingly with much more creditability and odd creativity.

The following 78 rpm Decca releases were released in album form. Libby, perhaps influenced by folk entities such as the Almanac Singers, including Woody Guthrie, Burl Ives, Leadbelly, and Josh White, indeed seems focused. More so, her vocal style, usually committed but sadly without vocal direction, as noted in some of her previous picks, is finally defined. The result is a fine collection of folk and blues, with a winning vocal style that is consistent in expression. To top all this off, she is backed by Josh White on guitar, a noted blues entity who, more so, adds more power to the whole recording project.

24. "Baby, Baby," Decca 18304. Credited to Rainey on its original 78 rpm release, its origin is not this title, but Ma Rainey's "See See Rider" on Paramount 12252. While it's still speculation to give creative credit to Libby to even record this ditty as "Baby Baby," it's more credible to include Josh White. In any case, Libby's vocal is very soulful and far less contrived than any of her previous recordings. Indeed—a focused and real blues entity that does not fail to please!
25. "Far Thee Well," Decca 18304. Josh White would also record this traditional ballad credited to 'Austin', on Ash 341 B, in a similar cool style. While Josh may be credited to leading her with his "blues guitar," it's Libby's strong vocal that lifts this somewhat weak material.
26. "Good Morning Blues," Decca 18305. The Jimmy Rushing vocal, on a Count Basie release (Decca 1446), is toned down and indeed found to be a totally cool performance.
27. "When the Sun Goes Down," Decca 18305. A fine Leroy Carr (Bluebird B 5877) release is resurrected into something indeed slicker and smoother.
28. "House of the Rising Sun," Decca 18306. This classic ditty had been a loose Texas Alexander rendering (Okeh 8673). There are also subsequent recordings by Leadbelly and Woody Guthrie (with the Almanac Singers) and, much later, in the British invasion, by the Animals. It's, moreover, interesting to hear and subsequently appreciate a committed female vocal, noting the subject matter about prostitution.
29. "Old Smoky Hansom Winsome Johnny," Decca 18306. These traditional ballads—Anglo-Saxon in origin—while a bit corny, benefit from Libby's cool and quiet vocal.

Lena Horne

The image of minority groups in American society, especially that of Afro-Americans, had been always been stereotyped by white racism in America. The advent of Lena Horne in the early 1940s, in conjunction with the event of WWII, did much to change all that. Indeed, the forces of technology, which had already created much myth, finally demanded a movie image of a beautiful black woman and one who would integrate herself into the mainstream as no one had before her. Luckily, "Lena Horne" was discovered! Moreover, she could dance, act, and, for the purposes of this book, sing. As a living icon at the end of the century, her link with the pre-rock world of entertainment was huge, and she may be considered a major cultural event in herself. What became a celebration of her career was her own 1980 Broadway entity *The Lady and Her Music*. As a self-documentation, the former chorus member of the Cotton Club, influenced by the likes of Adelaide Hall, Ivie Anderson, and, especially, Ethel Waters, recreated much of her own triumphs and, in speech, her struggles with racism. Indeed, Lena Horne, alias HeLena Horne, blazed a long trail. When following it, it is more than the obvious musical trail that contains a classic art form, which just must be followed.

➢ Lena Horne picks are as follows:

▪ Note: The following two titles, recorded with the jumpy Nobel Sissle Orchestra of 1936, provide the ear with a fine 1930s' band with a fair-sounding Lena, not yet defined as a vocalist. They are, however, interesting enough to be heard as well as to be compared with her subsequent releases.

1. "I Take It to You," Decca 778. This ditty, penned by Mack Gordon and Harry Warren, is a bit loose, with Lena's vocal, though a bit clumsy, backed ably by Noble Sissle.
2. "That's What Love Did to Me," Decca 847. This one, penned by Sammy Cahn and SaulChaplin, is a bit better, although Lena's search for a vocal style is somewhat lost.

Note: After completing a black exploitation film in the mid-1930s, *The Duke Is Tops*, Lena gave up show business for a while to return to an early Broadway appearance on *Blackbirds of 1939*. By 1940, with the era still in full "swing," Lena got herself hired by a white bandleader, Charlie Barnet. By this time, Lena's vocal was sultry, smooth, and wet, somewhat like that of the up-and-coming Dinah Shore. More than Dinah, however, her delivery was hotter, with an understatement that could also turn cool by the end of a lyric. This unique blend of Lena's vocal and the tight Barnet Orchestra produced some fine "big band" moments, netting the young band singer with much notice on radio as well. Like Ethel Waters before her, Lena could "sound" white. Or maybe her black image should have stopped her from singing?

♦ Barnet picks

3. "Good for Nothin, ' Joe," Bluebird B-11037. What a song! Penned by Rube Bloom and Ted Koehler, this sad tale is further embellished by Lena's sexy and smooth vocal. Indeed, this ditty marks the first of the classic Lena Horne vocals.

4. "The Captain and His Men," Bluebird B-11081. With Barnet's sweet band actually up-tempo and swinging a bit, this dance number, penned by Allen and Carrol, is further graced by Lena's articulate licks.
5. "Haunted Town," Bluebird B-11093. Lena again scores with a lot of voice on this ditty penned by Alex Fogarty and Nigel Altman, perfect for contemporary 1941 dance floors, in slow and holding mode.
6. "You're My Thrill," Bluebird B-11141. Lena again hits the heart as her sultry vocal (penned by Sidney Clare and Jay Gorney) indeed, generates sweat.

The following two picks are with another and more famous white bandleader of the era, Artie Shaw. Again, Lena finds no limits on company or material.

7. "Love Me a Little Little," Victor 27509. The always excellent Artie Shaw Orchestra is further graced by Lena's vocal. While this may be labeled "soft," this contrived dance ditty, penned by Ellen Orr, Howard Smith, and Horance Holmes, indeed works, as did a contemporary version Ginny Simms. Similar in soft vocal style? Check them both out!
8. "Don't Take Your Love from Me," Victor 27509. This ballad side, penned by Henry Nemo, is again effective and softly hits the heart.

   ➢ The following release was perhaps based upon Lena's contemporary 1941 film short *Boogie-Woogie Dream*, which also featured Teddy Wilson and His Orchestra.

9. "Out of Nowhere," Columbia 36737. The Bing Crosby and Ruth Etting classic of 1931 is done well with a fine Teddy Wilson arrangement.

   ♦ The following four (W. C. Handy) classics were recorded with the Dixieland Jazz Group of NBC (radio) Chamber Music Society of Lower Basin Street, conducted by Henry Levine. At this time (1941), this radio entity meant a lot to Lena as well as to contemporary listeners.

10. "Aunt Hagar's Blues," Victor 27544. The W. C. Handy's classic, originally known as "Aunt Hagar, Children," is indeed claimed by Lena.
11. "St. Louis Blues," Victor 27542.
12. "Beale Street Blues," Victor 275343.
13. "Careless Love," Victor 27545. This ditty, penned by Handy, Koenig, and Williams (as noted on the original 78 rpm label) is a cheerful update to many renderings, especially noting an acoustic version by Alberta Hunter.

   ♦ Backed by Lou Bring's Orchestra, with lush strings arranged by Ned Freeman, the following 1941 recordings perhaps defined the sultry Lena Horne style. The following eight ditties were all issued on the 78 rpm album *Moanin' Low—Torch Songs by* Lena Horne. (P 118).

14. "I Gotta Right to Sing the Blues," Victor 27817. Lena excels, as her smooth blues is a tale that is less full of sadness and has more of sultry regret. This vocal is indeed inviting and, in comparison with a Lee Wiley rendering, a challenge.

15. "Moanin' Low," Victor 27817. This update to the 1929 classic, introduced by Libby Holman, is, in contrast, sultry but smoother.
16. "Where or When," Victor 27818. The obvious invitation found in Lena's vocal adds some cool fire to this classic, penned by Rodgers and Hart, from Broadway's *Babes in Arms*, back in the mid-1930s. (Lena would rerecord this ditty later in the decade.)
17. "The Man I Love," Victor 27818. The Marion Harris original "torch" is passed on well.
18. "Ill Wind," Victor 27819. The perfection found is this heart-throbbing tale, penned by Harold Arlen and Ted Koehler, is overwhelming. Lena had been identified with this ditty in a previous 1934 Cotton Club revue, perhaps as a backup for Adelaide Hall, who, like Lena, did not produce a contemporary recording, although Harold Arlen did. This later 1941 rendering is, more so, definitive, and Lena finally defined it. (A subsequent rendering by Frank Sinatra in the 1950s challenges Lena's version.) Listen and compare!
19. "Stormy Weather," Victor 27819. As recorded (before) the film of the same name was to be produced, and Lena had already put some claims upon the Ethel Waters 1933 classic!
20. "Mad about the Boy," Victor 27820. Lena's slow, sultry vocal of this ditty, penned by Nowell Coward, truly defines it.
21. "What Is This Thing Called Love," Victor 27820. Lena's question, as found in the title of this Cole Porter-penned classic is smooth enough. More so, she redefines this previous Libby Holman entity. While questions of style are sometimes acquired taste, Lena's "modern" and smooth 1941 rendering, noting the test of time, survives in comparisons.

♦ The following three were recorded with Horace Henderson and His Orchestra in 1944. By this time, Lena had become a major film entity in such films as *Cabin in the Sky* and *Stormy Weather* and also a popular "pinup" for the servicemen of WWII.

22. "I Didn't Know about You," Victor 20-1616. This ditty penned by Duke Ellington and Bob Russell is classy and smooth singing. (So was a contemporary Count Basie release with a fine vocal by Thelma Carpenter, on Columbia 36766.)
23. "One for My Baby," Victor 20-1616. This ditty penned by Harold Arlen and Johnny Mercer was introduced by Fred Astaire in the contemporary film *The Sky's the Limit*. While Fred's visual of this ditty is OK, this Lena Horne vocal indeed saves it as a classical recording. While a Lena Horne visual is lacking, the sad barroom tale leaves much to the imagination, owing much to Lena's own commitment to lyrics. (A later Frank Sinatra version is also excellent, and almost redefines it.)
24. "As Long as I Live," Victor 20-1626. This ditty penned by Harold Arlen and Ted Koehler is yet another sultry vocal that Lena defines as a classic. As a danceable entity as well, Lena's smooth coasting into lyrics moreover defines just what to wear when it rains and just "how" to eat an apple—Lena's way!
25. "I Ain't Got Nothing but the Blues," Victor 20-1626. Lena's blues are soft and jazzy, although she does get a bit edgy, on this ditty, penned by Duke Ellington, Don George and Larry Fotine. Yeah, she's got 'em.

♦ *Black Rhythm Radio,* Sandy Hook 2091. This LP, breaking rules as a radio entity for the purposes of this book just had to be included! As MC, Lena's appearances on the wartime *Jubilee* (1944?) radio program were most inspiring. Along with

Ernie "Bubbles" Whiteman, Fletcher Henderson, the Charioteers, Anna Mae Windburn, Mel "Bugs Bunny" Blanc, Jerry Colonna, and others, Lena takes command! Especially noting live versions of the following:

26. "Honeysuckle Rose."
27. "Mad about the Boy."
28. "Good for Nothin' Joe."
29. "As Long as I Live"
30. "Deed I Do."
31. "How Long Has This Been Going On," Victor 45-001. Lena returned to the recording studio in 1945 with a small jazzy group, the Phil Moore Four. As the first of many Phil Moore arrangements, Lena's backup sound became jazzier, noting the changes of the mid-1940s and a drift toward louder sounds. This Gershwin Brothers-penned ditty finds Lena in good spirits as her smooth vocal notes the betrayal of a truly beautiful woman, who can really sing!

    - Lena's move to the smaller Black & White label fortunately kept her intact with Phil Moore.

32. "Old Fashioned Love," Black & White 816. Alberta Hunter's acoustic version is finally defined!
33. "Glad to Be Unhappy," Black & White 817. This ditty penned by Rodgers and Hart finds Lena's slick vocal cool, moody, and precise. So indeed is Phil Moore's backing, which allows Lena to be softly heard on this sensitive rendering. Defined?
34. "At Long Last Love," Black & White 817. This fine flip side of "Glad To Be Unhappy," also finds Lena in good vocal form. While obvious comparisons with contemporaries Dinah Shore and Peggy Lee may be found in vocal styles, Lena's vocal of this (Cole Porter) ditty is no slouch. At medium-tempo, Phil Moore's background leads Lena into some fine lyric-bending. Moreover, this "nightclub" setting works well as this vocal projects a fine visual image and defines this ditty as a classic.
35. "Blue Prelude," Black & White 818. While less dramatic than the Bing Crosby original from the early 1930s, Lena's effective version has assets, with Phil Moore providing excellent and smooth backup. While this ditty may or may not be about suicide, perhaps the breakup is too hard to take? In any case, this slick version ain't bad.
36. "Squeeze Me," Black & White 819. As "Squeeze Me but Don't Tease Me," this ditty penned by Duke Ellington and Lee Gaines just has to be a perfect pun for a piano player. More so is Lena's slick and sultry vocal with Phil Moore directing the jazzy orchestration. While it's a good bet that Phil was playing piano keys, this effective medium-tempo vocal again proves Lena's commitment to excellence, as well as a legit claim as a jazz vocalist.
37. "You Go to My Head," Black & White 819. While Helen Ward or Billie Holiday had perhaps already defined this ditty penned by Haven, Gillespie, and Coots as a classic, this more pop rendering, with Phil Moore's usual "nightclub" touch, also finds this version to be a winner.
38. "Hesitating Blues," Black & White 844. Another W. C. Handy classic !
39. "It's a Rainy Day," Black & White 846. This Phil Moore-penned ditty is packed with Lena's usual vocal qualities as her sultry and soft vocal style, noting a "rainy day," is

totally committed. Indeed, this classic rendering just could be the best of the Black & White releases, also noting that this ditty may be heard in dry weather as well.

40. "Deed I Do," MGM 10165. Backed by Luther Henderson, the classic Ruth Etting version of the 1920s is challenged, and certainly updated.

The following MGM releases mark a return to "pop" as accompanied by Lennie Hayton, the fine musician who had previously backed many, including Bing Crosby in the early 1930s. (Lena would, more so, marry the white bandleader, finding much dissent from her fans, both black as well as white., in the latter 1940s. A big deal? Considering the fact that some states prohibited marriage between the races—it was! In true retrospective, Lena's own personality was defined as bold, as popular music had exploited). Back to the music.

41. "Love of My Life," MGM 10165. This Cole Porter-penned ditty finds Lena returning to the likes of previous Victor releases, as Lennie Hayton's arrangement indicates.
42. "The Lady Is a Tramp," MGM 30171-A. This 1949 rendering of the already classic ditty penned by Rodgers and Hart, from the 1930s, also found Lena introducing it as a film entity in *Words and Music*. While some excellent recordings did exist before this recording, including the likes of a somewhat stiff Adelaide Hall version, recorded in England, Lena more than challenges any previous efforts. While credit is indeed merited to the fast tempo of Lennie Hayton's arrangement, it's Lena's clear and hot vocal that defined it, both on-screen and as a recording. (Frank Sinatra, would later claim it and, perhaps, challenges Lena's version.)
43. "Where or When," MGM 30171. The rerecording of her lush Victor rendering, also found in the film *Words and Music*, is up-tempo.

- After 1950, Lena's position in Hollywood, largely because of racism, slipped. As noted in her (later) *The Lady and Her Music* LP, also on CD release, the deck was stacked against her. While losing out in the (still) breakthrough 1949 Ethel Waters film *Pinky*, perhaps the stupidity of the MGM musical *Show Boat*, struck a chord. In true retrospective, the mulatto role introduced on Broadway in 1927 by Helen Morgan, the white diva of Canadian origin, was to be remade in 1951. While Helen Morgan's subsequent filmed versions were indeed good, many women of color could have pulled it off. (Moreover, in London, blues entity Alberta Hunter, among others, had.) More so, Lena Horne had already and successfully sung the *Show Boat* entity "Can't Help Lovin' That Man" in the 1946 MGM film *Til' the Clouds Roll By*. As an established "star" by 1951, and vocally perfect for the role, the talented but non-singer Ava Gardner got the role. In true retrospective, this 1951 film is a mess, and indeed a real miss for MGM as well as for Lena.
- Lena Horne releases in the 1950s found her put into the "adult" category, and mostly on LP. The following LP issues were well especially worth the search.

44-50. *Jamaica*, LOC 1036. This RCA Victor Broadway soundtrack from 1957 is a bright, hidden gem and costarred the likes of Adelaide Hall, Josephine Premice, as well as some forced vocals by Ossie Davis and Ricardo Montalban. Backed by a first-rate orchestra led by Lehman Engel, this venture found song ditties by the established team of Harold Arlen and E. Y. Harburg. Lena's vocals are inspired by this fine original soundtrack, with one entity revisited.

a. "Pretty to Walk With."
b. "Push the Button." The modern age is commented upon, luckily by Lena.
c. "Coconut Sweet." Lena's vocal is also very sweet!
d. "Take It Slow, Joe."
e. "Ain't It the Truth." This ditty, a noted outtake from the film *Cabin in the Sky*, had originally been Lena's. This newer version, moreover, does not disappoint its listeners.
f. "Napoleon." The French pasty, now a song ditty, remains sweet.

51-57. *Porgy and Bess*, LOP 1507. This (1959) release of the already famous (1935) Broadway entity, penned by the Gershwin Brothers and Du Boise Heyward, is revisited. While there was nothing wrong with the concept of using Charleston, South Carolina, as a base, the concept of poor black people singing European opera was ludicrous. Moreover, The efforts of original (black) cast members Todd Ducan, Anne Brown, Warren Coleman, and foot-tapping John Bubbles had, perhaps, been misused in a non-offensive manner. Not even the likes of real and (black) contemporary operatic vocalists such as Paul Robeson and Marion Anderson could have made it all any more real. Luckily, the excellent song ditties made a critical difference, with George Gershwin (who passed away in 1937) leaving behind, in true retrospective, his best work as a credited songwriter. While setting aside the boring operatic types, the contemporary (1930s) renderings of this Broadway entity had perhaps benefited most by the likes and voices of Bing Crosby, Billie Holiday, and Maxine Sullivan. Subsequent other versions of these songs followed in radio performances and recordings, especially noting Mabel Mercer (1942) and Ethel Waters (1947) recordings of "Summertime." The contemporary world (1959) found a film with the likes of Sidney Poitier, Dorothy Dandridge, Diahann Carroll, Pearl Bailey, and Sammy Davis Jr. in a soundtrack and film that could have and should have been better, considering all the "star" power. While it is only speculation, it still looks as if its European born director, Otto Preminger, was more intent upon honoring the Gershwins and Du Boise Heyward than creating something special. Perhaps this film adoption will be revisited again, with better results?

The idea of this RCA soundtrack was perhaps an excuse for a competitive one from the film, with Lena and the bright Harry Belafonte, then a major contemporary 1950s entity, indeed a major RCA Victor recording artist. (Moreover, this attempt at the "adult" LP market, noting the tremendous success already achieved by Belafonte, especially noting his Victor LP *Calypso*, on LPM 1248, did produce good results. Harry's subsequent vocals with Lena found her in good company. Perhaps they should have been in the contemporary 1959 film.)

- Picks that included Lena are as follows:

a. "I Wants to Stay Here." Lena "wants," but like all the rest of the stereotypes of speech, perhaps it just ain't right. (Latter-century "rap" artist could have a field day with these lyrics!)

b. "Bess, You Is My Woman." This duet is smooth enough. Harry sounds a lot like Nat King Cole(here), which perhaps betrays a pop singer. Perhaps his preparation with the famous Lena found Harry a bit buzzed? In any case, it all works well enough.
c. "It Ain't Necessarily So." Lena's update is also a winner.
d. "My Man's Gone Now."
e. "There's a Boat That's Leavin' Soon for New York." Unlike the rest of takeoff musical trends of the 1930s, this ditty finds the creative Lennie Hayton Orchestra providing some slick and jazzy backing. Lena's vocal is also on the mark, somewhat lifting Harry.
f. "Summertime." As perhaps, the most familiar of the lot, this well-crafted version rivals many.

- As time marched on, so did popular music. Like many of her contemporaries, Lena was largely left behind by the rock era despite some good recordings and (still) excellent nightclub appearances.

58-69. *The Lady and Her Music*, Quest 3597. As an LP, or a CD, this (later) Broadway entity works, even in old age! Lena scores, and she may also be described as true retrospective, in itself. While her 1940's voice is missing, spinning into the 1980s found Lena aging well, or "ageless." Lena also benefits as a (then) contemporary Quincy Jones product, with musical direction by Harold Wheeler, a sign of excellence in itself. As a visual as well, Lena's life experiences come alive with self-made historical dialog, which adds weight to this fine performance of a living legend.

- Picks. The whole concepts works, the following especially stand out:

a. "From This Moment On." This "moment" compliments Cole Porter.
b. "I Got a Name."
c. "I'm Glad There Is You."
d. "Cotton Club Revue." This includes

(1). "Copper Colored Gal." This ditty, penned by Benny Davis and J. Fred Coots, was originally featured in 1933s *Cotton Club Parade,* which featured Bill "Bo jangles" Robinson, Cab Calloway, Katherine Perry, Henry Wessels, the Berry Brothers and "fifty copper-colored gals." Was Lena one of the original "gals"? She may have been!
(2). "Raisin' The Rent."
(3). "As Long as I Live."
(4.) "Lady With a Fan."
(5). "Where or When"

e. "Yesterday When I Was Young."
f. "Life Goes On."
g. "A Lady Must Live."

70-72. *Cabin in the Sky*, CD Rhino R2 72245. This CD issue contains some fine material. Lena's best, from the historic film of the same-named 1943 film are as follows:

a. "Ain't It the Truth." Actually cut! What were they thinking? Moreover, this outtake is great and, more so, is the original performance! More in "Visual

Image" below. (Lena's official recording would later be part of her fine 1957 *Jamaica* soundtrack.)

b. "Life Is Full of Consequence." This duet with Eddie "Rochester" Anderson is fine.

c. "Honey in the Honeycomb."

➢ Visual Image.

- As already noted, the impact on twentieth-century entertainment that Lena Horne provided was a cultural event that sidelined much of her music. Luckily, and not so for most of her earlier influences and contemporaries, Lena is well captured in her youth on film. Later, her many television appearances also add relevance to her art. Musical highlights, as picks, are as follows:

73. "Just One of Those Things." Lena's hot version from *Panama Hattie*, 1942.
74. "Life Is Full of Consequences." Lena with Eddie Rochester Anderson in *Cabin in the Sky*.
75. "Ain't It the Truth." The "hot" shot of Lena in a bathtub was cut off from *Cabin in the Sky*. It was subsequently put into an MGM 1946 film short *Studio Visit*.
76. "The Lady Is a Tramp." The film *Words and Music* (1949) is highlighted by Lena's fab rendition, both seen and heard.
77. "Can't Help Lovin' That Man." Film *Till the Clouds Roll By*, 1946.
78. "Why Was I Born." Film *Till the Clouds Roll By*, 1946.

♦ "Stormy Weather,"1943. This Harold Arlen-penned ditty had been a standard since Ethel Waters at the Cotton Club in 1933. After the release of the 1933 Waters recording, the ditty became a "standard." Moreover, a film short had found Ivie Anderson introducing it in *A Bundle of Blues* with Duke Ellington. Subsequently, the full-length 1943 film of the same name found Lena's breathtaking version of

79. "Stormy Weather." Overshadowing all others, noting a lack of visual image, for Waters, and a short life of recognition for Anderson.
80. "Out of Nowhere." With Teddy Wilson and His Orchestra in *Boogie-Woogie Dream*. And her very best
81. "Unlucky Woman." This was featured in the 1941 film short *Boogie-Woogie Dream*. Backed by the excellent Teddy Wilson Orchestra, with backup by contemporary keyboard specialists Albert Ammons and Pete Johnson, Lena's visual image is indeed red hot! In great style, Lena belts out a slick and smooth blues entity and truly generates uncontrollable excitement that moreover remains whenever seen and heard! (This performance is truly amazing and rivals many (later) rock-era entities.)

Helen Humes

The swing era (of the mid-1930s through to 1942) may be considered the triumph of the bandleader over the identity of the vocalist. As the floors of ballrooms and dance halls of the entire nation were indeed engrossed by the swing era, most "divas," limited as canaries, became faceless and easy to replace. The durable vocals of Helen Humes may be considered pleasant, and her sweet vocals may be considered a melody to the ear, and less forgettable, and much like that of Ethel Waters. Moreover, she could identify with any type of material and perform it well. Helen (later) adapted well as a rhythm and blues entity and had a direct effect upon many, including the likes of Ruth Brown, Dakota Stanton, and Lavern Baker, all noted recording artists of the (later) 1950s. Picks include the following:

1. "Black Cat Blues," Okeh 8467. Along with Lonnie Johnson's guitar, this (self-penned ditty), like most "race" recordings of the latter 1920s, is campy and fun.
2. "If Papa Has Outside Lovin'," Okeh 8545. This tricky bit of nonsense ain't bad!
3. "Do What You Did Last Night," Okeh 8545. This ditty penned by Razaf and J. C. Johnson is fun and even rivals the contemporary Ethel Waters version, on Columbia 14380-D.
4. "Everybody Does It Now," Okeh 8529. Yes they do.
5. "Cross-Eyed Blues," Okeh 8825. A rural-sounding guitar blends in well with Helen's vocal of this crude but effective recording.
6. "Alligator Blues," Okeh 8529. Yes, it's an alligator!

Note: It would be about eleven years (between 1927 through 1938), before Helen would record again. After singing with local (Cincinnati) bands, she adapted her vocal style as a more sophisticated big band vocalist, who could sing "sweet" or "swing." Moreover, she thrust herself into the (white) band of Harry James and finally into the company of Count Basie, whose swing style generated even more heat.

7. "I Can Dream, Can't I," Brunswick 8038. Forget about the 1938 contemporary version, a Tommy Dorsey entity, with a stiff Jack Leonard vocal, on Victor 25741. Indeed, this Helen Humes vocal is perfect and makes the Harry James arrangement sparkle! (A later 1949 version by the Andrews Sisters, on Decca 24705, ain't bad.)
8. "It's the Dreamer in Me," Brunswick 8055. This fine sweet arrangement was a best-selling Harry James entity, penned by Jimmy Dorsey and James Van Heusen), graced further with Helen's very controlled vocal. Indeed, a far cry from the likes of Helen's earlier blues releases.
9. "Song of the Wanderer," Brunswick 8067. Helen (again) graces the band of Harry James.
10. "My Heart Belongs to Daddy," Decca 2249. The (contemporary) best seller, by Mary Martin, was penned by Cole Porter. This more-creative approach by Basie's arrangement and Helen's vocal is an interesting comparison.
11. "If I Could Be with You One Hour Tonight," Vocalion 4748. Helen's crisp vocal update of this 1920s classic is done well.
12. "And the Angels Sing," Vocalion 4784. This (1939) release with Count Basie at least matches the Martha Tilton vocal for Benny Goodman, on Victor 26170.
13. "If I Didn't Care," Vocalion 4784. Count Basie leaves Helen just enough time to "swing" along with this very hip and danceable entity. (While the contemporary Ink Spots version is miles away in style, as found on Decca 2286, it also may be noted for its lack of swing.)
14. "Sub Deb Blues." Vocalion 5010. This curious bit of swing features Helen in her (usual) high, little-girl type of vocal, indeed similar to that of contemporary Ella Fitzgerald. Penned by Skippy Martin, Al Sears, and George Mac Klinnon, this dance number perhaps had Helen adding or embellishing lyrics, among the slang, noting her

appreciation and admiration for Count Basie as well as for Vocalion Records (then part of American Records Corporation).

15. "Don't Worry 'bout Me," Conqueror 9214. This ditty, penned by Ted Koehler and Rube Bloom, finds itself very much energized by Helen's vocal, fueled by Basie's swing. From the "*Cotton Club Parade*, the World's Fair Edition," as stated on the original 1939 record label, this fine swing ditty was a fine musical keepsake from that New York City event. Moreover, in true retrospective, the performance still "swings." (A later version that also found the light of day was recorded by Frank Sinatra, with backing by Nelson Riddle, on Capital 2787—an interesting, different performance. Listen and compare!)
16. "Moonlight Seranade," Conqueror 9295. The huge instrumental hit by Glenn Miller and His Orchestra, on Bluebird 10214, is found to be fertile ground, noting the excellence of Count Basie. Penned by Mitchell Parish and Glenn Miller himself, it's a wonder that Miller had not pursued a vocal himself, although not having Helen to sing it was indeed a handicap.
17. "It's Square but It Rocks," Conqueror 9631. Swing or rock? Get it? Helen's vocal of this Carl Sigman and Freddie Slack penned ditty does not disappoint!
18. "Mound Bayou," Decca 8613. Helen left Basie, and by 1942, was freelancing with Pete Brown and His Band. This (urban) blues band is less of a "swing" and "dance" sound heard with Basie or at least not as high-powered as backing. Helen's vocal, however, adapts well, as a more polished embellishment of her original (1920s) blues style recalled for this ditty (penned by Leonard Feather and Andy Razaf) is effective.
19. "Unlucky Woman," Decca 8613. This flip side of "Mound Bayou" is more than good. This campy Leonard Feather's penned ditty is full-blown (urban) blues at its best with some vocal utterances, heard from Pete Brown's band, adding to the excitement of Helen's red-hot vocal. (Lena Horne's performace as seen and heard in 'Boogie Woogie Dream' is even more electric, although this author cannot find a contemporary recording by Lena).
20. "Gonna Buy Me a Telephone," Decca 8625. This bit of early rhythm and blues, penned by Williams, Sammy Price, and King, is a fast-paced performance, finding Helen's vocal and Pete Brown's band in perfect pacing tempo.
21. "Keep Your Mind on Me," Savoy 5514. This (great) rhythm and blues ditty, finds Helen Humes with Leonard Feather's Hiptet. Penned by Feather, it features a smoking and effective Humes vocal.
22. "He May Be Your Man," Philo 105. This updated and electric version of the early 1920s' classic, especially as by Edith Wilson on Columbia A 3653, may be considered a "classic" on solid ground as well as being much easier to hear.
23. "Blue Prelude," Philo 105. This (familiar) ditty from the 1930s had been a Bing Crosby success. Moreover, this ditty had been revived by many, including a smooth and contemporary Lena Horne version. Helen, as usual, finds her version very competitive, as this ditty, perhaps about a brooding suicide, is also done very well.
24. "Be-Baba-Leba," Philo 106. This bit of fast-paced rhythm and blues (with excellent backing by Bill Dogget's Octet and penned by Humes) was indeed explosive. In true retrospective, this style just had to have been an influence upon the young ears of Richard Penniman (or Little Richard) and Etta James, both of whom would popularize this vocal style in the 1950s as "rock and roll." Check it out!
25. "They Raided the Joint," Mercury 8056. Dan Burley's jumping bit of post WWII Chicago style rhythm and blues found Helen's easy transition from a jazz singer

perhsps brought her back to her earlier 1920s roots. More excellent postwar jump blues!

Alberta Hunter

- The raspy-voiced (Memphis born) Alberta Hunter was an early lounge (cabaret) singer, who got herself involved in black vaudeville as well. Like many contemporaries of color, including the likes of Mamie Smith, Edith Wilson, Eva Taylor, and Ethel Waters, the limits of racism had locked her out as a recording artist until the early 1920s. As an acoustic recording artist, subsequent recordings revealed a vocalist of versatility. Indeed, the early recordings of this blues queen sometimes reveal a jazzy style with a light vocal touch. It may also be observed, as well as heard, in an early (1930s) attempt at crooning, which was realized but, sadly, not pursued. Alas! The fate of the versatile performer!

  - The following picks are acoustic:

1. "How Long, Sweet Daddy, How Long," Black Swan 2008. This bit of novelty, penned by Jones and Taylor, like so many of the recordings of the 1921 era, is a bit bouncy and loose. Luckily, Alberta's vocal is solid. (A later version, as "How Long, How Long, Blues," featured a fine vocal by bluesman Leroy Carr, backed by Scrapper Blackwell on guitar and Leroy himself on a piano, generates more power on the electric recording, found on Vocalion 1191.)
2. "Someday, Sweetheart," Black Swan 2019. This classic ditty, penned by Spikes and Spikes, perhaps found itself defined by Alberta's fine raspy and sweet vocal. While Alberta would later (b.) rerecord it as an electric entity as well, some eighteen years later, on Decca 7727, this acoustic version is a foundation that nevertheless (still) generates a finer listening experience. Subsequent versions from the likes of Dolly Kay, and better-recorded electric renderings included an oddly just OK Ethel Waters version, a fine Gene Austin rendering, plus some excellent (later) crooning from Bing Crosby and Dick Todd.
3. "Don't Pan Me," Paramount 12001. This tired vaudevillian-styled vocal, penned by Gus Butler is at least backed by Eubie Blake's (piano) playing. While it's indeed Alberta's own vocal that provides this recording with a lift, a later (1931) Ethel Waters electric release as "Please Don't Talk About Me When I'm Gone," on Columbia 2409-D (credited to Sidney Clare, Sam Stept, and Bee Palmer) is better. (Who wrote this ditty?) Moreover, a (later 1939) rendering by Frankie "Half Pint" Jaxon, reverting back to Alberta's "Don't Pan Me" title, on Decca 7638, presents yet another interesting challenge in style—both vocal and backing.
4. "Down Hearted Blues," Paramount 12005. Alberta's efforts are backed by Eubie Blake's Orchestra, and Alberta indeed delivers a stylistic vocal to her self-penned classic. As a subsequent Bessie Smith version was released, on Columbia A 3844, the more-powerful Smith vocal style somewhat took away Alberta's original claims. While, indeed, the Bessie Smith version did define this ditty as a best seller, the contemporary differences between the smaller Paramount Record label and the established Columbia Records, for certain, gave Bessie the advantage.

5. "Jazzin' Baby Blues," Paramount 12006. This Alberta Hunter and Eubie Blake combination oddly contends with "Jazzing Babies Blues," a slightly earlier (1922) contemporary Ethel Waters release, on Black Swan 14117 (penned by Richard Jones).
6. "If You Want to Keep Your Daddy Home," Paramount 12016. Alberta is backed by the Original Memphis Five, an unusual racial mix (of a black vocalist and white band), in 1923. While not exploited, Alberta's vocal is fine and, indeed, generates much listening pleasure and interest.
7. "'T ain't Nobody's Bizness," Paramount 12016. The Original Memphis Five (again) backup on Alberta's jazzy vocal was hardly based on the older Bert Williams hit. Moreover, this ditty, penned by Porter Grainger and Everett Rickets, also associated with contemporaries like Edith Wilson, became a huge Bessie Smith classic as well as a standard for others, including, light-years away, for Billie Holiday.
8. "Loveless Love," Paramount 12019. This acoustic rendering of the (Handy) classic is well worth it! While a later electric version by Blanche Callaway is technically better, its subsequent renderings, as "Careless Love" by Lee Wiley and Ethel Waters, offer more challenges in style. Moreover, all are done well, with Alberta's own earlier acoustic version holding its own! Listen and learn!
8. "Bleeding Hearted Blues," Paramount 12021. Yes! Another classic, penned by Lovie Austin., a bit more "blue," and effectively backed by the all-white Original Memphis Five.

Note: The above-reviewed titles "'T ain't Nobody's Business" and "Bleeding Hearted Blues" would also be issued as a Mae Alix release, on Harmograph, with the Original Memphis Five.

It is, moreover, Alberta!

9. "Vamping Brown," Paramount 12020. Alberta (even) identifies herself as a brown-skinned woman from rural beginnings, penned by Lovie Austin-who was Paramount Records house pianist for its popular 'race' series. Moreover, this saloon-styled backing, perhaps by Fletcher Henderson, is indeed effective and contemporary for 1923.
10. "You Shall Reap Just What You Sow," Paramount 12021. This self-penned ditty is the gospel truth, and this spiritual remains an inspiration. (This side features Henderson's Novelty Orchestra, a fine Fletcher Henderson studio band.)
11. "Chirpin the Blues," Paramount 12017. Another self-penned ditty with Lovie Austin that made a lot of noise as well as heat. While a subsequent rerecording by Alberta in the electric age, on (b) Decca 7644, is indeed masterful, this original acoustic rendering defined it.
12. "Someone Else Will Take Your Place," Paramount 12017. Another tough song ditty with its own title explaining everything!

    - The following five acoustic recordings were released as "Red Onion Jazz Babies," with "Josephine Beatty," aka Alberta Hunter, as vocalist. (The band itself included Louis Armstrong, Lil Armstrong, Charlie Irvis, Sidney Bechet, and Buddy Christian.) These superb recordings defy the rules for most acoustic recordings, as Alberta's slick jazzy vocals burn the ear with fire, especially on "Nobody Known the Way I Feel Dis Morning." These "Gennett" recordings may also be considered the very best of Albertra's numerous acoustic recordings and, in true retrospective, define her a real jazz entity of the era.

13. "Everybody Loves My Baby," Gennett 5594. Alberta is given some fine and jazzy leads, and, moreover, her vocal of this classic fits. Eva Taylor would also do this ditty justice, as a contemporary release on Okeh 8181 with the Clarence Williams Blue Five, essentially the same studio band as the Red Onion Jazz Babies. A later electric rendering, by the Boswell Sisters, would redefine it.
14. "Texas Moaner Blues," Gennett 5594. Yup, she moans well enough. Perhaps it's Alberta's own, already familiar raspy vocal that finds this ditty, penned by Fae Barnes and Clarence Williams, so effectively.
15. "Cake Walking Babies," Gennett 5617. This ditty gives Alberta very little room as a vocalist, as the hot band and a duetting Clarence Todd drive this (Spencer Williams) classic with great vigor. Moreover, Alberta's slickness is skillful enough, with a bit of contemporary (black slang) adding much to the mix. (This ditty, penned by Clarence Williams, Chris Smith, and Henry Troy, was rerecorded within a year by the Clarence Williams Blue Five (also including Louis Armstrong, and Sidney Bechet, Clarence Williams, and vocalist, Eva Taylor) on Okeh 40321.
16. "Nobody Knows the Way I Feel Dis Morning," Gennett 5626. This truly awesome vocal is indeed a classic, penned by Tom Delany. Moreover, a contemporary Margret Johnson version, on Okeh 8162, is at least on par with Alberta's vocal.
17. "Early Every Mornin'," Gennett 5626. Alberta at least matches the earlier Virginia Liston version (Okeh 8187), penned by W. Benton Overstreet and Billy Higgins.
18. "Your Jelly Roll Is Good," Okeh 8268. This 1925's ditty has Perry Bradford's Mean Four backing Alberta up. Furthermore, the term "jelly roll," an obvious pun, is devilishly defined by Alberta's own enthusiasm.
17. "Old Fashioned Love," Paramount 12093. This title was indeed old-fashioned and dated for (even) 1924! Backed by the Elkins-Payne Jubilee Quartet, Alberta's fine and traditional vocal, more so, leads this sentimental schmaltz from (*Running Wild* starring Miller and Lyles) into something (still) worth hearing—as it's all real enough. (Contemporary Adelaide Hall had introduced this ditty on stage, but had not produced a contemporary recording.) Penned by Cecil Mack and James P. Johnson, a horrid Noble Sissle vocal, with (partner) Eubie Blake on piano (Victor 19253), it almost ruined it for others. In addition to Alberta's better recording (to listen to), contemporary Eva Taylor also laid better vocal claims to this ditty (Okeh 8114). Nevertheless, it was Frank Crumit's well-done rendering (Columbia-A3933) that became the better-known contemporary best seller. A later (electric) recording by Lena Horne, on Black & White 816, would define it. (Light-years later, Alberta would rerecord this ditty—later in review.)

- The following are 5 titles are (electric) Victor masters from the mid-1920s:

18. "I'll Forgive You Because I Love You," Victor 20497. This bit of blues is direct and, moreover, a tough and potent vocal.
19. "I'm Gonna Lose Myself Way Down in Louisville," Victor 20497. This very crude and rural-sounding rendering, while far from a jazzy outing, is, nevertheless, an effective tale by Alberta herself? Standing in the rain? Waiting for a train? Louisville, Kentucky? Is this "Vamping Brown" again?
20. "My Daddy's Got a New Brand New Way to Love," Victor 20651. As a typical 1927 race release, this ditty indeed skips around the country—Georgia, Maine, San Francisco, Alabama, London Bridge, or at least fragments of these places are noted by Alberta in this fine blues entity. (A fine variation of the ditty is found in a (later) 1928

Ethel Waters release, "My Baby Sure Knows How to Love," as another race release, on Columbia 14411 D.)

21. "Beale Street Blues," Victor 20771. This W. C. Handy classic had found its way to Broadway back in 1918 and was introduced by (white) vaudevillian Gilda Gray with a fine recording by Marion Harris in 1921. A subsequent acoustic version by (black) performer Esther Bigeou was also done well. Alberta perhaps found this more than interesting recording fodder as she was born in the area, before moving to Chicago. Her own subsequent electric recording, more so, found this ditty identifying with Fats Waller in the midst of his prolonged intro on pipe organ. Luckily, Alberta's vocal is on the mark and, indeed, worth the wait. A still later (1941) version by Lena Horne, more so, defined it. Listen to all!
22. "I'm Gonna See My Ma," Victor 21539. This crude ditty penned by Clarence Todd, is another tale about a train ride, this time to Omaha, Nebraska. "Ma" and "Pa" seem to rime with "Omaha"—well enough.
23. "Gimme All the Love You Got," Columbia 14450-D. Yes!

The 20s & 30s found Alberta touring and ending up on the English stage production of *The Show Boat*. While this notable event was not to appear in a filmed version, the noted Helen Morgan vehicle (a white diva of Canadian origin), about a personage of mixed race, was also to be passed over for its classic songs "Can't Help Lovin' Dat Man" and "Bill." The versatility of Alberta's vocals, however, provided her an opportunity to record for HMV, a British recording entity related to Victor.

The following HMV masters reveal a surprising and different vocalist. While Alberta had earlier demonstrated a softness in some of her earlier jazz vocals, the following, with Jack Jackson's Orchestra, from the Dorchester Hotel, indeed find the raspy-voiced Alberta adapting oddly and successfully into a sweet-voiced popular singer. Somehow, Alberta's loud (natural) voice succeeds in this attempt to "croon," and not in the crude original sense of the term. These recordings also left a lasting impression upon the contemporary 1934 (British) public, who were much impressed.

- Alberta's British releases are, moreover, a different product, and reveal a vocalist somehow "hidden." Perhaps Alberta's accent upon the likes of lyrics are suspect, but that makes it all the more interesting to hear, and investigate. The following are HMV master picks, noting the few (Victor) releases that were (also) released in the United States.

27. "Two Cigarettes in the Dark," HMV 6525. The contemporary Bing Crosby release, on Decca 245, is much better known. While its stupid lyrics are indeed novel, Crosby somehow succeeded to remain somber and made his version interesting, without breaking up. Alberta is also effective, benefiting from a different arrangement, and, more so, danceable.
28. "Miss Otis Regrets," HMV 6525. This ditty had originally been introduced on the London stage in *Hi Diddle Diddle*, as penned by Cole Porter. Led by Jack Jackson's cheerful and typical dance band arrangement, Alberta identifies herself as a maid, with a (male) vocal of perhaps an unknown band member. It is indeed a pun and a poke at British humor as this tale about the hanging of a scorned woman is oddly uplifted. (The contemporary (stateside) Ethel Waters release, on Decca 140, totally redefines this ditty as a more poignant type of pun—with a tongue-in-check vocal,

with a serious sense of drama. It is, moreover, an interesting comparison with Alberta's version as well as a totally differing tale.)

29. "When the Mountains Meet the Sea," HMV 6929.
30. "Soon," HMV 6530 This very fine sweet dance band number, penned by Frances Scottie Fitzgerald and Eddie Lisbona, should not be confused with a contemporary 1935 Bing Crosby title by the same name (penned by Rodgers and Hart and released on Decca 392). As Crosby's better-known title is crooned out well, the soft vocal tone achieved by Alberta's crooning is just as impressive as anything Bing ever did. Listen and compare!
31. "I Travel Alone," HMV 6535. Also issued on Victor 24835 in the States, this high-brow Noel Coward penned ditty is more ever crooned out to perfection in King's English style!
32. "A Lonely Singing Fool," HMV 6536.
33. "Stars Fell on Alabama," HMV 6542. Penned by Mitchell Parish and Frank Perkins, this soft piece of pop became a standard in the States as a Guy Lombardo release, on Decca 104, with a vocal by Carmen Lombadro, as well as a Richard Himber Orchestra release, on Victor 24745, with a vocal by Joey Nash. While it's obvious that Alberta's (British) version is better, it's also a sad commentary that most of her contemporaries did not know what they were missing.
34. "Long May We Love," HMV 6542.
35. "Two Flies on a Lump of Sugar," HMV 6541. Alberta's vocal is again on target, as the ditty penned by Irving Kahal and Sammy Frain also provides her a bit more opportunity to be "blue" despite the "pop" orchestration. Moreover, this near-miss somehow works.
36. "Be Still My Heart," HMV 6546. The contemporary Freddy Martin Orchestra release, penned by Jack Egan and Allan Flynn, (vocal by Elmer Feldkamp, on Brunswick 6998) is bettered. Moreover, the amazing vocal prowess as demonstrated by Alberta is again fun, noting lyrics just leaping out of her vocal cords that indicate English as English.

- The following find Alberta back in the United States and, more so, regulated back as a blues entity. Being a 'blues' entity is nt a bad thing, but being restricted from recording other types of recording fodder, in Alberta's case, just did not make any sense. While perhaps a creative step back, she did remain a fine blues entity, as the following releases indicate.

37. "You Can't Tell the Difference After Dark." This American Record Company recording found Alberta back in the United States, full of those down and dirty blues. While this pick breaks some rules of this book, this un-issued and bootlegged rendering cannot be dismissed! As noted in its title, this tale about a woman of color, noting a change after dark, is bluesy and nasty as ever and may indeed have been recorded to originally become an under-the-counter novel entity. Moreover, it sounds like Alberta's English experience did not faze her, as she sounds wild as ever!
38. "I'll See You Go," Decca 7644. This 1939 rendering is an awesome vocal, with some fine jazzy backings by the likes of Charlie Shavers, Buster Bailey, Lil Armstrong, and Wellman Braud.
39. "Yelpin' the Blues," Decca 7633. This very crude vocal is accompanied by some fine and jazzy accompaniment. Moreover, Alberta's blues are still tough enough, as her old acoustic style provides sparks on this 1939 electric recording.

40. "Someday Sweetheart," Decca 7727. This 1939 electric rerecording of her 1921 classic ain't bad.
41. "The Love I Have for You," Bluebird B-8539. On this self-penned ditty, Alberta croons out a soulful lament. Accompanied by pianist Eddie Heywood, this attempt at a cooler and jazzy style works. While much louder vocally than her English HMV renderings, this masterpiece again demonstrates versatility.
42. "My Castle's Rockin'," Bluebird B-8539. Alberta's rocking! Moreover, the piano backing by Eddie Heywood effectively leads Alberta into some fine slang that may be easily understood by her vocal.
43. "Boogie-Woogie Swing," Bluebird B-8485. Just how can Alberta, with only Eddie Heywood on piano, create a fine, danceable "boogie-swing" ditty? Contrived? Good-yes! More so, she even identifies Eddie by name, which must have pleased Eddie, on this 1940 classic.
44. "I Won't Let You Down," Bluebird B-8485. Alberta's blues are very much felt and again recalls her older acoustic vocal—loudly and effectively.
45. "Take Your Big Hands off It," Juke Box 510. This 1940's rendering, again "sounds" like a 1920s' entity. More so, as the title suggests, the suggestive Alberta's vocal smokes!
46. "He's Got a Punch Like Joe Lewis," Juke Box 510. This excuse for a Joe Louis tribute, the hero and (still) cultural icon of the era, is, moreover, full of wicked lyrics, indeed crudely and effectively vocalized by Alberta.

Alberta's long recording career, launched her into an excuse for "rhythm and blues" in 1950 through to (light-years away) 1980. While racism had figured into it all, so did Alberta's age. The following recordings, more so, reveal Alberta's vocals as durable and effective.

47. "I Got a Mind to Ramble," Regal 3252. This post-WWII ditty competes!

- The following (1980) LP release was a surprise, as well as a well-crafted product that found amazing sales! What a rediscovery!

48-56. *Amtrack Blues*, Columbia 36430. This LP concept (and eventual) CD is a another fine example of a recording project that is planned well and eventually works out well. Seemingly, a fine triumph for (aged) Columbia producer John Hammond as well (who had found Billie Holiday in the 1930s), Alberta had (again) been rediscovered as a plus-eighty-year-old vocalist! The following are fine picks, that indeed have been discovered by many grown-up baby boomers. The following are Alberta Hunter picks arefrom this well-done concept LP:

a. "The Darktown Strutters Ball." How can this pre-1920 entity sound great? The pop quality of Alberta is evident, and jazz is all digested very well.
b. "Nobody Knows You When You're Down and Out." How can Alberta compete with 1920's contemporary Bessie Smith, found on Columbia 14451-D? Just listen!
c. "I'm Having a Good Time."
d. "Always." This Irving Berlin-penned ditty had been crooned out well by Nick Lucas in 1926.
e. "My Handy Man Ain't Handy No More." This update of the 1920s classic is actually "My Handy Man," the Ethel Waters classic. (The real "My Handy Man

Ain't handy No More" was a different entity, recorded by Edith Wilson on Victor 38624.)

f. "Amtrack Blues." Great blues!
g. "Old Fashioned Love." A fine rerecording of Alberta's own Paramount acoustic rendering.
h. "Sweet Georgia Brown." This update of the Ethel Waters classic vocal of 1925, on Columbia 379-D, is good enough.

- "A Good Man Is Hard to Find." (Yes! This old ditty needed updating again! Indeed, both Marion Harris and Bessie Smith had got it right, and Alberta also does—some sixty years later!

   ➢ Visual Image.

A British film, *Radio Parade of 1935*, featured Alberta in a fine production number

57. "Blue Shadows."

The Ink Spots

The success of the Mills Brothers in the early 1930s led to the indirect development of rhythm and blues and, later, rock and roll itself. Among hundreds of would-be Mills Brothers were the "Ink Spots." Using tenor vocal leads were the merits of members Bill Kenny, Orville "Hoppy" Jones," Charlie Fuqua, and Ivory "Deek" Watson. (Jones was later replaced by Herb Kenny and Watson was later replaced by Billy Bowen). Was lead vocalist Bill Kenny an inspiration for Elvis Presley's "That's When Your Heartaches Begin?" Or was indeed Kenny (r and b entity) Jerry Butler's original idol? Was Charlie Fuqua a real "Ink Spot" or a "Moonglow," of the group "Moonglows"? This very influential vocal group, more so, recorded many standards, and if they were not always hipper versions, they were sung better, and even redefined as "group "entities. Or maybe a high tenor lead with vocal harmony was needed for popular songs in the latter 1930s? While the rhythm ditties were indeed done well, their slow ballads, especially when played on jukeboxes, seemed to define "home front" of WW II when played! Indeed, their successful efforts would be much initiated and emulated and, moreover, inspire much of the post-WWII "group" vocal boom of (later) 1950s rock and roll.

The following are Ink Spots picks:

1. "If I Didn't Care," Decca 2286. This (perhaps) clumsy Jack Lawrence-penned ditty became a best-selling entity of 1939, despite swing. Light-years away, this bit of nostalgia also found its place in the rock era as a fine (emulating) release by the Platters, on Mercury 71749.
2. "Knock Kneed Sal," Decca 2286. This clever novelty wins despite its sad message (penned by Zilner Randolph) about a "Mourner's Bench."
3. "Address Unknown," Decca 2707. A contemporary (1939) release, penned by Carmen Lombardo, Dedette Lee Hill, and Johnny Marks.

4. "My Prayer," Decca 2790. Some early followers of the rock era indeed found this ditty, penned by Jimmy Kennedy and Georges Boulanger, a redefined classic as recorded by the Platters, on Mercury 70893.
5. "Whispering Grass," Decca 3258. The slowness ain't bad in this ditty penned by Fred and Doris Fisher.
6. "Maybe," Decca 3258. Not to be confused with a previous Gershwin Brothers-penned ditty, this ditty (penned by Allan Flynn and Frank Madden), as the original flip side of "Whispering Grass," became a double hit and became even better known as a contemporary (1940) best-selling entity.
7. "Stop Pretending," Decca 3288. This upbeat ditty is less formal than swing; this Buddy Johnson-penned ditty is danceable.
8. "We'll Meet Again," Decca 3656. Unlike contemporaries Ginny Simms and Harry Babbit, on a Kay Kyser release on Columbia 35870, or a Peggy Lee vocal, as a Benny Goodman release, on Okeh 6644, this group vocal considers more voice. More so and advantage.
9. "We Three—My Echo, My Shadow, and Me," Decca 3379. This title may sound novel as this classic, penned by Dick Robertson, Nelson Cogane, and Sammy Mysels, benefits most by its group harmony.

(The above two ditties were particular favorites of the author's late mother, as by Vera Lynn and Ann Shelton, along with the Ink Spots versions.)

10. "Jave Jive," Decca 3432. This bit of rhythmic vocalizing, penned by Ben Oakland and Milton Drake, is uplifting and campy. Moreover, it `just could have been a major influence upon other contemporary groups, especially that of the Nat Cole Trio.
11. "Do I Worry," Decca 3432. This (1941) entity, penned by Stanley Cowan and Bobby Worth, became a best seller.
12. "That's When Your Heartaches Begin," Decca 3720. This classic bit of sentimental mush has became a (later) remained a rock-era entity. Penned by Fred Fisher, William Raskin, and Billy Hill, this exhausting bit of vocal edginess would later be somewhat emulated by Elvis himself (Victor 20 6870).
13. "Keep Cool, Fool," Decca 3958. This (usual) novelty is fun and un-swinging, while a contemporary Les Brown release, with a fine vocal by Doris Day (Okeh 6167), indeed does "swing!" Which is better? Or, which style does one feel like listening for? Are lyrics meant to be bent and vocally challenged?
14. "I Don't Want to Set the World on Fire," Decca 3987. Somehow, this ditty's boring lyrics, penned by Horace Heidt, Eddie Seiler, and Sol Marcus, work!
15. "Nothin, '" Decca 4045. This ditty rather "jumps" than "swings." As usual, the vocals offered are found to be in perfect harmony, as this fine novelty, penned by Hal Borne, Sid Kuller, and Ray Golden, is, indeed, good listening fun.
16. "Foo-Gee," Decca 4303. Penned by Erskine Butterfield, this bit of (early) 1940s' jive indeed refines slang.
17. "Don't Get Around Much Anymore," Decca 18503. The blues classic, penned by Duke Ellington and Bob Russell, finds a "group" sound!
18. "Cow Cow Boogie," Decca 18587. Ella Fitzgerald joins in the fun, adding even more voice! Moreover, this novelty, penned by Don Raye, Gene De Paul, and Benny Carter notes an interracial offspring and may be considered serious. (Ella Mae Morse, a contemporary white vocalist, also recorded a fine, but also exciting version.)

19. "Into Each Life Some Rain Must Fall," Decca 23356. Ella again provides some mellowness, although this ditty, penned by Allan Roberts and Doris Fisher, is far less entertaining and dated than "Cow Cow Boogie."
20. "I'm Beginning to See the Light," Decca 23399. Duke Ellington's contemporary (1945) band singer, Joya Sherrill, introduced this ditty, indeed showing off a mellow tone (Victor 20-1618). There is also a (like) Kitty Kallen vocal with a Harry James release (Columbia 36786). Contemporary comparisons, moreover, found the likes of Joya, Kitty, and Ella all well liked enough to become best-selling entities. This ditty, moreover, found Ella's own vocal perhaps a bit more familiar? Or perhaps the group vocal from the Ink Spots contributes a bit more to balance vocally this ditty, penned by Harry James, Duke Ellington, and Johnny Hodges, and Don George. A sleep-inducing ditty?
21. "That's the Way It Is," Decca 23399. How can Ella and the Ink Spots make it boring but still be interesting? Please listen to this ditty, penned by Alec C. Kramer, Mary Bourke, and Joan Whitney and find out!
22. "The Gypsy," Decca 18817. This much-recorded (Billy Reid-penned) ditty is most defined by this moody "group" sound.
23. "Prisoner of Love," Decca 18864. This ditty had found itself a major Russ Columbo classic, as on Victor 22867 in 1931. As a 1946 release, this version was perhaps a response to a contemporary Perry Como version, who indeed emulates the Columbo version. More so for another contemporary version as by Billy Eckstine, a deeper baritone. While it's all a bit confusing, making room for a (later) rock-era version by James Brown, this "group" effort is pleasant enough.
24. "I Cover the Waterfront," Decca 18864. The practice of covering pop standards may be a hard question for originality. This group sound, moreover, only challenges the previous versions, which is what creativity is all about. While the likes of such excellent previous renderings of this (Johnny Green and Ed Heyman) classic perhaps found both Connie Boswell (in 1933) and Billie Holiday's more contemporary (1944) version in fine form and updating this ditty, indeed finding its title and lyrics easily relating to the (then) WWII era. Like all the others, the Ink Spots' "group" effort differs and contributes to more listening pleasure and comparisons. (Oddly, just like "To Each it's Own," this film title was either cut, or not used in the actual film when released.)
25. "To Each His Own," Decca 23615. The (1946) film of the same name found this ditty, penned by Jay Livingston and Ray Evans, somehow left out. When compared to other contemporary versions, the group concept, when compared to a Tony Martin effort, along with an ever blander effort as by (singing-bandleader) Eddie Howard (again) saves a stiff song, at least in true retrospective!

Burl Ives

- Burl Ives was a bit of a "folksy" balladeer. While not exactly from the Bible belt of the South, his (Southern) Illinois upbringing from Jasper County was founded upon the hard work of farming and original American folk ballads. While it may be true that many of these ballads had origins from Europe, they were far from opera and, indeed, from the real folk of England, Scotland, Wales, and Ireland. Burl's simple vocal style just may be that of a baritone and with a light touch of crooning—much like that of the very pop renderings of Bing Crosby, but without Crosby's popular aspirations. Indeed, most of Burl's recordings are backed by vocal and his own guitar.

- Burl had started (professionally) as a vocalist with the likes of the somewhat "rebel" leanings of the Almanac Singers, in the late 1930s. While hardly an antiwar or union entity or a (real) communist, like his contemporary (1940s) friend Woody Guthrie, Burl did appreciate the absolute right (American) to protest anything. His subsequent solo recording are, moreover, rural, or even country, with less of a Southern accent. His many recordings, more so, consist of his simple protests of the poor, appreciations of religion, and his disdain for the powerful (indeed an icon for the later folk movement of the early 1960s).

    - The following are picks:

1. "Poor Wayfaring Stranger." This side is perhaps the religious (Methodist) ballad about a traveler traveling out of this world—to mother and God.
2. "Buck-eyed Jim," Ash 345-1A. This second ditty about Buck-eyed Jim seemingly finds him in demand! He also lies among blue jays and red birds. An old woman, who dies of a whoopin' cough, is also noted.
3. "The Bold Soldier." This side had English origins but with an American twist. While it seems that a young girl yearns to marry a soldier, her father has other concerns, about a dowry. Luckily, everything turns out.
4. "The Sow Took the Measles," Ash 345-1B. This second ditty is based upon the English ditty "The Red Herring." While this sow did die, it seems that its various parts, which included its nose, hide, tail, and feet, among others, were to be used to make clothes and even pickled feet. How crude! How real!
5. "The Foggy, Foggy Dew," Ash 345-2A. This traditional ballad from the British isles had perhaps been known by the Scotsman Robert Burns. While this tale is about a young maiden whose life is cut short from the winter's cold and fog, it's a good bet that it's from childbirth.
6. "Black Is the Color," Ash 345-2B. This Elizabethan-age tale about a young maiden with black hair is sincere enough.
7. "The Blue-Tail Fly," Ash 345-3A. Also known as "Jimmie Crack Corn," this very odd tale seemingly has origins of Afro-Americans and pre-Civil War slavery. It seems that this slave master takes a tumble off his horse, after the horse itself was bitten by a small blue-tail fly. Moreover, the master dies, with a humorous gravestone epitaph as a victim of a blue-tail fly. Justice for the slave?
8. "Henry Martyn," Ash 345-3B. This tale found three Scottish brothers casting lots on who should stay home and who should go abroad to be a pirate. Henry's subsequent trip in his (pirate) ship is a success in rampage and killing. What a guy!
9. "Lavender Blue Dilly Dilly," Decca 24547. This (Scottish) folk entity finds a young maiden in "lavender blue" waiting for her betrothed. It was, more so, featured in the 1949 Walt Disney film entity *So Dear to My Heart.* (A contemporary 1949 version by Dinah Shore, on Columbia 38299, is also done well.)
10. "Riders in the Sky," Columbia 38445. (Ghost) Riders in the sky. As penned by Stan Jones, this contrived bit of 'western' myth sort of became relivant, especialy when Burl tells it !
11. "On Top of Old Smoky," Columbia 39328. Another ditty of Scottish origins comes out of the mountains! (A subsequent later rendering, by the Weavers, who included a few of the (former) Almanac Singers (Decca 27515), would also become a popular best seller.)
12. "A Little Bitty Tear," Decca 31330. This light country ditty, penned by Hank Cochran is like enough. It fit in well with the contemporary (1961) folk revival. (A contemporary Wanda Jackson release, on Capital 4681, is also smooth.)

13. "Pearly Shells," Decca 31659. This updated original Hawaiian folk ditty, penned by Leon Pober and Webley Edwards is done well.
14. "A Holly Jolly Christmas," Decca 31695. In true retrospective, the perennial character of a snowman remained with baby boomers, as well as subsequent generations! A true friend of "Rudolph the Red Nosed Reindeer"-the TV kiddie program? For the young, this Johnny Marks penned ditty remains jolly enough!

➢ Visual Image.

This folk balladeer was also a fine actor. Burl had, moreover, appeared on Broadway in many roles, especially in the first run of the quality (Rodgers and Hart) 1938 musical production of *The Boys From Syracuse.* Burl was not limited to musicals, however, as his fine acting in the nonmusical (1958) *Cat on a Hot Tin Roof* indicates. Moreover, Burl, for most baby boomers, remained best known as a caricature, as a singing snowman.

Mahalia Jackson

The emergence of Mahalia Jackson, a singer of spirituals in the latter 1930s, found this young vocalist in a crowded field with little financial rewards. Indeed, this secular music was considered "square," and limited in marketability. As an Afro-American, the likes of the Fisk University Quartet, the Dinwiddie Colored Quartet, Washington Phillips, Homer A. Rodeheaver, "Blind" Willie and Angeline Johnson (his wife), J. C. Burnett, D. C. Rice, Arizona Dranes, the Biddleville Quintette, Bryants Jubilee Quartet, the Pilgrim Jubilee Singers, Silver Leaf Quartet, Dunham Jubilee Singers, Clara Ward, and, especially, Rosetta Tharpe, were indeed inspiring for her. Her secular world, found in the (Baptist) world of Chicago ministry, like so many others scattered about the country, was the principal center of the community, indeed the heart and soul of most contemporary Afro-American culture. The likes of all popular black successes were rooted and founded here. Alberta Hunter, Paul Robeson, Marion Anderson, Ethel Waters, and, especially bluesman, Tom Dorsey, who was perhaps best associated with Ma Rainey, all openly owed much to the music of the secular. In time, the return of Tom Dorsey to the Church, in 1932, would do much for the term "gospel music." Indeed, his own self-penned "Peace in the Valley" would become emulated by many, including the likes of (white) hillbilly acts as well. Moreover, the huge commercial success of Sister Rosetta Tharpe, basically a "rocking" idiom from the (black) Church itself, starting in the mid-1930s, had been something for the young Mahalia Jackson to directly emulate as well as to follow.

The emergence of Mahalia, when she found fame and recognition in the latter 1940s after a ten-year struggle, impacted upon popular culture as never before. While the post-WWII boom had much to do with the change, the aspects of body language, not visible on record, may be for certain found in churches, with hand clapping and Mahalia in lead vocal. Mahalia's own contemporaries, including the likes of Dinah Washington, Ruth Brown, and Ray Charles, would, like others before them, successfully integrate rhythm and blues with pop. Mahalia, however, stayed in the church and, in true retrospective, with record sales to verify, became identified as a "gospel" singer as well as with a vocal style that inspired the emergence of rock and roll.

1. "God's Gonna Separate the Wheat from the Tares," Decca 7341. This 1937 Decca master ain't bad, although it only reached the secular.
2. "Move on up a Little Higher," Apollo 164. This 1948 best seller (penned by W. Herbert Brewster and V. Davis) sold a million copies for the small label "Apollo."
3. "Get Away, Jordan," Apollo 240.
4. "The Lord's Prayer," Apollo 245. Sarah Vaughan also recorded a version of this tradition prayer.
5. "His Eye Is on the Sparrow," Apollo 246. Ethel Waters became associated with this (traditional) classic based upon the Gospel of Matthew, penned into song by Civilla D. Martin and Charles H, Gabriel, but this recording precedes it. Earlier renderings included a version by the Pace Jubilee Singers, on Brunswick 7008, which, perhaps, influenced Mahalia.
6. "It Is No Secret (What God Can Do)," Apollo 246. This classic ditty had been released by Stuart Hamblen, on Columbia 20724, who also penned it. While it's just very possible that a young Elvis Presley had heard Hamblen's version first, the later Presley version is most likely inspired by Mahalia's version, as it was widely believed that Elvis's mother, Gladys, collected Mahalia's recordings.
7. "Just as I Am," Apollo 248.
8. "In the Upper Room" (Parts one and two), Apollo 262.
9. "You Just Keep Still," Apollo 304.
10. "Walk Over God's Heaven," Columbia 40412. The move to Columbia Records aroused some to argue that Mahalia had lost some of her wildness and spirit. In reality, however, Mahalia clearly opened up to different musical approaches. This pleasant "rocker" moreover, retains the familiar Apollo style.
11. "Jesus Met the Woman at the Well," Columbia 40412. The gospel story is (again) wailed out, and Mahalia's vocal makes you want to hear more about it.
12. "A Satisfied Mind," Columbia 40554. This rare attempt at 1950s pop, in a religious vein, penned by Joe Hayes and Jack Rhodes is crafted well.
13. "Come Sunday," Columbia LP 1162. As a Duke Ellington's "concept" LP project, this obvious religious theme was perfect for Mahalia. The Duke had originally written this piece for a concert in 1943, and finally became realized in the mid-1950s. The original notes of this LP indeed indicate that Ellington asked Mahalia for her vocal as part of his "Black, Brown, and Beige" theme. All through her career, Mahalia had been asked to sing blues and jazz, and this stroke of typical Ellington genius links them all. Mahalia's vocal also adds the Twenty-Third psalm, and along with Ellington's full orchestra, this recording finds her vocal more than able. Indeed, her typical "gospel wailing" is replaced by a gentle and soft approach that is, indeed, jazzy. While speculation may always be suspect, the proof of a fine jazz entity is found in this recording and, in true retrospective, is not followed up.
14. "He's Got the Whole World in His Hands," Columbia 41150. Adapted by Geoff Love as a penned entity, this 1958 recording finds Mahalia wailing the "hell" out of it. A pop version, by Laurie London, on Capital 3891, ain't bad. (The election of John F. Kennedy in 1960 found many using this song ditty as a presidential theme.)
15. "Dig a Little Deeper," Grand Award 1025.

Papa Charlie Jackson

As a male vocalist, writer, and musician, this Paramount label entity is among the earliest of Afro-American influences and forces to shape the future of the twentieth century. With the likes of "Blind" Lemon Jefferson and "Blind" Blake on Paramount, Jackson's recordings find a place and time to introduce "rural blues," as an art form. The following are picks:

1. "Papa's Lawdy Lawdy Blues," Paramount 12219. This 1924 acoustic release identifies a crude banjo-playing vocalist. As also known as "Original Lawdy Lawdy Blues," this bit of slang, perhaps, also identifies a rich part of language, claimed by "Papa" Charlie himself. More ever, an earlier Paramount stable mat, blues queen Ida Cox, had previously claimed "Ida Cox's Lawdy Blues," on Paramount 12064, as hers.
2. "Airy Man Blues," Paramount 12219. This "man" entity is not by a blues queen and is, indeed, about a man. Just listen!

3, 4. "Salty Dog Blues," Paramount 12236. This bit of slang ain't bad. While this classic ditty itself does not imply a shared culture, within a few years, it would. Moreover, a later (1926) Freddie Keppard's Jazz Cardinals release, on Paramount 12399, also featured Charlie Jackson in a more sophisticated setting (b). This version identifies the usually rural Charlie Jackson as a bit of a jazz singer, as well as gives him identification as "Papa Charlie" by an unknown member of Keppard's jazzy orchestra. Indeed, Clara Smith's version (Columbia 14142-D) may have been recorded as a result of Papa Charlie's renderings. Subsequent versions found hillbilly recordings (although most likely *not*, in this case), prodded by Jackson's or Clara's success. They would include the likes of recordings as by the Allen Brothers (Austin and Lee) as "Salty Dog" (Columbia 15175-D), as "Laughin' and Crying Blues" (Columbia 14266 D), and into the 1930s as "New Salty Dog" (Victor 23514). Jimmie Davis's (1932) recording as "Davis' Salty Dog," on Victor 23674, put claims on this shared folk entity. (The post-WWII version by Papa Charlie Jackson's (1920s) contemporary blues entity Lizzie Miles (Capital 2341) is a successful attempt to reclaim it as a "blues" entity, although Lizzie (from New Orleans), may have been just as familiar with this ditty before Jackson's original (1924) recording or Clara Smith's later (1926) release.)

5. "Shave 'Em Dry," Paramount 12264. It ain't Ma Rainey (Paramount 12222), but it's still very fine.
6. "Shake That Thing," Paramount 12281. This original release of the blues classic is rural and gritty enough. So indeed was a better-known contemporary 1925 Ethel Waters release, on Columbia 14116-D, who, along with physical bumps and grinds, incorporated this ditty into her (risqué) personal appearances. (A later, post-WWII version, by Wynonie Harris, on King 4716, was to be a noted rhythm and blues entity, indeed to become a huge influence upon the up-and-coming rock era.)
7. "Mama Don't Allow It," Paramount 12296. As "Mama Don' Allow It (and She Ain't Gonna Have It Here)," this ditty is indeed a basic ingredient for the shared slang and culture of rural folk. (A cruder vocal yet more sophisticated dance recording with better electric sound found in a later (1933) rendering by Frankie "Half Pint" Jaxon (Vocalion 2603) is well worth noting and comparing. More so is a (1935?) hillbilly release finding "Mama" not so fond of fiddling in a well-done "string band" dance record by Leon's Lone Star Cowboys on Montgomery Ward 8015 release. While Leon's recording is credited to Davenport, it's more than obvious that "Papa" Charlie and "Half Pint" shared a culture claimed by all! Listen to all versions for good fun!

8. "Maxwell Street Blues," Paramount 12320. This "Maxwell Street" is most likely Chicago's own. "Chicago blues?" Perhaps these early Paramount releases, recorded in Chicago, indeed defined the term.
9. "All I Want Is a Spoonful," Paramount 12320.
10. "Your Baby Ain't Sweet Like Mine," Paramount 12383. This Ezra Shelton-penned ditty is hot jazz, with a bit of showmanship and vaudeville.
11. "She Belongs to Me Blues," Paramount 12461. This simple, banjo-strumming classic perhaps finds Charlie at his rural best.
12. "Butter and Egg Man Blues," Paramount 12358. Sexual virility was a principal theme in rural folklore. This crude ditty, penned by E. Murphy, more so, finds Papa Charlie personally greeting the opposite gender, as well as noting a specific sexual position. The term "butter and egg" certainly finds fertile ground here, although a later rendering, by Louis Armstrong and His Hot Five, as "Big Butter and Egg Man" (Okeh 8423), while still crude, is indeed more urban.
13. "The Judge Cliff Davis Blues," Paramount 12366. While most of these ditties are indeed an exercise in rural and crude entertainment, the term "blues" always implies the negative and the sad. This ditty, as penned by Harry Philwin, was more. As contemporary comment and indeed "protest," this bit of folk music is wholly Afro-American. It seems this Cliff Davis was a real character, a Memphis police official, who enforced the "Jim Crow" status with zeal. In true retrospective, Papa Charlie's crude vocal style is a mask for his obvious intelligence and his social concerns.
14. "Up the Way Bound," Paramount 12375. This "train" song rambles along well.
15. "Coal Man Blues," Paramount 12461. This entity has some identification as well as social commentary. (A contemporary Peg Leg Howell entity, on Columbia 14194-D, may be even more effective.)
16. "Bright Eyes," Paramount 12574. This rural and folk entity indeed invites an integrated audience.
17. "Blue Monday Morning Blues," Paramount 12574. This original flip side of "Bright Eyes," is a typical rural blues performance and is far more identified as Afro-American in vocal delivery.
18. "Hometown Skiffle," Paramount 21453. Papa Charlie is joined by fellow Paramount stable mats Blind Blake, Blind Lemon, Will Ezell, Charlie Spand, and the Hokum Boys in a promotional effort for the fleeting label (1930). While this effort may be considered, in true retrospective, a fair-sounding folk entity, these fabulous artists provide this recording with much historical interest. Indeed, the Great Depression, which had started in the stock market crash of October 1929, would doom Paramount itself.

Frankie "Half Pint" Jaxon

By (1926), Frankie "half pint" Jaxon, had finally become a "recording artist." As a vaudevillian of the pre-1920 acoustic era, this very short personage was known as "Half Pint." His emulation of his hero, Bert Williams, was well known. While the racism of that previous era had prevented him from becoming a recording artist, the new trends of jazz and blues found his "act" somewhat old hat. As a vocalist (who could at least carry a tune), his experience in dance and imitation (as a female impersonator), incorporated in Afro-American slang, at least made him interesting. He may be considered, as a black entity, the opposite end of (white) vaudevillian EmmetMiller, whose crudeness, nevertheless, combined early components of the musical styles of jazz and blues.

The following are picks:

1. "If That Don't Get It, This Sho' Will," Okeh 8359. This quirky piece of vaudeville, with some fine work on piano (female Blanche Smith Walton) could have also easily found its origins as a pre-Prohibition saloon entity.
2. "Can't Wait Till You Get Home," Gennett 6212. While this ditty sounds much like "old" Broadway and George M. Cohan, the "salty" lyrics about waiting in the parlor remain hokey and novel.
3. "Willie the Weeper," Black Patti 8048. This quirky and wordy entity, is at least spirited. It is also noteworthy that this ditty just could have inspired the (later) Cab Calloway entity "Minnie the Moocher."
4. "Corrine," Black Patti 8048. This bit of uninhibited vocal silliness has been divided, for the sake of musical listening, into two parts. The first (a) Black Patti release is more primitive. A later (b.) version (Vocalion 1539) finds clarinet and piano in a jazz setting. Both are very good, with perhaps the second release "rambling" down the line.
5. "Hit Ta Ditty Low Down," Vocalion 1226. While this reference to "mammy" finds more than some "jive," its crude message works. It seems a young lad from Louisiana may find out a few things about the world; this "dance" number may have been his most important lesson.
6. "Down at Jasper's Bar-B-Que," Vocalion 1226. As a reference to radio listening, a contemporary recording "It's Tight Like This," by Tampa Red and Georgia Tom, may have attended this Bar B Que. On the other hand, a "Chicago-style" bar-b-que was a real cultural event. In true retrospective, it still remains so.
7. "It's Tight Like That," Vocalion 1228. Both Hudson Whittaker (alias Tampa Red) and Tom Dorsey (alias Georgia Tom) made a duet of this ditty, on Vocalion 1216, before Frankie. While much like "Down at Jasper's Bar-B-Que," Frankie's usual antics (actually on a Tampa Red's Hokum Jug Band release) better the previous release. A later Louis Armstrong ditty "It's Tight Like This," on Okeh 8649, is also good, if a bit tame in comparisons.
8. "Fan It," Vocalion 1257. This version of this self-penned ditty, in true retrospective, became the best-known Jaxon entity. While his other versions are OK, including a contemporary one on Vocalion 2553, this Vocalion release is indeed more gutsy and finds Frankie's vocal tougher, even more explicit. More so, a high "female" voice is not to be heard on this ditty, but a somewhat danceable recording and a fuller sound.

   Moreover, there was indeed much emulation too, including, a (1931) Red Nichols release, with a fine vocal as by Red McKenzie on Brunswick 6160, which became a best seller.

   So did a 1935 recording, with Woody Herman's own vocal, on Decca 834.

   Subsequently, the "white" world of hillbilly found a creative version by Milton Brown and His Brownies, as a "western swing" entity, on Decca 5244. Another version, inspired by Brownie, found a Leon Chappelear version as "She's Got Me Worried," with an obvious title change.

9. "My Daddy Rocks Me with Steady Roll," Vocalion 1274. As a Tampa Red entity, this ditty finds Frankie's "hot" vocal a necessary ingredient to confirm its rock message. To be fair, however, an earlier acoustic version, as by Trixie Smith (Black Swan 14127), entitled "My Man Rocks Me with a Steady Roll," is just as "hot." It's also interesting to speculate if Frankie knew Trixie and even wanted to be her. (Yes, "her"!)
10. "Rock Me, Mama," Brunswick 4964. This ditty was released as a Banjo Ikey Robinson and His Bull Fiddle Band release. It's Jaxon's fine vocal, however, blended with this little-known band that is the highlight of this well-done entity. The term "rock" is also to be noted. Moreover, the sheer crudeness of this vocal, using the term "rock" as risqué slang, is certain to raise more than an eyebrow. Just listen.
11. "Let's Knock a Jug," Vocalion 1285. This vocal (again) hits the spot.
12. "Get the 'L' on Down the Road," Brunswick 7067. As vocalist for Bill Johnson's Louisiana Jug Band, this (very) crude bit of "jive" talk finds Jaxon duetting with his (female) voice and his own, in the midst of kazoo's. The "L" is Chicago mass transit? (This ditty may also have become an inspiration for a later R & B personality, Clarence "Frogman" Henry. While speculation about the "frog" may belong to Clarence, the remainder of "Ain't Got No Home," on Argo 5259, including the "female" part, just might be Frankie? Just listen.
13. "Don't Drink It in Here," Brunswick 7067. While also a Bill Johnson Louisiana Jug Band release, this ditty sounds a lot more urban. Moreover, this parody of the Prohibition era is a novel approach and defines much of the cultural taboo and culture that existed in 1929.
14. "Jive Man Blues," Vocalion 1539. This 1929 ditty just may define "hip." Indeed, Jaxon's vocal tricks are always obvious, as perhaps the "king" of the art itself.
15. "Take It Easy," Vocalion 1424. With a full (unknown) backing, this jazz ditty finds Frankie "Corrine Brown" (of Chicago) and "Jazz Bo Jones" (from somewhere else), in a flashy urban tale. While many a 1929 dance floor found this tale familiar, there's more. An obvious reference to "Shake That Thing" and "My Daddy Rocks Me with a Steady Roll" only begin to expand upon this tale. Perhaps the term "rocking" was meant to be transitory? Indeed, the term itself is well used. Just Listen.
16. "You Got to Wet It," Vocalion 1472. While it may be assumed that this tale, which eventually found its way to (yet) another dance floor, a comparison to a dry part of the (male) anatomy is also "rocking," and indeed invites much speculation. (Backed by Punches Delegates of Pleasure, another fine and little-known Chicago studio group, even then, also finds some collectors at odds.)
17. "Down Home in Kentucky," Vocalion 1472. This tale about a visit to Kentucky, without the modern 1929 conveniences of the city, finds Frankie seeking out a previous female companion, as well as skinny dipping and liquor. What a place! What a find!
18. "Scuddlin'," Vocalion 1583. Just what is this guy doing behind his door? While his mother asks, this crude tale, like almost all of Frankie's ditties, gets more involved and more into trouble! Is it worthy of masturbation? While his mother's voice may be suspect, this danceable ditty, finds Frankie capable of anything, including some fine vocal scats!
19. "Chocolate to the Bone," Vocalion 1583. While this ditty about a "brown skin," was an obvious ploy, this crude novelty has listening assets.
20. "Mama Don't Allow It," Vocalion 2603. This (full orchestra) backing indeed sounds a bit tame, at least for Frankie, bettering an earlier Papa Charlie rendering of a novel folk entity. While perhaps Frankie's own vocal indeed shies away from hillbillies, the shared culture was perhaps to become best described in a (1935?) real hillbilly string

band dance release by Leon's Lone Star Cowboys. Indeed, interesting listening is to be had when Papa Charlie, Jaxon, and Leon (identified as Leon Chappelear by the author) versions are all compared. A difference in culture? Just listen!

21. "When a Woman Gets the Blues," Decca 7363. This attempt at crooning, with xylophone, guitar, and piano backing, is yet another attempt at another style.
22. "Take It Easy, Greasy, You Got a Long Way to Slide," Decca 7304. The slang heard on this tale remains a fine ploy upon vocabulary.
23. "Riff It," Decca 7482. Jaxon is again relevant as his (1920s) vocal style, in 1938, remains hip and a uses a lively bit of slang.
24. "Some Sweet Day," Decca 7548. This slower but rhythmic ditty scores!
25. Don't Pan Me," Deccca 7638. While Alberta Hunter had claims upon this ditty from as far back as 1923, it's very possible that they had both known each other in the Dreamland Café in Chicago. While it's nothing like the acoustic Hunter version (Paramount 12001), it is (still) closer than the differing and defining (1931) Ethel Waters version as "Please Don't Talk About Me When I'm Gone" (Columbia 2409-D).
26. "Let Me Ride Your Train," Decca 7786. This (1940) vocal finds Jaxon in fine storytelling form.
27. "Be Your Natural Self," Decca 7786.
28. "You Can't Tell," Decca 7806.

Blind Lemon Jefferson

After finding Ma Rainey in 1923 and wanting more, the Paramount label stumbled upon the likes of a blind Mississippi Delta personage, Blind Lemon Jefferson. At first hearing, despite initial acoustic grit, the storytelling aspects of what could have been considered folk music, with primitive guitar backing and vocals, may be considered even more rural than Ma Rainey's already established legacy as a recording artist, as Lemon's renderings perhaps indicate an even poorer region of the Southland, more so of black Americans. Originality may also be questioned, as with Rainey, noting local tales and stories translated into self penned song entities and, moreover, challenge time itself. The forbidden act of race-mixing found the saga of life common for poor folk, both black and white. The recordings of Blind Lemon Jefferson sound much like a later generation of bluesmen, despite poor acoustics. Moreover, the likes of Blind Lemon's recordings are simple "Delta" entities, deep in mud and culture. Among most contemporary musicians, both black as well as white, a curious attitude developed. In separating the crude from the sophisticated, rural "blues" vocalists, led by Blind Lemon, were generally to be put down and ignored. In true retrospective, the latter-century aspects of rock and roll owe much more to Blind Lemon, as perhaps, the myth of (recorded) Mississippi Delta blues is originally found in his crude and effective vocals. The following are Blind Lemon picks:

1. "Got the Blues," Paramount 12354. Got the blues? Before BB King was around? Got 'em!
2. "Corinna Blues," Paramount 12367. While this ditty is indeed documented by Ma Rainey (as "See See Rider" on Paramount 12252), it's perhaps a shared cultural idiom, in common with fellow (Paramount) recording artist Ma Rainey. It's also very possible that Blind Lemon and Ma could have picked it up in the same tent show, or it could be (as in the case of blues queen Victoria Spivey (as "Black Snake Moan") a steal.

While it's still a word game indeed between the Tommy Johnson's "Maggie Campbell Blues" (on Victor 21409), a (later) 1950's entity (Chuck Willis on Atlantic 1130) claims "C C Rider." Raved-up (later) versions—by Mitch Ryder and Elvis Presley, as "See See Rider"—also fit into this mix, but it's for sure that Ma and Blind Lemon originally "found" it.

3. "Beggin' Back," Paramount 12394. While all Blind Lemon's blues are rural, this ditty is perhaps his most crude and is, perhaps, as much as a folk entity, as any black or white. While it's true that Blind Lemon could carry a tune much better than his white opposite A. P. Carter (of the Carter Family), the cultural split between the races of the (then) segregated Southland is, nevertheless, found on the back porch. This interesting tale about a man's suspicions about his woman's behavior (thirty days(in prison? It's all true grit—in true retrospective.
4. "That Black Snake Moan," Paramount 12407. The "shared" culture of Afro-Americanisms was never an exclusive opportunity for poor white Southern, copping culture with "folk" songs. This ditty is much like (contemporary) blues queen Victoria Spivey's own recording, on Okeh 8339. While Victoria may have a point indeed, at least in the title, Blind Lemon contributes more primitive language. In addition, questions may be found in the sources of Victoria herself. (Victoria's female moans do indeed please the authors of this book more than Blind Lemon, however). No time to debate Blind Lemon's ownership! This ditty was also recorded on (b) Okeh 8455, in which Bind Lemon is linked more directly to Victoria Spivey's version.

    ➢ Moreover, there's more. Bind Lemon's incidental vocal phrasing is indeed to be noted in that later rendering of Arthur Big Boy Crudup's "That's All Right, Mama (on Victor 20-2205) and (with more reworking) by Elvis Presley (on Sun 209). Elvis's recording credits Crudup. But it's also obvious that Elvis did not rip-off Blind Lemon! More so, if rip-offs are credited, is it more than possible that a fine (1930) Son House recording "My Black Mama," on Paramount 13042, obviously segregating its message, owes much to Blind Lemon? Or did both Blind Lemon and House attend the same rural Mississippi Delta tent-show entity?

5., 6. "Matchbox Blues," Paramount 12474. A. This ditty, more so than others, links into the rock era. The Carl Perkins hit, as a self-penned ditty on Sun 243, rocks as well as, perhaps, questions Carl. In emulation of Carl, the Beatles (Capital 5255) single release and LP recorded a fine version. This ditty had also found emulation by a rousing Billie Holiday vocal (Vocalion 3288) as "Billie's Blues" in the mid-1930s. Blind Lemon's Blues?

Note: b. This ditty was also recorded at Okeh, on Okeh 8455, with not much of a difference. As the flip side of (already) mentioned "Black Snake Moan," this seems to be Lemon's only other relevant master recording which differs from poor sound at Paramount.

7. "Right of Way Blues," Paramount 12510. Country folk were always in awe of trains, and this primitive "train" ditty, is also full of double meaning. In any case, the contemporary Carter Family ditty, on Victor 40317, as "Worried Man Blues," is just as primitive. Further investigation finds "Six White Horses" (in 1940 as by Bill Monroe) as well as "Mystery Train" (as by Little Junior Parker) less than a stretch. With more embellishment, Elvis Presley found this tale of a girl taking leave of him on a train

indeed had even more effect upon its passengers, in 1955. Just when Blind Lemon and A. P. Carter first became aware of this train is unclear, although it's a good bet that Blind Lemon boarded first, with the help of a porter, and he was seated in the "colored" section.

8. "Rambler Blues," Paramount 12541. This tale about a traveling guy (between Texas and Tennessee) is classic rural blues. Later blues entities such as Charlie Patton, Leroy Carr, Lonnie Johnson, Robert Johnson, Arthur Crudup, Sonny Boy Williamsons (both), Big Maceo, Roy Brown, Howlin' Wolf, and Muddy Waters (among many others), find the way through up the turnpike to find the "blues" of Jimmie Rodgers, Jimmie Davis, Roy Acuff, and Hank Williams, among others.
9. "One Dime Blues," Paramount 12578. Blind Lemon makes it clear that he's broke and possesses (for a while)—ten cents! Blind Lemon also so states "Mama He Treats Your Daughter Mean," which (in a way) developed into a huge rhythm and blues entity (as penned by Wallace and Lance), recorded by Ruth Brown (Atlantic 986), light-years away in the early '50s.
10. "Blind Lemon's Penitentiary Blues," Paramount 12666. The laments of blues vocalists is perhaps best captured here in this simple and crude tale about the evils of drinking (in the Prohibition era) and advice about bad behavior in a state penitentiary.
11. "Bed Springs Blues," Paramount 12872. This blind guy seems to know his way to the bedroom as well as the "sound" of bed-springs. Perhaps bluesman Josh White, in the early 1930s, took this ditty a bit more seriously?
12. "That Crawlin' Baby Blues," Paramount 12880. This tale just might be about a baby whose paternity is questioned. While this tale could be strange, it's Blind Lemon's simple usage of slang (as usual), which leaves the listener of this ditty no less the wiser.
13. "Hometown Skiffle," Paramount 21453. This (1930) ditty may be considered a promotional item for the Paramount label. With the effects of the Great Depression setting in, sales for records more than slipped, and not just for Paramount. The need for food greatly replaced the quest for recorded entertainment. It was in fact a time for another "media" to claim more listeners—that of radio. While the times were also finding debates for the negative aspects of the playing of commercial recordings on the radio (without purchasing), "live" radio established itself. In true retrospective, the recording industry (and the film industry as well) would reel until the mid-1930s. Blind Lemon is joined by Blind Blake, Will Ezell, Charlie Spand, the Hokum Boys, and Papa Charlie Jackson on this so-so folk-sounding recording. An historical entity, this early blues "promo" found few buyers especially for the even harder-hit black community. Since the early 1920s (beginning with Mamie Smith), the established train porters (all black), as well as the mail-order business, had provided for Afro-Americans a fairly good distribution system throughout the country. The Great Depression had generally put sales to a standstill, especially for Blind Lemon's contemporary label mates. (A noted exception would be Big Bill Broonzy, found as the "Hokum Boys," "Big Bill," or "Sammy Sampson.")

Lonnie Johnson

As the Paramount label was about to launch (male entities) Papa Charlie Jackson and Blind Lemon Jefferson in 1925, the blues field was already crowded with "blues queens." The Okeh label, which had ignited the whole "race" field, some five years earlier, with Mamie Smith, in turn, had similar impulses. Okeh session guitarist—although over thirty-six years old—Lonnie Johnson, was thus thrown into the race and, in hindsight, lasted far longer than both Jackson and Jefferson. Indeed, Lonnie would liven things up and, as a matter of fact, transcend the roles of a definitive "blues" picker, as well as "jazz." Indeed, he influenced many, including the likes of Charlie Christian, associated with Duke Ellington, as well as Eddie Lang, a white guitarist perhaps also known as "Blind" Willie Dunn, who would become famous for his recordings for many as well as a professional and personal influence upon Bing Crosby. More so, this guitarist could belt out some fine vocals, as well as croon.

The following are Lonnie Johnson picks:

1. "Mr. Johnson's Blues," Okeh 8252 As this dated (1925) title suggests, this "Mr. Johnson" is Lonnie himself, and his fine vocal and guitar playing are truly defined.
2. "Falling Rain Blues," Okeh 8252.
3. "Five O' Clock Blues," Okeh 8417.
4. "Oh Doctor, the Blues," Okeh 8391.
5. "Back Water Blues," Okeh 8466. As a real, honest-to-God and personal tale of the (1927) flooded area of the Mississippi Delta, Lonnie's original at least doesn't get drowned out with the author of this book. A regular theme throughout the rest of the century, this ditty finds its most famous rendition by Bessie Smith (on Columbia 14195 D). In addition to this ditty, Bessie also found the means to transform a pop ditty "Muddy Water" (on Columbia 14197-D), into something much more mournful than Gene Austin or Bing Crosby. Other contemporary ditties like, "Mississippi Heavy Water Blues" by Barbecue Bob (on Columbia 14222-D), and "High Water Everywhere" by Charlie Patton (on Paramount 12909), also address this "knee deep" event more than a casual concern. It is even interesting to speculate if one McKinley Morganfield (from the delta area in Rolling Fork, Mississippi,) found his name in these ditties, as "Muddy Waters." In any hearing, Lonnie's effort is poignant enough.
6. "Mean Old Bed Bug Blues," Okeh 8497. This ditty, also known as a later Bessie Smith classic, on Columbia 14250-D, found some good 1927contemporary rivalry by Betty Gray, on Lincoln 2714. A fine case may be made for this ditty as social commentary as these pests remained a nuisance for all, both the black-and white-skinned. While it's still a sure bet that Lonnie got it right the first time, a later hillbilly version by Ernest Tubb, on Bluebird 8899, is just as itchy. Indeed, Southern culture is shared, and these recordings, however novel, like the buggers themselves, also live in the north.
7. "Kansas City Blues," (Pt. 1 and 2) Okeh 8537. Lonnie's got the blues for this city twice as much as his (later) "Chicago Blues."
8. "Crowing Rooster Blues," Okeh 8574. Oh! It's time to get up. This "rooster" theme found its way through the likes of many, especially Charlie Patton's "Banty Rooster Blues," on Paramount 12792. It seems, as well that these roosters were still plentiful and productive for the rest of the century. For certain, bluesman Howling Wolf (alias Chester Burnett) found the Willie Dixon-penned "Little Red Rooster," on Chess 1804, more than an inspiration in the light-years through to the 1950s. More so, his imported tales would find much more emulation in England! Yes! The huge importance of these "rooster" themes indeed became a fable of rock music itself.

Indeed, the British "beat boom," resulting from the effects of the emulation of Afro-American culture, was founded in the "skiffle" music led by one Lonnie Donegan (as the name "Lonnie" is even an emulation of Lonnie Johnson himself). Influenced heavily by the imported likes of Lonnie Johnson, Robert Johnson, Leadbelly, Big Bill Broonzy, Howling Wolf, and Josh White, among others, as well as the musical boom of sales in America (led by Elvis Presley and his peculiar emulation of his Southern roots, black and white), the "rock" era shook Britain hard. Moreover, using recordings themselves, the emulations of sound found many would-be musicians purchasing electric guitars, harmonics, and percussion instruments, hoping to duplicate them. One such group consisted of Charlie Watts, Keith Richards, Brian Jones, Bill Wyman, and would-be vocalist Mick Jagger. (As a British entity, "Little Red Rooster," on Decca F 12014, became more than anthem for the Rolling Stones. More so, this musical statement had already been exploited by (real) black musicians. The likes of those who had inspired the British groups of the 1960s had already included a later generation, who included the likes of Elmore James, Jimmy Reed, Slim Harpo, and Muddy Waters, along with the already noted Howling Wolf and Willie Dixon, among others. In fact, Jagger's "Rolling Stones," found its origins in a 1950's recording by Muddy Waters (as "Rollin' Stone," on Chess 1426). While questions are also in doubt, it is a fact that a 1928 recording, by one Robert Wilkins, on Victor 12990, just may have influenced Muddy Waters himself (alias "McKinley Morganfield").

9. "Sweet Potato Blues," Okeh 8586. This play on lyrics was (and still is) what the blues can be.
10. "Wrong Woman Blues," Okeh 8601.
11. "New Black Snake Moan" (Pt 1 and 2), Okeh 8626. A vocal duet with Victoria Spivey was most likely a marketing effort that was deemed to be effective. As it turns out, that wailing blues queen is at least matched by Lonnie's fine exchange of views. As for the "black snake," perhaps the obvious is crude enough.
12. "It Feels So Good" (Pt 1 and 2), Okeh 8664. This duet with Spencer Williams is just what it is supposed to be, with Spencer in a female mood, as this novelty indeed works.
13. "Toothache Blues" (Pt. 1 and 2.), Okeh 8744. Another fine duet with Victoria Spivey that (again) crudely works.
14. "She's Making Whoopee in Hell Tonight," Okeh 8768. While Eddie Cantor's stupid Broadway entity "Making Whoopee"(on Victor 21862) is perhaps influencing this ditty's title, this hard-bitten blues tale is indeed not. This tale, in fact, condemns and more! Look out!
15. "No More Troubles Now," Okeh 8831. While this blues title is indeed perfect, this fine (dated) vocal also betrays crooning and pop aspirations, beyond the blues.
16. "Got the Blues for Murder Only," Okeh 8846. This tale of Mexico is a strange one and perhaps full of stereotypes. In any case, this old blues ditty (1930) is much like a Hollywood fable.
17. "Racketeers Blues," Okeh 8946. This familiar tale about greed and gangsters, in 1932, was at least in vogue with the likes of contemporaries like Al Capone, among others.
18. "Devil's Got the Blues," Decca 7427. This theme just does not end, but that's the "blues."
19. "The Lonesome Road," Bluebird 0714. The classic road is traveled much after the likes of Gene Austin and Louis Armstrong.
20. "Get Yourself Together," Bluebird 8530. After beginning with "Rocks in My Bed," a later 1941 Duke Ellington entity (with the excellent Ivie Anderson vocal on Victor 27639) comes to mind. Lonnie, moreover, makes his case known, with a rocking chair to spare.

21. "Don't Be No Fool," Bluebird B-8530. Good Advice!
22. "Chicago Blues," Bluebird B-8684. Lonnie had been around since the 1920s and no stranger for the great city, as this self-penned (as usual) ditty was even recorded there.
23. "Lazy Woman Blues," Bluebird 8748. This ditty finds Lonnie finding out that getting his beautiful woman to quit her job caused him some big problems. This lady doesn't seem to want to pick up anything, but at least she's got a lot to look at.
24. "In Love Again," Bluebird B-8748. Lonnie's crooning again, and it ain't too bad.

- Note: Postwar

25. "Tomorrow Night," King 4201. This postwar ditty may be considered a landmark event for the new, upstart "King Records" recording label, led by the enterprising Syd Nathan—as well as for Lonnie. As a pop entity in the 1930s this sweet band standard had already found its way into the pop mainstream. Earlier versions included a Horace Heidt release (with a vocal by the Heigh-Lights, on Columbia 35203) as well as one as by Ozzie Nelson, on Bluebird B-10420. Penned by the familiar Sam Coslow and Will Grosz (associated with many other recording artists the era—found within this book), this ditty was indeed an unlikely entity for bluesman Lonnie. Indeed, Lonnie had already reached his mid-fifties by this time, in 1947. Moreover, like many musicians and vocalists of the prewar period, competition from "new" rhythm and blues performers, including the likes of King Records' own Bull Moose Jackson and Wynonie Harris, found Lonnie largely forgotten.

As released on King, the record (unusually) did not credit Coslow or Grosz, and so stated "Lonnie Johnson's Theme Song." As Lonnie had indeed taken credit for most of his previous recordings as a writer, many assumed that Lonnie had penned the slow and effective ditty. As it stood, the crooning job by Lonnie was (and is) a fine piece of work, with a "blues" feeling that far out-distances it from any previous "sweet band" idiom. As a matter of fact, this ditty (even) broke into pop best-seller lists, which is what the small, independent labels (such as King) would continue to do—set "trends," with creative efforts not found in the likes of RCA Victor, Columbia, or Decca—the "established" companies. While Lonnie had always had a following among those in the Afro-American community and some white musicians, this ditty made Lonnie better known and more appreciated. It is a pity, despite some excellent later recordings, that Lonnie never attempted to do more with pop entities, as black contemporaries Nat Cole and Billy Eckstine.

Additional note: This song ditty would find its way into another small-label company, Sun. Like Nathan at King earlier, its owner Sam Phillips "found" creative ways and different (cheap) methods to market "new" product. It is also interesting to note that a major discovery of his, Elvis Presley, a young white part-time truck driver and a huge fan of Lonnie Johnson's recordings (among other rhythm and blues performers) recorded "Tomorrow Night," without success! When Sam sold (most) of his unreleased master recordings to RCA Victor, the Elvis version finally found itself released, in different forms—starting many years later, in 1965.

26. "What a Woman," King 4201.
27. "My Mother's Eyes" King 4510. This old and sentimental 'mother' theme had been penned by L. Wolf Gilbert and Abel Baer for the contemporary 1928 Broadway entity "Lucky". As introduced by George Jessell, it's pogiant message perhaps became an

attempt as a stiff croon. By the time Lonnie got it, around 1951, it's obvious his croon is vastly different, noting that this bit of mush did indeed retain some of it's universal appeal.

Some year later in 1964, a former fellow King Records blues entity, who just had to have been aware of Lonnie's vocal style, known as Mabel Scott, now calling herself 'Big Maybelle', rendered the same pop ditty. Was Maybelle's souful version on the Rojac label inspired by Lonnie's earlier recording ?

28. "Love Is the Answer," Alladin 197. Another fine postwar outing, with some "urban blues" that just seem to find a place to be emulated by all others to follow, especially the likes of B. B. King!
29. "Tomorrow Night," Paradise 110. Another, dreamy version (mid-1950s). (re recorded).

Robert Johnson

The mythology of the "blues" or "blues" singing existed way before the advent of "rock." In the attempt to explain the meaning of "blues," "jazz," "hillbilly," or even "pop" vocals, it is still best left to the listener, with added perceptions. Moreover, the purposes of this book try to keep things in full retrospective, noting obvious restrictions of time and place, not experienced by latter-day listeners Whether contrived or not, the idiom continues with embellishment. The recordings of one Robert Johnson (one of many Mississippi "Delta" bluesmen), especially seem to fit that mode. In fact, the progress of time (into the rock era) only adds to much of the speculation and myth that led to his "discovery." More so than many others, the Robert Johnson myth, which started with perhaps only a desire to record (emulating the success of Blind Lemon Jefferson), among others, remains knee deep.

The early success of Elvis Presley also found his music, in many places in the country, condemned as something bad or lewd. The sexual image, combined with the Hollywood images (of James Dean and Marlon Brando), indeed worked well for the young white Southerner from Mississippi. While the combinations of "blues," "country," "pop," "folk" and "gospel" dazzled the music world of the 1950s, the Elvis Presley explosion did much to topple the worlds of Irving Berlin, Bing Crosby, and the popular broadway music that had basically shut out bluesmen like Robert Johnson. Moreover, Presley was also condemned by many of his own. While contemporaries in 1950s C & W music had no use for his embellishment of black sounds, contemporary Pentecostal churches of the South (both black as well as white) called it the "devil's music." Despite a huge catalog of gospel ditties as well, Elvis, like many bluesmen, had sold out to the devil. The Robert Johnson myth, perhaps more powerful as a tool of Hollywood, in *Crossroads*, nevertheless remained with the latter century. Indeed, as the author can personally attest, from some Chicago area residents—indeed, transplanted Mississippians, the pursuit of the blues, instead of religion, remains the "devil's music." Picks are as follows:

1. "Kind Hearted Woman," Vocalion 03416. The bluesman and his strumming guitar had been previously best described as recordings as by Charlie Patton, on "Pony Blues" (Paramount 12792); Blind Willie McTell, on "Statesboro Blues"(Victor 38001); Sleepy John Estes, on "Divin' Duck Blues" (Victor 38549); Blind Blake, on "Diddie Wa Diddie" (Paramount 12888); Mississippi John Hurt, on "Candy Man

Blues" (Okeh 8654); Skip James, on "Illinois Blues" (Paramount 13072); Son House, on "My Black Mama" (Paramount 13042); and blues woman, Memphis Minnie, on "Bumble Bee" (Vocalion 1476)—all electric recordings. Indeed this theme about a "kind-hearted woman" is basic, but perhaps Robert, more so, defined it with his pleasant vocal.

2. "Terraplane Blues," Vocalion 03416. Like many other blues entities, the car (the "Terriplane," manufactured by the Hudson Motor Co., in the 1930s), is a good substitute for self.
3. "I Believe I'll Dust My Broom," Vocalion 03475. This ditty's good and also may be referenced to the previous Carl Rafferty rendering as "Mr. Carl's Blues," on Bluebird 5429. A later and hipper version, an Elmore James version (as "Dust My Broom" (Trumpet 146) by "Elmore James") is also better defined.
4. "Sweet Home, Chicago," Vocalion 03601. As luck would have it, Robert Johnson would gain fame for a song ditty about Chicago, Illinois, the urban center for many a fellow Mississippi black sharecropper, seeking a better life. Moreover, it is the fact that Robert never made it to Chicago, as this 1936 ditty was recorded in San Antonio, Texas!

As a latter-day discovery, this ditty was found to be much in favor of Chicago area musician and actor John Belushi, who, along with Dan Aykroyd, performed it with much vigor on television's *Saturday Night Live*, in 1979. As the "Blues Brothers," the act among baby boomers took off, both as recording fodder and as a major film, also called *The Blues Brothers*, in 1980. Indeed, Robert Johnson enjoyed none of this huge commercial success featuring his song, although his legacy, much embellished, owes much to both John and Dan. Moreover, the Johnson recording, despite the fine Blues Brothers version, remains a classic, and indeed "rocks," or "pre-rocks." As a further note, Robert most likely had heard Kokomo Arnold's previous "Old Original Kokomo Blues," on Decca 7026, or perhaps an earlier and similar recording by Blind Blake (Paramount 12479) as "One Time Blues," recorded in 1927.

5. "32-20 Blues," Vocalion 03445. This rambling ditty contains a fine vocal about guns. His girl has not come home and a decision has been made about shooting her. (A previous ditty, as "22-20 Blues," on Paramount 13066, by Skip James, may have been an inspiration for Robert; although, like most of these ditties, folk origins are always in question.)
6. "They're Red Hot," Vocalion 03563. This fast-paced tale has Robert duetting with himself. Just what's "hot," moreover, is easy to speculate upon.
7. "Dead Shrimp Blues," Vocalion 03475. This novelty is more than X-rated. But the listener must listen.
8. "Cross Road Blues," Vocalion 03519. The 1986 film entity *Crossroads* had a lot to do with the Hollywood exploitation. As previously noted, however, the myth of the rural folk should not be taken lightly, as some of the secular, both black and white, found this film to be an embellishment of something very real. Baby boomer acceptance, especially among guitarists, remains huge, although it should be noted that the film concentrated upon playing the guitar, and not vocalizing, or uttering sinfulness. Whether or not this bluesman, who died at the age of twenty-seven years, made a pact with the devil in order to play his guitar so well is one of high speculation. What is true, however, is that the story of the selling of a "soul" to the devil was (and is) a relevant tale for bluesmen. It's also very true that this fable did not begin or end Robert Johnson. As a matter of fact, a fine Peetie Wheatstraw recording, "The Devils

Son-in-Law," on Bluebird 5451, follows the theme, as well as Charlie Patton's "Devil Sent the Rain," on Paramount 13040, proceeded Robert. While this theme is indeed found in Shakespeare, the more primitive acoustic sounds on blues queen Clara Smith's 1923 "Done Sold My Soul to the Devil," on Columbia 14041 D, perhaps had more influence? Follow the logic? Or is it?

9. "Come on in My Kitchen," Vocalion 03563. As if the melody of "theme" may just be in the air, this excellent ditty never misses the (very different) theme (and vocal harmony) of the previous Mississippi Sheiks recording "Sitting on Top of the World," on Okeh 8784.
10. "Walking Blues," Vocalion 03601. Some very fine guitar pickin' is paced with perhaps a good long walk. An earlier walk taken by Ma Rainey (as "Walking Blues," Paramount 12082) just ain't the same!
11. "Preachin' the Blues Up Jumped the Devil," Vocalion 04630. It's that devil again! While Robert may have been familiar with the Son House version, on Paramount 12990, so what? Bessie Smith's rendering on Columbia 14195-D (almost) amounts to the same!
12. "Love in Vain," Vocalion 04630. This ditty's not in vain. A previous recording (Leroy Carr's "When the Sun Goes Down," on Bluebird 5877, may not be either. Perhaps a more powerful case may be heard in a later (light-years away) live entity, by the Rolling Stones, on LP, as released on the London label, London-NPS-5. While Mick Jagger's vocals always seemed to get to the heart of things (without the usual grit), he should be cheered on. The (1969) album title, *Get Yer Ya-Yas Out*, is also an item, as that of another early bluesman, Blind Boy Fuller (Vocalion 04519).
13. "Little Queen of Spades," Vocalion 04108. This sad tale about a girl who doesn't have to gamble because she's so hot does not lie. She's so good-looking that you'll give her all your money anyway—I'll bet!(A curious Peetie Wheatstraw recording "King of Spades," on (Conqueror 9028), may just be a good companion for this wordy game of slang, not entirely about cards.
14. "Malted Milk," Vocalion 03665.
15. "Me and the Devil, Blues," Vocalion 04108. Oh! At it again.
16. "Milk Cow's Calf Blues," Vocalion 03655. This (1937) rendering had been perhaps inspired by the better-known (1934) Kokomo Arnold entity as "Milkcow Blues," on Decca 7026. But, to be fair, without fences, these cows get around. The primitive aspects of this rural entity truly found raw vocals—indeed "raw"-with guitar. Such other "cows" perhaps seek ownership.

They include

- As claimed by Mr. Freddie Spuell on "Milk Cow Blues" (Okeh 8422), in 1926.
- As claimed by Charlie Patton as "Jersey Cow Blues" (Vocalion 02782), in 1934.
- As claimed by Pinewood Tom (alias Josh White) on Banner 33361, in 1934.

Moreover, a later post-WWII (1947) hillbilly version, by the Maddox Brothers and Rose, on 4 Star 1185, becomes a fine rhythmic novelty. The later (1954) Elvis Presley version, on Sun 215, is rhythmic and, nevertheless, as primitive as any, including the likes of any previous bluesman.

Al Jolson

The first great American recording artist to capture American popular tastes was Al Jolson. With an ethnic (Jewish) musical background, Jolson proceeded to take on contemporary musical stage, finding the art of George M. Cohan and the minstrel (blackface) traditions of Lew Dockstader's Minstrels. In the midst of the music of the "old" world of (Italian) opera recording star Enrico Caruso and the (Irish) tenor John McCormick, and a novel approach to the canned and primitive recording techniques of the era, perhaps, in true retrospective, perhaps the rage of "ragtime," as found in the better-sounding instrumental piano rolls of (Afro-American) Scott Joplin are more relevant. The era of the early 1900s, moreover, in addition to the already noted Caruso, Dockstader, and McCormick, belonged to the likes of Harry MacDonough, Billy Murray, the Hayden Quartet, Byron G. Harlan, Arthur Collins, Ada Jones, J. W. Myers, among many other white and European inspired vocalists. A few lone (real blackfaced) performers, Bert Williams and George Walker, did find some success in a likely hostile white society. The clowning and huge stereo-typing of blacks found success in the likes of "coon" songs, which indeed contributed to the brainwashing of Americana and founded much into the eventual development of Al Jolson himself. It would be a mistake to label Jolson a racist by choice, however. As a Jew, he was also an oddity, especially in the company of his own. Perhaps the lure of the musical stage, as documented light-years away in 1927's film *The Jazz Singer*, also found Jolson an outcast among many Jews, as the separations between secular and popular entertainment remained a huge issue.

The minstrel entertainer, indeed, became a showman, more than even George M. Cohan himself. Cohan had little regard for recording, and although he did record for the Victor label, he regarded contemporary recordings as a sideline. The bigger money in 1911 was in selling music, and Cohan sold a lot of it. From his first recordings, the energetic Jolson (disregarding a few ethnic recordings) founded a popular tenor-like vocal style, indeed perfect for acoustic recording. His "American" style, found the likes of the Broadway stage, vaudeville, and especially as a recording artist, a welcome and dynamic entity. By 1920, Jolson had become a huge chunk of American entertainment itself. Within time, and the advent of electric recordings, the tenor like Jolson, full of vocal tricks and quirks, adapted to a crooning style, also successful. Indeed, some of his Brunswick recordings of the 1920s note him as "The World's Greatest Entertainer," and contribute to a legacy of an arrogance of personality that would define even the best of his recordings. In true retrospective, his use of blackface earns him some sharp critics, especially from those of African American origins. The following picks seek to find some art, clouded by the likes of racism.

- Song Picks are as follows:

Most Al Jolson classic vocals were originally "live" on stage, usually on Broadway. The biggest were *Honeymoon Express*, *Sinbad*, and *Bombo*. In all of these, and his later "one and only" shows, *he* was the show. The Broadway "show" was used by Jolson to showcase himself. Contemporaries such as George Jessel and Eddie Cantor, although popular, were almost nonexistent clones, when compared to Jolson. (Jessel did make some recordings, his most popular called "My Mothers Eyes," on Victor 21852). The more talented Cantor, who made quite a few recordings, PA appearances, and (later) was a huge radio and film star (like Jolson), is covered in another section of this book). The most interesting thing about Al Jolson (whose long career started with the blackfaced teachings of Lew Dockstader's Minstrels from the turn of the century and ended after a tired trip entertaining American troops in the Korean Conflict, 1950) was his (seemingly) ageless maturity as a recording artist.

The "show" Jolson put on, with or without blackface, consisted of rolling articulate *r*'s, a flashy face with rolling eyeballs, and almost a magical spell put upon his audiences. His use of coon songs was, perhaps, more of a (personal) identity crisis and, sadly, a vehicle for the white racism of the era. The only time Jolson left the safe arena of "his" public, or fans, was when he made first sound film *The Jazz Singer,* at forty-one years of age, in 1927. By that time also, Jolson's voice was no longer that pleading tenor of the acoustic age; there was more of a tenor-baritone, with better vocal tricks and more of the type of vocals that are considered "modern" and technically better, even in (true) retrospective.

Jolson Picks are as follows:

1. "Snap Your Fingers," Victor 17075. While poor-sounding, Jolson's natural hipness works for this ditty by Harry von Tilzer and William Jerome.
2. "Asleep in the Deep," Victor 17915. Yup. Al actually sounds as if he's treading water, and losing!
3. "Ragging the Baby to Sleep," Victor 17081. Jolson's (odd) use of "ragtime" is (still) oddly entertaining (penned by Lewis F. Muir and L. Wolfe Gilbert).
4. "The Spaniard That Blighted My Life," Victor 17318. From Broadway's *Honeymoon Express*, penned by Billy Merson, Al seemingly gets operatic. Fortunately, it works.
5. "You Made Me Love You," Columbia A-1374. Also from Broadway's *Honeymoon Express*, this famous (1913) acoustic classic, penned by James Monaco and Joseph McCarthy, indeed needed Jolson to belt it out. (Years later, as "Dear Mister Gable," Judy Garland, hamming it up as a parody about film star Clark Gable, was indeed hamming it up in Jolson's vocal style. While all of this is OK, it's interesting to note that by (1938), the advent of "electric" recordings had found Jolson's style far less needed.
6. "Sister Susie's Sewing Shirts for Soldiers," Columbia A-1671. From Broadway's *Dancing Around*, this popular WWI entity, penned by H. Darewski and R. P. Weston, is quirky and novel enough.
7. "Rock-a-Bye Your Baby with a Dixie Melody," Columbia A-2560. As penned by Jean Schwartz. Joe Young and Sam M. Lewis in 1918 for Broadway's *Sinbad*, Al again belts out a winner, as well as a classic.
8. "I'll Say She Does," Columbia A-2746. As another *Sinbad* entity, this risqué lyric, penned by Gus Kahn, Bud De Sylva, and Al himself) finds Al hamming it up and, somehow, still succeeding in producing a fine acoustic rendering.
9. "I've Got My Captain Working for Me Now," Columbia A-2794. As a post-WWI novelty from *Ziegfeld Follies of 1919*, Eddie Cantor dad found himself a hit, penned by Irving Berlin. Jolson, however, steals it all, and well, considering Cantor's own Jolson-inspired vocal style.
10. "Tell Me," Columbia A-2821. As usual, the Jolson vocal improves upon a ballad. With a bit of personality, this ditty is indeed Jolson, as his quirkiness and embellishment of clumsy lyrics produces a (dated) winner.
11. "You Ain't Heard Nothin' Yet," Columbia A-2836. This best-selling ditty of 1919, penned Gus Kahn, Buddy De Sylva, and Jolson himself, ain't bad.
12. "Swanee," Columbia A-2884. As a *Sinbad* entity, this perfect antique of 1920, penned by George Gershwin and Irving Caesar, again demonstrates Al's belting vocal style vastly overcoming acoustic limits. (It also gave George Gershwin much recognition.)

13. "Avalon," Columbia A-2995. Jolson (again) pulls it off, as this ditty, penned by Bud De Sylva, Vincent Rose, and Al Jolson, is belted out well enough.
14. "Toot Toot Tootsie, Goo'bye," Columbia A-3705. This Broadway entity, from *Bombo*, penned by Gus Kahn, Ernie Erdman, and Dan Russo, finds clumsy lyrics that are more annoying than novel. Nevertheless, the bombastic Jolson vocal delivers and, indeed, personalizes this ditty.
15. "Waiting for the Evenin' Mail," Columbia A-3933. Al's attempt at blues, penned by Billy Baskett, succeeds! More so would a later (1923) Clara Smith version, on Columbia 13002-D.
16. "California, Here I Come," Brunswick 2569. Penned by Joseph Meyer, Bud De Sylva, and Jolson himself, this bit of stupid lyric, as usual, benefits from Jolson's theatrics.
17. "I'm Going South," Brunswick 2569. This flip side of "California, Here I Come," while not as popular, in retrospective, contains a better vocal. Moreover, this Brunswick recording far exceeds a previous Jolson version (b) on Columbia 61-D. Indeed, this 1924 ditty penned by Harry Woods and Abner Silver finds Jolson committed and, perhaps because of the excellent backing provided by Isham Jones, the vocal style is a bit tighter and closer to jazz. In true retrospective, Jolson would be labeled a "Jazz Singer," due to the film of the same name. Nevertheless, taking into consideration the huge leaps and bounds of the evolving musical term, Jolson did produce some fine vocals, and this ditty ain't bad. As a further note, Jolson himself (later) claimed that he himself had discovered "jazz," as in the form of the "Original Dixieland Jass' Band," a white band, led by a product of New Orleans's Italian immigrant population, one Nick La Rocca, while appearing in Chicago. While this all may be suspect, the younger Jolson had, indeed, been a patron of numerous houses of ill repute, and it's very possible that his first "jazz" had been heard in one of them.
18. "Steppin' Out," Brunswick 2567. This is (another) fab recording with the Isham Jones Orchestra, and Jolson indeed sounds inspired in this ditty penned by Con Conrad and Richard Howard.
19. "Mr. Radio Man," Brunswick 2582 Jolson (again) produces good product, as this 1924 entity—noting the emergence of commercial radio-penned by Ira Schuster, William Wilfred, and Cliff Friend, also accompanied by Isham Jones, wins out.
20. "Lazy," Brunswick 2595. This Irving Berlin classic title was later to be crooned out by Bing Crosby in 1942. Jolson's original, however, is faster and in great creative style—oddly, more than his earlier contemporary work. Accompanied by the Gene Rodemich Orchestra, who perhaps led him into this fine vocal, it's possible that Jolson's version is better, although the Crosby arrangement sounds different, indeed a different song altogether. Perhaps, if Irving Berlin was still around, someone could ask him? Or, does anyone care?

    Or what about a fine Blossom Seeley rendering (a longtime vaudevillian contemporary of Al's), released as a vocal on a (Georgians) recording on Columbia 114-D? Or what about a contemporary (1924) completely different sounding group rendering by the Brox Sisters on Victor 19298? Where the young Boswells listening?

21. "My Papa Don't Two Time No More," Brunswick 2595. This Walter Donaldson-penned ditty is tough, and Jolson's vocal prowess is indeed very effective.
22. "Hello, Tucky," Brunswick 2763. This ditty, penned by James F. Hanley, Joseph Meyer, and Bud De Sylva, is also tough despite its dumb title.

23. "Miami," Brunswick 3013. Al makes 'em all sound good, for his own Broadway entity from *Big Boy*, penned by Con Conrad, Bud De Sylva, and Al himself, works well enough.
24. "Tonight's My Night with Baby," Brunswick 3196. Jolson, backed by Carl Fenton and Orchestra, picks an Irving Ceasar, Joseph Meyer and Bobby Buttenuth penned ditty indeed sounds hip.
25. You Flew Away from the Nest," Brunswick 3014. Al emulates himself very well, as this 1925 ditty, penned by Harry Ruby and Bert Kalmar, scores.
26. "I'm Sitting on Top of the World," Brunswick 3014. This bit of a mouthful, penned by Ray Henderson, Sam M. Lewis, and Joe Young, is nevertheless a stimulating Jolson vocal.
27. "When the Red Red Robin Comes Bob-Bob-Bobin' Along," Brunswick 3222. This stupid and somewhat juvenile title, penned by Harry Woods, somehow works. More so, this ditty would oddly become contemporary recording fodder for (black) entity Eva Taylor.
28. "Blue River" Brunswick 3719. Jolson's vocal is a bit tough, and indeed turns in a fine and durable vocal. As penned by (Joseph Meyer and Al Bryran), this just could be Jolson at his very best, with good backing support as by Bill Wirges and Orchestra.
29. "Golden Gate," Brunswick 3775. This 1928 ditty, penned by Dave Dreyer, Joseph Meyer, Billy Rose, and Al himself, defines a typical showboating Jolson vocal
30. "Back in Your Own Backyard," Brunswick 3867. Jolson's tougher vocal style shines through. Penned by Dave Dreyer, Billy Rose, and Al himself, this ditty perhaps found a contemporary Ruth Etting rendering a bit better. A lesser-known Russ Columbo version is also better. (A later differing vocal and jazz style, as recorded by Billie Holiday in 1938, offers even more interest in this ditty.) Listen and compare.
31. "Dirty Hands, Dirty Face," Brunswick 3912. Penned by James Monaco, Grant Clark, Edgar Leslie, and Jolson himself, this effective lament was featured in the first major "talking" film *The Jazz Singer*.
32. "My Mammy," Brunswick 3912. This ditty, penned by Walter Donaldson, Sam M. Lewis, and Joe Young, is better seen and heard in *The Jazz Singer*. While in title alone, this bit of schmaltz (resurrected from Jolson's previous Broadway entity *Sinbad*) reeks in sentiment, the typical Jolson delivery (in blackface, on bended knee) sells it! The greatest parody of its time?
33. "There's a Rainbow Around My Shoulder," Brunswick 4033. While the 1928 Jolson film *The Singing Fool* is forgotten, this ditty from that film, penned by Billy Rose, Dave Dreyer, and Jolson himself, remains. While a bit fluffy, the Jolson vocal, typically full of confidence, succeeds.
34. "I'm in Seventh Heaven," Brunswick 4400. Penned by Lew Brown Buddy De Sylva, Ray Henderson, and Jolson himself, this ditty was featured in the Jolson film *Say It with Songs*. While this 1929 film is forgotten for good reason, this recording should not be.
35. "Let Me Sing and I'm Happy," Brunswick 4721. Jolson introduced this Irving Berlin-penned classic in his 1930's film Mammy. While a bit sappy, the Jolson style, also sappy, fits. A contemporary Ruth Etting version is also good and, indeed, a fine embellishment of Jolson's rendering, at least for a while. Moreover—Ruth's version is indeed better! Listen and compare.
36. "When the Little Red Roses Get the Blues for You," Brunswick 4721. This stupid title, penned by Al Dubin and Joe Burke, is actually better than its long title! (A contemporary version by the Boswell Sisters has been found to be far better, but as

(only) a radio aircheck, hardly heard and competitive in 1930. Perhaps this book has gotten it right, but who really cares?)

37. "Hallelujah, I'm a Bum," Brunswick 6500. This dumb title, penned by Rodgers and Hart, was also the title of his 1933 film. Somehow, despite its limitations, the typical Jolson style scores.
38. "Rock-a-Bye-Your Baby with a Dixie Melody," Brunswick 6502. Most of the time, rerecordings fail to score. Considering the previous acoustic age and the fine original recording Jolson had made in 1918, it's a good bet that Jolson figured he had something to prove. This (1933) rendering, casting off most of his previous acoustic inhibitions and style, finds Jolson attempting to croon and, oddly enough, succeeding. Moreover, this already old ditty, while full of schmaltzy lyric and fluff, perhaps defined Jolson—just as much.

- Jolson Recordings on Decca

The 1930s found Jolson competing less with the likes of crooning radio singers and the advent of swing music. While he did remain active in radio and film work, his activity as a recording entity literally stopped in 1933. The advent of WWII found Jolson, like many others, ready to contribute entertainment for USO shows and, in a great way, reintroduced Jolson into Americana. Following the war, radio was offered, as well as a Decca Records contract. The Decca masters generally consist of rerecordings and hits of the 1920s, indeed capitalizing on a successful 1946 film bio *The Jolson Story*. While the older performer could not play himself, the soundtrack featured a likable and durable Jolson vocal. In retrospective, the dubbing of actor Larry Parks in blackface in this post WW II period sadly put the face of previously accepted racism directly upon the Jolson legacy in the last phase of his career.

This last Decca period indeed found Jolson in good voice and, like his earlier Brunswick recordings, a polished package of crooning, with more than a lot of the Jolson personality hamming it up. The following Decca recordings have merit:

39. "Alexander's Ragtime Band," Decca 40038. This (1947) duet with Bing Crosby became a best seller.
40. "About a Quarter to Nine," Decca 24400. For some odd reasons, Jolson had not make a studio recording of his own 1935 film entity, *Go into Your Dance*. Indeed, this ditty penned by Harry Woods and Al Dubin, had been a fine film song and had been recording fodder for many, noting very fine version contemporary 1935 versions by Ozzie Nelson and Chick Bullock. Jolson, as committed as ever, perhaps even realizing his mistake, at last produced a fine recording and, moreover, claimed this fast-paced classic as his own (recording).
41. "Down Among the Sheltering Palms," Decca 24534. This much-recorded ditty found itself as a best-selling (acoustic) entity in 1915, rendered by the Lyric Quartet, on Victor 17778. It had also been successfully revived as a Boswell Sisters entity in the early 1930s. As part of his "comeback," this ditty, penned by Abe Olman and James Brockman, is given a great professional rendering which, in fact, is embellished by the addition of the Mills Brothers. In true retrospective, this interesting recording finally integrates Jolson as a recording artist, with a black group sound that didn't really need him.
42. "Is It True What They Say About Dixie," Decca 24534. As the flip side, penned by Irving Caesar, Sammy Lerner, and Gerald Marks, this ditty had been a best seller for

Ozzie Nelson in the mid-1930s. This rendering, further graced by the Mills Brothers "group" sound, contributes well to the Jolson legacy, as his older vocal holds his own with the multitalented group. (As a further note, for some reason, Jolson rerecorded this ditty, on Decca 24684), resulting in the sad result of the missing Mills Brothers vocals. Stupid? You bet!)

43. "Baby Face," Decca DL-5006. While Jolson was not seen, his vocals, using new Decca masters, were used in two bios, *The Jolson Story* (1946) and *Jolson Sings Again* (1949). Penned by Benny Davis and Harry Akst, this novel ditty had, more so, been well known as a (1926) Jan Garber release, featuring a spirited vocal from its coauthor, the contemporary vaudevillian Benny Davis. As well as many subsequent versions, especially noting an interesting rendering by "Whispering" Jack Smith. Perhaps Mary Eaton's well-done (1929) film could have defined it better, if a contemporary (Eaton) recording had followed? Noting that the original Benny Davis version had an obvious (vocal) debt to Jolson anyway, it's more than easy to find the newer Jolson version (finally) claiming it. (Later, in 1958, many young baby boomers, unfamiliar with all this, indeed found a (differing) Little Richard version quirky and rockin'.)
44. "Are You Lonesome Tonight," Decca 27043. This ain't great, but notable. This 1920s entity, penned by Ray Turk and Lou Handman had been recorded by many, including the likes of Vaughn De Leath. This (1950) recording, along with a contemporary Blue Barron release, with a vocal by Bobby Beers and the Blue Notes (MGM 10628), most likely had an effect upon a young Memphis teenager—Elvis Presley, who would later record and claim it.

Visual Image.

- *The Jazz Singer*, Warner Brothers,1927. The Jolson legacy, in true retrospective, is shot to pieces with his "blackface" image. As seen in the first film of commercial significance as a "talking picture" (a Jolson first), he is seen performing some earlier hits, especially with "Toot, Toot, Tootsie, Good-bye," as he is seen and heard singing with (embarrassing) bird calls to boot. The subsequent featured ethnic religious stuff and the previously introduced "My Mammy" are full of hooky, dated antics as well. *The Jazz Singer*, nevertheless, does find the contemporary Irving Berlin-penned ditty in a Jolson performance never attempted as a recording, nor actually finished in the film itself. In it, Al (not in blackface) intermittently breaks into

45. "Blue Skies." His totally committed performance is seen and heard to be quite sensational. Like an early Elvis Presley number, Jolson truly electrifies the screen. Moreover, if this is any indication of his (earlier) and younger days, it only proves a greater loss for later generations, as in the case of other performers not possessing the technology to capture the moment.

Louis Jordan

The term "rhythm and blues," in itself defines Louis Jordan. His combination of rhythmic singing, blowing away on his sax (with his Tympany Five) would help replace the age of "swing" and catch fire to the strong rhythmic patterns of musical taste. It was also this singing bandleader's vocals, while possessing no great qualities, which, nevertheless, captured the masses with a simple message of rhythmic style and danceable fun. Like Frankie "Half Pint" Jaxon before him, Jordan's vocabulary nourished upon the everyday words of the urban ghetto, with much hipness. More so, it was Louis, more than anyone before him, who combined slower, urban blues with a more-definable rhythmic beat, and more simple than "swing." While noting the influences of the already mentioned Jaxon, the likes of bandleaders Chick Webb and Cab Calloway, who had also figured hugely in his development, the artistic and commercial success of Louis Jordan would indeed directly influence many after WWII. In true retrospective, Jordan's own influence, despite a somewhat normal vocal, on all future rhythm and blues, rock and roll, and rap trends is still lingering, still relevant.

The following are Louis Jordan picks:

1. "Doug the Jitterbug," Decca 7590. Yeah! This danceable ditty, penned by Louis himself, is a fine excuse for a dance. Indeed, it works!
2. "Keep a-Knocking," Decca 7609. Noted as "Blues Vocal Fox Trot," this curious description takes on some fast-paced vocalization. Credited to Mays Bradford, a 1928 release by "Boodle It" Wiggins as "Keep A-Knockin' An' You Can't Come In" (Paramount 12662), comes into mind. More so does a later Little Richard release, on Speciality 611, which, while inspired by Louis Jordan, is more of an explosion!
3. "Fore Day Blues," Decca 7693 (Sepia Series). This "race" series by Decca of the 1930s was a backward step. Luckily, the series was dropped. This ditty, however, did give customers what they wanted, and indeed more.
4. "Pan Pan" Decca 8537 (Sepia Series). Novelty.
5. "Mama, Mama Blues," Decca 8626 (Sepia Series).
6. "What's the Use of Getting Sober (When You Gonna Get Drunk Again)," Decca 8645. Noted as a "Novelty Blues Vocal Chorus by Louis Jordan," this ditty, penned by Bubsy Meyers, notes social responsibility, or lack of it.
7. "The Chicks I Pick Are Slender and Tender and Tall," Decca 8645. This bit of slang, penned by Mike Jackson, is not hard to fully grasp, and also pleases the ear.
8. "You Can't Get Tat No More," Decca 8668.
9. "Mop Mop," Decca 8668. Penned by Claude De Metruis and J. M. Williams, this ditty may "rock," as well as "swing."
10. "Caldonia," Decca 8670. Louis, while still in a "novel" mood, rocks and rolls into something noteworthy, and danceable. (Bill Haley and His Comets, some ten years later, would also render this ditty).
11. "Is You Is or Is You Ain't My Baby," Decca 8659. This bit of urban slang, like so many of Jordan's efforts, was self-penned, along with Billy Austin. Moreover, this classic became a huge 1944 contemporary success as a filmed entity in *Follow the Boys*, and as a Bing Crosby and Andrews Sisters recording, released on Decca 23350. While the Vic Schoen Orchestra, which was featured on the Crosby and Andrews Sisters version, is no match for Jordan's Tympany Five, the Crosby and Andrews Sisters vocal, using slang, is excellent. More than likely, it's a good bet that Jordan very much enjoyed the Crosby and Andrews Sisters classic rendering, especially noting some of those royalty sales.
12. "G. I. Jive," Decca 8659. While Johnny Mercer's original, on Capital 141, ain't bad, the Jordan version provides a bit more bounce as well as (vocally) a bit more honest rendering of "jive" lyric.

13. "My Baby Said Yes," Decca 23417. This ditty, penned by Teddy Walters and Sydney Robin, was part of an attempt by Decca Records to par up its contemporary 1945 stable of recording artists. As Bing Crosby was then Decca's best-selling recording artist, it's also a good bet that even Bing was looking for something of substance. Moreover, for Jordan, more inroads into an integrated market provided for him more recognition. Luckily, everything seems to jell, as the very novel Crosby demonstrates his ability to use slang, and just as effectively as Jordan.
14. "Your Socks Don't Match," Decca 23417. Jordan and Bing, as in "My Baby Said Yes," are low key enough, as well as effective vocally, as they take on this fine novelty, penned by Leon Carr and Leo Corday. In true retrospective, it's more than a shame that the men did not produce more together, as they indeed match up well.
15. "Buzz Me," Decca 18734. There is more than the usual novelty here, as Louis creates a little (urban) blues theme (penned by Fleecie Moore and Danny Baxter). Moreover, this ditty caught the attention of (white) contemporary Ella Mae Morse, whose release on Capital 226 just may be better.
16. "Don't Let the Sun Catch You Cryin'," Decca 18818. This sentimental ditty, penned by Joe Greene, ain't bad. In true retrospective, a rock-era version by Gerry and Pacemakers, on Laurie 3251, is much better.
17. "Stone Cold Dead in the Market," Decca 23546. Louis and his old friend from the Chick Webb organization, Ella Fitzgerald, team up in a novel duet. While contrived with fake Caribbean accents, along with campy lyrics by Wilmouth Houdini, both Ella and Louis somehow meet the challenge and are convincing enough.
18. "Petootie Pie," Decca 23546. Louis and Ella again duet, with Ella again winning the vocal honors. Moreover, this ditty finds Ella scatting away, while Louis improvises upon some very hip lyrics, penned by L. Pack, F. Paparelli, and R. Leveen.
19. "That Chick's Too Young to Fry," Decca 23610. This bit of slang, penned by Tommy Edwards-the later 1950s performer and vocalist, ain't bad.
20. "Choo Choo Ch'Boogie," Decca 23610. This dumb dance number, penned by Vaughn Horton, Denver Darling, and Milt Gabler, nevertheless produced a fine excuse for the dance floor. (Bill Haley and his Comets would later use it, and just as effectively.)
21. "Let the Good Times Roll," Decca 23741. While a lot of respect for a Ray Charles version (Atlantic 2047) and a Shirley and Lee version (Alladin 3335) are still due, this Fleecie Moore-penned classic, as recorded by Louis Jordan, just had to influence all later recordings.
22. "Ain't Nobody Here But Us Chickens," Decca 23741. Yet another silly novelty, penned by Joan Whitney and Alec Kramer, that somewhat works.
23. "Run Joe," Decca 24448. Penned by Joe Willougnby, Walt Merrick, and Louis himself, this bit of playful novelty, addressed as "Calypso Afro Vocal Chorus by Louis Jordan and the Calypso Boys," while contrived and novel, still scores.
24. "Baby, It's Cold Outside," Decca 24644. Ella Fitzgerald (again) duets with Louis, and again scores!
25. "Saturday Night Fish Fry," Decca 24725. Is this ditty, penned by Ellis Lawrence Walch and Louis himself, perfect 1949 juke box fodder for a small café or roadhouse?

Helen Kane

- Is Helen Kane (a latter 1920s', baby-voiced flapper) "Betty Boop"? Her "pop" appeal was considerable, and she shared much in style, on more than a few recordings, as by contemporaries Ruth Etting, Annette Hanshaw, and Libby Holman. While always a bit contrived, Helen Kane could indeed sing and, on occasion, prove it. In any case, this wild flapper just might have had just claims upon the contemporary Max Fleischer cartoon voice, although Mae Questel, perhaps originally a Helen Kane emulator, would indeed stage further claims upon the Fleischer cartoon. Even so, the "little girl" vocal, a delight for many 1920s' recording companies, would be popular, as Helen's flirting vocals, more than suggestive, remain novel and, indeed, fun.

1. "Get Out and Get Under the Moon," Victor 21557. While noted on the original recording as a "Comedienne with orchestra," Helen projects more, as she literally plays with the lyrics, penned by Charles Tobias, Larry Shay, and William Jerome, as well as keeps in tempo with an accompanying Hawaiian guitar. (a contemporary and jazzy effort, released as a Paul Whiteman entity with a fine differing Bing Crosby vocal on Columbia 1402-D, also offers good vocal comparisons.)
2. "That's My Weakness Now," Victor 21557. Yeah, this lyric is loose and wild, as penned by Bud Green and Sammy Stept for the 1927 Broadway entity 'A Night In Spain", and the cool baby talk of Helen's is both spirited and sensual as a contemporary recording as it had been when Helen had originally introduced it in the same production? Or how do we know? Or-who cares?
3. "I Wanna Be Loved By You," Victor 21684. This title may, for many, be considered a tip-off for the style of "Betty Boop." Penned by Bert Kalmar, Harry Ruby, and Herbert Stothart, this bit of slang, noting perhaps "boop," "boop-a-doop" as the kind of language that a contemporary 1928 flapper, indeed, defined as an era, also defined as language. Helen had more ever introduced this ditty originally in the contemporary Broadway entity "Good Boy". (Other versions, including a fine version by Vaughn De Leath, as a Ben Selvin Orchestra release, on Columbia 1604 D, is also hip, although the edge goes to Helen.) Whether the stylistic origins may still be credited to black entertainers Baby Ester or Baby Cox is an open question. Did Helen and Vaughn bump into Ester or Cox? As a further note, a minor victory was achieved by Helen Kane in 1950s, when at about the age of forty-six years, her vocal was dubbed into a Fred Astaire film (about authors Kalmar and Ruby), again using her original 1920s' style for "I Wanna Be Loved by You."
4. "Is There Anything Wrong with That?" Victor 21684. Penned by Herb Magidson and Michael Cleary, this bit of suggestive tease remains fun.
5. "Me and the Man in the Moon," Victor 21830. Helen is always playful, and this bit of camp, penned by Edgar Leslie and Jimmy Monaco, may again be considered a classic, as well as a real "moon" song.
6. "Don't Be Like That," Victor 21830. Helen's attitude is infectious, as this ditty, penned by Archie Gottler, Charles Tobias, and Maceo Pincard, defines a "flapper" as well.
7. "Button Up Your Overcoat," Victor 21863. Penned by De Sylva, Brown, and Henderson, this 1929 ditty had become a classic flapper entity. Moreover, it's more than noteworthy that other versions, as by Ruth Etting and Vaughn De Leath, as a vocalist for Paul Whiteman, are basically sung in the same style, with Helen's version leading the way in sales.
8. "I Want To Be Bad," Victor 21863. Helen is so good that she's "bad," as she infuses humor into this fine ditty contemplating a bit of fun, penned by Buddy De Sylva, Lew Brown, and Ray Henderson.
9. "Do Something," Victor 21917. Helen indeed does "do something" with her flirtatious vocal in this ditty as penned by Bud Green and Sammy Stept.

10. "That's Why I'm Happy," Victor 21917. Helen indeed "sounds" happy, as these typicial lyrics of the jazz age of 1929, penned by Herb Magidson and Michael N. Cleary, make intentions clear.
11. "I'd Do Anything for You," Victor 22080. It seems that Helen's inviting vocal is loose enough, as this ditty penned by Cliff Friend and Lew Pollack indicates.
12. "He's So Unusual," Victor 22080. This ditty was penned by Al Lewis, Al Sherman, and Abner Silver for the 1929 film *Sweetie*, which featured Helen Kane. While the film is no gem, this recording again finds Helen flirting—which is not unusual! (Light years away, did rocker Cyndi Lauper resurrect this ditty?).
13. "I Have to Have You," Victor 22192. This breezy vocal is bright and bubbly and so is a similar contemporary version by Annette Hanshaw, on Okeh 41351. Contemporary 1929 speculation had it that Victor Records had been so upset about Annette Hanshaw, or Annette Hanshaw as Gay Ellis, similar 'lille gir' vocal style (on the same titles like this one) considered legal action. Penned by Richard Whiting and Leo Robin for the contemporary fim 'Pointless Heels' in which Helen herself introduced the ditty, this obvious clash of similar styles is also hard to figure.
14. "Ain'tcha," Victor 22192. The fun is still heard, and Helen (again) delivers the goods originally in the 1929 contemporary film 'Pointless Heels" with some harmless slang, as penned by Mack Gordon and Max Rich.
15. "Readin' Ritin' Rhythm'," Victor 22407. Helen's at school, and her rhythm is real (penned by Don Hartman and Victor Schertzinger).
16. "If I Knew You Better," Victor 22520. This slower tempo works for Helen (penned by Don Hartman and Victor Schertzinger). However, it seems that Helen cannot stop her bubbly personality, or at least contain it, as contemporaries Ruth Etting and Annette Hanshaw could and did.
17. "My Man Is on the Make," Victor 22475. The high-voiced contemporary Libby Holman version of this Richard Rogers and Lorenz Hart penned ditty, on Brunswick 4554, is slower, and better. So is a jazzy Eva Taylor version for the Knickerbockers, on Columbia 2067-D. Nevertheless, the quirky Kane vocal is full of her novelty and her own personality. In fact, with a bit of change in approach, noting a strong voice somewhere in Helen Kane, a more competitive release just could have been produced. Sadly, it was not, although this version is far from bad.

The following is not a Helen Kane vocal but is a pick, breaking the rules of this book, but for good reason. The following is a Mae Questal novelty recording review:

"The Music Goes 'Round and 'Round," Decca 680. This ditty is worth hearing and, indeed, the voice of Helen Kane is recalled, but it's not her!

NOTE : Speculation has it that Mae, at one time or another, in addition to Betty Boop, was the caracture voice of Popeye, Olive Oyl, Felix the Cat, Little Audrey and Casper the friendly ghost.

Frankie Laine

- Frankie Laine's bombastic approach to popular music, using a baritone-tenor-like pitch, adding drama to a story (usually related to cowboys and Western themes), found great favor with most popular music fans of the latter 1940s. The Laine approach is, moreover, a quirky one, which indicates that he could have been the type of vocalist who would have scored in the pre-electric age of acoustic recording. He, in fact, may have been influenced vocally by the erratic 1930's voice of "street singer" Arthur Tracy, but Laine's vocal is far more controlled, possibly influenced by the contemporary (1930s-40s) Italian recordings of Carlo Buti? For a while, Frankie Lane's recordings offered an interesting alternative for pop, although, in true retrospective, no one figured on the rise of rhythm and blues, which greatly overshadowed Laine's vocal and stylistic approach.

1. "Moonlight in Vermont," Atlas FL 156. This well-sung ditty, competing with the superb vocal by Margaret Whiting on a Billy Butterfield release, on Capital 182, ain't bad. While Margaret had, and still has, claims upon this classic, a later 1950s rendering, as by Frank Sinatra, on LP W 920 is stronger.
2. "That's My Desire," Mercury 5007. This recording, penned by Carroll Loveday, and Helmy Kresa, while dated, indeed defined a fine pop hit. A previous 1931 Nick Lucas version. (Brunswick 6147) is softer as well as an interesting comparison in vocal technique and effect.
3. "(What Did I Doto Be So) Black and Blue," Mercury 1026. This best-selling entity of 1947 is an odd piece of work, noting that this Afro-American entity, penned by Fats Waller, Harry Brooks, and Andy Razaf), is a lament about racism and, indeed, about how black folk themselves discriminate. Moreover, this 1928 ditty, from the all-black revue *Connie's Hot Chocolates,* had been recorded by its stars Edith Wilson, on Brunswick 4685 and by Louis Armstrong, on Okeh 8715. It had also been defined in 1930 as a dramatic Ethel Waters release, on Columbia 2184-D. Just why Laine decided to drop the race issue and turn the corner as a light attempt at jazz is unclear, and perhaps it's interesting to speculate if he even knew just what these lyrics were asking, as well as telling. Nevertheless, backed by the Carl Fisher Swingtet, this recording is vocally bombastic enough and, while confused, a fairly interesting vocal.
4. "Two Loves Have I," Mercury 5064. When heard, the obscure (1931) recording by Morton Downey, on HOW 1201, proves that *sometimes*, attempts at crooning from tenors can provide good listening. Or maybe it was just quirkiness of Downey's vocal prowess? Moreover, it would be Josephine Baker who would define this ditty in French, which was, for most Americans, even more obscure than Downey's rendering, who was a popular radio entity of those Depression-era times. For Laine, this ditty was not about Downey, Paris, or Josephine Baker. Like most ditties, Laine's own quirky (post-WWII) style is not always about lyrics, but emotional mood.
5. "Shine," Mercury 5091. This late 1940's attempt at rhythmic singing, with Carl Fishers Orchestra, just may have been inspired by Louis Prima, the white singing bandleader who loved and emulated Louis Armstrong, both as a trumpet player and a gritty vocalist. While not in the same league as the classic 1931 Armstrong vocal, on Okeh 41486, nor the Bing Crosby and Mills Brothers 1932 rendering, on Brunswick 6276, this fast-paced vocal is solid, and indeed scores.
6. "We'll Be Together Again," Mercury 5091. This unusual vocal style, demonstrates a willingness to be different, and this fine recording, penned by Carl Fisher and Frankie himself, also lends credit for Laine's own interest as a recording artist. Noting that Laine could not break through as a pre-WWII entity, the postwar world of 1948 seemingly proved that timing is everything, especially for the already middle-aged singer.

7. "You're All I Want for Christmas," Mercury 5177. This ditty penned, by Glen Moore and Seger Ellis, is full of the usual sentiments of Christmas blandness. While the sentiment is obvious, Laine's own edgy vocal delivers more, as well as something different for Christmas.
8. "That Lucky Old Sun," Mercury 5316. Frankie got lucky again, as this ditty, penned by Haven Gillespie and Beasley Smith, is well defined by his emotional rendering.
9. "Mule Train," Mercury 5345. Yeah, you can hear the whip and maybe the rolling of the wagons driven by mules. As a film entity, penned by Johnny Lange, Hy Heath, and Fred Gleckman for the forgotten film *Singin' Gun*, this contrived bit of nonsense ain't much. The Laine version, moreover, in addition to the gimmicks, is perfectly fit, in bombastic style, and, moreover, defines this ditty. (A contemporary Bing Crosby version, on Decca 24798, reveals a hidden strength in Crosby's voice, although, in comparison, with the Laine version, it is a bit lame.)
10. "The Cry of the Wild Goose," Mercury 5363. This interesting title, penned by Terry Gilkyson, is about all this ditty has going for it, except for the bombastic Laine style, which. indeed. saves it.
11. "South of the Border," Mercury 5892. The (1939) Gene Autry classic is resurrected!
12. "Jezebel," Columbia 39367. After generating huge sales for Mercury, Frankie Laine was lured into a better cash deal by Columbia. This classic tale of deception, penned by Wayne Shanklin, is a perfect for the Laine style, as well as very believable.
13. "High Noon," Columbia 39770. The Tex Ritter classic, penned for the contemporary 1952 Gary Cooper Western, had also been released by him, on Capital 2120. Both versions are sincere, although the original Ritter version, in comparison, is obviously less a drain upon the emotions, as Laine, as usual, adds more theatrics and drama.
14. "I Believe," Columbia 39903. This religious theme, penned by Erwin Drake, Irvin Graham, Jimmy Shirl, and Al Stillman, is well defined by Laine's style.
15. "Your Cheating Heart," Columbia 39903. This Hank Williams classic finds Frankie as committed as ever, with a vocal attempt at "soft" vocalizing. Indeed, he succeeds.
16. "Moonlight Gambler," Columbia 40780. This 1956 release again showcases an emotional vocal, with a contrived tale about a professional gambler, penned by Bob Hilliard and Phil Spriger. Moreover, this winner is deep into "cowboy" mythology and perhaps an inspiration for the likes of fellow C & W Columbia recording artist Marty Robbins.
17. "Lotus Land," Columbia 40780. Another fine and contrived tale, penned by Mitchell Parish and Cyril Scott, this time about a man lost in the middle of the desert. Effective? Thirsty?
18. "Love Is a Golden Ring," Columbia 40856. Penned by Richard Dehr, FrankMiller, and Terry Gilkyson, this somewhat conventional tale is "pop," and Lane scores—despite rock and roll.
19. "Way Down Yonder in New Orleans," Columbia 40116. (Duet with Jo Stafford).
20. "Cool Water." Columbia-40457.
21. "Rawhide," Columbia 41230. As introduced in the TV Western *Rawhide*, and penned by Ned Washington and Dimitri Tiomkin, this contrived tale is also noted for its gimmicky "whip" sound—much like the previous "mule train." Moreover, this television classic, which ran many years, and still in reruns, indeed preserves Lane's vocal, along with a young Clint Eastwood—part of Americana itself.
22. "You Gave Me a Mountain," ABC 11174. The late 1960s moved Laine into different directions as the effects of rock and the Beatles had shaken up pop as well. Penned by

Marty Robbins, it was odd that it had not been a single release by him. In any case, this sad tale, perfect for Laine's style, actually became a minor best seller, this late, in 1969.

Harlan Lattimore

The fame and fortunes of Bing Crosby in the early 1930s provided the foundation for the music called "pop," or "popular," music as no one before him. Indeed, his commercial success in the media of personal appearances, radio, films and "crooning" recordings found him to be a marketable wonder and, indeed, an institution. Others sought to be like him and, for a few decades more, the likes of many, adapted. As noted in other parts of this book, however, the evolution of Crosby did not take place overnight. Like contemporaries Russ Columbo, Ozzie Nelson, Harlan Lattimore, and others including Ruth Etting and Ethel Waters, the influence of Rudy Vallee had set an example. The newer technology of electronic recording, with megaphone and (newer) microphones, indeed founded a softer, more intimate vocal style. The need to be heard, as by tenors, and quirky voices of the acoustic age was blown away. Indeed the "love song" matured, as the enhanced listener was, more so, "adult." The likes of torch singers became popular, as though the vocalist was singing directly to its listeners, not at them. Harlan Lattimore was a fine vocalist, who could also "croon". Whether, like Russ Columbo, he sought to emulate Crosby is hard to prove. As a true contemporary of Crosby, it's a better bet that like Crosby, he evolved. Unlike Columbo, Harlan was Afro-American and, perhaps, Harlem's best-kept secret. Indeed, as a Connie's Inn live entity, he packed in crowds of mostly black patrons, "crooning" and electrifying his audiences, mostly as a featured vocalist with the fine Don Redman Orchestra. As demonstrated in many of the following picks, he indeed sounds much like contemporaries Crosby or Columbo. As the "black Crosby," his skin color also restricted his fame, although, perhaps, for many who had seen and heard him, a label for Bing Crosby as the "white Lattimore" is not without legitimate debate.

- The following are Harlan Lattimore picks:

1. "If It's True," Brunswick 6368. Don Redman plays, and Harlan croons out this Gus Bentley, Jule Primrose and Don Redman penned ditty.
2. "Underneath the Harlem Moon," Brunswick 6401. Penned by Mack Gorden and Harry Revel, this bit of questionable racial lyrics finds the slick crooner scoring. (A more rigorous and rousing version is found in the film short *Rufus Jones for President*, as by Ethel Waters. The Waters version, more of a "drug" song," moreover, never became a commercial recording.)
3. "Ain't I the Lucky One," Brunswick 6401. This Don Redman release, also penned by him, the flip side of "Underneath The Harlem Moon," also scores. Is it similar to the later 1950s Marty Robbins recording?
4. "Pagan Paradise," Brunswick 6412. This under-sung ditty is still hot crooning of this Ted Koehler and Kay Parker penned ditty perhaps penned for the 'Connies Inn' nightclub un which Harlan was it's resident performer in the early 1930s?
5. "That Blue-Eyed Baby from Memphis," Brunswick 6560. Don Redman's orchestra is on the fast track, and rhythmically challenges Harlan. Moreover, the fast-paced crooner pleasantly catches up, and this fine ditty, as penned by Palmer, is indeed made into a classic crooner rendering.

6. “Lazybones,” Brunswick 6622. Harlan croons out this Hoagy Carmichael and Johnny Mercer-penned classic, and without a racial stereotype that perhaps the contemporary Mildred Bailey version implies.
7. “I Found a New Way to Go to Town,” Brunswick 6684. Harlan’s fine crooning job on this mid-tempo ditty, penned by Harvey Brooks, Gladys DuBois aand Ben Ellison may be lost to most, but Mae West’s version in the contemporary 1933 film *I’m No Angel*, although found to be heard in filmed sequences, remains a sight to be seen!
8. “Lonely Cabin,” Brunswick 6935. This crooner seemingly wants to fill his cabin.
9. “You Told Me but Half the Story,” Brunswick 6935.
10. “Who Wants to Sing My Love Song,” Vocalion 3359.
11. “Got the South in My Soul,” Melotone 12417. The Lee Wiley original is more than challenged!
12. “Moonrise on the Lowlands,” Melotone 60709. Harlan’s smooth baritone vocal is a bit fast, as well as good, in this ditty penned by Al Neiburg and Jerry Levinson.
13. “Lazy Weather,” Melotone 60709. This delightful ballad, penned by Irving Kahal and Oscar Levant, is crooned out to perfection! Perhaps contemporary Perry Como, also a Crosby-influenced crooner, heard it? More so, a later Como “crooning” vocal as a Ted Weems release (Decca 822) ain’t bad.
14. “Poor Old Joe,” Victor 24008. This recording, a rare early 1930s Fletcher Henderson release, features another fine and novel crooning job.
15. “A Day without You,” Brunswick 6747. This Victor Young release, penned by Sam Coslow and Arthur Rebner, ain’t bad. It’s interesting to speculate how Young, who knew Bing Crosby well, felt about Harlan’s fine crooning vocal?
16. “Beloved,” Brunswick 6748. Another outing with Victor Young produced another good crooning job.
17. “How Do You Do It,” Brunswick 6380. This release from Ballyhoo is sung hauntingly for Abel Lyman’s Orchestra.
18. “Take Me in Your Arms,” Melotone M-12512. As recorded with the Owen Fallon Orchestra, this bit of crooning finds its mark. So does a contemporary crooned-out torch effort as by Ruth Etting, on Banner 32634.
19. “A Little Street Where Old Folks Meet,” Melotone M-12512. This ditty, penned by Gus Kahn and Harry Woods, perhaps had roots in Mexican folklore. In any case, this slow-crooning effort is appreciated.
20. “Some Day We’ll Meet Again,” Conqueror 8029. The challenge to the contemporary Bing Crosby version, on Brunswick 6427, is obvious, as this crooning job, as part of an Ed Lloyd release, is to be realized and appreciated.
21. “Just a Little Home for the Old Folks,” Conqueror 8029. Another mellow crooning ditty!
22. “With Summer Coming On,” Columbia 2671-D. Like many previous efforts, this bit of crooning matches Crosby at his best, as noted on Crosby’s contemporary release on Brunswick 6329. More so, this mushy song is lifted with sincere commitments by a vocal style that indeed identified with the Depression era. Listen to both recordings and decide “who”?
23. “Strange as It Seems,” Columbia 2671-D. This fine crooning job indeed beats out others, including a clumsy contemporary Adelaide Hall version on Brunswick 6375.
24. “I Wanna Be Loved”. Brunswick-6745. (This1934 croon job was later revived in1950 by the Andrews Sisters and Dinah Washington).

Leadbelly

The "blues" songs of America can easily be transformed into "folk," and the creation of an idiom just may become just another label on a "sound" product. In fact, the government of the United States (using the Library of Congress) may indeed be the subjective instrument to find or locate its own folklore, discarding commercial interests. Indeed, the efforts of John Lomax (and his son Alan), in the 1930s, found much of it, especially in the case of Leadbelly, aka Huddie Leadbetter.

> The real-life tale of Leadbelly is indeed a document in actual acts of violence that resulted in his imprisonment in both Texas and Louisiana. The influences of first-generation blues recordings also had to have had an impact, especially in the personage of Blind Lemon Jefferson, whose contemporary presence in east Texas just may have found both men aware of each other, with Blind Lemon's strumming, more than an inspiration. The legacy of Leadbelly recordings, both vocally and instrumentally, is primitive, with his latter recordings, in urban New York City, promoted as "folk." The following are picks of this highly influential vocalist, who died in 1949 and never lived to enjoy many commercial riches. More so, he never realized his contributions the future, noting the mid-1950s' "skiffle" movement of the UK (led by Britisher Lonnie Donnigan) and the following folk revival of the early 1960s.

Note: The huge output of the (uncommercial) Library of Congress recordings of Huddie are not found in review in this book. It should be noted, moreover, that many LIBOC recordings found their way to many of the commercial recordings, and are specific picks below.

1. "Looky, Looky, Yonder Black Betty Yellow Woman's Doorbells," Musicraft 223. This very powerful lyric just doesn't lie. The "Black Betty" segment is, perhaps, the ultimate hip statement about relationships. (Huddie also had a relationship with Southern prisons, and his incarnations, more so, to be more than familiar with black whips, or "Black Betty." A later rock-era entity of 1977 "Black Betty," as by Ram Jam, on Epic 50357, is very much inspired by the black girl, not the whip!
2. "Frankie and Albert," Musicraft 223. Is this the "folk" tale "Frankie and Johnny?—Yes!
3. "Bourgeois Blues," Musicraft 227. A slap at society?
4. "Midnight Special," Victor 27266. The addition of the Golden Gate Quartet also contributes to this ditty becoming special.
5. "Easy Rider," Bluebird 8570.
6. "New York City," Bluebird 8709. The staggering sites of the big apple is documented well by this very rural (from Mooringsport, Louisiana,) country entity.
7. "Leaving Blues," Bluebird 87913
8. "Take This Hammer," Ash 101. The rock pile of a prison must have been an inspiration to sing on this one. (Much later, Johnny Cash would also "pick" this hammer up.)
9. "Rock Island Line." Ash 102. This rambling tale of a train ride is indeed full of the drama of its effect. Once its listener is on board, the free ticket to travel and adventure is all true grit. This very fine recording, about an Illinois railroad, found its way across on ocean to Lonnie Donegan's version, on the (1956) American release (London

1650). Indeed, they do have trains in England, as well as Leadbelly reissues! Moreover, this train ride found an earthy version by Johnny Cash.

10. "Irene," Ash 343-2. "Goodnight, Irene" became a huge seller for the Weavers (Decca 27077) about a year after Leadbelly,—who penned this classic with John Lomax—was in his grave. While the commercial aspects of the Weavers recording reaped great rewards, perhaps the added "goodnight" in the title was, indeed, correct?
11. "John Henry," Ash 243-3. This traditional tale of the John Henry fable of a steel-driving man doesn't necessarily pertain to Afro-Americans. Certainly the later (1947) recording is just as interesting, noting a saga from East or West! (Preceding both Leadbelly and Travis, the stringy, captured (acoustic) sounds of Gid Tanner's vocal and fiddling and Riley Puckett's vocal and guitar-strumming produced a "folk" sound, then dubbed "hillbilly," on Columbia 15019-D in 1924.)
12. "On a Monday I'm Almost Gone," Ash 343-1. This ditty, credited as penned by John and Alan Lomax, is a contrived, up-tempo ditty that accurately exploits Huddie's own prison experience. This just may be the very best release by Huddie, aka Leadbelly, which also became the prototype for the (later) Johnny song ditty, "I Got Stripes," on Columbia 41427.
13. "Midnight Special," Disc 6043. This rerecording (of the Victor release) features Huddie with Woody Guthrie and Cisco Houston sharing vocal harmony.
14. "John Hardy," Musicraft 311. This tale of a murderer in West Virginia, with both mother and wife visiting, finds the prisoner resigned to die. (Among earlier recordings, a less forceful but good rendition may be found by Buell Kazee, a fine early (white) folk entity (dubbed "hillbilly"), on Brunswick 144 in 1927.
15. "In New Orleans," Musicraft 312. While the origins of this ditty are most likely based upon the fable and fiction of New Orleans nightlife, Huddie's version (credited to him) is found in the fragments of other blues entities, including that of Texas Alexander's House's "The Rising Sun," on Okeh 8673. It's also very possible that Huddie found his friend Woody Guthrie's "House of the Rising Sun" (General Album 5020) more than a raw inspiration for his own. So was a fine 1942 version of "House of the Rising Sun" by Libby Holman (Decca 18306). (While the pre-rock era is full of shadows for many such entities, the fine 1964 recording, by the British blues band—the Animals—release of "The House of the Rising Sun" (MGM 13264), more so redefined it.)

Julia Lee

Julie Lee was, for the most part, a lounge singer (from Kansas City), who specialized in risqué novelty songs. As part of her brother's jazzy George Lee band in the latter 1920s, her piano sounds and (sometimes) backing vocals were at least relevant. Her clear and crisp vocals may have been at first influenced by Ethel Waters and Alberta Hunter. Later, as a solo entity, and much like contemporary Cleo Brown, her soft and jazzy vocals produced good recorded efforts. As a regular at Milton's Tap Room in Kansas City, Julia's jazzy vocals became better known. By the mid-1940s, she adapted a more simple but effective rhythm and blues style, without losing her usual (own) jazzy piano lead. The following picks are mostly novelties, mixed with familiar pop song ditties:

➢ The following find Julia Lee vocals with George Lee and His Orchestra.

1. "Down Home Syncopated Blues," Merritt 2206. This attempt at jazz is good, along with other voices in the band.
2. "He's Tall, Dark, and Handsome," Brunswick 4761. Julia's voice is a bit strained, but she clearly gets her message across.
3. Won't You Come Over to My House," Brunswick 4761. Another band-intro finds Julia's somewhat stretched vocal effectively inviting her audience over to her house. While the results are mixed, the excuse to dance, in a pre-swing medium tempo, ain't bad.

➤ The following find Julia Lee vocals with the Tommy Douglas Orchestra.

4. "Show Me Missouri Blues," Premier 29012.
5. "Lotus Blossom," Premier 29013.

➤ The following find Julia Lee vocals are identified as "Julia Lee and Her Boyfriends." As postwar Capital label releases, the following also found an attempt at products for the newer rhythm and blues market. It was, moreover, a brilliant move, in true retrospective, as the clear-voiced and effective Julia Lee was versatile enough to pull it off. Moreover, as most of the following titles indicate, the contrived titles and contents of these risqué ditties just could have been dirty jokes, yet sung with fun and flare. Listen.

6. "Snatch and Grab It," Capital 40028. The blatant sexual references found in this ditty are nothing new, as this ditty, penned by Sharon A. Pease, may be considered tame in comparison with the likes of the already numerous recorded blues ditties of the 1920s. Nevertheless, this well-recorded and clear-voiced bit of smirk is telling, as well as electric.
7. "King Size Papa," Capital 40082. Yes! This guy's got it! Penned by J. Gomez and P. Vance, the obvious pun is harmless fun, although perhaps a reference to 1992 found this ditty dated?
8. "You Ain't Got It No More," Capital 40082. This original flip side of "King Size Papa," penned by M. H. Wax, finds Julia in a different and disappointed mood. Seems like a problem?
9. "Tell Me, Daddy," Capital 15144. This rhythmic ditty, penned by Bobby Black, is more than danceable; it's raved up!
10. "I Didn't Like It the First Time," Capital 15367. Also known as "The Spinach Song," penned by J. Gomez and B. Gordon, the obvious pun works!
11. "If it's Good," Mercury 8005

Peggy Lee

As a young band vocalist of the mid-1930s, Peggy Lee (real name Norma Jean Egstrom) of Jamestown, North Dakota, found herself surrounded by crowds of Midwesterners, craving for a danceable tune, accompanied by a crooning vocal. By the latter 1930s, Peggy found a well-known bandleader to sing for, and by 1941, with Benny Goodman, the "King of Swing" himself. In true retrospective, her (wartime) appearance with Goodman in the film *Stage Door Canteen* (unintentionally) stole the spotlight away from her bandleader-mentor! Peggy's vocal delivery, perhaps best inspired by recordings of Ella Fitzgerald, Maxine Sullivan, Jo Stafford, Billie Holiday, and the (cool) Lee Wiley, and Lil Green. As with

Goodman and subsequent others, including (her husband for a time), Dave Barbour, her style and creativity were obvious, as well as her "show-off" image, which reeked of sophistication, and perhaps unreal perceptions as a later solo recording entity. In any case, Peggy still produced some fine recordings, many of which were classic renderings.

Picks are as follows:

1. "That Did It, Marie," Okeh 6497. This bit of Goodman style swing is done well, as this danceable entity—penned by J.C. Higginbotham and F. Meadows—like so many of the era, just cannot stop its listeners from (at least) standing. Nor can Goodman steal Peggy's effective vocal, however limited.
2. "Somebody Else Is Taking My Place," Okeh 6497. This flip side of "That Did it, Marie," penned by Dick Howard, Bob Ellsworth, and Russ Morgan, is a fine swing title tune, with Peggy trying to find out just who she should attempt to emulate (vocally). In any case, even *if* Peggy was trying to be Jo Stafford for this ditty, it's not bad, and is a fine choice!
3. "Blues in the Night," Okeh 6553. While searching for a style, Peggy is (greatly) aided by a typical Benny Goodman arrangement which encourages vocal prowess, as well as timing, between his vocalist and band. Considering the huge Dinah Shore success, on her Bluebird 11436 best seller, Goodman also found this classic (penned by Arlen and Mercer) something to be even more to be worked upon. The resulting recording, with Peggy and band member Lou McGarrity, is perhaps an improvement, noting Shore's warmth and Lee's coolness. Among many other recordings of this (1941) film title, Cab Calloway's usual grit, found on Okeh 6422, competes in a different way.
4. "Where or When," Okeh 6553. This flip side of "Blues in the Night," is another stab at creativity with Goodman. Goodman (graciously) gives Peggy a chance at a real vocal performance. While this Richard Rodgers and Lorenz Hart ditty fails to match the (contemporary) Lena Horne version (Victor 27818), Peggy, perhaps in emulation of Lena, is indeed very cool and good.
5. "We'll Meet Again," Okeh 6644. This very fine ditty, penned by Ross Parker and Hughie Charles, had (1939) origins in England, as a bland Vera Lynn release, on Decca F-7268. As the war progressed, along with the London blitz, this ditty came to represent much more, along with Vera Lynn's BBC radio broadcasts for the home folks and the British Empire. (Vera's later postwar (1954) version, on London 1348, would finally provide for Vera a far better recording, which became a best-selling entity in the United States, as well as a huge American audience, unfamiliar with her war-release broadcasts. In the time after Lynn's (1939) version, American ears found versions by a best seller for Kay Kyser (featuring fine vocals by Ginny Simms and Harry Babbitt, on Columbia 35870), a creative Ink Spots release, on Decca 3656, and this fine Goodman release, featuring this excellent Peggy Lee vocal, also in 1941.
6. "Elmer's Tune," Columbia 36359. How does such an un-hip name like "Elmer" become hip? Perhaps it's because this typical Goodman number swings, and Peggy's crisp vocal of this ditty (penned by Elmer Albrecht, Sammy Gallop, and Dick Jurgens) is, for certain, sung far better, yet sold far less than contemporary Glenn Miller's version, released on Bluebird 11274, which featured passable vocals as by Ray Eberle and the Modernaaires.
7. "Full Moon," Okeh 6652. Goodman's Orchestra dominates this ditty penned by Bob Russell, Gonzalez Curiel, and Odette Jackson, but Peggy also contributes just enough vocally, and indeed effectively.

8. "I Threw a Kiss to the Ocean," Columbia 36590. Peggy's vocal again gels well with Goodman, as this (Irving Berlin) classic is ignited as a fast-paced swing entity.
9-10. "Why Don't You Do Right?" Columbia 36652. This 1942 (wartime) release establishes a cool tongue-in-cheek vocal style that finally got Peggy Lee best known. Peggy's appearance with Goodman in the film *Stage Door Canteen*, aping this ditty, penned by Joe Mc Coy, also helped—indeed, providing this cool blonde with a definitive visual image in a smoke-filled room! (An earlier version (perhaps better for many) by Lil Green (with Big Bill Broonzy on guitar), on Bluebird 08714, indeed gave Peggy much to emulate, or at least much to speculate (vocally) upon.) For many ears, she sounds *just* like Lil Green! Other differing but good versions of this ditty include a yet earlier (1936) version, by the Harlem Hamfats, known as "Weed Smokers Dream" with a vocal by Chicago bluesman "Hamfoot Ham" (perhaps a good pal of Big Bill's?) and released on Decca 7234. As a further note, Peggy's (b) a later recording (Capital 15118), while not as nostalgic, is still cool and sexy.
11. "What More Can a Woman Do," Capital 197. This edgy bit of pop, penned by Dave Barbour and Lee herself, is superb. (A contemporary Sarah Vaughan version, on Continental 6008, is a direct stylistic challenge for Peggy. Listen and compare.)
12. "You Was Right, Baby," Capital 197. This contrived use of slang, in this ditty penned by Barbour and Lee, works, as Peggy's hipness (perhaps due to listening to Billie Holiday) just cannot be challenged.
13. "Waitin' for the Train to Come In," Capital 218. This top seller for the fairly new Capital label sounds as if Peggy is intent upon emulating Mildred Bailey. If so, it's a fact that Peggy had more voice, as well as a better one on this contrived Sunny Skylar and Martin Black penned ditty that works.
14. "It's a Good Day," Capital 322. With (then) husband Dave Barbour, a creative pairing of songwriting and vocals, belonging to Lee, and a guitar lick, like that of contemporary Les Paul, belonging to Barbour), a vocal, perhaps emulating Dinah Shore (minus guitar), is pleasantly heard.
15. "He's Just My Kind," Capital 322. This flip side, of "It's a Good Day," penned by Mark McIntyre and Floyd Huddleston), is sung with more commitment. Peggy's cool and dry delivery is indeed very effective. Moreover, there's perhaps a hint of both Lena Horne's and Connie Boswell's influences—which, perhaps, hints a good (ear) on Peggy's part.
16. "For Every Man There's a Woman," Capital 15030. While becoming designated as a band singer, or a "canary" (in Peggy's case at this time), this could have been seen as a step down career-wise. Instead, based upon previous experience, Peggy's paring with Goodman meant for good music, and, indeed, as in earlier times, Goodman's arrangement and Lee's vocal of this Leo Robin, Harold Arlen and Axel Stordahl penned ditty, indeed mesh well.
17. "Save Your Sorrows for Tomorrow," Capital 810. The old weeping Gene Austin entity from the 1920s finds a fresher vocal on a dismal song ditty!
18. "Sugar," Capital 810. Peggy's first attempt at this old Ethel Waters standard from the 1920s ain't bad.
19. "It Takes a Long Long Train with a Red Caboose," Capital 8445. This ditty penned by Larry Marks and Dick Charles is another winner—this time, perhaps, competing with fellow Capital artist, Ella Mae Morse.
20. "Just an Old Love of Mine," Capital 8445. Penned by Lee and Barbour, this creative venture wins.
21. "Golden Earrings," Capital 15009. This ditty, from the 1947 film of the same name, penned by Jay Livingston, Ray Evans, and Victor Young, produced many

contemporary renderings. Moreover, Peggy indeed sings her heart out, with some effective guitar work (probably) from Dave Barbour and tambourines.

22. "I'll Dance at Your Wedding," Capital 15009. This dated novelty works, and this ditty penned by Ben Oakland and Herb Magidson also provided Peggy a fine best seller for 1948.
23. "Manana Is Good Enough for Me," Capital 15022. This well-crafted bit of fluff, penned by Dave Barbour and Peggy herself, with a Latin theme, also demonstrates Peggy's impeccable ability to vocalize fast-paced lyrics. Moreover, this novel 1948 release became for her a huge best seller and, in fact, her most popular thus far.
24. "Bubble-Loo, Bubble-Loo," Capital 15118. Peggy does well on this novel classic penned by Hoagy Carmichael and Paul Francis Webster.
25. "Just One of Those Things," Decca 28313. Not much happened to this 1935 Cole Porter ditty from Broadway's *Jubilee*, unless you count Lena Horne's sensational filmed version in 1942, *Panama Hattie*. As a recording, Lena seems to clinch it, although Frank Sinatra's contemporary version quickly put Peggy's version in second place. Ginny Simms? Mabel Mercer's (later) version? Listen and compare.
26. "Lover," Decca 28315. Greta Keller's previous soft and inviting 1933 (NYC) 'torch' recording of the (Rogers and Hart) penned ditty from the contemporary film "Love Me Tonight", successfully hiding her (natural German accent), had previously defined it. Lee's liquid vocal, a bit more moody and personable, perhaps re-defined it? Peggy or Greta?
27. "Little Jack Frost, Get Lost," Decca 28463. This Yule-time duet with Bing Crosby gave Peggy the opportunity to record with one of her idols. Moreover, Peggy's performance of this contrived bit of fluff penned by Al Stillman and Seger Ellis is good, noting Peggy's energy lifting (old) Bing!
28. "Love, You Didn't Do Right," Decca 29250. Included in the original soundtrack of the (1954) film *White Christmas*, this Irving Berlin-penned classic was indeed the highlight of the film. While Peggy herself did *not* appear in the film, it's obvious enough that a huge marketing error had occurred for the soundtrack of that film. Along with Bing Crosby, Danny Kaye, the Skylarks, and the Joseph Lilley Orchestra and chorus, Peggy was part of the original recording project, which was issued on this single, issued on 78 rpm and 45 rpm, as well as on 45 EP and LP, on Decca 8083. While this project, for some reason, perhaps contractual, did not include contemporary Rosemary Clooney, the film version did, and along with Clooney's own recorded version (Columbia 40305), she claimed this ditty as her own. As for Peggy's original, her coolness is still an asset and is a fine example of what good popular music, this late in the game—was. It is also interesting to compare the fine Clooney version with Lee's. It is indeed understated and edgy in delivery, much like Peggy's version, but, a bit softer in style. Listen and compare!

29-35. *Songs from Walt Disney's Lady and the Tramp* (10-inch LP), Decca 5557. Many of the original baby boomers in 1955 were introduced to Peggy Lee, via Walt Disney, although we never knew it! The same may be said for the grandchildren of these mid-1950s kids as in the subsequent reissues on tape and DVDs for *Lady and the Tramp*. This excellent film soundtrack also claims Peggy Lee as a vocalist and writer, with (Sonny Burke), as these classic song ditties come alive in cartoon images.

Titles include

a. "Bella Notte." Peggy is backed here by Victor Young (as well as on the next three titles).

This bit of fluff, especially for preteens, is well worth it and extremely entertaining. For the adult ear, Peggy is perhaps at her creative peak as a single vocalist, as she is clearly heard and appreciated, noting the absence of the filmed cartoon, just listening to the recording. Peggy's obvious commitment, in true retrospective, remains a timeless pleasure for all future generations!

b. "Peace on Earth," actually "Silent Night."
c. "What Is a Baby."
d. "La La Lu."
e. "The Siamese Cat Song." Although this title takes a bit to digest as a recording, it somehow fits. (Peggy is backed here by Oliver Wallace and the Disney Studio Orchestra).
f. "He's a Tramp." Actually a good blues song, as sung by Peggy Lee with the Pound Hounds and Rhythm Accompaniment.

36-37. *Pete Kelly's Blues*, Decca LP 8166. This 1955 film soundtrack features Peggy Lee and Ella Fitzgerald. Peggy may be heard singing her heart out on the following:

a. and b. "He Needs Me" and "Sugar." In this knockout combination, penned by Arthur Hamilton ("He Needs Me") and Maceo Pinkard and Edna Alexander ("Sugar"), this excellent and jazzy effort finds Peggy in good vocal form and prowess—her second recording of this classic from the 1920s. (As far as Ella is concerned, she took the title vocal "Pete Kelly's Blues." It's also worth noting that perhaps the sharing of this soundtrack for both Peggy and Ella was competitive, and both recording artists produced results that were excellent.)

38. "Fever," Capital 3998. This 1958 recording defines "cool" and demonstrates just what Peggy was capable of when bending a lyric, as penned by Jack Davenport and Eddie Cooley. As a Little Willie John original, on King 4935, this ditty had reeked of a capable R & B vocal performance. Peggy's version is more sultry and is also a jazzy performance, with her own personable attributes thrown in. It's hard to say if she had heard the Willie John original, but it is also obvious that her performance is seemingly not like Willie John's. The not-too-much-later Elvis Presley rendering in 1960, on RCA LP (LSP 2231), is also sultry, but in more of the R & B mode of Willie John. More so, less jazzy than Peggy, a rich Presley vocal, like Peggy's, scores! Listen and compare Willie John, Peggy, and Elvis!
39. "Is That All There Is," Capital 2602. Peggy's cool vocal fire scores high with a title penned by Jerry Leiber and Mike Stoller—indeed an unusual thing for the "rock" generation year of 1969.

Visual Image.

While Peggy's appearance in the film *Pete Kelly's Blues* is creditable, the hairstyles of this 1955 film provide an image of a much older woman. The (already noted) 1943 film *Stage Door Canteen*, more so, finds a younger Peggy, with Benny Goodman, as an excellent band singer, coolly singing

40. "Why Don't You Do Right" and, more so, stealing the spotlight from the bandleader himself.

Nick Lucas

- The "new" electric recording method of recording, from about 1926 for most, for a while in fact, carried many such acoustic (leftover) vocalists into electric and the (developing) microphone techniques of recording. One such survivor was Nick Lucas. Like such contemporaries as Frank Crumit, and Cliff Edwards, his 1920s' style became involved in "jazz," and a style sounding much dated after the emergence of electric recording. Moreover, the quirky Lucas vocal style, noting his own self-guitar-strumming, is still a bit novel to play and hear and (much like Crumit and Edwards), perhaps, defines novelty—without added vulgarity. More so—perhaps, baby boomers remember 1968 and the latter-day entity himself, Tiny Tim?

  - Picks are as follows:

1. "My Best Girl," Brunswick 2768. This Walter Donaldson-penned ditty is overly sentimental, but in this case, so what! Nick's own guitar-strumming (even) keeps the listener of this ditty from falling asleep.
2. "Brown Eyes, Why Are You Blue," Brunswick 2961. Nick and his guitar-strumming find this ditty, penned by Alfred Bryan and George Meyer, as faster paced and a less-sleepy challenge.
3. "Sleepy Time, Gal," Brunswick 2990. This simple ditty, penned by Ange Lorenzo, Richard Whiting, Joseph R. Alden, and Raymond B. Egan, is yet another sleepy vocal that works.
4. "A Cup of Coffee, a Sandwich, and You," Brunswick 3052. Nick breezes through this obvious stage novelty, penned for *Charlot's Revue of 1926* by Billy Rose, Al Dubin, and Joseph Meyer.
5. "Always," Brunswick 3088. This overly sentimental vocal of this (Irving Berlin) classic still scores.
6. "Bye, Bye, Blackbird," Brunswick 3184. This 1920s standard, shared by many—including a Gene Austin version—and penned by Ray Henderson and Mort Dixon, is quirky and a pleasant enough novelty.
7. "I'm Looking at the World Thru Rose Colored Glasses," Brunswick 3283. This simple ditty (penned by Tommy Malle and Jimmy Steiger), as its own title indicates, is a light and quirky entertainment that should be expected. More so, this lighthearted vocal does not disappoint.
8. "I've Got the Girl," Brunswick 3370. Contemporary crooner and rival Gene Austin's version on Victor 20397 is also good competition. (A contemporary 1926 Don Clark Biltmore Hotel Orchestra release of the (Walter Donaldson-penned ditty) that featured an unaccredited vocal refrain by Bing Crosby and Al Rinker was sadly flawed on release. Columbia 824-D.) Good thing Nick and Gene got it right!
9. "Hello Bluebird," Brunswick 3370. Another Roaring Twenties ditty, as penned by Cliff Friend.
10. "I'm Looking Over a Four Leaf Clover," Brunswick 3439. This ditty penned by Harry Woods and Mort Dixon may be considered a fine and contrived connection to Ireland that (still) works.
11. "Side by Side," Brunswick 3512. This very simple and well-sung vocal, penned by Harry Woods, is fine enough with some fine (guitar) strumming.
12. "Rosy Cheeks," Brunswick 3518. Did Annette Hanshaw's perky contemporary vocal do it better?

13. "Among My Souvenirs," Brunswick 3684-D. Among many other best sellers, this ditty (penned by Edgar Leslie and Horatio Nicholls) lingers.
14. "Together," Brunswick 3749. Another 1920s' standard, also shared by Cliff Edwards, that somehow ain't bad, if similar in style from either vocalist. (Dick Todd would later update it a decade later.)
15. "Without You Sweetheart," Brunswick 3773. This ditty (by Ray Henderson, Buddy De Sylva, and Lew Brown) is, like most of Nick's efforts, soft and full of sugar-coated vocal fluff. In true retrospective, this ditty defines "mush," and is not without its original appeal.
16. "Sunshine," Brunswick 3850. This bright vocal of this Irving Berlin-penned classic indeed shines. (A contemporary Paul Whiteman release, featuring a less-quirky vocal as by Bing Crosby, on Victor-21240, is perhaps a bit hipper, even considering its title.)
17. "I'm Waiting for Ships that Never Come In," Brunswick 3853. Later crooner Dick Todd would perhaps transform this ditty, penned by Jack Yellen and Abe Olman, into WWII, as lyrics could suggest!
18. "Singing in the Rain," Brunswick 4378. This attempt at the contemporary Cliff Edwards original (Columbia 1869 D) is indeed very similar in style. Moreover, the older Edwards just had to have been an earlier vocal influence upon Nick. While it is worth comparisons, it is also noteworthy that this light-crooning style, so juvenile and quirky in the earlier times, was beginning to get serious. Indeed, an "adult" approach to crooning was evolving, due largely to the progress of microphone vocals. Moreover, a more intimate style, for this ditty, did not appear, although a later vocal as by Valaida Snow, on Paraphone F-165, indeed had more depth.
19. "Tip-Toe Through the Tulips," Brunswick 4418. Introduced by Nick himself (in the 1929 film *Gold Diggers of Broadway*, the first of what was to be the "Gold diggers" films), this ditty, penned by Joe Burke and Al Dubin, indeed survived Nick's visual image, found in that forgotten film. More so, this ditty, more than any others, defines "quirkiness" and indeed an acoustic approach in the "electric" era of 1929. Numerous contemporary versions also appeared, with perhaps even better vocals as by Annette Hanshaw (as Gay Ellis) on Harmony 1012-D. (Nevertheless, the Lucas version remained the best known, until the unlikely arrival of Tiny Tim, on Reprise 0679, light-years away in a rock-era year of 1968—Beatles and all)!
20. "Painting the Clouds with Sunshine," Brunswick 4418. This flip side of "Tip-Toe Through the Tulips," also penned byJoe Burke and Al Dubin, is another gem, with Nick's high-floating vocals, guitar, and a (Brunswick) studio orchestra producing yet another quirky-sounding entity despite it being an electric recording.
21. "Don't Tell Her What Happened to Me," Brunswick 4896. This typical light-crooning job is an interesting comparison to a contemporary Ruth Etting version, of the Buddy DeSyvlia and Lew Brown ditty penned as "Don't Tell Him What Happened to Me," on Columbia 2280-D. While mushy, Etting's "torch singing" is exceptional, and indeed sparks fly—for those who listen to intimate speech.
22. "I'm Yours," Nick's crooning got it right, and so did contemporaries Johnny Marvin and (especially) Ruth Etting. (More than a decade later, in the 1940s, Billie Holiday would define this ditty.)
23. "You're Driving Me Crazy," Brunswick 4987. This Walter Donaldson-penned ditty finds Nick's vocal and guitar-strumming (with his Crooning Troubadours Orchestra) discovering a sweet band sound, with a fine jazz theme. While a contemporary Louis Armstrong and Lional Hampton version (on Okeh 41478) is more hip, this ditty retains its fine sound.

24. "Lady Play Your Mandolin," Brunswick 6013. This ditty penned by Oscar Levant and Irving Caesar is a contrived attempt at Latino (Cuban) tempo, and it succeeds. The Crooning Troubadours again find Nick, with his high-pitched but steady vocal style, with perhaps Nick's own mandolin-strumming
25. "Walking My Baby Back Home," Brunswick 6048. This 1931 rendering is smooth enough for its Depression-era time to remind many that it was and still is cheaper to walk than ride. Penned by Fred E. Ahlert, Roy Turk, and Harry Richmond, this was also to become a jazz classic. Among other contemporary versions, perhaps it's Annette Hanshaw's spirited version, with a fine unaccredited jazz backup (Clarion 5248-C) that's tops. Sorry, Nick! Among other contemporary versions, a Maurice Chevalier version (Victor 22634) finds the Frenchman, with his European music hall technique, discovering "jazz." Chevalier, at this time, was in the midst of exploring Hollywood film, and perhaps this ditty, in true retrospective, provided him with some very solid (American) musical influence.
26. "Falling in Love Again," Brunswick 2048. The contemporary Marlene Dietrich and Ruth Etting releases is crooned out well
27. "That's My Desire." Brunswick 6147. Another good bit of high-voiced crooning! This ditty, penned by Hemly. Kresa and Carroll Loveday, later found a more bombastic approach by Frankie Laine. Listen and compare.
28. "All of Me," *Hit of the Week* A-4-B-1. Indeed, all of the crooning ain't bad.
29. "An Evening in Carolina," *Hit of the Week* B-3-4. Penned by Walter Donaldson, this light-crooning job skims through some flowery lyrics, and moreover, makes it all sound relevant.

Visual Image.

Nick Lucas, like many, got lost in the rush into "talkies," although he did get a head start in 1929's *Gold Diggers of Broadway*. In it, Nick may be seen "live," introducing two of his biggest hits:

30. "Tip Toe Through the Tulips."
31. "Painting the Clouds with Sunshine."

Rose Maddox

The fusion of "hillbilly" to "country and western" in the 1940s was perhaps founded in the aspect of respect. The emergence of rural honky-tonk bars (after the repeal of Prohibition) and the placing of record-spinning jukeboxes, more so, gave live entities competition and cheaper dance music at lower prices. The likes of hillbilly crooners, founded in the likes of Ernest Tubb and Red Foley, found the latter 1930s also jumping with string band music, perhaps best promoted by the success of Bob Wills himself, the rural answer to the urban and "white" "swing" success of Benny Goodman and Artie Shaw.

Rose Maddox, a native of Boaz, Alabama, was, along with her musical brothers Fred (bass), Carl (rhythm guitar) and Henry (mandolin), somehow transplanted to Oakland, California, during the Great Depression. In 1936, at around eleven years of age, Rose, very much influenced by the yodeling success of Jimmy Rogers, and (especially) Patsy Montana, became the lead vocalist of The Maddox Brothers and Rose. As a principal means to make a buck, the family became well-known radio entities, mostly in California. While it would take another decade, and the end of WWII, the family would finally become recording artists in 1947, signing with the small label 4-Star, or Four Star.

By this time, the Maddox Brothers and Rose had matured enough in various honky-tonks and live radio to provide patrons what they wanted—good, weepy bar songs along with some upbeat boogie-woogie, played as dance music. Shades of Ella Mae Morse on Capital? Rose's vocals, minus the yodeling, were, moreover, tough enough to compete with any of the emerging (black) rhythm and blues entities, including the likes of Dinah Washington. She became known for her (signature) laugh, a crackling laugh, for the fun of it! Along with her brothers' "hot" string band, she became a fixture in "C & W," while generating major changes into rhythm music, along with contemporary (and acquaintance) Hank Williams. Rose founded the "country" aspects of what would emerge as "rock and roll" despite resistance from many of her peers.

- The following are Rose Maddox picks:

1. "Milk Cow Blues," 4-Star 1185. Milk it!
2. "Honky Tonkin'," 4-Star 1238. A raved-up Hank Williams? Yup!
3. "Tramp on the Street," 4-Star 1239. This ditty may be credited to Grady and Hazel Cole, a country act of the latter 1930s, who may have bumped into Rose and her brothers, which touring West Coast honky-tonks in the 1930s. This ditty's poignant lyrics, of a religious vein, were, more so, traced to a Dr. Addison Crabte, who published it in 1877. Baby boomers may know this title from Peter, Paul, and Mary, whose 1960s folk revival success became their own success. Rose, however, seems to have found it in a fine, contemporary 1947 Molly O' Day recording (Columbia 37559). Rose, more so, succeeds in recording a sobering rendition, without the wildness found in her up-tempo renderings. (Many references to this ditty as a Hank Williams (studio) recording are in error, although he may have rendered it on a radio program.)
4. "New Muleskinner Blues," 4-Star 1240. Inspired by Jimmy Rogers? Bill Monroe? A wilder rendition that would (much) later inspire the likes of Dolly Parton?
5. "Philadelphia Lawyer," 4-Star 1289. Rose just may have hear Woody Guthrie perform this ditty as "Reno Blues." Since Reno was the way to go to get a serious divorce, the fact was clear in the still young age for Rose in (1948/1949, at around twenty-four years of age). As contemporary jukebox fodder, this weepy bar song is full of raw emotion, as Rose's crude vocal, about just how lawyers do their thing, hits the spot! Another beer?
6. "George's Playhouse Boogie," 4-Star 1369. Perhaps this "Boogie-Woogie" rump was inspired from an actual (1940s) honky-tonk, as by the same name, in Stockton, California? In any case, Rose's (1949) vocal is hot, as is the cross talk heard between Rose and other band members, including her brothers.
7. "Sally Let Your Bangs Hang Down," 4-Star 1398. Folk songs always have a history, or mythology, that can be fixed or worked upon as time passes by. Credited to Clayton McMichen and Riley Puckett, it's still hard to find out where they found it. This speculation is, however, unwarranted, as Rose rips through some risqué lyrics as no one before her, some five to six years before the term "Rockabilly" could apply!
8. "Water Baby Blues," 4-Star 1507.
9. "I Gotta Go Get My Baby," Columbia 21375. It rocks, but it wasn't called "rock" at this time (1955).

10. "Wild, Wild Young Men," Columbia 31394. The contemporary (1953) Ruth Brown (R & B) hit on Atlantic 993, penned by (A. Nugetre), somehow caught Rose's attention. More so, Rose's own (1955) vocal is smokin' and gives (even) Ruth Brown some heavy competition. In retrospective, this type of material won Rose few friends, except perhaps a younger crowd of would-be C & W performers.

    - By the mid-1950s (and beyond the scope of this book), the emergence of "rock and roll" found the newly founded "Country and Western" establishment at odds. The influence of rhythm and blues found the older crowd in terror, which also found most of the elders of popular music panning it as well. For C & W, the ears of Elvis, Buddy Holly, Wanda Jackson, Carl Perkins, Johnny Cash, Jerry Lee Lewis, Gene Vincent, and Glen Glenn, among others, the already older recordings of Rose Maddox provided good listening fodder. Indeed, many of Rose's earlier 4-Star recordings were reissued on King Records, which, for many listeners, including this author, were thought to be newly released contemporary recordings.

11. "Hey Little Dream Boat," Columbia. 21490.
12. "Death of Rock and Roll," Columbia 21559. A parody of Elvis Presley's version of Ray Charles-penned "I Got a Woman" is nonsense. Just how this works is more than silly, but it does!
13. "Love Is Strange," Columbia 40895. The contemporary (1957) Mickey and Sylva hit (Groove) is covered very well.

Dean Martin

The Dean Martin story was first viewed by most baby boomers as either the other half of the extremely popular Dean Martin-Jerry Lewis comedy team, or the host of a highly rated TV variety show of the 1960s, which usually catered to adult tastes in music and "guest" stars. (Another possible recognition of Dean Martin could also have been the fact that he was the father of "Dino," who was part of the a mid-1960s rock act, "Dino, Desi, and Billy." The purposes of this book, however, should narrow into Dean's contributions to popular music, which were considerable—although, after 1950. Unlike Frank Sinatra, but like a few others, Dean Martin breaks the rules of this book, and, moreover while his pre-1950s material had little impact, his later 'rock' era era recordings did." His subsequent appearances in film, television, live gigs and 'pop' recordings, in an era of Elvis, the Beatles, and Motown found Martin laying claim upon much of the (past) entertainment of the pre-rock era. Moreover, his crooning style, perhaps an emulation of (early) Bing Crosby and Mills Brothers vocals, had nothing to owe to rock and roll. More so, he became an adult alternative against it.

The latter 1940s found a would-be boxer and Bing Crosby imitator (with a bit of an Al Jolson introduction), Dino Crocetti, team up with a struggling New York comic, Jerry Lewis. Dino Crocetti then changed his name to Dean Martin. His crooning vocals, with a somewhat lazy, masculine quality, perhaps founded in ethnic Italian upbringings, after teaming with Lewis, seemingly then were realized. Subsequent radio, film, and television appearances, finding Dean a fine straight man for Jerry as well, became hugely successful. Even more impressive was an emerging recording career that was popularized and marketed in films as well recordings. After the breakup between Martin and Lewis in 1956, and despite the emergence of rock and roll, the Dean Martin story continued as a TV personality, for about ten years, as well as a major film entity. More so, his popularity, as an "adult" entity, may truly be noted in 1964. Indeed, this rock-era year of the Beatles, and the British invasion of America, had found Martin's second version of an old Frank Sinatra release "Everybody Loves Somebody," on Reprise 0281, a competing best-selling entity, sung in a familiar, somewhat thought to be obsolete style. The following are Dean Martin picks:

1. "The Money Song," Capital 15249. This Harold Rome-penned ditty (somehow) works, with Jerry Lewis hamming it up.
2. "Powder Your Face with Sunshine," Capital 15351. This 1949 effort, penned by Carmen Lombardo and Stanley Rochinski and backed by Paul Weston's Orchestra, became Dean Martin's first best-selling entity.
3. "I Don't Care If the Sun Don't Shine," Capital 981. Penned by Mack David, this somewhat of a country ditty ain't bad. (Later, young Elvis Presley, on Sun 210, would attempt to rock it up a bit. Did Elvis hear the Martin version? Or was it the contemporary Patti Page version?)
4. "I'll Always Love You" Capital-1028. As penned by Jay Livingston & Ray Evans for the 1950 (Martin & Lewis) film "*My Friend Irma Goes West*", this ditty found deserved added publicity to 'discover' Dean's well done croon.
5. "You Belong To Me". Capital-2165. Dean's croon on this contemporary ditty is valid!
6. "I'm Yours". Capital EP-401. While both Ruth Etting and Billie Holiday had valid claims on this ditty, this crooning job of Martin's, also seen and heard in the 1952 Martin & Lewis film *The Stooge*, is indeed no slouch.
7. "There's My Lover". Capital-2378. Somehow Deans' excellent 1952 croon on this original ditty, penned by (Sylvia Dee & Sidney Lippman), did not become a best seller. Dean may have wondered just why his pleasing, intimate and soft vocal only sold moderately. In true retrospective, so does this author.
8. "If I Could Sing Like Bing". Capital-2555. This might be the ultimate Bing Crosby tribute, (penned by Victor G. Davis), as Dean rightfully acknowledges his crooning style.
9. "Thats Amore". Capital-2589. Penned by Jack Brooks and Harry Warren and featured in the highly popular Martin & Lewis film "*The Caddy*", this ditty, more than any other previous soundtrack entity, was a huge marketing and (even) creative success. The pleasant Martin crooning voice never sounded better, as this recording, much better than its film introduction, truly defined Dean as a voice to be more heard, and indeed more exploited.
10. "The Christmas Blues". Capital-2640. Yes—this bit of contrived seasonal theme, penned by Sammy Kahn and David Holt, indeed finds Dean in good holiday mode.
11. "I'd Cry Like A Baby". Capital-2749. Penned by Sammy Gallop and Howard Steiner, the smooth crooning style of Dean is further advanced, as well as appreciated.
12. "Money Burns A Hole In My Pocket". Capital-2818. Dean himself introduced this Jule Styne and Bob Hilliard penned ditty based upon an old saying, in the film "*Living It Up*", with Jerry Lewis. Dean again finds an excuse to croon and, more so, does it very well.
13. "Long Long Ago". Capital-2985. This modest duet with Nat King Cole, while not great, still ain't bad.

14. "Young And Foolish" Capital 3036. This vocal rendering, penned by Albert Hague and Arnold Horwitt, just may feature the Dean Martin vocal in its softest mode.
15. "Memories Are Made Of This" Capital 3295. Backed by the vocal group the Easy Riders, this very polished pop classic (1950s), as penned by Terry Gilkyson, Richard Dehr, and Frank Miller, is perhaps his best-remembered rendering, ,besides his later single release of "Everybody Loves Somebody". While the vocal group indeed contributes to the effort, the Martin vocal is seemingly led on, and subsequently catches up vocally, and lastly fades out, leaving the finished vocals back to the group.
16. "Im Gonna Steal Your Love Away". Capital 3468. This attempt at rock and roll, with an actual contemporary R&B group, the Nuggets, is at least interesting and a further attempt to be creative. While the orchestra of Dick Stabile seems to get in the way, this ditty, penned by Fred Speilman and Buddy Kaye, finds the vocals by Dean and the Nuggets in good time, indeed producing a fine product. It's interesting to speculate just why more of this stuff was not attempted, although it's most likely that Dean himself was a creature of another time. More so, Dean's musical tastes were of previous era—that of the pre-1950s.
17. "Return To Me". Capital-3894. This latter—1958 release, penned by Carmen Lombardo and Danny Di Minno, with some actual Italian lyrics, was a best selling crooning job, despite rock and roll.
18,19. Dean's (1959) LP *A Winter Romance*, Capital T 1285, could have been marketed better, although latter-century sales of its material on CD find it all very pleasing. For the purposes of this book, the following two titles made this package well worth it. a. "Out In The Cold Again". The older (Ruth Etting) standard is updated and challenged! Dean never crooned better! b. "It Won't Cool Off". Dean's wit and sexual appeal is evident on this ditty penned by Sammy Cahn and Ken Lane.
20. "Ain't That A Kick In The Head". Capital 4420. Yeah. This lesser known film ditty—from the Rat Pack film *Ocean's Eleven*, featuring Frank Sinatra, Sammy Davis Sr. and among others, Dean himself—is a novel attempt at creativity. Penned by (Jimmy Van Heusen and Sammy Cahn, this obvious play on lyrics also suggests other ideas that found this ditty basically banned from radio airplay in 1960? In true retrospective, this ditty should be considered a classic, with high marks for the clever Martin vocal.
21,22. "Everybody Loves Somebody". As noted in text, but not defined in text, Dean's 1962 original rendering of "Everybody Loves Somebody", (released on LP "*Dream With Dean*", on Reprise-RS-6123)—was a stripped down vocal, emulating Sinatra's original (Columbia) recording. b. In true retrospective, the (reviewed in text) best selling 2nd version released in 1964, on single release on (Reprise-0281) is brighter and sung in mid-tempo, and (almost) rocks, despite it's smaltzy title.
23-27. *"Everybody Loves Somebody" LP*. T Reprise RS 6130. The title song has been reviewed as (Reprise-0281). LP Picks: a. "Your Other Love". b. "Things". c. "Shutters And Boards". d. "Corrine Corrine". e. "Siesta Fiesta".
28. "Youre Nobody Till Somebody Loves You". Reprise 0333. Dean's resurrection of the old Russ Morgan release—featuring Russ's own vocal, (penned by Larry Stock, James Cavanough and Russ himself) is redefined!
29. "The Door Is Still Open To My Heart" Reprise 0307. As penned by blues entity Chuck Willis, this ditty had been a modest seller by the (r&b) Cardinals and 'pop' entity Don Cornell. Dean's update is more successful!
30-37. *Houston* (LP) Reprise 6181. As the best of the Dean Martin LP product, the reasons why are found in the Martin vocal style. Like Bing Crosby had done, and unlike Frank Sinatra or Tony Bennett, Dean Martin could croon out country-styled

entities, and do it very well. Moreover, the easy crooning style heard on this 1965 LP, with Jimmy Bowen, Bill Justis and the Jack Hallaran Singers, gels into a "pop-country" classic, more so, some fine competition for the "Nashville sound" of the era. Picks are as follows: a. "Houston". This (Lee Hazelwood) penned ditty, also a single release on (Reprise 0393), is smooth and convincing enough to transplant this Las Vegas entertainer, with bow tie and tux, into a Texas town. b. "Hammers And Nails". Re-building a relationship? A (Dick Glasser) penned entity benefits from Dean's sentimental croon! c. "Down Home". Dean's (Crosby like vocal approach) more than defines this (Rudy Clark) penned ditty. d. "I Will". As penned by (Dick Glasser), this title was also a best selling single release, on (Reprise 0415). e. "Snap Your Fingers". This contemporary rock era 1960s ditty, penned by (Grady Martin and Alex Zanetis), sounds more like a 1940s 'smokey' nightclub entity. It had more so been a best seller by (r&b) performers Joe Henderson & Barbara Lewis before Dean's well done croon. f. "Old Yellow Line". Dean's vocal of this mid-tempo ditty, penned by L.W. Hensen, Jimmy Bowen, and Amos & Kelly Smith is indeed a smooth ride. g. "Detour". This (Paul Westmoreland) penned ditty had been a 1946 Spade Cooley release, featuring a Tex Williams vocal. An early Patti Page version had more so been a best seller. With a newer 1960s backing, Dean (again) pulls off a winning vocal.

38. "Bumming Around". Reprise-0393. This old (C&W) 1953 Jimmie Dean standard, penned by Pete Graves, released on (4 Star-1613), had also found crooner Dick Todd—in a later age. Did Dick Todd's earlier croon influence Dean?

39-41. *The Dean Martin Christmas Album*. Reprise 6222. Another attempt at a Christmas product in (1965) LP works well. Picks include a. "Marshmallow World". b. "Blue Christmas". c. "Silver Bells".

42. "In The Chapel In The Moonlight". reprise 0601. The old Ruth Etting rendering, on Decca 1084, is crooned, and updated well.

43. "That Little Ole Wine Drinker, Me". Reprise 0608. Speculation had it that actor Robert Mitchum had penned this title. While his recording is well done, Dean's version clinched it.

Visual Image—The visual of Dean Martin was very familiar with the baby boomer generation. Along with his earlier films with Jerry Lewis, his 1960s television series was anthem for that television era. Highlights may include:

44. "That's Amore". The 1953 film *The Caddy*, with Jerry Lewis, found Dean crooning this ditty out with some distraction! While this film version is flawed, it's perhaps a bit more fun.
45. "Ain't That A Kick In The Head". From The (1960) Rat Pack film *Oceans 11*.
46. "S posin". As perhaps most familiar to later baby boomers, his (1960s-early 1970s) NBC television program found its place in many homes. A (1967?) clip of Dean crooning out this old Fats Waller standard perhaps best defined success with an older style of singing that had largely become passé, except for the likes of a few (especially of Dean), who could winningly pull it off.

Special note

Dean's pal Jerry Lewis continued his efforts to stamp out muscular dystrophy into another century.

Tony Martin

While this tenor-like vocalist cannot seem to find his way into much of an impression into the ears of later generations, Tony Martin was a creature of his times. Moreover, he was and should be acknowledged as a very popular vocalist, as well as a minor film entity, through the 1930s to the 1950s. As a band vocalist with the likes of Ray Noble, Abe Lyman, and others, he seemingly developed his own crooning style, although not always smooth, and sometimes tenor-like. The following titles, after much research, at least give Tony Martin a (slight) bump in recognition, which is deserved.

1. "My Walking Stick," Brunswick 8153. Backed by Ray Noble, this (Irving Berlin) novelty works well enough. A contemporary Louis Armstrong and Mills Brothers release, moreover, defines it.
2. "It's a Blue World," Decca 2932. Dorcas Cochran and Harold Grant penned this fine ditty that perhaps Martin best defines?
3. "South of the Border," Decca 2788. The contemporary Gene Autry best-seller is more than challenged.
4. "Fools Rush In," Decca 3119.
5. "When the Swallows Come Back to Capistrano," Decca 3246. Like so many others influenced by Bing Crosby, Tony "croons" out of this Leon Rene-penned ditty. (Light-years later, this title, resurfaced as a Pat Boone entity, on Dot 15660, who also aped Bing Crosby's crooning style, but with smoother results.)
6. "Below the Equator," Decca 3967. The tenor-like voice attempts to croon, penned by Cliff Friend and Charlles Tobias, with some good result.
7. "Tonight We Love," Decca 3988. While Tchaikovsky's music theme does indeed have something to do with this ditty, penned by Freddy Martin, Bobby Worth, and Ray Austin, it's also Tony's controlled, classy singing that produced this excellent recording.
8. "To Each His Own," Mercury 3022. Along with a vocal group "the Starlighters," Martin produces a fine product. Penned by Ray Evans and Jay Livingston for the film of the same name, this ditty was somehow dropped from the 1946 film. Another version, by contemporary singing bandleader, Eddie Howard, on Majestic 7188, was also popular, although not as good as Martin's. A contemporary Ink Spots rendering, on Decca 23615, however—was. (Sorry, Tony! Sorry, Eddie!)
9. "There's No Tomorrow," RCA Victor 20-3582. This bombastic 1949 approach to deal with a (real) Italian classic "O Sole Mio," especially notes the early acoustic release on Victor 87243 and almost succeeds. Some years later in 1960, as "It's Now or Never," on Victor 47-7777 as by Elvis Presley, this ditty became a huge best seller. Could Elvis sing? Yes, even by pre-1950s standards. Any doubts? Just compare Martin's "There's No Tomorrow"(credited to Leo Corday, Leon Carr, and Edurado De Capua) and "It's Now or Never",(Aaron Schroeder and Wally Gold) with the original Italian—"O Sole Mio"—just listen!
10. "Va Vie En Rose," RCA Victor 20-3819. French entity Edith Piaf's latter-1940s American tours found her act (sophisticated to Americans), in mostly French with some English—something new and different. More so, as penned by Edith herself and Louiguy, this ditty would eventually, in true retrospective, serve to identify Piaf as one of the world's most popular vocalists. Martin's contemporary (1950) version typically shows off his (bland) yet effective vocal abilities. Another contemporary version by Louis Armstrong, more so, offers his (usual) ability to sing it with grit and

get away with it in style. (Light-years later, rock-era pop entity Grace Jones would successfully adapt this ditty.)
Visual Image—Tony Martin's 1941 image in "Ziegfeld Girl" found the (Nacio Herb Brown & Gus Kahn) penned ditty

11. "You Stepped Out Of A Dream", exploiting the likes of beautiful Hollywood entities including Hedy Lamarr, Lana Turner, and Judy Garland easily stealing the spotlight from his (bland) vocal. Indeed, Martin must have loved his job! His earlier 1936 film "Banjo On My Knee", more so found him sharing the stage with Barbara Stanwyck in
12. "Where The Lazy River Goes By", as well as a fine solo performance of (another) Jimmy McHugh & Harold Adamson penned ditty
13. "There's Music In The Air".

Memphis Minnie (Lizzie Douglas)

- While Lizzie Douglas was indeed around when the likes of Mamie Smith, Ethel Waters, and Ma Rainey (among many others) had begun recording in the early 1920s, her recorded work didn't get its start until 1929. Like many other recording artists of the '20s, her style, while linked to others, may be considered original, as a recorded entity. The rather crude lady guitarist, seemingly matched some tough licks with a good tongue-lashing of words and tunes, many self penned. Her output of blues recordings, moreover, may be considered a true retrospective of the future rock era, and just as important as her guitarist contemporaries, including those of Blind Lemon Jefferson and Charlie Patton. As a matter of fact, Memphis Minnie (aka Lizzie Douglas) may indeed have been more influential as all her recorded works are electric recordings, covering through the '30s, '40s, and '50s.

The following picks were released as "Memphis Minnie and Kansas Joe" with combinations of her "jug band," "her combo" or "Kansas Joe" and "Memphis Minnie."

1. "Bumble Bee," Vocalion 1476. As recorded with a smoking guitar," Kansas Joe McCoy (one of her husbands), this (1929) ditty is a crude tale of a bumble bee, or better yet, a typical novelty item. An earlier version, on Columbia 14542-D, ain't bad, but it just cannot do what this version does. Nor does a later (1930) rendering, as part of a vocal, with Minnie included as a Memphis Jug Band release, on Victor V38599. (While bumble bees were indeed as common in the 1930s as well as at the turn of any century, the later blues ditty, as by Slim Harpo "I'm a King Bee" (Excello 2113), finds a neat hive—near Minnie's recording.)
2. "Frankie Jean (That Trottin' Fool)," Vocalion 1588. This self-penned ditty ain't nothin' but a folk tale. Its rural appeal even features Minnie whistling at times—something not usually appreciated by latter-day listeners. In any case, Minnie's tale about a family horse remains a simple and earthy story, all the way back to the barn.
3. "New Dirty Dozen," Vocalion 1618. This extreme reflection on rural morality is crudely graced. as (usual), by Minnie's guitar-pickin'.
4. "I Called You This Morning," Vocalion 1631. This vocal duet (with Kansas Joe McCoy) is a confused tale about his repeated phone calls to her in the early morning. While this is all very entertaining, it's too bad (in true retrospective) there was no voice mail to be found in 1930.

5. "North Memphis Blues," Vocalion 1550. Minnie's blues are about living in Memphis. This tale is, moreover, upbeat. This time, with a supply of coal for fuel, she seems to seek out her neighbors and, indeed, become a good neighbor. A local restaurant also seems to provide for more of her needs. But, just what about this put-on? Just what else is she getting?
6. "Tricks Ain't Walkin' No More," Vocalion 1653. This sad tale (actually continued by "Crazy Crying Blues") finds a woman in despair about performing "tricks." Indeed, this very effective statement also notes social issues.
7. "Crazy Cryin' Blues," Vocalion 1678. The drama (created by her guitar-strumming) finds this crude, wailing vocal, featuring a tale of a woe, without reason. Perhaps this is what the "blues" is all about?
8. "Soo Cow Soo," Vocalion 1658. The rural appeal of this ditty (along with some fine strumming guitar pickin') ain't bad at all.
9. "You Got to Move," Decca 7038. This vocal duet with Kansas City Joe is a fast-paced bit exchange of real problems, without real solutions. Will he move? She did make some money last week.
10. "Dirty Mother for You," Decca 7048. It seems some slang never changes. In true retrospective, this ditty still means what it says.
11. "Let Me Ride," Decca 7063. As "Gospel Minnie," this upbeat ditty tells a familiar tale of the gladness of redemption. The term used to describe Minnie "Gospel Minnie" just may be around the first time the term "gospel" is used, outside of Thomas Dorsey ("Georgia Tom"). This ditty also just may be an ear-full of inspiration for one Rosetta Tharpe, whose recording career would begin on Decca, within a year of this fine recording (with an unknown backing chorus), in 1935.
12. "When Somebody Loses," Vocalion 03197. As a "Bumble Bee Slim" entity, Minnie is identified as his duetting partner.
13. "Hoodoo Lady," Vocalion 03222. The mythology of a traveling "medicine show" is perhaps a way of saving grace—an absence of basic religion and the folklore of fortune-telling.
14. "Ice Man Come on Up," Vocalion 03222. The world before air conditioning (in true retrospective) did have its rewards. This tale about "struttin'" her stuff and loading up on ice—is more than novel.
15. "Caught Me Wrong Again," Vocalion 03258. Is Memphis Minnie baking bread? This novelty about money and infidelity is a crude slice of life, as well as campy.
16. "If You See My Rooster," Vocalion 3285. This rural tale is actually a familiar "rooster" tale. But this 1936 recording by Minnie remains an effective one.
17. "Good Morning," Vocalion 3436. The (apparent) slapping of the backside of her guitar blends in nicely as Minnie's off-key vocal produces a hard bitten "good morning."
18. "Man, You Won't Give Me No Money," Vocalion 3474. This self-penned ditty is typical of most of Minnie's blues—they are more hard-bitten than novel—and this tale of a woman needing some money to spend on herself is (still) an intriguing plea.
19. "Me and My Chauffeur Blues," Okeh 06288. By this time, in 1941, Minnie's legacy as a recording blues entity had become firmly established. This tale of the lady and her chauffer (penned by Lawler) ain't nothing but a story told with a boogie guitar beat—with Minnie's usual vocal grit that keeps its listener interested.
20. "Looking the World Over," Okeh 6707. Okeh 6702. Again, Minnie hits and misses all her options fromcontemporary Big Bill (Broonzy)?

Johnny Mercer

While this songwriter may be considered as one of the best of the early century (as well as the latter part of the century), it is often forgotten that he was a huge success at marketing records—as an owner of Capital in the 1940s and as a vocalist. As a voice, Mercer is no great shakes, although he was more than a competent vocalist. He more so used it to his advantage noting his language skills, which were considerable. Picks include:

1. "Sizzling One-Step Medley," Columbia 18002-D. The contemporary (1932) best-seller recordings of Bing Crosby and the Mills Brothers of "Dinah," "My Honey's Loving Arms," and the Mills Brothers rendering of "Nobody's Sweetheart" found Mercer scatting (much like Crosby), along with the nightcaps—Johnny, Helen Rowland, and Johnny Blake—scatting along, much like the Mills Brothers. Somehow, this Frank Trumbauer release, while full of emulation, remained a fine bit of jazz as the originals. Well done!
2. "There's a Cabin in the Pines," Varsity 8031. Another emulation of a (contemporary) Bing Crosby recording found Mercer's soft croon almost as good.
3. "Lazybones," Varsity 8031. A self-penned ditty credited as Mercer and Carmichael, this did find much contemporary notice, recorded by whites (including Mildred Bailey) and blacks (including Harlan Lattimore) alike. In true retrospective, it did imply racial bias. For newer listeners not aware of all this, just listen and enjoy a slow and simple put down for anyone so inclined to be perceived as lazy. Check out the better vocal releases of this ditty by Mildred and Harlan!
4. "Small Fry," Decca 1960. This novel 1938 release challenges the (very) witty Bing Crosby, who was, by this time, at the top of his game as a radio entity as well as an established film and recording entity. Penned by Hoagy Carmichael and Frank Loesser, for the Crosby film *Sing, You Singers*, this rather risqué and campy ditty had been thrown away in the film. In an age of innocence, the crude implications of these lyrics perhaps got over censorship. Moreover, this spirited exchange, with Mercer's Southern accent used superbly, at least matches (his idol) Crosby, as this tale of (suspected) child abuse is pure camp.
5. "I Lost My Sugar in Salt Lake City," Capital 122. The "new" Capital Records recording company was organized by Johnny Mercer himself in 1942. This recording by Mercer, with one of his own Freddie Slack Orchestra, may be defined as urban jazz, with a fair-voiced Mercer vocal. Penned by Leon Rene and Johnny Lange, one might speculate that if Mercer had used his principle female vocalist, Ella Mae Morse, a more exciting result would have been heard!
6. "G. I. Jive," Capital 141. This contrived self-penned Mercer penned title about contemporary World War II culture nevertheless works. This jive slang is colorful enough and perhaps found another version, by Louis Jordan, on Decca 8659, perhaps defining it better.
7. "San Fernando Valley," Capital 150. This Gordon Jenkins-penned ditty may be considered country and a good attempt at a then growing market. Moreover, Mercer's vocal, with a vocal group the "Berries," is simple enough to compete with contemporaries Bing Crosby and Roy Rogers.
8. "Accent on the Positive," Capital 180. Penned by Harold Arlen and Johnny Mercer, this ditty had been penned for the Crosby film *Here Come the Waves* in 1944. As yet another bit of wit, this fine classic had been wasted in the film, with this Mercer recording much improving upon it. Luckily, for Bing, however, a contemporary

recording with the Andrews Sisters, on Decca 23379, turned out to be a brilliant exchange of chatter, truly defining it as their own. Mercer must have been pleased by it all, especially noting sales.

9. "Candy," Capital 183. Jo Stafford, who Mercer had signed up for his label, indeed contributes a lot of voice in this shared vocal with him. While Johnny is sharp enough, Jo is both sharp and sultry. Other 1945 contemporary versions included a Dinah Shore version on Victor 20-1632, a King Sisters group rendering on Victor 20-1633 by Johnny Long's Orchestra, with a vocal by Dick Robertson on Decca 18661 and by the Jerry Wald Orchestra, with a vocal by Dick Merrick on Majestic 7129.
10. "Blues in the Night," Capital 1001. Both Johnny Mercer and Harold Arlen had penned this much-recorded song ditty for the (1941) film of the same name. This recording, along with Jo Stafford and the Pied Piper, was late in the game, as notable vocal recordings by Cab Calloway, Dinah Shore, Peggy Lee (as a Benny Goodman release), (unaccredited) Willie Smith (as a Jimmie Lunceford release), Hot Lips Page (as an Artie Shaw release), among others, offered many differing approaches and stylistic attitudes. Luckily, Jo Stafford's vocal helps, as she has the better voice as well as being just as slick as Mercer.
11. "On the Atchison, Topeka, and the Santa Fe," Capital 195. As another classic of the 1940s, this ditty penned by Harry Warren and Johnny Mercer was featured in the Judy Garland film *The Harvey Girls*. As Mercer indeed lays good claims on this ditty, as his vocal is truly inspiring enough, the Judy Garland vocal, both in the film and on recording release, on Decca 23436, is a clear winner. Moreover, a fine Bing Crosby version, on Decca 18690, also gels and competes with the Garland version.
12. "Conversation While Dancing," Capital 195. This contrived bit of wit, penned by Paul Weston and Mercer himself, again finds Mercer in the good company of Jo Stafford, which also produced another winning combination.
13. "Personality," Capital 230. Bing Crosby's contemporary version, on Decca 18790, perhaps defines this ditty penned by Jimmy Van Heusen and Johnny Burke their best, although Mercer's version is a fine and pleasant comparison. Dorothy Lamour had introduced this ditty in the contemporary film *The Road to Rio*.
14. "Zip-a-Dee-Doo-Dah," Capital 323. Many baby boomers might know this title from the 1947 Disney film classic *Song of the South*. In true retrospective, the Southern-accented Mercer still sounds like a winner and moreover truly defines this classic penned by Allie Wrubel and Ray Gilbert also a 1947 Academy Award winner. (This ditty also became a rock era entity by Bob B. Soxx and the Blue Jeans on Philles 107.)
15. "My Baby Likes to Be-Bop," Capital 15026. Mercer and Nat King Cole combine with the King Cole Trio in a contrived exchange of urban slang penned by Walter Bishop.
16. "Baby, It's Cold Outside," Capital 567. Penned by Frank Loesser for the film entity *Neptune's Daughter*, this original film entity truly outlasted the 1949 film. Scores of versions exist of this novelty, and luckily for Mercer, this rendering with Margaret Whiting indeed scores. Among the many recorded versions were: (a) A filmed version as introduced in the film by Ricardo Montalban (known by many baby boomers in the later television series *Fantasy Island*), Esther Williams, Red Skelton (known by baby boomers as a later television comic), and Betty Garrett—also later known as a television entity in *All in the Family*. (b) A recording by Dinah Shore and Buddy Clark on Columbia 38463. (c) A recording by Ella Fitzgerald and Louis Jordan on Decca 24644. (d) A Sammy Kaye orchestra version, with vocals by Don Cornell and

Laura Leslie on Victor 78-3448. A country Homer and Jethro version, on Victor 20-0078, which is so bad, it's good.

Mabel Mercer

This (British-born) cabaret singer was born to a (black) American vaudevillian and a (British) mother, who was also a vaudevillian. As a (black) personage growing up in England, her struggle was less of her (unknown) Afro-American father, eventually finding traditional British music halls a home. By the early 1920s, her traveling led her to Paris and, more so, finding comfort in the likes of Ada "Bricktop" Smith, a transplanted Afro-American blues entity, who oddly became a successful cabaret owner. Indeed, all of Europe was thrilled with the recordings of American jazz and blues, especially noting the "new" emergence of black American vocals, for the most part, previously not allowed to record before 1920.

The (real) black-faced Mercer's natural British accent sounded sophisticated when attempting pop standards of the day and hardly a blues entity. Mabel easily incorporated the popular contemporary show tunes of the era, especially including those of Irving Berlin, the Gershwins, and Cole Porter into her late-night cabaret shows, most of them at Bricktop's in Paris (1920-38). After landing up in New York City at thirty-eight years old in 1938, she again performed in cabaret. She would remain, for the most part, a NYC nightclub icon for over forty more years, despite her age, black face, and the new age of rock and roll.

After 1950, Mabel's vocal tones are far from sweet, nor are they of a high tone. Her ability to project her soft, accented voice (noting her nightclub origins were perfected without microphones) in Paris perhaps defined her success. It should also be noted that oddly this vocalist recorded very little material before 1950 and did find much American recognition as a recording artist in "old" age.

- ➢ The following picks are (1942) Liberty Music Shop recordings from the (Gershwin and Heyward) Broadway entity of *Porgy and Bess*.

1. "Summertime," LMS-362. Mabel's turned-on operatic depth easily and defines a classic.
2. "My Man's Gone Now," LMS L-361. Another fine ditty is done with highbrow know-how.
3. "I Loves You, Porgy," LMS-360. More so than "Summertime" and "My Man's Gone Now,"

   Mabel further defines this ditty as her own, a nightclub gem, as led by her (then) classy pianist from "Tony's Restaurant," Cy Walter.

- ➢ The following are selective ditties from (1950s) Atlantic LP masters, recorded after the age of fifty. Whatever Mabel had lost (vocally) from her youth must have been considerable. Yet somehow, the following picks merit good taste and were more so applauded by many of her (then) contemporaries, including the likes of Tony Bennett, Thelma Carpenter, and Frank Sinatra.

- *Songs by Mabel Mercer, Vol. 1*, ALS 402 (10 inch).

4. "Autumn Leaves." This contemporary ditty penned by Johnny Mercer, Prevert, and Kosma is indeed interesting to compare to the contemporary recording by Bing Crosby.
5. "End of a Love Affair." Perhaps the Frank Sinatra version clinched it, but this is no slouch!
6. "Ivory Tower." This contemporary 1951 Cory Cross-penned ditty is relevant!
7. "You Are Not My First Love." A heartbreaking title penned by pianist Bart Howard.
8. "Just One of Those Things." This already old 1935 (Cole Porter) Broadway entity is well done. Lena Horne (in film) and Peggy Lee (recording) had claimed it previously Frank Sinatra would (later) claim it in 1956.

- *Songs by Mabel Mercer Vol. Two*, ALS 403 (10 inch).

9. "By Myself." This ditty penned byHoward Dietz and Arthur Schwartz is finally defined.
10. "Let Me Love You." Yes! This ditty penned by Bart Howard is intimate enough!
11. "Some Fine Day." A fine day? This ditty penned by Cy Walter is indeed very fine!
12. "Did You Ever Cross Over to Sneden's?" A stupid title? After much searching, it's a good guess that the writer (Alec Wilder) penned this ditty for Mabel, who took vacations near Sneden's Landing in New York State in the 1950s. If not, it's still something pleasant enough. Listen!

- "The Art of Mabel Mercer," Atlantic ALS-408.

13. "It Was Worth It." Great! Another very well-penned entity by Bart Howard. Worth it? Yes.
14. "Thank You for the Flowers." Nightclub mythology had it that this silly ditty was penned by two patrons of Bricktop's (A. Crooms Johnson and Clarence Moore) in 1932. A Contemporary Greta Keller (British) recording followed. Thank you Mabel, for finally recording it (1953).
15. "While We Were Young." While recorded when Mabel was old, at around fifty-three, this Alec Wilder, Bill Engvick and Morty Palitz ditty had been penned in 1932 when she was young!

- *Mabel Mercer Sings Cole Porter*, Atlantic LP-1213 (12 inch).

16. "Looking At You." Not as good as the earlier (1940) Lee Wiley version but still a classic!
17. "Oh Where, Oh Where?" Lyrics drift by, but Mabel somehow catches up with them!
18. "It's De-lovely." Mabel speeds this up a bit, with great vocal skill.
19. "After You, Who?" Serious stuff? After what? After who?

Visual Image. Forget the old lady in Manhattan nightclubs! This early English film found Mabel taking a short leave from Bricktop in Paris, when perhaps in her zenith as a performer!

20. "Since Black Minnie's Got the Blues." The (1936) English film *Everything Is Rhythm* found showgirls tap dancing, Brit bandleader Harry Roy scatting (like Cab Calloway), along with young Mabel, whose (then) high soprano vocal, in a nightclub setting, indeed produces rhythm and excitement!

Ethel Merman

- The author of this book does not find Ethel Merman's loud projection of her (almost operatic) voice on most recordings very pleasing! Indeed, Merman's real power was as a stage performer, where loudness is more of an asset. Nevertheless, she did produce some very good recordings (noted below) and became a successful radio and film entity as well!

    - The following picks reflect both recordings and film:

1. "How Deep Is the Ocean," Victor 24146.
2. "Eadie Was a Lady," Brunswick 6456. Along the Victor Young orchestra, Ethel recreates her Broadway review of the early 1930s *Take a Chance*. Penned by B.G. De Sylvia, Richard b Whiting and Nacio Herb Brown, this ditty is about a sophisticated lady who liked to drink. While it's all interesting enough, this lady's novel story remains true enough. Cab Callaway's contemporary version on Melotone M-12583 is a bit hipper, with similar comparisons to Cab's familiar "Minnie the Moocher."
3. "An Earful of Music," Brunswick 6995. While Eddie Cantor can be described as a huge Broadway entity (like Ethel Merman) in 1934, he also achieved great success as a film entity. As a film, *Kid Millions*, which also featured Merman, this fine ditty penned by Gus Kahn and Walter Donaldson is an earful.
4. "I Get a Kick Out of You," Brunswick 7342. The Cole Porter-penned classic, direct from Ethel Merman's 1934 Broadway success *Anything Goes*, ain't bad. Light years later, on Capital (LP) H-488, Frank Sinatra would clearly define this classic.
5. "You're the Top," Brunswick 7342. As another Cole Porter-penned ditty from *Anything Goes*, this may be considered another standard. This contemporary (1934) lyric finds Merman's version noting the likes of many, including the likes of (India's) Mahatma Gandhi, (film star) Greta Garbo, (songwriter) Irving Berlin, and the (toothpaste product) Pepsodent.
6. "It's De-lovely," Liberty Music Shop 206. The stupid lyrics by Cole Porter somehow found him creating a word. In any case, Ethel is on par and makes it all sound very pleasant! In retrospective, it's a pity that Bob Hope, who had introduced this ditty from *Out of This World* on Broadway with Ethel, was not part of this fine recording. (Contemporary bandleader and vocalist Will Osborne recorded and adapted this ditty as his "theme" song.) Light years later, Mabel Mercer put some claims on it.
7. "Red Hot and Blue," Liberty Music Shop 207. Another classic Cole Porter-penned ditty done well!
8. "Make It Another Old-Fashioned, Please," Decca 23199. Ethel introduced this Cole Porter-penned ditty in the (1940) Broadway production of *Panama Hattie*. A fine drinking song for highbrows.
9. "Marching Through Berlin," Victor 20-1521. This (dated) World War II entity is (still) loaded with true patriotism.

10. "I Got Rhythm," Decca 24453. While a bit later after World War II, Ethel Merman got around to recording the (Gershwin) classic she had introduced on Broadway in 1930.
11. "You're Just in Love," Decca 27317. Ethel introduced this Irving Berlin penned from her own (1950) Broadway entity *Call Me Madam*. Luckily she also produced a decent (contemporary) recorded duet with Dick Haymes.

Visual Image

The very (dated) visual image of Ethel Merman in film (and later TV appearances) is limited in appeal. Even her earlier filmed appearances with the likes of Eddie Cantor and Bing Crosby lack much anticipated excitement; indeed, the magic of Broadway is gone.

> ➢ The exceptions are:
>
> A fine 1931 film short, *Be Like Me* finds Ethel in (perhaps) a border town of Mexico, working with a local Mexican girl in a seedy bar. The young Merman looks tough, with a tight-fitting skirt, and a fight develops between patrons of the bar, patrons that also are noted as integrated entities—indeed rare for the times. Within this background, Ethel belts out:

12. "Be Like Me," indeed a fine song ditty, with a tough and hot attitude and
13. "After You've Gone." The tough Afro-American penned classic by (Creamer and Layton) is given a superb rendering, as Ethel not only scores but smokes. In true retrospective, it's more than a pity that Ethel Merman did not record a contemporary recording duplicating this fine filmed performance.

➢ More visual image:

14. "I Got Rhythm." A newsreel performance finds Merman belting out this (Gershwin) classic in perhaps a 1930 radio broadcast. For some odd reason, a contemporary 1930 recording was not attempted by Ethel Merman. She waited until 1948, as noted above, on Decca 24453 to record the classic she had introduced. More so, the newsreel is better!
15. "Marching through Berlin." As introduced in the film *Stage Door Canteen* by George Jessel, this 1943 patriotic rendering is full of Merman's personal energy and vitality. Don't miss it, however dated!

Lizzie Miles

While Lizzie's New Orleans background helped, her initial recordings in early 1922 put her into a pack of hundreds of (Afro-American) would-be recording artists, who had, like her, been previously unable to record due to racism and also giving Mamie Smith, whose initial Okeh (1920) recordings promoted a demand for other black voices, a run for her newfound recognition and fame. Starting in 1922, Lizzie recorded on many labels, but her 1923 signing on major (contemporary) Victor and Brunswick labels (who had rejected Mamie Smith and others) found Lizzie's "race" recordings being officially issued in Europe and elsewhere, easily outselling imports (for a time) of contemporaries such as Ethel Waters, Alberta Hunter, Edith Wilson, and Mamie herself. Lizzie's subsequent recordings found a husky and low-toned vocal, with an occasional ability to sing a bit softer in mid-tempo. The following are picks:

1. "Muscle Shoals Blues," Okeh 8031. An interesting town (Muscle Shoals), penned by Geo. W. Thomas, is full of woe.
2. "He May Be Your Man, But He Comes to See Me Sometimes," Okeh 8037.
3. "Please Don't Tickle Me, Babe," Okeh 8039. This odd title penned by Q. Roscoe Snowden was also rendered by contemporary blues entity Josie Miles (no relation to Lizzie) on Black Swan 14121.
4. "Black Bottom Blues," Okeh 8050.
5. "Four O'Clock Blues," Emerson 10586. As an acoustic ditty, this recording has added interest in its (produced) sound effects. While a cuckoo clock surprisingly finds its cuckoo bird at (four cuckoos) to start Lizzie's tale of woe, as the sad vocal ends, a (real) train is heard leaving the station. Just listen!
6. "You've Gotta Come and See Mama Every Night," Emerson 10603.
7. "Haitian Blues," Emerson 10613. Its a long way but this ditty, penned by Spencer Willliams and Lizzie herself, find it interesting.
8. "Sweet-Smellin' Mama," Columbia A-3897. This (Bob Miller) penned ditty's title says enough! Or is it 'Poro Blues'.
9. "You're Always Messin' Round with My Man," Victor 19083. This (1923) recording, penned by Spencer Williams, was subsequently issued in Britain on HMV B-1703. (Reverse Victor side "I'm Going Away Just to Wear You off My Mind" features Edna Hicks, Lizzie's half-sister)?
10. "Family Trouble Blues," Columbia A-3920. Real family problems? Lizzie's family, was indeed well managed, as noted in this Olman J. Cobb penned ditty.
11. "Triflin' Man," Columbia A-3920. This novel dity, penned by Bob Miller, indeed identifies some kind of nasty behavour
12. "Black Man," Brunswick 2462. Also known as "Black Man (Be on Yo' Way)," this Spencer Williams-penned ditty was also found in Britain with the same Brunswick issue number. More so, Spencer's own piano lead is (crudely) but effectively joined by Lizzie's own (possible) Kazoo playing, following a tough vocal.
13. "Cotton Belt Blues," Victor 19124. Spencer Williams's poigent penned ditty finds Lizzie's crude commentary well worth hearing.

- Lizzie toured Europe, with a stay in Paris until around 1926. Subsequent recordings are all better-sounding electric recordings when she returned.

14. "Shake It Down," Banner 7128. A fine mid-tempo dance number penned by Spencer Williams!
15. "Banjo Papa," Domino 4152. As penned by Andy Razaf, this ditty, also known as "Banjo Papa (Stop Pickin' on Me)" is a somewhat lively tune, with a strumming banjo, and finds Lizzie a (willing) victim of a wife-pickin'—and beating banjo player.

- The following two recordings feature the Jasper Davis Orchestra (dance band) from 1929.

16. "Georgia Gigolo," Harmony 944. Lizzie's vocal lightens up, much like Ethel Waters or Eva Taylor, after a long and jazzy introduction for this Spencer Williams-penned ditty on this dance band release.
17. "It Feels So Good," Harmony 944. While the previous Lonnie Johnson and Spencer Williams vocal duet is a solid bit of novelty, released on Okeh 8664, this Spencer Williams-penned ditty finds Lizzie in a differing idiom, more so as in a mid-tempo jazzy, danceable mood.
18. "Don't Tell Me Nothin' About My Man," Victor V38571. Jelly Roll Morton's piano backing and credited songwriting abilities found Lizzie in a fast-paced vocal. Does Lizzie answer the knock on the door? Does she want to listen to stuff about her man? Just listen!
19. "I Hate a Man Like You," Victor V38571. Another Jelly Roll Morton-penned ditty finds Lizzie in a deep, depressing mood, sounding much like Bessie Smith, complaining about dice, cards, and all sorts of vices.
20. "My Man O'War," Victor 23281. This ditty penned by Spencer Williams and Andy Razaf finds Lizzie in a bold, novel mood, perhaps explaining just why she likes men prepared to give all they have. Lena Wilson's contemporary (1931) version on Columbia 14618-D finds Lena's lighter and less bold vocal an interesting contrast to Lizzie's (harsher) vocal style. Listen to both!
21. "Electrician Blues," Victor 23298. As with pianist Harry Brooks, this tale of a (good) electrician who fixes hall lights, fans, bells, and whatever else, after a phone call, because he's so busy he issues tickets, is pure camp. Just another interesting "Handy Man?"
22. "Good Time Papa," Victor 23306. A somber but (somewhat) lighter vocal is good enough.
23. "Don't Throw Away the Key," Victor 23306. Lizzie's vocal is led by a slick guitar lead, which speeds up toward the end of the recording when Lizzie sneaks in a snore. While it's just speculation, the (unaccredited) guitar picker finds himself in a gradual mid-tempo lead that (perhaps) helps many latter-day listeners to wake up. Stay up and listen.

- The following three ditties find the Melrose Stompers backing Lizzie in 1939.

24. "He's My Man," Vocalion 5260.
25. "He's Red Hot to Me," Vocalion 5325.
26. "Twenty Grand Blues," Vocalion 5392. About a racehorse, a sable, and a jockey!

- After some time out of recording and performing, Lizzie was rediscovered after World War II, finding work in (hometown) New Orleans clubs and (most) importantly on TV. The following 1950s recordings are of merit:

27. "Bill Baily Wont You Please Come Home". Capital-2243. The ragtime 'coon' song'of the early century as by the likes of Dan Quinn, Arthur Collins and Silas Leachman, amoung other is finally realized as 'jazz;, without racial stereotypes in lyrics, with 'Dixie land' backing by Sharkey's Kings Of Rhythm,. (For many, the song had sounded similar to "Daddy Wont You Please Come Home", especially noting Eva Taylor and Annette Hanshaw renderings.
28. "Salty Dog," Capital 2341.
29. "Eh La Bas," Jansco LP-6252. Sadly, by the time this bit of barrelhouse (in French) "Dixieland jazz" recorded in 1956 was officially released in 1966, both Lizzie and

bandleader Bob Scobey could not benefit from the (belated) applause from later generations. While late for Lizzie, this traditional ditty of Creole origins easily notes her own "Creole" roots with as much authority as good fun!

Emmett Miller

The recorded legacy left behind by vaudevillian Emmett Miller in the 1920s is very much appreciated. In direct contrast to others, this white Southern was a crude example of what entertainment could be, which in true retrospective, must be explored. Moreover, the terms "black face," "hillbilly," and "blues singer" also apply. While his "black face" minstrel idiom has (rightly) developed into social taboo, as well as the term "hillbilly," his blues recordings are far better. So do some of his country ditties, replacing the hillbilly description. Indeed Emmett Miller's recorded legacy predates most of these terms. The quirkiness of Miller's vocals do in fact remain entertaining, and his use of ditties with black ownership, noting the likes of. W.C. Handy, Roger Graham, Spencer Williams, Andy Razaf, Fats Waller, and J. C. Johnson material. Miller in fact does "sound" black, or is it really how many white and rural Southerners also spoke in speech? Spoken word? Is "race" so difficult? More so, the term jazz may also be applied and perhaps lift the somewhat crude and racist act into something better. For Emmet, perhaps the opportunity to emulate a bit more, perhaps, at times creating for him a carnival atmosphere, or a bit of fun. In true retrospective, Miller delivers, although his own vocals May be in question? Just listen!

Note: Picks for Emmet Miller: Emmett's (1928-29) electric backup band, then known as the "Georgia Crackers" were more so an Okeh recording house band. They have since been identified as an early Dorsey Brothers orchestra dance band.

1. "I Ain't Got Nobody," Okeh 40162. Emmett's quirky vocal tricks are very evident on his 1928 version, on this already familiar song ditty popularized by (white) entity Marion Harris's original 1916 acoustic recording, on Victor 18133, penned by the afro-American team of Roger Graham and Spencer Williams. Moreover, a contemporary Sophie Tucker version, on Okeh 40837 is extremely more contrived. Tucker, like Miller, had also been a "black face" performer. Unlike Miller, however, most of her later electric recordings reek of her loud acoustic style, while Emmett could almost croon. Listen and compare!

2, 3. "Lovesick Blues" (a) As an earlier vaudeville style song ditty penned by Clifford Friend and Irving Mills, this ditty became a 1922 acoustic entity for Elsie Clark as released on Okeh 4589, along with another by Jack Shea on Vocalion 14333. Emmett, the would-be minstrel performer with a "real" Southern Georgia accent likely had put it into his act and recorded it on Okeh 40465. (b) This second electric (1928) rerecording on Okeh 41062 found some quirky vocal dialog with musician Dan Fitch and an added jazzy backing by the "Georgia Crackers," as this ditty turned out to be something very special—better than *all* other versions, including the much later (1949) version by Hank Williams. Just listen.

3, 4. "Anytime" (a) This Herbert Lawson-penned ditty was originally an acoustic one, as released on Okeh 4039, in (1924) and perhaps his very first recording. (b) This finer 1928 electric version on Okeh 40195, again sharing a vocal with Dan Fitch, is novel and fun. (This version also beats out the later country crooning of Eddy Arnold and a pop-styled version by Eddie Fisher.)

5. "St. Louis Blues," Okeh 41095. A fine vocal of the Handy-penned classic, with equally solid and jazzy backing by Georgia Crackers.
6. "Take Your Tomorrow," Okeh 41135. This (1928) attempt at popular singing found more Afro-American penned material from Fats Waller, Andy Razaf, and J. C. Johnson and is indeed given a fine blues treatment by Emmett's crusty vocal, with the (usual) fine backing by the Georgia Crackers. More so, was this ditty a contemporary "answer" record to the ditty penned by Sherman and Sylva, also a Gene Austin recording of "No Sorrow (for Tomorrow)." Listen and compare if you care.
7. "Dusky Stevedore," Okeh 41135. This original "flip" side of "Take Your Tomorrow" is also rooted in Afro-American idiom penned by Andy Razaf and J. C Johnson. Emmett (again) scores and perhaps merges blues and jazz singing, noting his usual vocal crudeness as something to admire, as backed by the Georgia Crackers.
8. "She's Funny That Way," Okeh 41182. Emmett takes a stab at pop penned by Neil Moret and Richard Whiting perhaps using the contemporary Gene Austin rendering as his (vocal) inspiration.
9. "You're the Cream of My Coffee," Okeh 41182. Another attempt a popular (1929) song ditty betrays a crude attempt at "crooning." (Perhaps an interesting comparison to the more sophisticated contemporary Ruth Etting best seller?
10. "The Lion Tamers," Okeh 41205. This campy bit of vaudeville is full of stereotypes, more so a contrived bit of vaudeville, as penned by its vocal participants Emmett Miller and Dan Fitch. The racism is very much in evidence as a contemporary "minstrel show" lacking a black face.
11. "You Lose," Okeh 41205. A dice game is a game, despite obvious stereotypes!
12. "I Ain't Gonna Give Nobody None of This Jelly Roll," Okeh 41280. The perfect mood as created by the Georgia Crackers (again) provides the quirky Miller vocal an opening for another excuse for jazz, as penned by Clarence Williams and Spencer Williams.
13. "Right or Wrong," Okeh 41280. Emmett's vocals, when not in a quirky mode, while no great shakes, are at least honest as well as simple and earthy. As penned by Benny Davis, Billy Rose, and Harry Akst, this pop entity is transformed into reality. Just listen.
14. "Lovin' Sam (The Sheik of Alabam)," Okeh 41305. The earlier acoustic best seller by Nora Bayes, on Columbia A-3757, was penned by Jack Yellen and Milton Ager and had also been an early acoustic entity for Mamie Smith on Okeh 4253. This bolder and electric recording, while dated upon release, finds Miller in a capable and novel mood. It indeed scores better than all previous versions and is successfully revived and defined by Emmett, fortunately backed up by the jazzy Georgia Crackers.

15,16. "Big Bad Bill Is Sweet William Now" (a) As released on Okeh 40465, this contrived novelty, as penned by Jack Yellen and Milton Ager, identifies black women and slang, which may suggest some speculation into the origins of this ditty. More so, a contemporary "acoustic" (1924) version as a (nonblack) female recording artist Margaret Young on Brunswick 2736 does away with the slang, yet stuck with the lyric. (b) Emmett's own subsequent (1929) version adds more to the fun as Miller's vocal (almost) rocks, (again) backed with the jazzy "Georgia Crackers."

17, 18. "Sweet Mama (Papa's Getting Mad)," Okeh 41342. (a) This is perhaps a contrived ditty, as credited to the likes of Harold Frost, Billy Rose, and George Little for a (black?) sounding acoustic Marion Harris release on Columbia A-3300. While Marion is convincing enough, Emmett is always cruder; (b) As a 1929 electric rendering, along with the Georgia Crackers, Emmett redefines this ditty!

19. "The Ghost of the St. Louis Blues," Okeh 41342. How can this contrived rip-off of Handy's St. Louis Blues work? Perhaps both Billy Curtis and J. Russell Robinson, who penned this ditty didn't mind. Amazingly, it does, noting that the Miller's vocal tricks and a few contrived pranks by the Georgia Crackers are more than fun to listen for.
20. "The Blues Singer from Alabama," Okeh 41377. Yes, he's the man! As penned by Castletown and Williams, this rambling tale more so favors a man from Alabama. Or perhaps a woman as noted in a contemporary (1929) release from contemporary (black) vaudevillian Bessie Brown on Brunswick 4346.
21. "God's River Blues," Okeh 41438. Yup. Emmett was a real "blues' singer," as he is found at his soulful best in this Hackett-penned ditty. More so, this ditty reeks not of racism, but of regional and cultural sharing.

Mills Brothers

By all accounts, the (1931) original Mills Brothers should be considered the first rhythm and blues group, defining huge commercial success. Ranging from about fifteen to twenty years old, the young Mills brothers from Piqua, Ohio, John, Herbert, Harry, and Donald, after some work in local vaudeville, caught the attentions of Cincinnati, Ohio, radio. It seems that they found the ability to emulate instruments, including kazoos and trumpets, with their human voices. More so, they produced excellent vocal harmony and were indeed to be found more than just a novelty act. Their smooth and hip vocals, perfectly suitable for electric recordings, were to become highly influential and imitated. Their early duets with Bing Crosby perhaps defined jazz vocals for some time to come as well as signaling integration. As billed on their first records, unless accompanied by other vocalists or bands or orchestras, these "four boys and a guitar" made recording history.

- The following are Mills Brothers picks from 1931 to 1935:

1. "Tiger Rag," Brunswick 6197. While the term "rag" had origins before the start of the century, this interesting vocal became a fine update from this Harry Decosta-penned ditty claimed by La Rocca as well for his Original Dixieland Band of 1918. While other instruments followed, including a nonvocal Ethel Waters release in 1922, this 1931 electric release is differing and better. With just a guitar as an instrument, this (very) smooth rendering pioneered a group sound as never before, as the efforts of any previous barbershop quartets had never sounded so hip! This ditty more so, despite the Depression, became a best seller.
2. "Nobody's Sweetheart," Brunswick 6197. A bit smooth, this old barbershop quartet entity penned by Billy Meyers, Elmer Schoebel, Gus Kahn, and Ernie Erdman had been instrumental best sellers for Isham Jones in 1925 and Paul Whiteman in 1930. While more conventional than "Tiger Rag," this Mills' vocal indeed transforms this ditty into something a bit more hip (1931).
3. "You Rascal, You," Brunswick 6225. It is interesting to compare a wild Louis Armstrong version, on Okeh 41514, and any equally exciting Cab Calloway rendering, on Brunswick 6198. Indeed, the group song is less than wild, noting a cooler and effective vocal song, yet not lacking hip-ness.
4. "Baby, Won't You Please Come Home?" Brunswick 6225. This version of the ditty penned by Charles Warfieled and Clarence Williams, in comparison to the previous

acoustic versions by Eva Taylor and Bessie Smith version, is a cooler and slicker group sound, with better (electric) sound. As a jazzy standard, a contemporary and very hip Annette Hanshaw rendering is also a good version as well as an (electric) comparison.

5. "Dinah," Brunswick 6240. The earlier Ethel Waters acoustic 1925 version had been sweet as well as a light jazzy vocal that had found, to a large degree, white buyers. As part of Columbia's (pop) series, the recording "sounded" white. Just how a black person could sound this way on Columbia 487-D was beyond the culture, at least for whites. Most Afro-Americans knew better. This Mills Brothers and Bing Crosby pairing moreover is more than an update. As heard on the record, the interaction between Crosby and the Mills clan is truly inspiring. In true retrospective, the clever scatting and jazzy phrasing is based on mutual respect. While it's no surprise that the Afro-American Mills Brothers were indeed hip, the inspired Crosby is more than good!
6. "I Heard," Brunswick 6269. The Don Redman-penned ditty is heard well, as this group effort makes it all the more interesting to follow, noting all that smooth gossip is contrived. Or is it?
7. "How'm I Doing?" Brunswick 6269. As full of slang, this ditty penned by Lem Fowler and Don Redman is crooned out effectively, retaining an edge in true (black) vocal expression.
8. "Shine," Brunswick 6276. While a contemporary Louis Armstrong version on Okeh 41486 is indeed good competition and comparison, this very hip vocal performance between Bing Crosby and the Mills Brothers, if contrived, indeed succeeds. Exciting? Innovative? A major step in integration? Can the crooning Crosby, at his zenith in 1932, be taken serious as a jazz singer? Yes, on all accounts!
9. "Rockin' Chair," Brunswick 6278. The contemporary Louis Armstrong and Hoagy Carmichael version, on Okeh 8756, and a Mildred Bailey rendering, on Victor 24117, are somewhat challenged by a smooth group outing.
10. "Goodbye Blues," Brunswick 6278. As penned by the familiar Jimmy McHugh, Dorothy Fields, and Arnold Johnson, this cool rendering had been used as their "radio theme."
11. "Sweet Sue, Just You," Brunswick 6330. The curious vocal penned by Victor Young and Will J. Harris is jazzy enough. An earlier 1928 version, by Earl Burtnett and his Los Angeles Biltmore Hotel Orchestra, with a vocal by the Biltmore Trio on Columbia 1361-D is also a group rendering. It is interesting to speculate if the Mills Brothers influenced a bit (vocally) by this white trio, noting the black foursome to be a hipper in slang.
12. "The Old Man of the Mountain," Brunswick 6357. While a bit smaltzy, penned by Lew Brown and Victor Young, at least finds a vocal that makes it interesting.
13. "Bugle Call Rag," Brunswick 6357. As another "rag" is recalled, this bit of rhythmic sound, without a real bugle, indeed sounds like one. As penned by Jack Pettis, Billy Meyers, and Elmer Schoebel, this ditty had been around, but except for one word and some spoken words, had never sounded like this before or perhaps since.
14. "It Don't Mean a Thing (If It Ain't Got That Swing)," Brunswick 6377. Its interesting to compare this group record to the excellent original Ivie Anderson vocal as a Duke Ellington release on Brunswick 6265. It ain't Ivie, but it's interesting!

Note: The following three titles were part of a Depression-era recording project that was essentially a rerecording project of the (all-black) *Blackbirds of 1928* Broadway entity. While the Mills Brothers were not involved in recording in the original, their hipper group sound was fresh enough for the already dated material penned by Dorothy Fields and Jimmy McHugh.

15. "Doing the New Low-Down," Brunswick 6917. As part of the Broadway production of *Blackbirds of 1928*, this ditty had been introduced by tap dancing Bill "Bojangles" Robinson as released on Brunswick 4535; he had been backed by "Irving Mills and His Hotsy Totsy Gang,". While Bojangles's version is just spoken word vocally, it's a far better voice to hear than to endure a horrid rendering by Irving Mills himself (Ellington's manager) on Okeh 8602. Moreover, a well done and jazzy Elisabeth Welch vocal was also produced, which had more so defined this classic, on Brunswick 4014, which had involved Irving Mills and his "Hotsy Totsy Gang" and luckily without his voice (1928). This newer Mills Brothers attempt is also good and also included the likes of a scatting Cab Calloway (minus his orchestra), with a backing orchestra provided by Don Redman.
16. "Diga Diga Doo," Brunswick 6519. As part of a Brunswick records recording project in 1932-33, this group effort also included the Duke Ellington Orchestra. As an original Ellington effort as well as "Irving Mills and His Hotsy Totsy Gang," a fine and jazzy 1928 Elisabeth Welch vocal, on Brunswick 4014, had already been made. Nevertheless, this very hip Mills Brothers version of the ditty penned by Dorothy Fields and Jimmy McHugh indeed scores.
17. "I Can't Give You Anything but Love," Brunswick 6519. Like "Diga Diga Doo," this *Blackbirds of 1928* classic penned by the familiar Fields and McHugh had been recorded by many. Perhaps an edgy 1928 crooning job by Cliff Edwards on Columbia 1471-D had been one of the better ones. More interesting was the fact that while Adelaide Hall, who had introduced this ditty in the original *Blackbirds of 1928* production, as she had also introduced "Diga Diga Doo," had not recorded as contemporary 1928 recordings. This could have been rectified, somewhat, in this ambitious Brunswick project of 1932-33, but oddly was not. Moreover, as part of a project by Brunswick Records, this rerecording had also been assigned to Ethel Waters and her resulting vocal, with Ellington's backing, released on Brunswick 6517, perhaps defined it as jazz. It's interesting to compare all versions, also noting a (later) 1938 Adelaide Hall version, with Fats Waller, perhaps redefining it.
18. "Coney Island Washboard," Banner 33211. Another brilliant exercise in group harmony finds the old amusement park, as penned by Ned Nestor, Aude Shugart, Hampton Durand, and Jerry Adams, a playful novelty, with a creative ride.
19. "Smoke Rings," Brunswick 6525. Penned by Ned Washington and Gene Gifford, the creative young group sound is mellow enough, and no coughing is heard. While politically incorrect in the latter century, and beyond, it is indeed well worth hearing this tale of blowing smoke!
20. "My Honey's Lovin' Arms," Brunswick 6525. There's a lot of fun and good jazz to be heard on this 1933 classic recording with Bing Crosby. By now, all the vocal scats are now expected, and both Bing and the Mills Brothers do not disappoint their listeners. It is also interesting to speculate that if Crosby had hung around the Mills Brothers a bit more, his recorded legacy would have contained more jazzy punch. In any case, this classic update of the rougher acoustic 1922 Frank Crumit release, on Columbia A-3699, remains a fine gem for all involved.
21. "I Found a New Baby," Brunswick 6785. Indeed, the group sound of the Mills Brothers is a fine and differing update for the earlier (acoustic) and jazzy Ethel Waters version. The smooth scatting is more so understood as well as appreciated.

22. "Jungle Fever," Brunswick 6785. As penned by Howard Dietz and Walter Donaldson, this bit of rhythm lyric is smoothly controlled and effective.
23. "Swing It, Sister," Brunswick 6894. The contrived title nevertheless succeeds!
24. "Sleepy Head," Brunswick 6913. This 1934 rendering, as penned by Donaldson and Kahn, is yet another creative bit of group singing and moreover a jazzy one. This ditty is perhaps something to compare with a contemporary Boswell Sister entity "Lawd, You Made the Night Too Long," on Brunswick 20109, which is very similar in vocal style as well as a jazzy outing as well.
25. "Limehouse Blues," Decca 167.

Note: John Mills passed away in late 1935. Instead of breaking up, however, he was replaced by John Mills, Sr. (his father).

26. "Shoeshine Boy," Decca 961 (recorded in London,1936).
27. "Long About Midnight," Decca 1360 (recorded in England in 1936).
28. "Big Boy Blue," Decca 1148. When swing music was a rage in 1937, one of its chief "band singer" vocalists was young Ella Fitzgerald, also a Decca recording artist. As paired by Decca Records with the Mills Brothers, hopes of producing a fabulous rendering was huge. Moreover, this resulting recording succeeds. More so, Ella's own sense of rhythm is heard very clearly here, as she proves she doesn't need Chick Webb's Orchestra to bounce strong rhythmic phrases around. Moreover, the Mills Brothers seem to enjoy Ella's company, indeed defining cool rhythmic vocals themselves!
29. "Swing for Sale," Decca 1147. Another contrived excuse for swing, penned by Burton Lane and Harold Adamson works well.
30. "Flat Foot Floogie," Decca 1876. This 1938 duet, with fellow Decca artist Louis Armstrong as well as the following title, penned by Slim Gailard, Slam Stewart, and Bud Green, released on Decca 1892, was the result of another Decca effort to market their fine stable of recording artists. The outcome, as with Ella, was also a winner, noting a primitive-sounding Louis among the smooth Mills Brothers.
31. "My Walking Stick," Decca 1892. This (Irving Berlin) classic had been introduced in the contemporary Alice Faye film *Alexander's Ragtime Band*. This fluid exchange of vocals between Louis and the Mills Brothers, while perhaps not what Berlin expected, yet best defined it.
32. "Sixty Seconds Got Together," Decca 1964. As penned by Jerry Livingston and Mack David, this somewhat clever vocal is timeless (also released by contemporary Dick Todd).
33. "Asleep in the Deep," Decca 2804. As an acoustic Al Jolson release in 1912, this very odd tale of a drowning man, penned by H. W. Petrie and Arthur J. Lamb, is actually helped by poor acoustic techniques, as Jolson's own contrived attempt at vocalizing a man treading water somehow achieves success. This electric update also notes a vocal challenge, with vocal tricks intact. Moreover, the result is indeed better sounding than Jolson's noting the obvious technical advancements. Just why this recording was even attempted is also something to speculate upon, although, for some odd reason, it remains a bit interesting.
34. "WPA," Decca 3151. This vocal duet with Louis Armstrong was good as well as a political comment upon the Roosevelt administration of 1940. Political? Yes!
35. "Marie," Decca 3151. The (Irving Berlin) classic had been around for a while, as even the likes of Rudy Vallee had attempted it. This fresher group sound is better and a real foundation for the (later) era of 1954 R&B and the group sound of the Four Tunes on Jubilee 5128. Were the Four Tunes influenced by the Mills Brothers? Bet on it!

36. "By the Watermelon Vine, Lindy Lou," Decca 3545. This smaltzy ditty, penned by Thomas Allen, perhaps indicates an attitude indicating race. In any case, backed by Benny Carter and His Orchestra, this excuse for swing oddly fails while still noting an interesting vocal.
37. "Lazy River," Decca 4187. The perfect harmony achieved on this classic, penned by Sidney Arodin and Hoagy Carmichael, remains laid back and priceless listening.
38. "627 Stomp," Decca 4187. This flip side of "Lazy River" is no fluke. More so, this attempt at vocal swing, while contrived, as penned by Pete Johnson, Dave Dexter, and Roy Jacobs, is a true classic. This highly danceable gem is full of energy and also surpasses all previous Mills Brothers efforts—at least since John (senior's) appearance in 1935.
39. "Paper Doll," Decca 18318. This World War II released title, as penned by Johnny S. Black, was actually released twice during the war, noting the musicians' strike and the fact that this vocal group was not an orchestra. The vocal style heard on this best-selling ditty is more so a throwback to the barbershop quartets of the 1890s, with a bit of rhythmic style. As a creative entity, it ain't much. In true retrospective, this ditty was by far the best known Mills Brothers rendering, with sales surpassing perhaps all other contemporaries, except for Bing Crosby's 1942 original of "White Christmas." Indeed, this record was a huge marketing success, perhaps lending optimism for a war-weary public. (As a record hunter, this record is not hard to find, as it had become part of 1940s Americana itself. Common? Yes! Still worth it? Yes again!)
40. "I'll Be Around," Decca 18318. As the flip side of "Paper Doll," this Alec Wilder-penned ditty also enjoyed success as a double-sided success.
41. "You Always Hurt the One You Love," Decca 18599. This simple ditty penned by Doris Fisher and Allan Roberts is smooth and slow.
42. "Till Then," Decca 18599. This title, penned by Guy Wood, Eddy Seiler, and Sol Marcus, had obvious contemporary World War II implications.
43. "Don't Be a Baby, Baby," Decca 18753. A free use of slang, penned by Buddy Kaye amd Howard Steiner.
44. "I Guess I'll Get the Papers," Decca 23638. This bit of smaltz, penned by Hughie Prince, Dick Rodgers, and Hal Kenner, was at least effective enough.
45. "Down Among the Sheltering Pines," Decca 24534. Somehow, this (already) old entity was to be revived by the Mills Brothers and Al Jolson, who was on a post (World War II) comeback career. This professional recording, not sung as a novelty, is still fun to hear, as Al, without black face, meshes well with the Mills Brothers group sound. More so, by this time, the Mills Brothers did not need Jolson.
46. "Is It True What They Say About Dixie?" Decca 24534. As the original flip side of "Down Among the Sheltering Pines," this old ditty penned by Irving Caesar, Sam Lernar, and Joe Marks also featured an excellent and controlled Al Jolson duet vocal.
47. "I Love You So Much It Hurts," Decca 24550. The country and pop contemporary (1947) standard is challenged!
48. "I Gotta Have My Baby Back," Decca 24813. Ella Fitzgerald and the Mills Brothers still sound good together, even this late. As penned by country entity Floyd Tillman, who also released it on Columbia 20641, this ditty's leap into R&B is considerable!
49. "Daddy's Little Girl," Decca 24872. This wedding day musy stuff, penned by Horance Gerlich and Bobby Burke was perfect for brides and Mills Brothers sales.
50. "The Glow Worm," Decca 28384. More mushy stuff that became a huge 1952 best seller.

Visual Image

The visual image of the Mills Brothers is loaded with a long trail of films throughout the 1930-40s, more so much more in luck than most other back performers. Considering death and subsequent success, the enduring Mills Brothers became prototype for all "groups," both black and white. Their visual image, a huge part of their legacy, may be best found in:

- Note: The two following film entities are also noted Brunswick recordings listed above.

Both feature the (original) Mills Brothers in the 1932 Bing Crosby film *The Big Broadcast*.

51. "Goodbye Blues." A fine live version of the Brunswick pick, noted in the text above.
52. "Tiger Rag." A fine live version of the Brunswick pick, noted in the text above.

Note: The 1934 film *Twenty Million Sweethearts* was a Dick Powell entity, who was a very popular tenor-like personality, who had attempted to "croon" on occasion. As featured in his film, the (original) Mills Brothers are more so noted below in:

53. "How's I Doing?" A fine live version of the Brunswick pick, noted in the text above.
54. "Out for No Good." This ditty, penned by Al Dubin and Harry Warren, is a very effective duet matching the Mills Brothers with Dick Powell. As a matter of fact, Powell seems to take a very sensible approach to it all, and his interplay with the Mills Brothers is a brilliant bit of work, a breakthrough. It is also more than a pity that this ditty had not been a commercial recording.

Bill Monroe

The origins of country music were originally folk and thus mixed with many influences.

> Considering the forced segregation between white and black cultures, the shared music of the church, work songs, and the playing of instruments was considered normal. As a young (white) Southerner, Bill Monroe also found the playing of phonograph records a huge lift. While the vocals of Jimmie Rodgers and the Carter Family consistently dominated the commercial success of an emerging genre, the likes of string pickers such as (North Carolina's) Charlie Poole were more so to become taken seriously. Poole's own recordings such as "Good-bye, Sweet Liza Jane" found tradition ballads becoming good excuses to show off his brilliant (banjo) playing, with a lesser focus on his singing indeed led by strings. Along with the banjo sounds of vaudevillians Eddie Peabody and Roy Smeck, Poole's picking indeed helped commercial sales of the banjo before his death in 1931. All this rural appeal subsequently led itself into the repeal of Prohibition and the emergence of bar or honky-tonk songs. After Poole, among others, a newer wave of such popular entities as Milton Brownie, Leon Chappelear, Cliff Bruner, and Bob Wills, along with the "Monroe Brothers, would emerge." Noting that the (urban) success of such entities as Duke Ellington, Benny Goodman, and the Dorsey Brothers were as influential as important, the eventual and alternative commercial success of "Western swing" would emerge.

Caught up in the middle of all this was bluegrass music, yet another rural (1930s) alternative. As the sophisticated pick of banjos, fiddles, and mandolins are heard, more so are some crude (yodeling) vocal efforts that had produced recordings in the earlier acoustic era, noting the (even) cruder styles of Fiddling John Carson, Wendell Hall, Uncle Dave Macon, Carson Robinson, and Gil Tanner. While more seriously challenged by Carter Stanley, the emergence of Bill Monroe (as a group with his brothers Byron and Charlie as the "Monroe Brothers") in the late 1930s finally defined another aspect of what was then called "hillbilly music." The sound achieved may also be considered folk, as the simple vocals may be considered hick. The crude vocal moreover works well. The (solo) Bill Monroe vocal approach may be somewhat quirky, and in fast "picking" tempo, he tries to put in a few licks, playing mandolin, or guitar, spacing in a lyrics. The following are Bill Monroe vocal picks:

1. "Muleskinner Blues," Bluebird B-8568. Right off the bat, they say in American baseball, the influence of the awesome Jimmie Rodger's version, on Victor 23503, some ten years earlier, in 1930, is recalled. While the emulation is noted, this fast-paced version, with Bill on guitar and with "Kentucky bluegrass" country fiddling, adds depth. The whole arrangement (a staple of bluegrass) may be considered great listening, with a wistful breezy lift, full of creativity. Some years later, Rose Maddox's tough vocal added a rhythmic style on 4 Star 1288. Light years later, a 1960 version by the Fendermen, on Soma 1137, was somewhat the same, perhaps seeking the wildness and rhythmic nature of the Rose Maddox. An even later attempt by Dolly Parton, on RCA Victor 47-9863, may even be better.
2. "Dog House Blues," Bluebird B-8692. This bit of rural slang is perfect in approach as well as novel. As penned byJ. L. Frank and Pee Wee King, this just ain't for the dogs. A moaning dog, as a matter of fact, deems this ditty more palatable—in-between some awesome (fast-paced) yodeling.
3. "Orange Blossom Special," Bluebird B-8893. This "train" theme, as penned by Ervin Rouse, is a fast-paced fiddling bluegrass special as well. While it is very true that Bill is emulating the excellent Rouse Brothers version, on Bluebird B-8218, the slicker vocals by Pete Pyle and Bill himself make this a winner to ponder and hear. This train of the rural south speeds away with much imagination, as creative fiddling and whistles do not fail to satisfy its commuters. Other versions in the (later) rock era are numerous, noting a fine (1964) Johnny Cash entity on Columbia 43206.
4. "Blue Moon of Kentucky," Columbia 20370. This self-penned ditty by Bill himself is a bit of a "weeper," as this slow-paced vocal indicates a throwback to the 1800s and the state of Kentucky. A much hipper Elvis Presley version, on Sun 209, some years later, is perhaps more interesting.
5. "Little Cabin Home on a Hill," Columbia 20459. The crude vocals by Bill and guitarist Lester Flatt are offset with some hot (hick) strumming. Moreover, both Flatt and Monroe also take credit in the authorship of this bit of "folk."
6. "It's Mighty Hard to Travel," Columbia 20526. This self-penned ditty finds a (good) excuse for a shared vocal with Lester Flatt (who is also strumming on guitar) jamming away (with a group including Earl Scruggs's banjo), producing some fast-paced bluegrass music! (Flatt and Scruggs were later to become very well heard, playing for the 1960s (TV) sitcom *The Beverly Hillbillies*. Where's granny)?
7. "Kentucky Waltz," Columbia 36907. Yup, this "waltz" title is a bit smaltzy. Nevertheless, this self-penned "weeper" by Bill himself is still a winner. Go figure?

8. "Rocky Road Blues," Columbia 36907. A very fine (prerock) use of a vocal and also a self-penned excuse for "rock." Moreover, Bill and his bluegrass boys indeed deliver.
9. "Footprints in the Snow," Columbia 27151. While these 'rural' entities had dubious origins, this ditty, claimed by Rupert Jones, as speculation has it, had British origins?
10. "True Life Blues," Columbia 37151. A good jam with vocals!
11. "Uncle Penn," Decca 46283. Is this ditty really about Bill Monroe's (real) Uncle Penn? If it is it's so hard to understand (vocally) that it just may define smooth "crooning" in its purest and crudest form?

- More: Bill recorded many song ditties without using his own vocals. Among the most significant are:

  - ✓ "Six White Horses," Bluebird B-8568. This fast-moving ditty, with a vocal by band member Clyde Moody had been based upon the Carter Family's "Worried Man Blues" on Victor 40317. Earlier, Blind Lemon Jefferson's "Right of Way Blues" on Paramount 12510 may have inspired it. A folk entity? In any case, a later Little Jr. Parker release on Sun 192 by Parker and Sun owner Sam Phillips just had to have been influenced by these earlier efforts. A subsequent Sun release, by Elvis Presley, on Sun 223, perhaps defined it best.

Helen Morgan

This recording artist, however highbrow, had a tiney soprano vocal especially fit for Broadway, in the 1920s. Her audience appeal was perhaps of an earlier era, and her contemporary phonograph recordings indicate a style most influenced by the likes of European, semiclassical works, enhanced into highbrow pop by electric recordings. Like her many contemporaries, her art was also just right for "speak easy" nightspots and for the new media of radio and talking motion pictures. As one of the original torch singers, with the adapted contemporary likes of Ruth Etting, Annette Hanshaw, Libby Holman, Kate Smith, and Ethel Waters, among others, the act of singing jazz and influences of tradition musical theater was first considered a step above the act of crooning. Perhaps the development of the microphone changed these attitudes. The use of radio, as exploited heavily by the crooning Rudy Vallee, would make it all seem more sound a bit better, as by 1931, these early pioneers of electric recording would all define themselves. They would all more so define the act of crooning as respectable as on records, film and (especially) radio. Picks include:

1. "Me and My Shadow," Brunswick 104. Contemporary (1927) bandleader Ted Lewis used this bit of poor word construction (penned by Dave Dreyer, Billy Rose, and Al Jolson) as his theme. The contemporary best seller by the quirky "Whispering" Jack Smith on Victor 20626 remains the better known version, along with a Cliff Edwards's release and more so with a differing "group" version by the Keller Sisters and Lynch, on Apex 8620, all give differing ears something else to consider, along with the even lesser known Morgan version. While Helen cannot restrain her uppity vocal approach, her pianist Leslie A. Hutchinson is as lively as jazzy, indeed lifting Helen's vocal.
2. "When I Discover My Man," Brunswick 104. A fine Kern-penned ditty initially finds Helen (successfully) showboating her abilities at highbrow singing, indeed defining

her torch emotions as premium recording fodder. Sadly, as times changed, she would (rarely) deviate.

3. "A Tree in the Park," Brunswick 111. This ditty penned by Rodgers and Hart is poignant enough.
4. "Just Like a Butterfly," Brunswick 110. This ditty penned by Mort Dixon and Harry Woods had been released by many, including a slightly more hip version by Peggy English on Vocalion 15568 as well as the better version by Annette Hanshaw on Pathe 32267.
5. "Lazy Weather," Brunswick 113. Good and upbeat!
6. "Nothin' But," Brunswick 122. This stiff ditty penned by Henry Busse, Ferde Grofe, and Sam Ward, who were all musicians who had been members of Paul Whitemans contemporary orchestra, found Helen prepared.
7. "Do Do Do," Brunswick 129. This Gershwin-penned ditty found Helen's emulation of the original and operatic rendering of Gertrude Lawrence. (Contemporaries Ruth Etting and Annette Hanshaw had differing renderings to produce.) Listen to all and compare!
8. "Maybe," Brunswick 129. The (Gershwin) title is hardly good, as Helen, along with a group of studio voices perhaps imagine themselves on stage. What is interesting moreover is this recorded example of the pristine atmosphere of operatic utterances that at least defined Helen as (vocal) leader. Showboating before *Show Boat*? Listen and learn!

9, 10, 11. "Can't Help Lovin' Dat Man," Victor 23238. The ultimate tear jerker? Helen was destined to be associated with (Oscar Hammerstein II and Jerome Kern's) Broadway classic *Show Boat*. As introduced as a "mulatto" or a person of mixed racial background, this Canadian-born vocalist perhaps defined it all for the European influenced songwriters. This (first) 1928 longer version backed by Victor Baravalli, sung in Helen's very highbrow voice, is definitive—as a vocal, as a torch song, and as part of popular culture that has indeed endured! Subsequent versions (with the same flip side "Bill" on Victor 21238 (ABRIDGED) in (1928) and rerecorded on a 12 inch Brunswick 020115 with backing by Victor Young in 1932 indicate an almost identical rendering for both song ditties. (Later recordings as "Can't Help Lovin' Dat Man" or 'That Man" by Ethel Waters and Lena Horne provide listeners some fine listening as well as interesting comparisons in vocal styles.)

12, 13, 14. "Bill," Victor 23238-12 inch / 21238 10 inch. This 1928 flip side of the above is another but a somewhat lesser *Show Boat* entity. Helen's lament, about an ordinary man, penned by Jerome Kern, Hammerstein II, and P.G. Wodehouse perhaps found itself other audiences of men named "Bill." Dated? Yes! Sad and wistful? Still good? Yes!. Like it's flip side, this ditty was abriged to 10 inch and later re recorded on Brunswick 020115 in 1932.

15. "Mean to Me," Victor 21930. Helen actually gets a bit mid-tempo here, although the hearts and flowers and strings are evident. So were many other (contemporary) versions, especially noting the likes of a (less operatic) renderings from Ruth Etting and Annette Hanshaw.
16. "Who Cares What You Have Been?" Victor 21930. This dreary song ditty, as penned by L. Wolfe Gilbert and Martin Freed, is not for everyone, yet it's (still) a good bet that when Helen introduced it in *A Ziegfeld Midnight Frolic* (1929), it did induce emotional tears due to Helen's torch vocal style.
17. "What Wouldn't I Do for That Man?" Victor 22149. As penned by Jay Gorney and Yip Harburg, this ditty was introduced by Helen, on an all-white piano, in the 1929 film *Glorifying the American Girl*. In this sensational film appearance, Helen is perhaps

in her prime. As a title, this ditty perhaps says it all. Do women want to be liberated with ditties like these? In any case, Helen indeed sings her heart out. It's also interesting to note the contemporary Ruth Etting version, on Columbia 1801-D, which was considered a blues entity at the time, as Ruth's vocal is far less highbrow. Both more so define heart-rendering torch. Yet another contemporary Charleston Chaser version (with a bouncy vocal by Eva Taylor, hidden as vocal refrain) also hid her (real) blackface. In fact, Eva's vocal is far less than blues but perhaps jazz. These labels indeed cause problems, but as a listener, these differences are well-noted comparisons. Check them all out!

18. "More Than You Know," Victor 22149. This standard tear-jerker does not fail it's listener. Nor does a contemporary Ruth Etting version on Columbia 2038-D. More highbrow than Ruth? Yes!
19. Why Was I Born? Victor 22199. Helen introduced this ditty in the contemporary 1929 Broadway entity 'Sweet Adeline'. As penned by Jerome Kern and and Oscar Hammerstein II yet another heart-wrenched emotional plea also found a contemporary Libby Holman version on Brunswick 4910) 'torch' rendering. Moreover, both ladies are similar in vocal style, although not in actual voice. Moreover, later versions produced by Billie Holiday and Lena Horne (on film) offer differing styles and voices. Listen to all? Anyone care?
20. "Don't Ever Leave Me," Victor 22199. This early assault on women's lib may be a contradiction on the freedom achieved by women in the 1920s, much of it involving what would be called popular culture. This Jerome Kern and Oscar Hammerstein II, however stiff, is uplifted by Helen's original sober vocal performance (from Broadway's *'Sweet Adeline"*.
21. "Body and Soul," Victor 22532. As penned by Johnny Green, Frank Eyton, Edward Heyman, and Robert Sauer, this ditty Broadway entity had had origins in *Three's a Crowd*, with a contemporary Libby Holman original version in 1930. As usual, Libby and Helen's versions are close, with Helen's vocal tone less shaky, and pure. Other contemporary versions by both Ruth Etting and Annette Hanshaw find Helen too stiff and Libby's vocal pitch a bit too much. A Paul Whiteman release, with a Jack Fulton vocal, could be considered OK, but a vocal by Louis Armstrong, completely changed things. (In later years, both Lee Wiley and Sarah Vaughan would also interpret this classic in far different ways.)
22. "Something to Remember You By," Victor 22532. Mmm. This ditty, like "Body and Soul" shares the same contemporary flip side as on the original Libby Holman release on Brunswick 4910. Whether 1930 marketing competition was involved is not clear, although this oddity of same flip sides in a Depression year a good question. The obvious vocal style similarities between Helen and Libby do not clash, although a comparison between these releases de reveal a few higher notes hit on Helen's part. Moreover, these torch songs are emotional enough!
23. "Give Me a Heart to Sing To," Victor 24650. As a 1934 film soundtrack entity from *Frankie and Johnny*, Helen articulates this ditty out, as penned by Ned Washington and Victor Young, without a dry eye in the house. Other contemporary versions by Bing Crosby and Ethel Waters sounded hipper, although in true retrospective, they all sound very tired by the end of the song. Perhaps they all just sung the heart out of it? Check them all out!
24. "When He Comes Home to Me," Brunswick 6984. This guy means everything to her, and this very sentimental piece of work penned by Sam Coslow and Leo Robin, just may be a bit too much for those involved (light years away), in woman's lib. In any case, this typical torch song hits the heart, which is just what Helen was aiming for!

25. "Sand in My Shoes," Brunswick 6984. This somewhat faster backing for Helen in 1934 still finds Helen very able as penned by Louis Alter and Arthur Swanstrom, this ditty should not be confused with the later 1941 Connie Boswell classic rendering on Decca 3893, a different song, penned by Frank Loesser and Victor Schertzinger.
26. "Song of a Dreamer," Brunswick 7329. As introduced by Helen in the 1934 film *Marie Galante*, this bit of mush, penned by DonHartman and Jay Gorney, while well done, loses its punch.
27. "I See Two Lovers," Brunswick 7391. Helen seeks not to become overdramatic and seems to have even conformed to let up a little and croon. While this vulgar term for singing was to be avoided in the 1920s, by 1934, the likes of Bing Crosby and Russ Columbo had for certain changed all that. Russ Columbo did in fact record this ditty and moreover seeks to get more out of lyric (and tonsils) than Helen ever did. How can a dull song be interesting? Listen to Helen and Russ to find out. Still too slow?
28. "I Was Taken by Storm," Brunswick 7424. Perhaps this ditty's poignant message, as penned by Louis Alter and Edward Heyman found the torch aspect of singing as overblown. It's (still) interesting enough to find a "drama queen's" lament (almost) too much! Or perhaps a contemporary voice from Hal Kemp's sweet band orchestra, featuring Maxine Gray's vocal on Brunswick 7444 more so defines differing styles of singing? Listen to both and find out which version induces sleep the faster.
29. "The Little Things You Used to Do," Brunswick 7424. Helen herself introduced this ditty in the 1935 film "Go Into Your Dance". This ditty penned by Harry Warren and Al Dubin from 1935 is a bit dramatic. But aren't they all? As a matter of fact, the little things that Helen accomplishes with her voice, while perhaps a little looser than in 1929, are still very effective.

Visual Image

- Helen Morgan appeared in some of the first "talkies" and had great claims as one of the first important popular vocalists to become a film entity. The following perhaps define her best:

30. "What Wouldn't I Do for That Man?" Helen, as noted in the text above, may be seen sitting on a white piano, at the height of her fame in *Glorifying the American Girl* in 1929. Classic!
31. "Can't Help Lovin' Dat Man." This 1936 film production of the *Show Boat* finds Helen in a fine update of the ditty, along with Paul Robeson and Hattie Mc Daniel. (The author of this book could not find Helen's previous 1929 filmed version). Lena Horne would also provide a later and interesting filmed version in the 1946 film *Till the Clouds Roll By*.
32. "Song of the Dreamer." In a minor part, Helen plays a seedy bar singer, somewhere in South America, or perhaps the Caribbean. With fans and hungry male patrons, with their eyes popping, Helen delivers a fine torch performance. As seen in the forgotten film of 1934 *Marie Galante*, her recording (a pick noted above) is indeed enhanced and edgier. As a further note, unlike her other filmed appearances, the visual image, as seen for this ditty, moreover provides for its listeners a bit more excitement.
33. "Give Your Baby Lots Of Love" from *Applause*, 1929. As penned by (Joe Burke and Dolly Morse), this ditty was introduced only infragments, and more so wickedly pleasing, as Helen assumed a role of an over the hill entertainer. (A well done

contemporary Aileen Stanley recording just has to do, as Helen, oddly-never recorded this ditty).

34. "What Wouldn't I Do for That Man?" from *Applause*. The song ditty in fragments is still worth it.
35. "Bill," from *Show Boat*, 1936.
36. "I Can't Go on Like This," from *Roadhouse*, 1930, with the jazzy backing of Jimmy Durante and Lou Clayton. Too bad this ditty was not recorded!
37. "The Little Things You Used to Do" from *Go Into Your Dance*, 1935.

Ella Mae Morse

As founded by the crafty singer-songwriter Johnny Mercer, the Capital label in 1942 found talent and taste just waiting to be exploited. In addition to older bandleaders like Paul Whiteman, Mercer seemed to have had a good ear. After stealing the Nat King Cole Trio from Decca and a little (white) boogie-woogie pianist named Freddy Slack, who had worked with Ben Pollack, Jimmy Dorsey, and Will Bradley, Mercer perhaps knew which contemporary trends to exploit and market.

As impressed as ever with the likes of Decca's Louis Jordan, the trends toward boogie-woogie and rhythm and blues had been hot enough during the early 1940s. Perhaps following the lead of Ella Fitzgerald's work with Chick Webb, (white) canary Anita O'Day, backed by some wild drumming by Gene Krupa's Orchestra got it right on rhythm numbers. More so, popular balladeers like Dinah Shore and Jo Stafford, sounded tame, next to Anita's up-tempo releases. Why should only black entertainment be hip? What was considered something natural for the likes of Helen Humes and even Lena Horne, in some cases, was to be somehow lost to the likes of these white girls. Slack had also been a follower of the contemporary boogie-woogie pianist Albert Ammons in keyboard style.

In any case, the infectious beat produced by Freddie Slacks small bands did in fact compete with the rise of Louis Jordan's rhythm and blues and was indeed simpler than swing. It was also (very) danceable. The vocal approach of Ella Mae Morse, like Southern-accented vocal influence of Connie Boswell is a bit more intense. While Ella and Anita had challenged their bandleaders, Ella Mae, in many ways, would take a lead from Slack and take over. Ella Mae, by the end of her renderings, would usually dominate, as her exciting vocals, overtake the infectious beat that the (unselfish) Slack had provided her. More so than her white contemporaries, Ella Mae's vocal style sizzled with raw energy. Indeed, her authentic sultry Southern accent and mischievous delivery was ten years ahead of its time. Rock in 1942? The following are Ella Mae Morse's picks:

1. "Cow Cow Boogie," Capital 102. As a Freddie Slack release, with vocals by Ella Mae Morse, this unusual title told an equally bizarre tale of a racially mixed would-be hip cowboy. Penned byRaye and De Paul, this novelty is boosted by Ella Mae's spirited vocal, which adds spark to an already playful and exciting Freddie Slack arrangement. The sales of this Capital release helped found the "new" Johnny Mercer label. As a further note, the other Ella—Ella Fitzgerald, along with the Ink Spots, also found this ditty, as released on Decca 18587, a fine excuse for rhythmic singing. It is indeed another powerhouse of a recording. In comparison with Ella Mae, it is only fair to

observe and hear that the young Ella Mae competes. She indeed holds her own. Listen and compare!

2. "Mr. Five by Five," Capital 115. This Don Raye-Gene De Paul-penned novelty had also found success as a contemporary Andrews Sisters release on Decca 18470. While the Andrews Sisters rendering is almost rocking, with a fair Vic Schoen backing, Freddie Slack's backing is far hipper. More so, it is a fine Ella Mae's smoking vocal.
3. "Get on Board, Little Chillun," Capital 133. As credited to Don Raye and Gene De Paul, this perhaps questionable in origin ditty reeks of black church rhythms. It had indeed been defined in (1926) by Clara Smith on Columbia 14183-D, among others. Could it be a previously credited song ditty by Baptist minister John Chamberlain from the 1800s, as part of "The Gospel Train"? Or perhaps with origins in Britain? Perhaps Ella Mae had heard it while growing up in West Virginia. The Southern accented Ella Mae moreover is rhythmic enough and succeeds. Get on board!
4. "Old Rob Roy," Capital 133. While Freddie Slack sounds a bit more traditional, the very potent Ella Mae vocal wins out. As penned by Robert Emmett Dolan and Johnny Mercer, this somewhat contrived tale about a Scottish Robin Hood also finds Ella Mae clever enough to muddle through.
5. "Shoo-Shoo Baby," Capital 143. As an "Ella Mae Morse" release and backed this time by the Dick Walters Orchestra, this bit of World War II slang, penned by Phil Moore, is fast and full of excitement. Ella Mae again excels as her sultry vocal style explores and explodes. A fine contemporary Andrews Sisters version, as found on Decca 18572 also "rocks," noting a group style. It is indeed hard to choose between each version, although it does provide, for listeners, indeed something to very much enjoy.
6. "No Love No Nothin'," Capital 143. This original flip side of "Shoo Shoo Baby" also became a best seller in 1944. As penned by Leo Robin and Harry Warren, this bit of a ballad is found to be a blues rendering by Ella Mae's vocal.
7. "Milkman, Keep Those Bottles Quiet," Capital 151. While dated by the familiar Don Raye and Gene De Paul, this tale about a sexy World War II factory worker does not disappoint. Indeed, Ella Mae's lyrical prowess is sultry and edgy and must have given contemporary censors fits. Yes!
8. "Tess's Torch Song," Capital 151. Yeah, this ain't bad, as this ditty penned by Harold Arlen and Ted Koehler, as heard in Ella Mae's sultry vocal indeed delivers. Torch? You bet!
10. "The Patty Cake Man," Capital 163. Some potent lyrics, by Roy Jordan, somewhat sell a story about this stupid "Patty Cake Man" title. Even so, Ella Mae's vocal may really turn you on! Just listen!
11. "Invitation to the Blues," Capital 163. Ella Mae (again) holds her own, as a stylish, if contrived, blues entity with rhythm. As penned by Allan Roberts, Doris Fisher, and Arthur Gershwin, this ditty, in comparison with the likes of Lena Horne and Dinah Washington versions, finds Ella Mae in competitive fine comparisons of style.
12. "Captain Kidd," Capital 193. The contrived tale, penned by Roy Alfred and Marvin Fisher, as delivered by Ella Mae, again compliments her uninhibited style.
13. "Buzz Me," Capital 226. Ella Mae's delivery is still interesting; in fact, she even beats out a very fine Louis Jordan original on Decca 18734.
14. "The House of Blue Lights," Capital 251. This return with Freddie Slack also finds this ditty penned by Don Raye and Freddie Slack a serious contemporary attempt by the band to record "rhythm and blues." With Slack obviously following Louis Jordan's lead, this contrived yet potent ditty is full of slang and with a "boogie-woogie" beat,

Ella Mae's vocal, while a bit controlled, "rocks." Just what is the "House of Blue Lights"? Or just where is it? Ella Mae's slick and (very) hip vocal says it all!

15. "Hey, Mr. Postman," Capital 251. As the flip side of "The House of Blue Lights," this effort penned by Don Raye and Paul Weston, while controlled and slow, is an interesting tale about Ella Mae's need for news. From a (lucky) postman? Perhaps Ella Mae's sultry delivery is enough for any man. Just listen!
16. "Pig Foot Pete," Capital 278. Released as "Ella Mae Morse and Freddie Slack with Rhythm Section," this ditty penned by Don Raye and Gene De Paul delivers boogie-woogie, rock, and some fine slang. Moreover, the (usual) sultry Ella Mae vocal finds a way to make it all come together.
17. "Your Conscience Tells You So," Capital 278. This slower blues fins Ella Mae capable enough to adapt. As penned by Benny Carter, Gene De Paul and Don Raye, an impressive rhythm section, perhaps found in a dreamy and smoky urban bar, leads Ella Mae, while retaining her own sense of rhythmic timing.
18. "Early in the Morning," Capital 487. Penned by Leo Hickman, Louis Jordan, and Dallas Bartley and released as "Ella Mae Morse and Her Boogie Woogie Sextet Conducted by Dave Cavanaugh," this ditty ain't bad! As Ella Mae tells it, it seems this tale about a woman who is looking for her "friend" is a bit tired. Moreover, after trying this guy's family as well as another girlfriend and different nightspots, her hard luck remains with her "Early in the Morning." Is there more to the story? Just listen!
19. "Down the Road a Piece," Capital 15097. As an "Ella Mae Morse and Her Boogie Woogie Seven" titled release, Ella Mae again scores. As another Don Raye and Gene de Paul novelty, this fast-paced example of rhythmic singing, with some fine slang mixed in, is hip enough. An unaccredited male vocal is heard at the beginning. Perhaps it's Don Raye?
20. "The Blacksmith Blues," Capital 1922. This 1952 best seller, penned by Jack Holmes, also credits a more traditional "Ella Mae Morse with Orchestra Conducted by Nelson Riddle," also stating "Vocal with Orchestra." As a pre-Sinatra effort for Riddle, his touch is well heard, with Ella Mae indeed well under wraps vocally. Ella Mae also invokes a bit of "country," along with her (usual) rhythmic style. Somehow, everyone is in time, and this somewhat interesting tale about a blacksmith works.
21. "Oakie Boogie," Capital 2072. This bit of rhythmic singing, mixed with "country," due largely to Ella Mae's (real) Southern accent and Nelson Riddle, also works. Penned by Johnny Tyler, this ditty is also a fine link to pop and R&B, something that was "new" in the early 1950s.
22. "Love You Like Mad!" Capital 2072. This flip side of "Oakie Boogie," penned by Jules Fox and Sam Freidman, luckily finds Ella Mae very able to overcome perhaps a flaky lyric.
23. "False-Hearted Girl," Capital 2215. This pairing of the rising country tenor-Tennessee Ernie Ford with Ella Mae somewhat works. Penned by Alton and Raban Delmore, the Delmore Brothers, and backed by Cliffie Stone's Orchestra, this quirky country entity is a far leap from boogie-woogie. (Tennessee Ernie Ford, while starting before 1950, became a huge country and pop entity in the 1950s.)
24. "Greyhound," Capital 2276. This bit of pop penned by Rudolph Toombs may be considered another attempt at creative rhythmic singing. A dull song ditty made better by Ella Mae?

25-28. *Barrlhouse, Boogie, and the Blues*, Capital H-513 (10-inch issue in 1954) later released a 12-inch LP in 1957. This bit of mid-1950s recordings (also released as single release) is highlighted an LP. By this time, the bold, exciting new style of

Ella Mae of 1942 had basically been replaced with and by others, noting a direct link back to her. As this book takes great pains to a cut off 1950, Ella Mae *is* a huge part of the musical differences that occurred. It might even be considered fair game to cover Afro-American entities and replace rhythm and blues, a style adapted and successfully exploited by Ella Mae through to the likes of Bill Haley and Elvis Presley. The principle problem with all this is that by this time, performers, both black and white, were doing what Ella Mae and numerous others had already attempted. As noted in the picks below, the obvious aging of Ella Mae (a common problem for most all vocalists) and the "Big Dave" Cavanaugh orchestra often fail each other. When compared to the likes of mid-1950s contemporaries such as Ruth Brown, Lavern Baker, Dakota Stanton, and Etta James, Ella Mae is barely holding her own. The following picks are nevertheless Ella Mae's interesting versions on contemporary mid-1950s rhythm and blues:

a. "Goodnight, Sweetheart, Goodnight." The group Spaniels version penned by Calvin Carter and James Hudson, on Vee Jay 107, rules, but Ella Mae does well.
b. "5-10-15 Hours." Ella Mae does not surpass the classic Ruth Brown rendering, penned byRudy Toombs on Atlantic 962, yet she doesn't have to. Again, she proved a winner.
c. "Have Mercy, Baby." Not bad, as Ella Mae captures the spirits of the Domino's hit, penned by Billy Ward and Rose Marks, on Federal 12068.
d. "Money Honey." Ella Mae tackles the Drifters hit penned by Jesse Stone on Atlantic 1006, with mixed results. An up and coming Elvis Presley rendering on RCA LP 1254 and on 45EP, 78 and 45 rpm would more so provide it with more energy.

➢ Visual Image. Perhaps the best visual image finds Ella Mae, with Freddie Slack's backing, rocking out on:

29. "Cow Cow Boogie," featured in the (1943) film *Reveille with Beverly*.

Lee Morse

Lee Morse was one of many vaudevillians who sang well enough to become part of the new jazz age of the 1920s. She was more so a credited songwriter. While from the west, she had somewhat of a Southern accent, which is noticeable on many recordings. Her vocals are mostly low keyed, although a shrill vocal at times off key with some scatting can sometimes be noted in a higher tone. She was sometime mistaken for a man when drifting in 'low' mode. Like Libby Holman, in true retrospective, she had a lot of trouble controlling her voice, which also led this author to be very selective.

1. "Mail Man Blues," Pathe 32086. In true retrospective, the likes of "blues singers" or "hillbilly singers" did apply to both races, although "being blue" just could and can apply to popular song. This self-penned ditty finds Lee's vocal deep in the blues in 1924. Did young Jimmie Rodgers hear this ditty?
2. "Dallas Blues," Pathe 25162. Another fine blues performance penned by Hart Wand and Lloyd Garrett perhaps defined?
3. "Yes, Sir, That's My Baby," Pathe 025146. Lee produces a rhythmic, jazzy performance.

4. "I Wonder Where My Baby Is Tonight," Perfect 11599. This Walter Donaldson-penned ditty became a novel best seller by Henry Burr and Billy Murray on Victor 19864. Lee cools it off!
5. "I Love My Baby," Perfect 11602. Both (1926) contemporaries Aileen Stanley on Victor 19864 and Dolly Kay on Harmony 107-H are challenged by Lee's "low" vocal!
6. "Bolshevik":. Perfect-4722.
7. "Side by Side," Columbia 974-D. Unlike the Nick Lucas best seller, this slow blues with guitar is (almost) a different song! Check it out.
8. "Mollie, Make Up Your Mind," Columbia 939-D. Both low and occasional high overtones find Lee demonstrating her vocal trick and abilities on this self-penned ditty.
9. "Mississippi Mud," Columbia 1584-D. The contemporary Bing Crosby original is challenged!
10. "Let's Do It," Columbia 1659-D. The Cole Porter-penned ditty finds Lee's flat cool and jazzy vocal sounding very different from Bing Crosby's perky and more upbeat contemporary versions such as by Rudy Vallee. Is it a challenge to Lee Wiley's (later) update? Listen and compare!
11. "Love Me," Columbia 1972-D. This self-penned ditty finds Lee influenced much like Ruth Etting!
12. "He's a Good Man to Have Around," Columbia 1866-D. Contemporaries Sophie Tucker and Libby Holman both produced good versions. Is Libby's style closer to Lee's?
13. "Swinging in a Hammock," Columbia 2225-D. The contemporary Kate Smith version is challenged!
14. "Little White Lies," Columbia 2248-D. The perky Annette Hanshaw version differs, more so do all future versions, including those by Ella Fitzgerald and Dick Haymes. Listen and compare.
15. "Nobody Cares I'm Blue," Columbia 2248-D. This ditty penned by Harry Akst and Grant Clarke challenges Lee to find a smoother, but still edgy cool style. Contemporaries Marion Harris, Annette Hanshaw, and Gene Austin more so offered differing yet very good versions of this ditty. Hard to figure?
16. "Walking My Baby Back Home," Columbia 2417-D. Much different from Annette Hanshaw's version!
17. "Something in the Night," Columbia 2705-D. While hardly sweet, this husky voiced, but soft-edged vocal finds Lee scoring something good in this ditty penned by Paul Wenrick, Helmy Kresa, and Joe Young.
18. "I'm An Unemployed Sweetheart". Columbia-2997-D.

   - Visual Image. From the (1930) Paramount short *Song Service*. Lee sings these ditties smooth!

19. I'll Adore You." Lee drops much of her edgy style.
20. "Just Another Dream Gone Wrong." Another ditty, penned by Yip Harburg, sung straight!

Ozzie and Harriet Nelson

- Most baby boomers fondly remember the television sitcom *The Adventures of Ozzie and Harriet*, which had started as a radio entity of the later 1940s. While, in true retrospective, the older Ozzie and Harriet were usually boring, it was David and (especially) Ricky (their two sons in real life) who most interested the (new) audiences of 1950s television. Lasting way into the early 1960s, it was more fun to watch both David and Ricky grow up. The mid-1950s advent of rock and roll also found its way into the show, as Ricky (greatly influenced by the likes of Elvis Presley, Carl Perkins, and Fats Domino) actually became a major rock and roll entity, and the weekly sitcom may be credited as a major exponent of the (new) musical genre. While essentially white and "middle class," the Nelsons also helped neutralize the rougher image of rock and roll (especially meaning Elvis into mainstream homes (middle class) each week. For older viewers, however, Ozzie and Harriet had meant something more. Ozzie originally had been a bandleader who did his own vocals and was much influenced by the rise of Rudy Vallee. His softer baritone style can be considered "crooning," and along with the likes of Bing Crosby, Russ Columbo, and Harlan Lattimore, among others, he gradually surpassed Vallee. Harriet Hillard a vocalist perhaps influenced by many, including Mildred Bailey, got herself a job as one as Ozzie's band vocalists. (Harriet had also found film work without Ozzie.) Great success followed, and both married. By the 1940s, radio and (more) film work still found both Ozzie and Harriet. This success continued into the 1950s and into the baby boomer heaven of TV.

- The following are Ozzie and/or Harriet picks.

1. "I Still Get a Thrill," Brunswick 4897. The (1931) release on Brunswick, penned by Benny Davis and J. Fred Coots, is a somewhat weak crooning job but interesting. It is likewise more interesting to note "Ozzie Nelson and His Orchestra," termed musically as a "Fox-trot with Vocal Chorus" on this original Brunswick release.
2. "I Don't Mind Walking in the Rain," Brunswick 4897. As the original flip of "I Still Get a Thrill," this ditty penned by Max Rich and Al Hoffman is crooned out better.
3. "Dream a Little Dream of Me," Brunswick 6060. This soft and mushy stuff, penned by Fabian Andre, Wilbur Schwandt, and Gus Kahn, found Ozzie helping to introducing this standard, along with contemporary (1931) Ernie Burchill's vocal on a Wayne King release on Victor 22643. (Light years later, Cass Elliot, or the Mamas and the Papas, would revive it as rock idiom—even hipper.)
4. "On the Beach with You," Brunswick 6131. This (1931) ditty, penned by Tot Seymour and Jesse Greer, again finds Ozzie producing more sweet-band sounds as well as a serious vocal effort. (Contemporary bandleader Johnny Hamp also had a best seller with this ditty, on Victor 22730, with a vocal by Cliff Gamet.) Moreover, this ditty's theme also made it an official beach song, at least in true retrospective.
5. "Say It Isn't So," Brunswick 6372. Ozzie's vocal is (again) very good. Moreover, this ditty is on par with a contemporary Rudy Vallee version on Columbia 2714-D. It is still likewise to compare others, noting versions by Connie Boswell and Eva Taylor.
6. "About a Quarter to Nine," Brunswick 7425. The contemporary (1935) Al Jolson film *Go into Your Dance* somehow lacked a Jolson (contemporary) recording. Moreover, Ozzie, always able to produce a fine dance number, defined it better than contemporary Chick Bullock could. (Jolson would record this Harry Warren and ASl Dubin penned ditty about a decade later.)
7. "She's a Latin from Manhattan," Brunswick 7425. As penned for the contemporary (1935) Jolson film *Go Into Your Dance*, this ditty, penned by Harry Warren and Al Dubin, while perhaps a contrived bit of Latin rhythm, still scores.
8. "I Wished on the Moon," Brunswick 7485. This lively vocal penned by D. Parker and. Rainger more than matches the contemporary Bing Crosby crooning job on Decca 543.

9. "Double Trouble," Brunswick 7485. As the flip of "I Wished on the Moon," Ozzie injects a little (dated) humor in this fine vocal penned by Richard Whiting, Ralph Rainger, and Leo Robin.
10. "Get Thee Behind Me, Satan," Brunswick 7607. This Irving Berlin-penned ditty had been introduced by Harriet herself in the (1936) film *Follow the Fleet* (vocal Harriet-1).
11. "But Where Are You?" Brunswick 7607. As introduced in the film *Follow the Fleet*, Harriet looked great but vocally a bit shaky. This recording of this Irving Berlin-penned ditty is far better. Another contemporary version, by Jane Froman, on Decca 710, is a bit more highbrow (vocal Harriet-2).
12. "Once in a While," Bluebird B-7256. Harriet's vocal is OK, penned by Bud Green and Michael Edwards (vocal Harriet-3).
13. "Says My Heart," Bluebird B-7528. Harriet's film work was sketchy, and her appearance with such heavy weights like Fred Astaire and Ginger Rogers in *Follow the Fleet* (1936) had been much overlooked indeed by the sheer star power of this dynamic duo of the era. By 1938, Harriet was starred with Fred Mc Murray, among others, in the film *Coconut Grove*. While considered a minor contemporary effort and miscasting a likable Fred MacMurray, Harriet steals the show. More so, her vocal of this fine ditty penned by Frank Loesser and Burton Lane find Harriet in a bright and good mid-tempo vocal mode. As duplicated on record, with Ozzie—who should have been in the film—this danceable tune remains a fine and pleasant "sweet band effort" retaining Harriet's more than good vocal efforts (vocal Harriet-4).
14. "Change Partners," Bluebird B-7734.
15. "White Sails Beneath a Yellow Moon," Bluebird B-10311. Ozzie is pleasant enough on this vocal penned by Nick and Charles Kenny and Harry Archer.
16. "I Want the Waiter with the Water," Bluebird B-10365. As vocalists, Ozzie (not Harriet), comes close to the likes of Ella Fitzgerald. It's to Ozzie's credit that he somehow distances himself and sounds fresh. Moreover, his fast-paced arrangement seemingly drives his vocal cords into chaos, until he runs out of breath. Indeed, a campy and interesting recording penned by Sue and Kay Werner.
17. "Tomorrow Night," Bluebird B-10420. This soft bit of crooning found this very danceable entity, penned by Coslow and Grosz, pleasing to the ear. While Ozzie is good, a later, and (very) radical rerecording by bluesman Lonnie Johnson, on King 4201, may be considered a bolder effort at crooning. (Light years away, an Elvis Presley version would be influenced by the Johnson rendering.)
18. "I'm Looking for a Guy Who Plays Alto and Baritone, Doubles on Clarinet, and Wears a Size 37 Suit," Bluebird B-10666. As perhaps the longest title of the prerock era, this mouthful is worth hearing. As a matter of fact, Ozzie's vocal, as well as writing skills, as "spoken word," is understandable. (It is also understandable that Bluebird did not attempt to spell out "37" on the original record label release.)
19. "Jersey Jive," Bluebird B-11180. Ozzie's own self penned excuse to dance ditty also found a tribute to his New Jersey roots. (Ozzie was born in the state of New Jersey).

Visual Image

The Nelsons were perhaps the most recognized family of the postwar television era. Earlier, Harriet had been the most bankable attraction as a solo film entity, especially in:

20. "Says My Heart." Previously noted as a recording, Harriet lifts up the otherwise weak (1937) film *Coconut Grove* with this song ditty. (vocal-Harriet-5)
21. "Get Behind Thee, Satan." Harriett introduced this ditty in the Fred Astaire and Ginger Rogers 1936 film *Follow the Fleet*. (vocal-Harriet-6)

Anita O'Day

- As a band singer with Gene Krupa and later with Stan Kenton, she could easily sound like Jo Stafford or Dinah Shore, yet could also vocalize on rhythm titles, with an edge. While she may easily be accused emulating the likes of Ella Fitzgerald's rhythmic vocals with the Chick Webb Orchestra, there is no doubt her rhythmic style was genuine. So was the wild drumming of Orchestra leader Gene Krupa, a (white) musician who, in a different way, had been influenced by the likes of Chick Webb. Moreover, as the swinging and drumming Webb had been a mentor for Ella, Krupa, later in the swing era, had led and laid down some rhythmic impulse for Anita. In addition, Krupa's integrated orchestra included an Afro-American trumpeter, whose sidelining rhythmic vocals just had to have lifted Anita's own (vocals).

    - The following are Anita O'Day's picks:

1. "Just a Little Bit South of North Carolina," Okeh 6130. This bit of clever lyric, penned by Betty Cannon, Sunny Skylar and Arthur Shaftel is bent, as an excuse to swing by Anita.
2. "Let Me off Uptown," Okeh 6210. There is no need for an excuse for drumming, as this rhythmic pattern is set! More so, this ditty, penned by Redd Evans and Earl Bostic, has it all and is further highlighted by a bright exchange of jive chatter between Anita and Roy Eldridge.
3. "Green Eyes," Okeh 6222. While this is more traditional and Latin in origin, penned by Eddie Rivera, Eddie Woods and Nilo Menendez, Anita, along with a stiff-sounding Howard Du Lany, does her best on this original "Aquello s Ojos Verdes" theme as a rumba and fox-trot. While perhaps as a danceable item, this (1941) entity is a bit passé; it was indeed a contemporary success. Indeed another contemporary rendering as a Jimmy Dorsey release, on Decca 3689, featured a somewhat stiff vocal duet by Bob Eberly and Helen O'Connell, and it became a huge best-selling entity. In true retrospective, it just may find Anita's sultry vocal style, in comparisons, scoring well over the likes of Eberly, O'Connell, and Du Lany! As good as Chick Bullock's quirky croon about 10 years earlier? Just listen, if anyone should care anymore.
4. "Kick It," Okeh 6278. This bit of rhythmic nonsense, penned by Teddy Hill and Vernier Bauer, is also high powered. In addition to Gene's magnificent drumming and the rest of the band, including Roy's loud trumpet, Anita's rhythmic vocal indeed kicks as well as prerocks.
5. "Stop the Red Light," Okeh 6411. No! Don't stop! Sing it with a beat.
6. "I Take to You," Okeh 6187. As a Noble Sissle release in 1936, Lena Horne, on Decca 847, had made a somewhat clumsy attempt on this ditty. Anita attacks this ditty and indeed improves upon it. Sorry, Lena!
7. "Skylark," Okeh 6607. Competition for contemporaries Dinah Shore and Helen Forrest? Yo bet!

8. "Harlem on Parade," Okeh 6607. Gene Krupa and his Orchestra offend no one, despite this perhaps stereotyped title, penned by Benny Carter, Ray Evans, and Elton Hill. Does Anita swing or rock?
9. "Chickery Chick," Columbia 36877. While contrived, Anita's rhythmic vocal is contained a bit, noting a fine and swinging Krupa backing. As penned by Sylvia Dee and Sid Lippman, this use of slang, like most others, may label Anita not only hip but black. More so, white singers were not supposed to sing or sound like this. Indeed, a contemporary (white) singer, also a fan of Ella Fitzgerald, by the name of Ella Mae Morse, on the Capital label, had similar ideas too.
10. "Boogie Blues," Columbia 36986. Gene Krupa again scores in the way he is heard in beating it out on his drums! Nevertheless, penned by Alexis Bledel and Gene Krupa himself, this ditty needed a slick and hot vocal—indeed Anita's specialty.
11. "And Her Tears Flowed Like Wine," Capital 166. After leaving the Gene Krupa band, Anita hooked up with the (then) up and coming jazz bandleader, Stan Kenton. (Kenton became a huge musical entity in the later 1940s, working with the likes of Nat King Cole and the voices of June Christy and Chris Connor.) This earlier 1944 ditty penned by Joe Green, Charles Lawrence, and Stan Kenton himself, with Anita's rhythmic and sultry touch perhaps provided Kenton with a challenge of containment. Indeed, this ditty is well structured while allowing Anita to attack lyric at just the right time. (Lauren Bacall introduced this ditty in the contemporary film *"The Big Sleep"*).
12. "Are You Livin', Old Man?" Capital 187. This Stan Kenton entity, as penned by Redd Evans, is an interesting question. Luckily, the rhythmic Anita is asking it!
13. "Ace in the Hole," Signature 15127. Anita's (1947) approach to this ditty is totally uninhibited and more so an excuse to scat! This very surprising recording may or may not be a live entity as well. This time, Anita and her own band, "Alvie and his Little Band" produce some fast-paced and jazzy sounds that seemingly never find an end! Stand up and listen! Penned by George Mitchell and James Dempsey, this tale of gambling is far from the Cole Porter ditty of the same name. Another contemporary version, although less known, by Jessie Stone and his Orchestra, featuring Jessie's own vocal of "Ace in the Hole," on Victor 20-2554, is worth hearing as well as comparing to Anita's hotter and uninhibited vocal. Jessie Stone would more so influence the (later) rock era, as Charles Calhoun, with many of his own penned song ditties.
14. "Sometimes I'm Happy," Signature 15127. While this ditty is indeed slower, it is for sure a very different type of vocal (and orchestration) than any earlier versions. As penned by Irving Caesar, and Vincent Youmans, it had been a 1927 best-selling release for the Roger Kahn Orchestra, with a vocal by Franklyn Baur, although a contemporary Vaughn De Leath version was better. After Anita, perhaps the later Lee Wiley version would define it. Listen and compare.
15. "Hi Ho Trailus Boot Whip," Signature 15162. This postwar title is enough to blow away anyone, and, as usual, Anita does not disappoint her audience. As penned by Buster Harding, Jack Palmer, and Roger Ram Ramarez and backed by the Will Bradley Orchestra, Anita's rhythmic vocal more so makes sense out of this stupid and challenging title.
16. "What Is This Thing Called Love?" Signature 15162. Anita (somehow) doesn't run out of breath as she scats the hell out of this otherwise traditional Cole Porter-penned ditty. While it's a long shot, it is more than interesting to compare the earlier clumsy and sultry Libby Holman version (1930) to a more current (1944) deliberate and sultry Lena Horne version. Indeed, any review finds that these ladies had style!

Will Osborne

- This nasal baritone vocalist found the sweet band sounds of the late 1920s much to his liking. As a bandleader as well as a vocalist, his rise to popularity was to be derailed some way by a similar-sounding entity, one Rudy Vallee. Even so, this Canadian singer (like Helen Morgan) still found much fame as a radio entity of the later 1920s and early 1930s. More so, he was in good company, as the success of Vallee had found other contemporaries, such as Bing Crosby, Russ Columbo, and Ozzie Nelson, seeking a better and bolder style. In true retrospective, the "radio" feud with Vallee was a good marketing idea as a useful ploy to entertain his radio audiences as well as his own record sales.

- Picks include:

1. "On a Blue and Moonless Night," Columbia 2128-D. Along with Al Hoffman, Charles O'Flynn, Will himself set up a soft croon with a moon (finally) not to bee seen!
2. "So Beats My Heart for You," Columbia 2269-D. Another 'soft' song ditty of the 'heart', penned by Tom Waring. Pat Waring and Charles Henderson is crooned out well enough.
3. "Say It Isn't So," Perfect 12843. Contemporaries Annette Hanshaw, Morton Downey, and Sing Sam join Will in this Irving Berlin-penned ditty. While other versions are done very well, including those by Ozzie Nelson, Connie Boswell, and the Riffers (Eva Taylor), it's more than fortunate that Annette Hanshaw's added vocals cancel out the horrid sounds of Morton Downey and Singing Sam!
4. "Cocktails for Two," Melotone 12996. A fine ditty for an upper-crust dinner party, 1934, penned by Sam Coslow and Arthur Johnston seemingly needed a croon job.
5. "For All We Know," Perfect 15960. Again the "sweet band" effect finds Will in good form. This ditty penned by J. Fred Coots and Sam M. Lewis could be his best. As sung in (almost) mid-tempo, Will's vocal finds some fine direction from his orchestra, which makes for some pleasant and easy listening.
6. "Three's a Crowd," Perfect 15663. As penned by Al Dubin, Irving Kahal, and Harry Warren for the Broadway entity of the same name, this typical "sweet-band" sound is another (slow) dance floor winner. Moreover, Will does indeed croon out much like contemporary Rudy Vallee (again). Or did Rudy emulate Will?
7. "Lover," Perfect 16741. This ditty penned by Richard Rogers and Lorenz Hart, was introduced by) Maurice Chevalier in the contemporary 1932 film "Love Me Tonight". While Chevalier is pleasant enough, this ditty begged for a good crooning job. Osborne's vocal more so does indeed sound identical to that of Rudy Vallee, but it's all Will! Will Osborne! Really? Or what about Greta Keller's contemporary best seller?
8. "A Ghost of a Chance," Perfect 15741. This stiff vocal attempt at the contemporary Bing Crosby original is at least interesting, however lacking.
9. "Ev'ry Day," Conqueror 8477. As penned by Irving Kahal and Sammy Fain, the references to summer and a new marriage are typical for this type of smaltzy stuff.
10. "It's De-Lovely," Decca 1058. The (Cole Porter) hit found pleasant enough.
11. "Between 18th and 19th on Chestnut Street," Victor 8113. Mmm. Will changes style and discovers the likes of swing about five years too late. As penned by Dick Rogers and Will himself, this ditty is still better heard on Decca 2948 by Bing Crosby and Connie Boswell.

Patti Page

- The pop success of Patti Page on the independent Mercury label of the later 1940s generated enough revenue to help the "new" label become known as a major label by the end of the 1950s. The young Clara Ann Fowler, this Patti Page, had first become a regional voice through the growing media of radio in the latter 1940s. After briefly appearing with Benny Goodman (a jazz legend by 1948) she signed with the new Mercury label and began a singing career (despite rock and roll) which would establish her as a top-selling musical entity for more than a decade to follow.

1. "So In Love," Mercury 5230. This Cole Porter penned ditty found Patti's husky, deep vocal able to take on sophisticated material.
2. "With My Eyes Wide Open I'm Dreaming," Mercury 5344. With an odd notion to produce the "Patti Page Quartet," this old ditty penned by Harry Ravel and Mack Gordon finds Patti's vocal (as noted on the original 78 rpm record) being chopped up (electronically four ways) by her Mercury producer Jack Rael, resulting in the (admitted) gimmick becoming interesting. While not really (duet ting) with herself, this ditty does prove that this vocalist indeed had a great set of lungs.
3. "Oklahoma Blues," Mercury 5344. This ditty is not the old (1928) title as the (credited) Frankie Wallace version on Cameo 8328 had been. It was, however, contrived as something similar. As credited to Jack Rael, this mid-tempo tale of a "cowboys" blues finds a committed vocal pulled off by Patti. It is interesting that this (white) vocalist was producing recording fodder much like some of the material heard from the likes of contemporaries Kay Starr, Jo Stafford, and (especially) Ella Mae Morse, who had found the likes of current upbeat R&B and "country boogie" material good and trendy.
4. "I Don't Care If the Sun Don't Shine," Mercury 5396. Perhaps Dean Martin and (later) Elvis Presley was inspired by this best seller of 1950?
5. "All My Love," Mercury 5455. Maurice Ravel's French theme 'Bolero', penned by Mitchell Parish, Paul Dorand and Henri Contet found Patti's vocal more than a 'pop' compliment!
6. "Tennessee Waltz," Mercury 5534. While there is indeed distaste for "waltz" music for many, this wordy title penned by Redd Stewart and Pee Wee King is full of sentimentality, and it works! More so, considering an original country Pee Wee King version, on Victor 20-2680, the clear, straight, and low-keyed vocal performance by Patti is indeed a converted country weeper that made for its (1950) jukebox audience to get a bit teary-eyed. As a recording, Patti's version outsold the previous (Pee Wee King) version as well as all others that followed, including an excellent and similar rendering by a rival and vocal influence, Jo Stafford.
7. "Boogie Woogie Santa Claus," Mercury 5534. This side, the original "A" side of "Tennessee Waltz," reveals a fine rhythmic vocalist not limited by fluff. While, in true retrospective, it's more than a pity that the fine original Mabel Scott version, on Exclusive 75X, was less known as a contrived excuse for rhythm and blues, penned by Leon Rene, is no less of a challenge for Patti. Moreover, Patti proves she's no slouch at rhythm! (This ditty would be reissued later on Mercury 5729.)
8. "Long, Long Ago," Mercury 5534. The overwhelming success of "Tennessee Waltz," the original B side of "Boogie Woogie Santa Claus," found the Christmas of 1950 over, with the Christmas entity as it's flip side. Probably, because of seasonal concerns,

as well as the song ditty's listing on contemporary jukeboxes, this new side, penned by T.H. Bayle and Jack Rael, using the same record number, replaced it.

9. "Detour," Mercury 5682. This ditty penned by Paul Westmorland found its way to "country and western" jukeboxes as well as achieved pop success.
10. "Christmas Bells," Mercury 5729. While more modest than "Boogie Woogie Santa Claus," as reissued on its flip side, this seasonal ditty, penned by Harry Filler and Leonard Schroeder, figured well into contemporary (seasonal) marketing in 1951.
11. "Release Me". Jack Rael's vamping otchestra arraingement almost ruins this Coakey Robbins penned ditty that found Patti in a well done 'pop'duet with with Rusty Draper.
12. "You Belong to Me," Mercury 5899. Patti shared contemporary best-selling success with versions by Jo Stafford's initial recording and by Dean Martin. Listen and compare!
13. "Conquest". Mercury 70025. This Coakey Robbins penned ditty found Patti in vocal territory that perhaps tried to emulate the bombastic contemporary likes of Frankie Laine or Vic Damone. As an attempt at a Spanish style with perhaps an older Mexican theme, the mixed results of the almost horrid vocal performance a very unusual and unexpected result for her. What does make it all interesting however, are lyrics that perhaps imply a needed sexual satifaction from a woman's prospective? Woman's lib in the early 1950s?
14. "That Doggie in the Window," Mercury 70070. This bit of novelty penned by Bob Merrill had problems. While typical for the early 1950s, this seemingly harmless tale, about a child (trying) to find a pet and work for all concerned, led to a lot of family arguments. Moreover, a lot of young parents began to hate Patti Page. Perhaps a lot more pet store owners felt differently?
15. "Allegheny Moon". Mercury 70878. This sentimental 'moon' song, penned by Al Hoffman and Dick Manning, despite it's old style and some heavy competition from the likes of 1956 rock and roll led by Elvis, became a huge best selling entity for that year.
16. "A Poor Man's Roses Are A Rich Mans Gold". Mercury 71059. This ditty, penned by Bob Hilliard and Milton De Lugg is a traditional 'pop' entity, sung in mid tempo. What makes it all more ever interesting however, was a contemporary 1957 version by an up and coming 'county' entity, Patsy Cline. For many radio listeners at the time, Patsy was Patti ! In retrospective, Patsy just had to have been influenced by Patti, noting that Patsy cannot be a featured artist within this text, and the fact that Patti had just made it into this book as a 'cusp' artist, starting just bere 1950. As a further note, Patsy's vocal, while similar in style to Patti, had more vocal range and possibilities. Patti or Patsy? Listen to both versions.
17. "Old Cape Cod". Mercury 71101. This pleasant bit of non-rock alternative, penned by Claire Rothrucki, Milton Yukus and Allen Jeffrey sold well in 1957
18. "Dark Moon". Mercury 71870. Ned Miller's fine country entity had been popularized in 1957 by Bonnie Guitar and the older actress & (then) TV icon, Gale Storm. Patti's later 1961 version, which no means better, is pleasant enough. (This ditty was also released on a Mercury LP release MG 20615).
19. "Release Me And Let Me Love Again". Mercury (LP) MG 20615. Along with other song ditties considered 'country', including the single release of "Dark Moon", Patti's better than average vocal attempted to define the already old honky tonk song "Release Me", penned by Eddie Miller, Robert Yount and James Pebworth. As the song ditty was a 'standard' by 1961, the likes of many voices, including vocals by Eddie Miller,

Park Williams and Kitty Wells, had already made it popular. As juke box fodder, the Kitty Wells version, with blazing fiddles had more ever best defined it in 1954.

Patti's 'pop' vocal, however, in comparison with later versions, many only be considered interesting. This would especially include Little Ester Phillip's soufull rendering, with violins not called fiddles and the even later 1967 polished 'pop' version by (British) Engelbert Humperinck just blow away Patti-but maybe not Kitty? Listen to all and compare!(This ditty is not the previous Corky Robbins penned song that Patti had recorded with Rusty Draper). ditty).

20. "The Boy's Night Out". Mercury 72013. As a classy 1962 film title, this Sammy Cahn and Jimmy Van Heusen penned ditty found Patti more than able to deliver a 'pop' sound
21. "Hush Hush Hush Sweet Charlotte". Columbia 43251. By 1965, the world of popular music was dominated by the likes of the British invasion led by the Beatles, as well as the likes of the Motown label, as well as a 'country' sound founded in Nashville in the 1950s. As penned by Frank De Vol and Mack David, this ditty had more so been used for the title of the popular contemporary Bette Davis and Olivia de Havilland film, finding Patti more so introducing it. Because of all this publicity, along with Patti's excellent vocal, and despite all the changes noted, this ditty became a best selling entity in 1965.

Charlie Patton

- As a relative latecomer to recording, in 1929, this real entity of the Mississippi delta laid a huge claim to the music, both vocally and instrumentally. Like Blind Lemon Jefferson and Papa Charlie Jackson before him, a crude and loud vocalist emerges. Patton is rough sounding and perhaps a bit more folk than even Blind Lemon. As recorded in Richmond, Indiana and in Paramount's (new) and doomed facilities in Grafton, Wisconsin, Patton's tenure as Paramount's "King of the Delta Blues" was ended by the Depression, as Paramount Records became one of its early victims, 1930. Later recordings, on Vocalion, are also not bad but were never as influential as to contemporaries as those of Big Bill Broonzy's were. As a blues singer, some of these picks may be linked to the style of hillbilly blues singer Jimmie Rodgers, minus Rodger's yodeling. More so, the regional (Southern) culture was a shared experience marred by rigid segregation. Originally perhaps it existed while traveling down any rural road. In true retrospective, Patton became at least as famous as Broonzy by later century. Indeed, the newer rock generation discovered him and linked him to a style that lingers. The cruder the better. The following are Charlie Patton picks:

1. "Pony Blues," Paramount 12792. Like most of Patton's compositions and like his contempories at (Paramount), if suspect, they are a borrowed culture, and not stolen from unregistered song pluggers or copywrite extention limits. This ditty more ever rides along well.
2. "Banty Rooster Blues," Paramount 12792. The rooster was indeed a deal for rural folk and a sign of sexual prowess. Is this what Charlie is crudely singing about?
3. "Mississippi Bo Weevil Blues," Paramount 12805. If this title is contrived, Patton's grit and crudeness of voice is not.

4. "Shake It and Break It but Don't Let It Fall, Mama," Paramount 12869. This crude tale is suggestive enough. More so, Charlie delivers! Just listen.
5. "I'm Going Home," Paramount 12883. The bit of true folk is a crude expression for those ready to die. While "Fare Thee Well" was shared by both blacks and whites alike, this ditty finds Charlie ready.
6. "High Water Everywhere," Paramuont 12909. As "part one" and the other side "part two," this sad tale has a common (delta) one. Bessie Smith's previous "Back Water Blues" on Columbia 14195-D also addresses this subject and compares to Patton's vocal, a bit (less) crude!
7. "Running Wild," Paramount 12924. This tale about "running wild" sounds as if a fiddle is playing in the background. While always crude, the term "hillbilly" may be applied, noting Charlie's blackness. A shared culture? Just listen.
8. "Elder Green Blues," Paramount 12972. This crude vocal is backed by some funky fiddling! This tale about elder Green, indeed a man full of fight, is a well-rendered tale.
9. "I Shall Not Be Moved," Paramount 12986. The spiritual (pre-gospel) label is appropriate as well as Charlie's soulful rendering.
10. "Devil Sent the Rain," Paramount 13040. The religious theme is pursued and indeed believed!
11. "Frankie and Albert," Paramount 13110. Is this also Frankie and Johnny? Indeed, this folk tune got around.
12. "Jersey Bull Blues," Vocalion 02782.

Louis Prima

- The vocal abilities of Louis Prima were somewhat limited. While it may be subject to taste, it's also the case of such popular attractions as Louis Armstrong, Cab Calloway, Louis Jordan, and Fats Waller. While it is indeed possible to find error in the merits of this review itself, the vocals of Irving Mills (an early manager of Duke Ellington), Lee Morse, and Arthur Tracy ("the Street Singer") are found to be (still) lacking. Louis Prima was, however, a fine musician. While he never captured the popularity of his major vocal and musical influence, Louis Armstrong, he did in fact contribute much and with substance. His own compositions included "Sing, Sing, Sing (With a Swing)," which gave Benny Goodman (with drummer Gene Krupa) a major instrumental hit on Victor 25796 in 1937. More importantly, for the purposes of this book, he recorded some fine and uninhibited jazz vocals which (even) match him up with the likes of Cab Calloway, Louis Jordan, and Louis Armstrong himself. On top of all that, he did indeed play a mean trumpet.

- The following are Louis Prima picks:

1. "'Long About Midnight," Brunswick 7335. This ditty penned by Irving Mills and Alex Hill by "Louis Prima and His New Orleans Gang," is all about rhythm singing—and by a white Italian American, who truly loved Louis Armstrong.
2. "Stardust," Brunswick 7335. The Louis Armstrong rendering, on Okeh 41530, is the basis of this fine recording and interestingly not the Crosby one on Brunswick 6169.
3. "I'm Living in a Great Big Way," Brunswick 7419. The Dorothy Fields and Jimmy Mc Hugh penned ditty, with (President) Franklin D. Roosevelt in it's lyric, finds Louis's vocal read.

4. "Swing Me with Rhythm," Brunswick 7431. This dance number penned by Irving Mills and Louis Prima is sung faster than most. Contemporaries like Cab Calloway must have wondered how this white boy found all his energy?
5. "The Lady in Red," Brunswick 7448. This celebration of Dixieland jazz is no slouch. Penned by Allie Wrubel and Mort Dixon, its lyrics are pretty much shredded by Louis's vocal.
6. "It's the Rhythm in Me," Brunswick 7471. This ditty penned by Jimmy Kennedy and Michael Carr is pure jazz. While it's emulation of Louis Armstrong is absolute—so what?
7. "In a Little Gypsy Tea Room," Brunswick 7479. A smooth Bob Crosby vocal on Decca 478 in interesting to compare, considering style, in this Edgar Leslie and Johnny Burke penned ditty.
8. "Let's Get Together and Swing," Brunswick 7740. Indeed a contrived and effective excuse to swing, penned by Lin Hain and Louis himself. Morever, the Stafford Sisters -Jo, Christine and Pauline are providing background vocals for Louis on this energenic ditty!
9. "Dance with a Dolly," Variety 8245. This fine title, a fine if contrived excuse to dance, penned by Terry Shand, Jimmy Eaton, and Mickey Leder was adapted from the American folk entity "Buffalo Gals (Won't You Come Out Tonight)?" It had been a (1944) best-selling entity for many, and it perhaps led in sales popularity by a Russ Morgan release, Al Jennings vocal on Decca 18625. Louis, with his usual touch of Louis Armstrong, at least finds a bit of creativity with his vocal. (About ten years later, a Bill Haley vocal with his Saddle men, on Essex 305, produced a more simple vocal, with a simple but effective backbeat. Call it rock and roll?)
10. "Robin Hood," Hit 7083. Penned by Louis and Bob Miketta, this silly, rhythmic 1944 (World War II) entity somehow works.
11. "A Sunday Kind of Love," Majestic 1113. A contemporary Ella Fitzgerald version on Decca 23866 perhaps best defines this Anita Leonard, Stan Rhodes, Barbara Belle and Louis Prima-penned ditty.
12. "That Old Black Magic," Capital 4063. While perhaps the earlier 1942 vocal by Margaret Whiting as a Freddie Slack release on Capital 126 is vocally better, this later 1958 release, with Keely Smith's smooth vocal included is more energetic. More so, Louis's act with Keely Smith was perhaps the forerunner for the (later) rock act of Sonny and Cher?

Ma Rainey

- The later part of the 1800s found but a few Afro-American entertainers in the mainstream of popular music. While the secular had had appeal, the strong hard-core racial bigotry, actually cemented as a result of a Supreme Court decision in 1890, doomed and hid most of the deserved creditability that was contributed by black artists and performers. While the likes of a few, including the likes of composer Scot Joplin (the father of "ragtime") and entertainer Bert Williams, who actually made it as a recording artist and on "white" Broadway before 1920, the door was closed for the black-skinned person in an integrated society. The success of the white "minstrel" performer reflected racial bias as white-skinned superiority. While unknown to most whites, the racial attitudes of Afro-Americans was perhaps founded in slavery days. The "cakewalk," as part of black entertainment, was essentially a black observance and emulation of white entertainment. As an inside joke, it would be successfully used by many. Oddly, the use of "black face," not really needed, was used by black performers for black patrons.

Gertrude Pridgett, born in around 1886, was one such performer. As later married to William "Pa" Rainey, she was part of a traveling show (the Rabbit Foot Minstrels) throughout her native state of Georgia and the rest of the south. While not the first black person to sing the blues or even record, like most all before 1920, she was not allowed. Historically, "Ma" Rainey is credited as one of the first and best rural blues vocalists. Her eventual recording career with Paramount, between 1923 through 1929, with acoustic and electric recordings, demonstrates a fine musical legacy. Origins of folk are to be found and a bit of (forbidden) cultural sharing. Is this crude-sounding woman the true "mother of the blues"? The following picks seem to indicate just that:

1. "Walking Blues," Paramount 12082. As penned by Lovie Austin, the Afro-American musician writer and director of Paramount Records, this acoustic recording session is a (horny) one, noting Ma's crude and earthy vocal demanding to be heard.
2. "Ma Rainey's Mystery Record," Paramount 12200. This attempt at marketing a name works well. As penned by "Early" and "Georgia Tom" in reality blues man Thomas A. Dorsey, this mystery, while solved, is a creditable one.
3. "Lawd, Send Me a Man Blues," Paramount 12200. This side is novel and penned by "Ma" herself. Get the message?
4. "Shave 'Em Dry," Paramount 12222. Contempory 1924 Afro-American slang may refer to (much) sexuality, and indeed "Ma" lets it all fly. Contemporary Papa Charlie Jackson, on Paramount 12264, also recorded this ditty, and perhaps just as effectively, from a different point of view. By the mid-1930s, this ditty (interestingly) was emulated, perhaps in its original form, as a bit of hard-core porn. While the 1935 Bessie Jackson (also a one-time Paramount entity known as Lucile Bogan), on Banner 33475, among other legit (ARC) labels is much like "Ma." A vastly circulated bootlegged version more so defines the word *smut*. Indeed, later century "rappers," on hearing this ditty, would (even) be amazed. Wild? You bet!
5. "See See Rider Blues," Paramount 12252. Penned by Lena Arant and Ma herself, this ditty in its original form, with musicians Charlie Green, Buster Bailey, Charlie Dixon, Fletcher Henderson, and Louis Armstrong himself, is light years away from the likes of raved-up versions by latter-century artists such as Chuck Willis, Mitch Ryder, and Elvis Presley. In any case, it's not just a good record, and, despite acoustics, it's an influential one. Contemporary Blind Lemon Jefferson's "Corrina Blues," on Paramount 12369, is very much related to this "self-penned" ditty about a woman selling herself. So was a later creative 1942 attempt as "Baby Baby" by Libby Holman, on Decca 18304, who credited "Rainey."
6. "Jealous-Hearted Blues," Paramount 12252. This side is also good, and, while this claim of ownership is open in folk music, there is no denying "Ma" backed by the jazz backings of Green, Bailey, Henderson, and Louis Armstrong scores. It's also interesting enough to question a (later) Carter Family rendering "Jealous-Hearted Me" on Decca 5241.
7. "Courtin' the Blues," Paramount 12238. The listener can find any way to find the blues and dating? Is this bit of slang common enough?
8. "Jelly Bean Blues," Paramount 12238. "Ma" is wondering where her "daddy" has gone, indeed a common blues theme. Moreover, this answer to "See See Rider" is well worth it, despite the stupid title.

9. "Chain Gang Blues," Paramount 12338. These prisoners indeed did hard labor and had a reason to get the "blues." Crime and punishment?
10. "Stack O'Lee Blues," Paramount 12357. This bit of Americana is perhaps the story of "Frankie and Johnny" and more. As a very fine and rural performance, this version just may be at the top of a huge stack of other versions and variations. In this case, a huge explanation is warranted.

- As "Stagger Lee," the tune is a direct throwback to Ma, as a rock era entity, on ABC Paramount 9972, and its tale of a murder as a Lloyd Price best seller in 1959.
- While a question of authorship does not directly point out to Ma, as a 1904 entity "He Done Me Wrong," credits one Hughie Cannon, the "story," as recordings tend to drift within the same theme. A murder committed by a mulatto child of an ex-confederate general at least places this yarn after 1865. Is it dangerous to play cards and gamble?
- Recordings by Ma's contemporaries blues men Mississippi John Hurt on Okeh 8654 and by Furry Lewis on Vocalion 1132 as Stack O'Lee owes nothing to "Ma."
- Another folk entity, known as "Frankie," is more about a woman's revenge and could be more about folk (both black and white) in any age. As "Frankie and Johnny," this ditty finds itself with embellishment on stage and screen in numerous undertakings, especially noting a fab Mae West filmed version *Honky Tonk* in 1934. But what about 1929s "Frankie and Albert" on Paramount 13110 by Charlie Patton? It is indeed cruder than "Ma."
- As a further point, this common story of betrayal could be found all over rural Americana, ranging through the Carolinas through Missouri, Illinois, Tennessee, Texas, Mississippi, and possibly more. While speculation may also be a more historic journey to colonial days, it's best to note "Albert" in Huddie Ledbetter's fine 1939 version on Musicraft 223 and "Johnny" as found in a Jimmie Rodgers version on Victor 22134 in 1929. In another interesting twist, a 1959 Johnny Cash rendering as "Frankie's Man Johnny" on Columbia 41371 owed at least something to Jimmie Rodgers and perhaps Leadbelly's version.
- Polished up a bit? Indeed a fine 1938 Ethel Waters version on Bluebird B-10038 is uptown. So is a (later) 1963 Sam Cooke version on Victor 20-8215. A subsequent Elvis Presley version in 1966 on Victor 20-8780, with a full rhythm section of horns, takes this entity back to the Mississippi (as did his so-so 1966 film of the same name).

11. "Wringing and Twisting Blues," Paramount 12338. This tale of woe penned by P. Carter is about a visit to a gypsy and an apparent poisoning of a rival. As a further point, this "wringing and twisting" does not refer to dancing—to be sure!
12. "Don't Fish in My Sea," Paramount 12438. Ma sounds a lot like Bessie Smith on this electric recording. Or does Bessie sound like Ma? Does she "fish" in her sea?
13. "Ma Rainey's Black Bottom," Paramount 12590. This dance craze of the 1920s may or may not have had some origins with Ma herself in this self-penned ditty. Or was it Jelly Roll Morton's Black Bottom Stomp? In any case, the old lady's back bottom just may be the bottom of a muddy river. Or is it all so novel?
14. "Blues on Blues," Paramount 12566. This electric recording (self penned) is perhaps Ma's most effective blues rendering.
15. "Oh, Papa Blues," Paramount 12566. Mmm. "Oh Daddy"? Ethel Waters or Bessie Smith? Seemingly, this bit of slang is not contrived, as its own origins just could be older than its title.

16. "Prove It on Me Blues," Paramount 12668. This self-penned ditty is loaded with questions. Is this about a same-sex relationship? This ditty also features the sounds of "Ma's Tub Washboard Band," which includes the sounds of a kazoo, banjo, jug, and washboard.
17. "Black Cat Hoot Owl Blues," Paramount 12687. As assisted by her Jug band again, Ma again scores! This time, the sounds of a cat and an owl as a superstitious tale penned by Tom Dorsey and Ma herself unfolds.
18. "Daddy, Goodbye Blues," Paramount 12963. This self-penned ditty is backed up by Tom Dorsey on piano and Tampa Red on guitar. This sad tale, about a woman leaving her man a letter, while a familiar theme, is a good one.
19. "Black Eye Blues," Paramount 12963. The reality of the blues may amount to violence, as this ditty penned by Tom Dorsey indicates.

Tex Ritter

- This contrived "cowboy" stuff, a product of Hollywood since "silent" films, was nevertheless popular. While Maurice Woodward Ritter was college educated and perhaps a bit slick, he was indeed from Texas, and his adapted "Tex" surname fit just as much as his hat. As a radio performer, in the 1920s, his renderings were somewhat of a "crooner" type. As a singer of contrived "Western" songs on Broadway, as early as in 1931, it was more than obvious that this Texan was slick enough. His vocals were at best loud enough, which had oddly put him on among the many highbrows of Broadway in 1931. Moreover, his B-filmed Westerns had fanned the Hollywood myth, almost as much as contemporary Gene Autry. The following recordings may be termed "Western" and/or "hillbilly," subsequently "country and Western" by the later 1940s.

1. "Good-bye, Old Paint," Conquer 8073. This old traditional 'cowboy' song is at least authenic, with claims even later extending to Woody Guthrie. While myth emerges, the cattle drives and horse riding was indeed real enough.
2. "Rye Whiskey," Conquer 8144. While this traditional "drinking" song is contrived, it's still a good enough novelty. (A second recording on Capital 20068 is also done well.)
3. "A Riding Old Paint," Banner 32992. This horse gets around!
4. "Bill, the Bar Fly," Champion 45191. Yup. The end of Prohibition made it all legal again!
5. "Lady-Killing Cowboy," Decca 5076.
6. "Have I Stayed Away Too Long?" Capital 147. This poignant ditty penned by Frank Loesser is hardly a great vocal and, as usual, loud. However, like most other country idiom, its simple message about real people is perhaps all that is required.
7. "There's a New Moon over My Shoulder," Capital 174.
8. "Jealous Heart," Capital 179. A real "heart" song. Yes. As penned by Jenny Lou Carson, this weepy honky-tonk bar song hits the heart! This ditty would later be revived by many, including contemporary Al Morgan version and a later R&B entity by Ivory Joe Hunter. Still later, in the rock era, Connie Francis would also turn it into a best-selling pop entity.
9. "Green Grow the Lilacs," Capital 206. Tex had introduced this traditional "Western" entity on Broadway, actually using the title as the name of the (1930) production.

Oddly, he had not rendered a contemporary recording. In any case, this later (1945) effort should suffice.

10. "Long Time Gone," Capital 253. While far from cool, this slick bit of a honky-tonk ditty penned by Frank Hartford and Tex Ritter himself is more so slick. Just why this lady is gone makes no difference to Tex. Moreover, throughout rural diners and bars, its contrived message could not have been better.
11. "When You Leave, Don't Slam the Door," Capital 296. Perhaps crude in title, penned by Joe Allison, it's at least an entity that provides its listeners something expected. While piled-up dishes are more than a mess, there's more! More so, obvious jukebox ditty, like most, rings true.
12. "Have I Told You Lately That I Love You?" Capital 296.
13. "When My Blue Moon Turns to Gold Again," Capital 1977. This ditty penned by Wiley Walker and Gene Sullivan had been a best-selling (1941) entity by its authors, with Sullivan's lead vocal on Okeh 6374. Ritter's attempt is more so worth it! (Later, in 1956, Elvis Presley would resurrect this fine mid-tempo song.)
14. "Fort Worth Jail," Capital 48004.
15. "Let Me Go, Devil," Capital 1698. As mythology would have it, this Jenny Lou Carson-penned ditty, noting the evils of (serious) alcohol addiction, was perhaps to the problems of Hank Williams? Within a few years, this ditty, credited to Jenny Lou Carson and Al Hill, was to become known as "Let Me Go, Lover," a (serious) love song. Introduced on TV in 1954 by young Joan Weber, as part of a marketing ploy, Joan's own recording released at the time of the TV broadcast provided a huge best seller, as released on Columbia 40366.
16. "High Noon," Capital 2120. The somewhat bombastic vocal approach to this vocal is more so an asset for the 1952 Western *High Noon*. While contrived, this somewhat highbrow ditty penned by the sophisticated team of Dmitri Tiomkin and Ned Washington did indeed add to the excellent drama of this Cary Cooper entity, indeed a rare Western with creditability. (Contemporary pop vocalist Frankie Laine also recorded this ditty.)
17. "Wayward Wind," Capital 3430. Ritter's version has certainly got more grit than the contemporary (1956) version by Gogi Grant. (Gogi would subsequently lend her highbrow vocal attributes to ape Helen Morgan's voice in the film *The Helen Morgan Story*.) Penned by Stanley Lobowsky and Herb Newman, this contrived bit of Western idiom was more of a fit for Tex. Or does it all really matter?

Visual Image

Tex Ritter was featured in many B Westerns, much like Gene Autry and Roy Rogers, throughout the latter 1930s through the 1940s. Perhaps the best images are:

18. "Bo Weevil Song." Tex and Afro-American bit actor Manhattan Moreland (best known for his contemporary Charlie Chan film appearances) effectively share vocals on this real folk entity, *Riders of the Frontier*, 1939.
19. "You Are My Sunshine." Tex wails out this ditty slowly, and then picks up a little bit in mid-tempo, with backing provided by Western swing entity Bob Wills and His Texas Playboys, also in the movie *Take Me Back to Oklahoma*, 1940.

Paul Robeson

- Paul Robeson was one of the few Afro-American entities who became known for his bass-baritone operatic style. Born in 1898 to an (unusual) upper-class black family, he became a star athlete for Rutgers University in track, baseball, and American football. He also became a law student at Columbia Law School in 1920. By the mid-1920s, he had tried acting on the stage as well as becoming a recording artist. Robeson himself called his music folk songs, and while musical terms are always transitory, his excuse for secular "spirituals" were indeed a good link to folk. The recorded legacy of Paul Robeson may be considered a bit more personal. In fact, this book refuses to deal with most of it, as he is really a (very good) operatic singer. Indeed, his recordings, like those of Marion Anderson (another Afro-American), Morton Downey, Deanna Durbin, Lilly Pons, and Jeanette Mac Donald have little to do with the new music that was popular, or to be popular. More so, Robeson could seldom control his bass vocals. He was indeed clumsy, attempting pop ditties, and for the most part, tripped over his own lyrics. Nevertheless, Robeson, who probably has great claims to the term "politically incorrect" as a communist (but not a bad communist), did find his way into greater popularity on (British) stage, radio, and films in the 1930s. An un-hip and black American in America?

    - The following are Paul Robeson picks:

1. "Joshua Fit the Battle," Victor 19743 (with Lawrence Brown).
2. "Bye and Bye," Victor 19743 (with Lawrence Brown).
3. "Water Boy," Victor 19824. This old work song of the South penned by a white Southerner, Avery Robinson, who had heard a "chain gang" of black prisoners sing it, is a fine bit of social commentary as well. More so, Robeson's bass baritone vocal actually contributes to a strong and moody effort that succeeds.
4. "On Ma Journey," Victor 20013.
5. "Swing Low, Sweet Chariot," Victor 20068.
6. "Nobody Knows the Trouble I've Seen," Victor 20068. While this title had been around since slavery times, the success of a contemporary 1925 Marion Anderson recording, on Victor 19560, most likely led Paul to record it. Marion Anderson, years later in 1939, was requested by (then) first lady Eleanor Roosevelt to sing before the Lincoln Memorial in Washington DC, after a white group, "the daughters of the American Revolution," had refused to invite her. Marion did and caused quite a racial breakthrough. In true retrospective, it's amazing that the "daughters of the American Revolution" didn't know their own history. More so, like most Americans, they were unaware of Afro-American contributions, despite slavery).
7. "Deep River," Victor 20793. This classic is also good. A Marion Anderson version on Victor 19227 also preceded it.
8. "Ol' Man River," Victor 35912. This Broadway entity, from *Show Boat*, was first introduced by Afro-American Jules Bledsow in the original stage production in 1927. This recording, as a Paul Whiteman release, features a full-blown bass-baritone Robeson vocal. Robeson would soon take the Bledsow part, on stage, in London. The controversy of this classic by Oscar Hammerstein and Jerome Kern, originally using the "N" word in the original productions of *Show Boat*, is also negated by Robeson's stiff vocal omission. (A contemporary Al Jolson release, on Brunswick 3867, sadly, had no concerns for the future.) (A hipper and jazzier vocal, also a bouncier Paul

Whiteman release, on Victor 21218, with a vocal by Bing Crosby, omits racial slur and is sung better.)

9. "I Still Suits Me," Victor 25376. This 1935 British recording, with Elisabeth Welch, a transplanted black American, is a featured duet penned by Oscar Hammerstein and Jerome Kern. As usual, the Robeson bass baritone is stiff, as Paul had never really learned to sing a popular song. Luckily, the bright and clear singing of Elisabeth Welch is a big lift and perhaps contains Robeson enough to produce a fine record for both.

Visual Image

- Robeson's films of the 1930s, like most Afro-Americans, are spotty, as well as limited, for the most part. What he was able to achieve on stage, for American and European audiences, never really materialized. His British films, however, cast him with more respect and dignity. As this author finds his operatic tendencies over the top in recorded entities, his films are found to be flawed in contrive excuses for opera. Perhaps one film, for the purposes of this book, is worth more than a look:

- In the (1936) British film *Song of Freedom*, Robeson is cast as a dockworker, with operatic tendencies, which searches out his long-lost "African" roots. He is to be seen and heard with Elisabeth Welch, who plays his wife, and shares with him in this ditty penned by Erik Ansell and Robeson himself:

10. "Sleepy River."

- The 1936 film *Show Boat*:

11. "Old Man River." Better filmed than his recording!
12. "I Still Suites Me." Duet with Hattie Mc Daniel—not as good as his contemporary recording with Welch!

Jimmie Rodgers

The 1920s produced so many (new) recorded sounds that the scope of this book can only hope to outline, in true retrospective. The 1920s, because of the technical advances of electric recording and radio, contained first generation of contained musical identities. The success of Jimmie Rodgers, born in 1896, indeed founded changes. While there is much fault to be found with his (trademark) of yodeling, the (following) reviewed picks are indeed solid enough. In addition to playing and attempting somewhat crude vocals, Jimmie's earthy renderings about hardship, relationships, and sickness are perhaps as real enough as his own personal saga as a one-time hobo hopping trains. Even some of his more contrived renderings, as well as a jazzy outing (with that of Louis Armstrong's trumpet, Lil Hardin's piano, and Bob Sawyers Orchestra) remain interesting. His death in 1933, while final in human form, found him a huge commodity and part of Americana itself. Indeed, the image of the "singing brakeman" remains. The following are his picks:

1. "Mother Was a Lady," Victor 21433. As recorded in 1927, Jimmie's storytelling hits its mark as he tells an (already) old story about meeting up with a waitress in a diner, as penned by Edward B. Marks and Joseph Stern.
2. "Blue Yodel (T for Texas)," Victor 21142. This first blue yodel is a sad tale of a woman moving on. Jimmie's own guitar strumming, on this self-penned ditty, is also effective and proves that this rural what vocal was indeed full of the blues. The ditty seemingly had had an effect on the (later) Johnny Cash entity, on Sun 232, known as "Folsome Prison Blues," as well as subsequent Cash rerecordings on Columbia.
3. "Ben Dewberry's Final Run," Victor 21245. This 1927 recording about a doomed railroad engineer, penned by Andy Jenkins, indeed rambles along into an effective and adventurous tale.
4. "In the Jailhouse Now," Victor 21245. This traditional yarn, found Jimmy claiming it as self-penned, about the results of unlawful gambling is superb. Jimmie is also backed by steel guitar, mandolin, and ukulele and it all works!
5. "Never No Mo' Blues," Victor 40054. Jimmie again excels, crudely backing himself with guitar. Penned by Elsie Mc Williams and Jimmie himself, the origins of this ditty may be suspect, but it's all relative to the shared culture of the blues, both black and white.
6. "Waiting for a Train," Victor 40014. As backed by a full jazz band, this self-penned tale of woe, around a water tank, is somewhat spooky and real. While starting with a (contrived) whistle (about the only thing really contrived heard in this recording), this rendering of a drifter's travels is no myth, although perhaps the start of one.
7. "My Carolina Sunshine Girl," Victor 40096. Where is she? This sad rendering penned by Jimmie himself is an effective use of regional and rural location.
8. "Daddy and Home," Victor 21757. This tale penned by Elsie Mc Williams and Jimmie about a good daddy is almost as effective as the previous "Mother Was a Lady." Would it be the inspiration for the later Gene Autry ditty "That Silver-haired Daddy of Mine"?
9. "Frankie and Johnny," Victor 22134. Jimmie's adaptation of this already old tale, found elsewhere in this book, has its own gritty and rural appeal.
10. "Everyone Does It in Hawaii," Victor 22143. An awfully crude ditty penned by Elsie McWilliams and Rodgers himself that somehow works!
11. "High-Powered Mama," Victor 22523. Yeah, more (self-penned) earthy blues that became more than an inspiration for the likes of Jimmie Davis and Gene Autry. Just listen.
12. "Tuck Away My Lonesome Blues," Victor 22220. This ain't bad! As penned by Elsie Mc Williams, Joe Katipo, and Jimmie himself, this blues ditty scores!
13. "My Rough and Rowdy Ways," Victor 22220. Jimmie often described himself as a songwriter. Penned by Elsie McWilliams and Jimmie, this bit of self-admiration is a bit over the top, not doubting Jimmie's (real) toughness.
14. "Blue Yodel No. 6," Victor 22271. Don't let this stupid title stop the listener. While midnight turns to day, the "n" word is used in the crudest of rural slang (1930). Racism? In modern terms, yes! It is more so a blues rendering warning to approach a poor white Southerner, longing for his lost woman, the same way as a contemporary Afro-American—hardly at all! Moreover, this is hardly a derogatory "coon" song! If the listen can get through the yodeling, perhaps these mean blues are not bleached at all. Just listen and cringe!
15. "Any Old Time," Victor 22488. A self-penned ditty with a full-blown (sophisticated) 1930 orchestra!

16. "Hobo Bill's Last Ride," Victor 22421. Yet another hobo tale is done well as this Waldo O'Neal tale comes to life.
17. "Pistol-Packin' Papa," Victor 22554. This bit of gross humor penned by Waldo O'Neal and Jimmie himself somewhat works. More so, in true retrospective, it just could be rated "x." Or is it just some dirty blues?
18. "That Gambler's Blues," Victor 22554. This may be Jimmie's very best blues performance, as he solidly describes those blues.
19. "Jimmie's Mean Mama Blues," 23503. Jimmie is effectively backed by Bob Sawyer's jazz orchestra, as this contrived ditty penned by Waldo O'Neal and Bob Sawyer challenges it's listeners as just how to label it. Is this jazz? Blues?
20. "Blue Yodel No. 8 (Mule Skinner Blues)," Victor 23503. There were many "blue yodel" themes, and this somewhat horrid tale about rural living should nevertheless earn for its listeners a lesson about real and rural life. (Light years later, Bill Monroe, Rose Maddox, the Fenderman, and Dolly Parton, among others, would each redefine this (morbid) rural blues classic.
21. "T. B. Blues," Victor 23535. Jimmie was (slowly) dying of TB. He knew it. He had 'em.
22. "Mississippi River Blues," Victor 23535. Indeed, this river is a good theme.
23. "My Blue-Eyed Jane," Victor 23549. Bob Sawyer's orchestra (again) do well backing up Jimmie, in another (common) tale penned by Lulu Bell White and Jimmie himself.
24. ("Blue Yodel No. 9) Standing on the Corner," Victor 23580. Both Louis Armstrong and Lil' Hardin backed Jimmie up in a Los Angeles session. As a self-penned entity, this rendering is full of fight, and about a shooting in Memphis. More so, Jimmie's crude vocal scores as much as a Louis Armstrong vocal could have. As far as originality, Jimmie's (Southern) slang, is perhaps challenged by a Furry Lewis release on Victor 21664 as "Kassie Jones." A hustler's journey never ends, but it's an open question if Lewis or Rodgers knew of each other, but if each knew of this shared rural tale? (A later early 1950s recording, by Harmonica Frank "Rockin' Chair Daddy," on Sun 205, seems to emulate Jimmie.)
25. "Travelin' Blues," Victor 23564. Jimmie again scores, as this ditty penned by Shelly Lee Alley and Jimmie Rodgers travels far and wide.
26. "Jimmie Rodgers Visits the Carter Family," Victor 23574. The (contrived) bit of historic significance with the Carter family is corny but fun. It includes the title "A Hot Time in the Old Town Tonight."
27. "The Carter Family and Jimmie Rodgers in Texas," Bluebird B-23574. This was released posthumously in 1937. It included newer versions of "Blue Yodel" and "T for Texas."
28. "Looking for a New Mama," Victor 23580. Why are Afro-Americans always assigned to the "down home" dirty blues? Jimmie, especially on this ditty, crudely proves this myth wrong!
29. "What's It?" Victor 23609. This ditty penned by Jack Neville and Jimmie himself is real "trash," but it's so bad, that it's good! What's it? Just listen and you'll know.
30. "Let Me Be Your Sidetrack," Victor 23621. There's more self penned blues here—right from the soul.
31. "When the Cactus Is in Bloom," Victor 23636. This bit of Western music, seems like a contrived type of ditty formulated in a Hollywood film.
32. "Gambling Polka Dot Blues," Victor 23636. This dumb title penned by Raymond E. Hall and Rodgers further escapes into the contrived "old west."

33. "Ninety-Nine Year Blues," Victor 23669. A prison sentence is indeed enough for a blues song. Moreover, this contrived ditty penned by Raymond E. Hall and Rodgers is more than a lifetime.
34. "She Was Happy Till She Met You," Victor 23681. Who was it making this statement? Was it this married girl's mother? This song was claimed by McWilliams and Jimmie in 1929. This title however had acoustic origins before 1900 by Dan Quinn and S. H. Dudley. As penned by Charles Graham and Monroe H. Rosenfeld well before Jimmie was born. A yet older folk entity?
35. "Mississippi Moon," Victor 23796. Jimmie moans out an attempt at crooning, as penned by Elsie Mc Williams and Rodgers.
36. "Long Tall Mama Blues," Victor 23766. More blues, more self penned blues.
37. "Gambling Bar Room Blues," Victor 23777. This 1932 recording penned by Shelly Lee Alley and Rodgers would (almost) signal the end of Prohibition, which would happen in 1934. While Jimmy would not be alive to see it again, this ditty, as a (prelegal) honky-tonk entity, (again) reveals Jimmie's own realistic attitude toward life.
38. "My Good Gal's Gone Blues," Bluebird B-5942. This ditty, released after his death, is a self-penned expression of the blues, and, as this title indicates, a good reason to "have" the blues.
39. "The One Rose," Bluebird B-7280. This 1930 recording by Jimmy had eyes for the future. Penned by Lani Mc Intire, whose "Hawaiians" are heard backing this ditty, finds Jimmie's crude vocal and Lani's Hawaiian strings somehow meshing. In 1937, a somewhat prissy Bing Crosby vocal, on Decca 1201, became a best seller and revived this ditty. So did a Larry Clinton release, with a Bea Wain vocal. It was also a contemporary Midge William's release, similar in swing band style to Wain's. While they beat out Crosby's mush by far, it's just very possible that the crude and dead hillbilly singer (Rodgers) comes off more sincere and better.
40. "Somewhere Down Below the Mason Dixon Line," Victor 23840. As penned by Walter Ryan and Jimmie himself, this ditty's title, recorded in New York City (1933), was obviously directed elsewhere.

Visual Image

- The 1929 film short *The Singing Brakeman* tells it all. Jimmie, in a brakeman's train uniform, is invited to sit on the porch. He croons out:

40. "Waiting for a Train."
41. "Daddy and Home."
42. "T for Texas."

Ginger Rogers

- Ginger Rogers was oddly a musical film entity, whose subsequent success in musical films hardly produced any well-known musical recordings. When teamed with Fred Astaire, her obvious sex appeal, dancing ability (to keep up with Fred) and her (better) vocal abilities (when paired with Fred) seemed to indicate a load of fine recordings as well as best sellers. While it is obvious that Fred did produce (some) best sellers, in true retrospective, it's a real mystery that Ginger's legacy did not. The following picks in film and recordings, many already noted in the Fred Astaire section, are worth hearing:

1. "We're in the Money." The obvious assets of Ginger Rogers were perhaps best realized in the (1933) film *Gold Diggers of 1933*. Moreover, her spunky vocal introduction of this ditty penned by Al Dubin and Harry Warren remains something to still watch and hear. Was Ginger perhaps influenced (vocally) by the likes of contemporary Helen Kane?
2. "Carioca." As featured in the (1933) film *Flying Down to Rio*, Fred Astaire and Ginger squared off as a dancing pairing for the first time. While (also) sharing vocals with Dolores Del Rio and Etta Moten, Ginger scores!
3. "Music Makes Me." Another ditty from *Flying Down to Rio* finds Ginger more than able to croon out a lively tune.
4. "I'll String Along with You." In 1934, Ginger was paired with Dick Powell in *Twenty Million Sweethearts*. Moreover, this crooned-out vocal duet, penned by Al Dubin and Harry Warren with him proves her good voice, and indeed is a lift for Powell. (A contemporary Ted Fio Rito release on (Brunswick-6859)) featuring a vocal by Muzzy Marcellino, became a huge best seller.
5. "Out for No Good." This rhythmic ditty, penned by Al Dubin and Harry Warren, from *Twenty Million Sweethearts* is also a hot item that forms this contemporary platinum blonde who could also sing!

   - Many good-sounding film entities had good voices besides Ginger. While it's still quite a wonder as to how many film entities were to be cast into films and subsequently dubbed, it's very odd that the likes of Alice Faye, Martha Raye, and Dorothy Lamour, among others, did not become major recording entities. More so, it's odder that (most) commercial Ginger Rogers's recordings, although recorded in the USA, they were to be principally released in England. The following Decca F series releases, note an original and unique British entity.

6. "No Strings," Decca F-5746. Ginger's vocal is far better than Fred's film version from *Top Hat*, as well as Fred's own recording on Brunswick.
7. "Isn't It a Lovely Day?" Decca F-5746. Another *Top Hat* film ditty finds Ginger's vocal indeed very able.
8. "Piccolino," Decca F-5747. The dance number from *Top Hat* is also sung and claimed (vocally) by Ginger.
9. "Cheek to Cheek," Decca F-5747, from *Top Hat*. The Astaire vocal, one of his better ones, is (still) claimed upon by Ginger.
10. "I'm Putting All My Eggs in One Basket," Decca F-5963, from *Follow the Fleet*.
11. "Let You Go," Decca F-5963. Ginger had introduced this "hot" vocal and (dance) number in *Follow the Fleet*. This recording is also rhythmic!
12. "Eeny Meeny Miny Mo," Decca F-6822. The Johnny Mercer-penned ditty is rhythmic and fun. Contemporary renderings by Bob Crosby and Billie Holiday are interesting to compare!
13. "Out of Sight, Out of Mind," Decca F-6822.
14. "Pick You Up," with Fred in *Swing Time*.
15. "A Fine Romance," with Fred in *Swing Time*.
16. "The Way You Look Tonight," with Fred in *Swing Time*.
17. "They All Laughed." Ginger introduced this classic herself in *Shall We Dance*?
18. "Let's Call the Whole Thing Off," with Fred in *Shall We Dance*?
19. "The Yam," Bluebird B-7891. Ginger had introduced this ditty in *Carefree*. This subsequent recording is also done well, if better.

20. "Saga Of Jenny." Film 1944. Ginger in a musical without Fred-singing, dancing, and looking great in *Lady In The Dark.*

- The multitalented Ginger Rogers would find hard-core nonmusicals a challenge as well as something accessible. She would indeed become a respected Academy Award winner who could easily adapt into musicals or both. Moreover, her musical legacy, while huge (in films), was perhaps considered a sideline by her.

- Another oddity: Film: *Roxie Hart* (Fox) 1942. This stage entity was made into a film with high expectations. As based upon a (real) Chicago reporter's novel Maurine Watkins's *Chicago*, was about a murder and the whole (real) gangster element that had existed in the city that had famously and notoriously included the likes of Al Capone and Bugs Moran in the 1920s. Moreover, Ginger Rogers, who had just won a nonmusical Academy Award, was signed for the part. Indeed this part seemingly had everything, with risqué and snappy dialog, as well as some (tap) dancing. In reality, Ginger had (really) been a struggling would-be showgirl indeed perfect for the part. Sadly, despite the presence of such fine contemporary (1942) entities as George Montgomery, Adolphe Menjou, and William Frawley (years before he was "Fred" on the well-known Lucille Ball TV sitcom), no vocals were to be found! More so, the "roaring 20s" had produced a lot of good material, found in abundance within this book! Background music was to be heard, but not much else. The resulting film found Ginger able, with wisecracking jokes that got stale. Is this the worst film Ginger ever made? (Light years later, after the turn of the century, the musical film *Chicago* found musical vocals and dance with the capable likes of Catherine Zeta-Jones, Renee Zellweger, and Richard Gere. It seemingly took some fifty years to get it done right! Moreover, the (new) product would have been perfect for the (still young) Ginger in (1942). Or does anyone care?

Roy Rogers

As the third most important of the singing "cowboys," Leonard Slye (alias Roy Rogers) had been with a vocal group, "The Sons of the Pioneers" since the early 1930. As born in Cincinnati, Ohio, Roy had, early on, been a follower of popular music, as well as the enormous myth and image of the American "cowboy." What helped Roy Rogers most was, in true retrospective, his active participation in "b" westerns, radio, and (later) baby boomer television. More so, with his wife Dale Evans (a former band singer) had an appeal for young women, in the (huge) marketing game. Roy's vocals are nothing special, although, in the great scheme of things, just as useful, and more lasting than most of the film fodder produced.

- As a would-be vocalist specializing in "Western" music, mostly contrived, Leonard Slye found himself a member of "The Sons of the Pioneers," noting a vocal lead by Bob Nolan, a Canadian by birth. By the mid-1930s, the subsequent group releases (with Leonard), also known as "Dick Weston" for a while, were significant:

1. "Tumbling Tumbleweeds," Decca 5047. This (1934) rendering is a contrived bit of Western or really Southwestern folklore, set in the hot deserts of possibly Arizona, New Mexico, or Texas. More so, as penned by a cold Canadian (Bob Nolan), it nevertheless became part of the Western myth. A contemporary Gene Autry entity, on Romeo 5434, was also done well.
2. "Empty Saddles," Decca 5247. Penned by Billy Hill, from a poem by J. Keinan Brennan, this bit of mush, sung with fine harmony, is actually less than contrived.
3. "I'm an Old Cowhand," Decca 5247. The chance for Hollywood was realized in a 1935 Bing Crosby film *Rhythm on the Range*, as the Sons of the Pioneers, including Len, were to enjoy. As a "modern" Western, the crooning Crosby, an early vocal influence for all, including Len, moreover introduced this contrived ditty penned by Johnny Mercer and Louis Prima to the screen. Somehow, it all worked out well, and this item became a classic Crosby entity. While on the screen, the likes of the Songs of the Pioneers may be seen, along with the likes of Louis Prima, who was also in the film, did not appear on the subsequent Crosby recording, on Decca 871, backed by the Dorsey Brothers. This independent group effort, with a Bob Nolan vocal lead, ain't bad.

➢ The name of Roy Rogers would appear as a single entity on the following picks:

4. "Hi-Yo Silver," Vocalion 04190. Roy, while not the "Lone Ranger," would later be dubbed "the King of the Cowboys." Penned by Erik Erikson and Vaughn DeLeath, this silly novelty finds Roy on his horse and among some very smaltzy lyrics; it's somewhat of an oddity that Roy is not riding "Trigger." Interesting perhaps?

5, 6. "Don't Fence Me In." Oddly penned by Cole Porter, Roy's light-voiced attempt at crooning was very effective, noting his popular (1944) screen appearance in *Hollywood Canteen* (on his horse Trigger) introducing this well-done novelty. Indeed it's a sight to hear and see! More so was his contemporary recording on Victor 20-3073., that was more oddly not recorded until after the contemporary Bing Crosby version, much more raved up, would further so redefine this ditty as a classic, as a popular and contemporary Bing Crosby and the Andrews Sisters release on Decca 23364.

7, 8. "San Fernando Valley." (a) While more than a bit contrived for Roy's contemporary (1944) film of the same name, this bit of smaltz penned by Gordon Jenkins is pleasant enough. (b) So was his subsequent recording on Victor 20-3075, that had followed the notable 1944 Bing Crosby version on Decca 18586.

While the films and recordings were seemingly endless, the mass marketing of Roy Roger would even overtake the likes of both Gene Autry and Tex Ritter. Moreover, the sales of shirts, jeans, cowboy hats, (play) guns, and just about anything was popularized by Roy's media appeal to (young) fans. While in true retrospective, most of this may be considered rubbish, the following ditties have merit:

9, 10. "Blue Shadows on the Trail." (a) As featured in the creative Disney film *Melody Time*, this ditty penned by Eliot Daniel and Johnny Lange, while contrived, reunites Roy with the Sons of the Pioneers, with Roy in the lead. More so, as part of the "Pecos Bill" segment, it's Roy's successful attempt at leading the group that makes all sound like a winning combination. This ditty, however contrived, just also may have been the best of its kind. (b) A subsequent recording on Victor 20-2780 was also a winner. (A contemporary Bing Crosby version, on Decca 24433, was more so also done very well.)

11. "Pecos Bill," Victor 20-2780. Smaltzy? Juvenile? Indeed! As also a segment of the Disney (mostly) cartoon of 1948 *Melody Time*, this contrived ditty penned by Eliot Daniel and Johnny Lange, with a vocal lead by Roy, and accompanied by the Sons of the Pioneers, is nevertheless effective.

The visual image of Roy Rogers, Dale Evans, and Trigger remain a huge part of Americana. It is more so not so hard to disregard his many featured films, mostly for Republic, as more than junk. Even so, the effective marketing of the cowboy myth should not be dismissed. It is moreover found in early 1950s television, with both Roy and Dale Evans (the former band singer), becoming a televised event for many young baby boomers!

The hard facts of the real "west," for the most part, would remain hidden from the general public for a least a few generations. It is the fodder of broken dreams to imagine a group of happy (native) American Indian cowboys who didn't sweat and the (real) black and Hispanic cowboys who were at least mean enough to break crooked laws. The relevance of the American West is an endless bit of history, with the real likes of figures such as Daniel Boone, Davy Crockett, and Bat Masterson, and places like the Alamo and Boot Hill finding themselves in novels, comic books, song ditties, silent films, and talking pictures and singing cowboys. The settlement of the American west and perhaps the theft of Mexican lands may be countered by those of American Indians without tribal borders. So was the real slaughter of the food source of the American Indian, the buffalo. Indeed, the exploitation of Americana had nothing to do with Gene Autry, Tex Ritter, or Roy Rogers personally, although the Hollywood myth more so became largely identified with their images.

Visual Image II—Baby Boomer TV

The great success of the Roy Rogers and Dale Evans films for Republic were to be converted into a part of the emerging postwar television market, with a success that was very much a surprise! While perhaps the contrived images of cowboys became less appreciated by the children of baby boomers, perhaps the (closing) images of Roy and Dale Evans (who had married each other in 1947) singing 12. "Happy Trails to You," penned by Dale herself, remains a classic for many aging baby boomers.

Like the record release, it ain't bad. Perhaps some myths are not all that bad!

Note: *Dale Evans*. Before she met Roy, Dale was a radio entity and popular band singer with the likes of Ray Noble, Anson Weeks, and Abe Lyman Orchestras (see the radio section of this book). Oddly, she produced few recordings with them. Dale also appeared in over forty B films, most famously with Roy Rogers. Subsequently, her early TV appearance with Roy made her one of the best recognized women in America, despite fiction, known as "queen of the west."

Visual Image (*solo*) for Dale Evans:

1. Dale can be found with Anson Weeks in the (1945) film *The Big Show Off* singing her self-penned popular ditty "There's Only One of You."
2. Dale's (earlier) sexy image was indeed exploited in the (1945) film *Don't Fence Me In*. While wearing a (very) short skirt, her leggy introduction of the contemporary ditty "A

Kiss Goodnight" also merits an appreciation of her fine vocal talents. As recorded by the likes of contemporaries such on a Woody Herman release with a Frances Wayne vocal, a Freddie Slack release with a Liza Morrow vocal and a fine Ella Fitzgerald release, it's more than a shame that Dale did not produce a contemporary recording!

Jimmy Rushing

- The vocal style of Jimmy Rushing was perhaps (along with contemporary Joe Turner) the best known and most imitated of the pre-WWII (male) blues singers. While no disrespect for such great blues men as Blind Lemon Jefferson, Papa Charlie Jackson, and other rural blues men, it was the (urban) style of Rushing that was recognized and commercial. More so, Jimmie's full-blown baritone, with an accent on every vowel, fit in well with his mentor and friend, Count Basie. Jimmy was able, unlike most other, to overcome his "band singer" label and come to be recognized as "Jimmy Rushing."

Picks include:

1. "He Ain't Got Rhythm," Victor 25505. This Irving Berlin-penned ditty is (perhaps) one of the best Benny Goodman releases ever, moreover as good as those featuring Goodman and Billie Holiday. While Jimmie's fine vocal is held in check by Goodman's 1937 "big band" arrangement, there is no hiding Jimmie's strong and distinctive vocal prowess.
2. "Exactly Like You," Decca 1252.
3. "Boogie Woogie," Decca 1252. Base's "jump" blues, a highly danceable product, still owes much to Jimmie's ability to keep in tempo.
4. "Good Morning Blues," Decca 1446. Indeed a very influential recording. As penned by Eddie Durham, Count Basie and Jimmy himself, this ditty perhaps defines 'urban blues', finding many listeners transformed in small, smoke filled rooms digging it!
5. "How Long Blues," Vocalion 5010. This ditty penned by Count Basie and Jimmie himself, like all other blue label Vocalion releases, is of high quality, as Jimmy's fine vocal meshes well with the Basie orchestra.
6. "You Can't Run Around," Okeh 5673. While the Count could always swing, his (usual) devotion for urban blues is perfected in this ditty penned by Basie and Rushing that spins its own sad and familiar tale.
7. "Going to Chicago Blues," Okeh 6244. This ditty, more than any other Count Basie entity (perhaps), captures the spirit of the Basie band and, more importantly, provided for Jimmie his most recognized vocal performance. Penned by Basie and Jimmy himself, this classic captures all the true drama of urban blues, forever linking "Chicago," by word as well as in fact to blues mythology. (Indeed, the great Count Basie organization was originally a fine Kansas City one, and while he had played Chicago and was aware of the Chicago connection to New Orleans jazz, it's interesting to note the greater success that the Count, with Jimmy Rushing and Helen Humes, would find in New York City.)
8. "Driftin' Blues," Conquer 9632. (In true retrospective, this contrived bit of an excuse for a blues song has become more relevant.)
9. "I Want a Little Girl," Okeh 5773. Another classic, penned by Billy Moll and Murray Mencher, finds the big man looking around!

10. "I'm Gonna Move to the Outskirts of Town," Columbia 36601. It's interesting to compare contemporary pleading and moody Big Bill Broonzy vocal, and an attempt at crooning, found on a Josh White rendering compared with Jimmie's solid and cool version of this Casey Bill Weldon and Roy Jacobs Check them all out!
11. "Jimmy's Blues," Columbia 36831. A fine excuse in title that more so had solid claims to blues singing.
12. "Bye Bye, Baby," Victor 20-3051. A better vocal than the Fats Waller version? Yes!

Andy Russell

- Andy Russell was really Andy Rabajos and was also (really) of Mexican American origins. His later 1940s crooning efforts were a bit stiff but nevertheless delivered a huge nationwide audience of radio and record buyers for Capital records. Capital's original answer to Columbia's contemporary "hot" Frank Sinatra or Decca's Dick Haymes? Or like contemporary Billy Eckstine? Russell also had good looks, and it's more so a mystery that a limited film career existed in oddly shabby parts. In any case, the following song ditties merit review:

1. "Besame Mucho," Capital 149. The obvious Spanish Mexican influences are very much heard, as this ditty penned by Sunny Skylar and Consuelo Velazquez was also a huge contemporary Jimmy Dorsey 1944 best seller, with stiff vocal by Bob Eberly and Kitty Kallen on Decca 18574. Russell's soft vocal is more committed, much in a contemporary Frank Sinatra style. Andy contributes a bit extra with his Spanish as a soft and effective crooning job. Perhaps a later flat-sounding Coasters (rock-era) version, on Atco 6163, is more of a parody—but, perhaps, who noticed?
2. "Amor," Capital 156. Penned by Gabriel Ruiz and Sunny Skylar, this obvious Latino title reference (like "Besame Mucho") provided Andy comfort, as he again delivers!
3. "What a Difference a Day Made," Capital 167. The Hispanic origins of this ditty perhaps fit Russell's tastes, although this style remains very soft and Sinatra like.
4. "I Dream of You," Capital 167. Soon after Andy recorded this ditty (1944), Frank Sinatra crooned it out—indeed in much the same style. Who's cloning who?
5. "I Can't Begin to Tell You," Capital 221. As introduced by (World War II pinup) Betty Grable in *The Dolly Sisters*, in the 1945 film bio 'Dolly Sisters', (based upon the early century vaudville 'sister' act) associated with Ziegfeld among others), this ditty also found a solid recording by her on Columbia 36867 backed by Harry James. Russell's contemporary rendering is also done very well, although a surprisingly committed Bing Crosby version on Decca 23457 is better. Listen and compare.
6. "If I Had a Wishing Ring," Capital 234. Penned by Lou Alter and Marla Shelton, this ditty is successfully crooned out as softly as possible.
7. "Laughing on the Outside Crying on the Inside," Capital 252. This very pop-sounding entity penned by Ben Raleigh and Bernie Wayne is true enough, in title alone. Luckily, the softness of Russell's vocal makes it all work.
8. "Just a Memory," Capital-10085. This old ditty by Buddy De Sylva, Lew Brown, and Ray Henderson is much improved upon by Andy's rich baritone when compared with over the earlier (1927) version by Franklyn Bauer on Brunswick 3590.
9. "It's Too Soon to Know," Capital 15281. With Andy in the mellow-voiced lead, this ditty with the Pied Pipers, who had backed Frank Sinatra some six years earlier, as penned by Deborah Chessler, retains a smaltzy, yet effective soft sound.

10. "Imagination," Capital 30034. This pop standard by Johnny Burke and Jimmy Van Heusen, while lacking imagination, remains relevant enough by Russell's good singing.
11. "Marie Elena," Capital 20035. Speculation has it that this title had been inspired by a Mexican president's wife of the same name in the 1930s? Penned by S. K. Russell and Lorenzo Barcelata, this mellow Mexican tune had already been a Dick Todd rendering and huge 1941 best seller for Jimmy Dorsey, with a stiff vocal by Bob Eberly on Decca 3698. This mellow version by Andy was perhaps meant to produce a better vocal, and it obviously does!
12. "I'll See You in My Dreams," Capital 20036. Anyone who would want to push this old Marion Harris standard vocal as a contemporary Frank Sinatra rendering would find it a simple task—but who really cares? Or could it be Dick Haymes? Or is it all redundant over fifty years later?

Visual Image

- Andy Russell did appear in films, and he is perhaps best seen and heard in the 1946 film *Breakfast in Hollywood.* As named for a popular contemporary radio program of the same name, hosted by Tom Brennaman, where Andy, had previously been featured as a radio entity. He moreover delivers as softly and effectively croons out:

13. "If I Had a Wishing Ring" (already a pick above) for the (mostly) all-female (studio) audience.

Dinah Shore

- The female artist who produced the greatest amount of best sellers, of the prerock era, was Dinah Shore. She had been influenced by many before her, especially noting the vocals of Ginny Simms, a fine band singer for Kay Kyser. After scoring well on radio, she had made a few records with the Latin delight of the pre-WWII era—Xavier Cugat. It's interesting to also note, despite all her 1940s commercial success, it's her lesser-known recordings that seem to be of most interest, in true retrospective.

- The following picks reveal a fine vocalist:

1. "The Thrill of a New Romance," Victor 26299. As a "Xavier Cugat and his Waldorf Astoria Orchestra Vocal refrain by Dinah Shaw," original release, the label misspelled "Shore." Penned by Harold Adamson, Fausto Curbelo, and Xavier Cugat, this ditty reveals a fine and clear vocal, whose annunciation of lyric and a huskiness is reminiscent of Connie Boswell. More so, Dinah's vocal is well controlled by Cugat's sweltering (Latin) rhythms.
2. "I Thought About You," Bluebird 10473. This ditty penned by Johnny Mercer and Jimmy Van Heusen is indeed very well sung. It more so competes with a contemporary Mildred Bailey vocal as a Benny Goodman release on Columbia 35313.
3. "You Can't Brush Me Off," Bluebird 10720. In 1940, the "Canadian Crosby" Dick Todd, got together with Dinah and effectively crooned out this Irving Berlin-penned ditty.

4. "Outside of That I Love You," Bluebird 10720. Dick Todd and Dinah do well together, with Dinah again, holding her own the more experienced Todd on yet another Irving Berlin classic.
5. "How Come You Do Me Like You Do?" Bluebird 10824. This ditty penned by Gene Austin and Roy Bergere from the 1920s is surprisingly good.
6. "Do You Care?" Bluebird 11191. Another bit of fluff penned by Jack Elliott and Lew Quadling that finds Dinah's sultry and pleasing vocal indeed scoring. Other contemporary version included a current best-selling entity for Sam Donohue, with an OK vocal by Irene Day on Bluebird 11198 as well as a Bob Crosby entity, with a horrid vocal l by Eddie Miller on Decca 3860 in 1941.
7. "Blues in the Night," Bluebird 11436. The clear-voiced Shore vocal style is sultry and even more recognized, in the best-selling entity, penned by the recognized team of Harold Arlen and Johnny Mercer. Moreover, her (real) Southern accent adds reality to this somewhat contrived classic ditty. (Other contemporary versions included a fine Willie Smith vocal on a Jimmie Lunceford release, on Decca 4125 by Oran Hot Lips Page, on an Artie Shaw release on Victor 27609, a Cab Calloway version on Okeh 6422, as well as a cool Peggy Lee vocal as a Benny Goodman release on Okeh 6553. Indeed, the Peggy Lee version gives Dinah a most interesting vocal challenge, in comparisons.)
8. "Skylark," Bluebird 11473. This excellent ditty penned by Johnny Mercer and Hoagy Carmichael also invited (female) contemporaries Helen Forrest and Anita O'Day to sing it, along with vocal comparisons. If Anita is less "sweet" than Helen or Dinah, maybe (male) Billy Eckstine's less-known version defined it? Listen and compare these fine vocals!
9. "Mood Indigo," Victor 27302. This original Duke Ellington instrumental on Victor 22587 demanded a vocal version, and the group sound of the Boswell Sisters on Brunswick 6470 provided a classic rendering. So did a somewhat later Ivie Anderson vocal, on a Duke Ellington release, on Columbia 35427. Dinah's update vocal finds her committed, providing more tong to lyrics. Her backups, who consisted of Paul Lavel and his Woodwindy Ten, lack Ellington's tight control and leave Dinah with a surprisingly good result.
10. "Sophisticated Lady," Victor 27624. This attempt at Ellington material, also an original instrumental for the Duke penned by Irving Mills, Mitchell Parish, and the Duke himself on Brunswick 6527, is merited by Dinah's vocal.
11. "Chlo-E," Victor 27625. This ditty penned by Gus Kahn and Neil Moret had been around since the 1920s. Also known as "Song of the Swamp" it had been a Paul Whiteman release, with a so-so vocal by Austin Young on Victor 35921. While this ditty presented no great challenge for Dinah, her vocal commitment found her hitting high notes without (seemingly) much effort.
12. "He Wears a Pair of Silver Wings," Victor 27931. This ditty penned by Eric Maschwitz and Michael Carr is pure war propaganda. More so, it works! It is worth the speculation that Dinah featured in this ditty, along with a few other (World War II) entities noted below, on many touring USO tours).
13. "Mad About Him Sad without Him, How Can I Be without Him Blues," Victor 27940. This very ambiguous title, from the contemporary 1944 film *Follow the Boys*, penned by Larry Marks and Dick Charles, while somewhat novel, ain't bad.
14. "He's My Guy," Victor 27963. Wartime servicemen must have really dug this ditty. Moreover, a contemporary Ella Fitzgerald version on Decca 18472 is better. More so, this ditty penned by Don Raye and Gene De Paul just could sound like the Kern and Hammerstein *Show Boat* entity, a classic that Helen Morgan introduced "Cant Help Loving Dat Man"? Or does it? Just listen!

15. "Dearly Beloved," Victor 27963. OK, this sappy ditty, penned by Johnny Mercer and Jerome Kern somewhat works.
16. "Murder He Says," Victor 20-1519. This ditty penned by Frank Loesser and Jimmy Mc Hugh had been introduced in the contemporary 1943 film *Happy-Go-Lucky* by Betty Hutton.
17. "You'd Be So Nice to Come Home To," Victor 20-1519. Another World War II entity that indeed had relevance in its title alone, penned by Cole Porter.
18. "I'll Walk Alone," Victor 20-1586.
19. "Sleigh Ride in July," Victor 20-1617. A fine Johnny Burke and Jimmy Van Heusen penned ditty finds lyrics more than playful?
20. "The Gypsy," Columbia 36964. A fine and husky vocal scores for Dinah on this ditty. (A contemporary group version by the Ink Spots on Decca 18817 is a better vocal however. Sorry, Dinah!)
21. "Daddy-O," Columbia 38284. While this attempt at singing blues is marred by a stiff backing by Sonny Burke, Dinah's vocal of this novelty penned by Don Raye and Gene De Paul is a (minor) win.
22. "Far Away Places," Columbia 38356. As Bing Crosby had also recorded this ditty, penned by Joan Whitney and Alex Kramer, on Decca 24532, this study of Bing and blandness by Dinah still works.
23. "Shoo-Fly Pie and Apple Pan Dowdy," Columbia 36943. Penned by Sammy Gallop and Guy Wood, this is a pleasant novelty and indeed pleasantly sung. (As a jazzy, contemporary Stan Kenton entity, with a cooler June Christy vocal, this ditty is more than a novel effort. Does Shore's pop effort beat Christy's jazzy vocal? Just compare, if it still means anything!)
24. "Buttons and Bows," Columbia 38284. Along with "Her Happy Valley Boys," this contrived attempt at "country and western" is novel fluff. Penned by Jay Livingston and Ray Evans, for the contemporary 1948 film *The Paleface*, perhaps Bob Hope, in the film, did it a bit better.
25. "Lavender Blue," Columbia 38299. This bit of Scottish folk had been adapted into the contemporary Walt Disney film *So Dear to My Heart*. As credited to the Disney team of Morey and Daniel, this adoption of the folk ditty of "Dilly Dilly" all seems a bit dumb, and the commercial considerations of an orchestra led by Harry Zimmerman perhaps found Dinah, as usual, trapped by rubbish. This resulting (1949) recording, however, indicates a committed Shore, with a toned-down orchestra. Moreover, Dinah's fine vocal is stripped bare, and her excellent voice is exposed! (A contemporary Burl Ives version on Decca 24547 is a good comparison, with Dinah's version somehow competing).
26. "Baby, It's Cold Outside," Columbia 38463 (a fine duet with Buddy Clark).
27. "It's So Nice to Have a Man Around the House," Columbia 38689. This sultry vocal, a tongue-in-cheek performance, perhaps lifts this stupid attempt by Jack Elloit and Harold Spina at novelty.
28. "Getting to Know You," Victor 20-4286. This bit of smaltz, a Broadway entity penned by Richard Rodgers and Oscar Hammerstein II for the contemporary (1951) *The King and I* at least found Dinah more than able to introduce it as a recording for highbrows. Somehow it works for other ears as well.
29. "Facination". Victor-20-6980. This old Neopolitan melody had previous claims upon it by Maurice de Ferda vdy, F.D. Marchetti and Dick Manning. It had been perhaps defined by (cabaret) entity Le'o Marjane in (French), in about 1940? Luckily, the ditty found (contemporary) 1957 recognition from the film "Love In The Afternoon".

Dinah's soft approach more so redefined it, along with another and similar (mushy) rendering by Jane Morgan. (Not to be confused with contemporary Jayne P. Morgan). Soft and sleep inducing? With Jane or Dinah?

Visual Image

Note: While Dinah did become a bit of a minor film entity in the 1940s (including *Thank Your Lucky Stars, Follow the Boys, Up in Arms*, with Danny Kaye, and the horrid *Belle of the Yukon*, among others, it would be her work in (1950s) television that would attract the attentions of many ex-servicemen (including the author's (late) father, who saw her in a USO show) and their kids (many of us baby boomers). Her being dressed to the hilt in long gowns (for her women audiences) and her kiss off for the Chevy Motor Corporation became indeed a novel and fun thing to watch and hear.

30. "Thank Your Lucky Stars." As well as being a film title, this ditty penned by Frank Loesser and Arthur Schwartz was introduced by Dinah in the film. Dressed up to the hilt and wearing a huge hat, which luckily does not fail to hide the big band, backs her up. She is rhythmic, with a soft vocal style, which had much in common with her 1943 contemporaries Ginny Simms and Lena Horne. In any case, Dinah's vocal and image works well and definitively!

Ginny Simms

This vocalist had a very sweet vocal, which sometimes found perhaps a hidden desire to abandon pop and become an opera singer, emulating Helen Morgan, producing music for highbrows. In comparison with those who would follow her as a band singer, the influences of Ella Fitzgerald on upbeat material, area bit more substantial. Just how bandleader Kay Kyser was able to handle it all is oddly creative. Or perhaps the contemporary swing style had a lot of an effect upon Ginny's moods? Moreover, Ginny had a "show off" voice, something that most bandleaders who attempted to contain Ginny's style would more so become an influence upon many up and coming singers, especially noting much similar stylist emulation from the (later) likes of Dinah Shore and (even) Lena Horne, especially on slower material. Along with the likes of vocalists Harry Babbitt, Sully Mason, and Ish Kabibble, it would be Ginny's vocals that stood out as part of Kyser's "Kollege of Musical Knowledge on radio and film as well as on the recordings she did."

Note: Most of the following picks with Kay Kyser almost sound like separate radio programs:

1. "For Sentimental Reasons," Brunswick 7759. This ditty penned by Abner Silver, Al Sherman, and Edward Heyman perhaps first defined Ginny as a self-controlled vocalist who was perhaps much influenced by the previous torch recordings of Helen Morgan.
2. "Perfidia," Conqueror 9652. This ditty penned by Xavier Cugat, Milton Leeds, Will Heagney, and Alberto Dominguez also contains some well enough Spanish, as this vocal demonstrated Ginny's ability to overcome such fluffy material with her classy vocal.
3. "Music Maestro Please," Brunswick 8149.
4. "Don't Let That Moon Get Away," Brunswick 8181.

5. "Love of My Life," Brunswick 8201. This ditty penned by Artie Shaw and Johnny Mercer is sung to perfection in highbrow style.
6. "At Long Last Love," Brunswick 8209. A stuffy Cole Porter-penned ditty is done well.
7. "For No Rhyme or Reason," Brunswick 8209. Another Cole Porter-penned ditty is worth hearing.
8. "Have You Got What Gets Me?" Brunswick 8228. This ditty penned byLeo Robin and Ralph Rainger perhaps had Kay Kyser eager to use it on his contemporary radio program as novel material. This recording found Ginny picking up on Kyser's upbeat arrangements to fit her emerging (vocal) style.
9. "Two Sleepy People," Brunswick 8244. The vocal by Ginny is always excellent, while for Harry Babbitt, his own problem of sounding stiff almost ruins it. (This ditty, penned by Hoagy Carmichael and Frank Loesser, had been introduced in the contemporary 1939 film 'Thanks For The Memory" by Bob Hope and Shirley Ross in a fine duet, and had subsequently been recorded on Decca 2219)
10. "Three Little Fishes," Brunswick 8358. As part of the vocal chorus, Ginny and Harry Babbitt muddle through the novelty and antics of Sully Mason and Ish Kabibble. Penned by Saxie Dowell, this huge best-selling entity of May 1939, which included "Boop-Boop Dit-Tem Dot Tem What-Tem Chu" as part of its title on its original Brunswick release, perhaps did provide somewhat of a cheer, as war clouds in Europe would break in September of that fateful year.
11. "On the Road to Mandalay," Brunswick 8415. (Kipling is quoted)!
12. "With the Wind and Rain in Your Hair," Columbia 35380. This Jack Lawrence and Clara Edwards penned ditty pehaps put hair problems in a different prospective?
13. "Indian Summer," Columbia 35337. Very, very mellow! Indeed, the playful voice of Ginny found Al Dubin's redone Victor Herbert song melody "An American Idyll" with added (mushy) words the kind of material that she could show case 'show off' her great voice! Not an 'American Idol"!
14. "Blue Love Bird," Columbia 35488. Hoagy Carmichael and Ned Washington penned this bit of mush that perfectly 'fit' Ginny.
15. "I'd Know You Anywhere," Columbia 35761. Not only did Ginny first introduce this Johnny Mercer and Jimmy Mc Hugh bit of mush penned ditty in the 1940 film "You'll Find Out", she is also introduced as 'Ginny Simms' on the recording itself. That's class!
16. "I've Got a One-Track Mind," Columbia 35762. Ginny does very well with this penned by Johnny Mercer and Jimmy McHugh. Ginny also introduced this ditty in the film "You'll Find Out," along with Kay Kyser.
17. "We'll Meet Again," Columbia 35870 This Hugh Charles and Ross Parker penned ditty found Ginny (with the stiff voiced Harry Babbitt) providing a (lasting) WWII era song ditty, due to it's title alone.
18. "What Goes Up Must Come Down," Vocalion 4721. (An interesting comparison with the contemporary Ethel Waters version? Listen and compare!)
19. "Way Back in 1939 AD," Vocalion 5329 The show-off voice of Ginny leads in to a slow start with a familiar excuse to swing. Penned by Johnny Mercer and Hoagy Carmichael, this novelty dates itself, as released in 1940! While this ditty just may find Ginny sweetly explaining about how she had met a person she liked, the carefree ditty avoided the fact that World War II had started in Europe.
20. "Get Out of Town," Vocalion 4549. This Cole Porter-penned ditty suits Ginny's show-off vocal best of all. Her slow and brooding voice is only complimented by her own orchestra, most likely from the Kay Kyser orchestra, as a studio favor for Ginny.

21. "Please Come Out of Your Dream," Vocalion 4549. As the flip of "Get Out of Town," this Carl Sigman-penned ditty is slightly upbeat and also done very well.
22. "I Walk Alone," Vocalion 5140. It's not I'll Walk Alone', but it's good.
23. "Love Me a Little Little," Okeh 6259. A contemporary Charlie Barnet release of this ditty penned by Herbie Holmes, Howard Smith, and Ellen Orr found a bouncy and light Lena Horne vocal just as smooth as Ginny's. Listen to both versions and compare a shared vocal style.
24. "Someone's Rocking My Dreamboat," Okeh 6566. This ditty by Leon Rene, Emerson C. Scott, and Otis Rene effectively demonstrates a lesser than stiff attitude in vocal approach.
25. "Any Bonds Today?" Columbia 36228. Speculation has it that Irving Berlin's previous 1938 film entity "Any Yams Today' from "Carefree" became transformed into "Any Bonds Today? Like most, Kay Kyser and company found themselves in good company, as the patriotic appear to sell bonds from Ginny during the (then) peacetime draft of 1941 before the actual bombing of Pearl Harbor on December 7, later in that year).
26. "You and I," Columbia 36244.
27. "Why Don't We Do This More Often?" Columbia 36253. Indeed an interesting question penned by Allie Wrubel and Charles Newman, Ginny's tight vocal pun is appreciated. In true retrospective, this 1941 question was to find Ginny, for the most part, leaving the Kay Kyser organization as a band singer since 1935 and unofficially as a single entity.
28. "Irresistible You," Columbia 36693. This very typical ballad penned by Don Raye and Gene De Paul is noted on its original (red) Columbia label as "Vocal with Chorus." How true!
29. "Suddenly It's Spring," Columbia 36693. This ditty penned by Johnny Burke and Jimmy Van Heusen, as the flip side of "Irresistible You," while sung very well, can guarantee sleep as much as any other pop ballad of the era.
30. "Cuddle Up a Little Closer," Columbia 36797. The contemporary (1943) film *Coney Island* had found Betty Grable introducing this ditty penned by Ralph Rainger and Leo Robin. Luckily, Ginny's recording also made it interesting. (While Betty Grable's legs were indeed most popular during this exhausting war year, Ginny, in addition to have been appreciated for her talents as a contemporary singer, had become reveled as a contemporary pinup, along with USO shows and broadcasts.)
31. "They Say It's Wonderful," ARA 139. The lush backing of Lou Bring's orchestra works well with this slightly oversung vocal penned by Irving Berlin.
32. "Just One of Those Things," Sonora 1192. Another Cole Porter entity aced as a recording!

Visual Image

Speculation has it that Ginny Simms, despite her pinup status and proven vocal abilities as a band singer, found her temperament getting in the way of becoming a major film star. It's also evident that her reported "nose" job in 1940 had found her ambitious enough. She did, however, appear in enough films to generate interest and a lasting impression as a fine vocalist.

33. "I've Got a One-Track Mind." This (1940) ditty from the current film *You'll Find Out* finds Ginny and the whole Kay Kyser Organization live, doing their thing, indeed

more so like a recreated contemporary radio broadcast. (This ditty is also reviewed as a recorded entity above.)

34. "Can't Get Out of This Mood." This effective ditty penned by Loesser and McHugh found Ginny singing it in the contemporary (1942) Victor Mature and Lucille Ball film *Seven Day's Leave*.
35. "I'm Like a Fish Out of Water." Along with the Johnny Long Orchestra, Ginny is found to be singing this upbeat novelty in the contemporary Abbott and Costello film *Hit the Ice* in 1943.
36. "You're the Top." Ginny and Cary Grant are found pleasantly singing a duet in the (1946) film about Cole Porter *Night and Day*.

Ethel Shutta

Ethel Shutta was one of the many vaudevillian raised kids who learned the likes of show business from their parents. She could sing and dance as well as more than carry a tune. Her petite, cool blonde image is more so clearly showcased in the (1930) Eddie Cantor film *Whoopee*, even if she was unaccredited in the "Stetson Hat" song and dance segment of that film. She was by then hooked up as an early band singer with the popular, contemporary George Olsen dance band, a somewhat smaltzy and stiff organization that nevertheless produced best sellers, usually from show tunes. More so, the subsequent hiring by Jack Benny for his (1931) radio program of Olsen and his principle vocalist (Ethel) made them very well known to the public, and most likely kept Olsen's (mostly) sappy orchestra sound somewhat contemporary, at least until the mid-1930s. The following are Ethel Shutta picks:

1. "A Precious Little Thing Called Love," Victor 21832. This ditty penned by Lou Davis and J. Fred Coots is cool and poignant and became a huge (1929) best-selling entity. Perhaps the success of this ditty led to Ethel to become more than vocal refrain. She somehow gets enough of a vocal in despite Olsen's hog arrangement! (A contemporary (brighter) Annette Hanshaw version challenges Shutta's version.)
2. "South Sea Rose," Victor 22213. The very pleasing and pleasant bit of danceable fluff penned by Abel Baer perhaps finds Ethel aping Ruth Etting. (It's interesting to note that Ruth had costarred with Eddie Cantor on Broadway in *Whoopee*. For the subsequent (1930) film, Ruth was not to been seen, while Ethel Shutta was seen unaccredited. Fair? In true retrospective, no!
3. "There I Go Dreaming Again," Victor 22937. More fluffy, slow dance material penned by Lew Brown and Ray Henderson finds Shutta in a mellow vocal, however highbrow.
4. "And So To Bed," Victor 24125. Putting the kids to bed with stiff-sounding Paul Small? This vocal duet penned by Mack Gordon and Harry Revel only succeeds because of Shutta's better vocal.
5. "Rock-A-Bye Moon," Victor 24165. This ditty penned by Howard Johnson, Fred Steele, and Morton Lang became Jack Benny's first radio theme, as well as providing instant radio recognition to Shutta's pleasant vocal, perhaps inducing sleep. After a short while, Olsen and Shutta left the program for their own program, along this tune. In true retrospective, a major mistake for both, plus for this song's recognition.
6. "Ah, but I've Learned," Victor 24166. Shutta's mellow voice drops a little, yet this ditty penned by Roy Turk and J. Fred Coots still works.

7. "Underneath the Arches," Victor 24229. A slow but effective vocal finds this somewhat confused highbrow look at life; penned by Joseph McCarthy and Bud Flanagan, it somehow works. A contemporary Connie Boswell version is warmer. Listen and compare.
8. "Vas Villst Du Haben," Victor 24229. This German title breaks the rules of this book! Penned by Al Bryan and James V. Monaco, this lame ditty contains all the likes of a European music hall, something that was clearly outdated for contemporary material, except for an ethnic (German) meeting? With all this noted, Ethel's vocal puts up with it all and almost produces something (half-way) hip. Indeed, this clumsy song ditty proves that Shutta could be very skillful, with a winning performance, over stupid material.
9. "Stetson Hat," Hot and jazzy Ethel sings and tap dances in *Whoopee* (1930).

The marriage between (boss) George Olsen and Ethel produced great marketing and some kids along the way. Indeed, after the Jack Benny program, Olsen and company retained a huge Depression-era radio audience. Sadly, by the mid-1930s, they were divorced, which disappointed and discouraged many listeners. Olsen, a victim of changing musical tastes, foundered. Shutta, while still fairly young, about thirty-seven, in 1935 could not find much success as a vocalist. She would subsequently find work primarily as an actress, with a minor comeback on Broadway, in old age.

Frank Sinatra

The new popular music led by Crosby, in the early 1930s, was extended into popular music and culture by Frank Sinatra, into the 1990s, when most of that style had died out. Sinatra was nicknamed "the voice," in the 1940s and for a lot of good reasons. While Sinatra could bring an Italian American identity with him, he was rarely a tenor yet a great annunciator of spoken (American) lyrics. Sinatra moreover sounds best in the written old school of writers, who included the likes of Irving Berlin, the Gershwins, Harold Arlen, and Cole Porter. Sinatra more so kept a later school of songwriters in business, noting both Sammy Cahn and Jimmy Van Heusen. By his sheer arrogant nature, he dumped big bandleaders. Although some of the swooning girls were perhaps the work of a press agent, his effect upon the whole music industry was indeed unprecedented and real. By the mid-1940s Frank Sinatra was on his way to becoming an institution, much like his idol, and, sometimes mentor, Bing Crosby. By the age of twenty-nine, through most of 1945, he had already topped most all the existing media. A superstar? Bet upon it!

The following seven Frank Sinatra picks are as a band singer with Harry James, all recorded in 1939. Reissue numbers for single release are noted as they also became best sellers after Frank became a solo artist, noting the need to release material, due to the musicians' strike of 1942.

1. "From the Bottom of My Heart," Brunswick 8443. In mid-1939, Frank had gotten himself into the "big band" of Harry James. Since the mid-1930s, he had made several radio appearances on *Major Bowes Amateur Hour* with some of his buddies from Hoboken, New Jersey. After a bit of a struggle as a single, he seemingly found himself with a major band, moreover, as far as he could go. As a Harry James entity, this fine Brunswick release penned by Billy Hays, Albert Gibson, Morty Berk, and Harry

James himself, while not a classic, is classically sung. It would be later replaced by the new and red (color) Columbia label.

2. "Melacholy Mood," Brunswick 8443. The flip of "From the Bottom of My Heart" penned by Vick Knight and Walter Schuman, this vocal is also a fine one, with Frank already displaying vocal discipline and intonation.
3. "It's Funny to Everybody but Me," Columbia 35209. Another fine ditty penned by Jack Lawrence defined as "soft" remains as a sensitive bit of singing (reissued later on Columbia 36738).
4. "All or Nothing at All," Columbia 35587. As the first of many great ditties recorded by Frank, this ditty penned by Jack Lawrence and Arthur Altman is indeed defined by Sinatra's classy singing. It may also be considered the best of the early Harry James entities recorded by Frank. As a reissue in 1943, due to the current recording ban and (more likely) the contemporary success of Frank Sinatra, this ditty became a huge best-selling entity, using the same original Columbia release number, with Frank's name in larger print than the 1939 original release that had been largely ignored. While contemporary (reissues) from Freddy Martin's band singer Clyde Rogers on Victor 20-1537 and a Jimmy Dorsey release on Decca 2580, with a vocal by Bob Eberly did indeed meet some merits, Frank's better and dominating version ruled the roast as a vocal!
5. "On a Little Street in Singapore," Columbia 35261. Penned by Billy Hill and Pete De Rose, this ditty also found a (good) contemporary Buddy Clark release on Varsity 8101, among many other contemporary versions for competition. As a lesser known (1939) Harry James release, the smoother and nasal Sinatra vocal was better, if you had heard it! (As a 1944 reissue on Columbia 36700, this ditty became better known and associated with Frank's vocal.)
6. "Ciribiribin," Columbia 35316. The last of the Harry James recording titles was also a Harry James theme song claimed by Harry James, Jack Lawrence, and Alberto Pestalozza and defined by Frank's singing of the old Italian folk entity. Reissued on Columbia 37141, it is nevertheless rivaled by a fine contemporary Bing Crosby and Andrews Sisters version on Decca 2800. It was more so noted as the first release by this very successful combination of Bing and the girls. In comparison, a win for the elder man—Bing? Listen!
7. "Every Day of My Life," Columbia 35531. Another Harry James release penned by James, Beck, and Hayes, noted as a contemporary fox-trot may really be termed as a mellow vocal with music easy to dance along with slowly (later reissued in 1944 on Columbia 36700).

Note: The following Frank Sinatra picks are as a band singer for Tommy Dorsey and were recorded between 1940 through most of 1942. The vocal refrain by Frank Sinatra, as noted on original record releases, would, in time, prove to be too much for Frank's arrogant nature. In retrospective review moreover, Sinatra did learn a lot about music and how to vocalize "on the beat" and perhaps try to emulate band instruments. Tommy Dorsey's horn was to indeed be important for Frank as well as for the likes of other traveling vocalists, noting the group vocals of the Pied Pipers. It is more so important to note two other (Dorsey) contemporaries of Frank, who would also become a huge solo entity by the mid-1940s—Jo Stafford and Connie Haines.

8. "Too Romantic," Victor 26500. This ditty penned by Johnny Burke and James V. Monaco was originally a Bing Crosby entity, as released on Decca 2998. It is also the

first of many solo releases to compare between them that usually gives Frank's nasal vocal the edge. Indeed, this one is improved upon!

9. "I'll Be Seeing You," Victor 26539. A World War II entity before the bombing of Pearl Harbor in 1941 indeed! As originally penned by Sammy Fain and Irving Kahal for the Broadway entity *Right This Way*, the question of timing is essential. As this ditty had originally nothing to do with war, it's own sentimental title had found an audience in Canada, England, and elsewhere (already at war) since 1939. Contemporary (1940) recordings by Dick Todd and Frank Sinatra more so revived it into something special, and it was Frank's excellent version that found most notice as a best-selling entity. Later, as war did entangle America, this Tommy Dorsey release was reissued on Victor 20-1574 and (again) became popular. By 1944, other versions were recorded and among them were two very well-conceived and committed vocals that indeed challenged Frank's original. The valid contemporary best-selling Bing Crosby release on Decca 18595 may be considered one of his best (later) renderings. Moreover, a small label contemporary release by Billie Holiday on Commadore 553 may be considered a flawless performance! Choose.
10. "Polka Dots and Rainbows," Victor 26539. This dumb title penned by Johnny Burke and Jimmy Van Heusen somehow works.
11. "Fools Rush In," Victor 26593. This effective song penned by Johnny Mercer and Rube Bloom remains a classic, despite its many other interactions and another Sinatra version on a Columbia rerecording.
12. "Devil May Care," Victor 26593 A contemporary Glenn Miller release on Bluebird B-10717, featuring a Ray Eberle vocal may have put this ditty penned by Harry Warren and Johnny Burke on more (1940) jukeboxes as a best seller, but Frank, in true retrospective, *is* the better vocalist! Listen and learn.
13. "I'll Never Smile Again," Victor 26628. While all previous Jimmy Dorsey releases were to be of value, this Ruth Lowe-penned ditty became the bigger seller and thus gave Frank the most recognition, up to this time. As noted on the original record, "Vocal refrain by Frank Sinatra and the Pied Pipers," in small letters, this ballad had influence. It is more so interesting to note that this is truly a group rendering and not a real solo effort, despite Frank's lead.
14. "All This and Heaven Too," Victor 26653. Penned by Eddie De Lange and Jimmy Van Heusen, this bit of fluff was more so a contemporary film title. Moreover, contemporaries Dick Todd, on Bluebird B-10787, and a Jimmy Dorsey release, with a Bob Eberly vocal, on Decca 3259, as well as a Charlie Barnet release, with a Larry Taylor vocal, on Bluebird 10751, provided some stiff competition. (While Dick Todd gets the nod, it's all still, good listening.)
15. "The One I Love (Belongs to Somebody Else)," Victor 26660. Thankfully, Frank's vocal updates this mushy smatlz from the (1920s) into something! (Sarah Vaughan also recorded this ditty later.)
16. "Trade Winds," Victor 26666. The contemporary Bing Crosby version, as released on Decca 3299, is slow and surprisingly well done. While Frank's vocal of this ditty penned by Cliff Friend and Charles Tobias is edged out, it ain't by much.
17. "Our Love Affair," Victor 26736. Tommy and Frank mesh well indeed, and this ditty penned by Arthur Freed and Roger Edens outsold a fine contemporary Judy Garland rendering on Decca 3593. More so, comparisons in style and arrangement should be made, with the (younger) vocal of Garland's and Frank's (mature) adult dance record.

18. "We Three (My Echo, My Shadow and Me)," Victor 26747. A contemporary Ink Spots version, of this ditty penned by Dick Robertson, Nelson Gogane, and Sammy Mysels on Decca 3379 may be better, but Frank's vocal presence is no slouch.
19. "Stardust," Victor 27233. This classic by Hoagy Carmichael and Mitchell Parish is revisited, and indeed, Frank provides an excellent vocal. While in true retrospective considered "classic Sinatra" by many, it's the earlier versions, especially noting Bing's original on Brunswick 6159, that truly linger. Bing or Frank? It's Bing!
20. "You Might Have Belonged to Another," Victor 27274. As originally noted a foxtrot, this (radio) contest winner of Tommy Dorsey's *Fame and Fortune* program remains an icon as well as a bit of excellent singing. Penned by Pat West and Lucille Harmon, perhaps having origins in Mexican folklore (Puedes Haber Sido de Otro), this ditty, featuring vocals by Frank, Connie Haines, and the Pied Pipers somehow remains effective.
21. "Oh! Look At Me Now," Victor 27274. As the original flip side of "You Might Have Belonged to Another," this foxtrot and also a contest winner of Tommy Doresy's *Fame and Fortune* (radio) program, this vocal by Frank, Connie Haines, and the Pied Pipers again works. More so, this ditty penned by Joe Buskin and John Devries, while a bit sappy, is a better tune.
22. "Dolores," Victor 27317. Penned by Frank Loesser and Louis Alter, this ditty, for a bit, made it into a 1941 film *Las Vegas Nights*. As made into a recording, Frank is definitely in focus, more so defining this ditty.
23. "It's Always You," Victor 27345. The well done ditty penned by James Van Heusen and Johnny Burke had been (another) original Crosby entity, more recently from his contemporary film *Road to Zanzibar*. Frank's subsequent version as contemporary Tommy Dorsey fodder found better recognition a few years later in 1942 as reissued on Victor 20-1530. Like other song ditties of the era, the mid-1942 musicians' strike had a lot to do with it, along with the fact that Frank, indeed leaving Tommy Dorsey as a solo artist, had become even *more* popular. (As noted elsewhere in the text of this book, many previous Harry James and Tommy Dorsey re-releases enjoyed huge sales, subsequently exploiting Frank Sinatra.)
24. "Let's Get Away from It All, Victor" 27377 (with Connie Haines and Pied Pipers).
25. "Do I Worry?" Victor 27338. Contemporary recordings by a similar fox-trot arrangement by former band singer Bea Wain and by the (group) rendering of the (still) very danceable Ink Spots version offer good (vocal) comparisons.
26. "This Love of Mine," Victor 27508. Mmm. This fine ditty penned by Sol Parker, Hank Sanicola, and Frank Sinatra himself is indeed done well. (A subsequent re-recording would more so be better.)
27. "Everything Happens to Me," Victor 27359. Another bit of fluff, and done well, penned by Matt Dennis and Tom Adair, also finds Frank's vocal plea another winner.
28. "Blue Skies," Victor 27566. The Irving Berlin-penned ditty is smoothly rearraigned as a contemporary and danceable entity; it finds Frank perhaps almost as bright as the Maxine Sullivan update.
29. "How About You?" Victor 27749. The classic ditty penned by Arthur Freed and Burton Lane had also found a contemporary Dick Todd crooning effort on Bluebird B-11406 and the Judy Garland original on Decca 4072 stiff competition.
30. "Snootie Little Cutie," Victor 27875. As noted on original release, this vocal refrain by Frank Sinatra Connie Haines and the Pied Pipers, a somewhat rhythmic dance number, somehow works. Moreover, don't let the stupid title penned by Bobby Troup stop one from playing it!

31. "Street of Dreams," Victor 27903. As a serious and meaningful classic, this ditty penned by Sam Lewis and Victor Young had been defined some ten years earlier by Bing Crosby on Brunswick 6464. While falling a bit short of Crosby's excellent performance, this committed Sinatra vocal is nevertheless relevant.
32. "I'll Take Tallulah," Victor 27869. Penned by E. Y. Harburg and Burton Lane, Frank and the Pied Pipers actually swing out and are joined in by Tommy himself, in a rare vocal refrain.
33. "Be Careful, It's My Heart," Victor 27923. The contemporary (1942) Bing Crosby recording on Decca 27923 is indeed challenged by Frank's committed and careful vocal. Bing or Frank?
34. "In the Blue of the Evening," Victor 27947. While not "The Blue of the Night," this ditty penned by Tony Adair and Alfred D'Artega is more than good.
35. "There Are Such Things," Victor 27974. This ditty penned by Stanley Adams, Abel Baer, and George Meyers, while sappy, is defining.
36. "It Started All Over Again," Victor 20-1522. Somehow this fair Carl Fisher and Bill Carey penned title attracted the Dorsey organization. Luckily, Frank's vocal gives it class, as well as a lift.

Note: From this point on, from early 1942, except for reissues of previously recorded material, the name of Frank Sinatra is clearly stated on the record labels. The voice had learned his trade with the bandleaders and had also learned to vocalize in the style that he is recognized for, even till death. Frank Sinatra was essentially singing as though he was vocalizing through his nose, not his throat—and intonation through speech, as he had always had. The following are picks:

37. "Night and Day," Bluebird 11463. This 1932 entity penned by Cole Porter had been perhaps inspired by a Moslem's sung-out prayer in North Africa. As a pop entity, it had been introduced by Fred Astaire in Broadway's *Gay Divorce*. It would subsequently be made into a film *The Gay Divorcee*, with Fred and Ginger. As a recording, a Leo Reisman release featuring a Fred Astaire vocal, on Victor 24193, Fred actually sounds committed. Even so, the mixed result is less than powerful and un sexy without Ginger Rogers. While others, including the likes of crooners such as Crosby or Columbo, did not take a whack at it before Sinatra, Maxine Sullivan's (1938) version, on Victor 26132, had moreover defined it. Luckily, Sinatra's own (1941) solo entity is flawlessly sung. His committed vocal is more so total, and if he does not surpass Maxine's fine crooning job, its a close second. As this ditty has since been subsequently well done by others, including a later, Sinatra rerecording, it should not be confused with the (1944) reissue of this same (Bluebird) master released on Victor 20-1589. Frank had also been found rendering this ditty in the contemporary (1943) film *Reveille with Beverly*.
38. "The Lamplighter's Serenade," Bluebird 11515. Penned by Paul Francis Webster and Hoagy Carmichael, this bit of mellow pop is indeed a winner.

Frank signed up with Columbia Records in mid-1943. The following are hispicks:

39. "You'll Never Know," Columbia 36678. A contemporary 1943 Dick Haymes version, released on Decca 18556, penned by Mack Gordon and Harry Warren, sounds more than familiar. Indeed, both of these contemporaries featured a smooth singing style that matched in more ways than one. Within a few years, perhaps Mel Torme,

influenced by the same people who had effected Dick and Frank, could be counted as a Sinatra clone.

40. “Close to You,” Columbia 36678. What a good (marketing) title! Penned by Al Hoffman, Jerry Livingston, and Carl Lampi, this ditty, sung especially for the women in his audience, is also a winner.
41. “People Will Say We’re in Love,” Columbia 36682. As a classic bit of highbrow pop, this gem penned by Richard Rodgers and Oscar Hammerstein II from the contemporary (1943) Broadway entity *Oklahoma* would and indeed did provide a challenge for most other vocalists, including a contemporary version from Bing Crosby and Trudy Erwin. Frank, moreover, performs this ditty with zest and, despite its clumsy lyric, claims and defines it as his own. Bing or Frank?
42. “I Couldn’t Sleep a Wink Last Night,” Columbia 36687. This ditty became the lead song for the (1943) Frank Sinatra film entity *Higher and Higher*. Penned by Harold Adamson and Jimmy McHugh, it’s original Columbia release stated *Frank Sinatra* and was described as a vocal with chorus. The smooth vocals found on this rendering also betray a group sound, moreover unaccredited. Indeed, the soft tones are pleasant enough and indeed influenced by Frank’s previous work with Dorsey’s Pied Pipers.
43. “A Lovely Way to Spend an Evening,” Columbia 36687. Again, a marketing ploy toward young females found in Frank’s audiences, on film, on radio, in personal appearances, and on record delivers. Penned by Harold Adamson and Jimmy McHugh), this 1943 demonstration in smoothness and nose holding, while a bit sappy, is indeed another winner.
44. “White Christmas,” Columbia 36756. This attempt at the Crosby hit is indeed competitive.
45. “Saturday Night,” Columbia 36762. This very upbeat title, penned by Sammy Cahn and Jule Styne, is moderately simple and is ably backed by an orchestra directed by his early manager, Axel Stordahl.
46. “I Dream of You,” Columbia 36762. As a well-sung entity, this ditty penned by Marjorie Goetschius and Edna Osser further defines Frank’s smooth and pleasant vocal style.
47. “I Begged Her,” Columbia 36774. As an upbeat novelty, from the Sinatra film *Anchors Aweigh*, this ditty penned by the already familiar team of Jules Styne and Sammy Cahn sounds like a good plea for sex! Or love? More so, this 1944 entity, a wartime fixture, just had to provide, for many, a bit of inspiration. Or is it just another silly song ditty?
48. “Dream,” Columbia 36797. The very smooth rendering penned by Johnny Mercer is all Sinatra.
49. “Put Your Dreams Away,” Columbia 36814. This may be the very best of all of Frank’s Columbia picks. More so, Frank’s added vocal commitment is indeed enough and creates a more moody and meaningful edge, smothered with smoothness. Penned by Ruth Lowe, Stephen Weiss, and Paul Mann, this very interesting title is furthered by Frank’s own imagination.
50. “I Fall in Love Too Easy,” Columbia 36830. This ditty penned by Sammy Cahn and Jules Styne is a bit highbrow. Fortunately, Frank’s vocal approach is right.
51. “Don’t Forget Tonight Tomorrow,” Columbia 36854. Could this be a bit of R&B? While Frank himself seemingly did not like the new trend of the later 1940s, this recording, with a fine Afro-American group, proves otherwise! Penned by Jay Milton and Okie Sherin, this very effective recording indeed works and may even be considered hip for the times.

52. "Nancy," Columbia 36868. A special tribute to daughter, Nancy? This ditty was penned by two of Frank's talented friends, Jimmy Van Heusen and comic Phil Silvers. To say in the least that Frank is committed to this song is not surprising, as a smooth and (even) emotional rendering, however controlled, produces another winner. (Phil Silvers later became a familiar 1950s television entity for many baby boomers: *Sgt. Bilko.*)
53. "The House I Live In," Columbia 36886. As the subject of a film short by the same name, this pre-Civil Rights era entity of 1945 indeed hits the heart of American bigotry, both in religious and racial terms. Penned by Lewis Allan and Earl Robinson, the political fallout could have been huge. Apparently, all this didn't bother Frank, as his commitment and awareness are more projected to his audiences, as in the film, and on this recording. (A contemporary Josh White version, vastly stripped down to basics, released on Ash 348, is an interesting comparison.)
54. "I Don't Know Why," Columbia 36918. The crooned Russ Columbo version, on Victor 22801, most likely provided Frank with something to start with. As usual, Frank's commitment toward this classic by Roy Turk and Fred Ahlert produces a winner.
55. "Try a Little Tenderness," Columbia 36920. While Frank almost beats out Bing's classic (male) version on Brunswick 6480, it's a good bet that Harry Woods, Jimmy Campbell, and Reg Connelly were indeed pleased that Frank's fine effort is no slouch.
56. "Five Minutes More," Columbia 37048. This ditty penned by Sammy Cahn and Jule Styne is a fine and upbeat novelty. More so, Frank's vocal is exploitative, and his clear message of just what may happen in five minutes is more than a joke—it's an invitation!
57. "The Coffee Song," Columbia 37089. This novelty title is handled in a superior manner. Frank's vocal indicates he is for sure having fun, as he skillfully bends lyrics penned by Bob Hilliard and David Miles at will. More so, while this somewhat silly ditty had no real value, Frank's approach is indeed a lesson in singing, as he lifts this material into something more than regular. Perked up? Just listen!
58. "Begin the Beguine," Columbia 37064. While Cole Porter was always a bit highbrow, this ditty seemingly found the sophisticated Porter at a loss for words. "Beguine"? In any case, it's more so a bit of luck that Frank recorded this ditty, as his clear vocal indeed defined it.
59. "The Thing We Did Last Summer," Columbia 37089. This serious attempt at art and sentimentality penned by Sammy Cahn and Jule Styne just may be their best effort. It is also easy to figure out that Frank knew what he had when he recorded this gem. Moreover, this classic rendering by Sinatra is indeed special, as Frank's vocal, much influenced by these fine lyrics, claims another prolific entity. Frank's best (Columbia) recording?
60. "This Is the Night," Columbia 37193. Penned by Red Evans and Lewis Bellin, Frank again wins out, as this title suggests.
61. "That's How Much I Love You," Columbia 37231. The success of "country crooner" Eddy Arnold on Victor 20-1948 indeed found its way into the mainstream of 1946 pop. While hardly a country interpretation, Frank's medium tempo voiced attempt of this ditty penned by Wally Fowler, Graydon Hall and Eddy Arnold, while not great, is interesting enough.
62. "Mamselle," Columbia 37343. This somewhat novel ditty penned by Mack Gordon and Edmond Goulding is luckily saved by Frank's rendering.

63. "Stella by Starlight," Columbia 37343. As a fine example of classic pop, this ditty by Ned Washington and Victor Young first used as a contemporary film theme for *The Uninvited* is no slouch. More so, it is perfectly fit for Frank's vocal abilities. Moreover, this (typical) Sinatra rendering indeed defines yet another classic.
64. "Ain'tcha Ever Coming Back?" Columbia 375544. While a bit below standards Frank had set for himself, this ditty penned by Paul Weston, Axel Stordahl, and Irving Taylor was perhaps the result of a favor, of Frank's, to make a rendering out of it. Moreover, this resulting vocal, indeed a huge lift, became another Sinatra classic.
65. "I Have but One Heart," Columbia 37554. Young and new (clone of Frank himself) vocalist Vic Damone recorded this ditty exactly as Frank would have and did. This overbearing vocal is not for everyone, except for those who could attempt it. Listen and compare a classy vocal style shared by Frank and Vic.
66. "Christmas Dreaming," Columbia 37809. Mmm. While it is mostly forgotten by time, the contemporary smooth vocal styles of Frank Sinatra and Dick Haymes were very much the same and more so competitive. Penned by Mack Gordon and Lester Lee, this yule time entity had been a fine rendering for Dick Haymes on Decca 24169. In comparison, and indeed like the 1930s clash of clones between Crosby and Columbo, it is still a bit hard to figure who's who. It is also still interesting to find and make these comparisons—at least for some. Just listen!
67. "I've Got a Crush on You," Columbia 38151. This somewhat silly ditty penned by Gershwin brothers is also more than mushy. Luckily, the Sinatra vocal style, always committed, produces a winner. A previous cooler and poignant rendering by Lee Wiley on LMS 282 cut through the mush, but that's something Frank would learn later at Capital Records.
68. "All of Me," Columbia 38163. Penned by Seymour Simons and Gerald Marks, this ditty had already been rendered by many, including the likes of Mildred Bailey, as a Paul Whiteman release on Victor 22879, a hipper Louis Armstrong version on Columbia 2606 and a high-voiced crooning job by Russ Columbo on Victor 22903. Frank distances himself from the past and outsings this classic, without the gimmicks and quirks of all previous versions. More so, Frank (again) redefines a classic.
69. "Everybody Loves Somebody," Columbia 38225. This ditty penned by Irving Taylor and Ken Lane, light years away into the 1960s, became a huge entity for Dean Martin. This Sinatra original is a bit quieter than Dean's best-selling 1964 single, on Reprise 0281, although a previous Martin LP version had indeed emulated Frank.
70. "Autumn in New York," Columbia 38316. This fine Vernon Duke-penned ditty finds Frank at his creative best, as his tender voice greets Duke's lyrics and defines them.
71. "Sunflower," Columbia 38391. An interesting change in material, but not in vocal style, finds the always able Sinatra up for a challenge. Penned by Mack David, this ditty, as accompanied by a country string band, is indeed unusual for Frank. While Frank would never "sound" country, it's oddly country—his way.
72. "Why Can't You Behave?" Columbia 39393. Frank is backed by the Phil Moore Four, and as an early and odd attempt at R&B, that succeeds, it's also just as oddity that it's a Cole Porter-penned entity.
73. "Laura," Columbia 38472. Penned by Johnny Mercer and David Raskin from the 1945 film of the same name, this soft "name" song had already become a hit by Dick Haymes on Decca 1866. As usual, both Dick and Frank sound almost identical, which perhaps finds this fine ditty defined by both versions. Just listen!

74. "One for My Baby," Columbia 38474. This outstanding rendering of this ditty penned by Harold Arlen and Johnny Mercer is rivaled only by that of Lena Horne's contemporary version on Victor 20-1616.
75. "Sweet Lorraine," Columbia 37293. This already old ditty penned by Mitchell Parish and Cliff Burell is saved and updated. As backed by the "Metronome All-Stars," Nat King Cole may be heard playing on the piano keys. Was Frank a jazz singer? At least this attempt somewhat works.
76. "The Hucklebuck," Columbia 38486. This title penned by Roy Alfred and Andy Gibson, adapted from jazz great Charlie Parker's "Now's the Time," puts some fine lyrics into what became a dance craze, fueled by rhythm and blues in 1949. Frank's vocal is moreover up to the challenge, as this upbeat and somewhat rhythmic rendering indeed proves that Frank could become very hip, when he chose to be.
77. "It Happens Every Spring," Columbia 38486. The popular material that Sinatra recorded is so prolific that it boggles the mind. Penned by Mack Gordon and Josef Myrow, for a 1949 film title of the same name, this lush and mellow ditty, while a bit sappy, is masterfully sung. (As the film, which did not include Frank, is about American baseball, it's more than a reach, while later ears cannot relate to the film that the lyrics of this soft ditty are about the American past time. Indeed, contemporary 1949 listeners did make the connection, while later generations have no need.)
78. "A Little Learnin' Is a Dangerous Thing," Columbia 38362. As a fine vocal duet with Pearl Bailey, this original ditty by Sy Oliver and Al Jacobs finds Frank meddling into some mild R&B. Moreover, Pearl's Broadway touch does liven things up and perhaps inspires Frank?
79. "Bop! Goes My Heart," Columbia 38421. There is some brilliant innovation here, as Frank gets down with the Phil Moore Four. Penned by Walter Bishop and Jule Styne, this contrived bit of bebop works, largely due to the obvious fun that Frank and Phil Moore's guys were having. Just listen!
80. "Let Her Go, Let Her Go, Let Her Go," Columbia 38555. This Joe Marsala-penned title, also known as "Don't Cry, Joe," has fine vocal support provided by the "Pastels." As a fine 1949 entity, Frank's smooth vocal is somewhat crooned out and again demonstrates his ability to personalize material into something special, an accommodatingly soft backing provided by an orchestra led by Hugo Winterhalter. A contemporary (influenced by Frank) version by Johnny Desmond is also worth comparing vocally, as released on MGM 10518. So is a soft lesser known version by Rosemary Clooney.
81. "God's Country," Columbia 38708. While more than overboard in sentimentality, Frank's contemporary version of this ditty by Harold Arlen and Yip Harburg still produces a fine result.
82. "The Continental," Columbia 38997. As another highlight from a Fred Astaire and Ginger Rogers musical from the 1930s *The Gay Divorcee*, this ditty, like all the rest, did not translate well on to a contemporary recording. As a forgetful vocal, by Harold Van Emburgh and Roy Strom, in the "sweet" band of the Jolly Coburn Orchestra, on Victor 24735, as well as a vocal by Joe Host, of the Lud Gluskin Orchestra, on Columbia 2952-D, this ditty penned by Con Conrad and Herb Magidson had only scored as a contemporary 1934 instrumental by the Leo Reisman Orchestra on Brunswick 6973. This rather (late) Sinatra rendering, backed by the orchestra of George Siravo, provides Frank with a sway as well as a challenge. The resulting recording finds Frank in a bold mood, with a superior vocal style that flows and

sways, indeed keeping in perfect tempo with Siravo. In true retrospective, Frank sounds much like a 1935 vocalist, as if no one else had had claims upon this classic. A defining effort for 1950? Or perhaps the century? Just listen.

83. "Should I?" Columbia 38998. The Sinatra style is clearly defined by 1950 and is easy to figure upon, considering the contemporary rival sounds of R&B and C&W. This fast-paced vocal of another old standard penned by Arthur Freed and Nacio Herb Brown, backed by George Siravo, while excellent, was considered a bit stiff, for the times. (An earlier 1930s version, with a little-voiced vocal by Burt Lorin, a Victor Arden and Phil Ohman Orchestra released rendering, is only recognized by lyric, which, in true retrospective, after 1950, discovers that Frank's approach was right all along.
84. "Mama Will Bark," Columbia 39425. This vocal duet with a (then) current 1951 sexy bombshell Dagmar was considered by many as to be the absolute worst Sinatra release. Penned by Dick Manning, this attempt at novelty, egged on by (then) Columbia's Mitch Miller, was perhaps a cut below in quality for Frank. Even so, Frank had taken on some stupid material before, and for the most part, did well with it. There are also many previous recordings not found in this book as Sinatra picks, and this ditty with Dagmar indeed made it. More so, this recording ain't all that bad, and perhaps the contemporary effect upon the public about Frank's personal life and divorce from first wife, Nancy, had something to do with the negativity concerned about this release. A great recording? No. An interesting recording? Yes. Well enough. Just listen.
85. "Castle Rock," Columbia 39527. This contrived 1951 rendering penned by Irwin Drake, Jimmy Shirl, and Al Sears is a fast-paced, almost swinging entity. Backed by (a reuniting) Orchestra led by Harry James, Frank's obvious ease at faster tempo vocals, with a driving band remains a good example of competitive singing, and the word *rock* that replaces *swing* perhaps provides this ditty with more of a challenge for the future. Rock? What's that? What did Frank mean? The contemporary (small) label Essex release "Rock the Joint" penned by Harry Crafton, Wendell Don Kean, and Harry 'Doc 'Bagby found a "Bill Haley with the Saddlemen" rendering, on Essex 303, indeed found rock to be more of a hip phrase and a (new) musical expression, with style. Within some years, in 1954, a film entity *Blackboard Jungle* included perhaps an offshoot of "Rock the Joint," the ditty "Rock Around the Clock" penned by traditional songwriters Jimmy De Knight and Max C. Freeman. The subsequent recording, used as only a soundtrack, still found this Bill Haley and The Comets release on Decca 29124 very hip and most influential. While De Knight and Freeman would have been more pleased to give this ditty to Frank, in true retrospective, it's more than a stretch that Frank could not have pulled it off. Sorry, Frank.
86. "I Could Write a Book," Columbia 39652 (The Rodgers and Hart ditty was later recorded for Capital).
87. "Bim Bam Baby," Columbia 39819. This novelty is sung with a punch, as this attempt at the current trend of R&B at least finds Frank willing to become hip. Penned by George Mysels, this material is perhaps lowbrow for Sinatra, who nevertheless manages to make it a creditable performance, despite stupid lyrics.
88. "Tennessee Newsboy," Columbia 38787. Also known as "The Newsboy Blues," this ditty penned by Bob Manning and Percy Faith reeks of creativity, despite its contrived title. While Frank was never country, noting his previous attempts at "Sunflower" and "That's How Much I Love You," they are fine adapted pop titles—as Frank recorded them. The title finds Frank backed by a full orchestra by Axel Stordahl, and with a simple storytelling vocal, he again produces a winner.

By the early 1950s, Frank Sinatra had dropped out of Columbia. By all accounts, his personal life was on the skids and had affected his professional image. It also seemed that his recordings, although usually done very well, and his films were all perhaps a bit too familiar. Even a well-done film, *Meet Danny Wilson*, in its original release, had failed. Privately, suicidal tendencies would perhaps emerge. Fortunately, these negative aspects of show business would never get the best of him or his art. The breakthrough for Frank was to be twofold. One was the much-acclaimed role as an actor in *From Here to Eternity*, a non-singing role. Indeed, the best supporting actor Academy Award, a huge image builder, also gave him a recognition from those in the entertainment business that had otherwise been missing. The other, and more to the point, was his association with Capital Records.

From the (1953) start, although the talented Axel Stordahl was brought along from Columbia, the staff at Capital had big ideas and a lot of respect for Frank. While the label's founder Johnny Mercer had already sold out, the likes of Voyle Gilmore, Billy May, Gordon Jenkins, and especially Nelson Riddle, all formally "big band" musicians, had a liking for huge orchestra arrangements and bright vamping sounds. Like Nat King Cole, already a Capital entity, an "adult" market, an alternative to R&B and R&R was to be largely built upon Cole and Sinatra.

The following Capital recordings represent the most familiar of all Frank's renderings and much of the best. Except for but a few titles, most are rerecordings of earlier pop entities, as many of these titles are to be found elsewhere within this book. These recordings are nevertheless different, as the always committed Sinatra vocal is complimented as never before by a huge backing sound of orchestra arrangements that would never smother but enhance Frank's fine singing.

- The following are Capital picks:

89. "Lean Baby," Capital 2450. This bright 1952 start finds Frank's embellishment of this novelty penned by Billy May and Roy Alfred into something better. More so, backed by the familiar Axel Stordahl, Frank's sway is also a bit jazzy.
90. "I'm Walking Behind You," Capital 2450. Frank got stiff and younger competition from contemporary versions by Eddie Fisher and Vic Damone. Listen and compare.
91. "I've Got the World on a String," Capital 2505. The excellence of this vocal is perhaps enhanced by the set up arrangement by Nelson Riddle. As the 1933 Bing Crosby version, on Brunswick 6491, is a fine comparison, it's obvious that Frank's own vocal sway with Riddle truly is interested in something different. Moreover, the 1942 Lee Wiley rendering, on Schirmer 2009, is poignant and moody, much like Crosby's effort but more so. The more cheerful Sinatra and Riddle combination is indeed a winner, although the previous Crosby and Wiley versions are also notable. Who wins? It's a tough question. Does anyone even care?
92. "My One and Only Love," Capital 2505. This average pop entity penned by Guy Wood and Roberto Mellin is given a huge lift by Frank's vocal and Riddle's backing. Just listen!
93. "From Here to Eternity," Capital 2560. While this film title can be considered an acting triumph for Frank Sinatra, this song ditty, penned by Fred Karger and Robert Wells, is also a win. More so, Frank's vocal interest is, for some, better than his Academy Award-winning acting performance. Or maybe he should have won a "best song" award as well?

94. "South of the Border," Capital 2638. As (another) standard from the 1930s penned by (Jimmy Kennedy and Michael Carr, this ditty had already been a best seller for the Shep Fields Orchestra, with Hal Derwins vocal on Bluebird 10376, the Ambrose Orchestra, with a vocal by Denny Dennis on Decca 2732, by Tony Martin on Decca 2788, and especially by Gene Autry on Vocalion 5122, among others. A fine Bing Crosby 1939 radio version was sadly not released as a recording. More so, just a few years before, Frankie Laine added his usual vocal edge, producing a very fine recording on Mercury 5892. As now credited with the lush Billy May Orchestra, Sinatra renders a bright vocal, successfully challenging and (perhaps) redefines this classic. Listen and compare.
95. "Young at Heart," Capital 2703. This 1953 recording penned by Johnny Richards and Carolyn Leigh was indeed something new as a song ditty. While Riddle's arrangement is always superb, perhaps this one is his very best. As lyrics go, this intelligent and poetic bit of prose, seemingly a reject, impressed Frank enough to record it. Moreover, Frank's soft and precise vocal, as given a lush opening by Riddle, finds Frank at his perhaps supreme best. As an original classic, this popular ditty remains claimed by Frank. Just listen! (A later 1955 film, by the same name, would also feature Sinatra with Doris Day.)
96. "Don't Worry 'bout Me," Capital 2787. Don't worry or bother with a 1939 Hal Kemp release, with a vocal by Bob Allen. A Count Basie release, featuring a vocal by Helen Humes, had defined it. Moreover, Frank and Nelson Riddle again define creativity, as this old ditty penned by Rube Bloom and Ted Koehler, out of New York's famed 'Cotton Club' night club review, at it's 2nd location is redefined.
97. "Three Coins in a Fountain," Capital 2816. As a 1954 contemporary film title that did not feature Frank, this somewhat contrived soap opera of a film at least had the talents of the familiar Jules Styne and Sammy Cahn to pen a song ditty by the same name. Like *Young at Heart*, the Sinatra-Riddle combination works, although the mushy lyrics of this title could have been a disaster. Luckily, Frank's careful caressing voice is on the mark and give him claims upon another pop classic.
98. "The Gal that Got Away," Capital 2864. This excellent classic penned by Harold Arlen and Ira Gershwin is the male version of the contemporary 1954 Judy Garland release "The Man That Got Away." More so, as well as a compliment, it works.
99. "Half As Lovely (Twice As True)," Capital 2864. Lew Spence and Sammy Gallop penned this silly ditty that Frank makes into something great to listen!
100. "Learnin' the Blues," Capital 3102. This ditty is a favorite personal memory of the author (of this book) and perhaps the greatest of all Sinatra entities, which obviously is a lot. Penned by Dolores Vicki Silvers, perhaps related to comic Phil Silvers, this relatively unknown song ditty is a masterful composition. Frank's vocal swings, and Riddle, as usual, does his thing well. Moreover, Frank's commitment to lyrics is incredibly jazzy—or at least it all turns out that way. While not a jazz exponent, perhaps, in Frank's case, he never had to be.
101. "Love and Marriage," Capital 3260. As part of a contemporary 1955 television project, *Our Town*, this original Sammy Cahn and James Van Heusen is a pleasant bit of smaltzy pop that, like most other entities, benefits from the Sinatra and Riddle combination. More so, this somewhat swinging vocal, while not jazzy like "Learning the Blues," is yet another Sinatra classic as well as an enduring reminder of just how great this vocalist was. (A later 1980s TV sitcom *Married with Children* later revived interest in this ditty and interest in Frank.)

Note: While some of this material was issued on 78 rpm and 45 rpm, the huge popularity of the "Long Play" LP (chiefly by adults), in the early 1950s, just has to be noted. While the scope of this book is principally ending in 1950, this artist is a huge exception. Moreover, following the earlier lead of Nat King Cole, a Capital artist before Frank, the concept LP, a marketing ploy from the 78 rpm era, became much enhanced and indeed more popular.

While originally separate 10-inch LPs these Capital issues are noted. Both. "Swing Easy" on Capital H-528 and "Songs for Young Lovers" on Capital H-488 were combined on the 12-inch LP, Capital W-587.

102-117. "Swing Easy" and "Songs for Young Lovers," Capital W-587. As stated above, this LP was made up of the two 10-inch disks listed above. The titles are:

a. "Just One of Those Things." The Cole Porter-penned ditty is further defined, noting previous recordings from Ginny Simms and Peggy Lee as well as the 1942 filmed Lena Horne version is finally challenged!
b. "Sunday." This is pleasant enough, as this old ditty penned by Chester Conn, Ned Miller, Bennie Kruger, and Jule Styne is effective.
c. "All of Me." In a rare case, the earlier Columbia rendering may be better, but not by much.
d. "Get Happy." The classic by Harold Arlen and Ted Koehler had already been revived by Judy Garland, although this version is no slouch.
e. "I'm Gonna Sit Right Down and Write Myself a Letter." As a jazzy item, an earlier Fats Waller version was impressive. So was a Boswell Sisters effort. This "modern" 1954 effort is also done well. (A bit later, a Bing Crosby and a jazzy pop singing Billy Williams version would appear.)
f. "Taking a Chance on Love." The Ethel Waters title is updated and sparkling.
g. "Wrap Your Troubles in Dreams." The Bing Crosby title is updated.
h. "Jeepers Creepers." The Louis Armstrong and Ethel Waters versions are recalled well.
i. "Violets for You Furs." Penned by Tom Adair and Matt Dennis, this bit of snobbery and sophistication fortunately finds Frank as committed as ever.
j. "My Funny Valentine." This old show tune by Rodgers and Hart had been defined by Margaret Whiting, also a Capital artist, a few years before. This excellent version perhaps found inspiration from the Whiting version?
k. "The Girl Next Door." The earlier Judy Garland entity, "The Boy Next Door" penned by Hugh Martin and Ralph Blane is successfully exploited to a male point of view. More so is Frank's tender approach, obviously influenced by the Garland original.
l. "A Foggy Day." This ditty penned by George and Ira Gershwin is seriously dealt with, more so than any previous version. While a Fred Astaire film entity in a 1937 film *A Damsel in Distress* is OK, his recording on Brunswick 7982 is only passable. A contemporary Bob Crosby version, featuring a fine vocal by his band singer Kay Weber on Decca 1539 was better. This Sinatra and Riddle rendering is memorable and indeed redefines yet another classic for Frank.
m. "They Can't Take That Away from Me." Another (Gershwin Brothers) rendering from a Fred Astaire film (this time with Ginger Rogers in the 1937 *Shall We Dance*), this ditty found a best-selling but weak Astaire vocal attempt released

on Brunswick 7855. Indeed, like many filmed entities, the public image found on the film, and not just as found in Fred Astaire films, in true retrospective, just could not be duplicated. Sinatra and Riddle, however, had other ideas as well as perhaps a vision. Moreover, the bright Sinatra vocal truly defined this old film classic like no other.

n. "Like Someone in Love." As a ditty penned by Johnny Burke and Jimmy Van Heusen, a somewhat of a surprising 1945 Crosby version was known on Decca 18640. As a rule, while Bing had continued to produce best sellers, by this time, he was usually more prepared to golf than record. Frank was seemingly always prepared, and in this case, some years later in 1953, recorded this ditty. Moreover, the tired Crosby recording offers no contest, as Frank truly defines this old ditty. Had Crosby recorded this ditty with Brunswick, in the early 1930s, he could have provided Sinatra some competition.
o. "I Get a Kick Out of You." This classic Cole Porter-penned ditty is actually a "drug" culture entity, or at least the snorting of cocaine is seeming acceptable. In any case, the earlier Ethel Merman version, on Brunswick 7342, while worth it, finds Frank's personable touch, with some intelligent singing, a bit more commanding than even the bombastic Merman vocal. Redefined? You bet!
p. "Little Girl Blue." The previous Margaret Whiting version of this diity penned by Richard Rodgers and Lorenzo Hart just had to be an inspiration for this classic, redefined.

118-133. "*In the Wee Small Hours*," Capital W-581. This LP had been originally released as a two 10-inch set and subsequently released as a 12-inch, 16-track entity. As a concept LP, this ditty is superb and arguably the best of its kind. The painted blue original cover itself pictures Frank on a city street, late at night. Moreover, he is wearing a suit and a hat and is flashing a cigarette. His image is captured as a cool customer and, as projected in his (real) personal life, an observer of life as it is.

As it turns out, the great cover delivers. The Sinatra vocal, a bit cooler than his previous Capital LPs, remains committed as Frank. Frank establishes such moody contact with his listeners. As a contrived product, this whole effort, with Nelson Riddle remains, in true retrospective, an artistic reminder of good music—indeed the music of an older generation as released in to the (coming) new age of rock that no one had figured upon.

➢ The titles are:

a. "In the Wee Small Hours." A poignant title? Penned by Dave Mann and Bob Hilliard, this ditty is indeed a moody and substantive vocal performance. While it's a stretch if Frank had been involved in the Capital cover of this LP project, originally on Capital W581-1, the very believable Sinatra vocal, full of a bittersweet tale, is indeed one to be listened to and appreciated.
b. "Mood Indigo." The classic penned by Duke Ellington, Irving Mills, and Barney Bernard had already found jazzy interpretation from many, including a fine group version by the Boswell Sisters. This version is popular and sung with a coolness that is needed and perhaps missing. Moody and sad? With lush backing strings? Want to cry? Perfect!

c. "Glad to Be Unhappy." How could Richard Rodgers and Lorenz Hart have known that Frank was going to record this ditty? Indeed a serious challenge to the previous Lee Wiley version, on Gala 2, a poignant performance as well.
d. "I Get Along without You Very Well." What a theme! Writer Hoagy Carmichael must have been very pleased! While a competent 1939 crooning job by Dick Todd on Bluebird 10150 existed, this serious Sinatra vocal, along with Riddles orchestra, just blows all other versions away.
e. "Deep in a Dream." Penned by Eddie De Lange and Jimmy Van Heusen, a fine Connie Boswell version on Decca 2259 is indeed moody enough, although it's still a bit more interesting to speculate if Frank had finished his cigarette. A wet dream? In any case, it's an interesting one. Just listen!
f. "I See Your Face Before Me." A stiff Carmen Lombardo vocal, found on a 1937 Guy Lombardo release, on Victor 25684, just needed to be updated. Luckily, for the familiar team of Arthur Swartz and Howard Dietz, the creative Sinatra vocal hits its mark. Sad and poignant? Just listen! Be sad but pleased.
g. "Can't We Be Friends?" As an emotional edge is tested on each track of this LP, this old standard penned by Kay Swift and Paul Jones had sparks anyway. As a 1920s torch effort, the original Libby Holman version released on Brunswick 4606 had been one of her better and more focused recordings, as this wicked tale about a casual relationship is as poignant as it gets, so was a fine contemporary Bing Crosby effort released on Columbia 2001-D and much like Libby's. Frank and Nelson's newer attempt is also done extremely well, with perhaps Frank's bold vocal, with lush strings, taking things a bit further. In any case, a fine update!
h. "When Your Lover Has Gone." The original torch effort of Ethel Waters on Columbia 2409-D is revisited, and Frank's softer voiced vocal, perhaps inspired by Riddle's lush strings, produces a fine update. More so, as this title indicates, Frank is given a choice to become a wimp or produce a mature statement. As compared with Ethel's emotional and female plea, his masculinity is obvious, as he indeed provides his listeners with a solid claim upon this Edgar Swann-penned classic. i. "What Is This Thing Called Love?" As a torch entity for Libby Holman, on Brunswick 4700, this oddly sung Cole Porter entity found recognition. A later rendering, by Lena Horne in 1941, on Victor 27890, is a softer vocal, with a lush string section by Lou Bring. Moreover, it's obvious that Frank and Riddle were most influenced by the Lena Horne rendering. Nevertheless, Frank's equally mature vocal is just as moody as Lena's, which is indeed a desired result.
j. "Last Night When We Were Young." This ditty penned by Harold Arlen and E. Y. Harburg is defined by Frank's smooth and cool approach. Nasal? You bet!
k. "I'll Be Around." Frank truly was "around" and is as moody and poignant as ever. While this old pop effort penned by Alec Wilder had been a group effort by the Mills Brothers, on Decca 18318, it is more than obvious than Frank and Nelson had other ideas.
l. "Ill Wind." In the early 1930s, writer and musician Harold Arlen also rendered some notable recordings. As well as a competent vocal of his "Stormy Weather," a 1933 Leo Reisman release on Victor 24262, he recorded and released this ditty, a 1934 Eddie Duchin release, on Victor 24579. Both songs became standards, although it took a while for "Ill Wind." It just may be that Lena Horne, in the 1934 Cotton Club, in a (still) minor role as an entertainment entity had sung it as a backup for Adelaide Hall, sadly noting that a contemporary Hall recording cannot be found.

Much later, Lena produced a sultry, smooth, and moody 1941 version, with a lush string section provided by Lou Bring. In true retrospective and more so than "Stormy Weather," Lena had clearly defined this Harold Arlen and Ted Koehler masterpiece. Fortunately, both Frank and Nelson were ready to challenge Lena's classic rendering, producing a fine update.

m. "It Never Entered My Mind." This ditty penned by Richard Rodgers and Lorenzo Hart is very telling and true. Luckily, for them, Frank and Riddle produced something special.
n. "Dancing on the Ceiling." This title penned by Richard Rodgers and Lorenzo Hart finds Frank "dreaming" about "ceiling." Frank's mellow vocal is just right, and his mature rendering of this ditty, initially a fine excuse to be explicable novel, is not to be. While it is only speculation if Frank could keep a straight face while recording this ditty, it's due to Frank's approach that defines this ditty as a classic. If understated, it worked.
o. "I'll Never Be the Same." The mellow-voiced Sinatra again graces another "old" standard penned by Matty Malneck, Frank Signorelli, and Gus Kahn. While the previous efforts of Mildred Bailey and Ruth Etting are notable, this Sinatra effort, like so many other "old" standards found on this LP, is defining.
p. "This Love of Mine." Frank beats all previous versions and his own original, the Tommy Dorsey release on Victor 27508. Is Frank better in 1955? Yes!

134-149. *Songs for Swinging Lovers*, Capital W-653. This 1956 LP release, in contrast with his previous "Wee Small Hours" LP, is uplifting. A positive mood replaces gloom, and the theme of this project, with the vamping horns and strings of Nelson Riddle, results in another classic LP concept. In true retrospective, this LP concept is almost as good as "Wee Small Hours," although its original orange cover artwork, with a smiling Frank and a young embracing couple, is smaltzy and dumb. As "image," this LP cover is unlike the cool "Wee Small Hours" LP concept, perhaps too "adult" to attract (most) teenagers of the era of rock and Elvis.

➢ The titles are:

a. "You Make Me Feel So Young." As a 1946 Dick Haymes release (Frank's old rival), this ditty penned by Mack Gordon and Josef Myrow had been very similar in vocal style. A contemporary (1946) Martha Tilton version, with Paul Weston's backing, was brighter. While it is obvious that Frank's 1956 vocal depth had improved, Tilton's earlier vocal just may have inspired Frank. Ditto for Nelson's vamping Orchestra and Weston's fine arrangement. Moreover, Frank manages to inspire his listeners and define this old film ditty from *Three Little Girls in Blue.*
b. "It Happened in Monterey." The fine 1930 Ruth Etting version is recalled and updated.
c. "You're Getting to Be a Habit with Me." The well-done 1933 Bing Crosby version is recalled and updated.
d. "You Brought a New Kind of Love to Me." The fine (1930) versions of Bing Crosby, Ethel Waters, and Maurice Chevalier versions are recalled and updated. Listen to all differing versions!
e. "Too Marvelous for Words." The fine 1937 Bing Crosby version is recalled and updated.

f. "Old Devil Moon." The fine 1947 previously defind Margaret Whiting version is recalled and updated.
g. "Pennies from Heaven." Both fine Bing Crosby 1936 versions, including one including Louis Armstrong and Frances Langford, are recalled and updated.
h. "Love Is Here to Stay." While the excellent 1938 Bea Wain vocal with the Larry Clinton Orchestra is recalled, on Victor 25761, a more recent rendering, on Capital H 420, had Riddle doing (the same) with Nat King Cole. While Frank is excellent, perhaps Riddle, in true retrospective, could have been a bit more selective—or was it Frank? Or does it all really matter?
i. "I've Got You Under My Skin." Virginia Bruce's 1936 film introduction in *Born to Dance* had provided contemporary recording fodder for both Al Bowlly and Lee Wiley in the United States. More so, a (1937) rendering by Josephine Baker became well recognized as a classic, outside of the United States. Sadly, a surprisingly poor effort (1947) by Bing Crosby, on Decca 24201, did not do much for the song. Luckily, Frank redefines and claims this tired Cole Porter-penned ditty with a new energy and vigor!
j. "I Thought About You." The 1939 Mildred Bailey version, a Benny Goodman release, as well as a Dinah Shore version are recalled and updated.
k. "We'll Be Together Again." The fine 1947 Frankie Laine version is recalled and updated.
l. "Makin' Whoopee." This title penned by Walter W. Donaldson and Gus Kahn for the 1929 Broadway entity *Whoopee*, originally an Eddie Cantor novelty, is perhaps the one weak entity to be found on this LP. In true retrospective, the substitution for "sex" with "whoopee" was far less novel in 1956 and for later decades. Even so, Frank's approach is solid enough, which is indeed a lift, despite dumb lyrics.
m. "Swingin' Down the Lane." Penned by Gus Kahn and Isham Jones, this ditty had been around since a best selling 1923 accoustic instrumental, on Brunswick-2438. Jones would more so record it again in 1930, featuring an excellent (electric) crooning job by Frank Sylvano on Brunswick 6161. Frank's vocal perhaps defined the ditty because of Riddle's brighter arraingement? Frank or Frank?
n. "Anything Goes." This bright (Cole Porter) classic had been introduced by Ethel Merman as a Broadway entity in 1934 and subsequently by her in a 1936 film with Bing Crosby. A stiff 1934 vocal of Bob Lawrence, a Paul Whiteman release on Victor 24770 was less defining. Luckily for Porter, Frank finally defines this classic as a recording, as much so as he had defined others in later times, including the earlier Porter product "Night and Day."
o. "How About You?" Frank betters his own original recording with Tommy Dorsey, on Victor 27749, as well as other previous versions, noting a fine 1940 crooning job by Dick Todd and the Judy Garland original. This ditty penned by Ralph Freed and Burton Lane, from the 1941 Judy Garland and Mickey Rooney film *Babes in Arms*, also needed a little updating, as the politics of the Franklin Roosevelt era, indeed a dated issue in 1956, was far from relevant. In true retrospective, Frank's tribute to his (then) aging show business buddy Jimmy Durante, a fine contemporary (old) 1956 personality as well, produced an infectious and stimulating rendition. While all this still dates the recording, it all still works. How About You?

- Note: The following three titles represent an attempt at rock and roll and the teenage market:

150. "Two Hearts, Two Kisses," Capital 3084. This attempt at R&R penned by Henry Stone and Otis Williams is given much creditability with the contemporary (black) R&B group, The Nuggets. More so, he is backed up by an orchestra led by "Big Dave" Cavanaugh, who had been with Capital stable mate Ella Mae Morse, who had claimed the new movement of rhythm and blues for herself, basically since 1942. While the sound of "Big Dave" was nothing unique by 1955, noting the contemporary recordings of Ella Mae, they were good enough. Moreover, as Frank had already been adaptable to the likes of previous trends found in "The Hucklebuck" and "Bip Bam Baby," his vocal performance is indeed impressive.
151. "From the Bottom to the Top," Capital 3084. Backed by the Nuggets and "Big Dave," Frank again explores early R&R, as the ditty penned by Gee Wilson is serious enough.
152. "Hey, Jealous Lover," Capital 3552. Penned by Sammy Cahn, Bee Walker, and Kay Twomey, this 1956 release, without a backing vocal group identification, was produced by Nelson Riddle. By this time, the influences of contemporary Atlantic Records recording artists, noting such fine recording artists as Clyde Mc Phatter, Lavern Baker, and the Drifters, had produced best-selling winners. As of hearing them, it's not a long shot to discover that Nelson liked the supporting background music, initially the backbeat produced. More so, Frank's ditty sounds like a contemporary 1956 Atlantic release. Just listen.

It is really a pity that Frank had to criticize the "new" style. While he does sound best with the old standards of the 1930s and 1940s, as well as some newer titles written and expressed in the "old" style, a lot of bad will as well as a generation gap was created between the new baby boomers, who would represent more than half of the record buyers in the next decades—1950s, 1960s, and the "old."

- Hoping that rock and roll would go away, as many fads do, it just got bigger, despite the likes of Frank, Nat King Cole, and others.
- The traditional "singles" market would finish its transition from 78 rpm to 45 rpm by the end of 1959. For the most part, despite some success by Frank himself, the Elvis-led medium would become essentially rock and "Top 40."

  The LP market, despite some success by rock and roll, would remain pop, until the ascent of the Beatles-led "British invasion" in 1964. It was by this time that the fragmented country and rhythm and blues LP concept, while always seeing popular acceptance and crossover, split away. The popular acts of many, including those "easy listening" entities such as Tony Bennett Jack Jones, Dean Martin, Johnny Mathis, Della Reeves, Nancy Wilson, and Frank himself would hang on. More so, others, who were essentially "old school," were still influenced to some degree by the emergence of rock.

153-156. *High Society*, Capital W-750. This 1956 soundtrack LP boasts a Cole Porter score, with Johnny Green and the MGM Studio Orchestra.

- The Sinatra titles are reviewed:

a. "Who Wants to Be a Millionaire?" This duet with actress Celeste Holm, while a bit smaltzy and most highbrow, is somehow managed correctly.
b. "You're Sensational." Frank had produced many musicals in the 1940s. Perhaps his experience in these films gave Frank some insight. In any case, it's Frank's own sensational vocal that defines this ditty, both in film and as a recording.
c. "Well, Did You, Evah!" This non-radio duet with Bing Crosby, his one-time idol, was long overdue. Luckily, for record listeners, Bing's vocal is somewhat inspired, which was a little unusual for 1956. Frank is prepared. Moreover, it is a fine duet that overcomes smaltzy lyrics d. "Mind If I Make Love to You?" This ditty is easily the best of the Cole Porter ditties assigned to Frank in the film, featuring some clever lyrics graced by Frank's excellent interpretation.

157-161. *Pal Joey*, Capital W-912. This 1957 soundtrack is graced by a collection of standards penned by Richard Rodgers and Lorenz Hart recalling the previous 1940 Broadway entity that had featured Gene Kelly. The orchestra is led by Morris Stoloff, with sharing musical efforts by Rita Hayworth and Kim Novak, both dubbed. Even so, the strength of this soundtrack is Frank's innate ability to sing old songs and claim them as his own.

➢ The song titles are:

a. "I Didn't Know What Time It Was." The 1939 Benny Goodman entity, with a fine Louis Tobin vocal on Columbia 35230 is recalled. Frank does more and indeed claims this ditty in medium tempo style.
b. "There's a Small Hotel." A 1936 Paul Whiteman release, featuring Durelle Alexander, on Victor 25270, wasn't bad, although a Benny Goodman release, hiding a brilliant Helen Ward vocal on Victor 25363 defined it. A later Bing Crosby (V-Disc) was superb, yet not a commercial release. As a commercial entity, Frank again defines another classic as his own!
c. "I Could Write a Book." The 1941 Eddie Duchin release, with a stiff Tony Leonard vocal on Columbia 35941 had been bettered by Frank's Columbia release on Columbia 39652. This brighter version is, however, more than an embellishment of himself, as this vocal is superbly mature.
d. "The Lady Is a Tramp." The 1937 Tommy Dorsey entity, with a fine Edythe Wright vocal is recalled. So is a fine British release by Adelaide Hall. Frank's inspiration, however, has just got to be the defining 1949 Lena Horne release on MGM 3071.
e. "Bewitched." The 1941 Leo Reisman entity, with a fine Anita Boyer vocal on Victor 27344 is recalled. So are excellent (1950) versions by Doris Day and a Sinatra-like-sounding release by Mel Torme. Frank is bolder and brighter.

162. "All the Way," Capital 3793. This fine single release penned by Sammy Cahn and Jimmy Van Heusen finds Frank in fine voice, indeed an alternative to 1957 rock and roll that was effective and impressive. More so, in true retrospective, Frank's pop style, an icon of the old style, is further defined in a new age.
163. "Chicago," Capital 3793. As the flip side of "All the Way," this old Fred Fisher standard had been around since 1922, noting a fine but acoustic version by Aileen Stanley on Okeh 4792. Introduced by Frank as a vocal, from his contemporary 1957 film *The Joker Is Wild*, a film about a real 1920s performer Joe E. Lewis, it was deemed

more than this fast and jazzy ditty be used. Moreover, this ditty remarkably succeeded, despite its age!

164. "Witchcraft," Capital 3859. Penned by Carolyn Leigh and Cy Coleman, Frank and Riddle sway and swing, while Frank's bright vocal again defines a great song ditty, and more so!

165. "Tell Her You Love Her," Capital 3859. A very mature vocal again succeeds, as this ditty penned by Homer Dennison, Barry Parker, and Hugh Halliday also remains good advice.

166-170. *Close to You*, W Capital-W-789. This 1957 LP featured the Hollywood String Quartet and a backing vocal support, with Nelson Riddle's orchestra. Perhaps, as a rerecording of his previous (Columbia) single, this title got confused. Its best songs boast the following:

a. "It's Easy to Remember." The 1934 Bing Crosby crooning job is redone quite well. Moreover, the original Crosby classic had featured the Rhythettes and the Three Shades of Blue, who included some founding vocal support, with the Georgie Stoll Orchestra. Indeed, the original Decca 391 release had contained a lot of voice. Luckily, the Hollywood String Quartet was on par, with Riddle and his modern approach. A bit confusing? Perhaps! More so, it's Frank's professional and excellent vocal that holds it all together. Just listen!
b. "P.S. I Love You." Frank updates and claims this old Rudy Vallee standard, not to be confused with the (later) Beatles title by the same name.
c. "With Every Breath I Take." Another 1934 Crosby classic is revisited well.
d. "End of a Love Affair." Penned by Edward C. Redding, this highly charged ditty is full of the sop and smaltzy type of lyric that begs to become familiar or forgotten. Frank, however, is serious enough as he mesmerizes his listeners with substance and personal experience.
e. "Close to You." Frank is generally sharper on Capital, as he is on this ditty, although perhaps the Columbia original had more sentimental value.

171-182. *A Jolly Christmas from Frank Sinatra*, Capital W-894. The marketing of seasonal product had been realized by the likes of Decca records and (especially) Bing Crosby, as, since the 1940s, collections of previous Crosby singles were repackaged and sold (again) each year. The LP concept had boosted this marketing strategy to new heights, and adding to the pool came many, especially noting the success of Nat King Cole and Gene Autry.

- Although Frank had been a Capital artist since 1953, his success had found numerous Columbia reissues, often competing with his contemporary Capital releases. More so, a collection of previous Columbia singles "Christmas Dreaming" on Columbia CL-1032 was issued.
- Two seasonal titles, as original Columbia single issue, are found to be picks above, reissued on the Columbia "Christmas Dreaming" LP. They were the title "Christmas Dreaming" and "White Christmas."
- The new 1957 Capital recordings of Christmas ditties find Frank in excellent vocal expression, backed by the choir vocals by the credited Ralph Brewster Singers. While Nelson Riddle is gone, the very able Gordon Jenkins leads an orchestra with skill and bright arrangements.

- The original painted Capital cover portrays a smiling Frank with presents in a black background. While it all sounds a bit smaltzy, it is done in excellent taste, and more so, it's a traditional Christmas package, featuring Sinatra. Indeed, it's really all supposed to be this way.
- The following are picks:

    a. "Jingle Bells."
    b. "The Christmas Song."
    c. "Mistletoe and Holly." As an original part of the LP, this pleasant title finds Frank very much committed. As credited to Hank Sanicola, Dok Stanford, and Frank himself, this ditty is no slouch and indeed remains a Sinatra Christmas classic.
    d. "I'll Be Home for Christmas."
    e. "The Christmas Waltz." As another original, this classic penned by Sammy Cahn and Jimmy Van Heusen, while using that dreaded term "waltz," succeeds. Frank is as mellow as ever, with backing chorus and Gordon Jenkins producing a complicated piece of music, steep in tradition.
    f. "Have Yourself a Merry Little Christmas." While Frank had recorded this ditty back in the 1940s for Columbia, it's more than obvious that this edgier vocalist on Capital is exceptional and better. The mature Sinatra is also given perhaps a bit more by Gordon Jenkins's arrangement, as a lead in, and in time. While it's still a toss up compared to the original Judy Garland rendering, it's still another classic redefined by Frank. Just listen and compare.
    g. "The First Noel."
    h. "Hark the Herald Angel Sing."
    i. "O, Little Town of Bethlehem."
    j. "Adeste Fideles."
    k. "It Came Upon the Midnight Clear."
    l. "Silent Night."

183-194. *Come Fly with Me*, Capital W-920. This 1957 LP product is another concept and indeed a fine marketing ploy for the airline and vacation industry as well as for Frank.

- This cover portrait identifies Frank—with his hat, tie, suit coat, and thumb out—in front of an airport. Frank is indeed ready to travel, and far!
- The familiar Nelson Riddle is not to be found, although the equally Billy May and His Orchestra are.
- The titles of this classic 1957 entity are:

    a. "Come Fly with Me." This title penned by the familiar Sammy Cahn and Jimmy Van Heusen finds Frank in an excellent medium tempo voice, with a bright Billy May backing. More so, was it is a possible sound effect that perhaps sounded like a plane taking off? Or do gimmicks sometimes work?
    b. "Around the World." Bing Crosby had recorded this ditty penned by Victor Young and Harold Adamson only a few years earlier. More so, Bing was in an unusually good voice, although perhaps, the edge in comparisons provides Frank another redefined winner.
    c. "Isle of Capri." While a bit novel, Frank's attention is all that this ditty needed; this ditty penned by Will Croz and Jimmy Kennedy indeed works.

d. "Moonlight in Vermont." The exquisite Margaret Whiting classic rendering, on a 1945 Billy Butterfield release, is embellished and reexamined with great skill. Frank's vocal is in perfect step with Billy May's orchestra and, for many, amazingly better than with previous and lush Nelson Riddle arrangements.
e. "Autumn in New York." This classic by Vernon Duke had already received a classic Sinatra rendering as a previous Columbia 38316. While the Axel Stordahl backing is done well, the (newer) Billy May arrangement is brighter. And more so is the most mature Sinatra vocal, as Frank reinvents himself as a vocalist as well as redefines this Vernon Duke-penned ditty.
f. "On the Road to Mandalay." As it's British origins were obvious, this ditty credited to Rudyard Kipling, the poet, and Oley Speaks had become a mild music hall entity and an acoustic recording in 1913 on Columbia A-5441. The had also been an excellent Ginny Simms recording in the early 1940s. Frank and Billy May are moreover better and brighter, as they more so lift this material. Just listen.
g. "Let's Get Away from It All." The previous Tommy Dorsey release, with Connie Haines and the Pied Pipers on Victor 27377 is brightly updated! Frank and Billy May moreover find this ditty penned by Matt Dennis and Tom Adair more interesting, as Frank again re-defines another classic.
h. "April in Paris." As a 1933 entity, this title had been a Freddy Martin release, with a Russ Morgan vocal on Brunswick 6717 as well as a Henry King release, with a vocal by Joe Sudy on Victor 24478. Luckily, this excellent ditty penned by Vernon Duke and Yip Harburg was revived as a film title in 1952, with contemporary recordings by the film stars Doris Day, (Sinatra-like) Vic Damone, and a truly (French) version by Edith Piaf. More so, did this (still) later version define this ditty? Listen and compare!
i. "London by Night." This contrived ditty penned by Carroll Coates was fortunate to have found Frank.
j. "Brazil." Penned by Ary Barroso and S. K. Russell and associated with the numerous Latino dance crazes redefining rumba rhythms since 1911, this title had also been pursued by bandleader Xavier Cugat in the 1940s. Since then, the middle 1950s found the rumba again popular, despite rock and roll. In the midst of things, the R&B group sound of the Coasters, on Atco 6073, found this novelty a good parody and indeed injected some wicked ridicule. Frank, with his (usual) excellent elocution, found this novelty something to be narrated into something less than danceable and more of a ruse.
k. "Blue Hawaii." This original 1937 Bing Crosby hit is resurrected. By 1961, Elvis Presley would claim it.
l. "It's Nice to Go Traveling." This upbeat ditty penned by Sammy Cahn and Jule Styne finds Frank's vocal swaying and Billy May's orchestra producing a fine ingredient for this travel theme that succeeds.

195. "High Hopes," Capital 4214. This ditty was featured in the contemporary 1959 Sinatra film *A Hole in the Head*. As a single release, despite rock and roll, Frank's pleasing and medium tempo vocal is on the mark, with a couple of voices along with Nelson Riddle's usual vamping arrangement. As an original single, it sounded dated and much like the already usual step back into the popular music of the mid-1930s. Moreover, this ditty did impress many, with perhaps the dream of many others, especially noting the likes of songwriters Sammy Cahn and Jimmy Van Heusen, as a good replacement from the upstart rock-and-roll phase.

In true retrospective, this fine but old-style song ditty did find much more life but in a different aspect. Indeed, as something that presidential candidate John F. Kennedy found to be a catchy tune, this ditty became his 1960 campaign theme. Moreover, as a democrat at the time, Frank recorded it as a noncommercial entity, with new lyrics, and was used extensively in that winning campaign. Was Frank part of that history? Bet on it!

- While Frank continued to crank out best-selling ditties for Capital, times were changing. Whether It became an artistic move or ego, Frank left Capital Records in 1961. As part of his own investment, Reprise Records was founded. Musically, the old standbys of Nelson Riddle, Billy May, Gordon Jenkins, and others would still be Frank's own, and it is a credit to him that he would always demand the best musicians and material.
- While a bit redundant, Frank would continue to ignore the emergence of rock music and subsequently become identified with the "good" music before rock.
- The following "Reprise" releases are reviewed:

196. "The Second Time Around," Reprise 20001. This ditty penned by Sammy Cahn and Jimmy Van Heusen, despite being a latter-day Bing Crosby original entity, found greater recognition in this equally fine Sinatra rendering. Indeed, yet another redefined classic is claimed by Frank! What a guy!
197. "Pocketful of Miracles," Reprise 20040. This very pleasing ditty had been a film title penned by Sammy Cahn and Jimmy Van Heusen. Moreover, while not starring Frank, this ditty remains, more so than the film, another winner for Frank's vocal and Riddle's vamping arraignment.
198. "Everybody's Twistin'," Reprise 20063. This single release is indeed an odd one, as Frank actually attempts to cash in on the contemporary 1962 twist dance craze that had been started by Hank Ballard and Chubby Checker. What is also a bit strange is that two (very) popular songwriters, dating from the early 1930s, Rube Bloom and Ted Koehler, took credit for writing this ditty. Like most material, Frank's vocal is good enough, although since he had artistic control, as he had not had before, it is odd that he would attempt this material. Or perhaps, he just did it because he actually wanted to hear what he could do?
199. "Call Me Irresponsible," Reprise 20063. The old school of songwriting struck well in 1963, as Jack Jones, hugely influenced by Frank Sinatra, made this ditty penned by Sammy Cahn and Jimmy Van Heusen a modest best seller on Kapp 516. Frank's version, with familiar backing by Nelson Riddle, is also good and despite his age is committed totally.

200-201. *It Might As Well Be Swing*, Reprise FS-1012. Frank takes on some good song ditties with the (old) but still good Count Basie Orchestra with the younger and brilliant Quincy Jones arrangements. Picks, however, are few from this (stupidly named LP) issued in (1964). They are:

a. "Fly Me to the Moon." Oddly, this ditty became better identified with Frank much later, when, in true retrospective, the Apollo 11 space crew played Frank's version (up in space) when it landed on the moon in 1969. A huge and unknown audience?
b. "Wives and Lovers." This ditty penned by Burt Bacharach and Hal David had been a huge best seller for Jack Jones on Kapp 551 in 1963. Jack was one of those popular vocalists influenced by Frank and not involved in contemporary

rock idiom, also the son of (operatic) film entity Allan Jones. Moreover, Frank's rendering of this ditty, claiming newer songwriters, is perhaps just as good as Jack's?

- *Robin and the 7 Hoods*, Reprise FS-2021-LP. The talents of Sammy Davis Jr., Dean Martin, and Bing Crosby, as well as the arrangements of Nelson Riddle, all meshed together well for this highly entertaining 1964 film soundtrack. All song ditties were penned by Sammy Cahn and Jimmy Van Heusen. More so, the following picks note single release from this LP:

202. "My Kind of Town," Reprise 0279. While the city of Chicago just could be my kind of town, this ditty was and still is mixed up with perhaps a slightly similar Fred Fisher-penned ditty from 1924 *Chicago*. Moreover, Frank had recorded "Chicago" in his previous 1957 film *The Joker Is Wild*.
203. "I Like to Lead When I Dance." While the humor is a bit old, considering the Beatles had arrived in America in the same year of release, 1964, Frank is still quite good and bright in this vocal.

204-205. *12 Songs of Christmas by Bing Crosby, Frank Sinatra, Fred Waring*, Reprise F-2022. This excellent season product featured exceptional vocals by Frank and Bing, with some excellent backing provided by the elderly "sweet" bandleader Fred Waring. Moreover, for Frank's solo performances, Nelson Riddle is found to have arranged them. They are:

a. "An Old-Fashioned Christmas." While both Sammy Cahn and Jimmy Van Heusen were indeed "old-fashioned," in age and musical style, this seasonal ditty is found to be of substance, and with the committed Sinatra vocal, this effort succeeds well.
b. "I Heard the Bells on Christmas Day." While the somewhat excellent original 1956 Bing Crosby effort had largely been buried by his lesser season fodder, this ditty, based upon the writings of the poet (Longfellow) and cleverly made into a song ditty by Johnny Marks, had been a classic for those who had heard it. Frank is bolder, and this rendering is a fine updated, if not better than the Crosby, version.

205. "Softly As I Leave You," Reprise 0301. This tale about a dying person penned by Hal Shaper, Angelo De Vita, and Nick Calabrese may have been a bit morbid, but Frank's committed vocal pulls it off due largely to his usual eloquence.
206. "It Was a Very Good Year," Reprise 0429. Penned by Irvin Drake, this song ditty about life, at the height of Beatle mania, was new and Frank's vocal touchingly effective-indeed a good year for him!
207. "Strangers in the Night," Reprise 0470. In 1966, noting the age of Frank Sinatra, this oddity that sounded like older music, penned by Bert Kaempfert, Charles Singleton, and Eddie Synder, became a huge best seller. While written for the forgotten film *A Man Could Get Killed*, it's a huge mystery just to why Frank recorded this ditty, but, in true retrospective, it fit him perfectly. More so, this ditty, arraigned by Ernie Freeman, did indeed compete with the rock generation, as many teenagers upon hearing bought into this old vocal style. Or perhaps, it sounded "new" for many.

208. "Summer Wind," Reprise 0509. The Nelson Riddle style or arrangement finds this 1966 attempt much changed, with some funky background vocals, covering Frank's rendering of lyrics. Moreover, Frank's usual sway is more than a bit faster, with Nelson perhaps much influenced, by now, by the sounds of "Motown." Penned by the likes of Johnny Mercer and Henry Mayer, it's also obvious that Mercer is also a bit hipper, considering his age.
209. "That's Life," Reprise 0531. Arraigned by Ernie Freeman, this ditty penned by Dean Kay and Kelly Gordon, considering Frank's age, capitalizes upon it. As the master vocalist, Frank's fast-paced vocal, backed by some fine funky background female voices, is indeed done well. Moreover, the obvious cracks in his voice are acceptable for this gospel-influenced ditty. Frank adapts, as never before, to a "new" style, bettering all his old rivals as well as the few "newer" recording entities who were not recording rock music.
210. "Something Stupid," Reprise 0561. As a duet with his all grown-up daughter Nancy (perhaps with the smiling face?), Frank took a risk at ridicule. Nancy had become a bit of a rocker, but luckily a good one. Arranged by Billy Strange, this C. Carson Parks-penned ditty, a very hip and commercial 1967 release, became another huge seller. While Frank's voice is soft enough, his boldness is gone. For a while, Frank seems lost. Yet, it's Nancy's splendid vocal that leads him through and indeed defines a winning vocal combination.
211. "Cycles," Reprise 0764. Penned by Gayle Caldwell, another "life" song, noting Frank's sometimes failing vocal, still wins out.
212. "My Way," Reprise 0798. As a 1968 entity, this ditty penned by (rock era artist) Paul Anka, Claude Francois, Gilles Thibault, and Jacques Revaix perhaps found its European origins somewhat hidden. In any case, this ditty found Frank returning to the older style, which was originally influenced by other than America gospel, rhythm and blues and country. By now, the Sinatra vocal, while still the "Voice," was dubbed "The Chairman of the Board." On hearing, as compared to even Frank's earlier Reprise masters, a decline in voice in noticed. Nevertheless, it doesn't matter, as Frank is still very good, and his earned prestige towered him over his contemporaries, still singing this style. Moreover, despite Riddle's absence, the backings provided by Don Costa and Bill Miller are also excellent and signaled a successful return to the old style—and more so resurrected
213. "Something," Reprise 0981. The younger and arrogant Sinatra has started out dismissing rock and roll, but this contemporary 1970 Beatles entity, penned by Beatle (George Harrison), only proved him so very wrong. Moreover, Frank is truly committed and interested, and this vocal, however late, backed by Don Costa, is a fine performance.

Time and age finally gave Frank a reason to retire and come back (yet) again. While his vocals had held up well enough, as the previous Reprise picks indicate, they are still selective. Except for die-hards, the Sinatra voice gradually wore out, despite some success.

The 1980 release of the LP "Trilogy" on Reprise 3FS 2300 was a commercial celebration of sorts, as Frank had outlasted just about everybody; he also outlived Elvis, and, with the breakup of the Beatles, found himself, as a single entity, a living and breathing pop icon, without competition. This LP, however, is musically a huge disappointment, as Frank's tired vocals fair to cut it. All tracks are suspect of much tampering, as his attempt at "Love Me Tender," compared to a previous television version, is unsatisfactory. So is a horrid rerecording of the George Harrison-penned "Something." Moreover, his previous rendering, while already old, had been a brilliant effort. The following, also issued as a single, is, however, worth it. It is:

214. "Theme from New York, New York," Reprise 49233. As a film title with the same name, starring Liza Minnelli, the daughter of Frank's old friend Judy Garland, this old-style ditty had the original "Sinatra" style all over it. In addition, Nelson Riddle, with his familiar vamping orchestra, is again backing Frank up and in perfect time on the John Kander and Fred Ebb penned ditty. Voice? It's OK, and, with this type of material, so what? Frank is again triumphant!

- Later efforts, despite the likes of Quincy Jones, found Frank's fine vocals a bit flat or just worn out by time. Still, the die-hard fans kept coming to his "sold out" concerts, as the living icon, whose post-1950 output is considerable, just had to get the nod, noting the purposes of this book.

The 1990s found commercial success for *"Duets,"* using Capital masters with such latter-century "superstar" appeal. They included the likes of Charles Aznavour the French-Armenian pop performer, dubbed the 'Frank Sinatra' of France, Luther Vandross, Arethra Franklin, U2s Bono, Barbara Streisand, Liza Minnelli, Julio Igesias, Carly Simon, Gloria Estefan, Anita Baker, and a surprisingly fit Tony Bennett vocal. Perhaps this "Duets" package was a good enough marketing ploy, although perhaps this fake electronic stuff is a bit much?

   ➢ Special. Extra Stuff. Moreover, the original picks demonstrate, as listed above, that Frank was more than good.

◆ As a pioneer in television, his *Frank Sinatra Show* (1950), and especially his *Frank Sinatra Timex* shows, between 1959-60, were especially well done. As well as appearances with Bing Crosby, Ella Fitzgerald, Lena Horne, and Dean Martin, the following is especially noted:

215-216. "Love Me Tender-Witchcraft." The "Timex" appearance of Elvis Presley in 1960 found both idols at their best. This duet was part of that excellent show. Also featured are the "Rat Pack" members Sammy Davis, Jr. and Joey Bishop as well as a very young Elvis fan, the prerocker, Nancy Sinatra!

- Later specials and shows also made their mark, especially a 1966 entity *A Man and His Music*, which featured the backings of Nelson Riddle and Gordon Jenkins. His daughter Nancy, in the midst of starting up a rock career, was also a fine guest.

◆ The media of radio was also another accomplishment that Frank Sinatra excelled in, while in it. While his appearances with Harry James and Tommy Dorsey, before he was a solo entity, remain good, they are all a bit stiff.

- Frank's solo appearances were sensational, and his work on live radio programs such as *Hit Parade* (solo appearances 1943-49), and his own *Songs by Sinatra* (1943-47) may be considered well done, although numerous.

217. "A Lover Is Blue," with Tommy Dorsey Orchestra (1940).

218. "Pistol Packin' Mama"-"Hit Parade" (1943).
219. "My Sugar Is So Refined,"-"Songs by Sinatra" (1946).
220. "Exactly Like You,"-"Songs by Sinatra," duet with Nat King Cole (1946)
221. "I Found a New Baby," Songs by Sinatra (1946).

- The same may be said about his (V-Disc) output while always good, very numerous, and common.
- The very best of the Frank Sinatra radio programs, while compromising the purposes of this book, were the *Perfectly Frank* programs, which ran from 1953 through 1955. As a creative slice of radio, with footsteps and mood, perhaps as imagined on his 1955 LP "In the Wee Small Hours," Frank produced his finest radio product, and more so, some of the finest radio ever, However, so late in the game!

    - "To Be Perfectly Frank," Sandy Hook 2116. This LP includes:

222. "What Can I Say?"
223. "Love Me or Leave Me."
224. "You Took Advantage of Me."

- Musical films—Selective
- The Frank Sinatra film legacy, in true retrospective, found Frank to be a fine actor, who didn't need a musical ditty to provide a good performance, although it took a while to become realized.

    - A short (selective) review follows. Musical film picks are so numbered:

The film *Reveille with Beverly* found Frank defining the (Cole Porter) classic

225. "Night and Day."

- *Higher and Higher* (1944) featured:

226. "I Couldn't Sleep a Wink Last Night."

    - *The House I Live In* (1945). After some real junk (that still made some money), this excellent film short release, featuring Frank performing the title, is truly inspiring, and moreover, the filmed

227. *The House I Live In* also finds Frank's performance, as in his contemporary recording of its title, flawless.

    - *Meet Danny Wilson* (1952). After a lot of junk, this film failed at the box office. In true retrospective, this gem of a musical film had also failed noting Frank's own personal problems, as his divorce was highly publicized. Who was Frank? Was he a devoted family guy like Bing or somebody else? It took the public a while to digest and change it's perceptions of this very popular singer.

In any case, within a gangster plot that included the likes of Shelly Winters and Raymond Burr,

Frank sings his heart out on the following filmed versions:

228. "You're a Sweetheart."
229. "That Old Black Magic."
230. "I've Got a Crush on You."
231. "All of Me."
232. "She's Funny That Way."
233. "Lonesome Man Blues."
234. "How Deep Is the Ocean."
235. "A Good Man Is Hard to Find." A fine duet with Shelly Winters.

- After *From Here to Eternity*, some fine musicals, noted in record pick above. The following, however, perhaps, in true retrospective, serve Frank best as a filmed musical entity:

    - *High Society* (1956). Along with Bing Crosby, Louis Armstrong, Grace Kelly, and Celeste Holm, this highbrow (Cole Porter) score reeks of excellence. Frank is involved in:

236. "Who Wants to Be a Millionaire?" A fine duet with Celeste Holm.
237. "Well, Did You, Evah!" A fine duet with Bing Crosby.
238. "You're Sensational."
239. "Mind If I Make Love to You."

    - *Pal Joey*. (1957). The original 1940 Broadway entity had starred Gene Kelly. While it's hard to say if this film version is better, it's no mystery that Frank could sing much better than Gene. This film also featured Rita Hayworth (who may have been dubbed) and Kim Novak. Frank's filmed vocals of this ditty penned by Rogers and Hart musical included:

240. "There a Small Hotel."
241. "I Could Write a Book."
242. "The Lady Is a Tramp."
243. "I Didn't Know What Time It Was."
244. "Bewitched."

    - *The Joker Is Wild* (1957). The loose tale about a 1920s nightclub singer and comic Joe E. Lewis, which also featured Jeanne Craine, Mitzie Gaynor, Beverly Garland, and Eddie Albert, is yet another winner. Frank is involved in the following musical selections:

245. "All the Way."
246. "Chicago."

    - *A Hole in the Head*. While not meant as a musical, fine acting, along with Edward G. Robinson, Eleanor Parker, Carolyn Jones, Thelma Ritter, and young Eddie Hodges find this 1959 film entity a winner. It is Frank's vocal, with "a couple of kids":

247. "High Hopes."

- Other films followed, including the excellent 1960 entity *Ocean's Eleven*. As a rat pack feature, Frank's buddies Dean Martin, Sammy Davis Jr., Joey Bishop, Peter Lawford, and Angie Dickinson are effective and novel. Musically, it's Dean Martin who stole the show with "Ain't That a Kick in the Head?"
- More films followed, including the excellent acting role in *The Manchurian Candidate* in 1962.

Finally:

> ➢ *Robin and the 7 Hoods*. This 1964 film featured the Rat Pack members Dean Martin and Sammy Davis Jr., as well as the likes of Bing Crosby, Barbara Rush, (pre-Columbo) Peter Falk, and Edward G. Robinson. Frank was especially effective in:

248. "My Kind of Town."
249. "I Like to Lead When I Dance."

> ➢ More TV:

250. "Love and Marriage." The (1955) TV production of *Our Town*.
251. *Our Town*, as above.

- ◆ Image and Legacy
- The Frank Sinatra legacy of entertainment, most of it easily accessible, speaks for itself. While caution is advised on a good part of his output, his classy vocals remain. As the picks above note, there is a lot out there.
- Moreover, the music of Frank Sinatra became attached to the works of such writers as Arlen, Berlin, Cahn, Duke, the Gershwin brothers, Hart, Koehler, Mercer, Porter, Rogers, and Van Heusen, among others, and like no others. Despite the likes of Crosby and others, who had preceded him, the latter age of the rock era just had to hear him.
- A lucky survivor? An attempted suicide in the mid-1950s? Bad press? Arrogant. Swinging at reporters? Bad marriages? In the mob? While it's hard to answer all that, his great vocals and music indeed did survive—and largely because of him.

(More Frank Sinatra information is found throughout this book, especially noting the radio and LP sections.)

Bessie Smith

The stereotyped image of a huge black woman starts and ends with Bessie Smith. As a 1920s musical personality, her kind of vocals largely contributed to the development of the blues and as a recording artist defined the genre as no one before her. While her subsequent recordings do offer some attempts at diversity, with some jazz and popular titles, she is far less the vaudevillian than the likes of Mamie Smith, Alberta Hunter, Eva Taylor, Ethel Waters, and Bert Williams, among others. Even Bessie's own mentor, Ma Rainey, was to be overshadowed, as the mythology of "the empress of the blues" indeed stuck and would linger into the rock era—as a founder of the later rock era.

- The following picks reveal a rougher blues vocal style than had been heard by the likes of those Afro-American "blues queens" who had preceded her as a recording artist in 1923. Moreover, her powerful vocals are just as forbidding and mournful as a lightning storm, as this rural Southerner is indeed awesome.

1. "Down-Hearted Blues," Columbia A3844. Bessie's tales of woe indeed sound "down-hearted," but the public at large, both black and white, were mesmerized by the wailing vocal and Clarence Williams on the piano keys. The earlier version was by the raspy-voiced blues queen Alberta Hunter, on Paramount 12005, who also had claims in writing it, along with Lovie Austin. Moreover, the Hunter original was a powerhouse but lacked the distribution system of the established Columbia label.
2. "Golf Coast Blues," Columbia A3844. This flip side of "Down-Hearted Blues" had also found an earlier version on Okeh 3055 by Eva Taylor becoming overshadowed by Bessie's powerful vocal.
3. "Beal Street Mama," Columbia A3877. Along with her "Down Home Trio," which included trumpet, banjo, and piano, Bessie delivers a strong bit of lyrics and proves she is louder, as this tale about Beale Street penned by Roy Turk and J. Russell Robinson is made hard to dismiss.
4. "Baby, Won't You Please Come Home?" Columbia A3888. This bit of vocal grit is sometimes considered jazz, but it's more than obvious that Bessie's low-down mood, as heard in this rendition of this ditty penned by CharlesWarfield and Clarence Williams, is indeed blue. A previous rendition is a bit jazzier by Eva Taylor on Okeh 4740.
5. "Oh, Daddy Blues," Columbia A3898. Penned by Ed Herbert and William Russell, this version of an already established blues classic explores the somewhat limited possibilities of original acoustic masters as well as vocal style. More immediate are the examples of Ethel Waters, on Black Swan 2010, and of Eva Taylor and Clarence Williams, on Okeh 4740. (Interestingly enough, Bessie's own (1923) rendering would be challenged by her own mentor, Ma Rainey, in a 1927 electric rendering as "Oh Papa Blues" on Paramount 12566.
6. "T'Ain't Nobody's Bizness If I Do," Columbia A3898. As originally credited to "Williams," this ditty had claims upon it by Robert G. Price, Porter Grainger, and Everett Robbins. Indeed, the 1919 Bert Williams rendering as "It's Nobody's Business but My Own" on Columbia A-2750 had been a rare best seller as a show tune for *Ziegfeld's Midnight Frolic*. Alberta Hunter's (1923) version found her raspy vocal defining, while Bessie's gutsy and slightly later version attests a still stronger female point of view. (A much later electric Billie Holiday version on Decca 24726 owes much to Bessie.
7. "Midnight Blues," Columbia A3936. This ditty, about a midnight tryst penned by B. Thompson and Spencer Williams is interesting, as found in the earlier Ethel Waters version, on Black Swan 14146, backed by Fletcher Henderson on piano. Like always, Bessie's roughness is evident in comparison, although both versions are graced by Fletcher Henderson's backing.
8. "I'm Going Back to My Used to Be," Columbia 13007-D. This vocal duet with the already established blues queen Clara Smith interestingly pits two women together who indeed knew how to wail. Penned by James Cox, both explore lyrics, as "Bessie"

or "Clara," about their own feelings for the opposite sex. Although all this sounds a bit campy, both voices still note a serious tone, with subtle sarcasm.

9. "Easy Come, Easy Go Blues," Columbia 14005-D. While most of Bessie's renderings are loud and urban due to piano backing, this ditty has added strings (guitar) and thus a rural feel. Penned by W. Jackson and E. Ollie Brown, this ditty is easy enough, at least in Bessie's rough and tough style.
10. "Sorrowful Blues," Columbia 14020-D. Penned by Irving Johns and Bessie herself, this bit of grit is creatively pieced together with guitar and violin backing.
11. "Rocking Chair Blues," Columbia 14020-D. This ain't bad, and this rocking ditty penned by Irving Johns, and Bessie herself, with violin and piano backing, perhaps had some inkling, in title as well as in vocal style, for the latter century.
12. "Sing Sing Prison Blues," Columbia 14051-D. A popular place! Yet morer good commentary, penned by Porter Grainger and Freddie Johnson perhaps kept Bessie interested?
13. "St. Louis Blues," Columbia 14064-D. The drama created by Bessie's tough vocals is noteworthy. More so, this classic by W. C. Handy is defined. It should be noted that previous versions were done well, especially noting a fine 1920 Marion Harris rendering, followed by a fine Esther Bigeou rendering. For Bessie's harder vocal style, however, her ability to emulate (black) speech and slang indeed put Bessie into a mode much differing form Marion Harris as well as most of her (black) contemporaries, including Esther Bigeou. If any song had a fit for Bessie's masterful acoustic vocal style, this ditty was predestined. More so, the blues are further defined and are indeed sad and blue, with some superb trumpet backings by a young Louis Armstrong. Bessie's serious vocal style is indeed poignant, as this ditty, never a novelty, is to define this classic as no one had done before or perhaps since.

(Bessie's later 1929 film *St. Louis Blues* features Bessie's vocal in a fine visual in a bar. While the performance of this ditty is indeed awesome (and also available in bootleg form as a record), the original 1925 acoustic recording is just hard to beat. Subsequent creative recorded attempts of note include the likes of Bing Crosby, Louis Armstrong, Cab Calloway, Ethel Waters, and Milton Brown.

14. "Cold In Hand Blues," Columbia 14064-D. While this flip side of *St. Louis Blues* is somewhat buried by its A side, it's still full of raw power as well as being accompanied by Louis Armstrong. Penned by Jack Gee and Fred Longshaw, this play on slang has Bessie at her (usual) emotional best.
15. "The Yellow Dog Blues," Columbia 14075-D. Another classic by W, C, Handy is defined by Bessie's strong vocal. While the "Yellow Dog" origins perhaps linked to an actual train in the Yazoo delta in Mississippi before 1920, this folktale about a woman's search for a very good male friend is updated into something relevant.
16. "Ain't Gonna Play No Second Fiddle," Columbia 14090-D. She ain't, and she's tough enough to believe! These Perry Bradford penned lyrics get right to the point!
17. "I Ain't Got Nobody," Columbia 14095-D. The Marion Harris hit is finally challenged!
18. "Squeeze Me," Columbia 14133-D. This title is interesting enough. Moreover, it's Bessie's own vocal that delivers. Penned by Clarence Williams and Fats Waller, this obvious Afro-American ditty found its (1926) vocal definition by Bessie. (While origins of song ditties within the music industry are always dubious, mythology has it that Clarence Williams just might have put one over on (fellow) black songwriter,

Andy Razaf. Could black artists steal from one another? While it's truly possible, it's a better bet to just enjoy Bessie's performance!)

19. "Back Water Blues," Columbia 14195-D. Bessie's own tale of rain, dark clouds, wind, thunder, lightning, a rowboat, and trouble all combine to validate Bessie's contemporary (1927) tale of woe. Like always, her tough expressions have an effect, and this tale has more. There were (and are) many reasons why blues are found, and this perhaps self-penned tale about the great 1927 flood cannot be found contrived, as the earthy Bessie Smith vocal makes it all too real.
20. "Preachin' Blues," Columbia 14195-D. Did Ma Rainey teach her? Or is it Bessie's own personal experience while working Atlanta, Georgia nightclubs, as the (then) big and segregated city is indeed noted in her warning for other women of her era?
21. "Muddy Water," Columbia 14197-D. As one of the best known popular entities of the 1920s, the peppy Bing Cosby vocal, recorded as a Paul Whiteman release, on Victor 20508, was in itself jazzy and rhythmic. Bessie's approach to this bit of pop penned by Trent, De Rose, and Richman is of one of strong contrast. As usual, Bessie's wailings are full of woe, and this masterfully sung ditty is transformed into something downright awesome and serious, noting the "muddy" water of the (1927) great flood. Muddy water? While Jo Trent was himself (black), his (white) co-composer Peter De Rose was at least honest enough not to cheat him (Speculation has it that Jo Trent may also be a woman? This author however, believes this person to be a black man, sometimes referred to as 'Joe Trent'). While it's possible that (white) vocalist, bandleader Harry Richmond also had a hand in the lyric, his own contemporary version, on Brunswick 3435, is well done, as well as another contemporary claim upon the song ditty.
22. "Some of These Days," Columbia 14197-D. As a 1911 entity for Sophie Tucker, on Edison 10360, this ditty, penned by Shelton Brooks, openly claimed Afro-American origins. While Sophie herself was then a black-faced entertainer who performed "coon songs," it's more than obvious her gritty vocal sought out the real thing. It's also to Sophie's credit, in true retrospective, that Brooks had been openly promoted by her, in an era of hard-line segregation. As times changed, Tucker would seek the services of many Afro-Americans as vocal coaches, although it seems her pre-1920 vaudeville voice and act would remain with her for the rest of her life. As a recording artist, her value became far less or more of the same in future years, including a well done re-recorded (1927) electric version. Bessie's later 1927 version just may have been an answer or challenge to the contemporary Tucker version or a challenge to the 1911 Tucker original. In any case, (usual) Bessie Smith vocal style further defines this ditty, as perhaps declares in itself, the real thing.
23. "After You've Gone," Columbia 14197-D. As a (1918) Marion Harris release, this ditty had found the Afro-American origins of Henry Creamer and J. Turner Layton as credited writers. As a fine vocalist, Marion's version had been creditable, noting an adapted vocal style emulating blacks, with far better authority than the more novel Sophie Tucker style could hope to possess. Even so, Bessie's authority, in the 1927 electric age, further defines this sad tale.
24. "Alexander's Ragtime Band," Columbia 14219-D. Bessie's (1927) attempt at this popular standard from 1911 was indeed interesting enough. As a huge best seller in its day, noting the success of the acoustic releases of Arthur Collins and Byron Harlan, on many labels, including a best-selling Victor release, on Victor 16908, and a fine contemporary Billy Murray version, on Edison 10522, this ditty had been very influential. Penned by Irving Berlin, its own rhythmic form and time, as played, was

highly infectious. Whether the term "rag," a term from some eleven years earlier, had been stolen from (Afro-American) Scott Joplin, is conjecture; it was considered by many 1911 contemporaries as a coon song. While the identity of "Alexander" is indeed black, it does seem odd, as it seems as if Berlin is appreciative of his subject and not in any way demeaning. What was demeaning was the fact that except for a few black vaudevillians like Bert Williams, very few persons of color were allowed to recordt in 1911. This was hardly Berlin's fault, as much as it was Bert's own success. Bessie's vocal is somewhat spirited, with a somewhat rhythmic backing unusual for her. She is far less inspiring and rousing than previous versions and later recorded versions. In true retrospective, while not a great rendering, the Bessie Smith style is evident, and her claims upon this ditty may be considered personal.

25. "Mean Old Bed Bug Blues," Columbia 14250-D. How true! This ditty, penned by L. Wood, luckily had the tough voiced Bessie to explain the creepy situation.
26. "A Good Man Is Hard to Find," Columbia 14250-D. This fine tale tells no lies. Penned by Eddie Green, it became a 1919 release by Marion Harris on Victor 18535. While Marion's acoustic version ain't bad, it's not hard to figure what Bessie could have done with this ditty at that time—if she had been permitted to do so.
27. "Empty Bed Blues," Columbia 14312-D. (Parts 1and 2). Most baby boomers know this title from the late 1960s as performed by a young white blues singer, Janis Joplin. Indeed, Janis was a true fan of Bessie, noting her open emulation as a record collector as well as a vocalist. The cultural changes of the latter 1960s were noted in much musical product, and the success of Janis Joplin, noting the sexual contents of this ditty, were fully realized by Joplin, truly emulating Bessie's tough style.

Bessie's original 1928 recording penned by pianist J. C. Johnson is indeed descriptive, as the strong lyrics describe sexual activity in a poignant manner. Yet, Bessie is less crude, but explicative. While less than a pun, it's obvious that the sexual revolution started in the 1920s, something that Bessie successfully expresses. While the part about her girlfriend, contained in the lyric, gets a bit wild, it's a credit to Bessie's own style and timing that she pulls off this classic rendering with class, while talking some fine trash—without much slang.

28. "I'm Wild About That Thing," Columbia 14427-D. This ditty penned by Spencer Williams finds Bessie actually finding a mid-tempo vocal range. More so, her vocal is novel and playful enough, accompanied by some jazzy guitar licks, possibly by the excellent (white) guitarist, Eddie Lang? That thing? Just listen!
29. "Nobody Knows You When You're Down and Out," Columbia 14451-D. Yes, how true! This ditty penned by Jimmy Cox is truthful enough, and, luckily, Bessie's own vocal defines it. Nothing contrived! Just listen.
30. "On Revival Day (A Rhythmic Spiritual)," Columbia 14538-D. This Andy Razaf-penned ditty is a bit medium tempo and may be considered spiritual. As a rare foot tapped, Bessie is even backed by a vocal group, perhaps a leading piano played by James P. Johnson. A bit contrived? If so, this arrangement indeed had roots.
31. "Moan, You Moaners," Columbia 14538-D. This spiritual, as the flip side of "On Revival Day," penned by Spencer Williams also finds the excellent Bessemer Singers in backup vocal support.
32. "Don't Cry Baby," Columbia 14487-D. Bessie is full of advise, and this ditty, penned by (pianist) James P. Johntson, Bernie Saul, and Stella Unger, finds it all hard to forget.

33. "Black Mountain Blues," Columbia 14554-D. Those people who live on Black Mountain are really bad people! As Bessie tells it, as penned by J.C. Johnson, as wel as corrupt judges, bad moonshine, and good with guns, even the kids are raised mean!

Note. On the following (1933) recordings, Bessie found some real jazz, at least in the fine backup provided. It is very possible that such fine contemporaries such as Frank Newton, Jack Teagarden, Chu Berry, Bobby Johnson, Billy Taylor, Buck Washington, and Benny Goodman were included for this session? As Bessie had never been backed up as much before, in a recording session, it's obvious that the "empress of the blues" perhaps did have aspirations, despite the delicious grit and bite heard on these, to become a popular recording artist or at least a jazzy entity. While both of the following are excellent recordings, Bessie retains her blues, noting a more rhythmic style, which was sometimes attempted in earlier recordings.

34. "Do Your Duty," Okeh 8945. As this ditty, penned by Clyde Darnell and Wesley Wilson, is novel enough, Bessie's need for her man is direct enough to become as laughable as it is serious. This woman indeed needs satisfaction! Don't send some one else!
35. "Gimme A Pigfoot," Okeh 8949. As also known as 'Gimme A Pigfoot And A Bottle Of Beer". This ditty, penned by Wesley Wilson, finds Bessie in some prohibition era juke joint amoung the kind of company who put their weapons at the door-you hope! Reefer and gin are also plentiful! Since Bessie is so tough, it's a wonder her bar room friends don't leave?

Note: Both 'Do You Duty" and 'Gimme A Pigfoot" were to be recorded by Billie Holiday in the latter 1940s. While a vocal debt is linked to Bessie, it's obvious that Billie's vocal on these ditties is a less as rough vocal, but slicker. Listen to them all and compare!

- Note: After 1933, Bessie never again did any recording. In 1937, she was involved in an accident in Clarksdale, Mississippi, closer to the Mississippi Delta, from where she was originally from—which was Chattanooga, Tennessee.

  - Visual Image. (Unlike most other blues entities, Bessie was captured on film.)

36. "St. Louis Blues," The 1929 film captures the myth and provides reality. In true retrospective, Bessie did in fact live up to her image, and, despite musical changes, she remains an awesome figure to both see and hear.

Clara Smith

- The brooding vocals of Clara Smith perhaps found the ears of many contemporary (1923) record collectors at odds with blues styles. Indeed, her contemporary and fellow Columbia recording artist Bessie Smith was also to be found with a similar vocal style, with Bessie possibly with more vocal capacity to shout. While it's sometimes difficult to tell between Clara and Bessie, on some recordings, it's a hard case to prove any emulations or rip-offs of vocal styles. Like others, they emerged within a world of spirituals, vaudeville, tent shows, and racism. A vocal duet between Clara and Bessie, on Columbia 13007-D, "I'm Going Back to My Used to Be," finds only some subtle (vocal) differences. In any case, Clara's blues are true enough and the following picks:

1. "Every Woman's Blues," Columbia A-3943.
2. "I Want My Sweet Daddy Now," Columbia A-3991. This sad tale is essentially blues, as penned by Donald Heywood, with Clara's careful and even articulate vocal about a relationship gone lost. Moreover, this acoustic recording is very listenable, perhaps due to the sheer quality of Clara's vocal and Fletcher Henderson's (piano) backing.
3. "Awful Moanin' Blues," Columbia A-4000. Speculation as it that Clara was known as 'queen of the moaners', which perhaps originated with this recording, penned by Stanely S. Miller, as well by Columbia Records for promotional purposed.
4. "Waiting for the Evening Mail," Columbia 13002-D. This gutsy ditty penned by Billy Baskette perhaps finds the aspects of jail, and an incarcerated prisoner's anticipation of bail money had already been an oddly effective Al Jolson attempt at blues singing on Columbia A-3933—more so are Clara's blues.
5. "I'm Going Back to My Used to Be," Columbia 13007-D. This vocal duet, penned by James Cox, with Bessie Smith is indeed no clash of blues vocal styles! Bessie shouts best and Clara moans best.
6. "Chicago Blues," Columbia 14009-D. The fast-paced bit of rhythmic vocal action between Clara and her band, as penned by Paul Biese, Charlie Altiere, and Spencer Williams, did indeed define the great city during those wild Prohibition years! These blues are not sad. So what!
7. "Done Sold My Soul to the Devil (and My Heart's Done Turned to Stone)," Columbia 14041-D. The drift to commercialism found the contemporary (black) religious community suspicious—as this title itself indicates. As penned by Harold Gray, this ditty finds that the sad 'blues' are the opposite of secular religoun, as indicated in the shared culture of religious music, that had been founded by the early (white) settlers, usually of (British) Baptist sects. It should also be noted that Clara's lament abou the devil was more ever shared by many whites of similar religious beliefs, along with segregation. Later, the likes of others, including Charlie Patton and (especially) Robert Johnson, would take it all a bit more seriously. Or did they?
8. "Freight Train Blues," Columbia 14041-D. This 1924 ditty penned by Thomas Dorsey and Everett Umphrey, also recorded by contemporary Trixie Smith, should not be confused with the later hillbilly 1935 train ride penned by John Lair for Red Foley and Roy Acuff. In any case, Clara finds herself on a fast and wild ride! Get aboard!
9. "Nobody Knows the Way I Feel Dis Mornin'," Columbia 14058-D.
10. "Broken Busted Blues," Columbia 14062-D. There're broken, but Clara finds these crude lyrica by Sax Edgar Dowell a bit more edgier-she moreover succeeds!
11. "Kitchen Mechanic Blues," Columbia 14097-D. Did Clara's pianist Stanley Miller, who also penned this ditty, find work in the kitchen? Is he a good "handyman" or "electrician"? Perhaps contemporaries Ethel Waters, Edith Wilson, and Lizzie Miles had similar chores!
12. "Salty Dog," Columbia 14143-D.
13. "Get on Board," Columbia 14183-D (the Gospel Train's here)! Lem Fowler's claims upon this secular ditty was just about right, as least for 1926!
14. "Ain't Got Nobody to Grind My Coffee," Columbia 14368-D. Another domestic need? As penned by Bud Allen and Clarence Williams, this ditty in retrospective, perhaps reminds it's listeners that 'grinding van be a lot of fun?

Kate Smith

As a baby boomer growing up, this fat lady could be seen on numerous television shows, aping a ditty "When the Moon Comes Over the Mountain" and receiving much applause. While her dry vocal sounded OK to (already) rock-oriented ears, her "old" style was evident. Just "how" and "why" is hard to pin down. Her clear, smooth vocal was surely all she had going for her, but as her original recordings and successful radio shows of the early 1930s attest, Kate did have appeal. And more so, despite some heavy competition of singers who were better singers, it would be Kate Smith's programs that would outlast all others, for more than a decade.

Picks include:

1. "One Sweet Letter from You," Columbia 911-D. This "Charlestown Chasers" release of 1928 is suspected as fronting contemporary jazz master Red Nichols. Moreover, the young Kate Smith sounds inspired enough, as her vocal of this ditty penned by Sidney Clare and Lew Brown may be considered a true jazz entity, more so defining this fine ditty far better than Gene Austin could.
2. "Maybe Who Knows?" Diva 2970-G. Kate emulates Ruth Etting's recording, on Columbia 1801-D, with fine results.
3. "He's a Good Man to Have Around," Diva 2970-G. While it's a fact that Sophie Tucker had introduced this ditty in her (1929) film *Honky Tonk*, it's best left in that film. A contemporary Libby Holman recording on Brunswick 4447 is better. Kate's version is moreover done quite well and perhaps in style, not as high pitched as Libby's vocal. Yet another version by Lee Morse on Columbia 1866-D is jazzy enough but perhaps lacks Kate's vocal prowess.
4. "Waiting At the End of the Road," Velvet Tone 1999-V. While this recording finds Kate's vocal just as dry as the contemporary Ethel Waters version, the emulation is not of Waters but that of a Ruth Etting vocal, which is also very dry.
5. "Moanin' Low," Velvet Tone 1999-V. Very good results find Kate emulating contemporary Libby Holman's original recordings.
6. "Swinging in a Hammock," Velvet Tone 2191-V. Kate's jazzy vocals were far and few, and this very fine bit of it penned by Tot Seymour, Charles O'Flynn, and Pete Wending is no fluke. More so, Kate's timing again defined a jazz classic, despite a fine competing contemporary version by Lee Morse on Columbia 2225-D.
7. "I Don't Mind Walking in the Rain," Velvet Tone 2191-V. Penned by Max Rich and Al Hoffman, this jazzy classic, perhaps more than inspired by contemporary Ruth Etting's dry vocal style succeeds!
8. "Making Faces at the Man in the Moon," Clarion 5359-C. While a Ruth Etting vocal, dryness can still be heard; this "moon song" penned by Max Rich, Smith, Al Hoffman, and Ned Washington does define a "Kate Smith" vocal with ownership. The label notes Kate as "The Song Bird of the South with Her Swanee Music," strongly indicating her assertions to radio success and Depression era (1931). This ditty, moreover, despite its fluffy title, finds Kate in a jazzy mode, with fine and unaccredited backing, most likely from a Columbia studio band. (Columbia, at this time, owned Clarion, Diva, Harmony, and Velvet Tone.)
9. "When the Moon Comes Over the Mountain," Clarion 5359-C. This somewhat smaltzy title penned by Harry Woods, Howard Johnson, and Kate herself nevertheless became known as Kate's own radio program theme. On first spinning this Clarion release, as also released on the Harmony label, its "radio" identification was clear—and

surprisingly interesting. She is more so noted on the record label as "The Song Bird of the South with Her Swanee Music." More interesting is perhaps the fact that this ditty was rerecorded and released on Columbia 2516-D. The resulting confusion deemed the latter rendering more than boring and stiff. Find this original!

10. "You Try Somebody Else," Clarion 5405-C. This lively ditty is more than good. As a matter of fact, it's more upbeat than a fine contemporary Russ Columbo version on Victor 22861.
11. "River, Stay 'Way from My Door," Columbia 2578-D. While the Ethel Waters version, on Columbia 2511-D, is more poignant, Kate's version of this ditty penned by Dixon and Woods ain't bad.
12. "God Bless America," Victor 26198. While the storm clouds of war hung over Europe in 1939, Irving Berlin reworked his 1918 "Yip Yip Yaphank" and wrote "God Bless America." While it is only speculation that Berlin himself had Kate in mind to introduce it on her popular and contemporary radio show, its patriotic message, noting its smaltzy content, became Kate's most recognized recording. Moreover, as time progressed into World War II, it's Kate's version, above many hundreds of others, that became part of Americana itself. (Light years later, past rock and into a new century, this ditty and Kate would be fondly remembered on the steps of the Capitol in Washington DC. Patriotic? 9/11? You bet!)
13. "The Last Time I Saw Paris," Columbia 35802. Penned by the popular writing team of Jerome Kern and Oscar Hammerstein for the 1941 film *Lady Be Good*, this ditty had been associated with actress Ann Southern in that film. (A film entity, *The Last Time I Saw Paris*, came about later.) As a recording, Kate's version is predictably full of smaltzy, although as a World War II entity, noting the fall of France in 1940, its meaning and message had much contemporary impact.
14. "Seems Like Old Times," Columbia 36950.

- Kate is radio: Her numerous programs counting decades featured standards already noted. A key exception is her:

15. "Rockin The Town". This (Ted Koehler & Johnny Green) penned ditty had been introduced by (sultry) Gertrude Niesen in the 1937 film "Start Cheering", as well as a well done recording by Betty Allen, as a contemporary Hudson-De Lange recording. Did Gertrude, Betty and Kate "rock"? Yup!

- Kate's visual image, despite baby-boomer TV is earlier in the 1932 film "The Big Broadcast", crooning out:

16. "When The Moon Comes Over The Mountain".
17. "It Was So Beautiful".

Mamie Smith

As one of many talented back performers of the pre-1920 era, who had hoped especially to emulate the (limited) success of Bert Williams, Mamie Smith, perhaps by a fluke, was allowed to become a recording artist in 1920. While acoustic, her recordings were considered novel and most interesting. Just how could a black woman attempt to compete with the likes of white coon singers like Sophie Tucker, Nora Bayes, or the (better-sounding) Marion Harris? Or perhaps, just how could a person of color have a personality and sing as well as a white woman?

To be certain, a huge talent pool of the black contemporaries of Mamie Smith, known by black patrons of segregated white rip-off artists were also waiting. They would include the likes of Louis Armstrong, Eubie Blake, Perry Bradford, Adelaide Hall, Fletcher Henderson, Lucille Hegamin, Alberta Hunter, Florence Mills, Lizzie Miles, Ma Rainey, Noble Sissle, Bessie Smith, Mary Stafford, Eva Taylor, Ethel Waters, Clarence Williams, and Edith Wilson, among many. While it may have been inevitable that any one of these talented performers could have produced an entity that could change everything, it ended up being Mamie Smith.

- The following are Mamie Smith picks:

1. "That Thing Called Love," Okeh 4113. This ditty penned by Perry Bradford as well as its flip side was actually recorded with a white band as backup. Noting Bradford, the idea of black material was nothing new. While the (then) independent Okeh record label had been struggling to find something jazzy to compete with the likes of contemporary Marion Harris, the likes of Mamie Smith, a well-known (black) vaudevillian, was more of a gamble than a risk. This competent recording was indeed competed head-on with the "coon singing" of many white contemporaries. Moreover, the real thing was out of the bag, which would prove, over time, that these black and jazzy entertainers had always been a huge part of Americana itself.
2. "You Can't Keep a Good Man Down," Okeh 4113. The flip of "That Thing Called Love" is also another black enterprise penned by Perry Bradford and well sung by Mamie, noting the acoustic standards of 1920.
3. "Crazy Blues," Okeh 4169. While the release of Okeh 4113 (noted above) had generated some fair sales, its original release was one of mystery and suspicion. The general (white) public had heard that the artist was colored as well as the black community. Yet, could it be a white girl with the common name of "Mamie Smith"? It was this release that really broke the ice. This time she is accompanied by her jazz hounds, who just may have been Johnny Dunn, Dope Anderson, Ernest Elliott, Leroy Parker, and Willie "the Lion" Smith, no relation and all-black backing. In true retrospective, this first truly segregated and black entity, by choice, is the real thing. Penned by the already familiar (black) author Perry Bradford, the recognition of risqué lyric, often considered (black) and hip, was more so real—at least for the likes of his review 'Made In Harlem', that had began his association with Mamie.
4. "It's Right Here for You," Okeh 4169. As the flip side of the "Crazy Blues" this long title, with its limited acoustic sound, is somewhat more risqué than its flip side. Penned by Alex Belledna and Marion Dickerson, this Perry Bradford-owned ditty again demonstrates a sure winner, both for Bradford as well as Mamie.

   - The overwhelming 1920 marketing success of "Crazy Blues" led to the immediate realization by the other recording companies that big sales and a previously hidden market, hidden by racism, had to be explored and emulated. More so, many other persons of color were to be recorded and exploited.

5. "Lovin' Sam from Alabam," Okeh 4253. This ditty penned by Jack Yellen and Milton Ager is not much different from the contemporary coon-singing Nora Bayes release on Columbia A-3757. Nevertheless, Mamie's version of this clever novelty is just as

fun and, moreover, the real thing. A later and better-sounding electric recording by Emmitt Miller on Okeh 41305 is well done, despite the fact that Miller had been a (white) black-faced performer.

6. "Jazzbo Ball," Okeh 4295. This contrived bit of jazz penned by Marion Dickerson somehow works.
7. "Old Time Blues," Okeh 4296. Mamie took this Perry Bradford-penned ditty to the all-black (1921) review of "Put and Take." Within a year, Mamie left the show, and contemporary Edith Wilson took her place. Edith also recorded this ditty, which also calls for some interesting comparisons in vocals. While it is always more of a problem with acoustic renderings, the similar styles of Mamie and Edith refuse to clash. Perhaps Edith's vocal is a bit sweeter in pitch. Listen and compare!
8. "Sax-O-Phoney Blues," Okeh 4416.
9. "Wang Wang Blues," Okeh 4445. This song ditty penned by the white team of Gus Mueller, Leo Wood, Theron E. Buster Johnson and Henry Busse had already become known as a huge contemporary (1920) instrumental best seller for the Paul Whiteman Orchestra and destined for Broadway's *Ziegfeld Follies of 1921*. Somehow, Mamie, along with her own jazz band, had their own ideas of providing a fine *vocal* with music. While like most all acoustic endeavors, in true retrospective, this all now sounds a bit muddy; it's Mamie's version that pleases the ears. Just listen!
10. "Arkansas Blues," Okeh 4446. This recording, noted on its label as a "Popular Blues Vocal," penned by Anton Lada and Spencer Williams found itself pitted against a fine contemporary of Mamie's Lucille Hegamin on Black Swan 2032. In title, this ditty about a Southern state was considered appreciate enough, as both vocals are somewhat jazzy, with a vaudevillian touch and sound. (Mildred Bailey would later update this ditty electronically in 1939.)
11. "I Want a Jazzy Kiss," Okeh 4623. Yes! Yet another excuse for a contemporary jazz title, penned by Milo and Riga works again!
12. "Mean Daddy Blues," Okeh 4631. This just could be the best of the Mamie Smith releases. As credited to the unlikely (white) team of Fred Hamburger, Irving Bloom, Robert W. Ricketts and Jimmy Durante-the later radio, film and television personality, this contrived tale, with the use of contemporary slang, found Mamie and her jazz hounds more than ready. While acoustic, this vocal somehow comes off as clear and crisp, with some added handclapping and jazzy riffs from the band.
13. "Dem Knock-Out Blues," Okeh 4631. A fine use of slang penned by Geo Butts is evident.
14. "You Can Have Him, I Don't Want Him, Didn't Love Him Anyhow Blues," Okeh 4670. Another bit of crude ness, penned by Dan Dougherty and Willliam Tracey, is proclaimed!
15. "You've Got to See Mama Every Night (Or You Can't See Mama At All)," Okeh 4781.

Trixie Smith

As another of the (Afro-American) recording pioneers who had followed contemporary Mamie Smith, this "Smith" began recording in 1921. In true retrospective, while immediate impact was huge, her (1922) recording of "My Man Rocks Me (With One Steady Roll)" would later become anthem for the later rock generation. The following are picks:

1. "Trixie's Blues," Black Swan 2039. This self penned title indicated a good self identification and introduction.

2. "You Missed a Good Woman When You Picked All Over Me," Black Swan 2044. This Clarence Williams penned ditty may be a bit wordy, but Trixie's complaint ain't.
3. "Give Me That Old Slow Drag," Black Swan 14127. This old bit of slang, penned by Tom Delaney, is well worth hearing.
4. "My Man Rocks Me (With One Steady Roll)," Black Swan 14127. Penned by J. Berni Barbour, this (1922) penned ditty, full of novel sexual innuendo, was initially issued as the B-side of the Tom Delaney-penned "Give Me That Old Slow Drag." Within a few years, as both ditties were reissued on Paramount 12164, this B side became better known. In true retrospective, this title became a solid foundation, along with Frankie "Half Pint" Jaxon, (bluesman) Tampa Reds, indeed an anthem to *rock* music.
5. "Freight Train Blues," Paramount 12211. This ditty penned by Tom Dorsey and Everett Murphy is taken for a good ride with Trixie's mid-tempo vocal but perhaps not as bold as (1924) contemporary Clara Smith's version on Columbia 14041-D.
6. "You've Got to Beat Me to Keep Me," Paramount 12256. Abuse wanted? This Porter Grainger penned ditty, in retrospective, could put 'woman's lib' back about 100 years-although perhaps Trixie's vocal crude story was relivant? Listen and find out?
7. "Mining Camp Blues," Paramount 12256.
8. "The World's Jazz Crazy and So Am I," Paramount 12262. Yet another excuse for a 'Jazz'title, penned by Jimmy Blythe and William Henry Huff, also finds a good 'flapper era' title just right for Trixie.
9. "Railroad Blues," Paramount 12262. This (1925) recorded ditty was perhaps the inspiration for Bertha "Chippie" Hill's classic rendering of "Trouble in Mind" on Okeh 8312.
10. "How Come You Do Me Like You Do?" Paramount 12249. Penned by Gene Austin, this ditty became a huge (1924) best seller for Marion Harris. While taking away no due merits for Marion's fine vocal, the likes of Trixie and Edith Wilson (contemporary) release indeed provide some stiff competition.

Note: Original (Paramount) issues of this ditty credit Fletcher Henderson or Trixie's "Down Home Syncopators," although (on hearing) the (white) "Original Memphis Five" band has been so identified. Was this just a label mistake or was it a bold decision of integration, already successful for Alberta Hunter, on the same label, put off for Trixie?

Valaida Snow

This gifted vocalist was also a trumpet player. Among chiefly Afro-Americans in the United States, she was to be found with a huge following in pre-WWII Europe. Valaida's act featured a musicianship well crafted and well beyond any contemporaries, including that of one Louis Armstrong himself. As the "female" Louis Armstrong, her trumpet sound was no fluke, neither were her mimicking vocals of such fine personages as Ethel Waters, Louis Armstrong, Adelaide Hall, and (later), both BillieHoliday, and Dinah Washington. It's also interesting to compare her sweet-sung vocals complimenting a rougher sound coming from her own instrument (trumpet) on popular standards.

- Picks include:

- Note: This very active entertainer had first appeared on the Broadway stage in the early 1920s. She had been part of a musical family that later became part of a 'sister' act including Lavada, Hattie and Valaida (originally Valada). She had also seen the lights of Europe and the middle east before her recording debut in 1933.

1. "Maybe I'm to Blame," Brunswick A-9407. This Earl Hines release features Valaida showboating a high-pitched and mellow vocal style, influenced by both Ethel Waters and Adelaide Hall. This fine torch style is in fact a stylistic high, with the Earle Hines orchestra (letting) Valaida have her way on this ditty penned by Louis Dunlap, Charles Carpenter, and Hines. (This recording, made in New York, seemingly found commercial release only in Europe? This thus explains the odd Brunswick release number.)
2. "I Wish I Were Twins," Parlophone F-118. This (English recording) is the first of many European recordings as well as those designated as "Valaida, Queen of the Trumpet." More so, Valaida indeed delivers, with trumpet blaring and a fine vocal to boot! (This ditty for certain beats out Fats Waller's fine and better-known version on Victor 24641.
3. "I Can't Dance, I Got Ants in My Pants," Parlophone F-118. This flip side of the above, penned by Clarance Williams and Charlie Gaines may be even better. The scatting vocal from 'Valaida' is sensational as well as her own fine trumpet playing.
4. "It Had to Be You," Paraphone F-140. While this (already) old standard had found greater recognition in the twenties, especially in the recordings of Cliff Edwards on Pathe 032047 and Marion Harris on Brunswick 2610, it's Valaida's spirited (and electric) recording that beats out all other versions penned by Kahn and Jones.
5. "You Bring Out the Savage in Me," Paraphone F-140. Penned by the popular Sam Coslow, this rhythmic ditty is improved upon by Valaida's vocal and trumpet.
6. "Imagination," Parlophone F-230. This self-penned ditty by Valaida is very much influenced by Louis Armstrong's earlier 1930s Okeh ballads, in both vocals and trumpet playing. Again, Valaida scores.
7. "Sing, You Sinners," Paraphone F-230. This ditty penned by Sam Coslow and W. Franke Harling had found some success by the High Hatters on Victor 22322, after being introduced by Lillian Roth in the (1930) film *Honey*. (Too bad Roth did not produce a contemporary recording!) In any case, by the time Valaida recorded this ditty in 1935, the song needed a lift and more so got its due because of Valaida's energy.
8. "Singing in the Rain," Paraphone F-165. This famous ditty found its origins in the Cliff Edwards version, on Columbia 1869-D, which was also featured (by Cliff himself) in the film *Hollywood Review of 1929*. While the latter century found Gene Kelly's film version of the ditty, using the title in 1952 more memorable, it's Cliff's recording and Valaida's more peppy (1935) versions that sound best. Just listen and compare!
9. "Until the Real Thing Comes Along," Paraphone F-559. While the excellent contemporary (1936) version of this ditty penned by Sammy Cahn, Jule Styne, Saul Chaplin, and L.E. Freeman by Andy Kirk and his Twelve Clouds of Joy, with a vocal by Pha Terrell on Decca 809 was far and wide well known, Valaida's artistry trumps.
10. "High Hat, Trumpet and Rhythm," Paraphone F-559. Yes, this self-penned ditty is just full of it! 11. "I Want a Lot of Love," Paraphone F-559. Another self-penned ditty with plenty of novelty and rhythmic power. Valaida's vocal prowess is also found, with some toughness.
12. "I Must Have That Man," Parophone F-575. A fine challenge to Adelaide Hall's previous renderings.

13. "You Let Me Down," Paraphone F-605. Is it most likely that Valaida had heard this fine contemporary Billie Holiday vocal, of this Harry Warren-penned ditty as a Teddy Wilson release on Brunswick 7581. Even so, it's still the likes of Ethel Waters and Adelaide Hall's vocals that had most influenced Valaida as she had worked with both women on Broadway.
14. "Dixie Lee," Paraphone F-605. A good excuse to play and swing?
15. "Lovable and Sweet," Paraphone F-657. This ditty had penned by Sindey Clare and Oscar Levant for the 1929 film "Street Girl". It had been more ever saved for memory by a fine and pleasant recording by Annette Hanshaw. Is Valaida's (later) recording as lovable and sweet as Annette's version? Yes!
16. "You're Not the Kind," Paraphone F-631. The better-known Fats Waller version on Victor 25342 penned by Will Hudson and Irving Mills is bettered by Valaida's style. Just compare and listen.
17. "The Mood That I'm In," Paraphone F-867. Another fine ballad penned by Abner Silver and Al Sherman finds Valaida in a good singing mood and mode. Contemporary American version recorded by Dolly Dawn and Billie Holiday offer good (vocal) comparisons.
18. "Where Is the Sun?" Paraphone F-868. Speculation had it that this ditty penned by John Redman and David Lee had been part of a contemporary (1937) "*Cotton Club*" review at the new Broadway location, introduced by Ethel Waters. While it's very odd that Ethel never bothered to record this ditty, it is more so a very good recording produced by Valaida. While Valaida's vocals are always bright, her sweet and rhythmic vocal claims this ditty as her own.

Note: While Valaida did return to America, between touring and recording dates in Europe, it is significant that she would become better known abroad. While always welcome overseas, it seems she had overstayed her welcome while touring, in 1940. After some time in prison, by invading Nazi, she made her way back to the United States by 1942.

- The rest of Valaida's picks are all American releases and recordings. Noting the radical changes since the early 1930s, Valaida's creativity and artistic abilities adapted well into the popular and (then) rising musical rhythm and blues idioms.

19. "My Heart Is Such a Fool," Apollo 1185. This big band arrangement penned by Smith, Bobby Smith?) finds Valaida much inspired (vocally) by the likes of Ella Fitzgerald.
20. "Fool That I Am," Bel-Tone 7001. The dryness of the vocal heard on this ditty penned by Floyd Hunt is very much influenced vocally by the contemporary (1945) Billie Holiday renderings. She is also accompanied by a vocal group, the "Daydreamers."
21. "If Only I Had You," Bel-Tone 7002. Another Billie Holiday-inspired performance penned by Surrell is also done very well.
22. "Caravan," Bel-Tone 7008. This ditty penned by Duke Ellington, JuanTizol, and Irving Mills, an instrumental hit from 1937, sounds much like a film score than a regular pop entity. In any case, Valaida somehow delivers.
23. "Tell Me How Long This Train's Been Gone," Derby 729. This attempt at rhythm and blues is indeed very hip. As perhaps inspired (vocally) by the likes of Dinah Washington, this ditty is another winner.

24. "Coconut Head," Derby 735. Penned by Herrer, Newton, and Valaida herself, this "calypso" idiom, a current trend, is creative and (even) inspiring. In true retrospective, it should have been more appreciated.
    It's odd that Leonard Chess did not use the multitalented Valaida as a pop addition to his upstart blues and rhythm and blues label. Around this time (1950), the rival Atlantic label had signed the (European) Mabel Mercer as a popular vocalist, among "rhythm and blues" entities. Perhaps if Leonard had known whom he had signed, things would have been more interesting? Nevertheless, the following attempt at hard-core rhythm and blues is another success, as the creative and very adaptable Valaida again proves and demonstrates her great versatility. Perhaps, that's the problem.
25. "I Ain't Gonna Tell," Chess 1555. This rhythm and blues masterpiece penned by Rudy Toombs truly rocks. Sounding much like the very hip Dinah Washington, Valaida scores heavily as a fast-paced rhythmic rhythm and blues singer.
26. "If You Don't Mean It," Chess 1555. This flip side of "I Ain't Gonna Tell" penned by Singleton may have been considered a "rock-a ballad." It also amazingly works!

    Visual Image:

27. "My Sweet Heart". The sexy trumpet player also sings some jazz in the 1939 (French) film *"Pieges"*

Victoria Spivey

The defined divisions and styles within the (mostly) black community and "race" recording artists were to be noted by those especially within that community. Occasional white buyers were to become somewhat confused by releases of all types and kinds, springing up like weeds throughout the 1920s. The vocals of Victoria Spivey, a transplanted Texan, wailing out the blues in Chicago were to become, for a time, a reliable source for blues and more so highlighted by a surprise 1929 film appearance as a "good" girl.

- The following are Victoria Spivey picks:

1. "Black Snake Blues," Okeh 8338. This title implies a lot, and it delivers. Bluesman Blind Jefferson borrows (some) of Victoria's wordy licks on "Black Snake Moan" on Okeh 8455, and "That Black Snake Moan" on Paramount 12407. As in most of her recordings, it's her wailed-out moaning that wins the day, as her own vocals became easily recognized as "urban" and crude. While the Blind Lemon versions are a bit more difficult and perhaps rural, the sexual references that are implied within this ditty are to be taken literally. In this, Spivey's version, full of wailing is more than a pun as well as better than Blind Lemon.
2. "Long Gone Blues," Okeh 8351.
3. "Got the Blues So Bad," Okeh 8401. Yeah, the listener will get the blues too.
4. "Christmas Morning Blues," Okeh 8517. Yes, a sad 1927 Christmas ditty! This girl's man sent a letter explaining that he's in jail for murder, arriving to her door on Christmas Eve.
5. "Blood Thirsty Blues," Okeh 8531. This desperate woman ain't no vampire, although Victoria's mate is indeed a sad corpse.

6. "Dope Head Blues," Okeh 8531. This bit of cocaine sniffing is emotional enough as well as a bit over the top.
7. "Organ Grinder Blues," Okeh 8615. It's interesting to compare the contemporary 1928 Ethel Waters version, on Columbia 14365-D, with Victoria's vocal. Indeed, both vocals are gritty enough.
8. "New Black Snake Blues Parts 1 and 2," Okeh 8626. The vocal duet features Victoria and blues man Lonnie Johnson. This ditty sounds as if Victoria herself is playing the keyboard and Lonnie is strumming his guitar, but that's speculation. The fact that this fine duet is hot, however, is perhaps a crude understatement, despite its need for both sides of the original record.
9. "How Do They Do It?" Okeh 8713 (a good question).
10. "Toothache Blues," Okeh 8744 (Pt. 1 and 2). This traditional blues opens with Clarence Williams on the piano it seems. There are some hot vocal exchanges in lyric, as emulated by Victoria's moans (in a dentist chair as the patient) and Lonnie Johnson (playing the dentist!). While this dentist "theme" can indeed become a struggle, contemporary ditties such as "Dentist Chair Blues" by Hattie Mc Daniel on Paramount 12751 and Laura Bryant on QRS R7055 add up to a line of women seeking out this dentist!

(As a further note, a later Dinah Washington effort "Long John Blues" on Mercury 8148 is a fine update to the theme, although it's certain that Victoria's moans are indeed even wilder than Dinah's as well as these other fine ladies already accounted for.)

11. "Telephoning the Blues," Victor 38546. Victoria's phone call, also self penned, is of a suspicious nature, as she has a feeling that someone else may be visiting at her (male) friend's residence.
12. "Dirty T. B. Blues," Victor 38570. This sad tale self penned about the sick is (still) interesting and sad.

Visual Image

- The 1929 (all-black cast) of *Hallelujah* features Victoria (for about a minute or so) wailing out some good blues. They include:

15. "E I O." It's fun to hear the distinctive wailings of Victoria. Victoria is cast as the "good girl" as opposed to Nina Mae Mc Kinney as "bad girl." While it's at best mostly Nina Mae's show, the visual of Victoria is well worth noting.

Jo Stafford

Jo Stafford had been part of a sister act in Los Angeles radio since the early 1930s. As preceded by some excellent "canaries" (or female band singers) such as Kay Weber, Edythe Wright, and Anita Boyer, Jo Stafford, along with Connie Haines, became part of a newer vocal group concept, the "Pied Pipers," backing Tommy Dorsey's Orchestra. Jo became exceptionally good at bending a mellow lyric and, on occasion, led the pack with a soft and pleasing vocal tone. An addition of Frank Sinatra in 1940 made things a bit more noticeable, and by 1942, both Frank and Jo Stafford, on occasion, seemed to even dwarf Tommy and his orchestra. As (eventual) solo performers, Frank and Jo were destined for much acclaim and recognition. The following are Jo Stafford picks:

1. "For You," Victor 36399. The (original) 12-inch 78 rpm release takes some time before Jo blends in her mellow vocal on this ditty penned by Joe Burke and Al Dubin on this fine Tommy Dorsey release.
2. "Little Man with a Candy Cigar-F. T.," Victor 27338. Somehow, Jo's mellow-sounding vocal saves this ditty penned by Matt Dennis and Frank Killduff, noting not novel but stupid lyrics.
3. "A Boy in Khaki, A Girl in Lace," Victor 27947. This World War II era entity penned by Charles Newman and Allie Wrubel may be considered a real fox-trot and indeed found its way onto many contemporary ballroom floors. For those who didn't get up and slow dance, Jo's soft and mellow vocal, in true retrospective, retains its own pleasant sound. Just listen!
4. "Manhattan Serenade," Victor 27962. Jo gets in some soft vocal licks, again—as allowed by bandleader Tommy Dorsey, as this bit of fluff penned by Harold Adamson and Louis Alter succeeds.
5. "You Took My Love," Victor 20-1539. This Tommy Dorsey release penned by Tom Adair and Matt Dennis is a bit sophisticated. Seemingly, it's no problem for Jo's vocal touch, this time with a bit of prowess.

By 1944, after some notable musicians' strikes, the shift by record companies to vocals by solo and group sounds was progressing. Why shouldn't record companies save money? Why did recordings require so many musicians? Luckily, for Jo Stafford, the owner of a new recording entity Johnny Mercer had been aware of her fine vocal performances. The following picks are Capital masters by Jo Stafford:

6. "Long Ago (and Far Away)," Capital 153.
7. "It Could Happen to You," Capital 158. Penned by Johnny Burke and Jimmy Van Heusen for the contemporary 1944 film entity *And the Angels Sing*, this fine vocal recording indeed outlasts the film, as did a contemporary Bing Crosby version. A later version by June Christy defines this ditty. Listen and compare!
8. "Blues in the Night," Capital 1001. Jo, along with Johnny Mercer and the Pied Pipers, link up for this classic penned by Johnny Mercer and Harold Arlen.
9. "Candy," Capital 183. Along with Johnny Mercer and the Pied Pipers, this bit of novel and sultry singing penned by Mack David, Joan Whitney, and Alex Kramer, while full of smaltzy, ain't bad.
10. "Conversation While Dancing," Capital 195. The only thing wrong with this duet with Johnny Mercer is the (dumb) title-penned by Paul Weston and Mercer himself.
11. "A Friend of Yours," Capital 199. Forget about the contemporary Bing Crosby claimed film venture *The Great John L* and listen to this soft and mellow ditty penned by Johnny Burke and JimmyVan Heusen.
12. "That's for Me," Capital 213. Is this better than the contemporary Dick Haymes original?
13. "Ivy," Capital 388. The usual mellow sound works well for this Hoagy Carmichael-penned ditty.
14. "A Sunday Kind of Love," Capital 388. Another winner perhaps gave Jo her best ditty to record, thus far. Louis Prima's original is challenged by Jo, although a contemporary version by Ella Fitzgerald does indeed invite vocal comparisons of style. Jo or Ella?
15. "Some Enchanted Evening," Capital 544. This highbrow classic had been part of the contemporary (1949) musical *South Pacific* penned by Richard Rodgers and Oscar Hammerstein II. While recorded by countless others, Jo's vocal, not originally a

Broadway voice, defines this ditty best. Or perhaps a contemporary version by Perry Como?

16. "Diamonds Are A Girl's Best Friend," Capital 824. Penned by Jules Styne and Leo Robin for the Broadway entity of the same name, this bit of smaltzy product nevertheless found Jo's vocal to define it as a recording. As (vocally) accompanied by the "Starlighters," Jo's fine vocal lead is somewhat detracted, as the end result (still) could have been better. As a matter of fact, a later 1953 film, *Gentlemen Prefer Blondes*, found Marilyn Monroe's (dubbed?) sultry version, as on screen, doing it better?
17. "The Best Things In Life Are Free," Capital 15017. This breezy and brassy bit of free-spirited singing backed by Paul Weston's fine backing became a pleasant update, especially noting the 1927 comparison, a previous (stiff) vocal by Bob Borgen, as a 1927 George Olson release on Victor 20872.
18. "I Never Loved Anyone," Capital 15017. This slower-paced flip of "The Best Things In Life Are Free," penned by G. R. Brown is also sung well.
19. "Just Reminiscin'," Capital 15378. Backed up by the Starlighters (perhaps a clone of the Pied Pipers?), Jo produces a familiar mellow mood, as this ditty penned by Lorraine Harbin, Jimmy Shirl, and Ervin Drake scores well.

- The following three ditties were issued on the 78 rpm album: *Songs by Jo Stafford.*

20. "Over the Rainbow," Capital 20049. While Judy Garland's original remains as the best version, Jo's own soft stylistic version, sung through her nose, owes nothing to Judy. Listen and compare!
21. "Yesterdays," Capital 20050. The old 1930s standard from the film *Roberta* is given a fine update. While not as highbrow as Irene Dunne's stiff original or as definitive as Billie Holiday's more recent (1944) rendering, Jo's soft vocal, along with strings, while stiff, is pleasant enough.
22. "Carry Me Back to Old Virginny," Capital 20051. The obvious lyrics of this dated James A. Bland are dated with a typically submissive attitude toward the Southern state of Virginia, and its black citizens are perhaps a bit of confused history. Bland, an Afro-American himself, perhaps contributed to the racisms of the times, and he needed to make a buck, not considering a legacy. In any case, this stiff song entity became a huge 1915 best seller for soprano opera entity Alma Gluck on Victor 88481. This odd post-WWII attempt by Jo Stafford is stiff but somehow survives as a bit of good singing that lifts a tired bit of flawed lyrics.

- A jump to Columbia Records in 1951 found the following ditties to be of interest:

23. "Shrimp Boats," Columbia 39581. As the association with bandleader Paul Weston had (also) found a marriage between them, this ditty penned by Paul Mason Howard and Paul Weston himself produced soft and contemporary (1951) recording fodder that became a huge best seller.
24. "You Belong to Me," Columbia 39811. This ditty penned by Pee Wee King, Rodd Stewart, and Chilton Price was perhaps based upon an older 1916 operetta by Victor Herbert, *The Century Girl.* Jo's mellow and winning (1952) vocal was perhaps matched the likes of a Dean Martin rendering on Capital 2165, a Patti Page version on Mercury 5899, as well as a lesser-known version by Joni James on MGM 11295. All recordings produced the same style.

25. "Jambalaya," Columbia 39838. From out of the country came Hank Williams and his contemporary 1952 version about the Louisiana bayou on MGM 11283 had been defining and gritty. Nevertheless, this differing pop version by Jo is done well.
26. "Early Autumn," Columbia 39838. This flip side of "Jambalaya" penned by Ralph Burns, Woody Herman, and Johnny Mercer had already been a best seller for the Claude Thornhill Orchestra, with a fine vocal by Fran Warren on Columbia 37593. In comparison, perhaps the rich-voiced Jo Stafford wins out.
27. "Keep It a Secret," Columbia 39891. This very fine vocal penned by Jesse Mae Robinson was done well and no secret as a best-selling entity in 1953.
28. "Make Love to Me," Columbia 40143. Yeah, this is the right idea, as this mushy title penned Bill Norvas and A. Copeland works.
29. "Way Down Yonder in New Orleans," Columbia 40116. This (1953) duet with Frankie Laine revived the earlier (1923) best seller by vaudevillian Blossom Seeley, released on Columbia A3731, penned by the (Afro-American) team of John Turner Layton and Henry Creamer.
30. "Teach Me Tonight," Columbia 40351. (A softer alternative to the contemporary Dinah Washington version?)
31. "I Got a Sweetie," Columbia 40451. From out of the R&B field, this "stolen" gospel entity by Ray Charles, "I've Got a Woman," on Atlantic 1050, had generated some protest for Ray Charles from the black community. Jo's pop version is further tamed in "sweetie" as for gender changing. Still, Jo ain't bad. In about a year (1956), RCA released another version, hardly tamed and more so rougher than the Ray Charles original. As by Elvis Presley (another transitory figure, who, also like Ray Charles, is not covered in this book), his cannonball (vocal) delivery and raved-up finish would be issued on 45EP (EPA 747) and subsequent LP, 45 rpm and 78 rpm releases.
32. "Young and Foolish," Columbia 40495. Better than the contemporary Dean Martin title?

Kay Starr

The vocal talents of one Kay Starr (Katherine Starks), from Oklahoma, were considerable and ambitious enough. As a young radio vocalist in Memphis, Tennessee, Kay found an appetite for singing anything, which led to her association with the likes of the bandleading hogs such as Bob Crosby, Glenn Miller, and Charlie Barnet. More so, her clear vocals proved her more than able to sing with a band and indeed become a solo attraction.

- The following are Kay Starr picks:

1. "Baby Me," Bluebird 10372. A fine Glenn Miller release penned by Lou Handman, Harry Handman, and Archie Gottler. is a typical "sweet" band entity, with Kay finding (at least) a recording outlet as a fill in or relief for the (then) better known Marion Hutton, whose vocal best sellers, including "The Man with the Mandolin" on Bluebird 10358 and "The Woodpecker Song" on Bluebird 10598 became a huge part of the Glenn Miller "Sound" of the early 1940s.
2. "Love with a Capital 'You'," Bluebird 10383. Another Glenn Miller entity, somehow recorded, that sounds very danceable; it was penned by Leo Robin and Ralph Ranger.
3. "What a Diff'rence a Day Made," Decca 18620. Kay's version with Charlie Barnet's backing ain't bad. (Later, perhaps Sarah Vaughan and Dinah Washington would both do it again.)

4. "Come Out, Come Out, Wherever You Are," Decca 18620. A very fine flip side of "What a Difference a Day Made," this ditty penned by Jule Styne and Sammy Cahn provided some swing for Charlie Barnet and Kay's flawless vocal.
5. "You Always Hurt the One You Love," Decca 18638. Like its flip side (below), this ditty penned by Doris Fisher and Allen Fisher swings.
6. "Into Each Life Some Rain Must Fall," Decca 18638. The huge contrast between contemporary Ella Fitzgerald and Ink Spots version, on Decca 23356, is a curious question. Along with Charlie Barnet, Kay swings, while Ella, a huge vocal influence, does not. Go figure!
7. "Share Croppin' Blues," Decca 24264. This ditty penned by Ray Mayer and Willard Robinson is a fine urban blues item, with the backing of the very able Charlie Barnet orchestra. While it was common to sound black and sound good, this soulful rendering about Southern "sharecroppers" can also apply to poor whites. Kay lays out a lot of lyric here, and (perhaps) a soulfulness found in her American Indian heritage, like fellow Oklahoman Lee Wiley, contributes. While Kay's blues are less bold than Lee's, she's at least on par with "white" contemporaries (1944) Ella Mae Morse and Anita O'Day. A fine recording!

The following Capital (10-inch) LP was released in 1949. The former band singer found herself competing in a postwar market, attempting "rhythm and blues." Luckily, Kay's vocal abilities were up to the job, indeed competing with her contemporary (white) Capital recording artist, Ella Mae Morse. The following are picks:.

8. "Steady Daddy." This Vernon White-penned ditty found Kay emulating Billy Holiday, at least in the beginning. When the rhythm picks up, it's all Kay!
9. "You've Got to See Mama Every Night . . ." Kay's much newer electric version improves upon the earlier acoustic versions by Marion Harris, Sophie Tucker, Mamie Smith, and Lizzie Miles.
10. "Ya Gotta Buy, Buy, Buy for Baby." This gimmicky penned by Walter Kent and Walton Farrar is all about buying a woman Cadillac. Kay, more so, makes it work for her . . .
11. "Poor Papa (He's Got Nothin' At All)." This standard by Harry Woods and Billy Rose remains novel and improved upon this mid-1920s entity, including versions by Dolly Kay on Harmony 107-H and by a "Whispering" Jack Smith version on Victor 19978.
12. "You're the One I Care For." Kay takes good care of this old standard.
13. "It's the First Time (I've Given My Heart)" Did credited writers Alan Roberts and Lester Lee really mean to pen an obvious pun? An obvious pun? Kay proves she can be as slick as any contemporary, including the likes of Ella Mae Morse and Dinah Washington.
14. "Second Hand Lover." This ditty penned by Benny Carter and Paul Vance is hardly secondhand singing.
15. "Mercy, Mercy, Mercy." Kay again finds some rhythm and blues, as penned by Vernon White, to her liking and versatility.
16. "Hoop Dee Doo," Capital 20-3747. Is the contemporary (1950) Perry Como version (with the Fontaine Sisters) of this novelty improved upon?
17. "Bonaparte's Retreat," Capital 936. This ditty is country and novel. Penned for the country idiom by Pee Wee King, it is given a successful big-band approach, a dying art form for popular music in 1950, although no one realized it. Even so, it's Kay herself who sells this disk, as her crisp-clear vocal is well heard as well as sung.

18. "Wheel of Fortune," Capital 1677. This very fine 1952 pop ballad, penned by Bennie Benjamin and George Davis Weiss a huge best seller, finds Kay's emotionally pitched vocal something special, although she finds some very good competition in the Dinah Washington cover version on Mercury 8267.
19. "On a Honky Tonk Hardwood Floor," Capital 1856. This very fine country ditty is transformed into swing, thanks to Billy May, in a pre-Sinatra warm-up arraignment. Kay, as usual, is heard here at her best, as her skillful vocal prowess brightens up this ditty penned by Eddie Hazelwood and Scotty Harrell.
20. "Good-for-Nothing Joe," Modern 680. While it's a sure bet the Lena Horne's version, a Charlie Barnet entity on Bluebird 11037, still gets the nod, this version is done quite well. This seemingly live cut finds Kay starting to emulate Lena, for a time. More so, Kay's own bold embellishment of lyric about spouse beating is more than novel—it's wicked! As woman lib just may have a setback, in true retrospective, it's even more of a kick to listen for a recorded gasp of her live audience, which also gives the listeners of this ditty something to stand up and cheer for.
21. "Ain't Misbehavin'," Modern 680. As the live flip side of the "Good For Noting Joe," this well-sung version of the 1929 classic penned by Fats Waller and Andy Razaf is also something to appreciate.

Maxine Sullivan

- With her name associated with (white) bandleader, Claude Thornhill, the young and pretty (Afro- American) Maxine Sullivan offered a clear, crisp vocal style and more so the type of personality that was associated with film magazines and glamour. While Maxine did indeed appear in 1930s films, her early film image as a maid, like other contemporary 1930s black divas (with the supreme exception of Josephine Baker in French films), was not to be exploited, due to the rampant racism of the era. Fortunately, as far as a recording artist, she fared better, as Claude Thornhill, recognizing her vocal gifts above all else, made her his "canary." The following are Maxine Sullivan picks, noting many as Thornhill releases:

1. "Gone With The Wind," Vocalion 3595. This easy ballad ain't bad and not to be confused with the (later) film title as penned by Herb Magidson and Allie Wrubel.
2. "Stop! You're Breaking My Heart," Vocalion 3616. Maxine swings, rather like Ella on this ditty, and more so. Penned by Burton Lane and Ted Koehler), the easygoing Claude Thornhill backing is enough to put Maxine ahead, as her pleasant vocal indicates.
3. "Loch Lomond," Vocalion 3654. The contrived "Scottish" spirit is not lost to Claude Thornhill, as this excuse for swing finds Maxine more than capable and also sounding (vocally) for less like Ella.
4. "I'm Coming Virginia," Vocalion 3654. This update of the Ethel Waters hit of the 1927 on Columbia 14170-D adds rhythm, noting a bit of Ethel's vocal influence upon Maxine.
5. "Blue Skies," Vocalion 3679. Maxine's cheerful vocal lifts this version of the Irving Berlin-penned classic. Does Maxine's sweet vocal define this ditty?
6. "Don't Save Your Love for a Rainy Day," Brunswick 7957. While this title is more than ambiguous, it's a fine, if contrived, excuse for Claude Thornhill's Orchestra to swing, as the bright and pleasant-voiced Maxine easily explains it all. Penned by

Harold Spina and Walter Bullock, this very danceable ditty may be also noted for its perfect timing between vocalist and band.

7. "Nice Work If You Can Get It," Vocalion 3848. The Gershwin Brothers had put this ditty into a contemporary 1937 Fred Astaire film, *A Damsel in Distress*. While pleasant enough in the film (without Ginger Rogers), an awful Astaire rendering appeared on Brunswick 7983. While this ditty would remain a classic film entity, much better recordings would be produced, including a contemporary Billie Holiday vocal, with Teddy Wilson on Brunswick 8015. While noting the Billie Holiday vocal as done well, Maxine's brighter vocal is also perkier, as Maxine defines this ditty as her own.
8. "Easy To Love," Vocalion 3848. This Cole Porter classic had been somewhat crooned out by Al Bowlly, as a Ray Noble release on Victor 25422. A high-voiced Frances Langford attempt, on Decca 940, had also been tried before, with mixed results. A contemporary Billie Holiday rendering on Brunswick 7762 is jazzy enough, yet not sweet enough (vocally). Maxine's vocal is (predictably) brighter and produces more substantive style. Indeed, Maxine defines another ditty! Within a few years, Lee Wiley, in a bittersweet style, would challenge Maxine's version. Maxine or Lee?
9. "The Folks Who Live On The Hill," Vocalion 3885. Maxine's (sweet) vocal is (again) a pleasure, in this highbrow ditty penned by Oscar Hammerstein II and Jerome Kern.
10. "Darling Nellie Grey," Vocalion 3885. Maxine again excels, this time taking on tradition, as penned by Benjamin Hanby. As pre-Civil War tradition has it, this sad ditty originally noted a couple of escaped slaves, who's love story could not overcome re capture and separation-from each other. While it's a stretch that most 1930s record buyers ever consider this recording as anymore than a good love song, it's also a good bet that Maxine did know what she was singing about.
11. "Dark Eyes," Vocalion 4015. Maxine shows off her vocal gifts, like an operatic performer or perhaps as a showboater or "show off." Oddly, Maxine's vocal is in Russian, and more so, she makes this old (Czarist) Russian folk song penned by Yevhen Hrebinka (somehow) her own. A black Russian? Or Ukranian?
12. "Moments Like This," Victor 25802. This bit of mush penned by Frank Loesser and Burton Lane may be termed as so. And more so, it seems Maxine's vocal is full of good moments. Just listen!
13. "It Was A Lover and His Lass," Victor 25810. This old bit of novelty penned by Thomas Morley and William Shakespeare himself adds up to another British theme. While not another excuse to swing, this ballad is provided sweet backing as well by Maxine's sweet vocal.
14. "Down the Old Ox Road," Victor 25894. This bright-voiced trip down the "Old Ox Road" is just as breezy as Bing Crosby's original on Brunswick 6601 as well as a bit more jazzy.
15. "St. Louis Blues," Victor-25895. A soft vocal finds 'blues' bleached "pop".
16. "Say It with a Kiss," Victor 26124. In (1938), the (already) legendary Louis Armstrong and the (new) swing vocalist Maxine Sullivan herself were added to the contemporary Dick Powell film, *Going Places*, which also starred a very young Ronald Reagan. While latter-century standards would not consider this film anything special, the fact that both Louis and Maxine, who were both black, was a big deal.

While a maid, Maxine's musical part found her sharing vocals with Dick Powell and Louis on "Mutiny in the Nursery." While not involved with Louis and horse names "Jeepers Creepers" (also a song hit for Louis on Decca 2267, Maxine is given a fine ballad by Johnny Mercer and Harry Warren "Say It with a Kiss." While it's a mystery just "why" this ditty was cut from the film, the bright vocal of Maxine still may be found on her excellent recording. (An interesting and lower-toned contemporary version by Billie Holiday, backed by Teddy Wilson, on Brunswick 8270, is a fine comparison.)

17. "Kinda Lonesome," Victor 26124. Maxine is indeed lonesome, as her mellow style makes it all work for this ditty penned by Leo Robin and Sam Coslow for the (1938) film *St. Louis Blues*, which had featured Dorothy Lamour, along with Maxine. Lamour's own contemporary release of this same song ditty on Brunswick 8304 offers a similar soft vocal style, indeed good comparisons with Maxine's.
18. "It Ain't Necessarily So," Victor 26132. The 1935 ditty penned by Gershwin brothers and Du Bose Heyward was indeed a classic. As a Broadway entity for *Porgy and Bess*, this mixed bag of stereotyping dialog and lyric had not been accepted by many (black) contemporaries. As the originals by black Todd Duncan and John Bubbles had found their way on to a recording, on Brunswick 7562, the predictable stiffness of Broadway lingered. Moreover, a fine contemporary 1936 Bing Crosby version, on Decca 806, while serious enough, was better. Perhaps it's Maxine's own bright vocal style, considering a moody and gloomy lyric, that makes her version work best. While noting the ditty had originally been about Afro-Americans, penned by nonblacks, its obvious attempt at moodiness had been its chief asset, until Maxine had recorded it! While fences of race are noted, this has to be noted, at least until listening.
19. "Night and Day," Victor 26132. Maxine's vocal is far better than the Fred Astaire original, on Victor 24193, which is not much on Astaire's part. In true retrospective, a contemporary Frank Sinatra version, on Bluebird 11463, is fine competition for Maxine, who also did his best for this (Cole Porter) classic.
20. "I'm Happy About the Whole Thing," Victor 26237. Backed by Claude Thornhill, Maxine gets happily involved into a smooth and jazzy mood, as this ditty penned by Johnny Mercer and Harry Warren is effective and "happy" enough.
21. "Corn Pickin'," Victor 26237. Despite its dumb title, this ditty penned by Johnny Mercer and Harry Warren again provides with something smooth, noting most importantly, Maxine's own sweet and smooth style.
22. "The Hour of Parting," Columbia 36341. Maxine's vocalizing by (1940) usually found slow and cool-sounding ditties, as this one by Sammy Cahn and Mischa Spoliansky had European origins. While no German is spoken here, the title, also known as 'Old Berlin Schlanger', was the perfect type of contemporary juke box fodder for smoky jazz night clubs.
23. "Midnight," Bluebird B-11288. With this ditty (1941), Maxine becomes a band singer for (Afro-American) "Benny Carter and His Orchestra." While perhaps a step down for her as a singing entity, this bit of cool swing penned by Johnny Gomez and Charlie Parker is an effective bit of jive, however contrived.
24. "Just Like a Gypsy," Decca 3954. This update of the 1919 (acoustic) Nora Bayes release, on Columbia 6138, penned by Seymour Simons and Nora Bayes herself is more than good.
25. "My Blue Heaven," Decca 4154. This update of the Gene Austin release, on Victor 20964, sounds crisp and bright, which, in itself, defines the Maxine Sullivan touch.
26. "My Curly-Haired Baby," Decca 18349. This ditty had been a popular early 1900s 'coon' song; as "Little Nigger Baby", penned by George H. Clutson. Speculation also has it that this nursery rhyme had been adapted by Clutson from old 'cowboy' times, before he changed it? By the time Maxine rendered it, with obvious title change, her tender vocal became very endering-as well as an end to racism.

27. "My Ideal," Decca 18555. This update of the (already) old Maurice Chevalier ditty, is done well!.
28. "When Your Lover Has Gone," Decca 18555. A fine update of the Ethel Waters classic on Columbia 2409-D.

Visual Image

Like all (black) performers, Maxine was limited for screen appearances, although in the 1930s, she lucked out. As already noted in the text above, the young Maxine may be seen and heard in the 1938 film *Going Places*, with Louis Armstrong swinging out on:

29. "Mutiny in the Nursery."

Eva Taylor

The success achieved by the arrival of the (black) blues queens of the early 1920s, was also a mixed bag, with white vaudevillian influences, mixed with blues, as well as the playing of jazz and blues, noting the vocals could also be Afro-American. Perhaps one of the best known and versatile voices among the new wave was Eva Taylor, also known as Irene Gibbons. Like Ethel Waters, her fine and (very dry) vocals did not restrict her to blues and was more so a jazz entity, who was capable of performing any kind of material. While, for sure, the fact that her husband was the popular musician, bandleader, and music publisher Clarence Williams, had given her some fine advantages and material, her subsequent change from acoustic renderings to electric was more so successful, demonstrating her own vocal prowess and abilities.

Picks include:

- Note: "Vocal Chorus by Eva Taylor," on "Clarence Williams" "Blue Five" releases, or "Eva Taylor" And Clarence Williams "Blue Five."

1. "I Wish I Could Shimmy Like My Sister Kate," Okeh 4740. This (1922) recording of this danceable popular ditty, credited as penned by Afro-American (Armond J. Piron) indeed had pop aspirations noting the limits of the acoustic age. Moreover, the origins of this ditty may have been as an earlier New Orleans brothel entity, perhaps penned by Louis Armstrong as "Get Off Katie's Head," who subsequently sold it to Clarence Williams and Piron. The newer and somewhat cleaned up lyrics by Piron where more so to become a hot contemporary item, as well as a bankable dance band specialty. (The publishing interests of Clarence Williams should also be considered, which also figured into most of Eva's subsequent recordings.)
2. "Baby, Won't You Please Come Home?" Okeh 4740. This flip side of "I Wish I Could Shimmy Like My Sister Kate" again features Clarence Williams on piano as backup. Penned by Charles Warfield and Clarence Williams, this classic perhaps finds its true (vocal) jazz origins with Eva. (Bessie Smith would later claim it, so would many others, including a hipper group version by the Mills Brothers. More so would Annette Hanshaw as "Daddy, Won't You Please Come Home?")

For some, this ditty may have been similar to the older, turn of the century rag-time era best selling entity as penned by Hughie Cannon "Bill Bailey Wont You Pleae Come

Home" or as "Wont You Come Home Bill Bailey"? The 1902 ditty had indeed caused a stir on sheet music and on records and cylinder, including releases as by Dan Quinn on Victor-Monarch-1411, Arthur Collins on Edison-8112 and by Silas Lechman on Victor-Monarch—1458. (Lizzie Miles would later define "Bill Bailey Won't You Please Come Home" as a 'dixieland" song years later in the in the 1950s).

3. "You Missed a Good Woman When You Picked All Over Me," Okeh 8047. While (very) and ambiguous, this Clarence Williams-penned ditty is clever and novel enough.
4. "Last Go Around Blues," Columbia A-3834. As Irene Gibbons, this bit of blues, penned by Jimmy Cox, is far from being "last."
5. "That Da Da Strain," Columbia A-3834. As a hot dance item in the early 1920s, this dated approach to pop, in true retrospective, can be considered jazz. Penned by Mamie Medina and J. Edgar Dowell, this hard-to-hear acoustic classic had also been recorded by Ethel Waters on Black Swan 2021.
6. "You Can Have My Man," Okeh 8050. This ditty is actually an "answer" record, as its own perhaps origins had found the previous Edith Wilson renderings "He May Be Your Man (But He Comes to See Me Sometimes)," on Columbia A-3653, and "He Used to Be Your Man (But He's My Man Now)," on Columbia A-3787 well worth hearing, with vocal comparisons.
7. "Twelfth Street Rag," Okeh 4805. Euday L. Bowman's 1914 term "rag" had by the time of this 1923 recording been replaced by jazz, but this hot dance number is done well, by contemporary acoustical standards.
8. "Golf Coast Blues," Okeh 3055. The somewhat later Bessie Smith rendering on Columbia A-3844 became better known, in true retrospective, but it's a fine vocal by Eva and deserves a listening matchup, considering Bessie's shouting vocal style. Listen and compare, noting that Bessie is backed by Clarence Williams on piano, as well as holding the contemporary publishing rights. (Who says that only white publishers could play games with controlling interests? Or was Clarence just a good businessman?)
9. "Oh, Daddy Blues," Okeh 4927. This fine novel vocal duet, between Clarence Williams and Eva is perhaps a step more than the previous Ethel Waters "Oh, Daddy" (solo) on Black Swan 2010.
10. "I've Got the Yes! We Have No Banana Blues," Okeh 4927. The Eddie Cantor hit on Columbia A-3964 had been a popular answer for a contemporary Irving Kaufman vocal as a Ben Selvin release on Vocalion 14590, as well as a Billy Jones version on Edison 51183 and other labels. More so, the versatile Eva vocal ain't bad, considering the acoustic limits.
11. "Do It a Long Time, Papa," Okeh 8073. This title says it all—even for latter-century rap. Penned by W. Benton Overstreet, this 1923 entity suffers only from the poor technology of what was then acoustic. Having learned to overcome all this can be fun, as Eva's wild message, explicitly noted in the title, is convincing and intriguing.
12. "Tired of Waiting Blues," Okeh 8084. A fine duet with contemporary blues queen Sarah Martin.
13. "Old-Fashioned Love," Okeh 8114. This bit of sentimental smaltzy is almost ruined as Eva gets involved in a duet with the semi-operatic voice of Lawrence Lomax. Contemporary Alberta Hunter would produce a better (1924) version, as would Frank Crumit. Listen and compare.

14. "Jazzin' Babies Blues," Okeh 8129. The earlier Ethel Waters version on Black Swan 1417 finds Eva's flat vocal and better acoustics an interesting comparison. Listen and compare!
15. "Everybody Loves My Baby," Okeh 8181. This classic 1924 jazz ditty as a "Clarence Williams Blue Five," penned by Jack Palmer and Spencer Williams, gave Eva a limited but still important vocal chore. Oddly, a contemporary Red Onion Jazz Babies release on Gennett 5594, with a vocal by Josephine Beatty (actually Alberta Hunter), was also cut at the same time, changing vocalists (Eva to Alberta) as well as band names (Clarence Williams Blue Five to Red Onion Jazz Babies. For the purposes of this book, the vocal differences between Eva and Alberta find Alberta, while excellent, a bit tight.
16. "Terrible Blues," Okeh 8183. While this (terribly) dated vocal duet with (author) Clarence Williams is also crude, Eva's vocal, along with a strumming banjo, retains interest.
17. "Mandy, Make Up Your Mind," Okeh 40260. A fine and popular Broadway entity, penned by Geo. W. Meyer, Arthur Johnston, Grant Clark, and Roy Turk for the Broadway production *Dixie to Broadway*, this highbrow entity was ably challenged by Eva. By contemporary (1925) acoustical standards, it ain't bad.
18. "I'm a Little Blackbird Looking for a Bluebird," Okeh 40260. This bit of acoustic pop is encouraging. As a stage entity, penned by Grant Clarke, Roy Turk, George W. Meyer, and Arthur Johnston, this ditty had been introduced in 'Black Birds' by Afro-American dynamo Florence Mills. Just "why" Florence Mills never produced any commercial recordings is unclear, but this rendering by Eva, who was perhaps deep in admiration of Mills, is indeed done with class.

For most contemporaries of the era, Florence was considered most talanted Afro-American entity in the mid-1920s. As part of the "Panama Trio" before World War I (based upon Chicago's Panama nightspot), she was part of a spirited group that included Cora Green and redheaded Ada Smith, later known as "Bricktop." By the early 1920s, while both Cora and Ada found vaudeville and Broadway success, Florence was "found" by white producer Lew Leslie, who made her a star and very well known in Europe. It's also very odd that all three of these successful women who sang did not produce any well-known recordings, if any. Florence's subsequent early death due to appendix in 1927 was a huge shock as well as a well-attended funeral, rivaling the funeral of contemporary film entity Rudolph Valentino's the year before in 1926. Among others, popular tenor Vernon Dalhart's contemporary recording on Victor 20193, "There's a New Star in Heaven Tonight," penned by Keirn Brennan, Jimmy McHugh, and Irving Mills, was indeed a solemn piece of commercial work, something that 'country' entity Gene Autry would also subsequently emulation after the 1933 death of the popular rural entity, Jimmie Rodgers,. (Eva's own tribute recording about Florence Mills is noted below—pick no. 29.)

19. "Cake Walking Babies from Home," Okeh 40321. This bit of Afro-American slang had found its own history since slavery times. As a bit of observation, black servants found white socialization, with slow dancing and alcohol, somewhat amusing. After a bit of time, many servants in back rooms would emulate, embellish, and poke fun between themselves. This (1925) Clarence Williams Blue Five release had found Alberta Hunter's previous rendering, about a month before, as Josephine Beatty release with the Red Onion Jazz Babies, something to start with as well as to be embellished. As luck would have it, its jazzy message, considering Eva's limited vocal,

like Alberta, is well worth it, moreover, among interested white listeners, a cultural revelation.

20. "Get It Fixed," Okeh 8267. A playful Eva is novel and sexy, noting some risqué lyric from Clarence Williams in a positive way.
21. "Shake That Thing," Okeh 8267. The well-done Papa Charlie Jackson ditty, on Paramount 12281, had at least found Eva's attempt interesting enough but strangely tame. A bit later, a smoking Ethel Waters version, on Columbia 14116-D would more so define this ditty.
22. "I've Found a New Baby," Okeh 8286. This classic vocal had found a contemporary Ethel Waters version on Columbia 561-D perhaps even more jazzy. A contemporary Josephine Baker version recorded in France is also done well, although it's a good bet that neither Eva or Ethel were aware of Josephine's claims upon this fine bit of jazz.
23. "Charleston Hound," Okeh 40655. This attempt at a vocal for the dominate and lasting national dance craze of the "Roaring Twenties" had its origins, as an instrumental in the 1923 (black) review *"Running Wild."* As an instrumental, it was wildly danced by Elisabeth Welch, (later) to be important as a vocalist. As credited to the highly accomplished Afro-American pianist (James P. Johnson), it was to be further fueled by a contemporary 1925 Paul Whiteman instrumental release on Columbia 19671. While "hound" is for some not the same, the high-strung vocal by Eva is a danceable ditty and moreover articulate enough, for some, to guess if Eva is awhite flapper? More so, if the "Charleston" did want for contemporary lyrics, this ditty, penned by Fats Waller, Spencer Williams ans Clarence Williams is indeed a pleasant solution, as well as an excuse to get up and dance.
24. "When the Red, Red Robin Comes Bob, Bob, Bobbin' Along," Okeh 40671. This contemporary yet hardly known version of the contemporary 1926 Al Jolson best seller, on Brunswick 3222, more so defined Eva's own pop aspirations. Jolson had more ever introduced this silly ditty in the contemporary 'sound' film short 'Plantation Days" in blackface. In retrospective, the 'real' black face of Eva deliveres an improved (real blackfaced) performace of the happy but so-so song ditty penned by Harry Woods.
25. "Nobody but My Baby Is Getting My Love," Okeh 8407. Jazzy? Rhythmic? While dated, this danceable ditty, penned by Clarence Williams and Andy Razaf, perhaps focuses upon a flapper who could put over a 1926 contemporary tune!
26. "Candy Lips, I'm Stuck on You," Okeh 8414. This novel 'flapper' but clumsy 1926 ditty. penned by Jack Laurie and Mike Jackson is a bit rhythmic as well as pure and smaltzy dance number. Moreover, it works as another serious claim for Eva as a 'pop' entity or yet another firm excuse to get up and dance.
27. "If I Could Be with You," Okeh 8444. This ditty penned by Henry Creamer and Jimmy Johnson would also be known as "If I Could Be with You One Hour Tonight." Backed by "Clarence Williams Blue Five," this slow tempo could be another attempt at pop. Its jazzy background leads Eva's somewhat dry vocal to a somewhat mixed level of listening (1927). So would later notable versions. Within some years (1929), a raved-up best seller version by "McKinney's Cotton Pickers" scored. This recording included Don Redman, Coleman Hawkins, Fats Waller, Bill McKinney, and a vocal by band member George Thomas on Victor 38118. Another group version, with a vocal by bandleader George Lee, of "the George Lee Orchestra" on Brunswick 7132, also ain't bad. Julia Lee, a future 1940s R&B entity is to be heard only on piano on this disk. Another.version, as a huge contemporary best seller for Louis Armstrong, on Okeh 41448, whose changing slow to mid-tempo phrasing was to be something

expected. A Marion Harris version on Brunswick 4873, ain't bad. Moreover, a Ruth Etting version, on Columbia 2300-D, was also recorded, and perhaps her usual and expected medium to fast-paced attack on lyrics better defines this ditty.

28. "Red Hot Flo from Ko-Ko-Mo," Okeh 8463. While this ditty officially finds another lady to be a flapper, this rhythmic ditty, however dated, is successfully sung in a jazzy style. Just how hot is Flo? Does her doctor know? Is there anything she doesn't know? And what about the butcher, the baker, and the candlestick maker? Just listen!
29. "She's Gone to Join the Song Birds in Heaven," Okeh 8518. Florence Mills had been considered the brightest (black) entity on (segregated) Broadway as well as in London, where she had been seen and appreciated on tour. This tribute, while a bit slow and (even) a bore, is significant enough, as the event of Florence Mill's death in 1927 had been a huge event within the Afro-American community.
30. "Jeannie I Dream of Lilac Time," Columbia 14362-D. This fluffy and smaltzy ditty had been part of a previous (pre-jazz) era and had been somewhat revived by a (dull) 1928 Gene Austin best seller on Victor 21564. Just why Eva recorded this ditty is a mystery, as she makes no attempt to improvise. Moreover, the attempt at versatility still retains interest, as Eva again proves, as a vocalist, that she can take on any material and do a competent rendering.
31. "I'm Busy and You Can't Come In," Columbia 14362-D. This original flip side of "Jeannie I Dream of Lilac Time," penned by Clarence Williams, finds Eva in jazzier territory. Perhaps backed by the likes of Joe "King Oliver, Omer Simeon, Eddie Lang, and Clarence himself, this ditty is suspect by other versions." As by "Boot It" Wiggins on Paramount 12662, as "Keep A-Knockin' (but You Can't Come In)" Eva's ditty is tame, although far from lame. Later interest in this ditty by Louis Jordan and (light years later) by Little Richard may also be noted with the same speculation.

➢ The following are "Charlestown Chasers" releases, a white band, with various members at different times, was a free-spirited jazz group. The following six titles are (very) much unlike anything Eva had previously attempted. Although regulated as a band singer, largely unaccredited, these sides are smoking, with Eva's vocals adding even more power and punch.

32. "Ain't Misbehavin'," Columbia 1891-D. This hot vocal of the Fats Waller and Andy Razaf Broadway entity *Hot Chocolates* is indeed jazzed up as no other version. Indeed, a contemporary Louis Armstrong version, among others, is also hot, and while Louis's own horn should also be noted, Eva's vocal is even hotter. Other versions of the ditty were also notable, including a fair Vaughn De Leath version, along with one by Gene Austin. More so is a noted Ruth Etting version, which is sung sweet and turned into an effective bit of a (mushy) torch song.
33. "Moaning Low," Columbia 1891-D. The excellent original Libby Holman version is very much challenged, as Eva matches Libby with a sultry voice of her own. A tie?
34. "Turn on the Heat," Columbia 1989-D. Yeah, she does indeed! This jazzy ditty penned by Buddy De Sylva, Lew Brown, and Ray Henderson had been introduced by Sharon Lynn as an elaborate singing and dance sequence in the contemporary 1929 film *Sunny Side Up*. While it's true that 'flapper'Eva shows no leg in this recording, did her hot vocal inspire her bandmates to play it all a bit harder?
35. "What Wouldn't I Do for That Man?" Columbia 1989-D. Eva competes well with a fine contemporary Ruth Etting torch version on Columbia 1998-D.

36. "You're Lucky to Me," Columbia 2309-D. Eva at least matches the contemporary 1930 Ethel Waters torch version on Columbia 2288-D.
37. "Loving You the Way I Do," Columbia 2309-D. This Eubie Blake and Jack Scholl penned ditty is hot! It is also hotter when Eva, in free style 'flapper'style succeeds!
38. "My Man Is on the Make," Columbia 2067-D. While this ditty penned by Richard Rogers and Lorenz Hart had been introduced as a Broadway entity by Libby Holman, its jazzy backings and fine Holman vocal are far from dull. Moreover, despite a perky and contemporary Helen Kane version, Eva's version, on a Knickerbockers release, a white group, on Columbia 2067-D perhaps defines this ditty most as a jazz vocal.
39. "When I'm Housekeeping for You," Columbia 2072-D. Another bright and jazzy backing by the (white) Kolster Dance Orchestra finds Eva improving upon some stupid lyrics, and finds a "sweet band" vocal style much to her advantage.
40. "What Makes You Love Me So," Victor V38575. This somewhat pop vocal is somewhat sophisticated, and the capable Eva again pulls off another winner.
41. "You Don't Understand," Victor V38575. Another somewhat pop ditty is greatly enhanced by Eva's cool and jazzy vocal.
42. "Shout, Sister, Shout," Okeh 8821. This classic bit of jazz penned by J. Tim Byran, Alex Hill, and Clarence Williams himself is done well. An even jazzier Boswell Sisters version on Brunswick 6109 would later define it.

- ➢ The following two are "Riffers" releases. As a group sound, with Lil Hardin and Clarence Williams, it's interesting to note a vocal introduction by Clarence. Could this have originally been a radio transcription from a local (New York City) broadcast made into a commercial release? Just listen!

43. "Say It Isn't So; Papa De-Da Da," Columbia 14677-D. As a Riffers release, the vocals of Eva, Lil Hardin, and Clarence Williams are somewhat hidden. Nevertheless, this odd combination of the Irving Berlin "Say It Isn't So" and Clarence Williams "Papa De-Da-Da" ditties find Eva's lead vocal, scatting by Lil and some incidental voice by Clarence, an excellent combination.
44. "Rhapsody in Love." (Columbia-14677-D). As penned by (Clarence Williams), this light vocal approach is crooned out well. As another Riffers release, Eva's vocal lead is backed by a scatting performance by Lil Hardin (formerly married to Louis Armstrong), noting a scatting style that is soft in approach. More so, this is an effective crooning job! Listen!
45. "Chizzlin' Sam," Columbia 2829-D. As with "Clarence Williams Jug Band," Eva's vocal part is a welcome voice, perhaps joined by Lil Hardin.
46. "Uncle Sammy, Here I Am," Bluebird B-11368. It's almost a decade since "Chizzlin' Sam" and the World War II year of 1942. Patriotic? Just listen! Forgotten until found by this author.

- ➢ The filmed image of Eva Taylor is hard to find, although her success on commercial New York City (local) radio in the 1920s and 1930s is well known. It is also obvious that Eva should have seen more success, and it's worth speculating that, besides racism, the controlling interests of husband and musical publisher perhaps contained her from doing other opportunities as well as recording fodder.

Sister Rosetta Tharpe

- The (commercial) success of (previous) 1920s recording entities of "race music" had found the secular spiritual somewhat misplaced. While the efforts of many had found their way on to recordings, perhaps it had been personalities such as Arizona Dranes, Memphis Minnie, and Tom Dorsey (a converted blues man) who influenced (young) Rosetta as recording entities.

Rosetta's recording legacy (1936 and up) is one of a self-infectious beat, with clear-spoken worded vocals that are so personal that one may just want to stand up and cheer. Rosetta doesn't have to be novel or create a mood, as her performances are sheer energy, even on ballads. More so than (even) fellow vocal-guitarist Lonnie Johnson, Rosetta found (commercial) acceptance (despite even some resistance from traditional (black) churches) in the world of popular music. Indeed, the likes of (bandleaders) Cab Calloway and (especially) Lucky Millinder welcomed her. Rosetta's appeal, although mostly involved by choice in the secular, in true retrospective, would very much influence the rock generation to come, as heard in many vocals in her uninhibited style as well as upon (any) modern guitarists heard on her recordings. Picks are:

1. "The Lonesome Road," Decca 2243. This ditty from the 1920s, a Gene Austin release on Victor 21098, was subsequently rendered by many, including a hip version by Louis Armstrong. Rosetta's (even later) earthy vocal, sung in her usual high pitch, with more than a medium-tempo barrage of lyric, churns out of a fine sound. Better than all other versions?
2. "Rock Me," Decca 2243. This flip side of "The Lonesome Road" is another gem penned by Thomas A. Dorsey—"Georgia Tom," but it's still Rosetta who rocks (1938), which was plenty of time before anyone else did.

3, 4. "That's All," Decca 2503. (a) This self-penned ditty is most likely based upon a lot of folklore. A later Merle Travis rendering is no fluke. A shared culture in a segregated society? (b) Another version with contemporary bandleader Lucky Millender on Decca 18496 is less of a a folk ballad and more of an attempt at swing, which, in retrospective, is more of a prerock era statement! Who knew?

5. "This Train," Decca 2558. This self-penned ditty sounds as if its (actual) origins from pre-Civil War days. In any case, Rosetta and her guitar take the listener on a rocking trip, perhaps to the Promised Land itself. (This ditty just may have been Willie Dixon's penned inspiration for "My Babe" on Checker 811, an excellent Little Walter 1950s blues entity.)
6. "Sit Down," Decca 8538. This traditional spiritual won't let (the listener) "sit down." Perhaps its origins are as primitive as the south land was, but this earthy sound, without background orchestration of vocal backup, is true. More so, so real that one could be transported to a Mississippi porch! Indeed, a fine recording.
7. "Stand by Me," Decca 8548. This Thomas A. Dorsey-penned ditty, straight from Chicago's transplanted black sharecroppers of the south, would become part of the standard gospel tradition, for both black and white churches. Many other artist have indeed recorded this classic, although none are as fast-paced, or as rocking. More so Rosetta's approach, with her crisp and clear vocal, is more of a handclapping dance and indeed inspiring.

8. "There Is Something within Me," Decca 8548. The differences between (early) spirituals, which expressed hope, and those of the blues, which expressed despair, are clearly found within this ditty, as penned by K. B. Nubin and Rosetta herself.
9. "Just a Closer Walk with Thee," Decca 8594. Rosetta's rocking (with guitar) is very much infectious.
10. "Pure Religion," Decca 8634. More rockin' and more talking about a train, as this traditional ballad was the basis of (faster-paced) "This Train," the above pick. Moreover, this slower ride is still worth the trip!
11. "All Over This World," Decca 8639. This traditional (blues) theme is sure to note that "moaning" just might be over, indeed all "All Over This World." Blues?
12. "Singing in My Soul," Decca 8672. Penned by Katie Bell and Rosetta herself, this reference to "soul" had not originally been a referral to the (later) musical term. Nevertheless, this ditty more so does have claims upon the term.
13. "I Claim Jesus First," Decca 8672. This rocking ditty, with guitar, piano, and drum backing, in the prerock era, more so really does claim "Jesus" first. Just listen!
14. "Rock Daniel," Decca 3956. As a vocalist with (swing-band) Lucky Millinder's Orchestra, this (contrived) example of religion and "swing," finds Rosetta sounding much more like Ella Fitzgerald, that her (usual) earthy self. Penned by K. B. Nubin and Rosetta herself), this ditty still works, noting its stab at commercialism.
15. "Shout, Sister, Shout," Decca 18386. Rosetta's no slouch at swing, as this Lucky Millinder release resurrects the Clarence Williams ditty into something that (even) rivals likes the previous recordings featuring the likes of Eva Taylor and the Boswell Sisters.
16. "I Want a Tall Skinny Papa," Decca 18386. Another Lucky Millinder side finds Rosetta's slick vocal on a Millinder-penned excuse to swing ditty, backed up with great (if contrived) rhythm and band members, providing occasional group vocals.
17. "Strange Things Happening Each Day," Decca 48009.

    ➢ "Gospel Hymns," Sister Rosetta Tharpe, Decca A-527, Decca 48009. This 78 rpm album (1943) is a fine group of religious ditties, straight out of the black idiom. "Vocal with guitar, piano, bass, and drums." Indeed, this could have claims as the first rock album, as its rhythmic vocal and prominent guitar licks indicate. All eight titles are penned or adapted by Rosetta Tharpe, unless noted. (The traditional "God Don't Like It" is a rerecording.)

18. "Forgive Me, Lord, and Try Me One More Time." This bit of religious fever was penned by Katie Bell. Decca (72379).
19. "Jesus Taught Me How to Smile" Decca (72378.)
20. "God Don't Like It," Decca 48022. This ditty about the evils of drinking (moon-shine) had much rural appeal. As much as a folk entity as anything recorded by contemporaries Woody Guthrie or Josh White, this traditional ditty is also betrayed by its age. Moreover, it's much like Blind Willie Johnson's (1928) "God Don't Never Change," on Columbia 14490-D, which ain't a bad thing.
21. "What Is the Soul of a Man?" Decca 48022. (72380) penned by Katie Bell.
22. "Let That Liar Along," Decca 48023, penned by Taylor (71523).
23. "What's the News?" Decca 48023 (72016).
24. "Nobody Knows Nobody Cares," Decca 48024 (72377).
25. "The Devil Has Thrown Him Down," Decca 48024 (71524).

26. "Up Above My Head I Hear Music in the Air," Decca 48090. As by "Sister Rosetta Tharpe and Marie Knight with Sam Price Trio," this fast-paced duet (with Marie Knight) could have been rooted in an urban Chicago church, among other such places or worship.
27. "White Christmas," Decca 48119. The (Irving Berlin) penned classic is performed with much vocal depth and soul. It is more so noted on its original label release as "Gospel singing with Celeste, Drums and Bass."
28. "Silent Night," Decca 48119. The traditional Christmas ditty is given a vocal approach, as it had never been attempted before (1942). As backed by the "Rosette Gospel Singers," this secular vocal performance snuck into the popular mainstream, with huge stylistic differences. In true retrospective, this performance would become well excepted as an accepted vocal rendering, but it would take many years, well into the rock era, to become realized.
29. "Have a Little Talk with Jesus," Decca 29505. This (unusual) duet with country entity Red Foley, penned by Cleavent Derricks, ain't bad. (Integration in the church!)

- More on Rosetta Sharpe in the radio and LP sections of this book.

Martha Tilton

Following the lead of Helen Ward, who left Benny Goodman's Orchestra in 1936, Martha Tilton found Goodman a tough taskmaster, as Ward did. Luckily, Martha was up to the challenge, as her vocal was as clear as Helen's, with good looks to boot. She also was familiar with Helen Ward's pioneering radio sound, that, when given the chance, was heard very well. The following are Martha Tilton picks:

1. "Mama, That Moon Is Here Again," Victor 25720. This ditty penned by Leo Robin and Ralph Rainger also find Martha improving upon a filmed novelty ditty as introduced by Martha Raye in *The Big Broadcast of 1938*.
2. "You Took the Words Right Out of My Mouth," Victor 25720. Another ditty penned by Leo Robin and Ralph Rainger from *The Big Broadcast of 1938* is given the "Goodman" drill, fortunately along with Martha.
3. "I Let a Song Get Out of My Heart," Victor 25840. This ditty penned by Duke Ellington, Irving Mills, John Redman and Henry Nemo again finds Martha more than capable. (A contemporary Connie Boswell version is interesting enough, considering that Connie had been a vocal influence for Martha.)
4. "Why'd Ya Make Me Fall in Love?" Victor 25846. The Walter Donaldson-penned ditty swings.
5. "This Can't Be Love," Victor 26099. This may be Martha's best vocal, as this contemporary ditty penned by Richard Rogers and Lorenz Hart, from Broadway's *The Boys from Syracuse* is best introduced to the general public. A contemporary Adelaide Hall version in comparison is very highbrow. Later, in the 1950s, both Nat Cole and Judy Garland would attempt to define this ditty.
6. "Sing for Your Supper," Victor 26099. Another ditty penned by Richard Rogers and Lorenz Hart from the Broadway entity *The Boys from Syracuse* finds excellent recording fodder for Martha!

7. “And the Angels Sing,” Victor 26170. A contemporary Count Basie release, featuring Helen Humes, also swings. It’s also interesting to compare Martha’s and Helen’s vocals, which differ in tone, but not in excellence. Listen!

   - After leaving Goodman, Martha continued to record, along with becoming a huge radio entity.

8. “Easy Street,” Decca 3841. Backed by Gordon Jenkins, this Alan Rankin Jones-penned ditty finds Martha producing some quality recording fodder.
9. “There’s Good Blues Tonight,” Capital 244. Penned by Abe Osser and Edna Osser, this 1946 ditty has the bright Martha again scoring. It’s interesting to compare this vocal with a contemporary Tommy Dorsey release with a Sy Oliver vocal on Victor 20-1842 and, more importantly, with a contemporary Les Brown release on Columbia 36972, featuring a fine Doris Day vocal. (Yet another aspect to this ditty, is a contemporary 1946 film short, featuring Martha’s very capable sister, Liz Tilton. So far, this author cannot find a contemporary matching recording, as by Liz).
10. “You Make Me Feel So Young,” Capital 272. Maybe contemporary Dick Haymes got it right, but Martha is also superb. (So is Frank Sinatra, noting his defining version recorded over a decade later.)

Visual Image

11. “Say It with Love,” Film Master 1944. Penned by Jay Livingston, Ray Evans, and Lewis Ballin for this low-budget flick, this ditty rivals any big production, especially highlighting Martha’s great looks, with her voice to match (*Swing Hostess*, 1944).
12. “A Little Jive Is Good for You.” Penned by Sam Coslow and Josef Berne, this ditty was sung finding hot-looking Martha in a nurse’s uniform instructing her patients to get up and dance! (Soundie: 1941)

Dick Todd

This recording artist, like fellow Canadian-born Helen Morgan, had a huge impact upon American popular music before 1950. First known as the “Canadian Crosby” on Canadian radio, his vocal style of crooning may indeed be attributed directly to Bing Crosby’s commercial success. Subsequent successful recordings and radio identification in the United States between the latter 1930s-1940s did indeed highlight his fine vocal attributes. The following are picks:

1. “As Long as We’re Together,” Victor 25843. Todd’s warm crooning on this ditty penned by Cliff Friend and Dave Franklin is well worth noting his admitted debt to Bing Crosby.
2. “So Help Me,” Victor 26004. It’s another well-crooned job penned by Eddie De Lange and Jimmy Van Heusen, yet more so a hidden (1938) Larry Clinton release that makes this interesting listening.
3. “Change Partners,” Victor 26010. Ginger Rogers had introduced this ditty in the contemporary (1938) film *The Yam*. More interesting, however, is Dick Todd’s croon on this Larry Clinton compared to a contemporary croon as heard on a contemporary Ozzie Nelson release of the Irving Berlin-penned ditty.
4. “Sixty Seconds Got Together,” Victor 26057. A Mills Brothers rendering provides interesting comparisons.

5. "Thanks for the Memory," Bluebird B-7434. Originally conceived as a film entity for *The Big Broadcast of 1938*, this ditty penned by Leo Robin and Ralph Rainger had been released as the B side of "Two Sleepy People" on Decca 2219, with vocals from Bob Hope and Shirley Ross, who had introduced both ditties in the film. Moreover, a subsequent film *Thanks for the Memory* would star Hope and Ross.

An A side contemporary (1938) Shep Fields release, with a vocal by Bob Goday, became a best seller on Bluebird B-7318. For many, Dick's croon *was* Bing Crosby's contemporary version, although no one knew at the time that this ditty would stay with Bob Hope as his theme song on radio, personal appearances, and the (later) media of baby boomer television.

6. "Love Walked In," Bluebird B-7446. A lesser known Gershwin Brothers ditty that needed defining?
7. "Gardenias," Montgomery Ward M-7554. Another well-done soft croon find this smaltzy ditty penned by Harold Lawrence, Barry Nieson, and Jay Milton questions a preference for gardenias over roses? Cheaper?
8. "Deep Purple," Bluebird B-10072. While many versions exist, this rendering finds interesting and similar comparisons with the vocal influence of Bing Crosby, whose contemporary release on Decca 2372 was (also) an excellent croon. Dick or Bing?
9. "Penny Serenade," Bluebird B-10144. Penned by Hal Halifax and Melle Weersma, this fine (1939) excuse for a mid-tempo rumba is more so complimented by Dick's crooning. This ditty should *not* be confused with the weepy (1941) film of the same name, which starred Cary Grant and Irene Dunne.
10. "I Get Along without You Very Well," Bluebird B-10150. While a well-done Terry Allen vocal for a contemporary 1939 Red Novo rendering does exist, on Vocalion 4648, this well-crafted Hoagy Carmichael-penned ditty was defined by Todd, at least until the 1950s, when a supreme Frank Sinatra effort on LP Capital W-581 was released.! Dick or Frank?
11. "At a Little Hot Dog Stand," Bluebird 10183. It's not hard to speculate that this stupid title penned by Sam Coslow and Larry Spier could describe a cheap date! In any case, any listener of this ditty will find it pleasant enough and perhaps looking for a snack. Get one!
12. "You've Got Me Crying Again," Bluebird B-10217. Yet another (favorable) comparison with Bing Crosby may be found on Brunswick 6515.
13. "Blue Evening," Bluebird B-10234. This ditty penned by Gordon Jenkins and Joe Bishop may just be Dick's very best rendering. This husky voiced baritone vocal is truly fine, and by this time, 1939, it should be noted that Bing Crosby had effectively abandoned his earlier (1930s) baritone style.
14. "Why Begin Again?" Bluebird B-10234. The overly sentimental Dick Todd vocal blends in so well with the "The Three Reasons" backup vocal group, that it may have been considered a group outing. Penned by Artie Shaw, Don Raye, and Charles Shavers, this bit of fluff is effective, if not a very enjoyable bit of crooning.
15. "At a Table in a Corner," Bluebird B-10335. Dick's rich baritone creates a mellow feeling, as this sad ditty penned by Sam Coslow and Dana Suesse is more so a bit of a weeper.
16. "Manhattan," Bluebird B-10374. This just may be among the best (ever) versions of this classic Gershwin-penned ditty, Moreover, despite Dick's miss-spoken word for "girl," it is still a battle with a cooler Lee Wiley rendering.

17. "Blue Orchids," Bluebird B-10398. This (mostly) forgotten Hoagy Carmichael-penned ditty is far from a blues rendering, although blue still applies. Moreover, this smaltzy ditty about flowers is expertly crooned out.
18. "One Morning in May," Bluebird B-10431. Dick (again) excels, as this woeful tale as penned by Mitchell Parish and Hoagy Carmichael is equal to any previous torch song. As good as the previous Marion Harris version? Yes!
19. "Lazy River," Bluebird B-10431. Dick very skillfully takes this ditty penned by Hoagy Carmichael and Sidney Arodin for a good crooning.
20. "It's the Talk of the Town," Bluebird B-10559. The earlier Connie Boswell version, also crooned out well, is a fine comparison.
21. "I'll Be Seeing You," Bluebird B-10636. As a little known Broadway entity, this ditty was revived with great success by a contemporary (1940) Tommy Dorsey release featuring a well-done Frank Sinatra vocal and by Dick's excellent crooning . . .
22. "You Can't Brush Me Off," Bluebird B-10720. This fine duet with Dinah Shore finds Dick (tastefully) not overpowering Dinah's fine vocal of this Irving Berlin-penned ditty.
23. "Outside of That I Love You," Bluebird B-10720. Another duet with Dinah Shore, as well as another Irving Berlin-penned ditty, results in yet another winning combination.
24. "All This and Heaven Too," Bluebird B-10789. This ditty penned by Eddie De Lange and Jimmy Van Heusen was also a huge (1940) film entity that starred (non-singing) Betty Davis and Charles Boyer. In comparison with other contemporary recordings, only a Tommy Dorsey release, with a somewhat nasal vocal by Frank Sinatra, on Victor 26653, is anywhere as good. Listen and compare.
25. "Orchids for Remembrance," Bluebird B-10805. Peter De Rose and Mitchell Parish penned this classy title that found Dick's vocal more than up for the challenge. More expensive than gardenias? Yes!
26. "I'm Waiting for Ships That Never Come In," Bluebird B-10805. The earlier Nick Lucas best seller perhaps finds Todd more to speculate about with war in Europe? (A cruder rendition by Jimmie Davis is also worth it to compare and listen to.)
27. "Nightingale Sang in Berkley Square". Bluebird - B - 10912.
28. "Along the Santa Fe Trail," Bluebird B-10949. This ditty had been penned by Al Dubin, Edwina Coolidge and Will Grosz for the contemporary 1940 film *"Santa Fee Trail"*, which starred (non-singing) Errol Flynn, Olivia De Havilland and Ronald Reagan. At last, Dick beats out a contemporary Bing Crosby version on Decca 3565. In fact, Bing's recording, in his newer style, on Decca 3565, is so bad that it ain't even a "Crosby" pick. That's right!
29. "We Go Well Together," Bluebird B-11091. As a "Dick Todd with Orchestra and the Four Belles," (perhaps a "fourth" "Three Reason"?) release, this smaltzy ditty penned by Sid Robin and Arthur Kent still works.
30. "Worried Mind," Bluebird B-11142. The poignant country ditty penned by Jimmie Davis and Ted Daffon is well done, if done best. Worried?
31. "Together," Bluebird B-11156. Dick revives this (already) old ditty that had found similar styles from the likes of both Cliff Edwards and Nick Lucas. Listen more so to Dick's smoother croon!
32. "Marie Elena," Bluebird B-11156. While perhaps far too sentimental, this ditty penned by S. K. Russell and Lorenzo Barcelata of Mexican origins just might have made "Marie Elena" fall asleep. Nevertheless, it's still a well-done crooning job, if sleep does not overwhelm its listeners. Listen before bed.

33. "The White Cliffs of Dover," Bluebird B-11406. This sentimental 1941 entity had also been an effective propaganda tool for England and had been penned by Nat Burton and Walter Kent, who may not have even seen those famous white cliffs or the real bombs falling from the sky. There is another question about Bluebirds flying about in England? In any case, when Vera Lynn, who had already achieved recognition before the war, recorded this ditty as a British entity in England, the emotional effects of her fine vocal on Decca F-8110 and on the BBC achieved a propaganda triumphant. Why look for bluebirds when you could hear Vera Lynn, already dubbed as "the forces sweetheart"? To a lesser effect, Dick's crooning job is still effective, as the transplanted Canadian had indeed become very much known in Britain, with many of his American (Bluebird) recordings released on the (HMV) record label.
34. "How About You?" Bluebird B-11406. This original ditty is crooned out just right!
35. "'Tis Autumn," Bluebird B-11531. On this ditty penned by Henry Nemo, Dick playfully mentions Bing Crosby by name and even embellishes his vocal a bit more. (It is interesting to speculate if Bing Crosby had ever heard this fine Dick Todd rendering.)
36. "I'm Old-Fashioned," Bluebird B-11577. Yes, Dick Todd is old-fashioned. Yet noting this fine ditty penned by Johnny Mercer and Jerome Kern, it's easy to hear just why this sentimental bit of smaltzy and fluff, as crooned out so well by Dick Todd, works so well.
37. "When the Lights Go On Again," Bluebird B-11577. As (another) World War II-era song ditty by Eddie Seiler, Sol Marcus, and Bennie Benjamin, this plea for world peace is expertly crooned out, as was Vera Lynn's English recording released (over there) on Decca F-8241. As a best-selling entity (over here), bandleader-singer Vaughn Monroe's well-done (1942) version on Victor 27945 sold many more copies than both Dick or Vera, despite a similar tone of (real) vocal style and sentiment. Listen and compare.

Note: Like most vocalists of the prewar era, musical styles and the media of radio changed very rapidly, especially for the likes of aging crooners like Dick Todd finding themselves out of style and work. The two following post-WWII releases, however, do merit interesting listening.

38. "Oh, Happy Day," Decca 28506. This (postwar) ditty penned by Don Howard Kaplow, while sounding more dated than ever, is crooned out well.
39. "Bumming Around," Decca 28583.

Mel Torme

Most baby boomers remember him from the 1980s (TV) sitcom *Night Court*. While the plot of the story involved a (young) judge immersed in jazz music and an interest in Mel Torme, an "old" guy, somewhat involved in jazz. The original vocal style of Mel Torme had been influenced by many, including the likes of Ethel Waters and Bing Crosby, much like many of Mel's contemporaries. His own pop success, with his "MelTones," had been seemingly inspired by the likes of singing groups, as like the somewhat smaltzy "Pied Pipers." More so, the rise of the vocal groups had been accelerated by the musicians' strike of 1942, which found most record companies, including newer independents, cutting musician costs with vocal groups. As time went on, the likes of such pop groups such as "Six Hits and a Miss," the "Ken Darby Singers," the "Rhythmaires," and "The Song Spinners," among others, all became recognized, if faceless, voices on many of the contemporary popular recordings of the 1940s. Mel, with his Mel-Tones, was originally in the thick of things, and more importantly, noting his considerable jazzy musical talents, he would emerge as a solo vocal performer as well as a songwriter of considerable influence.

- The following are Mel Torme picks:

1. "Where Or When?" Jewel 4000. As recorded in 1944, this pop style, sounding much like earlier Pied Piper efforts (with Tommy Dorsey), is pleasant enough. As good as Lena Horne? No!
2. "A Stranger in Town," Decca 18653. As recorded by "Mel Torme and His MelTones," this self-penned ditty, while a bit fluffy, finds Mel's own vocal much like contemporaries Frank Sinatra or Dick Haymes.
3. "Day By Day," Decca 18746. As a Bing Crosby release, "Mel Torme and His MelTones," who had included Betty Beveridge, Ginny O'Connor, and Les Baxter, were fortunate to have landed onto Crosby land. Moreover, this ditty penned by Sammy Cahn, Alex Stordahl, and Paul Weston was, in true retrospective, luckily to have had Mel and his group sound backing Bing at this time, noting Crosby's less-than-interested attitude toward recording.
4. "Prove It By The Things You Do," Decca 18746. As the flip of the "Day by Day," this ditty penned by Doris Fisher and Allen Roberts finds Bing, with Mel's backing vocals, producing another effective recording.
5. "Willow Road," Musicraft 363. The vocal style found on this ditty is all Frank Sinatra, as this ditty penned by Jack Wells and Mel Torme himself is done well by Mel and his MelTones, backed by Sonny Burke.
6. "What Is This Thing Called Love?" Musicraft 390. As a 1946 Artie Shaw release, this old standard, perhaps already defined by Lena Horne, is still given a fine rendering by Mel and his MelTones.
7. "Born to Be Blue," Musicraft 397. Another Mel and MelTones effort finds another ditty penned by Jack Wells and Mel Torme another winner.
8. "Night and Day," Musicraft 538. It is at least interesting that Mel, still influenced vocally by Frank Sinatra, also adds some obvious Ella Fitzgerald influenced type scatting, noting a somewhat clumsy result.
9. "Do It Again," Musicraft 534. Mel (perhaps) reaches perfection as his vocal attempt on this ditty penned by George Gershwin and Buddy De Silva, to sound jazzy, indeed works.
10. "It's Dreamtime," Musicraft 15102. Credited to Mel and the Sonny Burke Orchestra, this ditty penned by Jack Brooks and Walter Schumann, obviously influenced vocally by the smooth contemporary vocal styles of Sinatra and Haymes, is good and no dream.
11. "Careless Hands," Capital 15379. Mel and the Sonny Burke Orchestra combined to successfully produce this fine 1949 best seller. Penned by Bob Hilliard and Carl Sigman, this somewhat novel ditty includes clapping hands, which almost spoiled the recording.
12. "Blue Moon," Capital 15428.
13. "Bewitched," Capital 1000.

In his chosen role as a songwriter, perhaps his greatest success was "The Christmas Song" for Nat King Cole. By the emergence of rock and roll and Elvis in the mid-1950s, his "adult" approach to music was somewhat dated, although newer pop vocalists, who included the likes of Vickie Carr, Edie Gorme, Steve Lawrence, Johnny Mathis, Della Reese, Dakota Stakota, Andy Williams, and Nancy Wilson, among others, like the (already) dated Mel, hoped the newer trend would fade away. While Mel's dilemma was not unique, he did attempt a newer style with the upstart Atlantic Records. Moreover, perhaps his timing was right, as Bobby Darin, a converted rock and roller who could mimic, much like he himself had in the 1940 Frank Sinatra, left the label in 1962.

❖ The following (Atlantic) releases are notable:

14. "Comin' Home, Baby," Atlantic 2165. Backed by an unaccredited black female group, Mel's vocal sounds a lot like Bobby Darin on this stimulating and serious ditty penned by Bob Dorough and Ben Tucker. More so, Mel's vocal, however contrived, is for sure hip, as his mature edge, in complete contrast to his earlier jazzy vocals, works to his advantage.
15. "Right Now," Atlantic 2165. As the flip side of "Comin' Home, Baby," Mel again sounds hip, as this fine ditty penned by Herbie Mann and Carl Sigman perhaps gave Mel a bit of a pause in his previous musical attitudes.

While Mel did prove that he could progress better than Sinatra, Martin, or Bennett, as to be found on his Atlantic renderings, Mel chose to revert back to jazz and pop, most likely because he felt more comfortable with the material? In true retrospective a creative mistake. Mel nevertheless continued to record, and his fans, and some new ones, were appreciative enough. More so, the fortunate break in the *Night Court* sitcom brought him back to interest, and his older attempts at jazz were (again) revived and appreciated.

Merle Travis

Guitarist and musician Merle Travis was a light-voiced vocalist, whose subsequent songwriting abilities, in true retrospective, would influence later generations of country and western, pop, and (even) rock. His (own) guitar picking perhaps founded more than a few rockabilly licks in a future era, and some "country twang" influence upon a slightly younger contemporary from the north, Bill Haley. Merle, who had worked in radio since the 1930s, did indeed produce some very significant (latter) 1940s recordings, as both country and western and folk. The following are picks:

1. "Cincinatti Lou," Capital 258. As a fine honky-tonk bar song penned by Cliffie Stone and Merle himself, this ditty finds a girl named Lou who finds nothing she will not do. Just how much beer does she drink? Does she roll her eyes like she rolls dice? Among other things, she has an effect upon roosters and Grandpa. Just listen, as many postwar honky-tonk patrons did when playing the jukebox, and find out.
2. "No Vacancy," Capital 258. Merle's self-penned ditty perhaps gives much to speculate upon in the post-WWII era. While still a typical bar song, this ditty about returned

veteran not able to find somewhere to live identified a huge housing shortage following the war. Social commentary?

3. "Divorce Me C.O.D," Capital 290. Perhaps one of the ultimate honky-tonk played songs. This ditty penned by Cliffie Stone, Eddie Kirk, and Merle Travis found a guy tired of his wife hardly home, deciding to move to Dallas, Texas, without waiting for a divorce. While this tale is indeed sad, its upbeat vocal makes it clear the guy is happy about it. After a few beers and a few plays of this recording, many listeners may still be happy or sad?
4. "So Round, So Firm, So Fully Packed," Capital 349. This (1947) best seller penned by Cliffie Stone, Eddie Kirk, and Merle was perhaps founded on a phrase picked up in a local honky-tonk. The great measurements of a fine-looking lady are proudly bragged about in a local bar it seems. Do barflies like to drink? Did teenagers like Frank Sinatra? Among blazing fiddles and steel guitar backing, this entity (still) wins. (Contemporary Ernest Tubb also recorded this ditty, providing a tougher vocal for many delighted jukebox listeners.)
5. "Sweet Temptation," Capital 349. As the original flip side to "So Round, So Firm, So Fully Packed," this ditty penned by Cliffie Stone and Merle is nothing to be overlooked! While describing a flirt, perhaps the (very) risqué lyrics seek to describe the term "diamond in the ruff" and another delicious "peach" in an outrageous and expletive manner. Or just join in the fun. Listen and decide.
6. "Three Times Seven," Capital 384. Is it time to have fun (legally) at twenty-one years old? Why? This Cliffie Stone and Travis penned ditty perhaps makes a man think about stuff?
7. "Fat Gal," Capital 40026. This ditty, Merle's own claimed composition, is crudely put together to poke fun at fat people. Or was it about a guy bragging about the merits of a fat partner? In winter? In summer?
8. "Merle's Boogie Woogie," Capital 40026. This self-penned ditty was just a good excuse to highlight Merle's guitar-playing skills and producing a fine and contemporary dance record for jukeboxes. As some girls with big legs were bound to join in, his swing band concept just had to find his "6 times 6 equals 36." It was perhaps later found on the 1952 recording on Essex 303 "Rock This Joint" by "Bill Haley and His Comets," formerly known as "Bill Haley and the Saddlemen."
9. "Alimony Bound," Capital 40115. Just another familiar subject for bar patrons.
10. "Blues Stay Away from Me," Capital 40254. The contemporary (original) Delmore Brothers recording on King 803 found the (already) well-known country group to become later known as an early attempt to commit itself into a differing postwar sound. Merle's subsequent rendering, while no better than the Delmore Brothers' smooth and slick vocal, documents a recorded excuse for a get-together with the likes of Merle's own fellow (Capital) recording artists identified as "Tennessee Ernie" Ford and (musician) Eddie Kirk as heard on the recording itself.

- Merle's (1947) 78 rpm album release "Folk Songs of the Hills" on Capital AD-50 found Merle claiming or adapting ditties for a planned and contrived set of contemporary folk entities for children on the Capital. In true retrospective, this contemporary (fair-selling) album found Merle's songwriting abilities returning to his (real) coal miner family in Kentucky. As with his own guitar, Merle more so created some fine and truthful material about the plight of the coal mining industry, with some other traditional folk song ditties that were (still) very well known to all inhabitants of the region. Note the following eight picks:

11. "Nine-Pound Hammer," Capital 48000.
12. "John Henry," Capital 48000.
13. "Sixteen Tons," Capital 48001. As a tale about coal miners, this claimed self-penned ditty perhaps found Merle's own heart and soul involved, as his immediate family were coal miners. It is even more odd, using latter-century logic, that this ditty was attacked as being pro-Communist in the early days of the cold war.

In true retrospective, Merle's light mid-tempo vocal, while done well, would largely be forgotten until the later (1955) Tennessee Ernie Ford version on Capital 3262 became a best-selling ditty. Indeed, it was Ford's hard-in-the-right-places tenor vocal, so much different from Merle's softer tone, sounding almost threatening and spooky, that produced a classic recording.

14. "Dark as a Dungeon," Capital 48001. Another "coal miner song," reintroduced (later) by Johnny Cash.
15. "That's All," Capital 48002. Merle's committed blue singing is far from contrived, noting a previous and differing version from Sister Rosetta Tharpe more so betrays an older folktale subsequently becoming a recorded entity.
16. "Over by Number Nine," Capital 48002. More stuff to know while working in the coal mine?
17. "I Am a Pilgrim," Capital 48003. Another traditional spiritual finds Merle's committed vocal special!
18. "Muskrat," Capital 48003. Yeah, can you make a guitar talk?
19. "Start Even," Capital 965. Another Travis-penned ditty finds his "slow-talking blues" vocal with his own gritty guitar something very special!
20. "Lost John Boogie," Capital 1737. As a "Whippoorwills" release, Merle's adaption of some local (Southern) blues finds a tale about a prisoner "John" from Bowling Green, Kentucky, perhaps trying to board a train out of town? This ditty had more ever been part of southern folklore, with evidence of a W.C. Handy sheet music in the early century. Speculation has it that both Handy and (more recently) Wayne Rainy) had claim put on the (shared) culture itself, and Merle's recording perhaps (finally) defined it?

Visual

21. "Re enlistment Blues" Merle's limited but well done rendering of his ditty, with guitar in the film *"From Here To Eternity"* is short but memorable!

Ernest Tubb

The effects of the post-Prohibition era, which started in 1933, affected the music industry as much as defining it. The rise of the bar song as well as live entertainment also founded the jukebox industry, which, in the absence of radio in the 1930s, significantly marketed recording artists, especially those of vocalists. More so, the rise of rural honky-tonks, along with diners and restaurants became, for observers and listeners, a huge cultural part of Americana. Ernest Tubb had been a rural Texan, born near the town of Crisp. Like most others, he was much influenced by the changes of the Roaring Twenties' and the expansion of the recording industry. More so, he became a follower and fan of Jimmie Rodgers, whose song ditties had founded the term "hillbilly" in a positive and marketable enterprise. By 1936, with the actual assistance of Jimmie Rodger's widow, Ernest became a radio entity and subsequent recording artist, aping as much of Jimmie Rodgers as he could. As a live entity and patron of rural honky-tonk life, he noted, as a writer and observer, the aspects of aspirations of patrons. While there were others, Tubb may be considered one of the best, as the local success he achieved became national. Moreover, along with Roy Acuff and Red Foley, among others, the term "hillbilly" matured into country. The following are Ernest Tubb picks:

1. "Mean Old Bed Bug Blues," Bluebird B-8899. The effects of Bessie Smith's own race recordings were huge, as her rendering on Columbia 14250-D is recalled, as well as a Jimmie Rodgers vocal style.
2. "I'll Get Along Somehow," Decca 5825. The 1940 self-penned rendering is crudely sincere.
3. "Walking the Floor Over You," Decca 5958. By 1941, after much frustration as a recording entity, as well as a local radio and live personality, this self-penned ditty made a huge impact. As a simple understatement, this novelty also defined Ernest Tubb. While crude, this vocal is believable and indeed sounds as if Ernest is indeed in a honky-tonk, in common with so many patrons. Moreover, as a jukebox entity, this recording especially meant good business. A fine and contemporary Bing Crosby version, on Decca 18371, with backing by Bob Crosby's Bearcats, is novel and swinging and may be considered a nightclub version. While the Crosby vocal is highly polished as compared with Tubb's crude vocal, it's also a good bet that Ernest was more than pleased about Crosby's rendering, noting the royalty payments of Ernest Tubb origin.
4. "Mean Mama Blues," Decca 5976. A crude and white blues singer? Indeed, except for a yodel, a lot less like Jimmie Rodgers, which is a good thing by this time!
5. "Try Me One More Time," Decca 6093. This simple message is full of self-pity, as this self-penned bar item just had to score! More so, for some, it still does.
6. "Soldier's Last Letter," Decca 6098. The great struggle of World War II finds a sympathetic and patriotic rendering as self-described and penned by Henry Stewart and Ernest himself.
7. "Tomorrow Never Comes," Decca 6106. What if "Tomorrow Never Comes"? Penned by Johnny Bond and Ernest himself, this murky and crude ditty somehow works!
8. "It's Been So Long, Darlin'," Decca 6112. While the Tubb vocal is always crude, this sincere rendering, also self-penned, is a true heart song. As with many country ditties, it's hard to figure just why these bar songs are so effective, noting the playing of this ditty in fact is at home on a turntable!
9. "Rainbow At Midnight," Decca 46018. A "Rainbow at Midnight"? Just how can one see all that in the dark? Penned by John A. Miller, this stupid title nevertheless works when heard.
10. "Drivin' Nails in My Coffin," Decca 46019. This oddly titled ditty penned by Jerry Irby directly relates to the social problems indeed found by the same regulars, in any given honky-tonk. Does anyone care? In decades since, perhaps informed adults make a choice? In any case, this novel and grim ditty may also be a good reason to stop, or even get a bit whacked.
11. "Filipino Baby," Decca 46019. This side is a lively tale penned by Billy Cox and Clarke Van Ness about an interracial World War II adventure in the Philippines,

also recorded by (1944) contemporary Cowboy Copas on King 505. Great Asian-American relations in a Southern and segregated society?

12. "So Round, So Full, So Fully Packed," Decca 46040. While "girl watching" was in true retrospective a favorite 1947 pastime, it remains for many the same. Penned by Merle Travis, Cliffie Stone, and Eddie Kirk, this fast-paced novelty was originally released by Merle Travis on Capital 349. While always crude, Ernest's vocal is a bit tougher.
13. "I'm Biting My Fingernails and Thinking of You," Decca 24592. The added vocals of the Andrews Sisters add much smoothness to this ditty penned by Roy West, Ernest Benedict, Lenny Saunders, and Ernest Tubb. In fact, Ernest's own vocal is held in check, as perhaps he understands his "understatement" as much as Bing Crosby did.
14. "Have You Ever Been Lonely". Decca-46144. The old 1933 dance band ditty, penned by Peter De Rose and George Brown, is transformed into a honky tonk weeper.
15. "Slippin' Around," Decca 46173. This very crude ditty penned by Floyd Tillman as well as a contemporary recording by him, on Columbia 20581, also reeks of real-life bar talk. More so was a softer approach found in the contemporary best seller featuring Margaret Whiting and Jimmy Wakely on Capital 40224.
16. "Warm Red Wine," Decca 46175. They don't just drink beer in honky-tonks. Or just for a special occasion? This gem penned by Cindy Walker makes it all go down easy enough.
17. "Tennessee Border No. 2," Decca 46200. This novel pairing with contemporary rival Red Foley, penned by Jimmy Work, Kenneth Burns, and Henry Haynes, does not disappoint.
18. "Blue Christmas," Decca 46186. Ernest's typically crude vocal defines the term "blue" as a bit sad—in true holiday spirit. A later rendering of this ditty penned by Billy Hayes and Jay Johnson and sung by Elvis Presley on Victor LP LOC 1035, as well subsequent 45EP and 45 rpm releases, in true retrospective, define the blues a bit more.
19. "Letters Have No Arms," Decca 46207. Honest to God, this weepy and even creepy bit of sop penned by Arbie Gibson and Ernest himself just had to have had its origins in a honky-tonk! Moreover, ditties like this defined 1949 country and still do.
20. "I Love You Because," Decca 46213. Ernest Tubb's version of the Leon Payne-penned ditty released by Leon on Capital 40238 is just as crude. Later, Elvis would croon it out and more so crudely and emotionally.

- Note: Ernest continued to record prolifically through rock and roll and latter-day country.

The following two ditties were recorded in 1960 and, as recorded by others, perhaps define the unlikely likable Ernest Tubb style.

21. "Let the Little Girl Dance," Decca 9-31119. Penned by Carl Spencer and Bert Lawrence, this ditty, already been a been a popular hit by Billy Bland on Old Town 1076, is great R&B style. While less hip and more hick by contemporary 1960s standards, this version remains interesting enough.
22. "Everybody's Somebody's Fool," Decca 31119. This ditty had became a huge best seller for Connie Francis on MGM 12899. Penned by Howard Greenfield and Jack Keller, this somewhat bit of smaltzy material is a bit rougher in Tubb's version.

Sophie Tucker

This performer, like Al Jolson, found emulation of black Americans very profitable, as her own blackface routines of the (pre-1920) era attest. Moreover, it's Sophie's own questions about race that found her (Afro-American) songwriter Shelton Brooks. Just how she had gotten a hold of the Brooks's composition "Some of These Days" is perhaps speculation. In any case, her commitment to Brooks and the song ditty itself had found her a very hip recording entity in 1911. She would subsequently seek out to emulate the forbidden black singing style, eventually perhaps, finding the likes of both Ethel Waters and Alberta Hunter to teach her. The Sophie Tucker attempt at singing was a ragged-voiced result. Noting the poor acoustic limits of the era, the Tucker recordings were also tough enough and even a bit ragtime. Others, influenced by her were better singers, including the likes of Marion Harris, soon to follow as a contemporary rival, finding and singing (real) black accredited composed songs.

After 1920 and the emergence of (real) black-faced vocalists, starting with Mamie Smith, the novel appeal of Sophie's singing style plummeted. Her overbearing quest to remain tough became novel and more than necessary. Later electric recordings of the 1920s did provide her some good material, yet Sophie would be stuck with a dated acoustic vocal style, moreover a novelty with personality. Despite these limits, she would continue on successfully and boldly, producing some fine 1920s best-selling entities, thus keeping for herself an audience of interested admirers.

1. "That Lovin' Rag," Edison 10360. Look out 1910! The perhaps stolen use of rag of ragtime and of Afro-American Scott Joplin (who had popularized the term some ten years earlier) was still the rage. This ditty penned by Bernard Adler and Victor H. Smalley finds Sophie's vocal rough and tough, indeed more than contemporary Nora Bayes known for her coon singing, as it was then defined. Bayes also produced a popular, best-selling rendering of this ditty on Victor 60023.
2. "That Lovin' Two-Step Man," Edison 10411. Credited to Stanley Murphy and Percy Wenrich, this attempt at (1910) contemporary dance music was considered and noted in this Edison cylinder release as a coon song.
3. "Some of These Days," Edison Amberol 691. The Shelton Brooks-penned classic found Sophie's rough vocal something of best-selling value. For sure, this sad lament about someone leaving somebody for someone else was common, but Sophie's harsh vocal, perfect for acoustic recordings, hits hard and lingers. Moreover, many 1911 music contemporaries were to question if Sophie was black. (A later electric recording on Columbia 826-D is easier to listen to, and, while not the event that the 1911 original had been, it is not a bad rendering.)
4. "Good Morning, Judge," Edison Amberol 10529. This ditty penned by Victor H. Smalley and Bernard Adler is yet another piece of smaltzy that somehow worked. More so, Sophie and some unidentified voices display some mischief, along with clearly identifying Sophie herself.
5. "Knock Wood," Edison Amberol 852. Another hard-hitting vocal, with stupid lyrics by Andrew B. Sterling and Harry Von Tilzer that somehow work.

As far as this author can find, Sophie relied upon her fame as a live vaudevillian than as a recording artist for the period of her last Edison recording sessions (1911) to signing with

Aeolian-Vocalion in 1918. As a stage performer, like many contemporaries, the ability to project a vocal on (acoustic) disks required certain skills, noting and identifying themselves to their followers and public. Sophie definitely found this ability. It is more so worth the speculation that Sophie's vaudevillian contemporary Mae West had a similar vocal style, with a risqué touch, although Sophie was more articulate. More so, Mae's looks matched her wit, as Sophie could only produce wit, in comparison to Mae. Indeed, Mae would later produce a few electric records, and she would primarily become a Broadway and film success, elapsing Sophie, defying age, in the 1930s. For the purposes of this book, however, Sophie did indeed become a very influential recording artist, as Mae did not. Did Mae and Sophie know each other? Did Mae produce some acoustic recordings that this author cannot find?

6. "Won't You Be a Dear, Dear Daddy to a Itta Bitta Doll Like Me," Aeolian Vocalion 12090. This long and stupid lyric, claimed by the Afro-American team of Henry Creamer and Turner Layton, must have appealed to Sophie for it's pure camp and fun. More so, unlike her previous Edison releases, Sophie's vocal, while still rough around the edges, betrays a voice.
7. "I'm Glad My Daddy's in a Uniform," Aeolian Vocalion 12090. Sophie, who had turned thirty some two years earlier, found this World War I era (1918) ditty penned by Carey Morhan and Charles McCarron something to become indeed patriotic for. Men in uniforms? Just listen!
8. "Everybody 'Shimmies Now'," Aeolian Vocalion 12099. Penned by Edmond J. Perray and Joe Gold, this 1919 ditty welcomed the current dance craze known as the "Shimmie." While attributed to contemporary Broadway entity Gilda Gray's loose shoulder strap, after shaking it up a bit (1918), this ditty found attributed to Afro-American origins, with shaking motions founded in (black) churches, transplanted into equally separated (black) vaudeville, by many, including the likes of contemporaries like Alberta Hunter and Ethel Waters, then still largely unknown to the general public. More so, other contemporaries of Sophie, including Bea Palmer and Mae West, used and put the tern into their vaudeville and stage acts, putting claims upon the new dance term. In any case, Sophie put her bold claim on the Shimmie by recording this ditty, with the jazzy backing of her "Five Kings of Syncopation."
9. "High Brown Blues," Okeh 4565. This attempt at blues penned by Milton Ager and Jack Yellen is a creditable (1922) performance, despite some real competition from contemporary Afro-American performers who suddenly were allowed to become recording entities.
10. "Jig Walk," Okeh 4590. This danceable entity penned by black entities Henry Creamer and Will Vodery is hip and full of fun, more so stated by Sophie's clear vocal, not to be confused with the later Duke Ellington and Jo Trent instrumental composition.
11. "Pick Me Up and Lay Me Down in Dear Old Dixieland," Okeh 4590. Penned by Bert Kalmar and Harry Ruby, this ditty of 1922 found Sophie having fun as well as fanning the fuel for the decade, later known, in true retrospective, as the Roaring Twenties. Vernon Dalhart's contemporary version on Columbia A-3575 is OK but in comparison to Sophie's vocal very un-hip and stiff.
12. "You've Got to See Mama Ev'ry Night (Or You Can't See Mama At All)," Okeh 4781. Credited to Con Conrad and Billy Rose, this ditty finds interesting comparisons to contemporary and (longtime rival Marion Harris's version on Brunswick 2410 as

well as the likes of three blues women, who had previously not been able to be in the game of recording), which included renderings by Mamie Smith on Okeh 4781 and Lizzie Miles on Emerson 10603 as "You've Gotta Come and See Mama Ev'ry Night."

13. "Old King Tut," Okeh 4830. This (1923) ditty penned by William Jerome and Harry Von Tilzer found a fast-paced and novel-tongued Sophie, perhaps scaring away any curse.
14. "Red Hot Mama," Okeh 40129. This ditty penned by Gilbert Wells, Bud Cooper, and Fred Rose indeed provided Sophie more creditable material to match the contemporary material of Afro-American blues queens.

Note: By the mid-1920s, the rush to electric recordings and talking films still found the already aged Sophie, reaching forty in 1926, also an icon, a fine and fitting nostalgic act. She had also become an acknowledged influence for many of the newer (white) musical performers, including the likes of Libby Holman and Lee Morse as well as upon her Broadway contemporary, Mae West.

15. "Fifty Million Frenchmen Can't Be Wrong," Okeh 40813. This bold novelty title penned by Billy Rose, Willie Raskin, and Fred Fisher is bold enough. Luckily, Sophie pulls it off.
16. "After You've Gone," Okeh 40827. The acoustic Marion Harris version is challenged, although the contemporary and electric Bessie Smith version is not. Even so, this rendering is no slough!
17. "I Ain't Got Nobody," Okeh 40837. This electric recording also gives Sophie some creditable updates to previous acoustic version by Marion Harris and Bessie Smith. A contemporary Emmett Smith version, however, is more of a challenge.
18. "There'll Be Some Changes Made," Okeh 40921. The previous Ethel Waters version on Black Swan 2021 is challenged only by better acoustics by this electric recording. Moreover, did Sophie herself take voice lessons from Ethel Waters and Alberta Hunter? Speculation?
19. "Some of These Days," Columbia 826-D. This is a fine 1927 electric rendering of Sophie's signature tune.

- The following three ditties penned by Jack Yellen and Milton Ager, as found in her early "talking" (1929) film *Honky Tonk*, are creditable:

20. "I'm Doing What I'm Doing for Love," Victor 21993.
21. "He's a Good Man to Have Around," Victor 21994.
22. "I'm the Last of the Red Hot Mamas," Victor 21994. Perhaps this title, a contrived claim of novel mischief, perfectly fit Sophie's own image of herself.
    - While on a tour of England in 1928, Sophie recorded a bit. Already known as a risqué entity, from her previous tour in 1922, she was more so known as a recording artist of long standing. The following rendering is well worth hearing:

23. "He Hadn't It Up Till Yesterday," Columbia 5064. This British release, as the title blatantly implies, is very risqué. Penned by Wright, Will G. Haines, and Jack Meskill, this contrived blues entity works. The committed Sophie is, as usual, very much influenced by contemporary and black-based blues, noting that most of her British audience was unaware. Even so, Sophie does provide spark, despite her age (about forty-one) and obvious vocal limits. It is more so interesting that the author cannot find a contemporary 1928 release in the United States.

24. (Sophie Tucker "for President". Mercury - 5839. The 1952 presidential election found the old icon without voice or vote. She did however compensate providing well done competition for the contemporary ethnic comic, Mickey Katz.)

Joe Turner

The inclusion into this book of blues-shouter Joe Turner might find many directly involved in the early tends of 1950s rock and roll, perhaps questioning his presence. In reality, Joe Turner had been into urban blues since the early 1930s, and by 1939 rivaled only by Jimmy Rushing in recognition and style. It's also found that his song writing with Pete Johnson on many song ditties became well known classics Later, as a middle-aged man, his association with Atlantic Records found him and his blues style perhaps a bit more rhythmic and mid-tempo, an appealing entity for young teenagers. Moreover, Joe Turner turned people's heads, including the likes of many would-be hip white entities, including the likes of Bill Haley and Elvis Presley.

Picks include:

1. "Wee Baby Blues," Decca 8526.
2. "Corrine Corrine," Decca 8563.
3. "Rock Me, Mama," Decca 8577.
4. "Rainy Day Blues," Decca 7824.
5. "Roll 'Em, Pete," Vocalion 4607. As Joe's early career is supported with the likes of some of the very best keyboard entities of the era (Art Tatum on the first four picks above and Pete Johnson until the 1950s), the "urban" blues is unmistakable. While it should be pointed out that the boogie-woogie style itself is very much admired by Tatum and Pete Johnson, had "started" with the very fine 1928 recording by "Pine Top" Smith's "Pine Top's Boogie Woogie" on Vocalion 1245. This very danceable music became rediscovered in the latter 1930s with "Kansas City" rivals such as Jimmy Rushing (with Count Basie himself on the keys) and Joe (with Pete Johnson) leading the way.
6. "Goin' Away Blues," Vocalion 4607. This flip side of the above is no slouch.
7. "Cherry Red," Vocalion 4997. This Pete Johnson release still features a blockbuster vocal by Joe.
8. "Lovin' Mama Blues," Vocalion 5186.
9. "Cafe Society Rag," Vocalion 5186. The term "rag," or "ragtime" had (already) been played out at the turn of the 1800s to 1900s. While the likes of Scott Joplin had been replaced by jazz and blues, the combinations of Albert Ammons, Meade Lux Lewis, and Pete Johnston's boogie-woogie piano workouts, with Joe's urban baritone vocals, give this rag energy and a good excuse their own written song ditty for the contemporary New York City Nightclub (of two locations).
10. "Joe Turner Blues," Okeh 6001. This Benny Carter release find Joe doing W.C. Handy's fine (already) old classic while this was not penned for *this* Joe Turner, Joe indeed takes ownership.
11. "Rebecca," Decca 11001. This spirited tale penned by Joe himself about a girl whose trip to pick berries in the woods ends without the berries, but with a smile; it is campy and fun.

12. "It's the Same Old Story," Decca 11001. This self penned tale is more sad, and a typical urban feel is heard in Joe's vocal.
13. "Pitney Brown Blues," Decca 18121. This term may just be the name of a local (Kansas City) nightclub that had featured Pete and Joe. Or was Pitney Brown a man who sold women's services on the corner of 18th and Vine ?
14. "I Got a Gal for Every Day of the Week," Decca 28042. This self penned ditty finds Joe's bragging? Or silly?

Note: The parting of pianist Pete Johnson left Joe, like many other contemporaries, in musical doldrums in 1950. A small, upstart, New York-based recording label, however, came to his rescue. While owner Ahmet Ertegun and Jerry Wexler didn't throw a lot of money around, it would turn out to be their new Atlantic recording label that would lead the way to huge profits and sales throughout the 1950s. The famous old blues vocalist would be transformed into a rock and roll entity, as Ertegun's and Wexler's creative and personal interest in Joe would reap profit. While Joe did still record a lot of urban blues with Atlantic, it's his upbeat tunes that win the day.

- The following recordings prove Joe's great versatility as a vocalist in a dawn of a new age of music:

15. "Chains of Love," Atlantic 939. This ditty, penned by George Ducas and Zack Turner, became a well known' rhythm and blues'entity.
16. "Honey Hush," Atlantic 1002. This ain't nothing but urban blues with a beat. Lu Willie Turner's penned ditty also notes an attitude toward women that's more tan demanding, Hi -yo hi-yo silver? Just listen, Better yet it's rhythm and blues with backbeat. It ain't "do-whop," but it's still (very early) rock and roll. (Speculation has it that Lu Willie Turner was Joe's wife).
17. "TV Mama," Atlantic 1016. Yet another attitude toward women finds Lu Willie Turner's penned ditty also founding a rhythmic excuse about the newest 1950s American past time-television!
18. "Shake, Rattle, and Roll," Atlantic 1026. Penned by "Charles Calhoun," alias Jesse Stone, back in the 1920s, its own origins just may have been for a small (black) Broadway production of the same name (1927) that had starred Adelaide Hall. In any case, this fast-paced bit of urban humor was risqué enough and would still break into the later R&B field as exciting and fresh. Moreover, Joe's rhythmic impulses find his vocal a clear message for the (new) times (1954). Subsequently, a fine and somewhat cleaned-up version by Bill Haley and His Comets on Decca 2168 generated more recognition. By 1956, an Elvis Presley rendering, released on 45EP, LP, 45, and on 78 rpm Victor 20-6642 would be more of a shock, as Elvis had reverted back to the original Joe Turner version.
19. "Flip Flop and Fly," Atlantic 1053. This high-flying vocal penned by Charles Calhoun, alias Jesse Stone and Joe himself is a simple tale of country living, with a bullfrog from the state of Mississippi at the end of Joe's tonsils.
20. "Chicken and the Hawk," Atlantic 1080. The lively backbeat is much like "Shake, Rattle, and Roll." While far less controversial, this gem penned by Jerry Leiber and Mike Stoller is novel and full of energy.
21. "Corrine Corrina," Atlantic 1088. This (second) better-sounding rerecording, a pick noted above, is also sung better. Credited to J. M. Williams, Bo Chatman, and Mitchell Parish, this rock and roll version really does liven things up.

Rudy Vallee

From out of New England, born in Island Pond, Vermont, in 1901, came Herbert Vallee, alias Rudy Vallee. Initially a horn player (clarinet), with his college band, the "Connecticut Yankees," he became a rage as well as a fad of the latter electric recording technique of the late 1920s. His clean-cut, highbrow appeal, especially for college entities, in fact, defined social class, even beyond transplanted Britishers and Broadway. Rudy's attempt to become a vocalist, after mastering a saxophone, also involved a playful use of a megaphone, trapping his vocal within sheets of paper, while much a norm for the pre-microphone era, and he soon found itself identified with Rudy. Along with his tonsils, nose, and throat, he indeed became identified with the era. Whether contemporary Will Osborne founded the style first will always remain a question. It is beyond any question, however, that Rudy, using the new media of electric recording, radio, and film, became the most popular vocalist of his time. Indeed, many attempted to croon like him, although perhaps the uppity Rudy himself was offended by the word. Many, including the likes of Bing Crosby, Russ Columbo, Ozzie Nelson, and (even) the ever-adaptable Ethel Waters, among others, would emulate his crooning style. While in substance, his recordings may be found lacking and far too novel for the most part, Rudy did rule, until the likes of Crosby's developed crooning eclipsed him . . .

The following are Rudy Vallee picks:

1. "Doin' the Raccoon," Velvet Tone 1759-V. The Roaring Twenties found many popular dance bands at many colleges throughout Americana. Rudy's own "Yale Men" loosen things up a bit, as this very hot dance number scores. With some typical and contemporary 1928 college slang, Rudy's vocal glides into some typically simple lyrics, as even the hipness of "Harlem" is noted. Penned by J. Fred Coots and Raymond Klages, this ditty perhaps notes raccoon coats, something that Rudy himself had worn! Vallee had indeed attended the University of Maine and Yale in the 1920s.
2. "Outside," Velvet Tone 1857-V. This stupid ditty penned by Frank Flynn is corny but slick. While this novelty about "outside" is more so evident, so indeed is a lyric that travels with a wild flapper, a married party girl! Rowing down in a lake via canoe? There's more!
3. "Let's Do It". Harmony 808-H. The contemporary Cole Porter title, full of racial slurs, more so found Rudy in a jazzy mood. (A contemporary Dorsey Brother release, featuring a fast paced Bing Crosby vocal, more so defined it, although no one had figured it-back in 1928.).
4. "If I Had You". Harmony 825-H. Rudy's offbeat croon, penned by Jimmy Campbell, Reg Connelly and Ted Shapiro if not perfect, is more ever backed up with jazz.
5. "Marie," Harmony 834-H. This harmless 1928 entity became a best seller. While Rudy's vocal prowess is perhaps a nonfactor of this Irving Berlin-penned ditty, future comparisons make it all very interesting. Rudy is at least ahead of other contemporaries as well as a later (1938) Dorsey arrangement, with an OK vocal by Jack Leonard on Victor 25523. A (still) later forerunner to rock; as by the Four Tunes on Jubilee 5128, it is (at last) so hipper.
6. "Bye And Bye Sweetheart". Harmony905-H. This bit of 1928 mush, found a weak but effective Vallee baritone vocal, penned by Buddy Valentine, Joseph Ford and Jack Yellen, being very much appreciated by young flapper age women. (Rudy would re record this ditty the following year on (Victor-21924) in the same style. Why?

7. "Youll Do It Someday So Why Not Now". Clarion-5182-C. This silly and wordy bit of risqué commentary aimed at young flappers is at least breezy and jazzy-something that would be largly missed on future Vallee recordings.
8. "Lover, Come Back to Me," Velvet Tone1881-V This intimate crooning jpb done by Rudy upon this Broadway entity by Sigmund Romberg and Oscar Hammerstein II, for the operetic "New Moon" is weakly sung but pleasant enough. Yawning? Staying awake?
9. "Weary River," Victor 21868. Well done! The Grant Clarke and Louis Sliver penned ditty had been also the name of a contemporary 1929 film of the same name. Speculation had it that actor Richard Barthelmess had been dubbed while introducing it. While recorded by many, Rudy does find a commited vocal, and more ever without his (usual) attitude.
10. "Deep Night," Victor 21868. This (1929) rendering penned by Charlie Henderson and Rudy himself is (really) deep. More so, Rudy demonstrates a serious side with creditable lyrics, as his committed rendering is indeed demonstrated.
11. "Honey". Victor-21869. As expected, this Richard Whiting, Seymour Simons and Havon Gillespie penned (contemporary) film title is a mushy bit of fluff that found Rudy's weak baritone just perfect for young flapper ears and 1929.
12. "Coquette," Victor 21880. This Irving Berlin-penned ditty, also a contemporary film title, was described as a waltz on its original release. While over the hill with such mush, its contemporary message was correct, which Rudy delivers.
13. "My Time Is Your Time," Victor 21924. The obvious intentions of this title, penned by Eric Little and Leo Dance, suggest more than intimate sweet talk. More so, the clever Vallee began to use it as an invitation to his female radio listeners and was welcome. It could also be found to be a reminder on just what time Rudy's broadcasts would begin, as this bit of smaltzy would indicate. In true re retrospective, this (1929) recording of this radio theme retains its original charms, if its listener doesn't fall asleep!
14. "I'm Just a Vagabond Lover," Victor 21967. Penned by Leon Zimmerman and Rudy himself, this ditty also became a self-starring film title in 1929. While smaltzy in both word and title, this effect recording, along with radio and personal appearances, pushed Vallee into a hugely popular single entity.
15. "Sposin'," Victor-21998. (This 1929 ditty would later become more identified with a Fats Waller (Victor) recording in 1936).
16. "Heigh Ho! Everybody, Heigh Ho!" Victor 22029. Rudy's appearances in NYC's "Heigh Ho Club" (1928-29) had generated even more interest than the club's planned remote radio hookup had anticipated. Indeed, Rudy's live crooning became even better known to the general public, providing Rudy with a technological advantage over all those young and popular before him and something to build upon for those who would come before the public after him. This ditty, penned by Harry Woods, was a typical jazz age roump, used as the simple greeting Rudy had used on radio while at the "Heigh Ho Club." Indeed a true remnant of the 1920s!
17. "A Little Kiss Each Morning," Victor 22193. As yet another intimate titled ditty this Harry Woods-penned entity is crooned out well enough.
18. "Stein Song," Victor 22321. As a New Englander, the appeal of this traditional college drinking song, perhaps with strong connections with the University of Maine, was also found to openly mock Prohibition. While far from great, this ditty could also be a good excuse to drink, or to play while drinking. Or not! Vallee had based this novel ditty on the (Emil Fenstad) march "Opie."

19. "Would You Like to Take a Walk?" Victor 22611. The innocence of this still suggestive title penned by Harry Warren, Mort Dixon, and Billy Rose indeed finds Rudy willing enough to record this bit of mush. More so was a similar crooning job from Skinnay Ennis on a current Hal Kemp release on Brunswick 6055 that just had to have followed Rudy's lead. Luckily, a contemporary Annette Hanshaw version on Velvet Tone 2315-V remains a more interesting alternative! Listen to all!
20. "Besides an Open Fireplace," Victor 22284. Rudy takes a possible gift from contemporary rival Will Osborne, as this crooning job penned by Paul Denniker and Will Osborne himself is very well done.
21. "When Your Hair Has Turned to Silver," Victor 22595. Another bit of smaltzy lyrics penned by P. De Rose and C. Tobias that perfectly fit into the early Depression years of 1930-31. This ditty was more so released as a duet by the likes of the rural appeal of "Bud and Joe Billings," who were to become identified by contemporaries Frank Luther and Carson Robinson.
22. When Yuba Playes The Rhumba On His Tuba". Victor 22742. Herman Hupfeld's penned novelty about a tuba player in Havana, Cuba more so offered the (then) very hip Rudy to provide good commentary on the contemporary cultural influences upon American dance and rhythmic song. (Havana was indeed a hot spot, as well as a legal place to buy a drink,(due to prohibition), as well as providing other vices, in 1930.
23. "Life Is Just a Bowl of Cherries," Victor 22783. Perhaps this Broadway entity from *George White's Scandals of 1931*), penned by Lew Brown and Ray Henderson, attempted to be novel despite the Great Depression was entertaining. Does Rudy imitate contemporary Willie Howard mimicking his vocal style?
24. "This Is The Missus". Victor 22783. Another Broadway entity that Rudy introduced from George White's Scandals of 1931 that ain't bad.
25. "As Time Goes By," Victor 22773. This moody title penned by Herman Hupfeld is notable in the career of Rudy Vallee. As a Broadway entity from *Everybody's Welcome*, the song ditty had also been a contemporary 1931 Jacques Renard release on Brunswick 6505. More so, it had also been crooned out by Bing Crosby (only) over the radio in the same year. This emotional bit of smaltzy had indeed been known well enough, and while perhaps even Vallee himself did not think much of it, it had been less than a novelty, which was something Rudy had perhaps been overly concerned with as recording fodder. This ditty, however smaltzy, had been solid material. (Crosby had missed this one!)

As luck would have it, the 1942 film *Casablanca*, with Humphrey Bogart, Ingrid Bergman, and singing at a piano, Dooley Wilson, had inserted "As Time Goes By" into the film. While done well by Dooley in the film, a musicians' strike had prevented a contemporary newer recording. More so, as the popularity of the film continued, a public demand from a weary World War II generation had found both the Renard and Vallee originals reissued. Amazingly, the (1943) Vallee reissue product on Victor 20-1526 sold. Moreover, it sold so well, that it became his biggest seller since 1929! For a time, the Rudy Vallee recording legacy, noting other reissues, also did well.

26. "Home," Hit of the Week-A-3-4. Another bit of fluffy (1932) crooning penned by Peter Van Steeden and Geoffrey Clarkson. It also seems that Rudy's mushy croon is a bit stronger, or had recording technics improved a bit?
27. "By the Sycamore Tree," Hit of the Week-B-1-2. What could be worked out by a Sycamore tree? This light (1932) crooning job penned by Haven Gillespie and

Peter Wendling explains it all. Is it just too much soft talk?(This ditty should not be confused with another song ditty, with the same title as penned by George V. Hubart and Max Hoffman, popular around the turn of the century in (1903). Amoung many versions, an acoustic 9 inch (Zone-o-phone) version by Bob Roberts found the subject about owls, and the sounds they make influencing girls named Sue? While all this stupidty was hard to hear, Rudy's mushy song is better, although it still seems Rudy must use a lot of lyric, including an example of birds getting together, to get where he wants to be)?

28. "Was That the Human Thing to Do," Hit of the Week C-1-2. (The Boswell Sisters did it better!)
29. "A Faded Summer Love," Hit of the Week-M-4-5. The contemporary Bing Crosby version, on Brunswick 6200, finds Rudy's crooning effort a bit stiffer, although just as mushy.
30. "The Wooden Soldier and the China Doll," Hit of the Week-C-2-3. This two-sided exercise of mushy crooning at least defined Rudy as someone that was very good at it! Penned by Charles Newman and Isham Jones, this two-sided (mushy) crooning effort finds its ambiguous title just too much for one side. Or maybe if the first side does not produce sleep, side two will do the trick?
31. "You Try Somebody Else," Hit of the Week-MM-4-5. Another Vallee effort to rival a well-done and jazzy contemporary Kate Smith rendering as well as a surprising fast-paced attempt by rival crooner, Russ Columbo.
32. "By the Fireside," Hit of the Week-D-2-3. While this ditty penned by Ray Noble, Jimmy Campbell, and Reg Connolly is perhaps all British, Rudy's creditable crooning job, noting a (British) version by Al Bowlly, finds a worthwhile comparison.
33. "Lovable," Hit of the Week-D-2-3. This ditty penned by Gus Kahn and Harry Woods was mushy enough to become a contemporary (1932) best seller as a Leo Reisman release, featuring a stiff vocal by Dick Robertson on Victor 22954. Rudy is just as soft but sung better if anyone had bothered to purchase this little-known recording as released on thin (cardboard like) Durium (Hit of the Week) release. Bing Crosby had perhaps sung it best in a contemporary film short, yet sadly did not officially record it. The title should not be confused with a ditty penned by Seymour Simons and Richard Whiting that had been a (1928) mid-tempo attempt at rhythmic jazz released by the former director of the University of North Carolina's orchestra, Hal Kemp. This recording had featured Kemp's drummer-singer Skinnay Ennis, who was to become (later) heard as an early crooner, much influenced by Rudy's 1928-29 contemporary success.
34. "Three's A Crowd". Columbia 2714-D. Did contemporary Will Osborne's version of the Broadway entity title sound like Rudy? Or did Rudy, with his picture on the (Columbia) release, sound like Will? Or were both dance bands the same?
35. "Let's Put Out the Lights," Columbia 2715-D. As far as lyrics are to be voiced, Rudy's own "Let's Put Out the Lights and Go to Bed" is somewhat toned down by a contemporary Bing Crosby version on Brunswick 6414, much as a slight title difference, "Let's Turn Out the Lights and Go to Sleep." While (still) a harmless bit of fluff, it's easy to figure, Rudy does succeed at making things a tad more interesting! Does Rudy mention (composer) Herman Hupfeld?
36. "Brother, Can You Spare a Dime?" Columbia 2725-D. As from the contemporary 1932 Broadway review *Americana* penned by Jay Gorney and "Yip" Harburg, this poignant ditty about the effects of the Great Depression (for most people) was considered a bit radical for the times. Perhaps a political statement as well, the

powerful lyrics indeed explore deeply into the hopeless situation of many Americans. While the highbrow image of Rudy Vallee would not have seemed to had possessed the abilities to make this ditty effective, he somehow does and with great clarity. In comparison, a fine and contemporary Bing Crosby version on Brunswick 6414 was to be considered a bit better. More so, it should also be noted that the Vallee version also had an effective spoken word introduction, something that Crosby had decided not to use.

37. "How Deep Is the Ocean," Columbia 2724-D. Rudy attempts to emulate Bing Crosby here, and while done well enough, the Crosby version on Brunswick 6406 beats him out.
38. "The Glory of Love," Melotone 6-06-09. This Billy Hill-penned ditty finds Rudy in good and typically stiff form. While this dated style may be considered a bit of fluff, Rudy is found to have been at least committed to this recording, which is also a fine sweet band effort. A contemporary Benny Goodman release with a fine vocal by Helen Ward is also done very well. As a further note, it's worthwhile to speculate on a later 1950s group sound recording by the "Five Keys" on Alladin 3099.
39. "A Jug Of Wine A Loaf Of Bread And Thou". Columbia-2730-D. (Thelma Carpenter would later define this ditty).
40. "Old Man Harlem," Columbia 2764-D. This fine excuse for "Harlem" hip-ness and a faster-paced vocal with his usual 1933 'sweet band arraingement ain't bad. While there could be some speculation raised upon who penned this ditty, it was credited to Hoagy Carmichael and Rudy himself. Did Rudy write this with Carmichael? Speculation has it that a deal with Carmichael was made? Moreover, a (later) Ethel Waters version, with a better vocal and swing arrangement by the lesser-known all-black Eddie Mallory Orchestra, would more so define this ditty.
41. "Meet Me In The Gloming" Columbia-2756-D. A bit of mushy lyric, penned by Al Goodhart, Al Hoffman and Arthur Freed meet Rudy's soft croon well enough.
42. "Everything I Have Is Yours," Victor 24458. A fine film entity more so defined by contemporary Ruth Etting on Brunswick 6719.
43. "Flying Down To Rio". Victor 24459. This title of the very successful 1933 Ginger Rogers and Fred Astaire film, penned by Edward Eliscu, Vincent Youmanns and Gus Kahn found Fred trying to sing it but mostly dancing. Luckily, Rudy's croon (somewhat emulated by Fred Astaire in the film), makes it even more pleasant mid tempo dance number as a contemporary recording.
44. "Puddin'Head Jones". Victor 24475. This Al Byron and Lou Handman penned ditty is more of a pun that later became a film title? Or just good fun?
45. "Ha Cha Cha". Victor 24722. This bit of slang was associated with comic Jimmy Durante as well as the contemporary 1934 Loretta Young and Charles Boyer film "Caravan", penned by Gus Kahn and Wearner Richard Heymann. As a mid-tempo 'fox trot', this very pleasant dance number found Rudy's croon as elegant as it was sophisticated.
46. "P.S. I Love You," Victor 24723. This early ditty penned by Johnny Mercer and Gordon Jenkins. Jenkins luckily found its way to Rudy. (Light years later in 1957, Frank Sinatra would finally define it!)
47. "To Be Or Not To Be", Bluebird-B-5118. The articulate vocal of Rudy nails this Allie Weubel & Elliot Grennard penned ditty. (Ethel Waters also rendered a contemporary version, just as articualate as the college educated Vallee. yet only as a lesser known radio performance).

48. "By A Waterfall". Bluebird-B-5171. The contemporary 1933 film "Footlight Parade", had found Dick Powell and Ruby Keeler introducing this Sammy Fain and Irving Kahal penned ditty shortly before a fabulous group of scantily clothed girls took a punge into a huge 'water' production. While the production was better than the stupid song, Rudy's croon and 'sweet band' finds a way to lift it.
49. "Shanghai Lil". Bluebird B-5172. This Harry Warren and Al Dubin penned ditty had been introduced in the contemporary 1933 film "Footlight Parade" by James Cagney. As Shanghai, China was then considered the most corrupt city in the world, the obvious pun, about a lady of the evening, "Shanghai Lil" more ever fit. As a recording, Rudy's own slicker vocal, made it an even better 'fit' for Rudy.
50. "Harbor Lights," Bluebird B-7067. In 1950, Bing Crosby would later revive Rudy's original 1930s croon of this ditty, penned by Will Grosz and Jimmy Kennedy. Listen to both and compare!
51. "Vieni Vieni", Bluebird-B-7069. As adapted from the European Neopolitan theme by Frenchman Vincent Scotto, Rudy, along with George Koger & H. Varna, somehow made this popular operatic based ditty, a contemporary continental hit by Erna Sack (the; German nightingale')., into a major U.S. best selling entity, casting aside the current 1937 'swing era'
52. "Whiffenpoof Song," Bluebird B-7135. Rudy's first recording of this sentimental ditty associated with Yale University and penned by Tod Galloway, Meade Minnigerode, and George S. Pomeroy, is still a dated piece of work but done well. Or perhaps Rudyard Kipling has something to do with the original lyrics?(Rudy would later re-record this ditty in the 1940s-with little difference).
53. "Mad Dogs and Englishmen," Bluebird B-7135. This attempt at novelty and highbrow humor actually works and perhaps because of the personality of Rudy Vallee himself. More so, this ditty perhaps personifies a huge longing of many wealthy Americans to indeed be Brits. For many contemporaries, this rendering was Rudy's own emulation of contemporary Britisher Noel Coward, who had claimed authorship for this ditty, with a U.S. release on on Victor-24332. While this ditty was speculative, it was also true for those interested in literature and Rudyard Kipling, that the pun, among others, in the British Empire was true. Sunburn?
54. Have You Met Ms. Jones?" Bluebird B-7238. This ditty penned by Rodgers and Hart is a sure classic.
55. "The Drunkard Song," Victor 24721. Drinking again? Rudy found this traditional drinking song known as "There's a Tavern In Town," penned by William H. Hills and Robert De Cormier in 1883, a perfect way for the public to celebrate (with him) the end of Prohibition. Another beer?
56. "Lost In A Fog". Victor-24721. While Connie Boswell defined this Dorothy Fields and Jimmy McHugh penned ditty, Rudy still croons it well enough?
57. "Evry Day". Victor-24827. It's interesting to compare this Sammy Fain and Irving Kahal penned ditty with a very similar vocal contemporary Will Osborne version. Listen and compare.
58. "The Way You Look Tonight". Conquer-8699. It aint Fred Astaire or as defining as Billie Holiday or Bing Crosby and Dixie Lee Crosby, yet Rudy's classy vocal is indeed done well!
59. "Lydia, the Tattooed Lady," Decca 2708. Rudy got this novelty penned by E.Y. Harburg and Harold Arlen from the contemporary 1939 Marx Brothers film *At the Circus*, and it had been introduced in fine and humorous flair by Groucho himself.

Moreover, Rudy's own interest in novel approach had already been proved, and those who had purchased this ditty would not be disappointed.

60. "Alouetta". Enterprise-181. This later, post war release in 1946 found Rudy's adaption of an older traditional French Canadian song ditty pleasing and pleasant enough. (The tune may be the basis of Eddie Cantor's previous release of the novel "The Man On The Flying Trapees")?
61. "Winchester Cathedral". Dot-(LP)-V-6005. Light-years away from Rudy's initial 1928 success at New York's "Heigh Ho" Club, without a microphone (but with a megaphone), Rudy (again) became at least became relivant in a time of rock and the "British invasion in 1966. As luck would have it, a young (British) songwriter, Geoff Stephens, a huge fan of many of Rudy's old recordings, found his cathedral in Winchester, Hampshire, England, something the write about. While it is unclear the subsequent best selling recording on (Fontana Records-F-1562), as recorded by the "New Vaudville Band", featured Geoff or a vocalist named John Carter or not, it is alleged that Carter did tour with the band, using a megaphone as a prop, in a well done imitation of Rudy. Or was Carter really aware of Rudy? While the new 'rock' age already had different founders, the forgotten Vallee style was to at least acknowledged, from some? Or who really cared? Or cared? Or did old photographs of Rudy in the 1920s (with a megaphone) clinch his visual image?

As all this developed, the aged Vallee just had to have enjoyed it. A subsequent (1967) LP release by Rudy, on Dot Records, found the old voice much less that what it had been, although his own recording of "Winchester Catherdal" is at least interesting enough. Does Rudy sound better in mono or stereo? This LP may find the silly answer?

Radio. As perhaps the *major* radio vocal entity from 1928 until the emergence of Bing Crosbyand Russ Columbo in 1931, the sophisticated and popular Vallee was not afraid to invite on his on his major network programs such contemporary (black) guests such as Ethel Waters, Midge Williams, Louis Armstrong and (visiting from France in 1935)-Josephine Baker, despite the extreme limits of racism of the times. In addition to many contemporary film entities, he pioneered and or helped introduce many 'new' vocalists, especially noting Alice Faye and Lee Wiley. He also helped the continental (Austrian born) cabaret and film entity Greta Keller become better known in the U.S. His social conscience also led him to feature a contemporary fan, (blind) Helen Keller in 1936—who, like most women, just loved him! The following "Fleishman" radio entities perhaps found Rudy at his best mushy crooning style in 1932:

62. "Babes in the Wood," This ditty penned by Jerome Kern and Schuyler Green had been around since 1916. More so, Rudy most likely figured that the song needed a good crooning.

Note: The following ditties are from the (then) contemporary 1932 Broadway entity *Ballyhoo*, which involved the likes of E.Y. Harburg, Louis Gensler, and a young Johnny Mercer in the production. While Rudy was not involved in the original production, his soft crooning indicates that he should have been!

63. "Thrill Me."
64. "Riddle Me This."

65. "How Do You Do It?" (Rival crooner Harlan Lattimore did produce a fine recording of this ditty.)

As a bandleader, Rudy more ever backed up the likes of many, especially noting Alice Faye, as well as the Stewart Sisters release of the contemporary 1935 Shirley Temple film ditty "On The Good Ship Lollypop". on Victor-24838.

Rudy continued to perform in radio, film, Broadway, and record. While a later appearance in a 1968 Elvis Presley film, *Live a Little Love a Little*, in a non-singing roll, had really no real merits, perhaps his natural wit in earlier films was, in true retrospective, to be taken more seriously than his singing. Moreover, as in recordings, the films of his rivals, especially noting those of Bing Crosby, reduced him as a major film entity. Indeed, his luck had been, in true retrospective, bigger and better as a major radio entity as far as contemporary media was concerned. Nevertheless, as a vocalist, perhaps a visual image in the following defined him at his best:

66. "I'm Just a Vagabond Lover," Rudy made an appearance in the 1929 film *Glorifying the American Girl*, as is captured perfectly, performing with megaphone and all at his peak. (Rudy also had a contemporary film out by the same name.)
67. "A Little Kiss Each Morning." In the film short *Radio Rhythm*, 1929.
68. "Don't Take Her Pooh Pooh Doo Away." In the film short *Radio Rhythm*.

- More found about Rudy Vallee in the record labels and Radio sections of this book.

Sarah Vaughan

The popular music of the 1940s is divided by the mid-1942 musicians' strike and the music subsequently produced after it in 1944. In was also a time of much creative endeavor by the likes of urban entities such as Dizzy Gillespie, J. C. Heard, Charlie "bird" Parker (also sax), and among others, the vocals of Billy Eckstine (with the Erskine Hawkins and Earle Hines Orchestras), and Sarah Vaughan. In true retrospective, the enormous popularity of the baritone-voiced Eckstine would become fully recognized after World War II (1945), more so as a black and urban alternative to the likes of Frank Sinatra and Dick Haymes. The subsequent career of Sarah Vaughan was to be more complicated—indeed a far different vocal than found in female contemporaries such as Dinah Shore or Jo Stafford as well as heard in Billie Holiday, Ella Fitzgerald, or Thelma Carpenter. As a showboating vocalist, Sarah had something more unique, as her vocal style, was all her own, indeed something very different. Moreover, on some renderings, she made the attempt to "double sing" or "over sing" lyric, something similar to the instrumental antics of Gillespie and Parker, who were also professional colleges and would appear on (some) early recordings. Picks include:

1. "I'll Wait and Pray," De Lux 2003. As a vocalist with Billy Eckstine's orchestra, this ditty penned by Gerald Valentine and George Tredwell, found Sarah's smoothness truly innovative (1944) as well as very "different" from any other contemporary vocalists.

Note: The rise of small recording labels in the mid-1940s found the smooth and cool Sarah trying to find luck with better than average productions, after her debut with Eckstine's equally small "De Lux" recording. While she would not see some big money for some time, she was in the good company of committed musicians, in the midst of the current bebop movement. The following releases create a dreamy (1940s) nightclub image and mood.

2. "Signing Off," Continental 6024. Sarah's creative edge (already heard on "I'll Wait and Pray" (noted above) is even further advanced with Dizzy Gillespie and Company and penned by Leonard Feather and Jessyca Russell.
3. "Interlude (Night in Tunisia)," Continental 6031. Some clever playing has Sarah (really) transporting her listeners from a (smoky) nightspot in urban Americana to the African port of Tunisia, with contrived and adapted Tunisian sounds penned by Frank Paparelli, Raymond Leveen, and Dizzy Gillespie.
4. "No Smoke Blues," Continental 6061. The (cigarette) smoke has cleared, and Sarah's vocal image (of nightclub action) penned by Sanderson is in sight, as well as Sarah's exciting vocal!
5. "East of the Sun," Continental 6031. Sarah indeed takes you "east of the sun" as the old standard penned by "Bowman" or Brooks Bowman is more so defined.
6. "Lover Man," Guild 1002. While this title had its greatest claims on a contemporary (1945) Billie Holiday vocal released on Decca 23391, it's more than interesting to compare Sarah's ((fuller) voice to that of Billie's shady vocal tones. A close call? (This guild master was later released on one side of Musicraft 499.
7. "What More Can a Woman Do?" Continental 6008. This version of the (then) contemporary Peggy Lee original entity on Capital 197 successfully challenges Peggy's coolness (in true retrospective), noting the differing excellence of the Lee style.
8. "I'd Rather Have a Memory Than a Dream," Continental 6008. This ditty penned by Leonard Feather and Bob Russell cannot help itself; its projection of a "memory of a dream" is (for sure) very real. Just listen!
9. "Mean to Me," Continental 6024. This (already) old ditty penned by Roy Turk and Fred Ahlert is challenged with a completely fresh and creative approach to the likes of others, especially noting the previous renderings of Ruth Etting, Helen Morgan, and Billie Holiday. More so with Gillespie backing, Sarah's vocal is indeed redefining, as she is seemingly harmonizing with herself, a mean feat in itself!
10. "Time and Again," Musicraft 337. This ditty features less bebop and more of a group sound. Dizzy Gillespie is gone, as this rendering features Sarah with "Stuff Smith and His Trio," penned by Stuff Smith himself.

The following four titles feature Sarah as a vocalist for "John Kirby and His Orchestra."

11. "I'm Scared," Crown 107. A very fine vocal penned by Raymond Leveen and Lou Singer.
12. "You Go to My Head," Crown 109. This Haven Gillespie and J. Fred Coots vocal is very much influenced by the earlier Billie Holiday release, on Vocalion 4126, noting no clash in style as was heard in the previous vocal comparisons found in "Lover Man."

13, 14. "I Could Make You Love Me," Crown 118. Sarah (again) scores, with style, as this commanding title penned by Pete De Rose and Bob Russell also fits Sarah's own command of lyric, which just must be heard! (This rendering must not to be confused with a rerecording, almost as good, on Musicraft 398 within a few months.)

15. "It Might as Well Be Spring," Crown 108. No one can sing this ditty penned by Richard Rodgers and Oscar Hammerstein II so beautifully, as her vocal just cannot be emulated by anybody else. Moreover, other versions are good, including those by 1946 contemporaries Dick Haymes on Decca 18706 and the excellent Margaret Whiting rendering, a Paul Weston release on Capital 214.
16. "All Too Soon," Gotham 105 This ditty penned by Duke Ellington and Carl Sigman benefits (greatly) by Sarah's vocal.
17. "We're Through," H.R.S. 1019. As by Sarah "With Dicky Wells' Big Seven," Sarah's vocal adds drama to this fine ditty penned by Tadd Dameron and Jesse Greer. Moreover, she is backed up by George Tredwell, with some excellent backing.
18. "If You Could See Me Now," Musicraft 380. While record buyers could only hear Sarah, this mellow bit of smaltzy penned by Tadd Dameron and Carl Sigman is indeed a beautiful experience to be heard, yet not to be seen.
19. "You're Not The Kind," Musicraft 380. This ditty penned by Will Hudson and Irving Mills, while dated, was well worth Sarah's efforts to record.
20. "You're Blase," Musicraft 394. Backed by "George Auld and His Orchestra," this ditty penned by Ord Hamilton and Bruce Siever may be considered the first of many stupid titles which Sarah would somehow lift by her (still) committed vocal.
21. "My Kinda Love," Musicraft 398. Sarah's update of the old Bing Crosby rendering from the 1920s on Okeh 4118 is more so a totally different vocal style, as this excellent ditty penned by Louis Alter and Jo Trent finds Sarah's vocal workout something very special. Jazzy (young) Bing or you and jazzy Sarah?
22. "September Song," Musicraft 446. Penned by Kurt Weill and Maxwell Anderson for the Broadway entity *Knickerbocker Holiday*, his straight-laced ditty was luckily challenged by Sarah, with fine and interesting backing by the Teddy Wilson Quartet. Sarah clearly scores here, as her very jazzy and sophisticated singing provides this ditty with a definitive rendering. Is this better than Frank Sinatra's better knowncontemporary version? Yes!
23. "Everything I Have Is Yours," Musicraft 494. Another attempt at an old standard more so betters the 1933 Rudy Vallee version as well as competes with the fine older style of Ruth Etting's version on Brunswick 6919. It is moreover a fine and interesting comparison in the Etting and Vaughan matchup, with the Vaughan version at least sounding more latter century (modern) than the older claims charm of Ruth Etting. Ruth or Sarah?
24. "Body and Soul," Musicraft 494. Sarah (almost) succeeds with this (already) old 1930 classic. More so, after starting off well enough with a traditional rendering, she challenges lyrics with her showboating vocal style and somehow gets lost and sadly never finishes. Nevertheless, while not achieving the success of other versions, as those of many, including the likes of divas Helen Morgan, Libby Holman, or Ruth Etting, this failure to define is still an interesting and entertaining listening experience.
25. "I'm Through with Love," Musicraft 499. As the original flip of "Body and Soul," another old Bing Crosby classic on Brunswick 6120 is challenged. Moreover, Sarah's confident showboating finds a successful result, noting the vast differences between the excellent early crooning of Crosby and the unique vocal prowess of Sarah. Bing or Sarah?
26. "I Cover the Waterfront," Musicraft 503. Sarah covers the "Waterfront" in style, as her newer style, in interesting comparisons with the likes of Connie Boswell and Billie Holiday, scores. A tough one to call.

27. "Tenderly," Musicraft 504. Sarah's first best seller (1947) also finds George Treadwell's excellent backing. Penned by Walter Gross and Jack Lawrence, this may be considered Sarah's own signature tune, betraying her soft mellow voice rendered tenderly.
28. "Don't Blame Me," Musicraft 504. The excellence of the older Ethel Waters version is challenged. Ethel or Sarah?
29. "The Lord's Prayer," Musicraft 525. This semi-opera rendering, with cello and harp backing provided by Ted Dale, finds a traditional arrangement claimed by Albert Hay Malotte. It is directly from the New Testament: Matthew 6:9-13 and Luke 11:2-4.
30. "Gentleman Friend," Musicraft 539. A sophisticated gentleman may be visiting. This ditty penned by Arnold B. Horwitt and Richard Levine just may provide a smirk, although Sarah's rich vocal is committed enough not to betray it.
31. "The One I Love Belongs to Somebody Else," Musicraft 552. Accompanied by "Ted Dale and Orchestra," Sarah achieves (another) vocal triumph, finally updating this old tired (1924) ditty a good and interesting vocal! Penned by Isham Jones and Gus Kahn, Sarah's commitment to this ditty remains relevant.
32. "What a Difference a Day Made!" Musicraft 552. While differences between vocalists are fun to find and compare, this old and traditional ditty of Latin origins had been previously known as "Cuando Vuelva a tu Lado." As a contemporary (1935) Bob Crosby vocal, on the Dorsey Brothers release on Decca 283 and a later rendering from Kay Starr, as a (1941) Charlie Barnet release, on Decca 18620, this ditty already achieved relevance as good recording fodder. Oddly, Sarah's own vocal, despite its excellence, somehow did not exploit or explode into recognition of this ditty claimed by Marie Grever and Stanley Adams. This ditty would more so become a best seller some ten years later as a fine Dinah Washington rendering, a contemporary rival of Sarah, on Mercury 71435.
33. "It's Magic," Musicraft 557. This vocal by Sarah just might be better than the smooth (contemporary) original version by Doris Day on Columbia 38188. Doris or Sarah?
34. "Nature Boy," Musicraft 567. This best seller of 1948 had been sung to perfection by contemporary Nat King Cole on Capital 15054. Is Sarah's version better or is it just another comparison of vocal ability and style?
35. "Black Coffee," Columbia 38462. As Sarah's first Columbia best seller (1949), this title penned by Paul Francis Webster and Sonny Burke is creative singing at its best. More so, its lyrics are stupid, as latter-century feminists would attest. In any case, it's hard to remain angry at Sarah!
36. "I'm Crazy To Love You," Columbia 38701. Sarah (perhaps) achieves her best side (for Columbia), as she successfully flirts with this ditty penned by Sue Werner, Kay Werner, and Karry Marino.
37. "Thinking Of You," Columbia 38925. Sarah again scores on this old standard penned by Bert Kalmar and Harry Ruby, more so better than contemporary Eddie Fisher. Listen and compare!
38. "The Nearness of You," Columbia 39071. Connie Boswell's (excellent) and previous version of this ditty is challenged!
39. "Deep Purple," Columbia 39370. This already old (1930s) entity penned by Mitchell Parish and PeteDe Rose had been introduced by Bea Wain, as a Larry Clinton release on Victor 26141. The haunting melody had found Wain's excellent version to become a best seller and, rendered by many others, include Bing Crosby. Sarah, as backed by Percy Faith's Orchestra, perhaps has the edge, as her natural voice, with a creative Percy Faith touch, is relevant and perfectly mellow.

40. "Mighty Lonesome Feelin'," Columbia 39873. While not as good as "Deep Purple," this Percy Faith-backed ditty penned by Sammy Gallop and Al Kent finds Sarah in a fine, somber, and moody voice.
41. "After Hours," Columbia 39494. A smoke-filled urban nightclub and Sarah (1950) may seem like a dream, as this ditty penned by Robert Gordon creates an atmosphere, however contrived. Close your eyes and dream. Or fall asleep. Perhaps contemporary Dinah Washington had other ideas!
42-49. "Sarah Vaughan," Columbia B-211. This early LP found Sarah, with George Tredwell and his All Stars, featuring Jimmy Jones, Bud Johnson, Benny Green, Tony Scott, Freddy Green, Mundell Lowe, Billy Taylor, and J. C Heard in good company on pop standards. Like always, Sarah's vocals claim these pop standards, especially the Frank Loesser and Jimmy McHugh ditty "Can't Get Out of This Mood." While it's reasonable that the likes of Dick Haymes, Margaret Whiting, Ella Fitzgerald, and others found Sarah's choice of the following song ditty more than a challenge, it's also a wonder why Sarah tackles her own previous versions of "Mean to Me," "East of the Sun," and "It Might as Well Be Spring. As in most cases, re recordings are not as good as original renderings, although Sarah's vocals do not lack quality. In any case, these Columbia masters include:

a. "East of the Sun."
b. "Nice Work If You Can Get It."
c. "Come Rain, Come Shine." d. "Mean to Me."
e. "It Might as Well Be Spring."
f. "Can't Get Out of This Mood" Frank Loesser and Jimmy Mc Hugh 's penned ditty tops this LP's best recording as Sarah moreover defines it as a 'modern' jazz classic.
g. "Goodnight, My Love."
h. "Ain't Misbehavin'."

50. "Once in a While," MGM 10549. Penned by Michael Edward and Bud Green, this version easily beats out on older Harriet Hilliard version as an Ozzie Nelson releaser on Bluebird 7256. Harriet or Sarah?
51. "I Can't Get Started," MGM 10762. Yeah, this is the same old ditty penned by Ira Gershwin and Vernon Duke, with Sarah doing her thing very well.
52. "I Love You," MGM 11144. Sarah is teamed with Billy Eckstine and both show off their vocal styles, with good-sounding results, as this old Cole Porter-penned standard is revived.
53. "Make Yourself Comfortable," Mercury 70469. This (1954) novelty penned by Bob Merrill is campy and predictably risqué. While the Vaughan showboating style is less obvious, this ditty by Sarah is well worth hearing. More so, this ditty sounds as if it has added sound effects—echo. Just why this was added to Sarah's recording is beyond reason, as he her natural voice is so unique. So why? Or perhaps does anyone still care?
54. "Idle Gossip," Mercury 70469. This very title had possibilities, and Sarah's vocal penned by Floyd Huddleston and Joseph Meyer is a fine popular rendering, despite the emergence of rock and roll.
55. "Whatever Lola Wants," Mercury 70534. The Broadway entity from *Damn Yankees* penned by Richard Adler and Jerry Ross is a contrived calypso number that works.
56. "It Happened Again," Mercury 70947. This ditty penned by Johnny Orlando and Jack Limber is sung without gimmicks and indeed very well!

57. "I Wanna Play House," Mercury 70947. This popular novelty penned by Bob Dane and Victor Paul ain't bad.
58. "Passing Strangers," Mercury 71030. This classic duet with Sarah's old friend and mentor, while very pop-sounding, finds Billy Eckstine in good voice.
59-67. "The Best of Irving Berlin," Mercury 20326 (Sarah and Billy Eckstine). At last, a duet LP with the two vocal pioneers of the bebop era! But wait! The likes of Gillespie, Charlie "bird" Parker, and Erskine Hawkins are sadly missing. Oh well, this collection of popular collection of old (Irving Berlin) standards just had to do. Fortunately (alone with a fine cover shot of Sarah and Billy), this LP does deliver some fine pop music, however aged. The bass baritone of Eckstine's vocal more so cuts through Sarah's (usual) showboating vocals. Her vocal finds itself secondary to Eckstine's lead, thus leaving Sarah with less to do, yet graciously. Indeed, there is no clash here, just good vocals with more than perfect pitch for interesting listening for (many) boring (old) songs. Highlights include:

    a. "Easter Parade."
    b. "You're Just in Love." Better than the previous duet with Dick Haymes and Ethel Merman? Yes!
    c. "Remember."
    d. "Isn't It a Lovely Day?"
    e. "I've Got My Love to Keep Me Warm." Yeah.
    f. "Alexander's Ragtime Band." Billy and Sarah drag a little, but (near the end), they make up for it!
    g. "Now It Can Be Told."
    h. "Cheek to Cheek."
    i. "Always."

68-74. "Sarah Vaughan," Mercury 20383. This live LP from the mid-1950s (still) sounds very personable. Moreover, the (contrived) small cabaret setting is real enough for Sarah to sound as if she is performing at a party in your living room.

    a. "Like Someone in Love."
    b. "Detour Ahead."
    c. "Three Little Words."
    d. "I'll String Along with You."
    e. "You'd Be Nice to Come Home To."
    f. "All of You" or "All of Me."
    g. "Thanks for the Memory."

75. "Broken-Hearted Melody," Mercury 7147. This (1959) recording penned by Hal David and Sherman Edwards is of high quality, with a backbeat and rhythmic tempo managed by the up and coming Quincy Jones. While some may have called it a piece of mellow rock, this ditty is perfectly harmonized by Sarah, blending in well with lyric. This attempt by Sarah to sound contemporary in 1959 is modern and perhaps defines vocal excellence and innovation itself.
76. "Misty". Mercury-7147. How can a truly great flipside be ignored? In this case "Broken Hearted Melody" just buried it, as this Errol Gardner and Johnny Burke penned ditty, as a single relese, just did not get enough contemporary 1959 airplay. Sarah, managed by Quincy Jones, is just supurb. In retrospective, while a younger

contemporary, Johnny Mathis put his own soft crooning claims upon it as an 'A' side the same year, for many, Sarah's well done vocal indeed defined it. (The later 1971 Clint Eastwood film "Play Misty For Me" refers to this ditty as the original instrumental by Gardner).

77. "Send In The Clowns". Mainstream (LP) MLR-412

- Note: Sarah continued to record numerous LPs and singles and is still ever present on numerous CDs. More so than other vocalists, she has remained known for her natural vocal (voice).
- *More* about Sarah Vaughan in the LP section of this book.

Bea Wain

A pleasant rhythmic lead from the fine contemporary sweet band of Larry Clinton indeed put vocalist Bea Wain in the spotlight. With a warm and dry vocal, her obvious bending of phrases produced a huge audience, leading to a solo career and a radio career as well. The following picks find Bea at her best:

1. "Wake Up and Sing," Banner 6-04-13 This attempt at rhythm penned by Cliff Friend, Carmen Lombardo, and Charles Tobias seems to work. Check it out!
2. "The One Rose That's Left in My Heart," Victor 25724. A good rendering!
3. "Old Folks," Victor 26056. This yarn penned by Dedette Lee Hill and Willard Robinson, is far from great, yet it's an interesting tale of an old Yankee or Confederate soldier, noting that many were still around and aging in (1938). Somehow, this song ditty found its way to the dance floor for (close) dancing partners. (Abraham Lincoln at Gettysburg? Just listen!)
4. "Dr. Rhythm," Victor 25768. The contemporary (1938) Bing Crosby film title, penned by Johnny Burke and James Monaco, just had to be defined as a recording. Since Crosby (mysteriously) didn't, Bea indeed did!
5. "Marta," Victor 25789. This very fine swing entity penned by C. Von-Flotow challenges Bea with a (very) wordy lyric, with Bea sneaking in a high note and holding it very well, meshed in between Larry Clinton's backing.
6. "I Dreamt I Dwelt in Marble Floors," Victor 25789. This contrived excuse to dance is obvious, and, penned by M. W. Balfe, succeeds. A light swing!
7. "You're An Education," Victor 25794. As this title penned by Al Dubin and Harry Warren suggests, an education is indeed important! Listen to this (important) ditty and become educated.
8. "My Reverie," Victor 26006. This ballad, adapted by Larry Clinton from the classical Claude Debussy piece, served them well. As a huge best seller of 1938, it indeed enhanced both Bea and Larry Clinton's value to RCA Victor.
9. "Heart and Soul," Victor 26046. Larry Clinton's orchestra perfectly meets Bea's soft vocal tone. A fine contemporary version by Connie Boswell, on Decca 1896, is also a winner. Bea or Connie?
10. "Deep Purple," Victor 26141. This classic song ditty is less than mush and is full of lyric substance, penned by Pete De Rose and May Singhi. Moreover, Bea's soft vocal is meaningful. Who says the color purple is not a deep one? Among others, contemporary crooning jobs by Bing Crosby on Decca 2374 and by Dick Todd on Bluebird B-10072 may be singled out as competitive comparisons with Bea's. Listen

and learn! Light years away, the rock era found versions by Billy Ward and the Dominos, on Liberty 55099, and the team of Nino Tempo and April Stevens on Atco 6294 might be more familiar for many baby boomers.

11. "I Get Along without You Very Well," Victor 26151. Bea's outstanding performance owes nothing to anyone, even noting contemporary (1939) renderings by Terry Allen as a Red Norvo release on Vocalion 4648 and an excellent crooning job by Dick Todd released on Bluebird B-10150. Perhaps this classic penned by Hoagy Carmichael would later find even more clarity by Frank Sinatra, light years away in the 1950s on Capital LP W-518.
12. "The Masquerade Is Over," Victor 26151. This ditty penned by Herb Magidson and Allie Wrubel isn't bad.
13. "Do I Worry?" Victor 27353. A contemporary Ink Spots release on Decca 3432 is perhaps better.
14. "You Can Depend on Me," Victor 27353. This flip side of the above is a fine (1941) update of the (1932) Louis Armstrong masterpiece, penned by Charles Carpenter, Louis Dunlap, and Earl Hines on Okeh 41538. While falling short of Louis, it's also interesting to compare the contemporary (1941) Art Jarret vocal on Victor 27580. Light years later in 1961, an excellent Brenda Lee version on Decca 31231 would become known by many baby boomers.

Fats Waller

- Thomas "Fats" Waller is often considered a great entity as an instrumentalist (piano and organ) as well as a composer. He had found success as a house band pianist at Vocalion Records in the as well as Broadway composer ("Ain't Misbehavin'"). More so, his personality may be found on many vocal efforts of his own. While limited (vocally), he nevertheless provided his listeners with some fine novelty renderings, many self-penned, and with some fine playing of a jazzy piano or pipe organ. While at first a songwriter, his subsequent and limited radio appearances found him attempting vocals or at least commenting (humorously) about lyrics.

Indeed, this huge piano player became popular and led to a commercial success as a novelty vocalist and as a (vocalist) recording artist as well. The following are picks:

1. "I'm Crazy About My Baby," Columbia 2428-D. The 1920s produced many fine bandleaders. The dance band of the (white) Ted Lewis ranked high, especially in terms of recordings and sales. The young Thomas "Fats" Waller, already a known sideman and pianist for many as well as a Broadway composer of "Ain't Misbehavin'," penned with Andy Razaf and Harry Brooks. While perhaps oddly matched with Lewis, a novel and jazzy result is to be heard, as both Ted and Fats, instrumentally and vocally, jell.
2. "Dallas Blues," Columbia 2527-D. This Louis Armstrong influenced vocal, found on Okeh 8774, ain't bad. Backed (again) by the able Ted Lewis, a fine jazz masterpiece is produced.
3. "Royal Garden Blues," Columbia 2527-D. Another Ted Lewis and Fats Waller combination works well! Perhaps Waller, totally committed, is to be appreciated on the Clarence Williams-penned classic.

4. "You Rascal You," Columbia 2558-D. Sharing some vocals with Jack Teagarden, a fine white bandleader who could also produce some fine vocals, also provided Fats with some challenges. This Teagarden release, yet another Louis Armstrong influenced performance, fins Fats in the thick of it.
5. "Mean Old Bed Bug Blues," Melotone 12457. This bit of novelty, a release by the (unidentified) Rhythmakers, gives punch to the already old Bessie Smith version on Columbia 14250-D.
6. "Yellow Dog Blues," Melotone 12481. More camp and nonsense from Fats and the Rhythmakers visit the (Handy) classic.

   - Note: The following picks, for the most part, find Fats Waller as a single entity. The following recordings also include some of his overseas recordings, which also added more relevance for his huge international appeal.

7. "I Wish I Were Twins," Victor 24641. This ditty penned by Eddie De Lange, Frank Loesser, and Joseph Meyer was given a fair bounce into best-seller territory (1934). A contemporary (English) release by Valaida Snow on Parophone F-118 is less novel, better sung, and far less known.
8. "Don't Let It Bother You," Victor 24714. The iceman? The undertaker? Fats and an unidentified member of his band talk up some good contemporary (1930s) urban slang, penned by Harry Revel and Mack Gordon for the Fred Astaire and Ginger Rogers film "The Gay Divorcee".
9. "Honeysuckle Rose," Victor 24826. While this (1934) rendition should not be confused with a later (1937) recording on Victor 25559, featuring Tommy Dorsey, Bunny Berigan, and Dick Mc Donough, this original is more than fine listening. This ditty penned by Andy Razaf and Fats himself would also be recorded by many others as well as for a (later) sultry-voiced radio air check for Lena Horne. A fine Fats Waller visual performance of this ditty is (later) found in the 1943 film *Stormy Weather*.
10. "I'm Gonna Sit Right Down and Write Myself a Letter," Victor 25039. This very influential rendering of this ditty penned by Joe Young and Fred Ahlert is an attempt at a smooth vocal style that resulted in a jazzy classic. Whatever Fats lacked in vocal ability is to be realized in his musicianship. Or if it was just a fluke, the result is highly appreciated and relevant. (A contemporary Boswell Sisters version on Decca 671 is also very good but less known. Later, in 1957, Bing Crosby actually recorded a fine and jazzy version with the Bob Scobey band on the Victor LP LPM 1473. Another fine rendering was another (1957) Billy Williams single release on Coral 61830.
11. "Lulu's Back in Town," Victor 25063. Fats cuts up this wordy and contrived novelty penned by Harry Warren and Al Dubin with ease.
12. "Truckin'," Victor 25116. This title penned by Rube Bloom and Ted Koehler became a huge best seller for Fats (1935). More so, this very influential bit of Harlem jive, while novel, just might describe both white songwriters Bloom and Koehler as hip. Just how much of this ditty was borrowed is perhaps worth some speculation. In any case, Waller was bound to get it right. Other versions by (black) contemporaries are also well worth noting. A Duke Ellington release, with a smoking Ivie Anderson vocal is better. So is a version by the Mills Blue Rhythm Band on Columbia 3078-D. Yet another rendering by the transplanted Adelaide Hall (in Europe), accompanied by Joe Turner on UI AP-1574 features a fine vocal along with her own dancing, which also may be heard on her recording.
13. "It's a Sin to Tell a Lie," Victor 25342.

14. "You're Not That Kind," Victor 25353.
15. "Bye Bye, Baby," Victor 25388. Pork Chops? Corn bread?
16. "Sposin'," Victor 25415. The previous (1929) best-selling Rudy Vallee recording penned by Paul Denniker and Andy Razaf is resurrected.
17. "The Joint Is Jumpin'," Victor 25689. This wild novelty penned by Andy Razaf, J. C. Johnson, and Fats himself also contains some novel sound effects. Listen for the sound effects of a siren! Somehow, it all works!
18. "That Old Feeling," HMV B-8849. As recorded in Europe in 1938, Fats bumped into his old Broadway contemporary and Harlem neighbor, Adelaide Hall. While the soprano Adelaide croons, Fats, playing a pipe organ, casually puts in a few words!

19, 20. "I Can't Give You Anything but Love," HMV B-8849. (a) Adelaide and Fats again combine, as they had in "That Old Feeling," and soprano Adelaide actually wins out on the jive talk, as this campy flip side scores well indeed. (b) Waller would also record this ditty with his fine-looking and fine-sounding radio protégé, Una Mae Carlisle, sounding very much less highbrow than Hall.

This ditty had been around for a long time as a ditty penned by Dorothy Fields and Frank McHugh for the all-black musical *Blackbirds of 1928*. Oddly, it had not been recorded by Hall and had gotten to be even better well known by a Cliff Edwards release on Columbia 1471-D. Within a few years, a Louis Armstrong version on Okeh 8669 revived it. An effective (1932) rendering by Ethel Waters on Brunswick 6517 had more so defined it. While it's a fact this Hall and Waller version was less known in the United States, it is a classic rendering, a good rival to the Waters version. Just listen!

(Speculation exists about the origins of this ditty, as perhaps speculation by Waller himself.)

21. "Hold Tight," Bluebird 10116. This 1939 title is very hip. The Andrews Sisters version on Decca 2214 is also very good but in this case gives a (slight) edge to Fats. More so, this contrived bit of slang penned by Leonard Kent, Jerry Brandow, Edward Robinson, Leonard Ware, and Willie Spotswood is still novel as well as rhythmic.
22. "Your Socks Don't Match," Bluebird 30-0814.
23. "Honeysuckle Rose." Great visual in film *Stormy Weather*.

> ➢ Note: Fats Waller's superb abilities as a musician may be heard as on many credited and unaccredited backings for many other vocalists. They include the likes of Gene Austin, Adelaide Hall, Ethel Waters, and Lee Wiley.

Helen Ward

The swing era, while founded in Ivie Anderson's vocal of "It Ain't Got the Swing" was considered a band release of Duke Ellington, although it's a good bet that without Ivie, the era would have missed a definition. Bandleader Benny Goodman, while obviously influenced by Ellington and Ivie, also had other ideas and more musical ground to cover. By the time Benny found young Helen Ward (1934), in addition to his notable work as a studio musician with Columbia Records in the late 1920s, his own band had recorded the likes of the established vocals of Ethel Waters and Mildred Bailey as well as a young and struggling Harlem nightclub singer, Billie Holiday.

As a (white) vocalist, Helen Ward's dry voice only needed a little prodding, along with some bright arrangements, usually lined up by Fletcher Henderson, another of Goodman's early influences. Along with his integrated band, which included the likes of Harry James, Gene Krupa, Lionel Hampton, and Teddy Wilson, Benny Goodman struck upon a rhythm section, with some disciplined rhythm singing that ushered in the swing era. For many, Goodman truly dug the music, although for most, the fine vocals of Helen Ward, who was also not bad to look at, defined Goodman's assent into fame, as in live personal appearances, with radio remote, throughout the nation.

1. "All Through The Night"-Columbia-2986-D. Somehow, Helen defines a Cole Porter penned ditty-without being mushy about it.
2. "Blue Moon," Columbia 3003-D. This ditty penned by Rogers and Hart also found a contemporary rendering by Connie Boswell. Listen and compare Helen with Connie's slight Southern accent.
3. "Goody Goody," Victor 25245. This ditty penned by Johnny Mercer and Matty Malneck perhaps found Helen exploiting the rhythm around her with satisfaction. This bit of smaltzy (later) became known to many baby boomers as a huge 1956 Frankie Lymon and The Teenagers.
4. "The Glory of Love," Victor 25316. Another fine vocal penned by Billy Hill, somehow gets a hearing, despite Goodman's Orchestra. (Another contemporary version by Rudy Vallee is also done very well. Listen and compare.)
5. "Sing Me a Swing Song and Let Me Dance," Victor 25340. Is Helen just as good as Ella on this contemporary swing entity?
6. "These Foolish Things Remind Me of You," Victor 25351. Is this Helen's mid tempo version best? Penned by Harry Link, Holt Marvell, and Jack Strachey, Helen sets the mood with excellent, disciplined singing. A Nat Brandywynne release with a Buddy Clark vocal, a (Teddy Wilson) release featuring Billie Holiday and a release from former vaudevillian Benny Fields on Decca-849 more so betray differences in contemporary (mid-1930s) vocal styles that (still) sound interesting. Later mid-1940s versions perhaps found a Thelma Carpenter version (somewhat influenced by Billie Holiday's earlier version), along with a release by a stiff Herb Jeffries version on Exclusive-93-x. Herb Jeffries was a noted band singer for Duke Ellington, and more so a contemporary (black) singing cowboy in film known by mainly by Afro-American audiences in a sadly segregated society. In any case-it's Thelma! Sorry Helen!
7. "There's a Small Hotel," Victor 25363 As in other cases, the bandleader hog, in true retrospective, almost erases Helen's own classic rendering of this classic penned by Rogers and Hart. Helen's 1936 contemporary Durelle Alexander's vocal on a Paul Whiteman release, on Victor 25270, did get a bit more recognition, as Whiteman was a bigger hog than Goodman! In any case, this recording, more than any others, defines Helen Ward as a premium vocal entity. Just listen! (As a recording, Frank Sinatra would later revive and claim this ditty in the 1950s.)
8. "You Turned the Tables on Me," Victor 25391. This wordy ditty penned by Louis Alter and Sidney Mitchell is defined well.
9. "When a Lady Meets a Gentleman Down South," Victor 25434. It takes a while to say the lyrics of this ditty, as Helen finds a way to do it very well; it was penned by Michael Cleary, Jacques Krakeur, and David Oppenheim. Did Lee Wiley later define this ditty? Or did Lee emulated Helen's original?
10. "Feeling High and Happy," Brunswick 8123. Does this ditty penned by Ted Koehler and Rube Bloom feel good? Can this title refer to reefer? While it's true that

bandleader Gene Krupa would eventually be linked to drugs, this fast-paced ditty turns out to become a good excuse to swing. High or happy?

11. "How Am I to Know?" Brunswick 7893. The (1929) Gene Austin hit is redone with style!
12. "One More Dream," Brunswick 8123. This dream penned by Maurice Sigler and J. Fred Coots again swings, as Helen's vocal and (drumming) Gene Krupa prove they can (even) challenge Ella and (drumming) Chick Webb.
13. "Day In, Day Out," Decca 2703. The jazz standard penned by Johnny Mercer and Rube Bloom found Helen's (1939) band singing with Bob Crosby a huge best-selling entity.
14. "I Take to You," Columbia 36174. Backed by Matty Malneck, this clear vocal swings as much as it pleases the ear! (An earlier version of this ditty penned by Mack Gordon and Harry Warren, as by Lena Horne in comparison, oddly finds Lena singing out of key. Listen and compare.)
15. "You're My Favorite Memory," Columbia 37637. Teddy Wilson's backing found Helen very able to produce a decent vocal on this ditty penned by Wilson and P. Johnson. (The flip side of this Red Columbia issue found Wilson backing Lena Horne on "Out of Nowhere.")

➢ Visual Image: Helen is both seen and heard with the Will Osborne Orchestra in a (1934) film short, singing:

16. "Midnight, the Stars and You." Film 1934. Watch closely, as Helen is not given much but takes what she can!

Dinah Washington

As born in Tuscaloosa, Alabama, young Ruth Jones alias Dinah Washington, became a transplanted resident of Chicago. As a member of St. Luke's Church on the south side, her gospel roots, like many Southerners, both black and white, trained her for other entertainment. As a performer in Chicago's Regal Theater, the Chicago answer to the New York City's Apollo, she developed into a fine (1940s) band singer with the likes of Joe Liggins and the Honeydrippers and Lionel Hampton's Orchestra. Dinah's own scope as a vocalist was much like that of Ethel Waters, being able to sound as tough or soft as required or as desired. While only lacking in Waters's sweetness, Dinah's eventual ability to adapt to contemporary pop was to eventually lead her into a fine ability to transform traditional ballads into songs of substance. Her attempts at jazz, rhythm and blues, and (eventually) rock and roll are also successful. This cusp vocalist had a major impact upon both R&B and R&R. She pioneered a loud, gospel-flavored style, an inspiration for all her contemporaries and those who would later become credited for the rock era itself. Indeed, her natural ability to sing with a cannonball effect, like Bessie Smith, and switch to a smoother jazzy style like Waters, further indicate Dinah's extraordinary vocal arsenal. The following are Dinah Washington picks:

1. "Evil Gal Blues," Keynote K-605. As a band singer for Lionel Hampton, Dinah explodes, yet adapts her gospel instincts, on this jazzy ditty penned by Leonard Feather, creating a blue mood with a band sound.

2. "I Only Know," Mercury 8163. This slow, solo effort is obviously pure gospel but without religious reference. Dinah's high shrill-pitched vocal is "in your face," despite the fact of the matter is that this is only a recording! Penned by Richard Johnson and Dinah herself, this ditty also retains much of its power and was perhaps more than an inspiration for the likes of a notable latter-century diva Patty Labelle.
3. "Baby, Get Lost," Mercury 8148. As a major seller in the R&B field in 1949-50 and penned by Billy Moore Jr., it's obvious that this uninhibited and overpowering vocal had found no problem in being heard when played on a contemporary jukebox, more so even with the volume turned off! Indeed a powerful performance!
4. "Long John Blues," Mercury 8148. This Tommy George-penned ditty is not just novel, it's gritty and fittingly a tale about a dentist visit. More so, Dinah's bold vocal style indicates that she likes such visits, as these campy and risqué lyrics say it all more clearly!
5. "I Wanna Be Loved". Mercury 8181. This old 1934 (Billy. Rose, Ed. Heyman & Johnny Green), penned show tune, should not be confused with Savannah Churchill's R&B 1946 best seller,(penned by Churchill) "I Want To Be Loved").
6. "I Cross My Fingers," Mercury 5488. As another attempt at pop, this ditty penned by Walter Kent and William Farrer had been a fluffy contemporary (1950) Bing Crosby best seller on Decca 27111. Dinah had other ideas, as her stylistic approach, when heard, is, in true retrospective, a far better rendering.
7. "Cold, Cold Heart," Mercury 5728. This (Hank Williams) masterpiece had already won the hearts of the American public on MGM 10904 despite much emulation, especially noting the likes of contemporary 1951 pop versions. Indeed a fine Tony Bennett version on Columbia 39449 was OK and gave Hank more deserved recognition. Moreover, Dinah's bold style, in her typical bombastic idiom, is a "crossover" into a shared culture. While perhaps Hank's simplicity could make listeners cry, Dinah's rendering is beautiful and could compel her own listeners to cry as well as become a bit edgy. Just listen!
8. "Mixed Emotions," Mercury 5728. Penned by F. Stuart Louchheim, this bit of creative pop had been well done by a soft Rosemary Clooney version on Columbia 39333. It's also a sure bet that Dinah's more emotional! Mixed emotions?
9. "Fast-Movin' Mama," Mercury-8207. This ditty penned by Washington is indeed fast! In it, Dinah clearly encourages her pepped-up listeners to come along for a ride! More so, this ditty provides much entertainment for its listeners. Take a ride!
10. "Juice Head Man of Mine," Mercury 8207. Penned by Jesse Stone, Tab Smith, and Dinah herself, perhaps define a good excuse for juice?
11. "Hey, Good Looking!" Mercury 8257. As another Hank Williams entity, another interesting venture into C&W is attempted. More so, the attempt has the added vocals of the contemporary R&B group sound of Jimmy Ricks and the Ravens. Moreover, this attempt at creativity turns the excellent Hank Williams version into something completely different, highlighted by some fine duet ting vocals by Dinah and Jimmy! Indeed a fantastic result that rocks!
12. "TV Is the Thing," Mercury 70214. This novelty penned by William Sanford and Phil Medley is a fast-paced adventure and, while dated, an historic statement noting the death of celebrity radio and the contemporary (1951) rise of television.
13. "Fat Daddy," Mercury 70214. As the subject of the shape of the human body has always been one of concern, this bit of slang penned by William Sandford and Phil Medley, this novelty about a fat man who scores isn't bad.

14. "No No No You Can't Have Two," Mercury 70392. How true! Dinah, as usually, wickedly notes this social problem penned by Mamie Terry and Eddie Kirkland with ease as well as a perceived smirk.
15. "Big Long Slidin' Thing," Mercury 70392. Dinah really explodes and excels on this reworking of the old acoustic Ethel Waters hit on Black Swan 14128 as, originally "Oh Joe, Play That Trombone." In comparison, the advantages of electric recording microphone technology dwarf Ethel's original but noting the jazzy Waters influence on Dinah. This ditty curiously notes Mamie Terry and Eddie Kirkland as songwriters for Dinah, and Edgar Dowell for Ethel.
16. "Trouble in Mind," Mercury 8269. Despite the fact that this original (1925) Bertha "Chippie" Hill rendering penned by Richard M. Jones on Okeh 8312 had yet to be surpassed as a blues classic recorded as an acoustic entity, this ditty had found an interesting (1937) rendering from the efforts of Leon's Lone Star Cowboys, a hillbilly string band attempt at blues, with an honest and simple Leon Chappelear vocal on Decca 5340. Dinah's version, while similar in style with Hill's original, may be considered a compliment.
17. "Wheel of Fortune," Mercury 8267. This 1952 pop hit by Kay Starr, on Capital 1964, penned by Bennie Benjamin and George David Weiss is no less complimented by Dinah's vocal. More so, as backed by Jimmy Cobb's orchestra, Dinah seemingly reverts back to a more controlled style, fully challenging the Kay Starr original.
18. "I Don't Hurt Anymore," Mercury 70439. This title penned by Jack. Rollins and Don Robertson became a major C&W best seller for a transplanted Canadian Hank Snow on Victor 20-5698. Backed by Hal Mooney's Orchestra, a completely different result is interestingly achieved. Indeed, Dinah rocks!
19. "Teach Me Tonight," Mercury 70497. The mid-tempo beat of the De Castro Sisters on Abbot 3001 group sound was considered by some 1954 contemporaries as R&R. In any case, a jazzy Dinah Washington version of this Gene De Paul and Sammy Cahn penned ditty is done very well.

20-23. "*After Hours with Ms. D*," EmArcy MG-26032. This original LP concept (a 10 inch) could be the ultimate urban jazz LP. While far less bombastic than most previous picks, Dinah reverts back to her band singer days and this time with a focus for the LP. Some will argue that this trip into modern jazz is a bit out of focus for the purposes of this book, but Dinah is a transitional entity, who just could not have been ignored or discarded. It should also be noted that, for many, the stated and credited work of musicians that included the likes of Clark Terry (trumpet), Rick Henderson (alto sax), Eddie "Lockjaw" Davis (tenor sax), Gus Chappell (trombone), Julian Mance (piano), Keener Betties (bass), and Ed Happen (drums) are considered more relevant for Dinah's vocals than as entities on to themselves. As noted throughout this book, while the creativity of backing musicians is sometimes critical for vocalists, it is, for the most part, a factor that all vocalists must interpret.

- The following four song ditties had been popular standards (before 1950) and are sung in a jazzy and softer style by Dinah. Most are more than five minutes long. All are innovative, different, and creatively vocalized by Dinah. They are:

    a. "Blue Skies."
    b. "Bye Bye Blues."
    c. "A Foggy Day."
    d. "I Let a Song Go Out of My Heart."

24. "Blue Gardenia," EMArcy MG 36011. From the LP "For Those in Love," this original Nat King Cole best seller benefits from a softer phrasing Dinah, and among (young) Quincy Jones arrangement.
25. "What a Difference a Day Made!" Mercury 71435. This ditty penned by Maria Grever and Stanley Adams was originally released on a single, in 1959, and scored huge sales in an already rock-dominated singles' market. It was also to be a successful LP entity as Mercury MG 20479 and won a Grammy award for best rhythm and Blues recording of 1959. While it's worth it to speculate if Dinah's soft tones and jazzy vocal, as found on this recording, really had anything to do with (contemporary) 1959 R&B, it's easy to spin a few of Dinah's earlier and tougher renderings that were indeed hipper to find more relevance. Indeed times had changed.

As a traditional Mexican folk ditty, this ditty was adapted as a pop rendering, as a Dorsey Brothers release, with a fair Bob Crosby vocal on Decca 283 in 1934. It was later to be resurrected by a Charlie Barnet release, with a better vocal by Kay Starr on Decca 18620. A 1944 Andy Russell version on Capital 167 sounds much like a Sinatra clone. Later, a more stylistic approach by Sarah Vaughan on Musicraft 552 was attempted. Oddly, it was Dinah's (later) soft version that finally defined this ditty.

25. "Baby, You've Got What It Takes," Mercury 71565. This vocal duet with R&B great Brook Benton is also a stylistic approach to rock and roll. Dinah's more controlled vocal could still become dynamic, as this 1960 ditty penned by Brook Benton, Clyde Otis and Murray Stein was a best-selling single entity purchased by teenagers and adults.
26. "A Rocking Good Way to Mess Around and Fall in Love," Mercury 71629. As a follow-up to the success of "Baby, You've Got What It Takes," Dinah, along with Brook Benton, overcame this somewhat ambiguous title penned by Luchi De Jesus and Clyde Otis and in medium-tempo rock!

27-29. *Unforgettable*, Mercury MG 20572. This LP, while not rocking, is excellent pop, with some toned blues titles, with an orchestra directed by Belford Hendricks. With lush strings, Dinah adapts a mellow tone, while somehow maintaining her personable and identifiable voice. Picks for this LP are:

   a. "Unforgettable." As the title track, Dinah matches the Nat King Cole version.
   b. "A Bad Case of the Blues." This Clyde Otis-penned title has Dinah in complete control of the lyrics, as she does not choose to overpower its message.
   c. "This Bitter Earth." Another Clyde Otis-penned gem finds a serious Dinah, committed and controlled.

   ➢ Note: Dinah was signed up with the Roulette label in the early 1960s and made quite a few recordings for them until 1963. While all are good, it seems her strides into rock and roll were abandoned, but for this release:

30. "Soulville," Roulette 4490. This is brilliant singing while not a huge-selling single.

   ✓ The early excitement of Dinah Washington was to be found on a (1945?) "Jubilee" *Radio* rendering of:

31. "And Her Tears Flowed Like Wine," with fine backing from Lionel Hampton. Better than the contemporary recordings of by Anita O'Day? Finally:

The Dinah Washington Story was tragically ended in late 1963 at about the young age of thirty-nine. R&B, C&W, R&R, pop, and jazz—Dinah's music? She did it all! Unmistakably!

- More about Dinah Washington in the LP section of this book.

Ethel Waters

Ethel Waters was the first African American superstar, in terms of modern popular music. Waters was about the fifth or sixth black woman to record, following the lead of contemporary Mamie Smith's 1920 breakthrough recording of "Crazy Blues" on Okeh 4169. Before this time, it was the decision of the major record companies that black people could not be marketable in a mostly white society. The principle exception to all this nonsense was the (black) and British West Indian-born Bert Williams. His success as the acoustic singer and writer of "Nobody" and others such as "Good Morning, Carrie" made inroads into the coon song of the early 1900s. So was his success with Flo Ziegfeld in the "white time" of segregated Broadway. While a character and a token, his dignity was maintained as were his recordings especially treasured by the (black) society of his time.

Ethel Waters was born in Chester, Pennysylvania, in 1896. While growing up poor in and around the Philadelphia area, she was for a time sent to a school run by a group of Catholic nuns. As well as religion, noting she was originally a Baptist, she was taught to speak in the proper form of the English language, with rolling Rs and articulation of her words, usually something for rich white kids to pick upon. Ethel took it all to heart and used it to dazzle her friends. More so, her command of proper grammar and street slang, as well as the diverse acoustic recordings of Bert Williams and those of (white) contemporaries such as Nora Bayes and Marion Harris, provided her natural, sweet, and articulate voice something to study and something to better. Later, as an already established recording entity in the 1920s, with the introduction of electric recording, she adapted a soft crooning style, which indeed competed and rivaled the likes of many, including her popular contemporaries Ruth Etting, Rudy Vallee, and Bing Crosby. She came to terms (on her own) terms with the labels of the early electric age of recording such as blues singer, jazz singer, crooner, and torch singer. They would all soon apply to this multitalented diva, who just happened to be black. In true retrospective, until the mid-1930s, she would dominate the entire idiom of black culture, as her performances in theater, vaudeville, film, and especially recordings, always popular in the black community, would sell themselves into a huge white following as well. Were black artists able to sound white? How could crude-sounding black performers able to articulate Broadway? Was this all possible?

- Ethel Waters Picks

The Ethel Waters recordings between 1921 and 1926 are acoustic, like all contemporary recordings of the era, and suffer greatly from poor quality of recording and poor backup sounds, despite great musicians. Nevertheless, the following Ethel Waters picks, especially noting the releases on the contemporary "Cardinal" and Afro-American-owned Black Swan label, immediately put Ethel a cut above her contemporaries. As perhaps the first real jazz singer, her adaptability and abilities are well noted.

1. "The New York Glide," Cardinal 2936. This hip (1921) ditty penned by Tom Delaney is a jazzy, if contrived, dance entity backed by Albury's Blue and Jazz Seven. Listen and glide!
2, 3. "At the New Jump Steady Ball," Cardinal 2036. A bootleggers meeting?(a) Another (1921) jazzy attempt with Albury's Blue and Jazz Seven as a contemporary dance entity penned by Tom Delaney and Sidney Easton works well enough; (b) A later (1922) rerecording is just about the same vocally, with similar backing from the "Jazz Masters," released on Black Swan 14218.

Black Swan originals recorded between 1921 and 1923 found Ethel labeled an instant blues queen in direct rivalry with contemporaries including Mamie Smith, who had (like her) previously not been able to record (due to racism) before 1920.

4. "Down Home Blues," Black Swan 2010. This gritty blues entity penned by Tom Delaney found Ethel hitting lyrics in her very (stylish) vocal, backed by the "Cordy Williams" jazz masters. Speculation that exists finds Black Swans's pianist Fletcher Henderson the actual leader of the jazz masters as well as the one who contributed on (most) other Black Swan masters, featuring Ethel and others between 1921 and 1923.
5. "Oh, Daddy," Black Swan 2010. The much-recorded ditty of the 1920s, penned by William Russell and Ed Herbert, found Ethel's (original) vocal as another attempt at a popular style. Despite the acoustics and the need to (almost) shout, she succeeds!
6. "There'll Be Some Changes Made," Black Swan 2021. This classic jazz entity penned by Billy Higgins and Benton Overstreet has since been recorded by many, noting Ethel's original rendering an edgy and jazzy performance, a huge influence for all (future) jazz vocalists. More so, despite its poor acoustics and many later acoustic and electric attempts by both back and white performers, this 1921 rendering truly defined it.
7. "One Man Nan," Black Swan 2021. An early dance number penned by William Russell and Ed Herbert.
8. "Dying with the Blues," Black Swan 2038. Fletcher Henderson penned this fine and novel blues entity for Ethel. (It should be noted that, like in other blues titles before this recording, including Ethel's own "Down Home Blues," blues indicated a down and low feeling expressed in popular song. More so, the term "blues singer" had applied to many white singers and would continue to be until the early 1930s, when record companies would (finally) designate the term for (mostly) Afro-American recording artists.
9. "Kiss Your Pretty Baby Nice," Black Swan 2038. This ditty penned by Corrine and Edgar Dowell is a crude blues entity that finds Ethel capable enough to lift her material to (her) liking.
10. "Jazzin' Babies Blues," Black Swan 14117. Ethel attacks these perhaps contrived lyrics penned by Richard Jones. Indeed, the terms of "jazz" and "blues" both benefit from Ethel's approach, which also asserts a vocal quality (despite poor acoustics) to a softer but bold jazz quality, indeed not found in most or her contemporaries.
11. "Kind Lovin' Blues," Black Swan 14117. This already familiar tale of lovemaking penned by the likes of Waters herself, Sidney Mitchell, and Fletcher Henderson is fun and novel.
12, 13. "Georgia Blues," Black Swan 14120. (a) Penned by Billy Higgins and W. Benton Overstreet, this contrived bit of crudeness is very effective; (b) Her later electric (1929) rerecording of this title, on Columbia 14565-D, benefits from better acoustics, with a still interested Ethel providing a nasty and clever vocal about a very much desired man from Georgia. Listen to both versions for both technical information and fun.

14. "That Da Da Strain," Black Swan 14120. (A fine dance number penned by Mamie Medina and Edgar Dowell also notes a contemporary (1922) "Harlem Renaissance" cultural movement in title.)
15. "Oh, Joe, Play That Trombone," Black Swan 14128. After the musical instrument "trombone" is slyly introduced by the Jazz Masters, Ethel's almost wicked vocal toys around with yet another meaning or purpose for the instrument. While not quite rated "X," penned by Edgar Dowell, this full of smut remains something full of fun. The late and electric updated Dinah Washington version, known as "Big Long Slidin' Thing" on Mercury 70392 just may be. Or is it the fact that Ethel's original is acoustic?
16. "Brown Baby," Black Swan 14145. While Ethel's previous race records could be directed at anyone, this title penned by Paul Henry and (Willie) William Grant (or known as William Grant still) was directly aimed at an Afro-American audience. It finds a vocal almost swaggering, as this fast-paced ditty almost rocks!
17. "Ain't Gonna Marry, Ain't Gonna Settle Down," Black Swan 14145. Was it just speculation that Ethel's (Black Swan) contract stipulated that she could not marry while employed? Perhaps this wordy, fast-paced ditty, with Fletcher Henderson on piano, somehow works.
18. "Midnight Blues," Black Swan 14146. Yeah. Penned by Thomas (Fats) Waller and Clarence Williams, Ethel's effective vocal again wins with the telling of a tall tale.
19. "Memphis Man," Black Swan 14146. As the flip side of "Midnight Blues," this exciting bit of acoustic grit penned by George Brashear, Edgar Campbell, Elmer Chambers, Paul Henry and William Grant is typically novel. As for the question about men from Memphis, it's a good bet that Ethel's smoky delivery of lyrics come from experience! Better than her previous man from Georgia in "Georgia Blues"? Or Joe in "Oh, Joe, Play That Trombone"? Or daddy in "Oh, Daddy"?
20. "If You Don't Think I'll Do, Sweet Pops, Just Try Me," Black Swan 14148. This bit of slang penned by CB and J. Armstrong as recording fodder is a bit substandard. Luckily, Ethel's very crude vocal succeeds.
21. "Long Lost Mama," Black Swan 14148. Ethel ain't shouting, but this fast-paced vocal penned by Harry Woods proves she's more than a contemporary mama-she's a flapper!

22, 23. "You Can't Do What My Last Man Did," Black Swan 14151. (a) Yeah. This (1923) dated bit of urban blues penned by A. C. Anderson and pianist J. C. Johnson tells a story in a culturally and purposely crude vocal performance, perhaps led (on piano) by the great J. C. Johnston himself; (b) Though not much later, better recorded (1925) rerecording on Columbia 14112-D finds an added but unaccredited duet that is also effective. Is contemporary actress Ethel Barrymore mentioned in the new version?

24. "Lost Out Blues," Black Swan 14151. You can have the blues penned by William Grant, and you can become very lost.
25. "Ethel Sings 'Em," Black Swan 14154. Ethel gets down and dirty and (actually) belts out a contemporary (1923) blues entity, more so clearly identified as her own! While not known as a contemporary shouter or wailer, this ditty (again) proves that her (vocal) versatility could successfully carry her to record any types of material she was interested in and to compose it as well!
26. "Sweet Man Blues," Black Swan 14154. This flip side of "Ethel Sings 'Em" (again) betrays a powerful vocal ability, not always to be revealed, led by contemporary (1923) pianist J. C. Johnson, who penned this ditty about a 'hot'contemporary flapper's lament.

The brief existence of the black-owned Black Swan label, while a failure, due to the poor distribution and racism of the times (1921-23) would perhaps become more realized in the development of Motown later in the century. During this creative time, while on a tour as a "Black Swan Troubadour," Ethel appeared as a radio vocalist on WGV in New Orleans. With this performance, she became the very first Afro-American vocalist to sing on radio.

The Black Swan masters were leased out and all reissued on Paramount label, the pioneering Chicago label. Moreover, Ethel did record some fine ditties for the label. The following picks are Paramount originals:

27. "Tell 'Em About Me," Paramount 12214. A fine storytelling entity about someone on the way to Tennessee, penned by Sidney Easton, finds Ethel in good spirits, with a spunky attitude. As a contemporary (1924) blues entity, Ethel is less than crude, as her personality and vocal adaptability also tells of her jazzy differences between her and most (black) contemporaries.
28. "You'll Need Me When I'm Gone," Paramount 12214. Another crude tale of the blues penned by Richard Carpenter is well worth hearing.
29. "Craving Blues," Paramount 12313. Penned and arranged by Paramont's house pianist Lovie Austin, this sad tale finds one of Ethel's tougher vocals a powerful force! Check it out!
30. "Black Spatch Blues," Paramount 12230. As another Paramount original, Ethel is again tough, and this tale of woe penned by M. Sudoth and J. Guy Suddoth finds Ethel explaining in no uncertain terms an experience in the kitchen. Dinner?
31. "I Want Somebody All My Own," Paramount 12230. As the flip side of "Black Spatch Blues" and also penned by J.G. Suddoth, this (1924) simple tale about a woman's dreams still works.

Note: The following two Vocalion recordings were recorded in New York City. These sides were also released on (Silvertone-3014) under the name of Mamie Jones, another contemporary black entity. It is also interesting to be noted that the name of 'Mamie Jones'had been used to issue some recordings by contemporary (white) vocalist Aileen Stanley, oddly on Black Swan-14116. These sides were "Honey Rose" and "Mandy N Me". Speculation has it that these sides had been Olympic (Records) masters purchased by Harry Pace (Afro-American owner of Black Swan, subsequently released in error.

32. "Pleasure Mad," Vocalion 14860. This hot and jazzy dance number of this mid-1920s, penned by Sidney Bechet and Rousseau Simmons, indeed made the decade roar! A contemporary (1924) (white) dance band Bennie Krueger Orchestra release, found on Brunswick 2667, perhaps defined it as an instrumental. Moreover, Ethel's subsequent vocal features a bright and rhythmic lead, just perfect for any flapper on any dance floor!
33. "Back Biting Mama," Vocalion 14860. This blues items penned by Thomas (Fats) Waller, who was also credited as the original label as backup (piano), is a tale full of black slang as well something that Ethel could produce quite well.

Columbia Records

Note: The following picks consist of Columbia masters, using its pop series (three numbers, with a dash and alpha), and its race series (five numbers, with a dash and alpha). While some mistakes in processing were made, it became an open secret on Columbia 487-D on

"Dinah" and its flip "Sweet Man" that this vocalist was passed (or sold) as a white recording artist. Just how could a colored girl sound so white? Or was it all racism?

Others, especially noting the dance number "Sweet Georgia Brown," more on the borderline, noting a wild style that white artists like Sophie Tucker and Marion Harris, once accepted surrogates for black culture, could by 1925 only hope to particularly emulate. While other entities such as "Shake That Thing" or "No Man's Mama" leave no doubts about Ethel's black heritage, the problem for Ethel and some others (noting Eva Taylor, Adelaide Hall, and Elisabeth Welch) was that of a stylish clash and difference, with that of the ultimate blues shouter—Bessie Smith. Attempts to do popular white material found much success for the jazzy Waters style, noting an incredible sweet and dry voice, often claiming white standards for herself as no one else.

As the latter 1920s moved on, Ethel would find herself in competition with (white) contemporaries successfully singing definitive love or torch songs encouraged by the newer electric recordings, talkies in films, the development of the microphone, and the expanding use of live radio. Among such contemporaries as Ruth Etting, Rudy Vallee, Annette Hanshaw Kate Smith, and Libby Holman, the crude term of "croon" or "crooner" was in itself to become reversed, with Waters (importantly) included.

34. "Sweet Georgia Brown," Columbia 379-D. As a dance entity, this original vocal penned by Ben Bernie, Maceo Pinkard, and Ken Casey became one of the many standards of the 1920s and of popular music offered by Ethel. While (white) bandleader Ben Bernie's contemporary hot (instrumental) version on Vocalion 15002 became a popular dance band favorite, it's Ethel's own (while still acoustic) rendering of a wild and uninhibited vocal, not unlike her performance in the previous "Pleasure Mad," that (still) roars when played or heard! Indeed, this novel tale about a contemporary 1920s flapper was provided with its hipper (black) origins and (white) acceptance largely due to the (landmark) Waters rendering. (Later recordings, including a bright and jazzy (1932) Bing Crosby version on Brunswick 6320 would revive it as a vocal. Still later, in 1948, adapted as the official theme of the Harlem Globetrotter's basketball team, by Brother Bones and His Shadows on Tempo 652, this tale about the (1920s) flapper "Georgia Brown" remained as hip as it seemed relevant. Or perhaps, light years away, an insignificant early 1960s rendering by an English rock band (the Beatles), who had more likely never heard the previous vocals, recorded it? Eventually released on Atco 6302, it would later provide listeners an interesting bit of rock.
35. "No One Can Love Me Like The Way You Do," Columbia 379-D. This flip side of the "Sweet Georgia Brown" is medium tempo and finds Ethel in a sweet voice, as this ditty penned by Clarence Williams is less known and still a winning vocal.
36. "Sympathetic Dan," Columbia 433-D. This dude Dan from Tennessee has got it all! While this crude tale of this wild guy is not for all, the ditty penned by Flatow and Cramer finds Ethel's usual explicative use of lyrics more than fun.
37. "Pickaninny Blues," Columbia 472-D. With a piano intro (as played by Pearl Wright), this ditty penned by (Kierman) drifts into Ethel's interesting vocal identification of Afro-American stereotypes that had been lingering in the culture since slavery days.
38. "Loud Speakin' Papa," Columbia 472-D. This ditty as credited and penned by the white entities Lew Pollack and Jack Yellen finds the subject of commercial (1925) radio, along with real black slang, effective.

39. "Dinah," Columbia 487-D. (a) Although acoustic, this (Columbia) master sounds almost as good as an electric recording. If this is a blues song, its backing by her "Plantation Orchestra" and its breezy and light sound is pure jazz, as much as Ethel's very sweet voice. Penned by the white team of Joe Young, Sam M. Lewis, and Harry Akst directly for the popular and contemporary (1925) "Plantation Club" nightclub, this popular tune had been recorded to duplicate the success of her own original introduction there. In true retrospective, when first heard, this recording found most listeners believing that they were hearing a white singer. As perhaps by a fluke, the contemporary Columbia race series found this early number a bit confused by nominal white buyers. Just how could a black singer sound so sweet and articulate? Is this the same singer that had recorded the uninhibited vocal on "Sweet Georgia Brown"? Was this a mistake? Or just racism? Ethel's best-selling success of this recording led others to contribute to the concept of producing song ditties, not just for "Broadway" but for nightclubs. It would also be used in Ethel's own stage act, including many (future) radio programs. It would also be exported to France, when Josephine Baker, who had been part of Ethel's original Plantation revue, left for Paris, along with Ethel's stage act, along with "Dinah"-which she subsequently recorded. While the radio entities will be noted elsewhere in the text, Ethel did produce two more commercial recordings; (b) The (1934) electric re-recording released on Decca 234 is good but surprisingly not as effective as the earlier acoustic rendering; and (c) A later post-WWII rerecording in 1947 finds Ethel's vocal being led by a newer jazz sound by J. C. Heard, producing a solid but hardly defining rendering.

Still other significant versions of this ditty after 1925 (besides Ethel's competing with herself) find an excellent (1931) Bing Crosby and Mills Brothers version on Brunswick 6240.

40. "Sweet Man," Columbia 487D. As the flip side of "Dinah," this ditty penned by Roy Turk and Maceo Pinkard cannot be ignored. Again, the sweet-voiced Ethel scores with a jazzy and soft medium tempo vocal. As a 'flapper' or high quality she's as "hot' as TNT? Or gasoline? (This ditty should not be confused with the raunchier styled (earlier) "Sweet Man Blues").
41. "I've Found a New Baby," Columbia 561-D. Another fine jazz vocal and a neglected classic penned by Jack Palmer and Clarence Williams finds Ethel's gliding a strong vocal defining.
42. "Go Back Where You Stayed Last Night," Columbia 14093-D. As another ditty that seemed to stay around in jazz circles, this ditty penned by Sidney Easton and Ethel Waters is a bit tougher sounding. Jazz or blues? (Light years away in the Kid Ory Creole Dixieland band in the 1940s, band singers Lee Sapphire and Joe Darensbourg successfully attempted it again, so would a later (rock era) Bill Haley and his Comets attempt in 1956.
43. "Maybe Not At All," Columbia 14116-D. Penned as by Sidney Easton and Ethel herself, this ditty reeks of an early attempt at marketing the black contemporary (1925) black community, perhaps inspired by a contemporary *Vanity Fair* article. As a large recording entity, Columbia had already provided Ethel with better distribution. This ditty finds Ethel paying tribute to her (black) contemporary Columbia stable mates (who were more so rivals) Clara Smith and Bessie Smith in mock emulations. Moreover Ethel's own mimic talents of both are considerable and admirable. As recorded, she unselfishly and formally proclaims Bessie Smith as empress of the blues.

More so, she (even) defines her own style, which makes this ditty a "must hear." Just listen!

44. "Shake That Thing," Columbia 14116-D. Yeah. The Papa Charlie Jackson-penned ditty, also a contemporary release for him on Paramount 12281 is realized and more so bettered! Ethel's hot and smoking vocal style on this ditty truly does shake things up and may be considered pre-rock! (Ethel would use this number in her contemporary (1927) stage show "Africana" in a reported hip-shaking frenzy, and while not stripping down as much as contemporary Josephine Baker in France, she did attract some censor. A few decades later in the postwar 1940s, blues entity Wynonie Harris would more so use this ditty, much as Ethel did, in his own hip-shaking stage act, which also found a contemporary recording on King.
45. "No Man's Mama," Columbia 14116-D. This ditty, as credited and penned by the (white) team of Lew Pollack and Jack Yellen, was meant to sound wild, although hardly a good song. More so, the use of black slang, in true retrospective, finds the futuristic term of woman's lib at least liberating.
46. "Make a Pallet on the Floor," Columbia 14125-D. This (very) dated piece of vaudeville penned by Shelton Brooks also features an unidentified male voice with some mean lyrics. Its contents are crudely noted with its own woman-beating theme becoming a drama! (Is this Handy's "Atlanta Blues")?
47. "Bring the Greenbacks," Columbia 14125-D. As a matter-of-fact vocal (poorly produced by Columbia), this ditty penned by Shelton Brooks finds in Ethel's blues more than a hint at the social reality of prostitution.

48, 49. "Throw Dirt in Your Face," Columbia 14132-D. (a) Another fine and tough novelty perhaps finds author Shelton Brooks on piano, backing Ethel's rough storytelling; (b) Ethel's (later) 1947 recording on Mary Howard MHR-112, while (still) stripped down, is better. Ethel would use this ditty in personal appearances (later) in her career.

50. "If You Can't Hold the Man You Love," Columbia 14134-D. Yes. It's true, and this fast-paced vocal penned by Sammy Fain and Irving Kahl, while hampered by poor acoustics, still works.
51. "Sugar," Columbia 14146-D. Another lost jazz vocal by Ethel finds her at her best. More so, this often imitated title never sounded better by anyone else, despite better recording techniques. Penned by Edna Alexander, Sidney Mitchell, and Maceo Pinkard, this very sad ditty is fully of substance, a woman's lament of something very much lost and desired.
52. "Heebie Jeebies," Columbia 14153-D. The contemporary Louis Armstrong version is better, as Ethel's somewhat wild style is partly ruined by the Columbia label's failure to provide her with better recording acoustics.
53. "Everybody Mess Around," Columbia 14153-D. This side also found a (better) contemporary Louis Armstrong version, with poor (Columbia) recording acoustics (again) almost ruining Ethel's rousing recording. Listen and compare.
54. "We Don't Need Each Other Anymore," Columbia 14162-D. This (crude) social statement penned by J.C. Johnson, while oddly hampered by a poor (Columbia) recording result, noting a more (modern) electric recording, still finds Ethel able to put over a fine rendering about splitting up.
55. "I'm Coming Virginia," Columbia 14170-D. With vocal accompanied by Will Marion Cook's Singing Orchestra, this dated but good vocal penned by Will Marion Cook and Donald Heywood found Ethel more than able to take lead of the many backing voices and effectively put them behind her vocal. Ethel would incorporate this ditty into her own contemporary Broadway reviews of "Africana" as well as another "Miss

Calico." A contemporary version as a Paul Whiteman release found a bouncy Bing Crosby vocal on Victor 20751 that is far jazzier than this Waters's version. Listen and compare!

56. "He Brought Joy to My Soul," Columbia 14170-D. This traditional "spiritual" title (1926) is truly an inspiration. Ethel's clear vocal is truly earthy, leading her "Ebony Four," who provide a more religious zeal. (The first of many religious song ditties that Ethel would be associated with!)
57. "Jersey Walk," Columbia 14182-D. As from the (1927) contemporary Broadway entity *Honeymoon Lane* and penned by the team of Henry Creamer, Eddie Dowling, and James F. Hanley for an all-white cast, this ditty had possibilities for a fast-paced dance record. Sadly, Ethel's red hot vocal is marred by a substandard (Columbia Records) production, something that is sadly to be found on most of her recordings after her great start in 1925.
58. "Home," Columbia 14214-D. Also known as "Home (Cradle of Happiness)," this dreary song ditty, penned by J.C. Johnson, finds some sort of redemption from Ethel's stripped-down vocal.
59. "I Want My Sweet Daddy Now," Columbia 14229-D. Ethel's (1926) technical recording flaws are especially brought to light when the earlier acoustic (1922) recording by contemporary Clara Smith on Columbia A-3991 simply sounds better than her electric update.
60. "Someday Sweetheart," Columbia 14264-D. Despite the fact her backing orchestra sounds out of tune, Ethel prevails. A better version, and oddly acoustic, had been released by contemporary Alberta Hunter on Black Swan 2019 in 1921. Subsequent versions by Gene Austin, Bing Crosby, Dick Todd, and an updated electric version by Alberta Hunter also find a better recorded product.
61. "My Handy Man," Columbia 14353. This risqué entity penned by Andy Razaf and Eubie Blake was to become very popular with Ethel's own (1928) crudely expressed version becoming the better known and best seller. Moreover, does this ditty prove that cleaning up has some advantages? Who says yard work is that yard? Oddly, the follow up song ditty "My Handy Man Ain't Handy No More," which was to be subsequently reported to be used by Ethel in her stage act, lacked a Waters recording. It was, however, to become known as a recording with a fine (1930) version by contemporary Edith Wilson released on Victor V38624.
62. "West End Blues," Columbia 14365-D. The contemporary Louis Armstrong version perhaps noses out Ethel's version, at least in historical significance. Nevertheless, this performance is full commitment, as the drama injected into this classic penned by Oliver and Williams still provides strong claims upon this strong urban tale of hopelessness.
63. "Organ Grinder Blues," Columbia 14365. Ethel's grit is more than obvious, as her strong blues vocal penned by Clarence Williams is more than appreciated.
64. "Do What You Did Last Night," Columbia 14380-D. Another attempt at risqué singing is a success, as this just passable ditty penned by Andy Razaf and J.C. Johnson suggests a bit more than mischief.
65. "Lonesome Swallow," Columbia 14411-D. An attempt at a softer vocal style works, as this ditty penned by Andy Razaf and J.C. Johnson is effective enough, despite a flawed backing.
66. "My Baby Sure Knows How to Love," Columbia 14411-D. Penned by Crawford and Rafe, this obvious risqué title does not disappoint its listeners.

67. "Am I Blue?" Columbia 1837-D. This contemporary (1929) release found this recording and its flip side l issued on Columbia's popular series, discarding the usually accounted race series of numbers. Penned by the familiar and white team of Grant Clarke and Harry Akst, this ditty would be introduced in the early all-talking film entity *On with the Show*, also finding Ethel in the same film performing it with perfection. Indeed, the sight of the young and beautiful jazz singer is historically caught forever! (More on this film in noted elsewhere in this text.)

As an (equally) important recording, this ditty perhaps leads the pack of the (many) song classics introduced or associated with Waters. Ethel's own vocal on this ditty finds her in her usual excellent voice, as her clear and jazzy vocal glides through a bouncy and rhythmic backing. Moreover, the lighthearted lyrics are more than greeted by Ethel's pleasant question as a croon. Though (unaccredited) speculation exists that the (Columbia) house band included both Tommy and Jimmy Dorsey, as well as Ben Selvin, indeed a bunch of (white) musicians who clearly dug Ethel!

68. "Birmingham Bertha," Columbia 1837-D. As the flip side of "Am I Blue?" this bouncy title from *On with the Show* also penned by Grant Clark and Harry Akst, although not the classic that "Am I Blue?" was to become, is a more contrived tale about a woman named Bertha, who is more than lonesome for her guy (in Chicago); it remains as novel as it is jazzy.
69. "True Blue Lou," Columbia 1871-D. This very dated (1929) film entity from *The Dance of Life* penned by Sam Coslow, Leo Robin, and Richard Whiting obviously tells a tale of a really loyal guy! While Ethel is (sadly) not to be seen in this film, it's lucky that her recording of this bit of smaltzy, with (perhaps) a cold in her throat, nevertheless delivers an effective performance, despite the weakness of lyrics.
70. "Do I Know What I'm Doing?" Columbia 1905-D. A bouncy vocal, with risqué lyrics, penned by Sam Coslow, Leo Robin, and Richard Whiting, nevertheless provides Ethel with a wordy challenge. Fortunately, her clever singing makes it all sound easy as well as pleasant and simple.
71. "Shoo Shoo Boogie Boo," Columbia 1905-D. Another bouncy novelty title penned by the already familiar white team of Sam Coslow, Leo Robin, and Richard Whiting finds Ethel's vocal overcoming some really stupid and smaltzy lyrics with her articulate phrasing, as the title itself indicates.
72. "I Like the Way He Does It," Columbia 14565-D. A very crude entity penned by (Dallavon) at least gets to the point. Is crudeness likable? Listen and decide.
73. "Waiting At the End of the Road," Columbia 1933-D. This Irving Berlin-penned ditty was introduced in an all-black contemporary (1929) film *Hallelujah*, which, oddly, did not include Ethel. This recording perhaps found Ethel performing it as the Dixie Jubilee Singers had, in a slow and passionate plea. While intending no disrespect to Waters, this ditty was to be recorded by many, including a few jazzier sounding performances in a Paul Whiteman release, featuring with a Bing Crosby vocal on Columbia 1974-D as well as a significant rendering by Kate Smith on Velvet Tone 1999-V. Listen and compare!
74. "Traveling All Alone," Columbia 1933-D. Credited to pianist J. C. Johnson, this weepy (1929) ballad is full of sentiment and emotion. (About ten years later, Billie Holiday would later record it, not as an emotional lament, but as a defining rhythm song. Compare and listen!)

75. "Long, Lean, Lanky Mama," Columbia 14458-D. By this time (1929), Ethel had been prolifically become a recording artist for eight years. This contrived blues entity penned by (Rich) is backed by a Columbia (white) unaccredited house band and hits its mark as any (black) jazz band ever could! More so, Ethel's savvy vocal is outstanding, as this tale about a "long, lean, and lanky mama" did in fact fit her own physical attributes at the time!

76, 77. "Porgy," Columbia 2184-D. (a) As a title of a contemporary (1920s) novel, "Porgy" had been written by a (white) Southerner from South Carolina, Du Bose Heywood. By 1927, the sentimental story about poor Afro-Americans in Charleston, South Carolina, made it to Broadway and a popular song ditty penned by Dorothy Fields and Jimmy McHugh emerged. Ethel's commitment to this weepy ballad is considerable, as this ditty if further enhanced by Ethel's strong performance. From out of this ditty came the further development of the later (1935) *Porgy and Bess*, with more development and interest from George and Ira Gershwin; (b) Ethel would rerecord this ditty with a credited Duke Ellington backing two years later in 1932 released on Brunswick 6521. This rendering as even in the subsequent reissue on Brunswick 6758) finds no vocal or much differing orchestra backing as the original (1930) release. In true retrospective, a wasted (second) performance that could have been supplemented by other contemporary fodder! Or does anyone still care? Listen and learn.

78. "(What Did I Do to Be So) Black and Blue," Columbia 2184-D. This title penned by Andy Razaf, Fats Waller, and Harry Brooks was originally recorded by Edith Wilson on Brunswick 4685 and Louis Armstrong on Okeh 8714. As a truly all-black enterprise from the contemporary (1928) review *Hot Chocolates*, its message still, in true retrospective, haunts Americans of any color. Indeed, its own crude exposure of racism, even within the black community, was and remains a powerful statement. More so, considering the fine and different efforts of Wilson and Armstrong, it's Ethel's (1930) version, a far more articulate rendering, that defines this ditty as a classic. With a strong vocal (with attitude) and in an added sense of drama of stark realism, perhaps Ethel's own case for equality, especially noted in (intelligent) black slang, remains a lingering question?

79. "My Kind of Man," Columbia 2222-D. This contemporary Marion Davies (1930) film ditty from "*The Florodora Girl*", all about the agony of relationships, provides fine recording fodder. As, in true retrospective, Ethel was setting standards for the future, this bit of torch, as betrayed in its title penned by Herbert Stothart, Clifford Grey, and Andy Rice is crooned out dryly and effectively as (another) untouchable Waters classic.

81. "You Brought a New Kind of Love to Me," Columbia 2222-D. This title penned by Sammy Fain, Irving Kahal, Pierre Connor and Norman had been lightheartedly introduced by the crafty Frenchman Maurice Chevalier in the (1930) film, *The Big Pond*. Chevalier's subsequent recording on Victor 22405 is also crooned out well, as is a bouncy Bing Crosby attempt, a Paul Whiteman release on Columbia 2171-D. While this very pleasant and pleasing Depression-era ditty (1930) did have a casual message, this Waters version is more so crooned out to perfection and indeed defining! Listen and compare.

82. "You're Lucky to Me," Columbia 2288-D. As introduced in the Broadway entity *Blackbirds of 1930*, which starred Ethel herself, this very fine bit of torch singing, and a jazzier Eva Taylor vocal as a "Charleston Chasers" release, is realized best by Ethel's

croon. Penned by Eubie Blake and Andy Razaf, this original (1930) truly (black) enterprise retains its soft and classy popular appeal.

83. "Memories of You," Columbia 2288-D. Great again! As another entity penned for Ethel's own *Blackbirds of 1930* Broadway review, this sentimental bit of torch finds Ethel perhaps influenced a bit by the likes of contemporary Al Jolson, although (much) softer, with a Rudy Vallee (like) croon. Ethel mimics an attitude of a highbrow, pulling off a popular song penned by (black) composers and defining it!
84. "I Got Rhythm," Columbia 2346-D. As noted in its own Gershwin Brothers—penned title, this highbrow Broadway entity from the 1930 entity *Girl Crazy* had been magnificently introduced by Ethel Merman. Oddly, this (other) Ethel did not produce a contemporary recording! Moreover, the loud-voiced Merman, perfect for the Broadway stage, just might have heard this fine contemporary Ethel Waters version. Indeed, the talented Waters takes on the Gershwin lyrics and exploits this rhythm song in an exciting, sensational, and scatting performance! With no disrespect to Merman, what if Ethel Waters had been allowed in *Girl Crazy*? This recording does indeed invite such speculation!
85. "Three Little Words," Columbia 2346-D. This title, written by Bert Kalmar and Harry Ruby, was originally a very unusual Duke Ellington release, as it featured an all-white vocal performance, as the "rhythm boys," included Bing Crosby, Harry Barris, and Al Rinker on Victor 22528. This unusually integrated meeting of black and white efforts also met with great success and was more so a step into further racial progress for the times (1930). Ethel's torch approach, with backing (white) musicians, differs greatly from the group effort, and if not as historical, it is a serious crooning effort, noting lyrics "I Love You" that still flicker.
86. "When Your Lover Has Gone," Columbia 2409-D. This Einar Aaron Swan-penned ditty aims for the heart. As an instrumental theme, its melody has been used in many films since 1931. A contemporary Gene Austin vocal, hardly challenges Ethel's excellent execution of language clarity. As its very title indicates, it's a wordy torch song that Ethel, as a vocalist, defines.
87. "Please Don't Talk About Me When I'm Gone," Columbia 2409-D. Penned by the team of Sam H. Stept and Sidney Clare, this wordy ditty may also be known as "Don't Pan Me" credited to Gus Butler. Indeed, the earlier and acoustic Alberta Hunter release, on Paramount 12001, in 1922, had indicated a somewhat clumsy lyric, saved only by Alberta's abilities and (perhaps) by the piano backing of Eubie Blake. Ethel's own "Please Don't Talk About Me When I'm Gone" differs (much) the Hunter vocal and is a clever, polished (vocal) performance. A contemporary 1930 stage performance by Bee Palmer, the (white) former "Ziegfeld girl," who had claimed the Shimmy, some ten years or so earlier, had also claimed this ditty as a contributing writer, on sheet music, with Sidney Claire and Sam Stept, yet without a contributing contemporary recording. Had they been familiar with Hunter or Butler? In any case, Ethel's version is aided as a (1931) electric recording, with artfully backed by the (all-white) Columbia (studio) house band, with speculation existing that musicians present included the likes of Manny Klein, Tommy Dorsey, Joe Venuti, Rube Bloom Eddie Lang, and Benny Goodman. Gene Austin also produced a contemporary version that hardly challenged Ethel's articulate vocal. A later (1939) version as "Don't Pan Me" by Frankie "Half Pint" Jaxon, offers even more differences, with Jaxon (even) subduing his quirky voice, ably backed by the very possible cooler jazz backings of Barney Bigard, Lil Armstrong, Wellman Braud, and Sid Catlett. Listen and compare!

88. "You Can't Stop Me from Loving You," Columbia 2481-D. Ethel perhaps defines jazz vocals, noting her vocal alertness and attitude capturing some challenging lyrics, penned by Mann Holiner and Alberta Nichols for Ethel's own Broadway review *Rhapsody in Black*. For many 1931 contemporaries (and in retrospective) many later listeners, this ditty perhaps finds the talented Waters challenging some very smart lyrics with ease and captures Ethel at her absolute zenith as a jazz vocalist! Just listen!
89. "Without That Gal," Columbia 2481-D. Sung as "Without That Man," this ditty penned by Walter Donaldson is a medium tempo bit of torch, finding Ethel's own crooning in an emotional overload, defining this ditty than a contemporary (1931) Ruth Etting version on Banner 2291. Listen and compare.
90. "River, Stay 'Way from My Door," Columbia 2511-D. While perhaps a bit dumb for a title, this ditty penned by Mort Dixon and Harry Woods betrays a committed vocal, which beautifully defined this (1931) song ditty, noting a differing vocal from a current Kate Smith version on Columbia 2578-D was also done so well. Listen and compare the vocal styles of these interesting (contemporary) divas. A bit boring?
91. "Shine On, Harvest Moon," Columbia 2511-D. This (already) old ditty, even by contemporary (1931) standards, had been around since the acoustic days of 1909, penned by the popular vaudevillians of the era, Nora Bayes and Jack Norworth. As associated with the aging Ziegfeld since 1927, the popular Ruth Etting was given the title to perform in a revival as in *Ziegfeld Follies of 1931*. More so, it was Ruth's own contemporary recording on Perfect 12737 that (perhaps) led Ethel to record it. Ethel's subsequent vocal finds her dragging it a bit, that is until the last part of the (bland) song, when her vocal speeds up and makes things sound a bit more interesting. Check it out.

Brunswick Records. Ethel Waters original Brunswick masters recorded between 1932 and 1934 were produced when Brunswick was part of the American Record Company or (ARC), which had also bought out the Columbia label.

92. "I Can't Give You Anything but Love," Brunswick 6517. This fine standard from Broadway's *Blackbirds of 1928* had been somewhat lost by its original black star contemporary Adelaide Hall, as she had not recorded it. While subsequent recordings by Cliff Edwards, and finally, Louis Armstrong, among others, were done well, this ditty penned by Dorothy Fields and Jimmy McHugh became part of a Brunswick Records (1932-33) project; it was given to Ethel, although Adelaide herself was part of the project and available. Backed by Duke Ellington and His Orchestra, Ethel croons out an effective recording and had a few (vocal) tricks to add! It would seem that Ethel was very much familiar with the (1929) Louis Armstrong version of this ditty released on Okeh 8669, and for about a third of her rendering, a surprisingly (good) emulation of Louis's vocal may be heard! (Adelaide Hall would later and finally lay claims upon this ditty, with Fats Waller in 1938.)
93. "St. Louis Blues," Brunswick 6521. (a) Speculation has it that Ethel had performed this ditty before 1920, way before black women were allowed to even record. This (1932) recording found Ethel oddly recording it for the first time as part of a Brunswick records project and was backed by the popular Cecil Mack Choir, providing a group sound. While it ain't bad, this vocal lacks discipline, as (perhaps) Ethel was distracted by the chorus. It is hardly the acoustic rendering that Marion Harris had produced nor as good as the defining previous acoustic release by Bessie Smith back in 1925 on Columbia 14064-D. Nor is it as good as many other

subsequent efforts, including a brilliant Louis Armstrong (1929) recording or a riveting contemporary Bing Crosby version, with fine backing from Duke Ellington; (b) While Ethel would continue to perform this ditty on radio, as a recording, her later (1947) Mary Howard Records Master subsequently released by Mercury Records on LP (MG 20051) and 45 EP (EP-1-3245) finds a fine, stripped-down, poignant vocal, well led by (pianist), Reginald Beane.

94. "Stormy Weather," Brunswick 6564. This title by Ted Koehler and Harold Arlen is probably Ethel's most popular torch song as she introduced it at the *Cotton Club* review in 1933. As a truly great song ditty with its own merits, Arlen himself recorded a somewhat good vocal for himself as a contemporary Leo Reisman release on Victor 24262.

While considered by many contemporaries as a blues song, or perhaps the ultimate torch song, it's Ethel's own total (vocal) commitment that identifies a classic recording, despite many other renderings by other singers. Moreover, this (rare) Depression-era best seller found its way into the (white) mainstream as no previous (Waters) recording had ever produced previously, noting her (already) acclaimed success.

Among many other versions, a (later) Ivie Anderson film short and the even better known (1943) film of the same name, featuring Lena Horne, laid some claims to the classic, further exploiting the title through a visual image that Ethel did not enjoy. Nevertheless, it's hard to take this ditty away from Ethel. Very hard! Listen and decide.

95. "Love Is the Thing," Brunswick 6564. The flip of "Stormy Weather," this is another intimate torch song that achieved greatness. As a ditty penned by Ned Washington and Victor Young, this impressive and serious tale of love again finds Ethel's flawless crooning vocal performance an artistic achievement.
96. "Don't Blame Me," Brunswick 6617. Another fine crooning job penned by Dorothy Fields and Jimmy McHugh finds the very able Waters on another emotional adventure in torch that does not fail to burn.
97. "Shadows on the Swanee," Brunswick 6617. This contrived title penned by Joe Young, Johnny Burke, and Harold Spina finds Ethel pleasantly crooning away in mid-tempo.

Note: The following two song ditties were penned by Irving Berlin for his (1933) Broadway entity *As Thousands Cheer*. As Berlin himself also hired Ethel Waters to perform these ditties in the same production, Ethel thus became the first black woman to appear in lights, as a credited act, with equal billing shared with white performers of an all-white cast. While both Berlin and Waters took heat from all this, this significant integration of Broadway must acclaim Ethel for another significant achievement, solely due to her own unique gifts and Berlin's own (personal) recognition of them.

98. "Heat Wave," Columbia 2826-D. As to what was to become a classic Broadway showstopper, as introduced in *As Thousands Cheer*, this rhythmic ditty, with a Latin rumba beat, remains yet another original Waters performance that became definitive. As officially backed by Benny Goodman, found on the original Columbia issue, it's also to be noted, as on the original flip side "Harlem on My Mind," the name "Ethel Waters" above that of Goodman's Orchestra.
99. "Harlem on My Mind," Columbia 2826-D. This ditty is another (Berlin) title from *As Thousands Cheer*. On hearing, its questionable lyrics on race are serious enough as

well as a cheery reference to Josephine Baker, who had been Ethel's own understudy at the Plantation Club before leaving off to fame in France in 1925. In any case, Ethel's clever vocal skills are articulately intact, noting a bit of French with Harlem slang, seemingly thrown in a simple pun. Indeed, another masterful performance!

100. "I Just Couldn't Take It, Baby," Columbia 2853-D. Ethel's blues sounded a bit sophisticated by this time in 1933. Penned by Mann Holiner and Alberta Nichols, this bit of risqué innuendo nevertheless still holds its listeners. Just listen!

101, 102. "A Hundred Years from Today," Columbia 2853-D. (a) Backed by "Benny Goodman and His Orchestra," with a rare sweet band arraignment, Ethel sings her heart out. More so, penned by the likes of Joe Young, Ned Washington and Victor Young, this classic torch ditty was to become greatly appreciated and emulated, noting a fine (Waters) influenced contemporary version by Lee Wiley on Brunswick 6775; (b) Ethel's lesser known subsequent postwar version released on Mary Howard Records MHR 108 finds Ethel, with only piano backing crooning out an affective rendering. With Benny or without Benny? Listen and compare.

103. "Come Up and See Me Sometime," Brunswick 6885. This novelty had been performed by Lillian Roth in the popular contemporary (1934) film version in *Take a Chance*. As a shimmy dancer, Roth's hot performance of this (obvious) novelty, penned by Arthur Swanstrom and Louis Alter in the film is as full of fun as it is playful. (As a recording by Roth, this ditty is hard to find, if it exists.) Oddly, a contemporary Mae West film found film *I'm No Angel* found (Mae) using language *similar*, but not the same lyric as from this ditty penned by Swanstrom and Alter as found in the Roth film. Subsequently, by the time Ethel took on this contrived bit of nonsense, she most likely attributed it to Mae West, although Mae had not sung it in her film as Ethel's own vocal indicates a clever bit of mimicking Mae West herself! Waters goes off a little more as she goes off on her own risqué attempt with perhaps some added (unaccredited lyrics) of her own. Is this Ethel at her steamy best? Are there any Eskimos around? Listen and learn from this (very) dated recording fodder.

104. "You've Seen Harlem At Its Best," Brunswick 6885. A wordy social statement crooned out just right still finds Dorothy Fields and Jimmy McHugh, who penned this ditty, many (black) stereotypes and sad (1934) commentary with racial conclusions clearly identified by Ethel's ever-sensitive vocal. In true retrospective, this ditty would be found in much displeasure for many later (1960s) radicals, conscience of the fact that racism was (then) tolerated and accepted. While it's true that Waters could have easily rejected this material as recording fodder, it's interesting to speculate why she recorded it. Was it ever pondered that Ethel's own struggle with racism had broken down many racial barriers?

Ethel's move to the newly formed (American) Decca group from Brunswick Records in 1934 led to some interesting recordings, if too few. She recorded a few interesting side of the independent Liberty Music Shop Record, also noted below.

105. "Miss Otis Regrets," Decca 140. This odd Cole Porter-penned ditty had British music hall origins. Moreover, Ethel's approach is serious enough as she effectively croons out the sad tale about a hanging of a distraught woman as more than the pun that was intended. More so is the pathos and drama created by Ethel's vocal as defining (another) classic.

106. "Moonglow," Decca 140. Penned by Will Hudson, Eddie De Lange, and Irving Mills for a contemporary "*Cotton Club*" review, this (1934) ditty emerged as an instrumental

for Cab Calloway. More so, and some light years later, it became known as the (1956) instrumental song "Theme from Picnic," used in the film so called *Picnic*. As a vocal, Ethel's crooning job, which may be only so described as melodious and mellow, provides for this ditty an ultimate recording, with lyric.

107 "I Ain't Gonna Sin No More," Decca 141. Ethel herself introduced this contrived bit of rhythm, penned by Con Conrad and Herb Magidson, in the 1934 film *Gift of Gab*.

108. "Trade Mark," Brunswick 02045. This ditty, perhaps a cast off from the film, *Gift of Gab*, as penned by Sidney Easton, had oddly found release, not in the United States, but as an original (1934) British release. As a contrived bit of risqué lyrics and rhythm, this tale of a raunchy prostitute finds Ethel (still) ready to take on this type of crude material with flare, just as she had in the 1920s. This (British) Brunswick release was the result of American (Decca) masters being released on (British) Brunswick releases. This also applied to contemporary Bing Crosby releases.

109. "Give Me a Heart to Sing To," Decca 141. The Helen Morgan original version penned by Victor Young and Ned Washington is sung in her (usual) emotionally high-pitch vocal. More so is Ethel's version and perhaps with a bit of mimicry of Morgan, her contemporary since the 1920s? (Another fine crooning job of this ditty notes a contemporary Bing Crosby release on Brunswick 6953.) Listen to all and compare vocals to this dull song pleading for passion while crying. A true bit or torch?

110. "You're Going to Leave the Old Home, Jim," Decca 234. This (1934) rendering was hardly the type of recording fodder that challenged Ethel, except that she is indeed in good voice. As a slow and dreary (mother) entity, this tradition (folk) ballad had seemingly been around Americana, also known as "The Tramp's Mother," more so as claimed by hillbilly Goebel Reeves (only with his guitar) on Okeh 45381 previously in 1929. As a pick, this ditty makes it interesting enough for Ethel, as she (fortunately) fails to yodel as Reeves had.

Note: The following two ditties penned by Howard Dietz and Arthur Schwartz were originally introduced in the (1935) Broadway entity *At Home and Abroad*, by Ethel, in another integrated production.

111. "Hottentot Potentate," Liberty Music Shops L-188. As a clever ploy on words, this ditty reeks of highbrow Broadway, with Ethel adapting to anything and masterfully defining yet another classic.

112. "Thief in the Night," Liberty Music Shops L-188. This well-crafted ditty is crooned out in good storytelling fashion. More so, while novel, it's still a fine torch entity as well. Just listen!

Note: After an unknown absence of about three years, despite continued success in nightclub work across the country, Ethel Waters returned to the recording studio in 1938. As the emergence of swing found its zenith in these times, Ethel perhaps found it a good challenge to put herself back in circulation. Much had changed. An industry that she had a lot of influence in had found newer divas, younger faces, fresher voices. The likes of the newer (black) entities such as Ivie Anderson, Billie Holiday, Ella Fitzgerald, and Maxine Sullivan, all provided the older Ethel some stiff competition. Within the times between 1938 through 1941, Ethel would nevertheless record some notable popular swing and Broadway classics by combining a bit of touring and a few triumphant Broadway entities *Mamba's Daughters* and *Cabin in the Sky*.

Note. All (Decca) and (Bluebird) masters reviewed as picks below are backed by the Eddie Mallory Orchestra, a fine contemporary (1938-39) black swing band that had become her touring band. Among good speculation, many (Bluebird) recordings find the likes of musicians Benny Carter and Regional Beane.

113. "You're a Sweetheart," Decca 1613. This ditty was penned for a contemporary Alice Faye film entity by Harold Adamson and Jimmy McHugh. Ethel's sweet-voiced vocal found some serious contemporary Dolly Dawn version, on Vocalion 3874, which is almost as sweet sounding. Listen and compare.
114. "I'll Get Along Somehow," Decca 1613. This bit of expressive regret penned by Buddy Fields and Gerald Marks finds Ethel's vocal getting along well and more so serious and sweet.
115. "How Can I Face This Wearied World Alone?" Decca 4410. A tale for those who question life and fate, penned by Roscoe McRae and Eddie Mallory, is masterfully told.
116. "Frankie and Johnnie," Bluebird B-10038. A fine updated version of the traditional bit of Americana is a 1938 excuse to swing? It more so succeeds!
117. "They Say," Bluebird B-10025. While a bit slow, this ditty penned by Edward Heyman, Paul Mann, and Stephan Weiss found Ethel's polished vocal in direct competition with the likes of contemporary Billie Holiday version, whose attempts to be smooth are impressive, as found on Brunswick 8270 featuring a jazzier arrangement by Teddy Wilson. Yet another contemporary version, as a Artie Shaw release, as with a fine and equally polished version by vocalist Helen Forrest on Bluebird 10075, offers more debate. Listen to all!
118. "Jeepers Creepers," Bluebird B-10025. This title written by Johnny Mercer and Harry Warren had been featured and introduced by Louis Armstrong in the 1938 film, *Going Places*, which starred a young actor, Ronald Reagan. A subsequent Armstrong recording, a smaltzy story about a racehorse in the film, ain't bad. Ethel (always the better singer) solidly beats out the Armstrong version with her bright rhythmic singing, with some fine swing backup. Listen and compare.
119. "Lonesome Walls," Bluebird B-10222. Penned by Jerome Kern and Du Bois Heyward, this superb Broadway entity, perhaps the only song ditty from Ethel's own (1939) Broadway triumphant *Mamba's Daughter*, is crooned out to perfection. (In true retrospective, perhaps one of the most forgotten gems ever penned from Kern and Du Bois Heyward!) Listen and do not forget.
120. "If You Ever Change Your Mind," Bluebird B-10222. Ethel's question is fair enough. Penned by Johnny Green, Marice Sigler, and Mayme Watts, this bit of fine singing again spotlights Ethel's vocal abilities.
121. "What Goes Up, Must Come Down," Bluebird B-10207. Another fine vocal penned by Ted Koehler and Rube Bloom, this bit of swing is more than a pleasure, as is a contemporary version by Ginny Simms. Listen and compare differing vocal styles.
122. "You Had It Coming to You," Bluebird B-10207. Penned by Sammy Lerner and Ben Oakland, this ditty again finds Ethel very able to fit lyrics to a soft but mid-tempo swing backup.
123. "Bread and Gravy," Bluebird B-10415. This Hoagy Carmichael-penned ditty describes the bare necessities of "Bread and Gravy." Ethel's fine abilities as a vocalist are again apparent, and this well-done performance just could be an excuse

to be played before dinner. (Ethel would more so use thing ditty in future personal appearances, which will be noted later in the text of this book.)

124. "Down in My Soul," Bluebird B-11284. Is this pre-Motown? The word *soul* is indeed sung very soulfully. Was this edgy vocal performance penned by Porter Grainger ahead of its time? Just listen!
125. "Georgia on My Mind," Bluebird B-11028. This title penned by Hoagey Carmichael and Stuart Gorrell is given a fine contemporary (1939) crooning job, indeed far from the likes of the previous Louis Armstrong gritty version found on Okeh 41441. Light years away, in 1960, Ray Charles would further define this already old ditty on ABC Paramount 10135. Listen to all and compare.
126. "Stop Myself from Worrying Over You," Bluebird B-11284. Penned by pianist Regional Beane and Ethel Waters herself, this bit of contrived swing cannot fail to please anyone, upon any dance floor.
127. "Old Man Harlem," Bluebird B-11028. High marks for this swing number! As Ethel's fine and jazzy vocal smokes, so does musician Benny Carter, blowing away! This long-neglected gem at least matches any of Ethel's swing contemporaries, including the likes Ivie Anderson, Dolly Dawn, Maxine Sullivan, Billie Holiday, and Helen Humes! As credited and penned by Hoagy Carmichael and Rudy Vallee, this contrived bit of Harlem jive is far more effective than the previous Rudy Vallee release, on Columbia 2764-D, which had just attempted to be hip. Or are Ethel and her band just better? Listen and decide.
128. "Push Out," Bluebird B-10415-Another moving swing number! Ethel's flawless and jazzy vocal and Benny Carter's horn again attract many listeners, as this ditty penned by Alex Lovejoy and Nat Reed indeed smokes!
129. "Baby, What Else Can I Do?" Bluebird B-10517. Is this a bit of "Harlem" slang? If so, it's worthy of Ethel to explain it! In any case, this wordy ditty penned by Gerald Marks and Walter Hirsh works.
130. "I Just Got a Letter," Bluebird B-10517. Ethel's fast-paced and novel vocal penned by David Franklin is a smoking novelty, with an energetic vocal equally matched by some fine swing!

Note: The following (1940) Liberty Music Shop recordings represent a grouping of an original Broadway soundtrack of 78 rpm records in album form, a new concept for its time.

131 "Love Turned the Light Out," Liberty Music Shops L-310. This moving ballad penned by John Latouche and Vernon Duke is sung in medium tempo and crooned out tenderly. (For some odd reason, this Broadway entity did not make it to the later film version.)

132, 133. "Taking a Chance on Love," Liberty Music Shops L-310. (a) As another classic Broadway entity penned by John Latouche, Vernon Duke, and Ted Fetter, this fast-paced piece of popular property was to become often recorded, after Ethel's initial and defining rendering. More so, a contemporary and jazzy (1941) Benny Goodman release, featuring a fine vocal by Helen Forrest on Columbia 35869 became a well-known best-selling entity, along with a reissue in 1943, when the film version was released, which also more than helped popularize the song ditty; (b) Continental 1006. Ethel's second recording in 1946, backed by the postwar jazz of J. C. Heard, find Ethel dropping her original Broadway idiom in a successful attempt to redefine herself. Her bright vocal is found to be less than bold, which perhaps found her being led by the (Heard) orchestra. In true retrospective, this author's ears favor the first (1940) original recording, noting the second version as far jazzier and no slouch! Listen and decide. Does it matter? What about Helen Forrest? (The filmed movie version will be subsequently noted, along with other renderings in radio and personal appearances.)

134. "Honey in the Honeycomb," Liberty Music Shops L-311. The very able Waters vocal for this ditty penned by John Latouche and Vernon Duke perhaps finds Ethel showboating. Or is it just a masterful voice and bright style becoming highlighted? (This ditty would later be reviewed subsequently as a film entity.)

135, 136. "Cabin in the Sky," Liberty Music Shops L-311. (a) This original title song from the Broadway classic of the same name, while obviously contrived, penned byJohn Latouche and Vernon Duke, fortunately benefited from Ethel's committed vocal. Indeed, this spirited crooning job about inspiration was to be considered a gospel entity, despite its (1940) Broadway origins. Like all other song ditties from the original Broadway production, this ditty would remain with Ethel as a radio entity and as a popular ditty in personal appearances. Her later (1943) film of the same name, also containing a version, will be reviewed subsequently in the text of this book; (b) Continental 1006. As far as a recording, her second rendering with J. C. Heard is far jazzier and makes for good comparisons. Prewar or postwar version—which is better?

Note: As age and American participation in World War II approached (1941), Ethel's own career at first found some success on USO tours, radio, and films. More so, the musical (1943) films *Stage Door Canteen* and her own *Cabin in the Sky* remain, in true retrospective, among the very best of the genre. However, her inability to manage money, age, temperament, and racism finally caught up with her.

The following (4) are (1946) Continental masters all penned by Leonard Feather. More so, they are all new titles backed by the jazzy postwar sound of J. C. Heard, with Reginald Beane on piano. (Subsequently, all Continental Masters were acquired and reissued in the Remington Record label). For any listener who might think that Ethel had lost it as a true jazz entity, these recordings prove otherwise.

137. "Man Wanted," Continental 1007. This stylish vocal achieves good and jazzy results.
138. "Honey in a Hurry," Continental 1009. Another jazzy trip again achieves interesting results with a committed Ethel.
139. "I Shoulda Quit," Continental 10009. This could be considered R&B, as a very energetic-voiced Ethel proves she's still no slouch at rhythmic songs, despite her age.
140. "You Took My Man," Continental 10008. Another excuse for a rhythmic entity pays off. Moreover, the committed Ethel (again) rocks.

The following are Mary Howard Records Masters that were issued as "Mary Howard Records" and (or) both on Mercury Records, which acquired masters (Mary Howard Records) and released them.

141. "Supper Time," Mary Howard Records 116. This is the missing vocal that Ethel never got around to recording from Irving Berlin's (1933) Broadway entity "As Thousands Cheer," where she more so had introduced it. As a bit of contemporary social commentary, Ethel is found to have set a place at her dinner table, even though her loved one had been lynched! Moreover, considering the risks that (Berlin) took to put

this type of drama into a musical, the reality of Ethel's real (blackface) rendering of this yarn was an eye opening for Americana itself. With a sob at the end (also heard on this recording), Waters took the culture into a Broadway stage as no other before her, and moreover in an active part in an otherwise segregated environment of shame. Subsequently, Ethel would perform this ditty in radio and on stage, yet oddly did not produce an official recording until her Mary Howard Records master. However late, this (1947) rendering finds Ethel ready to (again) experience the reality of racism, sharing her emotions of regret and despair for the many people (especially of color) around her.

142. "Summertime," Mary Howard Records 115. This Gershwin title from *Porgy and Bess* finds Ethel's edgy vocal on the popular song ditty she had not bothered to record since at least (1936), although she did in fact perform it on stage and on radio broadcasts. Indeed, earlier versions as by Billie Holiday and Bing Crosby had defined this ditty as a recorded classic, or did Ethel in fact redefine it with her stripped-down vocal of subtle emotion and pathos.

143. "Happiness Is a Thing Called Joe," Mary Howard Records 107. The 1942-43 recording ban had probably prevented Ethel from commercially recording this very fine ditty penned by Harold Arlen and E. Y. Harburg, more so an original film song ditty (not in the original Broadway entity of *Cabin in the Sky*) for the (1943) film version. Her very well-done introduction of this ditty in the film found Ethel in a sweet and somber mood, expressing her feelings about a guy named Joe; this would be nominated for an academy award for best song, though it lost. Ethel would perform this ditty on stage and on radio, before (finally) her own well-done (1947) recording.

144. "Little Black Boy," Mary Howard Records 117. Ethel had introduced this ditty on radio, as far back as in 1933. Yet this ditty's origins are deep. It may have been based upon a song ditty of older Scottish and English folklore as "Mighty Lak' a Rose." The titled ditty "Little Black Boy" penned by George Whiting and J.C. Johnson had (direct) race implications, with Ethel's own (black) experience lending a more than credible vocal. Ethel's control is obvious, as her advice to a small (black) child becomes as heart-wrenching as it is tender.

145-148. *The Favorite Songs of Ethel Waters*, Mercury LP-MG-20051. This mid-1950s Mercury LP release had been partially released on the "Mary Howard Records" label. The (below) titles find the remainder of the original (1947) titles (finally) released.

a. "The Crucifixion." Is this church music or true gospel? In any case, a fine performance.
b. "Sometimes I Feel Like a Motherless Child." Ethel had performed this traditional spiritual as a radio performance long before this fine recording.
c. "Paper Moon" or as "It's Only a Paper Moon," penned by Billy Rose, E.Y. Harburg, and Harold Arlen is revived with a pleasing spirit in a bright-voiced vocal.
d. "Cant Help Loving That Man". Did Ethel re-define this classic?

Note: A contemporary (1947) RCA Victor Album P-192 as a "Musical Smart Set" found Ethel sharing the concept with Louis Armstrong, Mildred Bailey, and Jack Teagarden. While this company of recording artists was indeed impressive, the concept found each recording artist recording with differing backup, contributing *one* two-sided 78 record. The set could also be ordered separately from Victor if requested. In Ethel's recordings, she finds a strong backing of (pianist) Herman Chittison, leader of his "Herman Chittison Trio." The jazzy group just had to have been heard by Waters long before Chittison's success in Europe before WWII? Luckily for Ethel, Chittison's jazzy backup is less than the (already) older sounds of swing and fits the sound of postwar jazz that she had (already) successfully produced with J. C Heard's contemporary band.

149. "Blues in My Heart," Victor 20-2459. This stylish vocal led by Herman Chittison was perhaps influenced by the popular style of contemporary (1947) vocalist and musician Nat King Cole. Penned by Irving Mills and Benny Carter, while contrived, it finds an interested Ethel in good spirits, more so producing a creative, jazzy expression in her vocal.
150. "Careless Love," Victor 20-2459. The already old standard is given a (newer) musical identity led by Chittison's Trio, along a shining and subdued vocal from Ethel, indeed a perfect fit for Chittison's modern jazz. Too bad this did not continue!

By the end of the 1940s, Ethel no longer slim and "Sweet Mama Stringbean," was more than overweight and down on her luck. Despite her Broadway and Hollywood success of the early 1940s, her own personal decisions, age, and a newer generation of musical tastes found her more than lost. Fortunately, her acting abilities (previously discovered on Broadway in 1939s *Mamba's Daughter*) finally led her (well-deserved) recognition in the non-singing (1949) film *Pinky*. As nominated for an academy award, which she lost, she then pursued another attempt at Broadway, with *Member of the Wedding*, along with a filmed version in 1952 that led to (even) more kudos for her acting. While nonmusical, the film did find Ethel singing the old spiritual "His Eyes Are on the Sparrow," which would subsequently become the title of her successful autobiography. This document would prove and remain a good source of information about her and the lesser documented time she had performed.

After 1950, Ethel's music was to be produced in a far lesser scale, except for reissued material. The following recordings, however, do merit review. Picks:

151. "Partners with God," Jubilee 5274. A self-penned ditty (with Eddie Stuart) on 78 and 45 rpm found this mid-1950s recording, if limited, a sincere and fine vocal professing her faith.
152. "His Eye Is on the Sparrow," Chancel CR-2002. While Ethel scored well as an old lady performing the traditional spiritual "His Eye Is on the Sparrow," she did not produce a contemporary recording that her contemporary friend Mahalia Jackson had with great success. Some years later, around 1957, Ethel became associated with Rev. Billy Graham and his religious movement. This resulting recording of "His Eye Is on the Sparrow" finds Ethel's committed vocal led by the "New York Crusade Choir." While hardly a commercial venture, this ditty and its flip side, "Just a Closer Walk with Thee" did indeed find Ethel's concerns about religion serious enough.
153. "Just a Closer Walk with Thee," Chancel CR-2002.

154-158. "His Eye Is on the Sparrow," Word 8044. While the front shot of Ethel is done in good taste, the back of this original (1957?) album betrays an aged sixty-one-year-old woman, hardly dignified. Other than this gross neglect of a dignified woman, this LP does have some assets. As accompanied by the "Paul Mickelson Orchestra and Choir," Ethel's vocal commitment is considerable, as many of these old ditties just had to be known to her when growing up earlier in the century. Picks include:

a. "Deep River." This title may have origins in slavery times, and Ethel strongly conveys them. While this traditional entity had been around a while, as a Marion Anderson entity on Victor 9227 and by Paul Robeson on Victor 20793, since the mid-1920s, this title has deeper roots.
b. "Mammy." This already old Will Marion Cook-credited title is truly an experience, as "told" by Ethel.
c. "I Just Can't Stay Here by Myself."
d. "In His Care." Ethel and Mickelson's church organ actually rock and roll, and—in an odd way, one hears Ethel duet with herself in some recording mix of wizardry. Somehow, the recorded result finds her singing into a playback surprisingly good, indeed "hot" gospel at its best. e. "Stand by Me."

159-167. *Ms. Ethel Waters*, Evergreen Monument MES-6812. This (later) 1950s recording captures the old lady with (only) Reggie Beane at the piano in a small live performance. While not the spectacular kind of show that Lena Horne would (later) put together in her old age, this captured performance does deliver a fine performance, with perhaps (even) some evidence of the much (younger) woman who was known as "Sweet Mama Stringbean." Picks include:

a. "Am I Blue?"
b. "I Ain't Gonna Sin No More."
c. "Dinah."
d. "Throw the Dirt."
e. "Trouble, Trouble" and "St. Louis Blues."
f. "Supper Time."
g. "Bready and Gravy" and "Oh, Lady, Be Good."
h. "Half of Me."
i. "Stormy Weather" and "Taking a Chance on Love."

168-170. *Reminisces*, Word 3173. This early (1960s) album found Ethel in a diminished vocal form and *not* accompanied by anyone except a piano player, who was most likely Regional Beane. The following renderings, however, do merit listening:

a. "I Am a Pilgrim."
b. "Crying Holy on to the Lord."
c. "Is It Well with Your Soul?"

171-187. *Who Said Blackbirds Are Blue?* Sandy Hook LP 2060. Somehow, this small label got a hold of some live material from perhaps the (early) 1950s? While not as good as "Miss Ethel Waters" nor as good a recording job, as a live entity, this ain't bad. Highlights include: a. "Who Said Blackbirds Are Blue?" b. "Young At Heart." c. "My Gal Sal" (duet with Reggie Beane). d. "How Are Things in Glocca Morra?" (duet with Reggie Beane). e. "Eli Eli." (This Hebrew lament had more so been part of (Waters) stage programs since the 1920s.) f. "Birth of the Blues." g. "My Man." h/i. "Come Rain or Shine" and "The Man I Love." j. "Blues in the Night." k. "That's What Harlem Means to Me." l. "I Got It Bad and That Ain't Good." m. "Easter Parade" (duet with Reggie Beane). n. "You Took Advantage of Me." o. "Yesterdays." p. "Smoke Gets in Your Eyes." q. "You're Just in Love" (duet with Reggie Beane).

- Special limited original release.

188. "When That Man is Dead and Gone," Hollywood 7391. This very effective (1942?) recording found Ethel producing a recording for the (British) Royal Navy, "with compliments of Samuel Goldwyn." The Irving Berlin-penned ditty about Germany's contemporary leader Adolph Hitler had already made the rounds as a popular Glenn Miller release, with a vocal by Tex Beneke, Paula Kelly and the Modernaires released on Bluebird-B-11069. More ironically, in England, crooner Al Bowlly, was soon killed, during a 1941 blitz, after recording it. As this dance ditty is far less novel because of its serious message for the world, its exposure must be brought to light, at least by the efforts of this author.

- Radio

As an early (1920s) performer, Ethel Waters was credited as the first woman of color to be heard over radio, as featured in a live broadcast in New Orleans in 1921. While always hardest on (black) performers, Ethel appeared on many live broadcasts as time progressed, including her own short-lived network program *American Review* of 1933-34. The following picks were to be discovered on numerous LP issues found on material with other recording artists, along with some vintage stuff captured by "Totem," "Sandy Hook," "Curtin Call," and "Sunbeam" record labels. There is also some material found from recordings found from primitive sources. Picks are:

189. "Stormy Weather," 1933, Rudy Vallee *Fleishman Program* (Sandy Hook 2027).
190. "Raisin' the Rent," 1933, *American Review* (Dorsey Brothers).
191. "To Be or Not to Be," 1933, *American Review* (Dorsey Brothers).
192. "Harlem on My Mind," 1933, *American Review* (Dorsey Brothers).
193. "Dinah," 1933, *American Review* (Dorsey Brothers).
194. "Give All Your Love to Me," 1933, *American Review* (Dorsey Brothers).
195. "Stormy Weather," 1933, *American Review* (Dorsey Brothers).
196. "Them Green Pastures," 1933, *American Review* (Totem 1041).
197. "There'll Be Some Changes Made," 1941, *Kraft Music Hall*, Bing Crosby (Totem 1041).
198. "St. Louis Blues," 1941, "*Jubilee-Forecast 12*," with Duke Ellington Orch (Sunbeam 214).
199. "Stormy Weather," 1941, "*Jubilee-Forecast 12*," with Duke Ellington Orch (Sunbeam 214).
200. "A Woman without a Man," 1942, "*Command Performance*," intro. Cary Grant (Totem 1041).
201. "Dinah," "*Command Performance*," 1942, Intro, Bob Hope (Totem 1041).
202. "Buds Won't Bud," 1943 MGM radio promo for contemporary film *Cairo*.
203. "Taking a Chance on Love," 1943. "*Treasury Song Parade*."
204. "Happiness Is Just a Thing Called Joe,"1943, "*Treasury Song Parade*."
205. "Summertime," 1943. "*Treasury Song Parade*."

206. "Smoke Gets in Your Eyes," 1944, *Rudy Vallee Drene Shampoo Program* (Totem 1041) (Benny Kreuger Orchestra, Regional Beane, piano).
207. "Summertime," 1947, "*Guest Star*," intro, Kenny Delmar (Herman Chittison Trio).
208. "Can't Help Lovin' Dat Man," 1949. "*Guest Star*," intro. John Conte (Totem 1041) (Fletcher Henderson, piano).

- Visual Image / Legacy

In 1993, the US Postal Service issued a stamp with the image of Ethel Waters. As seen, the image is of a smiling old matron of her latter days. The young flapper of the 1920s is sadly missing. The young Ethel Waters was much more than this. Her classic lovely nose and chin, the lovely hair, and the vibrancy of her youth, as witnessed by her contemporaries, is sadly lost!

209, 210. The (1929) film *On with the Show* found a thin-figured in a cotton field. With stereotypes pushed aside, it's not the cotton picking that's so hot and steamy, it's Ethel herself introducing (a) "Am I Blue?" Moreover, Ethel may be seen in a vaudeville act performing (b) "Birmingham Bertha."

211, 212, 213. A (1933) film short *Rufus Jones for President* perhaps captures Ethel Waters at the height of her fame. The following three titles are to be seen and heard: a. "Stay on the Right Side of the Fence." Ethel croons out this sad ditty to a young Sammy Davis Jr. b. "Am I Blue?" While not as good as in *On with the Show*, Ethel slowly reintroduces her hit. c. "Underneath the Harlem Moon." With great skill, Ethel turns this novelty title into a memorable musical experience that indeed still lingers! Did they smoke reefers? Were they Democrats? Was Ethel Waters the mother of a young president? Was Ethel Waters an exciting performer? Are there too many stereotypes? Watch and listen!

214. "Quicksand." The hard-core (1943) World War II drama *Stage Door Canteen* finds a heavier Ethel backed by Count Basie and his orchestra, in a knockout crooning performance. Class!

215, 216. The 1943 film release: *Cabin in the Sky.* Among the ditties from the original 1940 Broadway production (already reviewed), the latter visual images of the older Ethel Waters (still) generate interest. Picks include:

(a) "Lil Black Sheep" (in a church setting); (b) "Happiness Is a Thing Called Joe"; (c) "Cabin in the Sky" duet with Eddie Rochester Anderson; (d) "Dat Suits Me" duet with Butterfly McQueen; (e) "Taking a Chance on Love" numerous times; and (f) "Honey in the Honeycomb."

217. "His Eyes Is on the Sparrow." A (very) aged black woman is both heard and seen in the 1952 film *Member of the Wedding*.

218, 219. The aged and overweight diva found the aspects of income very slim, especially after 1960. Yet speculation does exist that admirers such as Bing Crosby (who in a 1960 interview with Tony Thomas professed great appreciation for her early talent and influence upon him), Sammy Davis Jr., and Frank Sinatra (an early influence upon him), Della Reeves, Pearl Bailey, Barbara McNair, Mike Douglas, and Johnny Carson were all (still) very much interested in her, along with Billy Graham's religious crusades. Ethel's 1969 (around seventy-three years old) appearance on the contemporary TV program *Hollywood Palace* found her linked up with the around twenty-five-year-old Diana Ross, just as she was splitting off from the Supremes. While the young Ross had already grown up in a tough environment, singing as a teenager as Ethel had in an earlier age, she (most likely) had no idea about just how important Ethel had previously been to the culture, especially her own. She was, however, aware that Ethel Waters was a great lady and an historic singer and actress. Ethel, who had for the most part ignored the new wave of the rock and roll and Motown, just had to be keenly aware of Diana's success, with contemporary radio blasting away with best-selling recordings clearly identified with Diana Ross. In any case, Ethel was prepared to sing a duet with (host) Ross and proceed with a (dated) rendition of: (a) "Supper Time," the ditty that Irving Berlin had produced for her in 1933 about a lynching. While all this proved to be good drama, in true retrospective; (b) the duet of "Bread and Gravy," another old ditty associated with Waters between Dinah and Ethel is most telling and interesting. While this author has no idea about any rehearsals, the live show found the professional Waters seemingly at ease, catching up on lyrics in a fine clear vocal. For the younger Diana, already a vet singer, her part of the exchange of lyrics betrays her well-done performance deeply in awe of the old diva (Waters). Watch, listen, and decide.

The ultimate diva of the 1920s and 1930s? Ethel achieved a record of greater success than any of her (black) contemporaries from the 1920s through to the 1940s. Moreover, she also competed with (white) contemporaries, indeed introducing many recorded standards on record, Broadway and films, despite the usual racial segregation.

Elisabeth Welch

- This largely unknown Afro-American had introduced the "Charleston" dance craze of the 1920s, in the off Broadway entity *Running Wild* (1923)? Later, using the music from the more lavish production *Blackbirds of 1928*, she introduced the ditties penned by Dorothy Fields and Jimmy McHugh "Diga Diga Do" and "Doing the New Low-Down" as recorded definitive recordings. The vocal style of Elisabeth Welch may be considered very highbrow, very polished. Her early vocal influences had more to do with all-white Broadway vaudeville following the lead of another Afro-American, Florence Mills. Moreover, Welch was still very much influenced by jazz and as versatile as any of her black contemporaries, who included the likes of Ethel Waters, Adelaide Hall, Josephine Baker, Edith Wilson, and Eva Taylor. She would indeed become most influenced by "white time" and, like Hall and Baker, become most celebrated in Europe, and, for the most part, live abroad and become most attached to the music of the traditional (European) music hall, BBC radio, and theater. Considering Elisabeth's British influences, the recordings left behind in her rich legacy, amazingly competing with the (white) world and winning.

Picks include:

1. "Diga Diga Do," Brunswick 4014. Backed by Irving Mills and His Hotsy-Totsy Gang (sometimes confused with the Duke Ellington Orchestra), Elisabeth's high vocal seemingly works well with fast-paced and terrific jazz background. Noting the slang involved, this down and dirty lyric is somehow sophisticated, noting the fine elocution found in Elisabeth's vocal.

2. "Doing the New Low-Down," Brunswick 4014. This flip side of "Diga Diga Do," another ditty penned by Fields and McHugh, from the Broadway review of *Blackbirds of 1928* is also jazzy. More so, this excuse for a dance tune works well as Welch's vocal with the "Irving Mills and His Hotsy-Totsy Gang" produce another early electric classic.
3. "Solomon," Victor 35226. The (very) highbrow Cole Porter-penned this ditty for the London stage production *Nymph Errant* (1933) that starred British Gertrude Lawrence and Elisabeth herself. Just how Elisabeth had been able to "star" in this all-white production is unclear, noting a step-up from American segregated productions. (Indeed, the same year in America, Ethel Waters had finally broken the Broadway color line in a major production *As Thousands Cheer*.) In any case, this ditty is not for everyone but still managed to make it as a pick, as its careful vocal still manages to infuse a bit of "Harlem," however highbrow. Nevertheless, the loudness of Welch's stage-struck voice, in the same way as Ethel Merman's although not the same voice as Merman's, demands patience for any listener. While not a shouter, this tale of King Solomon, however contrived, is perhaps a cruel pun. Did King Solomon really have a thousand wives? Did they all cheat? Was Solomon enough of a serial killer as to cut them up like poultry? Is this sick tale worth listening?
4-9. "Soft Light and Sweet Music Melody," HMV B-8144. This medley of hits found its mark with British audiences as part of BBC radio program. In this group of HMV (His Masters Voice) recordings, Elisabeth's accent is indeed found English. a. "Soft Lights and Sweet Music" (Irving Berlin). b. "Just Like a Melody from Out of the Sky" (Walter Donaldson). c. "When Day Is Done". Classy singing that had been penned by (Robert Katscher and B.G. De Silva) for the earlier 1926 British production "Madonna". d. "Darktown Strutter's Ball" (Shelton Brooks). e. "So Shy" (Allen Boretz and Walter G. Samuels). f. "I'll Never Be the Same (Little Buttercup)," Matty Malneck, Frank Signorelli, and Gus Kahn penned this ditty's same name for two titles. Elisabeth is joined by announcer Austen Croon Johnson (1934).
10. "I Still Suits Me," Victor 25375. This duet with Paul Robeson penned by O. Hammerstein II and J. Kern for the 1936 *Show Boat* film is perhaps the very best version of this very much recorded ditty. Elisabeth's own high vocal is perfect and indeed subdues Robeson's vocal tendencies to overblow it. While it's all perhaps a bit of interesting slang, in stereotypical fashion, it is also obvious that both Elisabeth and Paul are bright and articulate and adapt themselves well into lyrics.
11. "When Lights Are Low," Brunswick 7853. A visit to England paired bandleader Benny Carter with Elisabeth. Elisabeth's (less British) crooning style is evident and very much appreciated, perhaps influenced by Benny and penned by Carter and Williams.
12. "I Gotta Go," Vocalion S-16. This ditty penned by Benny Carter and Spencer Williams is crooned out well, and Benny's fine rhythm section that brings out the best within Elisabeth—even when overblown.
13. "Poor Butterfly," Vocalion 526. This high-voiced vocal is meshed well with Carter's low-key jazz, as penned by John Golden and Raymond Hubbell.
14. "That's How the First Song Was Born," Vocalion 526. This Alexander Hill penned ditty is all very straight laced, but it's (again) Benny Carter's backing that lifts Elisabeth.
15. "Harlem in My Heart," HMV B-8608. Elisabeth starred with Paul Robson in the British film *Big Fella* in 1937. This ditty penned by James Dyrenforth and Eric Ansel

for the film, is pleasant enough, with the curious British influence perhaps finding contemporary Adelaide Hall sounding much the same?

Visual Image

The beautiful images of Elisabeth Welch are scattered in film and in fact in many British productions. Perhaps the most interesting is her costarring role with Paul Robeson in the 1936 entity *Song of Freedom*. While limited in vocals in the film, her sharing of:

16. "Sleepy River" is done well. Indeed, as demonstrated in a previous recording, her bright vocal lifts Robeson's dreadful and deep baritone.
17 "Harlem in My Heart." Elizabeth singing this ditty in the film *Big Fella.*

Josh White

- This would-be blues singer somehow found his way through the blues folk, protest, pop, and religious. While his vocals are indeed effective, his recordings may be considered long journey in search of an idiom. Unlike other recording artists, black or white, Josh somehow never found one to categorize him—or at least define himself. His vocals are soft (an opposite to most blues entities), and his guitar playing, not containing the chords heard in entities after an accident in 1936, still become an intimate and well-told story to his audience. As "Pinewood Tom," Josh chooses to emulate such established entities as Blind Lemon Jefferson, Charlie Patton, and Big Bill Broonzy. As "The Singing Christian," Josh divides his Afro-American following as a singer of spirituals. The opposite appeals of fundamentalist Christian music, inspiring hope, and the "devil's music," in the despair of the blues, seemingly merge in the music presented on his fine recordings of the early 1930s. His later recordings as "Josh White," the non-delta blues singer and songwriter from South Carolina, drift to an intimate and personal version of pop as well as a real alternative.

Picks include:

1. "I Got a Home in That Rock," Banner 22419. As "The Singing Christian," Josh at least explains himself.
2. "Lazy Black Snake Blues," Banner 32527. This (already) familiar theme by Victoria Spivey on Okeh 8338 and Blind Lemon Jefferson as "Black Snake Moan" on Paramount-12407 is not wasted by Josh's matter-of-fact vocal.
3. "Howling Wolf Blues," Banner 32427. This theme is almost scary as well as hairy. As adapted from fellow bluesman "Funny Paper" Smith, on Vocalion 1558, this already familiar "creature" ain't all that bad.
4. "Greenville Sheik," ARC 6-05-63. The sexual prowess of this young man from Greenville, South Carolina, is very much exploited and found on this entity.
5. "Low Cotton," Banner 32858. This 1933 recording has a lot to do about the price of cotton in the Depression era, something that Josh felt deeply about picking "low cotton" meant a hand-and-knees effort, a task that straddled many a rural farmer, black and white, of that very hungry era.

6. "Welfare Blues," Banner 33024. The distribution of welfare, applied to the rural farmer as well as the urban dweller. Josh again hits home again at this tale of a bitter rural entity finding no luck at all in the big city, New York.
7. "Milk Cow Blues," Banner 33361.
8. "Bed Springs Blues," Perfect 0320. Josh clearly identifies himself as "Pinewood Tom," as this otherwise common but awesome blues theme is heard and appreciated. (Another contemporary "Bed Springs Blues" on Vocalion 2923, by George Noble also pleases the ears of its listeners. A somewhat earlier entity by Blind Lemon Jefferson on Paramount 12872 also entertains the ears of its listeners.)
9. "Black Man," Banner 33489. With a funky piano backing, Josh's slick (and soft) vocal provides the listener of this ditty a familiar (stereotyped?) tale of real black men.

- Note: Josh found himself shoved into the idiom of a blues entity by the end of the 1930s. While there was indeed no shame to this, Josh's soft, effective vocal tones made him more of a crooner (like contemporary blues entity Lonnie Johnson), with less urban trimmings. By 1939, while the Depression was still going on (especially for the black community), the recording industry had recovered enough for smaller, independent recording companies to emerge. (The Great Depression had wiped out most in the early 1930s.) It also would provide a better outlet for (recorded) creativity and change.
- While this would far exceed anything thought possible in the latter 1940s (after World War II), the most compelling and controversial entity was in fact recorded (for a small label) in 1939. Indeed, the original Billie Holiday version of "Strange Fruit," based upon a poem by Lewis Allen (a white personage), had been about a black man hanging on a tree in Georgia, a shameful and fairly common occurrence in 1939. Like many, the release of "Strange Fruit" also deeply affected Josh, as a later version by Josh himself will be noted. It was also to become part of a contemporary and urban folk movement, largely abandoned by Holiday, which consisted of such diverse contemporaries as the Almanac Singers, Woody Guthrie, Burl Ives, Leadbelly, and Josh White himself.

10. "Strange Fruit," Decca 23654. As a "vocal with guitar," this cool vocal, less shocking than the previous Billie Holiday version on Commodore 547, is still deeply felt. His vocal indignation is indeed felt but like most post-1939 recordings of his, the blues, as defined in numerous previous recordings, just where did they go? While Billie Holiday could safely escape into jazz or pop, Josh just can't. The blues are indeed bleached here, as Josh's vocal may be considered an urban sounding folk entity.
11. "Sometime," Decca 23654. As the original flip side of "Strange Fruit," this ditty differs with harmonica, bass, and drums, with the likes of Sonny Terry and Brownie McGhee.

Note: The following Ash label recordings were issued as a 78 rpm album called "Songs by Josh White," A 348. As a concept entity, this whole idea, featured Josh's soulful vocal of mostly (then) contemporary recordings. This collection very much succeeds, as Josh's renditions provide a better product or at least an alternative version for the ears of its listeners.

12. "I Got a Head Like a Rock," Ash 348-1A. The "singing Christian" is found again!
13. "Fare Thee Well," Ash 348-1B.

14. "Outskirts of Town," Ash 348-2A. This faster paced entity is most like his previous blues efforts.

As a matter of fact, the influence of Big Bill Broonzy's "I'm Gonna Move to the Outskirts of Town," on Columbia 30010, is more than obvious. Toward the end of this rendition, however, Josh finds a way to redeem himself.

15. "One Meat Ball," Ash 348-2B. Just how can a somewhat old, stupid novelty penned by Hy Zaret and Lou Singer, as noted in a popular vocal by the Andrews Sisters, on Decca 18636, become serious? While Josh just might be putting us on, this vocal is more than different.
16. "When I Lay Down and Die," Ash 348-3A.
17. "The House I Live In," Ash 348-3B. As a Frank Sinatra entity and as a recording on Columbia 36886 as a film (short), this material penned by Earl Robinson was (surprisingly) deep. A focus on racial and religious tolerance, (more) clearly seen and heard in the film, may be considered a major breakthrough in the social fiber of America (1945). This Josh White recording may also be considered a milestone as Josh turns this entity into something new as well as defining this ditty as an even more of a plea for racial equality.

Margaret Whiting

- As the daughter of a famous writer of popular music (Richard Whiting), whose many song ditties are to be found in this book, Margaret never needed to become a pop vocalist. The fact that she became one, and a very good one, is clearly found in the picks below:

1. "That Old Black Magic," Capital 126. While Capital's sensational and rhythmic vocalist Ella Mae Morse was not deemed available for this ditty penned by Johnny Mercer and Harold Arlen, the bright, clear, and sparkling vocal prowess of Margaret Whiting was. While not the type of vocalist who Ella Mae was, an adapting rhythmic backing by Freddie Slack somewhat works. A later version, well into the rock era (1958), found a fine Louis Prima and Keely Smith version, on Capital 4063, more novel.
2. "My Ideal," Capital 134. Penned by Newell Chase, Leo Robin, and Richard Whiting, Margaret's own father, this ditty had been a highbrow number for a Maurice Chevalier film *Playboy of Paris* (1930). Like many film entities that could at least carry a tune, Chevalier's recording, on Victor 22542, may be considered personable but certainly less than the film version. As a 1943 rendering, Margaret's vocal shines, although a contemporary Maxine Sullivan version, on Decca 18555, just may be tops. Listen and decide!
3. "Moonlight in Vermont," Capital 182. What defines mellow? Perhaps it's this fine Billy Butterfield release, in which his lush and moody arrangement sets up a huge gap for a fine vocal. More so, Margaret's approach is indeed on the mark, as her voice, as bright as ever, flows free and soft. The song itself is full of contradiction and without lyrical rhyme. While looking a bit weird, as in a song folio, the depth of this ditty is the success of Margaret's voice and Butterfield's mellow string section. More so, a (later) Frank Sinatra recording on Capital LP W-920 of this classic penned by Karl Suessdorf and John Blackburn also reeks of excellence, somewhat of an emulation of

Margaret's original. Indeed, Frank succeeds! (As a further note, Margaret rerecorded this ditty as a solo artist in 1954 on Capital 2681. While it is a good outing, the original rules.)

4. "There Goes That Song Again," Capital 182. This original flip side of "Moonlight in Vermont," penned by Sammy Cahn and Jule Styne, is another winner.
5. "It Might as Well Be Spring," Capital 214. Backed by Paul Weston, the mellow-sounding Margaret indeed rivaled contemporary Dick Haymes (original) version on Decca 18706. It is more interesting to compare a small label release by John Kirby, with a more defining and fresh vocal style by Sarah Vaughan on Crown 108.
5. "All Through the Day," Capital 240. The stuffy Oscar Hammerstein II and Jerome Kern's penned ditty found Margaret ready to make it sound more interesting, despite it's mushy lyrics.
6. "Younger Than Springtime," Capital 57-598. Just what is classic pop? For most latter-day followers, it's the classic Capital recordings of Frank Sinatra and Nat King Cole a decade later. While this is all nonsense, as this book attempts to prove and expose, this ditty penned by Rodgers and Hammerstein, like most Margaret Whiting renderings of the 1940s, is a real beginning, or start of that style, that myth. Backed by the mellow Frank De Vol, Margaret's dry and bright vocal softly eats up lyrics, and this overly sentimental ditty is defined.
7. "Come Rain or Shine," Capital 247. As introduced by Ruby Hill and Harold Nicholas (of the Nicholas Brothers, the famous Afro-American dancer act) in the Broadway entity *St. Louis Woman,* this classic ditty was a highlight. Penned by Johnny Mercer and Harold Arlen, this ditty had also been a fine recording by Hill and Nicholas and released on Capital 10055, as part of a 78 rpm soundtrack. A contemporary duetting Dick Haymes and Helen Forrest rendering on Decca 23548 also became better known and more so a best seller. Margaret's solo version is a bit more personable and intimate. While her passion for singing is held ably in check, by Paul Weston's backing, her soft and classy vocal tone, indeed a trademark, perhaps more than defines this ditty.
8. "Old Devil Moon," Capital 360. As a Broadway entity, this ditty penned by Yip Harburg and Burton Lane is passable. Luckily, Margaret recorded it and made it memorable.
9. "You Do," Capital 438.
10. "Pass That Peace Pip," Capital 15010. From the 1947 film "Good News"-the only thing good about it?)
11. "Little Girl Blue," Capital 20116. As a Broadway entity, and as penned by Richard Rodgers and Lorenz Hart, this classy ditty was seemingly something good for Margaret.
12. "A Tree in the Meadow," Capital 15122. Another classic rendering penned by Billy Reid gives Margaret yet another (signature) tune. Backed by a lush Frank De Vol arrangement, Margaret's patience is fitting and defining.
13. "I'm Sorry But I'm Glad," Capital 15122. This original flip side of "A Tree in the Meadow," penned by Buddy Pepper and Inez James, while not as classic, is soft and well sung.
14. "Baby, It's Cold Outside," Capital 567. This duet with Johnny Mercer ain't bad.
15. "Slippin' Around," Capital 40224. The combination of this "country and western" ditty with Jimmy Wakely, a fine rival to Ernest Tubb, found this cheater in best seller lists. Indeed less crude than (writer) Floyd Tillman's original, on Columbia 20581, or Ernest Tubb's version, on Decca 46173, this successful (1949) marketing ploy, in true

retrospective, is a bit clumsy. More so, as an attempt to become a hick rather than a hip rhythmic vocalist, Margaret's principal asset, her bright voice, is somewhat lost with Wakely. Somehow, it worked!

16. "I'll Never Slip Around Again," Capital 40246. The best-selling (1949) success of "Slippin' Around" with Wakely found that this ditty also produced recognition! From producing sophisticated lounge songs and honky tonk bar titles for juke boxes-that's the (versatile) Margaret!
17. "My Foolish Heart," Capital 934.
18. "I've Never Been in Love Before," Capital 1213. Another worthy and classic vocal is achieved, as this ditty penned by Frank Loesser was never to be sung as softly and poignantly.
19. "My Heart Stood Still," Capital 21015. This ditty penned by Rodgers and Hart is a classic rendering. Or did Hildegarde previously defines it?
20. "My Funny Valentine," Capital 21017. The bright and optimistic vocal of Margaret just has to cheer up this gloomy classic by Rodgers and Hart.

Lee Wiley

- The lesser known recordings of Lee Wiley were, in reality, concerned with a shot at perfection and vocal style of the whole pre-rock era. Lee Wiley had been a huge fan of Ethel Waters records, and, more so, had some of the same vocal elocution and dryness as the famous Waters voice. Lee's often bittersweet voice is strong, like that of Waters, yet with a distinct coolness. She was also able to sound jazzy on popular song ditties and a bit less husky than contemporary Connie Boswell. Lee was also able to become rhythmic and successfully more so than Mildred Bailey. Lee's faster-paced songs somehow sounded more intimate, with perhaps a fatal disregard to commercial success. In all, Lee Wiley was a perfectionist, and her love of singing, in true retrospective, perhaps makes most all her creative attempts at singing, especially noting the very first pop songbook 78RPM album concept of 1939, a special and pleasing listening experience.

From what may be known, the young, mid-teenager from Oklahoma (part American Indian) somehow got herself singing jobs in the nightlife atmosphere of New York City. While working hard into the Depression years of 1930 and 1931, she eventually got herself known and heard by the likes of many, including the likes of bandleader—Leo Reisman. She also got herself involved in radio, a major step into recognition.

➢ The following are Lee Wiley picks:

1. "Take It From Me," Victor 22757. This Leo Reisman release is a bit rhythmic, as Lee coolly finds in this simple ditty penned by Thomas Waller and Stanley Adams a bit more. Moreover, as its listeners are treated to a mellow instrumental, about halfway, a dry and deep Wiley vocal much excites the ears. Just listen!
2. "Time on My Hands," Victor 22839. This ditty penned by Harold Adamson, Mack Gordon, and Vincent Youmans had been made into a popular crooning entity by contemporary Russ Columbo. While Russ is good, perhaps the Wiley dryness of voice is a bit more effective.

3. "Got the South in My Soul," Victor 24048. Lee Wiley is partly credited with original lyrics, with the likes of Ned Washington and Victor Young. Moreover, this moving and powerful ditty is serious enough, as the "south" and "soul" finding a homesick Southerner, however contrived, sounding real enough. Lee's smoothness of voice is also evident, with a coolness that perhaps defined hip-ness, at least for 1932. More so, a creative touch remains on this third release. (This much-imitated title also found its way to Harlem, with a fine Harlan Lattimore crooning version, with a more than real claim upon this ditty as well as the south and soul.)
4. "You're an Old Smoothie," Brunswick 6484. As a tad rhythmic, this novelty penned by B.G. De Sylvia Richard Whiting and Nacio Herb Brown finds Lee in an able duet with Victor Young and band member Billy Hughes.
5. "A Hundred Years from Today," Brunswick 6775. While Glenn Grey and Orchestra provide a very mellow background, it's Lee's own commitment that perhaps challenges the contemporary (1934) Ethel Waters hit.
6. "Easy Come, Easy Go," Brunswick 6855. As a Johnny Green Orchestra release, Lee's coolness, perhaps an understatement of lyrics that would define her style, makes all of this ditty penned by Johnny Green and Edward Heyman very sustentative. A contemporary Ruth Etting version, sounding brighter yet dry in slow tempo, is interesting to compare. Ruth or Lee?
7. "Repeal the Blues," Brunswick 6855. This ditty penned by Johnny Green and James Dyrenforth is another Johnny Green release and perhaps a pun for the repeal of the Prohibition era, which occurred in the same year of this release (1934). As a spirited and rhythmic dance number, Lee's dry vocal somehow overcomes most of its own reserve, as Lee again demonstrates her unique vocal abilities.

- ➢ The following Decca releases finds Lee as a fully credited vocalist.

8. "Careless Love," Decca 132. This classic is perhaps blended into a bit of country. While slow and dated, Lee's emotion and edgy vocal is a fine, if different, update, as Lee claims a classic for her own.
9. "Motherless Child," Decca 132. The tradition (black) song of inspiration finds the creative Wiley attempting to be different. Perhaps as used as part of her radio experiences, this very cool vocal, with arrangements by (perhaps) Victor Young and Tommy Dorsey, definitely, is very different from any previous versions or future versions! Just listen and be totally entertained.
10. "Hands Across the Table," Decca 322. This slow material reeks of sentimentality, but Lee's stripped down vocal, penned by Jean Deletre and Mitchell Parish, somewhat succeeds.
11. "I'll Follow My Secret Love," Decca 322. Lee's attempt at a higher vocal is demonstrated well enough, as this semi-operatic rendering penned by the contemporary highbrow Englishman (Noel Coward) somehow holds listeners for a while, at least until nodding off to sleep.

Note: The following 2 ditties were originally released on a (rare) 12 inch 78.

12. "I've Got You Under My Skin," Decca 15034. This clever arrangement by Victor Young's backing (full-blown) concert orchestra finds Lee in a highbrow mode. Penned by Cole Porter, this vocal perhaps finds the able Lee toying with lyrics, yet stiffly, as found on Al Bowlly's vocal on the previous (1936) Roy Noble release. A competing

and contemporary Josephine Baker version was largely unknown in the States. (Light years later, Frank Sinatra, in a completely different arrangement, would redefine it.)

13. "What Is Love?" Decca 15034. This very highbrow entity penned by Victor Young, Leo Robin, and Ralph Rainger perhaps finds Lee showing off or showboating some of her high-strung vocal abilities. Moreover, despite a somewhat complicated arrangement that becomes cumbersome, Lee's showboating actually wins out.

Note: By the mid-1930s, Lee had made some progress as a popular vocalist, as a recording entity as well as a radio personality. Nevertheless, as well as illness, speculation has it that her independence led her to feud with this likes of many, including the (still) very influential bandleader, Paul Whiteman. More damaging was her stiffness with would-be radio sponsors, which would restrict her own commercial success in possible film and future national radio exposure.

➢ Nevertheless, Lee did win many friends, as her artful vocals were to be very much applauded and appreciated. After perhaps a dispute with Decca, she was signed up with an emerging small record label "Liberty Music Shop," which assured her of her own artistic control, with some of the finest (freelancing) musicians of the era (1939). As it all turned out, this change was to become the best decision of her career, as far as her eventual legacy indicates.

The following titles were part of a creative Liberty Music Shop project. While the classical music of Europe had for some time been marketed as songbooks, this idea of creating a songbook out of somewhat contemporary popular music composers was a brilliant marketing attempt to sell pop. More so was the concept of starting from scratch and grouping song ditties with a fresh studio orchestra or band, which in turn created its own moods and sounds. These early collections were made of some fine material by George and Ira Gershwin. Just who picked this material may be in question, but it is no question that each song ditty finds Lee and her musicians at their very best!

- This first Gershwin 78 rpm album release was backed by the Max Kaminsky Orchestra, which consisted of, at times, Max, Bud Freeman, Joe Buskin, Artie Shapiro, George Whetting, Pee Wee Russell, Eddie Condon, and "Maurice" on pipe organ, alias for Fats Waller. They were arranged by Brad Gowan.

14. "Sweet and Lowdown," LMS L-284. The excellent Max Kaminsky backing group blends in well with Lee's dry and crisp vocal. More so, Lee's sultry attitude is most evident as well as appreciated.
15. "But Not for Me," LMS L-284. This jazzy version of an otherwise gloomy ballad finds Lee defining it.
16. "How Long Has This Been Going On?" LMS L-281. This title has the Joe Buskin Orchestra, along with jazz great Eddie Condon on guitar. More so, the sparkling Lee Wiley vocal sparkles and much improves upon the earlier Libby Holman version.
17. "My One and Only," LMS L-281. This sexy and cool vocal perhaps mocks the lyrics. An earlier (1927) version was upbeat and jazz, and recorded by Jane Green on Victor 21145 is totally disregarded by Lee's approach. "My One and Only"? Come on! Not for this hot lady?

18. "I've Got a Crush on You." This mushy title is a bit hard to overcome as a (later) but well-sung Frank Sinatra rendering on Columbia 38151 attests. While it's possible that Frank, a young (1939) contemporary for Lee Wiley, had heard Lee's smoking and poignant version, it's more than too bad that he didn't attempt to emulate it.
19. "Someone to Watch Over Me," LMS L-282. While Broadway's Gertrude Lawrence highbrow rendition of 1927 was very good, on Victor 20331, it's Lee's cool and slickness while bending lyrics that truly define it. (A musician identified as "Maurice" on pipe organ just may be Fats Waller.)
20. "Sam and Delilah," LMS L-283. The battle of the sexes is cleverly put into prospective in lyrics. Moreover, this smoking Wiley vocal obviously makes it known just who the boss is! She is!
21. "'S Wonderful," LMS L-283. Any earlier versions, including a (1928) Scrappy Lambert vocal, as a Ipana Troubadours release, on Columbia 1213-D, had been jazzy enough. However, it's Lee's cool and successful showboating of her own gifted vocal style that (again) redefines this classic.

- The following titles were recorded for the small label "Gala." This time, sticking with the previous success of the songbook theme, the composed work of Rogers and Hart are met with Lee's creative edge.

22. "Baby's Awake Now," Gala 1. The sophisticated ditty penned by Rodgers and Hart could also be a bit crude, as this mocking tale about child rearing, with possible child abuse, is wildly and wickedly exploited by Lee's cool vocal. An interesting joke? Or is it a brilliant observation about a young woman's coming of age? Just listen!
23. "Here in My Arms," Gala 1. Lee's a little softer voiced here but no less the wild.
24. "I've Got Five Dollars," Gala 2. This Depression-era ditty had been perhaps best defined as a (1931) recording by bandleader Ben Pollack on Perfect 15431. Lee, moreover does it better, and perhaps her noting of "I've Got Five Dollars" and her subsequent lyric bending is more about the use of money for herself and her successful showboating than the Depression era. Moreover, Lee again redefines a classic.
25. "Glad to Be Unhappy," Gala 2. Lee again delivers with a title which perhaps defines her many listeners just how they feel after playing one of her recordings, especially this one. A later (1955) Frank Sinatra version, on LP, more so defined it.
26. "A Little Birdie Told Me So," Gala 3. Lee's cool style more than makes up for the utter stupidity of this title. Just listen!
27. "You Took Advantage of Me," Gala 3. Lee finds completely new ground, differing (completely) from the 1928 Paul Whiteman version, featuring a Bing Crosby vocal! Indeed, while Crosby did do it well enough, Lee's crafty vocal is more than inviting as if she really wants to be taken, again and again!
28. "As Though You Were There," Gala 4. Yes. This meaningful title luckily finds Wiley's coolness a major asset.
29. "Ship without a Sail," Gala 4. The previous Libby Holman version, on Brunswick 4700, while still an obvious vocal influence for Lee, had usually been more than a bit clumsy. Moreover, the controlled and controlling Wiley never had that problem! Moreover, this "Ship without a Sale" is finally defined as a well-crafted vocal.

- Note: The following are Cole Porter titles, released by the Liberty Music Shop label, as another in the series of songbooks.

30. "Looking At You," LMS L-294. A controlled high-pitched vocal (also very highbrow) results in a brilliant and moody entity. Perhaps this ditty should have been called "Listening to You, Lee."
31. "You Do Something to Me," LMS L-294. A previous (1930) Leo Reisman release, with a vocal by Frank Luther on Victor 2244 had been a bit stiff. It is perhaps well worth it to speculate if Lee would have recorded this Broadway entity with Reisman back then, as she was originally associated with him as a band singer, a better vocal would have been rendered. In any case, this (1940) arrangement with Paul Weston is set up very well, with the usual and the edgy Wiley vocal effectively pushing this Broadway entity into something more special, however highbrow.
32. "Easy to Love," LMS L-295. Perhaps an earlier crooning job by Al Bowlly on a previous 1936 Ray Noble release on Victor 25422 had been done well. More so was an easy and bright Maxine Sullivan rendering on Vocalion 3848. The cooler Wiley scores well in this updated, noting the opposite mood and tone, as compared with the cheer heard in the Sullivan version. While it is perhaps a toss-up between Maxine and Lee, perhaps all depends upon the mood of its listeners. Just listen and compare. (Put aside the stiffer Bowlly version.)
33. "Why Shouldn't I?" LMS 295. Why ask the question? Lee's poignant vocal is well worth it.
34. "Let's Fly Away," LMS L-296. This bit of escapism from Porter finds Lee coolly optimistic. Moreover, this ditty is serious enough. Fly away with Lee? Does she mean it? Along with some well-crafted vocal surprises, the effective Wiley scores!
35. "Find Me a Primitive Man," LMS L-296. The earlier (1929) Libby Holman release on Brunswick 4666 had been wickedly effective. Noting Libby's always deliberate sultry style, perhaps Lee found herself a challenge. As it turned out, the cool and sultry Wiley rendering is sultry and smoother, with a controlled vocal expression of novelty. Moreover, the lyrics of this ditty just could be a problem for the latter-century followers of "Woman's Lib," as both Libby and Lee were both fiercely independent artists, whose attempts at creativity are well noted and heard.
36. "Hot House Rose," LMS L-297. Perhaps the most explicit of all Cole Porter's lyrics perhaps find any easy substitute from "Hot House" to "Whore House." More so, Lee's cool and hot delivery smoothly sizzles with subtle innuendo and spark! Yes, this ditty is very risqué, with a bittersweet and moody Wiley vocal that is defining!
37. "Let's Do It," LMS L-297. Perhaps a few earlier and jazzy (1929) Bing Crosby attempts were brighter, especially a fine release on Okeh 41181 with the Dorsey Brothers. Another Lee (Lee Morse) featured colder vocal version than Bing. A sillier Rudy Vallee version was also popular, despite stereotypes. The always cooler Wiley tones it down, while remaining suggestive, with an equally impressive and different jazzy arrangement with Bunny Berigan, Joe Buskin, Sid Weiss, and George Wetting. Let's do it. I'm ready!

- Note: The following 2 sides were recorded for the small label, "Commodore," a 12-inch release.

38. "Down to Steamboat Tennessee," Commodore 1507. Penned by Jess Stacy, Willard Robinson, and Lee Wiley herself, this title, however contrived, works very well. As a truly compelling tale of a woman's chosen life of prostitution, the sensitive Wiley vocal is not novel and more of a reflection of what's real. Moreover, a sophisticated vocal, still full of the blues, is poignant and cool, indeed, proving that this (white) girl from Oklahoma was extremely versatile.

39. "Sugar," Commodore 1507. Lee again excels, again with blues, and succeeds very well indeed to update the 1926 acoustic Ethel Waters classic on Columbia 14146-D.

Note: Lee continued her (unconventional) recording career-not recording until she determined what was right for her, despite the record ban of mid-1942. The following Harold Arlen titles Moreover continue the songbook theme in 78 rpm album form. As recorded for another small label, "Schirmer," with subsequent reissues on other small labels, it is amazing that major labels, considering the creative results of the previous Wiley songbooks failed to sign her up. More so, Lee is again backed by some fine musicians for these ditties, noting the likes of the guitar rhythm of Eddie Condon, and with various members, including Billy Butterfield on trumpet, Dave Bowman on piano, Bob Haggart on bass, Ernie Caceres, and George Wetting as the "Eddie Condon Sextette." Moreover, other Condon shifts of personal occur.

40. "Down with Love," Schirmer 2008. While perhaps the title of this ditty, penned by Harold Arlen and E. Y. Harburg, is obviously moody and poignant in itself, it's also perfect for Lee to exploit. Surprisingly, this mid-tempo rendering is very rhythmic, with Lee coolly and effectively proving her jazzy smoothness and worthiness.
41. "Stormy Weather," Schirmer 2008. The influence of Ethel Waters on Brunswick 6564 is very much noted, along with Lee's added coolness.
42. "I've Got the World on a String," Schirmer 2009. Bing Crosby's version on Brunswick 6491 is recalled, although Lee (still) has were own agenda. More so, this fine update works!
43. "Between the Devil and the Deep Blue Sea," Schirmer 2009. The warm and jazzy group sound of the Boswell Sisters on Brunswick 6291 is matched, with Lee's (cold) and still jazzy approach.
44. "Fun to Be Fooled," Schirmer 2010. These lyrics credited to Ira Gershwin, E. Y. Harburg, and Harold Arlen find Lee's very smooth handling informative, as Lee also has a bit of fun showboating her fabulous voice.
45. "You Said It," Schirmer 2010. Harold Arlen and Jack Yellen had penned this ditty in 1931 for a Broadway entity of the same name. Lee's cool 1942 update is serious enough, as this obvious tale about being thrilled comes true! Being stupid or just thrilled? Just listen!
46. "Let's Fall in Love," Schirmer 2011. While the (cheerful) mood of Annette Hanshaw's (1931), version on Vocalion 2639 is in faster tempo as well as jazzy. Lee's cooler rendering is more of a smooth ballad as well is an interesting comparison.
47. "Moaning in the Morning," Schirmer 2011. The mature subject matter of this ditty could have been a pun by (writer) Harold Arlen? In any case, the creative vocal of Lee defines it! Moan about it Lee!

- The following singles were released from near the end of World War II and beyond.

48. "Wherever There's Love," Decca 23393. This 1944 effort penned by Eddie Condon and John De Vries is another attempt at a smooth and jazzy vocal style.
49. "It's Only a Paper Moon," Victor 20-1708. The old standard is given a fine (1945) Wiley lift, with a fine mid-tempo vocal.
50. "Body and Soul," Victor 2322. As recorded with Eric Siday, this smooth oldie had been done by many, especially noting the previous torch efforts of Helen Morgan, Libby Holman, Ruth Etting, and Annette Hanshaw as well as by Jack Fulton and

Louis Armstrong. Moreover, it's good to find a smooth Wiley version, who just might have performed this ditty as a struggling nightclub vocalist back in 1930.

51. "A Woman Alone with the Blues," Majestic 7258. This Willard Robinson-penned ditty, while contrived, is an effective bit of smooth and stylistic blues that results in another Wiley gem.
52. "Memories," Majestic 7259. As this ditty was originally released as "Memories of You," this ditty penned by Eubie Blake and Andy Razaf, originally defined by Ethel Waters in 1930 on Columbia 2288-D, is revived very well.

By the end of the 1940s, the obvious failure for Lee Wiley not rising into any films or lasting recording contracts remains a bit of a mystery. While not put down by racism, as all black artists were, perhaps her personal struggles with marriage, age, and the changing trends of rhythm and blues in the music business found Lee herself at odds with what to explore with her talents. Moreover, her vocal versatility, already proven, could have found an attempt at R&B, something special, had she had been interested.

As finally signed by the major (Columbia) label in (1950), her pop aspirations, still led by jazz, were realized. Moreover, the songbook concept, of popular music, so successful pioneered by Lee some eleven years earlier (1939), on 78 rpm, now perfectly fit into the new (Long Play) LP concept. The following three Columbia original 10-inch LP issues, noting initial release on 78 rpm and forty-five (extended play) album form must be noted.

53-60. "Night in Manhattan," Columbia CL-6169. This (1950) 10-inch LP is a fine and founding songbook entity on 33 and a third LP. Moreover, despite song fine efforts from such (1950) contemporaries such as Sarah Vaughan, June Christy, and Dinah Washington, Lee's classy and intimate style is proven to remain relevant. This "Night in Manhattan" theme concept attempts to showcase old standards in a nightclub setting. Picks include:

a. "Manhattan." This old classic penned by Rodgers and Hart is fabulous, while still noting a previous and warmer crooning job by Dick Todd on Bluebird 10374.

b. "A Ghost of a Chance." This Irving Berlin-penned ditty had been a poignant crooning job for Bing Crosby on Brunswick 6454.

c. "Oh, Look At Me Now." This version of the ditty penned by Joe Buskin and JohnDe Vries beats any others, including the likes of a Frank Sinatra vocal, an earlier Tommy Dorsey release on Victor 27274. Sorry Frank!
d. "Street of Dreams." Lee most likely found the previous poignant Bing Crosby version on Brunswick 6464 a good reference.
e. "A Woman's Intuition." Lee is (again) on track, as this ditty penned by Ned Washington and Victor Young perhaps had Lee herself keenly wanting to record it. More so, the resulting serious vocal rendering, perhaps perfectly exposes her own attitudes.
f. "Any Time, Any Day, Anywhere." Lee's own involvement in this ditty finds the likes of Ned Washington, Victor Young, and Lee herself as credited writers. Moreover, the resulting song ditty is really an intimate statement, sung smoothly and emotionally.

The following two ditties from this LP are done well, although they had previously been recorded by Lee. In true retrospective, a few previously unrecorded entities would have been better for this LP concept.

g. "Sugar" (rerecording).
h. "I've Got a Crush on You" (re-recording).

➢ The following two songbooks for Vincent Youmans and Irving Berlin, while good, seemingly lack preparation and indicate a rushed job.

61-63. "Lee Wiley Sings Vincent Youmans," Columbia CL-6215. This songbook is only highlighted by the following:

a. "More Than You Know." As an old torch song, this ditty penned by Youmans, Billy Rose, and Edward Eliscu had been more than good for Helen Morgan and Ruth Etting.
b. "Sometimes I'm Happy" (credited to Youmans, Irving Caesar).
c. "Rise n' Shine" (credited to Youmans and B.G. De Sylvia). d. "Should I Be Sweet?" This ditty had originally been penned by Youmans for the 1932 Broadway entity 'Take A Chance". Luckily, Lee took a chance with it and more so (finally) defined the ditty as here own. e. "Keepin' Myself for You" Another (Youmans and Sidney Clare) penned title fitting in well with Lee's sultry style.

64-65. "Lee Wiley Sings Irving Berlin," Columbia CL-6216.

a. "Soft Light and Sweet Music."
b. "Heat Wave." (The Ethel Waters original is updated well.)

66. "When A Lady Meets A Gentleman Down South:, Coral 61039. While Helen Ward's previous version had defined this ditty, Lee's well done vocal does put claims upon it.

The rest of the 1950s found Lee Wiley, like most of her contemporaries, pretty much displaced by rock and roll. Moreover, while the likes of Frank Sinatra and Ella Fitzgerald prospered, most others, did not. While the releases of two Victor LPs in 12-inch form appeared as "West of the Moon" on LPM 1408 and the stereo "A Touch of the Blues" on LSP or LPM 1566, many song ditties were rerecordings. More so, the RCA product (covers) found Lee a bit ragged, most unlike her earlier success at image at Columbia. Nevertheless, the following ditties should be noted as well as heard:

67-69. From the LP *A Touch of the Blues*, with backing by Billy Butterfield and Orchestra:

a. "I Don't Want To Walk Without You."
b. "Maybe You'll Be There." Penned by Sammy Gallop and Rube Bloom, this question of intimately in the cool by (now-dated) Wiley style works well enough in the 1950s,
c. "My Melancholy Baby."

- Radio and Unreleased

"Lee Wiley—On the Air," Totem 1021. The Lee Wiley product led through some flaky LP covers that compromise Lee's (early) sultry image as heard on her recordings. This LP fortunately rescues her image, with contemporary picks and (radio) performances matched up perfectly. Picks are:

70. "You Came to My Rescue," (1936) Freddie Rich Orchestra.
71. "Three Little Words," (1936) Freddie Rich Orchestra.
72. "You Turned the Tables on Me," (1936) Freddie Rich Orchestra.
73. "Here's Love in Your Eyes," (1936) Freddie Rich Orchestra.
74. "The South in My Soul," (1932) guest for Rudy Vallee/Fleichman Program.
75. "I'm Coming Virginia
76. "A Thousand Good Nights," (1934) guest for Paul Whiteman. (Penned by Walter Donaldson).
77-78. "Motherless Child / Swing Low, Sweet Chariot," (1934) guest for Rudy Vallee/ Fleichman Program.
79. "If I Love Again," (1934) guest for Paul Whiteman.
80. "The Little Things You Used to Do." Was Lee influenced by Helen Morgan? This rendition of the Morgan original on Brunswick 7424 indeed seems to indicate just that! Just listen! (1935)
81-82. "I'm Coming Virginia / Robins and Roses." (1936)
83. "When I'm with You," (1936).

Lee Wiley Early Recordings, Philomel 1000. This LP, featuring somewhat less of a cover than *Lee Wiley on the Air* also breaks the rules, for the principal concept of this book. While most radio shows are basically not covered, the following recorded outtakes had never been commercial entities. While not generally bothered with, these performances are just too good to ignore! The following feature Lee Wiley, as backed by the Dorsey Brothers (1933).

84. "You've Got Me Crying Again."
85. "I Gotta Right to Sing the Blues."
86. "Let's Call It a Day."(Penned by Lew Brown and Ray Henderson)

- More about Lee Wiley in the radio and LP sections of this book.

Hank Williams

This recording artist is far less forgotten than most others featured within this book. Moreover, his influence upon the future was great, noting that he is also dead center on the dividing line of this book, as he recorded between 1946 through 1952. As matter of fact, even considering those ears not inclined to hear that of the "country-western," his namesake and latter-century son (Hank Williams Jr.) was to be a known entity introducing football games!

More so, the short career of this rural and very poor country boy from Alabama had found many of his own musical influences as on the previous recordings of Emmett Miller, Jimmie Rodgers, Jimmie Davis, and Gene Autry. Hank's music may be described as blues, but his country twang may just be described as bleached blues. His easy attack on lyrics may be even more simple than the many previous honky-tonk bar songs, an environment he was to grow up in as well as to sing for. Most titles of Hank Williams are self-penned ditties and retain elements of poetry, with stark realisms. They are also personal statements, not always meant to be novel, about the hard and rural life in the 1940s southland. Hanks own limitations as a vocalist are considerable. Like Louis Armstrong, his vocals are meant to be personable and real. More so, he could be crude as well as soft-sounding. His rural appeal, even more so than his immediate predecessors, including Ernest Tubb, Red Foley, or Roy Acuff, somehow expanded far from (his) honky-tonk origins and the era of the 1940s. Seemingly, his own personality became his own words. Indeed, the words of Hank remain with us as well as his simple vocal style that stillretains an international appeal.

Picks include:

1. "Honky Tonkin'," Sterling 208. This vocal's a bit different from the later release on MGM 10171. Even so, this tale of barhopping remains a still interesting comparison!
2. "Fly Trouble," MGM 10073. Yes. For males especially, this can become an issue! While this very unusual song ditty penned by Honey Wilds, Bunny Biggs, and Fred Rose is not for everyone, it is the kind of song title that is hard to forget. Call it crude humor?
3. "Rootie Tootie," MGM 10124. As "Hank Williams with his drifting Cowboys" find themselves stuck in the middle of flashing fiddling and electric guitars (the norm for Hank), it's the simple up-tempo vocal that's delivered that makes this very un-hip title, penned by Fred Rose, work. Score this one for the country boys and hicks!
4. "My Sweet Love Ain't Around," MGM 10124. This B side of the above features Hank telling a story of rain pouring down and sweet love not being around. Maybe he will take a train to escape from it all, but that's Hank!
5. "Honky Tonkin'," MGM 10171. Hank's hitting all the bars, and he's telling his girl; this self-penned, up-tempo crowd-pleaser remains a winner. (Note: This ditty had also found a perhaps finer rhythmic rendering by Rose Maddox, as released by "The Maddox Brothers and Rose," on Four Star 1238). Moreover, Rose herself was a C&W contemporary of Hank Williams and may be considered a cusp entity for the reasons of this book. More so, Rose's impact, like Hanks's was huge, although Rose may also claim more of the later decade of the 1950s.
6. "I Saw the Light," MGM 10271. Perhaps he did see the light?
7. "Six More Miles," 10271. This ditty about a spooky trip to a graveyard is well worth the trip.
8. "The Blues Come Around," MGM 10212. Those crude, rural-sounding blues indeed come around, as this tale about real life by a (white) bluesman is far from contrived. At sundown?
9. "Lovesick Blues," MGM 10352. This ditty penned by Irving Mills and Clifford Friend had been around since 1922, especially noting vaudeville-type contemporary acoustic recordings by Elsie Clark, Jack Shea, and Emmet Miller. While it's possible that Hank had heard these renderings, it is a better bet that Emmett's later and quirky (1928) electric recording on Okeh 41062 turned him on. Or it could have been the more recent (1939) Rex Griffin recording on Decca 5570 that had gotten his attention. In any case, Hank's own (1948) vocal is full of plain-talking fire, purposely crooned out in mid-tempo as crudely as he could be! Somehow, all the vocal imperfections come together in fine harmony! Is this *the* perfect bar song? Or perhaps Hank's version struck the hour and the public at large?

(Note: Rex Griffin had also recorded "Everybody's Trying To Be My Baby", whch was to be subsequently re-done by in the 'rock' era by Carl Perkins in the 1950s and the Beatles in the 1960s.).

10. "Lost Highway," MGM 10506. Hank's lost in the middle of the dark. While it's perhaps poor pun that its author (Leon Payne) was blind, Hank's performance of this perhaps brilliant entity recognizes the utter reality travel on a very rural road. Or perhaps, just how lost a soul might be!
11. "Mind Your Own Business," MGM 10461. Perhaps this tale originated when a newspaper reporter asked Hank too many questions.
12. "I'm So Lonesome I Could Cry," MGM 10660. This slow and moving ballad really does make a man want to cry! Moreover, its own death wish, found in the lyric, is compelling and poignant. Tears?
13. "My Bucket's Got a Hole in It," MGM 10660. While the famous (Afro-American) musician and composer (Clarence Williams) had put claims upon this ditty before Hank got to record it in 1949, a previous (1927) rendering by Tom Gates on Gennett 6184 as "The Bucket's Got a Hole in It" more so found that this bucket without beer also lacked Clarence Williams. A later (1938) version known as "Bucket's Got a Hole In" by bluesman Washboard Sam on Bluebird B-7906 perhaps owes Clarence Williams only for his (1933) copyright of this old, rural folk ditty of Americana. While it's possible that Hank could have been given this ditty to record, he may have been familiar with this ditty from previous recordings or had heard it while growing up in Alabama. In any case, this rural pun by Hank remains a good enough explanation as to "why" things no longer work out! It's more so, in true retrospective, a hell of a honky-tonk entity!
14. "Long Gone Lonesome Blues," MGM 10645. (Later in (1964), the likes of son Hank Williams Jr. (light years away from TV's 'Monday Night Football") would record his father's song ditty-a fine tribute to his legacy!
15. "Why Don't You Love Me?" MGM 10696. Hank's simple plea is sincere. Even the string section (fiddles) is not sappy—just snappy?
16. "A House Without Love," MGM 10696. This ditty, like most of Hank's efforts, is a true reflection on life and its limitations. Unlike most others, however, this self-penned entity is far from novel—it's very serious.
17. "Too Many Parties For Too Many Pals," MGM 10718. Like "Lovesick Blues," this ditty had been known in the Prohibition times, before the legality of honky tonks. As a stiff (1925) rendering recorded by Irving Kaufman on Banner 6342, this kind of serious song ditty penned by Billy Rose, Mort Dixon, and Ray Henderson did consider the consequences of having a bit too much fun.

While it's not too much of a stretch that Hank had likely heard of the popular (1920s) recordings of "Lovesick Blues" by Emmet Miller, it's less likely that Hank had heard of Kaufman's recording nor of the later (1948) contemporary version on the small "Cowboy" label on Cowboy 1201, as a "Bill Haley and the Four Aces of Rhythm" record, featuring a duet with (then) hardly known. Barney Bernard and Bill Haley? In any case, Hank's (1950) recording indicates a choice to render a ditty about a person just like him and perhaps the idea to accept the parties and (new) hang-on friends.

18. "Moaning the Blues," MGM 10832. Moan 'em, Hank!
19. "No No Joe," MGM 10806. As an issued "Luke the Drifter" entity, this Fred Rose-penned ditty perhaps dates Hank Williams as a cold war advocate. More so,

this stupid commentary about the dictator of the (former) U.S.S.R. communist state, Joseph Stalin, is at least interesting stuff as well as an example of political commentary and the "red scare." Moreover, in true retrospective, Hank was right! This guy Joe really was, in true retrospective, a real bad guy!

20. "Cold Cold Heart," MGM 10904. This ditty deserves some speculation. Did Hank use these words on an ex-wife? This poignant tale is indeed sad and more so hits those with (warm) hearts. This ditty found its way into a contemporary (1951) release by mainstream pop artist Tony Bennett on Columbia 39449. While the Bennett version is good, an oddly contemporary version by Dinah Washington, on Mercury 5728, is by far better! Is it better than Hank's original?
21. "Men with Broken Hearts," MGM 10932. What a poem! Who says women were the only sex to even have a heart! Men? Grown up men? Listen and believe to this fine "Luke the Drifter" issued entity.
22. "I Can't Help It," MGM 10961. The sincerity of this ditty cannot be denied. Am I still in love with you?
23. "Howling At the Moon," MGM 10961. Hank's done wrong, and now he's in the (backyard?) doghouse. Hank's humor is always infectious, and this very rural entity remains a true pun!
24. "Hey, Good Lookin'," MGM 11000. This fast-paced ditty is full of country corn and, of course, Hank. Like this slick county entity finds rural slang a bit fun, it remains a good pickup line. A contemporary Dinah Washington version, on Mercury 8257, in comparison, sparkles, noting an easy exchange of Southern style slang that (vocally) works.
25. "Ramblin' Man," MGM 11120.
26. "Lonesome Whistle," MGM 11054. Claimed by Jimmie Davis and Hank himself, Hank even imitates a whistle, with some clever phrasing on the "w" in "whistle" as well as a bone-chilling performance.
27. "Half as Much," MGM 11202. While Hank's fiddlers back him up a little bit too much, this effective tale, penned by Curley Williams about a man baring his feelings about his other half, not caring as much as he does, is indeed a compelling rural tale.
28. "Honky Tonk Blues," MGM 11160. Hank's walk into a honky-tonk just cannot be explained—perhaps it's just another (bad) habit that won't leave.
29. "Jambalaya," MGM 11283. Hank adapted this ditty somewhere in Louisiana's bayou country. It is very upbeat, and his brilliant and joyous elocution of Cajun music, penned with contemporary Cajun pianist Moon Mulligan, based upon local folklore, prove that Hank's simple "country boy" image also may be a joyous occasion.
30. "Window Shopping," MGM 11283. Looking for a date in the rural southland? Or perhaps anywhere? Indeed, this very simple and effective ditty, penned by Marcel Joseph, however clumsy, works!
31. "Be Careful of the Stones You Throw," MGM 11309. Some Hank Williams releases were released by "Luke the Drifter." This "drifter" release may be entitled "Mind Your Own Business" (a pick noted above), but this time without any novel theme. As a matter of fact, this tale of gossip ends in a tragic accident and vindicates the dangers of category, this time about a young woman saving a child. In any case, this drifter entity is serious stuff—the stuff of life. Heavy stuff!
32. "Setting the Woods on Fire," MGM 11318. This ditty penned by Ed G. Nelson and Fred Rose is an up-tempo ditty that somehow works.
33. "You Win Again," MGM 11318. This very powerful message about shattered trust and confidence still remains effective, especially for (1952) honky tonk juke box fodder. Or even now?

34. "Take These Chains from My Heart," MGM 11416. Hank wants to leave, but he also wants to hear it spoken to him.
35. "I'll Never Get Out of This World Alive," MGM 11366. (Did Hank know he would die soon?)

> ➢ Hank Williams died, perhaps from excessive drinking, in the back of a motor vehicle, while on the way to a concert, in the early morning of New Year's Day 1953. The following are notable MGM recordings released after Hank's death.

36. "Your Cheatin' Heart," MGM 11416. This ditty, perhaps Hank's most famous ditty of all, was oddly released after his death. More so, this classic bit of Americana tells it like it was and (still) is. It also remains meaningful speculation on just how perceptive this "country boy" really was. Can one's heart tell on you? Just listen and weep. The contemporary (1953) pop market took note, especially noting the genuine grief and huge funeral provided for him. Among some very well-done versions are that of Frankie Laine on Columbia 39903 and Joni James on MGM 11426.
37. "Kaw-Ling," MGM 11416. Is this tale about a wooden Indian stupid? If so, just why is it so likable?
38. "Take These Chains From My Heart," MGM 11479. This classic penned by Fred Rose and Hy Heath remains another effective and simple gem.
39. "Weary Blues For Waitin'," MGM 11574. It's just possible that this self-penned ditty had been given to his friend Ray Price? More so, his (1951) release on Columbia 20883 ain't bad. This version, perhaps an unissued demo by Hank, is nevertheless defining.

- Enduring Legacy. The music of Hank Williams, as noted elsewhere within this book, had already found contemporary pop and R&B aspirations within the likes of many, including the likes diverse tastes of Jo Stafford and Dinah Washington. While Tony Bennett would soon follow, did the likes of younger listeners, such as Johnny Cash, Ray Charles, Jerry Lee Lewis, Carl Perkins, and Elvis Presley, among others, as it turned out, find a lot of Hank, in personality, within themselves? Or could it have been his very public funeral, in Montgomery, Alabama, in 1953? A major event? A cultural reflection upon a (still) segregated society? Indeed far more lasting than the fine (1953) tribute recording "The Death of Hank Williams" by songwriter and vocalist Jack Cardwell on King 1172! More so, the success of a dirt poor young Southerner upon the world?

Midge Williams

The focus of this book limits the nod and recognition toward the many talented vocalists not finding contemporary (pre-1950) audiences very much able to label and identify. Among many talented vocalists, the author of this book was fortunate to find the smooth and jazzy Midge Williams. It is interesting to speculate upon her appeal, as it did exist and had great influence upon the likes of thousands, especially noting those of pre-WWII China and Hirohito's Imperial Japan. She had found some success on radio, noting (1930s) West Coast radio and the Rudy Vallee program. While it still may be hard to find out what happened to her after World War II, her pleasant recordings attest to her tremendous talents.

1. "Organ Grinder's Swing" Columbia-3151-D. Midge's vocal 'swings' out well, as this simple dance floor entity, as penned by (Will Hudson, Mitchell Parish and Irving Mills), based upon "I Love Coffee, I Love Tea" succeeds! (A few years later, the Ink Spot's "Java Jive" would become a similar excuse 'swing')?

The following two ditties were penned for the contemporary 'Cotton Club Parade Of 1936) by (Benny Davis and J. Fred Coots). While Midge was not part of that production, the excuse to get up and dance is fully exploited!

2. "Copper Colored Gal". Melotone- 61217. (Better that Cab Calloway's contemporary release)
3. Alabama Barbacue". Banner-61217.
4. "How Could You?" Brunswick 7842. This smart-sounding recording penned by Harry Warren and Al Dubin finds Midge in a fine swing mood. Backed by always relevant Miff Mole's Mollers, Midge's sweet vocal sparkles, with a dry quality, much like the previous example of Ethel Waters and indeed much like the more contemporary Maxine Sullivan.
5. "Walking The Dog," Variety 519. Backed by her "jazz jesters," Midge and the guys score. In some aspects, this Shelton Brooks-penned ditty swings, with perhaps some debt (vocally) to many (1937) contemporary vocals by Billie Holiday.
6. "I'm Getting Sentimental Over You," Variety 566. Another sweet sound is found and appreciated as another jazzy entity, as penned by Ned Washington and George Bassman, which also swings.
7. "I Know Now," Variety 620. This attempt at swing in medium-tempo is indeed smooth and jazzy enough, as Midge (again) defines contemporary (1937) jazz in this ditty penned by Al Dubin and Harry Warren.
8. "That Old Feeling," Variety 620. Midge indeed puts her vocal claims on this fine ditty!
9. "I Was Born to Swing," Variety 639. Look out! Midge explodes with energy and rhythm, as this fine swing entity penned by Henry Nemo and Irving Mills tells it like it is!
10. "Oh, Miss. Hannah," Variety 639. This flip side is a contrived but effective excuse to swing.
11. "The One Rose That's Left in My Heart," Variety 670. The already old standard is successfully sung in mid-tempo and jazzed up.
12. "The Lady Is a Tramp," Vocalion 3865. This jazzy version of the classic by Rodgers and Hart smoothly (also) mentions contemporary (1937) film star Robert Taylor. Also claimed by many others, perhaps differing renderings by Adelaide Hall and (later) by Lena Horne provide very interesting comparisons.
13. "Fortune Tellin' Man," Vocalion 3865. This may be considered a fine effective blues rendering with an adapted and smooth vocal, as this contrived ditty, penned by Bill Davis and J. Fred Coots, is nevertheless a winner. (Later-Helen Humes would also give this ditty a whirl. Midge or Helen?
14. "Singin' the Blues Till My Daddy Comes Home," Vocalion 3900. Midge's sweet and smooth vocal is also very jazzy. (Is Marion Harris's previous update of the (1920) Aileen Stanley acoustic rendering better? Listen and compare!)
15. "Mama's Gone Goodbye," Vocalion 3900. This ditty was originally based upon a 1923 instrumental by Piron's New Orleans Orchestra, released on (Victor-19233) As penned by Armond Piron and Peter Bocage, this muic with vocal is radicially transformed into a contemporary 1938 excuse to swing!.

16. "The Greatest Mistake of My Life," Vocalion-3961. Penned by James Netson, this wordy and contrived excuse for swing in mid-tempo is hardly a mistake! For a completely differing version of this ditty, would a contemporary Jimmie Davis version become good vocal comparisons?
17. "I'm in a Happy Frame of Mind," Vocalion 04026. Midge again swings, along with with some fine scatting, as this fine ditty penned by Mitchell Parish and Rube Bloom is more so jazzy.
18. "Love Is Like Whiskey," Vocalion 04026. This contrived attempt at blues penned by Segure and Hughes finds the smooth-voiced Midge attempting to be a bit edgy. Moreover, this bright vocal succeeds.
19. "Don't Wake Up My Heart," Vocalion 4192. This smooth crooning job penned by Al Lewis, George W. Meyer, and Pete Wending showcases some fine and cheerful singing!

Edith Wilson

- Edith Wilson was (one) of many Afro-American vaudeville types of the early century who could have easily got the nod that (contemporary) Mamie Smith achieved as the first Afro-American woman to become an actual recording artist. Her art and craft sounds as pioneering and dated as many of those same contemporaries, including her sister-in-law Lena Wilson whose career included some acoustic gems in the likes of "Down South Blues," on Ajax 17014, through to the risqué electric recorded "Triflin' Blues" on Victor 19085. Indeed, the baggage of Edith Wilson is more fluid, as her vocals betray a more pop or popular vocal style.

The following are Edith Goodall Wilson picks:

1. "Vampin' Liza Jane," Columbia A-3479. This hard-to-hear acoustic ditty, penned by Perry Bradford, is nevertheless a contrived update for this Liza Jane lady! Moreover, it's effective enough.
2. "Old Time Blues," Columbia A-3506. As featured in the (1921) review, Edith rendered this Perry Bradford-penned ditty featured in the show. It is also interesting to compare Edith's somewhat sweeter vocal to the Mamie Smith original on Okeh 4296. It's also quite hard, as both voices, recorded acoustically, are similar in style and approach. Listen and compare!
3. "Birmingham Blues," Columbia A-3558. This ditty, penned by Charles Mc Cord and Artie Matthews, is a predictable tale of the Alabama city, with some good banjo licks to at least make it all sound palatable.
4. "Wicked Blues," Columbia A-3558. As the flip side of "Birmingham Blues," this Perry Bradford-penned ditty sounds much like its flip side, except its subject matter is a little more personal.
5. "Take It 'Cause It's All Yours," Columbia A-3634. This jazzier ditty, penned by M. Horsley and backed by "Johnny Dunn's Original Jazz Hounds," finally defines Edith's fine mid-range vocal style.
6. "Mammy, I'm Thinking of You," Columbia A-3634. Were all "Mammy" songs restricted to the minstrel traditions of (1923) contemporary Al Jolson? Apparently, the ditty, penned by Perry Bradford, who was a (black) entity more than proves otherwise. Moreover, Edith's somewhat somber vocal is nevertheless pleasing as well as (more) believable.

7. "Frankie," Columbia A-3506. This rhythmic and jazzy vocal penned by Perry Bradford is provided with some good support by "Johnny Dunn's Original Jazz Hounds."
8. "Rules and Regulations 'Signed Razor Jim'," Columbia A-3653. This interesting tale penned by Perry Bradford is tough and novel. Ever walk in a 1920s rural roadhouse?
9. "He May Be Your Man (But He Comes to See Me Sometimes)," Columbia A-3653. This novelty penned by Lemuel Fowler is interesting to hear, and, with the able aid of Johnny Dunn's trumpet, Edith's message may be taken very seriously. (Black contemporary Lucille Hegamin had also recorded this ditty on Arto 9129 and on Black Swan 2049.) Nevertheless, its Edith's version that further defined this ditty is, however, similar to Lucille's version.
10. "He Used to Be Your Man but He's My Man Now," Columbia 3787. The follow-up, penned by Perry Bradford, for the above ditty is hot!
11. "Daddy, Change Your Mind," Columbia 14008-D. Edith's rhythm vocal very clearly notes some good slang.
12. "I Don't Know And I Don't Care Blues," Columbia 14008-D. The wildness of this (1924) ditty is captured very well on this recording.
13. "How Come You Do Me Like You Do?" Columbia 14027-D. The obvious message of this ditty finds Edith's mid-range vocal flirting with the slang of Gene Austin's (white) pop music (1924). Or did it really belong to Marion Harris? Or what about another contemporary version from Edith's (black) contemporary Trixie Smith? Listen and compare.
14. "Muscle Shoals Blues," Columbia 14027-D. While blues queen Lizzie Miles had recorded this ditty some two years earlier on Okeh 8031, Edith seemingly takes nothing away from her contemporary 1922 rendering. This contrived tale of the Alabama town penned by George W. Thomas is backed by some crude guitar work, as the versatile Edith sounds as though she left the big city to record something way out in the sticks. Moreover, the adaptable Edith does in fact produce some fine rural blues.
15. "He's A Mean Mean Man," Columbia 14054-D. Edith's urban sound is more so slick and more so overcomes the canned effects of acoustic recording limits-penned by Perry Bradford.
16. "Double Crossin' Papa," Columbia 14054-D. This bit of slang penned by Perry Bradford is entertaining enough.
17. "It's Gonna Be a Cold Cold Winter," Columbia 14066-D. This (dated) vocal duet with Doc Strain is a successful attempt at novelty, however contrived.
18. "There'll Be Some Changes Made," Columbia-14066-D. Doc Strain (again) finds a vocal duet for Edith a novel success on the already older Ethel Waters classic.
19. "Black and Blue," Brunswick 4685. By the time of this recording (1929), Edith found herself in the musical review *Hot Choclates*, with Louis Armstrong, Fats Waller, and Andy Razaf, among others. While in this good and talented company, both Edith and Louis on Okeh 8714 recorded this bare and honest lament of Afro-American frustration. More so, its own reality, in true retrospective, finds its origins in real (black) comments penned by Harry Brooks, Fats Waller, and Andy Razaf. While noting Edith's performance as done well, a study of vocal style also finds both Armstrong and a contemporary Ethel Waters version on Columbia 2184-D more compelling. Moreover, the added drama, especially found in the Waters version, noting the social class structure within the black community, is more defining. Later, light years away, an odd version by (white) entity Frankie Laine, on Mercury 1026, while good, perhaps confuses this personable (Afro-American) message.

20. "My Man Is Good for Nothing but Love," Brunswick 4685. While not on the same level as its flip "Black and Blue," this ditty, also from *Hot Chocolates*, finds a mid-tempo Wilson vocal in excellent and jazzy form.
21. "The Penalty of Love," Victor 23010. This is a pop sound, and Edith's vocal handles it well.
22. "My Handy Man Ain't Handy No More," Victor 38624. For some odd reason, this follow-up to the Andy Razaf penned ditty "My Handy Man," by Ethel Waters, on Columbia 14353-D, was not recorded by Ethel. This fine recording by Edith, however, is (another) fine example of her versatility and ability to appeal to audiences beyond racial boundaries. Moreover, the salty lyrics of this ditty, like its predecessor, perhaps confirm the notion that being handy has its own rewards.

While the focus of this book is usually considered with recordings before (1950), this very fine LP just cannot be ignored.

23. "He May Be Your Man but He Comes to See Me Sometimes," Delmark 637 (LP). As a bonus, the latter-day release this (1970s?) LP is included. Like most recording artists of the 1920s, the career of Edith Wilson faded. After becoming *"Aunt Jemima"* for a long while, for the popular pancake syrup, this opportunity to record again, brought on by latter-day interest of record collectors and fans, found the (LP) and subsequent (CD) issue. Moreover, Edith is in very good spirit and voice! The following are picks:

    a. "Hesitating Blues."
    b. "Easing Away from Me."
    c. "That Same Dog." Edith is very feisty here, and this vocal duet with Little Brother Montgomery, with the fine backing by the "State Street Swingers," a very good latter-day Chicago blues band, is just as good as Edith's duet with Doc Straine in the mid-1920s but this time with a better-sounding backing, due to technology. (Edith is backed up by the likes of bluesman Little Brother Montgomery, who had been a 1920s contemporary of Edith's. Perhaps best known for his 1931 self-penned ditty "Louisiana Man" on Vocalion 02706, Little Brother was also known as "Eurreal Montgomery.")
    d. "Hey Hey Boogie." While Edith's hey-day had been more to do with the "black bottom" than the "boogie," she still creates some energy with this fine vocal.
    e. "Papa Mama Blues."
    f. "Twiddlin'." This ditty about the old folks not twiddling their thumbs ain't bad.
    g. "Slow Creepin' Blues."

ISSUED RECORDINGS AS BY ARTIST, OR ARTISTS,—TITLE,—RECORD NUMBER,—ORCHESTRA, BAND, OR OTHER,—& DECADE ISSUED

Note:	* vocal is recognized as a bandsinger or not at all				
Note:	NAP==Not a pick, but recognized as a recording, in text				
Note:	AC notes an accoustc recording				
Acuff Roy	Blue Eyes Crying In The Rain	Columbia - 37822	Smoky Mountain Boys	40s	
Acuff Roy	Blues On My Mind	Okeh - 6735	Smoky Mountain Boys	40s	
Acuff Roy	Freight Train Blues	Columbia - 20034	Smoky Mountain Boys	40s	
Acuff Roy	Great Speckled Bird	Vocalion - 04252	Crazy Tenneeseans, his	30s	
Acuff Roy	I'llForgive You But I Can't . . .	Okeh - 6723	Smoky Mountain Boys	40s	
Acuff Roy	Just To Ease My Worried Mind	Okeh - 05820	Smoky Mountain Boys	40s	
Acuff Roy	New Greenback Dollar	Vocalion - 03255	Crazy Tenneeseans, his	30s	
Acuff Roy	New Jole Blon	Columbia - 20106	Smoky Mountain Boys	40s	
Acuff Roy	Night Train To Memphis	Okeh - 06693	Smoky Mountain Boys	40s	
Acuff Roy	Precious Jewel, The	Okeh - 05956	Smoky Mountain Boys	40s	
Acuff Roy	Steamboat Whistle Blues	Vocalion - 03255	Crazy Tenneeseans, his	30s	
Acuff Roy	Steel Guitar Blues	Conqueror - 9086	Crazy Tenneeseans, his	30s	
Acuff Roy	Wabash Cannonball	Columbia - 20034	Smoky Mountain Boys	40s	
Acuff Roy	Worried Mind	Okeh - 06229	Smoky Mountain Boys	40s	
Acuff Roy	Wreck On The Highway	Okeh - 06685	Smoky Mountain Boys	40s	
Alexander George	Mighty Lak' A Rose - AC	Columbia - 1585		00s	
Alexander Texas	Risin' Sun The	Okeh - 8673		20s	
Allen Betty*	Rockin The Town	Brunswick-8023	Hudson-DeLange Orch.	30s	
Allen Brothers	Laughin And Cryin Blues	Columbia - 14266 - D		20s	
Allen Brothers	New Salty Dog	Victor - 23514		20s	
Allen Brothers	Salty Dog	Columbia - 15175 - D		20s	
Allen Henry (Red)*	Truckin	Columbia - 3078 - D	Mills Blue Rhythm Band	30s	
Allen Terry*	I Get Along Without You Very . . .	Vocalion - 4648	Norvo Red Orch	30s	
Almanac Singers	Away Rio	General - 5017 - A	Almanac Singers	40s	
Almanac Singers - W. Guthrie	Blow The Man Down	General - 5016 - A	Almanac Singers	40s	
Almanac Singers	Blow Ye Winds Heigh Ho	General - 5015 - A	Almanac Singers	40s	
Almanac Singers	Coast Of High Barbary The	General - 5017 - B	Almanac Singers	40s	
Almanac Singers	Dodger Song The	General - 5018 - A	Almanac Singers	40s	
Almanac Singers	Golden Vanity The	General - 5016 - B	Almanac Singers	40s	
Almanac Singers - W. Guthrie	Hard Aint It	General - 5019	Almanac Singers	40s	
Almanac Singers - W. Guthrie	House Of The Rising Sun	General - 5020	Almanac Singers	40s	
Almanac Singers - W. Guthrie	I Ride An Old Paint	General - 5020 - A	Almanac Singers	40s	
Almanac Singers	State Of Arkansas	General - 5019 - A	Almanac Singers	40s	
American Quartet	America I Love You - AC	Victor - 17902	American Quartet	10s	
American Quartet	Casey Jones - AC	Victor - 16483	American Quartet	10s	
American Quartet	It's a Long Long Way To . . . - AC	Victor - 17639	American Quartet	10s	
American Quartet	Ragtime Dream The - AC	Victor - 17535	American Quartet	10s	
American Quartet	Some Of These Days - AC	Columbia - 16834	American Quartet	10s	
American Quartet - NAP	When You Wore A Tulip - AC	Victor - 17652	American Quartet	10s	
Anderson Bill	Tip Of My Fingers The	Decca - 9- 31092		60s	
Anderson Ivie	All Gods Chillun Got Rhythm	Film Master - 1937	Her Band From Dixie &	30s	
Anderson Ivie	All Gods Chillun Got Rhythm	Variety - 591	Her Band From Dixie &	30s	
Anderson Ive*	At A Dixie Roadside Diner	Victor - 26719	Ellington Duke Orch.	40s	
Anderson Ive*	Chocolate Shake	Victor - 27531	Ellington Duke Orch.	40s	
Anderson Ive*	Cotton	Brunswick - 7514	Ellington Duke Orch.	30s	
Anderson Ive*	Five O'Clock Whistle	Victor - 26748	Ellington Duke Orch.	40s	
Anderson Ive*	Get Yourself A New Broom	Brunswick - 6607	Ellington Duke Orch.	30s	
Anderson Ive*	Happy Is The Day Is Long	Brunswick - 6571	Ellington Duke Orch.	30s	
Anderson Ivie	He's Tall, Dark And Handsome	Black & White - 823	Moore Phil Orch	40s	
Anderson Ive*	I Don't Mind	Victor - 20 - 1598	Ellington Duke Orch.	40s	
Anderson Ive*	I Got It Bad And That Aint Good	Victor - 27531	Ellington Duke Orch.	40s	
Anderson Ive*	Im Checking Out Goo'mBye	Columbia - 35208	Ellington Duke Orch.	40s	
Anderson Ive*	Isent Love The Strangest Thing	Brunswick - 7625	Ellington Duke Orch.	30s	
Anderson Ive*	It Don't Mean A Thing	Brunswick - 6265	Ellington Duke Orch.	30s	

Anderson Ive*	It Was A Sad Night In Harlem	Brunswick - 7710	Ellington Duke Orch.	30s	
Anderson Ive*	Killing Myself	Columbia - 35640	Ellington Duke Orch.	30s	
Anderson Ive*	Kissin' My Baby Goodnight	Brunswick - 7627	Ellington Duke Orch.	30s	
Anderson Ive*	Lonely Co - Ed A	Columbia - 35240	Ellington Duke Orch	30s	
Anderson Ive*	Love Is Like A Cigarette	Brunswick - 7626	Ellington Duke Orch.	30s	
Anderson Ive*	Me And You	Victor - 26598	Ellington Duke Orch.	40s	
Anderson Ivie	Mexico Joe	Exclusive - 3113	Burke Ceele Orch.	40s	
Anderson Ive*	My Old Flame	Victor - 24651	Ellington Duke Orch.	30s	
Anderson Ivie	Oh Babe Maybe Some Day	Film Master - 1937	Ellington Duke Orch.	30s	
Anderson Ive*	Oh Babe Maybe Someday	Brunswick - 7667	Ellington Duke Orch.	30s	
Anderson Ivie	Play Me The Blues	Exclusive - 3114	Burke Ceele Orch.	40s	
Anderson Ive*	Raising The Rent	Brunswick - 6571	Ellington Duke Orch.	30s	
Anderson Ive*	Rocks In My Bed	Victor - 27639	Ellington Duke Orch.	40s	
Anderson Ivie	Stormy Weather	Film Master - 1933	Ellington Duke Orch.	40s	
Anderson Ive*	Swingtime In Honolulu	Brunswick - 8131	Ellington Duke Orch.	30s	
Anderson Ive*	Theres A Lull In My Life	Master - 117	Ellington Duke Orch.	30s	
Anderson Ive*	Troubled Waters	Victor - 24651	Ellington Duke Orch.	40s	
Anderson Ive*	Truckin	Brunswick - 7514	Ellington Duke Orch.	30s	
Anderson Ivie	Voot Is Here To Stay The	Black & White - 772	Anderson I. & her All Stars	40s	
Anderson Ive*	When My Sugar Walks Down The Street	Brunswick - 8168	Ellington Duke Orch.	30s	
Anderson Ive*	You Gave Me The Gate	Brunswick - 8169	Ellington Duke Orch.	30s	
Anderson Lale	Girl Under the Lantern The	Electrola - 6996		30s	
Anderson Marion	Deep River - AC	Victor - 19227		20s	
Anderson Marion	Nobody Knows The T . . . - AC	Victor - 19560		20s	
Andrews Sisters	Beat Me Daddy Eight To The Bar	Decca - 3375	Schoen Vic Orch	40s	
Andrews Sisters	Beat Me Daddy Eight To The Bar	Film Master - 1941	Schoen Vic Orch	40s	
Andrews Sisters	Beer Barrel Polka	Decca - 2462	vocal with orch	30s	
Andrews Sisters	Bei Mir Bist Du Schoen	Decca - 1562	Schoen Vic Orch	30s	
Andrews Sisters	Boogie Woogie Bugle Boy	Decca - 3598	Schoen Vic Orch	40s	
Andrews Sisters	Boogie Woogie Bugle Boy	Film Master - 1941	Schoen Vic Orch	40s	
Andrews Sisters	Bounce Me Brother With A Solid Four	Decca - 3598	Schoen Vic Orch	40s	
Andrews Sisters	Christmas Island	Decca - 23722	Lombardo Guy Orch	40s	
Andrews Sisters	Daddy	Decca - 3821	Schoen Vic Orch	40s	
Andrews Sisters	Don't Sit Under The Apple Tree	Decca - 18312		40s	
Andrews Sisters	Gimme Some Skin My Friend	Decca - 3871	Schoen Vic Orch	40s	
Andrews Sisters	Hold Tight Hold Tight . . .	Decca - 2214	Dorsey Jimmy & his Orch.	30s	
Andrews Sisters	I Can Dream, Cant I	Decca - 24705	Jenkins Gordon Orch	40s	
Andrews Sisters	I Wanna Be Loved	Decca - 27007	Schoen Vic Orch	40s	
Andrews Sisters	Jammin'	Brunswick - 7863	Belasco Leon Orch.	30s	
Andrews Sisters	Joseph ! Joseph!	Decca - 1691	Schoen Vic Orch	30s	
Andrews Sisters	Massachusetts	Decca - 18497	Schoen Vic Orch	40s	
Andrews Sisters	Mister Five By Five	Decca - 18470	Schoen, Vic Orch	40s	
Andrews Sisters	Near You	Decca - 24171		40s	
Andrews Sisters	One Meat Ball	Decca - 18536	Schoen, Vic Orch	40s	
Andrews Sisters	Rhumbaboogie	Decca - 3097	Schoen Vic Orch	40s	
Andrews Sisters	Rum and Coca - Cola	Decca - 18636	Schoen Vic Orch	40s	
Andrews Sisters	Scrub Me Mama With A Boogie Beat	Decca - 3553	Schoen Vic Orch	40s	
Andrews Sisters	Shoo Shoo Baby	Decca - 18572	Schoen Vic Orch	40s	
Andrews Sisters	Shortenin Bread	Decca - 1734	Vocal with Orchestral.	30s	
Andrews Sisters	Them That Has - Gets	Decca - 23656	Heywood Eddie Orch	40s	
Andrews Sisters	We Just Couldent Say Goodbye	Decca - 24406		40s	
Andrews Sisters	Well All Right	Decca - 2462	vocal with orch	30s	
Arlan Harold*	Little Girl	Columbia - 2488 - D	Ventuti Joe & Orch	30s	
Arlen Harold*	Ill Wind	Victor - 24579	Duchin Eddy Orch	30s	
Arlen Harold*	Stormy Weather	Victor - 24262	Reisman Leo Orch	30s	
Armstrong Louis	Aint Misbehavin'	Okeh - 8714	Armstrong L. & His Orch	20s	
Armstrong Louis	All Of Me	Okeh - 41552	Armstrong, L. & His Orch	30s	
Armstrong Louis	Basin Street Blues	Okeh - 8690	Armstrong, L. & His Orh	20s	
Armstrong Louis & May Alix	Big Butter And Egg Man	Okeh - 8423	Armstrong L. & H. Hot 5	20s	
Armstrong Louis	Black And Blue	Okeh - 8714	Armstrong L. & His Orch	20s	
Armstrong Louis	Blue Again	Okeh - 41498	Armstrong L. & His Orch	30s	
Armstrong Louis	Blues For Yesterday	Victor - 20 - 2456	Hot Six His	40s	
Armstrong Louis	Blues In The South	Victor - 20 - 2456	Hot Six His	40s	
Armstrong Louis	Body And Soul	Okeh - 41468	Armstrong L. & His SNOOO	30s	
Armstrong Louis	Confessin That I Love You	Okeh - 41448	Armstrong L. & His SNCCO	30s	
Armstrong Louis	Dallas Blues	Okeh - 8774	Armstrong L. & His Orch	40s	
Armstrong L. & Mills Brothers	Flat Foot Floogie, (The)	Decca - 1876		30s	
Armstrong Louis	Georgia On My Mind	Okeh - 41541	Armstrong Louis & Orch	30s	
Armstrong Louis & Kid Ory	Gut Bucket Blues*	Okeh - 8261	Armstrong L. & His Hot 5	20s	
Armstrong Louis	Heebie Jeebies*	Okeh - 8300	Armstrong L. & His. Hot 5	20s	
Armstrong Louis	Hello Dolly	Kapp - 573	Armstrong L & His Orch	60s	
Armstrong Louis	Hobo You Cant Ride This Train	Victor - 24200	Armstrong L. & His Orch	30s	
Armstrong Louis	I Cant Give You Anything But Love	Okeh - 8669	Armstrong L. & His SB5	20s	

Armstrong Louis	I Gotta Right To Sing The Blues	Victor - 24233	Armstrong L. & His Orch	30s	
Armstrong Louis	I Surrender Dear	Okeh - 41496	Armstrong. L. & His Orch	30s	
Armstrong Louis	If I Could Be With You One . . .	Okeh - 41448	Armstrong L. & His SNCCO	30s	
Armstrong Louis	Jeepers Creepers	Decca - 2267	Armstrong Louis Orch.	30s	
Armstrong Louis	Jeepers Creepers	Film Master - 1938		30s	
Armstrong Louis	Just A Gigolo	Okeh - 41486	Armstrong L. & His SCCO	30s	
Armstrong Louis	Keeping Out Of Mischief	Okeh - 41560	Armstrong L. & His Orch.	20s	
Armstrong Louis	Kiss To Build A Dream On A	Decca - 27720	Oliver Sy Orchestra	50s	
Armstrong Louis	La Vie Rose	Decca - 27113	All Stars his	50s	
Armstrong Louis	Lawd You Made The Night Too Long	Okeh - 41560	Armstrong L. & His Orch	20s	
Armstrong Louis	Lazy River	Okeh - 41541	Armstrong L. & His Orch	30s	
Armstrong Louis	Little Joe	Okeh - 41501	Armstrong L. & His Orch	30s	
Armstrong Louis	Lonesome Road, (The)	Okeh - 41538	Armstrong L. & His Orch	30s	
Armstrong Louis	Monday Date A	Okeh - 8597	Armstrong L. & His. Hot 5	20s	
Armstrong Louis	My Sweet	Okeh - 41415	Armstrong, L. & His Orch	30s	
Armstrong L. & Mills Brothers	My Walking Stick	Decca - 1892		40s	
Armstrong Louis	Old Man Mose	Decca - 622	Armstrong L. & His Orch	30s	
Armstrong Louis	Penut Vendor, (The)	Okeh - 41478	Armstrong L. & His SNCCO	30s	
Armstrong Louis	Public Melody Number One	Decca - 1347	Armstrong, L. & his Orch	30s	
Armstrong L. & H. Carmichael	Rockin' Chair	Okeh - 8756	Armstrong, L. & His Orch	30s	
Armstrong Louis	Shine	Film Master - 1932	Armstrong, Louis & Orch	30s	
Armstrong Louis	Shine	Okeh - 41486	Armstrong, L. & His Orch	30s	
Armstrong Louis	Squeeze Me	Okeh - 8641	Armstrong L. & HisH.5	20s	
Armstrong Louis	St. James Infirmary	Okeh - 8657	Armstrong, L. & HisSH.5	20s	
Armstrong Louis	St. Louis Blues	Okeh - 41350	Armstrong, L. & His Orch	30s	
Armstrong Louis	Star Dust	Okeh - 41530	Armstrong, L. & His Orch	30s	
Armstrong Louis	Sweethearts On Parade	Columbia - 2688 - D	Armstrong. & His SNCCO	50s	
Armstrong L. & V. Middleton	That's My Desire	Decca - 28372	All Stars his	50s	
Armstrong Louis	Them There Eyes	Okeh - 41501	Armstrong, L. & His Orch	30s	
Armstrong Louis	Theme From A Three Penny . . .	Columbia - 40587		50s	
Armstrong Louis	Tight Like This	Okeh - 8649	Armstrong, L. & His SH5	20s	
Armstrong L. & Mills Brothers	W. P. A.	Decca - 3151		30s	
Armstrong Louis	Walkin My Baby Back Home	Okeh - 41497	Armstrong, L. & His Orch	30s	
Armstrong Louis	West End Blues	Film Master - 1946		40s	
Armstrong Louis	West End Blues	Okeh - 8597	Armstrong L. & H. Hot 5	20s	
Armstrong Louis	When Its Sleepy Time Down.	Okeh - 41504	Armstrong L. & His Orch	30s	
Armstrong Louis	When The Saints Go Marching In	Decca - 2230	Armstrong L. & his Orch	30s	
Armstrong Louis	When Your Lover Has Gone	Okeh - 41498	Armstrong L. & His Orch	30s	
Armstrong Louis	When Youre Smiling	Okeh - 8729	Armstrong L. & His Orch	20s	
Armstrong Louis	Where The Blues Were Born.	Victor - 20 - 2088	Armstrong L. & H. D. 7	40s	
Armstrong Louis	You Can Depend On Me	Okeh - 41538	Armstrong L. & His Orch	30s	
Armstrong Louis	You Rascal You	Film Master - 1932	Armstrong L. & His Orch	30s	
Armstrong Louis	You Rascal You	Okeh - 41504	Armstrong L. & His Orch	30s	
Armstrong L. & Lionel Hampton	Youre Driving Me Crazy	Okeh - 41478	Armstrong L. & His SNCCO	30s	
Arnell Amy*	I Don't Want To Set The World	Okeh - 6320	Tucker Tommy Orch.	30s	
Arnold Eddy	Anything That's Part Of You	Victor - 20 - 4569		50s	
Arnold Eddy	Anytime	Victor - 20 - 2700	Tennessee Plowboys, &	40s	
Arnold Eddy	Bouquet Of Roses	Victor - 20 - 2806	Tennessee Plowboys, &	40s	
Arnold Eddy	Cattle Call	Bluebird - 33 - 0527		40s	
Arnold Eddy	Cuddle Buggin Baby	Victor - 21 - 0342		50s	
Arnold Eddy	Easy Rockin Chair	Victor - 20 - 2481		40s	
Arnold Eddy	I Really Don't Want To Know	Victor - 20 - 5525		50s	
Arnold Eddy	I Walk Alone	Bluebird - 33 - 0535		40s	
Arnold Eddy	I Wanna Play House With You	Victor - 21 - 0473	& his guitar	50s	
Arnold Eddy	I'll Hold You In My Heart . . .	Victor - 20 - 2332	Tennessee Plowboys, &	40s	
Arnold Eddy	It's A Sin	Victor - 20 - 2241	Tennessee Plowboys, &	40s	
Arnold Eddy	Mommy Please Stay Home . . .	Bluebird - 33 - 0520		40s	
Arnold Eddy	Rocking Alone In An Old . . .	Victor - 20 - 2488		40s	
Arnold Eddy	Texarkana Baby	Victor - 20 - 2806	Tennessee Plowboys, &	40s	
Arnold Eddy	That's How Much I Love You	Victor - 20 - 1948	Tennessee Plowboys, &	40s	
Arnold Eddy	That's How Much I Love You - 2	Camden - LP - CAL - 471		50s	
Arnold Eddy	You Don't Know Me	Victor - 20 - 6502		50s	
Arnold Eddy	You Must Walk The Line	Bluebird - 33 - 0540		40s	
Arnold Eddy	Lay Some Happiness On Me	Victor LP LSP-3715		60s	
Arnold Eddy	Somebody Like You	Victor-8965		60s	
Arnold Eddy	Tip Of My Fingers The	Victor-8869		60s	
Arnold Kokomo	Milkcow Blues	Decca - 7026		30s	
Arnold Kokomo	Old Origional Kokomo Blues	Decca - 7026		30s	
Astaire Fred	Beautiful Faces Need Beautiful Cloths	Film Master - 1948		40s	
Astaire Fred	Change Partners	Film Master - 1937		30s	
Astaire Fred	Cheek To Cheek	Brunswick - 7486		30s	
Astaire Fred	Cheek To Cheek	Film Master - 1935		30s	

Astaire Fred	Continental, The	Film Master - 1934		30s	
Astaire Fred	Easter Parade	Film Master - 1948		40s	
Astaire Fred & Ginger Rogers	Fine Romance A	Film Master - 1936		30s	
Astaire Fred	Flying Down To Rio	Film Master - 1933		30s	
Astaire Fred	Happy Easter	Film Master - 1948		40s	
Astaire Fred	I Cant Tell A Lie	Film Master - 1942	Crosby Bob & His Orch.	40s	
Astaire Fred	I'll Be Hard To Handle	Film Master - 1935		30s	
Astaire Fred	Im Putting All My Eggs In One Basket	Film Master - 1936		30s	
Astaire Fred	It Only Happens When I Dance With You	Film Master - 1948		40s	
Astaire Fred & Ginger Rogers	Lets Call The Whole Thing Off	Film Master - 1937		30s	
Astaire Fred	Lets Face The Music And Dance	Film Master - 1936		30s	
Astaire Fred	Needle In A Haystack	Film Master - 1934		30s	
Astaire Fred*	Night and Day	Victor - 24193	Reisman Leo Orch	30s	
Astaire - Fred & Adele Astaire	Oh Lady Be Good Medley	Columbia - E - 3970		20s	
Astaire Fred & Ginger Rogers	Pick Yourself Up	Film Master - 1936		30s	
Astaire Fred	Since They Changed Lock Lomond Into Swing	Film Master - 1937		30s	
Astaire Fred	Slap That Bass	Film Master - 1937		30s	
Astaire Fred	They Cant Take That Away From Me	Film Master - 1937		30s	
Astaire Fred & Ginger Rogers	They Cant Take That Away From Me	Film Master - 1949		40s	
Astaire Fred	Top Hat White Tie And Tails	Film Master - 1935		30s	
Astaire Fred & Ginger Rogers	Way You Look Tonight The	Film Master - 1936		30s	
Astaire Fred	Yam The	Film Master - 1938		30s	
Astaire Fred	Youre Easy To Dance With	Film Master - 1942		40s	
Austin & Lee Allen	Laughin' And Cryin' Blues	Columbia - 14266 - D		20s	
Austin Gene	Ain't Misbehavin	Victor - 22068		30s	
Austin Gene	Ain't She Sweet - AC	Victor - 20568	Skilkret Nat & His Orch.	20s	
Austin Gene	Blue Sky Avenue	Film Master - 1934		30s	
Austin Gene	Blue Sky Avenue	Victor - 24725		30s	
Austin Gene	Bye Bye Blackbird - AC	Victor - 20044		20s	
Austin Gene	Carolina Moon	Victor - 21833		20s	
Austin Gene as (Billy Collins)	Cindy Cindy	Victor - 20873		20s	
Austin Gene	Easter Parade	Romeo - 2189		30s	
Austin Gene	Five Foot Two Eyes Of Blue - AC	Victor - 19899		20s	
Austin Gene	Flapper Wife The - AC	Victor - 19638	International Novelty Orch.	20s	
Austin Gene	Git It	Victor - 24663		30s	
Austin Gene	Guilty	Banner - 32285		20s	
Austin Gene	How Am I To Know	Victor - 22128		20s	
Austin Gene	Ive Got A Feeling Im Falling	Victor - 22033		20s	
Austin Gene	Ive Got The Girl - AC	Victor - 20397		20s	
Austin Gene	Just A Little Home For The . . .	Banner - 23614		30s	
Austin Gene	Little Street Where Old . . .	Banner - 32614		30s	
Austin Gene*	Lonesome Road Blues - AC	Vocalion - 14809	Reneau George	20s	
Austin Gene	Lonesome Road, (The)	Victor - 21098		20s	
Austin Gene	Love Letters In The Sand	Victor - 22806		20s	
Austin Gene	Maybe Its The Moon	Banner - 32256		30s	
Austin Gene	Melancholy Baby, My	Victor - 20977		20s	
Austin Gene	Muddy Water	Victor - 20569		20s	
Austin Gene	My Blue Heaven	Victor - 20964		20s	
Austin Gene	My Fate Is In Your Hands	Victor - 22223		20s	
Austin Gene	Nobody Cares If Im Blue	Victor - 22518		30s	
Austin Gene	Nothin'	Victor - 21080	Skilkret Nat & His Orch.	20s	
Austin Gene	One Sweet Letter From You - AC	Victor - 20730		30s	
Austin Gene	Please Don't Talk About Me . . .	Victor - 22635		30s	
Austin Gene	Ramona	Victor - 21334	Shilkret Nat & His Orch.	20s	
Austin Gene	Ridin Around In The Rain	Victor - 24663		30s	
Austin Gene	Rollin Down The River	Victor - 22451		30s	
Austin Gene	Save Your Sorrow For . . .	Victor - 19857		20s	
Austin Gene	Shes Funny That Way	Victor - 21779		30s	
Austin Gene	Sleepy Tme Gal - AC	Victor - 19899		20s	
Austin Gene*	Softly And Tenderly - AC	Vocalion - 14918	Reneau George	20s	
Austin Gene	Someday Sweetheart - AC	Victor - 20561		20s	
Austin Gene	St. James Infirmary Blues	Victor - 22299		30s	
Austin Gene	Sweet Child - AC	Victor - 19928		20s	
Austin Gene	That's What I Call Heaven	Victor - 21893		20s	
Austin Gene	Thinking Of You	Victor - 20411		20s	
Austin Gene	Tonight You Belong To Me	Victor - 20371		20s	
Austin Gene & C. Robinson	Way Down Home - AC	Victor - 19637		20s	
Austin Gene	Weary River	Victor - 21856		20s	
Austin Gene	Wedding Bells	Victor - 21893		20s	
Austin Gene & Aileen Stanley	When My Sugar Walks Down The Street - AC	Victor - 19585		20s	
Austin Gene	When Your Lover Has Gone	Victor - 22635		30s	
Austin Gene	Ya Gotta Know How To Love - AC	Victor - 20044		20s	

Austin Gene	Yes Sir That's My Baby - AC	Victor - 19656		20s	
Austin Gene	Garden In The Rain A	Victor - 21915		20s	
Autry Gene	Be Honest With Me	Okeh - 5980		40s	
Autry Gene	Blue Days	Banner - 32123		30s	
Autry Gene	Death Of Mother Jones The	Banner - 32133		30s	
Autry Gene	Deep In The Heart Of Texas	Okeh - 06643		40s	
Autry Gene	Dust Pan Blues	Diva - 6030 - G		20s	
Autry Gene	Frosty The Snowman	Columbia - 38907		40s	
Autry Gene	Goodby Little Darlin Goodby	Okeh - 05463		40s	
Autry Gene	Have I Told You Lately That . . .	Columbia - 37079		40s	
Autry Gene	Here Comes Santa Claus	Columbia - 20377		50s	
Autry Gene	High Steppin Mama Blues	Banner - 32473		30s	
Autry Gene	I Call On Oscar I Call On Pete	Film Master - 1935		30s	
Autry Gene	I'll Never Let You Go	Okeh - 06360		40s	
Autry Gene	Im Getting A Moons Eye . . .	Film Master - 1935		30s	
Autry Gene	Last Round Up The	Melotone - M - 12832		30s	
Autry Gene & Jimmy Long	Mississippi Valley Blues	Conqueror - 7908		30s	
Autry Gene	My Alabama Home	Victor - 40400		20s	
Autry Gene	My Dreaming Of You	Victor - 40400		20s	
Autry Gene	Nobody's Darlin But Mine	Perfect - 6 04 52		30s	
Autry Gene	Ole Faithful	Metotone - 13354		30s	
Autry Gene	Peter Cottontail	Columbia - 38750		50s	
Autry Gene	Rhythm Of The Range	Melotone - M - 7 12 60		30s	
Autry Gene	Rudolph The Red Nosed R . . .	Columbia - 38610		40s	
Autry Gene	Slu - Foot Lou	Diva - 6031 - G		20s	
Autry Gene	South Of the Border	Vocalion - 05122		30s	
Autry Gene	Stay Away From My Chicken.	Diva - 6032 - G		20s	
Autry Gene	Take Me Back To My Boots . . .	Vocalion - 04172		30s	
Autry Gene	That Silver Haired Daddy Of.	Film Master - 1935.		30s	
Autry Gene & Jimmy Long	That Silver Haired Daddy Of.	Conqueror - 7908		30s	
Autry Gene	That's How I Got My Start	Romeo - 5093		30s	
Autry Gene Trio	Tumbling Tumbleweeds	Romeo - 5434		30s	
Autry Gene	Uncle Noah's Arch	Film Master - 1934		30s	
Autry Gene (Sam Hill)	Why Dont You Come . . .	Van Dyke - 5119		20s	
Autry Gene	Yellow Rose Of Texas The	Perfect - 12912		30s	
Autry Gene	You Are My Sunshine	Okeh - 06274		40s	
Autry Gene	Youre The Only Star In My . . .	Conqueror - 9098		30s	
Babbit Harry*	Stairway To The Stars	Brunswick - 8381	Kyser Kay & His Orch.	30s	
Babbit Harry, Gloria Wood*	On A Slow Boat To China	Columbia - 38301	Kyser Kay & His Orch	40s	
Bacon Louis (unacredited)	Blues In My Heart	Brunswick - 6136	Webb Chick Orch	30s	
Baby Mack	What Kind Of Man Is That - AC	Okeh - 8313		20s	
Bacall Lauren	And Her Tears Fell Like Wine	Film Master - 1946		40s	
Bailey Mildred*	All Of Me	Victor - 22879	Whiteman Paul Orch	30s	
Bailey Mildred	Arkansas Blues	Vocalion - 4802	Oxford Greys, her	30s	
Bailey Mildred	Barrelhouse Music	Vocalion - 4802	Oxford Greys, her	30s	
Bailey Mildred*	Cant You See	Victor - 22828	Whiteman Paul Orch	30s	
Bailey Mildred*	Concentratin'	Victor - 22880	Whiteman Paul Orch	30s	
Bailey Mildred*	Darn That Dream	Columbia - 35331	Goodman Benny Orch	40s	
Bailey Mildred	Dear Old Mother Dixie	Victor - 24137	Whiteman Paul Orch	30s	
Bailey Mildred	Doing The Uptown Lowdown	Brunswick - 6680	Dorsey Brothers Orch.	30s	
Bailey Mildred	From The Land Of Sky Blue Water	Vocalion - 3982	Bailey Mildred Orch	30s	
Bailey Mildred	Give Me Liberty Or Give Me Love	Brunswick - 6680	Dorsey Brothers Orch.	30s	
Bailey Mildred	Harlem Lullaby	Brunswick - 6558	Dorsey Brothers Orch.	30s	
Bailey Mildred	I Don't Want To Miss Mississippi	Victor - 20 - 2457	Larkins Ellis Trio	40s	
Bailey Mildred*	I'll Never Be The Same	Victor - 24088	Whiteman Paul Orch	30s	
Bailey Mildred	Is That Religion	Brunswick - 6558	Dorsey Brothers Orch.	30s	
Bailey Mildred*	Junk Man	Columbia - 2892 - D	Goodman, Benny Orch.	30s	
Bailey Mildred	Lazy Bones	Brunswick - 6587	Dorsey Brothers Orch.	30s	
Bailey Mildred	Long About Midnight	Vocalion - 3378	Bailey Mildred & Her Orch	30s	
Bailey Mildred*	Love Me Tonight	Victor - 24117	Whiteman Paul Orch	30s	
Bailey M. & Delta Rhythm Boys	Lover Come Back To Me	Decca - 3953	Chittison Herman Trio	40s	
Bailey Mildred*	My Goodby To You	Victor - 22876	Whiteman Paul Orch	30s	
Bailey Mildred*	Ol Pappy	Columbia - 2892 - D	Goodman Benny Orch.	30s	
Bailey Mildred	Rockin' Chair	Victor - 24117		30s	
Bailey Mildred	Rockin' Chair	Vocalion - 3553		30s	
Bailey Mildred	Shouting In That Amen Corner	Brunswick - 6655	Dorsey Brothers Orch.	30s	
Bailey Mildred*	Smoke Dreams	Brunswick - 7815	Norvo Red Orch	30s	
Bailey Mildred	Snowball	Brunswick - 6655	Dorsey Brothers Orch.	30s	
Bailey Mildred	That Aint Right	Victor - 20 - 2457	Larkins Ellis Trio	40s	
Bailey Mildred	Theres A Cabin In The Pines	Brunswick - 6587	Dorsey Brothers Orch.	30s	
Bailey Mildred*	Too Late	Victor - 22874	Whiteman Paul Orch	30s	
Bailey Mildred	Trust In Me	Vocalion - 3449	Bailey Mildred Orch	30s	

Bailey Mildred*	We Just Couldent Say Goodbye	Victor - 24088	Whiteman Paul Orch.	30s	
Bailey Mildred*	Week End Of A Private . . .	Brunswick - 8088	Norvo Red Orch	30s	
Bailey Mildred*	When Its Sleepy Time Down.	Victor - 22828	Whiteman, Paul Orch	30s	
Bailey Mildred	When We're Alone . . .	Majestic - 1040	Dale Ted Orch	40s	
Bailey Mildred	You And Your Love	Vocalion - 5006	Bailey Mildred & Her Orch	30s	
Bailey Sisters*	No Mama No	Vocalion - 5087	Bernie Ben Orchestra	30s	
Baird Eugenie*	My Shining Hour	Decca - 18567	Casa Loma Orchestra	40s	
Baker Belle	Hard Hearted Hannah - AC	Victor - 19436		20s	
Baker Belle	Laughing At Life	Brunswick - 4962		30s	
Baker Belle	Youre The One I Care For	Brunswick - 5051		30s	
Baker Bonnie*	Oh Johnny, Oh Johnny	Columbia - 35228	Tucker Orrin Orch	30s	
Baker Elsie	Silent Night - AC	Victor - 17164		10s	
Baker Elsie	There's A Broken Heart - AC	Victor - 17943		10s	
Baker Josephine	After I Say Im Sorry	Odeon - 166032	pare Le Jacob's Jazz.	20s	
Baker Josephine	Blue Skies	Odeon - 166042	pare Le Jacob's Jazz.	20s	
Baker Josephine	Breezing Along With The Breeze	Odeon - 166041	pare Le Jacob's Jazz.	20s	
Baker Josephine	Bye Bye Blackbird	Odeon - 166033	pare Le Jacob's Jazz.	20s	
Baker Josephine	Dinah	Odeon - 49172		20s	
Baker Josephine	Dream Ship	Film Master - 1935		30s	
Baker Josephine	Hello Bluebird	Odeon - 166041	pare Le Jacob's Jazz.	20s	
Baker Josephine	He's The Last Word	Odeon - 166042	pare Le Jacob's Jazz.	20s	
Baker Josephine	I've Found A New Baby	Odeon - 49227		20s	
Baker Josephine	I Love My Baby	Odeon - 49226		20s	
Baker Josephine	I Wonder Where My Baby Is Tonight	Odeon - 49174		20s	
Baker Josephine	Ive Got You Under My Skin	Columbia - DF - 2130		30s	
Baker Josephine	Jai Deux Amours	Columbia - DF - 229	Le Molodic Jazz . . .	30s	
Baker Josephine	King For A Day	Columbia - DF - 407	Mahieux Edmond dir	30s	
Baker Josephine	Neath The Tropical Blue Skies	Film Master - 1935		30s	
Baker Josephine	Pretty Little Baby	Odeon - 166031	pare Le Jacob's Jazz.	20s	
Baker Josephine	Skeedleum	Odeon - 49229		20s	
Baker Josephine	Sleepy Tme Gal	Odeon - 49173		20s	
Baker Josephine	Suppose	Columbia - DF - 230		30s	
Baker Josephine	That Certain Feeling	Odeon - 49170		20s	
Baker Josephine	Then Ill Be Happy	Odeon - 166032	pare Le Jacob's Jazz.	20s	
Baker Josephine	Wher'd You Get Those Eyes	Odeon - 19931	pare Le Jacob's Jazz.	20s	
Baker Josephine	Who	Odeon - 49170		20s	
Baker Josephine	Youre Driving Me Crazy	Columbia - DF - 709		30s	
Baker Josephine	Youre The One I Care For	Columbia - DF - 709		30s	
Baker Kenny	Remember Me	Film Master - 1937		30s	
Baker Lavern	Tweedle Dee	Atlantic - 1047	Gliders the	50s	
Baker Two Ton & Trio*	Sioux City Sue	Decca - 18745	Hoosier Hot Shots	40s	
Ballew Smith*	Liza All The Clouds Roll Away	Columbia - 1903 - D	Ipana Troubadors	20s	
Barbecue Bob	Mississippi Heavy Water Blues	Columbia - 14222 - D		20s	
Batts Will	Highway 61	Vocalion - 13531		30s	
Baur Franklyn	Just A Memory	Brunswick - 3590		20s	
Baur Franklyn*	Hallelujah	Victor - 20599	Skilkret Nat & His Orch.	20s	
Baur Franklyn*	Sometimes Im Happy	Victor - 20599	Kahn Roger Wolfe Orch	20s	
Baur Franklyn*	Thinking Of You	Brunswick - 3704		20s	
Bayes Nora	Japaneese Sandman - AC	Columbia - A2997		20s	
Bayes Nora	Just Like A Gipsy - AC	Columbia - A6138		20s	
Bayes Nora	Lovin Sam The . . . - AC	Columbia - A3757		20s	
Bayes Nora	Over There - AC	Victor - 17639		10s	
Bayes Nora	Prohibition Blues - AC	Columbia - A2823		10s	
Bayes Nora	That Lovin Rag - AC	Victor - 60023		10s	
Bayes Nora	You Can't Get Lovin' Where. AC	Columbia - A2771		10s	
Beatles	Aint She Sweet	Atco - 6308	Beatles the	60s	
Beatles	Matchbox	Capital - 5255	Beatles the	60s	
Beatles	P S I Love You	Tollie - 9008	Beatles the	60s	
Beatles	Sweet Georgia Brown	Atco - 6302	Beatles the	60s	
Beatles	Everybodys Trying To Be My Baby	Capital - LP) - T - 2228		60s	
Beavers Richard - NAP	The Girl On The Magazine Cover	Film Master - 1948		40s	
Beers Bobby & Blue Notes . . .*	Are You Lonesome Tonight	MGM - 10628	Barron Blue & his Orch	40s	
Beneke Tex & Four Modernaires	Chattanooga Choo Choo	Bluebird - B - 11235	Miller Glenn Orch	40s	
Beneke Tex*	Ladys In Love With You The	Bluebird - B - 10229	Miller Glenn Orch	40s	
Bennett Tony	Autumn Leaves - Indian Summer	Columbia - CD - 66214	Sharon Ralph Trio	90s	
Bennett Tony	Because Of You	Columbia - 39362	Faith Percy Orch	50s	
Bennett Tony	Blue Velvet	Columbia - 39555	Faith Percy Orch	50s	
Bennett Tony	Body And Soul	Columbia - CD - 66214	Sharon Ralph Trio	90s	
Bennett Tony	Cold Cold Heart	Columbia - 39449	Faith Percy Orch	50s	
Bennett Tony	Fire Fly	Columbia - 41237	Ellis Ray & Orchestra	50s	
Bennett Tony	Fly Me To The Moon	Columbia - 43331.	Costa Don	60s	
Bennett Tony	I Left My Heart In San Francisco	Columbia - 42332	Manning Marty	60s	

Bennett Tony	I Wanna Be Around	Columbia - 42634	Manning Marty	60s	
Bennett Tony	In The Middle Of An Island	Columbia - 40965	Ellis Ray & Orchestra	50s	
Bennett Tony	It Had To Be You	Columbia - CD - 66214	Sharon Ralph Trio	90s	
Bennett Tony	Love Song - From Beauty And . . .	Columbia - 41086	Faith Percy Orch	50s	
Bennett Tony	Love Story theme	Columbia - 45316		70s	
Bennett Tony & K. D. Lang	Moonglow	Columbia - CD - 66214	Sharon Ralph Trio	90s	
Bennett Tony	Rags To Riches	Columbia - 40048	Faith Percy Orch	50s	
Bennett Tony	Speak Low	Columbia - CD - 66214	Sharon Ralph Trio	90s	
Bennett Tony	Steppin Out With My Baby	Columbia - CD - 66214	Sharon Ralph Trio	90s	
Bennett Tony	Stranger In Paradise	Columbia - 40121	Faith Percy Orch	50s	
Bennett Tony	That Ole Devil Moon	Columbia - CD - 66214	Sharon Ralph Trio	90s	
Bennett Tony & Elvis Costello	They Cant Take That Away From Me	Columbia - CD - 66214	Sharon Ralph Trio	90s	
Berry Chuck	Promised Land	Chess - 1916		60s	
Berry Chuck	Reeling And Rockin	Chess - 1683		50s	
Big Maybelle or Mabel Smith	My Mother's Eyes	Rojac - 1003		60s	
Bigeou Esther	Basin Street Blues - AC	Okeh - 8058		20s	
Bigeou Esther	Memphis Blues The - AC	Okeh - 8026	contralto Solo With Piano Acc.	30s	
Bigeou Esther	St Louis Blues - AC	Okeh - 8026		20s	
Biltmore Rhythm Boys*	Bye Bye Blues	Columbia - 2258 - D	Lown Bert Orch.	30s	
Biltmore Trio*	Sweet Sue Just You	Columbia - 1361 - D	Burtnett E. & LA. B. Orch	20s	
Black Ted	Love Letters In The Sand	Victor - 22799	Black Ted Orch	30s	
Blaine Vivian	That's For Me	Film Master - 1945		40s	
Blake Blind	Bad Feeling Blues	Paramount - 12497		20s	
Blake Blind - (as George Martin)	Diddie Wa Diddie	Broadway - 5105		20s	
Blake Blind	Doggin Me Mama Blues	Paramount - 12673	vocal and guitar	20s	
Blake Blind	Early Moring Blues	Paramount - 12387		20s	
Blake Blind	Hasting Street Blues	Paramount - 12863		20s	
Blake Blind	One Time Blues	Paramount - 12479	vocal guitar	20s	
Blake Blind	Rambling Mama Blues	Paramount - 12767		20s	
Blake Blind	West Coast Blues	Paramount - 12387		20s	
Blake Eubie	You Rascal You	Film Master - 1935	Blake Eubie Orch	30s	
Bland Billy	Let The Little Girl Dance	Old Town - 1076		60s	
Boles John	Song Of The Dawn	Film Master - 1930		30s	
Boone Pat	Love Letters in the sand	Dot - 15570		50s	
Boone Pat	Tennessee Saterday Night	Dot - 15377		50s	
Booze Bea	See See Rider Blues	Decca - 8633		30s	
Borgen Bob*	Best Things In Life Are Free The	Victor - 20872	Olson George Orch.	20s	
Boswell Connie	Boulevard Of Broken Dreams The	Brunswick - 6871		30s	
Boswell Connie	Blue Moon	Brunswick - 7363	Young Victor Orch	30s	
Boswell Connie	Blueberry Hill	Decca - 3366	Sosnik Harry Orch	30s	
Boswell Connie	Carioca	Brunswick - 6871		30s	
Boswell Connie	Concentratin' On You	Brunswick - 6210	Young Victor Orch	30s	
Boswell Connie	Dear Old Southland	Brunswick - 20110	Nichols Red & His Orch	30s	
Boswell Connie	Deep In A Dream	Decca - 2259	Herman Woody Orch	30s	
Boswell Connie	Dinner At Eight	Brunswick - 6640		30s	
Boswell Connie	Emperor Jones	Brunswick - 6640		30s	
Boswell Connie	Gypsy Love Song	Decca - 1678	Crosby Bob Orch	30s	
Boswell Connie	Heart And Soul	Decca - 2028	Sinatra Ray & Orch	30s	
Boswell Connie	Hummin' To Myself	Brunswick - 6332		30s	
Boswell Connie	I Cover The Waterfront	Brunswick - 6592	Young Victor Orch	30s	
Boswell Connie	I Let A Song Go Out Of My . . .	Decca - 1896	Sinatra Ray Orch	30s	
Boswell Connie	Im All Dressed Up With A Broken Heart	Brunswick - 6162	Young, Victor Orch	30s	
Boswell Connie	Im Gonna Cry - Crying Blues - AC	Victor - 19639		20s	
Boswell Connie	In A Little Second Hand Store	Brunswick - 6552		30s	
Boswell Connie	In Other Words We're Through	Brunswick - 6754		30s	
Boswell Connie	I'snt It A Shame	Brunswick - 7303	Grier Jimmy Orch	30s	
Boswell Connie	Its The Talk Of The Town	Brunswick - 6632		30s	
Boswell Connie	Let It Snow Let It Snow	Decca - 18741	Morgan Russ Orch	30s	
Boswell Connie	Lost In A Fog	Brunswick - 7303	Grier Jimmy Orch	30s	
Boswell Connie	Make Love To Me	Victor - LP - LPM - 1426	Origional Memphis Five	30s	
Boswell Connie	Me Minus You	Brunswick - 6405		30s	
Boswell Connie	Mighty Lak' A Rose	Decca - 18423	Young Victor Orch	40s	
Boswell Connie	Moon Over Miami	Decca - 657		40s	
Boswell Connie	My Lips Want Kisses	Brunswick - 6297		30s	
Boswell Connie	Nearness Of You The	Decca - 3366	Sosnik Harry Orch	40s	
Boswell Connie	Night When Love Was Born The	Brunswick - 6332		30s	
Boswell Connie	On The Beach At Bali Bali	Decca - 829	Crosby Bob Orch	40s	
Boswell Connie	On The Isle Of May	Decca - 3004		30s	
Boswell Connie	Rampart Street Blues	Brunswick - 20110	Nichols Red & His Orch	30s	
Boswell Connie	River Stay Way From My Door	Brunswick - 21000	Nichols Red & His Orch	30s	
Boswell Connie	Rivers Taking Care Of Me The	Brunswick - 6603		30s	
Boswell Connie	Sand In My Shoes	Decca - 3893	Young Victor Orch	40s	
Boswell Connie	Say It Isnt So	Brunswick - 6393		30s	

Boswell Connie	That Old Feeling	Decca - 1420	Pollack Ben Orch	30s	
Boswell Connie	They Cant Take That Away . . .	Decca - 2879	Young Victor Orch	30s	
Boswell Connie	Time On My Hands	Brunswick - 6210		40s	
Boswell Connie	Under A Blacket Of Blue	Brunswick - 6603		30s	
Boswell Connie	Underneath The Arches	Brunswick - 6483		30s	
Boswell Connie	Washboard Blues	Brunswick=20108	Casa Loma Orchestra	30s	
Boswell Connie	What Is It	Brunswick - 6162	Young Victor Orch	30s	
Boswell Connie	When My Sugar Walks Down The Street	Victor - LP - LPM - 1426	Origional Memphis Five	50s	
Boswell Connie	Where Are You	Decca - 1160	Pollack Ben Orch	30s	
Boswell Connie	Whispers In The Dark	Decca - 1420	Pollack Ben Orch	30s	
Boswell Connie	With Every Breath I Take	Brunswick - 7354		30s	
Boswell Sisters	Alexander's Ragtime Band	Brunswick - 7412		30s	
Boswell Sisters	An Evening In Carolina	Brunswick - 6218		30s	
Boswell Sisters	Between The Devil And The . . .	Brunswick - 6291	Dorsey Brothers Orch	30s	
Boswell Sisters	Charlie Two Step	Brunswick - 6418	Dorsey Brothers Orch	30s	
Boswell Sisters	Cheek To Cheek	Decca - 574		30s	
Boswell Sisters	Coffee In The Morning . . .	Brunswick - 6733.		30s	
Boswell Sisters	Crazy People	Film Master - 1932		30s	
Boswell Sisters	Darktown Strutters Ball	Columbia - DO - 1255		30s	
Boswell Sisters	Does My Baby Love	Radio Master - 1930		30s	
Boswell Sisters	Doggone I've Done It	Brunswick - 6335		30s	
Boswell Sisters	Don't Tell Him What Happened.	Okeh - 41470	Boswell Martha - piano	30s	
Boswell Sisters	Down Amoung The Sweltering.	Brunswick - 6418	Dorsey Brothers Orch	30s	
Boswell Sisters	Down On The Delta	Brunswick - 6395	Dorsey Brothers Orch	30s	
Boswell Sisters	Every Little Moment	Brunswick - 7454		30s	
Boswell Sisters	Everybody Loves My Baby	Brunswick - 6783		30s	
Boswell Sisters	Forty Second Street	Brunswick - 6545		30s	
Boswell Sisters	Hand Me Down My Walking Cane	Brunswick - 6335		30s	
Boswell Sisters	Heebie Jeebies	Brunswick - 6193	Dorsey Brothers Orch	30s	
Boswell Sisters	Heebie Jeebies	Okeh - 41444		30s	
Boswell Sisters	Heebie Jeebies	Radio Master - 1934		30s	
Boswell Sisters	I Found A Million Dollar Baby	Brunswick - 6128	Young Victor Orch	30s	
Boswell Sisters	I'll Never Say Never Again	Radio Master - 1935		30s	
Boswell Sisters	Im Gonna Sit Right Down & . . .	Decca - 671		20s	
Boswell Sisters	Im In Training For You	Radio Master - 1930		30s	
Boswell Sisters	Im On A Diet Of Love	Radio Master - 1930		30s	
Boswell Sisters	Its The Girl	Brunswick - 6151	Dorsey Brothers Orch	30s	
Boswell Sisters	Lawd You Made The Night Too . . .	Brunswick - 20109	Redman Don Orch	30s	
Boswell Sisters	Life Is Just A Bowl Of Cherries	Brunswick - 20102	Young Victor Orch	30s	
Boswell Sisters	Louisiana Hayride	Brunswick - 6470		30s	
Boswell Sisters	Minnie The Moochers Wedding.	Brunswick - 6442		30s	
Boswell Sisters	Minnie The Moochers Wedding.	Radio Master - 1933	Dorsey Brothers Orch.	30s	
Boswell Sisters	Mood Indigo	Brunswick - 6470		30s	
Boswell Sisters	Music Goes Round And Round The	Decca - 671		30s	
Boswell Sisters	Nights When Im Lonely - AC	Victor - 19639		20s	
Boswell Sisters & Jimmy Grier	Object Of My Affection, The	Brunswick - 7348	Grier Jimmy Orch	30s	
Boswell Sisters	Old Man Of The Mountain, The	Brunswick - 20112	Young Victor Orch	30s	
Boswell Sisters	Old Yazoo	Brunswick - 6360		30s	
Boswell Sisters	Puttin It On	Brunswick - 6625		30s	
Boswell Sisters	Rarin' To Go	Radio Master - 1930		30s	
Boswell Sisters	Rock And Roll	Brunswick - 7302	Grier Jimmy Orch	30s	
Boswell Sisters	Rock And Roll	Film Master - 1934		30s	
Boswell Sisters	Roll On Mississippi Roll On	Brunswick - 6109		30s	
Boswell Sisters	Shout Sister Shout	Brunswick - 6109		30s	
Boswell Sisters	Shout Sister Shout	Film Master - 1932		30s	
Boswell Sisters	Shuffle Off To Buffalo	Brunswick - 6545		30s	
Boswell Sisters	Sing A Little Jingle	Brunswick - 6128	Young Victor Orch	30s	
Boswell Sisters	Song Of The Dawn	Radio Master - 1930		30s	
Boswell Sisters	Stardust	Brunswick - 20100	Young Victor Orch	30s	
Boswell Sisters	Strange As It Seems	Brunswick - 20112	Young Victor Orch	30s	
Boswell Sisters	Swanee Mammy	Brunswick - 6625		30s	
Boswell Sisters	That's How Rhythm Was Born	Brunswick - 6650		30s	
Boswell Sisters	That's Love	Brunswick - 20102	Young Victor Orch	30s	
Boswell Sisters	There'll Be Some Changes Made	Brunswick - 6291	Dorsey Brothers Orch	30s	
Boswell Sisters	There's A Wah - Wah Gal In . . .	Radio Master - 1930		30s	
Boswell Sisters	This Is The Missus	Brunswick - 20102	Young Victor Orch	30s	
Boswell Sisters	Top Hat White Tie And Tails	Decca - 574		30s	
Boswell Sisters	Was That The Human Thing To Do	Brunswick - 6257		30s	
Boswell Sisters	Way Back Home	Brunswick - 7454		30s	
Boswell Sisters	We Just Couldent Say Goodby	Brunswick - 6360		30s	
Boswell Sisters	We're In The Money	Brunswick - 6596		30s	
Boswell Sisters	We're On The Highway To . . .	Victor - 22500	Taylor Jackie Orch	30s	
Boswell Sisters*	We're On The Highway To . . .	Victor - 22500	Taylor Jackie Orch	30s	

Boswell Sisters	Wha'd Do To Me	Brunswick - 6083	Dorsey Brothers Orch	30s	
Boswell Sisters	When I Take My Sugar To Tea	Brunswick - 6083	Dorsey Brothers Orch	30s	
Boswell Sisters	When Its Sleepy Time Down.	Film Master - 1932		30s	
Boswell Sisters	When The Little Red Roses . . .	Radio Master - 1930		30s	
Boswell Sisters	Why Don't You Practice What You . . .	Brunswick - 6929		30s	
Boswell Sisters	You Aught To Be In Pictures	Brunswick - 6798	Dorsey Brothers Orch	30s	
Bowlly Al*	All Of Me	Durium - EN - 8	Durium Dance Band	30s	
Bowlly Al*	Blue Moon	Victor - 24849	Noble Ray And His Orch	30s	
Bowlly Al*	By The Fireside	Durium - EN - 0	Durium Dance Band	30s	
Bowlly Al*	Close Your Eyes	Decca - F - 3783	Stone Lee Band	30s	
Bowlly Al*	Dinner For One Please James	Victor - 25187	Noble Ray And His Orch	30s	
Bowlly Al*	Easy To Love	Victor - 25422	Noble Ray and HisOrch	30s	
Bowlly Al	Goodnight Angel	HMV-BD-565		30s	
Bowlly Al*	Goodnight Sweetheart	Victor - 25016	Noble Ray and His Orch	30s	
Bowlly Al*	Goodnight Vienna	Durium - EN - 9	Durium Dance Band	30s	
Bowlly Al*	If You Love Me	Victor - 25240	Noble Ray and His Orch	30s	
Bowlly Al*	Isle Of Capri	Victor - 24777	Noble Ray And His Orch	30s	
Bowlly Al*	I've Got You Under My Skin	Victor - 25422	Noble Ray and His Orch	30s	
Bowlly Al*	Lady Of Spain	Victor - 22774	Noble Ray And His Orch	30s	
Bowlly Al*	Love Is The Sweetest Thing	Victor - 24333	Noble Ray And His Orch	30s	
Bowlly Al*	Midnight The Stars And You	Victor - 24700	Noble Ray And His Orch	30s	
Bowlly Al*	Red Sails In The Sunset	Victor - 25142	Noble Ray And His Orch	30s	
Bowlly Al*	Save The Last Dance For Me	Durium - EN - 8	Durium Dance Band	30s	
Bowlly Al*	Very Thought Of You The	Victor - 24657	Noble Ray And His Orch	30s	
Bowlly Al*	Was That The Human Thing To Do	Durium - EN - 10	Durium Dance Band	30s	
Bowlly Al*	Weep No More My Baby	Decca - F - 3783	Stone Lee Band	30s	
Bowlly Al*	When Im With You	Victor - 25336	Noble Ray And His Orch	30s	
Bowlly Al*	When You've Got A Little . . .	Victor - 24720	Noble Ray And His Orch	30s	
Bowlly Al*	You Can't Stop Me From Loving You	Decca - F - 2487	Fox Roy Band	30s	
Bowlly Al*	Youre My Thrill	Decca - F - 3980	Stone Lew Orch	30s	
Boyer Anita*	Bewitched	Victor - 27344	Reisman Leo Orch	40s	
Boyer Anita*	Love Of My Life	Victor - 26790	Shaw Artie & Orchestra	40s	
Bradley Nita*	Goodnight Angel	Brunswick-8054	Shaw Art and his new Music	30s	
Brennan Walter	Old Time Religion	Film Master - 1941		40s	
Brenston Jackie	Rocket 88	Chess - 113	Delta Cats his	50s	
Brice Fanny	Cooking Breakfast For The . . .	Victor - 22310		20s	
Brice Fanny	Id Rather Be Blue Over You	Victor - 21815		20s	
Brice Fanny	If You Want The Rainbow	Victor - 21815		20s	
Brice Fanny	My Man	Film Master - 1928		20s	
Brice Fanny	My Man	Victor - 21168		20s	
Brice Fanny	My Man - AC	Victor - 46263		20s	
Brice Fanny	Second Hand Rose - AC	Victor - 46263		20s	
Brice Fanny	Sheik Of Avenue B	Victor - 25323		20s	
Brice Fanny	When A Woman Loves A Man	Victor - 22310		20s	
Britt Elton	There's A Star Spangled . . .	Bluebird - B - 9000		40s	
Broonzy (Big Bill)	All By Myself	Okeh - 06427		30s	
Broonzy (Big Bill)	Baby I Done Got Wise	Vocalion - 04429		30s	
Broonzy - (Big Bill Johnson)	Big Bill Blues	Champion - 16426		30s	
Broonzy (Big Bill)	Big Bills Milk Cow No 2	Romeo - 6 - 07 - 57		30s	
Broonzy (Big Bill)*	Brown Skin Shuffle	Champion - 40074	Johnson Ans Smith	30s	
Broonzy (Big Bill)	Friendless Blues	Bluebird - B - 5535		30s	
Broonzy - (Big Bill & Thomps)	House Rent Stomp	Paramount - 12656		20s	
Broonzy - (Sammy Sampson)	I Cant Be Satisfied	Perfect - 157		30s	
Broonzy (Big Bill)	I Love My Whisky	Mercury - 8122		40s	
Broonzy (Big Bill)	I'll Be Back Home	Bluebird - B - 5998		30s	
Broonzy (Big Bill)	Im Gonna Move To The . . .	Okeh - 6651	Chicago Five his &	40s	
Broonzy (Big Bill)	Im Woke Up Now	Okeh - 6724	Chicago Five his &	40s	
Broonzy (Big Bill)	Key To The Highway	Okeh - 6242		40s	
Broonzy (Big Bill)	Living On Easy Street	Vocalion - 4429		30s	
Broonzy (Big Bill)	Millman Blues The	Vocalion - 4280		30s	
Broonzy - (Big Bill Johnson)	Mr. Conductor Man	Champion - 16426		30s	
Broonzy (Big Bill)	Roll Them Bones	Columbia - 36879		40s	
Broonzy (Big Bill)	Serve It To Me Right	Bluebird - B - 5674		30s	
Broonzy (Big Bill)	Southern Blues	Bluebird - B - 5998		30s	
Broonzy (Big Bill)	Unimployment Stomp	Vocalion - 4378		30s	
Brown Bessie - original B. B.	Blues Singer From Alabam.	Brunswick - 4346		20s	
Brown Cleo	Boogie Woogie	Decca - 477		30s	
Brown Cleo	Breakin' In A New Pair Of Shoes	Decca - 718		30s	
Brown Cleo	Here Comes Cookie	Decca - 409		30s	
Brown Cleo	Latch On	Decca - 795		30s	
Brown Cleo	Mama Don't Want No Peas.	Decca - 512		30s	
Brown Cleo	Me And My Wonderful One	Decca - 486		30s	

Brown Cleo	Never Too Tired To Love	Decca - 512		30s	
Brown Cleo	Slow Poke	Decca - 795		30s	
Brown Cleo	Stuff Is Here And Its Mellow The	Decca - 410		30s	
Brown Cleo	Tramp	Decca Master - 1936	Hollywood Hotshots	30s	
Brown Cleo	When	Decca - 632		30s	
Brown Cleo	When Hollywood Goes Black.	Decca - 632		30s	
Brown Cleo	Who'll Chop Your Chop Suey	Decca Master - 1936	Hollywood Hotshots	30s	
Brown Cleo	Youre A Heavenly Thing	Decca - 410		30s	
Brown Cleo	You're My Fever	Decca - 718		30s	
Brown Edna - NAP	Hush A Bye Ma Baby - AC	Victor - 18214		10s	
Brown James	I Wanna Be Around	Smash (LP) - 27058		60s	
Brown James	Prisoner Of Love	King - 5739		60s	
Brown Milton	St. Louis Blues	Decca - 5070	Brown M & his Brownies	30s	
Brown Ruth	Five, Ten, Fifteen 5 - 10 - 15 Hours	Atlantic - 962		50s	
Brown Ruth	Mama, He Treats Your . . .	Atlantic - 986		50s	
Brown Ruth	Wild Wild Young Men	Atlantic - 993		50s	
Brox Sisters	Lazy - AC	Victor - 19298	Johnston Arthur - piano	20s	
Brox Sisters	Who - AC	Victor - 19631		20s	
Brox Sisters, Rhythm Boys	Bench In The Park, A	Film Master - 1930		30s	
Bruce Virginia	I've Got You Under My Skin	Film Master - 1936		30s	
Bryant Laura	Dentist Chair Blues	QRS - R - 7055		20s	
Bullock Chick	About A Quarter To Nine	Melotone - M - 13389	Levee Loungers, & his	30s	
Bullock Chick	Alcoholic Ward Blues	Oriole - 1903	Levee Loungers, & his	30s	
Bullock Chick*	Annie Doesent Live Here . . .	Conqueror - 8279	Kahn Art Orchestra	30s	
Bullock Chick	Are You Making Any Money	Conqueror - 8217		30s	
Bullock Chick	Dixie Lee	Melotone - M - 12879	Levee Loungers, & his	30s	
Bullock Chick*	Green Eyes	Victor - 22729	Aspiazu Don And His . . .	30s	
Bullock Chick	Have You Ever Been Lonely	Melotone - M - 12680		30s	
Bullock Chick	House Is Haunted, The	Perfect - 15922	Rollins Todd And His Orch	30s	
Bullock Chick*	I Want You For Myself	Conqueror - 7779	Sanella Andy And His.	30s	
Bullock Chick	Im Living In A Great Big Way	Melotone - M - 13389	Levee Loungers, & his	30s	
Bullock Chick*	I'm One Of God's Children . . .	Victor - 22632	Shilkret Nat & the Victor Orch	30s	
Bullock Chick	In A Little Red Barn	Melotone - M - 13052	Levee Loungers, & his	30s	
Bullock Chick*	In A Shanty In Old Shanty Town	Victor - 24050	Black Ted Orch	30s	
Bullock Chick*	It's The Girl	Banner - 32236	Haring Bob And His Orch	30s	
Bullock Chick	Lazy Lou"siana Moon	Banner - 0671	Levee Loungers, & his	30s	
Bullock Chick & Three Waring Girls*	Let's Have Another Cup Of . . .	Victor - 22936	Waring Fred Pennsylvanians	30s	
Bullock Chick	Mighty River	Perfect - 15678	Levee Loungers, & his	30s	
Bullock Chick	My Gal Sal	Melotone - M - 6 06 10	Levee Loungers, & his	30s	
Bullock Chick	On The Banks Of The Wabash	Okeh - 6261	All Star Orchestra his	40s	
Bullock Chick - (High Hatters)	Singing The Blues	Victor - 22809	Joy Lenard Orch.	30s	
Bullock Chick	Smoke Gets In Your Eyes	Perfect - 15860	Levee Loungers, & his	30s	
Bullock Chick*	Stardust	Perfect - 11326	Smeck Roy Vita Trio	30s	
Bullock Chick	Stars Fell On Alabama	Perfect - 13078	Levee Loungers, & his	30s	
Bullock Chick*	Sugar Blues	Vocalion - 2805	Williams Clarence Orch	30s	
Bullock Chick	There Ought To Be Moonlight . . .	Perfect - 12718		30s	
Bullock Chick	Theres A Cabin In The Pines	Perfect - 15775	Levee Loungers, & his	30s	
Bullock Chick	Underneath The Harlem Moon	Perfect - 15678	Levee Loungers, & his	30s	
Bullock Chick	Wagon Wheels	Perfect - 15894	Levee Loungers, & his	30s	
Bullock Chick	When The New Moon Shines.	Banner - 33139	Levee Loungers, & his	30s	
Bullock Chick	Winter Wonderland	Perfect - 13103	Levee Loungers, & his	30s	
Bullock Chick	You've Got To Get High To Sing	Melotone - M - 6 06 13	Levee Loungers, & his	30s	
Burke Solomon	I Really Don't Want To Know	Atlantic - 2157		60s	
Burnett J C	Will The Circle Be Unbroken	Columbia - 14385 - D		20s	
Burr Henry	Are You Lonesome Tonight	Victor - 20873		20s	
Burr Henry	Come Down Ma Ev'ning Star - AC	Columbia - A1405		20s	
Burr Henry & A, Campbell - NAP	For Me And My Gal - AC	Pathe - 20163		00s	
Burr Henry & Billy Murray	I Wonder Where My Baby Is Tonight	Victor - 19864		20s	
Burr Henry	I Wonder who's Kissing Her Now - AC	Columbia - A707		00s	
Burr Henry	Mother A Word That Means. - AC	Victor - 17913		10s	
Burr Henry	Peg Of My Heart - AC	Columbia - 1404		10s	
Burr Henry	When You And I Were Young . . . - AC	Columbia - 5088		00s	
Butterbeans & Susie	He Likes It Slow - AC	Okeh - 8355		20s	
Cagney James	Shanghai Lil	Film - Master - 1933		30s	
Calloway Blanche	Blue Memories	Victor - 22896	Calloway B & Her Joy Boys	30s	
Calloway Blanche	Catch On	Perfect - 16054	Calloway B & Her Joy Boys	30s	
Calloway Blanche	Concentratin On You	Victor - 22862	Calloway B & Her Joy Boys	30s	
Calloway Blanche	Growlin' Dan	Victor - 22866	Calloway B & HerJoy Boys	30s	
Calloway Blanche	I Got What It Takes	Victor - 22866	Calloway B & Her Joy Boys	30s	
Calloway Blanche	I Need Lovin'	Victor - 22641	Calloway B & Her Joy Boys	30s	
Calloway Blanche	Im Getting Myself Ready For You	Victor - 22659	Calloway B & Her Joy Boys	30s	

Calloway Blanche	It's Right Here or You	Victor - 22717	Calloway B & Her Joy Boys	30s	
Calloway Blanche	Just A Crazy Song	Victor - 22661	Calloway B & Her Joy Boys	30s	
Calloway Blanche	Last Dollar	Victor - 22862	Calloway B & Her Joy Boys	30s	
Calloway Blanche	Lazy Womans Blues	Okeh - 8279		20s	
Calloway Blanche	Lonesome Lovesick Blues	Okeh - 8279		20s	
Calloway Blanche	Louisiana Liza	Vocalion - 3112	Calloway B & Her Orch	30s	
Calloway Blanche	Loveless Love (Careless Love)	Victor - 22659	Calloway B & Her Joy Boys	30s	
Calloway Blanche	Make Me Know It	Victor - 22736	Calloway B & Her Joy Boys	30s	
Calloway Blanche	What's A Poor Girl Gonna Do	Melotone - M - 13191	Calloway B & Her Orch	30s	
Calloway Blanche*	When I Cant Be With You	Timely Tunes - C - 1578	Armstrong F & His S.	30s	
Calloway Blanche	Without That Gal	Victor - 22733	Calloway B & Her Joy Boys	30s	
Calloway Cab	Black Rhythm	Brunswick - 6141	Calloway Cab Orch	30s	
Calloway Cab & Palmer Brothers	Blues In The Night	Okeh - 6422	Calloway Cab Orch	40s	
Calloway Cab	Cabin In The Cotton	Brunswick - 6292	Calloway Cab Orch	30s	
Calloway Cab	Chinese Rhythm	Brunswick - 6992	Calloway Cab Orch	30s	
Calloway Cab	Copper Colored Gal	Brunswick - 7748	Calloway Cab Orch	30s	
Calloway Cab & Mills Brothers*	Doing The New Low Down	Brunswick - 6513	Redman Don Orch	30s	
Calloway Cab	Eadie Was A Lady	Melotone - M - 12583	Calloway Cab Orch	30s	
Calloway Cab & Chick Bullock	Git Along	Perfect - 12843	Calloway Cab Orch+	30s	
Calloway Cab	Happy Feet	Banner - 0835	Calloway Cab Orch	30s	
Calloway Cab	I Gotta Right To Sing The Blues	Brunswick - 6460	Calloway Cab Orch	30s	
Calloway Cab	Is That Religion	Brunswick - 6020	Calloway Cab Orch	30s	
Calloway Cab	I've Got The World On A String	Brunswick - 6424	Calloway Cab Orch	30s	
Calloway Cab	Jitter Bug	Victor - 24592	Calloway Cab Orch	30s	
Calloway Cab	Kickin The Gong Around	Brunswick - 6209	Calloway Cab Orch	30s	
Calloway Cab	Kickin The Gong Around	Film Master - 1932	Calloway Cab Orch	30s	
Calloway Cab	Lady With A Fan, (The)	Film Master - 1933	Calloway Cab Orch	30s	
Calloway Cab	Lady With A Fan, (The)	Victor - 24451	Calloway Cab Orch	30s	
Calloway Cab	Man From Harlem, (The)	Banner - 32866	Calloway Cab Orch	30s	
Calloway Cab	Minnie The Moocher	Brunswick - 6074	Calloway Cab Orch	30s	
Calloway Cab	Minnie The Moocher	Film Master - 1932	Calloway Cab Orch	30s	
Calloway Cab	Minnie The Moocher	Film Master - 1980	Calloway Cab Orch	80s	
Calloway Cab	Minnie The Moochers Wedding.	Brunswick - 6321	Calloway Cab Orch	30s	
Calloway Cab	Reefer Man	Banner - 32944	Calloway Cab Orch	30s	
Calloway Cab	St James Infirmary	Film Master - 1933		30s	
Calloway Cab	St James Infirmery	Film Master - 1932	Calloway Cab Orch	30s	
Calloway Cab	St. James Infirmary	Brunswick - 6105	Calloway Cab Orch	30s	
Calloway Cab	St. Louis Blues	Brunswick - 4936	Calloway Cab Orch	30s	
Calloway Cab	Strictly Cullurd Affair	Brunswick - 6292	Calloway Cab Orch	30s	
Calloway Cab	Utt Da Zah - The Taylor Song	Vocalion - 5062	Calloway Cab Orch	30s	
Calloway Cab	Vipers Drag (The)	Perfect - 15412	Calloway Cab Orch	30s	
Calloway Cab	Virginia, Georgia And Caroline	Okeh - 6717	Calloway Cab Orch	40s	
Calloway Cab	You Rascal You	Brunswick - 6196	Calloway Cab Orch	30s	
Calloway Cab	Zaz - Zuh - Zaz	Victor - 24557	Calloway Cab Orch	30s	
Cantor Eddie	Argentines, the Portuges,. - AC	Emerson - 10200		20s	
Cantor Eddie	Ballyhoo Theme - Cheer Up	HOW - K - 6	Spitalny Phil dir. Orch	30s	
Cantor Eddie	Build A Little Home	Film - Master - 1933		30s	
Cantor Eddie	Dixie Made Us Jass Band. - AC	Emerson - 10263		20s	
Cantor Eddie	He Loves It - AC	Columbia - A3754		20s	
Cantor Eddie	I Faw Down And Go Boom	Victor - 21862		20s	
Cantor Eddie	If You Knew Susie - AC	Columbia - A364		20s	
Cantor Eddie	Ive Got The Yes We Have. - AC	Columbia - A3964		20s	
Cantor Eddie	Making Woopie - NAP	Victor - 21831	Shilkret Nat Orchestra	20s	
Cantor Eddie	Man On The Flying Trapeze The	Melotone - 13001		30s	
Cantor Eddie	Margie - AC	Emerson - 10301		20s	
Cantor Eddie	My Baby Just Cares For Me	Film Master - 1930		30s	
Cantor Eddie	No No Nora - AC	Columbia - A3964		20s	
Cantor Eddie	That's The Kind Of Baby For.	Aeolian Vocalion - 1220		10s	
Cantor Eddie	That's The Kind Of Baby For . . . - AC	Victor - 18342	Bourdon Rosario Orch	10s	
Cantor Eddie	There's Nothing Too Good For.	Victor - 28851	Arnheim Gus Orch	30s	
Cantor Eddie	When It Comes To Lovin . . . - AC	Emerson - 10105		10s	
Cantor Eddie	You Aint Heard Nothin Yet - AC	Emerson - 10134		10s	
Cantor Eddie	You Don't Need The W . . . - AC	Pathe - 22163		10s	
Cardinals the	Door Is Still Open	Atlantic-1054		50s	
Cardwell Jack	Death Of Hank Williams The	King - 1172		50s	
Carmichael Hoagy*	Washboard Blues	Victor - 35877	Whiteman Paul Orch.	20s	
Carpenter Thelma	All Of My Life	Musicraft - 330	Chittison Herman Trio	40s	
Carpenter Thelma & Four . . .	American Lullaby	Majestic - 7254	Wilson Garland Orch	40s	
Carpenter Thelma	Bali Ha'I	Victor - LK - 1008	Goodman Al Orch	50s	
Carpenter Thelma	Gypse Blues	Victor - (LP) - LPM - 3154	Blake Eubie Orch	50s	
Carpenter Thelma	Harlem On My Mind	Majestic - 1104	Wilson Garland Orch	40s	

Carpenter Thelma	Hurry Home	Majestic - 1023	Freeman Bud Orch	40s	
Carpenter Thelma*	I Dident Know About You	Columbia - 36766	Basie Count Orch	40s	
Carpenter Thelma	I'm A Fool About Someone	Columbia - 30141	Ayres Mitchell Orch	40s	
Carpenter Thelma	I'm Just Wild About Harry	Victor - (LP) - LPM - 3154	Blake Eubie Orch	50s	
Carpenter Thelma	Jug Of Wine A	Majestic - 1030	Sauter Eddie dir. Orch	40s	
Carpenter Thelma	Just A Sittin And A Rockin	Majestic - 1023	Shelton Earl dir Orch.	40s	
Carpenter Thelma	Just You Just Me	Columbia - 30141	Ayres Mitchell Orch	40s	
Carpenter Thelma*	Love Growns On The White . . .	Brunswick - 8455	Wilson Teddy Orch	30s	
Carpenter Thelma	My Guys Come Back	Majestic - 1017	Freeman Bud Orch	40s	
Carpenter Thelma	Pie In A Basket	Columbia - 30212	Henderson Luther dir	50s	
Carpenter Thelma	Seems Like Old Times	Majestic - 1030	Sauter Eddie dir. Orch	40s	
Carpenter Thelma*	She's Funny That Way	Bluebird - B - 10477	Hawkins Coleman Orch	30s	
Carpenter Thelma	These Foolish Things Remind.	Majestic - 1017	Freeman Bud Orch	40s	
Carpenter Thelma*	This Is The Moment	Brunswick - 8455	Wilson Teddy Orch	30s	
Carpenter Thelma	Yes Im Lonesome Tonight	Coral - 62241		60s	
Carr Dora	Cow Cow Blues - AC	Okeh - 8250		20s	
Carr Leroy	How Long How Long Blues	Vocalion - 1191		20s	
Carr Leroy	Shinnin' Pistol	Vocalion Master - 1934		30s	
Carr Leroy	Suicide Blues	Vocalion Master - 1934		30s	
Carr Leroy	When The Sun Goes Down	Bluebird - B - 5877		30s	
Carter Bo	Banana In Your Fruit Basket	Columbia - 14661 - D		30s	
Carter Bo	My Pencil Won't Write No.	Okeh - 8912		30s	
Carter Bo	Please Warm My Weiner	Bluebird - B - 6058		30s	
Carter Bo	Pussy Cat Blues	Columbia - 14661 - D		20s	
Carter Family & J. Rodgers	Blue Yodel - T For Texas	Bluebird - B - 6762	Carter Family, the	30s	
Carter Family, the	Can The Circle Be Unbroken	Banner - 3465	Carter Family, the	30s	
Carter Family, the	Cannon Ball Blues	Conquer - 8816	Carter Family, the	30s	
Carter Family, the	Hello Stranger	Decca - 5479	Carter Family, the	30s	
Carter Family, the	I Never Will Marry	Bluebird - B - 8350	Carter Family, the	30s	
Carter Family, the	Im Thinging Tonight Of My . . .	Perfect - 35 - 09 - 23	Carter Family, the	30s	
Carter Family, the	Jealous Hearted Me	Decca - 5241	Carter Family, the	30s	
Carter Family, the	Keep On The Sunny Side	Victor - 21434	Carter Family, the	20s	
Carter Family, the	Little Darlin Pal Of Mine	Victor - 23574	Carter Family, the	30s	
Carter Family, the	Lonesome Valley	Victor - 23541	Carter Family, the	30s	
Carter Family, the	My Clinch Mountain Home	Victor - 23574	Carter Family, the	30s	
Carter Family, the	My Clinch Mountain Home	Victor - V40058	Carter Family, the	20s	
Carter Family, the	No Depression	Decca - 5242	Carter Family, the	30s	
Carter Family, the	Wabash Cannonball	Victor - 23731	Carter Family, the	30s	
Carter Family, the	Wildwood Flower	Victor - V40000	Carter Family, the	20s	
Carter Family, the	Worried Man Blues	Victor - 40317	Carter Family, the	30s	
Caruso Enrico	O Sole Mio - AC	Victor - 87243		00s	
Casman Nellie	Yosel - AC	Emerson - 13238 - AC		10s	
Cash Johnny	Folsom Prison Blues	Sun - 232	Tennessee Two and	50s	
Cash Johnny	I Got Stripes	Columbia - 41427		50s	
Cash Johnny	Orange Blossom Special	Columbia - 43206		60s	
Chang Anna	How Can A Gal Say No	Film Master - 1931		30s	
Chappelear Leon - as Leon	I'm A Do Right Papa	Champion - 35174		30s	
Chappelear Leon - as Leon	Mama Don't Allow It	Montgomery Ward - 8015	Lone Star Cowboys - Leon's	30s	
Chappelear Leon - as Leon	Trouble In Mind	Decca - 5340	Lone Star Cowboys - Leon's	30s	
Charles Ray	Borne To Lose	ABC Paramount - 10330		60s	
Charles Ray	Georgia On My Mind	ABC Paramount - 10135		60s	
Charles Ray	Ive Got A Woman	Atlantic - 1050		50s	
Charles Ray	Let The Good Times Roll	Atlantic - 2047		50s	
Charles Ray	You Don't Know Me	ABC Paramount - 10345		60s	
Chester Charles*	Did I Remember	Bluebird - B - 6476	Fields Shep & his R . . .	30s	
Chevalier Maurice	Louise	Victor - 21819	Griselle Tom orch. dir	20s	
Chevalier Maurice	Love Me Tonight	Film Master - 1932		30s	
Chevalier Maurice	My Ideal	Victor - 22542		30s	
Chevalier Maurice	Walking My Baby Back Home	Victor - 22634		30s	
Chevalier Maurice	You Brought A New Kind Of Love To Me	Film Master - 1930		30s	
Chevalier Maurice	You Brought A New Kind Of Love To Me	Victor - 22405		30s	
Christian Little Delk	Sweethearts On Parade	Okeh - 8650		20s	
Christy June*	How High The Moon	Capital - 15117	Kenton Stan Orch	40s	
Christy June	I Should Care	Capital - LP - H - 516	Rugolo Pete Orch	50s	
Christy June	I'll Take Ramance	Capital - LP - H - 516	Rugolo Pete Orch	50s	
Christy June	It Could Happen To You	Capital - LP - H - 516	Rugolo Pete Orch	50s	
Christy June	Lonely House	Capital - LP - H - 516	Rugolo Pete Orch	50s	
Christy June	Midnight Sun	Capital - LP - H - 516	Rugolo Pete Orch	50s	
Christy June & Nat Cole	Nat Meets June	Columbia - 37293	Metronome All Stars	40s	
Christy June*	Shoo - Fly Pie And Apple Pan.	Capital - 235	Kenton, Stan Orch	40s	
Christy June	Something Cool	Capital - LP - H - 516	Rugolo Pete Orch	50s	
Christy June*	Soothe Me	Capital - 15031	Kenton Stan Orch	40s	
Christy June	Stranger Called The Blues A	Capital - LP - H - 516	Rugolo Pete Orch	50s	

Christy June*	Tampico	Capital - 202	Kenton Stan Orch	40s	
Christy June*	Willow Weep For Me	Capital - 15179	Kenton Stan Orch	40s	
Churchill Savannah	I Want To Be Loved	Manor - 1046	Sentimentalists &	40s	
Churchill Winston	This Was Their Finest Hour	HMV - 3200	SPOKEN WORD	40s	
Clark Buddy*	Chiquita Banana	Columbia - 37051	Cugat Xavier And His . . .	40s	
Clark Buddy	I Love You So Much It Hurts	Columbia - 38406	Hagen Earle Orch	40s	
Clark Buddy	Lets Be Buddies	Okeh - 5912	with Orchestra	40s	
Clark Buddy	Linda	Columbia - 37215	Noble Ray Orch	40s	
Clark Buddy	On A Little Street in Singapore	Varsity - 8101	with Orchestra	30s	
Clark Buddy* as 'vocal refrain'	On Your Toes	Brunswick - 7633	Newman Ruby Orch	30s	
Clark Buddy	Peg Of My Heart	Columbia - 37392	Ayres Mitchell Orch	40s	
Clark Buddy*	Rhythm Of The Rhumba, The	Columbia - 3013 - D	Gluskin Lud & His Cont.	30s	
Clark Buddy*	Sailboat In the Moonlight A	Variety - 586	Hodges Johnny Orch	30s	
Clark Buddy	Spring Is Here	Vocalion - 4191	with Orchestra	30s	
Clark Buddy*	These Foolish Things . . .	Brunswick - 7676	Brandywynne & His . . .	30s	
Clark Buddy*	We Could Make Such . . .	Victor - 27358	King Wayne & his Orch.	40s	
Clark Buddy	With Every Breath I Take	Banner - 33298		30s	
Clark Elsie	He Loves It - AC	Okeh - 4725		20s	
Clark Elsie	Lovesick Blues - AC	Okeh - 4589		20s	
Clark Helen & George W Ballard	Im Forever Blowing Bubbles - AC	Edison - 50534		10s	
Clark Roy	Tip Of My Finger The	Capital-4956		60s	
Cline Patsy	Have You Ever Been Lonely	Decca - 25718		50s	
Cline Patsy	Poor Mans Roses A	Decca - 30221		50s	
Clooney Rosemary*	At A Sidewalk Penny Arcade	Columbia - 38142	Pastor Tony Orch	40s	
Clooney R. (ClooneySisters)*	A - Youre Adorable	Columbia - 38449	Pastor Tony Orch	40s	
Clooney Rosemary	Be My Life's Companion	Columbia - 39631	Faith Percy Orch	50s	
Clooney Rosemary	Beautiful Brown Eyes	Columbia - 39212	Miller Mitch cond. Orch.	50s	
Clooney Rosemary & B. Crosby	Brazil	Victor - LP - LPM - 1854	May Billy Orch	50s	
Clooney Rosemary & B. Crosby	Calcutta	Victor - LP - LPM - 1854	May Billy Orch	50s	
Clooney Rosemary	Come On - A My House	Columbia - 39467	Miller Mitch dir. Orchestra	50s	
Clooney R. & Mellow Men	Count Your Blessings Instead . . .	Columbia - 40370	Weston Paul dir. Orch.	50s	
Clooney Rosemary & J. Boyd	Dennis The Menace	Columbia - 39988	Luboff Norman Orch	50s	
Clooney Rosemary & B. Crosby	Fancy Meeting You Here	Victor - LP - LPM - 1854	May Billy Orch	20s	
Clooney Rosemary*	Grieving For You	Columbia - 38383	Pastor Tony Orch	40s	
Clooney Rosemary	Half As Much	Columbia - 39710	Faith Percy Orch	50s	
Clooney Rosemary	Hey There	Columbia - 40266	Cole Buddy Orch.	50s	
Clooney Rosemary & B. Crosby	Hindustan	Victor - LP - LPM - 1854	May Billy Orch	50s	
Clooney Rosemary & B. Crosby	How About You	Victor - LP - LPM - 1854	May Billy Orch	50s	
Clooney Rosemary & B. Crosby	I Cant Get Started	Victor - LP - LPM - 1854	May Billy Orch	20s	
Clooney Rosemary & B. Crosby	Isle Of Capri	Victor - LP - LPM - 1854	May Billy Orch	50s	
Clooney Rosemary & B. Crosby	It Happened In Monterey	Victor - LP - LPM - 1854	May Billy Orch	50s	
Clooney Rosemary	Let Her Go Let Her Go	Harmony - 1071	Winterhalters Hugo Orch	40s	
Clooney Rosemary & B. Crosby	Love Wont Let You Get Away	Victor - LP - LPM - 1854	May Billy Orch	50s	
Clooney Rosemary	Love You Dident Do Right.	Film Master - 1954		50s	
Clooney Rosemary	Me And My Teddy Bear	Columbia - 38766	Faith Percy Orch	50s	
Clooney Rosemary	Mixed Emotions	Columbia - 29333	Faith Percy Orch	50s	
Clooney Rosemary & B. Crosby	On A Slow Boat To China	Victor - LP - LPM - 1854	May Billy Orch	20s	
Clooney Rosemary & T. Pastor*	Saturday Night Mood	Columbia - 38383	Pastor Tony Orch.	40s	
Clooney Rosemary & B. Crosby	Say Si Si Para vigo me voy	Victor - LP - LPM - 1854	May Billy Orch	50s	
Clooney R. (ClooneySisters)	Sisters	Columbia - 40305	Faith Percy Orch	50s	
Clooney Rosemary	Sooner Or Later	Cosmo - 721	Pastor Tony Orch	40s	
Clooney Rosemary	Suzy Snowflake	Columbia - 46255	Mattola Tony Orch	50s	
Clooney Rosemary	Tenderly	Columbia - 39648	Faith Percy Orch	50s	
Clooney Rosemary	There's A Broken Heart For.	Harmony - 1074	Winterhalters Hugo Orch	40s	
Clooney Rosemary	This Ole House	Columbia - 40266	Weston Paul dir. Orch.	50s	
Clooney R. (ClooneySisters)*	Who Killed 'Er	Columbia - 38142	Pastor Tony Orch	40s	
Clooney Rosemary & B. Crosby	You Came A Long Way From St. Louis	Victor - LP - LPM - 1854	May Billy Orch	50s	
Clooney Rosemary*	You Started Something	Columbia - 38297	Pastor Tony Orchestra	40s	
Clooney Rosemary	Zip Ah Dee Do Dah	Cosmo - 723	Pastor Tony Orchestra	40s	
Clovers	Blue Velvet	Atlantic - 1052	Clovers	50s	
Coasters	Zing Went The Strings Of My . . .	Atco - 6116	Coasters	30s	
Colbert Claudette	Give Me Liberty Or Give Me Love	Film Master - 1933		30s	
Cole Nat King	Adeste Fideles	Capital - LP - SW - 1967	Carmichael Ralph Orch	60s	
Cole Nat King	Almost Like Being In Love	Capital - LP - H - 430.	Riddle Nelson Orch	50s	
Cole Nat King	Always You	Capital - 1365	Baxter Les & Orch.	40s	

Cole Nat King	Answer Me My Love	Capital - 2687		50s	
Cole Nat King	Away In A Manger	Capital - LP - SW - 1967	Carmichael Ralph Orch	60s	
Cole Nat King	Because Of Rain	Capital - 1501	Rugolo Pete & Orch	50s	
Cole Nat King	Because Youre Mine	Capital - 2212		50s	
Cole Nat Cole Trio	Best Man, (The)	Capital - 304	Cole Nat Trio	40s	
Cole Nat King & Four Knights	Blossom Fell A	Capital - 3095	Riddle Nelson Orch	50s	
Cole Nat King	Blue Gardenia	Capital - 2389		50s	
Cole Nat King	Blue Gardinia	Film Master - 1951		50s	
Cole Nat King	Calypso Blues	Capital - 1627		40s	
Cole Nat King & Nellie Lutcher	Can I Come In For A Second	Capital - 847	Cole Nat Trio	50s	
Cole Nat King	Caroling, Caroling	Capital - LP - SW - 1967	Carmichael Ralph Orch	60s	
Cole Nat Cole Trio	Christmas Song, (The)	Capital - 3411	Cole Nat Trio	40s	
Cole Nat King	Christmas Song, (The)	Capital - 2955	Riddle Nelson Orch	50s	
Cole Nat King	Christmas Song, (The)	Capital - LP - SW - 1967	Carmichael Ralph Orch	60s	
Cole Nat King	Christmas Song, The	Capital - 2955	Riddle Nelson Orch	50s	
Cole Nat Cole Trio	Come To Baby Do	Capital - 224	Cole Nat Trio	40s	
Cole Nat King	Cradle In Bethlehem, (A)	Capital - LP - SW - 1967	Carmichael Ralph Orch	60s	
Cole Nat King	Deck The Halls	Capital - LP - SW - 1967	Carmichael Ralph Orch	60s	
Cole Nat King	Dinner For One Please James	Capital - LP - H - 430.	Riddle Nelson Orch	50s	
Cole Nat King	Don't Blame Me	Capital - 15110		50s	
Cole Nat King	First Noel, (The)	Capital - LP - SW - 1967	Carmichael Ralph Orch	60s	
Cole Nat King & Nellie Lutcher	For You My Love	Capital - 847	Cole Nat Trio	50s	
Cole Nat King	Friendless Blues	Capital - LP - W - 993	Riddle Nelson Orch	50s	
Cole Nat Cole Trio	Frim Fram Sauce, (The)	Capital - 224	Cole Nat Trio	40s	
Cole Nat Cole Trio	Gee Baby Aint I Good To You	Capital - 169	Cole Nat Trio	30s	
Cole Nat Cole Trio	Get Your Kicks On Route 66	Capital - 224	Cole Nat Trio	40s	
Cole Nat King	God Rest Ye Merry Gentlemen	Capital - LP - SW - 1444	Carmichael Ralph Orch	60s	
Cole Nat King	Handful Of Stars, (A)	Capital - LP - H - 430.	Riddle Nelson Orch	60s	
Cole Nat King	Hark The Herald Angel Sing	Capital - LP - SW - 1967	Carmichael Ralph Orch	60s	
Cole Nat Cole Trio	Hit That Jive Jack	Decca - 8630	Cole Nat Trio	40s	
Cole Nat Cole Trio	I Love You For Sentimental Reasons	Capital - 304	Cole Nat Trio	40s	
Cole Nat King	I Saw Three Ships	Capital - LP - SW - 1967	Carmichael Ralph Orch	60s	
Cole Nat King	I Was A Little Too Lonely	Film Master - 1956		50s	
Cole Nat King & Four Knights	If I May	Capital - 3095	Riddle Nelson Orch	50s	
Cole Nat King	In Other Words - Fly Me To . . .	Capital - LP - SW - 1675	Shearing George piano	60s	
Cole Nat King	It Is Better To Be By Yourself	Capital - 239	Cole Nat Trio	40s	
Cole Nat King	It Is Better To Be By Yourself	Film Master - 1946	Cole Nat Trio	40s	
Cole Nat King	Jet	Capital - 1365	Lipman Joe Orch	40s	
Cole Nat King	Joy To The World	Capital - LP - SW - 1967	Carmichael Ralph Orch	60s	
Cole Nat King	Little Boy That Santa Clause Forgot The	Capital - 2616	Riddle Nelson Orch	50s	
Cole Nat King	Little Christmas Tree	Capital - 1203	Riddle Nelson Orch	50s	
Cole Nat King	Little Girl	Capital - 15165		50s	
Cole Nat King	Little Street Where Old Folks Meet A	Capital - LP - H - 430.	Riddle Nelson Orch	50s	
Cole Nat King & Dean Martin	Long, Long Ago	Capital - 2985	May Billy Orch	50s	
Cole Nat King	Love Is Here To Stay	Capital - LP - H - 430.	Riddle Nelson Orch	60s	
Cole Nat King	Lush Life	Capital - 1672	Riddle, Nelson Orch	50s	
Cole Nat King	Memphis Blues	Capital - LP - W - 993	Riddle Nelson Orch	50s	
Cole Nat King	Mona Lisa	Capital - 1010	Baxter Les & Orch.	40s	
Cole Nat King	Mrs. Santa Clause	Capital - 2616	Riddle Nelson Orch	50s	
Cole Nat ColeTrio & J. Mercer	My Baby Likes To Be - Bop	Capital - 15026	Cole Nat Trio	40s	
Cole Nat King	My Flaming Heart	Film Master - 1953		50s	
Cole Nat King	Nature Boy	Capital - 15054	Cole Nat Trio	50s	
Cole Nat King	O Holy Night	Capital - LP - SW - 1967	Carmichael Ralph Orch	60s	
Cole Nat King	O Little Town Of Bethlehem	Capital - LP - SW - 1967	Carmichael Ralph Orch	60s	
Cole Nat King	Oh Tannenbaum	Capital - LP - SW - 1967	Carmichael Ralph Orch	60s	
Cole NatKing & D. Martin	Open Up The Doghouse - NAP	Capital - 2985		50s	
Cole Nat Cole Trio	Orange Colored Sky	Capital - 1184	Cole Nat Trio	30s	
Cole Nat King	Pretend	Capital - 2346	Riddle Nelson Orch	50s	
Cole Nat King	Ramblin Rose	Capital - 4804		60s	
Cole Nat King	Red Sails In The Sunset	Capital - 1468	Rugolo Pete & Orch	50s	
Cole Nat Cole Trio	Scotchin With The Soda	Decca - 8556	Cole Nat Trio	30s	
Cole Nat King	Send For Me	Capital - 3737		50s	
Cole Nat King	Silent Night	Capital - LP - SW - 1967	Carmichael Ralph Orch	60s	
Cole Nat Cole Trio	Slow Down	Decca - 8556	Cole Nat Trio	30s	
Cole Nat King	St. Louis Blues	Capital - LP - W - 993	Riddle Nelson Orch	50s	
Cole Nat Cole Trio	Streighten Up And Fly Right	Capital - 154	Cole Nat Trio	50s	
Cole Nat Cole Trio	Sweet Lorraine	Decca - 8520	Cole Nat Trio	40s	
Cole Nat King	Tenderly	Capital - LP - H - 430.	Riddle Nelson Orch	50s	
Cole Nat Cole Trio	That Aint Right	Decca - 8630	Cole Nat Trio	40s	
Cole Nat King	There Goes My Heart	Capital - LP - H - 430.	Riddle Nelson Orch	50s	
Cole Nat King	This Cant Be Love	Capital - LP - H - 430.	Riddle Nelson Orch	60s	
Cole Nat King	Too Young	Capital - 1449	Baxter Les & Orch.	50s	
Cole Nat King	Unforgettable	Capital - 1808	Riddle, Nelson Orch	50s	

Cole Nat King	When I Fall In Love	Film Master - 1956		50s	
Cole Nat King	Yellow Dog Blues	Capital - LP - W - 993	Riddle Nelson Orch	50s	
Cole Nat Cole Trio	You Call It Madness I Call It Love	Capital - 274	Cole Nat Trio	40s	
Collins Arthur	Bill Bailey Won't You Please . . . AC	Edison 8112		00s	
Collins Arthur	Preacher And The Bear The - AC	Edison - 900		00s	
Collins Arthur	Steamboat Bill-AC	Victor - 16937		10s	
Collins Arthur & Byron Harlan	Alexanders Ragtime Band - AC	Victor - 16908		10s	
Collins Arthur & Byron Harlan - NAP	All Coons Look Aloke To Me - AC	Edison - 7317	Ossman Vess - banjo	00s	
Collins Arthur & Byron Harlan	Cubanola Glide The - AC	Columbia - A800		10s	
Collins Arthur & Byron Harlan - NAP	Dark Town Shutters Ball, The - AC	Columbia - A2478		10s	
Collins Arthur & Byron Harlan	Memphis Blues The - AC	Columbia - A1721		10s	
Collins Arthur & Byron Harlan	Put Your Arms Around Me - AC	Zon - O - Phone - 5734		10s	
Collins Arthur & Byron Harlan - NAP	Snookey Ookums - AC	Indestructable - 3296		10s	
Collins Arthur & Vess Ossman - NAP	When The Midnight Choo . . . - AC	Edison Amberol - 1719	Ossman Vess - banjo	10s	
Columbo Russ	All Of Me	Victor - 22903		30s	
Columbo Russ	As You Desire Me	Victor - 24076	Columbo Russ & his Orch	30s	
Columbo Russ	Auf Weidersehen, My Dear	Victor - 22976		30s	
Columbo Russ	Back In Your Own Backyard	Okeh - 41037		20s	
Columbo Russ & C. Bennett	Coffee In The Morning . . .	Film Master - 1933		30s	
Columbo Russ	Easy Come Easy Go	Radio Master - 1934		30s	
Columbo Russ	Goodnight Sweetheart	Victor - 22826	Joy Leonard Orchestra	30s	
Columbo Russ	Guilty	Victor - 22801		30s	
Columbo Russ	House Is Haunted, The	Radio Master - 1934		30s	
Columbo Russ (unacredited)	How Am I To Know	Film Master - 1929		20s	
Columbo Russ	I Don't Know Why	Victor - 22801		30s	
Columbo Russ	I See Two Lovers	Special Edition - 5001	Grier Jimmy Orch	30s	
Columbo Russ	Im Not Crazy Im Dreaming	Radio Master - 1934		30s	
Columbo Russ	Ive Had My Moments	Radio Master - 1934		30s	
Columbo Russ	Just Friends	Victor - 22903	Joy Leonard Orchestra	30s	
Columbo Russ	Kisses In The Dark	Radio Master - 1933		30s	
Columbo Russ	Lady I Love, The	Victor - 24076	Columbo Russ & his Orch	30s	
Columbo Russ	Lets Pretend There's A Moon	Brunswick - 6872	Grier Jimmy Orch	30s	
Columbo Russ	Living In Dreams	Victor - 22976	Columbo Russ & his Orch	30s	
Columbo Russ	Lonesome Me	Victor - 24077	Columbo Russ & his Orch	30s	
Columbo Russ	Lover	Radio Master - 1933		30s	
Columbo Russ	Make Love The King	Victor - 24195		30s	
Columbo Russ	More Than You Know	Radio Master - 1933		30s	
Columbo Russ	My Love	Victor - 24077	Columbo Russ & his Orch	30s	
Columbo Russ	Paradise	Victor - 22976		30s	
Columbo R. & C. Cummings	Pizzicato	Film Master - 1933		30s	
Columbo Russ	Prisioner Of Love	Film Master - 1933		30s	
Columbo Russ	Prisoner Of Love	Victor - 22867	Shilkret Nat Orchestra	30s	
Columbo Russ	Rolling In Love	Radio Master - 1934		30s	
Columbo Russ	Save The Last Dance For Me	Victor - 22903		30s	
Columbo Russ	Stardust	Radio Master - 1934		30s	
Columbo Russ	Street Of Dreams	Victor - 24194		30s	
Columbo Russ	Sweet And Lovely	Victor - 22802	Shilkret Nat Orchestra	30s	
Columbo Russ	Time On My Hands	Radio Master - 1933		30s	
Columbo Russ	Time On My Hands	Victor - 22826		30s	
Columbo Russ	Too Beautiful For Words	Film Master - 1934	Grier Jimmy Orch	30s	
Columbo Russ	Too Beautiful For Words	Special Edition - 5001	Grier Jimmy Orch	30s	
Columbo Russ	True	Radio Master - 1934		30s	
Columbo Russ	When Youre In Love	Brunswick - 6972	Grier Jimmy Orch	30s	
Columbo Russ & June Knight	When You're In Love	Film Master - 1934	Grier Jimmy Orch	30s	
Columbo Russ	Where The Blue Of The Night	Victor - 22867	Shilkret Nat Orchestra	30s	
Columbo Russ	With My Eyes Wide Open . . .	Radio Master - 1934		30s	
Columbo Russ	You Call It Madness . . .	Radio Master - 1933		30s	
Columbo Russ	You Call It Madness . . .	Victor - 22802	Shilkret Nat Orchestra	30s	
Columbo Russ	You Try Somebody Else	Victor - 22861		30s	
Columbo Russ	Youre My Past Present And.	Film Master - 1933		30s	
Columbo Russ	Youre My Past Present And.	Radio Master - 1933		30s	
Como Perry	A Hubba Hubba Hubba	Film Master - 1945		40s	
Como Perry & Satisfiers	A Hubba Hubba Hubba	Victor - 20 - 1750	Case Russ Orch	40s	
Como Perry	Bali Ha'I	Victor - 20 - 3402	Ayres Mitchell Orch	40s	
Como Perry	Blue Room	Film Master - 1949		40s	
Como Perry	Blue Room	Victor - 20 - 3329	Rene' Henri Orch	40s	
Como Perry & Ray Charles Singers	Catch A Falling Star	Victor - 20 - 7128	Ayres Mitchell Orch	50s	
Como Perry	Christmas Symphony, The	Victor - 20 - 3933	Ayres Mitchell Orch	50s	

Como Perry & Ramblers	Don't Let The Stars Get In Your Eyes	Victor - 20 - 5064	Winterhalters Hugo Orch	50s	
Como Perry*	Fooled By The Moon	Decca - 921	Weems Ted Orch	40s	
Como Perry*	Goodnight Sweet Dreams Goodnight	Decca - 1704	Weems Ted Orch	40s	
Como Perry*	Gypsy Told Me A	Decca - 1695	Weems Ted Orch	30s	
Como Perry & Ray Charles Singers	Home For The Holidays	Victor - 20 - 5950	Ayres Mitchell Orch	50s	
Como Perry & Ray Charles Singers	Hot Diggity Ziggity Boom	Victor - 20 - 6427	Ayres Mitchell Orch	50s	
Como Perry*	In My Little Red Book	Decca - 1695	Weems Ted Orch	50s	
Como Perry*	It All Comes Back To Me Now	Decca - 3627	Weems Ted Orch	30s	
Como Perry	Its Impossible	Victor - 74 - 0387		70s	
Como Perry*	Lazy Weather	Decca - 822	Weems Ted Orch	40s	
Como Perry	Long Ago And Far Away	Victor - 20 - 1569		50s	
Como Perry & Ray Charles Singers	Love Makes The World Go . . .	Victor - 47 - 7353	Ayres Mitchell Orch	50s	
Como Perry & Ray Charles Singers	Magic Moments	Victor - 20 - 7128	Ayres Mitchell Orch	50s	
Como Perry*	May I Never Love Again	Decca - 3627	Weems Ted Orch	30s	
Como Perry	Missouri Waltz	Victor - 20 - 2216	Rene' Henri Orch	40s	
Como Perry*	Ollie Ollie Outs In Free	Decca - 4138	Weems Ted Orch	40s	
Como Perry & Ray Charles Singers	Papa Loves Mambo	Victor - 20 - 5857	Ayres Mitchell Orch	40s	
Como Perry	Prisoner Of Love	Victor - 20 - 1814	Kostelanetz Andre Orch	40s	
Como Perry	Rambling Rose	Victor - 20 - 2947	Case Russ Orch	40s	
Como Perry & Ray Charles Singers	Round And Round	Victor - 20 - 6815	Ayres Mitchell Orch	50s	
Como Perry	Some Enchanted Evening	Victor - 20 - 3402	Ayres Mitchell Orch	40s	
Como Perry	Temptation	Victor - 20 - 1658	Steele Ted Orch.	40s	
Como Perry	There Is No Christmas Like A . . .	Victor - 20 - 3933	Ayres Mitchell Orch	40s	
Como Perry	Till The End Of Time	Victor - 20 - 1709	Case Russ Orch	50s	
Como Perry & Satisfiers	When You Where Sweet . . .	Victor - 20 - 2259	Shaffer Lloyd Orch	50s	
Como Perry & Satisfiers	Winter Wonderland	Victor - 20 - 1968	Ayres Mitchell Orch	40s	
Como Perry*	Wonder Who's Kissing Her . . . I	Decca - 2919	Weems Ted Orch	30s	
Como Perry & Fontane Sisters	Youre Just In Love	Victor - 20 - 3945	Ayres Mitchell Orch	50s	
Cooke Sam	There Ive Said It Again	Keen - 8 - 2105		50s	
Coolidge Calvin	Welcomes Col. Lindberg.	Victor - 35836	SPOKEN WORD	20s	
Coon Carlton & Joe Sanders	Darktown Shutters Ball, The	Victor - 22342	Coon - Sanders N. Orch	30s	
Coon Carlton & Joe Sanders	Flaming Mamie	Victor - 19922	Coon - Sanders N. Orch	20s	
Coon Carlton & Joe Sanders	Here Comes My Ball And Chain	Victor - 21812	Coon - Sanders N. Orch	20s	
Coon Carlton & Joe Sanders	I Got A Great Big Date	Victor - 22123	Coon - Sanders N. Orch	20s	
Coon Carlton & Joe Sanders	I Need Loving - AC	Victor - 20408	Coon - Sanders N. Orch	20s	
Coon Carlton & Joe Sanders	Is She My Girl Friend	Victor - 21148	Coon - Sanders N. Orch	20s	
Coon Carlton & Joe Sanders	Kansas City Kitty	Victor - 21939	Coon - Sanders N. Orch	20s	
Coon Carlton & Joe Sanders	Little Orphan Annie	Victor - 21895	Coon - Sanders N. Orch	20s	
Coon Carlton & Joe Sanders	My Baby Knows How - AC	Victor - 20390	Coon - Sanders N. Orch	20s	
Coon Carlton & Joe Sanders	Night Hawk Blues - AC	Victor - 19316	Coon - Sanders N. Orch	20s	
Coon Carlton & Joe Sanders	Red Hot Mama - AC	Victor - 19316	Coon - Sanders N. Orch	20s	
Coon Carlton & Joe Sanders	Stay Out Of The South	Victor - 21258	Coon - Sanders N. Orch	20s	
Coon Carlton & Joe Sanders	Yes Sir That's My Baby - AC	Victor - 19745	Coon - Sanders N. Orch	20s	
Copas Cowboy	Filipino Baby	King - 505		40s	
Cornell Don	Im Yours	Coral - 60690		50s	
Cornell Don	Love Is A Many Splendered . . .	Coral - 61467		50s	
Cornell Don	Door Is Still Open	Coral- 61393		50s	
Cornell Don & Laura Leslie*	Baby Its Cold Outside	Victor - 20 - 3448	Kaye Sammy Orch	40s	
Costello Billy	I'm Popeye the Sailor Man	Melotone - 92005		30s	
Coward Noel	Mad Dogs And Englishmen	Victor - 24332		30s	
Cox Baby, G. Goodwin* - NAP	I Cant Give You Anything But Love	Victor - 38008	Ellington Duke Orch	20s	
Cox Ida	Ida Cox's Lawdy Lawdy, - AC	Paramount - 12064	Blues Serenaders her &	20s	
Cox Ida	Mistreatin' Daddy Blues - AC	Paramount - 12298	Austin Lovie Blues S.	20s	
Crawford Joan	Everything I Have Is Yours	Film Master - 1933		30s	
Crosby Bing & Ken Darby Singers	Abraham	Decca - 18425	Trotter John Scott Orch	40s	
Crosby Bing & Andrews Sisters	Ac - Cent - Tchu - Ate - The Positive	Decca - 23379	Schoen Vic Orch	40s	
Crosby Bing & Guardsmen	Adeste Fideles	Decca - 621	Young Victor Orch.	30s	
Crosby Bing	After Sundown	Brunswick - 6694	Hayton Lennie Orch	30s	
Crosby Bing	After Sundown	Film Master - 1933		30s	
Crosby Bing*	After You've Gone	Columbia - 2098 - D	Whiteman Paul Orch	20s	
Crosby B. & Connie Boswell	Alexanders Ragtime Band	Decca - 1887	Young Victor Orch	30s	
Crosby Bing & Al Jolson	Alexanders Ragtime Band	Decca - 40038	Stoloff Morris Orch	40s	
Crosby Bing	All You Want To Do Is Dance	Decca - 1376	Trotter John Scott Orch	30s	
Crosby Bing & Andrews Sisters	Along The Navajo Trail	Decca - 23437	Schoen Vic Orch	40s	
Crosby Bing	Along The Way To Waikaki	Victor - LP - LPM - 1473	Scobey Bob band	50s	
Crosby B. & Connie Boswell	An Apple For The Teacher	Decca - 2640	Trotter John Scott Orch	30s	
Crosby B & Andrews S. & D. Haymes	Anything You Can Do I Can Do Better	Decca - 40039	Schoen Vic Orch	30s	

Crosby Bing	Arent You Glad You're You	Decca - 18720	Trotter John Scott Orch	40s	
Crosby Bing	Around The World	Decca - 30262	Cole Buddy Orch.	50s	
Crosby Bing	As Time Goes By	Radio Master - 1931		30s	
Crosby Bing	At Your Command	Brunswick - 6145	& orch	30s	
Crosby Bing	At Your Command	Film Master - 1931		30s	
Crosby Bing	Auf Wiedersehen My Dear	Film Master - 1931		30s	
Crosby Bing	Autumn Leaves	Decca - 27231	Stordahl Alex Orch.	50s	
Crosby Bing	Baby Where Can You Be	Columbia - 1851 - D		20s	
Crosby B. & Connie Boswell	Basin Street Blues	Decca - 1483	Trotter John Scott Orch	30s	
Crosby Bing	Be Careful Its My Heart	Decca - 14824	Trotter John Scott Orch	40s	
Crosby Bing	Be Honest With Me Dear	Decca - 3856	Trotter John Scott Orch	40s	
Crosby Bing	Beautiful Girl	Brunswick - 6694	Hayton Lennie Orch	30s	
Crosby Bing	Beautiful Girl	Film Master - 1933		30s	
Crosby B. & R. Boys, Brox Sisters	Bench In The Park A	Columbia - 2223 - D	Whiteman Paul Orch	30s	
Crosby B. (Rhythm Boys)*	Bench In The Park A	Columbia - 2223 - D	Whiteman Paul Orch	30s	
Crosby B. & Connie Boswell	Between 18th & 19th On Chestnut Street	Decca - 2948	Trotter John Scott Orch	40s	
Crosby Bing	Beyond Compare	Decca - 912	Young Victor Orch	30s	
Crosby Bing & Lyn Murray Chorus	Beyond The Reef	Decca - 27219	Murray Lynn Orch	50s	
Crosby Bing	Birth Of The Blues	Decca - 3970	Teagarden Jack Orch	40s	
Crosby Bing	Black Moonlight	Brunswick - 6643	Grier Jimmy Orch.	30s	
Crosby Bing	Blue Hawaii	Decca - 1175	McIntyre Lani & his Hawaiians	30s	
Crosby Bing	Blue Prelude	Brunswick - 6601	Grier Jimmy Orch.	30s	
Crosby Bing	Blue Room	Verve - LP - V - 2020	Bregman Buddy Orch.	50s	
Crosby B. & Ken Darby Singers	Blue Shadows On The Trail	Decca - 24433	Young Victor Orch.	30s	
Crosby Bing & Trudy Erwin	Blue Skies	Decca - 23646	Trotter John Scott Orch	30s	
Crosby Bing	Blues Seranade A	Decca Master - 1936	Malneck Matty	30s	
Crosby Bing	Blues Seranade A	Decca - 1933	Malneck Matty	30s	
Crosby B. & Connie Boswell	Bob White	Decca - 1483	Trotter John Scott Orch	30s	
Crosby Bing	Brother Can You Spare A Dime	Brunswick - 6414	& orch	30s	
Crosby Bing	But Beautiful	Decca - 24283	Young Victor Orch	40s	
Crosby Bing	But Beautiful	Film Master - 1946		40s	
Crosby Bing	Cabin In The Cotton	Brunswick - 6329	& orch	30s	
Crosby Bing	Cant We Be Friends	Columbia - 2001		20s	
Crosby Bing	Cant We Talk It Over	Brunswick - 6240	Crawford Helen	30s	
Crosby Bing	Christmas Carols Melodies	Decca - 24670	Rady Simon Orch	40s	
Crosby Bing	Christmas Song, (The)	Decca - 24144	Trotter John Scott Orch	40s	
Crosby Bing & Andrews Sisters	Ciribiribini	Decca - 2800	Venuti Joe Orch	30s	
Crosby Bing	Conchita, Marquita, Lolita, Pepita, Rosita, Juanita, Lopez	Decca - 4343	Schoen Vic Orch	40s	
Crosby Bing & Judy Garland	Connecticut	Decca - 23804	Lilly Joseph Orch	40s	
Crosby Bing*	Coquette	Columbia - 1775 - D	Whiteman Paul Orch	20s	
Crosby Bing	Dancing In The Dark	Brunswick - 6169	& orch	30s	
Crosby B. & M. Torme - MelTones	Day By Day	Decca - 18746	Trotter John Scott	40s	
Crosby Bing	Day You Came Along The	Brunswick - 6644	Grier Jimmy Orch.	30s	
Crosby Bing & J. Conlon' Rhythmaires	Dear Hearts & Gentle People	Decca - 24798	Botkin Perry guitar	40s	
Crosby Bing	Deep Purple	Decca - 2374	Malneck Matty	30s	
Crosby Bing	Did You Ever See A Dream Walking	Brunswick - 6724	Hayton Lennie Orch	30s	
Crosby Bing & Mills Brothers	Dinah	Brunswick - 6240	& orch	30s	
Crosby Bing & Patty Andrews	Dissertation On The State.	Decca - ED - (EP - 2186	Lilley Joseph Orch	50s	
Crosby Bing	Do You Hear What I Hear	Capital - 5088	Carmichael Ralph Orch	60s	
Crosby Bing	Don't Be That Way	Decca - 1794	Trotter John Scott Orch	40s	
Crosby Bing & Andrews Sisters	Don't Fence Me In	Decca - 23364	Schoen Vic Orch	40s	
Crosby Bing	Down By The River	Decca - 392	Stoll Georgie Orch	30s	
Crosby Bing	Down The Old Ox Road	Brunswick - 6601	Grier Jimmy Orch.	30s	
Crosby Bing	Down The Old Ox Road	Film Master - 1933		30s	
Crosby Bing	Dream A Little Dream Of Me	Victor - LP - LPM - 1473	Scobey Bob band	50s	
Crosby Bing	Easter Parade	Decca - 18425	Trotter John Scott Orch	40s	
Crosby Bing	Evelina	Decca - 18635	Camarata	40s	
Crosby Bing	Exactly Like You	Victor - LP - LPM - 1473	Scobey Bob band	50s	
Crosby Bing	Face The Music Medley - Soft Lights and Sweet Music	Brunswick - 20106	Young Victor Orch	30s	
Crosby Bing	Faded Summer Love A	Brunswick - 6200	& orch	30s	
Crosby Bing	Far Away Places	Decca - 24532	Darby Ken Choir	40s	
Crosby Bing	Fellow With An Umbrella A	Decca - 24433	Trotter John Scott Orch	40s	
Crosby Bing	Feudin & Fighting	Decca - 23975	Haggart Bob & Jesters	30s	
Crosby B. & Dixie Lee Crosby	Fine Romance A	Decca - 907	Young Victor Orch.	30s	
Crosby Bing*	Fool Me Some More	Victor - 22561	Arnheim Gus Orch	30s	
Crosby B. (Rhythm Boys)*	From Monday On	Victor - 21274	Whiteman Paul Orch	20s	
Crosby Bing	From The Top Of Your Head	Decca - 547	Dorsey Brothers Orch	30s	
Crosby Bing	Galway Bay	Decca - 24295	Young Victor Orch.	40s	

Crosby Bing	Gay Love	Columbia - 2001 - D		20s	
Crosby B. & Boswell S., Mills Bro.	Gems From George White's.	Brunswick - 20102	Young Victor Orch	30s	
Crosby Bing*	Get Out And Get Under The Moon	Columbia - 1402 - D	Whiteman Paul Orch	20s	
Crosby Bing	Ghost Of A Chance A	Brunswick - 6454	& orch	30s	
Crosby Bing	Give Me A Heart To Sing To	Brunswick - 6953	Aaronson Irving Orch	30s	
Crosby Bing	Go Fly A Kite	Decca - 2641	Trotter John Scott Orch	30s	
Crosby Bing & Max Terr's Chorus	God Rest Ye Merry Gentlemen	Decca - 18511	Trotter John Scott Orch	40s	
Crosby Bing	Going Hollywood	Film Master - 1933		30s	
Crosby Bing	Goodby Little Darlin Goodby	Decca - 3856	Trotter John Scott Orch	40s	
Crosby Bing	Goodby, My Lover Goodby	Decca - 23975	Haggart Bob & Jesters	40s	
Crosby Bing	Goodnight Lovely Little Lady	Brunswick - 6854	Finston Nat Orch.	30s	
Crosby Bing	Goodnight Sweetheart	Brunswick - 6203	Young Victor Orch	30s	
Crosby Bing	Got The Moon In My Pocket	Decca - 18354	Trotter John Scott Orch	40s	
Crosby B. (Rhythm Boys)*	Great Day	Columbia - 2023 - D	Whiteman Paul Orch	20s	
Crosby Bing & F. Langford	Gypsy Love Song - NAP	Decca - 2316	Young Victor Orch	30s	
Crosby Bing	Happy Birthday - Auld Lang Syne	Decca - 24273	Young Victor Orch	40s	
Crosby B. (Rhythm Boys)*	Happy Feet	Columbia - 2164 - D	Whiteman Paul Orch	30s	
Crosby Bing	Happy Go Lucky You	Brunswick - 6306	Jones Isham Orch	30s	
Crosby Bing & Music Maids	Happy Holiday	Decca - 18424	Trotter John Scott Orch	30s	
Crosby Bing & Lyn Murray Chorus	Harbor Lights	Decca - 27219	Murray Lynn Orch	40s	
Crosby Bing	Have You Met Miss Jones	Verve - LP - V - 2020	Bregman Buddy Orch	50s	
Crosby Bing	Here Is My Heart	Brunswick Master - 1933	Dorsey Brothers Orch	30s	
Crosby Bing	Here Lies Love	Brunswick - 6406	& orch	30s	
Crosby Bing	Here Lies Love	Radio Master - 1932		30s	
Crosby Bing*	High Water	Victor - 35992	Whiteman Paul Orch	20s	
Crosby B.* & Loyce Whiteman	Ho Hum	Victor - 22691	Arnheim Gus Orch	30s	
Crosby Bing	Holly And The Ivy, (The)	Warner Bro - LP - 1484	vocal	60s	
Crosby Bing	Home On The Range	Brunswick - 6663	Hayton Lennie Orch	30s	
Crosby Bing & J. Alexander C.	Horse Told Me The	Decca - 24875	Young Victor Orch	50s	
Crosby Bing	House Is Haunted, The	Radio Master - 1934	Stoll Georgie Orch	30s	
Crosby Bing	House That Jack Built For Jill The	Decca - 905	Dorsey Jimmy Orch	30s	
Crosby Bing	How Deep Is The Ocean	Brunswick - 6406	& orch	30s	
Crosby Bing & Arthur Norman Choir	How Lively Is Christmas	Kapp - 196x	& Orch	50s	
Crosby Bing	How Long Will It Last	Brunswick - 6259	& orch	30s	
Crosby Bing	I Apologize	Brunswick - 6179	& orch	30s	
Crosby Bing	I Cant Begin To Tell You	Decca - 32457	Cavallero Carmen - piano	40s	
Crosby Bing	I Cant Escape From You	Decca - 871	Dorsey Jimmy Orch.	30s	
Crosby Bing	I Don't Want To Walk Without You	Decca - 4184	Trotter John Scott Orch	40s	
Crosby Bing	I Found A Million Dollar Baby	Brunswick - 6140	& orch	30s	
Crosby Bing	I Found You	Brunswick - 6248	Crawford Helen	30s	
Crosby Bing	I Got Plenty Of Nuttin	Decca - 806	Young Victor Orch	30s	
Crosby Bing	I Guess It Had To Be That Way	Brunswick - 6644	Grier Jimmy Orch.	30s	
Crosby Bing	I Heard The Bells On Christmas . . .	Decca - 30126	Cole Buddy Orch.	50s	
Crosby Bing	I Kiss Your Hand Madame	Columbia - 1851 - D		20s	
Crosby Bing	I Knew You When	Radio Master - 1934	Stoll Georgie Orch	30s	
Crosby B. (Rhythm Boys)*	I Like To Do Things For You	Columbia - 2170 - D	Whiteman Paul Orch	30s	
Crosby Bing	I Never Realized	Decca - 1186	Young Victor	30s	
Crosby Bing & Lee Wiley	I Still Suits Me - NAP	Decca - 241100		40s	
Crosby Bing	I Surrender Dear	Film Master - 1931		30s	
Crosby Bing	I Surrender Dear	Radio Master - 1931		30s	
Crosby Bing*	I Surrender Dear	Victor - 22618	Arnheim Gus Orch	20s	
Crosby Bing	I Want My Mama	Decca - 18316	Hermann Woody Orch	40s	
Crosby Bing	I Wish I Were Alladin	Decca - 547	Dorsey Brothers Orch	30s	
Crosby Bing	I Wish You A Merry Christmas	Warner Bro - LP - 1484	vocal	60s	
Crosby Bing	I Wished On The Moon	Decca - 543	Dorsey Brothers Orch	30s	
Crosby Bing	I Wished On The Moon - T	Decca Master - 1935	Dorsey Brothers Orch	30s	
Crosby Bing	I Would If I Could But I Cant	Brunswick - 6623	Grier Jimmy Orch.	30s	
Crosby Bing & Rhythmaires	Ichabod	Decca - 24703	Schoen Vic Orch	40s	
Crosby Bing*	If I Had A Talking Picture Of You	Columbia - 2110 - D	Whiteman Paul Orch	20s	
Crosby Bing	If You Should Ever Leave Me	Brunswick - 6090	& orch	30s	
Crosby Bing	If You Stub Your Toe On . . .	Decca - 24524	Young Victor Orch	40s	
Crosby Bing	I'll Be Home For Christmas	Decca - 18570	Trotter John Scott Orch	30s	
Crosby Bing	I'll Be Seeing You	Decca - 18595	Trotter John Scott Orch	40s	
Crosby B., F. Astaire, M. Lenhart	I'll Capture Your Heart	Decca - 18427	Crosby Bob & Orch	40s	
Crosby Bing* (unacredited)	I'll Get By	Columbia - 1694 - D	Ipana Troubadours	20s	
Crosby Bing	I'll Follow You	Brunswick - 6427	& orch	30s	
Crosby Bing & Trudy Erwin	I'll See You In Cuba	Decca - 23646	Trotter John Scott Orch	30s	
Crosby Bing	Im An Old Cowhand	Decca - 871	Dorsey Jimmy Orch.	30s	
Crosby B. (Rhythm Boys)*	Im Coming Virginia	Victor - 20751	Whiteman Paul Orch	20s	
Crosby Bing*	Im Crazy Over You	Okeh - 41228	Lanin Sam Orch	20s	

Crosby Bing*	Im Gonna Get You	Victor - 22691	Arnheim Gus Orch	30s	
Crosby Bing	Im Humming Im Whistling Im.	Brunswick - 6953	Aaronson Irving Orch	30s	
Crosby Bing	Im Humming Im Whistling Im.	Radio Master - 1934	Stoll Georgie Orch	30s	
Crosby Bing	Im Playing With Fire	Brunswick - 6480		30s	
Crosby Bing	Im Sorry Dear	Brunswick - 6226	& orch	30s	
Crosby Bing	Im Thinking Of My Blue . . .	Decca - 18316	Hermann Woody Orch	40s	
Crosby Bing	Im Through With Love	Brunswick - 6140	& orch	30s	
Crosby Bing	Im Through With Love	Radio Master - 1931		30s	
Crosby B. (Rhythm Boys)*	Im Winging Home	Victor - 21365	Whiteman Paul Orch	20s	
Crosby Bing	In My Merry Oldsmobile	Decca - 2700	Trotter John Scott Orch	30s	
Crosby B. & Jane Wyman	In The Cool Cool Cool Of . . .	Decca - 27678		50s	
Crosby Bing	Iowa	Radio Master - 1944?	Wilson Meridith Orch	40s	
Crosby Bing & Andrews Sisters	Is You Is Or Is You Aint My Baby	Decca - 23350	Schoen Vic Orch	40s	
Crosby Bing	It Aint Necessarily So	Decca - 806	Young Victor Orch	30s	
Crosby Bing	It Could Happen To You	Decca - 18580	Trotter John Scott Orch	40s	
Crosby Bing	It Makes No Difference Now	Decca - 3590	Crosby Bob & Orch	40s	
Crosby Bing*	It Must Be True	Victor - 22561	Arnheim Gus Orch	20s	
Crosby Bing	Its Always You	Decca - 3636	Trotter John Scott Orch	40s	
Crosby Bing	Its Been A Long Long Time	Decca - 18708	Paul Les Trio	40s	
Crosby B & Rythmettes, three.	Its Easy To Remember	Decca - 391	Stoll Georgie Orch	30s	
Crosby Bing	Its Easy To Remember	Radio Master - 1934	Stoll Georgie Orch	30s	
Crosby Bing	Its Mine Its Yours	Decca - (EP) - ED - 2187	Lilley Joseph Orch	50s	
Crosby Bing	Its The Natural Thing To Do	Decca - 1376	Trotter John Scott Orch	30s	
Crosby Bing	Its Within Your Power	Brunswick - 6464	& orch	30s	
Crosby Bing	Ive Got A Pocket Full Of Dreams	Decca - 1933	Trotter John Scott Orch	40s	
Crosby Bing	Ive Got Five Dollars	Verve - LP - V - 2020	Bregman Buddy Orch	50s	
Crosby Bing	Ive Got Plenty To Be Thankful For	Decca - 18426	Crosby Bob & Orch	40s	
Crosby Bing & Al Rinker* - NAP	Ive Got The Girl - AC	Columbia - 824 - D	Clark Don & His B. Orch	20s	
Crosby Bing	Ive Got The World On A String	Brunswick - 6491	& orch	30s	
Crosby Bing	Ive Got To Pass Your House	Brunswick - 6610	Grier Jimmy Orch.	30s	
Crosby Bing	Ive Got To Sing A Torch Song	Brunswick - 6599	Grier Jimmy Orch.	30s	
Crosby Bing & Music Maids	Jimmy Valentine - T (Medley)	Decca Master - 1939	Trotter John Scott Orch	30s	
Crosby Bing & Andrews Sisters	Jingle Bells - T	Decca Master - 1943	Schoen Vic Orch	40s	
Crosby Bing	June In January	Decca - 310	Stoll Georgie Orch	30s	
Crosby Bing	Just A Gigolo	Victor - 22701	Barris Harry & acc. orch.	30s	
Crosby Bing	Just A Wearing For You	Decca - 100	Stoll Georgie Orch	30s	
Crosby Bing	Just An Echo In The Valley	Brunswick - 6454	& orch	30s	
Crosby Bing	Just One More Chance	Brunswick - 6120	Young Victor Orch	30s	
Crosby Bing	Just One More Chance	Radio Master - 1931	& orch	30s	
Crosby Bing & Skylarks	Kokomo Indiana	Decca - 24100	Trotter John Scott Orch	40s	
Crosby Bing	Land Around Us The	Decca - (EP) - ED - 2187	Lilley Joseph Orch	50s	
Crosby Bing	Last Night On The Back Porch	Victor - LPM - 1453	Scobey Bob band	50s	
Crosby Bing	Last Round - Up The	Brunswick - 6663	Hayton Lennie Orch	30s	
Crosby Bing & Boswell Sisters	Lawd You Made The Night Too Long	Brunswick - 20109	Redman Don Orch	30s	
Crosby Bing	Lazy	Decca - 18427	Crosby Bob & Orch	40s	
Crosby Bing	Lazy Day	Brunswick - 6306	Jones Isham Orch	30s	
Crosby Bing	Learn To Croon	Brunswick - 6594	Grier Jimmy Orch.	30s	
Crosby Bing	Learn To Croon	Film Master - 1934		30s	
Crosby Bing	Let A Smile be Your Umbrella	Victor - LP - LPM - 1473	Scobey Bob band	50s	
Crosby Bing	Let's Call A Heart A Heart	Decca - 947	Stoll Georgie Orch	30s	
Crosby B. (Rhythm Boys)*	Lets Do It	Columbia - 1701 - D	Whiteman Paul Orch	20s	
Crosby Bing*	Lets Do It	Okeh - 41181	Dorsey Brothers Orch	20s	
Crosby Bing	Lets Put Out The Lights And . . .	Brunswick - 6414	& orch	30s	
Crosby Bing	Lets Spend An Evening At Home	Brunswick - 6724	Hayton Lennie Orch	30s	
Crosby Bing	Lets Start The New Year Right	Decca - 18429	Crosby Bob & Orch	40s	
Crosby Bing	Lets Start The New Year Right	Film Master - 1942		40s	
Crosby Bing	Lets Try Again	Brunswick - 6320	Jones Isham Orch	30s	
Crosby Bing	Linger A Little Longer In The Twilight	Brunswick - 6491	& orch	30s	
Crosby Bing	Little Drummer Boy, (The)	Warner Bro - LP - 1484	vocal	60s	
Crosby Bing & David Bowie	Little Drummer Boy and Peace On Earth	Film (TV) Master - 1977		70s	
Crosby Bing	Little Dutch Mill	Brunswick - 6794	Grier Jimmy Orch.	30s	
Crosby Bing & Peggy Lee	Little Jack Frost Get Lost	Decca - 28463		50s	
Crosby Bing	Littleist Angel, (The)	Warner Bro - LP - 1484	vocal	60s	
Crosby Bing*	Livin In The Sunlight Lovin In . . .	Columbia - 2171 - D	Whiteman Paul Orch	30s	
Crosby Bing & Lee Gordan Singers	Looks Like A Cold Cold . . .	Decca - 27230	Burke Sonny Orch	50s	
Crosby B. (Rhythm Boys)*	Louise	Columbia - 1819 - D	Whiteman Paul Orch	20s	
Crosby Bing*	Louise	Columbia - 1771 - D	Whiteman Paul Orch	20s	
Crosby B. (Rhythm Boys)*	Lousiana	Victor - 21438	Whiteman Paul Orch	20s	
Crosby Bing	Lovable	Film Master - 1933		30s	
Crosby Bing	Love In Bloom	Brunswick - 6936	Aaronson Irving Orch	30s	
Crosby Bing	Love In Bloom	Radio Master - 1934	Stoll Georgie Orch	30s	

Crosby Bing	Love Is Just Around The Corner	Decca - 310	Stoll Georgie Orch	50s	
Crosby Bing	Love Me Tonight	Brunswick - 6351	& orch	30s	
Crosby Bing	Love Thy Neighbor	Brunswick - 6852	Finston Nat Orch.	30s	
Crosby Bing	Love You Funny Thing	Brunswick - 6268	& orch	30s	
Crosby Bing	Lullaby Of Broadway	Radio Master - 1934	Stoll Georgie Orch	30s	
Crosby Bing	Mack The Knife	Victor - LP - LPM - 1473	Scobey Bob band	50s	
Crosby B. (Rhythm Boys)*	Magnolia	Victor - 20679	Whiteman Paul Orch	20s	
Crosby Bing	Mairzy Doats	Film Master - 1944		40s	
Crosby Bing	Mama Loves Pappa	Victor - LP - LPM - 1473	Scobey Bob band	50s	
Crosby Bing	Man On Fire	Capital - 3695	Riddle Nelson Orch.	50s	
Crosby Bing	Many Happy Returns Of The Day	Brunswick - 6145	& orch	30s	
Crosby Bing & Lee Gordan Singers	Marshmallow World A	Decca - 27230	Burke Sonny Orch	50s	
Crosby Bing*	Mary What Are You Waiting For	Victor - 21103	Whiteman Paul Orch	20s	
Crosby Bing	May I	Brunswick - 6853	Finston Nat Orch.	30s	
Crosby Bing	Maybe I'm Wrong Again	Decca - 309	Stoll Georgie Orch	30s	
Crosby Bing	Me And The Moon	Decca - 912	Young Victor Orch	30s	
Crosby Bing & Andrews Sisters	Mele Kalikaka	Decca - 27228	Schoen Vic Orch	50s	
Crosby Bing & J. Conlon' Rhythmaires	Memories Are Made Of This	Decca - LP - DL - 8352	Pleis Jack Orch.	50s	
Crosby Bing	Mississippi Mud	Decca - 38031	Cole Budy & his Trio	50s	
Crosby Bing & R. Boys. & I. Taylor*	Mississippi Mud	Victor - 21274	Whiteman Paul Orch	20s	
Crosby Bing*	Mississippi Mud	Okeh - 40979	Trumbauer Frank Orch	20s	
Crosby B. (Rhythm Boys)*	Mississippi Mud - I Left My Sugar Standing In The Rain	Victor - 20783	Whiteman Paul Orch	20s	
Crosby Bing	Moon Got In My Eyes The	Decca - 1375	Trotter John Scott Orch	30s	
Crosby Bing	Moon Of Manakoora The	Decca - 1649	Trotter John Scott Orch	30s	
Crosby Bing	Moon Was Yellow The	Decca - 179	Stoll Georgie Orch	30s	
Crosby Bing	Moonburn	Decca - 617	Young Victor Orch.	30s	
Crosby Bing	Moonlight And Shadows	Decca - 1186	Young Victor Orch	30s	
Crosby Bing	Moonlight Becomes You	Decca - 18513	Trotter John Scott Orch	40s	
Crosby Bing	Moonlight Cocktail	Decca - 4184	Trotter John Scott Orch	40s	
Crosby Bing	Moonstruck	Brunswick - 6594	Grier Jimmy Orch.	30s	
Crosby Bing	Moonstruck	Film Master - 1933		30s	
Crosby Bing	Mountain Greenery	Verve - LP - V - 2020	Bregman Buddy Orch	50s	
Crosby Bing*	Muddy Water - AC	Victor - 20508	Whiteman Paul Orch	20s	
Crosby Bing	Mule Train	Decca - 24798	Botkin's Perry String Band	40s	
Crosby Bing & Louis Jordan	My Baby Said Yes	Decca - 23417	Jordan L & his Tympany Five	40s	
Crosby Bing	My Heart And I	Decca - 631	Stoll Georgie Orch	30s	
Crosby Bing	My Heart Is Taking Lessons	Decca - 1648	Trotter John Scott Orch	30s	
Crosby Bing & Mills Brothers	My Honeys Lovin Arms	Brunswick - 6525		30s	
Crosby Bing*	My Kinda Love	Okeh - 41188	Dorsey Brothers Orch	20s	
Crosby Bing	My Love	Brunswick - 6623	Grier Jimmy Orch.	30s	
Crosby Bing	My Woman	Brunswick - 6268	& orch	30s	
Crosby Bing	Never In A Million Years	Decca - 1210	Dorsey Jimmy Orch.	30s	
Crosby Bing	Nobody's Darlin But Mine	Decca - 18391	Young Victor	40s	
Crosby Bing	Now Is The Hour	Decca - 24279		40s	
Crosby Bing	Now That You've Gone	Brunswick - 6200	& orch	30s	
Crosby Bing & Louis Armstrong	Now You Has Jazz	Capital - LP - W - 750		30s	
Crosby Bing & Louis Armstrong	Now You Has Jazz	Film Master - 1956	Armstrong Louis Orch	50s	
Crosby Bing	Old Faithful	Radio Master - 1934	Stoll Georgie Orch	30s	
Crosby Bing*	Old Man River	Victor - 21218	Whiteman Paul Orch	20s	
Crosby B. & Six Hits & A Miss	On The Atcheson Topeka . . .	Decca - 18690	Trotter John Scott Orch	40s	
Crosby Bing	On The Sentimental Side	Decca=1648	Trotter John Scott Orch	30s	
Crosby Bing	On Treasure Island	Decca - 617	Young Victor Orch	30s	
Crosby Bing	Once In A Blue Moon	Brunswick - 6854	Finston Nat Orch.	30s	
Crosby Bing*	One More Time	Victor - 22700	Arnheim Gus Orch	30s	
Crosby Bing	One Rose The - NAP	Decca - 1201	Young Victor Orch	30s	
Crosby Bing	One Two Button Your Shoe	Decca - 948	Stoll Georgie Orch	30s	
Crosby Bing	One Two Button Your Shoe	Film Master - 1936		50s	
Crosby Bing	Our Big Love Scene	Brunswick - 6696	Hayton Lennie Orch	30s	
Crosby Bing	Our Big Love Scene	Film Master - 1933		30s	
Crosby Bing	Out Of Nowhere	Brunswick - 6090	& orch	30s	
Crosby Bing	Out Of Nowhere	Film Master - 1931		30s	
Crosby Bing	Out Of Nowhere	Radio Master - 1931	Arnheim Gus Orch	30s	
Crosby Bing	Paradise	Brunswick - 6285	& orch	30s	
Crosby Bing	Pat - A Pan	Warner Bro - LP - 1484	vocal	60s	
Crosby Bing	Peckin	Decca - 1301	Dorsey Jimmy Orch	30s	
Crosby Bing	Pennies From Heaven	Decca - 947	Stoll Georgie Orch	30s	
Crosby Bing	Pennies From Heaven	Film Master - 1936		30s	
Crosby B., Armstrong, Langford	Pennies From Heaven II	Decca - 15027	Dorsey Jimmy & His Orch	30s	

Crosby B., Armstrong, Langford	Pennies From Heaven Medley	Decca - 15027	Dorsey Jimmy & His Orch	30s	
Crosby Bing & Trudy Erwin	People Will Say We're In Love	Decca - 18564	Sportsman's Glee Club	40s	
Crosby Bing	Personality	Decca - 18790	Condon Eddie Band	40s	
Crosby Bing	Pinetops Boogie Woogie	Decca - 23843	Hampton Lionel & Orch	40s	
Crosby Bing & Andrews Sisters	Pistol Packing Mama	Decca - 23277	Schoen Vic Orch	40s	
Crosby Bing	Please	Brunswick - 6394	Weeks Anson Orch	30s	
Crosby Bing	Please	Radio Master - 1932		30s	
Crosby Bing	Porter The Waiter And . . .	Decca - 3970	Teagarden Jack Orch	40s	
Crosby B. & M. Torme - MelTones	Proove It By The Things You Do	Decca - 18746	Trotter John Scott	40s	
Crosby Bing & Andrews Sisters	Quicksilver	Decca - 24827	Schoen Vic Orch	40s	
Crosby Bing	Red Sails In The Sunset	Decca - 616	Young Victor Orch.	30s	
Crosby Bing	Remember Me	Decca - 1451	Trotter John Scott Orch	30s	
Crosby Bing	Rhythm On The River	Decca - 3309	Trotter John Scott Orch	40s	
Crosby Bing	Riding Around In The Rain	Brunswick - 6852	Grier Jimmy Orch.	30s	
Crosby Bing	Riding Around In The Rain	Radio Master - 1934	Stoll Georgie Orch	30s	
Crosby Bing & Bob Hope	Road To Morocco The	Decca - 18514	Schoen Vic Orch	40s	
Crosby Bing	Robins And Roses	Decca Master - 1936	Young Victor Orch	30s	
Crosby Bing	Robins And Roses	Decca - 791	Young Victor Orch	30s	
Crosby Bing	Rolliking Rockaway Raoul	Brunswick Master - 1933		30s	
Crosby Bing	San Fernado Valley	Decca - 18586	Trotter John Scott Orch	40s	
Crosby Bing	Search Is Through The	Decca - (EP) - ED - 2187	Lilley Joseph Orch	50s	
Crosby Bing	Second Time Around The	MGM - K - 12946	King Pete & Orchestra	60s	
Crosby Bing	Seven Nights A Week	Capital - 3695	Riddle Nelson Orch.	50s	
Crosby Bing	Seventh Air Force - T	Radio Master - 1943		40s	
Crosby Bing	Shadow Waltz	Brunswick - 6599	Grier Jimmy Orch.	30s	
Crosby Bing	Shadows On The Window	Brunswick - 6276	& orch	30s	
Crosby Bing	She Reminds Me Of You	Brunswick - 6853	Grier Jimmy Orch.	30s	
Crosby Bing & Mills Brothers	Shine	Brunswick - 6276	& orch	30s	
Crosby Bing	Shoo Shoo Baby	Radio Master - 1944		40s	
Crosby Bing & Al Rinker*	Side By Side	Victor - 20570	Whiteman Paul Orch	20s	
Crosby Bing	Sierra Sue	Decca - 3133	Trotter John Scott Orch	40s	
Crosby Bing & Guardsmen	Silent Night	Decca - 621	Young Victor Orch.	40s	
Crosby Bing & Carol Richards	Silver Bells	Decca - 27229	Trotter John Scott Orch	50s	
Crosby Bing	Sing A Song Of Sunbeams	Decca - 2359	Trotter John Scott Orch	30s	
Crosby Bing & Jesters	Sioux City Sue	Decca - 23508	Haggart Bob Orch	40s	
Crosby Bing & J. Conlon's R.	Sleigh Ride	Decca - 28463	Trotter John Scott Orch	50s	
Crosby Bing & J. Mercer	Small Fry	Decca - 1960	Young Victor(S. F.)	30s	
Crosby Bing	Smarty	Decca - 1375	Trotter John Scott Orch	30s	
Crosby Bing	Snuggled On Your Shoulder	Brunswick - 6248	& orch	30s	
Crosby Bing	So Do I	Decca - 948	Stoll Georgie Orch	30s	
Crosby Bing	So Do I	Film Master - 1936		30s	
Crosby B. (Rhythm Boys)*	So The Bluebirds And The . . .	Columbia - 1819 - D	Whiteman Paul Orch	20s	
Crosby Bing	Some Of These Days	Brunswick - 6351	& orch	30s	
Crosby Bing	Some Sunny Day	Victor - LP - LPM - 1473	Scobey Bob band	50s	
Crosby Bing	Someday Sweetheart	Decca - 101	Stoll Georgie Orch	50s	
Crosby Bing	Someday Well Meet Again	Brunswick - 6427	& orch	30s	
Crosby Bing	Someone Stole Gabriels Horn	Brunswick - 6533	Dorsey Brothers Orch.	30s	
Crosby Bing	Song Of Freedom	Decca - 18426	Crosby Bob Orch	40s	
Crosby Bing	Soon	Decca - 392	Stoll Georgie Orch	30s	
Crosby Bing & Andrews Sisters	South America Take It Away	Decca - 23569	Schoen Vic Orch	40s	
Crosby Bing	South Of The Border	Radio Master - 1939	Trotter John Scott Orch	30s	
Crosby Bing*	Spell Of The Blues, (The)	Okeh - 41181	Dorsey Brothers Orch	20s	
Crosby Bing	St. Louis Blues	Brunswick - 20102	Ellington Duke Orch	40s	
Crosby Bing	Star Dust	Brunswick - 6169	& orch	30s	
Crosby Bing	Stardust	Decca - 2374	Malneck Matty	30s	
Crosby Bing	Starlight	Brunswick - 6259	& orch	30s	
Crosby B. & Connie Boswell	Start The Day Right	Decca - 2626	Trotter John Scott Orch	30s	
Crosby Bing	Stay On The Right Side Ofr The Road	Brunswick - 6533	Dorsey Brothers Orch.	30s	
Crosby Bing	Straight From The Shoulder	Brunswick - 6936	Aaronson Irving Orch	30s	
Crosby Bing	Street Of Dreams	Brunswick - 6464	& orch	30s	
Crosby Bing	Summertime	Decca - 2147	Malneck Matty	40s	
Crosby Bing & K. Darby Singers	Sunday Monday Or Always	Decca - 18561		40s	
Crosby B. (Rhythm Boys)*	Sunshine	Victor - 21240	Whiteman Paul Orch	30s	
Crosby Bing & Carole Richards	Sunshine Cake	Decca - 24875	Young Victor Orch.	30s	
Crosby Bing	Sweet And Lovely	Brunswick - 6179	& orch	30s	
Crosby Bing	Sweet Georgia Brown	Brunswick - 6320	Jones Isham Orch	30s	
Crosby Bing	Sweet Lelani - NAP	Decca - 1175	McIntyre & his Hawaiians	30s	
Crosby Bing	Sweet Sue Just You	BrunswickMaster - 1933	Hayton Lennie Orch	30s	
Crosby Bing	Swing Low Sweet Chariot	Decca - 1819	Choristers Paul Taylor	30s	

Crosby Bing & Williams Bro. Q.	Swinging On A Star	Decca - 18597	Trotter John Scott Orch	40s	
Crosby Bing	Takes Two To Make A Bargin	Decca - 548	Dorsey Brothers Orch	30s	
Crosby Bing & Andrews Sisters	Tallahassee	Decca - 23885	Schoen Vic Orch	40s	
Crosby B. & Connie Boswell	Tea For Two	Decca - 3689	Crosby Bob & Bearcats	40s	
Crosby Bing	Temptation	Brunswick - 6695	Hayton Lennie Orch	30s	
Crosby Bing	Thanks	Brunswick - 6643	Grier Jimmy Orch.	30s	
Crosby Bing	Thanks	Radio Master - 1933		30s	
Crosby Bing & J. Conlon' Rhythmaires	Thanks For The Memory	Decca - LP - DL - 8352	Pleis Jack Orch.	50s	
Crosby Bing*	Thanks To You	Victor - 22700	Arnheim Gus Orch	30s	
Crosby Bing	That's For Me	Decca - 3309	Trotter John Scott Orch	40s	
Crosby B. (Rhythm Boys)*	That's Grandma	Columbia - 1455 - D	Whiteman Paul Orch	20s	
Crosby B. (Rhythm Boys)*	That's Grandma	Victor - 27688	Whiteman Paul Orch	30s	
Crosby B. (Rhythm Boys)*	Them There Eyes	Victor - 22580	Arnheim Gus Orch	20s	
Crosby B. (Rhythm Boys)*	There Aint No Sweet Man . . .	Victor - 21464	Whiteman Paul Orch	20s	
Crosby Bing & Andrews Sisters	Therell Be A Hot Time In The Town Of Berlin	Decca - 23350	Schoen Vic Orch	40s	
Crosby Bing	Theres A Cabin In The Pines	Brunswick - 6610	Grier Jimmy Orch.	30s	
Crosby Bing & Andrews Sisters	There's A Fellow Waiting In Poughkeepsie	Decca - 23379	Schoen Vic Orch	40s	
Crosby Bing, intro B. Hope	There's A Small Hotel	V - Disc - 700	Duchin Eddie pianist	40s	
Crosby Bing	Thousand Goodnights A	Radio Master - 1934	Stoll Georgie Orch	30s	
Crosby Bing & Andrews Sisters	Three Caballeros, (The)	Decca - 23364	Schoen Vic Orch	40s	
Crosby B. (Rhythm Boys)*	Three Little Words	Victor - 22528	Ellington Duke Orch	30s	
Crosby Bing	Time On My Hands	Radio Master - 1937		30s	
Crosby Bing	Too Late	Brunswick - 6203	Young Victor Orch	30s	
Crosby Bing	Too Marvelous For Words	Decca - 1185	Dorsey Jimmy Orch	30s	
Crosby Bing	Too Romantic	Decca - 2998	Trotter John Scott Orch	30s	
Crosby Bing	Trade Winds	Decca - 3299	McIntire Dick	30s	
Crosby B. & Grace Kelly	True Love	Capital - LP - W - 750	Green John & MGM Orch	50s	
Crosby Bing	Try a Little Tenderness	Brunswick - 6480		30s	
Crosby Bing	Two Cigarettes In The Dark	Decca - 245	Stoll Georgie Orch	30s	
Crosby Bing	Two For Tonight	Decca - 543	Stoll Georgie Orch	30s	
Crosby Bing	Very Thought Of You The	Decca - 179	Stoll Georgie Orch	30s	
Crosby Bing*	Waiting At The End Of The Road	Columbia - 1974 - D	Whiteman Paul Orch	20s	
Crosby Bing	Walking The Floor Over You	Decca - 18371	Crosby Bob & Bearcats	40s	
Crosby Bing	Waltzing In A Dream	Brunswick - 6394	Weeks Anson Orch	30s	
Crosby Bing & Glee Club	Way Back Home	Decca - 24800	Waring Fred Orch	40s	
Crosby B. & Dixie Lee Crosby	Way You Look Tonight The	Decca - 907	Young Victor Orch.	40s	
Crosby Bing & F. Sinatra	Well Did You Evah	Capital - LP - W - 750	Green John & MGM Orch	50s	
Crosby Bing	Well Make Hay While The . . .	Brunswick - 6695	Hayton Lennie Orch	30s	
Crosby Bing & Marion Davies	Well Make Hay While The . . .	Film Master - 1933		30s	
Crosby Bing	Were A Couple Of Soldiers	Brunswick - 6696	Hayton Lennie Orch	30s	
Crosby Bing	Were You Sincere	Brunswick - 6120	Young Victor Orch	30s	
Crosby Bing	What Am I Gonna Do About You	Decca - 23850	Paul Les Trio	40s	
Crosby Bing	What Child Is This	Warner Bro - LP - 1484	vocal	60s	
Crosby Bing	What Do I Care Its Home	Brunswick - 6515	& orch	30s	
Crosby Bing & L. Whitman	What Is It	Radio Master - 1931	Arnheim Gus Orch	30s	
Crosby Bing	What Will I Tell My Heart	Decca - 1185	Dorsey Jimmy Orch	30s	
Crosby Bing	Whats New	Decca - 2671	Trotter John Scott Orch	40s	
Crosby Bing	When My Dreamboat Comes Home	Decca - 18371	Crosby Bob & Bearcats	40s	
Crosby Bing	When The Folks Up High Do . . .	Film Master - 1930		30s	
Crosby Bing	Where The Blue Of The Night	Brunswick - 6226	& orch	30s	
Crosby Bing	Where The Blue Of The Night	Radio Master - 1934	Stoll Georgie Orch	30s	
Crosby Bing & Murial Lane	Whistlers Mother In Law, (The)	Decca - 3971	Hermann Woody Orch	40s	
Crosby Bing	White Christmas	Film Master - 1942		40s	
Crosby Bing & Ken Darby Singers	White Christmas	Decca - 18429	Trotter John Scott Orch	40s	
Crosby Bing & Ken Darby Singers	White Christmas - 2nd -	Decca - 23778	Trotter John Scott Orch	40s	
Crosby Bing	White Christmas - 3rd	Decca - 29342	Lilly, Joseph Orch.	50s	
Crosby Bing	Whos Dream Are You	Decca - 18708	Paul Les Trio	40s	
Crosby Bing & Al Rinker*	Wistful And Blue	Victor - 20418	Whiteman Paul Orch	20s	
Crosby Bing	With Every Breath I Take	Decca - 309	Stoll Georgie Orch	30s	
Crosby Bing	With Every Breath I Take	Film Master - 1935		30s	
Crosby Bing	With Every Breath I Take	Decca - 309	Stoll Georgie Orch	30s	
Crosby Bing	With My Eyes Wide Open . . .	Radio Master - 1934	Stoll Georgie Orch	30s	
Crosby Bing	With Summer Coming On	Brunswick - 6329	& orch	30s	
Crosby Bing	Without A Word Of Warning	Decca - 548	Dorsey Brothers Orch	30s	
Crosby Bing	Would You	Decca - 756	Young Victor Orch	30s	
Crosby Bing	Wrap Your Troubles In Dreams	Decca Master - 1939	Trotter John Scott Orch	30s	
Crosby Bing	Wrap Your Troubles In Dreams	Victor - 22701	orch & H. Barris, piano	30s	
Crosby B. & Connie Boswell	Yes Indeed	Decca - 3689	Crosby Bob & Bearcats	40s	

Crosby B. & Andrews Sisters - NAP	Yodelin Jive	Decca - 2800		30s	
Crosby Bing	You Are My Sunshine	Decca - 3952	Young Victor	40s	
Crosby Bing	You Belong To My Heart	Decca - 23413	Cugat Xavier Orch	30s	
Crosby Bing*	You Brought A New Kind Of Love To Me	Columbia - 2171 - D	Whiteman Paul Orch	30s	
Crosby Bing & Andrews Sisters	You Don't Have To Know . . .	Decca - 24282	Schoen Vic Orch	40s	
Crosby Bing & Andrews Sisters	You Don't Have To Know . . .	Film Master - 1948	Schoen Vic Orch	40s	
Crosby B. (Rhythm Boys)*	You Got Love	Film Master - 1930		30s	
Crosby Bing	You Must Have Been A Beautiful Baby	Decca - 2147	Crosby Bob and his orch.	40s	
Crosby Bing & Jesters	You Sang My Love Song To Somebody Else	Decca - 23508	Haggart Bob Orch	40s	
Crosby Bing*	You Took Advantage Of Me	Victor - 21398	Whiteman Paul Orch	20s	
Crosby Bing	You've Got Me Crying Again	Brunswick - 6515	& orch	30s	
Crosby Bing & Judy Garland	You've Got Me Where You Want Me	Decca - 23410	Lilley Joseph Orchestra	40s	
Crosby Bing	Young And Healthy	Brunswick - 6472	Lombardo Guy Orch.	30s	
Crosby Bing & Louis Jordan	Your Socks Don't Match	Decca - 23417	Jordan L & his Tympany Five	40s	
Crosby Bing	Youre Beautiful Tonight, My Dear	Brunswick - 6477	Lombardo Guy Orch.	30s	
Crosby Bing	Youre Getting To Be A Habit With Me	Brunswick - 6472	Lombardo Guy Orch.	30s	
Crosby Bing	Youre Still In My Heart	Brunswick - 6285	& orch	30s	
Crosby B. & Jane Wyman	Zing A Little Song	Decca - 28255		50s	
Crosby Bob*	Eeny Meeny Miney Mo	Decca - 633	Crosby, Bob and his orch.	30s	
Crosby Bob*	Here Is My Heart	Decca - 331	Dorsey Brothers Orch	30s	
Crosby Bob*	I Believe In Miracles	Decca-335	Dorsey Brothers Orch	30s	
Crosby Bob*	In A Little Gypsy Tea Room	Decca - 478	Crosby Bob & His Orch.	30s	
Crosby Bob*	Lullaby Of Broadway	Decca - 370	Dorsey Brothers Orch.	30s	
Crosby Bob*	What A Difference A Day Made	Decca - 283	Dorsey Brothers Orch.	30s	
Cross Hugh	Wabash Cannonball	Columbia - 15439 - D		20s	
Crudup Arthur	Cool Disposition	Bluebird - 34 - 0738		40s	
Crudup Arthur	Crudup's After Hours	Victor - 20 - 2205		50s	
Crudup Arthur	Gonna Follow My Baby Blues	Bluebird - 34 - 0704		40s	
Crudup Arthur	If I Get Lucky	Bluebird - B - 8858		40s	
Crudup Arthur	Kind Lover Blues	Bluebird - B - 8896		40s	
Crudup Arthur	Mean Old Frisco Blues	Bluebird - 34 - 0704		40s	
Crudup Arthur	My Baby Left Me	Victor - 22 - 0109		50s	
Crudup Arthur	Rock Me Mama	Bluebird - 34 - 0725		40s	
Crudup Arthur	So Glad You're Mine	Victor - 20 - 1949		40s	
Crudup Arthur	That's All Right Mama	Victor - 20 - 2205		40s	
Crumit Frank	Abdul Abulbul Amir	Victor - 20715		20s	
Crumit Frank	Gay Caballero A	Victor - 21735		20s	
Crumit Frank	Girl Friend, The	Victor - 20124		20s	
Crumit Frank	I Learned About Women From.	Victor - 21735		20s	
Crumit Frank	Little Brown Jug	Victor - 24092		20s	
Crumit Frank	Love Nest The - AC	Columbia - A2973		20s	
Crumit Frank	Margie - AC	Columbia - A3332		20s	
Crumit Frank	Mountain Greenery	Victor - 20124		20s	
Crumit Frank	My Honeys Lovin Arms - AC	Columbia - A3699	Miller Ray Novelty Orch	20s	
Crumit Frank	My Little Bimbo Down . . . - AC	Columbia - A2981.		30s	
Crumit Frank	Nagasaki	Victor - 21603		20s	
Crumit Frank	Old Fashioned Love - AC	ColumbiaA3997		20s	
Crumit Frank	Song Of The Prune, The	Victor - 21430		20s	
Crumit Frank	The Return Of Abdul Abulbul. AC	Victor - 22482		20s	
Crumit Frank	Ukelele Lady - AC	Victor - 19701		20s	
Dalhart Vernon	Cindy Cindy - AC	Challenge - 405		20s	
Dalhart Vernon	Lindbergh The Eagle Of The USA	Columbia - 1000 - D		20s	
Dalhart Vernon	Lucky Lindy	Columbia - 1000 - D		20s	
Dalhart Vernon	Pick Me Up And Lay Me . . . - AC	Columbia - A3575		20s	
Dalhart Vernon	Prisioners Song, The - AC	Victor - 19427		20s	
Dalhart Vernon	There's A New Star In Heaven.	Victor - 21093		20s	
Dalhart Vernon	Wreck Of The Old 97, The - AC	Victor - 19427		20s	
Damone Vic	April In Paris	Mercury - 70022	Siravo George Orch	50s	
Damone Vic	I Have But One Heart	Mercury - 5053	Gray Jerry Orch	40s	
Damone Vic	I Love You So Much It Hurts	Mercury - 5261	Osser Glenn Orch	40s	
Damone Vic	I'm Walking Behind You	Mercury - 70128	Carroll David Orch	50s	
Damone Vic	In The Still Of The Night	Mercury - 5350	Osser Glenn Orch	50s	
Damone Vic	My Heart Cries For You	Mercury - 5563	Sirabo George Orch	50s	
Damone Vic	On The Street Where You . . .	Columbia - 40654	Faith Percy Orch	50s	
Damone Vic	Take Me In Your Arms	Mercury - 5486		50s	
Damone Vic	Why Was I Born	Mercury - 5326	Osser Glenn Orch	50s	
Damone Vic	Youre Breaking My Heart	Mercury - 5261	Osser Glenn Orch	40s	
Dandridge Dorothy	Jungle Jive	Film Master - 1942		40s	
Darby & Tarlton	Columbus Stockade Blues	Columbia - 15212 - D	Darby & Tarlton	20s	
Darin Bobby	Mack The Knife	Atco - 6147		50s	
Darin Bobby	Sorrow Tomorrow	Atco - LP - 33 - 146		60s	

Davies Ramona*	Are You Making Any Money	Victor - 24365	Whiteman Paul Orch	30s	
Davis Benny*	Baby Face	Victor - 22809	Garber Jan & His Orch.	20s	
Davis Betty	They're Either Too Young Or.	Film Master - 1943		40s	
Davis Jimmie	Alimony Blues	Bluebird - B - 5635		30s	
Davis Jimmie	Arabella Blues	Victor - 23517		30s	
Davis Jimmie	Bang Bang	Decca - 46016		40s	
Davis Jimmie	Barroom Message The	Victor - V - 40154		20s	
Davis Jimmie	Bear Cat Mama From . . .	Victor - 23517		30s	
Davis Jimmie	Columbus Stockade Blues	Decca - 6083		40s	
Davis Jimmie	Come On Over To My House	Decca - 5249		30s	
Davis Jimmie	Davis Salty Dog	Victor - 23674		30s	
Davis Jimmie	Doggone That Train	Victor - V - 40286		30s	
Davis Jimmie	Grieving My Heart Out For You	Decca - 18756		40s	
Davis Jimmie	Honky Tonk Blues	Decca - 5400	Brown's Musical Brownies	30s	
Davis Jimmie	I Just Dropped In To Say Goodbye	Decca - 46066		40s	
Davis Jimmie	I Wonder Who's Kissing Her . . .	Decca - 5363		30s	
Davis Jimmie	Im Waiting For Ships That . . .	Decca - 5867		30s	
Davis Jimmie	In Arkansas	Victor - 23525		30s	
Davis Jimmie	It Makes No Difference Now	Decca - 5620		30s	
Davis Jimmy	It's All Coming Home To You	Bluebird - B - 5156		30s	
Davis Jimmie	Live And Let Live	Decca - 6053		40s	
Davis Jimmie	Lonely Hobo	Victor - 23648		30s	
Davis Jimmie	Mama's Getting Hot And . . .	Decca - 5249		30s	
Davis Jimmie	My Blue Heaven	Decca - 5779		30s	
Davis Jimmie	My Louisiana Girl	Victor - V - 40302		30s	
Davis Jimmie	Nobody's Darlin But Mine	Decca - 5090		30s	
Davis Jimmie	Organ Grinder Blues	Victor - 23763		30s	
Davis Jimmie	Out of Town	Victor - V - 40215		20s	
Davis Jimmie	She's A Hum Dum Dinger . . .	Victor - 23587		30s	
Davis Jimmie	Sweethearts Or Strangers	Decca - 5902	Mitchell Charles Orch	40s	
Davis Jimmie	Theres A New Moon Over My.	Decca - 6105		40s	
Davis Jimmie	Tired Of Crying Over You	Decca - 18832	Welk Lawrence Orch	40s	
Davis Jimmie	Tom Cat And Pussy Blues	Victor - 23763		30s	
Davis Jimmy	Walkin' My Blues Away	Decca - 6083		40s	
Davis Jimmie	Woman's Blues, A	Victor - 23544		30s	
Davis Jimmie	You Are My Sunshine	Decca - 6813	Mitchell Charles Orch	40s	
Davis Jr. Sammy	Bang Bang	Film Master - 1964		60s	
Davis Jr. Sammy	Bang Bang	Reprise - LP - 2021		60s	
Davis Jr. Sammy	Be - Bop The Beguine	Capital - 70022		40s	
Davis Jr. Sammy	Candy Man, The	MGM - 14360		70s	
Davis Jr. S. & Carmen McRae	Happy To Make Your Acquaintence	Decca - LP - 8490		50s	
Davis Jr. Sammy	Hey There	Decca - 29199		50s	
Davis Jr. Sammy	I Do I Do	Film Master - 1933		30s	
Davis Jr. Sammy	I Don't Care Who Knows	Capital - 15390		40s	
Davis Jr. Sammy	Ive Gotta Be Me	Reprise - 20779		60s	
Davis Jr. Sammy	Mr. Booze	Reprise - LP - 2021		60s	
Davis Jr. Sammy	Singing In The Rain	Casablanca - LP - 1296	Severinsen Doc Orch.	70s	
Davis Jr. Sammy	That Old Black Magic	Decca - 29541		50s	
Davis Jr. S. & Carmen McRae	They Dident Believe Me	Decca - LP - 8490		50s	
Davis Jr Sammy	Too Close For Comfort	Decca - 29861		50s	
Davis Jr. S. (Shorty Muggins)	We're Gonna Roll	Capital - 70052		50s	
Davis Jr. Sammy	What Kind Of Fool Am I	Reprise - 20048		60s	
Davis Jr. Sammy	You Rascal You	Film Master - 1933		30s	
Dawn Dolly*	Have You Got Any Castles . . .	Variety - 621	Hall George Orch	30s	
Dawn Dolly	How Could You	Bluebird - B - 6797	Hall George Orch	30s	
Dawn Dolly	How'd Ya Like To Love Me	Vocalion - 4018	Dolly Dawn & Her Dawn P.	30s	
Dawn Dolly*	I Never Saw A Better Night	Bluebird - B - 6016	Hall George Orch	30s	
Dawn Dolly*	It's a Sin To Tell A Lie	Bluebird - B - 6378	Hall George Orch	30s	
Dawn Dolly*	Mood That I'm In The	Bluebird - B - 6861	Hall George Orch	30s	
Dawn Dolly*	No Strings	Bluebird - B - 6098	Hall George Orch	30s	
Dawn Dolly*	Remember Me	Variety - 623	Hall George Orch	30s	
Dawn Dolly*	Robins And Roses	Bluebird - B - 6381	Hall George Orch	30s	
Dawn Dolly*	Says My Heart	Vocalion - 4098	Hall George Orch	30s	
Dawn Dolly*	Shine	Bluebird - B - 6170	Hall George Orch	30s	
Dawn Dolly*	Sing A Song Of Nonsence . . .	Bluebird - B - 6576	Hall George Orch	30s	
Dawn Dolly	There Wont Be A Shortage . . .	Elite - 5018	Dolly Dawn & Her Dawn P.	40s	
Dawn Dolly*	Weatherman	Bluebird - B - 6017	Hall George Orch	30s	
Dawn Dolly*	You Cant Pull The Wool . . .	Bluebird - B - 6382	Hall George Orch	30s	
Dawn Dolly	You Can't Stop Me From . . .	Variety - 652	Dawn Dolly & Her Dawn P.	30s	
Dawn Dolly*	Youre A Sweetheart	Vocalion - 3874	Hall George Orch	30s	
Day Doris*	Aren't You Glad You're You	Columbia - 36875	Brown Les & His Orch	40s	
Day Doris	At The Café Rendezvous	Columbia - 38517	Raring John Orch	40s	
Day Doris*	Beau Night In Hotchkiss C . . .	Okeh - 6098	Brown Les & His Orch	40s	

Day Doris	Bewitched	Columbia - 38698		40s	
Day Doris*	Broomstreet	Okeh - 6049	Brown Les & His Orch	40s	
Day Doris*	Come To Baby Do	Columbia - 36884	Brown Les Orch	40s	
Day Doris*	Day By Day	Columbia - 36945	Brown Les & His Orch	40s	
Day Doris*	Dig It	Okeh - 5964	Brown Les & His Orch	40s	
Day Doris	Domino	Columbia - 39596	Weston Paul Orch	50s	
Day Doris	Everybody Loves A Lover	Columbia - 41195	De Vol Frank Orch.	50s	
Day Doris	If I Give My Heart To You	Columbia - 40300		50s	
Day Doris	Ill Never Stop Loving You	Columbia - LP - CL - 710	Faith Percy Orch	50s	
Day Doris	Its A Great Feeling	Columbia - 38517	Raring John Orch	40s	
Day Doris	Its Magic	Columbia - 38188	Siravo George Orch	40s	
Day Doris*	I've Got The Sun In The Morning	Columbia - 36977	Brown Les & His Orch	40s	
Day Doris*	Keep Cool Fool	Okeh - 6167	Brown Les & His Orch	40s	
Day Doris*	Lets Be Buddies	Okeh - 5937	Brown Les & His Orch	40s	
Day Doris	Love Me Or Leave Me	Columbia - LP - CL - 710	Faith Percy Orch	50s	
Day Doris	Mean To Me	Columbia - LP - CL - 710	Faith Percy Orch	50s	
Day Doris*	My Dreams Are Getting Better All The Time	Columbia - 36779	Brown Les & His Orch	40s	
Day Doris	My Lost Horizon	Film Master - 1941	Brown Les Orchestra	40s	
Day Doris	Never Look Back	Columbia - LP - CL - 710	Faith Percy Orch	50s	
Day Doris	Secret Love	Columbia - 40108	Heindorf Ray Orch	50s	
Day Doris*	Sentimental Journey	Columbia - 36769	Brown Les & His Orch	40s	
Day Doris	Song is You, The	Columbia - LP - CL - 142	Weston, Paul & His Orch.	50s	
Day Doris & Frankie Laine - NAP	Sugarbush	Columbia - 39693		50s	
Day Doris*	T'Aint Me	Columbia - 36804	Brown Les & His Orch	40s	
Day Doris	Ten Cents A Dance	Columbia - LP - CL - 710	Faith Percy Orch	50s	
Day Doris*	There's Good Blues Tonight	Columbia - 36972	Brown Les & His Orch	40s	
Day Doris*	Till The End Of Time	Columbia - 36828	Brown Les & His Orch	40s	
Day Doris*	We'll Be Together Again	Columbia - 36875	Brown Les & His Orch	40s	
Day Doris	Whatever Will Be Will Be	Columbia - 40704	De Vol Frank Orch.	50s	
Day Doris	Whatever Will Be Will Be	Film Master - 1956		50s	
Day Doris	When I Fall In Love	Columbia - 39786	Faith Percy dir. orch.	50s	
Day Irene*	Do You Care	Bluebird - B - 11198	Donahue Sam Orch	40s	
De Castro Sisters	Teach Me Tonight	Abbott - 3001		50s	
De Leath Vaughn(Betty Brown)	Aint Misbehavin'	Grey Gull - 2501		20s	
De Leath Vaughn	All By My Lonesome Blues - AC	Okeh - 4492		20s	
De Leath Vaughn	All By Myself - AC	Okeh - 4355		20s	
De Leath Vaughn*	Aloha Oe Blues	Columbia - 1251 - D	Moana Orchestra	20s	
De Leath Vaughn	Are You Lonesome Tonight	Edison - 52044		20s	
De Leath Vaughn	Baby Your Mother	Victor - 20873		20s	
De Leath Vaughn	Blue Skies	Okeh - 40750		20s	
De Leath Vaughn*	Button Up Your Overcoat	Columbia - 1736 - D	Whiteman Paul Orch	20s	
De Leath Vaughn	Bye Bye Blackbird - AC	Cameo - 963		20s	
De Leath Vaughn(Gloria Geer)	Bye Bye Blackbird - AC	Romeo - 240		20s	
De Leath Vaughn	Crazy Words Crazy Tune	Brunswick - 3443		20s	
De Leath Vaughn	Here Comes Fatima	Champion - 15178	Broadway Strollers	20s	
De Leath Vaughn & Tom Stacks	Honolulu Moon	Columbia - 1026 - D	Clicquot Club Eskimos	20s	
De Leath Vaughn*	I Wanna Be Loved By You	Columbia - 1604 - D	Broadway Nitelites	30s	
De Leath Vaughn	Im Just Wild About Harry - AC	Gennett - 4905		20s	
De Leath Vaughn	Like An Angel You Flew Into . . .	Victor - 20674		20s	
De Leath Vaughn	Lovin Sam The Sheik Of . . . - AC	Bell - P - 182		20s	
De Leath Vaughn*	Man I Love The	Columbia - 50058 - D	Whiteman Paul Orch	20s	
De Leath Vaughn	Sometimes Im Happy	Brunswick - 3608		20s	
De Leath Vaughn	Toymakers Dream, The	Victor - 21975		20s	
De Leath Vaughn	Ukelele Lady - AC	Columbia - 361 - D		50s	
De Leath Vaughn	Where'd You Get Those Eyes	Gennett - 3347		20s	
De Leath Vaughn	Whisper Song The	Okeh - 40814		20s	
Dean Jimmie	Bumming Around	Four Star - 1613		50s	
Delmare Brothers	Blues Stay Away From Me	King - 803	Delmare Brothers	40s	
Delta Rhythm Boys	Dry Bones	Decca - 4406		40s	
Delta Rhythm Boys	Gee Baby Aint I Good To You	Decca - 18650		40s	
Delta Rhythm Boys	Just A Sittin And Rockin	Decca - 18739		40s	
Delta Rhythm Boys	One O'Clock Jump	Victor - 20 - 2463		40s	
Delta Rhythm Boys	Praise The Lord & Pass . . .	Decca - 4406		40s	
Delta Rhythm Boys	September Song	Victor - 20 - 2460		40s	
Delta Rhythm Boys	Take The A Train	Victor - 20 - 2461		40s	
Dennis Dennis* - NAP	South Of The Border	Decca - 2732	Ambrose & His Orch	30s	
Derwin Hal*	South Of The Border	Bluebird - B - 10376	Fields Shep & HRR Orch	30s	
Desmond Johnny	Let Her Go, Let Her Go	MGM - 10518		40s	
Destine Jean Leon	Congo Noundong	Decca - 40027	Dunham. K. & Ensemble	40s	
Destine Jean Leon	Soli Ohi	Decca - 40026	Dunham. K. & Ensemble	40s	

Dexter Al	Pistol Packin'Mama	Okeh - 6708	Dexter Al and his Troopers	40s	
Dietrich Marlene	Boys In The Backroom, The	Film Master 1939		30s	
Dietrich Marlene	Falling In Love Again	Film Master - 1930		30s	
Dietrich Marlene	Falling In Love Again	Victor - 22593	Comedienne with orch	30s	
Dietrich Marlene	Laziest Gal In Town The	Film Master 1949		40s	
Dietrich Marlene	Lily Marlene	Radio Master 1944?		40s	
Dietrich Marlene	Lili Marlene	Decca - 23456	Magnante Charles Orch.	40s	
Dietrich Marlene	Naughty Lola	Film Master - 1930		30s	
Dinning Sisters	I Wonder Who's Kissing Her Now	Capital - 433		20s	
Dinwiddie Quartet	Poor Mourner - AC	Victor - 1715		10s	
Dixie Jubilee Singers	Waiting At The End Of The . . .	Film Master - 1929		20s	
Domino Fats	Blueberry Hill	Imperial - 5407		50s	
Domino Fats	My Blue Heaven	Imperial - 5386		50s	
Domino Fats	When My Dreamboat Comes.	Imperial - 5396		50s	
Dominos	Have Mercy Baby	Federal - 12068		50s	
Dominos - Billy Ward	I Really Don't Want To Know	King - 1368	Dominos the	50s	
Donegan Lonnie	Rock Island Line	London - 1650	& His Skiffle Group	50s	
Downey Morton	Two Loves Have I	HOW - 1201		30s	
Downey Morton	Auf Weidersehen, My. - NAP	Melotone - M - 12319		30s	
Drifters the	Money Honey	Atlantic - 1006		50s	
Drifters the	Save The Last Dance For Me	Atlantic - 2071		60s	
Duncan & Bubbles	It Aint Necessarily So	Brunswick - 7562		30s	
Dudley S.H.	She was Happy Till... - AC	Berliner - 1961		0os	
Duncan Tommy*	Worried Mind	Okeh - 06101	Willis, B & his Texas Playboys.	40s	
Dunham K. & J. L. Destine	Choucounne	Decca - 40028	Dunham. K. & Ensemble	40s	
Dunham K. & J. L. Destine	Nago	Decca - 40029	Dunham. K. & Ensemble	40s	
Dunham Katherine	Batucada	Decca - 40026	Dunham. K. & Ensemble	40s	
Dunham Katherine	Callate	Decca - 40027	Dunham. K. & Ensemble	40s	
Dunlap Margurite	Mighty Lak' A Rose - AC - NAP	Victor - 5837		11s	
Dunne Irene	After The Ball	Film Master - 1936		30s	
Dunne Irene	Cant Help Lovin That Man	Film Master - 1936		30s	
Dunne Irene	Smoke Gets In Your Eyes	Film Master - 1935		30s	
Dunne Irene	Yesterdays	Film Master - 1935		30s	
Durante Jimmy	Inka Dinka Doo	Brunswick - 6774	Durante Jimmy Orch	30s	
Durante Jimmy	Inka Dinka Doo	Film Master - 1934		30s	
East Texas Serenaders, the	Shannon WaltzAC	Brunswick - 282	East Texas Serenaders	20s	
Eaton Mary	Baby Face	Film Master - 1929		20s	
Eberle Ray & Modernaires*	Elmer's Tune - NAP	Bluebird - B - 11274	Miller Glenn Orch	40s	
Eberle Ray*	Devil May Care	Bluebird - B - 10717	Miller Glenn Orch	40s	
Eberle Ray*	Blueberry Hill	Bluebird - B - 10768	Miller Glenn Orch	30s	
Eberle Ray*	My Prayer	Bluebird - B - 10404	Miller Glenn Orch	40s	
Eberle Ray*	Nightingale Sang in . . .	Bluebird -B - 10931	Miller Glenn Orch.	40s	
Eberly Bob & Kitty Kallen*	Besame Mucho	Decca - 18574	Dorsey Jimmy Orch	40s	
Eberly Bob with H. O'Connell*	Green Eyes	Decca - 3698	Dorsey Jimmy Orch	40s	
Eberly Bob*	All Or Nothing At All	Decca - 2580	Dorsey Jimmy Orch.	40s	
Eberly Bob*	All This And Heaven Too	Decca - 3259	Dorsey Jimmy Orch	40s	
Eberly Bob*	Chasing Shadows	Decca - 476	Dorsey Brothers Orch	30s	
Eberly Bob*	I Dident Know What Time It Was	Decca - 2813	Dorsey Jimmy Orch	30s	
Eberly Bob*	Marie Elena	Decca - 3698	Dorsey Jimmy Orch	40s	
Eckstine Billy & Sarah Vaughan	Alexanders Ragetime Band	Mercury - LP - 203161		50s	
Eckstine Billy & Sarah Vaughan	Always	Mercury - LP - 203161		50s	
Eckstine Billy	Blue Moon	MGM - 10311	vocal	30s	
Eckstine Billy & Sarah Vaughan	Cheek To Cheek	Mercury - LP - 203161		50s	
Eckstine Billy	Cottage For Sale A	National - 9014		40s	
Eckstine Billy & Sarah Vaughan	Easter Parade	Mercury - LP - 203161		50s	
Eckstine Billy	Good Jelly Blues	De - Lux - 2000	Eckstine Billy Orch.	40s	
Eckstine Billy	Here Comes The Blues	MGM - 10916	Herman Woody Orch	40s	
Eckstine Billy	I Do - Do You	National - 9086	vocal	40s	
Eckstine Billy	I Left My Hat In Hati	MGM - 10916	Herman Woody Orch	40s	
Eckstine Billy & Sarah Vaughan	I Love You	MGM - 11144		50s	
Eckstine Billy	I Want To Talk About You	De - Lux - 2003	Eckstine Billy Orch.	40s	
Eckstine Billy & Sarah Vaughan	Isent This A Lovely Day	Mercury - LP - 203161		50s	
Eckstine Billy & Sarah Vaughan	Ive Got My Love To Keep Me Warm	Mercury - LP - 203161		50s	
Eckstine Billy	Jelly Jelly	National - 9021	Eckstine Billy Orch.	40s	
Eckstine Billy*	Jelly Jelly Blues	Bluebird - B - 11065	Hines Earle Orch	40s	
Eckstine Billy*	Jitny Man, (The)	Bluebird - B - 11535	Hines Earle Orch	40s	
Eckstine Billy*	My Heart Beats For You	Victor - 20 - 2636	Hines Earle Orch	40s	
Eckstine Billy & Sarah Vaughan	Now It Can Be Told	Mercury - LP - 203161		50s	

Eckstine Billy & Sarah Vaughan	Passing Strangers	Mercury - 71120		50s	
Eckstine Billy & Sarah Vaughan	Remember	Mercury - LP - 203161		50s	
Eckstine Billy*	Skylark	Bluebird - B - 11512	Hines Earle Orch.	40s	
Eckstine Billy*	Somehow	Bluebird - B - 11432	Hines Earle Orch	40s	
Eckstine Billy*	Stormy Monday Blues	Bluebird - B - 11567	Hines Earle Orch	40s	
Eckstine Billy*	Water Boy	Bluebird - B - 11329	Hines Earle Orch.	40s	
Eckstine Billy	You Call It Madness But I Call It Love	National - 9019		40s	
Eckstine Billy & Sarah Vaughan	Youre Just In Love	Mercury - LP - 203161		50s	
Edwards Cliff	After My Laughter Came Tears	Columbia - 1254 - D		20s	
Edwards Cliff	Anita	Columbia - 1609 - D.		20s	
Edwards Cliff	Come Back Chiquita	Columbia - 1514 - D		20s	
Edwards Cliff	Halfway To Heaven	Columbia - 1523 - D		20s	
Edwards Cliff	I Cant Give You Anything But Love	Columbia - 1471 - D		20s	
Edwards Cliff	I Want To Call You Sweet Mama	Vocalion - 2578		30s	
Edwards Cliff	I'll Buy The Ring - AC	Pathe - 025131		20s	
Edwards Cliff	I'll See You In My Dreams	Columbia - 2169 - D		30s	
Edwards Cliff	Im A Bear In A Lady's . . .	ARC Master		30s	
Edwards Cliff	Im Gonna Give It To Mary . . .	ARC Master		30s	
Edwards Cliff	Its Only A Paper Moon	Vocalion - 2587		30s	
Edwards Cliff	Just You Just Me	Columbia - 1907 - D		20s	
Edwards Cliff	Keep Croonin' A Tune - AC	Pathe - 25164	Hot Combination & his	20s	
Edwards Cliff	Lonesomest Girl In Town The	Perfect - 11594	Hot Combination & his	20s	
Edwards Cliff	Love Is Just Around The Corner	Romeo - 2428		30s	
Edwards Cliff	Mary Ann	Columbia - 1295 - D		20s	
Edwards Cliff	Me And The Man In The Moon	Columbia - 1705 - D		20s	
Edwards Cliff	Meadow Lark - AC	Perfect - 11633	Hot Combination & his	20s	
Edwards Cliff	Night Is Young And You're So.	Decca - 1106	Iona Andy & his Hawaiians	30s	
Edwards Cliff	Orage Blossom Time	Columbia - 1869 - D		20s	
Edwards Cliff	Paddlin' Madelin' Home - AC	Pathe - 025149		20s	
Edwards Cliff	Singing In The Rain	Columbia - 1869 - D		20s	
Edwards Cliff	Singing In The Rain	Film Master - 1929		20s	
Edwards Cliff	That's My Weakness Now	Columbia - 1471 - D		20s	
Edwards Cliff	Together	Columbia - 1295 - D		20s	
Edwards Cliff	When You And I Were Young.	Radio Master - 1934		30s	
Edwards Cliff	When You Wish Upon A Star	Victor - 26477		40s	
Edwards Cliff	Where The Lazy Daisies . . . - AC	Regal - 9620		20s	
Edwards Cliff - (Ukulele Ike)	Alabamy Bound - AC	Pathe - 025127		20s	
Edwards Cliff - (Ukulele Ike)	Charlie My Boy - AC	Pathe - 025122		20s	
Edwards Cliff - (Ukulele Ike)	Clap Hands Here Comes . . . - AC	Pathe - 025167		20s	
Edwards Cliff - (Ukulele Ike)	Facinating Rhythm - AC	Pathe - 025126		20s	
Edwards Cliff - (Ukulele Ike)	Great Big Bunch Of You A	Brunswick - 6319		30s	
Edwards Cliff - (Ukulele Ike)	Hard Hearted Hannah - AC	Pathe - 032054		20s	
Edwards Cliff - (Ukulele Ike)	Heart Breaking Creole Rose - AC	Pathe - 025153		20s	
Edwards Cliff - (Ukulele Ike)	I Can't Believe That Youre . . .	Perfect - 11638		20s	
Edwards Cliff - (Ukulele Ike)	He's The Hottest Man In . . . - AC	Pathe - 025123		20s	
Edwards Cliff - (Ukulele Ike)	I Can't Get The One That I.	Perfect - 12354		20s	
Edwards Cliff - (Ukulele Ike)	I Don't Want Nobody But You - AC	Perfect - 11626		20s	
Edwards Cliff - (Ukulele Ike)	I Want To Walk In Again Blues	Pathe - 032041		20s	
Edwards Cliff - (Ukulele Ike)	I Wonder What's Become . . . - AC	Pathe - 025122		20s	
Edwards Cliff - (Ukulele Ike)	Im Tellin' The Birds Im Tellin . . .	Perfect - 11634		20s	
Edwards Cliff - (Ukulele Ike)	Insufficient Sweetie - AC	Pathe - 025121		20s	
Edwards Cliff - (Ukulele Ike)	It Had To Be You - AC	Pathe - 032047		20s	
Edwards Cliff - (Ukulele Ike)	Me And My Shadow	Perfect - 11643		20s	
Edwards Cliff - (Ukulele Ike)	My Best Girl - AC	Pathe - 025123		20s	
Edwards Cliff - (Ukulele Ike)	Oh Lady Be Good - AC	Pathe - 025130		20s	
Edwards Cliff - (Ukulele Ike)	Remember - AC	Perfect - 11611		20s	
Edwards Cliff - (Ukulele Ike)	Say Who Is That Baby Doll - AC	Perfect - 11593		20s	
Edwards Cliff - (Ukulele Ike)	She's My Sheba Im Her . . . - AC	Pathe - 10882		20s	
Edwards Cliff - (Ukulele Ike)	Somebody Loves Me - AC	Pathe - 032073		20s	
Edwards Cliff - (Ukulele Ike)	What Does It Matter - AC	Pathe - 25207		20s	
Edwards Cliff - (Ukulele Ike)	Whisper Song The	Perfect - 25206		20s	
Edwards Cliff - (Ukulele Ike)	Youre So Cute	Perfect - 11553		20s	
Edwards Cliff*	Virginia Blues - AC	Gennett - 4843	Ladd's Black Aves	20s	
Edwards Cliff* unacredited	Bringing Home The Bacon	Perfect - 14282	Fred Ozarks Jug Blowers	20s	
Ellis Seger	Aint Misbehavin'	Okeh - 41291	Ellis Seger Orch	30s	
English Peggy	Just Like A Butterfly	Vocallion - 15568		20s	
Ennis Skinnay*	Lovable	Brunswick - 3937	Kemp Hal Orchestra	20s	
Ennis Skinnay*	When Im With You	Brunswick - 7745	Kemp Hal Orchestra	20s	
Ennis Skinnay*	Where Or When	Brunswick - 7856	Kemp Hal Orchestra	30s	
Estes Jon	Street Car Blues	Victor - V38614		20s	
Estes Sleepy John	Airplane Blues	Decca - 7354		30s	

Estes Sleepy John	Divin Duck Blues	Victor - V38549		20s	
Estes Sleepy John	Milk Cow Blues	Victor - V38614		30s	
Estrada La Rosita	Toitica	Decca - 20028	Dunham. K. & Ensemble	40s	
Etting Ruth	Aint Misbehavin'	Columbia - 1958 - D		20s	
Etting Ruth	At Twilight	Columbia - 1958 - D		20s	
Etting Ruth	Back In Your Own Backyard	Columbia - 1288 - D		20s	
Etting Ruth	Because My Baby Don't Mean Maybe Now	Columbia - 1420 - D		20s	
Etting Ruth	Body And Soul	Columbia - 2300 - D		30s	
Etting Ruth	Build A Little Home	Brunswick - 6697		30s	
Etting Ruth	Button Up Your Overcoat	Columbia - 1762 - D		20s	
Etting Ruth	Cigarettes, Cigars	Perfect - 12737		30s	
Etting Ruth	Close Your Eyes	Brunswick - 6657		30s	
Etting Ruth	Cottage For Sale A	Columbia - 2172 - D		20s	
Etting Ruth	Could I ? I Certainly Could - AC	Columbia - 633 - D		20s	
Etting Ruth	Crying For The Carolinas	Columbia - 2073 - D		20s	
Etting Ruth	Cuban Love Song	Columbia - 2580 - D		30s	
Etting Ruth	Dancing With Tears In My Eyes	Columbia - 2216 - D		30s	
Etting Ruth	Dancing With Tears In My Eyes	Film Master - 1930		30s	
Etting Ruth	Dancing With Tears In My Eyes	Radio Master - 1930	Selvin Ben Orch	30s	
Etting Ruth	Deed I Do	Columbia - 865 - D		20s	
Etting Ruth	Deep Night	Columbia - 1801 - D		20s	
Etting Ruth	Don't Tell Him What Happened.	Columbia - 2280 - D		30s	
Etting Ruth	Easy Come Easy Go	Brunswick - 6892		30s	
Etting Ruth	Everything I Have Is Yours	Brunswick - 6719		30s	
Etting Ruth	Exactly Like You	Columbia - 2199 - D		30s	
Etting Ruth	Falling In Love Again	Columbia - 2445 - D		30s	
Etting Ruth	Funny Dear What Love Can Do	Columbia - 2146 - D		30s	
Etting Ruth	Glad Rag Doll	Columbia - 1733 - D		20s	
Etting Ruth	Goodnight My Love	Decca - 1107		30s	
Etting Ruth	Guilty	Columbia - 2529 - D		30s	
Etting Ruth	Happy Days And Lonely Nights	Columbia - 1454 - D		20s	
Etting Ruth	Hold Me	Banner - 32739		30s	
Etting Ruth	Holiday Sweethearts	Rex - 8881		30s	
Etting Ruth	If I Could Be With You One . . .	Columbia - 2300 - D		30s	
Etting Ruth	I'll Be Blue Just Thinking of You	Columbia - 2307 - D		30s	
Etting Ruth	I'll Get By As Long As.	Columbia - 1733 - D		20s	
Etting Ruth	I'll Never Be The Same	Banner - 32499		30s	
Etting Ruth	Im Good For Nothing But Love	Columbia - 2505 - D		30s	
Etting Ruth	Im Nobodys Baby	Columbia - 1104 - D		20s	
Etting Ruth	Im Walking Around In A . . .	Columbia - 1830 - D		20s	
Etting Ruth	Im Yours	Columbia - 2318 - D		30s	
Etting Ruth	In The Chapel In The Moonlight	Decca - 1084		30s	
Etting Ruth	It All Belongs To Me	Columbia - 1113 - D		20s	
Etting Ruth	It All Depends On You	Columbia - 908 - D		20s	
Etting Ruth	It Happened In Monterey	Columbia - 2199 - D		30s	
Etting Ruth	it's a Sin To Tell A Lie	Rex - 8853	Wilbur Jay Orchestra	30s	
Etting Ruth	Its Swell Of You	Decca - 1212		30s	
Etting Ruth	Ive Got An Invitation To . . .	Columbia - 2985 - D		30s	
Etting Ruth	Just A Little Closer	Columbia - 2307 - D		30s	
Etting Ruth	Laughing At Life	Columbia - 2318 - D		30s	
Etting Ruth	Lazy Day	Banner - 32448		30s	
Etting Ruth	Let Me Sing And Im Happy	Columbia - 2172 - D		30s	
Etting Ruth	Let Me Sing And Im Happy	Film Master - 1930		30s	
Etting Ruth	Linger A Little Longer In The Twilight	Banner - 32714		30s	
Etting Ruth	Lonesome And Sorry - AC	Columbia - 644 - D		20s	
Etting Ruth	Love Letters In The Sand	Conqueror - 7823		30s	
Etting Ruth	Love Me Or Leave Me	Columbia - 1680 - D		20s	
Etting Ruth	March Winds And April . . .	Columbia - 3014 - D		30s	
Etting Ruth	Maybe Who Knows	Columbia - 1801 - D		20s	
Etting Ruth	Mean To Me	Columbia - 1762 - D		20s	
Etting Ruth	More Than You Know	Columbia - 2038 - D		20s	
Etting Ruth	My Man	Columbia - 995 - D		20s	
Etting Ruth	Needle In A Haystack A	Columbia - 2979 - D		30s	
Etting Ruth	Nevertheless	Oriole - 2291		30s	
Etting Ruth	Night When Love Was Born The	Columbia - 2681 - D		30s	
Etting Ruth	No More Love	Brunswick - 6697		30s	
Etting Ruth	No More Love	Film Master - 1933		30s	
Etting Ruth	Nothing Else To Do - AC	Columbia - 580 - D		20s	
Etting Ruth	On A Dew - Dew - Dewy Day	Columbia - 979 - D		20s	
Etting Ruth	Out In The Cold Again	Columbia - 2955 - D		30s	
Etting Ruth	Out Of Nowhere	Columbia - 2454 - D		30s	
Etting Ruth	Reaching For The Moon	Columbia - 2377 - D		30s	
Etting Ruth	Shaking The Blues Away	Columbia - 1113 - D		20s	

Etting Ruth	Shine On Harvest Moon	Perfect - 12737		30s	
Etting Ruth	Smoke Gets In You Eyes	Brunswick - 6769		30s	
Etting Ruth	Stay As Sweet As You Are	Columbia - 2979 - D		30s	
Etting Ruth	Take Me In Your Arms	Banner - 32634		30s	
Etting Ruth	Talkin To Myself	Columbia - 2954 - D	Grier Jimmy Orch.	30s	
Etting Ruth	Talkin To Myself	Film Master - 1934		30s	
Etting Ruth	Ten Cents A Dance	Columbia - 2146 - D		30s	
Etting Ruth	Song Is Ended The	Columbia - 1196 - D		20s	
Etting Ruth	Things Might Have Been So.	Columbia - 3014 - D		30s	
Etting Ruth	Tormented - (Stormy Weather)	Radio Master - 1936	Black Frank Orch	30s	
Etting Ruth	Try A Little Tenderness	Melotone - M - 12625		30s	
Etting Ruth	Varsity Drag, The	Columbia - 1237 - D		20s	
Etting Ruth	What Wouldent I Do For That Man	Columbia - 1998 - D		20s	
Etting Ruth	When Wer're Alone . . .	Columbia - 2630 - D		30s	
Etting Ruth	When Youre With Somebody.	Columbia - 1288 - D		20s	
Etting Ruth	Where You Sincere	Columbia - 2445 - D		30s	
Etting Ruth	Where Your Ears Burning . . .	Brunswick - 6941		30s	
Etting Ruth	Whos Honey Are You	Radio Master - 1935	Young Victor Orch	30s	
Etting Ruth	Wistful And Blue	Columbia - 924 - D		20s	
Etting Ruth	With My Eyes Wide Open . . .	Brunswick - 6914		30s	
Etting Ruth	Without That Gal	Oriole - 2291		30s	
Etting Ruth	You've Got Me Crying Again	Conqueror - 8154		30s	
Etting Ruth	Youre The Cream In My Coffee	Columbia - 1707 - D		20s	
Etting Ruth	Zing Went The Strings Of My . . .	Radio Master - 1935	Young Victor Orch	30s	
Etting Ruth	Sam The Old Accordian Man	Columbia - 908 - D		20s	
Etting Ruth	Youre The One I Care For	Columbia - 2398 - D		30s	
Etting Ruth*	Dancing With Tears In My Eyes	Columbia - 2206 - D	Selvin Ben Orch	30s	
Etting Ruth*	Hello Baby - AC	Columbia - 716 - D	Kahn Art Orch	20s	
Etting Ruth*	Keep The Cobwebs Off The Moon	Columbia - 1242 - D	Lewis Ted Orch	20s	
Eton Boys (unacredited)	Betty Boop	HOW - F - 3 - 4	Spitalny's Music - Phil	30s	
Evans Dale	Kiss Goodnight A	Film Master - 1945		40s	
Evans Dale	There's Only One Of You	Film Master - 1945	Weeks Anson Orchestra	40s	
Evans Edith	Kansas City Kitty	Brunswick - 4291		20s	
Farrar Geraldine	Mighty Lak' A Rose - AC - NAP	Victor - 88537		10s	
Faye Alice	According To The Moonlight	Romeo - 2483		30s	
Faye Alice	Goodnight My Love	Brunswick - 7821	Feuer Cy dir. Orchestra	30s	
Faye Alice*	Honeymoon Hotel	Bluebird - B - 5171	Connecticut Yankees	30s	
Faye Alice	Here's The Key To My Heart	Brunswick - B - 099	Martin Freddy Orch	30s	
Faye Alice	I'm Just Wild About Harry	Film Master - 1939		30s	
Faye Alice	Im Shooting High	Melotone - M - 6 03 08	Feuer Cy dir. Orchestra	30s	
Faye Alice	It's Swell Of You	Brunswick - 7860		30s	
Faye Alice	Ive Got My Fingers Crossed	Melotone - M - 6 03 09	Feuer Cy dir. Orchestra	30s	
Faye Alice	My Future Star	Film Master - 1934		30s	
Faye Alice	Nasty Man	Film Master - 1933	Vallee Rudy cond. Orch.	30s	
Faye Alice	Nasty Man	Brunswick - B - 099	Martin Freddy Orch	30s	
Faye Alice	Never In A Million Years	Brunswick - 7860		30s	
Faye Alice*	Shame On You	Bluebird - B - 5175	Connecticut Yankees	30s	
Faye Alice	Slumming On Park Avenue	Brunswick - 7825		30s	
Faye Alice	Spreadin Rhythm Around	Melotone - M - 60308	Feuer Cy dir. Orchestra	30s	
Faye Alice	There's A Lull In My Life	Brunswick - 7876	Feuer Cy dir. Orchestra	30s	
Faye Alice	This Years Kisses	Brunswick - 7825	Feuer Cy dir. Orchestra	30s	
Faye Alice	Wake Up And Live	Brunswick - 7876		30s	
Faye Alice	Yes To You	Film Master - 1934		30s	
Faye Alice	Yes To You	Romeo - 2407		30s	
Faye Alice	Youll Never Know	Film Master - 1943		40s	
Faye Alice	Youre A Sweetheart	Film Master - 1938		30s	
Feldkamp Elmer*	Be Still My Heart - NAP	Brunswick - 6998	Martin Freddy Orch	30s	
Feldkamp Elmer*	There's Nothing Too Good For.	Oriole - 2348	Kirkeby Eddie Orch	30s	
Fields Arthur & Peerless Quartet	Keep Your Head Down . . . - AC	Columbia - A2600		10s	
Fields Benny	These Foolish Things . . .	Decca - 849		30s	
Fields Gracie	Machine Gun Song	Film Master - 1943		40s	
Fishe Eddie	Lady Of Spain	Victor - 20 - 4953	Winterhaulter Hugo Orch	50s	
Fisher Eddie	Cindy Oh Cindy	Victor - 20 - - 6677		50s	
Fisher Eddie	I Need You Now	Victor - 20 - 5830	Winterhaulter Hugo Orch	50s	
Fisher Eddie & Sally Sweetland	I'm Walking Behind You	Victor - 20 - 5293	Winterhaulter Hugo Orch	50s	
Fisher Eddie	Im Yours	Victor - 20 - 4574	Winterhaulter Hugo Orch	50s	
Fisher Eddie	Thinking Of You	Victor - 20 - 3901	Winterhaulter Hugo Orch	50s	
Fisher Eddie	Wish You Were Here	Victor - 20 - 4830	Winterhaulter Hugo Orch	50s	
Fisher Eddie	With These Hands	Victor -20 - 5365	Winterhaulter Hugo Orch	50s	
Fisher Eddie - NAP	Oh ! My Pa Pa - NAP	Victor - 20 - 5552	Winterhaulter Hugo Orch	50s	
Fisk University Jubilee Quartet	Swing Low Sweet Chariot - AC	Victor - 16453		10s	
Fitzgerald Ella*	All My Life	Brunswick - 7640	Wilson Teddy Orch	30s	

Fitzgerald Ella	Away In A Manger	Capital - LP - ST - 2805	Carmichael Ralph Orch	60s	
Fitzgerald Ella & Louis Jordan	Baby Its Cold Outside	Decca - 24644	Jordan Louis & his T. Five	40s	
Fitzgerald Ella	Bennys Come Home On Saterday	Decca - 18713	Brooks Randy Orch	40s	
Fitzgerald Ella & Mills Brothers	Big Boy Blue	Decca - 1148		40s	
Fitzgerald Ella*	Chew Chew Chew Your Bubble Gum	Decca - 2389	Webb Chick Orchestra	30s	
Fitzgerald Ella & Ink Spots	Cow Cow Boogie	Decca - 18587		40s	
Fitzgerald Ella*	Everybody Step	Decca - 1894	Webb Chick Orchestra	30s	
Fitzgerald Ella	Five O'Clock Whistle	Decca - 3420	& her famous orchestra	40s	
Fitzgerald Ella	Flying Home	Decca - 23956	Schoen Vic Orch	40s	
Fitzgerald Ella & L. Armstrong	Frim Fram Sauce, (The)	Decca - 23496		40s	
Fitzgerald Ella	Good Morning Blues	Verve - (LP) - V - 4042	De Vol Frank Orch.	50s	
Fitzgerald Ella*	Goodnight My Love	Victor - 25461	Goodman Benny Orch.	30s	
Fitzgerald Ella	Guilty	Decca - 23844	Heywood Eddie Orch	40s	
Fitzgerald Ella & the Llittle Chicks*	Hallelujah	Decca - 15039	Webb Chick Orchestra	30s	
Fitxgerald Ella	Hard Hearted Hannah	Decca - LP - 8166		50s	
Fitzgerald Ella	Have Yourself A Merry Little C.	Verve - (LP) - V - 4042	De Vol Frank Orch.	50s	
Fitzgerald Ella	He's My Guy	Decca - 18472		40s	
Fitzgerald Ella	I Dident Mean A Word I Said	Decca - 18814	Kyle Billy And His Orch	40s	
Fitzgerald Ella & Mills Brothers	I Gotta Have My Baby Back	Decca - 24813		40s	
Fitzgerald Ella	I Put A Four Leave Clover In Your Pocket	Decca - 18472	Four Keys her &	50s	
Fitzgerald Ella*	I Want The Waiter With The Water	Decca - 2628	Webb Chick Orchestra	30s	
Fitzgerald Ella*	I Want The Water With The . . .	Radio Master - 1939	Webb Chick Orchestra	30s	
Fitzgerlad Ella & The Little Chicks*	I Want To Be Happy	Decca - 15039	Webb Chick Orchestra	30s	
Fitzgerald Ella	If Anything Happened To You	Decca - 2481	Savoy Eight & her	30s	
Fitzgerald Ella	If You Ever Change Your Mind	Decca - 2481	Savoy Eight & her	30s	
Fitzgerald Ella*	I'll Chase The Blues Away	Decca - 494	Webb Chick Orchestra	30s	
Fitzgerald & Ink Spots	Im Beginning To See The Light	Decca - 23399		40s	
Fitzgerald Ella	I'm Getting'Mighty Lonesome.	Decca - 4315	Five Keys & her	40s	
Fitzgerald Ella*	Im Just A Jitterbug	Decca - 1899	Webb Chick Orchestra	30s	
Fitzgerald Ella	Im Just A Lucky So And So	Decca - 18814	Kyle Billy And His Orch	40s	
Fitzgerald Ella & Ink Spots	Into Each Life Some Rain Must.	Decca - 23356		40s	
Fitzgerald Ella & Delta R. Boys	Its Only A Paper Moon	Decca - 23425		40s	
Fitzgerald Ella	It's Too Soon To Know	Decca - 24497		40s	
Fitzgerald Ella	Jingle Bells	Verve - (LP) - V - 4042	De Vol Frank Orch.	50s	
Fitzgerald Ella	Kiss Goodnight A	Decca - 18713		40s	
Fitzgerald Ella*	Little Bit Later On A	Decca - 831	Webb Chick Orchestra	30s	
Fitzgerald Ella	Little White Lies	Decca - 2556	Savoy Eight her &	40s	
Fitzgerald Ella*	Love And Kisses	Decca - 494	Webb Chick Orchestra	30s	
Fitzgerald Ella	Mack The Knife	Verve - LP - 4041		60s	
Fitzgerald Ella	My Baby Likes To Be - Bop	Decca - 24332		40s	
Fitzgerald Ella	My Happiness	Decca - 24446	Song Spinners	40s	
Fitzgerald Ella	My Heart And I Decieded	Decca - 18530	Four Keys her &	40s	
Fitzgerald Ella*	My Melancholy Baby	Brunswick - 7729	Wilson Teddy Orch	30s	
Fitzgerald Ella*	Oh Johnny Oh Johnny	Radio Master - 1939	Webb Chick Orchestra	30s	
Fitzgerald Ella	Oh Lady Be Good	Decca - 23956	Haggart Bob Orch	40s	
Fitzgerald Ella & Joe Williams	Party Blues	Verve - CD - 835 - 329 - 2	Basie Count Orch	50s	
Fitzgerald Ella	Pete Kelly's Blues	Decca - LP - 8166		50s	
Fitzgerald Ella & Louis Jordan	Petootie Pie	Decca - 23546	Jordan Louis & his T. Five	40s	
Fitzgerald Ella*	Rhythm And Romance	Decca - 588	Webb Chick Orchestra	30s	
Fitzgerald Ella*	Rock It For Me	Decca - 1586	Webb Chick Orchestra	30s	
Fitzgerald Ella	Rudolph The Red Nosed . . .	Verve - (LP) - V - 4042	De Vol Frank Orch.	50s	
Fitzgerald Ella	Santa Clause Is Coming To T.	Verve - (LP) V - 4042	De Vol Frank Orch.	50s	
Fitzgerald Ella*	Sing Me A Swing Song And Let Me Dance	Decca - 830	Webb Chick Orchestra	30s	
Fitzgerald Ella	Sleep My Little Jesus	Capital - LP - ST - 2805	Carmichael Ralph Orch	60s	
Fitzgerald Ella	Sleigh Ride	Verve - (LP) - V - 4042	De Vol Frank Orch.	50s	
Fitzgerald Ella	Stairway To The Stars	Decca - 2598	Webb Chick Orchestra	30s	
Fitzgerald Ella & Louis Jordan	Stone Cold Dead In The Market	Decca - 23546	Jordan Louis & hisT. Five	40s	
Fitzgerald Ella & A. Love Quintet	Sunday Kind Of Love A	Decca - 23866	Haggart Bob Orch	40s	
Fitzgerald Ella*	Taint What You Do	Decca - 2310	Webb Chick Orchestra	30s	
Fitzgerald Ella*	Take Another Guess Oh Yes	Decca - 1123	Webb Chick Orchestra	30s	
Fitzgerald Ella*	Take Another Guess Oh Yes	Victor - 25461	Goodman Benny Orch.	30s	
Fitzgerald Ella	Taking A Chance On Love	Decca - 3490	Orchestra, & her	40s	
Fitzgerald Ella & the Ink Spots	That's The Way It Is	Decca - 23399		40s	
Fitzgerald Ella*	Tisket A Tasket A	Decca - 1840	Webb Chick Orchestra	30s	
Fitzgerald Ella	Tisket A Tasket A	Film Master - 1942		40s	
Fitzgerald Ella & Joe Williams	Too Close For Comfort	Verve - CD - 835 - 329 - 2	Basie Count Orch	50s	
Fitzgerald Ella*	Undecieded	Decca - 2323	Webb Chick Orchestra	30s	
Fitzgerald Ella*	Vote For Mr. Rhythm	Decca - 1032	Webb Chick Orchestra	30s	
Fitzgerald Ella*	Wacky Dust	Decca - 2021	Webb Chick Orchestra	30s	
Fitzgerald Ella	We Three Kings	Capital - LP - ST - 2805	Carmichael Ralph Orch	60s	

Fitzgerald Ella	What Are You Doing New . . .	Verve - (LP) V - 4042	De Vol Frank Orch.	50s	
Fitzgerald Ella & L. Armstrong	You Wont Be Satisified Until . . .	Decca - 23496		40s	
Five Keys	Glory Of Love The	Alladin - 3099		50s	
Five Satins	In The Still Of The Night	Ember - 1005		50s	
Foley Red	Atomic Power	Decca - 46014	Ross Roy And his Ramblers	40s	
Foley Red	Candy Kisses	Decca - 46151		40s	
Foley Red	Chattanoga Shoe Shine Boy	Decca - 46205		50s	
Foley Red	Freight Train Boogie	Decca - 46035		40s	
Foley Red	Hang Your Head In Shame	Decca - 16698		40s	
Foley Red	I Got The Freight Train Blues	Conquer - 8285	Cumberland Ridger R. &	30s	
Foley Red	Midnight	Decca - 28420		50s	
Foley Red	Never Trust A Woman	Decca - 46074	Cumberland Valley Boys	40s	
Foley Red	Old Shep	Decca - 5944	Ross Roy And his Ramblers	40s	
Foley Red	Old Shep	Melotone - 6 - 03 - 53		30s	
Foley Red	Smoke On The Water	Decca - 6102	Cumberland Valley Boys	40s	
Foley Red	Sunday Down In Tennessee	Decca - 36197		40s	
Foley Red	Tennessee Border	Decca - 46151		40s	
Foley Red	Tennessee Saterday Night	Decca - 46136	Cumberland Valley Boys	40s	
Foley Red	The 1936 Flood	Vocalion - 8676		30s	
Foley Red & Ernest Tubb	Tennessee Border No 2	Decca - 46200		50s	
Foley Red*	Shame On You	Decca - 18698	Welk Lawrence Orch	40s	
Ford Mary*	How High The Moon	Capital - 1451	Les Paul & Mary Ford	50s	
Ford Tennessee Ernie	Sixteen Tons	Capital - 3262		50s	
Forrest Helen	Baby, What You Do To Me	Decca - 18778	Paul Les Trio	40s	
Forrest Helen	Time Waits For No One	Decca - 18600	Camarata orch. Dir.	40s	
Forrest Helen & Dick Haymes	Come Rain Or Shine	Decca - 23548		40s	
Forrest Helen & Dick Haymes	Ill Buy That Dream	Decca - 23434		40s	
Forrest Helen*	Any Old Time	Victor - 20 - 1575	Shaw Artie Orch	40s	
Forrest Helen*	Between A Kiss And A Sigh	Bluebird - B - 10055	Shaw Artie Orch	30s	
Forrest Helen*	How High The Moon	Columbia - 35391	Goodman Benny Orch.	30s	
Forrest Helen*	I Had The Craziest Dream	Columbia - 36659	Harry James & His Orch.	40s	
Forrest Helen*	I Remember You	Columbia - 36518	James Harry Orch	40s	
Forrest Helen*	Ive Heard That Song Before	Columbia - 36644	Harry James & His Orch.	40s	
Forrest Helen*	Mr. Five By Five	Columbia - 36650	James Harry Orch	40s	
Forrest Helen*	Skylark	Columbia - 36533	James Harry Orch	40s	
Forrest Helen*	Taking A Chance On Love	Columbia - 35869	Goodman Benny Orch	40s	
Forrest Helen*	They Say	Bluebird - B - 10075	Shaw Artie Orch	30s	
Foster Allen*	Remember Pearl Harbor	Victor - 27738	Kaye Sammy Orch.	40s	
Four Aces	Love Is A Many Splendered . . .	Decca - 29625		50s	
Four Aces	Garden In The Rain A	Decca - 27860		50s	
Four Tunes	Marie	Jubilee - 5128		50s	
Four Vagabonds	Coming In On A Wing And A . . .	Bluebird - B - 0815		40s	
Francis Connie	Everybody's Somebody's Fool	MGM - 12899		60s	
Francis Connie	MGM-12588	Who's Sorry Now	Lipman Joe dir. Orch	50s	
Froman Jane	Baby Mine	Columbia - 36460		40s	
Froman Jane	Be Still My Heart	Capital (LP) H - 354	Feller Sid cond. Orch	50s	
Froman Jane	Boy What Love Done To Me	Columbia - 36414		40s	
Froman Jane	But Where Are You	Decca - 710		30s	
Froman Jane	For You For Me Evermore	Majestic - 1086		40s	
Froman Jane	Garden In the Rain A	Majestic - 1086		40s	
Froman Jane	Garden In The Rain A (re-issue)	Royale - 350		50s	
Froman Jane	Hands Across The Table	Capital (LP) H - 354	Feller Sid cond. Orch	50s	
Froman Jane	How About You	Capital (LP) H - 354	Feller Sid cond. Orch	50s	
Froman Jane	I Got Lost In His Arms	Majestic - 1049	Gray Jerry And His Orch	40s	
Froman Jane	I Only Have Eyes For You	Decca - 181		30s	
Froman Jane*	June Kisses	Victor - 22460	Thies Henry Orchestra	30s	
Froman Jane	Little Kiss Each Morning A	Capital (LP) H - 354	Feller Sid cond. Orch	50s	
Froman Jane	Lost In A Fog	Decca - 180		30s	
Froman Jane	More Than You Know	Capital (LP) H - 354	Feller Sid cond. Orch	50s	
Froman Jane	Please Believe Me	Decca - 710		30s	
Froman Jane*	Sharing	Victor - 22461	Thies Henry Orchestra	30s	
Froman Jane	Song From Desiree	Capital - F - 2979	Feller Sid orch.	50s	
Froman Jane	There's A Lull In My Life	Capital (LP) H - 354	Feller Sid cond. Orch	50s	
Froman Jane	Tonight We Love	Columbia - 36414	Goodman Al dir. Orch	40s	
Froman Jane	What Is There To Say	Capital (LP) H - 354	Feller Sid cond. Orch	50s	
Froman Jane	When I See An Elephant Fly	Columbia - 36460		40s	
Froman Jane	With A Song In My Heart	Capital - 2044	Feller Sid cond. Orch	50s	
Fuller Blind Boy	Get Yer Ya Yas Out	Vocalion - 04519		30s	
Fuller Blind Boy	Where My Woman Usta Lay	Decca - 7903		30s	
Fulton Jack & chorus	Christmas Melodies	Columbia - 50070	Whiteman Paul Orch	20s	
Fulton Jack*	Body And Soul	Columbia - 2297 - D	Whiteman Paul Orch	30s	
Fulton Jack*	It Happened In Monterey	Columbia - 2199 - D	Whiteman Paul Orch	20s	
Gable Clark	Who's Afraid Of The Big Bad . . .	Film Master 1934		30s	

Garland Judy	All Gods Chillun Got Rhythm	Decca - 1432		30s	
Garland Judy	Better Luck Next Time	Film Master - 1948		40s	
Garland Judy	Better Luck Next Time	MGM - 30187		40s	
Garland Judy	Birthday Of A King, The	Decca - 4050		40s	
Garland Judy	Boy Next Door The	Decca - 23362		40s	
Garland Judy	Broadway Melody	Film Master - 1943		40s	
Garland Judy	Buds Wont Bud	Decca - 3174	Sherwood Bobby Orch	40s	
Garland Judy	Changing My Tune	Decca - 23688	Jenkins Gordon & Orch	40s	
Garland Judy	Chicago	Capital - LP - 1569		60s	
Garland J. & Mickey Rooney	Could You Use Me	Decca - 23308	Stoll Georgie & his Orch	40s	
Garland Judy & Fred Astaire	Couple Of Swells A	Film Master - 1948		40s	
Garland Judy	Dear Mr. Gable	Decca - 1463		30s	
Garland Judy	Do It Again	Capital - LP - 1569		60s	
Garland Judy	Easter Parade	MGM - 30185		40s	
Garland Judy & Fred Astaire	Easter Parade	Film Master - 1948		40s	
Garland Judy	Embraceable You	Decca - 23308	Stoll Georgie Orch	40s	
Garland Judy	Every Little Movement Has A Meaning Of Its Own	Film Master - 1943		40s	
Garland Judy	Everybodys Doing It	Film Master - 1948		40s	
Garland Judy & Fred Astaire	Fella With An Umbrella A	Film Master - 1948		40s	
Garland Judy	Foggy Day A	Capital - LP - 1569		60s	
Garland Judy & Fred Astaire	For Me And My Gal	Decca - 18480	Stoll Georgie Orch	40s	
Garland Judy & Gene Kelly	For Me And My Gal	Decca - 18480	Rose David Orch	40s	
Garland Judy	Get Happy	MGM - 30254		50s	
Garland Judy	Gotta Have You Go With Me	Columbia - 8005	Heindorf Ray Orch	50s	
Garland Judy	Gotta Have You Go With Me	Film Master - 1954		50s	
Garland Judy	Have Yourself A Merry Little Christmas	Decca - 23362	Stoll Georgie Orch	40s	
Garland Judy	How About You	Decca - 4072		40s	
Garland Judy	I Feel a Song Coming On	Capital - LP - T - 734	Riddle Nelson Orch	60s	
Garland Judy & Fred Astaire	I Love A Piano	Film Master - 1948		40s	
Garland Judy	I Want To Go Back To Michigan	Film Master - 1948		40s	
Garland Judy	I Will Come Back	Capital - LP - T - 734	Riddle Nelson Orch	50s	
Garland Judy & Gene Kelly	If You Wore A Tulip . . .	Decca - 18480	Rose David Orch	40s	
Garland Judy	Im Nobodys Baby	Decca - 3174	Sherwood Bobby Orch	40s	
Garland Judy	Its A New World	Columbia - 8008	Heindorf Ray Orch	20s	
Garland Judy	Its A New World	Film Master - 1954		40s	
Garland Judy	Jitterbug, The	Decca - 2672	Young Victor Orch	40s	
Garland Judy* (Gumm Sisters)	La Curaracha	Film Master - 1936		30s	
Garland Judy	Last Night When We Were Young	Capital - LP - T - 734	Riddle Nelson Orch	50s	
Garland Judy - NAP	Last Night When We Were Young	MGM - 30432		40s	
Garland Judy	Life Is Just a Bowl Of Cherries	Capital - LP - T - 734	Riddle Nelson Orch	60s	
Garland Judy	Look For The Silver Lining	Film Master - 1946		40s	
Garland Judy	Man That Got Away The	Columbia - 40270	Heindorf Ray Orch	50s	
Garland Judy	Man That Got Away The	Film Master - 1954		40s	
Garland Judy	Meet Me Is St. Louis, Louis	Decca - 23360	Stoll Georgie Orch	40s	
Garland Judy	Memories Of You	Capital - LP - T - 734	Riddle Nelson Orch	50s	
Garland Judy & Merry Macs	On The Atchison, Topeka, & The . . .	Decca - 23436	Murray Lynn Orch	40s	
Garland Judy	Our Love Affair	Decca - 3593		40s	
Garland Judy	Over The Rainbow	Decca - 2672	Young Victor Orch	30s	
Garland Judy	Over The Rainbow	Film Master - 1939		30s	
Garland Judy & Fred Astaire	Ragetime Violin	Film Master - 1948		40s	
Garland Judy	Star Of The East, The	Decca - 4050		40s	
Garland Judy	Stompin At The Savoy	Decca - 848	Crosby Bob Orch	30s	
Garland Judy	Swing Mister Swing	Decca - 848	Crosby Bob Orch	30s	
Garland Judy	This Cant Be Love	Capital - LP - 1569		60s	
Garland Judy	Three O'Clock In The Morning	Film Master - 1943		40s	
Garland Judy	Trolly Song The	Decca - 23361	Stoll Georgie Orch	40s	
Garland Judy & Fred Astaire	When The Midnight Choo Choo Leaves For Alabam	Film Master - 1948		40s	
Garland Judy & Fred Astaire	When You Wore A Tulip	Decca - 18480	Stoll Georgie Orch	40s	
Garland Judy	Who	Film Master - 1946		40s	
Garland Judy	Zing Went The Strings Of My Heart	Decca - 18543	Young Victor Orch	40s	
Garry Sid*	Blue Again	Victor - 22603	Ellington Duke Orch	30s	
Gaskin George J.	When You Where Sweet . . . - AC	Columbia - 4281		00s	
Gaskin George J.	On The Banks Of The . . . - AC	Edison - 1570		oo	
Gately Buddy*	Lovely Lady	Victor - 25216	Dorsey Tommy Orch	30s	
Gates Tom	Bucket's Got A Hole In It The	Gennett - 6184		20s	
Gaynor Janet	If I Had A Talking Picture Of You	Film Master - 1929		20s	
Gaynor Janet	I'm A Dreamer Are'nt We All	Film Master - 1929		20s	
Gaynor Janet	Sunny Side Up	Film Master - 1929		20s	
George Gladys	In A Shantly In Old Shanty . . .	Film Master 1939		30s	
Gerry & The Pacemakers	Don't Let The Sun Catch . . .	Laurie - 3251	Pacemakers the	60s	
Glee Club*	Praise The Lord & Pass The . . .	Columbia - 36640	Kyser Kay Orch	40s	
Gib Parker*	Winter Wonderland	Columbia - 2976 - D	Weems Ted Orch	30s	

Gibbs Georgia	Tweedle Dee	Mercury - 7017	Osser Glenn	50s	
Gibbs Georgia	Kiss Of Fire	Mercury - 5823	Osser Glenn	50s	
Gibson Fredda*	Laziest Gal In Town	Varsity - 8225	Trumbauer Frankie and his Orch.	40s	
Gibson Fredda*/	Not On The First Night Baby	Varsity - 8223	Trumbauer Frankie and his Orch.	40s	
Glinn Lillian	Doggin Me Blues	Columbia - 14275 - D	vocal, novelty acomp.	20s	
Gluck Alma	Carry Me Back To . . . AC	Victor - 88481		11s	
Goday Bob*	Thanks For The Memory	Bluebird - B - 7318	Fields Shep & His R. R. Orch.	30s	
Golden Billy	Turkey In The Straw-AC	Columbia - 7703		00s	
Grable Betty	Cuddle Up A Little Closer	Film Master - 1942		40s	
Grable Betty	I Cant Begin To Tell You	Film Master - 1945		40s	
Grable Betty*	I Cant Begin To Tell You	Columbia - 36867	James Harry & His Orch	40s	
Grant Coot	Find Me At The Greasy . . . - AC	Paramount - 12337		20s	
Grant Gogi	Wayword Wind	Era - 3046		50s	
Gray Betty	Mean Old Bed Bug Blues	Lincoln - 2714		20s	
Gray Jane	He's Tall Dark And Handsome	Harmony - 548 - H		20s	
Gray Lawrence	My Kind Of Girl	Film Master - 1930		30s	
Grayson Carl*	Der Fuehrers Face	RCA Victor - 20 - 2611	Jones Spike & City. S.	40s	
Green Jane	Mine All Mine	Victor - 21145		20s	
Green Jane	My One And Only	Victor - 21145		20s	
Green Jane*	Mama Loves Papa - AC	Victor - 19215	Virginians the	20s	
Green Lil	Why Don't You Do Right	Bluebird - B - 08714		40s	
Grey Maxine*	I Was Taken By Storm	Brunswick - 7404	Kemp Hal Orchestra	30s	
Griffin Rex	Lovesick Blues	Decca - 5570		30s	
Griffin Rex	Everybodys Tryin To Be My Baby	Decca - 5294		30s	
Gunther Arthur	Baby Lets Play House	Excello - 2047		50s	
Guthrie Jack	Oklahoma Hills	Capital - 201	Oklahomans & his	40s	
Guthrie Woody	Blowin Down This Road	Victor - 26619		40s	
Guthrie Woody	Car Song	Cub - 3A		40s	
Guthrie Woody	Do Re Mi	Victor - 26620		40s	
Guthrie Woody	Dust Bowl Refugee	Victor - 26623		40s	
Guthrie Woody	Dust Cant Kill Me	Victor - 26620		40s	
Guthrie Woody	Dust Pneumonia Blues	Victor - 26623		40s	
Guthrie Woody	Dusty Old Dust	Victor - 26622		40s	
Guthrie Woody	Great Dust Storm The	Victor - 26622		40s	
Guthrie Woody	I Aint Got No Home In This . . .	Victor - 26624		40s	
Guthrie Woody	Pastures Of Plenty	Disc - 5010		40s	
Guthrie Woody	Pretty Boy Floyd	Asch - 360 - 1		40s	
Guthrie Woody	Talkin Dust Bowl Blues	Victor - 26619		40s	
Guthrie Woody	This Land Is Your Land	Folkways - LP - FP - 27		50s	
Guthrie Woody	Tom Joad - Pt 1 & 2	Victor - 26621		40s	
Guthrie Woody	Vigilante Man	Victor - 26624		40s	
Guitar Bonnie	Dark Moon	Dot - 15550		50s	
Haines Connie*	Buds Wont Bud	Victor - 26609	Dorsey Tommy Orch	40s	
Haines Connie & Alan Dale	Darktown Shutters Ball, The	Signiture - 15197		40s	
Haines Connie	Do You Love Me	Mercury - 2063	Warrington Johnny Orch	40s	
Haines Connie* & P. P.	Kiss The Boys Goodby	Victor - 27461	Dorsey Tommy Orch	40s	
Haines Connie	She's Funny That Way	Mercury - 3006	Warrington Johnny Orch	40s	
Haines Connie*	Swingtime Up In Harlem	Victor - 27249	Dorsey Tommy Orch	40s	
Haines Connie*	Will You Still Be Mine	Victor - 27421	Dorsey Tommy Orch	40s	
Hale Sonnie	Tinkle Tinkle	Film Master - 1934		30s	
Haley Bill	Rock The Joint	Essex - 303	Comets & the	50s	
Haley Bill	Rocket 88	Essex - 381	Saddlemen & the	50s	
Haley Bill	Rocket 88	Holiday - 105	Saddlemen & the	50s	
Haley Bill	Shake Rattle And Roll	Decca - 2168	Comets & the	50s	
Haley Bill, & B. Bernard	Too Many Parties And Too . . .	Cowboy - CR - 1201	Haley B & his Four Aces.	40s	
Hall Adelaide*	Blues I Love To Sing The	Victor - 21490	Ellington Duke Orch	20s	
Hall Adelaide	Aint It A Shame About Mame	Decca - F - 7709		30s	
Hall Adelaide	As Time Goes By	Decca - - 8202	Wilbur Jay Orchestra	40s	
Hall Adelaide	Baby	Brunswick - 4031	Leslie's Lew, Blackbirds Orch	20s	
Hall Adelaide	Baby	Brunswick - 6518	Ellington Duke Orch.	30s	
Hall Adelaide* - vocal refrain	Chicago Stompdown	Okeh - 8675	Ellington Duke Orch.	20s	
Hall Adelaide* - vocal refrain	Creole Love Call	Victor - 21137	Ellington Duke Orch.	20s	
Hall Adelaide	Deep Purple	Decca - F - 7095	vocal	30s	
Hall Adelaide	Diga Diga Do	Monmouth - Ev - LP - 7080		70s	
Hall Adelaide	Drop Me Off In Harlem	Victor Master - 1934	Mills Blue Rhythm Band	30s	
Hall Adelaide	East Of The Sun	Ultraphone - AP - 1575	Ellsworth John Orch	30s	
Hall Adelaide	For Every Fish	Victor - LP - LOC - 1036	Engel Lehman Orch	50s	
Hall Adelaide	Have You Met Miss Jones	Decca - F - 7305		30s	
Hall Adelaide & Fats Waller	I Cant Give You Anything . . .	HMV - B - 8849	Waller Fats organ	30s	
Hall Adelaide	I Must Have That Man	Brunswick - 4031	Leslie's Lew, Blackbirds Orch	20s	
Hall Adelaide	I Must Have That Man	Brunswick - 6518	Ellington Duke Orch.	30s	
Hall Adelaide	ILL Wind	Monmouth - Ev - LP - 7080		70s	
Hall Adelaide	Im In The Mood For Love	Ultraphone - AP - 1574	Turner Joe piano	30s	

Hall Adelaide	Lady Is A Tramp The	Decca - F - 7345	vocal	30s	
Hall Adelaide	Minnie The Moocher	Brunswick - 01217		30s	
Hall Adelaide	Old Fashioned Love	Monmouth - Ev - LP - 7080		70s	
Hall Adelaide	Reaching Fot The Cotton Moon	Victor Master - 1934	Mills Blue Rhythm Band	30s	
Hall Adelaide	Rhapsody In Love	Brunswick - 01217		30s	
Hall Adelaide	Savannahs Wedding	Victor - LP - LOC - 1036	Engel Lehman Orch	50s	
Hall Adelaide	Strange As It Seems	Brunswick - 6376	vocal -	30s	
Hall Adelaide	Taint What You Do	Decca - F - 7121	vocal	30s	
Hall Adelaide & Fats Waller	That Old Feeling	HMV - B - 8849	Waller Fats organ	30s	
Hall Adelaide	This Cant Be Love	Decca - F - 7501	vocal	30s	
Hall Adelaide	To Love You Again	Film Master - 1935		30s	
Hall Adelaide	Too Darn Fickle	Oriole - P - 108	vocal -	20s	
Hall Adelaide	Truckin	Ultraphone - AP - 1574	Turner Joe piano	30s	
Hall Adelaide	Where Or When	Tono Radio - K - 6002	Ewans Kai	30s	
Hall Wendell	It Ain't Gonna Rain No Mo' - AC	Victor - 19171		20s	
Hamblin Stuart	This Ole House	Victor - 20 - 5739		50s	
Hamfoot Ham*	Weed Smokers Dream	Decca - 7234	Harlem Hamfats	30s	
Hanlon Clare*	Little White Lies	Victor - 22494	Waring Fred Orch	30s	
Hanshaw Annette	After My Laughter Came Tears	Perfect - 14940	Gold Lou Orch.	20s	
Hanshaw Annette	Ain't Cha	Harmony - 1075 - H	Auburn Frank & His Orch.	20s	
Hanshaw Annette	Aint He Sweet	Pathe - 32240	vocal	20s	
Hanshaw Annette	Am I Blue	Harmony - 940 - H	New Englanders acc.	20s	
Hanshaw Annette	Aw Gee Don't Be That Way Now	Pathe - 32267	vocal	30s	
Hanshaw Annette	Big City Blues	Columbia - 1812 - D	vocal	20s	
Hanshaw Annette	Black Bottom	Pathe - 32207	Brodsky Ivan piano	20s	
Hanshaw Annette	Body And Soul	Harmony - 1224 - H		20s	
Hanshaw Annette	Daddy Wont You Please Come Home	Velvet - Tone - 1940 - V	vocal	20s	
Hanshaw Annette	Do Do Do	Pathe - 32226	vocal	20s	
Hanshaw Annette	Don't Take That Black Bottom Away	Pathe - 32213	Redheads the	20s	
Hanshaw Annette	Fit As A Fiddle	Perfect - 12866		30s	
Hanshaw Annette	For Old Times Sake	Harmony - 666 - H		20s	
Hanshaw Annette	Happy Days Are Here Again	Diva - 3106 - G		30s	
Hanshaw Annette	Here Or There	Pathe - 32235	Brodsky Ivan piano	20s	
Hanshaw Annette	He's The Last Word	Pathe - 32240		20s	
Hanshaw Annette	Ho Hum	Harmony - 1324 - H		30s	
Hanshaw Annette	I Get The Blues When It Rains	Velvet - Tone - 1910 - V	New Englanders acc.	20s	
Hanshaw Annette	I Have To Have You	Okeh - 41351	vocal	20s	
Hanshaw Annette - (Gay Ellis)	I Must Have That Man	Harmony - 706 - H	& Her novelty orch.	20s	
Hanshaw Annette	If I Had A Talking Picture Of.	Diva - 3066 - G	Three Blue Streaks . . .	30s	
Hanshaw Annette	I'm A Dreamer Are'nt We All	Diva - 3066 - G	Three Blue Streaks . . .	20s	
Hanshaw Annette - (Gay Ellis)	In A Great Big Way	Harmony - 859 - H	vocal	30s	
Hanshaw Annette	Ive Got A Feeling Im Falling	Diva - 1915	New Englanders acc.	20s	
Hanshaw Annette	Ive Got To Get Myself Somebody To Love	Pathe - 32235	vocal	30s	
Hanshaw Annette	Japaneese Sandman	Pathe - 36796		20s	
Hanshaw Annette	Just Like A Butterfly	Pathe - 32267		20s	
Hanshaw Annette	Lazy Lou'siana Moon	Velvet Tone - 2121 - V	Ferera Frank Hawaiian T	20s	
Hanshaw Annette	Lets Fall In Love	Vocalion - 2635		30s	
Hanshaw Annette	Little White Lies	Diva - 3196 - G		30s	
Hanshaw Annette	Love Me Tonight	Banner - 32541	vocal	30s	
Hanshaw Annette	Lover Come Back To Me	Columbia - 1769 - D		20s	
Hanshaw Annette	Mean To Me	Diva - 2859	New England Yankees	20s	
Hanshaw Annette	Mine All Mine	Pathe - 32320		20s	
Hanshaw Annette	Miss Annabelle Lee	Perfect - 12362		20s	
Hanshaw Annette	Moaning Low	Okeh - 41292	vocal	30s	
Hanshaw Annette	Nobody Cares If Im Blue	Harmony - 1196 - D		20s	
Hanshaw Annette	Nothin	Pathe - 11471	Original Memphis Five	30s	
Hanshaw Annette*	Pagan Love Song	Diva - 2945 - D	Ferera Frank Hawaiian T	20s	
Hanshaw Annette	Pale Blue Waters	Velvet Tone - 2121	Ferera Frank Hawaiian T	20s	
Hanshaw Annette	Precious Little Thing Called Love A	Diva - 2859 - G	New England Yankees	20s	
Hanshaw Annette	Right Kind Of Man The	Okeh - 41327		20s	
Hanshaw Annette	Rosey Cheeks	Pathe - 32259		20s	
Hanshaw, Annette, & others	Say It Isn't So	Perfect - 12843	Osborne Will & his Orch.	30s	
Hanshaw Annette	Six Feet Of Pappa	Pathe - 32211	Brodsky Ivan piano	30s	
Hanshaw Annette	Song Is Ended The	Pathe - 32314	vocal	30s	
Hanshaw Annette	That's The Way I Feel Today	Clarion - 5037 - C	vocal	20s	
Hanshaw Annette	That's You Baby	Columbia - 1812 - D	vocal	30s	
Hanshaw Annette	This Little Piggie	Vocalion - 2635		30s	
Hanshaw Annette - (Gay Ellis)	Tip Toe Through The Tulips	Harmony - 1012 - H		20s	
Hanshaw Annette*	Ua Like No A Like	Diva - 2945 - D	Ferera Frank Hawaiian T	20s	
Hanshaw Annette	Walkin My Baby Back Home	Clarion - 5248 - C		30s	
Hanshaw Annette	We Just Couldent Say . . .	Banner - 32541		20s	
Hanshaw Annette	We Just Couldent Say . . .	Film Master - 1933		30s	
Hanshaw Annette	We Love It	Perfect - 12444		20s	

Hanshaw Annette	What Do I Care	Pathe - 36623	Original Memphis Five	30s	
Hanshaw Annette	Who's That Knockin At My . . .	Pathe - 32293	Sizzlin' Synopators her	30s	
Hanshaw Annette	Wistful And Blue	Pathe - 36623	Orginal Memphis Five	20s	
Hanshaw Annette	Would You Like To Take A W	Velvet Tone - 2315 - V		30s	
Hanshaw Annette	You Wouldent Fool Me Would You	Columbia - 1769 - D	vocal	30s	
Hare Ernest & Billy Jones*	Barney Google - AC	Edison - 51155	Happiness Boys the	20s	
Hare Ernest & Billy Jones*	Does Your Spearmint . . . - AC	Cameo - 504	Happiness Boys the	20s	
Hare Ernest & Billy Jones*	Don't Bring Lulu - AC	Edison - 51555	Happiness Boys the	20s	
Hare Ernest & Billy Jones*	How Do You Do - AC	Edison - 51500	Happiness Boys the	20s	
Hare Ernest & Billy Jones*	Last Night On The Back . . . - AC	Okeh - 4948	Happiness Boys the	20s	
Harlan Byron & Frank Stanley	Battle Cty Of Freedom The	Victor - 16165		10s	
Harmonica Frank	Rockin Chair Daddy	Sun - 205		50s	
Harris Frank (Irving Kaufman)	After I Say Im Sorry - AC	Columbia - A607 - D		20s	
Harris Marion	After You've Gone - AC	Victor - 18509	Pasternack Joseph Orch	10s	
Harris Marion	Basin Street Blues - AC	Columbia - A3474		20s	
Harris Marion	Blue Again	Brunswick - 6016		20s	
Harris Marion	Blue - AC	Brunswick - 2310	Jones Isham Orch	20s	
Harris Marion	Carolina In The Morning - AC	Brunswick - 2329	Fenton Carl And Orch	20s	
Harris Marion	Charleston Charlie - AC	Brunswick - 2735		20s	
Harris Marion	Did You Mean It	Victor - 21116		20s	
Harris Marion	Don't Leave Me Daddy - AC	Victor - 18185		10s	
Harris Marion	Everybody But Me - AC	Columbia - A - 2939		30s	
Harris Marion	Everybodys Crazy About . . . - AC	Victor - 18443		10s	
Harris Marion	Funny Dear What Love Can Do	Brunswick - 4663		30s	
Harris Marion	Good Man Is Hard To Find A - AC	Victor - 18535	Pasternack Joseph Orch	10s	
Harris Marion	Good - Bye Alexander . . . - AC	Victor - 18492		10s	
Harris Marion	How Come You Do Me Like . . .	Brunswick - 2610	Fenton Carl And Orch	20s	
Harris Marion	I Ain't Got Nobody Much - AC	Victor - 18133		10s	
Harris Marion	I Aint Got Nobody - AC	Columbia - A3371	Prince Charles A Orch	20s	
Harris Marrion & Billy Murray	I Wonder Why - AC	Victor - 18270		10s	
Harris Marion	If I Could Be With You One . . .	Brunswick - 4873		20s	
Harris Marion	I'll See You In My Dreams - AC	Brunswick - 2784	Fenton Carl And Orch	20s	
Harris Marion	Im Just Wild About Harry - AC	Brunswick - 2309	Jones Isham Orch	20s	
Harris Marion	I'm Nobodys Baby - AC	Columbia - A3433		20s	
Harris Marion	It Had To Be You - AC	Brunswick - 2610	Ohman Phil	20s	
Harris Marion	Jazz Baby - AC	Victor - 18555		10s	
Harris Marion	Little White Lies	Brunswick - 4873		30s	
Harris Marion	Look For The Silver Lining - AC	Columbia - A3367	Prince Charles A Orch	20s	
Harris Marion	Mammy's Chocolate . . . - AC	Victor - 18493		10s	
Harris Marion	Man I Love The	Victor - 21116		20s	
Harris Marion	Memphis Blues The - AC	Columbia - A3474		20s	
Harris Marion	My Canary Has Circles Under . . .	Columbia - DB - 4563	Mason Billy Café de Paris	30s	
Harris Marion	My Fate Is In Your Hands	Brunswick - 4681		30s	
Harris Marion	Nobody Cares If Im Blue	Brunswick - 4812		30s	
Harris Marion	One Morning In May	Decca - F - 3954		30s	
Harris Marion	OO - OO - !Honey What You . . .	Decca - F - 5160		30s	
Harris Marion	Paradise Blues - AC	Victor - 18152		10s	
Harris Marion	Rose Of The Rio Grande - AC	Brunswick - 2330		20s	
Harris Marion	Singing The Blues Till . . .	Decca - F - 5160		30s	
Harris Marion	Some Sunny Day - AC	Columbia - A3593	Prince Charles A Orch	20s	
Harris Marion	Somebody Loves Me - AC	Brunswick - 2735	Fenton Carl And Orch	20s	
Harris Marion	St. Louis Blues - AC	Columbia - A - 2944	Prince Charles A Orch	20s	
Harris Marion	Sweet Indiana Home - AC	Brunswick - 2310	Jones Isham Orchestra	20s	
Harris Marion	Sweet Mama, Papa's . . . - AC	Columbia - A - 3300	Prince Charles A Orch	20s	
Harris Marion	Take Me To The Land . . . - AC	Victor - 18993		20s	
Harris Marion	Tea For Two - AC	Brunswick - 2747	Fenton Carl And Orch	20s	
Harris Marion	There'll Be Some . . . - AC	Brunswick - 2651		20s	
Harris Marion	When I Hear That Jazz . . ._AC	Victor - 18398		10s	
Harris Marion	You Do Something To Me	Brunswick - 4806		30s	
Harris Marion	You've Gotta Come . . . - AC	Brunswick - 2410		20s	
Harris Wynonie	Shake That Thing	King - 4616		40s	
Harvey Morton	I Didn't Raise My Boy To Be, - AC	Victor - 17716		10s	
Hatcher Sam*	Freight Train Blues	Conquer - 9121	Crazy Tennesseans his	30s	
Hatcher Sam*	Wabash Callon Ball	Conquer - 9121	Crazy Tennesseans his	30s	
Hayes Grace	I Cant Give You Anything . . .	Victor - 21571	Comedian with orch.	20s	
Hayes Grace	I Must Have That Man	Victor - 21571	Comedian with orch.	20s	
Haymes Dick	Christmas Dreaming	Decca - 24169	Jenkins Gordon Orch.	40s	
Haymes Dick & Helen Forrest*	Come Rain Or Shine	Decca - 23548		40s	
Haymes Dick & Helen Forrest*	Devil Sat Down And Cried The	Columbia - 36466	James Harry Orch	30s	
Haymes Dick	Easy To Love	Decca - 23780	Dant Charles orch dir	40s	
Haymes Dick	How Are Thing In Glocca Morra	Decca - 23830		40s	
Haymes Dick	I Wish I Dident Love You So.	Decca - 23977		40s	

Haymes Dick*	Idaho	Columbia - 36613	Goodman Benny Orch	40s	
Haymes Dick & Helen Forrest	I'll Buy Thay Dream	Decca - 23434	Young Victor	40s	
Haymes Dick*	I'll Get By	Columbia - 36285	James Harry Orch	40s	
Haymes Dick & Song Spinners	It Cant Be Wrong	Decca-18557		40s	
Haymes Dick	It Might As Well Be Spring	Film Master - 1945		40s	
Haymes Dick	It Might As Well Be Spring	Decca - 18706	Hagen Earle Orch	40s	
Haymes Dick	Laura	Decca - 18666	Young Victor orch dir	40s	
Haymes Dick & Six Hits & A Miss	Little White Lies	Decca - 24280	Jenkins Gordon Orch	40s	
Haymes Dick	Long Ago And Far Away	Decca - 23317	Camarata orch directed	40s	
Haymes Dick	Love Letters	Decca - 18699	Young Victor orch dir	40s	
Haymes Dick	More I See You The	Decca - 18662	Young Victor Orch	40s	
Haymes Dick	Put Your Arms Around Me Honey	Decca - 18565		40s	
Haymes Dick & Helen Forrest	Some Sunday Morning	Decca - 23434	Jenkins Gordon Orch.	40s	
Haymes Dick	That's For Me	Decca - 18706	Hagen Earle Orch	40s	
Haymes Dick	You Make Me Feel So Young	Decca - 18914	Jenkins Gordon Orch	40s	
Haymes Dick	Youll Never Know	Decca - 18556		40s	
Haymes Dick & Ethel Merman	You're Just In Love	Decca - 27317		50s	
Hegamin Lucille	Arkansas Blues - AC	Black Swan - 2032	"Soprano woth Orch."	20s	
Hegamin Lucille	Beale St, Mama - AC	Cameo - 270	"Vocal Blues"	40s	
Hegamin Lucille	He May Be Your Man . . . - AC	Arto - 9129		20s	
Henderson Joe	Snap Your Fingers	Todd-1072		60s	
Hendrickson Al*	On A Slow Boat To China	Capital - 15208	Goodman Benny Orch	40s	
Henry Clarence - Frog Man	Aint Got No Home	Argo - 5259.		50s	
Hermann Woody*	Fan It	Decca - 834	Hermann Woody Orch	30s	
Hibbler Al*	Im Just A Lucky So And So	Victor - 20 - 1799	Ellington Duke Orch.	40s	
Hicks Edna	I'm Going Away - AC	Victor - 19083		20s	
Hildegarde	Ace In The Hole	Decca - 23242	Sosnik Harry Orch.	40s	
Hildegarde	All of a Sudden my Heart Sing	Decca 23348	Sosnik Harry Orch.	40s	
Hildegarde	All The Things You Love	Decca 23115		40s	
Hildegarde	Believe In Miracles I	Columbia - DO-1381		30s	
Hildegarde	Bon Soir	Columbia - FB- 1841		30s	
Hildegarde	Dance Little Lady, Dance!	Decca 23099	Sinatra Ray Orch.	30s	
Hildegarde*	Darling Je Vous Aime Beaucoup	Pathe - 5381	Rein Hardt Djengo	30s	
Hildegarde	Darling Je Vous Aime Beaucoup	Columbia - 258 - M	Gibbons Carol & His . . .	30s	
Hildegarde	Ev'rything I Love	Decca - 23242	Sosnik Harry Orch	40s	
Hildegarde	Everything I Got	Decca 23254	Sosnik Harry Orch.	40s	
Hildegarde	Every Time We Say Goodbye	Decca 23378	Sosnik Harry Orch.	40s	
Hildegarde	Farming	Decca - 23244	Sosnik Harry Orch	40s	
Hildegarde	For You For Me	Columbia - 258 - M	Gibbons Carol	30s	
Hildegarde	Gloomy Sunday	Columbia - FB - 1366	Sandler Elbert Trio	30s	
Hildegarde	Hate You Darling	Decca - 23244	Sosnik Harry Orch	40s	
Hildegarde	Honey Coloured Moon	Columbia - FB - 1123	Hall Henry BBC Orch.	30s	
Hildegarde	I'll Close my Eyes	Decca - 23756	Faith Percy Orch.	40s	
Hildegarde	Isn't it Romantic	Decca - 23135	Sinatra Ray Orch.	30s	
Hildegarde & Buddy Clark	I've Told Every Little Star	Decca - 23662		40s	
Hildegarde	Leave us Face it . . .	Decca - 23297	Sosnik Henry Orch.	40s	
Hildegarde	Lili Marlene	Decca - 23348	Sosnik Henry Orch.	40s	
Hildegarde	Little Rumba Numba A	Decca - 23243	Sosnik Harry Orch	40s	
Hildegarde	Love is a Dancing . . . Thing	Columbia - FB 1266	Mantovani & Pipica Orch.	30s	
Hildegarde	Love Walked In	Columbia - FB - 1992	Gibbons Carroll & Savoy Orpheans	30s	
Hildegarde	My Heart Stood Still	Decca - 23133	Sinatra Ray Orch.	30s	
Hildegarde	My Ship	Decca - 23208	Sosnik Harry Orch	40s	
Hildegarde	Nobody's Heart	Decca - 23254	Sosnik Henry Orch.	40s	
Hildegarde	Pennies From Heaven	Columbia - 1598 - D	Wirges William Orch.	30s	
Hildegarde	Pink Cocktail for a Blue Lady	Decca - 23245	Grant Bob Orch.	40s	
Hildegarde	Room with a View	Decca - 23101	Sinatra Ray Orch.	30s	
Hildegarde	There's A Small Hotel	Columbia FB-1598	Gibbons Carrol Orch	30s	
Hildegarde	You Irritate Me So	Decca - 23243	Sosnik Harry Orch	40s	
Hildegarde	Was in the Mood I	Columbia - DB- 1247	Wood George Scott Orch.	30s	
Hildegarde	What is There to Say?	Decca - 23163	Duke Vernon?	40s	
Hildegarde	With a Song in My Heart	Decca - 23135	Sinatra Ray Orch.	30s	
Hildegarde	Will You Remember	Columbia - FB - 1700	Mantovani Orchestra	30s	
Hill Bertha Chippie	Georgia Man - AC	Okeh - 8312		20s	
Hill Bertha Chippie	Pleadin' For The Blues - AC	Okeh - 8420		20s	
Hill Bertha Chippie	Trouble In Mind - AC	Okeh - 8812	Contralto with piano	20s	
Hill Ruby & Harold Nicholas	Come Rain Or Shine	Capital - 10055		40s	
Hogsed Roy	Cocaine Blues	Coast - 262.	Rainbow Riders & The	40s	
Hogsed Roy	Loafer's Song	Coast - 262.	Rainbow Riders & The	40s	
Holiday Billie	Ain't Nobody's Business If I Do	Decca - 24726	vocal	40s	
Holiday Billie*	Any Old Time	Bluebird - B - 7759	Shaw Artie Orch.	30s	
Holiday Billie*	April In My Heart	Brunswick - 8265	Wilson Teddy Orch	30s	
Holiday Billie	As Time Goes By	Commadore - 7520	vocal	40s	

Holiday Billie	Autumn In New York	Clef - 89108		50s	
Holiday Billie	Back In Your Own Backyard	Vocalion - 4029	Holiday Billie & Her Orch	30s	
Holiday Billie	Big Stuff	Decca - 23463		40s	
Holiday Billie	Billies Blues - I Love My Man	Vocalion - 3288	Holiday Billie Orch.	30s	
Holiday Billie	Billie's Blue - I Love My Man - 2	Commadore - 614	vocal	40s	
Holiday Billie	Blues Are Brewin The	Decca - 23463	Simmons John Orch.	40s	
Holiday Billie	Blues Are Brewin The	Film Master - 1946		40s	
Holiday Billie	Crazy He Calls Me	Decca - 24796	vocal	40s	
Holiday Billie	Detour Ahead	Alladin - 3094	Grimes Tiny Sextet	50s	
Holiday Billie	Did I Remember	Vocalion - 3276	Holiday Billie & Her Orch	30s	
Holiday Billie	Don't Explain	Decca - 23565		40s	
Holiday Billie	Easy Living	Decca - 24138	Haggart Bob & His Orch	40s	
Holiday Billie*	Easy Living	Brunswick - 7911	Wilson Teddy Orch.	30s	
Holiday Billie*	Easy To Love	Brunswick - 7762	Wilson Teddy Orch	30s	
Holiday Billie*	Eeny Meeny Miney Mo	Brunswick - 7554	Wilson Teddy Orch	30s	
Holiday Billie	Embraceable You	Commadore - 7520		40s	
Holiday Billie*	Everybodys Laughing	Brunswick - 8259	Wilson Teddy Orch	30s	
Holiday Billie	Fine And Mellow	Commodore - 526	Newton Frankie - trumpet	40s	
Holiday Billie	Fine And Mellow - I Love My . . .	Film (TV) Master - 1957		50s	
Holiday Billie	Fine Romance A	Vocalion - 3333	Holiday Billie & Her Orch	30s	
Holiday Billie	Getting Some Fun Out Of Life	Vocalion - 3701	Holiday Billie & Her Orch	30s	
Holiday Billie	Gimme A Pigfoot	Decca - 24947	vocal	40s	
Holiday Billie	Gloomy Sunday	Okeh - 6451	Holiday Billie Orch.	30s	
Holiday Billie	God Bless The Child	Decca - 249272	Jenkins Gordon	40s	
Holiday Billie	God Bless The Child	Okeh - 6279	Holiday Billie Orch.	40s	
Holiday Billie	Good Morning Heartache	Decca - 23676	Stegmeyer Bill Orch	40s	
Holiday Billie*	He Ain't Got Rhythm	Brunswick - 7824	Wilson Teddy Orch	30s	
Holiday Billie*	Here It Is Tomorrow Again	Brunswick - 8259	Wilson Teddy Orch	30s	
Holiday Billie	He's Funny That Way	Commadore - 569		40s	
Holiday Billie	How Am I To Know	Commadore - 569		40s	
Holiday Billie	Hymm Of Sorrow A	Film Master - 1934	Ellington Duke Orch	30s	
Holiday Billie	I Can't Believe That Youre . . .	Columbia - 36335		30s	
Holiday Billie*	I Cant Get Started	Radio Master - 1938	Basie Count Orch	30s	
Holiday Billie*	I Cant Give You Anything . . .	Brunswick - 7781	Wilson Teddy Orch	30s	
Holiday Billie	I Cover The Waterfront	Columbia - 37493	vocal	30s	
Holiday Billie	I Cover The Waterfront	Commadore - 559	vocal	40s	
Holiday Billie*	I Wished On The Moon	Brunswick - 7501	Wilson Teddy Orch.	30s	
Holiday Billie	I'll Be Seeing You	Commadore - 553		40s	
Holiday Billie	If The Moon Turns Green	Clef - 89108		50s	
Holiday Billie	I'll Get By	Commadore - 553	vocal	40s	
Holiday Billie*	I'll Get By	Brunswick - 7903	Wilson Teddy Orch	30s	
Holiday Billie	I'm Gonna Lock My Heart	Vocalion - 4238	Holiday Billie & Her Orch	30s	
Holiday Billie*	Im Painting The Town Red	Brunswick - 7511	Wilson Teddy Orch	30s	
Holiday Billie	Im Yours	Commodore - 585	vocal	40s	
Holiday Billie*	Its Too Hot For Words	Brunswick - 7511	Wilson Teddy Orch.	40s	
Holiday Billie	I've Got My Love To Keep Me Warm	Vocalion - 3431	Holiday Billie & Her Orch	30s	
Holiday Billie	Let's Call The Whole Thing Off	Vocalion - 3520	Holiday Billie & Her Orch	30s	
Holiday Billie	Long Gone Blues	Columbia - 37586	Holiday Billie & Her Orch	30s	
Holiday Billie	Love Me Or Leave Me	Okeh - 6369		40s	
Holiday Billie	Lover Man	Decca - 23391	Camarata orch. Dir.	40s	
Holiday Billie*	Mean To Me	Brunswick - 7903	Wilson Teddy Orch	30s	
Holiday Billie*	Miss Brown To You	Brunswick - 7501	Wilson Teddy Orch.	20s	
Holiday Billie	My Man	Brunswick - 8008	Wilson Teddy Orch	30s	
Holiday Billie	My Old Flame	Commadore - 585		40s	
Holiday Billie*	Nice Work If You Can Get It	Brunswick - 8015	Wilson Teddy Orch	30s	
Holiday Billie	No Regrets	Vocalion - 3276	Holiday Billie & Her Orch	30s	
Holiday Billie	Now Or Never	Decca - 24947	Oliver Cy orch. Dir.	50s	
Holiday Billie	Now They Call It Swing	Vocalion - 3988	Holiday Billie Orch.	30s	
Holiday Billie	On The Sentimental Side	Vocalion - 3947.	Holiday Billie Orch.	30s	
Holiday Billie*	Pennies From Heaven	Brunswick - 7789	Wilson Teddy Orch	30s	
Holiday Billie	Porgy	Decca - 24638	Tucker Bobby Trio . . .	40s	
Holiday Billie*	Riffin The Scotch	Columbia - 2867 - D.	Goodman Benny Orch.	30s	
Holiday Billie	Sailboat In the Moonlight A	Vocalion - 3605	Holiday Billie & Her Orch	30s	
Holiday Billie*	Say It With A Kiss	Brunswick - 8270	Wilson Teddy Orch	30s	
Holiday Billie	Solitude	Decca - 23853	Haggart Bob & His Orch	40s	
Holiday Billie	Solitude	Okeh - 6270	Holiday Billie Orch.	30s	
Holiday Billie	Some Other Spring	Vocalion - 5021	Holiday Billie & her Orch	30s	
Holiday Billie*	Spreadin' Rhythm Around	Brunswick - 7581	Wilson Teddy Orch.	30s	
Holiday Billie	Strange Fruit	Commodore - 526	White Sonny - piano/	30s	
Holiday Billie	Summertime	Vocalion - 3288		30s	
Holiday Billie*	Sunbonnet Blue A	Brunswick - 7498	Wilson Teddy Orch.	30s	
Holiday Billie*	Swing Brother Swing	Radio Master - 1938	Basie Count Orch	30s	
Holiday Billie	That Ole Devil Called Love	Decca - 23391	Camarata orch directed	40s	

Holiday Billie	Them There Eyes	Film TV Master - 1955	Henderson Skitch	50s	
Holiday Billie	Them There Eyes	Vocalion - 5021	Holiday Billie & her Orch	30s	
Holiday Billie	There Is No Greater Love	Decca - 23853	Haggart Bob & his Orch	40s	
Holiday Billie*	These Foolish Things . . .	Brunswick - 7699	Wilson Teddy Orch	30s	
Holiday Billie	They Can't Take That Away . . .	Brunswick - 3520	Holiday Billie & Her Orch	30s	
Holiday Billie*	They Say	Brunswick - 8270	Wilson Teddy Orch	30s	
Holiday Billie*	This Is My Last Affair	Brunswick - 7840	Wilson Teddy Orch	30s	
Holiday Billie*	This Years Kisses	Brunswick - 7824	Wilson Teddy Orch	30s	
Holiday Billie - as Lady Day*	Travelin Light	Capital - 116	Whiteman Paul Orch	40s	
Holiday Billie	Traveling All Alone	Vocalion - 3748	Holiday Billie Orch.	30s	
Holiday Billie*	Twenty Four Hours A Day	Brunswick - 7550	Wilson Teddy Orch.	30s	
Holiday Billie	Very Thought Of You The	Vocalion - 4457	Holiday Billie Orch.	30s	
Holiday Billie*	Way You Look Tonight The	Brunswick - 7762	Wilson Teddy Orch	30s	
Holiday Billie	Weep No More	Decca - 24551		40s	
Holiday Billie*	What A Little Moonlight Can Do	Brunswick - 7498	Wilson Teddy Orch.	30s	
Holiday Billie*	What A Night What A Moon	Brunswick - 7511	Wilson Teddy Orch.	30s	
Holiday Billie	When A Woman Loves A Man	Vocalion - 4029	Holiday Billie & her Orch	30s	
Holiday Billie*	Why Was I Born	Brunswick - 7859	Wilson Teddy Orch	30s	
Holiday Billie*	Yankee Doodle Never . . .	Brunswick - 7550	Wilson Teddy Orch	30s	
Holiday Billie	Yesterdays	Commadore - 527		40s	
Holiday Billie	You Better Go Now	Decca - 23565	Haggart Bob & his Orch	40s	
Holiday Billie	You Go To My Head	Vocalion - 4126	Holiday Billie Orch.	30s	
Holiday Billie*	You Let Me Down	Brunswick - 7581	Wilson Teddy Orch	30s	
Holiday Billie & Louis Armstrong	You Sweet Hunk Of Trash	Decca - 24785	Oliver Sy orch dir	40s	
Holiday Billie*	Youre Mothers Son In Law	Columbia - 2856 - D	Goodman Benny Orch.	30s	
Holly Buddy	I Wanna Play House With You	Coral - (LP) - 57463		50s	
Holman Libby	Baby Baby	Decca - 18304	White Josh guitar	40s	
Holman Libby	Body And Soul	Brunswick - 4910		30s	
Holman Libby	Cant We Be Friends	Brunswick - 4506		20s	
Holman Libby	Carefree	Brunswick - 3667		20s	
Holman Libby	Cooking Breakfast For The . . .	Brunswick - 4699	Kahn R. W. Orchestra	30s	
Holman Libby	Fare Thee Well	Decca - 18304	White Josh guitar	40s	
Holman Libby	Find Me A Primitive Man	Brunswick - 4666	Colonial Club Orchestra	20s	
Holman Libby	Good Mornin' Blues	Decca - 18305	White Josh guitar	40s	
Holman Libby	Hansom'Winsome Johnny . . .	Decca - 18306	White Josh guitar	40s	
Holman Libby	Happy Because Im In Love	Brunswick - 4613		20s	
Holman Libby	He's A Good Man To Have Around	Brunswick - 4447		20s	
Holman Libby	House Of The Risin' Sun	Decca - 18306	White Josh guitar	40s	
Holman Libby	I May Be Wrong But I . . .	Brunswick - 4506		20s	
Holman Libby	I'm Doing What Im Doing For.	Brunswick - 4453	Colonial Club Orchestra	20s	
Holman Libby	I'm One Of God's Children . . .	Brunswick - 6044	Colonial Club Orchestra	30s	
Holman Libby	Love For Sale	Brunswick - 6044	Colonial Club Orchestra	30s	
Holman Libby	Moanin Low	Brunswick - 4445		20s	
Holman Libby*	Moanin Low	Brunswick - 4446	Cotton Pickers	20s	
Holman Libby	My Man Is On The Make	Brunswick - 4554		20s	
Holman Libby	Ship Without A Sail A	Brunswick - 4700		30s	
Holman Libby	Something To Remember . . .	Brunswick - 4910		30s	
Holman Libby	There Aint No Sweet Man . . .	Brunswick - 3798		20s	
Holman Libby	Way He Loves Is Just . . .	Brunswick - 3798		20s	
Holman Libby	What Is This Thing Called . . .	Brunswick - 4700		30s	
Holman Libby	When A Woman Loves A Man	Brunswick - 4699	Kahn R. W. Orchestra	30s	
Holman Libby	When The Sun Goes Down	Decca - 18305	White Josh guitar	40s	
Holman Libby	Whos That Knockin At My . . .	Brunswick - 3667		20s	
Holman Libby	Why Was I Born	Brunswick - 4570		20s	
Holman Libby	You Are The Night And The . . .	Victor - 24839	Himber Richard Orch	30s	
Homer & Jethro	Baby Its Cold Outside	Victor - 20 - 0078		40s	
Hoosier Hot Shots	I Like Bananas Because . . .	Conquer - 8592	vocal group, novelty	20s	
Hope Bob & Marilyn Maxwell	Silver Bells	Film Master - 1949		40s	
Hope Bob - & Shirley Ross	Thanks For The Memory	Decca - 2219	Sosnik Harry	30s	
Hope Bob - & Shirley Ross	Thanks For The Memory	Film Master - 1938		30s	
Hope Bob & Shirley Ross	Two Sleepy People	Film Master - 1938		30s	
Hope Bob - & Shirley Ross	Two Sleepy People	Decca - 2219	Sosnik Harry	30s	
Horne Lena	Aint It The Truth	Film Master - 1946		40s	
Horne Lena	Aint It The Truth	Victor - LP - LOC - 1036	Engel Lehman Orch	50s	
Horne Lena	As Long As I Live	Quest - (LP) - 3597	Wheeler Harold M. Dir.	80s	
Horne Lena	As Long As I Live	Radio Master - 1944	Henderson Fletcher Orch	40s	
Horne Lena	As Long As I Live	Victor - 20 - 1626	Henderson Horance Or	40s	
horne Lena	At Long Last Love	Black & White - 817	Moore Phil Four	40s	
Horne Lena	Aunt Hagar's Blues	Victor - 27544	Levine Henry CMS . . .	40s	
Horne Lena	Beale Street Blues	Victor - 27543	Levine Henry CMS . . .	40s	
Horne Lena & Harry Belafonte	Bess, You Is My Woman	Victor - LP - LOP - 1507	Hayton Lenny Orch	50s	

Horne Lena	Blue Prelude	Black & White - 818	Moore Phil Four	40s	
Horne Lena	Cant Help Lovin That Man	Film Master - 1946		40s	
Horne Lena*	Captain And His Men The	Bluebird - B - 11081	Barnet Charlie Orch	40s	
Horne Lena	Careless Love	Victor - 27545	Dixieland Jazz Group.	40s	
Horne Lena	Cocoanut Sweet	Victor - LP - LOC - 1036	Engel Lehman Orch	40s	
Horne Lena	Copper Colored Gal	Quest - (LP) - 3597	Wheeler Harold M. Dir.	80s	
Horne Lena	Deed I Do	MGM - 10165	Henderson Luther Orch	40s	
Horne Lena	Deed I Do	Radio Master - 1944	Henderson Fletcher Orch	40s	
Horne Lena & Cab Callaway	Diga Diga Do	Film Master - 1943	Callaway Cab Orch	40s	
Horne Lena*	Don't Take Your Love From Me	Victor - 27505	Shaw Artie Orch	40s	
Horne Lena	From This Moment On	Quest - (LP) - 3597	Wheeler Harold M. Dir.	80s	
Horne Lena	Glad To Be Unhappy	Black & White - 817	Moore Phil Four	40s	
Horne Lena	Good For Nothin Joe	Radio Master - 1944	Henderson Fletcher Orch	40s	
Horne Lena*	Good For Nothin Joe	Bluebird - B - 11037	Barnet Charlie Orch	40s	
Horne Lena*	Haunted Town	Bluebird - B - 11093	Barnet Charlie Orch	40s	
Horne Lena	Hesitating Blues	Black & White - 844	Moore Phil Four	40s	
Horne Lena	Honey In The Honeycomb	Film Master - 1943		40s	
Horne Lena	Honeysuckle Rose	Radio Master - 1944	Henderson Fletcher Orch	50s	
Horne Lena	How Long Has This Been . . .	Victor - 45 - 001	Moore Phil Four	40s	
Horne Lena	I Aint Got Nothing But The Blues	Victor - 20 - 1626	Henderson Horance Or	40s	
Horne Lena	I Dident Know About You	Victor - 20 - 1616	Henderson Horance Or	40s	
Horne Lena	I Got A Name	Quest - (LP) - 3597	Wheeler Harold M. Dir.	80s	
Horne Lena	I Gotta Right To Sing The Blues	Victor - 27817	Bring Lou Orch	40s	
Horne Lena*	I Take To You	Decca - 778	Sissle Nobel Orch	40s	
Horne Lena	I Wants To Stay Here	Victor - LP - LOP - 1507	Hayton Lenny Orch	50s	
Horne Lena	Ill Wind	Victor - 27819	Bring Lou Orch	40s	
Horne Lena	Im Glad There Is You	Quest - (LP) - 3597	Wheeler Harold M. Dir.	80s	
Horne Lena	It Aint Necessarily So	Victor - LP - LOP - 1507	Hayton Lenny Orch	50s	
Horne Lena	Its A Rainy Day	Black & White - 846	Moore Phil Four	40s	
Horne Lena	Just One Of Those Things	Film Master 1942		40s	
Horne Lena	Lady Is A Tramp The	Film Master - 1949	Hayton Lenny Orch.	40s	
Horne Lena	Lady Is A Tramp The	MGM - 30171	Hayton Lennie Orch	40s	
Horne Lena	Lady Must Live A	Quest - (LP) - 3597	Wheeler Harold M. Dir.	80s	
Horne Lena	Lady With A Fan	Quest - (LP) - 3597	Wheeler Harold M. Dir.	80s	
Horne Lena	Life Goes On	Quest - (LP) - 3597	Wheeler Harold M. Dir.	80s	
Horne Lena & Rochester	Life Is Full Of Consquences	Film Master - 1943		40s	
Horne Lena	Life's Full On Consequences	Film Master - 1943		40s	
Horne Lena*	Love Me A Little Little	Victor - 27509	Shaw Artie Orch	30s	
Horne Lena	Love Of My Life	MGM - 10165	Hayton Lennie Orch	40s	
Horne Lena	Mad About The Boy	Radio Master - 1944	Henderson Fletcher Orch	40s	
Horne Lena	Mad About The Boy	Victor - 27820	Bring Lou Orch	40s	
Horne Lena	Man I Love The	Victor - 27818	Bring Lou Orch	40s	
Horne Lena	Moaning Low	Victor - 27817	Bring Lou Orch	40s	
Horne Lena	My Mans Gone Now	Victor - LP - LOP - 1507	Hayton Lenny Orch	50s	
Horne Lena	Napoleon	Victor - LP - LOC - 1036	Engel Lehman Orch	50s	
Horne Lena	Old Fashioned Love	Black & White - 816	Moore Phil	40s	
Horne Lena	One For My Baby	Victor - 20 - 1616	Henderson Horance Or	40s	
Horne Lena	Out Of Nowhere	Columbia - 36737	Wilson Teddy Orch	40s	
Horne Lena	Pretty To Walk With	Victor - LP - LOC - 1036	Engel Lehman Orch	40s	
Horne Lena	Push The Button	Victor - LP - LOC - 1036	Engel Lehman Orch	40s	
Horne Lena	Raisin The Rent	Quest - (LP) - 3597	Wheeler Harold M. Dir.	80s	
Horne Lena	Squeeze Me	Black & White - 819	Moore Phil Four	40s	
Horne Lena	St. Louis Blues	Victor - 27542	Levine Henry CMS . . .	40s	
Horne Lena	Stormy Weather	Film Master - 1943		40s	
Horne Lena	Stormy Weather	Victor - 27819	Bring Lou Orch	40s	
Horne Lena	Summertime	Victor - LP - LOP - 1507	Hayton Lenny Orch	50s	
Horne Lena	Take It Slow, Joe	Victor - LP - LOC - 1036	Engel Lehman Orch	50s	
Horne Lena*	That's What Love Did To Me	Decca - 847	Sissle Nobel Orch	30s	
Horne Lena & Harry Belafonte	Theres A Boat That's Leavin . . .	Victor - LP - LOP - 1507	Hayton Lenny Orch	50s	
Horne Lena	Unlucky Woman	Film Master - 1942	Wilson Teddy Orch	40s	
Horne Lena	What Is This Thing Called Love	Victor - 27820	Bring Lou Orch	40s	
Horne Lena	Where Or When	MGM - 30171		40s	
Horne Lena	Where Or When	Quest - (LP) - 3597	Wheeler Harold M. Dir.	80s	
Horne Lena	Where Or When	Victor - 27818	Bring Lou Orch	40s	
Horne Lena	Why Was I Born	Film Master - 1946		40s	
Horne Lena	Yesterday When I Was Young	Quest - (LP) - 3597	Wheeler Harold M. Dir.	80s	
Horne Lena	You Go To My Head	Black & White - 919	Moore Phil Four	40s	
Horne Lena*	Youre My Thrill	Bluebird - B - 11142	Barnet Charlie Orch	40s	
Host Joe*	Continental, (The)	Columbia - 2952	Gluskin Lud & His Orch	30s	
Hotel Pennsylvania Trio - vocal	Blue Again	Crown - 3042	Hotel Pennsylvania Trio	30s	
House Son	Preachin The Blues	Paramount - 13013		20s	
Howard Eddie	To Each His Own - NAP	Majestic - 7188	Howard Eddie Orch	40s	
Humes Helen	Alligator Blues	Okeh - 8529		20s	

Humes Helen*	And The Angels Sing	Vocalion - 4784	Basie Count Orch	30s	
Humes Helen	Be - Baba - Leba	Philo - 106	Doggett Bill Octet	40s	
Humes Helen	Black Cat Blues	Okeh - 8467		20s	
Humes Helen	Blue Prelude	Philo - 105	Doggett Bill Octet	40s	
Humes Helen	Cross - Eyed Blues	Okeh - 8825		20s	
Humes Helen	Do What You Did Last Night	Okeh - 8545		20s	
Humes Helen*	Don't Worry 'Bout Me	Conqueror - 9214	Basie Count Orch	30s	
Humes Helen	Everybody Does It Now	Okeh - 8529		20s	
Humes Helen*	Gonna Buy Me A Telephone	Decca - 8625	Brown Pete Band	40s	
Humes Helen	He May Be Your Man	Philo - 105	Dogget Bill Octet	40s	
Humes Helen*	I Can Dream, Cant I	Brunswick - 8038	James Harry Orch	30s	
Humes Helen*	If I Could Be With You One . . .	Vocalion - 4748	Basie Count Orch	30s	
Humes Helen*	If I Dident Care	Vocalion - 4784	Basie Count Orch	30s	
Humes Helen	If Papa Has Outside Lovin'	Okeh - 8545		20s	
Humes Helen*	It's Square But It Rocks	Conquer - 9631	Basie Count Orch	40s	
Humes Helen*	It's The Dreamer In Me	Brunswick - 8055	James Harry Orch	30s	
Humes Helen	Keep Your Mind On Me	Savoy - 5514	Feather Leonard Hiptet	40s	
Humes Helen*	Moonlight Seranade	Conqueror - 9295	Basie Count Orch	30s	
Humes Helen*	Mound Bayou	Decca - 8613	Brown Pete Band	40s	
Humes Helen*	My Heart Belongs To Daddy	Decca - 2249	Basie Count Orch	30s	
Humes Helen*	Song Of The Wanderer	Brunswick - 8067	James Harry Orch	30s	
Humes Helen*	Sub - Deb Blues	Vocalion - 5010	Basie Count Orch	40s	
Humes Helen	They Raided The Joint	Mercury - 8056		40s	
Humes Helen*	Unlucky Woman	Decca - 8613	Brown Pete Band	40s	
Humperdinck Engelbert	Release Me	Parrot - 40011		60s	
Hunter Alberta	Always	Columbia - CD - 36430		80s	
Hunter Alberta	Amtrack Blues	Columbia - CD - 36430		80s	
Hunter Alberta*	Be Still My Heart	HMV - B - 6546	Jackson Jack Orch	30s	
Hunter Alberta	Beale Street Blues	Victor - 20771	Waller Fats organ	20s	
Hunter Alberta	Bleeding Hearted Blues - AC	Paramount - 12021	Original Memphis Five	20s	
Hunter Alberta (May Alix)	Bleeding Hearted Blues - AC	Harmograph - 816	Original Memphis Five	20s	
Hunter Alberta	Blue Shadows	Film Master - 1934		30s	
Hunter Alberta	Boogie Woogie Swing	Bluebird - B - 8485	Heywood Eddie	40s	
Hunter A. (Josephine Beaty*)	Cake Walkin Babies - AC	Gennett - 5627	Red Onion Jazz Babies	20s	
Hunter Alberta	Chirpin The Blues - AC	Paramount - 12017	Henderson's Dance Orch	20s	
Hunter Alberta (May Alix)	Chirpin The Blues - AC	Harmograph - 801	Henderson Fletcher	20s	
Hunter Alberta	Darktown Shutter Ball	Columbia - CD - 36430		80s	
Hunter Alberta	Don't Pan Me - AC	Paramount - 12001	Blake Eubie & Orch	20s	
Hunter Alberta	Down Hearted Blues - AC	Paramount - 12005	vocal	20s	
Hunter A. (Josephine Beaty*)	Early Every Morn - AC	Gennett - 5626	Red Onion Jazz Babies	20s	
Hunter Alberta	Gimme All The Love You Got	Columbia - 14450 - D		20s	
Hunter Alberta	Good Man Is Hard To Find A	Columbia - CD - 36430		80s	
Hunter Alberta	He's Got A Punch Like Joe . . .	Juke Box - 510		40s	
Hunter Alberta	How Long Sweet Daddy . . . - AC	Black Swan - 2008	Hendersons Novelty Or	20s	
Hunter Alberta	I Got A Mind To Ramble	Regal - 3252		50s	
Hunter Alberta*	I Travel Alone	Victor - 24835	Jackson Jack Orch	30s	
Hunter Alberta	I Wont Let You Down	Bluebird - B - 8485	Heywood Eddie	40s	
Hunter Alberta	If You Want To Keep . . . - AC	Paramount - 12016	Original Memphis Five	20s	
Hunter Alberta	Ill Forgive You Cause I Love . . .	Victor - 20497		20s	
Hunter Alberta	Ill See You Go	Decca - 7644		30s	
Hunter Alberta	Im Going To Se My Ma	Victor - 21539	Waller Fats organ	20s	
Hunter Alberta	Im Gonna Lose My Way To . . .	Victor - 20497		20s	
Hunter Alberta	Im Having A Goodtime	Columbia - CD - 36430		80s	
Hunter Alberta	Jazzin Baby Blues - AC	Paramount - 12006	Blake Eubie & Orch	20s	
Hunter Alberta*	Lonely Singing Fool A	HMV - B - 6536	Jackson Jack Orch	30s	
Hunter Alberta*	Long May We Love	HMV - B - 6542	Jackson Jack Orch	30s	
Hunter Alberta	Love I Have For You The	Bluebird - B - 8539	Heywood Eddie	40s	
Hunter Alberta	Loveless Love - AC	Paramount - 12019	Henderson's Dance Orch	20s	
Hunter Alberta*	Miss Otis Regrets	HMV - B - 6525	Jackson Jack Orch	30s	
Hunter Alberta	My Castles Rockin	Bluebird - B - 8539	Heywood Eddie	40s	
Hunter Alberta	My Handy Man Aint Handy . . .	Columbia - CD - 36430		80s	
Hunter Alberta	My Old Daddys Got A New . . .	Victor - 20651		20s	
Hunter Alberta	Nobody Knows You When . . .	Columbia - CD - 36430		80s	
Hunter A. (Josephine Beaty*)	Nobody Knows - AC	Gennett - 5626	Red Onion Jazz Babies	20s	
Hunter Alberta	Old Fashioned Love	Columbia - CD - 36430		80s	
Hunter Alberta	Old Fashioned Love - AC	Paramount - 12093	Elkins Payne Jubilee Q.	20s	
Hunter Alberta	Someday Sweetheart	Decca - 7727		30s	
Hunter Alberta	Someday Sweetheart - AC	Black Swan - 2019		20s	
Hunter Alberta	Someone Else Will Take . . . AC	Paramount - 12017	Henderson Fletcher	20s	
Hunter Alberta*	Soon	HMV - B - 6530	Jackson Jack Orch	30s	
Hunter Alberta*	Stars Fell On Alabama	HMV - B - 6542	Jackson Jack Orch	30s	
Hunter Alberta	Sweet Georgia Brown	Columbia - CD - 36430		80s	
Hunter Alberta	Take Your Big Hands Off It	Juke Box - 510		40s	

Hunter Alberta*	Two Cigarettes In The Dark	HMV - B - 6525	Jackson Jack Orch	30s	
Hunter Alberta*	Two Flies On A Lump Of Sugar	HMV - B - 6541	Jackson Jack Orch	30s	
Hunter Alberta	Vamping Brown - AC	Paramount - 12020	Henderson Fletcher	20s	
Hunter Alberta*	When The Mountains Meet . . .	HMV - B - 6529	Jackson Jack Orch	30s	
Hunter Alberta	Yelpin The Blues	Decca - 7633		30s	
Hunter Alberta	You Cant Tell The Difference . . .	ARC Master - 1935	unknown	30s	
Hunter Alberta	You Gotta Reap What . . . AC	Paramount - 12021	Hendersons Novelty Or	20s	
Hunter Alberta	Your Jelly Roll Is Good - AC	Okeh - 8286	Bradford Perry Mean Four	20s	
Hurt Mississippi John	Candy Man Blues	Okeh - 8654		20s	
Hurt Mississippi John	Stack "O Lee Blues	Okeh - 8654		20s	
Hutton Ina Ray	Doing The Suzie Q	Film Master - 1937	Melodears her	30s	
Hutton Ina Ray	Truckin	Film Master - 1935	Melodears her	30s	
Hutton Marion*	Five O'Clock Whistle	Bluebird - B - 10900	Miller Glen Orchestra	40s	
Hutton Marion*	Man With The Mandolin, The	Bluebird - B - 10358	Miller Glen Orchestra	40s	
Hutton Marion, Modernaires*	Ive Lost A Gal In Kalamazoo	Victor - 27934	Miller Glen Orchestra	40s	
Ingle Red & Aileen Carlisle	Glow Worm The	Victor - 20 - 1893	Jones Spike & C. S.	40s	
Ink Spots	Address Unknown	Decca - 2707		30s	
Ink Spots	Do I Worry	Decca - 3432		40s	
Ink Spots	Don't Get Around Much Anymore	Decca - 18503		40s	
Ink Spots	Foo - Gee	Decca - 4303		40s	
Ink Spots	Gypsy The	Decca - 18817		40s	
Ink Spots	I Cover The Waterfront	Decca - 18864		40s	
Ink Spots	I Don't Want To Start The.	Decca - 3987		40s	
Ink Spots	If I Dident Care	Decca - 2286		30s	
Ink Spots	Java Jive	Decca - 3432		40s	
Ink Spots	Keep Cool Fool	Decca - 3958		40s	
Ink Spots	Knock Kneed Sal	Decca - 2286		40s	
Ink Spots	Maybe	Decca - 3258		40s	
Ink Spots	My Prayer	Decca - 2790		30s	
Ink Spots	Nothin'	Decca - 4045		40s	
Ink Spots	Prisoner Of Love	Decca - 18864		40s	
Ink Spots	That's When Youre Heart . . .	Decca - 3720		40s	
Ink Spots	To Each His Own	Decca - 23615		40s	
Ink Spots	We Three - My Echo . . .	Decca - 3379		40s	
Ink Spots	We'll Meet Again	Decca - 3656		40s	
Ink Spots	Whispering Grass	Decca - 3258		40s	
Ives Burl	Black Is The Color	Ash - 345 - 2B		40s	
Ives Burl	Blue Tail Fly, The	Ash - 345 - 3A		40s	
Ives Burl	Bold Soldier, The	Ash - 345 - 1B		40s	
Ives Burl	Buckeyed Jim	Ash - 345 - 1A		40s	
Ives Burl	Foggy Foggy Dew	Ash - 345 - 2A		40s	
Ives Burl	Henry Martyn	Ash - 345 - 3B		40s	
Ives Burl	Holly Jolly Christmas The	Decca - 31695		60s	
Ives Burl	Lavender Blue - Dilly Dilly	Decca - 24547		40s	
Ives Burl	Little Bitty Tear, A	Decca - 31330		60s	
Ives Burl	On Top Of Old Smokey	Columbia - 39328		40s	
Ives Burl	Pearly Shells	Decca - 31659		60s	
Ives Burl	Poor Warefaring Stranger	Ash - 345 - 1A		40s	
Ives Burl	Riders In The Sky	Decca - 38445		40s	
Ives Burl	Sow Took The Measles The	Ash - 345 - 1B		40s	
Jackson Aunt Molly	Kentucky Miners Wife - Ragged	Columbia - 15731 - D		30s	
Jackson Bessie - (L. Bogan)	Shave "Em Dry	Melotone - M - 13442		30s	
Jackson Bessie - (L. Bogan)	Shave 'em Dry	ARC Master - 1935		30s	
Jackson Mahalia	Come Sunday - 23rd Pslam -	Columbia - LP - 1162.	Ellington Duke Orch.	50s	
Jackson Mahalia	Dig A Little Deeper	Grand Award - 1025		50s	
Jackson Mahalia	Get Away Jordan	Apollo - 240		50s	
Jackson Mahalia	God's Gonna Separate The . . .	Decca - 7341		30s	
Jackson Mahalia	He's Got The Whole World In.	Columbia - 41150		50s	
Jackson Mahalia	His Eye Is On The Sparrow	Apollo - 246		50s	
Jackson Mahalia	In The Upper Room - PT 1 & 2	Apollo - 262		50s	
Jackson Mahalia	It Is No Secret . . .	Apollo - 246		50s	
Jackson Mahalia	Jesus Met The Woman At . . .	Columbia - 40412		50s	
Jackson Mahalia	Just As I Am	Apollo - 248		50s	
Jackson Mahalia	Lords Prayer The	Apollo - 245		50s	
Jackson Mahalia	Move On Up A Little Higher	Apollo - 164		40s	
Jackson Mahalia	Satisified Mind A	Columbia - 40554		50s	
Jackson Mahalia	Walk Over God's Heaven	Columbia - 40412		50s	
Jackson Mahalia	You Just Keep Still	Apollo - 304		50s	
Jackson Papa Charlie	Airy Man Blues - AC	Paramount - 12219		20s	
Jackson Papa Charlie	All I Want Is A Spoonful - AC	Paramount - 12320		20s	
Jackson Papa Charlie	Blue Monday Morning Blues	Paramount - 12574		20s	
Jackson Papa Charlie	Bright Eyes	Paramount - 12574		20s	
Jackson Papa Charlie	Butter and Egg Man Blues - AC	Paramount - 12358		20s	

Jackson Papa Charlie	Coal Man Blues	Paramount - 12461		20s	
Jackson Papa Charlie	Judge Cliff Davis Blues, The - AC	Paramount - 12366		20s	
Jackson Papa Charlie	Mama Don't Allow It - AC	Paramount - 12296		20s	
Jackson Papa Charlie	Maxwell Street Blues - AC	Paramount - 12320		20s	
Jackson Papa Charlie	Papa's Lawdy Lawdy . . . - AC	Paramount - 12219		20s	
Jackson Papa Charlie	Salty Dog Blues - AC	Paramount - 12236		20s	
Jackson Papa Charlie*	Salty Dog Blues - AC	Paramount - 12399	Keppard's, F. Jazz Cardinals	20s	
Jackson Papa Charlie	Shake That Thing - AC	Paramount - 12281		20s	
Jackson Papa Charlie	She Belongs To Me Blues	Paramount - 12461		20s	
Jackson Papa Charlie	Up The Way Bound - AC	Paramount - 12375		20s	
Jackson Papa Charlie	Your Baby Aint Sweet . . . - AC	Paramount - 12383		20s	
Jagger Mike*	Get Yer Ya Yas Out	London LP - NPS - 5	Rolling Stones	60s	
Jagger Mike*	Little Red Rooster	Decca - F - 12014	Rolling Stones	60s	
Jagger Mike*	Love In Vain	London LP - NPS - 5	Rolling Stones	60s	
James Elmore	Dust My Broom	Trumpet - 146		40s	
James Etta	At Last	Argo - 5380		60s	
James Etta	Trust In Me	Argo - 5385		60s	
James Etta	Wall FlowerThe	Modern Records - 947	Peaches the	50s	
James Joni	Your Cheatin Heart	MGM - 11426		50s	
James Skip	Twenty Twenty 22 - 20 Blues	Paramount - 13066		20s	
Jarrett Art*	My Baby Just Cares For Me	Victor - 22499	Weems Ted & His Orch	30s	
Jaxton Frankie - Half Pint	Chocolate To The Bone	Vocalion - 1583	Punches Delegates Of	30s	
Jaxton Frankie - Half Pint	Corinne	Black Pattie - 8048		20s	
Jaxton Frankie - Half Pint	Corrine	Vocalion - 1539		20s	
Jaxton Frankie - Half Pint*	Don't Drink It In Here	Brunswick - 7067	Johnson's Bill L. Jug B.	20s	
Jaxton Frankie - Half Pint	Don't Pan Me	Decca - 7638		30s	
Jaxton Frankie - Half Pint	Down At Jaspers Bar B Que	Vocalion - 1226		20s	
Jaxton Frankie - Half Pint	Down Home In Kentuck	Vocalion - 1472	Punches Delegates Of	20s	
Jaxton Frankie - Half Pint	Fan It	Perfect - 0210		20s	
Jaxton Frankie - Half Pint	Fan It	Vocalion - 1257		20s	
Jaxton Frankie - Half Pint	Fan It	Vocalion - 2553	acc, by His Hot Shots	30s	
Jaxton Frankie - Half Pint*	Get The L Down The Road	Brunswick - 7067	Johnson's Bill L. Jug B.	20s	
Jaxton Frankie - Half Pint	Hit The Ditty Low Down	Vocalion - 1226		20s	
Jaxton Frankie - (F. Jackson)*	If That Don't Get It This . . .	Okeh - 8359	Jackson Frankie	20s	
Jaxton Frankie - Half Pint*	It's Tight Like That	Vocalion - 1228	Tampa Reds H. Jug . . .	20s	
Jaxton Frankie - Half Pint	Jive Man Blues	Vocalion - 1539		20s	
Jaxton Frankie - Half Pint	Let Me Ride Your Train	Decca - 7786		40s	
Jaxton Frankie - Half Pint*	Lets Knock A Jug	Vocalion - 1285		20s	
Jaxton Frankie - Half Pint	Mama Don't Allow It	Vocalion - 2603	acc, by His Hot Shots	30s	
Jaxton Frankie - Half Pint*	My Daddy Rocks Me With A.	Vocalion - 1274	Tampa Reds H. Jug . . .	20s	
Jaxton Frankie - Half Pint	Riff It	Decca - 7482	Harlem Mamfats	30s	
Jaxton Frankie - Half Pint*	Rock Me Mama	Brunswick - 4964	Robinson Banjo Ikey . . .	20s	
Jaxton Frankie - Half Pint	Scuddlin	Vocalion - 1583		30s	
Jaxton Frankie - Half Pint	Some Sweet Day	Decca - 7548	Harlem Mamfats	30s	
Jaxton Frankie - Half Pint	Take It Easy	Vocalion - 1424		20s	
Jaxton Frankie - Half - Pint*	When A Woman Gets The . . .	Decca - 7363	Prince Budda & his Boys	30s	
Jaxton Frankie - Half Pint	Willie The Weeper	Black Pattie - 8048		20s	
Jaxton Frankie - Half Pint	You Cant Tell	Decca - 7806		40s	
Jaxton Frankie - Half Pint	You Got To Get It Wet	Vocalion - 1472	Punches Delegates Of	20s	
Jefferson Blind Lemon	Bed Springs Blues	Paramount - 12872		20s	
Jefferson Blind Lemon	Beggin 'Back - AC	Paramount - 12394		20s	
Jefferson Blind Lemon	Black Snake Moan	Okeh - 8455		20s	
Jefferson Blind Lemon	Blind Lemon's Penitentary . . .	Paramount - 12666		20s	
Jefferson Blind Lemon	Corrina Blues - AC	Paramount - 12367		20s	
Jefferson Blind Lemon	Got The Blues - AC	Paramount - 12354		20s	
Jefferson Blind Lemon	Matchbox Blues	Okeh - 8455		20s	
Jefferson Blind Lemon	Matchbox Blues	Paramount - 12474		20s	
Jefferson Blind Lemon	One Dime Blues	Paramount - 12578		20s	
Jefferson Blind Lemon	Rambler Blues	Paramount - 12541		20s	
Jefferson Blind Lemon	Right Of Way Blues	Paramount - 12510		20s	
Jefferson Blind Lemon	That Black Snake Moan - AC	Paramount - 12407		20s	
Jefferson Blind Lemon	That Crawlin' Baby Blues	Paramount - 12880		20s	
Jeffries Herb*	Flamingo	Victor - 27326	Ellington Duke Orch	40s	
Jeffries Herb	These Foolish Things . . .	Exclusive - 93 - x		40s	
Jennings Al*	Dance With A Dolly	Decca - 18625	Morgan Russ & Orch	40s	
Jessell George	My Mother's Eyes	Victor - 21852		20s	
John Little Willie	Fever	King - 4935		50s	
Johnson Blind Willie	God Don't Never Change	Columbia - 14490 - D	guitar accomp.	30s	
Johnson Blind Willie	Let Your Light Shine On Me	Columbia - 14490 - D	guitar accomp.	20s	
Johnson Lonnie	Back Water Blues	Okeh - 8466		20s	
Johnson Lonnie	Chicago Blues	Bluebird - B - 8684		30s	
Johnson Lonnie	Crowing Rooster Blues	Okeh - 8574		20s	
Johnson Lonnie	Devils Got The Blues	Decca - 7427		30s	

Johnson Lonnie	Don't Be No Fool	Bluebird - B - 8530		30s	
Johnson Lonnie	Five O Clock Blues	Okeh - 8417		20s	
Johnson Lonnie	Get Yourself Together	Bluebird - B - 8530		30s	
Johnson Lonnie	Got The Blues For Murder . . .	Okeh - 8846		30s	
Johnson Lonnie	Im In Love Again	Bluebird - B - 8747		40s	
Johnson Lonnie & S. Williams	It Feels So Good	Okeh - 8664	vocal duet piano & guitar	20s	
Johnson Lonnie	Kansas City Blues - Pt 1 & 2.	Okeh - 8537		20s	
Johnson Lonnie	Lazy Woman Blues	Bluebird - B - 8747		40s	
Johnson Lonnie	Lonesome Road, The	Bluebird - B - - 0714		30s	
Johnson Lonnie	Love Is The Answer	Alladin - 197		40s	
Johnson Lonnie	Mean Old Bed Bug Blues	Okeh - 8497		20s	
Johnson Lonnie	Mr Johnsons Blues	Okeh - 8253		20s	
Johnson Lonnie	My Mother's Eyes	King - 4510		40s	
Johnson Lonnie	No More Troubles Now	Okeh - 8831		30s	
Johnson Lonnie	Oh Doctor The Blues	Okeh - 8391		20s	
Johnson Lonnie	Racketeers Blues	Okeh - 8946		30s	
Johnson Lonnie	Shes Making Woopie In Hell . . .	Okeh - 8768		20s	
Johnson Lonnie	Sweet Potato Blues	Okeh - 8586		20s	
Johnson Lonnie	Tomorrow Night	King - 4201		40s	
Johnson Lonnie	Tomorrow Night	Paradise - 110		50s	
Johnson Lonnie	Very Lonesome Blues	Okeh - 8282		20s	
Johnson Lonnie	What A Woman	King - 4201		40s	
Johnson Lonnie	Wrong Woman Blues	Okeh - 8601		20s	
Johnson Margret	Mama's All Alone Blues - AC	Okeh - 8185		20s	
Johnson Margret	Nobody Knows The Way . . . AC	Okeh - 8162		20s	
Johnson Robert	Thirty Two Twenty 32 - 20 Blues	Vocalion - 03445		30s	
Johnson Robert	Come On In My Kitchen	Vocalion - 03563		30s	
Johnson Robert	Cross Roads Blues	Vocalion - 03519		30s	
Johnson Robert	Dead Shrimp Blues	Vocalion - 03475		30s	
Johnson Robert	I Believe Ill Dust My Broom	Vocalion - 03475		30s	
Johnson Robert	Kind Hearted Woman	Vocalion - 03416		30s	
Johnson Robert	Little Queen Of Spades	Vocalion - 04108		30s	
Johnson Robert	Love In Vain	Vocalion - 04630		30s	
Johnson Robert	Malted Milk	Vocalion - 03665		30s	
Johnson Robert	Me And The Devil Blues	Vocalion - 04108		30s	
Johnson Robert	Milkcows Calf Blues	Vocalion - 03665		30s	
Johnson Robert	Preaching The Blues Up . . .	Vocalion - 04630		30s	
Johnson Robert	Sweet Home Chicago	Vocalion - 03601		30s	
Johnson Robert	Terraplane Blues	Vocalion - 03416		30s	
Johnson Robert	Ther're Red Hot	Vocalion - 03563		30s	
Johnson Robert	Walking Blues	Vocalion - 03601		30s	
Johnson Tommy	Maggie Campbell Blues	Victor - 21409		20s	
Jolson Al	Spaniard That Blighted. - AC	Victor - 17318		10s	
Jolson Al	About A Quarter To Nine	Decca - 24400	Stoloff Morris Orch.	40s	
Jolson Al & Bing Crosby	Alexanders Ragetime Band	Decca - 40038	Trotter John Scott Orch	40s	
Jolson Al	April Showers	Brunswick - 6502	Lombardo Guy Orch	20s	
Jolson Al	April Showers - AC	Columbia - A3500		20s	
Jolson Al	Asleep In The Deep - AC	Victor - 17915		10s	
Jolson Al	Avalon - AC	Columbia - A2995		10s	
Jolson Al	Baby Face	Decca DL - 5006		40s	
Jolson Al	Back In Your Own Backyard	Brunswick - 3867	Wirges Bill Orch	20s	
Jolson Al	Blue River	Brunswick - 3719	Wirges Bill Orch	20s	
Jolson Al	Blue Skies	Film Master - 1927		20s	
Jolson Al	California Here I Come - AC	Brunswick - 2569	Jones Isham Orch	20s	
Jolson Al	Dirty Hands Dirty Face	Brunswick - 3912	Lyman Abe Orch	20s	
Jolson Al & Mills Brothers	Down Amoung The Sheltering.	Decca - 24534	vocal with guitar	40s	
Jolson Al	Golden Gate	Brunswick - 3775	Wirges Bill Orch	20s	
Jolson Al	Hallelujah Im A Bum	Brunswick - 6500	Young Victor Orch	30s	
Jolson Al	Hello Tucky - AC	Brunswick - 2763	Miller Ray Orch	20s	
Jolson Al	Ill Say She Does - AC	Columbia - A2746		10s	
Jolson Al	Im Going South - AC	Brunswick - 2569	Jones Isham Orch	20s	
Jolson Al	Im In Seventh Heaven	Brunswick - 4400		20s	
Jolson Al	Im Sitting On Top Of The World	Brunswick - 3014	Fenton Carl Orch	20s	
Jolson Al & Mills Brothers	Is It True What They Say About	Decca - 24534	vocal with guitar	40s	
Jolson Al	Is It True What They Say . . .	Decca - 24684	Stoloff Morris Orch.	40s	
Jolson Al	Ive Got My Captain . . . - AC	Columbia - A2794		10s	
Jolson Al	Lazy - AC	Brunswick - 2595	Jones Isham Orch	20s	
Jolson Al	Let Me Sing When Im Happy	Brunswick - 4721		30s	
Jolson Al	Miami - AC	Brunswick - 3013	Fenton Carl Orch	20s	
Jolson Al	Mr. Radio Man - AC	Brunswick - 2582	Jones Isham Orch	20s	
Jolson Al	My Papa Don't Two Time . . . - AC	Brunswick - 2595	Jones Isham Orch	20s	
Jolson Al	Ragging The Baby To Sleep - AC	Victor - 17081		10s	
Jolson Al	Rock - A - Bye Your Baby With. AC	Columbia - A2560		20s	

Jolson Al	Rock - A - Bye Your Baby With . . .	Brunswick - 6502	Lombardo Guy Orch	30s	
Jolson Al	Sister Susies Sewing . . . AC	Columbia - A1617		10s	
Jolson Al	Snap Your Fingers - AC	Victor - 17075		10s	
Jolson Al	Sonny Boy - NAP	Brunswick - 4033		20s	
Jolson Al	Stepping Out - AC	Brunswick - 2567	Jones Isham Orch	20s	
Jolson Al	Swanee - AC	Columbia - A - 2884		20s	
Jolson Al	Tell Me - AC	Columbia - A2821		20s	
Jolson Al	Theres A Rainbow Around My.	Brunswick - 4033		20s	
Jolson Al	Tonights My Night With . . . AC	Brunswick - 3196	Fenton Carl Orch	20s	
Jolson Al	Toot Toot Tootsie Goodby - AC	Columbia - A - 3705		10s	
Jolson Al	Toot Toot Tootsie Goodbye	Film Master - 1927		20s	
Jolson Al	Waitin' For The Evening Mail - AC	Columbia - A - 3933		20s	
Jolson Al	When The Little Red Roses . . .	Brunswick - 4721		30s	
Jolson Al	When The Red Red Robin . . .	Brunswick - 3222	Fenton Carl Orch	20s	
Jolson Al	You Aint Heard Nothin Yet - AC	Columbia - A2836		10s	
Jolson Al	You Flew Away From The. - AC	Brunswick - 3013	Fenton Carl Orch	20s	
Jolson Al	You Made Me Love You - AC	Columbia - A1374		20s	
Jones Ada	By The Light Of The Silv . . . - AC	Edison - 10362		10s	
Jones Ada - NAP	If The Man In The Moon . . . - AC	Edison - 9372		00s	
Jones Ada	If They'd Only Move To . . . - AC	Victor - 17576		10s	
Jones Ada - NAP	Put Your Arms Around Me Honey - AC	Edison - Amber - 669		10s	
Jones Ada & Billy Murray	Come Josephine In My . . . - AC	Victor - 16844		10s	
Jones Ada & Billy Murray	Shine On Harvest Moon - AC	Edison - 10134		00s	
Jones Billy	Bye Bye Blackbird - AC	Banner - 1808		20s	
Jones Jack	Wives And Lovers	Kapp - 551		60s	
Jones Maggie	Thunderstorm Blues - AC	Columbia - 14050 - D		20s	
Jones Tom	With These Hands	Parrot - 9787	Reed Les dir	60s	
Jordan Louis	Aint Nobody Here But Us Chickens	Decca - 23741	Jordan Louis & H. T. Five	40s	
Jordan Louis	Buzz Me	Decca - 18734	Jordan Louis & H. T. Five	40s	
Jordan Louis	Caladonia	Decca - 8670	Jordan Louis & H. T. Five	40s	
Jordan Louis	Chicks I Pick Are Slender And . . .	Decca - 8645	Jordan Louis & H. T. Five	40s	
Jordan Louis	Choo Choo Ch'Boogie	Decca - 23610	Jordan Louis & H. T. Five	40s	
Jordan Louis	Don't Let The Sun Catch . . .	Decca - 18818	Jordan Louis & H. T. Five	40s	
Jordan Louis	Doug The Jitter Bug	Decca - 7590	Jordan Louis & H. T. Five	30s	
Jordan Louis	Fore Day Blues	Decca - 7693	Jordan Louis & H. T. Five	30s	
Jordan Louis	G. I Jive	Decca - 8659	Jordan Louis & H. T. Five	40s	
Jordan Louis	Is You Is Or Is You Aint My Baby	Decca - 8659	Jordan Louis & H. T. Five	40s	
Jordan Louis	Keep A Knocking	Decca - 7609	Jordan Louis & H. T. Five	30s	
Jordan Louis	Let The Good Times Roll	Decca - 23741	Jordan Louis & H. T. Five	40s	
Jordan Louis	Mama Mama Blues	Decca - 8626	Jordan Louis & H. T. Five	30s	
Jordan Louis	Mop Mop	Decca - 8668	Jordan Louis & H. T. Five	40s	
Jordan Louis	Pan Pan	Decca - 8537	Jordan Louis & H. T. Five	30s	
Jordan Louis & Calypso Boys	Run Joe	Decca - 24448	Jordan Louis & H. T. Five	40s	
Jordan Louis	Saturday Night Fish Fry	Decca - 24745	Jordan Louis & H. T. Five	40s	
Jordan Louis	That Chicks Too Young To Fry	Decca - 23610	Jordan Louis & H. T. Five	40s	
Jordan Louis	Whats The Use Of Getting Sober	Decca - 8645	Jordan Louis & H. T. Five	40s	
Jordan Louis	You Cant Get Tat No More	Decca - 8668	Jordan Louis & H. T. Five	40s	
Kallen Kitty*	Im Beginning To See The Light	Columbia - 36758	Harry James & His Orch.	40s	
Kallen Kitty*	They're Either Too Young Or.	Decca - 18571	Dorsey Jimmy Orch	40s	
Kane Helen	Aintcha	Victor - 22192		20s	
Kane Helen	Button Up Your Overcoat	Victor - 21863		20s	
Kane Helen	Do Something	Victor - 21917		20s	
Kane Helen	Don't Be Like That	Victor - 21830		20s	
Kane Helen	Get Out And Get Under The Moon	Victor - 21557	Shilkret Nat & his Orch.	20s	
Kane Helen	He's So Unusual	Victor - 22080		20s	
Kane Helen	I Have To Have You	Victor - 22192		20s	
Kane Helen	I Wanna Be Loved By You	Victor - 21684	Joy Lenard Orch	20s	
Kane Helen	I Want To Be Bad	Victor - 21830		20s	
Kane Helen	Id Do Anything For You	Victor - 22080		20s	
Kane Helen	If You Knew Better	Victor - 22407		30s	
Kane Helen	Is There Anything Wrong with That	Victor - 21684		20s	
Kane Helen	Me And The Man In The Moon	Victor - 21830		20s	
Kane Helen	My Man Is On The Make	Victor - 22475		30s	
Kane Helen	Readin Ritin' Rhythm	Victor - 22407		20s	
Kane Helen	That's My Weakness Now	Victor - 21557	Skilkret Nat & his Orch	20s	
Kane Helen	That's Why Im Happy	Victor - 21917		20s	
Kaufields - Three Kaufields -	I'll See You In Cuba - AC	Emerson - 10158		20s	
Kaufman Irving*	Miss Annabelle Lee	Columbia - 1088 - D	Knickerbockers	20s	
Kaufman Irving*	Mr. Jazz Himself=AC	Columbia - A2460		10s	
Kaufman Irving*	Too Many Parties For Too . . .	Banner - 1668		20s	
Kay Dolly	Hard Hearted Hannah - AC	Columbia - 151 - D		20s	
Kay Dolly	Magnolia	Harmony - 449 - H		20s	
Kay Dolly	Poor Papa	Harmony - 107 - H		20s	

Kay Dolly	Some Day Sweetheart - AC	Columbia - 117 - D	Georgians the	20s	
Kaye Danny	Thumbelina	Decca - 28380	Jenkins Gordon Orch	50s	
Kazee Buell	John Hardy - AC	Brunswick - 144		20s	
Keaton Diane	Seems Like Old Times	Film Master - 1977		70s	
Keeshan Chuck*	Borne To Lose	Okeh - 6706	Daffan Ted Texans his	40s	
Keeshan Chuck*	Worried Mind	Conqueror - 9699	Daffan Ted Texans his	40s	
Keller Sisters & Lynch	Me And My Shadow	Apex - 8620		20s	
Keller Greta	Willow Weep For Me	Brunswick - 6506		30s	
Keller Greta	Blues In My Heart	Decca - F - 2592		30s	
Keller Greta	Lover	Brunswick-6544		30s	
Keller Greta	Thank You For The Flowers	Decca - M - 418		30s	
Kelly Gene	Singing In The Rain	Film Master - 1952		50s	
Kelly Paula & Tex Beneke . . .	When That Man Is Done And.	Bluebird - B - 11069	Miller Glen Orch	40s	
Kelly Willie	Coming In On A Wing And A . . .	Hit - 7046	Kelly Willie Orch	40s	
King Charles	Happy Days Are Here Again	Brunswick - 4615		30s	
King Charles & Louis Groody	Sometimes I'm Happy	Victor - 20609		20s	
King Edward VIII	Kings Farewell Speech	Brunswick - 7810	SPOKEN WORD	30s	
King George VI	Broadcast From Buckingham.	HMV - 8969	SPOKEN WORD	30s	
King Sisters	Candy	Victor - 20 - 1633	Cole Buddy Orch	40s	
King Sisters	Mairzy Doats	Bluebird - B - 0822	Rey Alvino - Rhythm Reys	40s	
King Yvonne*	Idaho	Bluebird - B - 11331	Rey Alvino - Rhythm Reys	40s	
Knight Evelyn	Little Bird Told Me So A	Decca - 24514	Stardusters	40s	
Laine Frankie	Black And Blue	Mercury - 1026	Fisher Carl Swingtet	40s	
Laine Frankie	Cool Water	Columbia-40457	Weston Paul &Mello men	50s	
Laine Frankie	Cry Of The Wild Goose, The	Mercury - 5363	Geller Harry Orch.	50s	
Laine Frankie	High Noon	Columbia - 39570	Carroll Jimmy Orch.	50s	
Laine Frankie & Doris Day	How Lovely Cooks The Meat - NAP	Columbia - 39693	Fisher Carl Orch	50s	
Laine Frankie & N. Luboff Choir	I Believe	Columbia - 39938	Weston Paul Orch	50s	
Laine Frankie	Jezebel	Columbia - 39367	Miller Mitch Orch.	50s	
Laine Frankie	Lotus Land	Columbia - 40780	Faith Percy Orch	50s	
Laine Frankie	Love Is A Golden Ring	Columbia - 40856	Easy Riders	50s	
Laine Frankie	Moonlight Gambler	Columbia - 40780	Conniff Ray Orch	50s	
Laine Frankie	Moonlight In Vermont	Atlas - FL - 156	Dunlap Paul Orchestra	40s	
Laine Frankie	Mule Train	Mercury - 5345	Muleskinners &	40s	
Laine Frankie	Rawhide	Columbia - 41230		50s	
Laine Frankie	Shine	Mercury - 5091	Fisher Carl Orch	40s	
Laine Frankie	South Of The Border	Mercury - 5892	Fisher Carl Orch	50s	
Laine Frankie	That Lucky Old Sun	Mercury - 5316	Geller Harry Orch.	40s	
Laine Frankie	That's My Desire	Mercury - 5007	Klein Manny All Stars	40s	
Laine Frankie	Two Loves Have I	Mercury - 5064		40s	
Laine Frankie & Jo Stafford	Way Down Yonder in New . . .	Columbia - 40116	Weston Paul Orch.	50s	
Laine Frankie	We'll Be Together Again	Mercury - 5091	Fisher Carl Orch.	40s	
Laine Frankie	You Gave Me A Mountain	ABC - 11174		60s	
Laine Frankie	Youre All I Want For Christmas	Mercury - 5177	Fisher Carl Orch	40s	
Laine Frankie & N. Luboff Choir	Youre Cheatin Heart	Columbia - 39938	Weston Paul Orch	50s	
Lambert Scrappy & Billy Hillpot*	Aint She Sweet	Brunswick - 3444	Bernie Ben Orch	20s	
Lambert Scrappy (unacredited)	Go Home And Tell Your Mother	HOW - 1091	Voorhees Don Orch	30s	
Lambert Scrappy*	How Am I To Know	Victor - 22111	Arden - Ohman Orch	20s	
Lambert Scrappy*	S'Wonderful	Columbia - 1213 - D	Ipana Troubadors Orch	20s	
Lamm Bob*	Near You	Bullet - 1001	Craig Francis Orch	40s	
Lamour Dorothy	Kinda Lonesome	Brunswick - 8304		30s	
Lamour Dorothy	Moonlight And Shadows	Brunswick - 7829		30s	
Lamour Dorothy	Personality	Film Master - 1946		40s	
Lane Buddy	Too Late	Crown - 3231		30s	
Lane Pricilla	Im Just Wild About Harry	Film Master - 1939		30s	
Lane Pricilla	It Had To Be You	Film Master 1939		30s	
Lane Pricilla	Melancholy Baby, My	Film Master 1939		30s	
Langford Frances	I Feel a Song Coming On	Brunswick - 7512		30s	
Langford Frances	Once In A While	Decca - 1542	Sosnik Harry	30s	
Lanza Mario	Be My Love	Victor - 78 - 1561		50s	
Larson Snooky* - NAP	By The Light Of The Silvery . . .	Columbia - 36479	Noble Ray Orchestra	40s	
Larson Snooky* - NAP	I Wonder Who's Kissing Her Now	Columbia - 37544	Noble Ray Orch	30s	
Lattimore Harlan*	Aint I The Lucky One	Brunswick - 6401	Redman Don Orch	30s	
Lattimore Harlan*	Beloved	Brunswick - 6768	Young Victor Orch	30s	
Lattimore Harlan*	Blue Eyed Baby From Memphis, That	Brunswick - 6560	Redman Don Orch	30s	
Lattimore Harlan*	Day Without You A	Brunswick - 6747	Young Victor Orch	30s	
Lattimore Harlan*	Got The South In My Soul	Melotone - M - 12417	Redman Don Orch	30s	
Lattimore Harlan*	How Do You Do It	Brunswick - 6380	Lyman Abe Orch	30s	
Lattimore Harlan*	I Found A New Way To Go To Town	Brunswick - 6684	Redman Don Orch	30s	
Lattimore Harlan	I Love You I Do	King - 4359	Glover Henry Orch	40s	
Lattimore Harlan*	I Wanna Be Loved	Brunswick - 6745	Redman Don Orch	30s	

Lattimore Harlan*	If Its True	Brunswick - 6368	Redman Don Orch	30s	
Lattimore Harlan*	Just A Little Home For The . . .	Conqueror - 8029	Loyd Ed Orch	30s	
Lattimore Harlan*	Lazy Weather	Melotone - M - 6 07 09	Redman Don Orch	30s	
Lattimore Harlan*	Lazybones	Brunswick - 6622	Redman Don Orch	30s	
Lattimore Harlan*	Little Street Where Old . . .	Melotone - M - 12512	Fallon Owen Orch	30s	
Lattimore Harlan*	Lonely Cabin	Brunswick - 6935	Redman Don Orch	30s	
Lattimore Harlan*	Moonrise On The Lowlands	Melotone - M - 6 07 09	Redman Don Orch	30s	
Lattimore Harlan*	Pagan Paradise	Brunswick - 6412	Redman Don Orch	30s	
Lattimore Harlan*	Poor Old Joe	Victor - 24008	Henderson Fletcher Or	30s	
Lattimore Harlan*	Some Day We'll Meet Again	Conqueror - 8029	Loyd Ed Orch	30s	
Lattimore Harlan	Strange As It Seems	Columbia - 2671 - D		30s	
Lattimore Harlan*	Take Me In Your Arms	Melotone - M - 12512	Fallon Owen Orch	30s	
Lattimore Harlan*	Underneath The Harlem Moon	Brunswick - 6401	Redman Don Orch	30s	
Lattimore Harlan*	Who Wants To Sing My Love Song	Vocalion - 3359	Redman Don Orch	30s	
Lattimore Harlan	With Summer Coming On	Columbia - 2671 - D		30s	
Lattimore Harlan*	You Told Me But Half The Story	Brunswick - 6935	Redman Don Orch	30s	
Laurenz John	My Happiness	Mercury - 5144		30s	
Lawrence Bob* - NAP	Wagon Wheels	Victor - 24517	Whiteman Paul Orch	30s	
Lawrence Gertrude	Do Do Do	Victor - 20331		20s	
Lawrence Gertrude	Someone To Watch Over Me	Victor - 20331		20s	
Leachman Silas	Bill Bailey Wont You Please - AC	Victor - Monarch - 1458		00s	
Leadbelly	Bourgeois Blues, The	Musicraft - 227		30s	
Leadbelly	Easy Rider	Bluebird - B - 8570		40s	
Leadbelly	Frankie And Albert	Musicraft - 223		30s	
Leadbelly	Irene	Ash - 343 - 1		40s	
Leadbelly	John Hardy	Musicraft - 311		40s	
Leadbelly	John Henry	Ash - 343 - 3		40s	
Leadbelly	Leaving Blues	Bluebird - B - 8791		40s	
Leadbelly	Looky Looky Yonder Black . . .	Musicraft - 223		30s	
Lead Belly, W. Guthrie, C. Houston	Midnight Special	Disc - 6043		40s	
Leadbelly & Golden Gate Quartet	Midnight Special	Victor - 27266		40s	
Leadbelly	New Orleans	Musicraft - 312		40s	
Leadbelly	New York City	Bluebird - B - 8750		30s	
Leadbelly	On A Monday Im Almost Gone	Ash - 343 - 1		40s	
Leadbelly	Rock Island Line	Ash - 102		40s	
Leadbelly	Take This Hammer	Ash - 101		40s	
Lee Bertha	Mind Reader's Blues	Vocalion - 02652		30s	
Lee Brenda	Some Of These Days	Decca - 30885		50s	
Lee Brenda	You Can Depend On Me	Decca - 31231		60s	
Lee George*	If I Could Be With You One . . .	Brunswick - 7132	Lee George Orch	20s	
Lee Julia*	Down Home Syncopated Blues	Merrit - 2206	Lee George Orch	30s	
Lee Julia*	He's Tall Dark And Handsome	Brunswick - 4761	Lee George Orch	30s	
Lee Julia	I Dident Like It The First Time	Capital - 15367	Her Boy Friends &	40s	
Lee Julie	If Its Good	Mercury - 8005		40s	
Lee Julia	King Size Papa	Capital - 40082	Her Boy Friends & her	40s	
Lee Julia*	Lotus Blossom	Premier - 29013	Douglas Tommy Orch	30s	
Lee Julia*	Show Me Missouri Blues	Premier - 29012	Douglas Tommy Orch	30s	
Lee Julia	Snatch And Grab It	Capital - 40028	Her Boy Friends &	40s	
Lee Julia	Tell Me Daddy	Capital - 15144	Her Boy Friends &	40s	
Lee Julia*	Won't You Come Over To . . .	Brunswick - 4761	Lee George Orch	30s	
Lee Julia	You Aint Got It No More	Capital - 40028	Her Boy Friends &	40s	
Lee Loretta*	Young And Healthy	Bluebird - B - 5022	Hall George Orch	30s	
Lee Peggy	Bella Notte	Decca - LP - DL - 5557	Young Victor Orch	50s	
Lee Peggy*	Blues In The Night	Okeh - 6553	Goodman Benny Sextet	40s	
Lee Peggy	Bubble - Loo Bubble - Loo	Capital - 15118	Barbour Dave & His Orch	40s	
Lee Peggy*	Elmer's Tune	Columbia - 36359	Goodman Benny Orch	40s	
Lee Peggy	Fever	Capital - 3998	Marshall Jack dir	50s	x
Lee Peggy*	For Every Man There's A . . .	Capital - 15030	Goodman Benny Orch	40s	
Lee Peggy*	Full Moon	Okeh - 6652	Goodman Benny Orch.	40s	
Lee Peggy	Golden Earrings	Capital - 15009	Barbour Dave & his Orch	40s	
Lee Peggy	He Needs Me - Sugar	Decca - LP - DL - 8166	Webb Jack	50s	
Lee Peggy	He's A Tramp	Decca - LP - DL - 5557	Pound Hounds the	50s	
Lee Peggy	He's Just My Kind	Capital - 322	Barbour Dave & His Orch	40s	
Lee Peggy	He's Just My Kind	Capital - 322	Barbour Dave & His Orch	40s	
Lee Peggy*	I Threw A Kiss To The Ocean	Columbia - 36590	Goodman Benny Orch.	40s	
Lee Peggy	I'll Dance At Your Wedding	Capital - 15009	Barbour Dave & his Orch	40s	
Lee Peggy	Is That All There Is	Capital - 2602	Newman Randy dir.	60s	x
Lee Peggy	It Takes A Long Long Train With A Red Caboose	Capital - 8445	Barbour Dave His Orch	40s	
Lee Peggy	Its A Good Day	Capital - 322	Barbour Dave & His Orch	40s	
Lee Peggy	Just An Old Love Of Mine	Capital - 8445	Barbour Dave & His Orch	40s	
Lee Peggy	Just One Of Those Things	Decca - 28313		50s	

Lee Peggy	La La La	Decca - LP - DL - 5557	Young Victor Orch	50s	
Lee Peggy	Love You Dident Do Right	Decca - 29250	Lilley Joseph Orch	50s	
Lee Peggy	Lover	Decca - 28215	Jenkins Gordon Orch	50s	
Lee Peggy	Manana Is Good Enough For Me	Capital - 15022	Barbour Dave & His Orch	40s	
Lee Peggy	Peace On Earth	Decca - LP - DL - 5557	Young Victor Orch	50s	
Lee Peggy	Save Your Sorrow For Tomorrow	Capital - 810	Rugola Pete Orchestra	40s	
Lee Peggy	Siamese Cat Song The	Decca - LP - DL - 5557	Wallace Oliver & D. S. O.	50s	
Lee Peggy*	Somebody Else Is Taking . . .	Okeh - 6497	Goodman Benny Orch	40s	
Lee Peggy	Sugar	Capital - 810		40s	
Lee Peggy*	That Did It Marie	Okeh - 6497	Goodman Benny Orch	40s	
Lee Peggy	Waiting For The Train To Come In	Capital - 218	Barbour Dave & His Orch	40s	
Lee Peggy*	We'll Meet Again	Okeh - 6644	Goodman Benny Orch	40s	
Lee Peggy	What Is A Baby	Decca - LP - DL - 5557	Young Victor Orch	50s	
Lee Peggy	What More Can A Woman Do	Capital - 197	Barbour Dave & His Orch	40s	
Lee Peggy*	Where Or When	Okeh - 6553	Goodman Benny Sextet	40s	
Lee Peggy	Why Don't You Do Right	Capital - 15118	Barbour Dave & His Orch	40s	
Lee Peggy	Why Don't You Do Right	Film Master - 1943	Goodman Benny Orch	40s	
Lee Peggy*	Why Don't You Do Right	Columbia - 36652	Goodman Benny Orch.	40s	
Lee Peggy	You Was Right Baby	Capital - 197	Barbour Dave & His Orch	40s	
Leonard Jack - NAP	I Can Dream, Cant I	Victor - 25741	Dorsey Tommy Orch	30s	
Leonard Jack*	In The Still Of The Night	Victor - 25663	Dorsey Tommy Orch	30s	
Leonard Jack*	Marie	Victor - 25523	Dorsey Tommy Orch	30s	
Lester Kitty	Love Letters	Era - 3068		60s	
Lewis Barbara	Snap Your Fingers	Atlantic-2214		60s	
Lewis Furry	Kassie Jones	Victor - 21664		20s	
Lewis Ted	In A Shanty In Old Shanty Town	Columbia - 2652 - D	Lewis Ted Orch.	30s	
Lewis Ted	Just A Gigolo	Columbia - 2378 - D	Lewis Ted Orch.	30s	
Lewis Ted	When My Baby Smiles At Me - AC	Columbia - A2908	Lewis Ted Orch.	20s	
Lewis Ted	Where'd You Get Those Eyes	Columbia - 667 - D	Lewis Ted Orch.	20s	
Liggins Jimmy	Cadallac Boogie	Speciality - 521	Drops Of Joy his	40s	
Light Crust Dough Boys	Pussy Pussy Pussy	Vocalion - 04560		30s	
Lindberg Col.	Colonel Lindberg Replies	Victor - 35836	SPOKEN WORD	20s	
Liston Virginia	Early In The Mornin - AC	Okeh - 8187		20s	
Little Jack Little	You Aught To Be In Pictures	Columbia - 2895 - D	Little Jack Little Orch	30s	
Little Richard - (Penniman)	Baby Face	Specialty - 645		50s	
Little Richard - (Penniman)	Keep A Knockin	Specialty - 611		50s	
Little Walter	My Babe	Checker - 811		50s	
Logan Ella & Al Bowlly	By The Old Oak Tree	Decca - F - 2206	Bowlly Al, guitar	30s	
Logan Ella	How Are Things In Glocca Mora	Columbia - MM - 686		40s	
Lombardo Carmen* - NAP	Sailboat In the Moonlight A	Victor - 25594	Lombardo Guy Orch	30s	
Lombardo Carmen* - NAP	Stars Fell On Alabama	Decca - 104	Lombardo Guy Orch	30s	
London Laurie	He's Got The Whole World In.	Capital - 3891		50s	
Lonzo & Oscar	Im My Own Grandpa	Victor - 20 - 2563	Winston County Pea Pickers	40s	
Lorin Burt*	Bashful Baby	Victor - 22074	Pollack Ben Orch	20s	
Lorin Burt*	Should I	Victor - 22255	Arden & Ohman Orch	20s	
Lucas Nick	A Cup Of Coffee A . . . - AC.	Brunswick - 3052		20s	
Lucas Nick	All Of Me	HOW - A - 4 - B	& Crooning Troubadors	30s	
Lucas Nick	Always - AC	Brunswick - 3088		20s	
Lucas Nick	Among My Soveniers	Brunswick - 3684		20s	
Lucas Nick	An Evening In Carolina	HOW - B - 3 - 4	Crooning Troubadors &	30s	
Lucas Nick	Brown Eyes Why Are . . . - AC	Brunswick - 2961		20s	
Lucas Nick	Bye Bye Blackbird - AC	Brunswick - 3184		20s	
Lucas Nick	Don't Tell Her What Happened.	Brunswick - 4896		30s	
Lucus Nick	Falling In Love Again	Brunswick - 6048		30s	
Lucas Nick	Hello Bluebird	Brunswick - 3370		20s	
Lucas Nick	Im Looking Over A Four Leaf . . .	Brunswick - 3439		20s	
Lucas Nick	Im Waiting For Ships That . . .	Brunswick - 3853		20s	
Lucus Nick	Im Yours	Brunswick - 4960		30s	
Lucas Nick	Lady Play Your Mandolin	Brunswick - 6013	Crooning Troubadors &	30s	
Lucas Nick	My Best Girl - AC	Brunswick - 2768		20s	
Lucus Nick	Painting The Clouds With . . .	Film Master - 1929		20s	
Lucas Nick	Painting The Clouds With . . .	Brunswick - 4418		20s	
Lucas Nick	Rosey Cheeks	Brunswick - 3518		20s	
Lucas Nick	Side By Side - AC	Brunswick - 3512		20s	
Lucus Nick	Singing In The Rain	Brunswick - 4378		20s	
Lucas Nick	Sleepy Time Gal - AC	Brunswick - 2990		20s	
Lucus Nick	Sunshine	Brunswick - 3850		20s	
Lucas Nick	That's My Desire	Brunswick - 6147		30s	
Lucas Nick	Tip Toe Through The Tulips	Brunswick - 4418		20s	
Lucas Nick	Tip Toe Through The Tulips	Film Master - 1929		20s	
Lucas Nick	Together	Brunswick - 3749		20s	
Lucas Nick	Walkin My Baby Back Home	Brunswick - 6048		30s	
Lucas Nick	Without You Sweetheart	Brunswick - 3773		20s	

Lucas Nick	Youre Driving Me Crazy	Brunswick - 4987	Crooning Troubadors &	30s	
Lulu Belle & Scotty	Time Will Tell	Vogue - R - 720		40s	
Lund Art	Mona Lisa	MGM - 10689		40s	
Luther F. as J. Billings, C. Robinson	When Your Hair Has Turned.	Victor - 22588		30s	
Luther Frank*	My Baby Just Cares For Me	HOW - 1 - 10	Rito Firo Ted Orchestra	30s	
Lynn Sharon	Turn On The Heat	Film Master - 1929		20s	
Lynn Vera	Under the Latern	Radio Master - 1942?		40s	
Lynn Vera	Nightingale Sang in . . .	Decca - F - 7507		40s	
Lynn Vera	Well Meet Again	Decca - F - 7268	Young Arthur on.	30s	
Lynn Vera	Well Meet Again	London - 1348	Shaw Roland Orch.	50s	
Lynn Vera	When The Light Go On Again	Decca - F - 8241		40s	
Lynn Vera	White Cliffs Of Dover The	Decca - F - 8110	Mantovani Orch.	40s	
Lyric Quartet*	Down Amoung The Sheltering.	Victor - 17778	Lyric Quartet	10s	
Mac Donough Harry - NAP	Girl In The Magazine Cover. - AC	Victor - 17945		10s	
Mac Donough Harry - NAP	Shine On Harvest Moon - AC	Victor - 16259		10s	
Mac Murray Fred*	After A Million Dreams	Victor - 22248	Olson George Orchestra	30s	
MacDonald Jeanette	San Francisco	Film Master - 1936		30s	
MacDonough Harry - NAP	When You Where Sweet Sixteen - AC	Victor - 769		00s	
Machin Arto*	El Manisero	Victor - 22483	Azpiazu D. & HisH. C. A.	20s	
Maddox Rose*	Death Of Rock And Roll	Columbia - 21559	Maddox Bros. & Rose	50s	
Maddox Rose*	George's Playhouse Boogie	Four Star - 1369	Maddox Bros. & Rose	40s	
Maddox Rose	Hey Little Dream Boat	Columbia - 21490	Maddox Bros. & Rose	50s	
Maddox Rose*	Honky Tonkin'	Four Star - 1238	Maddox Bros. & Rose	40s	
Maddox Rose*	I Gotta Go Get My Baby	Columbia - 21375	Maddox Bros. & Rose	50s	
Maddox Rose*	Love Is Strange	Columbia - 40895	Maddox Bros. & Rose	50s	
Maddox Rose*	Milk Cow Blues	Four Star - 1185	Maddox Bros. & Rose	40s	
Maddox Rose*	New Muleskinner Blues	Four Star - 1288	Maddox Bros. & Rose	40s	
Maddox Rose*	Philadelphia Lawyer	Four Star - 1289	Maddox Bros. & Rose	40s	
Maddox Rose*	Sally Let Your Bangs Hang . . .	Four Star - 1398	Maddox Bros. & Rose	40s	
Maddox Rose*	Tramp On The Street	Four Star - 1239	Maddox Bros. & Rose	40s	
Maddox Rose*	Water Baby Blues	Four Star - 1507	Maddox Bros. & Rose	40s	
Maddox Rose	Wild Wild Young Men	Columbia - 21394	Maddox Bros. & Rose	50s	
Mahoney Jer	When You Where . . . - AC - NAP	Edison - 7410		20s	
Mama Cass (Elliot)	Dream A little Dream Of Me	Dunhill - 4145	Mamas & The Papas	60s	
Mann Belle*	Buy Buy Buy For Baby	Victor - 21743	Pollock Ben Orch	20s	
Mann Peggy*	Because Of You	Bluebird - B - 11094	Clinton Larry Orch	40s	
Marjane Le`o	Facination	Disque Gramophone-2322		40s	
Marlin Sisters	My Happiness	Columbia - 38217		40s	
Marsh Lucy Isabelle	Glow Worm The - AC	Columbia - 3791		00s	
Martin Dean	Aint That A Kick In The Head	Capital - 4420		60s	
Martin Dean	Ain't That A Kick In The Head	Film Master - 1960		60s	
Martin Dean	Blue Christmas	Reprise - LP - 6222		60s	
Martin Dean	Corrine Corrine	Reprise - LP - 6130	Freeman Ernie	60s	
Martin Dean	Bumming Around	Reprise - 0393	Freeman Ernie	60s	
Martin Dean	Christmas Blues, The	Capital - 2640		50s	
Martin Dean	Detour	Reprise - LP - 6181		60s	
Martin Dean	Door Is Still Open...	Reprise - 0307	Freeman Ernie orch.	60s	
Martin Dean	Down Home	Reprise - LP - 6181		60s	
Martin Dean	Everybody Loves Somebody	Reprise - 0281		60s	
Martin Dean	Everybody Loves Somebody-1	Reprise LP - 6123		60s	
Martin Dean	Hammers And Nails	Reprise - LP - 6181		60s	
Martin Dean	Houston	Reprise - LP - 6181	Justis Bill	60s	
Martin Dean	I Don't Care If The Sun Don't . . .	Capital - 981	Weston Paul Orch	50s	
Martin Dean	I Will	Reprise - LP - 6181		60s	
Martin Dean	Id Cry Like A Baby	Capital - 2749		50s	
Martin Dean	If I Could Sing Like Bing	Capital - 2555		50s	
Martin Dean	I'll Always Love You	Capital - 1028	Weston Paul Orch	50s	
Martin Dean & Nuggetts	Im Gonna Steal Your Love . . .	Capital - 3468	Stabile Dick Orch	50s	
Martin Dean	Im Yours	Capital - EP - 401	Levene Gus Orch	50s	
Martin Dean	In The Chapel In The Moonlight	Reprise - 0601		60s	
Martin Dean	It Wont Cool Off	Capital - LP) - T - 1285	Levene Gus Orch	50s	
Martin Dean	Marshmellow World	Reprise - LP - 6222		60s	
Martin Dean & Easy Riders	Memories Are Made Of This	Capital - 3295		50s	
Martin Dean	Money Burns A Hole In My Pocket	Capital - 2818	Stabile Dick Orch	50s	
Martin Dean & Jerry Lewis	Money Song, The	Capital - 15249		50s	
Martin Dean	Old Yellow Line	Reprise - LP - 6181		60s	
Martin Dean	Out In The Cold Again	Capital - LP) - T - 1285	Levene Gus Orch	50s	
Martin Dean	Powder Your Face With Sunshine	Capital - 15351	Weston Paul Orch	40s	
Martin Dean	Return To Me	Capital - 3894	Levene Gus Orch	50s	
Martin Dean	Shutters And Boards	Reprise - LP - 6130	Freeman Ernie	60s	
Martin Dean	Siesta Fiesta	Reprise - LP - 613	Freeman Ernie	60s	
Martin Dean	Silver Bells	Reprise - LP - 6222		60s	

Martin Dean	Snap Your Fingers	Reprise - LP - 6181		60s	
Martin Dean	S'posin	Film Master - 1967	Lane Ken piano	60s	
Martin Dean	That Little Ole Wine Drinker Me	Reprise - 0698		60s	
Martin Dean	That's Amore	Capital - 2589	Stabile Dick Orch	50s	
Martin Dean	That's Amore	Film Master - 1953		50s	
Martin Dean	There's My Lover	Capital - 2378	Stabile Dick Orch	50s	
Martin Dean	Things	Reprise - LP6130	Freeman Ernie	60s	
Martin Dean	You Belong To Me	Capital - 2165		50s	
Martin Dean	Young And Foolish	Capital - 3036	Stabile Dick Orch	50s	
Martin Dean	Youre Nobody Till...	Reprise-0333	Freeman Ernie Orch	60s	
Martin Dean	Your Other Love	Reprise-LP-6130	Freeman Ernie	60s	
Martin Mary	My Heart Belongs To Daddy	Decca - 8282	Duchin Eddie Orch	30s	
Martin Sarah	Joe Turner Blues - AC	Okeh - 8058	"contralto Solo With Piano Acc.	20s	
Martin Sarah	Yes Sit That's My Baby - AC	Okeh - 8262		20s	
Martin Steve	Old King Tut	Warners - 8677		70s	
Martin Tony	Below The Equator	Decca - 3969		30s	
Martin Tony	Fools Rush In	Decca - 3119	Sinatra Ray Orch	30s	
Martin Tony	Its A Blue World	Decca - 2932		30s	
Martin Tony	La Vie En Rose	Victor - 20 - 3819		50s	
Martin Tony*	My Walking Stick	Brunswick - 8153	Noble Ray Orch	30s	
Martin Tony	South Of The Borber	Decca - 2788	Lyman Abe Orch	30s	
Martin Tony	There's No Tomorrow	Victor - 20 - 3582		40s	
Martin Tony	There's Something In The Air	Film Master - 1936		30s	
Martin Tony	To Each His Own	Mercury - 3022		40s	
Martin Tony	Tonight We Love	Decca - 3988		40s	
Martin Tony & B.Stanwyck	When The Lazy River..	Film Master - 1936		30s	
Martin Tony	When The Swallows Come . . .	Decca - 3246		30s	
Martin Tony	You Stepped Out As A..	Film Master - 1941		40s	
Marvin Johnny	Deed I Do	Edison - 51928		20s	
Marvin Johnny	Breezing Along With The Breeze	Columbia - 699 - D		20s	
Marvin Johnny	Little Birdie Told Me So A	Victor - 20493	Kahn Roger Wolf Orch	20s	
Marvin Johnny	Im Yours	Victor - 22555		20s	
Marx Groucho	Lydia, The Tattooed Lady	Film Master - 1939		30s	
Mathews Jessie	Daddy Won't Buy Me.	Film Master - 1934		30s	
Mathews Jessie	Dancing On The Ceiling	Film Master - 1934		30s	
Mathews Jessie	When You've Got A Little . . .	Film Master - 1934		30s	
Mathis Johnny	Misty	Columbia - 41483		50s	
Mc Cormack John	Killarney	Victor - 74157		20s	
Mc Cormack John	Star Spangled Banner, (The) - AC	Victor - 64664		20s	
Mc Daniel Hattie	Dentist Chair Blues	Paramount - 12751		20s	
Mc Daniel Hattie	I Thought Id Do It	Okeh - 8569	vocal with piano	20s	
Mc Daniel Hattie	Just One Sorrowing Heart	Okeh - 8569	vocal with piano	20s	
Mc Kenzie Red*	Fan It	Brunswick - 6160	Nichols, Red & Five P.	30s	
Mc Kinney Nina Mae	Everything Ive Got Belongs.,	Film Master - 1935	Blake Eubie Orch	30s	
Mc Kinney Nina Mae	Half Of Me	Film Master - 1935		30s	
Mc Kinney Nina Mae	Swanee Shuffle	Film Master - 1929		20s	
Mc Phatter Clyde	Hot Ziggity	Atlantic - 1070		50s	
Mc Tell Blind Willie	Statesboro Blues	Victor - V38001		20s	
Mecum Dudley*	Forty Second Street - NAP	Victor - 24253	Bestor Don Orch	10s	
Mendez Julio	Affrincomon	Decca - 40029	Dunham. K. & Ensemble	40s	
Mercer Johnny & Pied Piepers	Accent On The Positive	Capital - 180	Weston Paul Orch	40s	
Mercer Johnny & M. Whiting	Baby Its Cold Outside	Capital - 567	Weston Paul Orch	40s	
Mercer J., J. Stafford. P. Pipers	Blues In The Night	Capital - 1001	Weston Paul Orch	40s	
Mercer Johnny & Jo Stafford	Candy	Capital - 183	Weston. Paul Orch	40s	
Mercer Johnny & Jo Stafford	Conversation While Dancing	Capital - 195	Weston Paul Orch	40s	
Mercer Johnny	G. I Jive	Capital - 141	Weston Paul Orch	40s	
Mercer Johnny	I Lost My Sugar In Salt Lake.	Capital - 122	Slack Freddie Orch	40s	
Mercer Johnny	Lazybones	Varsity - 8031	Vocal with Piano Acc.	30s	
Mercer Johnny & Pied Piepers	On The Atchison, Topeka, & The Santa Fee	Capital - 195	Weston Paul Orch	40s	
Mercer Johnny	Personality	Capital - 230		40s	
Mercer Johnny	San Fernando Valley	Capital - 150		40s	
Mercer Johnny - (Nitecaps)*	Sizzling One Step Medley	Columbia - 18002 - D	Trumbauer Frank Orch	30s	
Mercer Johnny	There's A Cabin In The Pines	Varsity - 8031	Vocal with piano	30s	
Mercer Johnny	Zip A Dee - Doo Dah	Capital - 323		40s	
Mercer Mabel	After You	Atlantic - LP - 1213		50s	
Mercer Mabel	Autumn Leaves	Atlantic - ALS - 402		50s	
Mercer Mabel	By Myself	Atlantic - ALS - 403		50s	
Mercer Mabel	Did You Ever Cross Over To.	Atlantic - ALS - 403		50s	
Mercer Mabel	End Of A Love Affair The	Atlantic ALS - 408		50s	
Mercer Mabel	I Loves You Porgy	LMS - 362 to LMS - 360	Walter Cy piano	40s	
Mercer Mabel	It Was Worth It	Atlantic - ALS - 408		50s	
Mercer Mabel	It's De Lovely	Atlantic - LP - 1213		50s	

Mercer Mabel	Ivory Tower	Atlantic - ALS - 402		50s	
Mercer Mabel	Just One Of Those Things	Atlantic - ALS - 402		50s	
Mercer Mabel	Let Me Love You	Atlantic - ALS - 403		50s	
Mercer Mabel	Looking At You	Atlantic LP - 1213		50s	
Mercer Mabel	My Mans Gone Now	LMS - L - 361	Walter Cy piano	40s	
Mercer Mabel & Harry Roy	Since Black Minnie's Got The.	Film Master - 1936	Roy Harry Orchestra	30s	
Mercer Mabel	Some Fine Day	Atlantic - ALS - 403		50s	
Mercer Mabel	Summertime	LMS - 360 to LMS - 362	Walter Cy piano	40s	
Mercer Mabel	Thank You For The Flowers	Altantic - ALS - 408		50s	
Mercer Mabel	Where Oh Where	Atlantic LP - 1213		50s	
Mercer Mabel	While We Were Young	Atlantic - ALS - 408		50s	
Mercer Mabel	You Are Not My First Love	Atlantic - ALS - 402		50s	
Merman Ethel	After You've Gone	Film Master - 1931		30s	
Merman Ethel	An Earful Of Music	Brunswick - 6995		30s	
Merman Ethel	Be Like Me	Film Master - 1931		30s	
Merman Ethel	Eadie Was A Lady	Brunswick - 6456	Young Victor Orch	30s	
Merman Ethel	How Deep Is The Ocean	Victor - 24146	Skilkret Nat Orch	30s	
Merman Ethel	I Get a Kick Out Of You	Brunswick - 7342	Green Johnny Orch	30s	
Merman Ethel	I Got Rhythm	Decca - 24453		40s	
Merman Ethel	I Got Rhythm	Radio Master - 1931		30s	
Merman Ethel	Its De Lovely	LMS - 206		30s	
Merman Ethel	Make It Another Old Fashioned . . .	Decca - 32199		40s	
Merman Ethel	Marching Through Berlin	Film Master - 1943		40s	
Merman Ethel	Marching Through Berlin	Victor - 20 - 1521		40s	
Merman Ethel	Red Hot Amd Blue	LMS - 207		30s	
Merman Ethel	Youre The Top	Brunswick - 7342	Green Johnny Orch	30s	
Merrick Dick*	Candy	Majestic - 7129	Wald Jerry Orch	40s	
Merry Macs	Mairzy Doats	Decca - 18588		40s	
Merry Macs	Praise The Lord And Pass . . .	Decca - 18498		40s	
Meyers John W.	When You Where. - AC - NAP	Victor - 3135		00s	
Midler Bette	Boogie Woogie Bugle Boy	Atlantic - 2964		70s	
Midnighters	Work With Me Annie	Federal - 12169		50s	
Miles Josie	Please Don't Tickle Me . . . - AC	Black Swan - 14121	Snowden Q Roscoe piano	20s	
Miles Lizzie	Banjo Papa	Domino - 4152		20s	
Miles Lizzie	Bill Bailey Wont You Please . . .	Capital - 2243	Sharkey's Kings	50s	
Miles Lizzie	Black Bottom Blues The - AC	Okeh - 8050		20s	
Miles Lizzie	Black Man Be On Yo Way - AC	Brunswick - 2462	Williams Spencer - piano	20s	
Miles Lizzie	Cotton Belt Blues - AC	Victor - 19124		20s	
Miles Lizzie	Done Throw Away The Key	Victor - 23306		30s	
Miles Lizzie	Don't Tell Me Nothin Bout My Man	Victor - V38571	Morton Jelly Roll - piano	20s	
Miles Lizzie	Eh La Bas	Jansco - (LP) - 6250	Scobey Bob Band	50s	
Miles Lizzie	Electrician Blues	Victor - 23298	Brooks Harrypiano	30s	
Miles Lizzie	Family Trouble Blues - AC	Columbia - A3920	Williams Clarence; piano	20s	
Miles Lizzie	Four O'Clock Blues - AC	Emerson - 10586	Creole Jazz Hounds her	20s	
Miles Lizzie*	Georgia Gigolo	Harmony - 944 - H	Davis Jasper And His Orch	20s	
Miles Lizzie	Good Time Papa	Victor - V38607		30s	
Miles Lizzie	Haitian Blues - AC	Emerson - 10613	Creole Jazz Hounds her	20s	
Miles Lizzie	He May Be Your Man But. - AC	Okeh - 8037		20s	
Miles Lizzie*	He's My Man	Vocalion - 5260	Melrose Stompers	30s	
Miles Lizzie*	He's Red Hot To Me	Vocalion - 5325	Melrose Stompers	30s	
Miles Lizzie	I Hate A Man Like You	Victor - V38571	Morton Jelly Roll piano	20s	
Miles Lizzie*	It Feels So Good	Harmony - 944 - H	Davis Jasper And His Orch	20s	
Miles Lizzie	Muscle Shoals Blues - AC	Okeh - 8031		20s	
Miles Lizzie	My Man O' War	Victor - 23281		30s	
Miles Lizzie	Please Don't Tickle Me . . . - AC	Okeh - 8039		20s	
Miles Lizzie	Salty Dog	Capital - 2341	Sharkey's Kings	50s	
Miles Lizzie	Shake It Down	Banner - 7128		20s	
Miles Lizzie	Sweet Smellin Mama - AC	Columbia - A - 3897		20s	
Miles Lizzie	Triflin Blues - AC	Columbia - A3920	Clarence Johnson at the piano	20s	
Miles Lizzie*	Twenty Grand Blues	Vocalion - 5392	Melrose Stompers	30s	
Miles Lizzie	You're Always Messin . . . - AC	Victor - 19083	Williams Clarence piano	20s	
Miles Lizzie	You've Gotta Come And . . . - AC	Emerson - 10603	Creole Jazz Hounds her	20s	
Miller Bob*	Do You Care - NAP	Decca - 3860	Crosby Bob and his orch.	40s	
Miller Eddie	Release Me	Four Star - 1407	Oklahomans his	50s	
Miller Emmett	Anytime	Okeh - 41095		20s	
Miller Emmett	Big Bad Bill Is Sweet William.	Okeh - 41305	Georgia Crackers the	20s	
Miller Emmett	Blues Singer From Alabam . . .	Okeh - 41377	Georgia Crackers the	20s	
Miller Emmett	Dusky Stevedore	Okeh - 41135	Georgia Crackers the	20s	
Miller Emmett	Ghost Of The St. Louis Blues,	Okeh - 41342		20s	
Miller Emmett	God's River Blues	Okeh - 41438		20s	
Miller Emmett	I Aint Gonna Give Nobody . . .	Okeh - 41280	Georgia Crackers the	20s	
Miller Emmett	I Aint Got Nobody	Okeh - 41062		20s	
Miller Emmett & Dan Fitch	Lion Tamers The	Okeh - 41205		20s	

Miller Emmett & Dan Fitch	Lovesick Blues	Okeh - 41062	Georgia Crackers the	20s	
Miller Emmett	Lovesick Blues - AC	Okeh - 40465		20s	
Miller Emmett	Lovin Sam The Shiek Of . . .	Okeh - 41305	Georgia Crackers the	20s	
Miller Emmett	Right Or Wrong	Okeh - 41280 .	Georgia Crackers the	20s	
Miller Emmett	Shes Funny That Way	Okeh - 41182	Georgia Crackers, the	20s	
Miller Emmett	St. Louis Blues	Okeh - 41095	Georgia Crackers the	20s	
Miller Emmett	Sweet Mama Papa's Getting . . .	Okeh - 41342	Georgia Crackers the	20s	
Miller Emmett	Take Your Tomorrows	Okeh - 41135	Georgia Crackers the	20s	
Miller Emmett & Charles Chiles	You Loose	Okeh - 41205.		20s	
Miller Emmett	Youre The Cream Of My C . . .	Okeh - 41182	Georgia Crackers the	20s	
Miller Mitch & chorus - NAP	Yellow Rose Of Texas, The	Columbia - 40540		50s	
Mills Brothers	Asleep In The Deep	Decca - 2804		30s	
Mills Brothers	Baby Wont You Please Come Home	Brunswick - 6225		30s	
Mills Brothers	Bugle Call Rag	Brunswick - 6357		30s	
Mills Bothers	By The Watermellon Vine . . .	Decca - 3545	Carter Benny Orch.	40s	
Mills Brothers	Coney Island Washboard	Banner - 33211		30s	
Mills Brothers	Diga Diga Doo	Brunswick - 6519	Ellington Duke Orch	30s	
Mills Brothers	Doing The New Low Down	Brunswick - 6917	Redman Don Orch	30s	
Mills Brothers	Don't Be A Baby, Baby	Decca - 18753		40s	
Mills Brothers	Glow Worm The	Decca - 28384	McIntyre Hal Orch	50s	
Mills Brothers	Good Bye Blues	Brunswick - 6278		30s	
Mills Brothers	Goodby Blues	Film Master - 1932		30s	
Mills Brothers	How'm I Doing	Brunswick - 6969		30s	
Mills Brothers	How'm I Doing	Film Master - 1934		30s	
Mills Brothers	I Cant Give You Anything But Lole	Brunswick - 6519	Ellington Duke Orch	30s	
Mills Brothers	I Found A New Baby	Brunswick - 6785		30s	
Mills Brothers	I Guess Ill Get The Papers	Decca - 23638		40s	
Mills Brothers	I Heard	Brunswick - 6269		30s	
Mills Brothers	I Love You So Much It Hurts	Decca - 24550		40s	
Mills Brothers	Ill Be Around	Decca - 18318		30s	
Mills Brothers & Dick Powell	Is My Baby Out For No Good	Film Master - 1934.		30s	
Mills Brothers	It Don't Mean A Thing If It . . .	Brunswick - 6377		30s	
Mills Brothers	Jungle Fever	Brunswick - 6785		30s	
Mills Brothers	Lazy River	Decca - 4187		40s	
Mills Brothers	Limehouse Blues	Decca - 167		30s	
Mills Brothers	Long About Midnight	Decca - 1360		30s	
Mills Brothers	Nobodys Sweetheart	Brunswick - 6197		30s	
Mills Brothers	Old Man Of The Mountain, The	Brunswick - 6357		30s	
Mills Brothers	Paper Doll	Decca - 18318		30s	
Mills Brothers	Rockin Chair	Brunswick - 6278		30s	
Mills Bothers	Six Twenty Seven - 627 Stomp	Decca - 4187		40s	
Mills Brothers	Sixty Seconds Got Together	Decca - 1964		40s	
Mills Brothers	Smoke Rings	Brunswick - 6525		30s	
Mills Brothers	Sweet Sue Just You	Brunswick - 6330		30s	
Mills Brothers	Swing For Sale	Decca - 1147		30s	
Mills Brothers	Swing It Sister	Brunswick - 6894		30s	
Mills Brothers	Tiger Rag	Brunswick - 6197		00s	
Mills Brothers	Tiger Rag	Film Master - 1932		30s	
Mills Brothers	Till Then	Decca - 18599		40s	
Mills Brothers	You Always Hurt The One You Love	Decca - 18599		30s	
Mills Brothers	You Rascal You	Brunswick - 6197	Mills Brothers	30s	
Mills Brothers	You Rascal You	Brunswick - 6225		30s	
Mimiced voices	Who Killed Cock Robin	Film Master 1935		30s	
Minnie Memphis	Bumble Bee	Vocalion - 1476		30s	
Minnie Memphis*	Bumble Bee Blues	Victor - V - 38599	Memphis Jug Band	30s	
Minnie Memphis	Cought Me Wrong Again	Vocalion - 3258		30s	
Minnie Memphis	Crazy Cryin Blues	Vocalion - 1678		30s	
Minnie Memphis	Dirty Mother For You	Decca - 7048		30s	
Minnie Memphis	Frankie Jean	Vocalion - 1588		30s	
Minnie Memphis	Good Morning	Vocalion - 3436		30s	
Minnie Memphis	Hoodo Lady	Vocalion - 3222		30s	
Minnie Memphis & Kansas Joe	I Called You This Morning	Vocalion - 1631		30s	
Minnie Memphis	Ice Man Come On Up	Vocalion - 3222		30s	
Minnie Memphis	If You See My Rooster	Vocalion - 3285		30s	
Minnie Memphis	Its Hard To Be Mistreated	Vocalion - 03474	Vocal Blues	30s	
Minnie "Gospel" Memphis	Let Me Ride	Decca - 7063		30s	
Minnie Memphis	Man You Wont Give Me No . . .	Vocalion - 4295		30s	
Minnie Memphis	Me And My Chauffeur Blues	Okeh - 06288	Blues singer with guitar	40s	
Minnie Memphis	New Dirty Dozen	Vocalion - 1618		30s	
Minnie Memphis & Kansas Joe	North Memphis Blues	Vocalion - 1550		30s	
Minnie Memphis	Soo Cow Soo	Vocalion - 1658		30s	
Minnie Memphis	Tricks Aint Walkin No More	Vocalion - 1653		30s	

Minnie Memphis & Kansas Joe	You Got To Move	Decca - 7038		30s	
Miranda Carmen	Mana Euquero - I Want My . . .	Decca - 23132		40s	
Mississippi Sheiks	Bootlegger's Blues	Okeh - 8843		30s	
Mississippi Sheiks	Sitting On Top Of The World	Okeh - 8784		30s	
Mitchell Guy	My Heart Cries For You	Columbia - 39067		50s	
Mitchell Sue*	Get It Southern Style	Variety - 596	Bigard B. & Jazzopators	30s	
Mitchell Sue*	If Youre Ever In My Arms Again	Variety - 596	Bigard B. & Jazzopators	30s	
Modernaires the	Perfidia	Bluebird - B - 11095	Miller Glenn Orch	30s	
Monroe Bill	Blue Moon Of Kentucky	Columbia - 20370		40s	
Monroe Bill	Dog House Blues	Bluebird - B - 8693		40s	
Monroe Bill	Footprints In The Snow	Columbia - 27151	Blue Grass Boys his/	40s	
Monroe Bill	It's Might Hard To Travel	Columbia - 20526	Blue Grass Boys his/	40s	
Monroe Bill	Kentucky Waltz	Columbia - 36907	Blue Grass Boys his/	40s	
Monroe Bill	Little Cabin Home On A Hill	Columbia - 20459		40s	
Monroe Bill	Muleskinner Blues	Bluebird - B - 8568		40s	
Monroe Bill	Orange Blossom Special	Bluebird - B - 8893		40s	
Monroe Bill	Rock Road Blues	Columbia - 36907		40s	
Monroe Bill	Six White Horses	Bluebird - B - 8568		40s	
Monroe Bill	True Life Blues	Columbia - 37151		40s	
Monroe Bill	Uncle Penn	Decca - 46283		50s	
Monroe Marilyn - dubbed/	Diamonds Are a Girl's Best.	Film Master - 1953		50s	
Monroe Marilyn - dubbed/	Heat Wave	Film Master - 1954		50s	
Monroe Vaughn	Seems Like Old Times	Victor - 20 - 1811	Monroe Vaughn & Orch.	40s	
Monroe Vaughn	When The Lights Go On . . .	Victor - 27945	Monroe Vaughn & Orch.	40s	
Montana Patsy	I Want To Be A Cowboys . . .	Vocalion - 03010		30s	
Montez Chris	The More I See You	A & M - 796		60s	
Montgomery E.	Louisiana Blues	Vocalion - 2706		30s	
Moore Ann*	Jivin Joe Jackson	Columbia - 36889	Basie Count Orch	40s	
Moore Monette	Memphis Blues The - AC	Ajax - 17124		20s	
Moore Williaml	Old Country Rock	Paramount - 12761		20s	
Morgan Betty	After I Say Im Sorry	Perfect - 12245		20s	
Morgan Helen	Bill - 1st	Victor - 23238	Baravalli Victor dir. Orch.	20s	
Morgan Helen	Bill - 2nd	Victor - 21238		20s	x
Morgan Helen	Bill - 3rd	Brunswick - 20115	Young Victor Orch	30s	
Morgan Helen	Body And Soul	Victor - 22532	Joy Leonard Orch	30s	
Morgan Helen, Robeson, Mc Daniel	Cant Help Lovin Dat Man	Film Master - 1936		30s	
Morgan Helen	Cant Help Lovin Dat Man - 1st	Victor - 23238	Baravalli Victor dir. Orch.	20s	
Morgan Helen	Cant Help Lovin Dat Man - 2nd	Victor - 21238		20s	x
Morgan Helen	Cant Help Lovin Dat Man - 3rd	Brunswick - 20115	Young Victor Orch	30s	
Morgan Helen	Do Do Do	Brunswick - 129		20s	
Morgan Helen	Don't Ever Leave Me	Victor - 22199	Joy Leonard Orch	30s	
Morgan Helen	Give Me A Heart To Sing To	Victor - 24650	Skilkret Nat Orch	30s	
Morgan Helen	Give Your Baby Lots Of Lovin	Film Master - 1929		20s	
Morgan Helen	I Can't Go On Like This	Film Master - 1930	Durante J. & L. Clayton Orch.	30s	
Morgan Helen	I See Two Lovers	Brunswick - 7391	Bakaleinikoff Constantin	30s	
Morgan Helen	I Was Taken By Storm	Brunswick - 7424	Bakaleinikoff Constantin	30s	
Morgan Helen	Just Like A Butterfly	Brunswick - 110		20s	
Morgan Helen	Lazy Weather	Brunswick - 113		20s	
Morgan Helen	Little Things You Used . . .	Brunswick - 7424	Bakaleinikoff Constantin	30s	
Morgan Helen	Maybe	Brunswick - 129	Hutchinson Leslie A - piano	20s	
Morgan Helen	Me And My Shadow	Brunswick - 104	Hutchinson Leslie A - piano	20s	
Morgan Helen	Mean To Me	Victor - 21930		20s	
Morgan Helen	More Than You Know	Victor - 22149	Joy Leonard Orch	20s	
Morgan Helen	Nothing But	Brunswick - 122		20s	
Morgan Helen	Sand In My Shoe	Brunswick - 6984		30s	
Morgan Helen	Something To Remember . . .	Victor - 22532	Joy Leonard Orch	30s	
Morgan Helen	Song Of A Dreamer	Brunswick - 7328		30s	
Morgan Helen	Song Of A Dreamer	Film Master - 1934		30s	
Morgan Helen	Tree In The Park A	Brunswick - 111		20s	
Morgan Helen	What Wouldent I Do For . . .	Film Master - 1929	(with backing)	20s	
Morgan Helen	What Wouldent I Do For . . .	Victor - 22149		20s	
Morgan Helen	What Wouldn't I Do For . . .	Film Master - 1929	(without backing)	20s	
Morgan Helen	When He Comes Home To . . .	Brunswick - 6984		30s	
Morgan Helen	When I Discover My Man	Brunswick - 104	Hutchinson Leslie A - piano	20s	
Morgan Helen	Who Cares What You Have . . .	Victor - 21930	Joy Leonard Orch	20s	
Morgan Helen	Why Was I Born	Victor - 22199	Joy Leonard Orch	30s	
Morgan Helen	Winter Over Night	Brunswick - 7391	Grier Jimmie Orch	30s	
Morgan Jane	Facination	Kapp-151		50s	
Morgan Jayne P.	Life Is Just a Bowl Of Cherries	Derby - 837		40s	
Morgan Russ	You're Nobody Till...	Decca-18744	Morgan Russ Orch.	40s	
Morrison Joe	Last Round Up, The	Columbia - 2791 - D		30s	
Morrison Joe	Last Round Up, The	Film Master - 1935		30s	

Morrow Liza*	Kiss Goodnight A	Capital - 203	Slack Freddie Orch	40s	
Morse Ella Mae	Blacksmith Blues, The	Capital - 1922	Riddle Nelson Orch	50s	
Morse Ella Mae	Buzz Me	Capital - 226	May Billy Orch	40s	
Morse Ella Mae	Captain Kidd	Capital - 193	May Billy Orch	40s	
Morse Ella Mae	Cow Cow Boogie	Film Master - 1943	Slack Freddy Orch	40s	
Morse Ella Mae*	Cow Cow Boogie	Capital - 102	Slack Freddy Orch	40s	
Morse Ella Mae	Early In The Morning	Capital - 487	Her Boogie Woogie S. &	40s	
Morse Ella Mae & T. Ernie Ford	False Hearted Girl	Capital - 2215	Stone Cliffie Orch	50s	
Morse Ella Mae	Five Ten Fifteen - 5 - 10 - 15 Hours	Capital - LP - H - 513	Dave Big Orch	50s	
Morse Ella Mae*	Get On Board Little Chillun	Capital - 133	Slack Freddie Orch	40s	
Morse Ella Mae	Goodnight Sweetheart Goodnight	Capital - LP - H - 513	Dave Big Orch	50s	
Morse Ella Mae	Greyhound	Capital - 2276		50s	
Morse Ella Mae	Have Mercy Baby	Capital - LP - H - 513	Dave Big Orch	50s	
Morse Ella Mae*	Hey Mr. Postman	Capital 151	Slack Freddie Orch	40s	
Morse Ella Mae & Don Raye*	House Of Blue Lights The	Capital - 251	Slack Freddie Orch	40s	
Morse Ella Mae & T. Ernie Ford	Im Hog Tied Over You	Capital - 2215	Stone Cliffie Orch	50s	
Morse Ella Mae	Invitation To The Blues	Capital - 163		40s	
Morse Ella Mae	Little Further Down The Road	Capital - 15097	Her Boogie Woogie S. &	40s	
Morse Ella Mae	Love You Like Mad	Capital - 2072	Riddle Nelson Orch	50s	
Morse Ella Mae	Milkman Keep Those Bottles.	Capital - 151	Walters Dick Orch	40s	
Morse Ella Mae	Money Honey	Capital - LP - H - 513	Dave Big Orch	50s	
Morse Ella Mae*	Mr. Five By Five	Capital - 115	Slack Freddie Orch	40s	
Morse Ella Mae	No Love No Nothin	Capital - 143	Walters Dick Orch	40s	
Morse Ella Mae	Oakie Boogie	Capital - 2072	Riddle Nelson Orch	50s	
Morse Ella Mae*	Old Rob Roy	Capital - 133	Slack Freddie Orch	40s	
Morse Ella Mae	Patty Cake Man The	Capital - 163		40s	
Morse Ella Mae	Pig Foot Pete	Capital - 278	Slack Freddie Orch	40s	
Morse Ella Mae	Shoo Shoo Baby	Capital - 143	Walters Dick Orch	40s	
Morse Ella Mae*	Tess's Torch Song	Capital - 151		40s	
Morse Ella Mae*	Thrill Is Gone The	Capital - 115	Slack Freddie Orch	40s	
Morse Ella Mae	Your Conscience Tells You So	Capital - 278		40s	
Morse Lee	Dallas Blues - AC	Pathe - 25162		20s	
Morse Lee	He's A Good Man To Have . . .	Columbia - 1866 - D	Blue Grass Boys & her	20s	
Morse Lee	I Love My Baby	Perfect - 11602	Blue Grass Boys & her	20s	
Morse Lee	I Wonder Where My Baby Is Tonight	Perfect - 11599	Blue Grass Boys & her	20s	
Morse Lee	I'll Adore You	Film Master - 1930		30s	
Morse Lee	I'm Am Unemployed Sweetheart	Columbia - 2497 - D		30s	
Morse Lee	Just Another Dream Gone Wrong	Film Master - 1930		30s	
Morse Lee	Let's Do It	Columbia - 1659 - D	Blue Grass Boys & her	20s	
Morse Lee	Little White Lies	Columbia - 2248 - D	Blue Grass Boys & her	30s	
Morse Lee	Love Me	Columbia - 1972 - D	Blue Grass Boys & her	20s	
Morse Lee	Mail Man Blues - AC	Pathe - 32086		20s	
Morse Lee	Mississippi Mud	Columbia01584 - D	Blue Grass Boys & her	20s	
Morse Lee	Mollie Make Up Your Mind	Columbia - 939 - D	Southern Seraneders, & her	20s	
Morse Lee	Nobody Knows Im Blue	Columbia - 2248 - D	Blue Grass Boys & her	30s	
Morse Lee	Side By Side - AC	Columbia - 974 - D		20s	
Morse Lee	Something In The Night	Columkbia - 2705 - D		30s	
Morse Lee	Swinging In A Hammock	Columbia - 2225 - D	Blue Grass Boys & her	20s	
Morse Lee	Walkin My Baby Back Home	Columbia - 2417 - D		20s	
Morse Lee	Yes Sir That's My Baby	Perfect - 11580		20s	
Morse Lee	Bolshevik	Perfect - 4722		20s	
Morse Lee	I'm An Unemployed Sweetheart . . .	Columbia - 2497 - D		30s	
Moten Etta	Carioca The	Film Master - 1933		30s	
Moten Etta & Joan Blondel	My Forgotten Man	Film Master - 1933		30s	
Mullican Moon	New Pretty Blond	King - 578	Showboys - Moon Mullican	40s	
Mullican Moon*	Truck Driving Blues	Decca - 5725	Bruner Cliff Texans	30s	
Murray Billy	Bedelia - AC	Edison - 8550		00s	
Murray Billy & Haydn Quartet	By The Light Of The Silv . . . - AC	Victor - 16460		10s	
Murray Billy & Haydn Quartet	Budweisers A Friend Of . . . - AC	Victor - 16049		10s	
Murray Billy - NAP	For Me And My Gal - AC	Edison - 50407		00s	
Murray Billy	I Love A Piano - AC	Victor - 17945		10s	
Murray Billy	I Wonder Who's Kissing Her Now - AC	Victor - 16426		10s	
Murray Billy	In My Merry Oldsmobile - AC	Victor - 4467		10s	
Murray Billy - NAP	Meet Me In St. Louis, Louis - AC	Edison - 8722		00s	
Murray Billy & Haydn Quartet	Take Me Out To The Ball. - AC	Victor - 5570		00s	
Myers J. W.	Meet Me In St. Louis, Louis - AC	Columbia - 1848		00s	
Myers J. W.	My Wild Irish Rose - AC	Columbia - A3615		00s	
Nance Ray*	Slip Of The Lip A	Victor - 20 - 1528	Ellington Duke Orch	40s	
Nash Joey* - NAP	Stars Fell On Alabama	Victor - 24745	Himber Richard Orch	30s	
Negri Pola	Paradise	Film Master-1931		30s	
Negri Pola	Paradise	Ultraphone-AP-989		30s	
Nelson Harriet (Hilliard)	But Where Are You	Brunswick - 7607	Nelson Ozzie Orch	30s	

Nelson Harriet (Hilliard)	Get Thee Behind Me Satan	Brunswick - 7607	Nelson Ozzie Orch	30s	
Nelson Harriet (Hilliard)	Once In A While	Bluebird - B - 7256	Nelson Ozzie Orch	30s	
Nelson Harriet (Hilliard)	Says My Heart	Bluebird - B - 7528	Nelson Ozzie Orch	30s	
Nelson Harriet (Hillard)	Says My Heart	Film Master - 1937		30s	
Nelson Ozzie	About A Quarter To Nine	Brunswick - 7425	Nelson Ozzie Orch	30s	
Nelson Ozzie	Change Partners	Bluebird - B - 7734	Nelson Ozzie Orch	30s	
Nelson Ozzie	Double Trouble	Brunswick - 7485	Nelson Ozzie Orch	30s	
Nelson Ozzie	Dream A Little Dream Of Me	Brunswick - 6060	Nleson Ozzie Orch	30s	
Nelson Ozzie	I Don't Mind Walking In The Rain	Brunswick - 4897	Nelson Ozzie Orch	30s	
Nelson Ozzie	I Still Get A Thrill	Brunswick - 4897	Nelson Ozzie Orch	30s	
Nelson Ozzie	I Want The Water With The . . .	Bluebird - B - 10365	Nelson Ozzie Orch.	30s	
Nelson Ozzie	I Wished On The Moon	Brunswick - 7485	Nelson Ozzie Orch	30s	
Nelson Ozzie	Im Looking For A Guy Who . . .	Bluebird - B - 10666	Nelson Ozzie Orch	30s	
Nelson Ozzie	Jersey Jive	Bluebird - B - 11180	Nelson Ozzie Orch.	40s	
Nelson Ozzie	On The Beach With You	Brunswick - 6131	Nelson Ozzie Orch	30s	
Nelson Ozzie	Say It Isent So	Brunswick - 6372	Nelson Ozzie Orch	30s	
Nelson Ozzie	She's A Latin From Manhattan	Brunswick - 7425	Nelson Ozzie Orch	30s	
Nelson Ozzie	Tomorrow Night	Bluebird - B - 10420	Nelson Ozzie Orch	30s	
Nelson Ozzie	White Sails Beneath A Yellow Moon	Bluebird - B - 10311	Nelson Ozzie Orch	30s	
Nelson Willie	Blue Eyes Crying In The Rain	Columbia - 33482		70s	
New Vaudville Band	Winchester Cathedral	Fontana - F - 1562	New Vaudville Band	60s	
Nicholas Brothers	Lucky Number	Film Master - 1935		30s	
Niesen Gertrude	I Wanna Get married-NAP	Decca - 23382	Sosnik Harry Orch	40s	
Niesen Gertrude	Legalize My Name	Decca - 23499	Ludlow Ben Orchestra	40s	
Niesen Gertrude	Rockin The Town	Film Master-1937	Green Johnny Orch.	30s	
Niesen Gertrude	Supper Time	Victor - 24435	Jones Isham Orch	30s	
Niesen Gertrude	Where Are You	Brunswick - 7837	Feuer Cy. Orchestra	30s	
Noble George	Bed Springs Blues	Vocalion - 2923		30s	
Nolan Bob*	Cool Water	Decca-5939	Sons Of The Pioneers	40s	
Novis Donald	Trees	Film Master - 1932		30s	
Oakland Will	When You And I Were Young - AC	Edison - 9980		00s	
O'Connell Helen & Bob Eberly*	Green Eyes	Decca - 3698	Dorsey Jimmy & his orch.	40s	
O'Connell Helen & Bob Eberly	Green Eyes	Film Master - 1947		40s	
O'Connell Helen*	Boog - It	Decca - 3152	Dorsey Jimmy & his orch.	30s	
O'Connell Helen*	Embraceable You	Decca - 3928	Dorsey Jimmy Orch	40s	
O'Connell Helen*	Especially For You	Decca - 2554	Dorsey Jimmy & his orch.	30s	
O'Connor George - NAP	Nigger Blues - AC	Columbia - A2064		10s	
O'Day Anita*	And Her Tears Flowed Like Wine	Capital - 166	Kenton Stan Orch.	40s	
O'Day Anita*	Are You Living Old Man	Capital - 187	Kenton Stan Orch.	40s	
O'Day Anita*	Boogie Blues	Columbia - 36986	Krupa Gene Orch	40s	
O'Day Anita*	Chickery Chick	Columbia - 36877	Krupa Gene Orch	40s	
O'Day Anita*	Green Eyes	Okeh - 6222	Krupa Gene Orch	40s	
O'Day Anita*	Harlem On Parade	Okeh - 6607	Krupa Gene Orch	40s	
O'Day Anita	Hi Ho Trailus Boot Whip	Signiture - 15162	Bradley Will Orch	40s	
O'Day Anita*	I Take To You	Okeh - 6187	Krupa Gene Orch	40s	
O'Day Anita*	Just A Little Bit South Of North Carloina	Okeh - 6130	Krupa Gene Orch	40s	
O'Day Anita*	Kick It	Okeh - 6278	Krupa Gene Orch	40s	
O'Day Anita*	Let Me Off Uptown	Okeh - 6210	Krupa Gene Orch	40s	
O'Day Anita*	Massachusetts	Okeh - 6695	Krupa Gene Orch	40s	
O'Day Anita*	Skylark	Okeh - 6607	Krupa Gene Orch	40s	
O'Day Anita	Sometimes Im Happy	Signiture - 15127	Alvie & his Little Band	40s	
O'Day Anita*	Stop The Red Light	Okeh - 6411	Krupa Gene Orch	40s	
O'Day Anita	What Is This Thing Called Love	Signature - 15162	Bradley Will Orch	40s	
O'Day Molly	Tramp On The Street	Columbia - 37559	Cumberland Mountain Folks	40s	
Oliver Sy*	There's Good Blues Tonight	Victor - 20 - 1842	Dorsey Tommy Orch	40s	
Osborne Will	Between 18th And 19th On.	Victor - 8113	Osborne Will & his orch.	40s	
Osborne Will	Cocktails For Two	Melotone - M - 12996	Osborne Will & his orch.	30s	
Osborne Will	Ev ry Day	Conqueror - 8477	Osborne Will & his orch.	30s	
Osborne Will	For All We Know	Perfect - 15960	Osborne Will & his orch.	30s	
Osborne Will	Ghost Of A Chance A	Perfect - 15741	Osborne Will And His Orchestra/ - A his orch.	30s	
Osborne Will	It's De Lovely	Decca - 1058	Osborne Will & his orch.	30s	
Osborne Will	Lover	Perfect - 15741	Osborne Will & his orch.	30s	
Osborne Will	On A Blue And Moonless . . .	Columbia - 2128 - D	Osborne Will & his orch.	20s	
Osborne Will	So Beats My Heart For You	Columbia - 2269 - D	Osborne Will & his orch.	20s	
Osborne Will	Three's A Crowd	Perfect - 15663	Osborne Will & his orch.	30s	
Pace Jubilee Singers	His Eye Is On The Sparrow	Brunswick - 7008		20s	
Page Orin "Hot Lips"*	Blues In The Night	Victor - 27609	Shaw Artie Orch	40s	
Page Patti	Allegheny Moon	Mercury - 70878	Schoen Vic Orch.	50s	
Page Patti	All My Love	Mercury - 5455		50s	
Page Patti	Boogie Woogie Santa Clause	Mercury - 5534		50s	
Page Patti	Boys Night Out The	Mercury - 72013	Kennedy Jerry dir Orch.	60s	

Page Patti	Christmas Bells	Mercury - 5729		50s	
Page Patti	Conquest	Mercury - 70025		50s	
Page Patti	Dark Moon	Mercury - 71870	Parman Cliff Arr.	50s	
Page Patti	Detour	Mercury - 5682	Rael Jack Orch	50s	
Page Patti	Hush Hush Hush Sweet Charlote	Columbua - 43251	Mersey Robert Orch.	60s	
Page Patti	I Don't Care If The Sun Don't . . .	Mercury - 5396	Rael Jack Orch	50s	
Page Patti	Long Long Ago	Mercury - 5534	Rael Jack Orch	50s	
Page Patti - NAP	Mockin Bird Hill	Mercury - 5595	Carroll Jimmy Orch.	50s	
Page Patti	Oklahoma Blues	Mercury - 5344	Rael Septet	40s	
Page Patti	Old Cap Cod	Mercury - 71101	Schoen Vic Orch.	50s	
Page Patti	Poor Man's Roses A	Mercury - 71059	Schoen Vic Orch.	50s	
Page Patti	Release Me	Mercury - LP - MG - 20615	Kennedy Jerry dir Orch.	60s	
Page Patti & Rusty Draper	Release Me Let Me Bee . . .	Mercury - 5895	Rael Jack Orch	50s	
Page Patti	So In Love	Mercury - 5230		40s	
Page Patti	Tennessee Waltz, The	Mercury - 5534	Rael Jack Orch	50s	
Page Patti	That Doggie In The Window	Mercury - 70070	Rael Jack Orch	50s	
Page Patti (x4)	With My Eyes Wide Open . . .	Mercury - 5344	Pattie Page Quartet	40s	
Page Patti	You Belong To Me	Mercury - 5899	Rael Jack Orch	50s	
Parker Johnny*	Kiss To Build A Dream On A	Victor - 20 - 4455	Winterhalter Hugo Orch	50s	
Parker Junior	Mystery Train	Sun - 192		50s	
Parton Dolly	Muleskinner Blues	Victor - 47 - 9863		70s	
Pastor Tony*_NAP	I Poured My Heart Into A . . .	Bluebird - B - 10307	Shaw Artie & Orchestra	30s	
Patton Charlie	Banty Rooster Blues	Paramount - 12792		20s	
Patton Charlie	Devil Sent The Rain	Paramount - 13040		20s	
Patton Charlie	Elder Green Blues	Paramount - 12972		20s	
Patton Charlie	Frankie And Albert	Paramount - 13110		20s	
Patton Charlie	High Water Everywhere	Paramount - 12909		20s	
Patton Charlie	I Shall Not Be Moved	Paramount - 12986		20s	
Patton Charlie	Im Going Home	Paramount - 12883		20s	
Patton Charlie	Jersey Bull Blues	Vocalion - 02782		30s	
Patton Charlie	Mississippi Bo Weivel Blues	Paramount - 12805		20s	
Patton Charlie	Pony Blues	Paramount - 12792		20s	
Patton Charlie	Running Wild	Paramount - 12924		20s	
Patton Charlie	Shake It And Break It But . . .	Paramount - 12869		20s	
Paul Les & Mary Ford	How High The Moon	Capital - 1451	Paul Les. Mary Ford/	50s	
Payne Leon	I Love You Because	Capital - 40238		40s	
Peary Commander Robert E	Discovery Of The North Pole	Victor - 70012	SPOKEN WORD	10s	
Peerless Quartet	Along Thw Way To Wakiki - AC	Victor - 18326		10s	
Peerless Quartet	By The Light Of The Silv . . . - AC	Columbia - A799		10s	
Peerless Quartet	I Didnt Raise My Boy To . . . - AC	Columbia - A1697		10s	
Perkins Carl	Matchbox	Sun - 243		50s	
Perkins Carl	Everybodys Trying To Be My Baby	Sun - (LP) - 1225		50s	x
Pershing General John J.	From The Battlefields Of.	Nation's Forum - 69333	SPOKEN WORD	10s	
Phillips "Little" Esther	Release Me	Lennox - 5555		60s	
Phillips "Little" Esther	I Really Don't Want To Know	Lenox - 5560		60s	
Piaf Edith	April In Paris - Les Amants de Paris	Columbia - BF - 189	Chauvigny Robert Orch	50s	
Piaf Edith	La Vie En Rose	Columbia - DF - 3152		40s	
Pickens Sisters	Was That The Human Thing.	Victor - 22929		30s	
Pine Ridge Boys	You Are My Sunshine	Bluebird - B - 8263	sing with giutar	30s	
Platters, the	If I Dident Care	Mercury - 71749		60s	
Platters	My Prayer	Mercury - 70893		50s	
Platters	Smoke Gets In Your Eyes	Mercury - 71383		50s	
Platters, the	Smoke Gets In Your Eyes	Mercury - 71383		50s	
Pollack Ben & band	Peckin	Variety - 556	Pollack Ben Orch	30s	
Pollack Ben*	Ive Got Five Dollars	Perfect - 15431		30s	
Ponce Sisters	Black Bottom	Lincoln - 2588		20s	
Ponce Sisters	To-Night You Belong To Me	Columbia - 791 - D		20s	
Poole Charlie	Goodbye Liza Jane	Columbia - 15601 - D	Ramblers his N. Carolina	30s	
Powell Dick & Ruby Keeler	By A Waterfall	Film Master - 1933		30s	
Powell Dick	Ive Got To Sing A Torch Song	Film Master - 1933		30s	
Powell Dick	Shadow Waltz	Film Master - 1933		30s	
Presley Elvis	Anything That's Part Of You	Victor - 47 - 7992		60s	
Presley Elvis	Blue Moon	Victor - LP - LPM - 1254		50s	
Presley Elvis	Blue Moon Of Kentucky	Sun - 209	Scotty & Bill	50s	
Presley Elvis	Baby Lets Play House	Sun - 217	Scotty & Bill	50s	
Presley Elvis	Blue Hawaii	Victor - LP - LSP - 2426		60s	
Presley Elvis	Fever	Victor - LP - LPM - 2231		60s	
Presley Elvis	I Don't Care If The Sun Don't Shine	Sun - 210	Scotty & Bill	50s	
Presley Elvis	Its Now Or Never	Victor - 47 - 7777		60s	
Presley Elvis	Ive Got A Woman	Victor - EPA - 747		50s	
Presley Elvis	Love Letters	Victor - 47 - 8870		60s	
Presley Elvis	Milkcow Blues	Sun - 215	Scotty & Bill	50s	
Presley Elvis	Mystery Train	Sun - 223	Scotty & Bill	50s	

Presley Elvis	Shake Rattle And Roll	Victor - 20 - 6642		50s	
Presley Elvis	That's All Right Mama	Sun - 209	Scotty & Bill	50s	
Presley Elvis	That's When Youre Heart . . .	Victor - 20 - 6870		50s	
Presley Elvis	White Christmas	RCA - LP - LOC - 1035		50s	
Presley Elvis	You Don't Know Me	Victor - 47 - 9341		60s	
Preston Johnny	Running Bear	Mercury - 71474		60s	
Prima Louis	Dance With A Dolly	Variety - 8245		30s	
Prima Louis	Im Living In A Great Big Way	Brunswick - 7413		30s	
Prima Louis	In A Little Gypsy Tea Room	Brunswick - 7479		30s	
Prima Louis	It's The Rhythm In Me	Brunswick - 7471		30s	
Prima Louis	Lady In Red, The	Brunswick - 7448		30s	
Prima Louis	Lets Get Together And Swing	Brunswick - 7740		30s	
Prima Louis	Long About Midnight	Brunswick - 7335		40s	
Prima Louis	Robin Hood	Hit - 7083		30s	
Prima Louis	Stardust	Brunswick - 7335		30s	
Prima Louis	Sunday Kind Of Love A	Majestic - 1113		40s	
Prima Louis	Swing Me With Rhythm	Brunswick - 7431		30s	
Prima Louis & Keely Smith	That Old Black Magic	Capital - 4063		50s	
Puckett Riley	Cindy Cindy	Columbia - 15232 - D		20s	
Puckett Riley	Ol Faithful	Bluebird - B - 6313		30s	
Puckett Riley	When You And I Were Young.	Columbia - 15005 - D		30s	
Puckett Riley	Wish I Were Single Again I - AC	Columbia - 15036-D	own guitar	20s	
Puckett Riley & Gid Tanner	John Henry - AC	Columbia - 15019 - D		20s	
Questal Mae	Music Goes Round And Round	Decca - 680		30s	
Quinn Dan	Football - AC	Victor - 4603		00s	
Quinn Dan	Hot Time In The Old Town. - AC	Berliner - 527z		00s	
Quinn Dan	Bill Bailey Wont You Please - AC	Victor - Monarch - 1411		00s	
Radio Franks	I Found A Million Dollar Baby	Champion - 15178	piano accomp.	20s	
Rafferty Carl	Mr. Carls Blues	Bluebird - B - 5429		30s	
Rainey Ma	Black Cat Hoot Owl Blues	Paramount - 12687	Tub Jug Washboard Band.	20s	
Rainey Ma	Black Eye Blues	Paramount - 12963		20s	
Rainey Ma	Blues On Blues	Paramount - 12566	Georgia Band her	20s	
Rainey Ma	Chain Gang Blues - AC	Paramount - 12338	Georgia Band her	20s	
Rainey Ma	Courtin' The Blues - AC	Paramount - 12238	Georgia Jazz Band	20s	
Rainey Ma	Daddy Goodbye Blues	Paramount - 12963		20s	
Rainey Ma	Don't Fish In My Sea	Paramount - 12438	Georgia Band her	20s	
Rainey Ma	Jealous Hearted Blues - AC	Paramount - 12252	Georgia Jazz Band	20s	
Rainey Ma	Jelly Bean Blues - AC	Paramount - 12238	Georgia Jazz Band	20s	
Rainey Ma	Lawd Send Me A Man . . . AC	Paramount - 12200	Austin Lovie Blues S	20s	
Rainey Ma	Ma Raineys Black Bottom	Paramount - 12590	Georgia Band her	20s	
Rainey Ma	Ma Raineys Mystery . . . AC	Paramount - 12200	Austin Lovie Blues S	20s	
Rainey Ma	Oh Papa Blues - AC	Paramount - 12566	Georgia Jazz Band	20s	
Rainey Ma	Prove It On Me Blues	Paramount - 12668	Tub Jug Washboard Band.	20s	
Rainey Ma	See See Rider Blues - AC	Paramount - 12252	Georgia Band her	20s	
Rainey Ma	Shave 'Em Dry - AC	Paramount - 12222		20s	
Rainey Ma	Stack O' Lee Blues - AC	Paramount - 12357		20s	
Rainey Ma	Walkin Blues - AC	Paramount - 12082	Austin Lovie Blues S	20s	
Rainey Ma	Wringing And Twisting . . . AC	Paramount - 12338	Georgia Band her	20s	
Ram Jam	Black Betty	Epic - 50357		70s	
Ray Johnnie	Little White Cloud That Cried The	Okeh - 6840		50s	
Ray Johnnie	Cry	Okeh - 6840		50s	
Redding Ottis	Try A Little Tenderness	Volt - 141		60s	
Reeves Goebel	Tramp's MotherThe	Okeh - 45381		20s	
Renard Jacques*	As Time Goes By	Brunswick - 6205	Renard Jacques Orchestra	60s	
Revelers	Blue Room, The	Victor - 20082		20s	
Revelers, the	Birth Of The Blues, The	Victor - 20111		20s	
Rhodes Dusty*	Happy Days Are Here Again	Brunswick - 4709	Meroff Benny Orch	30s	
Rice Brothers Gang	You Are My Sunshine	Decca - 5763		30s	
Richmond Harry	Birth Of The Blues, The	Vocalion - 15412		20s	
Richmond June*	I Havent Changed A Thing	Decca - 1961	Dorsey Jimmy & his orch.	30s	
Riley Joe & Eddie Farley*	Music Goes Round And Round.	Decca - 678	Riley & Farley Orch.	30s	
Ritter Tex	Bill The Bar Fly	Champion - 45191		30s	
Ritter Tex & Mantan Moreland	Bo Weevil Song The	Film Master - 1939		30s	
Ritter Tex	Fort Worth Jail	Capital - 48004		40s	
Ritter Tex	Goodby Old Paint	Conquer - 8073		30s	
Ritter Tex	Green Grow The Lilacs	Capital - 206		40s	
Ritter Tex	Have I Stayed Away Too Long	Capital - 147	Texans his	40s	
Ritter Tex	Have I Told You Lately That.	Capital - 296		40s	
Ritter Tex	High Noon	Capital - 2120		50s	
Ritter Tex	Jealous Heart	Capital - 179.		40s	
Ritter Tex	Lady Killing Cowboy	Decca - 5076		30s	
Ritter Tex	Let Me Go Devil	Capital - 1698		50s	

Ritter Tex	Long Time Gone	Capital - 253		40s	
Ritter Tex	Riding Old Paint A	Banner - 32992		30s	
Ritter Tex	Rye Wiskey	Conquer - 8144		30s	
Ritter Tex	Wayward Wind	Capital - 3430		50s	
Ritter Tex	When My Blue Moon Turns.	Capital - 1977	Baxter Les Orch	40s	
Ritter Tex	When You Leave Don't Slam.	Capital - 296		40s	
Ritter Tex	You Are My Sunshine	Film Master - 1940	Wills Bob & Texas Play Boys	40s	
Roberts Charles*	From Now On	Victor - 22158	Pollack Ben Orch	20s	
Roberts Charles*	Keep Your Undershirt On	Victor - 22267	Pollack Ben Orch	20s	
Roberts Bob	Bye The Sycamore Tree - AC	Zon o Phone - C - 5788		00s	
Roberts Bob	Ragtime Cowboy Joe - AC	Victor - 17090		10s	
Roberts Bob	Shine On Harvest Moon - AC	Columbia - 668		00s	
Robertson Dick & American Four	We Did It Before And We'll . . .	Decca - 4117		40s	
Robertson Dick*	Blue Again	Brunswick 6014	Nichols Red & His F. Pennies	30s	
Robertson Dick*	Candy	Decca - 18661	Long Johnny Orch	40s	
Robertson Dick*	Lovable	Victor - 22954	Reisman Leo Orch	30s	
Robertson Dick*	Youre Lucky To Me - NAP	Victor - 23017	Ellington Duke Orch	20s	
Robeson P. & Elisabeth Welch	Ah Still Suites Me	Victor - 35376		30s	
Robeson Paul	Ah Still Suites Me	Film Master - 1936		30s	
Robeson Paul & L. Brown	Bye And Bye - AC	Victor - 19743		20s	
Robeson Paul	Deep River - AC	Victor - 20793		20s	
Robeson Paul & L. Brown	Joshua Fit The Battle - AC	Victor - 19743		20s	
Robeson Paul - NAP	King Joe Pt 1 & 2	Okeh - 6475	Basie Count Orchestra	30s	
Robeson Paul	Nobody Knows The T . . . - AC	Victor - 20068		20s	
Robeson Paul	O'l Man River	Film Master - 1936		30s	
Robeson Paul	O'l Man River	Victor - 35912	Whiteman Paul Orch	20s	
Robeson Paul	On Ma Journey - AC	Victor - 20013		20s	
Robeson P. & Elisabeth Welch	Sleepy River	Film Master - 1936		30s	
Robeson Paul	Swing Low Sweet Chariot - AC	Victor - 20068		20s	
Robeson Paul	Water Boy - AC	Victor - 19824		20s	
Robinson Carson	My Carolina Home	Victor - 20795		20s	
Roche Betty	Take The A Train	Columbia - B1566	Ellington Duke Orch	50s	
Roche Betty	Take The A Train	Film Master - 1943		40s	
Rodgers Jimmie	Any Old Time	Victor - 22488		20s	
Rodgers Jimmie	Ben Dewberry's Final Run	Victor - 21245		20s	
Rodgers Jimmie	Blue Yodel No 6	Victor - 22271		30s	
Rodgers Jimmie	Daddy And Home	Film Master - 1929		20s	
Rodgers Jimmie	Daddy And Home	Victor - 21757		20s	
Rodgers Jimmie	Everybody Does It In Hawaii	Victor - 22143		20s	
Rodgers Jimmie	Frankie And Johnny	Victor - 22143		20s	
Rodgers Jimmie	Gambling Bar Room Blues	Victor - 23766		30s	
Rodgers Jimmie	Gambling Polka Dot Blues	Victor - 23636		30s	
Rodgers Jimmie	High Powered Mama	Victor - 22523		20s	
Rodgers Jimmie	Hobo Bill's Last Ride	Victor - 22421		20s	
Rodgers J. & the Carter Family	Hot Time In The Old Town.	Victor - 23574	Carter Family the	30s	
Rodgers Jimmie	In The Jailhouse Now	Victor - 21245		20s	
Rodgers Jimmie	Jimmie's Mean Mama Blues	Victor - 23503	Sawyer Bob Orchestra	30s	
Rodgers Jimmie	Let Me Be Your Sidetrack	Victor - 23621		30s	
Rodgers Jimmie	Long Tall Mama Blues	Victor - 23766		30s	
Rodgers Jimmie	Looking For A New Mama	Victor - 23580		30s	
Rodgers Jimmie	Mississippi Moon	Victor - 23696		20s	
Rodgers Jimmie	Mississippi River Blues	Victor - 23535		20s	
Rodgers Jimmie	Mother Was A Lady	Victor - 21433		20s	
Rodgers Jimmie	Mule Skinner Blues - B. Y.	Victor - 23503		30s	
Rodgers Jimmie	My Blue Eyed Jane	Victor - 23549	Sawyer Bob Orchestra	30s	
Rodgers Jimmie	My Carolina Sunshine Girl	Victor - V40096		20s	
Rodgers Jimmie	My Good Gals Gone Blues	Bluebird - B - 5942	Louisville Jug Band	30s	
Rodgers Jimmie	My Rough And Rowdy Ways	Victor - 22220		20s	
Rodgers Jimmie	Never No Mo Blues	Victor - 21531		20s	
Rodgers Jimmie	Ninety - Nine Years Blues	Victor - 23669		30s	
Rodgers Jimmie	One Rose The	Bluebird - B - 7280		30s	
Rodgers Jimmie	Pistol Packin Papa	Victor - 22554		30s	
Rodgers Jimmie	She Was Happy Till She Met You	victor - 23681		30s	
Rodgers Jimmie	Somewhere Down Below The . . .	Victor - 23840		30s	
Rodgers Jimmie	Standing On The Corner - B. Y.	Victor - 23580		30s	
Rodgers Jimmie	T For Texas - (B. Yodel)	Victor - 21142		20s	
Rodgers Jimmie	T. B. Blues	Victor - 23535		30s	
Rodgers Jimmie	Those Gambler's Blues	Victor - 22554		30s	
Rodgers Jimmie	Travellin Blues	Victor - 23564		30s	
Rodgers Jimmie	Tuck Away My Lonesome Blues	Victor - 22220		20s	
Rodgers Jimmie	Waiting For A Train	Film Master - 1929		20s	
Rodgers Jimmie	Waiting For A Train	Victor - 40014		20s	

Rodgers Jimmie	What's It	Victor - 23609		30s	
Rodgers Jimmie	When The Cactus Is In Bloom	Victor - 23636		30s	
Rodney Don & the Lombard Trio*	Seems Like Old Times	Decca - 18737	Lombardo Guy Orch	40s	
Rogers Clyde*	All Or Noting At All	Victor - 20 - 1537	Martin Freddy Orch	40s	
Rogers Clyde*	Theres A Breeze On Lake . . .	Bluebird - B - 11437	Martin Freddy Orch	40s	
Rogers Ginger	Carioca The	Film Master - 1933		30s	
Rogers Ginger	Cheek To Cheek	Decca - F - 5747		30s	
Rogers Ginger	Did You Ever See A Dream.	Film Master - 1933		30s	
Rogers Ginger & Johnny Mercer	Eeny Meeny Miney Mo	Decca - F - 6822		30s	
Rogers Ginger	I'll String Along With You	Film Master - 1934		30s	
Rogers Ginger	Isent It A Lovely Day	Decca - F - 5746		30s	
Rogers Ginger	Let Yourself Go	Film Master - 1936		30s	
Rogers Ginger	Music Make Me	Film Master - 1933		30s	
Rogers Ginger	No Strings	Decca - F - 5746		30s	
Rogers Ginger	Out For No Good	Film Master - 1934		30s	
Rogers Ginger	Out Of Sight Out Of Mind	Decca - F - 6822		30s	
Rogers Ginger	Piccilino, The	Decca - F - 5747		30s	
Rogers Ginger	Saga Of Jenny The	Film Master - 1944		40s	
Rogers Ginger	They All Laughed	Film Master - 1937		30s	
Rogers Ginger	We're In The Money	Film Master - 1933		30s	
Rogers Ginger	Yam, The	Bluebird - B - 7891		30s	
Rogers Ginger	Yam, The	Film Master - 1938		30s	
Rogers Roy	Blue Shadows On The Trail	Film Master - 1948	Sons Of The Pioneers	40s	
Rogers Roy	Blue Shadows On The Trail	Victor - 20 - 2780	Sons Of The Pioneers	40s	
Rogers Roy	Don't Fence Me In	Film Master - 1944	Sons Of The Pioneers	40s	
Rogers Roy	Don't Fence Me In	Victor - 20 - 3073		40s	
Rogers Roy* (as Lenard Sly - chorus)	Empty Saddles	Decca - 5247	Sons Of The Pioneers	30s	
Rogers Roy & Dale Evens	Happy Trails To You	Film (TV) Master - 1954		50s	
Rogers Roy	Hi Yo Silver	Vocalion - 04190		30s	
Rogers Roy* (chorus)	Im An Old Cowhand	Decca - 5247	Sons Of The Pioneers	30s	
Rogers Roy	Pecos Bill	Victor - 20 - 2780	Sons Of The Pioneers	40s	
Rogers Roy	San Fernando Valley	Victor - 20 - 3075		40s	
Rogers Roy* (chorus)	Tumbling Tumbleweeds	Decca - 5047	Sons Of The Pioneers	30s	
Romainn Manual	I Wonder Who's Kissing Her Now - AC	Edison - 10287		30s	
Romay Lena*	Chica Chica Boom Chic	Columbia - 35995	Cugot Xavoir Orchestra	40s	
Romay Lina	She's A Bombshell From . . .	Film Master - 1943	Cugot Xavoir Orchestra	40s	
Roosevelt Franklin D.	Oath Of Office & Inagural.	Columbia - 50348 - D	SPOKEN WORD	30s	
Roosevelt Franklin D.	War Message To Congress	Columbia - 36516	SPOKEN WORD	40s	
Ross Lanny	Stay As Sweet As You Are	Brunswick - 7318		30s	
Roth Lilian & Jack Oakie	This Must Be Illegal	Film Master - 1930		30s	
Roth Lillian	Come Up And See Me Sometime	Film Master - 1933		30s	
Roth Lillian	Im So Unhappy Without You	Film Master - 1931		30s	
Roth Lillian	Sing You Sinners	Film Master - 1930		30s	
Rouse Brothers	Orange Blossom Special	Bluebird - B - 8218		30s	
Rushing Jimmy*	Boogie Woogie	Decca - 1252	Basie Count Orch	30s	
Rushing Jimmy*	Bye Bye Baby	Victor - 20 - 3051	Basie Count Orch	40s	
Rushing Jimmy*	Draftin' Blues	Conquer - 9632	Basie Count Orch	40s	
Rushing Jimmy*	Exactly Like You	Decca - 1252	Basie Count Orch	30s	
Rushing Jimmy*	Going To Chicago Blues	Okeh - 6244	Basie Count Orch	30s	
Rushing Jimmy*	Good Morning Blues	Decca - 1446	Basie Count Orch	30s	
Rushing Jimmy*	He Aint Got Rhythm	Victor - 25505	Goodman Benny Orch	30s	
Rushing Jimmy*	How Long Blues	Vocalion - 5010	Basie Count Orch	30s	
Rushing Jimmy*	I Want A Little Girl	Okeh - 5773	Basie Count Orch	40s	
Rushing Jimmy*	Im Gonna Move To The Out . . .	Columbia - 36601	Basie Count Orch	40s	
Rushing Jimmy*	Jimmy's Blues	Columbia - 36831	Basie Count Orch	30s	
Rushing Jimmy	Take Me Back Baby	Film Master 1941	Basie Count Orchestra	40s	
Rushing Jimmy*	You Cant Run Around	Okeh - 5673	Basie Count Orch	30s	
Russell Andy	Amor	Capital - 156		40s	
Russell Andy	Besame Mucho	Capital - 149	Sack Al Orch. & his	40s	
Russell Andy	Can't Begin To Tell You I	Captial - 221		40s	
Russell Andy	Dream Of You I	Captial - 167		40s	
Russell Andy	If I Had A Wishing Ring	Capital - 234		40s	
Russell Andy	If I Had A Wishing Ring	Film Master - 1946		40s	
Russell Andy	I'll See You In My Dreams	Capital - 20036	with orchestra	40s	
Russell Andy	Imagination	Capital - 20034	with orchestra	40s	
Russell Andy & Pied Pipers	It's Too Soon To Know	Capital - 15281	& Orchestra accomp.	40s	
Russell Andy	Just A Memory	Capital - 10085	Weston Paul Orch	40s	
Russell Andy	Laughing On The Inside . . .	Capital - 252		40s	
Russell Andy	Marie Elena	Captial - 20035	with orchestra	40s	
Russell Andy	What A Difference A Day Made	Capital - 167	Weston Paul Orch	40s	
Ryan Tommy*	Nightingale Sang in . . .	Victor - 26795	Kay Sammy Orch.	40s	

Sam Singing	Lawd You Made The Night . . .	Perfect - 2409		30s	
Sargent Kenny*	House Is Haunted The	Brunswick - 6858	Gray Glenn And His Casa.	30s	
Schuyler Sonny*	Santa Clause Is Comin To Town	Bluebird - B - 5711	Hall George Hall H. T. Orch	30s	
Scott Mabel	Boogie Woogie Santa Claus	Exclusive - 75x	Davis Maxwell Orch	40s	x
Seeley Blossom	Bringin' Home the Bacon - AC	Columbia - 136 - D		20s	
Seeley Blossom	Yes Sir That's My Baby - AC	Columbia - 386 - D		20s	
Seeley Blossom*	Lazy - AC	Columbia - 114 - D	Georgians the	20s	
Seeley Blossom*	Way Down Yonder In . . . - AC	Columbia - A3731	Georgians the	20s	
Segar Charlie	Key To The Highway	Okeh - 5441		40s	
Serrano Rosita	Babalu	Decca-C-16036		50s	
Serrano Rosita	La Paloma	Telefunken-A- 2563		40s	
Shannon Four	I Want To Be Happy	Columbia - 222 - D		20s	
Shay Dorothy	Feudin And Fightin	Columbia - 37189	Park Avenue Hillbillies	40s	
Shea Jack	Lovesick Blues - AC	Vocalion - 14333		20s	
Shelton Ann	Don't Want to Set the . . .	Decca F - 3652	Ambrose Burt Orch.	40s	
Shelton Ann	Lili Marlene	Decca - F - 8434		40s	
Sherman Lynn*	All Of Me	Columbia - 36675	Basie Count Orch	40s	
Sherrill Joya*	Come To Baby Do	Victor - 20 - 1748	Ellington Duke Orch	40s	
Sherrill Joya*	Im Beginning To See The Light	Victor - 20 - 1618	Ellington Duke Orch	40s	
Sherwood Lew* - NAP	Lovely To Look At	Victor - 24871	Duchin Eddie Orch	30s	
Shirelles	Everybody Loves A Lover	Specter - 1243		60s	
Shirley And Lee	Let The Good Times Roll	Aladdin - 3325		50s	
Shore Dinah & Buddy Clark	Baby Its Cold Outside	Columbia - 38463	Dale Ted Orch	40s	
Shore Dinah	Blues In The Night	Bluebird - B - 11436	Joy Lenard Orch	40s	
Shore Dinah	Buttons And Bows	Columbia - 38284	Happiness Boys, & Her	40s	
Shore Dinah	Chlo - E - (Song Of The Swamp)	Victor - 27625	Lavel Paul & his W. Ten.	40s	
Shore Dinah	Daddy - O	Columbia - 38284	Burke Sonny Orch	40s	
Shore Dinah	Dearly Beloved	Victor - 27963		40s	
Shore Dinah	Do You Care	Bluebird - B - 22291	Wetstein Paul orch	40s	
Shore Dinah	Facination	Victor-20-6980		50s	
Shore Dinah	Far Away Places	Columbia - 38356		40s	
Shore Dinah	Getting To Know You	Victor - 20 - 4286		50s	
Shore Dinah	Gypsy The	Columbia - 36964	Burke Sonny Orch	40s	
Shore Dinah	He's My Guy	Victor - 27963		40s	
Shore Dinah	How Come You Do Me Like . . .	Bluebird - B - 10824	Wetstein Paul orch	40s	
Shore Dinah	I Thought About You	Bluebird - B - 10473		40s	
Shore Dinah	Ill Walk Alone	Victor - 20 - 1586		40s	
Shore Dinah	Its So Nice To Have A Man Around The House	Columbia - 38689		50s	
Shore Dinah	Lavender Blue - Dilly Dilly	Columbia - 38299	Zimmerman Harry Orch	40s	
Shore Dinah	Mad About Him Sad Without.	Victor - 27940		40s	
Shore Dinah	Mood Indigo	Victor - 27302	Lavel Paul & hisW. Ten.	40s	
Shore Dinah	Murder Her Says	Victor - 20 - 1519		40s	
Shore Dinah & Dick Todd	Outside Of That I Love You	Bluebird - B - 10720	Joy Lenard Orch	40s	
Shore Dinah	Shoo - Fly Pie And Apple Pan Dowdy	Columbia - 36943	Burke Sonny Orch	40s	
Shore Dinah	Skylark	Bluebird - B - 11473		40s	
Shore Dinah	Sleigh Ride In July	Victor - 20 - 1617		40s	
Shore Dinah	Sophisticated Lady	Victor - 27624	Levine Henry & his . . .	40s	
Shore Dinah	Thank Your Lucky Stars	Film Master - 1943		40s	
Shore Dinah* (as Dinah Shaw)	Thrill Of A New Romance The	Victor - 26299	Cugat Xavior Orch	30s	
Shore Dinah	Wonderful Guy A	Columbia - 38460		40s	
Shore Dinah & Dick Todd	You Cant Brush Me Off	Bluebird - B - 10720	Joy Lenard Orchestra	40s	
Shore Dinah	Youd Be So Nice To Come . . .	Victor - 20 - 1519		40s	
Shutta Ethel*	Ah But What Ive Learned	Victor - 24166	Olsen George & His Music	30s	
Shutta Ethel & Paul Small*	And So To Bed	Victor - 24125	Olsen George & His Music Orch	30s	
Shutta Ethel*	Precious Little Thing Called Love	Victor - 21832	Olsen George & His Music Orch	20s	
Shutta Ethel*	Rock A Bye Moon	Victor - 24165	Olsen George & His Music	30s	
Shutta Ethel*	South Sea Rose	Victor - 22213	Olsen George & His Music	30s	
Shutta Ethel*	Stetson Hat	Film Master - 1931		30s	
Shutta Ethel*	There I Go Dreaming Again	Victor - 22937	Olsen George & His Music	30s	
Shutta Ethel*	Underneath The Arches	Victor - 24229	Olsen George & His Music	30s	
Shutta Ethel*	Vas Villst Du Haben	Victor - 24229	Olsen George & His Music	30s	
Silly Symphony	Who's Afraid Of The Big Bad . . .	Film Master 1933		30s	
Silver Monroe	Cohen On His Honeymoon - AC	Victor - 18501		10s	
Simms Ginny*	Any Bonds Today	Columbia - 36228	Kyser Kay and his orch.	40s	
Simms Ginny*	At Long Last Love	Brunswick - 8209	Kyser Kay and his orch.	30s	
Simms Giny*	Blue Love Bird	Columbia - 35488	Kyser Kay and his orch.	40s	
Simms Ginny	Can't Get Out Of This Mood	Film Master - 1942		40s	
Simms Ginny	Cuddle Up A Little Closer	Columbia - 36796	Fairchild Edgar & His Orch	40s	
Simms Ginny*	Don't Let That Moon Get Away	Brunswick - 8181	Kyser Kay and his orch.	30s	
Simms Ginny*	For No Rhythm Or Reason	Brunswick - 8209	Kyser Kay and his orch.	30s	
Simms Ginny*	For Sentimental Reasons	Brunswick - 7759	Kyser Kay and his orch.	30s	
Simms Ginny	Get Out Of Town	Vocalion - 4549	Simms Ginny & Orch	40s	

Simms Ginny*	Have You Got What Gets Me	Brunswick - 8228	Kyser Kay and his orch.	30s	
Simms Ginny	I Walk Alone	Vocalion - 5140	Simms Ginny & Orch	40s	
Simms Ginny	I'm Like A Fish Out Of Water	Film Master - 1943	Long Johnny Orch	40s	
Simms Ginny*	Indian Summer	Columbia - 35337	Kyser Kay and his orch.	30s	
Simms Ginny	Irrestiable You	Columbia - 36693	& orch	40s	
Simms Ginny*	Ive Got A One Track Mind	Columbia - 35762	Kyser Kay and his orch.	40s	
Simmy Ginny & others	Ive Got A One Track Mind	Film Master - 1940	Kyser Kay and his orch.	40s	
Simms Ginny	Just One Of Those Things	Sonora - 1192		40s	
Simms Ginny	Love Me A Little Little	Okeh - 6259	Simms Ginny & Orch	40s	
Simms Ginny*	Love Of My Life	Brunswick - 8201	Kyser Kay and his orch.	30s	
Simms Ginny*	Music Maestro Please	Brunswick - 8149	Kyser Kay and his orch.	30s	
Simms Ginny*	On The Road To Mandalay	Brunswick - 8415	Kyser Kay and his orch.	30s	
Simms Ginny*	Perfidia (Tonight)	Conqueror - 9652	vocal with Orch.	30s	
Simms Ginny	Please Come Out Of Your . . .	Vocalion - 4549	Simms Ginny & Orch	40s	
Simms Ginny	Someone's Rocking My Dreamboat	Okeh - 6566	Simms Ginny & Orch	40s	
Simmy Ginny	Suddenly Its Spring	Columbia - 36693	& orch	40s	
Simmy Ginny	They Say Its Wonderful	ARA - 139	& orch	40s	
Simms Ginny* & others	Three Little Fishes	Brunswick - 8368	Kyser Kay and his orch.	30s	
Simms Ginny & Harry Babbit*	Two Sleepy People	Brunswick - 8244	Kyser Kay and his orch	30s	
Simms Ginny	Way Back In 1939 AD	Vocalion - 5329	Vocal with Orchestra	40s	
Simms Ginny & Harry Babbit*	We'll Meet Again	Columbia - 35870	Kyser Kay and his orch.	30s	
Simms Ginny	What Goes Up Must Come Down	Vocalion - 4721	Simms Ginny & Orch	30s	
Simms Ginny*	Why Don't We Do More Of . . .	Colunbia - 36253	Kyser Kay and his orch.	40s	
Simms Ginny*	With The Wind And The Rain	Columbia - 35350	Kyser Kay and his orch.	30s	
Simms Ginny*	You And I	Columbia - 36244	Kyser Kay and his orch.	40s	
Simms Ginny & Cary Grant	You're The Top	Film Master - 1946		40s	
Sinatra Frank	Adeste Fideles	Capital - LP - W - 894	Jenkins Gordon Orch	50s	
Sinatra Frank	Aint cha Ever Coming Back	Columbia - 37554	vocal	40s	
Sinatra Frank	All Of Me	Columbia - 38163	vocal	40s	
Sinatra Frank	All Of Me	Film Master - 1952		50s	
Sinatra Frank	All Of Me - II	Capital - LP - W - 587	Riddle Nelson Orch	50s	
Sinatra Frank*	All Or Nothing At All	Columbia - 35587	James Harry Orch	30s	
Sinatra Frank	All The Way	Capital - 3793	Riddle Nelson Orch	50s	
Sinatra Frank	All The Way	Film Master - 1957		50s	
Sinatra Frank*	All This And Heaven Too	Victor - 26653	Dorsey Tommy Orch	40s	
Sinatra Frank	An Old Fashioned Christmas	Reprise - LP - 2022	Waring Fred Orch	60s	
Sinatra Frank	Anything Goes	Capital - LP - W - 653	Riddle Nelson Orch	50s	
Sinatra Frank	April In Paris	Capital - LP - W - 920	May Billy Orch	50s	
Sinatra Frank	Around The World	Capital - LP - W - 920	May Billy Orch	50s	
Sinatra Frank	Autumn In New York	Capital - LP - W - 920	May Billy Orch	50s	
Sinatra Frank	Autumn In New York	Columbia - 38316	Stordahl Axel Orch	40s	
Sinatra Frank*	Be Careful It's My Heart	Victor - 27923	Dorsey Tommy Orch	40s	
Sinatra Frank	Begin The Beguine	Columbia - 37064	vocal	40s	
Sinatra Frank	Bewitched	Capital - LP - W - 912	Stoloff Morris Orch	50s	
Sinatra Frank	Bewitched	Film Master - 1957		50s	
Sinatra Frank	Bim Bam Baby	Columbia - 39819	vocal	40s	
Sinatra Frank	Blue Hawaii	Capital - LP - W - 920	May Billy Orch	50s	
Sinatra Frank*	Blue Skies	Victor - 27566	Dorsey Tommy Orch	40s	
Sinatra, F. & Phil Moore Four	Bop Goes My Heart	Columbia - 38421	Moore Phil Four	20s	
Sinatra Frank	Brazil	Capital - LP - W - 920	May Billy Orch	50s	
Sinatra Frank	Call Me Irrespossible	Reprise - 20063	vocal	60s	
Sinatra Frank	Cant We Be Friends	Capital - LP - W - 581	Riddle Nelson Orch	50s	
Sinatra Frank	Castle Rock	Columbia - 39527	James Harry Orch	50s	
Sinatra Frank	Chicago	Capital - 3793	Riddle Nelson Orch	50s	
Sinatra Frank	Chicago	Film Master - 1957		50s	
Sinatra Frank	Christmas Dreaming	Columbia - 37809	vocal	40s	
Sinatra Frank	Christmas Song, (The)	Capital - LP - W - 894	Jenkins Gordon Orch	50s	
Sinatra Frank	Christmas Waltz, (The)	Capital - LP - W - 894	Jenkins Gordon Orch	50s	
Sinatra Frank*	Ciribiribin	Columbia - 35316	James Harry Orch	30s	
Sinatra Frank	Close To You	Capital - LP - W - 789	Riddle Nelson Orch	50s	
Sinatra Frank	Close To You	Columbia - 36678	vocal	40s	
Sinatra Frank	Coffee Song, (The)	Columbia - 37089	vocal	40s	
Sinatra Frank	Come Fly With Me	Capital - LP - W - 920	May Billy Orch	50s	
Sinatra Frank	Continental, (The)	Columbia - 38997	Siravo George Orch	50s	
Sinatra Frank	Cycles	Reprise - 0764		60s	
Sinatra Frank	Dancing On The Ceiling	Capital - LP - W - 581	Riddle Nelson Orch	50s	
Sinatra Frank	Deep In A Dream	Capital - LP - W - 581	Riddle Nelson Orch	50s	
Sinatra Frank*	Devil May Care	Victor - 26593	Dorsey Tommy Orch	40s	
Sinatra Frank*	Dolores	Victor - 27317	Dorsey Tommy Orch	40s	
Sinatra Frank & Charioteers	Don't Forget Tonight Tomorrow	Columbia - 36854	musical accompaniment	40s	
Sinatra Frank	Don't Worry Bout Me	Capital - 2787	Riddle Nelson Orch	50s	
Sinatra Frank	Dream	Columbia - 36797	Stordahl Axel Orch	40s	
Sinatra Frank	End Of A Love Affair (The)	Capital - LP - W - 789		50s	

Sinatra Frank*	Every Day Of My Life	Columbia - 35531	James Harry Orch	30s	
Sinatra Frank	Everybody Loves Somebody	Columbia - 38225	Stordahl Axel Orch	40s	
Sinatra Frank*	Everything Happens To Me	Victor - 27359	Dorsey Tommy Orch	40s	
Sinatra Frank	Evry Bodys Twisting	Reprise - 20063	Riddle Nelson Orch	60s	
Sinatra Frank & Nat Cole	Exactly Like You	Radio Master - 1946	Nat Cole Trio	40s	
Sinatra Frank	First Noel, (The)	Capital - LP - W - 894	Jenkins Gordon Orch	50s	
Sinatra Frank	Five Minutes More	Columbia - 37048	Stordahl Axel Orch	40s	
Sinatra Frank	Fly Me To The Moon	Reprise - LP - 1012	Basie Count Orch	60s	
Sinatra Frank	Foggy Day A	Capital - LP - W - 587	Riddle Nelson Orch	50s	
Sinatra Frank*	Fools Rush In	Victor - 26593	Dorsey Tommy Orch	30s	
Sinatra Frank	From Here To Eternity	Capital - 2560	Riddle Nelson Orch	50s	
Sinatra Frank*	From The Bottom Of My Heart	Brunswick - 8443	James Harry Orch	30s	
Sinatra Frank & Nuggetts	From The Bottom To The Top	Capital - 3084	Big Daves Music	50s	
Sinatra Frank	Gal That Got Away The	Capital - 2864		50s	
Sinatra Frank	Get Happy	Capital - LP - W - 587	Riddle Nelson Orch	50s	
Sinatra Frank	Girl Next Door The	Capital - LP - W - 587	Riddle Nelson Orch	50s	
Sinatra Frank	Glad To Be Unhappy	Capital - LP - W - 581	Riddle Nelson Orch	50s	
Sinatra, F. & J. Alexander Choir	Gods Country	Columbia - 38708	Stordahl Axel Orch	50s	
Sinatra Frank & Shelly Winters	Good Man Is Hard To Find A	Film Master - 1952		50s	
Sinatra Frank	Hark The Herald Angels Sing	Capital - LP - W - 894	Jenkins Gordon Orch	50s	
Sinatra Frank	Have Yourself A Merry Little Christmas	Capital - LP - W - 894	Jenkins Gordon Orch	50s	
Sinatra Frank	Hey Jealous Lover	Capital - 3552	Riddle Nelson Orch	50s	
Sinatra Frank	High Hopes	Capital - 4214	Riddle Nelson Orch	50s	
Sinatra Frank	High Hopes	Film Master - 1959		50s	
Sinatra Frank	House I Live In The	Columbia - 36886	vocal	40s	
Sinatra Frank	House I Live In The	Film Master - 1945		40s	
Sinatra Frank	How About You	Capital - LP - W - 653	Riddle Nelson Orch	50s	
Sinatra Frank*	How About You	Victor - 27749	Dorsey Tommy Orch	40s	
Sinatra Frank	How Deep Is The Ocean	Film Master - 1952		50s	
Sinatra Frank & Ken Laine Quintel	Hucklebuck, (The)	Columbia - 38486	Stordahl Axel Orch	40s	
Sinatra Frank	I Begged Her	Columbia - 36774	Stordahl Alex Orch	40s	
Sinatra Frank	I Could Write A Book	Capital - LP - W - 912	Stoloff Morris Orch	50s	
Sinatra Frank	I Could Write A Book	Columbia - 39652	Stordahl Axel Orch	50s	
Sinatra Frank	I Could Write A Book	Film Master - 1957		50s	
Sinatra Frank	I Couldent Sleep A Wink Last Night	Columbia - 36687	vocal with Chorus	40s	
Sinatra Frank	I Couldent Sleep A Wink Last Night	Film Master - 1944	Bakaleinikoff Constantin	40s	
Sinatra Frank	I Dident Know What Time It Was	Capital - LP - W - 912	Stoloff Morris Orch	50s	
Sinatra Frank	I Dident Know What Time It Was	Film Master - 1957		50s	
Sinatra Frank	I Don't Know Why	Columbia - 36918	Stordahl Axel Oech	40s	
Sinatra Frank	I Dream Of You	Columbia - 36762		40s	
Sinatra Frank	I Fall In Love Too Easily	Columbia - 36830	Stordahl Axel Orch	40s	
Sinatra Frank	I Found A New Baby	Radio Master - 1946	Nat Cole Trio	40s	
Sinatra Frank	I Get A Kick Out Of You	Capital - LP - W - 587	Riddle Nelson Orch	50s	
Sinatra Frank	I Get Along Without You Very Well	Capital - LP - W - 581	Riddle Nelson Orch	50s	
Sinatra Frank	I Have But One Heart	Columbia - 37343		40s	
Sinatra Frank	I Heard The Bells On Christmas Day	Reprise - LP - 2022	Waring Fred Orch	60s	
Sinatra Frank	I Like To Lead When I Dance	Reprise - LP - 2021	vocal	60s	
Sinatra Frank	I Likle To Lead When I Dance	Film Master - 1964		60s	
Sinatra Frank	I See Your Face Before Me	Capital - LP - W - 581	Riddle Nelson Orch	50s	
Sinatra Frank	I Thought About You	Capital - LP - W - 653	Riddle Nelson Orch	50s	
Sinatra Frank	I'll Never Be The Same	Capital - LP - W - 581	Riddle Nelson Orch	50s	
Sinatra Frank & Pied Pipers*	I'll Never Smile Again	Victor - 26628	Dorsey Tommy Orch	40s	
Sinatra Frank*	I'll Take Tallulah	Victor - 27869	Dorsey Tommy Orch	40s	
Sinatra Frank	Ill Wind	Capital - LP - W - 581	Riddle Nelson Orch	50s	
Sinatra Frank	I'lll Be Around	Capital - LP - W - 581	Riddle Nelson Orch	50s	
Sinatra Frank	I'lll Be Home For Christmas	Capital - LP - W - 894	Jenkins Gordon Orch	50s	
Sinatra Frank*	I'lll Be Seeing You	Victor - 26539	Dorsey Tommy Orch	40s	
Sinatra Frank	I'm Gonna Sit Right Down And Write Myself A Letter	Capital - LP - W - 587	Riddle Nelson Orch	50s	
Sinatra Frank	I'm Walking Behind You	Capital - 2450	Stordahl Axel Orch	50s	
Sinatra Frank*	In The Blue Of The Evening	Victor - 27947	Dorsey Tommy Orch	40s	
Sinatra Frank	In The Wee Small Hours	Capital - LP - W - 581	Riddle Nelson Orch	50s	
Sinatra Frank	Isle Of Capri	Capital - LP - W - 920	May Billy Orch	50s	
Sinatra Frank	It Came Upon The Midnight Clear	Capital - LP - W - 894	Jenkins Gordon Orch	50s	
Sinatra Frank	It Happened In Monterey	Capital - LP - W - 653	Riddle Nelson Orch	50s	
Sinatra Frank	It Happens Every Spring	Columbia - 38486	vocal	40s	
Sinatra Frank	It Never Entered My Mind	Capital - LP - W - 581	Riddle Nelson Orch	50s	
Sinatra Frank	It Never Entered My Mind	Columbia - 38475	Stordahl Axel Orch	40s	
Sinatra Frank*	It Started All Over Again	Victor - 20 - 1522	Dorsey Tommy Orch	40s	
Sinatra Frank	It Was A Very Good Year	Reprise - 0429		60s	
Sinatra Frank*	It's Always You	Victor - 27345	Dorsey Tommy Orch	40s	
Sinatra Frank	Its Easy To Remember	Capital - LP - W - 789		50s	

Sinatra Frank*	It's Funny To Everybody But . . .	Columbia - 35209	James Harry Orch	30s	
Sinatra Frank	Its Nice To Go Traveling	Capital - LP - W - 920	May Billy Orch	50s	
Sinatra Frank	Ive Got A Crush On You	Columbia - 38151	vocal	40s	
Sinatra Frank	Ive Got A Crush On You	Film Master - 1952		50s	
Sinatra Frank	Ive Got The World On A String	Capital - 2505	Riddle Nelson Orch	50s	
Sinatra Frank	Ive Got You Under My Skin	Capital - LP - W - 653	Riddle Nelson Orch	50s	
Sinatra Frank	Jeepers Creepers	Capital - LP - W - 587	Riddle Nelson Orch	50s	
Sinatra Frank	Jingle Bells	Capital - LP - W - 894	Jenkins Gordon Orch	50s	
Sinatra Frank	Just One Of Those Things	Capital - LP - W - 587	Riddle Nelson Orch	50s	
Sinatra Frank	Lady Is A Tramp The	Capital - LP - W - 912	Stoloff Morris Orch	50s	
Sinatra Frank	Lady Is A Tramp The	Film Master - 1957		50s	
Sinatra Frank	Lamplighters Serenade The	Bluebird - B - 11515	vocal	40s	
Sinatra Frank	Lamplighters Serenade The	Bluebird - B - 11515	Stordahl Axel Orch	40s	
Sinatra Frank	Last Night When We Were Young	Capital - LP - W - 581	Riddle Nelson Orch	40s	
Sinatra Frank	Laura	Columbia - 38472	Stordahl Axel Orch	40s	
Sinatra Frank	Lean Baby	Capital - 2450	Stordahl Axel Orch	50s	
Sinatra Frank	Learning The Blues	Capital - 3102	Riddle Nelson Orch	50s	
Sinatra Frank & Pastels	Let Her Go Let Her Go	Columbia - 38555	Winterhalter Hugo Orch	40s	
Sinatra Frank	Let's Get Away From It All	Capital - LP - W - 920	May Billy Orch	50s	
Sinatra Frank & Connie Haines*	Let's Get Away From It All	Victor - 27377	Dorsey Tommy Orch	40s	
Sinatra Frank & Doris Day	Let's Take An Old Fasion Walk	Columbia - 38513	Stordahl Axel Orch	40s	
Sinatra Frank	Like Someone In Love	Capital - LP - W - 587	Riddle Nelson Orch	50s	
Sinatra Frank	Little Drummer Boy, (The)	Reprise - LP - 2022	Waring Fred Orch	60s	
Sinatra Frank	Little Girl Blue	Capital - LP - W - 587	Riddle Nelson Orch	50s	
Sinatra Frank & Pearl Bailey	Little Learning Is A Dangerous.	Columbia - 38362	Stordahl Axel Orch	50s	
Sinatra Frank	London By Night	Capital - LP - W - 920	May Billy Orch	50s	
Sinatra Frank	Lonesome Man Blues	Film Master - 1952		50s	
Sinatra Frank	Love And Marriage	Capital - 3260	Riddle Nelson Orch	50s	
Sinatra Frank	Love And Marriage	Film(TV) Master - 1955	Riddle Nelson Orch	50s	
Sinatra Frank	Love Is Here To Stay	Capital - LP - W - 653	Riddle Nelson Orch	50s	
Sinatra Frank	Love Me Or Leave Me	Radio Master - 1954		50s	
Sinatra Frank & Elvis Presley	Love Me Tender - Witchcraft	Film (TV) Master - 1960	Riddle Nelson Orch	60s	
Sinatra Frank	Lovely Way To Spend An Evening	Columbia - 36687	vocal with Chorus	40s	
Sinatra Frank*	Lover Is Blue A	Radio Master - 1940	Dorsey Tommy Orch	40s	
Sinatra Frank	Makin Whoopee	Capital - LP - W - 653	Riddle Nelson Orch	50s	
Sinatra Frank & Dagmar	Mama Will Bark	Columbia - 39425	vocal duet	50s	
Sinatra Frank	Mamselle	Columbia - 37343	vocal	40s	
Sinatra Frank*	Melacholy Mood	Brunswick - 8443	James Harry Orch	30s	
Sinatra Frank	Mind If I Make Love To You	Capital - LP - W - 750	Green John & MGM Orch	50s	
Sinatra Frank	Mind If I Make Love To You	Film Master - 1956		50s	
Sinatra Frank	Mistletoe And Holly	Capital - LP - W - 894	Jenkins Gordon Orch	50s	
Sinatra Frank	Mood Indigo	Capital - LP - W - 581	Riddle Nelson Orch	50s	
Sinatra Frank	Moonlight In Vermont	Capital - LP - W - 920	May Billy Orch	50s	
Sinatra Frank	My Cousin Louella	Columbia - 38045		40s	
Sinatra Frank	My Funny Valentine	Capital - LP - W - 587	Riddle Nelson Orch	50s	
Sinatra Frank	My Kind Of Town	Film Master - 1964		60s	
Sinatra Frank	My Kind Of Town	Reprise - 0279	Riddle Nelson Orch	60s	
Sinatra Frank	My One And Only Love	Capital - 2505	Riddle Nelson Orch	40s	
Sinatra Frank	My Sugar Is So Refined	Radio Master - 1946		40s	
Sinatra Frank	My Way	Reprise - 0798		60s	
Sinatra Frank	Nancy	Columbia - 36868	vocal	40s	
Sinatra Frank	New York, New York - (Theme)	Reprise - 49233	Riddle Nelson Orch	80s	
Sinatra Frank	Night And Day	Bluebird - B - 11463	Stordahl Axel Orch	40s	
Sinatra Frank	Night And Day	Film Master - 1943		40s	
Sinatra Frank	O Little Town Of Bethleham	Capital - LP - W - 894	Jenkins Gordon Orch	50s	
Sinatra Frank* & Connie Haines	Oh Look At Me Now	Victor - 27274	Dorsey Tommy Orch	40s	
Sinatra Frank	Old Devil Moon	Capital - LP - W - 653	Riddle Nelson Orch	50s	
Sinatra Frank*	On A Little Street In Singapore	Columbia - 35261	James Harry Orch	30s	
Sinatra Frank	On The Road To Mandalay	Capital - LP - W - 920	May Billy Orch	50s	
Sinatra Frank	One For My Baby	Columbia - 38474	Stordahl Axel	40s	
Sinatra Frank*	One I Love Belongs To Some . . .	Victor - 2660	Dorsey Tommy Orch	40s	
Sinatra Frank*	Our Love Affair	Victor - 26736	Dorsey Tommy Orch	40s	
Sinatra Frank	Our Town	Film(TV) Master - 1955	Riddle Nelson Orch	50s	
Sinatra Frank	P S I Love You	Capital - LP - W - 789		50s	
Sinatra Frank	Paradise	Columbia - LP - CL - 743	vocal	40s	
Sinatra Frank	Pennies From Heaven	Capital - LP - W - 653	Riddle Nelson Orch	50s	
Sinatra Frank	People Will Say We're In Love	Columbia - 36682		40s	
Sinatra Frank	Pistol Packin Mama	Radio Master - 1943		40s	
Sinatra Frank	Pocket Full Of Miricles	Reprise - 20040		60s	
Sinatra Frank*	Polka Dots And Rainbows	Victor - 26539	Dorsey Tommy Orch	40s	
Sinatra Frank	Put Your Dreams Away	Columbia - 36814	Stordahl Axel Orch	40s	
Sinatra Frank	Santa Clause Is Comin To Town	Columbia - LP - CL - 1032		40s	

Sinatra Frank	Saturday Night	Columbia - 36762	Stordahl Axel Orch	40s	
Sinatra Frank	Second Time Around, (The)	Reprise - 20001	Slatkin Felix Orch	60s	
Sinatra Frank	September Song	Columbia - 37161	Stordahl Axel Orch	40s	
Sinatra Frank	She's Funny That Way	Film Master - 1952		50s	
Sinatra Frank	Should I	Columbia - 38998	Siravo George Orch	50s	
Sinatra Frank	Silent Night	Capital - LP - W - 894	Jenkins Gordon Orch	50s	
Sinatra Frank* & Connie Haines	Snootie Little Cutie	Victor - 27875	Dorsey Tommy Orch	40s	
Sinatra Frank	Something	Reprise - 0981		70s	
Sinatra Frank & Nancy Sinatra	Something Stupid	Reprise - 0561	vocal duet	60s	
Sinatra Frank	Sorftly As I Leave You	Reprise - 0301		60s	
Sinatra Frank	South Of The Border	Capital - 2638	May Billy Orch	50s	
Sinatra Frank	Spring Is Here	Columbia - LP - CL - 743	vocal	50s	
Sinatra Frank & Pied Pipers*	Stardust	Victor - 27233	Dorsey Tommy Orch	40s	
Sinatra Frank	Stella By Starlight	Columbia - 37343	Stordahl Axel	40s	
Sinatra Frank	Strangers In The Night	Reprise - 0470	Freeman Ernie Orch	60s	
Sinatra Frank & Pied Pipers*	Street Of Dreams	Victor - 27903	Dorsey Tommy Orch	40s	
Sinatra Frank	Summer Wind	Reprise - 0509		60s	
Sinatra Frank	Sunday	Capital - LP - W - 587	Riddle Nelson Orch	50s	
Sinatra Frank	Sunflower	Columbia - 38391	vocal	40s	
Sinatra Frank	Sweet Lorraine	Columbia - 37293	Metronome All Stars	40s	
Sinatra Frank	Swinging Down The Lane	Capital - LP - W - 653		50s	
Sinatra Frank	Taking A Chance On Love	Capital - LP - W - 587	Riddle Nelson Orch	50s	
Sinatra Frank	Tell Her You Love Her	Capital - 3859	Riddle Nelson Orch	50s	
Sinatra Frank	Tennessee Newsboy	Columbia - 38787	Stordah Axel Orch	50s	
Sinatra Frank	That Old Black Magic	Film Master - 1951		50s	
Sinatra Frank	That's How Much I Love You	Columbia - 37231	Cavanaugh Page Trio	40s	
Sinatra Frank	That's Life	Reprise - 0531		60s	
Sinatra Frank*	There Are Such Things	Victor - 27974	Dorsey Tommy Orch	40s	
Sinatra Frank	There's A Small Hotel	Film Master - 1957		50s	
Sinatra Frank	Theres A Small Hotel	Capital - LP - W - 912	Stoloff Morris Orch	50s	
Sinatra Frank	They Cant Take That Away From Me	Capital - LP - W - 587	Riddle Nelson Orch	50s	
Sinatra Frank	Things We Said Last Summer	Columbia - 37089	vocal	40s	
Sinatra Frank	This Is The Night	Columbia - 37197	vocal	40s	
Sinatra Frank	This Love Of Mine	Capital - LP - W - 581	Riddle Nelson Orch	50s	
Sinatra Frank*	This Love Of Mine	Victor - 27508	Dorsey Tommy Orch	40s	
Sinatra Frank	Three Coins In A Fountain	Capital - 2816	Riddle Nelson Orch	50s	
Sinatra Frank	Too Marvelous For Words	Capital - LP - W - 653	Riddle Nelson Orch	50s	
Sinatra Frank*	Too Romantic	Victor - 26500	Dorsey Tommy Orch	40s	
Sinatra Frank*	Trade Winds	Victor - 26666	Dorsey Tommy Orch	40s	
Sinatra Frank	Try A Little Tenderness	Columbia - 36920	Stordahl Alxel Orch	40s	
Sinatra Frank & Nuggetts	Two Hearts, Two Kisses	Capital - 3084	Big Dave	50s	
Sinatra Frank	Violets For You Furs	Capital - LP - W - 587	Riddle Nelson Orch	50s	
Sinatra Frank*	We Three - My Echo My . . .	Victor - 26747	Dorsey Tommy Orch	40s	
Sinatra Frank	We'll Be Together Again	Capital - LP - W - 653	Riddle Nelson Orch	50s	
Sinatra Frank	What Can I Say	Radio Master - 1954		50s	
Sinatra Frank	What Do I Care For A Dame	Capital - LP - W - 912	Stoloff Morris Orch	50s	
Sinatra Frank	What Is This Thing Called Love	Capital - LP - W - 581	Riddle Nelson Orch	50s	
Sinatra Frank	When Your Lover Has Gone	Capital - LP - W - 581	Riddle Nelson Orch	50s	
Sinatra Frank	White Christmas	Columbia - 36756	Stordahl Alex Orch	40s	
Sinatra, F. & Celeste Holm	Who Wants To Be A Millionaire	Capital - LP - W - 750	Green John & MGM Orch	50s	
Sinatra Frank	Why Cant You Behave	Columbia - 39393		40s	
Sinatra, F. & Phil Moore Four	Why Cant You Behave	Columbia - 38393	Phil Moore Four	40s	
Sinatra Frank	Witchcraft	Capital - 3859	Riddle Nelson Orch	50s	
Sinatra Frank	With Every Breath I Take	Capital - LP - W - 789		50s	
Sinatra Frank	Wives And Lovers	Reprise - LP - 1012	Basie Count Orch	60s	
Sinatra Frank	Wrap Your Troubles In Dreams	Capital - LP - W - 587	Riddle, Nelson Orch	50s	
Sinatra Frank	You Brought A New Kind Of Love To Me	Capital - LP - W - 653	Riddle Nelson Orch	50s	
Sinatra Frank	You Make Me Feel So Young	Capital - LP - W - 653	Riddle Nelson Orch	50s	
Sinatra Frank* & Connie Haines	You Might Have Belonged . . .	Victor - 27274	Dorsey Tommy Orch	40s	
Sinatra Frank	You Took Advantage Of Me	Radio Master - 1954		50s	
Sinatra Frank	Youll Never Know	Columbia - 36678	vocal	40s	
Sinatra Frank	Young At Heart	Capital - 2703	Riddle Nelson Orch	50s	
Sinatra Frank	Youre A Sweetheart	Film Master - 1952		50s	
Sinatra Frank	Youre Getting To Be A Habit With Me	Capital - LP - W - 653	Riddle Nelson Orch	50s	
Sinatra Frank	Youre Sensational	Capital - LP - W - 750	Green John & MGM Orch	50s	
Sinatra Frank	Youre Sensational	Film Master - 1956		50s	
Singing Sophmores	Breezing Along With The Breeze	Columbia - 4234 - D		20s	
Singing Sophmores	Sweet And Low Down	Columbia - 568 - D		20s	
Sissle Noble - NAP	Old Fashioned Love - AC	Victor - 19253	Blake Eubie at the piano	20s	
Sissle Noble & Eubie Blake - NAP	Crazy Blues - AC	Emerson - 10326		20s	
Six Hits & A Miss	Youd Be So Nice To Come . . .	Capital - 127		40s	

Slim Bumble Bee - (& M. Minnie)	When Somebody Loses	Vocalion - 3197		30s	
Small Paul*	I've Told Every Little Star	Victor - 24183	Denny Jack W. A Orch.	30s	
Small Paul*	Song is You The	Victor - 24183	Denny Jack W. A. Orch.	30s	
Smith Bessie	After You've Gone	Columbia - 14197 - D		20s	
Smith Bessie	Aint Gonna Play No Second Fiddle - AC	Columbia - 14090 - D	vocal, blues	20s	
Smith Bessie	Alexanders Ragetime Band	Columbia - 14219 - D	Blue Boys - her	20s	
Smith Bessie	Baby Wont You Please Come Home - AC	Columbia - A3888	Williams Clarence piano	20s	
Smith Bessie	Back Water Blues - AC	Columbia - 14197 - D	vocal, blues	20s	
Smith Bessie	Beale St. Mama - AC	Columbia - A3877	Down Home Trio her	20s	
Smith Bessie	Black Mountain Blues	Columbia - 14451 - D.	vocal, blues	20s	
Smith Bessie	Cold In Hand Blues - AC	Columbia - 14064 - D	Armstrong Louis cornet	20s	
Smith Bessie	Do Your Duty	Okeh - 8945	Buck And his band	30s	
Smith Bessie	Don't Cry Baby	Columbia - 14451 - D.	vocal, blues	30s	
Smith Bessie	Down Hearted Blues - AC	Columbia - A3844	vocal, blues	20s	
Smith Bessie	Easy Come Easy Go Blues - AC	Columbia - 14005 - D	vocal, blues	20s	
Smith Bessie	Empty Bed Blues - (PtI & II)	Columbia - 14312 - D	vocal, blues	20s	
Smith Bessie	Gimme A Pigfoot	Okeh - 8949	Buck And his band	30s	
Smith Bessie	Golf Coast Blues - AC	Columbia - A3844	vocal, blues	20s	
Smith Bessie	Good Man Is Hard To Find A	Columbia - 14250 - D	vocal, blues	20s	
Smith Bessie & Clara Smith	Im Going Back To My Used To Be - AC	Columbia - 13007 - D	Henderson Fletcher piano	20s	
Smith Bessie	I'm Wild About That Thing	Columbia - 14427 - D		20s	
Smith Bessie	Mean Old Bed Bug Blues	Columbia - 14250 - D	vocal, blues	20s	
Smith Bessie	Midnight Blues - AC	Columbia - A3936.	vocal, blues	20s	
Smith Bessie & Bessmer Singers	Moan You Moarners	Columbia - 14538 - D		20s	
Smith Bessie	Muddy Water - AC	Columbia - 14197 - D	vocal, blues	20s	
Smith Bessie	Nobody Knows You When Youre Down And Out	Columbia - 14451 - D.	vocal, blues	20s	
Smith Bessie	Oh Daddy Blues - AC	Columbia - A3898	Williams Clarence piano	20s	
Smith Bessie & Bessmer Singers	On Ravival Day . . .	Columbia - 14538 - D		20s	
Smith Bessie	PreachinThe Blues - AC	Columbia - 14195 - D		20s	
Smith Bessie	Rocking Chair Blues - AC	Columbia - 14020 - D	vocal, blues	20s	
Smith Bessie	Sing Sing Blues - AC	Columbia - 14051 - D		20s	
Smith Bessie	Some Of These Days	Columbia - 14197 - D	vocal, blues	20s	
Smith Bessie	Sorrowful Blues - AC	Columbia - 14020 - D	vocal, blues	20s	
Smith Bessie	St. Louis Blues	Film Master - 1929		20s	
Smith Bessie	St. Louis Blues - AC	Columbia - 14064 - D	Armstrong Louis cornet	20s	
Smith Bessie	T'Aint Nobodys Biz Ness If I Do - AC	Columbia - A3898	vocal, blues	20s	
Smith Bessie	Yellow Dog Blues The - AC	Columbia - 14075 - D	Henderson's Hot Six	20s	
Smith Bessie Mae	Dead Sea Blues	Okeh - 8553		20s	
Smith Clara	Ain't Got Nobody To Grind . . .	Columbia - 14368 - D		20s	
Smith Clara	Awful Moanin'Blues - AC	Columbia - A - 4000	Henderson Fletcher piano	20s	
Smith Clara	Broken Busted Blues - AC	Columbia - 14062 - D		20s	
Smith Clara	Chicago Blues - AC	Columbia - 14009 - D	her Jazz Band, &	20s	
Smith Clara	Done Sold My Soul To The . . .	Coumbia - 14041 - D	with her Jazz Trio	20s	
Smith Clara	Every Woman's Blues - AC	Columbia - A - 3943	Henderson Fletcher piano	20s	
Smith Clara	Freight Train Blues - AC	Columbia - 14041 - D	with her Jazz Trio	20s	
Smith Clara	Get On Board	Columbia - 14183 - D		20s	
Smith Clara	I Want My Sweet Daddy - AC	Columbia - A - 3991	Henderson Fletcher piano	20s	
Smith Clara	Kitchen Mechanic Blues	Columbia - 14097 - D	and her band	20s	
Smith Clara	Nobody Knows The Way . . . - AC	Columbia - 14058 - D		20s	
Smith Clara	Salty Dog	Columbia - 14143 - D	Henderson Fletcher piano	20s	
Smith Clara	Waitin For The Evenin' Mail	Columbia - 14002 - D	Henderson Fletcher piano	20s	
Smith Funny Paper -	Howling Wolf Blues	Vocalion - 1558		30s	
Smith Kate	God Bless America	Victor - 26198		30s	
Smith Kate	He's A Good Man To Have . . .	Diva - 2970 - D	Harmonians the	20s	
Smith Kate	I Don't Mind Walkin In The Rain	Velvet Tone - 2191 - V	Harmonians the	20s	
Smith Kate	Last Time I Saw Paris The	Columbia - 35802		40s	
Smith Kate	Making Faces At The Man In The Moon	Clarion - 5359 - C	Swanee Music her/	30s	
Smith Kate	Maybe Who Knows	Diva - 2970 - D	Harmonians the	30s	
Smith Kate	Moanin Low	Velvet Tone - 1999 - V	Harmonians the	20s	
Smith Kate*	One Sweet Letter From You	Columbia - 911 - D	Charleston Chasers	20s	
Smith Kate	River Stay Way From My Door	Columbia - 2578 - D	Lombardo Guy Orch	30s	
Smith Kate	Rockin The Town	Radio Master-1938		30s	
Smith Kate	Seems Like Old Times	Columbia - 36950		40s	
Smith Kate	Swinging In A Hammock	Velvet Tone - 2191 - V	Harmonians the	20s	
Smith Kate	Waiting At The End Of The Road	Velvet Tone - 1999 - V	Harmonians the	20s	
Smith Kate	When The Moon Comes Over The Mountain	Film Master - 1932		30s	
Smith Kate	When The Moon Comes Over The.	Columbia - 2516 - D		30s	
Smith Kate	When The Moon Comes Over.	Clarion - 5359 - C	Swanee Music her/	30s	
Smith Kate	You Try Somebody Else	Clarion - 5405 - C		30s	
Smith Mamie	Arkansas Blues - AC	Okeh - 4446	Jazz Hounds & her	20s	

Smith Mamie	Crazy Blues - AC	Okeh - 4169	Jazz Hounds	20s	
Smith Mamie	Dem Knock Out Blues - AC	Okeh - 4631	Jazz Hounds & her	20s	
Smith Mamie	Down Home Blues - AC	Okeh - 4446	Jazz Hounds & her	20s	
Smith Mamie	I Want A Jazzy Kiss - AC	Okeh - 4623	Jazz Hounds	20s	
Smith Mamie	It's Right Here For You - AC	Okeh - 4169	Jazz Hounds her	20s	
Smith Mamie	Jazzbo Ball - AC	Okeh - 4295	Jazz Hounds & her	20s	
Smith Mamie	Lovin Sam From Alabam - AC	Okeh - 4253	Jazz Hounds & her	20s	
Smith Mamie	Mean Daddy Blues - AC	Okeh - 4631	Jazz Hounds & her	20s	
Smith Mamie	Old Time Blues	Okeh - 4296	Jazz Hounds	20s	
Smith Mamie	Sax - O - Phoney Blues - AC	Okeh - 4416	Jazz Hounds & her	20s	
Smith Mamie	That Thing Called Love - AC	Okeh - 4113	Rega Orch	20s	
Smith Mamie	Wang Wang Blues - AC	Okeh - 4445	Jazz band her	20s	
Smith Mamie	You Can Have Him I Don't. AC	Okeh - 4670	Jazz Hounds & her	20s	
Smith Mamie	You Cant Keep A Good . . . - AC	Okeh - 4113	Rega Orch	20s	
Smith Mamie	You've Gotta See Mama_AC	Okeh - 4781		20s	
Smith Trixie	Freight Train Blues - AC	Paramont - 12211	Down Home Sycopators	20s	
Smith Trixie	Give Me That Old Slow Drag - AC	Black Swan - 14127	Jazz Masters the	20s	
Smith Trixie	Hoe Come You Do Me Like. - AC	Paramount - 12249	Henderson Fletcher?	20s	
Smith Trixie	Mining Camp Blues - AC	Paramount - 12256	Down Home Sycopators	20s	
Smith Trixie	My Man Rocks Me With . . . - AC	Black Swan - 14127	Jazz Masters the	20s	
Smith Trixie	Railroad Blues - AC	Paramount - 12262	Down Home Sycopators	20s	
Smith Trixie	Worlds Gone Jazz . . . - AC	Paramount - 12262	Down Home Sycopators	20s	
Smith Trixie	You Missed A Good Woman . . . AC	Black Swan - 2044	Harmony Eight J. P. Johnson's	20s	
Smith Trixie	You've Got To Beat Me - AC	Paramount - 12256	Down Home Sycopators	20s	
Smith Whispering Jack	Baby Face	Victor - 20229		20s	
Smith Whispering Jack	Me And My Shadow	Victor - 20626		20s	
Smith Whispering Jack	Poor Papa	Victor - 19978		20s	
Smith Whispering Jack	Then Ill Be Happy	Victor - 19856		20s	
Smith Willie*	Blues In The Night	Decca - 4125	Lunceford Jimmy Orch	40s	
Snow Hank	I Don't Hurt Anymore	Victor - 20 - 5698		50s	
Snow Valaida	Caravan	Bel - Tone - 7008	Sanns R. J. Orchestra.	40s	
Snow Valaida	Chlo-e	Parlophone - F - 1048		30s	
Snow Valaida	Coconut Head	Derby - 735	Mundy Jimmy Orch	40s	
Snow Valaida	Dixie Lee	Paraphone - F - 605	With Swing Acc.	30s	
Snow Valaida	Fool That I Am	Bel - Tone - 7001	Adlam Buzz Orch	40s	
Snow Valaida	Here Comes The Sun	Parlophone - F - 868	With Swing Acc.	30s	
Snow Valaida	High Hat Trumpet And Rhhythm	Paraphone - F - 559	With Swing Acc.	30s	
Snow Valaida	I Ain't Gonna Tell	Chess - 1555		50s	
Snow Valaida	I Cant Dance With Ants In My.	Parlophone - F - 118	Mason Billy & his Orch	30s	
Snow Valaida	I Must Have That Man	Parlophone - F - 575	With Swing Acc.	30s	
Snow Valaida	I Want A Lot Of Love	Paraphone - F - 575	With Swing Acc.	30s	
Snow Valaida	I Wish I Were Twins	Parlophone - F - 118	Mason Billy & his Orch	30s	
Snow Valaida	If I Only Had You	Bel - Tone - 7002	Adlam Buzz Orch	40s	
Snow Valaida	If You Don't Mean It	Chess - 1555		50s	
Snow Valaida	Imagination	Parlophone - F - 230	Mason Billy & his Orch	30s	
Snow Valaida	It Had To Be You	Parlophone - F - 140	Mason Billy & his Orch	30s	
Snow Valaida	Lovable And Sweet	Paraphone - F - 657	With Swing Acc.	30s	
Snow Valaida*	Maybe Im To Blame	Brunswick - A - 9407	Hines Earle Orch	30s	
Snow Valaida	Mood That I'm In The	Paraphone - F - 867	With Swing Acc.	30s	
Snow Valaida	My Heart Is Such A Fool	Apollo - 1185	Smith Bobby & Orch	40s	
Snow Valaida	Sing You Sinners	Paraphone - F - 230	Mason Billy & his Orch	30s	
Snow Valaida	Singing In The Rain	Paraphone - F - 165	Mason Billy & his Orch	30s	
Snow Valaida	Tell Me How Long This . . .	Derby - 729	Mundy Jimmy Orch	40s	
Snow Valaida	Until The Real Thing Comes.	Paraphone - F - 559	With Swing Acc.	30s	
Snow Valaida	You Bring Out The Savage In.	Parlophone - F - 140	Mason Billy & his Orch	30s	
Snow Valaida	You Let Me Down	Paraphone - F - 605	With Swing Acc.	30s	
Snow Valaida	Youre Not The Kind	Paraphone - F - 631	With Swing Acc.	30s	
Son House	My Black Mama	Paramount - 13042		30s	
Song Spinners	Coming In On A Wing And A . . .	Decca - 18553		40s	
Southern Ann	The Last Time I Saw Paris	Film Master - 1940		40s	
Southern Jeri	When I Fall In Love	Decca - 28224	Young Victor dir. Orch.	50s	
Spanials	Goodnight Sweetheart Goodnight	Vee - Jay - 107		50s	
Spencer Len	Arkansaw Traveler	Victor - Monarch - 1101		00s	
Spencer Len - NAP	Con Clancy's Christening - AC	Columbia - A31634		00s	
Spivey Victoria	Black Snake Blues	Okeh - 8338		20s	
Spivey Victoria	Blood Thirsty Blues	Okeh - 8531		20s	
Spivey Victoria	Christmas Morning Blues	Okeh - 8517		20s	
Spivey Victoria	Dirty T. B. Blues	Victor - 38570		30s	
Spivey Victoria	Dope Head Blues	Okeh - 8531		20s	
Spivey Victoria	E I O	Film Master - 1929		20s	
Spivey Victoria	Got The Blues So Bad	Okeh - 8401		20s	
Spivey Victoria	How Do They Do It	Okeh - 8713		20s	
Spivey Victoria	Long Gone Blues	Okeh - 8351		20s	

Spivey Victoria & L. Johnson	New Black Snake Blues	Okeh - 8626	vocal duet piano & guitar	20s	
Spivery Victoria*	Organ Grinder Blues	Okeh - 8620	Williams Clarence B 5	20s	
Spivey Victoria	Telephoning The Blues	Victor - 38646		20s	
Spivery Victoria & L. Johnson	Toothache Blues	Okeh - 8744		20s	
Sprague Carl T.	When The Works All . . . - AC	Victor - 19747		20s	
Stacks Tom"	Santa Clause Is Comin To Town	Decca - 264	Reser Harry Orch	30s	
Stacks Tom*	My One And Only	Columbia - 1213 - D	Clicquot Club Eskimos	20s	
Stafford Jo	Best Things In Life Are . . .	Capital - 15017	Weston Paul Orch	40s	
Stafford Jo*	Boy In Khaki a Girl In Lace A	Victor - 27947	Dorsey Tommy Orch	40s	
Stafford Jo	Carry Me Back To Old Virginny	Capital - 20051	Weston Paul Orch	40s	
Stafford Jo & Starlighters	Diamonds Are a Girl's Best.	Capital - 824		40s	
Stafford Jo	Early Autumn	Columbia - 39838	Weston Paul Orch	40s	
Stafford Jo*	For You	Victor - 36399	Dorsey Tommy Orch	40s	
Stafford Jo	Friend Of Yours A	Capital - 199	Weston Paul Orch	40s	
Stafford Jo	I Got A Sweetie	Columbia - 40451	Weston Paul Orch	50s	
Stafford Jo	I Love You	Capital - 153	Weston Paul Orch	40s	
Stafford Jo	I Never Loved Anyone	Capital - 15017	Weston Paul Orch	40s	
Stafford Jo	Im My Own Grandmaw	Capital - 15017		40s	
Stafford Jo	It Could Happen To You	Capital - 158		40s	
Stafford Jo	Ivy	Capital - 388	Weston Paul Orch	40s	
Stafford Jo	Jambalaya	Columbia - 39838	Weston Paul Orch	50s	
Stafford Jo & Starlighters	Just Reminiscin'	Capital - 15378	Weston Paul Orch.	40s	
Stafford Jo	Keep It A Secret	Columbia - 39891	Weston Paul Orch	50s	
Stafford Jo*	Little Man With A Candy C . . .	Victor - 27338	Dorsey Tommy Orch	40s	
Stafford Jo	Long Ago And Far Away	Capital - 153	Weston Paul Orch	40s	
Stafford Jo	Make Love To Me	Columbia - 40143		50s	
Stafford Jo*	Manhattan Seranade	Victor - 27962	Dorsey Tommy Orch	40s	
Stafford Jo	Over The Rainbow	Capital - 20049	Weston Paul Orch	40s	
Stafford Jo	Shrimp Boats	Columbia - 39581	Weston Paul Orch	50s	
Stafford Jo	Some Enchanted Evening	Capital - 544	Weston Paul Orch	40s	
Stafford Jo	Sunday Kind Of Love A	Capital - 388	Weston Paul Orch	40s	
Stafford Jo	Teach Me Tonight	Columbia - 40351	Weston Paul Orch	50s	
Stafford Jo*(C. G. Stump)	Temptation - NAP	Capital - 412	Ingel Red & the Natural 7	40s	
Stafford Jo*	That's for Me	Capital - 213	Weston Paul Orch	40s	
Stafford Jo	Yesterdays	Capital - 20050	Weston Paul Orch	40s	
Stafford Jo	You Belong To Me	Columbia - 39811	Weston Paul Orch	50s	
Stafford Jo*	You Took My Love	Victor - 20 - 1539	Dorsey Tommy Orch	40s	
Stafford Jo	Young And Foolish	Columbia - 40495		50s	
Stanley Aileen	Chicago - AC	Okeh - 4792		20s	
Stanley Aileen	Flaming Mamie - AC	Victor - 19283	Carpenter Billy 'Uke'	20s	
Stanley Aileen	Give Your Baby Lots Of Lovin	Victor - 21874		20s	
Stanley Aileen	Honey Rose - AC	Olympic - 14109		20s	
Stanley Aileen as Mamie Jones	Honey Rose - AC	Black Swan - 14116		20s	
Stanley Aileen & Billy Murray	I'm Gonna Dance With The Guy	Victor - 20822		20s	
Stanley Aileen	I Love My Baby - AC	Victor - 19950		20s	
Stanley Aileen	Im Nobodys Baby - AC	Vocalion - 14172		20s	
Stanley Aileen	Mandy 'N Me - AC	Olympic - 14113		20s	
Stanley Aileen as Mamie Jones	Mandy 'N Me - AC	Black Swan - 14116		20s	
Stanley Aileen	Singing The Blues Till . . . - AC	Victor - 18703		20s	
Stanley Frank & Henry Burr	Shine On Harvest Moon - AC	Zon - O - Phone - 5509		00s	
Star Kay	Steady Daddy	Capital(LP) - H211	Cavanaugh Dave	40s	x
Starr Kay	Ain't Misbehavin'	Modern - 680		50s	
Starr Kay	Bonapartes Retreat	Capital - 936	Busch Lou Orch.	50s	
Starr Kay	Hoop Dee Doo	Capital - 980.	De Vol Frank Orch.	50s	
Starr Kay	Good For Nothin Joe	Modern - 680		50s	
Starr Kay	It's The First Time	Capital - (LP) - H211		40s	
Starr Kay	Mercy Mercy Mercy	Capital - (LP) - H211		40s	
Starr Kay	On A Honky Tonk Hardwood Floor	Capital - 1856		50s	
Starr Kay	Poor Papa He's Got Nothin' . . .	Capital - (LP) - H211		40s	
Starr Kay	Second Hand Love	Capital - (LP) - H211		40s	
Starr Kay	Stop Dancing Up There	Film Master 1941		40s	
Starr Kay	Wheel Of Fortune	Capital - 1964	Mooney Hal Orch.	50s	
Starr Kay	Ya Gotta Buy Buy Buy For.	Capital - (LP) - H211		40s	
Starr Kay	You've Got To See Mama . . .	Capital - (LP) - H211		40s	
Starr Kay	You're The One I Care For	Capital - (LP) - H211		40s	
Starr Kay*	What A Difference A Day Made	Decca - 18620	Barnet Charlie Orch	40s	
Starr Kay*	Baby Me	Bluebird - B - 10372	Miller Glen Orch	40s	
Starr Kay*	Come Out Come Out Wherever.	Decca - 18620	Barnet Charlie Orch	40s	
Starr Kay*	Into Each Life Some Rain Must.	Decca - 18638	Barnet Charlie Orch	40s	
Starr Kay*	Share Croppin Blues	Decca - 24264	Barnet Charlie Orch	40s	
Starr Kay*	You Always Hurt The One You Love	Decca - 18638	Barnet Charlie Orch	40s	
Steel John	Whispering - AC	Victor - 18695		20s	
Steele Jon & Sondra	My Happiness	Damon - 11133		40s	

Stewart Cal	Uncle Josh Playing Golf - AC	Victor - 16226		10s	
Stewart Larry*	Sweet Dreams Sweetheart	Columbia - 36765	Nobel Ray Orchestra	40s	
Stewart Sisters*	On The Good Ship Lollipop	Victor - 24838	Connecticut Yankees	30s	
Stone Jessie	Ace In The Hole	Victor - 20 - 2554	Stone Jessie Orchestra	40s	
Stoneman Ernest	Titanic, The	Okeh - 40288		20s	
Storm Gale	Dark Moon	Dot - 15558		50s	
Storm Roy*	Continental The	Victor - 24735	Coburn Jolly & His Orch	30s	
Streisand Barbara	Keeping Out Of mischief	Columbia - CL - 2007		60s	
Streisand Barbara	My Man	Columbia - 3322		60s	
Streisand Barbara	Second Hand Rose	Columbia - 43469		60s	
Streisand Barbara	Who's Afraid Of The Big Bad . . .	Columbia - LP - CL - 2007		60s	
Strewart Redd*	Tennessee Waltrz	Victor - 20 - 2680	King Pee Wee & his G. W. C.	40s	
Sullivan Gene & Wiley Walker	When My Blue Moon Turns.	Okeh - 6374		40s	
Sullivan Maxine	Blue Skies	Vocalion - 3654		30s	
Sullivan Maxine	Brown Bird Singing, A	Vocalion - 4068		30s	
Sullivan Maxine	Corn Pickin	Victor - 26237	Thornhill Claude Orch.	30s	
Sullivan Maxine	Dark Eyes	Vocalion - 4015	Thornhill Claude Orch	30s	
Sullivan Maxine	Darling Nellie Gray	Vocalion - 3885	Thornhill Claude Orch	30s	
Sullivan Maxine	Easy To Love	Vocalion - 3848		30s	
Sullivan Maxine	Folks Who Love On The.	Vocalion - 3885	Thornhill Claude Orch	30s	
Sullivan Maxine	Hour Of Parting The	Columbia - 36341	Kirby John Orch.	40s	
Sullivan Maxine	Im Coming Virginia	Vocalion - 3654	Thornhill Claude	40s	
Sullivan Maxine	Im Happy About The Whole . . .	Victor - 26237	Thornhill Claude Orch.	30s	
Sullivan Maxine	It Aint Necessarily So	Victor - 26132		30s	
Sullivan Maxine	It Was A Lover And His Lass	Victor - 25810	Thornhill Claude Orch	30s	
Sullivan Maxine	Just Like A Gipsy	Decca - 3954		40s	
Sullivan Maxine	Kinda Lonesome	Victor - 26124		30s	
Sullivan Maxine	L'Amour, Toujours. L'Amour	Victor - 25895	Thornhill, Claude	30s	
Sullivan Maxine	Loch Lomond	Vocalion - 3654	Thornhill Claude	30s	
Sullivan Maxine	Moments Like This	Victor - 25802		30s	
Sullivan Maxine	Mutiny In The Nursery	Film Master - 1938	Armstrong Louis Orch	30s	
Sullivan Maxine	My Blue Heaven	Decca - 4154	vocal with orch.	40s	
Sullivan Maxine	My Curly Haired Baby	Decca - 18349		40s	
Sullivan Maxine	My Ideal	Decca - 18555		40s	
Sullivan Maxine	Nice Work If You Can Get It	Vocalion - 3848	Thornhill Claude	40s	
Sullivan Maxine	Night And Day	Victor - 26132		40s	
Sullivan Maxine	Say It With A Kiss	Victor - 26124		30s	
Sullivan Maxine	St. Louis Blues	Victor - 25895		30s	
Sullivan Maxine	When Your Lover Has Gone	Decca - 18555		30s	
Sullivan Maxine*	Don't Save Your Love For A . . .	Brunswick - 7957	Thornhill Claude Orch	30s	
Sullivan Maxine*	Down The Old Ox Road	Victor - 25894	Thornhill Claude Orch	30s	
Sullivan Maxine*	Gone With The Wind	Vocalion - 3595	Thornhill Claude Orch	30s	
Sullivan Maxine*	Midnight	Bluebird - B - 11288	Carter Benny Orch.	40s	
Sullivan Maxine*	Stop Youre Breaking My Heart	Vocalion - 3616	Thornhill Claude	30s	
Sunshine Boys-II	Don't Cry In My Beer	Okeh-06150		40s	
Sunshine Boys	I'm Crooning A Tune About June	Columbia-1834-D		20s	
Sunshine Boys	My Troubles Are Over	Columbia-1790-D		20s	
Sylvano Frank*	I'll Be Blue Just Thinking Of You	Brunswick - 4914	Jones Isham Orch	30s	
Sylvano Frank*	Swinging Down The Lane	Brunswick - 6161	Jones Isham Orch	30s	
Taft William Howard	Labor And Its Rights	Victor - 5553	SPOKEN WORD	10s	
Tampa Red	Let Me Play With Your Poodle	Bluebird - B - 37 - 0700		40s	
Tampa Red & Georgia Tom	It's Tight Like That	Vocalion - 1216		20s	
Taylor Eva	Baby Wont You Please Come	Okeh - 4740	Williams Clarence	20s	
Taylor Eva	Candy Lips(Im Stuck On You)	Okeh - 8484	Williams Clarence B. S.	20s	
Taylor Eva	Chloe-NAP	Okeh - 8585		20s	
Taylor Eva	Do It A Long Time Papa - AC	Okeh - 8073	Williams Clarence B. F.	20s	
Taylor Eva	I Wish I Could Skimmy Like . . .	Okeh - 4740	Williams Clarence	20s	
Taylor Eva	I've Found A New Baby	Okeh - 8286		20s	
Taylor Eva	Ive Got The Yes We Have . . .	Okeh - 4927	Williams Clarence B. F.	20s	
Taylor Eva	Jazzin Babies Blues - AC	Okeh - 8129	Williams Clarence Trio	20s	
Taylor Eva	Red Hot Flo (From Ko Ko Mo)	Okeh - 8463	Williams Clarence B. F.	20s	
Taylor Eva	She's Gone To Join The Song.	Okeh - 8518		20s	
Taylor Eva	Terrible Blues - AC	Okeh - 8183	Williams Clarence B. F.	20s	
Taylor Eva	Twelveth Street Rag - AC	Okeh - 8051	Williams Clarence	20s	
Taylor Eva	Uncle Sammy Here I Am	Bluebird - B - 11368	Williams Clarence B. F.	40s	
Taylor Eva	When The Red Red Robin . . .	Okeh - 40671	Williams Clarence B. F.	20s	
Taylor Eva	You Can Have My Man - AC	Okeh - 8050	Williams Clarence	20s	
Taylor Eva	You Don't Understand	Victor - V38575		20s	
Taylor Eva	You Missed A Good Woman . . .	Okeh - 8047	Williams Clarence	20s	
Taylor Eva	If I Could Be With You . . .	Okeh - 8444	Williams Clarence	20s	
Taylor Eva	What Makes You Love Me So	Victor - V38575		20s	
Taylor Eva & Clarence Williams	Oh Daddy Blues - AC	Okeh - 4927	Williams Clarence B. F.	20s	

Taylor Eva & Lawrence Lomax	Old Fashioned Love	Okeh - 8114		20s	
Taylor Eva*	Aint Misbehavin'	Columbia - 1891 - D	Charleston Chasers	20s	
Taylor Eva*	Cake Walking Babies From Home - AC	Okeh - 40321	Williams Clarence B. F.	20s	
Taylor Eva*	Everybody Loves My Baby - AC	Okeh - 8181	Williams Clarence B. F.	20s	
Taylor Eva*	Get It Fixed - AC	Okeh - 8267	Williams Clarence B. F.	20s	
Taylor Eva*	Im A Little Bluebird Looking . . .	Okeh - 40260	Williams Clarence	20s	
Taylor Eva*	Loving You The Way I Do	Columbia - 2309 - D	Charleston Chasers	20s	
Taylor Eva*	Mandy Make Up Your Mind - AC	Okeh - 40260	Williams Clarence B. F.	20s	
Taylor Eva*	Moanin Low	Columbia - 1891 - D	Charlestown Chasers	20s	
Taylor Eva*	My Man Is On The Make	Columbia - 2067 - D	Knickerbockers	30s	
Taylor Eva*	Shake That Thing - AC	Okeh - 8267	Williams Clarence B. F.	20s	
Taylor Eva*	Shout, Sister Shout !	Okeh - 8821	Williams Clarence W. Band	30s	
Taylor Eva*	Turn On The Heat	Columbia - 1989 - D	Charleston Chasers	20s	
Taylor Eva*	What Wouldent I Do For That Man	Columbia - 1989 - D	Charleston Chasers	20s	
Taylor Eva*	When Im Houskeeping For . . .	Columbia - 2072 - D	Kolster Dance Orch	30s	
Taylor Eva*	Youre Lucky To Me	Columbia - 2309 - D	Charleston Chasers	20s	
Taylor Eva* & Lil Hardin	Chizzlin Sam	Columbia - 2829 - D	Williams Clarence Jug Band	30s	
Taylor Eva* & Lil Hardin, others	Rhapsody In Love	Columbia - 14677 - D	Riffers	30s	
Taylor Eva* & Lil Hardin, others	Say It Isent So; Papa De Da.	Columbia - 14677 - D	Riffers	30s	
Taylor Eva - as Irene Gibbons	Im Busy And You Cant Come In	Columbia - 14362 - D	Williams Clarence J. B.	20s	
Taylor Eva - as Irene Gibbons	Jeannie I Dream Of Lilac Time	Columbia - 14362 - D	Williams Clarence J. B.	20s	
Taylor Eva - as Irene Gibbons	Last Go Round Blues - AC	Columbia - A - 3834	Williams Clarence	20s	
Taylor Eva - as Irene Gibbons	That Da Da Strain - AC	Columbia - A - 3834	Williams Clarence B. F.	20s	
Taylor Irene	No More Love	Vocalion - 2597		30s	
Taylor Irene*	Willow Weep For Me	Victor - 24187	Whiteman Paul Orch	30s	
Taylor Larry*	All This And Heaven Too	Bluebird - B - 10751	Barnet Charlie Orch	40s	
Taylor Tommy*	Little Girl	Bluebird - B - 10627	Ayres Mitchell & HFIM	40s	
Teagarden Jack	Blues After Hours	RCA Victor - 20 - 2458	vocal refrain & trombone by J. T.	20s	
Teagarden Jack & M. Blake	Sheik Of Araby	Brunswick - 8370	Teagarden Jack	40s	
Temple Shirley	That's What I Want for . . .	Film Master - 1936		30s	
Temple Shirley	On The Good Ship Lollipop	Film Master - 1934		30s	
Tharpe Rosetta	All Over This World	Decca - 8639		30s	
Tharpe Rosetta	God Don't Like It	Decca - 48022		40s	
Tharpe Rosetta	I Claim Jesus First	Decca - 8672	Vocal with guitar, bass, drums	30s	
Tharpe Rosetta	Just A Closer Walk With Thee	Decca - 8594		30s	
Tharpe Rosetta	Lonesome Road The	Decca - 2243		30s	
Tharpe Rosetta	Pure Religion	Decca - 8634		30s	
Tharpe Rosetta	Rock Me	Decca - 2243		30s	
Tharpe Rosetta	Silent Night	Decca - 48119		40s	
Tharpe Rosetta	Singing In My Soul	Decca - 8672	Vocal with guitar, bass, drums	30s	
Tharpe Rosetta	Sit Down	Decca - 8538		30s	
Tharpe Rosetta	Stand By Me	Decca - 8548		30s	
Tharpe Rosetta	That's All	Decca - 18496	Millinder Lucky Orch	40s	
Tharpe Rosetta	That's All	Decca - 2503		30s	
Tharpe Rosetta	There Is Something Within Me	Decca - 8548		30s	
Tharpe Rosetta	This Train	Decca - 2558		30s	
Tharpe Rosetta	White Christmas	Decca - 48119		40s	
Tharpe Rosetta & Red Foley	Have A Little Talk With Jesus	Decca - 29505		50s	
Tharpe Rosetta*	I Want A Tall Skinny Papa	Decca - 18386	Millinder Lucky Orch	40s	
Tharpe Rosetta*	Rock Daniel	Decca - 3956	Millinder Lucky Orch	40s	
Tharpe Rosetta*	Shout Sister Shout	Decca - 18386	Millinder Lucky Orch	40s	
Tharpe S. R. & Marie Knight	Up Above My Head There is . . .	Decca - 48090	Sam Price Trio with.	40s	
Tharpe Sister Rosetta	Devil Has Thrown Him Down	Decca - 48024		40s	
Tharpe Sister Rosetta	Forgive Me Lord And Try . . .	Decca - 48021		40s	
Tharpe Sister Rosetta	Jesus Taught Me How To Smile	Decca - 48021		40s	
Tharpe Sister Rosetta	Let That Liar Alone	Decca - 48023		40s	
Tharpe Sister Rosetta	Nobody Knows Nobody Cares	Decca - 48024		40s	
Tharpe Sister Rosetta	Strange Things Happening . . .	Decca - 48009		40s	
Tharpe Sister Rosetta	What Is The Soul Of A Man	Decca - 48022		40s	
Tharpe Sister Rosetta	What's The News	Decca - 48023		40s	
That Girl Quartet	Put Your Arms Around Me. - AC	Victor - 5827		40s	
Thomas George*	If I Could Be With You One . . .	Victor - 38118	McKinney's Cotton P.	20s	
Thomas Hociel	Adam And Eve Had The . . . - AC	Okeh - 8713		20s	
Tillman Floyd	I Gotta Have My Baby Back	Columbia - 20641		40s	
Tillman Floyd	Slippin Around	Columbia - 20581		40s	
Tilton Liz	There's Good Blues Tonight	Film Master - 1946		40s	
Tilton Martha*	And The Angels Sing	Victor - 26170	Goodman Benny Orch	30s	
Tilton Martha	Easy Street	Decca - 3843	Jenkins Gordon Orch	40s	
Tilton Martha*	I Let A Song Get Out Of My	Victor - 25840	Goodman Benny Orch.	30s	
Tilton Martha	Little Jive Is Good For You, A	Film Master - 1941		40s	
Tilton Martha*	Mama The Moon Is Here Again	Victor - 25720	Goodman Benny Orch	30s	
Tilton Martha	Say It With Love	Film Master - 1944		40s	

Tilton Martha*	Sing For Your Supper	Victor - 26099	Goodman Benny Orch	30s	
Tilton Martha	There's Good Blues Tonight	Capital - 244		40s	
Tilton Martha*	This Cant Be Love	Victor - 26099	Goodman Benny Orch.	30s	
Tilton Martha*	Whyd Ya Make Me Fall In	Victor - 25846	Goodman Benny Orch.	30s	
Tilton Martha	You Make Me Feel So Young	Capital - 272	Weston Paul Orch	40s	
Tilton Martha *	You Took The Words . . .	Victor - 25720	Goodman Benny Orch	30s	
Tim Tiny	Tip Toe Through The Tulips	Reprise - 0679		60s	
Tobin Louise*	I Dident Know What Time It Was	Columbia - 35211	Goodman Benny Orch.	30s	
Todd Dick	All This And Heaven Too	Bluebird - B - 10789		40s	
Todd Dick	Along The Santa Fe Trail	Bluebird - B - 10949		40s	
Todd Dick	As Long As We're Together	Victor - 25843		30s	
Todd Dick & the Three Reasons	At A Little Hot Dog Stand	Bluebird - B - 10183		30s	
Todd Dick	At A Table In A Corner	Bluebird - B - 10335		30s	
Todd Dick & the Three Reasons	Blue Evening	Bluebird - B - 10234		30s	
Todd Dick	Blue Orchids	Bluebird - B - 10397		30s	
Todd Dick	Bumming Around	Decca - 28583	Commanders	50s	
Todd Dick*	Change Partners	Victor - 26010	Clinton Larry Orchestra	30s	
Todd Dick	Deep Purple	Bluebird - B - 10072		30s	
Todd Dick	Gardenias	M. Ward. - M - 7554		30s	
Todd Dick & the Three Reasons	I Get Along Without You Very Well	Bluebird - B - 10150		30s	
Todd Dick	I'll Be Seeing You	Bluebird - B - 10636		40s	
Todd Dick	Im Old Fashioned	Bluebird - B - 11577		40s	
Todd Dick	Its The Talk Of The Town	Bluebird - B - 10559		30s	
Todd Dick	Lazy River	Bluebird - B - 10431		30s	
Todd Dick	Love Walked In	Bluebird - B - 7446		30s	
Todd Dick	Manhattan	Bluebird - B - 10374		30s	
Todd Dick	Marie Elena	Bluebird - B - 11156		40s	
Todd Dick	Nightingale Sang in . . .	Bluebird - B - 10912		40s	
Todd Dick	Oh Happy Day	Decca - 28506	Jerome Jerry	40s	
Todd Dick	One Morning In May	Bluebird - B - 10431		30s	
Todd Dick	Orchids For Remberance	Bluebird - B - 10805		40s	
Todd Dick & the Three Reasons	Penny Seranade	Bluebird - B - 10144		30s	
Todd Dick	Sixty Seconds Got Together	Victor - 26057	Joy Leonard Orch.	30s	
Todd Dick*	So Help Me	Victor - 26004	Clinton Larry Orchestra	30s	
Todd Dick	Thanks For The Memory	Bluebird - B - 7434		30s	
Todd Dick	Tis Autumn	Bluebird - B - 11531		40s	
Todd Dick	Together	Bluebird - B - 11156		40s	
Todd Dick $Four Bells	We Go Well Together	Bluebird - B - 11091		40s	
Todd Dick	When The Lights Go On Again	Bluebird - B - 11577		40s	
Todd Dick	White Cliffs Of Dover The	Bluebird - B - 11406		40s	
Todd Dick & the Three Reasons	Why Begin Again	Bluebird - B - 10234		30s	
Todd Dick	Worried Mind	Bluebird - B - 11142		40s	
Todd Dick	You've Got Me Crying Again	Bluebird - B - 10217		30s	
Tomlin Pinky	Im Gonna Swing While I'm . . .	Film Master - 1937		30s	
Tomlin Pinky	Ragtime Cowboy Joe	Decca - 2014	Sosnik Harry	30s	
Tomlin Pinky*	Object Of My Affection The	Brunswick - 7308	Grier Jimmy Orch	30s	
Torme Mel	Bewitched	Capital - 1000		50s	
Torme Mel	Blue Moon	Capital - 15428		50s	
Torme Mel - (Mel - Tones)	Born To Be Blue	Musicraft - 397	Burke Sonny Orch	40s	
Torme Mel	Careless Hands	Capital - 15379	Burke Sonny Orch	40s	
Torme Mel	Christmas Song The	Telaec - CD - 0000		90s	
Torme Mel	Comin Home Baby	Atlantic - 2165		60s	
Torme Mel	Do It Again	Musicraft - 534		40s	
Torme Mel	Its Dreamtime	Musicraft - 15102	Burke Sonny Orch	40s	
Torme Mel	Night And Day	Musicraft - 538		40s	
Torme Mel	Right Now	Atlantic - 2165		60s	
Torme Mel - (Mel - Tones)	Stranger In Town A	Decca - 18653		40s	
Torme Mel - (Mel - Tones)	What is This Thing Called Love	Musicraft - 390	Shaw Artie Orch	40s	
Torme Mel - (Mel - Tones)	Where Or When	Jewel - 4000		40s	
Torme Mel	White Christmas	Telaec - CD - 0000		90s	
Torme Mel - (Mel - Tones)	Willow Road	Musicraft - 363	Burke Sonny Orch	40s	
Tracy Arthur NAP	Marta Rambling Rosr Of The.	Brunswick - 6216		30s	
Travis Merle	Alimony Bound	Capital - 40115	vocal with country band	40s	
Travis Merle	Blues Stay Away From Me	Capital - 40254	vocal with country band	40s	
Travis Merle	Cincinatti Lou	Capital - 258	vocal with country band	40s	
Travis Merle	Dark As A Dungeon	Capital - 48001		40s	
Travis Merle	Divorce Me COD	Capital - 290	vocal with country band	40s	
Travis Merle	Fat Gal	Capital - 40026	vocal with country band	40s	
Travis Merle	I Am A Pilgrim	Capital - 48003		40s	
Travis Merle	John Henry	Capital - 48000		40s	

Travis Merle	Lost John Blues	Capital - 1737	Whippoorwills	50s	
Travis Merle	Merle's Boogie Woogie	Capital - 40026	vocal with country band	40s	
Travis Merle	Muscrat	Capital - 48003		40s	
Travis Merle	Nine Pound Hammer	Capital - 48000		40s	
Travis Merle	No Vacancy	Capital - 258	vocal with country band	40s	
Travis Merle	Over by Number Nine	Capital - 48002		40s	
Travis Merle	Sixteen Tons	Capital - 48001		40s	
Travis Merle	So Round So Firm So Fully . . .	Capital - 349	vocal with country band	40s	
Travis Merle	Start Even	Capital - 965	vocal with country band	40s	
Travis Merle	Sweet Temptation	Capital - 349	vocal with country band	40s	
Travis Merle	That's All	Capital - 48002		40s	
Travis Merle	Three Times Seven	Capital - 384	vocal with country band	40s	
Trinity Choir	Stand Up For Jesus - AC	Victor - 723		00s	
Tubb Ernest & Andrews Sisters	Bitin My Fingernails And . . .	Decca - 24592	Texas Troubadours &	40s	
Tubb Ernest	Blue Christmas	Decca - 46186	Texas Troubadours &	40s	
Tubb Ernest	Drivin Nails In My Coffin	Decca - 46019	Texas Troubadours &	40s	
Tubb Ernest	Everybody's Somebody's Fool	Decca - (45EP) - 31119	Texas Troubadours &	50s	
Tubb Ernest	Have You Ever Been Lonely	Decca - 24592	Texas Troubadours &	40s	
Tubb Ernest	I Love You Because	Decca - 46213		40s	
Tubb Ernest	Ill Get Along Somehow	Decca - 5825		40s	
Tubb Ernest	Its Been So Long Darlin	Decca - 6112	Texas Troubadours &	40s	
Tubb Ernest	Let The Little Girl Dance	Decca - (45EP) - 31119	Texas Troubadours &	50s	
Tubb Ernest	Letters Have No Arms	Decca - 46207		40s	
Tubb Ernest	Mean Mama Blues	Decca - 5976	Texas Troubadours &	40s	
Tubb Ernest	Mean Old Bed Bug Blues	Bluebird - B - 8899		30s	
Tubb Ernest	Rainbow At Midnight	Decca - 46018		40s	
Tubb Ernest	Slippin Around	Decca - 46173	Texas Troubadours &	40s	
Tubb Ernest	So Round So Firm So Fully . . .	Decca - 46040	Texas Troubadours &	40s	
Tubb Ernest	Soldier's Last Letter	Decca - 6098		40s	
Tubb Ernest & Red Foley	Tennessee Border 2	Decca - 46200		40s	
Tubb Ernest	Throw Your Love My Way	Decca - 46213	Texas Troubadours &	40s	
Tubb Ernest	Tomorrow Never Comes	Decca - 6106		40s	
Tubb Ernest	Try Me One More Time	Decca - 6093	Texas Troubadours &	40s	
Tubb Ernest	Walking The Floor Over You	Decca - 5958		40s	
Tubb Ernest	Warm Red Wine	Decca - 46175	Texas Troubadours &	40s	
Tucke Sophie	Some Of These Days	Columbia - 826 - D	Lewis Ted Orchestra	20s	
Tucker Sophie	After You've Gone	Okeh - 40827		20s	
Tucker Sophie	Ev'Ry Body Shimmies - AC	Aeolian - Vocalion - 12099	Five Kings Of Syncopation	10s	
Tucker Sophie	Fifty Million Frenchmen Cant.	Okeh - 40813		20s	
Tucker Sophie	Good Morning Judge - AC	Edison - 10529		10s	
Tucker Sophie	He Hadn't It Up Till Yesterday	Columbia - 5064		20s	
Tucker Sophie	He's A Good Man To Have Around	Victor - 21994		20s	
Tucker Sophie	High Brown Blues - AC	Okeh - 4565		20s	
Tucker Sophie	I Aint Got Nobody	Okeh - 40837		20s	
Tucker Sophie	Im Doing What Im Doing For.	Victor - 21993		20s	
Tucker Sophie	Im Glad My Daddy's In. - AC	Aeolian - Vocalion - 12090	Five Kings Of Syncopation	10s	
Tucker Sophie	Im The Last Of The Red Hot.	Victor - 21994		20s	
Tucker Sophie	Jig Walk - AC	Oheh - 4590		20s	
Tucker Sophie	Knock Wood - AC	Edison - Amberol - 10411		10s	
Tucker Sophie	Old King Tut - AC	Okeh - 4839	Rega Orchestra	20s	
Tucker Sophie	Pick Me Up And Lay Me. - AC	Okeh - 4590		20s	
Tucker Sophie	Red Hot Mama - AC	Okeh - 40129		20s	
Tucker Sophie	Some Of These Days - AC	Edison Amberol - 691		10s	
Tucker Sophie	Sophie Tucker for President	Mercury - 5839	Shapiro Ted/ piano	50s	
Tucker Sophie	That Lovin Rag - AC	Edison - 10630		10s	
Tucker Sophie	That Lovin Two - Step Man - AC	Edison - 10411		10s	
Tucker Sophie	Therell Be Some Changes Made	Okeh - 40813		20s	
Tucker Sophie	Wont You Be A Dear . . . - AC	Aeolian - Vocalion - 12090	Five Kings Of Syncopation	10s	
Tucker Sophie	You've Got To See Mama - AC	Okeh - 4817		20s	
Turner Joe*	Café Society Rag	Vocalion - 5186		30s	
Turner Joe*	Cherry Red	Vocalion - 4997	Johnson Pete & Boogie.	30s	
Turner Joe	Corrine Corrine	Atlantic - 1088		50s	
Turner Joe*	Corrine Corrine	Decca - 8563	Tatum Art & His Orch.	30s	
Turner Joe	Flip Flop And Fly	Atlantic - 1053		50s	
Turner Joe & Pete Johnson	Going Away Blues	Vocalion - 4607		40s	
Turner Joe	Honey Hush	Átlantic - 1001	& his band	50s	
Turner Joe	I Got A Gal For Every Night . . .	Decca - 28042	Johnson Pete trio	40s	
Turner Joe	Its The Same Old Story	Decca - 11001	Johnson Pete trio	40s	
Turner Joe*	Lovin Mama Blues	Vocalion - 5186	Johnson Pete & Boogie.	30s	
Turner Joe	Pitney Brown Blues	Decca - 18121	Fly Cats - and his/	40s	
Turner Joe*	Rainey Day Blues	Decca - 7824	Tatum Art & His Orch.	30s	
Turner Joe & Pete Johnson Trio	Rebecca	Decca - 11001	Johnson Pete trio	40s	

Turner Joe*	Rock Me Mama	Decca - 8577	Tatum Art & His Orch.	30s	
Turner Joe & Pete Johnson	Roll Em Pete	Vocalion - 4607		40s	
Turner Joe	Shake Rattle And Roll	Atlantic - 1026	Blue Kings & his	50s	
Turner Joe*	Six Twenty Seven 627 Stomp	Decca - 18121	Johnson Pete trio	40s	
Turner Joe	TV Mama	Atlantic - 1016		50s	
Turner Joe*	Wee Baby Blues	Decca - 8526	Tatum Art & His Orch.	30s	
Tuskegee Institute Singers	Nobody Knows The Trouble. AC	Victor - 18237		10s	
Tuskegee Institute Singers	Old Time Religion, The - AC	Victor - 18075		10s	
Twitty Conway	Mona Lisa	MGM - 12804		40s	
Vale Jerry	You Don't Know Me	Columbia - 40710		50s	
Vallee Rudy & Sportsmen	Alouetta	Enterprise - 181	Orchestra and	40s	
Vallee Rudy	As Time Goes By	Victor - 22773	Connecticut Yankees	30s	
Vallee Rudy	As Time Goes By - re - issue	Victor - 20 - 1526	Connecticut Yankees	40s	
Vallee Rudy	Babes In The Wood	Radio Master - 1932	Connecticut Yankees	30s	
Vallee Rudy	Besides An Open Fireplace	Victor - 22284	Connecticut Yankees	30s	
Vallee Rudy	Brother Can You Spare A Dime	Columbia - 2725 - D	Vallee Rudy Orch. & his	30s	
Vallee Rudy	By A Waterfall	Bluebird - B - 5171	Connecticut Yankees	30s	
Vallee Rudy	By The Fireside	HOW - D - 2 - 3	Vallee Rudy Orch. & his	30s	
Vallee Rudy	By The Sycamore Tree	HOW - B - 1 - 2	Connecticut Yankees	30s	
Vallee Rudy	Bye Aand Bye Sweetheart	Harmony - 905 - H	Connecticut Yankees	20s	
Vallee Rudy	Coquette	Victor - 21880	Connecticut Yankees	20s	
Vallee Rudy	Deep Night	Victor - 21868	Connecticut Yankees	40s	
Vallee Rudy	Doing The Raccoon	Velvet Tone - 1759 - V	Yale Men His	20s	
Vallee Rudy & Mae Questre	Don't Take Her Pooh Poop.	Film Master - 1931		30s	
Vallee Rudy	Drunkard Song The	Victor - 24721		30s	
Vallee Rudy	Everything I Have Is Yours	Victor - 24458		30s	
Vallee Rudy	Evry Day	Victor - 24827	Connecticut Yankees	30s	
Vallee Rudy	Faded Summer Love A	HOW - M - 4 - 5	Connecticut Yankees	30s	
Vallee Rudy	Flying Down To Rio	Victor - 24459	Connecticut Yankees	30s	
Vallee Rudy	Glory Of Love The	Melotone - M - 6 06 09	Connecticut Yankees	30s	
Vallee Rudy & Debutantes	Ha Cha Cha	Victor - 24722	Connecticut Yankees	30s	
Vallee Rudy	Harbor Lights	Bluebird - B - 7067	Connecticut Yankees	30s	
Vallee Rudy	Have You Met Miss Jones	Bluebird - B - 7238	Connecticut Yankees	30s	
Vallee Rudy	Heigh Ho Everybody Heigh Ho	Victor - 22029	Connecticut Yankees	20s	
Vallee Rudy	Home	HOW - A - 3 - 4	Connecticut Yankees	30s	
Vallee Rudy	Honey	Victor - 21869	Connecticut Yankees	20s	
Vallee Rudy	How Deep Is The Ocean	Columbia - 2724 - D	Connecticut Yankees	30s	
Vallee Rudy	How Do You Do It	Radio Master - 1932	Connecticut Yankees	30s	
Vallee Rudy	If I Had You	Harmony - 825 - H	Connecticut Yankees	20s	
Vallee Rudy	Im Just A Vagabond Lover	Victor - 21967	Connecticut Yankees	20s	
Vallee Rudy	Im Just A Vagabond Lover	Film Master - 1929		20s	
Vallee Rudy	Jug Of Wine A	Columbia - 2730 - D		30s	
Vallee Rudy	Lets Do It	Harmony - 808 - H	Connecticut Yankees	20s	
Vallee Rudy	Lets Put Out The Lights And.	Columbia - 2715 - D		30s	
Vallee Rudy	Life Is Just a Bowl Of Cherries	Victor - 22783	Connecticut Yankees	30s	
Vallee Rudy	Little Kiss Each Morning A	Film Master - 1931		30s	
Vallee Rudy	Little Kiss Each Morning A	Victor - 22193	Connecticut Yankees	30s	
Vallee Rudy	Lost In A Fog	Victor - 24721	Connecticut Yankees	30s	
Vallee Rudy	Lovable	HOW - D - 2 - 3	Connecticut Yankees	30s	
Vallee Rudy	Lover Come Back To Me	Velvet Tone - 1881 - V	Connecticut Yankees	20s	
Vallee Rudy	Lydia, The Tattooed Lady	Decca - 2708		30s	
Vallee Rudy & Gentlemen Songsters	Mad Dogs And Englishmen	Bluebird - B - 7135	Connecticut Yankees	30s	
Vallee Rudy	Marie	Harmony - 834 - H	Connecticut Yankees	20s	
Vallee Rudy	Meet Me In The Gloaming	Columbia - 2756 - D		30s	
Vallee Rudy	My Time Is Your Time	Victor - 21924	Connecticut Yankees	20s	
Vallee Rudy	Old Man Harlem	Columbia - 2764 - D	Connecticut Yankees	30s	
Vallee Rudy	Outside	Velvet Tone - 1857 - D	Connecticut Yankees	20s	
Vallee Rudy	P S I Love You	Victor - 24723	Connecticut Yankees	30s	
Vallee Rudy	Puddin Head Jones	Victor - 24475	Connecticut Yankees	30s	
Vallee Rudy	Riddle Me This	Radio Master - 1932	Connecticut Yankees	30s	
Vallee Rudy	S'posin'	Victor - 21998	Connecticut Yankees	20s	
Vallee Rudy	Shanghai Lil	Bluebird - B - 5172	Connecticut Yankees	30s	
Vallee Rudy	Stein Song	Victor - 22321	Connecticut Yankees	30s	
Vallee Rudy	This Is the Missus	Victor - 22783	Connecticut Yankees	30s	
Vallee Rudy	Three's A Crowd	Columbia - 2714 - D		30s	
Vallee Rudy	Thrill Me	Radio Master - 1932	Connecticut Yankees	30s	
Vallee Rudy	To Be Or Not To Be	Bluebird - B - 5118	Connecticut Yankees	30s	
Vallee Rudy & Gentlemen Songsters	Vieni Vieni	Bluebird - B - 7069	Connecticut Yankees	30s	
Vallee Rudy	Was That The Human Thing.	HOW - C - 1 - 2	Connecticut Yankees	30s	
Vallee Rudy	Way You Look Tonight The	Conquer - 8699	Connecticut Yankees	30s	
Vallee Rudy	Weary River	Victor - 21868	Connecticut Yankees	20s	
Vallee Rudy	When Your Hair Has Turned . . .	Victor - 22595	Connecticut Yankees	30s	

Vallee Rudy	When Yuba Plays The Rhumba.	Victor - 22742	Connecticut Yankees	30s	
Vallee Rudy & Gentlemen Songsters	Wiffenpoof Song, The	Bluebird - B - 7135	Connecticut Yankees	30s	
Vallee Rudy	Winchester Cathedral	Dot - (LP) - V - 6005		60s	
Vallee Rudy	Wooden Soldier And The . . .	HOW - C - 1 - 2	Connecticut Yankees	30s	
Vallee Rudy	Would You Like To Take A . . .	Victor - 22611	Connecticut Yankees	30s	
Vallee Rudy	You Try Somebody Else	HOW - MM - 4 - 5	Connecticut Yankees	30s	
Vallee Rudy	Youll Do It Some Day	Clarion - 5182 - C		20s	
Van & Schenck	For Me And My Gal - AC	Victor - 18258		11s	
Van & Schenck	When You And I Were Young - AC	Columbia - 3694 - D		20s	
Vance June*	This Little Piggie	Brunswick - 6747	Young Victor Orch	30s	
VanEmburgh H & R. Strom*	Continental, (The)	Victor - 24735	Coburn Jolly & His Orch	30s	
Vaughan Sarah	After Hours	Columbia - 39494		50s	
Vaughan Sarah	Aint Misbehavin'	Columbia - (45EP) - B - 211	Tredwell George All Stars	50s	
Vaughan Sarah	All Of You - (All Of Me)	Mercury - LP - 20383		50s	
Vaughan Sarah*	All Too Soon	Gotham - 105	Scott Tony & His D. B. C. S	40s	
Vaughan Sarah	Black Coffee	Columbia - 38462	Lippman Joe Orch.	30s	
Vaughan Sarah	Body And Soul	Musicraft - 494	Treadwell George Orch	40s	
Vaughan Sarah	Broken Hearted Melody	Mercury - 7147		50s	
Vaughan Sarah	Cant Get Out Of This Mood	Columbia - (45EP) - B - 211	Tredwell George All Stars	50s	
Vaughan Sarah	Come Rain Or Shine	Columbia - (45EP) - B - 211	Tredwell George All Stars	50s	
Vaughan Sarah	Deep Purple	Columbia - 39370	Faith Percy Orch	40s	
Vaughan Sarah	Detour Ahead	Mercury - LP - 20383		50s	
Vaughan Sarah	Don't Blame Me	Musicraft - 504	Treadwell George Orch	40s	
Vaughan Sarah	East Of The Sun	Columbia - (45EP) - B - 211	Tredwell George All Stars	50s	
Vaughan Sarah	East Of The Sun	Continental - 6031	Gillespie Dizzy Orch	40s	
Vaughan Sarah	Everything I Have Is Yours	Musicraft - 494	Treadwell George Orch	40s	
Vaughan Sarah	Goodniight My Love	Columbia - (45EP) - B - 211	Tredwell George All Stars	50s	
Vaughan Sarah	I Cant Get Started	MGM - 10762	Dale Ted Orch	50s	
Vaughan Sarah*	I Could Make You Love Me	Crown - 118	Kirby John Orch.	40s	
Vaughan Sarah	I Cover The Waterfront	Musicraft - 503	Treadwell George Orch	40s	
Vaughan Sarah	I Wanna Play House	Mercury - 70947	Peretti Hugo Orch	50s	
Vaughan Sarah	Id Rather Have A Memory Than A Dream	Continental - 6008	Birks J - (Dizzy Gillespie	40s	
Vaughan Sarah	Idle Gossip	Mercury - 70469	Peretti Hugo Orch	50s	
Vaughan Sarah	If You Could See Me Now	Musicraft - 380	Dameron Tadd Orch.	40s	
Vaughan Sarah	I'LL String Along With You	Mercury - LP - 20383		50s	
Vaughan Sarah*	I'LL Wait And Pray	De - Luxe - 2003	Eckstine Billy Orch	40s	
Vaughan Sarah	Im Crazy To Love You	Columbia - 38701	Lippman Joe Orch.	50s	
Vaughan Sarah*	Im Scared	Crown - 107	Kirby John Orch.	40s	
Vaughan Sarah	Im Through With Love	Musicraft - 499	Treadwell George Orch	40s	
Vaughan Sarah	Interlude	Continental - 6031	Gillespie Dizzy Orch	40s	
Vaughan Sarah	It Happened Again	Mercury - 70947	Peretti Hugo Orch	50s	
Vaughan Sarah	It Might As Well Be Spring	Columbia - (45EP) - B - 211	Tredwell George All Stars	50s	
Vaughan Sarah*	It Might As Well Be Spring	Crown - 108	Kirby John Orch.	40s	
Vaughan Sarah	Its Magic	Musicraft - 557	Maltby Richard Orch.	40s	
Vaughan Sarah	Like Someone In Love	Mercury - LP - 20383		50s	
Vaughan Sarah	Love Me Or Leave Me	Musicraft - 539		40s	
Vaughan Sarah	Lover Man	Guild - 1002	Gillespie D & All Star Q.	40s	
Vaughan Sarah	Make Yourself Comfortable	Mercury - 70469	Peretti Hugo Orch	40s	
Vaughan Sarah	Mean To Me	Continental - 6024	Birks, J - (Dizzy Gillespie	40s	
Vaughan Sarah	Mighty Lonesome Feeling	Columbia - 39873	Faith Percy Orch	50s	
Vaughan Sarah	Misty	Mercury - 7147		50s	
Vaughan Sarah	My Kinda Love	Musicraft - 398	Dameron Tadd Orch.	40s	
Vaughan Sarah	Nature Boy	Musicraft - 567		40s	
Vaughan Sarah	No Smoke Blues	Continental - 6061	Gillespie Dizzy Orch	40s	
Vaughan Sarah	Once In A While	MGM - 10549	Orch accompaniment	50s	
Vaughan Sarah	One I Love Belongs To Somebody . . .	Musicraft - 552	Dale Ted Orch	40s	
Vaughan Sarah	Send In The Clowns	Mainstream - MLR - 412	Griffin Paul arr.	70s	
Vaughan Sarah	September Song	Musicraft - 446	Wilson Teddy Quartet	40s	
Vaughan Sarah	Signing Off	Continental - 6024	Gillespie Dizzy Orch	40s	
Vaughan Sarah	Speak Low	Mercury - LP - 20383		50s	
Vaughan Sarah	Tenderly	Musicraft - 504	Treadwell George Orch	40s	
Vaughan Sarah	Thanks For The Memory	Mercury - LP - 20383		50s	
Vaughan Sarah	Thinking Of You	Columbia - 38925	Leyden Norman Orch.	50s	
Vaughan Sarah	Three Little Words	Mercury - LP - 20383		50s	
Vaughan Sarah	Time and Again	Musicraft - 337	Smith Stuff & His Trio	40s	
Vaughan Sarah	We're Through	H. R. S. - 1019	Wells Dicky Big Seven	40s	
Vaughan Sarah	What A Difference A Day Made	Musicraft - 552	Jones Jimmy Quartet	40s	
Vaughan Sarah	What More Can A Woman Do	Continental - 6008	Birks J - (Dizzy Gillespie	40s	
Vaughan Sarah	Whatever Lola Wants	Mercury - 70595		50s	
Vaughan Sarah*	You Go To My Head	Crown - 109	Kirby John Orch.	40s	
Vaughan Sarah	Youd Be So Nice To Come Home To	Mercury - LP - 20383		50s	
Vaughan Sarah	Youre Blasé	Musicraft - 394	Auld George Orch	40s	

Vaughan Sarah	Youre Not The Kind	Musicraft - 380	Dameron Tadd Orch.	40s	
Vinton Bobby	Blue Velvet	Epic - 9614		60s	
Vinton Bobby	There Ive Said It Again	Epic - 9638		60s	
vocal refrain*	Singing In The Bathtub	Brunswick - 4610	Bernie Ben Orch	20s	
Vocal refrain*	Who's Afraid Of The Big Bad . . .	Victor - 24410	Bestor Don Orchestra	30s	
Wain Bea*	Deep Purple	Victor - 26141	Clinton Larry Orcherstra	30s	
Wain Bea	Do I Worry	Victor - 27353		40s	
Wain Bea*	Dr. Rhythm	Victor - 25768	Clinton Larry Orchestra	30s	
Wain Bea*	Heart And Soul	Victor - 26046	Clinton Larry Orchestra	30s	
Wain Bea*	I Dreampt I Dwelt Im Marble Floors	Victor - 25789	Clinton Larry Orchestra	30s	
Wain Bea*	I Get Along Without You Very Well	Victor - 26151	Clinton Larry Orchestra	30s	
Wain Bea*	Marta	Victor - 25789	Clinton Larry Orchestra	30s	
Wain Bea*	Masquerade Is Over, The	Victor - 26151	Clinton Larry Orchestra	30s	
Wain Bea*	My Reverie	Victor - 26006	Clinton Larry Orchestra	30s	
Wain Bea*	Old Folks	Victor - 26056	Clinton Larry Orchestra	30s	
Wain Bea*	One Rose The	Victor - 25724	Clinton Larry Orchestra	30s	
Wain Bea*	Wake Up And Sing	Banner - 5 - 04 - 13	Kardos Gene & his Orch.	30s	
Wain Bea	You Can Depend On Me	Victor - 27353		40s	
Wain Bea*	You're An Education	Victor - 25794	Clinton Larry Orchestra	30s	
Wakely Jimmy	Beautiful Brown Eyes	Capital - 1393	Baxter Les Orchestra	50s	
Wakely Jimmy	I Love You So Much It Hurts	Capital - 15243		40s	
Wakely Jimmy	My Heart Cries For You	Capital - 1328		50s	
Wallace Frankie	Oklahoma Blues	Cameo - 8328	guitar his	20s	
Wallace Jerry	Shutters And Boards	Challenge - 9171	Levine Gus	60s	
Wallace Sippie	Dead Drunk Blues - AC	Okeh - 8449		20s	
Wallace Sippie	Jack O'Diamond Blues	Okeh - 8328		20s	x
Wallace Sippie	Jack Of Diamond Blues - AC	Okeh - 8328		20s	
Wallace Sippie	Lazy Man Blues - AC	Okeh - 8470		20s	
Wallace Sippie	Special Delivery Blues - AC	Okeh - 8328		20s	
Wallace Sippie	Up The Country Blues	Okeh - 8106		20s	
Waller Fats	Bye Bye Baby	Victor - 25388	Waller Fats & H. G. C. O. R	30s	
Waller Fats*	Dallas Blues	Columbia - 2527 - D	Lewis Ted Orch.	30s	
Waller Fats	Don't Let It Bother You	Victor - 24714	Waller Fats H. G. C. O. R	30s	
Waller Fats	Hold Tight, Hold Tight	Bluebird - B - 10116	Waller Fats & H. G. C. O. R	30s	
Waller Fats	Honeysuckle Rose	Film Master - 1943	on piano	40s	
Waller Fats	Honeysuckle Rose	Victor - 24826	Waller Fats & H. G. C. O. R	30s	
Waller Fats	Honeysuckle Rose	Victor - 25559	WallerFats & H. G. C. O. R	30s	
Waller Fats & Una Mae Carlisle	I Cant Give You Anything But Love	Victor - 20 - 1582	Waller Fats H. G. C. O. R	30s	
Waller Fats	I Wish I Were Twins	Victor - 24641	Waller Fats & H. G. C. O. R	30s	
Waller Fats	Im Crazy About My Baby	Columbia - 2428 - D		30s	
Waller Fats	Im Gonna Sit Right Down And	Victor - 25039	Waller Fats & H. G. C. O. R	30s	
Waller Fats	It's A Sin To Tell A Lie	Victor - 25342	Waller Fats & H. G. C. O. R	30s	
Waller Fats	Joint Is Jumping The	Victor - 25689	Waller Fats & H. G. C. O. R	30s	
Waller Fats	Lulu's Back In Town	Victor - 25063	Waller Fats & H. G. C. O. R	30s	
Waller Fats*(Rhythmakers)	Mean Old Bedbug Blues	Melotone - M - 12457	Rhythmakers Orch	30s	
Waller Fats*	Royal Garden Blues	Columbia - 2527 - D	Lewis Ted Orch	30s	
Waller Fats	S'posin'	Victor - 24515		30s	
Waller Fats	Truckin	Victor - 25116	Waller Fats & H. G. C. O. R	30s	
Waller Fats*(Rhythmakers)	Yellow Dog Blues	Melotone - M - 12481	Rhythmakers Orch	30s	
Waller Fats & J. Teagarden	You Rascal You	Columbia - 2558 - D	Teagarden Jack Orch	30s	
Waller Fats	Your Socks Don't Match	Bluebird - 30 - 0814		40s	
Waller Fats	Youre Not The Kind	Victor - 25353	Waller Fats & H. G. C. O. R	30s	
Walters Teddy*	There Ive Said It Again	Decca - 18670	Dorsey Jimmy Orch	40s	
Walters Teddy*	You Do Something To Me	Musicraft - 391	Shaw Artie Orch	40s	
Ward Helen*	All Through The Night	Columbia-2986-D	Rosenthal Harry Orch.	30s	
Ward Helen*	Blue Moon	Columbia - 3003 - D	Goodman Benny Orch.	30s	
Ward Helen*	Day In Day Out	Decca - 2703	Crosby Bob & His Orch.	30s	
Ward Helen*	Feeling Hight And Happy	Brunswick - 8123	Krupa Gene Orch	30s	
Ward Helen*	Glory Of Love The	Victor - 24316	Goodman Benny Trio.	30s	
Ward Helen*	Goody, Goody	Victor - 25245	Goodman Benny Trio.	30s	
Ward Helen*	How Am I To Know	Brunswick - 7893	Wilson Teddy Quartet	30s	
Ward Helen*	I Take To You	Columbia - 36174	Malneck Matty	40s	
Ward Helen*	One More Dream	Brunswick - 8123	Krupa Gene Orch	30s	
Ward Helen*	Sing Me A Swing Song And . . .	Victor - 25340	Goodman Benny Orch	30s	
Ward Helen*	There's A Small Hotel	Victor - 25363	Goodman Benny Orch	30s	
Ward Helen*	These Foolish Things Remind.	Victor - 25351	Goodman Benny Trio.	30s	
Ward Helen*	When A Lady Meeets A . . .	Victor - 25434	Goodman Benny Trio.	30s	
Ward Helen*	You Turned The Tables On Me	Victor - 25391	Goodman Benny Trio.	30s	
Ward Helen*	You're My Favorite Memory	Columbia - 36737	Wilson Teddy Quartet	40s	
Ward Helen*	Midnight - The Stars And You	Film Master - 1934	Osborne Will Orchestra	30s	
Ware Ozzie & Goodie Goodwin	Diga Diga Doo	Victor - 38008	Ellington Duke Orch	20s	
Ware Ozzie*	Bandanna Babies	Victor - 38007	Ellington Duke Orch	20s	
Warren Fran*	Early Autumn	Columbia - 37593	Thornhill Claude Orch	30s	

Washboard Sam	Bucket's Got A Hole In It	Bluebird - B - 7906	Washboard Band	30s	
Washington Dinah	And Her Tears Fell Like Wine	Radio Master - 1945	Hampton Lional Orch	40s	
Washington Dinah	Baby Get Lost	Mercury - 8148	blues vocal	40s	
Washington D. & Brook Benton	Baby You've Got What It Takes	Mercury - 71565		50s	
Washington Dinah	Bad Case Of The Blues, A	Mercury - LP - 20572		50s	
Washington Dinah	Big Long Slidin Thing	Mercury - 70392		50s	
Washington Dinah	Blue Gardinia	Mercury - LP - 36001		50s	
Washington Dinah	Blue Skies	Emarcy - 26032		50s	
Washington Dinah	Bye Bye Blues	Emarcy - 26032		50s	
Washington Dinah	Cold Cold Heart	Mercury - 5728	with orchestra	50s	
Washington Dinah	Evil Gal Blues	Keynote - K - 605	Hampton Lional Orch	40s	
Washington Dinah	Fast Movin Mama	Mercury - 5488	Stewart Teddy Orch	50s	
Washington Dinah	Fat Daddy	Mercury - 70214		50s	
Washington Dinah	Foggy Day A	Emarcy - 26032		50s	
Washington Dinah & Ravens	Hey Good Lookin	Mercury - 8257	with orchestra	50s	
Washington Dinah	I Cross My Fingers	Mercury - 5488	Carroll Jimmy Orch	50s	
Washington Dinah	I Don't Hurt Anymore	Mercury - 70439	Mooney Hal Orchestra	50s	
Washington Dinah	I Let A Song Get Out OF My Heart	Emarcy - 26032		50s	
Washington Dinah	I Only Know	Mercury - 8163	Stewart Teddy Orch.	40s	
Washington Dinah	I Wanna Be Loved	Mercury 8181	Jackson Chubby Q.	50s	
Washington Dinah	Juice Head Man Of Mine	Mercury - 8207	Stewart Teddy Orch.	50s	
Washington Dinah	Long John Blues	Mercury - 8148	blues vocal	40s	
Washington Dinah	Mixed Emotions	Mercury - 5728	with orchestra	50s	
Washington Dinah	No No No You Cant Have Two	Mercury - 70392		50s	
Washington D. & Brook Benton	Rockin Good Way A	Mercury - 71629		60s	
Washington Dinah	Soulville	Roulette - 4490		60s	
Washington Dinah	Teach Me Tonight	Mercury - 70497		50s	
Washington Dinah	This Bitter Earth	Mercury - LP - 20572		50s	
Washington Dinah	Trouble In Mind	Mercury - 8269	Cobb Jimmy Orchestra	50s	
Washington Dinah	TV Is The Thing	Mercury - 70214		50s	
Washington Dinah	Unforgettable	Mercury - LP - 20572		50s	
Washington Dinah	What A Difference A Day Made	Mercury - 71435		50s	
Washington Dinah	Wheel Of Fortune	Mercury - 8267	Cobb Jimmy Orchestra	50s	
Washington Laura *	Fool That I Am	Victor - 20 - 2470	Hawkins Erskine*	40s	
Waters Ethel	Aint Gonna Marry Aint . . . - AC	Black Swan - 14145	Henderson F. H. piano	20s	
Waters Ethel	Am I Blue	Columbia - 1837 - D	vocal	20s	
Waters Ethel	Am I Blue	Film Master - 1933		30s	
Waters Ethel	Am I Blue	Film Master - 1929		20s	
Waters Ethel	At The New Jump Steady Ball - AC	Black Swan - 14128	Jazz Masters & her	20s	
Waters Ethel	At The New Jump Steady Ball - AC	Cardinal - 2036	Albury's Blue & Jazz Seven	20s	
Waters Ethel	Baby What Else Can I Do	Bluebird - B - 10517	Mallory Edward Orch.	30s	
Waters Ethel	Back Bitin'Mama - AC	Vocalion - 14860	Waller Thomas piano	20s	
Waters Ethel	Birmingham Bertha	Columbia - 1837 - D	vocal	20s	
Waters Ethel	Birmingham Bertha	Film Master - 1929		20s	
Waters Ethel	Birth Of The Blues The	Sandy Hook - LP - 2060		50s	
Waters Ethel	Black Spatch Blues - AC	Paramount - 12230	Austin Lovie - Blues S.	20s	
Waters Ethel	Blues In My Heart	Victor - 20 - 2459	Chittison Herman Trio	40s	
Waters Ethel	Blues In The Night	Sandy Hook - LP - 2060		50s	
Waters Ethel & Diana Ross	Bread And Gravy	Film (TV) Master - 1969		60s	
Waters Ethel	Bread And Gravy	Bluebird - B - 10415	Mallory Edward Orch.	30s	
Waters Ethel	Bring The Greenbacks	Columbia - 14125 - D		20s	
Waters Ethel	Brown Baby - AC	Black Swan - 14145	Jazz Masters & the	20s	
Waters Ethel	Buds Won't Bud	Radio Master - 1943		40s	
Waters Ethel	Cabin In The Sky	LMS - L - 311	Meth Max Orch.	40s	
Waters Ethel & Rochester	Cabin In The Sky	Film Master - 1943		40s	
Waters Ethel	Cant Help Lovin That Man	Mercury - LP - 20051	Bean Regional - piano	40s	
Waters Ethel	Cant Help Lovin That Man	Radio Master - 1950	Henderson Fletcher piano	50s	
Waters Ethel	Careless Love	Victor - 20 - 2459	Chittison Herman Trio	40s	
Waters Ethel	Come Rain Or Shine/ Man I Love.	Sandy Hook - LP - 2060		50s	
Waters Ethel	Come Up And See Me Sometime	Brunswick - 6885	vocal	30s	
Waters Ethel	Craving Blues - AC	Paramount - 12313	Austin Lovie - Blues S.	20s	
Waters Ethel	Crucifixion, (The)	Mercury - LP - 20051	Beane Regional - piano	40s	
Waters Ethel	Crying Holy Onto The Lord	Word - 3173		60s	
Waters Ethel & B. McQueen	Dat Suits Me	Film Master - 1943	vocal - film	40s	
Waters Ethel	Deep River	Word - LP - 3100	Mickelson Paul Orch	50s	
Waters Ethel	Dinah	Radio Master - 1942		40s	
Waters Ethel	Dinah	Radio Master - 1933	Dorsey Brothers Orch	30s	
Waters Ethel	Dinah - AC	Columbia - 487 - D	Plantation Orch & her	20s	
Waters Ethel	Do I Know What Im Doing	Columbia - 1905 - D	vocal	20s	
Waters Ethel	Do What You Did Last . . . - AC	Columbia - 14380 - D	Johnson James P. piano	20s	
Waters Ethel	Don't Blame Me	Brunswick - 6617	vocal	30s	
Waters Ethel	Down Home Blues - AC	Black Swan - 2010	Williams Cody Jazz Masters	20s	
Waters Ethel	Down In My Soul	Bluebird - B - 11284	Mallory Edward Orch.	30s	

Waters Ethel	Dying With The Blues - AC	Black Swan - 2038	Jazz Masters & her	20s	
Waters Ethel & Reginal Beane	Easter Parade	Sandy Hook LP - 2060		50s	
Waters Ethel	Eli Eli	Sandy Hook - LP - 2060		50s	
Waters Ethel	Ethel Sings Em - AC	Black Swan - 14154	Johnson J. C. piano	20s	
Waters Ethel	Everybody Mess Around - AC	Columbia - 14153 - D	vocal	20s	
Waters Ethel	Frankie And Johnnie	Bluebird - B - 10038	Mallory Edward Orch.	30s	
Waters Ethel	Georgia Blues (II)	Columbia - 14565 - D		20s	
Waters Ethel	Georgia Blues - AC	Black Swan - 14120	Jazz Masters & her	20s	
Waters Ethel	Georgia On My Mind	Bluebird - B - 11028	Mallory Edward Orch.	30s	
Waters Ethel	Give All Your Love To Me	Radio Master - 1933	Dorsey Brothers Orch	30s	
Waters Ethel	Give Me A Heart To Sing To	Decca - 141	vocal	30s	
Waters Ethel	Go Back Where You . . . - AC	Columbia - 14093 - D	Ebony Four her	20s	
Waters Ethel	Happiness Is A Thing Called Joe	Film Master - 1943	vocal - film	40s	
Waters Ethel	Happiness Is A Thing Called Joe	MHR - 107	Beane Regional - piano	40s	
Waters Ethel	Happiness Is A Thing Called Joe	Radio Master - 1943		40s	
Waters Ethel	Harlem On My Mind	Columbia - 2826 - D	vocal	30s	
Waters Ethel	Harlem On My Mind	Radio Master - 1933	Dorsey Brothers Orch	30s	
Waters Ethel	He Brought Joy To My Soul - AC	Columbia - 14170 - D	vocal	20s	
Waters Ethel	Heat Wave	Columbia - 2826 - D	vocal	30s	
Waters Ethel	Heebie Jeebies - AC	Columbia - 14153 - D		20s	
Waters Ethel	His Eye Is On The Sparrow	Chancel - 2005	New York Crusade . . .	50s	
Waters Ethel	His Eye Is On The Sparrow	Film Master - 1952		50s	
Waters Ethel	Home	Columbia - 14214 - D		20s	
Waters Ethel	Honey In A Hurry	Continental - 1009	Heard J. C. Orch	40s	
Waters Ethel	Honey In The Honeycomb	Film Master - 1943		40s	
Waters Ethel	Honey In The Honeycomb	LMS - L - 311	Meth Max Orch.	40s	
Waters Ethel	Hottentot Potentate	LMS - L - 188	Wooding Russell Orch	30s	
Waters Ethel & Reginal Beane	How Are Things In Glocca Mora	Sandy Hook - LP - 2060		50s	
Waters Ethel	How Can I Face This Wearied World Alone	Decca - 4410	Mallory Edward Orch.	30s	
Waters Ethel	Hundred Years From Today A	Columbia - 2853 - D	Goodman Benny Orch.	30s	
Waters Ethel	Hundred Years From Today, A	MHR - 108	Beane Reginal piano	40s	
Waters Ethel	I Aint Gonna Sin No More	Decca - 141	vocal	30s	
Waters Ethel	I Am A Pilgrim	Word - LP - 3173	Beane Reginal piano	60s	
Waters Ethel	I Cant Give You Anything But . . .	Brunswick - 6517	Ellington Duke Orch	30s	
Waters Ethel	I Got It Bad And That Ain't Good	Sandy Hook - LP - 2060		50s	
Waters Ethel	I Got Rhythm	Columbia - 2346 - D	vocal	30s	
Waters Ethel	I Just Cant Stay Here By Myself	Word - LP - 8044	Mickelson Paul Orch	50s	
Waters Ethel	I Just Couldent Take It Baby	Columbia - 2853 - D	Goodman Benny Orch.	30s	
Waters Ethel	I Just Got A Letter	Bluebird - B - 10517	Mallory Edward Orch.	30s	
Waters Ethel	I Like The Way He Does It	Columbia - 14565 - D		20s	
Waters Ethel	I Shoulda Quit	Continental - 1009	Heard J. C. Orch	40s	
Waters Ethel	I Want My Sweet Daddy Now	Columbia - 14229 - D	vocal	20s	
Waters Ethel	I Want Somebody All . . . - AC	Paramount - 12230	Austin Lovie - Blues S.	20s	
Waters Ethel	If You Cant Hold The Man - AC	Columbia - 14134 - D	vocal	20s	
Waters Ethel	If You Don't Think I'll Do . . . - AC	Black Swan - 14148	Henderson Fletcher piano	20s	
Waters Ethel	If You Ever Change Your Mind	Bluebird - B - 10222	Mallory Edward Orch.	30s	
Waters Ethel	I'll Get Along Somehow	Decca - 1613	Mallory Edward Orch.	30s	
Waters Ethel	Im Coming Virginia	Columbia - 14170 - D	vocal	20s	
Waters Ethel	In His Care	Word - LP - 8044	Mickelson Paul Orch	50s	
Waters Ethel	Is It Well With Your Soul	Word - 3173	Beane Reginal piano	60s	
Waters Ethel	Its Only A Paper Moon	Mercury - LP - 20051	Beane Regional - piano	40s	
Waters Ethel	Ive Found A New Baby - AC	Columbia - 561 - D		20s	
Waters Ethel	Jazzin Babies Blues - AC	Black Swan - 14117	Smith Joe Jazz Masters	20s	
Waters Ethel	Jeeper Creepers	Bluebird - B - 10025	Mallory Edward Orch.	30s	
Waters Ethel	Jersey Walk	Columbia - 14182 - D		20s	
Waters Ethel	Kind Lovin Blues - AC	Black Swan - 14117	Smith Joe Jazz Masters	20s	
Waters Ethel	Kiss Your Pretty Baby Nice - AC	Black Swan - 2038	Jazz Masters & her	20s	
Waters Ethel	Little Black Boy	MHR - 117	Beane Regional - piano	40s	
Waters Ethel & Hall J. Choir	Little Black Sheep	Film Master - 1943	vocal - film	40s	
Waters Ethel	Lonesome Swallow	Columbia - 14411 - D	Johnson James P. piano	20s	
Waters Ethel	Lonesome Walls	Bluebird - B - 10222	Mallory Edward Orch.	30s	
Waters Ethel	Long Lean Lanky Mama	Columbia - 14458 - D	vocal	20s	
Waters Ethel	Long Lost Mama - AC	Black Swan - 14148	Jazz Masters & her	20s	
Waters Ethel	Lost Out Blues - AC	Black Swan - 14151	Jazz Masters	20s	
Waters Ethel	Loud Speakin Papa - AC	Columbia - 472 - D	Ebony Four her	20s	
Waters Ethel	Love Is The Thing	Brunswick - 6564	vocal	30s	
Waters Ethel	Love Turned The Light Out	LMS - L - 310	Meth Max Orch.	40s	
Waters Ethel	Make A Pallet On The . . . - AC	Columbia - 14125 - D		20s	
Waters Ethel	Mammy	Word - LP - 8044	Mickelson Paul Orch	50s	
Waters Ethel	Man Wanted	Continental - 1007	Heard J. C. Orch	40s	
Waters Ethel	Maybe Not At All - AC	Columbia - 14112 - D	Ebony Four her	30s	
Waters Ethel	Memories Of You	Columbia - 2288 - D	vocal	20s	
Waters Ethel	Memphis Man - AC	Black Swan - 14146	Jazz Masters	20s	

Waters Ethel	Midnight Blues - AC	Black Swan - 14146	Jazz Masters	20s	
Waters Ethel	Miss Otis Regrets	Decca - 140	vocal	30s	
Waters Ethel	Moonglow	Decca - 140	vocal	30s	
Waters Ethel	My Baby Shure Knows How To.	Columbia - 14411 - D	vocal	20s	
Waters Ethel & R. Beane	My Gal Sal	Sandy Hook - LP - 2060		50s	
Waters Ethel	My Handy Man	Columbia - 14353 - D	vocal	20s	
Waters Ethel	My Kind Of Man	Columbia - 2222 - D	vocal	30s	
Waters Ethel	My Man	Sandy Hook - LP - 2060		50s	
Waters Ethel	New York Glide, The - AC	Cardinal - 2036	Albury's Blue & Jazz Seven	20s	
Waters Ethel	No Mans Mama - AC	Columbia - 14116 - D	Ebony Four her	20s	
Waters Ethel	No One Can Love Me Like. - AC	Columbia - 379 - D	Ebony Four her	20s	
Waters Ethel	Oh Daddy Blues - AC	Black Swan - 2010	William's Cody Jazz Masters	20s	
Waters Ethel	Oh Joe Play That Trombone - AC	Black Swan - 14128	Jazz Masters & her	20s	
Waters Ethel & R. Bean	Oh Lady Be Good	Evergreen - LP - 6812	Beane Reginal piano	50s	
Waters Ethel	Old Man Harlem	Bluebird - B - 11028	Mallory Edward Orch.	30s	
Waters Ethel	One Man Nan - AC	Black Swan - 2121	Jazz Masters the	20s	
Waters Ethel	Organ Grinder Blues	Columbia - 14365 - D	Williams Clarence piano	20s	
Waters Ethel	Partners With God	Jubilee - 5274	Beane Reginal piano	50s	
Waters Ethel	Pichaninnay Blues - AC	Columbia - 472 - D		30s	
Waters Ethel	Please Don't Talk About Me When Im Gone	Columbia - 2409 - D	vocal	30s	
Waters Ethel	Pleasure Mad - AC	Vocalion - 14860	Bechet Sidney piano	20s	
Waters Ethel	Porgy	Columbia - 2184 - D	vocal	30s	
Waters Ethel	Porgy - (2nd recording)	Brunswick - 6521	Ellington Duke Orch	30s	
Waters Ethel	Push Out	Bluebird - B - 10415	Mallory Edward Orch.	30s	
Waters Ethel	Quicksands	Film Master - 1943	Basie Count Orch.	40s	
Waters Ethel	Raisin The Rent	Radio Master - 1933	Dorsey Brothers Orch	30s	
Waters Ethel	River Stay Way From My Door	Columbia - 2511 - D	vocal	30s	
Waters Ethel	Shadows On The Swanee	Brunswick - 6617	vocal	30s	
Waters Ethel	Shake That Thing - AC	Columbia - 14116 - D	Wright Pearl piano	20s	
Waters Ethel	Shine On Harvest Moon	Columbia - 2511 - D		30s	
Waters Ethel	Shoo Shoo Boogie Boo	Columbia - 1905 - D	vocal	20s	
Waters Ethel	Smile	Columbia - 12229 - D		20s	
Waters Ethel	Smoke Gets In Your Eyes	Radio Master - 1944	Kreuger Benny Orch	40s	
Waters Ethel	Some Day Sweetheart	Columbia - 14264 - D	vocal	20s	
Waters Ethel	Sometimes I Feel Like A Motherless Child	Mercury - LP - 20051	Beane Reginal piano	40s	
Waters Ethel	St. Louis Blues	Radio Master - 1941	Ellington Duke Orch	40s	
Waters Ethel	St. Louis Blues	Brunswick - 6521		30s	
Waters Ethel	Stand By Me	Word - LP - 8044	Mickelson Paul Orch	50s	
Waters Ethel	Stay On The Right Side . . .	Film Master - 1933		30s	
Waters Ethel	Stop Myself From Worrying Over You	Bluebird - B - 11284	Mallory Edward Orch.	30s	
Waters Ethel	Stormy Weather	Brunswick - 6564	vocal	30s	
Waters Ethel	Stormy Weather	Radio Master - 1941	Ellington Duke Orch	40s	
Waters Ethel	Stormy Weather	Radio Master - 1933	Connecticut Yankees	30s	
Waters Ethel	Stormy Weather	Radio Master - 1933	Dorsey Brothers Orch	30s	
Waters Ethel	Sugar - AC	Columbia - 14146 - D	vocal	20s	
Waters Ethel	Summertime	Radio Master - 1943		40s	
Waters Ethel	Summertime	MHR - 115	Beane Reginal piano	40s	
Waters Ethel	Supper Time	Film (TV) Master - 1969		60s	
Waters Ethel	Supper Time	MHR - 116	Beane Reginal piano	40s	
Waters Ethel	Sweet Georgia Brown - AC	Columbia - 379 - D	Ebony Four her	20s	
Waters Ethel	Sweet Man Blues - AC	Black Swan - 14154	Johnson J. C. piano	20s	
Waters Ethel	Sweet Man - AC	Columbia - 487 - D	Plantation Orch & her	20s	
Waters Ethel	Sympathetic Dan - AC	Columbia - 433 - D	Ebony Four her	20s	
Waters Ethel	Taking A Chance On Love	Radio Master - 1943		40s	
Waters Ethel	Taking A Chance On Love	LMS - L - 310	Meth Max Orch.	40s	
Waters Ethel & Rochester	Taking A Chance On Love	Film Master - 1943	vocal - film	40s	
Waters Ethel	Tell Em About Me - AC	Paramount - 12214	vocal	20s	
Waters Ethel	That Da Da Strain - AC	Black Swan - 14120	Jazz Masters & her	20s	
Waters Ethel	That's What Harlem Means To.	Sandy Hook - LP - 2060		50s	
Waters Ethel	Them Green Pastures	Radio Master - 1933	Dorsey Brothers Orch	30s	
Waters Ethel	There'll Be Some . . . - AC	Black Swan - 2021	Jazz Masters the	20s	
Waters Ethel	There'll Be Some Changes . . .	Radio Master - 1941	Trotter John Scott Orch	40s	
Waters Ethel	They Say	Bluebird - B - 10025	Mallory Edward Orch.	30s	
Waters Ethel	Thief In The Night	LMS - L - 188	Wooding Russell Orch	30s	
Waters Ethel	Three Little Words	Columbia - 2346 - D	vocal	20s	
Waters Ethel	Throw Dirt In Your Face	Evergreen - LP - 6812	Beane Reginal piano	50s	
Waters Ethel	Throw Dirt In Your Face - AC	Columbia - 14132 - D		20s	
Waters Ethel	To Be Or Not To Be	Radio Master - 1933	Dorsey Brothers Orch	30s	
Waters Ethel	Trade Mark	Brunswick - 02045		30s	
Waters Ethel	Traveling All Alone	Columbia - 1933 - D	vocal	20s	
Waters Ethel	True Blue Lou	Columbia - 1871 - D	vocal	20s	
Waters Ethel	Underneath The Harlem Moon	Film Master - 1933		30s	

Waters Ethel	Waiting At The End Of The Road	Columbia - 1933 - D	vocal	20s	
Waters Ethel	We Don't Need Each . . . - AC	Columbia - 14162 - D	vocal	20s	
Waters Ethel	West End Blues	Columbia - 14365 - D	Williams Clarence piano	20s	
Waters Ethel	What Did I Do To Be So Black And Blue	Columbia - 2184 - D	vocal	30s	
Waters Ethel	What Goes Up Must Come Down	Bluebird - B - 10207	Mallory Edward Orch.	30s	
Waters Ethel	What Goes Up Must . . .	Bluebird - B - 10207		30s	
Waters Ethel	When That Man Is Dead And Gone	Hollywood - 7391		40s	
Waters Ethel	When Your Lover Has Gone	Columbia - 2409 - D	vocal	20s	
Waters Ethel	Who Said Blackbirds Are Blue	Sandy Hook - LP - 2060	vocal, live	40s	
Waters Ethel	Without That Gal (Man)	Columbia - 2481 - D	vocal	30s	
Waters Ethel	Woman Without A Man A	Radio Master - 1942	vocal	40s	
Waters Ethel	Yesterdays	Sandy Hook - LP - 2060		50s	
Waters Ethel	You Brought A New Kind Of Love To Me	Columbia - 2222 - D	vocal	20s	
Waters Ethel	You Cant Do What My . . . - AC	Black Swan - 14151	Jazz Masters & her	20s	
Waters Ethel & male vocal	You Cant Do What My . . . - AC	Columbia - 14112 - D	Ebony Four her	20s	
Waters Ethel	You Cant Stop Me From Loving You	Columbia - 2481 - D	vocal	30s	
Waters Ethel	You Had It Coming To You	Bluebird - B - 10207	Mallory Edward Orch.	30s	
Waters Ethel	You Took Advantage Of Me	Sandy Hook - LP - 2060		50s	
Waters Ethel	You Took My Man	Continental - 1008	Heard J. C. Orch	40s	
Waters Ethel	You've Seen Harlem At Its Best	Brunswick - 6885	vocal	30s	
Waters Ethel	You'll Need Me When Im - AC	Paramount - 12214		20s	
Waters Ethel	Young At Heart	Sandy Hook - LP - 2060		50s	
Waters Ethel	Youre A Sweetheart	Decca - 1613	Mallory Edward Orch.	30s	
Waters Ethel	You're Going To Leave The . . .	Decca - 234		30s	
Waters Ethel & Reginal Beane	You're Just In Love	Sandy Hook - LP - 2060	Beane Reginal piano	50s	
Waters Ethel	Youre Lucky To Me	Columbia - 2288 - D	vocal	20s	
Waters Muddy	Rollin Stone	Chess - 1426		50s	
Watson El	Pot Licker Blues	Victor - 20951		30s	
Wayne Frances*	Kiss Goodnight A	Columbia - 36815	Herman Woody Orch	40s	
Weavers	Goodnight Irene	Decca - 27077		50s	
Webb Clifton*	Easter Parade	Victor - 24418	Reisman. Leo Orch	30s	
Weber Joan	Let Me Go Lover	Columbia - 40366		50s	
Weber Kay*	Foggy Day A	Decca - 1539	Crosby Bob & His Orch.	40s	
Weber Kay*	Welcome Stranger	Decca - 768	Dorsey Jimmy & His Orch.	30s	
Weber Kay*	Rhythm Of The Rain	Decca - 358	Dorsey Brothers Orch.	30s	
Weeks Ran*	With A Song In My Heart	Victor - 21923	Reisman. Leo Orch	20s	
Welch Elisabeth	Darktown Strutters Ball	HMV - B - 8144		30s	
Welch Elisabeth	Diga Diga Do	Brunswick - 4014	Hotsy Totsy Gang	20s	
Welch Elisabeth	Doing The New Low Down	Brunswick - 4014	Hotsy Totsy Gang	20s	
Welch Elisabeth	Harlem In My Heart	HMV - B - 8609		30s	
Welch Elisabeth	I Gotta Go	Vocalion - S - 16	Carter Benny Orch	30s	
Welch Elisabeth	Little Buttercup - Ill Never Be . . .	HMV - B - 8144		30s	
Welch Elisabeth	Poor Butterfly	Vocalion - 526	Carter Benny Orch	30s	
Welch Elisabeth	So Shy	HMV - B - 8144		30s	
Welch Elisabeth	Solomon	Victor - 35226	Noble Ray Orch.	30s	
Welch Elisabeth	Soft Lights And Sweet . . .	HMV - B - 8144	Noble Ray Orch.	30s	
Welch Elisabeth	That's How The First Song . . .	Vocalion - 526	Carter Benny Orch	30s	
Welch Elisabeth	When Day Is Done	HMV - B - 8144		30s	
Welch Elisabeth	When Lights Are Low	Brunswick - 7853	Carter Benny Orch	30s	
Welch Elisabeth	Just Like A Melody From . . .	HMV - B - 8144		30s	
Wells Kitty	Release Me	Decca - 29023		50s	
Wells Kitty & Red Foley	One By One	Decca - 29065		50s	
West Mae	I Found A New Way To Go . . .	Film Master - 1933		30s	
West Mae	Memphis Blues	Film Master - 1934	Ellington Duke Orch	30s	
West Mae	My Old Flame	Biltmore - 1014	Ellington Duke Orch	30s	
West Mae	My Old Flame	Film Master - 1934	Ellington Duke Orch	30s	
West Mae	Troubled Waters	Biltmore - 1014	Ellington Duke Orch	30s	
West Mae	Troubled Waters	Film Master - 1934	Ellington, Duke Orch	30s	
West Mae	When A St. Louis Woman . . .	Film Master - 1934	Ellington Duke Orch	30s	
Weston Cliff*	Alone	Victor - 25191	Dorsey Tommy Orch	30s	
Wheatshaw Peetie	Devil's Son In Law	Bluebird - B - 5451		30s	
Wheatshaw Peetie	King Of Spades	Conquer - 9028		30s	
White Josh - Pinewood Tom	Bed Springs Blues	Banner - 33404		30s	
White Josh - Pinewood Tom	Black Man	Banner - 33489		30s	
White Josh	Fare Thee Well	Ash - 348 - 1B		40s	
White Josh - Pinewood Tom	Greenville Sheik	ARC 6 - 05 - 63		30s	
White Josh	House I Live In The	Ash - 348 - 3B		40s	
White Josh	Howling Wolf Blues	Oriole - 8139		30s	
White Josh	I Got A Head Like A Rock	Ash - 348 - 1A		40s	
White Josh - Singing Christian	I Got A Home In That Rock	Banner - 22419		30s	
White Josh	Lazy Black Snake Blues	Oriole - 8159		30s	
White Josh	Low Cotton	Banner - 32858		30s	

White Josh - Pinewood Tom	Milkcow Blues	Banner - 33361		30s	
White Josh	One Meat Ball	Ash - 348 - 2B		40s	
White Josh	Outskirts Of Town	Ash - 348 - 2A		40s	
White Josh	Sometime	Decca - 23654		40s	
White Josh	Strange Fruit	Decca - 23654		40s	
White Josh - Pinewood Tom	Welfare Blues	Banner - 33024		30s	
White Josh	When I Lay Down And Die	Ash - 348 - 3A		40s	
Whiting Margaret	All Through The Day	Capital - 240	Kress Carl Orch	40s	
Whiting Margaret	Come Rain Or Shine	Capital - 247		40s	
Whiting Margaret & J. Wakely	Ill Never Slip Around Again	Capital - 40246		40s	
Whiting Margaret	Im Sorry But Im Glad	Capital - 15122	De Vol Frank & Orch	40s	
Whiting Margaret*	It Might As Well Be Spring	Capital - 214	Weston Paul Orch	40s	
Whiting Margaret	Ive Never Been In Love Before	Capital - 1213		50s	
Whiting Margaret	Little Girl Blue	Capital - 20116		40s	
Whiting Margaret*	Moonlight In Vermont	Capital - 182	Butterfield Billy & Orch	40s	
Whiting Margaret	My Foolish Heart	Capital - 934	De Vol Frank & Orch	50s	
Whiting Margaret	My Funny Valentine	Capital - 21017		40s	
Whiting Margaret	My Heart Stood Still	Capital - 21015		40s	
Whiting Margaret*	My Ideal	Capital - 134	Butterfield Billy & Orch	40s	
Whiting Margaret	Old Devil Moon	Capital - 360		40s	
Whiting Margaret	Pass The Peace Pipe	Capital - 15010		40s	
Whiting Margaret & J. Wakely	Slippin Around	Capital - 40224		50s	
Whiting Margaret*	That Old Black Magic	Capital - 126	Slack Freddie & Orch	40s	
Whiting Margaret	There Goes That Song Again	Capital - 182	Butterfield Billy & Orch	40s	
Whiting Margaret	Tree In The Meadow A	Capital - 15122	De Vol Frank orch	40s	
Whiting Margaret	You Do	Capital - 438		40s	
Whiting Margaret	Younger Than Springtime	Capital - 57 - 598	De Vol Frank orch	40s	
Whitney Joan*	In The Still Of The Night	Decca - 1467	Osborne Will & his orch.	40s	
Wiggins "Boodle It"	Keep A Knockin An You . . .	Paramount - 12662		20s	
Wiley Lee	Any Time, Any Day, Anywhere	Columbia - LP - 6169	Buskin Joe & his Strings	50s	
Wiley Lee	As Though You Were There	Gala - 4	Kaminsky Max Orch	40s	
Wiley Lee	Babys Awake Now	Gala - 1.	Buskin Joe Orch	40s	
Wiley Lee	Between The Devil And The . . .	Schirmer - 2009	Condon Eddie. (Quintette)	40s	
Wiley Lee	Body And Soul	Victor - 20 - 2322	Siday Eric Orch	40s	
Wiley Lee	But Not For Me	LMS - L - 284	Kaminsky Max Orch	30s	
Wiley Lee	Careless Love	Decca - 132		30s	
Wiley Lee	Down To Steamboat Tennessee	Commadore - 1507	Spanier M. & J. Stacy	40s	
Wiley Lee	Down With Love	Schirmer - 2008	Condon Eddie. (Sextette)	40s	
Wiley Lee*	Easy Come Easy Go	Brunswick - 6855	Green Johnny Orch	30s	
Wiley Lee	Easy To Love	LMS - L - 295	Weston Paul Orch	40s	
Wiley Lee	Find Me A Primitive Man	LMS - L - 296	Berigan Bunny Music	40s	
Wiley Lee	Fun To Be Fooled	Schirmer - 2010	Condon Eddie Orch	40s	
Wiley Lee	Funny Little World	Radio Master - 1934		30s	
Wiley Lee	Ghost Of A Chance A	Columbia - LP - CL - 6169	Buskin Joe & his. Strings	50s	
Wiley Lee	Glad To Be Unhappy	Gala - 2.	Kaminsky Max Orch	40s	
Wiley Lee	Got The South In My Soul	Radio Master - 1932	Connecticut Yankees	30s	
Wiley Lee*	Got The South In My Soul	Victor - 24048	Young Victor Orch	30s	
Wiley Lee	Hands Across The Table	Decca - 322		30s	
Wiley Lee	Heat Wave	Columbia - LP - CL - 6216	Freeman Stan & Walker, Cr	50s	
Wiley Lee	Here In My Arms	Gala - 1.	Kaminsky Max Orch	40s	
Wiley Lee	Here's Love In Your Eye	Radio Master - 1936	Rich Freddy Orch.	30s	
Wiley Lee	Hot - House Rose	LMS - L - 297	Berigan Bunny Music	40s	
Wiley Lee	How Long Has This Been Going On	LMS - L - 281	Kaminsky, Max Orch	30s	
Wiley Lee*	Hundred Years From Today A	Brunswick - 6775	Gray Glen Orch	30s	
Wiley Lee	I Don't Want To Walk Without You	Victor - LP - LSP - 1566	Butterfield Billy & Orch	50s	
Wiley Lee	I Gotta Right To Sing The Blues	Brunswick Master - 1933	Dorsey Brothers Orch.	30s	
Wiley Lee	If I Love Again	Radio Master - 1934		30s	
Wiley Lee	Im Coming Virgina	Radio Master - 1934	Whiteman Paul Orch	30s	
Wiley Lee	Its Only A Paper Moon	Victor - 20 - 1707	Stacy Jess	40s	
Wiley Lee	Ive Got Five Dollars	Gala - 2.	Buskin Joe Orch	40s	
Wiley Lee	Ive Got The World On A String	Schirmer - 2009	Condon Eddie. (Quintette)	40s	
Wiley Lee	Ive Got You Under My Skin	Decca - 15034	Young Victor Orch	30s	
Wiley Lee	Keeping Myself For You	Columbia - LP - CL - 6215	Freeman Stan & Walker, Cr	50s	
Wiley Lee	Lets Call It a Day	Brunswick Master - 1933	Dorsey Brothers Orch.	30s	
Wiley Lee	Lets Do It	LMS - L - 297	Berigan Bunny Music	40s	
Wiley Lee	Lets Fall In Love	Schirmer - 2011	Condon Eddie Orch	40s	
Wiley Lee	Lets Fly Away	LMS - L - 296	Berigan, Bunny Music	40s	
Wiley Lee	Little Birdie Told Me So A	Gala - 3	Buskin Joe Orch	40s	
Wiley Lee	Little Things You Used To Do	Radio Master - 1935		30s	
Wiley Lee	Looking At You	LMS - L - 294	Weston Paul Orch	40s	
Wiley Lee	Manhattan	Columbia - LP - 6169	Buskin Joe & his. Strings	50s	
Wiley Lee	Maybe Youll Be There	Victor - LP - LSP - 1566	Butterfield Billy & Orch	50s	
Wiley Lee	Memories - (Memories Of You)	Majestic - 7258	Stacy Jess	40s	

Wiley Lee	Moaning In The Morning	Schirmer - 2011	Condon Eddie Orch	40s	
Wiley Lee	Motherless Child	Decca - 132		30s	
Wiley Lee	Motherless Child - Swing Low.	Radio Master - 1934	Connecticut Yankees	30s	
Wiley Lee	My Melancholy Baby	Victor - LP - LSP - 1566	Butterfield Billy & Orch	50s	
Wiley Lee	My One And Only	LMS - L - 281	Kaminsky Max Orch	30s	
Wiley Lee	Oh Look At Me Now	Columbia - LP - 6169	Buskin Joe & his. Strings	50s	
Wiley Lee*	Repeal The Blues	Brunswick - 6855	Green Johnny Orch	30s	
Wiley Lee	Rise N Shine	Columbia - LP - CL - 6215	Freeman Stan & Walker, Cr	50s	
Wiley Lee	Robins And Roses	Radio Master - 1936		30s	
Wiley Lee	Sam And Delilah	LMS - L - 282	Kaminsky Max Orch	30s	
Wiley Lee	Ship Without A Sail A	Gala - 4	Kaminsky Max Orch	40s	
Wiley Lee	Should I Be Sweet	Columbia - LP - CL - 6215	Freeman Stan & Walker, Cr	50s	
Wiley Lee	Soft Lights And Sweet Music	Columbia - LP - CL - 6216	Freeman Stan & Walker, Cr	50s	
Wiley Lee	Someone To Watch Over Me	LMS - L - 282	Kaminsky Max Orch	30s	
Wiley Lee	Sometimes Im Happy	Columbia - LP - CL - 6215	Freeman Stan & Walker, Cr	50s	
Wiley Lee	Stormy Weather	Schirmer - 2008	Condon Eddie. (Sextette)	40s	
Wiley Lee	Street Of Dreams	Columbia - LP - 6169	Buskin Joe & his. Strings	50s	
Wiley Lee	Sugar	Commadore - 1507	Spanier M. & J. Stacy	40s	
Wiley Lee	Sweet And Low Down	LMS - L - 284	Kaminsky Max Orch	30s	
Wiley Lee	Swing Low Sweet Chariot	Radio Master - 1934		30s	
Wiley Lee	S'Wonderful	LMS - L - 282	Kaminsky Max Orch	30s	
Wiley Lee*	Take It From Me	Victor - 22757	Reisman. Leo Orch	30s	
Wiley Lee	Thousand Goodnights A	Radio Master - 1934	Whiteman Paul Orch	30s	
Wiley Lee	Three Little Words	Radio Master - 1936	Rich Freddy Orch.	30s	
Wiley Lee*	Time On My Hands	Victor - 22839	Reisman. Leo Orch	30s	
Wiley Lee	What Is Love	Decca - 15034	Young Victor Orch	30s	
Wiley Lee	When A Lady Meets A . . .	Coral - 61039	Prager Carol dir. Orch.	50s	
Wiley Lee	When Im With You	Radio Master - 1936		30s	
Wiley Lee	Wherever There's Love	Decca - 23393	Condon Eddie Orch	40s	
Wiley Lee	Why Shouldn't I	LMS - L - 295	Weston Paul Orch	40s	
Wiley Lee	Woman Alone With The Blues, A	Majestic - 7258	Stacy Jess	40s	
Wiley Lee	Woman's Intuition A	Columbia - LP - 6169	Buskin Joe & his. Strings	50s	
Wiley Lee	You Came To My Rescue	Radio Master - 1936	Rich Freddy Orch.	30s	
Wiley Lee	You Do Something To Me	LMS - L - 294	Weston Paul Orch	40s	
Wiley Lee	You Said It	Schirmer - 2010	Condon Eddie Orch	40s	
Wiley Lee	You Took Advantage Of Me	Gala - 3	Buskin Joe Orch	40s	
Wiley Lee	You Turned The Tables On Me	Radio Master - 1936	Rich Freddy Orch.	30s	
Wiley Lee	You've Got Me Crying Again	Brunswick Master - 1933	Dorsey Brothers Orch.	30s	
Wiley Lee & Billy Hughes	Youre An Old Smoothie	Brunswick - 6484	Young Victor Orch	30s	
Williams Andy	Love Story - theme	Columbia - 45317		70s	
Wilkins Robert	Rolling Stone	Victor - 21741		20s	
Williams Bert	Evry Body Wants A Key. - AC	Columbia - A2750		20s	
Williams Bert	Its Nobodys Business . . . - AC	Columbia - A - 2750		10s	
Williams Bert	Let It Alone - AC	Columbia - A3504		20s	
Williams Bert	Lonesome Alimony Blues - AC	Columbia - A2979	"Comedian"	20s	
Williams Bert	Nobody - AC	Columbia - A3423		10s	
Williams Bert & George Walker	Good Morning Carrie - AC	Victor - 997		00s	
Williams Frances	Doing The Uptown Lowdown	Film Master - 1933		30s	
Williams H. - Luke the Drifter	Be Careful Of The Stones Y . . .	MGM - 11309	Drifting Cowboys, with	50s	
Williams Hank	Blues Come Around The	MGM - 10212	Drifting Cowboys, with	40s	
Williams Hank	Cold Cold Heart	MGM - 10904	Drifting Cowboys, with	50s	
Williams Hank	Fly Trouble	MGM - 10073	Drifting Cowboys, with	40s	
Williams Hank	Half As Much	MGM - 11202	Drifting Cowboys, with	50s	
Williams Hank	Hey Good Lookin	MGM - 11000	Drifting Cowboys, with	50s	
Williams Hank	Honky Tonk Blues	MGM - 11160	Drifting Cowboys, with	50s	
Williams Hank	Honky Tonkin'	MGM - 10171	Drifting Cowboys, with	40s	
Williams Hank	Honky Tonkin'	Sterling - 210	Drifting Cowboys, with	40s	
Williams Hank	House Without Love A	MGM - 10696	Drifting Cowboys, with	50s	
Williams Hank	Howlin At The Moon	MGM - 10961	Drifting Cowboys, with	50s	
Williams Hank	I Cant Help It	MGM - 10961	Drifting Cowboys, with	50s	
Williams Hank	I Saw The Light	MGM - 10171	Drifting Cowboys, with	40s	
Williams Hank	Ill Never Get Out Of This W . . .	MGM - 11366	Drifting Cowboys, with	50s	
Williams Hank	Im So Lonesome I Could Cry	MGM - 10660	Drifting Cowboys, with	50s	
Williams Hank	Jambalaya	MGM - 11283	Drifting Cowboys, with	50s	
Williams Hank	Kaw - Liga	MGM - 11416	Drifting Cowboys, with	50s	
Williams Hank	Lonesome Whistle	MGM - 11054	Drifting Cowboys, with	50s	
Williams Hank	Long Gone Lonesome Blues	MGM - 10645	Drifting Cowboys, with	50s	
Williams Hank	Lost Highway	MGM - 10506	Drifting Cowboys, with	40s	
Williams Hank	Lovesick Blues	MGM - 10352	Drifting Cowboys, with	40s	
Williams H. - Luke the Drifter	Men With Broken Hearts	MGM - 10932	Drifting Cowboys, with	50s	
Williams Hank	Mind Your Own Business	MGM - 10461	Drifting Cowboys, with	40s	
Williams Hank	Moanin' The Blues	MGM - 10832	Drifting Cowboys, with	50s	

Williams Hank	My Bucket's Got A Hole In It	MGM - 10560	Drifting Cowboys, with	40s	
Williams Hank	My Sweet Love Aint Around	MGM - 10124	Drifting Cowboys, with	40s	
Williams H. - Luke the Drifter	No No, Joe	MGM - 10806	Drifting Cowboys, with	50s	
Williams H. - Luke the Drifter	Ramblin'Man	MGM - 11120	Drifting Cowboys, with	50s	
Williams Hank	Rootie Tootie	MGM - 10124	Drifting Cowboys, with	40s	
Williams Hank	Settin The Woods On Fire	MGM - 11318	Drifting Cowboys, with	50s	
Williams Hank	Six More Miles	MGM - 10271	Drifting Cowboys, with	40s	
Williams Hank	Take These Chains From My.	MGM - 11416	Drifting Cowboys, with	50s	
Williams Hank	Too Many Parties And Too . . .	MGM - 10718	Drifting Cowboys, with	50s	
Williams Hank	Wedding Bells	MGM - 10401	Drifting Cowboys, with	40s	
Williams Hank	Why Don't You Love Me	MGM - 10696	Drifting Cowboys, with	50s	
Williams Hank	Window Shopping	MGM - 11283	Drifting Cowboys, with	50s	
Williams Hank	You Win Again	MGM - 11318	Drifting Cowboys, with	50s	
Williams Hank	Your Cheatin Heart	MGM - 11416	Drifting Cowboys, with	50s	
Williams Leona	Sugar Blues - AC	Columbia - A3696	Dixie Band and her	20s	
Williams Midge*	Alabama Barbecue	Banner61217	Freeman Jerry Orch.	30s	
Williams Midge*	Copper Colored Gal	Melotone- 61217	Freeman Jerry Orch.	30s	
Williams Midge	Dinah	Radio Master-1936		30s	
Williams Midge	Don't Wake Up My Heart	Variety - 4192	Jazz Jesters, And Her	30s	
Williams Midge	Fortune Tellin Man	Variety - 3865	Jazz Jesters, And Her	30s	
Williams Midge	Greatest Mistake Of My Life.	Variety - 3961	Jazz Jesters, And Her	30s	
Williams Midge*	How Could You	Brunswick - 7842	Miff Mole's Molers	30s	
Williams Midge	I Know Now	Variety - 620	Jazz Jesters, And Her	30s	
Williams Midge	I Was Born To Swing	Variety - 639	Jazz Jesters And Her	30s	
Williams Midge	Im Getting Sentimental Over . . .	Variety - 566	Jazz Jesters And Her	30s	
Williams Midge	Im In A Happy Frame Of Mind	Variety - 04026	Jazz Jesters And Her	30s	
Williams Midge	Lady Is A Tramp, The	Variety - 3865	Jazz Jesters And Her	30s	
Williams Midge*	Lazybones	Columbia Master	Missman Tommy Orch.	30s	
Williams Midge	Love Is Like Wiskey	Variety - 04026	Jazz Jesters And Her	30s	
Williams Midge	Mama's Gone Goodby	Variety - 3900	Jazz Jesters And Her	30s	
Williams Midge	Oh Miss Hannah	Variety - 639	Jazz Jesters, And Her	30s	
Williams Midge	One Rose The	Variety - 670	Jazz Jesters And Her	30s	
Williams Midge	Singing The Blues Till . . .	Variety - 3900	Jazz Jesters And Her	30s	
Williams Midge	That Old Feeling	Variety - 620	Jazz Jesters And Her	30s	
Williams Midge	Walkin' The Dog	Variety - 519	Jazz Jesters And Her	30s	
Williams Midge*	Organ Grinder's Swing	Columbia - 3151 - D	Froeba Frank Swing Band	30s	
Williams Midge*	Lazybones	Nippon-Columbia Master		30s	
Williams Midge	Dinah	Radio Master-1938		30s	
Williams Midge	Lazybones	Radio Master-1938		30s	
Williams Sisters	He's The Last Word	Victor - 20425	Pollack Ben Californians his	20s	
Williams Sisters	Sam The Old Accordian Man	Victor - 20452	Missman Tommy Orch.	20s	
Williams Tex	Shame On You	Okeh - 6731	Cooley Spade	40s	
Williams Tex*	Detour	Columbia-36935	Cooley Spade	40s	
Williamson Sonny Boy	Wee Wee Hours	Decca - 7898	Blues Singing	40s	
Williamson Sonny Boy	Worried Life Blues	Decca - 7888	Blues Singing	40s	
Willis Chuck	C C Rider	Atlantic - 1130		50s	
Wilson Dooley	As Time Goes By	Decca - 40006		40s	
Wilson Dooley	As Time Goes By	Film Master - 1942		40s	
Wilson Dooley	Knock On Wood	Decca - 4008		40s	
Wilson Dooley	Knock On Wood	Film Master - 1942		40s	
Wilson Edith	Birmingham Blues - AC	Columbia - A - 3558	Original Jazz Hounds &	20s	
Wilson Edith	Black And Blue	Brunswick - 4385		40s	
Wilson Edith	Daddy Change Your Mind - AC	Columbia - 14008 - D	Jazz Band her	20s	
Wilson Edith	Double Crossin' Papa - AC	Columbia - 14054 - D	Jazz Hounds & her	20s	
Wilson Edith	Easing Away From Me	Delmark (LP) - 637		70s	
Wilson Edith	Frankie - AC	Columbia - A - 3506	Dunn's Johnny Jazz H	20s	
Wilson Edith	He May Be Your Man - AC	Columbia - A - 3635	Dunn's Johnny Jazz H	20s	
Wilson Edith	He's A Mean Mean Man - AC	Columbia - 14054 - D	Jazz Hounds & her	20s	
Wilson Edith	Hesitating Blues	Delmark (LP) - 637		70s	
Wilson Edith	Hey Hey Boogie	Delmark (LP) - 637		70s	
Wilson Edith	How Come You Like Me . . . - AC	Columbia - 14027 - D	Jazz Hounds & her	20s	
Wilson Edith	I Don't Care And I Don't - AC	Columbia - 14008 - D	Jazz Band	20s	
Wilson Edith & Doc Strain	It's Gonna Be A Cold . . . - AC	Columbia - 14066 - D	Jazz Hounds & her	20s	
Wilson Edith	Mammy Im Thinking Of . . . - AC	Columbia - A - 2634	Dunn's Johnny Jazz H	20s	
Wilson Edith	Muscle Sholes Blues - AC	Columbia - 14027 - D	Jazz Hounds & her	20s	
Wilson Edith	My Handy Man Aint Handy . . .	Delmark (LP) - 637		70s	
Wilson Edith	My Handy Man Aint Handy . . .	Victor - 38624		30s	
Wilson Edith	My Man Is Good For Nothing.	Brunswick - 4685		20s	
Wilson Edith	Old Time Blues	Columbia - A - 3506		20s	
Wilson Edith	Penalty Of Love The	Victor - 23010	Milage Makers	20s	
Wilson Edith	Poppa Mamma Blues	Delmark (LP) - 637		70s	
Wilson Edith	Rules And Regulations . . . - AC	Columbia - A - 3653	Dunn's Johnny Jazz H	20s	
Wilson Edith	Slow Creepin Blues	Delmark (LP) - 637		70s	

Wilson Edith	Take It Cause Its All Yours - AC	Columbia - A - 3634	Dunn's Johnny Jazz H	20s	
Wilson Edith	That Same Dog	Delmark (LP) - 637		70s	
Wilson Edith & Doc Strain	There'll Be Some Changes Made	Columbia - 14066 - D		20s	
Wilson Edith	Twiddlin	Delmark (LP) - 637		70s	
Wilson Edith	Vamping Liza Jane - AC	Columbia - A - 3479	Origional Jazz Hounds &	20s	
Wilson Edith	Wicked Blues - AC	Columbia - A - 3558	Origional Jazz Hounds. &	20s	
Wilson Lena	My Man O' War	Columbia - 14618 - D		30s	
Wilson Lena	Taint Nobodys Buz - ness . . . AC	Victor - 19085	Porter Grainger piano	20s	
Wilson Lena	Triflin Blues - AC	Victor - 19085	Porter Grainger piano	20s	
Wilson Nancy	That's What I Want for . . .	Capital - 5084		60s	
Wolf Howling	Little Red Rooster	Chess - 1804		50s	
Wood Gloria*	Woody Wood - Pecker	Columbia - 38197	Kyser Kay and his Orch.	40s	
Wright Edythe & Cliff Weston*	Santa Clause Is Coming To Town	Victor - 25145	Dorsey Tommy Orch	30s	
Wright Edythe*	Did I Remember	Victor - 25341	Dorsey Tommy Orch	30s	
Wright Edythe*	Music Goes Round And Round	Victor - 25201	Dorsey Tommy Orch	30s	
Wright Edythe*	On Treasure Island	Victor - 25144	Dorsey Tommy Orch	30s	
Wright Edythe*	Big Apple The	Victor - 25652	Dorsey Tommy Orch	30s	
Wynn Nan*	Whats New	Victor - 26336	Kemp Hal	30s	
Young Margaret	Big Bad Bill Is Sweet . . . - AC	Brunswick - 2736		20s	
Young Margaret	Ukulele Lady - AC	Brunswick - 2861		20s	

PRINTED SOURCES—BOOKS, MAGAZINES & OTHERS—IN ADDITION TO THE PREVIOUSLY NOTED "MEDIA LOCATIONS" WITHIN TEXT. /

Allen, Walter C., 1973	Hendersonia, The Music of . . .	Jazz Monographics, NJ	Highland Park, NJ	Book
Anderson, Jervis 1982	This Was Harlem 1900 - 1950.	Farrar Straus Giroux, New York, NY.		Book
Baumerger, Rob 1992	Syncopating Harmonists. Boswell S.	Take Two Records, Los Angeles, CA.		CD NOTES
Briggs, Asa 1965	Golden Age Of Wireless, The	Oxford Univ. Press, New York, Toronto		Book
C. Escott, G. Merritt & W. MacEwen	Hank Williams - The Biography	Little Brown And Company1994	Boston, New York, London	Book
Carroll Renee 1933 (Carroll had been a hat check girl for Vincent Sardi-owner of Sardi's Restaurnat in NYC).	In Your Hat	Macaulay Pub	New York, NY.	Book
Castle Irene 1958	Castles In The Air.	Doubleday & Co, Inc. Garden City, NY.		Book
Cohn, Lawrence - edited 1993	Nothing But The Blues	Abbeville Press 1993	New York, London, Paris	Book
Dance, Stanley - Notes in CD 1987	Essential Count Basie, The	Columbia - CK - 40608	New York, NY	CD NOTES
Davis, Frances 1995	History Of The Blues The	Hyperion, NY 1995	New York, New York	Book
Elder, Jane Lenz, 2002	Alice Faye, A Life Beyond The Silver Screen,	University Press Of Mississippi, Jackson, MS.		Book
Erenberg, Lewis A. 1998	Swinging The Dream	Univ. Of Chicago Press, Chicago, London		Book
Feather, Leonard 1955	Encyclopedia Of Jazz	Horizon Press 1955	New York, NY	Book
Feather, Leonard 1966	The Blues From Then Till Now	RCA Victor LP - PRM - 235	Printed In USA	LP NOTES
Friedwald, Will 2002	Stardust Melodies	Pantheon Books, NY	New York, New York	Book
Giants Of Jazz CD - 53281	Rainey, Gertrude "Ma" Madam	Promo Sound AG		CD NOTES
Giddins, Gary 2001	Bing Crosby - A Pocket Full Of Dreams	Little, Brown And Company	Boston - New York - London	book
Godrich J. & R. M. W. Dixon	Blues & Gospel Records 1902 - 42	Storyville Publications	London	Book
Granlund Nils T., S. Feller & R. Handcock 1957 (Granlund, also noted in text as (N.T.G), was famously a Theater & night club proprioter in NYC and Los Angeles).	Blonds, Brunettes & Bullets.	D.Mc Kay Pub.	New York, NY	Book
Harrison, Daphne Duval 1988	Black Pearls - Blues Queens . . .	Rutgers Univ. Press	New Brunswick, London	Book
Hirschhorn, Clive 1981	Hollywood Musical The /1927 - 79	Crown Publishers	New York, NY	Book
Holiday Billie & William Duffy 1956	Lady Sings The Blues 1956	Penquin Books	New York, NY	Book
Johnson James Wendon	Black Manhattan	Alfred A Knopf, NYC, NY	New York, NY	Book
Joslin Gene	Joslin's Jazz Journals	self published	Parsons, Kansas	Journal
Kay, Lenny 2004	You Call it Madness	Villard Books, NY.	New York, NY.	Book
Klingaman William K 1989	Year Of The Great Crash The, 1929	Harper & Row, NY, Grand Rapids, Philadelphia, St. louis, San Francisco, London, Singapore, Sydney, Tokyo		
L. Maslon & M. Kantor 2004	Broadway - The American Musical - PBS	Bulfinch Press	New York, Boston	Book
Loescher Greg/publisher	Goldmine /Various issues	Krause Publications, Iola, Wi		magazine
Lomax, Alan 1960	Folk Songs Of North America	Doubleday, NY, London	New York, London, Toronto	Book
Lomax, Alan 1993	The Land where The Blues Began	Pantheon Books, NY	New York	Book
M. Waller & A. Calabrese1977	Fats Waller	Schirmer Books, NY, NY.		Book
Malone Bill C 1981	Classic Country Music/Smithsonian	Smithsonian Inst.	Washington, DC	LP NOTES
Mattfeld Julius, edited by Abel Green Julius Mattfeld-music librarian/ Abel Green-the very influencial (high-brow) Variety magazine editor, (1930s-60s).	Variety Music Cavalcade, 2nd edition. Of Vocal and Instrumental Music-2nd edition	Prentiss-Hall, 1966	Highland Park, NJ	Book
Maxwell Gibbert 1974	Helen Morgan Her Life And Legend	Hawthorn Books	New York	Book

Mello, Ed & Mc Bride, Tom 1950	Crosby On Record, 1926 - 1950	Mellows Music	San Francisco, Ca	Book
Mezzrow M, & B. Wolfe 1946	Really The Blues	Random House, New York, NY		Book
Miller, P & Gingrich, A - edited & introd	Esquires Jazz Book - 1944	JJ Little & Ives Company	New York, NY	Book
Miller, P & Gingrich, A - edited & introd	Esquires Jazz Book - 1945	JJ Little & Ives Company	New York, NY	Book
Mize, Dr. J. T. H. 1946	Bing Crosby Style The - Crosbyana	Who Is Who In Music Inc LTD	Chicago, Il	Book
Morgenstern, D. 1974	Rainey, Ma	Milestone M - 47021	Berkeley, Ca	LP NOTES
Morgenstern, D. 2004	Living With Jazz	Pantheon Books, NY		Book
Murry, Albert.1985	Good Morning Blues - Autobiography Of Count Basie	Random House, New York, NY		Book
Numerous articals	Billboard	New York, NY.		Magazine
Numerous articals	Cash Box	New York, NY.		magazine
Numerous articals	Down Beat	New York, NY.		magazine
Numerous articals	Melody Maker	London, England		magazine
Numerous articals	Metrodome	New York, NY.		magazine
Osborne, J. P.1977 - 1978	Record Digest - Bi - Weekly	Osborne, J. P. - Publisher & Editor, Prescott, AZ		Publication
Perry, Hamilton Darby, 1983	Libby Holman, Body And Soul	Little, Brown & Co.	Boston, Toranto	Book
Pleasants, Henry 1974	Great American Pop Singers The	Simon & Schuster	New York, NY	Book
Porterfield, Nolan 1992	Rodgers, Jimmie	Bear Family Records	Germany	CD NOTES
Puch, Ronnie, 1996	Ernest Tubb - The Texas Troubadour	Duke University Press	Durham, London	Book
Raymond, Jack 1982	Show Music On Record, 1890s - 1980s	Fred Ungar Publishing	New York, NY	Book
Rosen, Jody.2002	White Christmas - The Story of	SCRIBNER, NY, 2002	New York,	Book
Ross Nathaniel Lester 1976	Mills Brothers - Four BoysAnd A Guitar	Sunbeam Records, Van Nuy, CA. (MFC - 15)		LP NOTES
Rust, Brian - 1997	Fabulous **Lena Horne** The	Living EraAJA5238	ASV LTD London	CD NOTES
Sanjek. R & D. Sanjek - update - 1996	Pennies From Heaven	DA Capo Press, NY, NY(Russel & David Sanjek)		Book
Sann, Paul 1957	Lawless Decade The	Bonanza Books	New York, NY	Book
Schaden, Chuck 2003	Speaking Of Radio	Nostalgia Digest Press, Morton Grove, IL		Book
Schenker, Anatol 1997	Sarah Vaughan1944 - 1946	CLASSICS RECORDS	Classics958 - France	CD NOTES
Smulyan, Susan 1994	Selling Radio 1920 - 1934	Smithsonian Inst. Press. Washington, London		Book
Stambler Irwin 1965	Encyclopedia Of Popular Music	St Martin's Press	New York, NY	Book
Thorndike Joseph J - editor - 1965/	American Heritage - Special 1920s	American Heritage Pub. Co., NY, NY/Aug.1965/		Magazine
Travis Dempsey 1983	Autobiography Of Black Jazz An	Urban Research Institute Inc		Book
Vallee, Rudy & GilMckean, 1962	My Time Is Your Time - Rudy Vallee	Ivan Obolensky, INC	New York, NY	Book
Vanguard Records, 1997	Century Of Ragtime A	Various Contributers	Santa Monica, CA	CD NOTES
Various Record Catalog listings	Various Record Companies			catalog
Various Record Catalog sleeves	Various Record Companies			sleeves
Walker, Leo, 1964	Wonderful Era Of The Great Dance Bands	Doubleday & Co, Inc, Garden City, NY.		Book
Walker, Stanley 1933	Night Club Era, The	Frederick A Stokes C0, NY. NY 0		Book
Waterhouse, Don - adapted 1993	Ella Fitzgerald - The Young Ella	Jazz ArchivesN66	EPM Paris, France	CD NOTES
Waterhouse, D - textof Jean Buzelin	Sister Rosetta Tharpe . . .	Fremeaux & assoc 1994	FA017 Vincennes France	CD NOTES
Waters, Ethel, with C. Samuels 1951	His Eye Is On The Sparrow	Doubleday & Co.	Garden City, NY	Book
Whitburn, Joel 1973	Top Pop Records 1955 - 72	Record Research Inc	Menomonee Falls, Wi	Book
Whitburn, Joel 1986	Pop - Memories - 1890 - 54	Record Research Inc	Menomonee Falls, WI	Book
Williams, Iain Cameron, 2002	Underneath A Harlem Moon	Continuum	London, New York	Book
Wlaschin Ken 1979	Illistrated Encyclopedia Of The World's Great Movie Stars The	Salamander Book, Harmony Books, NY, NY		Book
Wolfe, Charles K., 1999	Good Natured Riot A - The Birth of . . .	CM Foundation & Vanderbilt . . .	Nashville, TN	Book
Wolfe, C - Intro Johnny Cash 2000	Carter Family, In The Shadow . . .	Bear Family Records	Germany	CD NOTES
Wondrich David 2003	Stomp And Swerve American Music Gets Hot 1843 - 1924	A Cappella Books, Chicago Review Press		Book
Work, John W. 1940	American Negro Songs And Spirituals	Bonanza Books - Crown	New York, NY	Book
Wright Laurie - editor 1966+	Storyville - numerous issues/	Storyville Publications, London, England		magazine
Wyman, Billwith R. Havers2001	Bill Wyman's Blues Odyssey	DK Publishing, NY2001	New York, NY	Book

INDEX—SUPPLEMENT MUSICIANS ACCOMP./ARTIST & REPERTOIRE—RELATED TO TEXT

Aaron Al/trumpet/studio bands/Georgie Auld/	**Sarah Vaughan/**
Aaronson Irving /pianist/studio bands/ & his Commanders/	**Bing Crosby**
Abbott Larry/clarinet/kazoo/studio bands/	**Lee Morse/Annette Hanshaw/**
Acuff Roy/fiddle/vocals/his Crazy Tennesseans/his Smoky Mountain Boys/	**Roy Acuff/**
Addison Bernard/guitar/studio bands/Billie Holiday/	**Edith Wilson/Mills Brothers/Billie Holiday/Ella Fitzgerald/**
Adlam Buzz - Buzz Adlam's Band/	**Valaida Snow/**
Adler Henry/drums/studio bands/Larry Clinton/	**Bea Wain/Dick Todd/**
Adler Larry/harmonica/pianist/studio bands/	**Ruth Etting/**
Ahern Bob/jazz guitar/studio bands/Stan Kenton/Metronome All Star/	**Nat King Cole/June Christy/ Frank Sinatra/**
Aiken Bud/trombone/studio bands/Ethel Waters Jazz Masters/	**Ethel Waters/**
Aiken Gus/clarinet/studio bands/Ethel Waters Jazz Masters/	**Ethel Waters/**
Albright Max/drum/studio bands/Nelson Riddle/	**Frank Sinatra/**
Albury's Blue And Jazz Seven/	Lucille Hegamin/**Ethel Waters/**
Alderman Myrl/pianist/Studio bands/radio masters / - possible studio recordings - Ruth Etting?/	**Ruth Etting?**
Aless Tony/pianist/ studio band	**Dinah Washington**
Alexander Charlie/pianist/studio bands/Louis Armstrong/	**Louis Armstrong/**
Alexander Texas/own guitar/studio bands/	Texas Alexander/
Alexy Bob/trumpet/studio bands/Tommy Dorsey/	**Frank Sinatra/Jo Stafford/Connie Haines/**
All Stars - and her - Ivie Anderson/studio band/	**Ivie Anderson/**
Allen Ed/trumpet/studio bands/	**Bessie Smith/**
Allen George/clarinet/studio bands/Louisville Jug Band/	**Jimmie Rodgers/**
Allen Henry/as 'Red'/trumpet/studio bands/Louis Armstrong/Don Redman/ Artie Shaw/	**Louis Armstrong/Victoria Spivey/**Hoagy Carmichael/**Harlan Lattimore/ Lena Horne/**
Allen Tracy/trombone/studio Bands/Georgie Auld/	**Sarah Vaughan/**
Alley Shirley Lee/fiddle/studio bands/songwriter/	**Jimmie Rodgers/**
Almanac Singers/incl. Woody Guthrie	Almanac Singers/**Woody Guthrie/**
Alpert (Trigger) Herman/bass/studio bands/Glenn Miller/Axel Stordahl/	Tex Beneke/Paula Kelly/Modernaires/**Ella Fitzgerald/Frank Sinatra/**
Alter Louis/pianist/studio bands/	**Helen Morgan/Ruth Etting/**
Alvie And His Little Band/	**Anita O'Day/**
Ambrose Burt/dance band/studio bands/own Orch./(British)	Dennis Dennis/Ann Shelton/
American Quartet/	American Quartet/Billy Murry/
Ammons Albert/pianist/arrainger/1941 film - released 1944/	**Lena Horne/**
Ammons Albert/pianist/arrainger/studio bands/	**Joe Turner/**
Ammons Gene/tenor saxophone/studio bands/Billy Eckstine/	**Billy Eckstine/Sarah Vaughan/**
Anderson Don/trumpet/studio bands/Freddie Slack/	**Ella Mae Morse/ Johnny Mercer/**
Anderson Gene/pianist/studio bands/	**Victoria Spivey/**
Andrews Dope/trombone/studio bands/M. S. Jazz Hounds/	**Mamie Smith/**
Anthens Bill/tronbone/studio bands/Freddie Slack/	**Ella Mae Morse/**
Anthony Ray/trumpet/studio bands/Glenn Miller/	Tex Beneke/Paula Kelly/Modernaires/
Arbello Fernando/trombone/studio bands/M. W. Jazz Jesters/	**Midge Williams/**
Arden - Ohman Orchestra/(Victor Arden & Phil Ohman)/studio band/	Snappy Lambert/Burt Lorin
Arkarov James/cello/studio bands/Nelson Riddle/	**Nat King Cole/**
Arlen Harold/pianist/songwriter/arrainger/some vocals/	Harold Arlen/
Armstead Lester/pianist/studio bands/	**Ethel Waters/**
Armstrong Lil/as - (Lil Hardin) Armstrong/pianist/studio bands/Louis Armstrong's Hot Seven/	**Louis Armstrong/Eva Taylor/Alberta Hunter/Jimmie Rodgers/**
Armstrong Louis & Orchestra/ - Film Masters - 1932/1932/1938/1946/1956/	**Louis Armstrong/Maxine Sullivan/Billie Holiday/Bing Crosby/**
Armstrong Louis/ & his hot Five/trumpet/own vocals	**Louis Armstrong**May Alex/Kid Ory/
Armstrong Louis/ & His Hot Seven/trumpet/own vocals	**Louis Armstrong**
Armstrong Louis/ & his Orchestra//trumpet/own vocals	**Louis Armstrong/**Hoagy Carmichael/**Mills Brothers/**
Armstrong Louis/ & his Sebastian New Cotton Club/trumpet/own vocals	**Louis Armstrong/**Lional Hampton/
Armstrong Louis/cornet accomp/ studio bands/	Baby Mack//Virginia Liston/Sippie Wallace/Maggie Jones//Hociel Thomas/
Armstrong Louis/cornet accomp/studio bands/	**Blanche Calloway/Alberta Hunter/Eva Taylor/Ma Rainey/Victoria Spivey/ Jimmie Rodgers/**

Armstrong Louis/cornet accomp/studio bands/	Butterbeans & Susie/Ida Cox/Coot Grant/Bertha Chippie Hill/**Bessie Smith/ Trixie Smith/Clara Smith/**
Armstrong Louis/studio band/ & His All Stars/his Orch./	**Louis Armstrong/**Velma Middleton/**Bing Crosby/**
Arnheim Gus Orchestra/hotel band/dance band/ - Radio Master - 1931/1931/	**Bing Crosby/**Loyce Whitman/
Arnheim Gus/pianist/studio bands/Ambassador Hotel Cocoanut Grove Orch./	**Russ Columbo/Bing Crosby/**Loyce Whiteman/Rhythm Boys/**Eddie Cantor/**
Arnold Kokomo/own guitar/	Kokomo Arnold/
Arnspiger Herman/steel guitar/studio bands/Light Crust Dough Boys/Bob Wills/	Tommy Duncan/
Arodin Sidney/clarinet/studio bands/Louis Prima/	**Louis Prima/**
Arus George/trombone/studio bands/Artie Shaw/Tommy Dorsey/L. Shaffer/G. Siravo/	**Billie Holiday/Frank Sinatra/Jo Stafford/Connie Haines/Perry Como/**
Asby Irving/jazz guitar/studio bands/Nat Cole Trio/	**Nat King Cole/**Nellie Luther/
Ashford Bo/trumpet/studio bands/Ozzie Nelson/	**Ozzie Nelson/Harriet Hilliard/**
Atchison Tex/fiddle/studio bands/Gene Autry Trio/Patsy Montans Prarie Ramblers/	**Gene Autry/**Patsy Montana/
Atkins Chet/guitar/arrainger/Red Foley/radio/studio bands/	**Red Foley/**Homer And Jethro/(later) Carter Family/Hank Snow/**Eddy Arnold/**
Attlesey Bob or (as Bob Shelton)/ukelule/studio bands/	Shelton Brothers/**Jimmie Davis/**Leon Chappelear/
Attlesey Joe or (as Joe Shelton)/mandolin/studio bands/	Shelton Brothers/**Jimmie Davis/**Leon Chappelear/
Auburn Frank & His Orchestra/	**Annette Hanshaw/**
Augustine John/violin/studio band/Dick Stabile/	**Dean Martin**
Auld Georgie/tenor sax/arrainger/studio bands/Dizzy Gillespie/A. Shaw/	**Billie Holiday/Helen Forrest/Sarah Vaughan/**
Austin Gene/pianist/vocals/studio bands/	**Gene Austin/**
Austin Lovie/pianist/arrainger/ - Lovie Austin's Blues Serenaders/studio bands/	Ida Cox/**Ma Rainey/Ethel Waters/**
Austin Willie/pianist/studio bands/Louis Jordan Timpany Five/	**Louis Jordan/**
Autrey Herman/trumpet/studio bands/Fats Waller/	**Fats Waller/**
Autry Gene/own guitar/Film Master - 1934/with Gene Autry Trio/	**Gene Autry**
Autry Gene/own guitar/studio band/led Gene Autry Trio/	**Gene Autry**
Avola Al/jazz guitar/studio bands/Tommy Dorsey/Ardie Shaw/	**Haines/Helen Forrest/Billie Holiday/Frank Sinatra/Jo Stafford/Connie Haines/**
Ayres Mitchell/violin/arrainger/studio bands/own Orch./	Fontaine Sisters/Ray Charles Singers/
Ayres Mitchell/violin/arrainger/studio bands/own Orch./	**Perry Como/**Tommy Taylor/**Thelma Carpenter/Buddy Clark/**Tommy Taylor/
Azpiazu Don/ & His Havana Casino Orchestra/ - Cuban band -	Arturo Machin/
Bacon Louis/trumpet/studio bands/Louis Armstrong/	**Louis Armstrong/**
Bailey Joe/string bass/studio bands/Louis Armstrong Sebastian New Cotton Club Orch./	**Louis Armstrong/**
Bailey Mildred & Her Orch./studio band - same as Red Norvo Orch./	**Mildred Bailey/**
Baily Buster/clarinet/arrainger/studio bands/Claude Thornhill/M. W. Jazz Jesters/	**/Midge Williams/Maxine Sullivan/Sarah Vaughan/**
Baily Buster/clarinet/arrainger/studio bands/F. Henderson's Hot Six/	**Mamie Smith/Ma Rainey/Trixie Smith/Bessie Smith/Eva Taylor/Billie Holiday/**
Bain Robert/jazz guitar/studio bands/Phil Moore/Gordon Jenkins/	**Lena Horne/Frank Sinatra/Billie Holiday/**
Baine Bob/jazz guitar/studio bands/Gordon Jenkins/	**Billie Holiday/**
Bakaleinikoff Constantin/arrainger/cond. Orchestra/	**Helen Morgan**
Bakaleinikoff Constantin/arrainger/cond. Orchestra/Film - 1944/	**Frank Sinatra**
Baker Abbie/bass/studio bands/Blanche Calloway Orch./	**Blanche Calloway/**
Baker Arthur/saxophone/studio bands/Lloyde Shaffer/	**Perry Como/**
Baker Phil/pianist/accordian/songwriter/studio bands/	**Marion Harris/**
Ball Wilbur/guitar/studio bands/	**Jimmie Rodgers/**
Ballard Red/trombone/studio bands/Benny Goodman/	**Helen Ward/Mildred Bailey/Martha Tilton/**
Baltimore Jessie/drums/studio bands/E. W. Plantation Orch./Lew Leslie's Blackbirds Orch./	**Ethel Waters/Adelaide Hall/**
Banat Gabriel/violin/studio bands/violin/studio bands/Joe Bushkin/	**Lee Wiley/**
Banata Frank/pianist/srudio bands/	**Frank Crumit/**
Baravalli Victor/cond. own Orch./	**Helen Morgan/**
Barbarian Paul/drums/studio bands/Louis Armstrong Savoy Ballroom Five/	**Louis Armstrong/**Hoagy Caemichael/
Barbecue Bob/own guitar/	Barbecue Bob/
Barber Cliff/trumpet/studio bands/Jimmy Grier/	**Boswell Sisters/**
Barbour Dave/jazz guitar/studio bands/Benny Goodman/Axel Stordahl/ own Orch./	**Mildred Bailey/Anita O'Day/Frank Sinatra/Peggy Lee/Dick Haymes/**
Barefield/Eddie/alto saxophone/trumpet/studio bands/Cab Calloway/	**Cab Calloway/Chick Bullock/Ella Fitzgerald/**
Bargy Roy/pianist/studio bands/Isham Jones/Paul Whiteman/	**Marion Harris/Bing Crosby/**
Barker Danny/jazz guitar/studio bands/Eddie Mallory/M. W. Jazz Jesters/Cab Calloway/	**Ethel Waters/Midge Williams/Cab Calloway/**
Barksdale Everett/jazz guitar/studio bands/ Herman Chittison Trio/Sy Oliver/	**Mildred Bailey/Thelma Carpenter/Ethel Waters/Billie Holiday/**
Barnes Lloyd/pianist/studio bands/	**Victoria Spivey/**
Barnet Charlie/pianist/alto saxophone/arrainger/studio bands/own Orch./	**Lena Horne/Kay Starr/**Larry Taylor/**Nat King Cole/**Nellie Luther/
Barr Alfred/viola/studio bands/Nelson Riddle/	**Nat King Cole/Frank Sinatra/**
Barris Harry/pianist/accomp/vocals/studio bands/Paul Whiteman/Rhythm Boys/	Rhythm Boys/**Bing Crosby/**
Barron Blue/arrainger/studio bands/ & His Orchestra/	Bobby Beers, Blue Notes/
Barth Harry/tuba/studio bands/Ted Lewis/	Ted Lewis/**Sophie Tucker/Ruth Etting/**
Basie Count Orchestra - Film Master - 1941/1943/	**Jimmy Rushing/Ethel Waters/**
Basie Count Orchestra - Radio Master - 1938	**Billie Holiday**

Basie Count/ pianist/arrainger/studio bands/dance band/ & his Orch./	**Helen Humes/Jimmy Rushing/Thelma Carpenter/**
Basie Count/pianist/arrainger/studio bands/own Orch.//	**/Ella Fitzgerald/**Joe Williams/**Frank Sinatra/**Ann Moore/**Paul Robeson/** Lynn Sherman/
Bassey Bus/tenor saxophone/studio bands/Benny Goodman/	**Mildred Bailey/**
Battle Edgar/trumpet/studio bands/Blanche Calloway Orch./	**Blanche Calloway/**
Bauduc Ray/drums/studio bands/Louis Prima/Bob Crosby/	**Annette Hanshaw/Louis Prima/**Bob Crosby/**Bing Crosby/Connie Boswell/ Helen Ward/**
Bauer Abel/pianist/studio bands/	**Gene Austin/**
Bauer Billy/jazz guitar/studio band/	**Dinah Washington**
1st column: Bauer Joe/trumpet/studio bands/Hudson-DeLange Orch./	Betty Allen/
Baum Clyde/mandolin/studio bands/	**Hank Williams**
Baumel Herb/violin/studio bands/Joe Bushkin/	**Lee Wiley/**
Bauza Mario/trumpet/studio bands/Chick Webb/	**Ella Fitzgerald/**
Bavaralli Victor Orchestra/	**Helen Morgan/**
Baxter Les/studio bands/ & His Orch./	**Tex Ritter/Nat King Cole/**
Bay Victor/violin/studio bands/Nelson Riddle/Dick Stabile/	**Nat King Cole/Frank Sinatra/Dean Martin**
Beach Frank/trumpet/studio bands/Bob Scobey/	**Bing Crosby/**
Beal Charlie/pianist/studio bands/	**Louis Armstrong/**
Beane Reginal/pianist/arrainger/studio bands/	**Ethel Waters/**
Beane Reginal/pianist/ - Radio Master - 1944/	**Ethel Waters**
Beasley Walter/guitar/studio bands/	**Helen Humes/**
Beason Bill/drums/studio bands/John Kirby/	**Sarah Vaughan/**
Beau Heinie/ternor saxophone/clarinet/studio bands/Tommy Dorsey/Dave Barbour/	**Frank Sinatra/Jo Stafford/Connie Haines/Peggy Lee/**
Bechet Sidney/trumpet/arrainger/Clarence Williams/Noble Sissle/	**Eva Taylor/Ethel Waters/Alberta Hunter/Lena Horne/**
Beiderbecke Bix/clarinet/studio bands/ Paul Whiteman Orch./	**Bing Crosby/**
Beilman Peter/trombone/studio bands/Axel Stordahl/	**Frank Sinatra/**
Belasco Leon/studio bands/own Orch./	**Andrews Sisters/**
Beller Alex/violin/studio bands/Nelson Riddle/	**Nat King Cole/Frank Sinatra/**
Beneke Tex/tenor saxophone/some vocals/with Modinaires/studio bands/Glenn Miller/	Tex Beneke**/Paula Kelly/Modinaires/Kay Starr/**
Benford Bill/bass/studio bands/Plantation Orch./	**Ethel Waters/**
Benjamin Joe/bass/studio bands/Sy Oliver/	**Billie Holiday/**
Benner Bill/fiddle/studio bands/	**Tex Ritter/**
Benskin Sammy/pianist/studio bands/	**Billie Holiday/**
Berg Carl/trumpet/studio bands/Les Brown/	**Doris Day/**
Benson Walter/trombone/studio band/	**Mel Torme/Frank Sinatra**
Berg George/tenor saxophone/studio bands/Benny Goodman/Dick Haymes/	**Dick Haymes/Peggy Lee/**
Berigan Bunny/trumpet/arrainger/studio bands/Dorsey Brothers/Benny Goodman/own Orch./	**/Boswell Sisters/Mildred Baily/Billie Holiday/Lee Wiley/Frank Sinatra/Jo Stafford/Connie Haines**
Berigan Bunny/trumpet/arrainger/studio bands/Dorsey Brothers/Rudy Vallee/ Phil Spivey/	**Rudy Vallee/Bing Crosby/Mills Brothers/Ethel Waters/Eddie Cantor/ Chick Bullock/**
Berman Ruth/harp/studio bands/Russ Case/	**Perry Como/**
Bernard Cy/cello/studio bands/Axel Stordahl/	**Frank Sinatra/**
Bernardi Noni/alto saxophone/studio bands/Benny Goodman/	**Martha Tilton/**
Bernhart Milt/trombone/studio bnads/Nelson Riddle/	**Nat King Cole/**
Bernie Ben/pianist/arrainger/hotel orch./own Orch./	Snappy Lambert/Billy Hillpot/
Bernke Harold/cello/studio bands/Tommy Dorsey/	**Frank Sinatra/Jo Stafford/Connie Haines/**
Bernstein Artie/bass/studio bands/Benny Goodman/Teddy Wilson/ R. Norvo/ Claude Thornhill/	**/Cleo Brown//Maxine Sullivan/Mildred Bailey/Billie Holiday/**
Bernstein Artie/bass/studio bands/Dorsey Brothers/Benny Goodman/	**Annette Hanshaw/Boswell Sisters/Bing Crosby/Ethel Waters/Boswell Sisters/Mills Brothers/**
Berry Chu/tenor saxophone/studio bands/Buck And his Band/Cab Calloway/ Teddy Wilson/	**Bessie Smith/Cab Calloway/Billie Holiday/Mildred Bailey/**
Berry Emmett/trumpet/studio bands/Billie Holiday/	**Billie Holiday/**
Berry Hough/clarinet/studio bands/Leon's Lone Star Cowboys/	Leon Chappelear/
Berry Milton 'Muddy'/drum/studio bands/Kay Kyser/	**Ginny Simms/**
Berton Vic/drum/studio bands/Paul Whiteman/Miff Mole/Sam Lanin/Cliff Edwards/	Rhythm Boys**/Bing Crosby/Sophie Tucker/Cliff Edwards/Cleo Brown/**
Berv Henry/violin/studio bands/Lloyd Shaffer/	**Perry Como/**
Best Denzil/drums/studio bands/Leonard Feather's Hiptet/	**Helen Humes/Billie Holiday/**
Best John/trumpet/studio bands/Artie Shaw/Glenn Miller/Billy May/	**Billie Holiday/**Tex Beneke/Marion Hutton/Paula Kelly/Modernaires/**Nat King Cole/Dean Martin/**
Bester Don/arrainger/studio bands/own Orch./	Dudley Mechum/
Betts Kester/bass/studio bands/	**Dinah Washington/**
Bibbs Leonard/bass/studio bands/	**Cleo Brown/**
Biese Paul/saxophone/studio bands/own Orch./	**Marion Harris/**
Biesacker Carl/tenor saxophone/Gene Krupa/	**Helen Ward/**
Bigard Barney/clarinet/saxophone/ studio bands/Duke Ellington/	**Louis Armstrong/**Baby Cox/Irving Mills/Ozzie Ware/Rhythm Boys/
Bigard Barney/clarinet/saxophone/ studio bands/Duke Ellington/His Jazzopators/	**/Ivie Anderson/Adelaide Hall/Ethel Waters/Bing Crosby/**Sue Mitchell/
Bigelow Jack/trombone/studio bands/Larry Clinton/	**Bea Wain/Dick Todd/**

Binyon Larry/tenor saxophone/flute/studio bands/Dorsey Brothers/Jess Stacy/T. Camarata/	**Bing Crosby/Ethel Waters/Boswell Sisters/Mills Brothers/Billie Holiday/ Mildred Baily/Lee Wiley**
Biondi Ray/bass guitar/studio bands/Gene Krupa/	**Helen Ward/**
Bishop Joe/trumpet/fuglehorn/arrainger/songwriter/Isham Jones/Woody Herman/	**Bing Crosby/Connie Boswell/**Woody Hermann/Muriel Lane/
Bishop Wallace/drums/studio bands/	**Billie Holiday/**
Black Bob/pianist/studio bands/	**Memphis Minnie**/Washboard Sam/
Black Frank Orchestra - Radio Master - 1936/	**Ruth Etting/**
Black Ted & His Orchestra/own vocals on some/	Ted Black/**Chick Bullock/**
Blackwell Scrapper/guitar/studio bands/some vocals/	Leroy Carr/
Blake Blind/own guitar/Paramount studio bands	**Blind Blake/**
Blake Charlie/drums/studio bands/Larry Clinton/	**Bea Wain/**
Blake Eubie Orchestra/ - Film Master - 1935/1935/	Eubie Blake/Nina Mae Mc Kinney/
Blake Eubie/pianist/arrainger/songwriter/ & His Orch./	Eubie Blake/**Alberta Hunter**/Nobel Sissle/**Thelma Carpenter/**
Blake Jerry/alto saxophone/studio bands/Teddy Wilson/	**Ella Fitzgerald/**
Blake Jimmy/trumpet/studio bands/Cab Calloway/Tommy Dorsey/	**Cab Calloway/Frank Sinatra/Jo Stafford/Connie Haines/**
Blakey Art/drums/studio bands/Billy Eckstine/	**Billy Eckstine/Sarah Vaughan/**
Blanchette Jack/jazz guitar/studio bands/Casa Loma Orch./	**Connie Boswell/Lee Wiley/**
Blanton Jimmy/bass/guitar/studio bands/Duke Ellington/Red Norvo/	**Ivie Anderson/Mildred Bailey/**
Blind Blake/own guitar/vocals/	**Blind Blake/**
Bliss Helen/harp/studio bands/Dick Stabeli	**Dean Martin**
Bloom Kurt/tenor saxophone/studio bands/Charlie Barnet/	**Lena Horne/**
Bloom Mikey/trumpet/cornet/studio bands/	**Ruth Etting/**
Bloom Rube/pianist/studio bands/	**Ruth Etting/Lee Morse/Bing Crosby/Annette Hanhaw/Ethel Waters/**
Bloom William/violin/studio bands/Axel Stordahl/	**Frank Sinatra/**
Blowers Johnny/drums/studio bands/Russ Case/Axel Stordahl/	**Perry Como/Billie Holiday/Frank Sinatra/**
Blue Barron/arrainger/studio band/own Orch/	Bobby Beers/Blue Notes/
Blue Boys her - Bessie Smith/studio band/	**Bessie Smith/**
Blue Danny/trumpet/studio bands/Georgie Auld/	**Sarah Vaughan/**
Blue Grass Boys - & her - Lee Morse/studio band - incl. (Dorsey Brothers)/	**Lee Morse/**
Blue Grass Boys his - Bill Monroe - own vocals, (lead - guitar, mandolin/	**Bill Monroe/**
Blue Kings & his/	**Joe Turner/**
Blue Seranaders her - Ida Cox/	Ida Cox/
Bluestone Harry/violin/studio bands/Nelson Riddle/	**Nat King Cole/Frank Sinatra/**
Blythe Jimmy/pianist/studio bands/	**Ma Rainey/**
Bochco Rudolph/violin/studio bands/Russ Case/	**Perry Como/**
Bochme Dave/fiddle/studio bands/	**Roy Rogers/**
Bohn George/clarinet/studio bands/	**Annette Hanshaw/**
Bolar Abe/string bass/studio bands/Pete Johnson/	**Joe Turner/**
Boling Arnold/as "scrippy'/clarinet/studio bands/M. W. Jazz Jesters/	**Fats Waller/Midge Williams/**
Bonano Joseph/as 'Sharkey'/trumpet/studio bands/own band/	**Lizzie Miles/**
Bond Johnny/guitar/studio bands/Al Dexter/Pinafores/own band with vocals/	**Gene Autry/Jimmie Davis/Tex Ritter**/Johnny Bond/
Bonne Don/clarinet/studio bands/	**Frankie Laine**
Bonniface Marcel/accordian/studio bands/Joe Bushkin/	**Lee Wiley/**
Boone Lester/clarinet/alto saxophone/studio bands/Louis Armstrong/	**Louis Armstrong/Billie Holiday/**
Booze Bea/own guitar/	Bea Booze/
Borodin Abe/cello/studio bands/Artie Shaw/	**Lena Horne/**
Borodkin Herb/cello/studio bands/	**Gene Austin/**
Borowski Johnny/fiddle/studio bands/Brown's Musical Brownies/	**Jimmie Davis/**
Borsody Emil/cello/studio bands/Ted Steele/Lloyd Shaffer/	**Perry Como/**
Bose Sterling/trumpet/studio bands/Dorsey Brothers/Lennie Hayton/	**Annette Hanshaw/Bing Crosby/Ethel Waters/Boswell Sisters/Lee Wiley/**
Bostic Earle/alto saxophone/studio bands/arrainger/Cab Calloway/own Orch./	**Cab Calloway/**
Boswell Connie/pianist/cello/saxophone/Boswell Sisters/	**Boswell Sisters/Connie Boswell/Bing Crosby/**
Boswell Martha/pianist/vocals/arrainger/Boswell Sisters/Connie Boswell/	**Boswell Sisters/Connie Boswell/Bing Crosby/**
Boswell Sisters/ - Helvetia/Vet//Martha/Connie/vocal group/	**Boswell Sisters/Connie Boswell/Bing Crosby/**
Boswell Vet/or Helvetia/violin/guitar/vocals/Boswell Sisters/Connie Boswell/	**Boswell Sisters/Connie Boswell/Bing Crosby/**
Botkin Perry/jazz guitar/banjo/ukulele/studio bands/Irving Mills/Dorsey Brothers/ Victor Young/J. Scott Trotter/Alex Stordahl/	**Annette Hanshaw/Bing Crosby/Boswell Sisters/Cleo Brown/Frank Sinatra/ Roy Rogers/Johnny Mercer/Frankie Laine/**
Bourdon Rosario/violin/cello/studio bands/ Orch./	**Marion Harris/Eddie Cantor/**
Boutelje Phil/pianist/studio bands/	**Nick Lucas/**
Bowen Claude/trumpet/studio bands/Artie Shaw/Harry James/	**Billie Holiday/Frank Sinatra/**
Bowlly Al/guitar/banjo/vocalist/European studio bands/ (British)	**Al Bowlly/**
Bowman Dave/pianist/studio bands/Russ Case/Eddie Condon/	**Lee Wiley/Perry Como/Billie Holiday/Frank Sinatra/**
Boy Friends - her - Julia Lee/studio band/	**Julia Lee/**
Boyd Bill/studio bands/Cowboy Ramblers/	**Jimmie Rodgers/**
Boyd Roger/alto sax/studio nbands/Blanche Calloway Orch./	**Blanche Calloway/**
Bradford Perry/pianist/arrainger/songwriter/	**Mamie Smith/Alberta Hunter/**
Bradley Julius/alto saxophone/studio bands/Jess Stacy/	**Lee Wiley/**
Bradley Owen/pianist/studio bands/radio/	**Ernest Tubb/Red Foley/**Kitty Wells/Patsy Cline/Brenda Lee/
Bradley Will /trombone/studio bands/ Ray Noble/Jessa Stacy/Russ Case/his Orch./	**Bing Crosby/Boswell Sisters/Lee Wiley/Al Bowlly/Perry Como/Anita O'Day/Margaret Whiting/**
Bradshae Curley/guitar/studio bands/Blue Grass Boys/	**Bill Monroe/**

Brady Pat/bass/studio bands/Sons Of Pioneers/	Bob Nolan/Tim Spencer/Lloyd Perryman/**Roy Rogers/**
Brandywynne Nat /arrainger/studio bands/hotel bands/ & His Stork Club Orch./	**Ginny Simms/Buddy Clark/**
Brashear George/trombone/studio bands/Joe Smith's Jazz Masters/	**Ethel Waters/Alberta Hunter/**
Brassfield Herschel/alto saxophone/studio bands/M/Smith Jazz Hounds/	**Mamie Smith/**
Braud Wellman/bass/arrainger/studio bands/Duke Ellington/	**Alberta Hunter/**Rhythm Boys/**Ivie Anderson/Ethel Waters/Bing Crosby/**
Braud Wellman/bass/arrainger/studio bands/Duke Ellington/Jungle Band/	**Adelaide Hall/Baby Cox/**Ozzie Ware/Irving Mills/
Braun Lester/bass/studio bands/	Elton Britt/
Brecher Sidney/violin/studio bands/Percy Faith/	**Tony Bennett/**
Breeden Gene/guitar/studio bands/Maddox Brothers & Rose/	**Rose Maddox/**
Breen Larry/bass/studio bands/	**Mel Torme**
Bregman Buddy/arrainger/studio bands/own Orch./	**Bing Crosby/**
Brereton Clarence/trumpet/studio bands/John Kirby/	**Sarah Vaughan/**
Briedis Victor/pianist/studio bands/Irving Mills/	**Ruth Etting/Elisabeth Welch/**Williams Sisters/
Briggs James/clarinet/studio bands/Jimmie Grier Orch./	**Bing Crosby/Boswell Sisters/**
Briggs Pete/bass/studio bands/Louis Armstrong's Hot Seven/	**Louia Armstrong/**
Briglia Tony/drums/studio bands/Casa Loma Orch./	**Connie Boswell/Lee Wiley/**
Brillhart Arnold/clarinet/studio bands/Dorsey Brothers/	**Bing Crosby/**
Bring Lou/arrainger/studio bands/his Orch./	**Lena Horne/Ginny Simms**
Britt Elton/guitar/vocals/studio bands/	Elton Britt/
Broadway Nitelites/studio band	**Vaughn De Leath/**
Broadway Strollers/studio band/	**Vaughn De Leath/**
Brockman Gail/tuba/studio bands/Billy Eckstine/	**Billy Eckstine/Sarah Vaughan/**
Brodsky Irvingpianist/studio bands/	**Lee Morse/**
Brodsky Ivan/pianist/studio bands/	**Annette Hanshaw/**
Brooks Harry/pianist/studio bands/	**Lizzie Miles/**
Brooks Harvey/pianist/studio bands/Louis Armstrong Sebastian New Cotton Club Orch./	**Louis Armstrong/**
Brooks Randy /trumpet/arrainger/studio bands/ & Orch./Les Brown/	**Ella Fitzgerald/Doris Day/**
Brooks Shelton/pianist/arrainger/songwriter/studio bands/	**Ethel Waters/**
Broonzy Bil Bill/as 'Big Bill'/own guitar/studio bands/with S. Smith - banjo/ & His Chicago Five/	**Big Bill Broonzy/**Washboard Sam/
Brown Andrew/tenor saxophone/reeds/studio bands/Cab Calloway/	**Cab Calloway/Chick Bullock/**
Brown Blaude/trumphet/studio bands/Artie Shaw/	**Billie Holiday**
Brown Cleo/pianist/arrainger/vocals/studio bands/	**Cleo Brown/**
Brown Durwood/guitar/Milton Brown/Brown's Musical Brownies/	**Jimmie Davis/**
Brown George/viola/studio bands/Mitchell Ayres/	**Perry Como/**
Brown John/alto saxophone/studio bands/Bill Doggett/	**Helen Humes/**
Brown Lawrence/trombone/studio bands/Louis Armstrong/Duke Ellington/	**Louis Armstrong/**Rhythm Boys/**Ivie Anderson/Ethel Waters/Adelaide Hall/Bing Crosby/**
Brown Lawrence/trombone/studio bands/Metronome All Stars/	**Nat King Cole/June Christy/Frank Sinatra/**
Brown Les Orchestra - Film Master - 1941/1941/	**Doris Day/Martha Tilton/**
Brown Les/clarinet/arrainger/studio bands/ & His Band Of Renown/his Orch./	**Doris Day/**
Brown Lew/pianist/studio bands/Billy May/	**Nat King Cole/Dean Martin/**
Brown Maurice/cello/studio bands/Axel Stordahl/	**Frank Sinatra/**
Brown Milton/ & His Brownies/vocal/ - as Browns Musical Brownies - after Milton's death/	Milton Brown**/Jimmie Davis/**
Brown Pete/arrainger/trumpet/pianist/alto saxophone/studio bands/C. Thornhill/ own band/	**Maxine Sullivan/Midge Williams/Helen Humes/**
Brown Ray/bass/studio bands/Teddy Stewart/	**Dinah Washington/Billie Holiday/**
Brown Russell/trombone/studio bands/Harry James/	**Frank Sinatra**
Brown Vernon/trombone/studio bands/Benny Goodman/Eddie Condon/	**Mildred Bailey/Lee Wiley/**
Bruner Cliff/fiddle/studio bands/Texas Wanderers/	**Jimmie Davis/**Moon Mullican/
Brunis George/trombone/arrainger/studio bands/ Ted Lewis/Louis Prima/	Ted Lewis/**Ruth Etting/Fats Waller/Louis Prima/**
Bryan Dean/guitar/studio bands/	**Jimmie Rodgers/**
Bryant Hoyt 'Slim'/guitar/studio bands/	**Jimmie Rodgers/**
Buchanan 'Buck'/fiddle/studio bands/Brown's Musical Brownies/	**Jimmie Davis/**
Buck And His Band/studio band for Bessie Smith/leader: "Buck" Washington/	**Bessie Smith/**
Buckman Sid/trumpet/studio bands/	**Al Bowlly/**
Buckner Milt/pianist/studio bands/Lionel Hampton/	**Dinah Washington/**
Buldrino Fred/violin/studio bands/Axel Stordahl/	**Frank Sinatra/**
Buller Buddy/steel guitar/studio bands/Ted Daffan's Texans/	Chuck Keeshan/Leon Seago/
Bulllock Chick & His Orchestra/own vocals/ studio band	**Chick Bullock**
Bunn Teddy/guitar/studio bands/	**Lizzie Miles/**
Buono Nick/trumpet/studio bands/Harry James/	**Frank Sinatra/**
Burbeck Charles/saxophone/Ozzie Nelson/	**Ozzie Nelson/Harriet Hilliard/**
Burke Ceele/jazz guitar/banjo/arrainger/Louis Armstrong/own Orch./	**Louis Armstrong/Ivie Anderson**
Burke Sonny /pianist/violin/arrainger/studio bands/ & His Orch./	**Bing Crosby/Billy Eckstine/Mel Torme/Dinah Shore/**
Burkes Billy/guitar/studio bands/	**Jimmie Rodgers/**
Burkes Weldon/guitar/studio bands/	**Jimmie Rodgers/**
Burness Lester/pianist/studio bands/Artie Shaw/	**Billie Holiday/**
Burnet Robert/trumpet/studio bands/Charlie Barnet/	**Lena Horne/**

Burnette Smiley/accordian/studio bands/Gene Autry Trio/	**Gene Autry/**
Burtnett Earl & His Los Angeles Biltmore Hotel Orchestra/	Biltmore Trio/
Burwell Cliff/pianist/studio bands/Rudy Vallee & his Connecticut Yankees/	**Rudy Vallee/**
Busch Lou - (as also known as 'Joe Fingers Carr)/pianist/studio bands/own Orch./	**Kay Starr/**
Bushell Garvin/clarinet/studio bands/Ethel Waters Jazz Masters/Johnny Dunn/ Chick Webb/	**Ethel Waters/Edith Wilson/**Lena Wilson/**Cab Calloway/Ella Fitzgerald/**
Buskin Joe/pianist/trumpet/arrainger/studio bands/Tommy Dorsey/And His StringsOrch./	**Billie Holiday/Lee Wiley/Frank Sinatra/Connie Haines/Jo Stafford/**
Busse Henry/trumpet/studio bands/Payl Whiteman/	Rhythm Boys/**Bing Crosby/**
Butler Bill/steel guitar/studio bands/	**Tex Ritter/**
Butler Ross/trumpet/studio bands/Bill Doggett/	**Helen Humes/**
Butterfield Billy/trumpet/arrainger/studio bands/Benny Goodman/Les Brown/ Russ Case/	**Doris Day/Peggy Lee/Perry Como/**
Butterfield Billy/trumpet/arrainger/studio bands/Bob Crosby/Jess Stacy/Les Brown/G. Siravo	**Bing Crosby/Lee Wiley/Billie Holiday/Margaret Whiting/Frank Sinatra/**
Butterfield Charlie/trombone/studio bands/Lennie Hayton/Dorsey Brothers/	**Ruth Etting/Annette Hanshaw/Bing Crosby/Boswell Sisters/**
Butterman Lou/bass/studio bands/Gordon Jenjins/	**Billie Holiday/**
Byfield Jack/cello/British studio bands/	**Hildegarde/**
Byrd Eddie/drims/studio bands/Louis Jordan Tympany Five/	**Louis Jordan/Bing Crosby/**
Byrd Jerry/steel guitar/studio bands/Drifting Cowboys/	**Hank Williams/**
Byrne Bobby/trombone/studio bands/Jimmy Dorsey/Mitchell Ayres/	**Louis Armstrong/Bing Crosby/**Frances Langford/**Billie Holiday/Perry Como/**
Caceres Ernie/alto saxophone/studio bands/Glenn Miller/A. Stordahl/B. Goodman/E. Condon/	Tex Beneke/Paula Kelly/Modernaires/**Lee Wiley/Frank Sinatra/Peggy Lee/**
Caiazza Nicholas/saxophone/studio bands/Lloyd Shaffer/	**Perry Como/**
Caldwell Albert/'as 'Happy'/tenor saxophone/studio bands/	**Mamie Smith/Louis Armstrong/**
Calhoun Fred/pianist/studio bands/Milton Brown/Brown's Musical Brownies/	**Jimmie Davis/**
Cali John/studio bands/Cliff Edwards/	**Cliff Edwards/Lee Morse/Jimmie Rodgers/**
Callender Red/bass/studio bands/Maxine Sullivan/Bob Scobey/	**Maxine Sullivan/Louis Armstrong/Bing Crosby/**
Calloway Blanche/own vocals./ & Her Joy Boys/led own Orch./	**Blanche Calloway/**
Calloway Cab/ & His Orchestra/own vocals/as Jungle Band/	**Cab Calloway/Chick Bullock/**Palmer Brothers/
Calloway Cab/ & His Orchestra - Film Master - 1932/1933/1934/1980/1943/	**Cab Calloway/Lena Horne/**
Camarata Tutti or Toots/trumpet/arrainger/studio bands/Jimmy Dorsey/own Orch./	**Bing Crosby/Helen Forrest/Dick Haymes/Billie Holiday/**
Camarata Tutti or Toots/trumpet/studio bands/arrainger/Jimmy Dorsey/own Orch./	**Louis Armstrong/Bing Crosby/**Frances Langford/Helen O'Connell//Bob Eberly/
Cambell Edgar/clarinet/studio bands/Ethel Waters Jazz Masters/	**Ethel Waters/**
Camero Candido/bongos/conga drums/studio bands/	**Dinah Washington/**
Camgros Armound/tenor saxophone/studio bands/	**Billie Holiday/**
Campbell Chuck/trombone/studio bands/	**Boswell Sisters/**
Cannon Gus/banjo/his jug band/stomper/own vocals/	Gus Cannon/
Candido Johnny/as 'Candy"/bass/studio bands/	**Gene Austin/**
Canova Pete/studio bands/	**Gene Autry/**
Cara Mancy/banjo/studio bands/Louis Armstrong Savoy Ballroom Five/	**Louis Armstrong/Victoria Spivey/**
Carlisle Cliff/steel guitar/studio bands/	**Jimmie Rodgers/**
Carlisle Una Mae/pianist/studio bands/some vocals/arrainger/Fats Waller/	Una Mae Carlisle/**Fats Waller/**
Carlson Frank/drums/studio bands/Woody Herman/	**Bing Crosby/**Woody Herman/Murial Lane/
Carmichael Hoagy/pianist/arrainger/songwriter/actor/vocals/	HoagyCarmichael /**Louis Armstrong/**
Carmichael Ralph/ arrainger/studio bands/own Orch./	**Nat King Cole/Bing Crosby/Ella Fitzgerald/**
Carneel Jess/saxophone/studio bands/Russ Case/	**Perry Como/**
Carney Harry/clarinet/saxophone/studio bands/Duke Ellington/	**Adelaide Hall/**Rhythm Boys/**Bing Crosby/**
Carney Harry/clarinet/saxophone/studio bands/Duke Ellington/Metronome All Stars/	**/Ivie Anderson/Ethel Waters/Nat King Cole/June Christy/Frank Sinatra/**
Carpenter Billy 'Uke'/ - ukule/studio bands/	Aileen Stanley/**Gene Austin/**
Carr Leroy/pianist/vocals/songwriter/studio bands/	Leroy Carr/
Carrol Jimmy/studio bands/hisOrch./	**Dinah Washington/Frankie Laine/**
Carroll David/arrainger/studio bands/	**Vic Damone/**
Carroll Frank/bass/studio bands/Axel Stordahl/Lloyde Shaffer/Percy Faith/	**Frank Sinatra/Perry Como/Rosemary Clooney/Tony Bennett/**
Carroll Robert/tenor saxophone/studio bands/Don Redman Orch./	Don Redman/**Harlan Lattimore/Bing Crosby/Boswell Sisters/**
Carter Benny/trumpet/saxophone/arrainger/studio bands/Gene Krupa/his Orch./	**/Thelma Carpenter//Maxine Sullivan/Ethel Waters/Anita O'Day/Peggy Lee/**
Carter Benny/trumpet/saxophone/arrainger/studio bands/Teddy Wilson/Artie Shaw/	**Mills Brothers/Adelaide Hall/Billie Holiday/Lena Horne/Elisabeth Welch**
Carter Bo/or Bo Chatman/own guitar/	Bo Carter/
Carter Family/AP Carter/ & Sara / & /Maybelle - vocal & guitar/	**Carter Family/Jimmie Rodgers/**
Carter Frances J./pianist/studio bands/	**Adelaide Hall/**
Carter Maybelle/guitar/bass guitar/some vocals/Carter Family/	**Carter Family/Jimmie Rodgers/**
Carter Sara/guitar/autoharp/vocals/Carter Family/	**Carter Family/Jimmie Rodgers/**
Caruana Frank/bass/studio bands/Ted Steele/	**Perry Como/**
Casa Loma Orchestra/ - leader Glen Gray/hotel dance band/studio band/	**Connie Boswell/Mildred Bailey/**Kenny Sargent/**Lee Wiley/**
Case Russ/trumpet/studio bands/T. Camarata/own Orch./	**Boswell Sisters/Perry Como/**Satisfiers/**Billie Holiday/**
Casey Albert/jazz guitar/studio bands/Teddy Wilson/Fats Waller/	**Alberta Hunter/Fats Waller/Billie Holiday/**
Castaldo Charles/trombone/studio bands/Benny Goodman/	**Peggy Lee/Dick Haymes/**
Castaldo Lee/trumpet/studio bands/Tommy Dorsey/	Edythe Wright/Jack Leonard/**Frank Sinatra/Jo Stafford/Connie Haines/**
Catlett Big Sid/drums/studio bands/ Teddy Wilson /Benny Goodman/	**Billie Holiday/Martha Tilton/Helen Forrest/Peggy Lee/Sarah Vaughan/**

Cauldwell Happy/tenor saxophone/studio bands/	**Edith Wilson/**
Cavallaro Carmen/classical pianist/studio bands/own orch./	**Bing Crosby/**
Cavanaugh Dave or 'Big Dav'/tenor saxophone/studio bands/	**Ella Mae Morse/Frank Sinatra/**
Cavanaugh Page/pianist/studio bands/his Trio/	**Frank Sinatra/Doris Day/**
Cave John/french horn/studio bands/Nelson Riddle/	**Nat King Cole/Frank Sinatra/**
Ceppos Mac/violin/studio bands/Alex Stordahl/Ted Steele/Lloyd Shaffer/Mitchell Ayres/	**Annette Hanshaw/**Elton Britt/**Frank Sinatra/Perry Como/**
Chabama J./reeds/studio bands/Cab Calloway/	**Cab Calloway/**
Challis Bill/arrainger/dance bands/studio bands/Paul Whiteman/	Rhythm Boys/**Bing Crosby/**
Chaloffbar Serge/pianist/studio bands/Georgie Auld/	**Sarah Vaughan/**
Chambers Elmer/cornet/clarinet/studio bands/Jazz Masters/	**Clara Smith/Edith Wilson/Ethel Waters/**
Chambers Henderson/trombone/studio bands/	**Billie Holiday/**
Chapman Paul/jazz guitar/studio bands/Billie Holiday/	**Billie Holiday/**
Chappelear Leon/guitar/studio bands/Shelton Brothers/Lone Star Cowboys/ Charles Mitchell/	Leon Chappelear/**Jimmie Davis/**
Chappell Gus/trombone/studio bands/	**Dinah Washington/**
Charlestown Chasers/studo band - var. members incl. J. Dorsey/B. Goodman/M. Mole/	**Kate Smith/Eva Taylor/**
Chauvigny Robert/ arrainger/studio bands/Joe Buskin/his Orch./	**Lee Wiley/**Edith Pifat/
Cheatham Doc/trumpet/studio bands/Cab Calloway/Eddie Heywood/	**Cab Calloway/Chick Bullock/Billie Holiday/**
Cherwin Dick/string bass/studio bands/Dorsey Brothers/	**Gene Austin/Boswell Sisters/**
Chesleigh Jack/jazz guitar/studio bands/Larry Clinton/	**Bea Wain/Dick Todd/**
Chicago Five - his Big Bill (Broonzy/his guitar/	**Big Bill Broonzy/**
Childers Buddy/trumpet/studio bands/Stan Kenton/	**June Christy/**
Chittison Herman Trio/pianist/studio bands/his Trio/	**Mildred Bailey/Thelma Carpenter/Ethel Waters/**
Chittison Herman Trio - Radio Master - 1947	**Ethel Waters**
Christian Buddy/banjo/studio bands/Clarence Williams/	**Clara Smith/Eva Taylor/**
Christian Charlie/jazz guitar/studio bands/Benny Goodman/	**Helen Forrest/Peggy Lee/**
Clanton Sam/pianist/arrainger/studio bands/	**Alberta Hunter/**
Clark Dick/tenor saxophone/studio bands/B. Goodman/	**Helen Ward**
Clark Don/saxophone/dance bands/studio bands/ & own Orch./	**Bing Crosby.** Al Rinker/
Clark Pete/clarinet/studio bands/Louis Armstrong/	**Louis Armstrong/Billie Holiday/**
Clarkson Geoff/piano/studio bands/Les Brown/	**Doris Day/**
Clay Shirleytrumpet/studio bands/Don Redman//Benny Goodman/	**Harlan Lattimore/Mills Brothers/Billie Holiday/**
Clay Shirleytrumpet/studio bands/Don Redman/Eddie Mallory/Benny Goodman/	Don Redman/**Ma Rainey/Harlan Latimore/Bing Crosby/Boswell Sisters/ Ethel Waters/**
Clayton Buck/trumpet/studio bands/Count Basie/	**Billie Holiday/Jimmy Rushing/Helen Humes/**
Cleveland Jimmy/trombone/studio bands/	**Dinah Washington/**
Clinton Larry/trumpet/trombone/arrainger/studio bands/songwriter/Dorsey Brothers/His Orch.	**Bea Wain/Dick Todd/**Peggy Mann/
Cliquot Club Escomos/ name from radio program - studio band/led by Harry Reser/	**Vaughn De Leath/**Tom Stacks/
Cobb Arnett/tenor saxophone/studio bands/Lionel Hampton/	**Dinah Washington/**
Cobb Jimmy/drums/studio band/own Orch./	**Dinah Washington/**
Coburn Jolly & His Orchestra/	Harold Van Emburgh/Roy Storm/
Coffman Wanna/bass/studio bands/Milton Brownie/Brownie's Musical Brownies/	Milton Brown/**Jimmie Davis/**
Cohen Murray/saxophone/studio bands/Russ Case/	**Perry Como/**
Cohn Al/tenor saxophone/studio bands/Georgie Auld/	**Sarah Vaughan/**
Cole Buddy/pianist /celeste/arrainger/studio bands/Dave Baubour/Nelson Riddle/ own Orch./	**Bing Crosby/Mel Torme/**King Sisters/**Peggy Lee/Rosemary Clooney/Nat King Cole/**
Cole Cozy/drums/studio bands/Blanche Calloway/Cab Calloway/Teddy Wilson/	**Blanche Calloway/Mildred Bailey/Billie Holiday/Ella Fitzgerald/Cab Calloway/**
Cole Nat Trio/Film Master - 1946	**Nat King Cole**
Cole Nat Trio/Radio Master - 1946	**Nat King Cole/Frank Sinatra**
Cole Rupert/alto saxophone/studio bands/Don Redman/Teddy Stewart/	Don Redman/**Harlan Lattimore/Bing Crosby/Boswell Sisters/Dinah Washington/**
Cole Trio - Nat Cole Trio. Nat Cole lead vocal/or pianist/Metronome All Stars/	**Nat King Cole/Anita O'Day/Johnny Mercer/June Christy/Frank Sinatra/**
Coletta Harold/viola/studio bands/Axel Stordahl/	**Frank Sinatra/**
Collins John/jazz guitar/arrainger/Art Tatum/Nelson Riddle/Billy May/	**Joe Turner/Nat King Cole/Nat King Cole/Dean Martin/**
Collins Shad/trumpet/studio bands/Cab Calloway/	**Cab Calloway/Billie Holiday/**
Calonna Jerry/trombone/studio bands/John Scott Trotter/	**Bing Crosby?/**
Colonial Club Orchestra/	**Libby Holman/**
Colucci Tony/jazz guitar/studio bands/	**Annette Hanshaw/Ethel Waters/Jimmie Rodgers/**
Columbo Russ/violinist/studio band/Gus Arnheim/his Orchestra/	**Russ Columbo/Bing Crosby?/**
Columbus Christopher/drums/studio bands/Louis Jordan Tympany Five/	**Louis Jordan/**
Colvard Jessie/steel guitar/studio bands/	**Roy Rogers/**
Comfort Joe/bass/studio bands/Nelson Riddle/	**Nat King Cole/**Nellie Luther/**Frank Sinatra/**
Comstock Frank/arrainger/studio bands/Les Brown/	**Doris Day/**
Conaway Lincoln/guitar/studio bands/	**Bessie Smith/Clara Smith/**
Conden Eddie/jazz guitar/banjo/arrainger studio bands/Louis Armstrong/his Orch./	**Louis Armstrong/Lee Wiley/Bing Crosby/**

Coniff Ray/trombone/arrainger/studio bands/Artie Shaw/Bob Crosby/Harry James/his Orch/	**Bing Crosby/Helen Forrest/Frankie Laine/Frank Sinatra/**
Connant Nat/trumpet/studio bands/	**Bing Crosby/**
Connecticut Yankees/Rudy Vallee leader - clarinet/saxophone/ & vocalist/dance band/	**Rudy Vallee/**
Connecticut Yankees/Rudy Vallee's/ - Radio Master - 1932/1933	**Rudy Vallee/Lee Wiley/Ethel Waters/**
Conrad Lew/violin/studio bands/Leo Reisman/	**Lee Wiley/**
Consumano Bob/trumpet/studio bands/Larry Clinton/	**Bea Wain/**
Cook Phil/trumpet/studio bands/Harry James/	**Frank Sinatra/**
Cook Will Marion/violin/arrainger/songwriter/	**Ethel Waters/**
Cooley Spade/fiddle/studio bands/string band leader/	**Gene Autry/Roy Rogers/**Tex Williams/
Coon Carlton/drums/studio bands/dance band/Coon - Sanders Orch./	**Carleton Coon, Joe Sanders**
Coon - Sanders Orchestra/ - Carleton Coon & Joe Sanders	**Carleton Coon, Joe Sanders**
Cooper L. Z./pianist/studio bands/Louis Armstrong/	**Louis Armstrong/**
Cooper Sid/alto saxophone/studio bands/	**Billie Holiday/Louis Armstrong/**
Cordaro Joe/clarinet/studio bands/	**Annette Hanshaw/**
Cordova Mike/string bass/studio bands/	**Jimmie Rodgers/**
Cornell Rich/drums/studio bands/Freddie Slack/	**Ella Mae Morse/**
Costa Don/arrainger/studio bands/	**Tony Bennett/**
Cotner Carl/fiddle/studio bands/Pinafores/	**Gene Autry/**
Cotton Pickers/ studio band	**Libby Holman/**
Courtney Freddy/accondian/studio bands/Ted Daffan's Texans/	Chuck Keeshan/Leon Seago/
Cousin Wilbur/ - Willie Egbert/studio bands/Blue Grass Boys/	**Bill Monroe/**
Covarrubias Arnold/jazz guitar/studio bands/Benny Goodman/	**Mildred Bailey/**
Covetti Frenchy/string bass/studio bands/Herman Chittison/	**Mildred Bailey/**
Covington Warren/trombone/studio bands/Les Brown/	**Doris Day/**
Cowans Herbert/drums/studio bands/Billie Holiday/	**Billie Holiday/**
Cozzens Ellsworth T./mandolin/steel guitar/studio bands/	**Jimmie Rodgers/**
Craig Al/drums/British studio band/	**Adelaide Hall/**
Craig Frances/pianist/arrainger/studio bansa/ own Orch/	Bob Lamm/
Crawford Helen/pipe organ/	**Bing Crosby/**
Crawford Jimmy/drums/studio bands/Dicky Wells/Sy Oliver/	**Sarah Vaughan/Louis Armstrong/Billie Holiday/Rosemary Clooney/**
Crazy Tennesseans his/ - leader Roy Acuff - vocals & fiddle//some vocals - Sam Hatcher/	**Roy Acuff/**Sam Hatcher/
Creole Jazz Hounds her - Lizzie Miles/	**Lizzie Miles/**
Cressey Jack/alto saxophone/studio bands/Camarata dir. Orch/	**Billie Holiday/**
Crockett Alan/fiddle/studio bands/	**Gene Autry/**
Crooning Troubadors & / Nick Lucas	**Nick Lucas/**
Crosby Bob Orchestra - Film Master - 1942	**Fred Astaire**
Crosby Bob/arrainger/studio bands/own Orch./Bobcats/	**Fred Astaire/**Margaret Lemhart/
Crosby Bob/arrangements/own vocal/studio bands/Dorsey Brothers/	Bob Crosby/Kay Weber/Frank Tennille/**Bing Crosby/**Marion Mann/
Crosby Bob/arrangements/own vocal/studio bands/own Orch./his Bob - Cats	**/Helen Ward//Connie Boswell/Judy Garland/**Bob Miller/
Crosby Israel/bass/studio bands/Gene Krupa/	**Helen Ward/**
Crudup Arthur/own guitar/vocals/studio bands/	**Arthur Crudup/**
Cuffee Ed/trombone/studio bands/	**Victoria Spivey/**
Cugat Xavier Orchestra - Film Master - 1943	Lina Romay/
Cugat Xavier/violin/arrainger/dance band/ his Hotel Waldorf - Astoria Orchestra/ & his Orch./	**Bing Crosby/Buddy Clark/Dinah Shore/**Lina Romay/
Cullen Boyce/trombone/studio bands/Paul Whiteman/	Rhythm Boys/**Bing Crosby/**
Cumberland Mountain Folks/	Molly O'Day/
Cumberland Valley Boys/ his - Red Foley/	**Red Foley**
Cunningham Ed/bass/studio bands/George Auld/	**Sarah Vaughan/**
Curl Langston/trumpet/studio bands/Don Redman Orch./	Don Redman/**Harlan Latimore/Bing Crosby/Boswell Sisters/Mills Brothers/**
Cutshall Cutty/trombone/studio bands/Benny Goodman/Billy Butterfield/	**Peggy Lee/Margaret Whiting/**
Cyr John/drum/studio bands/Freddie Slack/	**Ella Mae Morse/Johnny Mercer/**
Dacus 'Smokey' William/drums/studio bands/Bob Wills & his Texas Playboys/	Tommy Duncan/
Daffan Ted/steel guitar/songwriter/studio bands/his Texans/	Chuck Keeshan/Leon Seago/
D'Agustino/trombone/studio bands/Mitchell Ayres/Lloyd Shaffer/Axel Stordahl/	**Perry Como/Frank Sinatra/**
Dale Alan/arrainger/some vocals/studio bands/own Orch./	Alan Dale/**Connie Haines/**
Dale Joe/drums/studio bands/Mitchell Ayres/	**Perry Como/**
Dale Ted /Orchestra/	**Mildred Bailey/Sarah Vaughan/Dinah Shore/Buddy Clark/**
Dalhart Vernon/harmonica/kazoo/own vocals/studio bands/	Vernon Dalhart/**Cliff Edwards/**
Dameron Tad/pianist/arrainger/songwriter/studio bands/his Orch./	**Sarah Vaughan/**
D'Almaine Charles/violin/arrainger/	Len Spencer/
D'Amico/Hank/clarinet/alto saxophone/studio bands/Bob Crosby//Russ Case/	**Connie Boswell/Bing Crosby/Perry Como/**
D'Amico/Hank/clarinet/alto saxophone/studio bands/Bob Crosby/Red Norvo/	**Mildred Bailey/**Bob Crosby/Kay Weber/Marion Mann/**Helen Ward/**
Dant Charles dir. Orchestra/	**Dick Haymes/**
Darby & Tarlton/Tom Darby - vocal, guitar/Jimmie Tarlton - vocal, guitar/	Darby & Tarlton
Daugherty Eddie/drums/studio bands/	**Billie Holiday/**
Davies Howaed 'Bud'/drums/Benny Goodman/	**Peggy Lee/**

Davis Al/trumpet/studio bands/Benny Goodman/	**Peggy Lee/**
Davis Art/fiddle/studio bands/	**Gene Autry/**
Davis Ed/guitar/studio bands/	**Jimmie Davis/**
Davis Eddie 'Lockjaw'/tenor saxophone/Lucky Millander/studio bands/	**Sister Rosetta Tharpe/Dinah Washington/**
Davis Jackie/organ/studio bands/	**Dinah Washington/**
Davis Jasper & His Orchestra/	**Lizzie Miles/**
Davis Leonard/trumphet/studio bands/Don Redmon/	Don Redmon/**Harlan Lattimore/Bing Crosby/Boswell Sisters/Mills Brothers/**
Davis Lem/alto saxophone/studio bands/	**Billie Holiday/**
Davis Maxwell/tenor sax/studio bands/own Orchestra/	Mabel Scott/
Davis Miles/trumpet/studio bands/	**Billy Eckstine/Sarah Vaughn/**
Davis Pat/tenor saxophone/studio bands/Casa Loma Orch./	**Connie Boswell/Lee Wiley/**
Davis Pike/trumpet/studio bands/Lew Leslie's Blackbirds Orch./	**Adelaide Hall/**
Davison 'Wild' Bill/pianist/cornet/studio bands/Louis Jordan/Eddie Condon/	**Louis Jordan/Bing Crosby/**
Dawn Dolly & Her Dawn Patrol/own vocals/mostly (George Hall Orch.)	**Dolly Dawn/**
Dean Demas/trumpet/studio bands/Lew Leslie's Blackbirds Orch./	**Adelaide Hall/**
DeArango Bill/jazz guitar/studio bands/	**Sarah Vaughan/**
Decker James/french horn/studio bands/Nelson Riddle/	**Frank Sinatra/**
Deems Barret/drums/studio bands/arrainger/	**Louis Armstrong/Bing Crosby/**
Dees Allen/guitar/studio bands/	**Jimmie Davis/**
DeFranco Buddy/clarinet/studio bands/Gene Krupa/Charlie Barnet/	**Anita O'Day/Kay Starr/**
DeKnight Rene/pianist/vocals/studio bands/Delta Rhythm Boys/	**Delta** Rhythm Boys/**Mildred Bailey/Ella Fitzgerald/**
Delmare Brothers/Alton - vocal & guitar/Rabon - vocal & guitar/songwriters/	Delmare Brothers/
Delta Rhythm Boys/bass/ lead by vocals of Kelsey Parr/var/members/	**Delta** Rhythm Boys/**Mildred Bailey/Ella Fitzgerald/**
DeLange Eddie/songwriter/arranger/studio bands/Hudson-DeLange Orch./	Betty Allen/
DeLuca Rude/trombone/studio bands/Georgie Auld/	**Sarah Vaughan/**
DeLugg Milton/accordian/studio bands/arrainger/songwriter/Matt Mattlock/	**Bing Crosby/**
Dennis Matt/pianist/songwriter/Tommy Dorsey/own Orch./	**Frank Sinatra/Connie Haines/Jo Stafford/Dick Haymes/**
Dennis Stanley/bass/studio bands/Casa Loma Orch./	**Connie Boswell/Lee Wiley/**
Denny Jack/arranger/studio band/his Waldorf Astoria Orchestra/	Paul Small/
DeParis Sidney/trumpet/studio bands/Don Redman Orch./	Don Redman/**Harlan Latimore/Bing Crosby/Boswell Sisters/**
DePew Bill/alto saxophone/studio bands/Denny Goodman/	**Helen Ward/Ella Fitzgerald/**
DeParis Wilbur/trombone/studio bands/Louis Armstrong/	**Louis Armstrong/Ella Fitzgerald/**
DeRosa Vince/french horn/studio bands/Nelson Riddle/	**Nat King Cole/Frank Sinatra/**
DeRose Pete/pianist/studio bands/	**Annette Hanshaw/**
Dessinger George/clarinet/studio bands/Larry Clinton/	**Bea Wain/Dick Todd/**
DeSylvia Buddy/ukulele/studio bands/songwriter/Isham Jones/	**Al Jolson/**
Deutsch Solomon/viola/studio bands/Artie Shaw/Alex Stordahl/	**Lena Horne/Frank Sinatra/**
DeVol Frank/violin/saxophone/studio bands/his Orch./	**Ella Fitzgerald/Margaret Whiting/Kay Starr/Rosemary Clooney/Doris Day/Nat King Cole/**
DeVooet John Peter/violin/studio bands/	**Dean Martin/**
DeVorzon Jules/violin/studio bands/Rudy Vallee/	**Rudy Vallee/**
Dexter Al/steel guitar/studio bands/some vocals/his Troopers/	Al Dexter/
Dial Harry/drums/studio bands//F. Waller And His Rhythm/	**Fats Waller/**
DiCarlo Torn/trumpet/studio bands/Gene Krupa/	**Helen Ward/**
Dickerson R/Q./trombone/studio bands/Cab Calloway/	**Cab Calloway/**
Dickinson Vic/trombone/studio bands/	**Louis Armstrong/**
Dickler Dick or Richard/viola/studio bands/Joe Bushkin/Percy Faith/	**Lee Wiley/Tony Bennett/**
Dieterle Kurt/violin/studio bands/Paul Whiteman/	**Bing Crosby/**
Dinkin Alvin/viola/studio bands/Nelson Riddle/	**Frank Sinatra/**
Dixie Band - & her - Leona Williams/	Leona Williams/
Dixie - her band from (Ivie Anderson) (associated with Duke Ellington)	**Ivie Anderson**
Dixon Charlie/banjo/studio bands/F. Henderson's Hot Six/	**Alberta Hunter/Ma Rainey/Trixie Smith/Edith Wilson/Bessie Smith/ Clara Smith/**
Dixon Gus/trombone/studio bands/Georgie Auld/	**Sarah Vaughan/**
Dixon Joe/clarinet/studio bands/Eddie Condon/	**Bing Crosby/**
Dodds Baby/drums/studio bands/Louis Armstrong's Hot Seven/	**Louis Armstrong/**
Dodds Johnny/clarinet/studio bands/Louis Armstrong's Hot Seven/	**Louis Armstrong**/Hociel Thomas/
Dodson Bert/bass/studio bands/Pinafores/	**Gene Autry/**
Dogget Bill/pianist/studio bands/Bill Doggett Octet/	**Helen Humes/**
Donahue Sam/tenor saxophone/studio bands/Benny Goodman/	Irene Day/
Dornbach Fred/saxophone/studio bands/Ted Steel/	**Perry Como/**
Dorsey Bob/tenor saxophone/studio bands/	**Billie Holiday/**
Dorsey Brother Orch./ - Radio Master - 1933/	**Ethel Waters/Boswell Sisters/**
Dorsey Brothers - Jimmy & Tommy/own orch./ - uncredited & credited/	**Lee Morse/Emmett Miller/Bing Crosby/Chick Bullock/Bob Crosby/**Bob Eberly/Kay Weber/Greta Keller?/
Dorsey Brothers - Jimmy & Tommy/own orch./ - uncredited & credited/	**Mills Brothers/Boswell Sisters/Connie Boswell/Mildred Bailey/**
Dorsey Brothers - Jimmy - clarinet/alto sax/Tommy - trumpet/trombone - unacredited/	**Ruth Etting/Bing Crosby/Ethel Waters/Annette Hanshaw/Mildred Bailey/** Harold Arlen/
Dorsey Jimmy Orch./studio bands/dance band/with own designated bandsingers	Helen O'Connell/June Richmond/Bob Eberly/Kitty Kallen/Teddy Walters/ Frances Langford

Dorsey Jimmy Orch./with others/ & own designated bandsingers	**Andrews Sisters/Louis Armstrong/**Frances Langford/
Dorsey Jimmy/clarinet/alto saxophone/studio bands/P. Whiteman//Dorsey Brothers/	**Sophie Tucker/Cliff Edwards/Ruth Etting/Annette Hanshaw/Eva Taylor/**
Dorsey Jimmy/clarinet/alto saxophone/studio bands/P. Whiteman/Miff Mole Molers/D. Brothers/	**Bing Crosby/Ethel Waters/Chick Bullock/**
Dorsey Thomas A./ - as Georgia Tom Dorsey/pianist/songwriter/some vocals/	**Ma Rainey/**Tampa Red/
Dorsey Tommy Orch./studio band/dance band/ own designated bandsingers/	**Frank Sinatra/Jo Stafford/Connie Haines/**Teddy Walters/June Hutton/
Dorsey Tommy Orch./studio band/dance band/with own designated bandsingers/	/Edythe Wright/Cliff Weston/Jack Leonard/Pied Pipers/Buddy Gately/Sy Oliver/Cliff Weston/
Dorsey Tommy/studio bands - unacredited/Sizzling Syncopators/Lennie Hayton/	**Annette Hanshaw/Eva Taylor/Bing Crosby/**
Dorsey Tommy/trumpet/trombone/studio bands/Paul Whiteman/Dorsey Brothers/	**Bing Crosby/Ethel Waters/Boswell Sisters/Chick Bullock/**
Doty Mike/clarinet/studio bands/Larry Clinton/	**Bea Wain/**
Dougherty Eddie/drums/arrainger/M. B. Oxford Grey's/Pete Johnson/Art Tatum/	**Mildred Bailey/Joe Turner/**
Douglas Mark/saxophone/studio bands/Les Brown/	**Doris Day/**
Douglas Tommy Orchestra/	**Julia Lee/**
Down Home Syncopators her/	**Trixie Smith/**
Down Home Trio her - Bessie Smith/	**Bessie Smith/**
Downey Rob/pianist/studio bands/	**Lee Morse/**
Dowell Saxie/tenor saxophone/studio bands/Hal Kemp/	Skinnay Ennis/Maxine Gray/
Downing Rex/trombone/studio bands/dance band/Coon0Sanders Orch./	**Carlton Coon/Joe Sanders/**
Drayton Charlie/bass/studio bands/Louis Jordan/Pete Brown/	**Louis Jordan/Helen Humes/**
Drellinger Art/tenor saxophone/studio bands/Sy Oliver/Gordon Jenkins/George Siravo/	**Billie Holiday/Louis Armstrong/Peggy Lee/Frank Sinatra/**
Dreyer Les/alto saxophone/studio bands/	**Bing Crosby/**
Drifting Cowboys - Hank Williams & His Drifting Cowboys/	**Hank Williams**
Duchin Eddy/pianist/Leo Reisman/own Central Park Casino Orch./on V - Disc/	Harold Arlen/Lew Sherwood/Mary Martin/**Bing Crosby/**
Duffy Al/violin/studio bands/	**Ruth Etting/**
Duke Vernon/pianist/song writer/studio bands/	**Hildegarde**
Dumas Prentis/giutar/studio bands/	**Jimmie Davis/**
Duncan Bud/steel guitar/studio bands/Maddox Brothers & Rose/	**Rose Maddox/**
Dunham Sonny/trumbone/studio bands/Casa Loma Orchestra/	**Connie Boswell/Lee Wiley/**
Dunlap Paul Orchestra/	**Frankie Laine/**
Dunn Johnny /cornet//arrainger/studio bands/Johnny Dunn's Jazz Hounds	**Mamie Smith/Edith Wilson/**
Durante Jimmy/pianist/with Lou Clayton & Eddie Jackson in jazz band/novelty/	Jimmy Durante/
Durante Jimmy/pianist/with Lou Clayton - Film Master - 1930	**Helen Morgan/**
Durham Eddie/trombone/guitar/studio bands/Count Basie/	**Jimmy Rushing/Helen Humes/**
Durium Dance Band/ (British band)	**Al Bowlly/**
Duvivier George/bass/studio bands/	**Billie Holiday/**
Easterday Jess/guitar/studio bands/Roy Acuff/	**Roy Acuff/**
Ebony Four her - Ethel Waters/	**Ethel Waters/**
Eckles Dick 'Dent'/tenor saxophone/flute/studio bands/Gordon Jenkins/	**Billie Holiday/**
Eckstine Billy/ trumpet/trombone/studio bands/Earl Hines/ & His Orchestra. own vocals/	**Billy Eckstine/Sarah Vaughan/**
Edelstein Walter/violin/studio bands/Dorsey Brothers/Axel Stordahl/Nelson Riddle/	**Bing Crosby/Ethel Waters/Boswell Sisters/Frank Sinatra/Nat King Cole/**
Edison Harry/trumpet/studio bands/Count Basie/Nelson Riddle/	**Jimmy Rushing/Helen Humes/Frank Sinatra/**
Edlin Louis/violinist/studio bands/Artie Shaw/	**Lena Horne/**
Edwards Bass/tuba/studio bands/Lew Leslie's Blackbirds Orch./	**Adelaide Hall/**
Edwards Cliff - Ukulele Ike - /vocals/ukele/	**Cliff Edwards/**
Effros Bob/trumpet/studio bands/Sam Lanin & His Famous Players/Phil Spivey/	**Bing Crosby/Annette Hanshaw/Ethel Waters/Eddie Cantor/**
Elder Joe/clarinet/studio bands/Ethel Waters Jazz Masters/	**Ethel Waters/**
Eldridge Al/pianist/studio bands/Isham Jones/	**Marion Harris/**
Eldridge Roy/trumpet/studio bands/some vocals/Teddy Wilson/Gene Krupa/ others	**Billie Holiday/Anita O'Day/**
Eldridge Roy - Film (TV) Master - 1957	**Billie Holiday**
Elkins Leon/trumpet/studio bands/Louis Armstrong Sebastian New Cotton Club Orch./	**Louis Armstrong/**
Elkins - Payne Jubilee Quartet/	**Alberta Hunter/**
Ellington Duke Orchestra - Film Master/1934/1937/1941/	**Billie Holiday/Mae West/Ivie Anderson/**
Ellington Duke Orch./also known as '/'Hotsy - Totsey Gang'/or Jungle Band/ Cotton Club	**Adelaide Hall/**Irving Mills/Baby Cox/Irving Mills/Ozzie Ware/ Dick Robertson/
Ellington Duke Orchestra - Radio Master - 1941	**Ethel Waters/**
Ellington Duke/'pianist/arrainger/songwriter/studio band/dance band/led his Famous Orch./	**Ivie Anderson/**/Rhythm Boys/**Ethel Waters/Mills Brothers/Bing Crosby/**/ Mae West/
Ellington Duke/pianist/arrainger/songwriter/studio bands/ Orchestra/ 1940s & later/	Joya Sherill/Ray Nance/Herb Jeffries/Betty Roche/Al Hibbler/**Mahalia Jackson/**
Elliot Ernest/clarinet/studio bands/	**Mamie Smith/Edith Wilson/**
Ellis Peter/violin/studio bands/Axel Stordahl/	**Frank Sinatra/**
Ellis Ray/arrainger/studio bands/	**Tony Bennett/**
Ellis Seger/pianist/arrainger /own vocals/studio bands/Orch./	Seger Ellis/
Ellsworth John/(European) Orch./	**Adelaide Hall/**

Elman Ziggy/trumpet/arrainger/studio bands/Benny Goodman/Tommy Dorsey/	**Mildred Bailey/Helen Ward/Martha Tilton/Frank Sinatra/Jo Stafford/ Connie Haines/Frankie Laine/Mel Torme/**
Engel Lehman Orcxh/	**Lena Horne/Adelaide Hall/**
Engund Ernie/trumpet/studio bands/Les Brown/	**Doris Day/**
Ennis Skinnay/drums/vocals/Hal Kemp/	Skinnay Ennis/
Erby John/pianist/studio bands/	**Victoria Spivey/**
Erti Bus/jazz guitar/studio bands/Charlie Barnet/	**Lena Horne/**
Erwin 'Pee Wee' George/trumpet/studio bands/R. Noble/B. Goodman/Jess Stacy/R. Case/	**Al Bowlly/Helen Ward/Lee Wiley/Perry Como/**
Escudero Ralph/bass/studio bands/Alburys Blue And Jazz Seven/F. Henderson's Hot Six/	Lucille Hegamin/**Ethel Waters/Bessie Smith/Ma Rainey/**
Esposito George/trumpet/studio bands/Charlie Barnet/	**Lena Horne/**
Estep Floyd/saxophone/studio bands/Coon Sanders Orch./	**Carleton Coon, Joe Sanders**
Estep Pop/tuba/studio bands/dance bands/Coon - Sanders Orch./	**Carlton Coon/Joe Sanders/**
Estes Buff/alto saxophone/studio bands/Benny Goodman/	**Mildred Bailey/**
Estron Joe/alto saxophone/studio bands/Woody Herman/	**Connie Boswell/**
Evans Henry/flute/studio bands/Freddie Slack/	**Ella Mae Morse/Johnny Mercer/**
Evans Hershel/tenor saxophone/studio bands/Teddy Wilson/Count Basie/	**Billie Holiday/Helen Humes/Jimmy Rushing/**
Ewan Kai/own Orchestra/in Europe/	**Adelaide Hall/**
Fairchild Edgar & His Orchestra/	**Ginny Simms/**
Faith Percy/arrainger/studio bands/ & His Orch./	**Rosemary Clooney/Doris Day/Sarah Vaughan/Frankie Laine/Tony Bennett/Hildegarde**
Fallon Owen/arrainger/his Californians/ Orchestra/	**Harlan Lattimore/**
Farberman Hymie/trumpet/studio bands/	**Lee Morse/**
Farley Ed/trumphet/some vocal/studio bands/Bert Lown/Will Osborne/	Ed Farley/Baltimore Rhythm Boys/Mike Riley/**Will Osborne**
Farley Max/saxophone/studio bands/Paul Whiteman/	Rhythm Boys/**Bing Crosby/**
Farr Hugh/fiddle/studio bands/Sons Of Pioneers/	Bob Nolan/Tim Spencer/Lloyd Perryman/**Roy Rogers/**
Farr Karl/guitar/studio bands/Sons Of Pioneers/	Bob Nolan/Tim Spencer/Lloyd Perryman/**Roy Rogers**/
Fasco Tony/trumpet/studio bands/Benny Goodman/Les Brown/	**Peggy Lee/Dick Haymes/Doris Day/**
Fatool Nick/drum/studio bands/George Hall/Benny Goodman/Dave Baubour/ Gordon Jenkins/	**Dolly Dawn/**Sonny Schuyler/Loretta Lee/**Mildred Bailey/Bing Crosby/ Peggy Lee/Billie Holiday/Johnny Mercer/Frank Sinatra/**Charioteers/
Faulkner Lawrence/pianist/studio bands/	**Ethel Waters/**
Fazola Irving/clarinet/studio bands/Bob Crosby/Claude Thornhill/	Bob Crosby/Kay Weber/Marion Mann/**Bing Crosby/Helen Ward/Billie Holiday/Maxine Sullivan/**
Feather Leonard/pianist/arrainger/studio bands/Leonard Feather's Hiptet/ songwriter/	**Louis Armstrong/Helen Humes/Sarah Vaughan/Ethel Waters/Dinah Washington**
Feld Morey/drums/studio bands/	**Lee Wiley/Sarah Vaughan/**
Feldman Harold/saxophone/studio bands/Axel Stordahl/	**Frank Sinatra/**
Feller Sid /arrainger/Orchestra/	**Jane Froman/**
Felline Tommy/jazz guitar/studio bands/	**Annette Hanshaw/**
Fenton Carl/pianist/studio bands/his Orch./	**Al Jolson/Marion Harris/**
Ferera Frank/Hawaiian guitar/ Hawaiian Trio/	**Annette Hanshaw/**
Ferguson Joe/saxophone/studio bands/Bob Wills & his Texas Playboys/	Tommy Duncan/
Ferguson Maynard/trumpet/studio bands/Stan Kenton/	**June Christy/Nat King Cole/**
Ferretti Andrew/trumpet/studio bands/Axel Stordahl/	**Frank Sinatra/**
Ferrie Joe/trombone/studio bands/(British)/	**Al Bowlly/**
Feuer Cy/studio bands/dir. Orch./	**Alice Faye/**Gertrude Niesen
Fields Eugene/jazz guitar/	**Mildred Bailey/**
Fields Herbie/clarinet/studio bands/Leonard Feather/	**Helen Humes/**
Fields Shep And His Rippling Rhythm Orchestra/	Charles Chester/Hal Derwin/
Finston Nat/ his Paramount Orchestra/	**Bing Crosby/**
Fiorito Ted/pianist/studio bands/	**Nick Lucas/**
Fisher Carl/pianist/arrainger/studio bands/his Orch./his /Swingtet/	**Frankie Laine/Jo Stafford/Doris Day/**
Fisher Shug/string bass/studio bands/Sons Of Pioneers/	**Roy Rogers/**
Fishkin Arnold/bass/studio bands/Jack Teagarden/Les Brown/	**Doris Day/**
Five Kings Of Sycopation/	**Sophie Tucker/**
Flatt Lester/guitar/studio bands/	**Bill Monroe/**
Fleming Herb/tronbone/studio bands/Johnny Dunn/Lew Leslie's Blackbirds Orch./	**Edith Wilson/**Lena Wilson/**Adelaide Hall/**
Fly Cats & his - Joe Turner/	**Joe Turner/**
Flynn Frank/vibraphone/studio bands/Nelson Riddle/	**Frank Sinatra/**
Foley Red/guitar/studio bands/radio/	**Red Foley/**
Ford Mary/guitar/studio bands/Les Paul/	Mary Ford/
Forsdick Dudley/mello phone/studio bands/Irving Mills	**Elisabeth Welch/**
Foster Pops/string bass/studio bands/Louis Armstrong Savoy Five/	**Louis Armstrong/Victoria Spivey/Lizzie Miles/**Hoagy Carmichael/
Four Keys/ & her - Ella Fitzgerald/	**Ella Fitzgerald**
Fowler Lemuel/pianist/studio bands/	**Clara Smith/**
Fox Curly/fiddle/studio bands/	**Jimmie Davis/**
Fox Roy/trumpet/studio bands/led own band - American led British band/	**Nick Lucas/Al Bowlly/**
Fransella Sal/saxophone/studio bands/Ted Steele/	**Perry Como/**
Franz William/tenor saxophone/Louis Armstrong Sebastian New Cotton Club Orch./	**Louis Armstrong/**

Franzella Sal/clarinet/studio bands/Jess Stacy/	**Lee Wiley/**
Frasier Earl/pianist/studio bands/	**Edith Wilson/**
Frazier Bill/tenor saxophone/studio bands/Billy Eckstine/	**Billy Eckstine/Sarah Vaughan/**
Frazier Charles/tenor sax/studio bands/Blanche Calloway Orch./	**Blanche Calloway/**
Freda Robert/violin/studio bands/Ted Steel/Lloyd Shaffer/	**Perry Como/**
Freed Samuel Jr/violin/studio bands/Axel Stordahl/	**Frank Sinatra/**
Freeman Bud/tenor saxophone/studio bands/Ray Noble/M. Sullivan studio band/ own Orch./	**Al Bowlly/Maxine Sullivan/Lee Wiley/Bing Crosby/Thelma Carpenter/**
Freeman Ernie/studio bands/ Orchestra/	**Frank Sinatra/Dean Martin/**
Freeman Hank/alto saxophone/studio bands/Artie Shaw/	**Billie Holiday/**
Freeman Jerry/arranger/studio bands/	**Midge Williams/**
Freeman Stan/pianist/harpsichord/arrainger/studio bands/Eric Siday/	**Lee Wiley/Rosemary Clooney/**
Freeman Tinker/A&R - arranger/pianist/	**Dinah Shore/**
Frey Fran/alto sax/some vocals/studio Bands/George Olsen Orch/	**Ethel Shutta/Boswell Sisters/Mills Brothers/**
Friede Elias/cello/studio bands/Dick Stabile/	**Dean Martin/**
Frisina David/violin/studio bands/Axel Stordahl/	**Frank Sinatra/**
Froeba Frank/pianist/studio bands/Benny Goodman/own band/	**Helen Ward/Midge Williams/**
Fuller Bob/clarinet/studio bands/	**Clara Smith/Lizzie Miles/**
Fulton Jack/trombone/some vocals/Paul Whiteman/	Jack Fulton/Rhythm Boys/**Bing Crosby/**
Fulton John/clarinet/flute/studio bands/Gordon Jenkins/	**Billie Holiday/**
Fuqua Charlie/guitar/studio bands/Ink Spots/	**Ink Spots/Ella Firzgerald/**
Furmansky Harold/viola/violin/studio bands/Axel Stordahl/Russ Case/	**Frank Sinatra/Perry Como/**
Galbraith Barry/jazz guitar/studio bands/Georgie Auld/	**Sarah Vaughan/Dinah Washington/**
Garber Jan/violin/dance band/studio bands/own Orch./	Benny Davis/
Garbler Milton/A&R - arranger/commodores/decca/	**Lee Wiley/Billie Holiday/Peggy Lee/**
Garcia Jake/string bass/studio bands/Jimmy Grier/	**Boswell Sisters/**
Garen Amos/bass/studio bands/Blue Grass Boys/	**Bill Monroe/**
Gasselin Jack/violin/studio bands/Russ Case/	**Perry Como/**
Gaylord Charles/violin/studio bands/Paul Whiteman/	Rhythm Boys/**Bing Crosby/**
Gail Paul/trumpet/studio bands/	**Mel Torme/**
Geller Larry/arrainger/studio bands/	**Frankie Laine/**
Gentry Chuck/baritone saxophone/studio bands/Benny Goodman/Billy May/	**Peggy Lee/Nat King Cole/Frank Sinatra/Dean Martin/**
Georgia Band & her - Ma Rainey/usual leader - pianist - 'Georgia" Tom Dorsey/	**Ma Rainey/**
Georgia Crackers the/studio band/ - actually (Dorsey Brothers)/	**Emmett Miller/**Dan Fitch/
Georgians/studio band/	Dolly Kay/Blossom Seeley/
Gerhardi Tony/guitar/banjo/studio bands/Ted Lewis/	Ted Lewis/**Sophie Tucker/Ruth Etting/Fats Waller/**
Gershman Manny/clarinet/studio bands/Tommy Dorsey/	**Frank Sinatra/Connie Haines/Jo Stafford/**
Getz Stan/saxophone/studio bands/Gene Krupa/Stan Kenton/	**Anita O'Day/**
Gibbons Caroll/pianist/studio bands/ & His Orch, / (British band)	**Hildegarde/**
Gibbs Ernie/trombone/studio bands/Leo Reisman/	**Lee Wiley/**
Gibbs Parker/tenor saxophone/studio bands/Ted Weems/	**Perry Como/**
Gilbert Edgar/cello/studio bands/Nelson Riddle/	**Frank Sinatra/**
Gillespie Dizzy /cornet/trumpet/studio bands/Cab Calloway/Pete Brown/All Star Quintet/Orch.	**Cab Calloway/Helen Humes/Sarah Vaughan/**
Glascoe Percy/clarinet/studio bands/	**Edith Wilson/**
Glenn Tyree/trombone/studio bands/with Eddie Mallory/Cab Calloway/	**Ethel Waters/Cab Calloway/**
Glickman Harry/violin/studio bands/Mitchell Ayres/	**Perry Como/**
Glover Pete/drums/studio bands/Stuff Smith Trio/	**Sarah Vaughan/**
Gluskin Lud/drums/arrainger/studio bands/dance band/ & His Orchestra/	**Buddy Clark/J**oe Host/
Goerner Fred/cello/studio bands/Axel Stordahl/	**Frank Sinatra/**
Gold Lou/arrainger/studio bands/his Orchestra/	**Annette Hanshaw/**
Goldberg Dick/bass/studio bands/George Hall/	**Dolly Dawn/**Sonny Schuyler/Loretta Lee/
Golder Gate Quartet/	Golden Gate Quartet/**Leadbelly/**
Goldstein Lenard/studio bands/	**Mildred Bailey/**
Golizio Matty/jazz guitar/studio bands/Axel Stordahl/	**Frank Sinatra/**
Gomar/drums/studio bands/Dorsey Brothers/	**Bing Crosby/Boswell Sisters/Lee Wiley/**
Gonella Nat/trumpet/studio bands - British/	**Al Bowlly/**
Gonzales Louis/jazz guitar/studio bands/Freddie Slack/	**Ella Mae Morse/Johnny Mercer/**
Gonsoulin Tom/trumpet/studio bands/Gene Krupa/	**Helen Ward/**
Goodall Bill/bass/studio bands/Joe Bushkin/	**Lee Wiley/**
Gooden Cal/guitar/studio bands/Les Paul/	**Bing Crosby/**
Goodman Al/pianist/studio bands/ his Orch./	**Libby Holman/Jane Froman/Thelma Carpenter/**
Goodman Benny Orchestra - Film Master - 1943	**Peggy Lee/**
Goodman Benny/ Quartet/his Sextet/ - regular bandsingers	**Jimmy Rushing/Billie Holiday/Helen Ward//Martha Tilton/Helen Forrest/ Dick Haymes/Peggy Lee**
Goodman Benny/clarinet/arrainger/studio bands/own Orch./	**/Boswell Sisters/**Harold Arlen//**Mildred Bailey/**Louise Tobin/**Ella Fitzgerald/**Al Hendrickson/
Goodman Benny/clarinet/studio bands/dance bands/Charlestown Chasers/Johnny Green/	**/Eva Taylor/Bessie Smith/Lee Morse/Bing Crosby//Lee Wiley/**
Goodman Benny/clarinet/studio bands/dance bands/Ted Lewis/Ben Pollack/	Ted Lewis/Williams Sisters/**Fats Waller/Ruth Etting/Annette Hanshaw/Lee Morse/Ethel Waters/**

Goodman Harry/bass/studio bands/Irving Mills/Benny Goodman/	**Elisabeth Welch/Helen Ward/Ella Fiitzgerald/Martha Tilton/**
Goodman Irving/trumpet/studio bands/Benny Goodman/	**Martha Tilton/**
Gorden Dexter/tenor saxophone/studio bands/Billy Eckstine/	**Billy Eckstine/Sarah Vaughan/**
Gottlieb Victor/cello/studio bands/Nelson Riddle/	**Nat King Cole/**
Gottuso Tony/guitar/studio bands/	Elton Britt/
Gould Dick/trombone/studio bands/Les Brown/	**Doris Day**
Gowans Brad/trombone/studio bands/Eddie Condon/	**Bing Crosby/**
Gozzo Conrad/trumpet/studio bands/Billy May/Nelson Riddle/	**Nat King Cole/Frank Sinatra/Dean Martin/**
Graham A William/trumpet/studio bands/Ted Steele/	**Perry Como/**Elton Britt/
Graham Leonard/trumpet/studio bands/Louis Jordan Timpany Five/	**Louis Jordan/**
Grainger Porter/pianist/kazoo/songwriter/studio bands/	**Bessie Smith/Clara Smith/**Lena Wilson/**Lizzie Miles/**
Gralufek Isodore/violin/studio bands/Ted Steele/	**Perry Como/**
Grande Vincent/tronbone/studio bands/Miff Mole's Molers/	**Midge Williams/**
Grant Bob/pianist/studio bands/and his Savoy Plaza Orchestra/	**Hildegarde**
Graver Luther/trombone/studio bands/Louis Armstrong/	**Louis Armstrong/**
Gray Glenn/alto saxophone/hotel dance bands/studio bands/led Casa Loma Orch./	Kenny Sargent/**Mildred Bailey/Connie Boswell/Lee Wiley/**
Gray Jerry/arranger/studio bands/Artie Shaw/Glenn Miller/	Ray Eberly/Marrion Hutton/Tex Beneke/**Vic Damone/Jane Froman/**
Gray Wardell/tenor saxophone/studio bands/Jimmy Cobb/	**Dinah Washington/**
Green Benny/trombone/studio bands/George Tredwell/	**Sarah Vaughan/**
Green Charlie/trombone/studio bands/HF. Henderson's Hot Six/Louis Armstrong/	**Ma Rainey/Trixie Smith/Bessie Smith/Louis Armstrong/Clara Smith/**
Green Freddie/jazz guitar/ Count Basie/studio bands/George Tredwell/Teddy Stewart/	**Billie Holiday/Jimmy Rushing/Helen Humes/Sarah Vaughan/Dinah Washington/**
Green Gordon/clarinet/tenor saxophone/Jimmy Grier/	**Boswell Sisters/**
Green Johnny/pianist/studio bands/radio/Leo Reisman/own Orch./MGM Orch./	**Lee Wiley/ Ethel Merman/Bing Crosby/Frank Sinatra/**Grace Kelly/Celeste Holm/
Green Lil/pianist/arrainger/songwriter/some vocals/studio bands/	Lil Green/**Big Bill Broonzy/**
Green Ray/drums/Ethel Waters Jazz Masters/	**Ethel Waters/**
Green Stan/trumpet/studio bands/Jimmy Grier/	**Boswell Sisters/**
Green Wynton/pianist/studio bands/	**Dinah Washington/**
Greenberg Jack/saxophone/studio bands/Gordon Jenkins/	**Peggy Lee/**
Greenwood Clifford/(British) Orchestra/	**Paul Robeson/Elisabeth Welch/**
Greer Sonny/drum/studio bands Duke Ellington/	/Rhythm Boys/**Ivie Anderson/Ethel Waters//Mills Brothers/Bing Crosby/**
Greer Sonny/drum/studio bands Duke Ellington/I. Mills & His Hotsey Totsey Gang/	**Adelaide Hall/**Baby Cox/Ozzie Ware/Irving Mills/
Grier Art/clarinet/tenor saxophone/studio bands/Jimmy Grier/	**Boswell Sisters/**
Grier Jimmy Orchestra - Film Master - 1934	**Russ Columbo/**June Knight/
Grier Jimmy/clarinet/arranger/some vocals/studio bands/Gus Arnheim/radio/own Orch./	**/Boswell Sisters/Connie Boswell/Helen Morgan/Ruth Etting/**PinkyTomlin/
Grier Jimmy/clarinet/some vocals/studio bands/own Orch./	Jimmy Grier/**Bing Crosby/Russ Columbo/**
Griffin Cris/trumpet/studio bands/Benny Goodman/Axel Stordahl/Billy Butterfield/G. Siravo/	**Martha Tilton/Frank Sinatra/Margaret Whiting/**
Griffin Gordon/trumpet/studio bands/Miff Mole's Molers/B. Goodman/Axel Stordahl/	**Martha Tilton/Billie Holiday/Midge Williams/Frank Sinatra/**
Griffin John/guitar/studio bands/	**Bessie Smith/**
Grimes Charlie/alto saxophone/studio bands/	**Lizzie Miles/**
Grimes Tiny/jazz guitar/studio bands/Tiny Grimes Sextet/	**Billie Holiday/**
Griselle Tom/arrainger/Orchestra/	Maurice Chevalier/
Grishaw James/guitar/studio bands/Drifting Cowboys/	**Hank Williams**
Grofe's Ferde/arrainger/studio bands/Paul Whiteman/	Rhythm Boys/**Bing Crosby/**
Guarante Frank/trumpet/studio bands/	**Bing Crosby/**
Guarnieri John/pianist/studio bands/George Hall/Axel Stordahl/	**Dolly Dawn/Frank Sinatra/**
Guthrie Jack/guitar/voclas/studio bands/songwriter/his Oklahomans/	Jack Guthrie/
Guthrie Woody/guitarharmonica//vocal/songwriter/studio bands/	**Woody Guthrie/**
Guy Fred/jazz guitar/trombone/studio bands/Duke Ellington/	**Adelaide Hall/**Rhythm Boys/**Ivie Anderson/Ethel Waters/Bing Crosby/**
Guy Joe/trombone/studio bands/	**Billie Holiday/**
Hackett/Bobby/trumpet/arrainger/studio bands/Claude Thornhill/Joe Ventuti/Axel Stordahl/	**Maxine Sullivan/Andrews Sisters/Bing Crosby/Lee Wiley/Frank Sinatra/ Billie Holiday/**Johnny Desmond/
Hag Al/pianist/studio bands/	**Sarah Vaughan/**
Hagan Earle/trombone/studio bands/Ray Noble/own Orch./	**Buddy Clark/Dick Haymes/**
Hagan Ray/drum/studio bands/Axel Stordahl/	**Frank Sinatra/**
Haggart Bob/pianist/trumpet/bass/arrainger/studio bands/ & his Jesters/Orch./	**Bing Crosby/Helen Ward/Billie Holiday/Connie Boswell/Ella Fitzgerald/ Louis Jordan/**Jesters/
Haggart Bob/pianist/trumpet/bass/arrainger/studio bands/Russ Case/Billy Butterfield/	**Perry Como/Margaret Whiting/Lee Wiley/Rosemary Clooney/**
Haig Al/pianist/studio bands/Dizzie Gillespie/	**Sarah Vaughan/**
Halbert Howard/violin/studio bands/Axel Stordahl/	**Frank Sinatra/**
Haley Bill / & His Comets/guitar/Saddlemen/His Four Aces/	Bill Haley/
Hall Alfred/string bass/studio bands/M. W. Jazz Jesters/	**Midge Williams/**
Hall Ed/clarinet/studio bands/arrainger/Billie Holiday/Teddy Wilson/M/W/Jazz Jesters/	**Billie Holiday/Midge Williams/Louis Armstrong/Bing Crosby/Joe Turner/**
Hall George/violin/studio bands/ his Arcadians/his Music/his Hotel Taft Orch./	**Dolly Dawn/**Sonny Schuyler/Loretta Lee/

Hall Joe/pianist/studio bands/Casa Loma Orch./	**Connie Boswell/Lee Wiley/**
Hall Lonnie/fiddle/studio bands/Leon's Lone Star Cowboys/Charles Mitchell's Texans/	**Jimmie Davis**/Leon Chappelear/
Hall Minor/drums/studio bands/	**Louis Armstrong/**
Hall Nelson/jazz guitar/banjo/studio bands/Gus Arnheim Orch./	**Russ Columbo/**
Hall Tubby/drums/studio bands/Louis Armstrong/	**Louis Armstrong/Cleo Brown/**
Hall Wendell/ukelele/studio bands/radio/	Wendell Hall/
Hall Wilbur/jazz guitar/studio bands/Paul Whiteman/	Rhythm Boys/**Bing Crosby/**
Halloran Jack/arrainger/studio bands/	**Bing Crosby/**
Hamilton Jimmy/clarinet/studio bands/Pete Brown/	**Billie Holiday/Helen Humes/**
Hammond John/A&R - arranger/ARC - Columbia/Okeh/	**Billie Holiday/Helen Humes/Jimmy Rushing/Thelma Carpenter/**
Hampton Lionel/ - Radio Master - 1945	**Dinah Washington/**
Hampton Lionel/drum/arrainger/vibraphone/saxophone/studio bands/L. Armstrong/own Orch/	**Louis Armstrong/Bing Crosby/Dinah Washington/**
Hanlon Allen/jazz guitar/studio bands/Red Norvo/Lloyd Shaffer/Percy Faith/	**Mildred Bailey/Perry Como/Tony Bennett/**
Hanty Bill/drums/studio bands/	**Al Bowlly/**
Happiness Boys & her - Dinah Shore/	**Dinah Shore/**
Happiness Boys - Ernest Hare & Billy Jones own vocals/	Ernest Hare & Billy Jones/
Harbert Slim/bass/studio bands/Leon's Lone Star Cowboys/	Leon Chappelear/
Hardman Walter/bass/studio bands/Larry Clinton/	**Bea Wain/Dick Todd/**
Hardwick Otto/clarinet/studio band/with Duke Ellington/	**Adelaide Hall/Ivie Anderson/**
Haring Bob/arrainger/songwriter/led Colonial Club Orch/own Orch/	**Libby Holman/**
Harland Don/saxophone/studio bands/Bob Wills & his Texas Playboys/	Tommy Duncan/
Harlem Hamfats/studio band/	Ham Hamfoot/**Frankie Half Pint Jaxton/**
Harminians her - Kate Smith/	**Kate Smith/**
Harmony Eight/ - James P. Johnson's/	**Trixie Smith/**
Harper Buddy/jazz guitar/studio bands/	**Ivie Anderson/**
Harris Arville/clarinet/alto saxophone/studio bands/Cab Calloway/	**Cab Calloway/Chick Bullock/**
Harris Charles/drums/studio bands/Bill Doggett/	**Helen Humes/**
Harris Charlie/bass/studio bands/Nelson Riddle/Billy May/	**Nat King Cole/Dean Martin/**
Harris Clarence/studio bands/Alburys Blues And Jazz Seven/	Lucille Hegamin/**Ethel Waters/**
Harris Dave/trombone/tenor saxophone/studio bands/M. W. Jazz Jesters/	**Midge Williams/Billie Holiday/**
Harris Dickie/trombone/studio bands/with J C Heard/	**Ethel Waters**
Harris George/jazz guitar/studio bands/	**Bing Crosby/**
Harris Leroy/alto saxophone/studio bands/Tadd Dameron/	**Sarah Vaughan/**
Harris Sidney/violin/studio bands/Axel Stordahl/Ted Steele/Mitchell Ayres/	**Frank Sinatra/Perry Como/**
Harris Stanley/viola/studio bands/Nelson Riddle/	**Nat King Cole/**
Harrison Jimmy/trombone/studio bands/	**Bessie Smith/**
Harry Bert/trumpet/studio bands/Freddie Slack/	**Ella Mae Morse/Johnny Mercer/**
Harshman Allen/viola/studio bands/Axel Stordahl/	**Frank Sinatra/**
Hart Clyde/pianist/studio bands/Blanche Calloway/Billie Holiday/	**Blanche Calloway/Billie Holiday/**
Hartman Leonard/saxophone/studio bands/Axel Stordahl/	**Frank Sinatra/**
Harvey Johnny/clarinet/studio bands/Leon's Lone Star Cowboys/	Leon Chappelear/
Harvey Roy/studio bands/folk/C. Poole North Carolina Ramblers/	Charlie Poole/
Haughton Chauncey/clarinet/sax/studio bands/Duke Ellington/Chick Webb/	**Ivie Anderson/Ella Fitzgerald/**
Hawes Pete/guitar/some vocals/studio bands/Almanac Singers/	Almanac Singers/**Woody Guthrie/**
Hawkins Coleman/bass//tenor saxophone/studio bands/Benny Goodman/ Metronome All Stars/	**/Mildred Bailey/Thelma Carpenter/Nat King Cole/June Christy/Frank Sinatra/**
Hawkins Coleman/bass//tenor saxophone/studio bands/F. Henderson's Hot Six/ & Orch./	**Mamie Smith/Ethel Waters/Ma Rainey/Bessie Smith/**
Hawkins Coleman - Film (TV) Master - 1957	**Billie Holiday**
Hawkins Erskine/arrainger/trumpet/ studio bands/his Orch./	Laura Washington/
Hawkins Skipper/bass/studio bands/Leon's Lone Star Cowboys/	Leon Chappelear/
Haworski Harry/violin/studio bands/Gus Arnheim/	**Bing Crosby/**
Hayes Clancy/jazz guitar/studio bands/Bob Scobey/	**Bing Crosby/Lizzie Miles/**
Hayes Clifford/fiddle/studio bands/Louisville Jug Band/	**Jimmie Rodgers/**
Hayes Clyde 'spider'/pianist/studio bands/M/W. Jazz Jesters/	**Midge Williams/**
Hayes Edgar/pianist/arranger/Mills Rhythm Band/Blue Ribbon Boys/	**Chick Bullock/Adalaide Hall/**
Haymer Herbie/tenor saxophone/studio bands/Red Norvo/Axel Stordahl/	**Mildred Bailey/Frank Sinatra/Peggy Lee/**
Hayton Lennie/Orchestra - Film Master - 1946	**Lena Horne**
Hayton Lennie/pianist/arrainger/studio bands/Paul Whiteman/ & own Orch./	**Bing Crosby/Lena Horne/**Harry Belefonte/
Hazel Marion 'Boonie'/tuba/studio bands/Billy Eckstine/	**Billy Eckstine/Sarah Vaughan/**
Hazlett Chet/clarinet/alto saxophone/studio bands/Paul Whiteman/Dorsey Brothers/	Rhythm Boys/**Bing Crosby/Boswell Sisters/**
Heard J C/ jazz guitar/drums/studio bands/Teddy Wilson/his Orch./George Tredwell/	**Billie Holiday/Sarah Vaughan/Ethel Waters/**
Hefti Neal/trumpet/arrainger/studio bands/Georgie Auld/	**Sarah Vaughan/**
Hegamin Bill/pianist/studio bands/	Lucille Hegamin/
Heglin Wally/jazz guitar/studio bands/Jimmy Grier/	**Boswell Sisters/**
Heimel Otto/as 'Coco'/guitar/studio bands/	**Gene Austin/**
Hein Wes/trombone/studio bands/	**Mildred Bailey/**

Heindorf Ray/arranger/studio bands/own Orch./	**Doris Day/Judy Garland/**
Heising Louise/fiddle/violin/studio bands/Pinafores/	**Gene Autry/**
Heller Ben/guitar/studio bands/Benny Goodman/	**Martha Tilton/**
Hellman Edwin/saxophone/studio bands/Ted Steel/Lloyd Shaffer/	**Perry Como/**
Henderson Fletcher Orchestra/pianist/ - Radio Master - 1944	**Lena Horne/Ethel Waters**
Henderson Fletcher/Henderson's Dance Orchestra/Novelty Orchestra/	**Alberta Hunter/Clara Smith/**
Henderson Fletcher/pianist/arrainger/studio bands/dance bands/Jazz Masters/Hot Six/Benny Goodman/	**Ethel Waters/Trixie Smith/Bessie Smith/Ma Rainey/Josie Miles/Harlan Lattimore/Mildred Bailey/Helen Ward/**
Henderson Horance/pianist/studio bands/Don Redman/Orch./own Orch./	Don Redman/**Harlan Lattimore/Bing Crosby/Boswell Sisters/Billie Holiday/Lena Horne/**
Henderson Luther/arrainger/studio bands/own Orch./	**Lena Horne/Thelma Carpenter/**
Henderson Rickie/alto saxophone/studio bands/	**Dinah Washington/**
Henderson Skitch/pianist/studio bands/Philco Show - radio/Steve Allen TV - Tonight Show/	**Bing Crosby/Billie Holiday/**
Hendrickson Alton/jazz guitar/studio bands/Freddie Slack/Nelson Riddle/	**Ella Mae Morse/Nat King Cole/Frank Sinatra/**
Henry Frances/jazz guitar/studio bands/with Guy Lombardo & His Royal Canadians Orch./	**Bing Crosby/**Carmen Lombardo**Andrews Sisters/Al Jolson/**
Henry Heywood/tenor saxophone/studio bands/Tiny Grimes Sextett/	**Billie Holiday/**
Hereford Fletcher/clarinet/studio bands/Larry Clinton/	**Bea Wain/**
Herfert Skeets/clarinet/alto saxophone/studio bands/Jimmy Dorsey/Billy May/N, Riddle/	**Louis Armstrong/Bing Crosby/**Frances Langford/**Mel Torme/Nat King Cole/Frank Sinatra/Dean Martin/**
Herman Max/trumpet/studio bands/Bob Crosby/	**Connie Boswell/Bing Crosby/**
Herman Woody/saxophone/clarinet/some vocals/G. Arnheim/ I. Jones/his Woodchoppers/s	Woody Hermann/Muriel Lane/**Connie Boswell//Bing Crosby/Billy Eckstine/**Frances Wayne/
Herriford Leon/alto saxophone/studio bands/Louis Armstrong/	**Louis Armstrong/**
Hershaft Maurice/violin/studio bands/Axel Stordahl/	**Frank Sinatra/**
Heywood Eddie - Jr/pianist/arrainger/studio bands/own Orch/	**Alberta Hunter/Ella Fitzgerald/Billie Holiday/Andrews Sisters/**
Heywood Eddie - Sr./pianist/studio bands/	Sippy Wallace/
Hicks Billy/trombone/trumpet/studio bands/Louis Armstrong/M. W. Jazz Jesters/	**Louis Armstrong/Midge Williams/**
Hicks Henry/trombone/studio bands/Jasper Davis Orch./	**Lizzie Miles/**
Higginbotham J. C./trombone/studio bands/Louis Armstrong Savoy Ballroom Five/A. Shaw/	**Louis Armstrong/Victoria Spivey/**Hoagy Carmichael/**Lena Horne/**
Higgins Bob/trumpet/studio bands/Les Brown/	**Doris Day/**
Hildegarde/or Loretta Sell/vocalist & pianist/also with Harry Sosnik/	**Hildegarde**
Hill Cliff/bass/studio bands/Benny Goodman/	**Peggy Lee/**
Hill Ruth/harp/studio bands/Tommy Dorsey/Ted Steele/	**Frank Sinatra/Jo Stafford/Connie Haines/Perry Como/**
Hill Teddy/tenor saxophone/studio bands/Louis Armstrong Savoy Ballroom Five/	**Louis Armstrong/Victoria Spivey/**Hoagy Carmichael/
Hilliard Jimmy/A&R- arranger/Mercury/	**Frankie Laine/Patti Page/**
Hillman Roscoe/jazz guitar/studio bands/Jimmy Dorsey/	**Louis Armstrong/Bing Crosby/**Frances Langford/
Himber Richardviolin//studio bands/dance band/ his Ritz - Canton Orch./ Orchestra/	**Libby Holman/**Joey Nash/
Hines Earl/pianist/arrainger/studio bands/Louis Armstrong/ & own Orch./	**Louis Armstrong/Valaida Snow/Billy Eckstine/**
Hinton Milt/bass/studio bands/Eddie Mallory/Cab Calloway/	**Ethel Waters/Cab Calloway/Billie Holiday/**
Hite Les/alto saxophone/studio bands/Louis Armstrong/	**Louis Armstrong/**
Hodges Johnny /clarinet//alto saxophone/arrainger/Duke Ellington/	Rhythm Boys/**Ethel Waters/Ivie Anderson/Bing Crosby/**
Hodges Johnny /clarinet//alto saxophone/arrainger/Duke Ellington/own Orchestra/Metronome All Stars/	**/Buddy Clark/Billie Holiday/Nat King Cole/June Christy/Frank Sinatra**
Hoffman Harry/violin/studio bands/Dorsey Brothers/Russ Case/	**Bing Crosby/Ethel Waters/Boswell Sisters/Perry Como/**
Hogan Carl/electric guitar/studio bands/Louis Jordan Tympany Five/	**Louis Jordan/Bing Crosby/**
Hogg Jack/electric guitar/studio bands/Rudy Sooter's Ranchmem/	**Jimmie Davis/**
Holiday Billie & Her Orchestra/studio band only - usually led by Teddy Wilson/	**Billie Holiday/**
Hollinger Harry/trumpet/studio bands/Al Dexter's Troopers/	Al Dexter/
Hollon Kenneth/tenor saxophone/studio bands/	**Billie Holiday/**
Hollywood Hotshots her - Cleo Brown/	**Cleo Brown/**
Holmes Charlie/clarinet/alto saxophone/studio bands/Louis Armstrong Savoy Ballroom Five/	**Louis Armstrong/Victoria Spivey/**Hoagy Carmichael/**Lizzie Miles/**
Holmes Horance/clarinet/studio bands/E. W. Plantation Orch./	**Ethel Waters/**
Holmes Salty/guitat/studio bands/Gene Autry Trio/	**Gene Autry/**
Homer Ben/arrainger/studio bands/songwrtier/Les Brown/	**Doris Day/**
Hooper Louis/pianist/studio bands/	**Ethel Waters/Lizzie Miles/**
Hoosier Hot Shots/	Two Ton Baker/
Hopsoner Ray/alto saxophone/studio bands/Woody Herman/	**Connie Boswell/**
Hopkins Claude/pianist/studio bands/	**Ma Rainey/Josephine Baker/**
Horvath Jimmy/saxophone/studio bands/George Siravo/	**Frank Sinatra/**
Hoskins Jimmy/drums/studio bands/	**Mildred Bailey/**
Hot Combination his/Cliff Edwards	**Cliff Edwards/**
Hotel Pennsylvania Trio/	Hotel Pennsylvanis Trio/
House Art/trumpet/studio bands/Georgie Auld/	**Sarah Vaughan/**
Howard Eddie & His Orchestra/own vocals/	Eddie Howard/
Howard Francis/trombone/studio bands/Nelson Riddle/	**Mel Torme/Frank Sinatra/**
Howard Joe/trombone/studio bands/Nelson Riddle/	**Frank Sinatra/**
Howe Bones/drums/arrainger/studio bands/Billy May/	**Bing Crosby/Rosemary Clooney/**

Hudson Bruce/trumpet/studio bands/Axel Stordahl/	**Frank Sinatra/**
Hudson George/trumpet/studio bands/	**Dinah Washington/**
Hudson Will/ arranger/songwriter/studio bands/Hudson-DeLange Orch/	Betty Allen/
Hughes John/pianist/studio bands/	**Lonnie Johnson/**
Hummel Fritz/trombone/studio bands/Casa Loma Orch./	**Connie Boswell/Lee Wiley/**
Humphries Conn/alto saxpphone/studio bands/Charlie Barnet/	**Lena Horne/**
Hunt George/trombone/studio bands/Count Basie/	**Jimmy Rushing/Helen Humes/**
Hunt Louis/trumpet/studio bands/Louis Armstrong/	**Louis Armstrong/**
Hunt Pee Wee/trombone/studio bands/Casa Loma Orch./	**Connie Boswell/Lee Wiley/**
Hunter Chuck/fiddle/studio bands/	**Roy Rogers/**
Hurley Clyde/trumpet/studio bands/Glenn Miller/Freddie Slack/Axel Stordahl/	Marion Hutton/Ray Eberle/Tex Beneke/**Ella Mae Morse/Frank Sinatra/**
Hurt Chick/mandolin/studio bands/Gene Autrry Trio/	**Gene Autry/**
Hutchenrider Clarence/clarinet/alto saxophone/studio bands/Casa Loma Orch./	**Connie Boswell/Lee Wiley/**
Hutchinson Leslie A - 'Hutch' /pianist/some vocals/studio bands/(British)	**Helen Morgan/**
Hutchison C. L./cornet/studio bands/	**Jimmie Rodgers/**
Hyde Earl/drims/studio bands/	**Nat King Cole/**Nellie Luther/
Hyland Bill/trumpet/studio bands/Red Norvo/	**Mildred Bailey/**
Ingle Ed/clarinet/flute/studio bands/Don Redman/	Don Redman/**Harlan Lattimore/Bing Crosby/Boswell Sisters/**
Ingle Red/saxophone/studio bands/Ted Weems/Paul Weston/own Orch./	**Perry Como/Jo Stafford/**
Ink Spots/O. Happy Jones/ Bill or Herb Kenny/Deek Watson/Billy Bowen/ guitar - C. Fuqua/	**Ink Spots/Ella Fitzgerald/**
Innes Louis/guitar/studio bands/Drifting Cowboys/	**Hank Williams**
International Novelty Orchestra/	**Gene Austin/**
Iona Andy and his Islanders/Cliff Edwards/	**Cliff Edwards/**
Ipana Troubadors - named from product sold on radio/	**Bing Crosby/**Smith Ballew/Snappy Lambert/
Irvis Charlie/trombone/studio bands/Clarence Williams/	**Eva Taylor/Louis Armstrong/**
Ives Burl/guitar/vocals/songwriter/	**Burl Ives/**
Izenhall Aaron/trumpet/studio bands/Louis Jordan Tympany Five/	**Louis Jordan/**
Jackson Alex/alto saxophone/studio bands/	**Ethel Waters/**
Jackson Andy/jazz guitar/studio bands/Blanche Calloway Orch./	**Blanche Calloway/**
Jackson Chubby Q. /bass/studio bands/	**Dinah Washington/**
Jackson Cliff/pianist/studio bands/	**Lizzie Miles/**Lena Wilson/
Jackson Jack /arrainger/studio band/Orchestra/ (British band) - Dorchester Hotel/	**Alberta Hunter/**
Jackson John/alto saxophone/studio bands/Billy Eckstine /	**Billy Eckstine/Sarah Vaughan/**
Jackson Joshua/tenor saxophone/studio bands/Louis Jordan Tympany Five/	**Louis Jordan/Bing Crosby/**
Jackson Mike/pianist/studio bands/	**Alberta Hunter/**
Jackson Papa Charlie/banjo/guitar/vocals/studio bands/	**Papa Charlie Jackson/**
Jackson Preston/trombone/studio bands/Louis Armstrong/	**Louis Armstrong/**
Jackson Quntin/trombone/studio bands/Cab Calloway/Don Redman/	**Cab Calloway/Harlan Lattimore/**
Jackson Rudy/clarinet/tenor saxophone/studio bands/Duke Ellington/	**Adelaide Hall/**
Jackson Tommy/fiddle/studio bands/	**Hank Williams**
Jacobs Dave/trombone/studio bands/Tommy Dorsey/	**Frank Sinatra/Connie Haines/**
Jacobs Leon/trumpet/studio bands/Le Jacob's Jazz/(France)	**Josephine Baker/**
Jacquet Illinois/tenor saxophone/studio bands/Horance Henderson/	**Lena Horne/**
Jaeger Harry/drums/studio bands/Gordon Jenkins/	**Peggy Lee/**
James Benny/banjo/studio bands/Lew Leslie's Blackbirds Orch./	**Adelaide Hall/**
James Elmer/string bass/studio bands/Louis Armstrong/	**Louis Armstrong/**
James George/clarinet/studio bands/Louis Armstrong/	**Louis Armstrong/**
James Harry/trumpet/arrainger/studio bands/Benny Goodman/own Orch/	**/Frank Sinatra/Connie Haines/Helen Forrest/Dick Haymes/Helen Humes/** Betty Grable/
James Harry/trumpet/arrainger/studio bands/Miff Moles Molers/B. Goodman/T. Wilson/	**Midge Williams/Billie Holiday/Ella Fitzgerald/Jimmy Rushing/Martha Tilton/**
Jarrett Art/banjo/guitar/some vocals/studio bands/Ted Weems/	Art Jarrett/**Perry Como/**
Jaworski Henry/violin/studio bands/Jimmy Grier/	**Boswell Sisters/**
Jaxton Frankie - Frankie Jaxton & His Hot Shots/	**Frankie Half Pint Jaxton/**
Jazz Band her/her Band - Clara Smith/	**Clara Smith/**
Jazz Band her - Edith Wilson/	**Edith Wilson/**
Jazz Hounds & Her - Mamie Smith/	**Mamie Smith/**
Jazz Hounds her - Okeh studio band for Mamie Smith	**Mamie Smith**
Jazz Jesters her - Midge Williams/	**Midge Williams/**
Jazz Masters & her - Black Swan studio & touring band for Ethel Waters/	**Ethel Waters/**
Jazz Masters Her - Black Swan Studio band/ - Trixie Smith/	**Trixie Smith/**
Jecker Walter/string bass/studio bands/	**Gene Autry/**
Jefferson Blind Lemon/own guitar/	**Blind Lemon Jefferson/**
Jefferson Freddy/pianist/studio bands/Stuff Smith Trio/	**Sarah Vaughan/**
Jefferson Hilton/alto saxophone/sStudio bands/Bubber Miley/Cab Calloway/ Teddy Wilson/	**Edith Wilson/Cab Calloway/Billie Holiday/**
Jefferson Maceo/banjo/studio bands/	**Ethel Waters/**
Jejo Carmello/clarinet/studio bands/Lew Leslie's Blackbirds Orch./	**Adelaide Hall/**
Jenkins Freddie/trumpet/studio bands/Duke Ellington/	**Adelaide Hall/**Rhythm Boys/**Ivie Anderson/Ethel Waters/Bing Crosby/**
Jenkins Gordon/arrangements./studio bands/ his orch./	**Billie Holiday/Dick Haymes/Frank Sinatra/Peggy Lee/**

Jenkins Gordon/arrangements./studio bands/ his orchestra/ - more	**Martha Tilton/Andrews Sisters/Judy Garland/Ethel Merman/**Danny Kaye/
Jenkins Les/trombone/studio bands/Artie Shaw/Tommy Dorsey/	**Helen Forrest/Frank Sinatra/Jo Stafford/Connie Haines/**
Jenner Russ/trombone/studio bands/	**Boswell Sisters/**
Jenny Jack/trombone/studio bands/Isham Jones/Artie Shaw/Benny Goodman/ own Orch/	**Bing Crosby/Lena Horne/Peggy Lee/Dick Haymes**
Jenssen Mel/violin/studio bands/Casa Loma Orch./	**Connie Boswell/Lee Wiley/**
Jerome Jerry/tenor saxophone/arrainger/studio bands/Red Norvo/B. Goodman/G. Siravo/	**Mildred Bailey/Martha Tilton/Dick Todd/Peggy Lee/Dick Haymes/Frank Sinatra/**
John Pete/tenor saxophone/studio band/Woody Hermann/	**Connie Boswell/**
Johnson Plas/saxophone/studio band/Nelson Riddle/	**Frank Sinatra/**
Johns Irving/pianist/studio bands/	**Bessie Smith/**
Johnson (J. C.) Clarence/pianist/arrainger/studio bands/	Spencer Williams/**Ethel Waters/Helen Humes/Lonnie Johnson/**
Johnson Arthur/pianist/studio bands/	Brox Sisters/
Johnson Bill/bass/Bill Johnson's Louisiana Jug Band/	**Frankie Half Pint Jaxton/**
Johnson Bobby/guitar/studio bands/Buck And His Band/	**Bessie Smith/**
Johnson Bud/tenor saxophone/trumpet/studio bands/Gus Arnheim/George Tredwell/	**Sarah Vaughan/Billie Holiday/ Rosemary Clooney/**
Johnson Chink/trombone/studio bands/Ethel Waters Jazz Masters/	**Mamie Smith/Ethel Waters/Alberta Hunter/**
Johnson Clarence/pianist/arrainger/studio bands/Louis Jordan/	**Lizzie Miles/Louis Jordan/**
Johnson Harry/trumpet/studio bands/Ozzie Nelson/	**Ozzie Nelson/Harriet Hilliard/**
Johnson James P./pianist/studio bands/songwriter/James P Johnson's Harmony Eight/	**Trixie Smith/Bessie Smith/Ethel Waters/Eva Taylor/**
Johnson Johnny/bass/studio bands/Ted Daffan's Texans/	Chuck Keeshan/Leon Seago/
Johnson Keg/trombone/studio bands/Cab Calloway/	**Cab Calloway/**
Johnson Lemuel/tenor saxophone/studio bands/Louis Jordan/	**Louis Jordan/**
Johnson Lonnie/own guitar/studio bands/Louis Armstrong Savoy Ballroom Five/	**Lonnie Johnson/Victoria Spivey/**Spencer Williams/**Louis Armstrong/Helen Humes/**
Johnson Manzie/drums/studio bands/	Don Redman/**Harlan Lattimore/Bing Crosby/Boswell Sisters/**
Johnson Margaret 'Countess'/pianist/studio bands/Billie Holiday/	**Billie Holiday/**
Johnson Marvin/alto saxophone/studio bands/Louis Armstrong/	**Louis Armstrong/**
Johnson Otis/trumpet/studio bands/Louis Armstrong/	**Louis Armstrong/**Hoagy Carmichael/
Johnson Pete/pianist/arainger/Film1944/	**Lena Horne/**
Johnson Pete/pianist/arrainger/ome vocals/studio bands/ & His Trio/	**Joe Turner/**
Johnson Robert/own guitar/	**Robert Johnson/**
Johnson Wayne/clarinet/studio bands/Bob Wills & his Texas Playboys/	Tommy Duncan/
Johnson Wesley/trumpet/studio bands/Albury's Blue and Jazz Seven/	Lucille Hegamin/**Ethel Waters/**
Johnson Will/jazz guitar/studio bands/Louis Armstrong/	**Louis Armstrong/Victoria Spivey/**Hoagy Carmichael/
Johnston Arthur/pianist/studio bands/	Brox Sisters/
Johnston Jimmy/saxophone/studio bands/	**Lee Morse/**
Jones Bobby/trumpet/studio bands/Casa Loma Orch./	**Connie Boswell/Lee Wiley/**
Jones Buddy/guitar/studio bands/	**Jimmie Davis/**
Jones Charlie/clarinet/studio bands/Louis Armstrong/	**Louis Armstrong/**
Jones Claude/trombone/Don Redman/ Chick Webb/studio bands/	**Harlan Lattimore/Bing Crosby/Boswell Sisters/**Don Redman/**Ella Fitzgerald/**
Jones Isham/saxophone/violin//arrainger/ his Orchestra/	**Marion Harris/Al Jolson/Bing Crosby/**Frank Sylvano/Gertrude Niesen
Jones Jimmy/pianist/guitar/arranger/studio band/Jimmy Jones Quartet/Tony Scott/George Tredwell/	**Sarah Vaughan/**
Jones Jonah/drum/studio bands/Teddy Wilson/Count Basie/Cab Calloway/	**Billie Holiday/Jinny Rushing/Helen Humes/Cab Calloway/**
Jones Leroy/clarinet/guitar/studio bands/M. W. Jazz Jesters/	**Alberta Hunter/Midge Williams/**
Jones Orville 'Happy'/cello/vocals/Ink Spots/	**Ink Spots/**
Jones Quincy/trumpet/arrainger/ - (especially) only noting only pre - rock era recording artists/	**Sarah Vaughan/Dinah Washington/Frank Sinatra/Lena Horne**
Jones Quinton/trombone/studio bands/Don Redman/	Don Redman/**Harlan Lattimore/**
Jones Red/string bass/studio bands/Roy Acuff/	**Roy Acuff/**
Jones Reggie/bass/studio bands/Louis Armstrong Sebastian New Cotton Club Orch./	**Louis Armstrong/**
Jones Richard M./pianist/studio bands/	Bertha Chippie Hill/**Blanche Calloway/**
Jones 'Shrimp' Ralph/violin/studio bands/	**Ethel Waters/**
Jones Spike /drum/arrainger/studio bands/John S. Trotter/Ted Daffan/His City Slickers Orch./	**Bing Crosby/**Leon Seago/Carl Grayson/Red Ingle/Aileen Carlisle/Willie Sticker/
Jones Wardell/saxophone/studio bands/Duke Ellington/	**Ivie Anderson/**
Jordan Louis/alto saxophone/studio bands/own vocals/Chick Webb/his Tympany Five/	**Louis Jordan/Bing Crosby/Ella Fitzgerald/**
Jordan Taft/trumpet/studio bands/with Chick Webb/Ella Fitzgerald & her Savoy Eight/	**Ethel Waters/Ella Fitzgerald/**
Jorden Al/trombone/studio bands/Jimmy Dorsey/	**Helen Forrest/**
Joy Leonard/accomp./studio bands/ & his Orch./	**Fanny Brice/Helen Morgan/Helen Kane/Jimmie Rodgers/Russ Columbo/ Dick Todd/Dinah Shore**
Joyce Gerald/violin/studio bnads/Axel Stordahl/	**Frank Sinatra/**
Julyie Kathryn/harp/studio bands/Nelson Riddle/	**Nat King Cole/Frank Sinatra/**
Kabibble Ish (Merwyn Bogue)/trumpet/actor/studio bands/Kay Kyser/	**Ginny Simms/**

Kafton Arthur/cello/studio bands/Axel Stordahl/	**Frank Sinatra/**
Kahn Art/pianist/ studio bands/own Orch./	**Ruth Etting/**
Kahn Leo/pianist/studio bands/	**Hildegarde**
Khan Lee/violinist/studio band/Artie Shaw/	**Lena Horne/**
Kahn Roger Wolfe/alto saxophone/ & own Orch./	Franklyn Baur/**Libby Holman/**
Kahn Walter/cornet/studio bands/Ted Lewis/	**Ruth Etting/**
Kaipo Joe/steel guitar/studio bands/	**Jimmie Rodgers/**
Kama Charles/steel guitar/studio bands/	**Jimmie Rodgers/**
Kaminsky Anatole/violin/studio bands/Nelson Riddle/	**Nat King Cole/**
Kaminsky Max/trumpet/arrainger/ studio bands/ & His Orch./	**Lee Wiley/**
Kane Sol/alto saxophone/studio band/Benny Goodman/	**Peggy Lee/**
Kansas Joe/ - (or Joe McCoy)/guitar/vocals with Memphis Minnie/studio bands/	**Memphis Minnie/**Kansas Joe/
Kaproff Armand/cello/studio bands/Axel Stordahl/Nelson Riddle/	**Nat King Cole/Frank Sinatra/Dean Martin/**
Kapp Dave/A&R - arranger/Decca/Kapp Records/	**Jimmie Davis/**Stewart Hamlin/Sons of the Pioneers/**Andrew Sisters/Ink Spots/ Ernest Tubb/Bing Crosby/**
Kapp Jack/A&R - arranger/Brunswick/ARC/Decca/	**Al Jolson/Bing Crosby/Boswell Sisters/Connie Boswell/Ethel Waters/Mills Brothers/**
Kardos Gene/saxophone/ & His Orchestra/	**Bea Wain/**
Karle Art/tenor saxophone/studio bands/Benny Goodman/	**Ethel Waters/Billie Holiday//Mildred Bailey/**Louise Tobin/**Ella Fitzgerald/ Jimmy Rushing/**
Kazebrier Nate/trumpet/studio band/Benny Goodman/	**Helen Ward/**
Katzman Harry/violin/studio bands/Axel Stordahl/	**Frank Sinatra/**
Kaufman Bernard/tenor saxophone/studio bands/AxelStordahl/Mitchell Ayres/	**Billie Holiday/Frank Sinatra/Perry Como/**
Kay Howard/viola/studio bands/Mitchell Ayres/	**Perry Como/**
Kaye Lenard/alto saxophone/studio bands/Tommy Dorsey/	**Jo Stafford/**Teddy Walters/
Kaye Sammy/clarinet/arrainger/studio bands/own Orch./	Don Cornell/Laurie Leslie/Allen Foster/Tommy Ryan/
Kayser George/fiddle/studio bands/	**Roy Rogers/**
Kazee Buell/banjo/folk/	Buell Kazee/
Keeshan Chuck/guitar/some vocals/studio bands/Ted Daffan's Texans/	Chuck Keeshan/Leon Seago/
Kellner Murray/violin/studio bands/	**Gene Austin/Ruth Etting/Annette Hanshaw/**
Kelly Monty/trumpet/studio bands/Paul Whiteman/	**Billie Holiday/**
Kelly Willie/own vocals/his Orch/	Willie Kelly/
Kelly Wynton/pianist/studio bands/Jimmy Cobb Orch./	**Dinah Washington/**
Kemp Hal /pianist/trumpet/collrge bands/ his Orch.	Skinnay Ennis/Maxine Grey/Nan Wynn/
Kent Red/jazz guitar/studio band/Harry James/	**Frank Sinatra/**
Kenton Stan/pianist/arrainger/studio bands/Gus Arnheim/ & own Orch./	**Anita O'Day/June Christy/Nat King Cole/**
Keppard Freddie//cornet/studio bands/leader - Freddie Keppard Jazz Cardinals/	**Ethel Waters/Papa Charlie Jackson/**
Kessler Barney/jazz guitar/studio band/	**Mel Torme/Billie Holiday/**
Kiezman Louis/viola/studio band/	**Dean Martin/**
Kersey Kenny/pianist/studio bands/	**Billie Holiday/**
Killirn Al/trumpet/studio bands/Count Basie/	**Jimmy Rushing/Helen Humess/**
Kincaide Deane/tenor saxophone/arrainger/studio bands/Bob Crosby/Tommy Dorsey/	Bob Crosby/**Bing Crosby/Connie Boswell/**Edythe Wright/Jack Leonard// **Pied Pipers/**
Kincaide Deane/tenor saxophone/arrainger/studio bands/Bob Crosby/Tommy Dorsey/	**Frank Sinatra/Jo Stafford/Connie Haines/**
King Eddie or Edward/drums/studio bands/dir Orch./	**Marion Harris/**
King Oliver/cornet/studio bands/own band/	**Eva Taylor/Victoria Spivey/**
King Pee Wee/accordian/songwriter/studio bands/his Golden West Cowboys/	Pee Wee King/Redd Stewart/
King Pete/arrainger/studio bands/	**Bing Crosby/**
King Stan/drums/studio bands/Dorsey Brothers/Charlestown Chasers/	**Annette Hanshaw/Lee Morse/Ethel Waters/Eva Taylor/Bing Crosby/Mills Brothers/**
King Stan/drums/studio bands/Dorsey Brothers/Louis Prima/	**Boswell Sisters/Eva Taylor/Mildred Bailey/Louis Prima/**
King Vernon/bass/studio bands/Lionel Hampton/	**Dinah Washington/**
King Wayne/altosaxophone/songwriter/studio bands/his Orch./	**Buddy Clark/**
Kirby John/ - John Kirby Sextet/ trombone/tuba/string bass/arrainger/ studio bands/Orch./	**Mildred Bailey/Maxine Sullivan/Billie Holiday/Midge Williams/Sarah Vaughan/**
Kirby Beecher Ray or Pete Bashful Bob Oswald/dobro/studio bands/Smoky Mountain Boys/	**Roy Acuff/**
Kirk Andy/studio bands/Blanche Calloway Orch./	**Blanche Calloway/**
Kirkeby Eddie/studio bands/his Orch/	Elmer Feldkamp/
Kirkeby Eddie/A&R - arranger/Edison/Victor/Bluebird/	Earnest Hare?/Billy Jones?/Vernon Dalhart/**Fats Waller/**
Kirkpatrick Don/pianist/studio bands/Louis Armstrong/	**Louis Armstrong/**
Kirsner Sylvan/violin/studio bands/ Axel Stordahl/	**Frank Sinatra/**
Kitsis Bob/pianist/studio bands/Artie Shaw/Axel Stordahl/	**Billie Holiday/Helen Forrest/Frank Sinatra/**
Klee Harry/flute/alto saxophone/studio bands/Nelson Riddle/Billy May/	**Nat King Cole/Frank Sinatra/Dean Martin/**
Klein Dave/cornet/trumpet/studio bands/Ted Lewis/	Ted Lewis/**Ruth Etting/Fats Waller/**
Klein Frances/trumpet/studio bands/film/with Ina Ray Hutton's Melodears - all girl//	Ina Ray Hutton/
Klein Franklin August/accordian/studio bands/	**Roy Rogers/**
Klein Manny/trumpet/studio bands/ & Sizzling Syncopators/Dorsey Brothers/ Benny Goodman/	**Ruth Etting/Annette Hanshaw/Lee Morse/Ethel Waters/Bing Crosby/ Adelaide Hall/**
Klein Manny/trumpet/studio bands//Dorsey Brothers/	**/Ethel Waters/Bing Crosby/Adelaide Hall/Boswell Sisters/**

Klein Manny/trumpet/studio bands/Claude Thornhill//Axel Stordahl/his All Stars/Billy May/	**/Mildred Bailey/Maxine Sullivan//Frank Sinatra/Frankie Laine/Nat King Cole/Dean Martin/**
Klein Sol/pianist/studio bands/Ted Lewis Orch/	Ted Lewis/**Sophie Tucker/Ruth Etting/Fats Waller/**
Klink Al/alto saxophone/tenor saxophone/studio bands/Glenn Miller/	Tex Beneke/Paula Kelly/Modernaires/**Billie Holiday/Perry Como/**
Knickerbockers/jazz group/assoc. with Ben Selvin/	Irving Kaufman/ **Eva Taylor/**
Knowles Leigh/trumpet/studio band/Glenn Miller/	Ray Eberle/Marrion Hutton/Tex Beneke/Modernaires/
Knowling Ransom/bass/sstudio bands/	**Arthur Crudup/**
Knox Harold/trumpet/studio bands/George E. Lee/	**Julia Lee/**
Kolster Dance Orchestra/assoc. with Ben Selvin?/	**Eva Taylor/**
Koone Fred/string bass/studio bands/	**Jimmie Rodgers/**
Kosloff Lou/violin/studio bands/Dorsey Brothers/	**Bing Crosby/Ethel Waters/Boswell Sisters/**
Kostelanetz Andre/arrainger/studio bands/ His Orchestra/	**Perry Como/**
Kosterlarsky Sergei/violin/studio bands/Dorsey Brothers/Artie Shaw/	**Bing Crosby/Boswell Sisters/Lee Wiley/Lena Horne/**
Koutzem George/cello/studio bands/Joe Bushkin/	**Lee Wiley/**
Kral Roy/pianist/studio bands/Georgie Auld/	**Sarah Vaughan/**
Kress Carl/jazz guitar/studio bands/arrainger/Miff Mole's Molers/ his Orch./	**Gene Austin/Lee Morse/Boswell Sisters/Midge Williams/Margaret Whiting/Billie Holiday/**
Kruczek Leo/violin/studio bands/Axel Stordahl/Russ Case/	**Frank Sinatra/Perry Como/**
Krueger Bennie Orchestra - Radio Master - 1944	**Ethel Waters/**
Krueger Bennie/alto saxophone/Carl Fenton/Dorsey Brothers/his Orch./	**Marion Harris/Bing Crosby/Boswell Sisters/Mildred Bailey/Lee Wiley/ Harlan Lattimore/**
Krupa Gene/drummer /studio bands/Dorsey Brothers/Benny Goodman/ & own Orch./	**/Billie Holiday/**Roy Eldridge/**Anita O'Day/**Irene Daye/
Krupa Gene/drummer /studio bands/Dorsey Brothers/Benny Goodman/Teddy Wilson/	**Emmett Miller/Ethel Waters/Mildred Bailey/Helen Ward/Cleo Brown/ Martha Tilton/**
Kusby Ed/trombone/studio bands/Freddie Slack/Billy May/Nelson Riddle/	**Ella Mae Morse/Nat King Cole/Dean Martin/Frank Sinatra/Mel Torme/**
Kruscbak Leo/violinist/studio band/Artie Shaw/	**Lena Horne**
Kyle Billy/pianist/arrainger/studio bands/John Kirby/his Orch, /M. W. Jazz Jesters/	**Maxine Sullivan/Ella Fitzgerald/Midge Williams/Sarah Vaughan//**
Kyle Billy/pianist/arrainger/studio bands/John Kirby/Sy Oliver/own Orch, /	**Billie Holiday/Louis Armstrong/Bing Crosby/**
Kyle Wilson/pianist/studio bands/Alburys Blue And Jazz Seven/	**Ethel Waters/**
Kyser Kay /arrainger/studio bands/radio/his Orchestra/	**Ginny Simms/** Harry Babbit/Gloria Wood/Glee Club/
Kyser Kay Orchestra - Film Master - 1940	**Ginny Simms**
La Vere Charles/pianist/studio bands/Gordon Jenkins/	**Billie Holiday/**
Lacey Jack/trombone/studio bands/Claude Thornhill/	**Maxine Sullivan/**
Ladds' Black Aces/jazz band/unicredited Cliff Edwards/	**Cliff Edwards/**
Ladnier Tommy/cornet/studio bands/Lovie Austin/	**Ethel Waters/Ma Rainey/**
Lamare James/alto saxophone/studio bamnds/Charlie Barnet/	**Lena Horne/**
Lamarre Nappy Hilton(or La Marre)/jazz guitar/studio bands/Louis Prima/Bob Crosby/	**Louis Prima/**Bob Crosby/**Connie Boswell/Bing Crosby/Helen Ward/Peggy Lee/Johnny Mercer/June Hutton/**
Lane Ken/pianist/arraigner/studio bands/songwriter/led 'Ken Lane Singers'/	**Frank Sinatra/**
Lane Ken/pianist - Film TV Master - 1967	**Dean Martin/**
Lang Eddie/jazz guitar/studio bands/arranger/Irving Mills/Dorsey Brothers/	**Elisabeth Welch/Ethel/Annette Hanshaw/Eva Taylor/Boswell Sisters/**
Lang Eddie/jazz guitar/studio bands/arraigner/Roger Wolf Kahn/Lenny Hayton/G. Lombardo/	**/Bessie Smith/Nick Lucas/Libby Holman/Bing Crosby/Mildred Bailey/**
Lang Eddie/jazz guitar/studio bands/arrainger/Dorsey Brothers/	**Ruth Etting/Emmett Miller/Lee Morse/Victoria Spivey/Ethel Waters/**
Lanin Sam/clarinet/violinist/arraigner/studio band/ & His Famous Players/Orch./	**Bing Crosby/**
Lanphere Charlie/tenor saxophone/studio bands/	**Mildred Bailey/**
Lansford Son/bass/studio bands/Bob Willis & his Texas Playboys/	Tommy Duncan/
Larkins Ellis/pianist/arrainger/lead of Trio/	**Mildred Bailey/**
Lathrop Jack/jazz guitar/studio bands/Glenn Miller/	Tex Beneke/Paula Kelly/Modernaires/
Lattimore Harlan/And His Connies Inn Orch. - actully the Don Redman Orch./	**Harlan Lattimore/**
Lavel Paul/clarinet/saxophone/arrainger/studio bands/radio/	**Dinah Shore/**
Lavola Al/jazz guitar/studio bands/Artie Shaw/	**Billie Holiday/**
Lawrence Lucielle/harp/studio bands/Mitchell Ayres/	**Perry Como/**
Lawson Bob/saxophone/studio bands/Dave Barbour/	**Peggy Lee/Mel Torme/**
Lawson Harold/saxophone/clarinet/studio bands/Axel Stordahl/Dave Barbour/	**Frank Sinatra/Peggy Lee/**
Lawson John 'Yank'/trumpet/studio bands/Bob Crosby/	**/Helen Ward//Fred Astaire/Connie Boswell/Judy Garland/Bob Miller/**
Lawson John 'Yank'/trumpet/studio bands/Bob Crosby/	Bob Crosby/Kay Weber/Frank Tennille/**Bing Crosby/**Marion Mann/**Billie Holiday/Maxine Sullivan/**
Lay Ward/string bass/studio bands/Charlestown Chasers/	**Eva Taylor/**
Layton Skip/trombone/studio bands/ Paul Whiteman/	**Billie Holiday/**
Le Molodic Jazz/ - (French) studio jazz band/	**Josephine Baker/**
Leadbelly - (Huddie Leadbetter)/ - own guitar/vocals/songwriter/studio bands/	**Leadbelly/**
Leary Ford/trombone/tenor saxophone/studio bands/Larry Clinton/Charlie Barnet/	**Bea Wain/ Lena Horne/**
Lee E. George/dance band/studio band/ & his Novelty Singing Orch./	**Julia Lee/**
Lee Julia/pianist/vocals/studio bands/George E. Lee & His Novelty Singing Orch/ own band/	**Julia Lee/**
Lee Sonny/trombone/studio bands/Benny Goodman/	**Mildred Bailey/**
Leeman Cliff/drums/studio bands/Artie Shaw/Charlie Barnet/	**Billie Holiday/Lena Horne/**
Lehman Engel Orchestra/	**Adelaide Hall/Lena Horne/**

Leidbrook Min/tuba/studio bands//Paul Whiteman/Frank Trumbauer/	Rhythm Boys/**Bing Crosby/**
Leighton Bernie/pianist/studio bands/Gordon Jenkins/	**Billie Holiday/Peggy Lee/**
Leighton Skip/trombone/studio bands/Paul Whiteman/	**Billie Holiday/**
Leininger Bob/bass/studio bands/Les Brown/	**Doris Day/**
Leithner Frank/pianist/studio bands/Axel Stordahl/	**Frank Sinatra/**
LeMasters/guitar/studio bands/Maddox Brothers & Rose/	**Rose Maddox/**
Leonard Harvey/pianist/studio bands/Georgie Auld/	**Sarah Vaughan/**
Leonard Herbert/harmonica/studio bands/	**Clara Smith/**
Leon's Lone Star Cowboys/Leon Chappelear (identified)/guitar/vocals/led string band/	Leon Chappelear
Lesberg Jack/bass/studio bands/Dizzy Gillespie/Gordon Jenkins/	**Sarah Vaughan/Billie Holiday/Peggy Lee/**
Leslie Lew/studio band of Broadway promoter/	**Adelaide Hall/**
Levee Loungers - his Chick Bullock/studio band/	**Chick Bullock/**
Levine Gus/studio bands/dir - Orchestra/Les Baxter/Dick Stabile/	**Nat King Cole/Dean Martin/**
Levine Henry/trumpet/Chamber Music Society Of Lower Basin Street/ studio band/radio/	**Lena Horne/Dinah Shore/**
Levine Samuel/violin/studio bands/Axel Stordahl/	**Frank Sinatra/**
Levy John/bass/studio bands/	**Billie Holiday/**
Lewis Cappy/cornet/studio bands/W. Herman Woodchopers/	**Connie Boswell/Bing Crosby/**
Lewis Ed/trumpet/studio bands/Count Basie/	**Jimmy Rushing/Helen Humes/**
Lewis Furry/own guitar/	Furry Lewis/
Lewis Meade Lux/pianist/studio bands/Pete Johnson/	**Joe Turner/**
Lewis Noah/harmonica/Gus Cannon/Jug/stompers/	Gus Cannon/
Lewis Ted /clarinet/arrainger/some vocals/dance bands/ & His Orch./	Ted Lewis/**Ruth Etting/Sophie Tucker/Fats Waller/**
Lewis Tubby/trumpet/studio bands/Bob Wills & his Texas Playboys/	Tommy Duncan/
Ley Ward/bass/studio bands/	**Ruth Etting/**
Leyden Norman Orchestra/	**Sarah Vaughan/**
Leyton Bernie/pianist/studio bands/	**Frank Sinatra/**
Liddel Frank/fiddle/studio bands/Rudy Sooter's Ranchmen/	**Jimmie Davis/**
Light Crust Doughboys/a radio band using sponsor name/many members/	Milton Brown/ Tommy Duncan/
Lilley Joseph/arrainger/studio bands/his Orch./	**Bing Crosby/Judy Garland/Peggy Lee/**Patty Andrews of **Andrews Sisters/**
Lincoln Abe/trombone/studio bands/Ozzie Nelson/John Scott Trotter/Bob Scobey/	**Ozzie Nelson/Harriet Hilliard/Bing Crosby/**
Linder Don/trumpet/studio bands/	**Jimmie Davis/**
Linder Sol/violin/studio bands/Axel Stordahl/	**Frank Sinatra/**
Lindsay John/string bass/studio bands/Louis Armstrong/	**Louis Armstrong/**
Linehan Tommy/pianist/studio bands/Woody Herman/	**Connie Boswell/Bing Crosby/**Woody Herman/Murial Lane/
Linn Ray/trumpet/studio bands/Tommy Dorsey/Axel Stordahl/Dave Barbour/	**Jo Stafford/Connie Haines/Frank Sinatra/Peggy Lee/Mel Torme/**
Linville Charlie/fiddle/studio bands/	**Tex Ritter/**
Lipkins Steve/trumpet/studio bands/George Siravo/	**Frank Sinatra/**
Lippman Joe/pianist/arrainger/studio bands/Jimmy Dorsey/own Orch./	Bob Eberly/Helen O'Connell/**Sarah Vaughan/Nat King Cole/Perry Como/**
Liss Joe/pianist/studio bands/Red Norvo/	**Mildred Bailey/**
Little Little Jack/arrainger/ & His Orchestra/own vocals	Little Jack Little/
Little Son Joe/ruitar/studio bands/	**Memphis Minnie/**
Livingston Fud/clarinet/studio bands/Irving Mills/Ben Pollack/Paul Whiteman/ Dorsey Brothers/Jimmy Dorsey/	**Elisabeth Welch/**William's Sisters/**Bing Crosby/Louis Armstrong/**Frances Langford/
Lloyd Ivor/trumpet/studio bands/Larry Clinton/	**Bea Wain/**
Lockwood William/violin/studio bands/Lloyde Shaffer/	**Perry Como/**
Lodice Don/tenor saxophone/studio bands/Tommy Dorsey/Axel Stordahl/	**Frank Sinatra/Jo Stafford/Connie Haines/**
Lomax Allan/A&R - arranger/victor/library of congress/	**Lead Belly/Woody Guthrie/**
Loeffler Carl/trombone/studio bands/Axel Stordahl/	**Frank Sinatra/**
Loguidice Don/saxophone/Axel Stordahl/	**Frank Sinatra/**
Lombardo Carmen/saxophone/some vocals/Royal Canadians Orch./	Carmen Lombardo/**Bing Crosby/Andrews Sisters/Al Jolson/**Don Rodney/
Lombardo Guy/pianist/violin/ & His Royal Canadians/Orchestra/	Carmen Lombardo/**Bing Crosby/Andrews Sisters/Al Jolson/**Don Rodney/
Lombardo Lebert/trumpet/Royal Canadians/Orch./	Carmen Lombardo/**Bing Crosby/Andrews Sisters/Al Jolson/**Don Rodney/
Lombardo Victor/flute/Royal Canadians Orch./	Carmen Lombardo/**Bing Crosby/Andrews Sisters/Al Jolson/**Don Rodney/
Long Avan /arrainger/studio bands/own Orch./	**Thelma Carpenter/**
Long Johnny Orchestra - Film Master - 1943	**Ginny Simms**
Long Johnny/studio bands/ own Orch./	Dick Robertson/
Longshaw Fred/pianist/studio bands/	**Bessie Smith/**
Louisville Jug Band/studio band/	**Jimmie Rodgers/**
Love Frances/tenor saxophone/studio bands/Benny Goodman/	**Mildred Bailey/**
Lowe Mundell/jazz guitar/studio bands/George Tredwell/Mitch Miller/	**Sarah Vaughan/Billie Holiday/Rosemary Clooney/**
Lown Bert/pianist/studio band/	Biltmore Rhythm Boys/
Lowy Manny/violin/studio bands/Rudy Vallee/	**Rudy Vallee/**
Lloyd Ed or Loyd Ed/studio bands/ own Orch, /	**Harlan Lattimore/**
Luboff Norman/arrainger/some vocals/Choir/	**Clooney Rosemary/Frankie Laine/**
Lucas Nick/guitar/banjo/own vocals/studio bands/Carl Fenton Orch./his own Troubadors/	**Nick Lucas/Marion Harris/**
Lucie Lawrence/jazz guitar/studio bands/Teddy Wilson/Pete Johnson/	**Billie Holiday/Joe Turner/**
Lucus John/drums/studio bands/Ted Lewis/	Ted Lewis/**Sophie Tucker/Ruth Etting/Fats Waller/**
Ludlow Ben/arrainger/studio bands	Gertrude Niesen

Lulu Belle/(Mertle Eleanor Coopper)/ & Scotty (Scotty Weisman/radio/studio/	Lulu Belle & Scotty/
Lunceford Jimmie/arrainger/studio bands/ & His Orch./	Willie Smith/
Lutcher Nellie/pianist/arrainger/vocals	Nellie Lutcher/**Nat King Cole/**
Lyman Abe /drums/ his California Ambassador Hotel Orchestra/ his Orch./	**Al Jolson/Harlan Lattimore/Tony Martin/**
Lyric Quartet/	Lyric Quartet/
Lytell Jimmy/clarinet/ 'Original Memphis Five'/studio bands/Claude Thornhill/ Joe Bushkin/	Phil Napoleon/**Alberta Hunter/Trixie Smith/Maxine Sullivan/Lee Wiley/**
MacGregor Chummy/pianist/studio bands/Glenn Miller/	Tex Beneke/Paula Kelly/Modernaires/
Mack Clarence/bass/studio band/	**Lonnie Johnson/**
Mach Lenard/trumpet/studio bands/Axel Stordahl/	**Frank Sinatra/**
Mack Al/pianist/studio bands/	**Jimmie Davis/**
MacMillan/string bass/studio bands/	**Jimmie Rodgers/**
MacMurray Fred/alto saxophone/some vocals// - the actor/studio bands/George Olson/Gus Arnheim/	Fred Mac Murray/**Bing Crosby?/Ethel Shutta?/**
Maddox Brothers/studio band/various members/	**Rose Maddox/**
Maddox Cal/guitar/harmonica/studio bands/Maddox Brothers & Rose/	**Rose Maddox/**
Maddox Don/fifddle/studio bands/Maddox Brothers & Rose/	**Rose Maddox/**
Maddox Fred/bass/studio bands/Maddox Brothers & Rose/	**Rose Maddox/**
Maddox Henry/guitar/mandolin/studio bands/Maddox Brothers & Rose/	**Rose Maddox/**
Madrick Steve/alto saxophone/Les Brown/	**Doris Day/**
Magnante Charles/pianist/accordian/studio bands/	**Annette Hanshaw/**Marlene Dietrich/
Magness Tommy/fiddle/studio bands/R. Acuff Smokey Mountain Boys/Blue Grass Boys/	**Roy Acuff/Bill Monroe/**
Malachi John/pianist/studio bands/Billy Eckstine/	**Billy Eckstine/Sarah Vaughan/**
Mallory Edward //trumpet/ /arrainger/studio bands/ & Orch./	**Cab Calloway/Ethel Waters/**
Malneck Matt/viola/violin/arrainger/songwriter/Paul Whiteman/Benny Goodman/own Orch./	Rhythm Boys/**Bing Crosby/Mildred Bailey/Helen Ward/**
Maltby Richard Orchestra/	**Sarah Vaughan/**
Mance Juiian/pianist/studio bands/	**Dinah Washington/**
Mandel Johnny/trombone/studio bands/Georgie Auld/	**Sarah Vaughan/**
Mangano Mickey/trumpet/studio band/Nelson Riddle/	**Frank Sinatra/**
Manne Shelly/drums/studio bands/Stan Kenton/	**June Christy/Peggy Lee/**
Manners Artie/clarinet/studio bands/Joe Bushkin/	**Lee Wiley/**
Manning Marty/arrainger/studio bands/	**Tony Bennett/Vic Damone/**
Mantovani A./violinist/British studio band/Pipica Orchestra	**Hildegarde/**Vera Lynn/
Mansfield Saxie/tenor sax/studio bands/Isham Jones Orch./W. Hermann/	**Bing Crosby/Connie Boswell/**
Manson Eddy/harmonica/studio bands/Percy Faith/	**Rosemary Clooney/**
Marcus Bill/drums/studio bands/Jimmy Grier/	**Boswell Sisters/**
Marcus Reuben/viola/studio band/Axel Stordahl/Dick Stabile/	**Frank Sinatra/Dean Martin/**
Mardigan/drums/studio bands/Georgie Auld/	**Sarah Vaughan/**
Margulis (or Margolies?) Charlie/trumpet/studio bands/Paul Whiteman/Benny Goodman/	Rhythm Boys/**Bing CrosbyMildred Bailey/**
Marshall Kaiser/drums/studio bands/Alburys Blue And Jazz Seven/	Lucille Hegamin/**Ethel Waters/Clara Smith/**
Martel Johnny/trumpet/studio bands/Benny Goodman/	**Mildred Bailey/**
Martin Carrol/trombone/studio bands/dance bands/Isham Jones/	**Marion Harris/**
Martin Freddy/tenor saxophone/studio bands/ his Orch./	**Alice Faye/**Elmer Feldkamp/Clyde Rogers/
Martin Kelly/drum/studio bands/	**Billie Holiday/**
Martin Lowell/trombone/studio bands/Tommy Dorsey/	**Frank Sinatra/Jo Stafford/Connie Haines/**
Martin Skip/alto saxophone/studio bands/Benny Goodman/	**Peggy Lee/**
Martin Walter/drums/studio bands/Louis Jordan/	**Louis Jordan/**
Marvin Frankie/guitar/steel guitar/some vocals/studio bands/	Frankie Marvin/**Gene Autry/Tex Ritter/**
Marvin Johnny/ukule/vocalist/songwriter/studio bands/	Johnny Marvin/
Mason Ann/harp/studio bands/Axel Stordahl/	**Frank Sinatra/**
Mason Billy /studio bands/own Café e Paris Orch/ (British)/	**Marion Harris/Valaida Snow/**
Mason Henry/trumpet/studio bands/Blanche Calloway Orch./	**Blanche Calloway/**
Mason Paul/tenor saxophone/studio bands/Tommy Dorsey/	**Frank Sinatra/Jo Stafford/Connie Haines/**
Mastren Al/trombone/studio bands/Glenn Miller/	**Mildred Bailey/**Marion Hutton/Tex Beneke/**Kay Starr/**
Mastren Carmen/jazz guitar/studio bands/Teddy Wilson/Tommy Dorsey/	Edythe Wright/Jack Leonard/**Billie Holiday/Frank Sinatra/Jo Stafford/ Connie Haines/**
Mathews George/trombone/studio bands/	**Billie Holiday/**
Matlock Matty/clarinet/alto saxophone/studio bands/Bob Crosby/Billy Butterfield/P. Weston/	Bob Crosby/**Bing Crosby/Connie Boswell/Margaret Whiting/Johnny Mercer/**Pied Pipers/
Matthews Al/bass/studio bands/	**Alberta Hunter/**
Mattison Don/trombone/studio bands/Jimmy Dorsey/	**Louis Armstrong/Bing Crosby/**Frances Langford/**Billie Holiday/**
Matz Peter/arrainger/studio bands/	**Bing Crosby/**
Maurice Brown/cello/studio bands/Mitchell Ayres/	**Perry Como/**
Maxey Leroy/drums/studio bands/Cab Calloway/	**Cab Calloway/Chick Bullock/**
Maxwell James/trumpet/studio bands/Benny Goodman/Mitchell Ayres/	**Mildred Bailey/Peggy Lee/Perry Como/**
May Billy/trumpet/arrainger/studio bands//Dave Barbour/ & own Orch./	**/Peggy Lee/Ella Mae Morse/Nat King Cole/Frank Sinatra/Dean Martin/**
May Billy/trumpet/arrainger/studio bands/Glenn Miller/Dave Barbour/ & own Orch./	Tex Beneke/Paula Kelly/Modernaires/**Rosemary Clooney/Bing Crosby/Kay Star**
Mayhew Jack/saxophone/studio bands/John Scott Trotter/	**Bing Crosby/ Kay Starr/Connie Boswell/**

Mayhew John/flute/studio bands/Axel Stordahl/	**Frank Sinatra/**
Mayhew Wendel 'Gus'/trombone/studio bands/Hal Kemp/	Skinnay Ennis/Maxine Grey/
McAfee Johnny/tenor saxophone/studio bands/Tony Pastor/	Clooney Sisters/**Rosemary Clooney/**
McAuliffe/steel guitar/studio bands/Bob Willis/	Tommy Duncan/
McCamish Charles/trombone/studio band/Gene Krupa/	**Helen Ward/**
McConnell Shorty/tuba/studio bands/Billy Eckstine/	**Billy Eckstine/Sarah Vaughan/**
McCord Castor/clarinet/studio bands/Eddie Mallory/	**Ethel Waters/**
McCoy Charlie/guitar/mandolin/studio bands/	**Memphis Minnie/**
McCoy Joe/jazz guitar/studio bands/Benny Goodman/	**Peggy Lee/**
McDonald Earl/jug/studio bands/Louisville Jug Band/	**Jimmie Rodgers/**
McDonough Dick/jazz guitar/studio bands/Dorsey Brothers/Benny Goodman/	**/Boswell Sisters/Mills Brothers/Mildred Bailey/Billie Holiday/**
McDonough Dick/jazz guitar/studio bands/Dorsey Brothers/Benny Goodman//	**Cliff Edwards/Ruth Etting/Annette Hanshaw/Bing Crosby/Ethel Waters/ Adelaide Hall/**
McEachern Murray/trombone/studio bands/Paul Whiteman/Billy May/	**Helen Ward/Billie Holiday/Nat King Cole/Dean Martin/**
McGarity Lou/trombone/studio bands/Benny Goodman/Eddie Condon/	**Peggy Lee/Dick Haymes/Lee Wiley/**
McHargue Rosey/clarinet/studio bands/Ted Weems/	**Perry Como/**
McGrath Fulton/jazz pianist/studio bands/Dorsey Brothers/	**/Mildred Bailey/Lee Wiley/Billie Holiday/**
McGrath Fulton/jazz pianist/studio bands/Dorsey Brothers//	**Bing Crosby/Ethel Waters/Boswell Sisters/Mills Brothers/**
McIntyre Dick/hawaiian guitar/songwriter/studio bands/	**Bing Crosby/**
McIntyre Hal/alto saxophone/ studio bands/Glenn Miller/his Orch./	Tex Beneke/Paula Kelly/Modernaires/**Mills Brothers/**
McIntyre Lani/hawaiian guitar/songwriter/studio bands/ & His Hawaiians/	**Jimmie Rodgers/Bing Crosby/**
McIntyre Mark/pianist/studio bands/Axel Stordahl/	**Frank Sinatra/**
McKendrick Mike/banjo/guitar/studio bands/Louis Armstrong/	**Louis Armstrong/Cleo Brown/**
McKibbon Al/drum/bass/studio bands/Dicky Wells/	**Ethel Waters/Sarah Vaughan/**
McKinley Ray/drums/studio bands/Jimmy Dorsey/	**Louis Armstrong/Bing Crosby/**Frances Langford/
McKinney's Cotton Pickers/studio band/	George Thomas/
McLin James/jazz guitar/studio bands/M. W. Jazz Jesters/	**Billie Holiday/Midge Williams/**
McMichen Clayton/fiddle/studio bands/	**Jimmie Rodgers/**
McMickle Dale/trumpet/studio bands/Glenn Miller/Axel Stordahl/	Marion Hutton/**Kay Starr/**Tex Beneke/Paula Kelly/Modernaires/**Frank Sinatra/**
McNally Zeb/saxophone/studio bands/Bob Wills & his Texas Playboys/	Tommy Duncan/
McNatt/fiddle/studio bands/Tennessee Plowboys/	**Eddy Arnold/**
McPartland Jimmy/trumpet/studio band/Irving Mills/Ben Pollack/	**Elisabeth Welch/**Williams Sisters/
McRae Ted/clarinet/bass/reeds/studio bands/Chick Webb/Ella Fitzgerald Savoy Eight/	**Ella Fitzgerald/Cab Calloway/**
McRea Dave/string bass/studio bands/	**Billie Holiday/**
McVey William/trombone/studio bands/dance bands/Isham Jones/	**Marion Harris/**
McWinders Oddie/banjo/studio bands/	**Jimmie Rodgers/**
Meisel Ken/trombone/studio band/Les Brown/	**Doris Day/**
Melnikoff Harry/violin/studio bands/Mitchell Ayres/	**Perry Como/**
Melodears /(all woman band of Ina Ray Hutton/	Ina Ray Hutton/
Melrose Stompers/	**Lizzie Miles/**
Memphis Jug Band/her - Memphis Minnie/	**Memphis Minnie/**
Memphis Minnie/(Minnie Douglas) guitar/own vocal/her jug band/	**Memphis Minnie/**
Menge Homer/trombone/studio bands/Jimmie Grier Orch./	**Bing Crosby/Boswell Sisters/**
Mercer Johnny/ pianist/arrainger/songwriter/vocalist/studio bands/	**Johnny Mercer/**
Mercurio Walter/trombone/studio bands/Tommy Dorsey/	**Frank Sinatra/Jo Stafford/Connie Haines/**
Meresco Joe/pianist/studio bands/	**Annette Hanshaw/Bing Crosby/**
Meroff Benny Orchestra/	Dusty Rhodes/
Metcalf Louis/trumpet/studio bands/Duke Ellington/	**Adelaide Hall/**
Meth Max Theatre Orchestra/	**Ethel Waters/**
Metronome All Stars/	**Frank Sinatra/Nat King Cole /June Christy/**
Meyer Bob/string bass/studio bands/Les Paul/	**Bing Crosby/**
Meyers Bumps/tenor saxophone/studio bands/Freddie Slack/	**Ella Mae Morse/Margaret Whiting/Johnny Mercer/**
Mezzrow Mez/clarinet/studio bands/Louis Armstrong/	**Louis Armstrong/**
Michaels Ray/drums/studio bands/Larry Clinton/	**Bea Wain/**
Mickelson Paul/arrainger/his Orch./	**Ethel Waters/**
Miff Mole /violin/trombone/studio bands/Ray Miller/Miff Mole's Molers/	**Frank Crumit/Al Jolson/Annette Hanshaw/Midge Williams/**
Milage Makers/Bubby Miley & his/	**Edith Wilson/**
Milazzo James/trumpet/studio bands/Mitchell Ayres/	**Perry Como/**
Miles Lizzie/kazoo/vocals/	**Lizzie Miles/**
Miley Bubber/trumpet/arrainger/Duke Ellington/ & his Milage Makers/Leo Reisman Orch./	**Edith Wilson/Adelaide Hall/**Baby Cox/Ozzie Ware/Irving Mills/**Lee Wiley/**
Miller Bill/jazz guitar/studio bands/Red Norvo/	**Mildred Bailey/**
Miller Bob/pianist/studio bands/	**Gene Autry**
Miller Eddie/tenor saxophone/studio bands/Louis Prima/John Scott Trotter/Bob Crosby/Billy Butterfield/	**Louis Prima/Helen Ward/**Marion Mann/Bob Crosby/**Connie Boswell/Bing Crosby/Johnny Mercer/Margaret Whiting/**
Miller Frank/cello/studio bands/Axel Stordahl/	**Frank Sinatra/**
Miller Glenn/trombone/studio bands/arrainger/Dorsey Brothers/Miff Moles Molers/ & His Orch./	**/Midge Williams/**Tex Beneke/Modernaires/Paula Kelly/Ray Eberle/Marion Hutton/**Kay Starr/**

Miller Glenn/trombone/studio bands/arrainger/songwriter/Ben Pollack/Dorsey Brothers/Ray Noble/	Williams Sisters/**Bing Crosby/Boswell Sisters/Lee Wiley/Al Bowlly/**
Miller Joe/tenor saxophone/studio bands/Rudy Vallee/	**Rudy Vallee/**
Miller Johnny/bass/studio band/Nat Cole Trio/	**Nat King Cole/**
Miller Mitchell - Mitch/oboe/arrainger//Maxine Sullivan/Axel Stordahl/own vocal group/Orch./	**Maxine Sullivan/Frank Sinatra/Rosemary Clooney/Frankie Laine/Tony Bennett/Lee Wiley**
Miller Ray Novelty Orchestra/	**Frank Crumit/Al Jolson/**
Miller Stanley/pianist/studio bands/	**Clara Smith/**
Millinder Lucky/arrianger/studio bands/Mills Blues Band/led own Orch/	**Rosetta Tharpe/**
Mills Blue Rhythm Band/Jimmy Lunceford/	Red Allan/**Adelaide Hall/**
Mills Brothers/group vocals & guitar/John Jr - later John Sr. after death/Herb/ Harry/Donald/	**Mills Brothers/Cab Calloway/Bing Crosby/Ella Fitzgerald/Louis Armstrong/**
Mills Irving/violin/arranger/some vocals/his Hotsy Totsy Gang/	Irving Mills/Ozzie Ware/**Elisabeth Welch/**
Mills Jackie/drum/studio bands/Harry James/	**Frank Sinatra/**
Mills John/guitar/(Mills Brothers)/	**Mills Brothers/Cab Calloway/Bing Crosby/**
Mince Johnny/clarinet/alto saxophone/studio bands/Cy Oliver/	**Louis Armstrong/Billie Holiday/**
Mince Johnny/clarinet/alto saxophone/studio bands/Tommy Dorsey/Cy Oliver/	Edythe Wright/Jack Leonard/**Frank Sinatra/Jo Stafford/Connie Haines/**
Mineo Sam/pianist/studio bands/Larry Clinton/	**Bea Wain/Dick Todd/**
Minor Dan/trombone/studio bands/Count Basie/	**Jimmy Rushing/Helen Humes/**
Missman Tommy/clarinet/Japanese studio bands/	**Midge Williams/**
Mitchell Alex 'Razz'/drums/studio bands/Louis Jordan Timpany Five/	**Louis Jordan/Bing Crosby/**
Mitchell Charles/electric guitar/studio bands/songwriter/ & His Texans(string band)/	**Jimmie Davis/**
Mitchell John/banjo/studio bands/Jazz Masters/	**Ethel Waters/Edith Wilson/**Lena Wilson/
Moana Orchestra/studio band/	**Vaughn De Leath/**
Mole Miff/trombone/studio bands/Charlestown Chasers/Molers/B. Goodman/	**Kate Smith/Eva Taylor/Midge Williams/Peggy Lee/**
Mole Miff/trombone/studio bands/O. Memphis Five/Molers/	Phil Napoleon/**Alberta Hunter/Trixie Smith/Sophie Tucker//Cliff Edwards/**
Moncur Grachan/bass/studio bands/Billie Holiday/	**Billie Holiday/**
Mondello Toots/alto saxophone/studio bands/Miff Mole's Molers/Claude Thornhill/B. Goodman/P. Faith/	**Helen Ward/Maxine Sullivan/Midge Williams/Billie Holiday/Mildred Bailey/ Tony Bennett/**
Monroe Bill/mandolin/guitar/some vocals/	**Bill Monroe/**
Monroe Charles/guitar/studio bands/Bill Monroe/	**Bill Monroe/**
Monroe Vaughn /trumpet/studio bands/vocals/own Orch./	Vaughn Monroe/
Montgomery Little Brother/pianist/arrainger/some vocals/	Little Brother Montgomery/**Edith Wilson/**
Moody Clyde/guitar/studio bands/Blue Grass Boys/	**Bill Monroe/**
Mooney Hal (or Harold)/pianist/studio bands/John Scott Trotter/studio bands/ his Orch./	**Bing Crosby/Kay Starr/Dinah Washington/**
Moore Alfred/bass/studio bands/Bill Doggett/	**Helen Humes/**
Moore Alton/trombone/studio bands/Blanche Calloway Orch./	**Blanche Calloway/**
Moore Cass/tuba/studio band/	**Lizzie Miles/**
Moore Bill/trumpet/studio bands/Rudy Vallee/	**Rudy Vallee/**
Moore Bobby/trumpet/studio bands/Count Basie/	**Jimmy Rushing/Helen Humes/**
Moore Oscar/jazz guitar/arrainger/studio bands/ Nat Cole Trio/	**Nat King Cole/Joe Turner/**
Moore Phil/arrainger/ Freddie Slack/Phil Moore Four/	**Ella Mae Morse/Lena Horne/Ivie Anderson/Frank Sinatra/**
Moore Sol/string bass/studio bands/	**Billie Holiday/**
Moore 'Wild Bill'/tenor saxophone/studio bands/Bill Doggett/	**Helen Humes/**
Morehouse Chauncey/drums/studio bands/Dorsey Brothers/Roger Wolf Kahn/C. Thornhill/	**Bing Crosby/Libby Holman/Ethel Waters/Boswell Sisters/Maxine Sullivan/**
Morgan Al/string bass/studio bands/arrainger/Cab Calloway/Louis Jordan Timpany Five/	**Cab Calloway/Chick Bullock/Louis Jordan/Bing Crosby/**
Morgan Russ/pianist/trombone/clarinet/studio bands/ & His Orchestra/	**Connie Boswell/**Al Jennings/
Morgan Tommy/jazz guitar/studio bands/Benny Goodman/	**Peggy Lee/**
Morris Jie/trumpet/studio bands/Lionel Hampton/	**Dinah Washington/**
Morrow Bob/violin/studio bands/Jimmy Grier/	**Boswell Sisters/**
Morrow Buddy/trombone/studio bands/Bob Crosby/Axel Stordahl/Eddie Condon/	Bob Crosby/**Helen Ward/Bing Crosby/Lee Wiley/Frank Sinatra/**
Morrow Fred/tenor saxophone/studio bands/Cliff Edwards/	**Cliff Edwards/**
Morse Lee/own guitar/kazoo/songwriter/studio bands/her Blue Grass Boys/	**Lee Morse/**
Morton Benny/trombone/studio bands/Don Redman/Teddy Wilson/	**Don Redman/Harlan Lattimore/Bing Crosby/Boswell Sisters/Billie Holiday/Ella Fitzgerald/**
Morton Jelly Roll/pianist/ songwriter/pianist/dir. Orchestra/	**Lizzie Miles/**
Mosiello Mike/trumpet/studio bands/	**Ruth Etting/**
Mott Tiny/saxophone/studio bands/Bob Wills & his Texas Playboys/	Tommy Duncan/
Mottola Tony/jazz guitar/drums/studio bands/	**Dolly Dawn/Frank Sinatra/Billie Holiday/Rosemary Clooney/**Johnny Desmond/
Mullican Moon/pianist/arrainger/songwriter/some vocals/studio bands/Cliff Bruner/	Moon Mullican/**Jimmie Davis/**
Mulligan Gerry/saxophone/pianist/arrainger/ - Film (TV) Master - 1957	**Billie Holiday**
Muma Dwightviolin/studio bands/Jimmy Grier/	**Boswell Sisters/**
Munday Jimmy/tenor saxophone/arrainger/songwriter/B. Goodman/ & Orchestra/	**Helen Ward/Billie Holiday/Valaida Snow/**
Murphy Leo/violin/studio bands/dance band/Isham Jones/	**Marion Harris/**
Murphy Lyle 'Spud'/trombone/saxophone/arrainger/Charlie Barnet/led band/	**Lena Horne/**

Murphy Timothy/trombone/studio bands/Ted Steele/	**Perry Como/**
Murray Alex/violin/studio bands/Nelson Riddle/	**Frank Sinatra/**
Murray Lyn/vocal arrainger/studio bands/ Orchestra/	**Judy Garland/Bing Crosby/**
Musso Vido/clarinet/tenor saxophone/studio bands/Harry James/Benny Goodman/	**Billie Holiday/Frank Sinatra/Helen Forrest/Peggy Lee/June Christy/**
Nance Ray/trumpet/studio bands/some vocals/Duke Ellington/	**Ivie Anderson/**Ray Nance/
Nanton Joe - as Tricky Sam Nanton - /trombone/studio bands/Duke Ellington/	**Adelaide Hall/Elisabeth Welch/**Rhythm Boys/**Ivie Anderson/Ethel Waters/ Bing Crosby/**
Napoleon Phil/trumpet/led 'Original Memphis Five"/some vocals/studio bands/ Dorsey Brothers	Phil Napoleon/**Alberta Hunter/Trixie Smith/Bing Crosby/Annette Hanshaw/Lee Morse/Eva Taylor/**
Napton John/trumpet/studio band/Benny Goodman/	**Peggy Lee/**
Nash Joey/alto saxophone/studio band/	**Rudy Vallee/**
Nash Ted/flute/alto saxophone/studio bands/Les Brown/Nelson Riddle/Billy May/	**Doris Day/Nat King Cole/Frank Sinatra/Dean Martin/**
Nat Cole Trio/Nay - vocal & pianist/Oscar Moore - bass/Wesley Prince - bass/ - Original group/	**Nat King Cole/**
Nathan Ray/drums/studio bands/Pete Brown/	**Helen Humes/**
Nation Buck/studio bands/	**Tex Ritter/**
Natoli Nat/trumpet/studio bands/Paul Whiteman/Lennie Hayton/Russ Case/	Rhythm Boys/**Bing Crosby/Perry Como/**
Navarro Fats/trumpet/studio bands/	**Billy Eckstine/**
Neagley Clint/alto saxophone/studio bands/Benny Goodman/	**Peggy Lee/**
Neary Jerry/trumpet/studio bands/Woody Hermann/	Woody Hermann/Murial Clare/**Connie Boswell/Bing Crosby/**
Neill Larry/trumpet/studio bands/Paul Whiteman/	**Billie Holiday/**
Nelson Horance/trumpet/studio bands/Axel Stordahl/	**Frank Sinatra/**
Nelson Ken/A&R - arranger/capital	**Merle Travis/**
Nelson Ozzie /tenor saxophone//own vocals/college bands/ his Orch./	**Ozzie Nelson/Harriet Hilliard/**
Neufeld Erno/violin/studio bands/Nelson Riddle/	**Frank Sinatra/**
New England Yankees/studio band/	**Annette Hanshaw/**
New Englanders/studio band/	**Annette Hanshaw/**
Newman Ruby/ violinist/arrainger/studio bands/own Orchestra/	**Buddy Clark/**
Newton Frankie/trumpet/studio bands/Teddy Wilson/M. W. Jazz Jesters/own Orch./	**Bessie Smith/Billie Holiday/Ella Fitzgerald/Maxine Sullivan/Midge Williams/**
Newell Laura/harp/studio band/Artie Shaw/	**Lena Horne/**
Nichols Albert/alto saxophone/Louis Armstrong Savoy Ballroom Five/	**Louis Armstrong/**Hoagy Carmichael/
Nichols Red/cornet/studio bands/ & His Five Pennies/Charlestown Chasers/ own Orch./	**Kate Smith/Connie Boswell/**Red McKenzie/Dick Robertson/
Nichols Red/cornet/studio bands/Redheads/ P. Whiteman/Miff Mole's Molers/ Five Pennies	**Sophie Tucker/Cliff Edwards/Bing Crosby/**Al Rinker/**Annette Hanshaw/ Lee Morse/**
Nicholson Ed/drums/studio bands/Tony Scott/	**Sarah Vaughan/**
Nickols Roy/guitar/studio bands/Maddox Brothers & Rose/	**Rose Maddox/**
Nidoff Jack/pianist/studio bands/Percy Faith/	**Tony Bennett/**
Ninde Julian R./guitar/studio bands/	**Jimmie Rodgers/**
Nizza Pat/tenor saxophone/studio bands/Sy Oliver/	**Louis Armstrong/Billie Holiday/**
Noble Ray/arrainger/studio bands/His Orch./ (originally British)	**Al Bowlly/Elisabeth Welch/Buddy Clark/Tony Martin/**Larry Stewart/ Snooky Larson/
Noel Dick/trombone/studio band/Les Brown/	**Doris Day/**
Nolan Bob/guitar/songwriter/arrainger/vocals/studio bands/Sons Of Pioneers/	Bob Nolan/Tim Spencer/Lloyd Perryman/**Roy Rogers/**
Norman Dave/violinist/studio band/Artie Shaw/	**Lena Horne/**
Nordquist Clinton/string bass/studio bands/Les Paul/	**Bing Crosby/**
Norvo Red/vibraphone/xylophone/arrainger/studio bands/Paul Whiteman/own Orch./	**Mildred Bailey/**Terry Allen/**Peggy Lee/**
Nottingham Jimmy/trumpet/studio bands/	**Billie Holiday/**
O'Brien Floyd/trombone/studio bands/Bob Crosby/	**Connie Boswell/Bing Crosby/**
O'Bryant Jimmy/clarinet/studio bands/Lovie Austin/	Ida Cox/**Ethel Waters/**
Ockner George/violin/studio bands/Percy Faith/	**Tony Bennett/**
Ocko Bernie/violin/studio bands/Russ Case/	**Perry Como/**
O'Day Molly/guitar/vocals/studio bands/Cumberland Mountain Folks/	Molly O'Day/
Oberstein Eli/A&R- arranger/Victor/Bluebird/Majestic/	**Ernest Tubb/Bill Monroe/**Patsy Montana/**Perry Como/Louis Prima/**Eddie Howard/
Ohman Phil/pianist/studio bands/Carl Fenton/Arden and Ohman/	**Marion Harris/**Frank/Snappy Lambert/Bert Lorin/
Oklahomans his - Jack Guthrie on guitar/studio band/	Jack Guthrie/
Oliver Earl/trumpet/studio bands/	**Lee Morse/**
Oliver Joe Ting/hornet/studio band/	**Eva Taylor/Lizzie Miles/Victoria Spivey/**
Oliver Howard/banjo/studio bands/Leon's Lone Satar Cowboys/	Leon Chappelear/
Oliver Sy/trumpet/arrainger/some vocals/songwriter/studio bands/Tommy Dorsey/ own Orch./Metronome All Star/	Sy Oliver/**Billie Holiday/Louis Arstrong/Nat King Cole/Frank Sinatra/**
Olson George/drums. studio bands/dance band/ & His Music/ & His Orch./	**Ethel Shutta/**Fran Fay/Joe Morrison/Bob Borgen/Fred MacMurray/
O'Neal Spencer/drums/studio bands/M. W. Jazz Jesters/	**Midge Williams/**
Orendorff George/trumpet/studio bands/Louis Armstrong/	**Louis Armstrong/**
Original Jazz Hounds/studio band/	**Edith Wilson/**
Original Memphis Five/Phil Napoleon leader/ - trumpet & some vocals/	Phil Napoleon/**Alberta Hunter/Trixie Smith/Annette Hanshaw/**
Orlewitz Felix/violin/studio bands/Axel Stordahl/Mitchell Ayres/	**Frank Sinatra/Perry Como/**
Ortolano Joe/trombone/studio bands/Larry Clinton/	**Bea Wain/Dick Todd/**

Ory Kid/trombone/studio bands/Louis Armstrong And His Hot Five/	**Louis Armstrong/Ma Rainey/**
Osborne Mary/jazz guitar/studio bands/	**Ethel Waters/**
Osborne Will Orchestra - Film Master - 1934	**Helen Ward/**
Osborne Will/pianist/ & His Orchestra/own vocals/	**Will Osborne/ Annette Hanshaw/**Joan Whitney/
Ossman Vess/banjo/arrainger/studio bands/	Arthur Collins/
Osser Glenn/alto sax/clarinet/studio bands/own Orchestra/	**Vic Damone/**Georgia Gibbs
Owens Arthur/saxophone/studio bands/Ted Steel/Lloyd Shaffer/	**Perry Como/**
Owens John/trumpet/studio bands/Lloyd Shaffer/	**Perry Como/**
Oxford Greys her/Mildrerd Bailey/	**Mildred Bailey/**
Ozark Fred Jug Blowers/featured unacredited vocal by Cliff Edwards/	**Cliff Edwards/**
Pace Harry/A&R - arranger/Black Swan/	**Alberta Hunter/Ethel Waters/**
Page Bob/trumpet/studio bands/dance bands/Coon - Sanders Orch./	**Carlton Coon/Joe Sanders/**
Page Orin - Hot Lips Page/trumpet/vocals/studio bands/Teddy Wilson/Artie Shaw/	**Joe Turner/Billie Holiday/**Hot Lips Page/
Page Walter/bass/arrainger/studio bands/Teddy Wilson/Count Basie/	**Jimmy Rushing/Helen Humes/Billie Holiday/**
Palange Joseph/flute/studio bands/Nelson Riddle/	**Frank Sinatra/**
Palmer Jack/trumpet/studio band/Harry James/	**Frank Sinatra/**
Panelli Charlie/trombone/with 'Original Memphis Five'/studio bands/	Phil Napoleon/**Alberta Hunter/**
Panico Louis/cornet/studio bands/dance bands/Isham Jones/	**Marion Harris/**
pare Le Jacobs's Jazz/ - (French) studio jazz band)/	**Josephine Baker/**
Parham Tiny/pianist/studio bands/	Hattie McDaniels/
Park Avenue Hillbillies/her Dorothy Shay	Dorothy Shay/
Parker Charlie - as 'bird'/alto saxophone/studio bands/Dizzy Gillespie/	**Sarah Vaughan/**
Parker Leroy/violin/studio bands/M. S. Jazz Hounds/	**Mamie Smith/**
Parshley Tom/saxophone/studio bands/Gordon Jenkins/	**Peggy Lee/**
Pasternack Josef/violin/studio bands/with Orch./	**Marion Harris/**Billy Murray/
Pastor Tony/tenor saxophone/studio bands/Artie Shaw/ & His Orch./	**Billie Holiday/**Clooney Sisters/**Rosemary Clooney/Helen Forrest**
Patent Harry/bass/studio bands/Rudy Vallee/	**Rudy Vallee/**
Patton Charlie/ own guitar/	**Charlie Patton/**
Paul Les/electric guitar/ accomp/studio bands/his Trio/	**Andrews Sisters/Bing Crosby/Helen Forrest/**Mary Ford/
Paxton George/saxophone/studio bands/George Hall/	**Dolly Dawn/**Sonny Schuyler/Loretta Lee/
Payne Bennie/pianist/studio bands/Cab Calloway/	**Cab Calloway/Chick Bullock/**
Payne Cecil/string bass/studio bands/Teddy Stewart/	**Dinah Washington/**
Payne Leon/guitar/own vocals/songwriter/studio bands/	Leon Payne/
Payne Stanley/tenor saxophone/studio bands/	**Billie Holiday/**
Peabody Eddie/banjo/guitar/studio bands/	Billy Murray/
Peer Beverly A./bass/studio bands/with Chick Webb/Ella Fitzgerald & Her Savoy Eight/	**Ella Fitzgerald/Mildred Bailey/**
Peer Ralph/A&R - arranger/Okeh/Victor-Bluebird/	**Mamie Smith/Carter Family/Jimmie Rodgers/**
Pepper Art/alto saxophone/clarinet/studio bands/Stan Kenton/	**Anita O'Day/June Christy/Nat King Cole/**
Pepper Art/pianist/studio bands/Gus Arnheim/	**Bing Crosby/**Loyce Whitman/
Peretti Hugo Orchestra/	**Sarah Vaughan/**
Perkins Bill/banjo/studio bands/Louis Armstrong/	**Louis Armstrong/**
Perkins Wilson 'Lefty'/electric guitar/studio bands/Brownies' Musical Brownies/	**Jimmie Davis/**
Perlmutter Maurice/viola/studio bands/Axel Stordahl/	**Frank Sinatra/**
Perri Danny/jazz guitar/studio bands/Eric Siday/Mitchell Ayres/	**Lee Wiley/Perry Como/Anita O'Day/**
Perrotti Anthony/violin/studio bands/Axel Stordahl/	**Frank Sinatra/**
Perry Joe/A&R-arranger/Brunswick/Decca/studio band/	**Connie Boswell?/Bing Crosby/Louis Armstrong/Francis Langford/Ernest Tubb**
Perry Mario/accordian/studio bands/	**Ruth Etting/**
Perry Ray/alto saxophone/studio band with J. C. Heard/	**Ethel Waters**
Perry Ron/tenor saxophone/studio bands/Artie Shaw/	**Billie Holiday/**
Perrymam Lloyd/string bass/studio bands/Rudy Sooter's Ranchmen/Sons Of Pioneers/	**Jimmie Davis/Roy Rogers/**Bob Nolan/Llord Perryman/Tim Spencer/
Persoff Samuel/viola/studio bands/Ted Steele/Lloyd Shaffer/Mitchell Ayres/	**Perry Como/**
Peterson Charles/banjo/studio bands/Rudy Vallee/	**Rudy Vallee/**
Peterson Charlie/trumpet/studio bands/Artie Shaw/Tommy Dorsey/	**Billie Holiday/Frank Sinatra/Jo Stafford/Connie Haines/**
Peterson 'Pete' Arthur/bass/studio bands/	**Mildred Bailey/Billie Holiday/**
Peterson Oscar/pianist/studio band/	**Billie Holiday/**
Peterson Tommy/trombone/studio band/Billie May/	**Frank Sinatra/**
Pettiford Oscar/bass/studio bands/Leonard Feather/	**Helen Humes/**
Pettis Jack/cello/arranger/Irving Mills/	**Elisabeth Welch/**
Philburn Al/trombone/studio band/Bert Lown/	Biltmore Rhythm Boys/
Phillips Flip/tenor saxophone/studio bands/	**Sarah Vaughan/**
Phillips Phil pianist/studio bands/	Dolly Kay/
Piarulli Luisa/violin/studio bands/Lloyde Shaffer/	**Perry Como/**
Pierce Alex/violin/studio bands/Joe Bushkin/	**Lee Wiley/**
Pinafores/studio band/	**Gene Autry/**
Pine Ridge Boys/vocals & guitar/	Pine Ridge Boys/
Pingatore Mike/banjo/jazz guitar/studio bands/PaulWhiteman Orch./	Rhythm Boys/**Bing Crosby/**
Pisani Nick/violin/studio bands/Axel Stordahl/Nelson Riddle/Dick Stabile/	**Frank Sinatra/Dean Martin/**
Pitt Merle/violin/studio bands/Axel Stordahl/	**Frank Sinatra/**

Plantation Orchestra her - Ethel Waters/	**Ethel Waters/**
Pleis Jack/pianist/arrainger/studio bands/ & Orch./	**Bing Crosby/Sammy Davis Jr.**/Carmen McRae/
Pletcher Stew/trumpet/studio bands/	**Mildred Bailey/**
Poliakin Raoul/violin/studio bands/Axel Stordahl/Mitchell Ayres/	**Frank Sinatra/Perry Como/**
Pollack Ben /drum/studio bands/some vocals with band/Irving Mills/& His Orchestra/	Ben Pollack/William Sisters/Irving Mills/Scrappy Lambert/**Elisabeth Welch/** Belle Mann/**Connie Boswell/**
Pollard Nat/drums/studio bands/Hudson-DeLange Orch./	Betty Allen/
Poole Charlie/banjo/folk/his North Carolina Ramblers/	Charlie Poole/
Porcino Al/trumpet/studio bands/Georgie Auld/	**Sarah Vaughan/**
Porpora Steve/string bass/Carmen Cavallaro/	**Bing Crosby/**
Porter Del/clarinet/studio band/Spike Jones/	Carl Grayson/
Porter Yank/drums/studio bands/	**Joe Turner/**
Potter Tommy/bass/studio bands/Billy Eckstine/	**Billy Eckstine/Sarah Vaughan/**
Pottinger Warren/dobro/studio bands/	**Jimmie Davis/**
Pound Hounds/	**Peggy Lee/**
Powell Benny/trombone/studio bands/Teddy Stewart/	**Dinah Washington/**
Powell Bud/pianist/studio bands/Tadd Dameron/	**Sarah Vaughan/**
Powell Carl/bass/studio bands/Herman Chittison Trio/	**Mildred Bailey/Thelma Carpenter/Ethel Waters/**
Powell Eddie/flute/studio bands/Claude Thornhill/	**Maxine Sullivan/**
Powell Ernie/alto saxophone/studio bands/	**Billie Holiday/**
Powell Jimmy/alto saxophone/studio bands/	**Billie Holiday/**
Powell Mel/pianist/studio bands/Benny Goodman/	**Peggy Lee/Dick Haymes/**
Powell Rudy/clarinet/alto saxophone/studio bands/	**Fats Waller/Billie Holiday/**
Powell Specs/drum/studio bands/	**Billie Holiday/**
Prager Irving/violin/studio bands/Russ Case/	**Perry Como/**
Prager Sammy/pianist/studio bands/	**Annette Hanshaw/**
Pratt Lloyd/bass/studio bands/Page Cavanaugh/	**Frank Sinatra/Doris Day/**
Prentice Charles/arranger/British studio band/	**Paul Robeson/Elisabeth Welch/**
Price Sam/pianist/studio bands/Leonard Feather/ his Trio/	**Rosetta Tharpe**/Marie Knight/**Helen Humes/**
Priddy Jimmy/trombone/studio bands/Glenn Miller/Nelson Riddle/	Tex Beneke/Paula Kelly/Modernaires/**Frank Sinatra/**
Prima Louis/trumpet/arrainger/vocals/songwriter/	**Louis Prima/**
Prince Budda And His Boys/studio bands/	**Frankie Half Pint Jaxton/**
Prince Charles/pianist/Victor studio bands. Prince's Orchestra/dir./Charles Prince And Orch./	**Al Jolson/Marion Harris/**
Prince Earres/pianist/studio bands/Cab Calloway/	**Cab Calloway/**
Prince Henry/pianist/studio bands/Louis Armstrong/	**Louis Armstrong/**
Prince Wesley/bass/studio bands/with Nat Cole Trio/	**Nat King Cole/**
Prisby Lou/tenor saxophone/studio bands/Georgie Auld/	**Sarah Vaughan/**
Pritchard William/trombone/studio bands/Axel Stordahl/	**Frank Sinatra/**
Privin Bernie/trumpet/studio bands/Charlie Barnet/Benny Goodman/Lloyd Shaffer/	**Lena Horne/Billie Holiday/Louis Armstrong/Peggy Lee/Dick Haymes/ Perry Como/**
Procope Russell/alto saxophone/studio bands/M. W. Jazz Jesters/	**Midge Williams/**
Prysock Red/tenor saxophone/studio band/	**Lonnie Johnson/**
Puckett Riley/guitar/vocals/	Riley Puckett/
Pugh Ray/pianist/studio bands/Leo Reisman/	**Lee Wiley/**
Pumiglio Pete/clarinet/studio bands/M. W. Jazz Jesters/	**Midge Williams/**
Punches Deligates Of Pleasyre/	**Frankie Half Pint Jaxton/**
Purce Ernest/alto saxophone/studio bands/	**Blanche Calloway/**
Purtill Maurice/drums/studio bands/Tommy Dorsey/Red Norvo/Glenn Miller/	Edythe Wright/**Mildred Bailey/**Tex Beneke/Paula Kelly/Modernaires/
Quadri Joseph/violin/studio band/	**Dean Martin/**
Quealey Chelsea/trumpet/studio bands/	**Bing Crosby/**
Quinichette Paul/tenor saxophone/studio bands/	**Dinah Washington/**
Quinn Snoozer/jazz guitar/studio bands/Paul Whiteman/	**Bing Crosby/**
Raderman Harry/trombone/violin/studio bands/Ted Lewis/	**Gene Austin/**Ted Lewis/**Ruth Etting/**
Radio Franks/named from radio program/Frank Bessinger/guitar/vocals/Frank Wright/vocals/	Frank Bessinger/Frank Wright
Rady Simon/arrainger/studio bands/Bill May/own Orchestra/	**Bing Crosby/Rosemary Clooney/**
Rael Jack/alto saxophone/studio band/	**Patty Page/**
Rassell Don/alto saxophone/studio band/	**Mel Torme/**
Rainbow Riders/studio string band/	Roy Hogsed/
Rainwater Carl/steel guitar/studio bands/Leon's Lone Star Cowboys/	Leon Chappelear/
Ralston Art/odbe/alto saxophone/studio bands/Casa Loma Orch./Dean Goodman/	**Connie Boswell/Lee Wiley/Peggy Lee/**
Ramey Gene/bass/studio bands/Tony Scott/	**Sarah Vaughan/**
Ramsey Ian/trumpet/studio bands/Axel Stordahl/	**Frank Sinatra/**
Rand Samuel/violin/studio bands/Ted Steel/Mitchell Ayres/	**Perry Como/**
Randolf Zilmer/trumpet/studio bands/Louis Armstrong/	**Louis Armstrong/**
Randolph Irving 'Mouse"/trumpet/studio bands/	**Billie Holliday/**
Rank Bill/trombone/studio bands/Paul Whiteman/	**Bing Crosby/**
Raring John/arrainger/studio bands/	**Doris Day/**
Raskin Milt/pianist/studio bands/Gene Krupa/Tommy Dorsey/Dave Barbour/	**Helen Ward/Frank Sinatra/Jo Stafford/Connie Haines/Peggy Lee/**

Rauch Billy/trombone/studio bands/Caasa Loma Orch./	**Connie Boswell/Lee Wiley/**
Raymond Irving/violin/studio bands/Tommy Dorsey/	**Frank Sinatra/Jo Stafford/Connie Haines/**
Red Onion Jazz Babies/Alberta Hunter also as 'Josephine Beatty'/	**Alberta Hunter/**
Redheads/the/studio band - assoc. with Red Nichols/	**Annette Hanshaw/**
Redman Don /alto saxophone/arrainger/somevocals/studio bands/ F. Henderson/ own Orch./	Don Redman/**Bessie Smith/Clara Smith/Ethel Waters/Ma Rainey/Bing Crosby/Boswell Sisters**
Redman Don /alto saxophone/arrainger/studio bands/somevocals/ & own Orch./	**/Mills Brothers/Cab Calloway/Connie Boswell/Harlan Lattimore/**
Reed Neal/trombone/studio band/Woody Hermann/	**Connie Boswell/**
Reese Rostelle/trumpet/studio bands/	**Billie Holiday/**
Reeves Goebel/own guitar/studio bands/	Goebel Reeves/
Reeves Reuben/trumpet/studio bands/Cab Calloway/	**Cab Calloway/**
Reeves Talcott/jazz guitar/studio bands/Don Redman/	**Don Redman/Harlan Lattimore/Bing Crosby/Boswell Sisters/**
Reevy James/trombone/studio bands/Alburys Blue And Jazz Seven/	Lucille Hegamin/**Ethel Waters/**
Rega Orchestra/ - Okeh studio band/	**Mamie Smith/Sophie Tucker/**
Reid Neal/trombone/studio bands/W. Herman Woodchopers/	**Connie Boswell/Bing Crosby/**
Reinhart Dick/string bass/studio bands/	**Gene Autry/**
Reinhardt Django/jazz guitar/studio band/	**Hildegarde/Adelaide Hall?/**
Reis Les/pianist/some vocals/studio bands/	Les Reis/
Reisman Leo/violin/dance bands/arrainger/own Orch, /	Dick Robertson/Harold Arlen/**Fred Astaire**/Ran Weeks/**Lee Wiley/C**lifton Webb/Anita Boyer/
Renard Jacques/violin/ & His Orchestra/own vocal/	Jacques Renard/
Ren'e Henri/dance bands/arrainger/studio bands/own Orch./	**Perry Como/**
Reneau George/guitar/harmonica/accomp./some vocals/studio bands/	**Gene Austin/**
Reo Thomas/trombone/studio bands/Ted Steel/	**Perry Como/**
Repay Ted/pianist/studio bands/Jimmy Grier/	**Boswell Sisters/**
Reser Harry/banjo/arrainger/studio bands/Carl Fenton/Bill Wirges/Clicquot Club Eskimos/	**Marion Harris/Al Jolson/Vaughan De Leath/Lee Morse/**Tom Stacks/
Reuss Allen/jazz guitar/studio bands/Teddy Wilson/Harry James/George Siravo/	**Helen Ward/Billie Holiday/Frank Sinatra/**
Rey Alvino/electric guitar/studio mbands/Rhythm 'Reys'/	King Sisters/Yvonne King/
Reynolds Blake/alto saxophone/studio bands/Freddie Slack/	**Ella Mae Morse/**
Reynolds Dick/pianist/studio bands/Ted Lewis Orch./	**Ruth Etting/**
Ricci George/cello/studio bands/Axel Stordahl/	**Frank Sinatra/**
Ricci Paul/clarinet/alto saxophone/studio bands/Miff Mole's Molers/	**Midge Williams/Billie Holiday/**
Rich Buddy/drum/arrainger/studio bands/Claude Thornhill/Tommy Dorsey/Artie Shaw/own Orch./Metronome All Stars/	**Maxine Sullivan/Jo Stafford/Connie Haines/Nat King Cole/Helen Forrest/ June Christy/Frank Sinatra/**
Rich Freddie Orchestra - Radio Master - 1936/	**Lee Wiley**
Rich Sonny/trumpet/studio bands/Georgie Auld/	**Sarah Vaughan/**
Richmond Harry & His Orchestra/own vocals/	Harry Richmond/
Richolson Joe/trumpet/studio bands/dance bands/Coon - Sanders Orch./	**Carlton Coon/Joe Sanders/**
Rickard James/clarinet/studio bands/	**Jimmie Rodgers/**
Ricketts Bob/pianist/studio bands/	**Lizzie Miles/**
Ricks Jimmy/bass/studio bands/vocals - led Ravens/	Jimmy Ricks/**Dinah Washington/**
Rickson George/pianist/studio bands/Lew Leslie's Blackbird Orch./	**Edith Wilson/Adelaide Hall/**
Riddle Jimmy/harmonica/studio bands/Roy Acuff And His Smokry Mountain Boys/	**Roy Acuff/**
Riddle Nelson Orchestra - Film TV Master - 1955/1955/1960/	**Frank Sinatra/**Elvis Presley/
Riddle Nelson/arrainger/studio bands/ & His Orch.	**Nat King Cole/Frank Sinatra/Ella Mae Morse/Judy Garland/Bing Crosby/** Four Knights/
Riffers - Clarance Williqams band/Lil Armstrong pianist & some vocal/oyjrts/	**Eva Taylor/**Lil Armstrong/
Riley Judge/drums/studio bands/	**Arthur Crudup/**
Riley Mike/trombone/studio band/Will Osborne/Rudy Vallee/Riley and Farley/	**Rudy Vallee/Will Osborne/**Riley and Farley/
Ring Justin/trumpet/cello/studio band/his band/	**Lee Wiley/**
Rito Ted Fio & His Orchestra/	Frank Luther/
Ritter/Tex/own guitar/radio vocals/	**Tex Ritter/**
Ridiello Nick/saxophone/flute/studio band/Les Brown/	**Doris Day/**
Roach Max/drums/studio bands/	**Sarah Vaughan/**
Roane Eddie/trumpet/studio bands/Louis Jordan Tympany Five/	**Louis Jordan/**
Robbins Robert/violin/studio bands/	**Bessie Smith/**
Roberts Dick/electric string guitar/studio bands/	**Jimmie Davis/**
Roberts George/trombone/studio bands/Nelson Riddle/	**Frank Sinatra/**
Robertson Bill/trombone/studio bands/Charlie Barnet/	**Lena Horne/**
Robertson Don/pianist/songwriter/studio bands/Nelson Riddle/	**Nat King Cole/**
Robinson Carson/own guitar/studio bands/radio/some vocals/	Carson Robinson/Wendell Hall/Vernon Dalhart/**Gene Austin/**
Robinson Clarence/clarinet/studio bands/Ethel Waters Jazz Masters/	**Ethel Waters/**
Robinson Fred/trombone/studio bands/Louis Armstrong/Don Redman Orch./	**Louis Armstrong/Victoria Spivey/**Don Redman/**Harlan Lattimore/Bing Crosby/Boswell Sisters/**
Robinson Ikey Banjo & His Bull Fiddle Band/	**Frankie Half Pint Jaxton/**
Robinson J. Russell/pianist/studio band/	**Lizzie Miles/**
Robinson Les/alto saxophone/studio bands/Artie Shaw/	**Billie Holiday/**
Robinson Prince/clarinet/tenor saxophone/studio bands/Teddy Wilsin/Leonard Feather/	**Billie Holiday/Helen Humes/**
Robinson Willard/pianist/studio bands/	**Annette Hanshaw/**

Rockwell Tommy/A&R-arranger/okeh/ARC/Decca/	**Helen Humes/Louis Armstrong/Bing Crosby/Mills Brothers/**Bob Crosby/
Rodemich Gene/pianist/studio bands/	**Al Jolson/**
Rodgers Harry or Harry Rogers /trombone/studio bands/	**Helen Forrest/ Billie Holiday/**
RodgersJimmie/own guitar/ - Film Master - 1929/	**Jimmie Rodgers/**
RodgersJimmie/own guitar/ukulele/	**Jimmie Rodgers**
Rodin Gil/clarinet/flute/arrainger/studio bands/Bob Crosby/	**/Helen Ward//Fred Astaire/Connie Boswell/Judy Garland/**Bob Miller/
Rodin Gil/clarinet/saxophone/flute/arrainger/studio bands/Ben Pollack/Bob Crosby/	Scrappy Lambert/Bob Crosby/Kay Weber/Frank Tennille/**Bing Crosby/** Marion Mann/
Rodriguez Willie/drums/studio bands/Paul Whiteman/	**Billie Holiday/**
Rogers Roy - also known as Dick Weston) - /guitar/vocals/studio band - Sons Of Pioneers/	**Roy Rogers/Dale Evans/**Songs Of The Pioneers/
Rogers Walter/clarinet/studio bands/	**Al Jolson?/**Alma Gluck/
Rogers Shorty/trumpet/studio bands/Stan Kenton/	**June Christy/Nat King Cole/**
Rollini Adrian/saxophone/bass/harmonica/studio bands/her Sizzling Synopators/	**Cliff Edwards/Annette Hanshaw/Lee Morse/**
Rollini Arthur/tenor saxophone/studio bands/Benny Goodman/	**Helen Ward/Ella Fitzgerald/Jimmy Rushing/Martha Tilton/**
Rollins Horance/bass/pianist/studio band/Gene Krupa/	**Helen Ward/**
Rose David/pianist/arranger/studio band/own Orchestra/	**Judy Garland/**Gene Kelly/
Rosengarden Robert/drums/studio bands/Mitchell Ayres/	**Perry Como/**
Rosenthal Harry/pianist/studio bands/	**Helen Ward/**
Ross Hank/clarinet/tenor saxophone/studio bands/Jess Stacy/Russ Case/Tadd Dameron/	**Lee Wiley/Anita O'Day/Perry Como/Billie Holiday/Sarah Vaughan/**
Ross Nathan/violin/studio bands/Nelson Riddle/	**Nat King Cole/Frank Sinatra/**
Ross Roy /arrainger/studio band/radio/ & His Ramblers/	**Red Foley/**
Ross Sam/viola/studio bands/Tommy Dorsey/	**Frank Sinatra/Jo Stafford/Connie Haines/**
Roth Irv/tenor saxophone/studio bands/Georgie Auld/	**Sarah Vaughan/**
Roth Jack/drums/with 'Original Memphis Five'/studio bands/	Phil Napoleon/**Alberta Hunter/Trixie Smith/**
Rothschild Irving/violin/studio bands/	**Sophie Tucker/**
Rothwell Walt/pianist/studio band/	**Emmett Miller/**
Rowland Henry/pianist/studio bands/Lloyde Shaffer/Mitchell Ayres/	**Perry Como/**
Roy Harry/arranger/some vocals/ - (British Band)	Harry Roy/**Mabel Mercer/**
Roy Harry Orchestra - Film Master - 1936	**Mabel Mercer**
Royal Ernie/trumpet/studio bands/	**Nat King Cole/**Nellie Luther/
Royal Marshall/clarinet/studio bands/Phil Moore/	**Lena Horne/Frank Sinatra/**
Rubinoff David/pianist/studio bands/	**Nick Lucas/**
Rugolo Pete/arrainger/studio bands/Stan Kenton/own Orch./	**June Christy/Nat King Cole/Dean Martin/Peggy Lee/**
Ruppersberg Don/trombone/studio bands/Charlie Barnet/	**Lena Horne/**
Rush Art/ A&R/Victor Records/ studio bands/manager/	**Roy Rogers/ Dale Evans/ Sons Of Pioneers/**
Russell Dillon 'Curley'/bass/studio bands/	**Sarah Vaughan/**
Russell Louis/pianist/studio bands/Louis Armstrong Savoy Ballroom Five/	**Louis Armstrong/Victoria Spivey/**Hoagy Carmichael/
Russell Mischa/violin/fiddle/studio bands/Axel Stordahl/Nelson Riddle/	**Gene Autry/Frank Sinatra/Nat King Cole/**
Russell 'Pee Wee'/clarinet/studio bands/Louis Prima/	**Louis Prima/**
Russin Babe/tenor saxophone/studio bands/C. Chasers/Teddy Wilson/M. Ayres/G. Siravo/Nelson Riddle/	**Eva Taylor/Maxine Sullivan/Billie Holiday/Mel Torme/Perry Como/Frank Sinatra/Frankie Laine/**
Russo Al/trombone/studio bands/Larry Clinton/	**Bea Wain/**
Rutherfolrd Rudy/clarinet/studio bands/Lionel Hampton/	**Dinah Washington/**
Ryan John or Jack/bass/studio bands/Axel Stordahl/Paul Weston/	**Frank Sinatra/Johnny Mercer/**Pied Pipers/June Hutton/
Ryerson Art/jazz guitar/studio bands/Gordon Jenkins/Percy Faith/	**Peggy Lee/Tony Bennett/**
Rythmakers Orch/ - studio band assoc. with Fats Waller/	**Fats Waller/**
Sack Al & His Orchestra/	**Andy Russell/**
Sacks Aaron/clarinet/studio bands/with Dizzie Gillespie/	**Sarah Vaughan**
Safransky Eddie/bass/studio bands/Metronome All Stars/	**Nat King Cole/June Christy/Frank Sinatra/**
Salazar M. T/guitar./studio bands/	**Jimmie Rodgers/**
Sall Ann/ - Wilene Forrester/accordian/studio bands/Blue Grass Boys/	**Bill Monroe/**
Salvador San/jazz guitar/studio bands/	**Rosemary Clooney/**
Sampson Edgar/clarinet/alto saxophone/studio bands/Chick Webb/Teddy Wilson/	**Louis Armstrong/Ethel Waters/Ella Fitzgerald/Billie Holiday/**
Sanders Joe/pianist/studio bands/dance band/Coon - Sanders Orch./	**Carlton Coon/Joe Sanders/**
Sandler Albert/violin/studio band/	**Hildegarde/**
Sannella Andy/clarinet/alto saxophone/violin/studio bands/	**Gene Austin/Ruth Etting/Annette Hanshaw/Eva Taylor/**
Sanns R J /studio bands/hisOrchestra/	**Valaida Snow/**
Saracco Frank/trombone/studio bands/Lloyd Shaffer/	**Perry Como/**
Sargent Charles/guitar/studio bands/	**Gene Autry/**
Sargent Kenny/alto saxophone/some vocals/studio bands/Casa Loma Orch./	Kenny Sargent/**Connie Boswell/Lee Wiley/**
Satterfield Jack/trombone/studio bands/Jess Stacy/	**Lee Wiley/**
Satherley Art/A&R-arranger/Paramont/Columbia/	**Ma Rainey/Gene Autry/Roy Aucuff/**
Sauter Eddie/trumpet/arrainger/studio bands/ Red Norvo/ownOrch./	**Mildred Bailey/Thelma Carpenter/**
Savitt Pinky/trumpet/studio bands/George Siravo/	**Frank Sinatra/**
Savoy Eight & her - Ella Fitzgerald/	**Ella Fitzgerald/**
Sawyer Bob/studio bands/Bob Sawyer's Jazz Band/	**Jimmie Rodgers/**
Saxe Phil/clarinet/violin/some vocals/studio bands/Irving Aaronson & his Commanders/	**Bing Crosby/**
Schacter Julious/violin/studio bands/Mitchell Ayres/Percy Faith/	**Perry Como/Tony Bennett/**

Schaffer "Dizzy Head" Ed /guitar/studio bands/	**Jimmie Davis/**
Schertzer Hymie/alto saxophone/studio bands/Benny Goodman/Jess Stacy/	**Billie Holiday/Helen Ward/Martha Tilton/Lee Wiley/Peggy Lee/Dick Haymes/**
Schmit Incion/solo/studio band/Artie Shaw/	**Lena Horne/**
Schmitt Lucien/cello/studio bands/Mitchell Ayres/	**Perry Como/**
Schoen Vic Orchestra - Film Master - 1941/1948	**Andrews Sisters/Bing Crosby/Andrews Sisters/**
Schoen Vic/studio bands/his Orch./	**Andrews Sisters/Bing Crosby/Dick Haymes/Ella Fitzgerald/**Bob Hope/ Rhythmaires/ **Patti Page**
Schroeder Gene/pianist/studio bands/Eddie Condon/	**Bing Crosby/**
Schuchmann Hatty/alto saxophone/studio bands/Tommy Dorsey/	**Frank Sinatra/Jo Stafford/Connie Haines/**
Schulman Sylvan/violin/studio bands/Lloyd Shaffer/Mitchell Ayres/	**Perry Como/**
Schumacher Frank/clarinet/alto saxophone/Jimmy Grier/	**Boswell Sisters/**
Schutt Arthur/pianist/studio bands/Dorsey Brothers/Charlestown Chasers/Benny Goodman/	**Emmett Miller/Bing Crosby/Cliff Edwards/Annette Hanshaw/Eva Taylor/ Mildred Bailey/Helen Ward/**
Schutz Buddy/drum/studio bands/Benny Goodman/Jimmy Dorsey/	**Martha Tilton**/Bob Eberly/Helen O'Connell/
Schwartz George/trumpet/studio bands/George Auld/	**Sarah Vaughan/**
Schwartz Phil/pianist/studio bands/	**Ruth Etting/**
Schwartz Willbur/clarinet/alto saxophone/studio band/Glenn Miller	Ray Eberly/ Marion Hutton/Tex Beneke/Paula Kelley/Modern Aires/
Schwartz Willie/flute/studio bands/Nelson Riddle/	**Frank Sinatra/**
Scobey Bob /trumpet/arrainger/studio bands/ led own Band - Frisco Band/	**Lizzie Miles/Bing Crosby/**
Scott Bud/jazz guitar/studio bands/	**Louis Armstrong**/Sippy Wallace/
Scott Cecil/clarinet/srudio bnads/Teddy Wilson/	**Clara Smith/Billie Holiday/**
Scott Harold/trumpet/studio bands/Louis Armstrong/	**Louis Armstrong/**
Scott Raymond/pianist/studio bands/M. W. Jazz Jesters/	**Midge Williams/**
Scott Tony/clarinet/studio bands/his Down Beat Club Septet/George Tredwell/	**Sarah Vaughan/**
Scruggs Earl/banjo/studio bands/	**Bill Monroe/**
Seaberg George/trumpet/studio band/	**Mel Torme/**
Seago Leon/fiddle/some vocals/studio bands/Ted Daffan's Texans/	Leon Seago/
Secrest Andy/tumpet/studio bands/Paul Whiteman/V. Young/Ted Weems/John Scott Trotter/	**Bing Crosby/Connie Boswell/Perry Como/**
Sedric Gene 'Honey Bear'/tenor saxophone/studio bands/	**Fats Waller/**
Seeger Pete/guitar/banjo/studio bands/songwriter/Almanac Singers/Weavers/	Pete Seeger/**Woody Guthrie/**
Segar Charlie/pianist/studio bands/	**Memphis Minnie/**
Sells Paul/accordian/studio bands/Al Dexter's Troopers/	Al Dexter/
Selvin Ben Orchestra - Radio Master - 1930/	**Ruth Etting**
Selvin Ben/violin/pianist/arrainger/studio bands/own Orch./	**Annette Hanshaw/Ethel Waters/Eva Taylor/**
Selvin Ben/violin/pianist/arrainger/studio bands/own Orch./	Irving Kaufman/**Vaughn De Leath/Ruth Etting/Bing Crosby/**
Senofsky Max/violin/studio bands/Lloyd Shaffer/	**Perry Como/**
Severnsen Doc/trumpet/studio bands/TV - Tonight Show/	Vaughn Monroe/**Sammy Davis Jr./**
Sewell Jack/cello/studio bands/Axel Stordahl/	**Frank Sinatra/**
Sexton James/trumpet/studio bands/Larry Clinton/	**Bea Wain/Dick Todd/**
Shaffer Lloyd /studio bands/his Orchestra/	**Perry Como/**Satisfiers/
Shamblin Eldon/guitar/studio bands/Bob Wills & his Texas Playboys/	Tommy Duncan/
Shanahan John/drums/studio bands/	**Bing Crosby/**
Shanahan Dick/drums/studio band/Les Brown/	**Doris Day/**
Shapiro Arthur/string bass/studio bands/L. Prima/M. Kaminsky/A. Stordahl/P. Whiteman/	**Louis Prima/Lee Wiley/Billie Holiday/Frank Sinatra/Peggy Lee/**
Shapiro Sam/violin/studio bands/Ted Lewis/	Ted Lewis/**Fats Waller/**
Shapiro Ted/pianist/studio bands/Miff Mole'sMolers/	**Sophie Tucker/**
Sharkeys Kings/ led by Joseph Sharkey Bonano/trumpet/arrainger/	**Lizzie Miles/**
Sharon Ralph/pianist/studio bands. led trio - C. Cameron, D. Richardson/	**Tony Bennett/**
Shavers Charlie/trumpet/arrainger/studio bands/Claude Thornhill/John Kirby/ Metronome All Stars/	**Maxine Sullivan/Billie Holiday/Midge Williams/Nat King Cole/June Christy/Frank Sinatra/**
Shaw Artie/clarinet/arrainger/studio bands/His Orch./more	**Lena Horne/Mel Torme/**Tony Pastor/Teddy Walters/Hot Lips Page/Anita Boyer/Nita Bradley/
Shaw Artie/clarinet/arrainger/studio bands/Lennie Hayton/Benny Goodman/ own Orch, /	**Bing Crosby/Mildred Bailey/Boswell Sisters/Helen Forrest/Billie Holiday/**
Shaw Arvell/bass/arrainger/studio bands/	**Louis Armstrong/Bing Crosby/**
Shaw Roland/arranger/British studio band/	Vera Lynn/
Shawker Norris 'Bunny'/drum/studio bands/Axel Stordahl/	**Billie Holiday/Frank Sinatra/**
Shea Dorothy Shay & Her Park Avenue Hillbillies/	Dorothy Shea/
Shellenburger George/trumpet/studio bands/Ted Steele/	**Perry Como/**
Shelton Bob/(Attlesey)/guitar/studio bands/Shelton Brothers/	Shelton Brothers/**Jimmie Davis/**
Shelton Earle/atudio bands/dir. Orch/	**Thelma Carpenter/**
Shelton Joe/(Attesey) mandolin/studio bands/Shelton Brothers/	Shelton Brothers/**Jimmie Davis/**
Shepard Jr. Ernest/bass/studio bands/Phil Moore/	**Lena Horne/Frank Sinatra/**
Sherlock Shorty/trumpet/studio bands/Tommy Dorsey/	**Connie Haines/**
Sherman James/pianist/studio bands/Billie Holiday/	**Billie Holiday/Frank Sinatra/**Charioteers/
Shertzer Hymie/saxophone/studio bands/Axel Stordahl/Russ Case/George Siravo/	**Frank Sinatra/Perry Como/**
Sherwood Bobby /jazz guitar/studio bands/own Orch./	**Bing Crosby/Cleo BrownJudy Garland/**
Shield Leroy/studio bands/dir. Orch./	**Marion Harris/**
Shields Calvin/drums/studio band/	**Lonnie Johnson/**

Shiffman Bud/alto saxophone/studio bands/Benny Goodman/	**Peggy Lee/Dick Haymes/**
Shilkret Jack/pianist/celeste/studio bands/Nat Shilkret/Leo Reisman/	**Frank Crumit/Gene Austin/Russ Columbo/Lee Wiley/**
Shilkret Nat/clarinet/Victor studio bands/ & His Orch./	Aileen Stanley/Johnny Marvin/Billy Murray/**Russ Columbo/Chick Bullock/ Ethel Merman/Ethel Shutta/**
Shilkret Nat/clarinet/Victor studio bands/ & His Orch./	**Gene Austin/Helen Kane/Helen Morgan/**Charles King/Louis Groody/
Shirley Jimmy/jazz guitar/studio band/Artie Shaw/	**Lena Horne/**
Shine Bill/alto saxophone/studio bands/Tommy Dorsey/	**Frank Sinatra/Connie Haines/**
Shoffner Bob/cornet/studio bands/Lovie Austin/	Ida Cox/
Sholes Steve/A&R - arranger/Victor/Bluebird/	**Eddy Arnold/**
Shoobe Lou/string bass/studio bands/M. W. Jazz Jesters/	**Midge Williams/**
Showboats his/ - Moon Mullican/	Moon Mullican/
Shure Paul/violin/studio bands/Nelson Riddle/	**Nat King Cole/Frank Sinatra/**
Shutt Arthur/pianist/studio bands/	**Ruth Etting/**
Siday Eric/violin/studio bands/ Orch./	**Lee Wiley/**
Signorelli Frank/pianist/studio bands/ 'Original Memphis Five'/Charlestown Chasers/	Phil Napoleon/**Alberta Hunter/Trixie Smith/Ruth Etting/Lee Morse/Eva Taylor/**
Signorelli Frank/pianist/studio bands/ 'Original Memphis Five'/Miff Mole's Molers/	**Ethel Waters/Midge Williams/**
Silvers Louis/studio bands/dir/ his Orch./	**Al Jolson/**
Simeon Omer/clarinet/studio bands/	**Eva Taylor/Victoria Spivey/**
Simeone Frank/clarinet/Altosaxophone/studio bands/Red Norvo/	**Mildred Bailey/**
Simmons John/bass/trumpet/studio bands/Benny Goodman/own Orch./	**Billie Holiday/Peggy Lee/**
Simms Ginny & Her Orchesyra/ studio band - Kay Kyser Orchestra/	**Ginny Simms/**
Simon Freddie/tenor saxophone/studio bands/Louis Jordan Timpany Five/	**Louis Jordan/Bing Crosby/**
Simpkins Po/bass/studio bands/Louis Jordan Tympany Five/	**Louis Jordan/Bing Crosby/**
Sims Zoot/tenor saxophone/studio bands/Benny Goodman/	**Peggy Lee/**
Sinatra Ray/arrainger/studio bands/ & His Orchestra/	**Connie Boswell/Tony Martin/Hildegarde/**
Singer Joseph/trumpet/studio bands/Axel Stordahl/	**Frank Sinatra/**
Singer Lou/drums/studio band/	**Dinah Washington/**
Silverman Max/violinist/studio band/Artie Shaw/	**Lena Horne/**
Singleton Zutty/drums/studio bands/with Louis Armstrong Orch./	**Louis Armstrong/Victoria Spivey/**Hoagy Carmichael/
Siravo George/alto saxophone/studio bands/Gene Krupa/own Orch./	**Helen Ward/Frank Sinatra/Doris Day/Vic Damone/**
Sissle Noble/arrainger/ songwriter/ & His Orchestra/	**Lena Horne/**
Sizzlin' Syncopators her/studio band for Annette Hanshaw	**Annette Hanshaw/**
Skiles Jimmy/trombone/studio bands/Tommy Dorsey/Axel Stotdahl/	**Frank Sinatra/Jo Stafford/Connie Haines/**
Slack Freddie Orchestra - Film Master - 1943	**Ella Mae Morse**
Slack Freddie/pianist/studio bands/Jimmy Dorsey/his Orch./	**Ella Mae Morse/Johnny Mercer/Margaret Whiting/**Don Raye/Lisa Morrow/
Slatkin Felix/violin/studio bands/Nelson Riddle/own Orch./	**Nat King Cole/Frank Sinatra/**
Small Paul/viola/some vocals/studio bands/Phil Spitalny/	**Eddie Cantor/**
Smalle Dick/kazoo/studio bands/Fred Azark's Jug Band/	**Cliff Edwards/**
Smeck Roy/guitar/steel guitar/banjo/arrainger/ & His Vita Trio/	**Gene AutryChick Bullock/Harlan Lattimore/**
Smirnoff Zelly/violin/studio bands/Mitchell Ayres/Axel Stordahl/	**Perry Como/Frank Sinatra/**
Smith Art/flute/studio bands/Freddie Slack/	**Ella Mae Morse/**
Smith Bobby Orchestra/	**Valaida Snow/**
Smith Buster/altosaxophone/studio bands/Pete Johnson/	**Joe Turner/**
Smith Cal/guitar/studio bands/Louisville Jug Band/	**Jimmie Rodgers/**
Smith Charlie/drums/studio bands/Joe Bushkin/	**Lee Wiley/**
Smith Clarence/trumpet/studio bands/Blanche Calloway Orch./	**Blanche Calloway/**
Smith Fay 'Smitty'/electric guitar/studio bands/Texas Troubadours/	**Ernest Tubb/**
Smith Floyd/jazz guitar/studio bands/M. B. Oxford Grey's/	**Mildred Bailey/**
Smith Fred/guitar/studio bands/Louisville Jug Band/	**Jimmie Rodgers/**
Smith George/tenor saxophone/studio band/Nelson Riddle/	**Frank Sinatra/**
Smith Harold/pianist/studio bands/Isham Jones/	**Bing Crosby/**
Smith Howard/pianist/studio bands/Isham Jones/Tommy Dorsey/	Edythe Wright/Jack Leonard/**Bing Crosby/Frank Sinatra/Jo Stafford/ Connie Haines/**Pied Pipers/
Smith Jabbo/trumpet/studio bands/Duke Ellington/	**Adelaide Hall/Eva Taylor/**
Smith Jess/clarinet/alto saxophone/studio bands/Leo Reisman/	**Lee Wiley/**
Smith Jimmy/string bass/studio bands/Cab Calloway/	**Cab Calloway/**
Smith Joe/cornet/studio bands/Joe Smith's Jazz Masters/F. Henderson's Hot Six/ Ebony Four/	**Ethel Waters/Bessie Smith/Ma Rainey/**
Smith Odell/fiddle//studio bands/studio bands/	Charlie Poole/
Smith Paul/pianist/studio band/	**Frank Sinatra/Ella Fitzgerald/**
Smith Ralph/piano/studio bands/Ted Daffan's Texans/	Chuck Keeshan/Leon Seago/
Smith Russell/trumpet/studio bands/Cab Calloway/	**Cab Calloway/**
Smith Stuff /pianist/studio bands/ & His Trio/	**Sarah Vaughan/**
Smith Tab/soprano saxophone/arrainger/studio bands/Count Basie/	**Billie Holiday/Jimmy Rushing/Helen Humes/**
Smith Walter/trumpet/studio bands/Larry Clinton/	**Bea Wain/Dick Todd/**
Smith Warren/trombone/studio bands/Bob Crosby/	Bob Crosby/**Bing Crosby/**Marion Mann/
Smith Willie/alto - sax/some vocals/studio bands/Jimmy Lunceford/	**Ivie Anderson/**
Smith Willie - the Lion/pianist/studio bands/	**Mamie Smith/Joe Turner/**
Smithers Elmer/trombone/studio bands/Axel Stordahl/Dave Baubour/	**Frank Sinatra/Peggy Lee/**

Smokey Mountain Boys/ lead - Roy Acuff/; most vocals & fiddle/	**Roy Acuff/**
Snow Valaida/trumpet/vocals/studio bands/Earle Hines/Billy Mason/Jimmy Munday/	**Valaida Snow/**
Snowden Elmer/banjo/studio bands/	**Lizzie Miles/**
Snowden Roscoe Q./pianist/studio bands/	Josie Miles/
Snyder Terry/drums/studio bands/Ted Steele/Lloyd Shaffer/Mitchell Ayres/Mitch Miller/	**Perry Como/Rosemary Clooney/**
Soccarras Alberto/alto saxophone/studio bands/Lew Leslie's Blackbirds Orch./	**Adelaide Hall/Lizzie Miles/Eva Taylor/**
Solomon Melven/trumpet/studio bands/Ted Steel/Mitchell Ayres/	**Perry Como/**
Song Spinners the/	**Ella Fitzgerald/**
Sons Of The Pioneers /Film Master - 1944/1946/	**Roy Rogers**
Sons Of The Pioneers/var. members incl. - Lenard Sly - (Roy Rogers/Bob Nolan/	Sons Of The Pioneers/**Lenard Sly - Roy Rogers/**Bob Nolan/Tim Spencer/
Sooson Marshall/violin/studio bands/Nelson Riddle/	**Frank Sinatra/**
Sooter Rudy/guitar/studio bands/as lead Rudy Sooter's Ranchmem/	**Jimmie Davis/**
Sosnik Harry /pianist/arraingerstudio bands/own Orch./	**Connie Boswell/Hildegarde/**Pinky Tomlin/Bob Hope/Shirley Ross/Gertrude Niesen
South Eddie/violin/studio bands/	**Marion Harris/**
Southern Seranaders her - Lee Morse/	**Lee Morse/**
Sowande Fela/organ/European studio band/	**Adelaide Hall**
Spanier Mugsy/trumpet/arrainger/studio bands/Ted Lewis/Bob Crosby/Ben Pollack/	Ted Lewis/**Fats Waller/Ethel Waters/Lee Wiley/Bing Crosby/Connie Boswell/**
Speed Samuel/banjo/studio bands/M. Smith Jazz Hounds/	**Mamie Smith/**
Speledore Thomas/pianist/studio bands/Ted Steele/	**Perry Como/**
Spencer Herb/tenor saxophone/studio bands/Dorsey Brothers/	**Bing Crosby/**
Sperzel John/bass/studio bands/Paul Whiteman/	Rhythm Boys/**Bing Crosby/**
Spiegelman Stan/viola/studio bands/Nelson Riddle/	**Nat King Cole/Frank Sinatra/**
Spitalny Phil/clarinet/studio bands/radio/own Orch/	**Eddie Cantor/**
Spivak Charlie/trumpet/studio bands/Dorsey Brothers/Ray Noble/Claude Thornhill/	**Ruth Etting/Bing Crosby/Boswell Sisters/Al Bowlly/Maxine Sullivan/**
Springer Joe/pianist/studio bands/	**Billie Holiday/**
Squires Bruce/trombone/studio band/Gene Krupa/	**Helen Ward/**
St. Cyr Johnny/banjo/guitar/studio bands/Louis Armstrong's Hot Seven/	**Louis Armstrong/**Hersal Thomas/
Stabile Dick/alto saxophone/arrainger/studio bands/ & His Orchestra	**Dean Martin/**Nuggets/
Stacy Jack/clarinet/studio bands/Jimmy Dorsey/	**Louis Armstrong/Bing Crosby/**Frances Langford/**Billie Holiday/**
Stacks Tom/drums/some vocals/studio bands/Cliquot Club Eskimos/	Tom Stacks/**Vaughn De Leath/Lee Morse/**
Stacey Jess/pianist/studio bands/Bob Crosby/Benny Goodman/own Orch./	**Martha Tilton/Bing Crosby/**Marion Mann/**Helen Ward/Lee Wiley/Connie Boswell/**
Stagliano James/cornet/studio bands/Axel Stordahl/	**Frank Sinatra/**
Staigers Del/trumpet/studio bands/	**Gene Austin/**
Stark Bobby/trumpet/studio bands/Chick Webb/Leonard Feather/	**Ella Fitzgerald/Helen Humes/**
Stark Willie/alto saxophone/studio bands/Louis Armstrong/	**Louis Armstrong/**
Starks Artie/clarinet/studio bands/Louis Armstrong/	Sippy Wallace/
Stearns Al/trumpet/studio bands/Tommy Dorsey/	**Frank Sinatra/Connie Haines/**
Steel Alphonse/drums/studio bands/Teddy Wilson/	**Billie Holiday/**
Steel Joe/pianist/studio bands/	**Ethel Waters/**
Steel Ted/studio bands/arrainger/own Orch./	**Perry Como/**
Stegmeyer Bill/alto saxophone/studio bands/his Orch./	**Billie Holiday/**
Stein Maury/clarinet/studio bands/Dave Barbour/	**Peggy Lee/**
Steiner William/alto saxophone/studio bands/Eddie Mallory/	**Ethel Waters/**
Stenofsky Max/violin/studio bands/Ted Steele/	**Perry Como/**
Stephens Haig/bass/studio bands/T. Camarata./	**Billie Holiday/**
Stephens Phil/string bass/studio bands/Charlie Barnet/Freddie Slack/George Siravo/	**Bing Crosby/Lena Horne/Ella Mae Morse/Peggy Lee/Frank Sinatra/ Frankie Laine/**
Stept Sammy/pianist/studio bands/	**Nick Lucas/**
Sterkin David/viola/studio bands/Alex Stordahl/Nelson Riddle/	**Frank Sinatra/**
Stern Hank/tuba/studio bands/Dorsey Brothers/	**Annette Hanshaw/Bing Crosby/**
Stevenson George/trombone/studio bands/	**Billie Holiday/**
Stewart Redd/fiddle/vocals/studio bands/Pee Wee King & his Golden West Cowboys/	Redd Stewart/
Stewart Rex/cornet/saxophone/studio bands	**Ivie Anderson/**
Stewart Teddy/drum/studio bands/own Orch, /	**Dinah Washington/**
Still William Grant/or as Willie Grant/A&R- arranger/songwriter/Paul Whiteman/	**Ethel Waters?/Bing Crosby/**
Stockard Ocie/banjo/studio bands/Milton Brown/Brownie's Musical Brownies/	Milton Brown/**Jimmie Davis/**
Stoll Georgie & His Orchestra - Radio Master - 1934/	**Bing Crosby/**
Stoll Georgie/violinist/ studio bands/ & His Orch./	**Bing Crosby/Judy Garland/Fred Astaire/**Mickey Rooney/Rhythmettes/ **Doris Day/**
Stoller Alvin/drums/studio bands/Benny Goodman/	**Peggy Lee/Dick Haymes/Mel Torme/Billie Holiday/**
Stoloff Morris/studio bands/dirOrch./	**Al Jolson/Bing Crosby/ Frank Sinatra/**
Stone Butch/saxophone/studio band/Les Brown/	**Doris Day/**
Stone Cliffie/string bass/songwriter/studio bands/own Orch./	**Tex Ritter/Merle Travis/Ella Mae Morse/**Ernie Ford/
Stone Eddie/violin/studio bands/Isham Jones Orch./	**Bing Crosby/**
Stone Jessie/pianist/or as Charles Calhoun/George Lee Orch./arrainger/ songwriter/	**Julia Lee/**Jessie Stone/

Stone Lew/pianist/studio bands/ & His Orch. (British band) /	**Al Bowlly/**
Stoneburn Sid/clarinet/studio bands/Dorsey Brothers/	**Bing Crosby/Boswell Sisters/Lee Wiley/**
Stoneman Ernest V/harmonica/autoharp/vocals/studio bands/	Ernest Stoneman/
Stordahl Axel Orchestra/trumpet/arrainger/studio bands/Own Orch./	**Frank Sinatra/**Pearl Baily/Dagmar/**Bing Crosby/**
Stout Russ/banjo/studio bands/dance bands/Coon - Sanders Orch./	**Carlton Coon/Joe Sanders/**
Stover Everett/trumpet/studio bands/Bob Wills & his Texas Playboys/	Tommy Duncan/
Straub Bill/pianist/studio bands/Larry Clinton/	**Bea Wain/**
Strayhorn Billy/pianist/arrainger/songwriter/Duke Ellington/	**Ivie Anderson/**Joya Sherill/Betty Roche/Herb Jeffries/
Stricklin Al/pianist/studio bands/Bob Wills & his Rexas Playboys/	Tommy Duncan/
Stringbean/or Stringbeans/ - David Akeman/banjo/studio bands/Blue Grass Boys/	**Bill Monroe/**
Strong Jimmy/clarinet/studio bands/Louis Armstrong/	**Louis Armstrong/Victoria Spivey/**Hoagy Carmichael/
Stulce Fred/alto saxophone/studio bands/Tommy Dorsey/Axel Stordahl/	**Frank Sinatra/Jo Stafford/Connie Haines/**Pied Pipers/
Sullivan Gene/steel guitar/studio bands/some vocals/Leon's Lone Star Cowboys/W. Walker/	Leon Chappelear/Gene Sullivan/Wiley Walker/
Sullivan Joe/pianist/arrainger/studio bands/Benny Goodman/Bob Crosby/	**Bing Crosby/Russ Columbo/Ozzie Nelson/Ethel Waters/Billie Holiday/**
Sullivan Maxine Orchestra/(Claude Thornhill Orchestra as studio band/	**Maxine Sullivan/**
Summers Thomas C/drums/studio bands/	**Roy Rogers/**
Summery James Clell/steel guitar/studio bands/Roy Acuff Craxy Tennesseans/	**Roy Acuff/**
Sutton Ralph/pianist/studio bands/Bob Scobey/	**Bing Crosby/**
Swain Loyce Bud 'Tex'/guitar/studio bands/Charles Mitchell's Texans/	**Jimmie Davis/**
Swanee Music her - Kate Smith/	**Kate Smith/**
Swayzee Edwin//trumpet/studio bands/Cab Calloway/	**Cab Calloway/Chick Bullock/**
Taft Jim/string bass/studio bands/Jimmy Dorsey/	**Louis Armstrong/Bing Crosby/**Frances Langford/
Tampa Red's Hukum Jug Band/guitar/kazoo/studio bands/	**Frankie Half Pint Jaxton/Ma Rainey/**
Taninbaum Wolf/saxophone/studio bands/Axel Stordahl/	**Frank Sinatra/**
Tanner Gid/fiddle/studio bands/	Riley Puckett/
Tanner Paul/trombone/studio bands/Glenn Miller/Nelson Riddle/	Marion Hutton/Tex Beneke/**Kay Starr/**Paula Kelly/Modernaires/**Nat King Cole/**
Tarto Joe/string bass/studio bands/Dorsey Brothers/Miff Moler's Molers/C. Chasers/	**Cliff Edwards/Eva Taylor/Ethel Waters/Alberta Hunter/**
Tarto Joe/string bass/studio bands/Dorsey Brothers/Miff Moler's Molers/Roger Wolf Kahn/	**Sophie Tucker/Ruth Etting/Emmett Miller/Libby Holman/Annette Hanshaw/**
Tate Harry/clarinet/studio bands/E. W. Plantation Orch./	**Ethel Waters/**
Tatum Art/pianist/arrainger/studio bands/ & own Orch./	**Adelaide Hall/Joe Turner/**
Taylor Al/flute/studio bands/Freddie Slack/	**Ella Mae Morse/Margaret Whiting/**
Taylor Billy/bass/arrainger/studio bands/Art Tatum/Chick Webb/Artie Shaw/	**Lena Horne/Sarah Vaughan/**
Taylor Billy/bass/arrainger/studio bands/Art Tatum/Chick Webb/Fats Waller/D. Ellington/	**Bessie Smith/Ivie Anderson/Ella Fitzgerald/Joe Turner/Fats Waller/Billie Holiday/**
Taylor Jack/string bass/studio bands/Gene Autry Trio/	**Gene Autry/**
Taylor Jackie / & His Orchestra/	**Boswell Sisters/Connie Boswell/**
Tayne Woolf/clarinet/studio bands/Larry Clinton/	**Bea Wain/**
Teagarden Charlie/studio bands/Ben Pollack/Benny Goodman/	Scappy Lambert/**Billie Holiday/**
Teagarden Jack /trombone//studio bands/Ben Pollack/Paul Whiteman/Dorsey Brothers/Benny Goodman/	Scrappy Lambert/**Bing Crosby/Emmett Miller/Fats Waller/Annette Hanshaw/Bessie Smith/Ethel Waters/Billie Holiday/**
Teagarden Jack /trombone/arrainger/studio bands/some vocals/own Orch./	**Mildred Bailey/**/Mary Martin/Jack Teagarden/
Tennessee Plowboys his/led Eddy Arnold - guitar/	**Eddy Arnold/**
Terr Max/pianist/studio bands/Lee Morse/Max Terr's Mixed Chorus/	**Lee Morse/Bing Crosby/**
Terri Vincent/jazz guitar/studio band/	**Dean Martin/**
Terrill Harry/saxophone/studio bands/Mitchell Ayres/	**Perry Como/**
Terry Clark/trumpet/studio bands/	**Dinah Washington/**
Texans his/ - Tex Ritter/	**Tex Ritter/**
Texas Troubadors his - leader - Ernest Tubb/guitar/	**Ernest Tubb/**
Thall Willie/bass/studio bands/Drifting Cowboys/	**Hank Williams**
Tharpe Rosetta/guitar/electric guitar/studio bands/Lucky Millinder Orch./	**Rosetta Tharpe/**
Theis Henry/violin/studio bands/ his Orch.	**Jane Froman/**
Thiel Joe/saxophone/studio bands/dance band/Coon - Sanders Orch./	**Carlton Coon/Joe Sanders/**
Thiell Harold/saxophone/studio bands/dance band/Coon - Sanders Orch./	**Carlton Coon/Joe Sanders/**
Thippen Ben/drums/studio bands/	**Blanche Calloway/Dinah Washington/**
Thomas Hershal/pianist/studio bands/Louis Armstrong/	**Louis Armstrong/**Hociel Thomas/Sippy Wallace/
Thomas Joe/trumpet/alto saxophone/arrainger/studio bands/Art Tatum/Teddy Wilson/	**Joe Turner/Billie Holiday/**
Thomas John/trombone/studio bands/Louis Armstrong's Hot Seven/	**Louis Armstrong/**
Thomas Walter/alto saxophone/studio bands/Cab Calloway/	**Cab Calloway/Chick Bullock/**
Thompson Bob/arrainger/studio bands/	**Bing Crosby/**
Thompson Lucky/tenor - sax/studio bands/	**Ivie Anderson/**
Thornhill Claude/pianist/studio bands/Louis Prima/Teddy Wilson/ & own Orch, /	**Louis Prima/Billie Holiday/Maxine Sullivan/**Fran Warren/
Thow George/trumpet/studio bands/Isham Jones/Jimmy Dorsey/	**Bing Crosby/Louis Armstrong/**Frances Langford/
Three Blue Streaks/	**Annette Hanshaw/**
Tice Larry/clarinet/studio bands/	**Annette Hanshaw/**
Tierney Louis/saxophone/studio bands/Bob Wills & his Texas Playboys/	Tommy Duncan/
Tizol Juan/trombone/violin/studio bands/Duke Ellington/Nelson Riddle/	Rhythm Boys/**Ivie Anderson/Ethel Waters/Bing Crosby/Nat King Cole/**

Toland Ray/drum/studio bands/Rudy Vallee/	**Rudy Vallee/**
Tompkins Eddie/trumpet/studio bands/Teddy Wilson/	**Billie Holiday/**
Torme Mel/pianist/drums/vocalist/arrainger/songwriter/Mel Tones/	**Mel Torme/Bing Crosby/**
Torres Gilbert/jazz guitar/studio bands/	**Ruth Etting/**
Tortomas Tony/trumpet/studio bands/Miff Mole's Molers/	**Midge Williams/**
Toscarelli Mario/drums/studio bands/Jess Stacy/	**Lee Wiley/**
Tough Dave/drums/studio bands/Charlestown Chasers/	**Eva Taylor/**
Traettino Rick/trumpet/studio bands/Larry Clinton/	**Bea Wain/Dick Todd/**
Travis Merle/guitar/arrainger/vocals/studio bands/	**Merle Travis/**
Traxler Gene/stringbass/studio bands/Tommy Dorsey/	Edythe Wright/Jack Leonard/**Frank Sinatra/Jo Stafford/Connie Haines/**
Tredwell George /trumpet/arrainger/studio bands/J. C. Heard/his All Stars/his Orch./	**Sarah Vaughan/Ethel Waters/**
Trotter John Scott Orchestra - Radio Master - 1939/1941/	**Bing Crosby/Ethel Waters/**
Trotter John Scott/pianist/college bands/arrainger/studio bands/Hal Kemp/	Skinnay Ennis/Maxine Gray/**Bing Crosby/Connie Boswell/**Trudy Erwin/**Mel Torme/Al Jolson/Peggy Lee/**
Trotter John Scott/pianist/Decca studio bands/arrainger/dir. orchestra/	Music Maids/Ken Darby Singers/Six Hits & A Miss/Carol Richards/Skylarks/ Max Terr Chorus
Trotter John Scott/pianist/Decca studio bands/arringer//dir. orch.	Williams Brothers - Andy Williams/Hal Hopper/
Trueheart John/jazz guitar/arrainger/studio bands/Chick Webb/E. Fitzgerald Savoy Eight/	**Louis Armstrong/Billie Holiday/Ella Fitzgerald/**
Trumbauer Frank/saxophone/arrainger/studio bands/Paul Whiteman/own Orch./	Rhythm Boys/**Bing Crosby/Johnny Mercer/**Fredda Gibson
Tubb Ernest/guitar/arrainger/songwriter/his Texas Troubadors/	**Ernest Tubb/**
Tucker Bobbypianist/studio bands/his Trio/	**Billie Holiday/**
Tucker Gabe/guitar/studio bands/Tennessee Plowboys/	**Eddy Arnold/**
Tucker Orrin/saxophone/studio bands/own Orch./	Bonnie Baker/
Tucker Tommy/pianiststudio bands/his Orch./	Amy Arnell/
Tudor Eddie/guitar/studio bands/	**Gene Autry/**
Tug Jug Washboard Band/banjo/jug/kazoo/	**Ma Rainey/**
Turner Charles/string bass/studio bands/Fats Waller/Eddie Mallory/	**Fats Waller/Ethel Waters/**
Turner Joe/pianist/some vocals/studio bands/ - NOT 'Big Joe' Turner/	Joe Turner/**Aldelaide Hall/**
Turner Ray/pianist/studio bands/Nelson Riddle/	**Nat King Cole/**
Tympany Five - Louis Jordan/mostlyown vocal	**Louis Jordan/Bing Crosby/Ella Fitzgerald/**
Urbont Harry/violin/studio bands/Artie Shaw/Axel Stordahl/	**Lena Horne/Frank Sinatra/**
Usera Ramone/tenor saxophone/studio bands/Lew Leslie's Blackbirds Orch./	**Adelaide Hall/**
Vail Olcott/violin/studio bands/Nelson Riddle/	**Nat King Cole/**
Vallee Rudy/alto saxophone/vocalist/college bands/studio bands/led Connecicut Yankees	**Rudy Vallee/Alice Faye/**
Van Epps Bobby/pianist//studio bands/Jimmy Dorsey/	**Louis Armstrong/Bing Crosby/**Frances Langford/
Van Epps George/jazz guitar/string bass/studio bands/Axel Stordahl/	**Louis Prima/Jo Stafford/Frank Sinatra/Frankie Laine/**
Van Eps John/trumpet/studio bands/Larry Clinton/	**Bea Wain/**
Vanasek Arthur J/violin/studio bands/dance bands/Isham Jones/	**Marion Harris/**
Varsalona Bart/trombone/studio bands/Mitchell Ayres/	**Perry Como/**
Vaughan Sarah/piano/organ/vocals/studio bands/	**Sarah Vaughan/**
Ventura Charlie/tenor saxophone/studio bands/Gene Krupa/	**Anita O'Day/**
Ventuti Joe/violin/studio bands/arrainger/Joe Venuti's Blue Four/Dorsey Brothers/ own Orch.	**Ruth Etting/Annette Hanshaw/Libby Holman/Rudy Vallee/Eddie Cantor/** Harold Arlen/
Ventuti Joe/violin/studio bands/arrainger/Paul Whiteman/Dorsey Brothers/own Orch.	**Bing Crosby//Ethel Waters/Boswell Sisters/Connie Boswell/Andrews Sisters/Lee Wiley/**
Vesly Ted/trombone/studio bands/Artie Shaw/Benny Goodman/	**Billie Holiday/Mildred Bailey/**
Victor Victor Orchestra - Radio Master - 1935/	**Boswell Sisters/Ruth Etting/**
Vinci Gerald/violin/studio bands/Nelson Riddle/	**Nat King Cole/Frank Sinatra/**
Viola Al/jazz guitar/studio bands/Page Cavanaugh/	**Frank Sinatra/Doris Day/**
Virginians the/ Orchestra/assoc. with Paul Whiteman/	Jane Green/
Vito - Ricci Elaine/harp/sytudio bands/Axel Stordahl/	**Frank Sinatra/**
Voorhees Don/pianist/studio band/	Scrappy Lambert?/
Vorzon Jules/tenor saxopjhone/studio bands/Rudy Vallee/	**Rudy Vallee/**
Vunk Lyman/trumpet/studio bands/Charlie Barnet/	**Lena Horne/**
Waddilove Don/trumpet/studio bands/Paul Whiteman/	**Billie Holiday/**
Wade Dave/trumpet/studio bands/M. W. Jazz Jesters/	**Midge Williams/**
Wainwright Connie/jazz guitar/studio bands/Billy Eckstine/	**Billy Eckstine/Sarah Vaughan/**
Wakely Jimmy/string bass/studio bands/ own band with vocals/	**Jimmie Davis/**Jimmy Wakely/**Margaret Whiting/**
Wald Jerry/clarinet/alto sax/studio bands/own Orchestra/	Dick Merrick/**Frank Sinatra/Frankie Laine/**
Walker Frank/A&R - arranger/Columbia/MGM/	**Bessie Smith/Ethel Waters/Ruth Etting/**Riley Puckett/Willard Robinson/ Allen Brothers/**Hank Williams/**
Walker T - Bone/electric guitar/studio bands/some vocals/Freddie Slack/	**Ella Mae Morse/**
Walker Wiley/fiddle/some vocals/studio bands/ & Gene Sullivan/	Wiley Walker/Gene Sullivan/
Wall Phil/pianist/studio band/	**Annette Hanshaw/**
Wallace Cedric/bass/studio bands/	**Fats Waller/**
Wallace Frankie/guitar/	Frankie Wallace/
Wallace Oliver/organist/studio bands/conduct dir/film orchestra/	**Peggy Lee/**
Waller Fats/pianist/pipe organ/accomp./or own vocal/ - also known as Maurice	**Lee Wiley**
Waller Fats/pianist/pipe organ/accomp./vocals/studio bands/ & His Rhythm/	/Una Mae Carlise/Jack Teagarden/**Adelaide Hall/**

Waller Fats/pianist/pipe organ/accomp. vocals/own vocals/satudio bands/Ted Lewis/	**Gene Austin/Alberta Hunter/Ethel Waters/**/Ted Lewis/**Fats Waller/**
Walter Cy/pianist/arrainger/studio bands/	**Mabel Mercer/Lee Wiley/**
Walters Dick/arrainger/studio bands/own Orchestra/	**Ella Mae Morse/**
Walters Teddy/jazz guitar/studio bands/Eddie Heywood/	**Billie Holiday/**
Waring Fred/banjo/guitar/college bands/hisF. Warings Pennsysvanians/ & Glee Club/	Clare Hanlon/**Chick Bullock &** Three Waring Girls/**Bing Crosby/Frank Sinatra/**
Warner Elmer/jazz guitar/studio bands/Bill Doggett/	**Helen Humes/**
Warren Earle/alto saxophone/studio bands/Count Basie/	**Jimmy Rushing/Helen Humes/**
Warrington Johnny/arrainger/studio bands/own Orchestra/	**Connie Haines/**
Washboard Sam/ own washboard/dubbed a blues singer/	Washboard Sam/
Washborne Country/tuba/studio bands/Ted Weems/	**Perry Como/**
Washington Albert/clarinet/studio bands/Louis Armstrong/	**Louis Armstrong/**
Washington Ford Lee/as 'Buck'/pianist/trumpet/studio bands/actor/L. Armstrong/ own band/	**Louis Armstrong/Bessie Smith/Billie Holiday**
Washington Jack/saxophone/studio bands/Count Basie/	**Jimmy Rushing/Helen Humes/ Thelma Carpenter/**
Waters Muddy/own guitar/studio bands/	Muddy Waters/
Watson El/harmonica/some vocals/studio bands/	El Watson/
Watson Ivory Deek/guitsr/ukuele/vocals/studio bands/Ink Spots/	**Ink Spots/Mildred Bailey/Ella Fitzgerald/**
Watt Don/clarinet/studio bands/Larry Clinton/	**Bea Wain/**
Watts Grady/trumpet/studio bands/Casa Loma Orch./	**Connie Boswell/Lee Wiley/**
Watts Howard/bass/studio bands/Blue Grass Boys/	**Bill Monroe/**
Watts Jake/harmonica/studio bands/	**Tex Ritter/**
Wayland Hank/string bass/studio bands/Larry Clinton/	**Bea Wain/**
Wayne Chuck/jazz guitar/studio bands/Leonard Feather/Dizzie Gillespie/	**Helen Humes/Sarah Vaughan**
Weaver Sylvester/pianist/arrainger/studio bands/	**Helen Humes/**
Webb Chick Orchestra - Radio Master - 1939	**Ella Fitzgerald**
Webb Chick/drumer/studio bands/Louis Armstrong/own Orch./	**Louis Armstrong/Ella Fitzgerald**
Webb Jack/dir/ Orchestra/	**Peggy Lee/**
Webb Stanley/string bass/saxophone/studio bands/Mitchell Ayres/	**Billie Holiday/Perry Como/**
Webb Warren/flute/studio bands/Nelson Riddle/	**Frank Sinatra/**
Weber Dick/violin/studio bands/Jimmy Grier/	**Boswell Sisters/**
Webster Ben/tenor saxophone/studio band/Teddy Wilson/Duke Ellington/Tony Scott/	**Billie Holiday/Ivie Anderson/Sarah Vaughan/Dinah Washington/**
Webster Ben - Film (tV) Master - 1957	**Billie Holiday**
Webster Freddy/trumpet/studio bands/Tadd Dameron/	**Sarah Vaughan/**
Weed Buddy/pianist/studio bands/Paul Whiteman/	**Billie Holiday/**
Weeks Anson Orchestra/Film Master - 1945	**Dale Evans**
Weeks Anson/hotel dance bands/studio bands/arrainger/ & his Orch./	**Bing Crosby**
Weems Art/trumpet/studio bands/Ted Weems/	**Perry Como/**Art Jarrett/
Weems Ted/trombone/arrainger/studio bands/ & His Orch./	Parker Gibbs/**Perry Como/**Art Jarrett/
Weidler George/alto saxophone/studio bands/Les Brown/	**Doris Day/**
Weinstock Manny/trumpet/studio bands/Dorsey Brothers/Lloyd Shaffer/	**Boswell Sisters/Perry Como/**
Weisman Scotty/guitar/banjo/radio/songwriter/Lulu Belle & Scotty/	Lulu Belle & Scotty/
Weiss Sam/drums/studio bands/Miff Mole's Molers/	**Midge Williams/**
Weiss Sid/string bass/studio bands/Artie Shaw/Benny Goodman/	**Helen Forrest/Peggy Lee/ Dick Haymes/**
Weiss Sid/string bass/studio bands/Miff Mole's Molers/Tommy Dorsey/Bunny Berrigan/	**Midge Williams/Billie Holiday/Lee Wiley/Jo Stafford/Frank Sinatra/ Connie Haines/**
Welk Lawrence/pianist/arrainger/accordian/ own Orch./	**Jimmie Davis/Red Foley/**
Wells Dicky/trombone/arrainger/studio bands/Count Basie/ - Dicky Wells Big Seven/	**Jimmy Rushing/Helen Humes/Sarah Vaughan/Billie Holiday/**
Wendt George/trumpet/studio bands/Freddie Slack/	**Ella Mae Morse/Johnny Mercer/**
Westhler Walter/pianist/studio band/	**Mel Torme/**
Westbrook John/steel guitar/studio bands/	**Jimmie Rodgers/**
Weston Don/guitar/studio bands/	**Gene Autry/**
Weston Paul /studio bands/arrainger/ & His Orch, /	**Johnny Mercer/Doris Day//Dean Martin/Margaret Whiting/Rosemary Clooney/**Betty Clooney/ **Frankie Laine**
Weston Paul/college bands/studio bands/arrainger/ & His Orch./	**Lee Wiley/Jo Stafford/Andy Russell/Martha Tilton/Dinah Shore/**Pied Pipers/June Hutton/
Westhington Crawford/clarinet/alto saxophone/studio band/Mills Blue Rhythm band/Blue Ribbon Boys/	**Adelaide Hall/Chick Bullock/**
Wettling George/drums/studio bands/Red Norvo/Max Kaminsky/Eddie Condon/	**Mildred Bailey/Bing Crosby/Lee Wiley/Billie Holiday/**
Wheatstraw Peetie/pianist/some vocals/studio bands/	Peetie Wheatshaw/
Wheeler De Priest/trombone/studio bands/Cab Calloway/	**Cab Calloway/Chick Bullock/**
Wheeler Harold/musical director/studio bands/	**Lena Horne/**
Whestsel Arthur/trumpet/satudio bands/Duke Ellington//	Baby Cox/Irving Mills/Ozzie Ware/Rhythm Boys/**Adelaide Hall/**
Whestsel Arthur/trumpet/studio bands/Duke Ellington/	**Ivie Anderson/Ethel Waters/Bing Crosby/**
Whiperwillows/country band/	**Merle Travis/**
Whistler Al/string bass/studio bands/Larry Clinton/	**Bea Wain/**
White Ernie/tenor saxophone/studio bands/Dorsey Brothers/	**Bing Crosby/Boswell Sisters/Lee Wiley/**
White Harry/trombone/studio bands/Cab Calloway/	**Cab Calloway/Chick Bullock/**
White Hy/jazz guitar/Studio bands/Woody Herman/Les Brown/	**Connie Boswell/Bing Crosby/**Woody Herman/Murial Lane/**Doris Day/**

White Josh/vocalist. own guitar/accomp./also known - as Singing Christian/ Pinewood Tom/	**Josh White/Libby Holman/**
White Leo/alto saxophone/studio bands/Charlie Barnet/	**Lena Horne/**
White Morris/banjo/studio bands/Cab Calloway/	**Cab Calloway/Chick Bullock/**
White Sonny/piano/studio bands/with Teddy Wilson/	**Billie Holiday/**
Whiteman Paul/violin/viola/arrainger/studio bands/dance band/his Orch/	Irene Taylor/Ramona/**Vaughn De Leath/Paul Robeson/**Dolores Del Rio/
Whiteman Paul/violin/viola/arrainger/studio bands/dance band/his Orch/	Jack Fulton/Charles Gaylord/Austin Young/Rhythm Boys - **Bing Crosby/**Al Rinker/Harry Barris/
Whiteman Paul/violin/viola/arrainger/studio bands/his Orch/	**Mildred Bailey/Billie Holiday/**
Whiting Fred/bass/studio bands/Freddie Slack/	**Ella Mae Morse/**
Whittet Ben/clarinet/studio bands/	**Fats Waller/**
Wiggins Ivan L./Hawaiian steel guitar/studio bands/Tennessee Plowboys/	**Eddy Arnold/**
Wilbur Jay/studio band/dance band/ Orchestra/ (British band)	Vera Lynn/**Ruth Etting/Adelaide Hall/**
Wilkins Ernie/alto saxophone/studio bands/Teddy Stewart/	**Dinah Washington/**
Willard Clarence/trumpet/studio bands/Woody Hermann/	**Woody Hermann/Murial Clare/Connie Boswell/Bing Crosby/**
Williams Bob/trumpet/studio bands/	**Billie Holiday/**
Williams Burt - NOT the broadway entity/flute/oboe/bassoon/studio bands/Leo Reisman/	**Lee Wiley/**
Williams Clarance/pianist/arrainger/songwriter/Blue Five/Blue Seven/Jug Band/ his Orch./	**Eva Taylor/**Dora Carr/**Louis Armstrong/Victoria Spivery/Ethel Waters/** Riffers/
Williams Clarance/pianist/arrainger/songwriter/own Orch./	**Lonnie Johnson//Chick Bullock/**
Williams Cootie/trumpet/studio bands/ Duke Ellington/	Ozzie Ware/Irving Mills/Rhythm Boys/**Ivie Anderson/Bing Crosby/Ethel Waters/**
Williams Cootie/trumpet/studio bands/ Duke Ellington/Benny Goodman/	**/Helen Forrest/Dick Haymes/Peggy Lee/**
Williams Cordy/violin/Cordy Williams Jazz Masters/	**Ethel Waters/**
Williams Elmer/tenor saxophone/studio bands/Louis Armstrong/	**Louis Armstrong/**
Williams Fred/tenor saxophone/studio bands/	**Billie Holiday/**
Williams J. Mayo Ink/A&R- arranger/Paramont/okeh/Blackpatty/vocalion/ Brunswick/decca/	**Papa Charlie Jackson, Frankie Half Pint Jaxton/**Leroy Carr/**Sister Rosetta Tharpe/**
Williams Johnny/string bass/studio bands/M. W. Jazz Jesters/B. H. Orch./M. B. Oxford Greys/	**Billie Holiday/Midge Williams/Mildred Bailey/**
Williams Mary Lou/pianist/arrainger/songwriter/Blanche Calloway Orch./M. B. Oxford Greys/	**Blanche Calloway/Maxine Sullivan/Mildred Bailey/**Mary Lou Williams/
Williams Midge/And Her Jazz Jesters/studio band/own vocals/	**Midge Williams/**
Williams Murray/alto saxophone/studio band/Gene Krupa/	**Helen Ward/**
Williams Sandy/trombone/trombone/studio bands/Chick Webb/	**Ethel Waters/Ella Fitzgerald/**
Williams Spencer/pianist/songwriter/some vocals/studio band/	Spencer Williams/**Lonnie Johnson/Lizzie Miles/**
Williamson James/flute/studio bands/Nelson Riddle/	**Nat King Cole/**
Wills Bob & His Texas Playboys - Film Master - 1940/	**Tex Ritter/**
Wills Bob fiddle/arrainger/songwriter/string band leader/ & His Texas Playboys/	Tommy Duncan/
Wills Johnny Lee/banjo/studio bands/Bob Wills & his Texas Playboys/	Tommy Duncan/
Wilson Garland Orchestra/	**Thelma Carpenter/**
Wilson Lonnie/guitar/studio bands/Roy Acuff And His Smokey Mountain Boys/	**Roy Acuff/**
Wilson Meridith Orchestra - Radio Master - 1944/	**Bing Crosby**
Wilson Shadow/drum/studio bands/	**Billie Holiday/**
Wilson Teddy Orchestra - Film Master - 1944	**Lena Horne/**
Wilson Teddy/pianist/arrainger/studio band/ & His Orchestra/his Quartet/	**/Lena Horne/Thelma Carpenter/Sarah Vaughan/**
Wilson Teddy/pianist/arrainger/studio band/Louis Armstrong/Benny Goodman/ ownOrch./	**Louis Armstrong/Billie Holiday/Helen Ward/Ella Fitzgerald/Mildred Bailey/**
Winding Kai/trombone/studio bands/Stan Kenton/	**June Christy/**
Winfield Herbert H/trombone/studio bands/Russ Case/	**Perry Como/**
Winkle Jimmy/guitar/studio bands/Maddox Brothers & Rose/	**Rose Maddox/**
Winston County Pea Pickers/	Lonzo & Oscar/
Winter Paul/violin/studio bands/Mitchell Ayres/	**Perry Como/**
Winterhaulter Hugo/saxophone/violinist/studio bands/Larry Clinton/own Orch./	**Bea Wain/Eddie FisherPerry Como/Frank Sinatra/Rosemary Clooney/** Satisfiers/
Wirges Bill or William/pianist/studio bands/own Orch./	**Al Jolson/Nick Lucas/Libby Holman/Hildegarde/**
Wise Chubby/fiddle/studio bands/	**Bill Monroe/**
Wolfson Herman/tenor saxophone/studio bands/	**Bing Crosby/**
Woodal Hershal/string bass/studio bands/Charles Mitchell's Texans/	**Jimmie Davis/**
Wooding Russell /arrainger/studio bands/own Orch./	**Ethel Waters**
Wood George Scott/pianist/British studio band/	**Hildegarde/**
Woods Oscar/guitar/studio bands/	**Jimmie Davis/**
Wooten Art/fiddle/banjo/guitar/studio bands/Blue Grass Boys/	**Bill Monroe/**
Worde Phil/pianist/studio bands/M. Smith Jazz Band/	**Mamie Smith/**
Worrell Frank/jazz guitar/studio bands/Jess Stacy/Russ Case/	**Lee Wiley/Perry Como/**
Wrighsman Stan/pianist/studio bands/Paul Weston/	**Johnny Mercer/**Pied Pipers/June Hutton/
Wright James/tenor saxophone/Louis Jordan/	**Louis Jordan/**
Wright Lammar/trumpet/studio bands/Cab Calloway/	**Cab Calloway/Chick Bullock/**
Wright Pearl/pianist/arrainger/studio bands with Ethel Waters/	**Ethel Waters/**
Yaner Milt/clarinet/alto saxophone/studio bands/Gordon Jenkins/	**Billie Holiday/Peggy Lee/**

Yocum Clark/guitar/studio bands/Tommy Dorsey/Nelson Riddle/	**Frank Sinatra/Jo Stafford/Connie Haines/Nat King Cole/**
Yoder Walter/string bass/studio bands/Woody Herman/	**Bing Crosby/**Woody Herman/Murial Lane/
Young Arthur/nova achord/arranger/British studio bands/	Vera Lynn/
Young Austin 'Skin"/banjo/studio bands/Paul Whiteman/	Rhythm Boys/**Bing Crosby/**
Young Jr. Leonidas/drums/studio bands/Phil Moore/	**Lena Horne/Frank Sinatra/**
Young Lee/drums/studio bands/Nelson Riddle/Billy May/	**Ivie Anderson/Nat King Cole/Dean Martin/**
Young Lester/clarinet/tenor saxophone/studio bands/Teddy Wilson/Count Basie/	**Billie Holiday/Jimmy Rushing/Helen Humes/**
Young Lester - Film (TV) Film Master - 1957/	**Billie Holiday/**
Young Sterling/violin/studio bands/Gus Arnheim/	**Bing Crosby/**
Young Trummy/trombone/arrainger/studio bands/songwriter/with Count Basie/	**Jimmy Rushing/Helen Humes/Thelma Carpenter/**
Young Trummy/trombone/studio bands/Tont Scott/Louis Armstrong/	**Louis Armstrong/Bing Crosby/Sarah Vaughan/**
Young Trummy/trombone - Film Master - 1956/	**Louis Armstrong/Bing Crosby/**
Young Victor /arrainger/studio band & orchestra - more/	Dixie Lee Crosby/Guardsmen/**Connie Boswell/Dick Haymes/Peggy Lee/ Ethel Merman/**June Vance/
Young Victor /arrainger/studio band/his Serenaders/ & orch./	**/Mills Brothers/Cliff Edwards/Judy Garland/Al Jolson/Lee Wiley/**Billy Hughes/
Young Victor/arrainger/studio bands/ & Orch./	**Helen Morgan/Bing Crosby/Ethel Waters/ Harlan Lattimore/Al Jolson/ Johnny Mercer/**
Ysaguirre Bob/tuba/studio bands/Don Redman/	Don Redman/**Harlan Lattimore/Bing Crosby/Boswell Sisters/**
Yukl Joe/trombone/studio bands/Jimmy Dorsey/	**Louis Armstrong/Bing Crosby/**Frances Langford/**Billie Holiday/**
Yumansen Eddie/trumpet/studio bands/Larry Clinton/	**Bea Wain/Dick Todd/**
Zanoni Gene/alto saxophone/studio bands/Georgie Auld/	**Sarah Vaughan/**
Zarchy Rubin/trumpet/studio bands/Axel Stordahl/	**Frank Sinatra/**
Zayde Jack/violin/studio bands/Axel Stordahl/Mitchell Ayres/	**Frank Sinatra/Perry Como/**
Zenter Si/ytombone/studio bands/Les Brown/Dave Baubour/Billy May/	**Doris Day/Peggy Lee/Frank Sinatra/Nat King Cole/Dean Matin/Mel Torme/**
Zimmerman Fred/bass/studio band/Artie Shaw/	**Lena Horne/**
Zimmerman Harry/studio bands/his Orch./	**Dinah Shore/**
Zimmers Tony/clarinet/studio bands/Larry Clinton/	**Bea Wain/Dick Todd/**
Zinkan Joe/bass/studio bands/Roy Acuff And His Smoky Mountain Boys/	**Roy Acuff/**
Zir Isadore/viola/studio bands/Mitchell Ayres/	**Perry Como/**
Zittman Sam/alto saxophone/studio bands/Georgie Auld/	**Sarah Vaughan/**
Zolkind Phillip/saxophone/studio bands/Mitchell Ayres/	**Perry Como/**
Zurke Bob/pianist/studio bands/Bob Crosby/	Bob Crosby/Marion Mann/**Helen Ward/Bing Crosby/Connie Boswell/**
NOTE - ONE - Musicians, bands or Orchestra listed ONLY apply to recordings featured in text/	
NOTE - TWO - Musicians, bands or Orchestra listed as RADIO MASTER apply only to airchecks selected within the text./	
NOTE - THREE - Musicians, bands or Orchestra listed as FILM MASTER only apply to those FILMS selected within the text./	
NOTE FOUR - Musicians, bands or Orchestra listed are MOSTLY identified by the author from actual record releases./	
NOTE - FIVE - Musicians, bands or Orchestra listed are SOMETIMES identified in FILMS by the author, or friends of the author. All opinions are speculative.	
NOTE - SIX - Vocalists in BOLD are premium FEATURED recording artists within the text of this book.	
NOTE - SEVEN - Vocalists NOT in BOLD are NOTED, not FEATURED within the text of this book.	
NOTE - EIGHT - ADDITIONAL informatiom about RADIO musicians, bands or Orchestra & vocalists may be found in the RADIO section of this book.	
NOTE - NINE - ADDITIONAL information about FILMS featuring musicians, bands or Orchestra & vocalists may be found in the FILM section of this book.	
NOTE - TEN - Some re - issued 78RPM records, as well as subsequent 33/1/3PRM /45RPM note many musicians NOT mentioned on originals/	
NOTE - ELEVEN - Information found about many musicians in ESQUIRE Jazz Book/1944ed/1945ed/	
NOTE - TWELVE - Much information about musicians & vocalists were found as in the MEDIA & NEWSPRINT entities listed.	

ON THE CUSP VOCALISTS

- The purposes of this book find the dividing line of 1950 something far more of a chore than the earlier dividing line between acoustic recording artists and the subsequent emergence of electric product. The following recording artists emerged as potential carriers of the types of popular musical idiom that had been established before them in the 1940s. They would moreover, due to the likes the unexpected explosion of rhythm and blues and rock music, become voices of an earlier generation, and more so considered part of a regressive part of a music industry that refused to change. They would moreover represent an adult alternative to a youth culture that had basically could not and would not accept put downs. Indeed the snobbery that existed against young rock artists was severe in the beginning, which is kind of sad, considering the struggles the elders themselves had experienced, and are noted within this book. This would more so become more than a generation thing, as there were more (baby boomer) teenagers than the adults. The same could be said about the emergence of "country and western." Obvious marketing product to the teenager, like never before in history, was to be founded in the growing idiom of rock. A fad? A fad that has lasted more than fifty years? Like all others, the changes in rock have been considerable but not yet replaced.
- The following recording artists, as featured artists who had recorded before 1939, also recorded after 1950. They would include the likes of Roy Acuff, the Andrews Sisters, Louis Armstrong, Fred Astaire, Gene Austin, Gene Autry, Connie Boswell, Big Bill Broonzy, Blanche Callaway, Cab Callaway, Eddie Cantor, Nat King Cole, Perry Como, Bing Crosby, Jimmie Davis, Sammy Davis Jr., Billy Eckstine, Ruth Etting (a few), Ella Fitzgerald, Red Foley, Jane Froman, Judy Garland, Woody Guthrie, Adelaide Hall, Dick Haymes, Billie Holiday, Libby Holman, Lena Horne, Helen Humes, Alberta Hunter, the Ink Spots, Mahalia Jackson, Robert Johnson, Al Jolson, Louis Jordan, Helen Kane, Nick Lucas, Tony Martin, Memphis Minnie, Johnny Mercer, Ethel Merman, the Mills Brothers, Bill Monroe, Louis Prima, Tex Ritter, Ginger Rogers, Roy Rogers, Jimmy Rushing, Ginny Simms, Frank Sinatra, Kate Smith, Valaida Snow, Victoria Spivey, Jo Stafford, Maxine Sullivan, Rosetta Tharpe, Mel Torme, Ernest Tubb, Sophie Tucker, Joe Turner, Sarah Vaughan, Rudy Vallee, Ethel Waters, Elisabeth Welch, Lee Wiley, Edith Wilson. It is more so obvious that some were more popular than most. Hopefully, this book sorted things out right and will help the serious listener!

- ➢ This listing above may also serve as a reference for evidence of rerecorded material, which the author of this book seeks to avoid. It is another warning to music consumers to bank on originals, in most all, but not all, as noted within the text of this book.

- The following recording artists, as featured artists, who had began recording in the 1940s, are the "cusp" artists that made it into this book. They include: Eddy Arnold, Tony Bennett, Rosemary Clooney, Vic Damone, Eddie Fisher, Red Foley, Burl Ives, Frankie Laine, Rose Maddox, Dean Martin, Ella Mae Morse, Anita O'Day, Patti Page, Dinah Shore, Kay Starr, Sarah Vaughan, Dinah Washington, Margaret Whiting, Hank Williams. Indeed, these recording artists fared better than most contemporaries when the "rock era" began.
- Then following recording artists, fairly or unfairly, were linked to the older idioms of the prerock era. Most would find success but were to find much of their success limited to an adult market, with limited teenager interest in their record product. The noted exclusing within this text of the young and (white) Johnny Ray, who's 1951 (Okeh) release of "Cry' and "The Little White Cloud That Cried" was just the type of original 'blues' that 'passed' for a 'black' rooted sound, finds the same typr of emotion found in Lonnie Johnson's "Tomorrow Night", that is more ever included in this text. Just right for the ears of a young, impressionable teenager, Elvis Presley? You bet! While an exception was made for Joe Turner, who was indeed a (later) rock and roll performer, and while Billy Haley is noted in text, comparions should beas noted and as heard. Featured artists within this book led by rhythmic 'boogie woogie', deeply rooted in black church music, found the intergrated likes of Rosetta Tharpe, Louis Jordan, Ella Mae Morse, Rose Maddox, Dinah Washington and Hank Williams the kind of styles that could have become, but were not rock and rollers. A principle exceptionwould have to be Dinah Washington, who's jazz, rhythm and blues, pop, and (later) rock styles easily blended into the new 'rock'era. While it is true that the elder likes of Frank Sinatra, Bing Crosby, Nat King Cole, and Perry Como would find success in the new media of television, the aging process, as not the case in radio, would betray them. More so were the elder and (Afro-American) 'guest' stars like Louis Armstrong, Ella Fitzgerald, and Lena Horne, who would endure a later racism. The newer singers had different problems, although racism would still plague black artists. The same may apply to country and blues performers, who coped with much contempt for simplicity of their art. For the most part, the 'older' performers openly shunned them. Sammy Davis Jr., while not the exception that Dinah Washington was, nevertheless a voice and style of the older crowd, that remained successful. Both Dean Martin and Tony Bennett (both "cusp" artists who are nevertheless featured artists in this book) perhaps did achieve Sinatra-like status—but for the most part, most others would not or could not.

- ➢ Again, beware of rerecorded material from many of these artists!

- ◆ Recording artists on the cusp between the mid-1940s and 1950s, however talented, are not featured artists within the scope of this book. Some are, however, indeed mentioned within the text, and for a specific recording that is featured within this book. They include:

- Ed Ames (also with the Ames Brothers—with Thelma Carpenter before becoming a solo performer).
- Harry Belafonte, featured with Lena Horne in text.
- Theresa Brewer
- Vikki Carr
- Barbara Cook
- Chris Connor
- Don Cornell
- Alan Dale
- Blossom Dearie
- Johnny Desmond
- Rusty Draper
- Tennessee Ernie Ford, featured in text with Ella Mae Morse
- Lefty Frizzell
- Merv Griffin
- Edie Gorme
- Joanie James
- Damita Jo
- Roy Hamilton
- Teddi King
- Eartha Kitt
- Abby Lane
- Steve Lawrence
- Julie London
- Al Martino
- Johnny Mathis (the Afro-American pop performer).
- Johnny Mathis (the C&W performer).
- Gisele Mac Kenzie
- Gordon Mac Rae
- Phyllis Mc Guire (of the Mc Guire Sisters)
- Bette Mc Laurin
- Carmen McRae, featured a bit in the text with Sammy Davis Jr.
- Vaughan Monroe
- Guy Mitchell
- Jayne P. Morgan
- Leon Payne
- Webb Pierce
- Johnny Ray
- Della Reese
- Bobby Short
- Nina Simone
- Hank Snow
- Jeri Southland
- Dakota Stanton
- Hank Thompson
- Floyd Tillman
- Jerry Vale
- Teddy Walters
- Kitty Wells

- Kitty White
- Slim Whitman
- Andy Williams (Andy had been part of the "Williams Brothers," with Bing Crosby in the 1940s)
- Billy Williams
- Joe Williams, featured a bit in the text with Ella Fitzgerald
- Nancy Wilson

& many others.

After the Cusp to the 1960s and Beyond

- The effects of rock music took their toll before the end of the decade. So did the lingering categories of rhythm and blues and country and western." While the age of rock also changed, the arrangements of artists of the pre-rock crowd such as Frank Sinatra, Dean Martin, Mel Torme, and even Bing Crosby are notably changed. In reality, the old style of singing perhaps escaped to the Broadway stage—when popular music had found its original popularity. The emergence of bright singers (of old songs) such as Vicky Carr, Shirley Horne, Jack Jones, Barbra Streisand, and Nancy Wilson perhaps saved it for many. Others, who were capable, such as Aretha Franklin (whose first LP was a pop effort that failed to catch on), Etta James, Patti LaBelle, or Dionne Warwick were sadly put into another category. Or did they care? Did Patsy Cline or Diana Ross? So were many such fine vocalists who could do it all and whose versatility tagged them, in true retrospective, as pigeon holed to nowhere. The emergence of Motown clinched it for jazz, along with perhaps a hipper and more sophisticated version of R&B, with rock appeal! What a merge!
- The likes of Elvis and his versions of "It's Now or Never" and "Are You Lonesome Tonight?" were not to be appreciated by those older or snootier. Nor was a very fine Beatles attempt at Broadway's entity *Till There Was You from Music Man.* Streisand's 1965 rendering of "My Man," got it right—but Fannie Brice did it twice, both acoustically and electronically, in the 1920s. When alive, Bobby Darin was considered an upstart rock and roller, despite his brilliant 1959 version of "Mack the Knife." Forget his emulations of Frank Sinatra and Johnny Mercer! Darin mimicked his own contemporaries, including Elvis as well as C&W singer Marty Robbins. He loved Ray Charles. Like Elvis, Wilbert Harrison and (later) the Beatles, some of Darin's success was linked to the likes of the hip rock songs of Jerry Leiber and Mike Stoller! And what of the 1963 original "On Broadway," by the Drifters on Atlantic 2237? Moreover, the likes of Leiber and Stroller song ditties did indeed (finally) make it to Broadway's lights by the latter end of the century. What about Peggy Lee's late success with their "Is That All There Is"? It's all in the "way" it was sung! Go figure! The snobs of Broadway just got to listen as all the (now) grown-up kids did. And what about James Brown's version of "Prisoner of Love"? Isn't it just great? Or is it just courageously different?

ALBUMS SELECTIVE (1933-44)

Original 78 Album Concepts

The scope of this book cannot reach or cover everyone. While the author of this book is selective, so is the quest to find originality. When the inevitable concept of a 78 rpm album sprung forth in the early 1930s, the Great Depression, like the introduction of the 331/3 speed, it put the brakes on everything. The idea of the album, perhaps already common for opera followers, nevertheless found issue as early as 1933, with the (Brunswick) package of the *Blackbirds of 1928* album, oddly consisting of all Afro-American entities: show tunes, film soundtracks, classical music, not covered in this book, and (some) recording sessions by various bandleaders and vocalists.

- ➢ The following fifteen album picks must meet the following criteria:

    - must always include vocals
    - should *not* be operatic release
    - will not usually include reissued product, unless used as part of a theme or concept
    - must be an *original concept* of a recording session for a contemporary Broadway entity or film or of an idea that grew into a concept.

- ➢ The following picks were originally released on album sets, usually in poor packaging, which in many cases helped crack the records they contained, although that's another matter.

    (Many of the following, after initial release, were to be subsequently reissued in LP format, with some label change.)

- 1. *Blackbirds of 1928*. This 1933 album release was a collection of rerecordings from the 1928 all-black Broadway entity as well as a few from *Blackbirds of 1930*. As released at the height of the Great Depression, when records were bought far less than in 1929, and most people could not find a job, this concept, nevertheless, worked. (Brunswick 6516, 6517, 6518, 6519, 6520, 6521). Moreover, this collection penned by Jimmy McHugh and Dorothy Fields, with a few exceptions, is superb and does indeed give its listener a feeling of being there.

    - Included are:

* Blackbird Melody: "I Can't Give You Anything but Love," "Doing the New Low-Down," "I Must Have That Man," "Baby," "Dixie," "Diga Diga Do," "Porgy," "I Can't Give You Anything but Love." This is an instrumental theme by the Duke Ellington Orchestra (Part 1 and 2).
* "I Can't Give You Anything but Love," Ethel Waters vocal, Duke Ellington Orchestra (pick in Ethel Waters).
* "Doing the New Low Down": the Mills Brothers and Cab Calloway do vocals, and Don Redman's Orchestra (not Cab's orchestra) provide the orchestra (pick in Cab Calloway).
* "I Must Have That Man," Adelaide Hall vocal, Duke Ellington Orchestra (pick in Adelaide Hall).
* "Baby," Adelaide Hall vocal, Duke Ellington orchestra (pick in Adelaide Hall).
* "Diga Diga Do," Mills Brothers vocals, Duke Ellington Orchestra (pick in Mills Brothers).
* "I Can't Give You Anything but Love," Mills Brothers vocal (pick in Mills Brothers).
* "Doin' the New Low-Down," Bill Robinson's tap dancing! Don Redman Orchestra.
* "Shuffle Your Feet and Just Roll Along," Bandana Babies, Harry and Donald Mills of the Mills Brothers vocal, Don Redman Orchestra (pick in Mills Brothers).
* "Porgy," Ethel Waters vocal, Duke Ellington Orchestra (pick in Ethel Waters).
* "St. Louis Blues," Ethel Waters and Cecil Mack Choir vocal (pick in Ethel Waters).

▪ Note: The Following Lee Wiley entities were among the first ever to become songbooks of popular contemporary songwriters such as the Gershwin Brothers, Cole Porter, Rodgers and Hart, and Harold Arlen. They were subsequently issued between 1939 through 1944. What later became popular as LP concepts were in reality created earlier, with Lee Wiley, already a noted record and radio entity leading the pack. Moreover, the cool Wiley approach is fabulous, noting some fine musicians backing her.

- 2. *George and Ira Gershwin*. Lee Wiley, Max Kaminsky, the Joe Buskin Orchestra, and other musicians are found to be freelancing for the small Liberty Music Shop label. Liberty Music Shop LMS 281, 282, 283, 284.

o All titles are reviewed in depth in the Lee Wiley section.

* "How Long Has This Been Goin' On?"
* "My One and Only."
* "I've Got a Crush on You."
* "Someone to Watch Over Me." (Perhaps Fats Waller is on pipe organ.)
* "Sam and Delilah."
* "'S Wonderful."
* "But Not for Me."
* "Sweet and Low Down."

- 3. *Rodgers and Hart Lee Wiley*. With Max Kaminsky Orchestra, Joe Buskin Orchestra, with freelancing musicians unidentified (Gala 1, 2, 3, 4).

- All titles are reviewed in depth in the Lee Wiley section.

    * "Here in My Arms."
    * "Baby's Awake Now."
    * "I've Got Five Dollars."
    * "Glad to Be Unhappy."
    * "A Little Birdie Told Me So."
    * "You Took Advantage of Me."
    * "A Ship without a Sail."
    * "As Though You Were There."

- 4. *Cole Porter*. Lee Wiley with Bunny Berigan, Joe Buskin, George Wettling, Paul Weston Orchestra, and others—freelancing musicians—(Liberty Music Shop LMS 294, 295, 296, 297).

    - All titles are reviewed in depth in the Lee Wiley section.

        * "Looking At You."
        * "You Do Something to Me."
        * "Easy to Love."
        * "Why Shouldn't I?"
        * "Let's Fly Away."
        * "Find Me a Primitive Man."
        * "Hot House Rose."
        * "Let's Do It."

- 5. *Harold Arlan*. Lee Wiley with combinations of Eddie Condon's Quentet or Sextet, with Billy Butterfield, Bob Haggart, George Wettling, others (Schirmer 2008, 2009, 2010).

    - All titles are reviewed in depth in the Lee Wiley section.

        * "Down with Love" (Arlen and E. Y. Harburg).
        * "Stormy Weather" (Arlen and Koehler).
        * "I've Got the World on a String" (Arlen and Koehler).
        * "Between the Devil and the Deep Blue Sea" (Arlen and Koehler).
        * "Fun to Be Fooled" (Arlen, Harburg, and Gershwin).
        * "You Said It" (Arlen and Yellen).
        * "Let's Fall in Love" (Arlen and Koehler).
        * "Moaning in the Morning" (Arlen and Harburg).

- 6. *Cabin in the Sky* (Ethel Waters, Max Meth Orchestra). This original and contemporary Broadway soundtrack was among the first of its kind (1940). Released on the Liberty Music Shop Label on LMS 310, 311, 312, this classy soundtrack featured titles written by John Latouche, Ted Fetter, and Vernon Duke and for Ethel Waters herself. (The later 1943 film of the same name used all original titles except "Love Turned the Light Out.")

    - All titles are reviewed in depth in the Ethel Waters section.

        * "Taking a Chance on Love" (Latouche-Fetter and Duke) (pick in Ethel Waters section).

  * "Love Turned the Light Out" (Latouche and Duke) (pick in Ethel Waters section).
  * "Cabin in the Sky" (Latouche and Duke) (pick in Ethel Waters section).
  * "Honey in the Honeycomb" (Latouche and Duke) (pick in Ethel Waters section).
  * "Cabin in the Sky"—Overture—Parts One and Two—(Latouche-Fetter and Duke)—Max Meth theatre orchestra (instrumental).

- 7. "Blues Till Dawn," sung by Libby Holman, guitar accompaniment by Josh White. Decca 18304, 18305, 18306. This (late) 1942 album release found 1920s torch entity Libby Holman attempting a career comeback after much public scandal since the early 1930s. It is unlike anything Libby had attempted before and indeed remains a creditable and creative group of recordings. These recordings consist of Afro-American blues as well as shared folk ditties. Just how Libby linked up with Josh White is unclear, but his guitar strumming provides this integrated effort even more relevance. If this album did have any regrets, it could have had provided a vocal duet. In any case, Libby's vocals are clear and focused, indeed better than her vocal inconsistencies found in her earlier recordings.

  o All titles are reviewed in depth in the Libby Holman section.

  * "Baby Baby" (based upon Ma Rainey's "See See Rider").
  * "Fare Thee Well" (the traditional religious theme).
  * "Good Morning Blues" (based upon the popular blues ditty, popularized by Jimmy Rushing).
  * "When the Sun Goes Down" (based upon the popular blues entity by Leroy Carr).
  * "House of the Rising Sun" (based upon the already old New Orleans entity, loosely done by many, including Texas Alexander).
  * "Old Smokey," Handsome, Winsome Johnny (traditional folk ballad).

- 8. *Let's Face It*, Hildegarde, Decca 291. This stiff 1941 Cole Porter Broadway score is transformed from the usual snobbery into a breezy and pleasant vocal performance. More so, this album's release preceded the *original* Broadway cast release with Gertrude Lawrence, which was, for its time, thought to be theft! Luckily, Hildegarde was up to the chore as a top-notch vocalist in her prime. (This original cover notes the long gloves on Hildegarde, her own trademark!)

  o All titles are reviewed in depth in the Hildegarde section.

  * "Ace in the Hole."
  * "Ev'rything I Love."
  * "You Irritate Me So."
  * "A Little Rumba Numba."
  * "Farming."
  * "I Hate You, Darling."

- 9. *Dust Bowl Ballads Vol. 1.*, Victor Album P-27. Woody Guthrie. Victor 26619, 26620, 26621. Released in 1940, this bit of American social commentary (in songs) is an event in itself. While Woody's own acoustic guitar and harmonica are evident, it's also evident it's not the type of chuck wagon yarns about the myth of American film and cowboys. This album and its companion (Part 2) is rich in social commentary and has Woody's own personal observations of the great dust bowl disasters that swept throughout western America in the early 1930s. If these recordings were originally a contrived idea of Woody's to emulate the contemporary John Steinbeck novel (also a film) *The Grapes of Wrath*, the powerful messages and images that they project are a stroke of genius.

- o All titles are reviewed in depth in the Woody Guthrie section.

  - * "Talking Dust Bowl Blues."
  - * "Blowin' Down This Road."
  - * "Do Re Mi."
  - * "Dust Can't Kill Me."
  - * "Tom Joad," Pt. 1 and 2, both sides.

- 10. *Dust Bowl Ballads Vol. 2.*, Victor album P-28. Woody Guthrie. Victor 26622, 26623, 26624. The companion (1940) volume as noted above.

- o All titles are reviewed in depth in the Woody Guthrie section.

  - * "The Great Dust Storm."
  - * "Dusty Old Dust."
  - * "Dust Bowl Refugee."
  - * "I Ain't Got No Home in This World Anymore."
  - * "Vigilante Man."

- 11. *The Wayfaring Stranger*, Ash Records (1944?) Ash 345A, Ash 345B, Ash 346A, Ash 346B. Folk singer Burl Ives, already a popular radio entity in urban New York City, put together a fine and effective group of soft tradition ballads for this indeed relevant album concept.

- o All titles are reviewed in depth in the Burl Ives section.

  - * "Poor Wayfaring Stranger."
  - * "Buckeye Jim."
  - * "Black is the Color."
  - * "Foggy, Foggy Dew."
  - * "The Bold Soldier."
  - * "Sow Has the Measles."
  - * "Blue Tail Fly"
  - * "Henry Martin."

- 12. *Gospel Hymns. Sister Rosetta Tharpe*, Decca A-527. Decca 48021, 48022, 48023, 48024. This (1943) collection is quite good and is more so given much relevance by Sister Rosetta Tharpe's committed vocals. Does she rock? Is this the first rock album? Rosetta's own added guitar licks seem to indicate just that!

- o All titles are reviewed in the Sister Rosetta Tharpe section.

  - * "Forgive Me, Lord, and Try Me One More Time."
  - * "Jesus Taught Me How to Smile."
  - * "God Don't Like It."
  - * "What Is the Soul of Man."
  - * "Let That Liar Alone."

 * "What's the News?"
 * "The Devil Has Thrown Him Down."
 * "Nobody Knows, Nobody Cares."

- 13. *Holiday Inn—Bing Crosby*, Decca 306. Decca 18424, 18425, 18426, 18427, 18429. (1942). This Crosby flick boasts a fine Irving Berlin score and is perhaps the most commercially successful 78 rpm album released in its time. (Perhaps some of Bing's earlier soundtracks on Brunswick Records may have been better, but none were released originally as 78 rpm albums.) While many Crosby concepts indeed proved to become popular sellers, including those of Hawaiian, country-western, religious, Spanish, and later ethnic (Irish) themes, the inclusion of White Christmas in *this* album, became the forerunner of the most profitable and subsequent package of a good number of Christmas songs and endless reissue products. For this album, Bing is in (surprising) good (1942) voice, in both the film and recordings.

o All titles are reviewed in depth in the Bing Crosby and Fred Astaire sections.

 * "Be Careful, It's My Heart" (Bing with John Scott Trotter and His Orchestra).
 * "Happy Holiday" (Bing with the Music Maids and Hal and John Scott Trotter and His Orchestra).
 * "Easter Parade" (Bing with John Scott Trotter and His Orchestra).
 * "Abraham" (Bing with John Scott Trotter and His Orchestra).
 * "I've Got Plenty to Be Thankful For" (Bing with Bob Crosby and His Orchestra).
 * "Lazy" (Bing with Bob Crosby and His Orchestra).
 * "I Can't Tell a Lie," Fred Astaire with Bob Crosby and His Orchestra.
 * "I'll Capture Your Heart." This duet with Crosby and Astaire and the unheralded Decca studio vocalist Margaret Lenhart was very conventional as a recording. Moreover, Lenhart dubbed in the vocals of Marjorie Reynolds in the film. (Bing backed by Bob Crosby and His Orchestra).
 * "Let's Start the New Year Right." (Bing with Bob Crosby and His Orchestra)
 * "Song of Freedom." Bing with John Scott Trotter and His Orchestra. *
 * "White Christmas." The original Decca recording DLA 3009 matrix and best known Bing Crosby classic recording was originally found here. *
 * "You're Easy to Dance With." Fred Astaire with Bob Crosby and His Orchestra.

(With Ken Darby Singers and John Scott Trotter and His Orchestra).

✓ As a further note: This original 78 rpm album was oddly compromised as a later release (Album No. A-534). This later release, with the same cover, omits "White Christmas," "Lazy," "I've Got Plenty to Be Thankful For," and "Easter Parade." Why? Does it really matter? Did it matter?

- 14. *Songs by Josh White*, Ash A-348. Josh White's soft soulful vocal is put to the test in this attempt at (then) contemporary (1946) popular recordings (Ash 1A,1B, 2A, 2B, 3A, 3B). The success of this collection rests on Josh's earthy, alternative and folksy approach.

- o All titles are reviewed in depth in the Josh White section.
    - * "Got a Head Like a Rock."
    - * "Fare Thee Well." (Josh's guitar had backed up a Libby Holman vocal on this same ditty some years before.)
    - * "Outskirts of Town."
    - * "One Meat Ball."
    - * "When I Lay Down and Die."
    - * "The House I Live In." (The contemporary Frank Sinatra version is indeed different.)

- 15. *Moaning Low—Torch Songs by* Lena Horne, Victor P-118. This sultry and silky vocals of Lena Horne, backed by Victor's (1941) studio bandleader Lou Bring Orchestra, with strings arranged by Ned Freeman is indeed a well-crafted piece of work. Lena's highly disciplined voice carries off good versions of all these (previously) released song ditties. While, in most cases, it cannot be claimed that Lena's versions are better than all previous versions, Lena's (newer) and softer vocal style does challenge all previous versions. Ethel Waters, Ivie Anderson, Libby Holman beware! (The later 10-inch Victor LP LPT 3061 reissue is also relevant, more so featuring a steamy cover pic of Lena while noting the original 78 release lacks even a picture!)

    - o All titles are reviewed in depth in the Lena Horne section.
        - * "Moaning Low."
        - * "I Gotta Right to Sing the Blues."
        - * "The Man I Love."
        - * "Stormy Weather."
        - * "Mad About the Boy."
        - * "Where or When?" (Lena would later rerecord this ditty.)
        - * "I'll Wind." This ditty penned by Arlen and Koehler had perhaps been introduced by Lena as a backup for Adelaide Hall, in the Cotton Club, some years before. While both ladies did not attempt a subsequent contemporary 1934 recording, this later 1941 recording clinches it for Lena. Much later, Frank Sinatra would somewhat challenge Lena.
        - * "What Is This Thing Called Love?"

Extra

- The following original 78 rpm album just could not be ignored. While not a featured recording artist within this book, Katherine Dunham's creativity is something that just could not be ignored!
- *Afro-Caribbean Songs and Rhythms—Katherine Dunham*. Decca 40026, 40027, 40028, 40029. Just how a young, black Afro-American dancer (among many other talents) found the time to explore Caribbean music boggles the mind. While in 1940s the Latin rhythms of popular vocalists like Carmen Miranda (Mamae Euquero "I Want My Mama" on Decca 23132) and Xavier Cugat, especially on "Chica, Chica, Boom Chic," with a vocal by Lena Romay on Columbia 35995, were novel, as it always had been, the great creativity was overshadowed. Moreover, within this time period, the sounds of Dizzy Gillespie would indeed make a more credible stab at a music that had combined the race mix of French, Spanish, and Portuguese with African slaves; these Katherine

Dunhan selections, which most likely began as a study in dance customs, are, however, in true retrospective, sadly overlooked.

* "Batucada." This dance somba penned by Don Alfonso-Trinidade-Stillman is sung in Portuguese by Katherine Dunham. Like other enities sung in other languages besides English, noted below, this ditty is worth hearing, even when not getting up to shake off a few pounds. In reality, Katherine found the word "Batuque" to be an actual African tribe in origin, and this dance number is about the charms of a dancer somewhere in Brazil.
* "Soleil Oh!" This traditional ditty from Haiti is sung in French patois by Jean Léon Destiné. An ancient gods of Africa is named "Damballa," and this semireligious ditty is voodoo all the way.
* "Callate (S-sh be Quiet Guaracha)." Penned by Candido Vicenty, this ditty is sung by Katherine Dunham herself in Spanish. This Cuban enity is about a young lady looking for a man. This ditty's theme is actually nothing new, until heard.
* d. "Congo Moundong." This Haitian Congo cult ditty is sung by Jean Léon Destiné in French patois, may be enough to give its listener the willies. Its subject is about communicating with an evil spirit.
* "Choucounne." This Haitian Merengue is sung in French patois by Katherine Dunham and Jean Léon Destiné. This tale of romance is not as serious as the previous selection.
* "Toitica La Negra." This ditty penned by Ritmo Santo-Cubano is sung in Spanish by La Rosa Estrada and (a very young) Eartha Kitt. This folk ditty (common and similar in Cuba and Haiti) asks where a girl Caridad is.
* "Aferincomon." Penned by Nanigo, this Afro-Cuban cult chant is sung in Spanish by Julio Mendez. There is no real translation to this Afro-Cuban chant. What is it? To be sure the evils of slavery are part of it—in any language.
* "Nago." This Hatian Voudun cult entity is sung in French patois by Katherine Dunham and Jean Léon Destiné. It is another folktale about a young man trying to communicate with the beyond.

- Note: The Katherine Dunham and Ensemble:

The tight sound used piano by Noro Morales, muted trumpet by Juan Ramirez, string Bass by Louis Richko, a three-stringed guitar (Tres) by Candido Vicenty, and a variety of drums, such as Claves, Marcas, Calabasse, Cha-cha, and bongos—among others—played by others, including the creative Katherine Dunham herself.

ALBUMS SELECTIVE—1945-55

- The Long Play (LP). The earlier Victor attempt at marketing this 331/3 speed concept had failed in the early 1930s due to the Great Depression. After World War II, consumers had more spending money. By 1948, the likes of 331/3 rpm, long play or LP, appeared in 10-inch form, the same size as the usual 78 rpm single. It would largely compete with the already popular 78 rpm album—a collection of single 78s in album form. By 1950, the 45 rpm single appeared to compete with the &*RPM single as well as 45 extended play of (EP) box to compete with the 78 rpm album as well as the newer 331/3 rpm LP. Luckily, record players quickly adapted, with flip needles to play 78 rpm as well. The first long play or LP records were mostly the same size as the 78 rpm 10 inch. By 1955, at the eve of the new rock era, the LP size expanded to 12 inch, with the ability to contain up to (sometimes) sixteen songs! What a deal!

- As well as continuing the concept of 78 rpm, the format had the ability to expand. Reissues were also a huge undertaking, with some original 78 rpm performances subsequently ruined by added echo and (later) reprocessed stereo.
- Many subsequent 10-inch reissue album releases retained the same original artwork as found on the 78 rpm album issue. Some did not.
- An added stab at creativity was also to be found in LP format design. Many subsequent LP issues were found to have some interesting covers. Those with *both* great music and covers more so do not disappoint listeners!
- Many 10-inch LPs were also issued as 45 rpm extended play or EP sets.
- Most 10-inch LPs would later be issued in the later 12-inch format, with more songs. Sometimes they remained faithful to their original theme and artwork and sometimes not.

  - The following ten *album* format picks include the original 78 rpm album or equal to the 10-inch LP or equal 45EP Long Play or LP release and are highly recommended picks within this format. (Many were also issued as single release as well.) This list uses (LP) issued numbers. Reissued 78 rpm product finds *original* issued numbers replaced with *new* numbers. Hard-core 78 rpm collectors *beware.*

    - 1. *Night In Manhattan*, Columbia CL-6169. This 10-inch Lee Wiley (1951) LP was excellent (more detail in the Lee Wiley section).

- 2. *Sarah Vaughan*, Columbia B-211. This 45 rpm box set is well worth it, despite three rerecordings from the "divine" Sarah (more detail in the Sarah Vaughan section).
- 3. *Two in Love*, Capital H-420. This 10-inch Nat King Cole release is soft pop, with fine color artwork on its cover (more detail in the Nat King Cole section).
- 4. *After Hours with Ms. D*, EmArcy MG26032. This hot and jazzy Dinah Washington product is well worth it (1954?) (more detail in the Dinah Washington section).
- 5. *Songs For Young Lovers*, Capital H-488. This Frank Sinatra theme also remains a classic (more detail in the Frank Sinatra section).
- 6. "*In The Wee Small Hours*, Capital H-581 PT 1 and 2. Perhaps this is the most brilliant pop LP ever produced? In addition to its superb song selection, its artwork is especially exceptional. If so, it has its problems. Eventually these two 10-inch records, both containing eight song ditties, would merge. Luckily, until the late 1950s, the original 1955 concept remained intact (more detail in the Frank Sinatra section).
- 7. *Lady And The Tramp*, Decca DL-557. Peggy Lee's jazzy vocals are part of this fine 1955 Disney flick. Its cartoon artwork also works (more detail in the Peggy Lee section).
- 8. *Nat King Cole—The Christmas Song*, Capital EAP-1-9026. As well as fine cover artwork, this Nat King Cole EP release is flawed by on ditty "Frosty the Snowman," as he is backed up by the stupid "singing Pussycats." Luckily, the other songs featured, including his second version, with "Nelson Riddles Orchestra of Christmas Song," overcome the ear fodder! (more detail in the Nat King Cole section).
- 9. *Something Cool*, Capital H-516. June Christy, with the Pete Rugolo Orchestra. A great and jazzy voiced June Christy indeed succeeds at defining cool (more detail in the June Christy section).
- 10. *Swing Easy*, Capital H-528. This Frank Sinatra release, despite its smaltzy title, is a winner (more detail in the Frank Sinatra section).

➢ More (1940s-55) *mixed original* and notable *reissue* products from 78 rpm *album* release. After 1948, many would be issued on the new LP (33&1/3 rpm) or on (45EP) box album sets. Moreover, like the list above, many releases would be released on *all* speeds and formats, until about 1957. By this time, the 78 rpm album was, for the most part, not issued at all, with the newer 12-inch 33&1/3 rpm album. The following LP are pop collections issues of 78 rpm, 33&1/3 rpm or 45 rpm origins. This list moreover *does* contain some notable reissued 78 rpm singles and even some unissued takes. While some are indeed excellent releases, the newer LP format very often contain added echo and sound enhancements, which tend to make the ears of most original 78 rpm collectors cringe. The following are selective and were often issued as other formats as well.

- *Art of Mabel Mercer*, Atlantic AlS-408. This 10-inch LP contains three picks.
- *Barrelhouse Boogie and the Blues*, Capital H-513. Ella Mae Morse. This 10-inch LP original concept of current R&B contains four picks found in the Ella Mae Morse section of this book.
- *Billy Eckstine Sings*, National NPL-2001. This 10-inch LP (1950?) reissue of original (1940s) National singles contains three picks found in the Billy Eckstine section of this book.
- *Shuffle along.* Victor LPM—3154. Thelma Carpenter perks up a revive 1921 Broadway entity electronically on this 10 inch LP issued in 1953.
- *Bing Crosby—A Collection of His Early Recordings*, Brunswick BL-58000. This 10-inch LP (1950) reissue of original (1930s) Brunswick singles contains eight picks found in the Bing Crosby section. It had been issued before as a Decca owned Brunswick masters collection (Brunswick album B 1012—Decca owned).
- *Bing Crosby—A Collection of His Early Recordings, Vol. 2.*, Brunswick BL-58001. This 10-inch LP (1949) reissue of original Brunswick singles contains eight picks found in the Bing Crosby section. It had been issued before as a Decca owned Brunswick masters collection (Brunswick album B 1015)—Decca owned).
- *Crosby Classics*, Columbia CL-6027. This 10-inch (1949) reissue of original (1930s) Brunswick singles contains eight picks found in the Bing Crosby section of this book. It had been issued before as a Columbia owned reissue 78 collection as well.
- *Crosby Classics Vol. 2*, Columbia 6105. This 10-inch LP (1949) reissue of original Brunswick singles contains eight picks, including some outtake found in the Bing Crosby section. It had been issued before as a Columbia owned many reissue 78 collection as well.
- *Der Bingle*, Columbia CL-2502. This 10-inch (1954?) reissue of original (1930s) Brunswick singles contains six picks found in the Bing Crosby section. (These are Columbia owned Brunswick masters reissue products.)
- *Merry Christmas*, Bing Crosby. Decca 550. This original 1945 78 rpm collection of previous Crosby Christmas song ditties may just be most marketable and profitable of all time! Its reissue value, escaping form the original "Holiday Inn" album concept was a stroke of genius as well as a subsequent 10-inch format on Decca DPL-5019. This 10-inch Christmas collection of Crosby singles and 78 rpm album from the 1940s later became the basis of the popular 12-inch (1957) Decca LP on DL 8128. By

late-century standards, reissues on cassette and CD remained part of the music business well after the turn of the century in 2000. Contains four picks found in the Bing Crosby section.

- *Christmas Greetings*, Bing Crosby. Decca 5020. This 10-inch LP Christmas collection of Crosby singles and 78 rpm album from the 1940s was, like the LP "Merry Christmas," to be reissued in many formats. Contains three picks found in the Bing Crosby section.
- *Dry Bones*, RCA Victor LPM 3085. The Delta Rhythm Boys are featured in this reissue of 78 rpm issued recordings on LP (contains four picks).
- *Fats Waller Favorites*, Victor P-151. Contains reissued four picks, plus one original.
- *Favoritos*, Andy Russell. Capital BD-13. This original 78 rpm pop collection contains three picks from the Andy Russell section.
- *Folk Songs of the Hills*, Capital AD-50. A Merle Travis collection of 78 rpm includes the following picks "Sixteen Tons," "Dark as a Dungeon," "I Am a Pilgrim."
- *Judy at the Palace*. Decca DL-6020. Despite its title, this is not a live album but a fine reissue collection of previous Judy Garland pick singles.
- *Helen Morgan*, Victor P-102. This 78 rpm pop reissue collection contains eight picks found in the Helen Morgan section.
- *Roy Rogers Souvenir Album*, Victor LPM-3041. This 10-inch singles collection had been issued on 78 rpm and retained its album artwork. It contains two picks found in the Roy Rogers section.
- *Songs by Kay Starr*, Capital H-211. This original LP contains eight picks.
- *Songs by Mabel Mercer, Vol. 1*, Atlantic ALS-402. This 10-inch LP contains four picks. (Vol. 2 on Atlantic ALS 403 contains two picks.)
- *Songs by Jo Stafford*, Capital B-D-23. This original 78 rpm pop collection contains three picks in the Jo Stafford section.
- *Songs Made Famous by the Golden Voice of Russ Columbo*, Victor P-95. This 78 rpm pop reissue collection contains seven picks from the Russ Columbo section.
- *Supper Club Favorites*, Perry Como. Victor LPM-3044. This 10-inch LP special edition for Como's (radio) listeners of the Chesterfield-sponsored show features a singles collection. It contains four picks featured in the Perry Como section.
- *Lee Wiley Sings Irving Berlin*, Columbia CL-6216. This 10-inch original finds Lee Wiley on two picks found in the Lee Wiley section.
- *Lee Wiley Sings Vincent Youmans*, Columbia CL-6215. This 10-inch original finds Lee Wiley on five picks found in the Lee Wiley section.
- *Little Girl Blue*, Black and White A-70. This Lena Horne 78 rpm original contains three picks.
- *Lover Man*, Billie Holiday. Decca DL-5345. This 10-inch LP reissue featured a singles collection of Decca masters. As also released in 78 rpm album form, the same fine artwork is retained on both issues. Contains four picks found in the Billie Holiday section.
- *Moanin' Low*, Lena Horne. Tops Masterpieces-L-931. This 10-inch LP of the early 1950s features original Black and White masters (contains three picks found in the Lena Horne section, not to be confused with the previous Victor masters product)!

- *Party Time*, Capital H-228. Julia Lee's reissued LP product was indeed hot
- Thelma Carpenter And The Ames Brothers. Royale-EP-212. This 45 EP contains 3 picks. noting the original (Majestic masters) had used the name 'Four Amory Brothers' on "American Lullaby"
- *Shades of Blue*, Remington RLP-1025. This 10-inch LP (1951) reissue of the previous Continental 78 rpm album from collection on CON 33 contains three picks found in the Ethel Waters section.
- *Sarah Vaughan and Orchestra*, Royale 18149. This 10-inch LP reissue of Musicraft maters contains two picks found in the Sarah Vaughan section.
- *Sarah Vaughan—The All-Star Band*, Remington RPL-1024. This 10-inch LP (1951) of previous Continental 78 rpm masters finds all of its seven titles as picks in the Sarah Vaughan section.
- *Ink Spots*, Decca A-477. This Decca 78 rpm reissue collection contains four picks found in the Ink Spots section. A later Decca 10-inch release on DL 5056 used the same picture cover.
- *Unforgettable. Nat King Cole*, Capital H-357. While using "Unforgettable" as a lead song title, this otherwise 10-inch reissue LP title truly is "unforgettable" for at least six picks to be found in the Nat King Cole section.
- *Yours Alone*, Jane Froman. Capital H-345. Jane Froman successfully covers eight original standards that she had not recorded back in the 1930s (seven picks).

ALBUMS SELECTIVE 12 INCH (1955+)

- ➢ The following are Original concept 12-inch album or 45EP album releases starting in 1956 are usually noted elsewhere within this book. Comments are selective.
- ➢ *A Touch Of The Blues*, Victor 1566. This original LP features three picks found in the Lee Wiley section.

- *A Jolly Christmas from Frank Sinatra*, Capital W-894. Original concept. Frank Sinatra. 1957.
- *Amtrack Blues*, Alberta Hunter. Columbia 36430. 1980.
- *Best of Irving Berlin*, Mercury 20326. Billy Eckstine and Sarah Vaughan. Original concept. 1958.
- *Bing Crosby—Just for You*, Broadway Intermission BR-134. This contains some booted material.
- *Bing with a Beat*, Victor LPM 1473. Original concept. Bing Crosby. 1957.
- *Black Rhythm Radio*, Sandy Hook 2091. Radio programs from 1944. Lena Horne.
- *Close to You*, Capital W-789. Frank Sinatra. 1957.
- *Come Fly with Me*, Capital W-920. Original concept. Frank Sinatra. 1958.
- *Compact Jazz*, Count Basie, Joe Williams. Verve-835.829. With Ella Fitzgerald and Joe Williams duets.
- *Connie Boswell and the Original Memphis Five in Hi-Fi*, Victor-LPM-1426.
- *Both Sides of Bing Crosby*, Curtin Calls 100/102/. The bootleg of Crosby is indeed a laughing matter. It covers outtakes and radio, 1930s, 1940s.
- *Dean Martin Christmas Album*, Reprise 6222. Dean Martin. Contains three picks.
- *Ella Wishes You a Swinging Christmas*, Verve 4042. Original concept. 1961. Ella Fitzgerald.
- *Fancy Meeting You Here*, Victor LPM-1854. Original concept. Bing Crosby, Rosemary Clooney. 1957.
- *Ernest Tubb*, Decca 9-3119. 45 rpm EP issue. 1959.
- *For Those in Love*, EmArcy MG-26032. Dinah Washington.
- *Ella Fitzgerald's Christmas*, Capital ST-2805. 1967.
- *Ella Sings, Chick Swings*, Olympic Records 7119. A fine (1939) radio live remote set preserves the original excitement of Ella and perhaps the ultimate swing bandleader, Chick Webb.

- o *Elvis Presley*, Victor LPM-1254. Hardly covered within the scope of this book, this LP, also originally found on 45 rpm EP and reissued single 45 rpm, may be considered the antithesis for any LP issued before it. Its crudeness speaks for itself, especially noting in comparison with the contemporary (reviewed) 1956 Frank Sinatra LP, *Songs for Swinging Lovers*. It is more so interesting that any subsequent release by Elvis is far less as radical. (If there are any doubters, the edgy Presley vocal on the ditty "Blue Moon" penned by Rodgers and Hart, a Victor issue of a Sun label original master (Memphis), is more than poignant and revealing!

- *High Society*, Capital W 750. Original film soundtrack featuring Louis Armstrong, Bing Crosby, Frank Sinatra, and Grace Kelly,. 1856. (Was Grace Kelly dubbed)?
- *Houston*, Reprise 6181. Dean Martin. Original pop LP. Contains seven picks.
- *I Wish You a Merry Christmas*, Warner Brothers W 1484. Original concept. Bing Crosby. 1962.
- *Jamaica*, Victor LOC 1036. Original Broadway soundtrack. Lena Horne, Adelaide Hall, Josephine Premice, others. 1957.
- *Lee Wiley on the Air*." Totem 1021. A collection of excellent Lee Wiley radio program broadcasts from the 1930s.
- *Love Me or Leave Me*, Columbia CL-710. Original 1955 film soundtrack bio of Ruth Etting featuring Doris Day vocals.
- *Mabel Mercer Sings Cole Porter*, Atlantic LP-1213. This original LP contains two picks. 1956.
- *Mack the Knife-Ella in Berlin*, Verve 4041. Original live concept. 1961. Ella Fitzgerald.
- *Merry Christmas*, Decca DL-8128. The 1957 12-inch Crosby collection of previously released Decca mastered Christmas songs.
- *Miss Ethel Waters Performing in Person . . .*" Monmouth-Evergreen. MES-6812. Original Live Concert, 1957.
- *Pal Joey*, Capital W-912. Original film soundtrack, adapted loosely from the earlier Broadway entity. Frank Sinatra, Rita Hayworth, Kim Novak. 1957.
- *Pete Kelly's Blues*, Decca DL-8166. Jazzy TV soundtrack featuring Ella Fitzgerald and Peggy Lee.
- *Porgy and Bess*, Victor LOP-1507. Lena Horne, Harry Belafonte. 1959 LP concept version of the Broadway entity.
- *Ruth Etting—America's Radio Sweetheart*, Totem 1018. Contains fine Ruth Etting radio airchecks.
- *Russ Columbo on the Air*, Totem 1031 (1930s radio broadcasts. From Russ).
- *Robin and the Seven Hoods*, Reprise FS-2021. Original film Soundtrack. Frank Sinatra, Dean Martin, Sammy Davis Jr., Bing Crosby. 1964. (Rat pack guys Frank, Dean, and Sammy, plus Bing Crosby and Peter Falk on cover)!
- *Sarah Vaughan. Live*, Mercury 20383. Sarah Vaughan. Original live concept. 1950s.
- *Songs for Swinging Lovers*, Capital W-653. Original concept. Frank Sinatra. 1956.
- *Songs I Wish I Had Sung*, Decca DL-8352. Original concept. 1956. Bing Crosby.
- *St. Louis Blues*, Capital W-993. Nat King Cole. 1958.
- *The Christmas Song*, Capital 1967. Original concept. Nat King Cole. 1962.

- *The Lady and Her Music*, Quest 3597. Original live Broadway concept, Lena Horne. 1981.
- *Thirties Girls*. Contains original airchecks from featured artist Mildred Bailey, Alice Faye, Libby Holman, Ethel Merman, and Ethel Waters. Also included are the likes of contemporaries Josephine Baker and Ella Logan (1932-36).
- *Trilogy*. Original concept. Frank Sinatra. Reprise FS-2300. Frank Sinatra. 1980.
- *To Be Perfectly Frank,* Sandy Hook 2112. A collection of 1953-54? radio shows—Frank Sinatra.
- *Twelve (12) Songs of Christmas*, Reprise FS-2022. Original concept. Frank Sinatra, Bing Crosby. 1964.
- *Unforgettable*, Mercury MG-20572. Dinah Washington. 1959.
- *What a Difference a Day Made*, Mercury MG-20479. Dinah Washington. 1959.
- *Where the Blue of the Night . . .* , Biograph BLP-M-1. This LP contains the soundtracks for the Mack Sennett film shorts as well as for "Reaching for the Moon." While hardly recordings, these filmed song showcases, all recorded before 1932, would become fodder for bootleggers, as early as 1934, on 78 rpm. This later and legit 1977 LP collection ain't bad, capturing Bing in his prime. (Better, however, are the actual films, which will feature both sight and sound.)

SELECTIVE AND NOTABLE 12-INCH ALBUM REISSUE

- *Strange Fruit*, Atlantic SD-1614. This 1972 Atlantic release of Commodore masters and outtakes from 1939 to 1944 is excellent material. It more so contains excellent notes by Leonard Feather as well as from the legendary original Commodore owner Milt Gabler. (reviewed in the Billie Holiday section).
- *The Father of Rock and Roll.* Arthur Big Boy Crudup. Victor LPV-573. A fine reissue collection of Arthur's Bluebird and Victor singles.
- *Ma Rainey*, Milestone M-47021. This spotty reissue product of original Ma Rainey, mostly made it appreciated in Europe, was finally realized in this 1974 (American) small label Milestone release. Excellent notes by Dan Morgenstern (contains eleven picks found in the Ma Rainey section).

  - Notable LPs of original radio broadcasts
  - Broadcasting limits of American Radio as noted on commercial record sleeves
  - These contemporary 1930s 78 rpm record sleeve samples contained warnings to buyers, noting that it was illegal, within the USA, to play them for commercial reasons on the radio.

ORIGINAL CD FORMAT

- It's hard to figure out the best and worst, although it seems that labels originating outside of the United States are done better. Many reissued 78 rpm originals have subsequently been issues *as is*, with poor acoustics, scratches, and even skips. For purists, it's all good stuff. For most others, used to better technical mastering, it's all hard to swallow. While some CD issues are just as bad as their earlier LP reissue products, some are also done well.
- Another key factor should be album liner notes. While some product is consistently well done, with accurate notes and recording information, some are completely bogus. Hopefully, the readers of this book will benefit with some added knowledge to identify original recordings as well as rerecordings. It is moreover a chore to find misinformation, especially about record labels. The most common is the use of red-label (CBS) Columbia reissued 78 rpm product for the older (pre-1939) Columbia label.
- This CD list consists of many latter-day reissue LP labels not listed in the *record label* section. Indeed many were originally just LP reissues until good quality control was demanded by consumers.
- There *is* one original concept CD listed. All others are reissue products.
- The following latter-century CD labels are noted, with some comments and relevant recording artists to be found on the label.

- *American Legends*. Delta Music. (USA). Jazz, pop, country, R&B remastered originals, OK liner notes (Bing Crosby, Billie Holiday, Jimmie Rodgers, Bessie Smith, Ethel Waters).
- *Arkadia Chansons 75103*. J'Ai Deux Amours. Josephine Baker masters. 1930-37.
- *Archeophone Records* (CDs). (USA). Early acoustic jazz, pop, and blues in excellent remastering. Ditto for excellent liner notes. Marion Harris, Mamie Smith, Sophie Tucker.
- *Baldwin Street Music*, formerly *Tono Records* (Canada). Jazz, blues, remastered. Good liner notes. Lee Wiley.
- *Bear Family Records* (CDs). (Germany). Jazz, pop, blues, country, remastered originals. Excellent liner notes.
- The Carter Family Bear Family, BCD 15865
- *Best of Jazz-The Swing Era*. (France). Jazz-great originals, remastered. Good liner notes.

- *Castle Pulse*. Santuary Records Group (CDs). (England). Jazz, pop, country, remastered. Lacks liner notes. (Louis Armstrong, Cab Calloway, Billie Holiday, Ethel Waters, Fats Waller)
- Ivie Anderson Best of Jazz 4020
- *Blues Roots. Time Life-Sony Music Special Products.* (USA). Blues, remastered. Excellent liner notes. Ma Rainey, Bessie Smith, Mamie Smith, Victoria Spivey, Charlie Patton.
- *BMG. RCA (Victor*). Jazz, pop, blues, country, remastered. Good liner notes. Ivie Anderson, Carter Family, Helen Forrest, Lena Horne, Jimmie Rodgers, Dinah Shore, Maxine Sullivan.
- *Capital Records* (CDs). Capital-EMI. (USA). Jazz, pop, country, R&B. The earlier CD products were duds that had followed previous reissued LP products. Products from 1991 on are excellent, with remastered originals as well as issues with original sleeves and artwork. Moreover, the efforts in liner notes are also done very well. Nat King Cole, Sammy Davis Jr., Dean Martin, Frank Sinatra, Jo Stafford, Peggy Lee, Margaret Whiting.
- CBS 466151 2 Bravo A Josephine Baker. Contains 1926-27 masters. Great cover!
- *Collector Series-Sony Corp Columbia Records* (CD). Jazz, pop, remastered. Excellent line notes. Other SONY products noted.
- *Cocktail Hour*. Allegro Corp Jazz, pop, great originals, remastered. Good liner notes.
- (Ivie Anderson Andrews Sisters, Louis Armstrong, Boswell Sisters, Mildred Bailey, Eddie Cantor, Cab Calloway, June Christy, Rosemary Clooney, Perry Como, Doris Day, Vic Damone, Judy Garland, Billie Holiday, Lena Horne, Peggy Lee, the Mills Brothers, Anita O'Day, Louis Prima, Dinah Shore, Jo Stafford, Mel Torme, Ethel Waters, Dinah Washington).
- *Columbia-Legacy*. Columbia Records—Sony Corp (CDs). Jazz, blues, pop, remastered. Good liner notes. Mildred Bailey, Rosemary Clooney, Ella Fitzgerald, Billie Holiday, Memphis Minnie, Sarah Vaughan, Ethel Waters, Josh White.

    - ✓ Emmett Miller. *The Minstrel Man from Georgia*. Columbia/LEGACY. Roots n' Blues. CK 66999.
    - ✓ Memphis Minnie Hoodoo Lady. 1933-1937. Columbia/Legacy Roots N Blues CK 46775.

        - ➢ MTV. "Unplugged." Columbia Tony Bennett, original concept. Reviewed in Bennett section.

- *Classic Hits. Charlie International.* (England). Jazz, pop, remastered. Lacks liner notes.
- *Classic Years in Digital Stereo. Louisiana Red Hot.* (USA-England). Jazz, pop, remastered in stereo! While some purists may balk, this is carefully done. Good liner notes. Helen Kane.
- *Classics.* (France). Jazz, blues, R&B, with great originals. Not remastered, excellent liner notes. Nat King Cole, Billy Eckstine, Ella Fitzgerald, Helen Humes, Bessie Smith, Valaida Snow, Maxine Sullivan, Sarah Vaughan, Fats Waller, Ethel Waters, Muddy Waters, Midge Williams.
- *Definition Records* (CDs). (Spain). Jazz, remastered, with good liner notes). (Ethel Waters, Lee Wiley).

    - ✓ *Helen Humes 1927-45. Classics 892*

- ✓ *Valaida Snow 1933-36. Classics 1158*
- ✓ *Midge Williams 1937-38. Classics 745*

- Delmark Records. USA. Edith Wilson.
- *Document. (Austria*). Jazz, blues, with great originals. Not remastered for true purists. Mostly good liner notes. Blind Blake, Alberta Hunter, Papa Charlie Jackson, Frankie "Half Pint" Jaxon, Blind Lemon Jefferson, Eva Taylor. Clara Smith, Mamie Smith, Edith Wilson, Lena Wilson. *Papa Charlie Jackson, Febuary 1926 to September 1928. Document DOCDb5088*

  - ✓ Frankie "Half Pint" Jaxon. Vol. May 1926 to July 1929. Document DOCD 5258

- *DRG Records Incorporated. EMI Records Limited.* (USA-Canada). Jazz, pop, remastered. Good liner notes. Alberta Hunter.
- *Edsel Records* (CD). England. Red Foley.
- *EMI Records, Ltd.* (CDs). (England). Jazz, pop, country, remastered. Fair liner notes.
- *Fabulous.* Acrobat Music and Media Limited. (England). Jazz, blues, remastered. Good liner notes.

Memphis Minnie.

- *Flair Records* (CDs). (England). Jazz, pop, remastered. Very good liner notes. Connie Boswell.

  - ✓ Connie Boswell-Flare-ROYCD-223."

- *Flapper. Pavilion Records.* (England-Germany). Jazz, pop, remastered. Very good liner notes. Lena Horne, Elisabeth Welch.
- *Fremeaux and Associates.* (France). Jazz, blues, gospel, remastered. Good liner notes. Billie Holiday, Sister Rosetta Tharpe.
- *Frog.* (England). Jazz, blues, remastered. Very good liner notes.
- *Giant of Jazz. Cedar. (Italy*). Jazz, with great originals remastered. Good liner notes. (Ma Rainey, Ethel Waters).
- *Goldenlane Records.* (USA). Jazz, pop, blues, folk, remastered originals. Poor liner notes. Leadbelly.
- *Hallmark.* (England). Jazz, pop, blues, remastered originals. Fair liner notes. Louis Prima.

  - ✓ *Rhythm Man Louis Prima 308662.*

- *Happy Days Series.* Cedar. (England). Jazz, pop, remastered. Good liner notes. Adelaide Hall.
- *Hep Records* (CDs). (England). Jazz, pop, remastered. Good liner notes. Cleo Brown.

  - ✓ *Here Comes Cleo Brown HEP CD 1034*

- *History. Trumpets of Jericho*, Ltd. (Germany). Jazz, pop, remastered. Lonnie Johnson, Memphis Minnie, Ma Rainey.
- *Indigo Recordings Ltd.* (England). Jazz, blues, remastered. OK liner notes.

- *Intersound Inc.* Platinum Entertainment. (USA-Canada). Jazz, pop, remastered. Good liner notes. Al Jolson.
- *Jasmine Records* (CDs). Cedar. (England-Czech Republic). Jazz, blues, pop, remastered. Good liner notes. Ivie Anderson, Annette Hanshaw, Libby Holman.
- *Jazz Archives* (France). Jazz, remastered. Good liner notes. Ivie Anderson, Louis Armstrong, Cab Calloway, Ella Fitzgerald, Adelaide Hall, Billie Holiday.

  ✓ Adelaide Hall Crooning Blackbird Jazz Archives N-60

- *Jazz Classics* (USA?). Jazz, remastered. Good liner notes. Lee Wiley.
- *Jazz Legends* (USA). *Allegro Corp.* Jazz, pop, great originals, remastered. Good liner notes. (Ethel Waters).
- *L'Art Vocal. France Telcom Foundation.* Cedar. (France). Jazz, blues, remastered. Excellent liner notes. Boswell Sisters, Billie Holiday, Frank Sinatra, Bessie Smith, Lee Wiley.
- *Legacy International.* (USA). Jazz, pop, folk, remastered. Fair liner notes.
- *Living Era.* (England). Jazz, blues, pop, great originals, remastered. Good liner notes. Rot Acuff, Connie Boswell, Russ Columbo, Bing Crosby, Annette Hanshaw, Lena Horne, Bill Monroe, Dick Todd, Ethel Waters.

  ✓ Nick Lucas. The Crooning Troubadour. Living Era. CD AJDA 5329.
  ✓ Bill Monroe and His Blue Grass Boys 1940-1947. CD AJA 5298.
  ✓ Dick Todd. The Canadian Crosby. Living Era. CD AJA 5179.

- *Memphis Archives.* (USA). Blues, remastered. Good liner notes. Ma Rainey, Bessie Smith, Clara Smith, Ethel Waters.
- *Magic Collection. ARC Records* (CDs). Telesonic. (Holland). Jazz, pop, remastered. Lacks liner notes.
- *Mojo Records* (CDs). (USA?). Jazz, blues, pop, remastered. Very good liner notes. Alberta Hunter.
- *Nostalgia Naxos.* HNH International. (Canada). Jazz, pop, remastered. Good liner notes. Frank Crumit.
- *Origin Jazz Library.* (USA). Jazz, country, remastered. Good liner notes.
- *Pair Records Portraits.* ESX Entertainment. (USA). Jazz, gospel, remastered. Very good liner notes. Mahalia Jackson.
- *Prism Leisure Corp.* (England). Jazz, pop, blues, folk, remastered. Good liner notes. Almanac Singers, Woody Guthrie.

  ✓ *Woody Guthrie Prism PLATBX-2234.*

- *Proarte Digital Compact Disc. Fanfare.* (USA). Jazz, pop originals, remastered. Lacks liner notes.
- *Reflections.* (Denmark). Jazz, pop, remastered. Good liner notes. Nat King Cole, Judy Garland, Ethel Waters.
- *Rhino Movie Music and Turner Classic Movies.* (USA). Excellent remastered film soundtracks, with equally impressive liner notes.
- *Roots n' Blues. Sony Music Entertainment.* Blues, pop, country, remastered. Excellent liner notes. Gene Autry, Emmett Miller, Josh White.

- *Sony Music Entertainment. Custom Marketing Group.* (USA). Jazz, pop, remastered. Good liner notes. Helen Morgan, Ethel Waters.
- *Take Two Records* (CDs). (USA). Jazz, pop, remastered. Good liner notes. Boswell Sisters, Ruth Etting, Libby Holman.
- *Timeless Records* (CDs). Chris Barber Collections. (Holland). Jazz, pop, remastered. Good liner notes (Bing Crosby, Ethel Waters).
- *Yazoo. Division of Shanachie Records Corp.* (USA). Jazz, blues, remastered originals. Good liner notes. Charlie Patton.

    ✓ King of the Delta Blues. Charlie Patton. Yazoo 2001.

RECORDED THEME TITLES. (1920-1950+) (ALL VOCALS)

Selective group titles of various subjects / plus twenty outrageous, risqué, and explicative titles, including booted material

- * Designates a featured recording artist within this book.
- o Not a contemporary song title by a featured recording artist within the text of this book, although the title itself may or may not have been noted.

➢ Man

* 1. "Lover Man," Decca 23391. Billie Holiday.
* 2. "My Man Is on the Make," Brunswick 4554. Libby Holman.
* 3. "Find Me a Primitive Man," LMS 296. Lee Wiley.
* 4. "My Man," Victor 21168. Fannie Brice.
* 5. "What Wouldn't I Do for That Man," Victor 22149. Helen. Morgan

➢ Woman

* 6. "Lazy Woman's Blues," Okeh 8279. Blanche Calloway.
* 7. "A Woman Alone with the Blues," Majestic 7258. Lee Wiley, Jesse Stacy.
* 8. "Unlucky Woman," Decca 8613. Helen Humes.
* 9. "Never Trust a Woman," Decca 46074. Red Foley.
* 10. "What More Can a Woman Do?" Continental 6008. Sarah Vaughan.

➢ Daddy

* 11. "Oh Daddy," Black Swan 2010. Ethel Waters (acoustic).
* 12. "That Silver Haired Daddy of Mine," Conquer 7908. Gene Autry.
* 13. "Daddy and Home," Victor 21757. Jimmie Rodgers.
* 14. "Mean Daddy Blues," Okeh 4631. Mamie Smith (acoustic).
* 15. "Daddy," Decca 3821. Andrews Sisters.

- Mama

  * 16. "That's All Right Mama," Victor 20-2205. Arthur Crudup.
  * 17. "High Steppin' Mama Blues," Banner 32473. Gene Autry.
  * 18. "Doggin' Me Mama Blues," Paramount 12673. Blind Blake.
  * 19. "Long Tall Mama Blues," Victor 23766. Jimmie Rodgers.
  * 20. "Mama Don't Allow It," Vocalion 2603. Frankie "Half Pint" Jaxon.

- Baby

  * 21. "Don't Be a Baby, Baby," Decca 18753. Mills Brothers.
  * 22. "You Must Have Been a Beautiful Baby," Decca 2147. Bing Crosby.
  * 23. "That Crawling Baby Blues," Paramount 12880. Blind Lemon Jefferson.
  * 24. "Baby's Awake Now," Gala 1. Lee Wiley.
  * 25. "Yes, Sir, That's My Baby," Victor 19656. Gene Austin.

- Men's Names (Interesting Descriptions)

  * 26. "Lovin' Sam the Sheik of Alabam," Okeh 41305. Emmett Miller.
  * 27. "Willie the Weeper," Black Patti 8048. Frankie "Half Pint" Jaxon.
  * 28. "Abdul Abulbul Amir," Victor 20715. Frank Crumit.
  * 29. "Good-For-Nothin' Joe," Bluebird B-11037. Lena Horne, Charlie Barnet Orch.
  * 30. "True Blue Lou," Columbia 1871-D. Ethel Waters

- Women's Names (Interesting Descriptions)

  * 31. "Minnie the Moocher," Brunswick 6074. Cab Calloway.
  * 32. "Hot House Rose," Liberty Music Shop L-297. Lee Wiley.
  * 33. "Red Hot Flo from Ko-Ko-Mo," Okeh 8463. Eva Taylor.
  * 34. "Hard Hearted Hannah," Pathe 032054. Cliff Edwards (acoustic).
  * 35. "Sweet Georgia Brown," Columbia 379-D. Ethel Waters (acoustic).

Heart

  * 36. "Down-Hearted Blues," Paramount 12005. Alberta Hunter (acoustic).
  * 37. "Be Careful, It's My Heart," Decca 14824. Bing Crosby.
  * 38. "Says My Heart," Bluebird B-7528. Harriet Hilliard.
  * 39. "My Heart and I Decided," Decca 18530. Ella Fitzgerald and her Four Keys.
  * 40. "Your Cheatin' Heart," MGM 11416. Hank Williams.

- Love

  * 41. "Love Is Like a Cigarette," Brunswick 7626. Ive Anderson, Duke Ellington Orch.
  * 42. "I Love You So Much It Hurts," Mercury 5261. Vic Damone.
  * 43. "What Is This Thing Called Love?" Victor 27820. Lena Horne.
  * 44. "Love Me or Leave Me," Columbia 1680-D. Ruth Etting.
  * 45. "Lovesick Blues," Okeh 41062. Emmett Miller.

➢ Parts of the (Upper) Body

* 46. "Cheek to Cheek," Brunswick 7486. Fred Astaire.
* 47. "I'm Thinking Tonight of My Blue Eyes," Perfect 35-09-23. Carter Family.
* 48. "Candy Lips Stuck on You," Okeh 8484. Eva Taylor, Clarence Williams Blue Five.
* 49. "Cold in Hand Blues," Columbia 14064-D. Bessie Smith (acoustic).
* 50. "Toothache Blues," Okeh 8744. Lonnie Johnson and Victoria Spivey.

➢ Farm Animals

* 51. "Banty Rooster Blues," Paramount 12792. Charlie Patton.
* 52. "Milkcow Blues," Banner 33361. Josh White (Pinewood Tom).
* 53. "Muleskinner Blues," Victor 23503. Jimmie Rodgers.
* 54. "Soo Cow Soo," Vocalion 01658. Memphis Minnie.
* 55. "Pony Blues," Paramount-12792. Charlie Patton.

➢ Birds

* 56. "Bye Bye, Blackbird," Victor 20044. Gene Austin.
* 57. "I'm a Little Bluebird," Okeh 40260. Eva Taylor.
* 58. "When the Red Red Robin Goes Bob Bob Bobbin' Along," Brunswick 3222. Al Jolson.
* 59. "Great Speckled Bird," Vocalion 04252. Roy Acuff.
* 60. "When the Swallows Come Back to Capistrano," Decca 3246. Tony Martin.

➢ Reptiles, Fish, and Insects

* 61. "Alligator Blues," Okeh 8529. Helen Humes.
* 62. "Bo Weevil Blues," Paramount 12080. Ma Rainey.
* 63. "Bumble Bee," Vocalion 1476. Memphis Minnie . . .
* 64 "Mean Old Bed Bug Blues," Columbia 14250-D. Bessie Smith.
* 65. "Black Snake Blues," Okeh 8338. Victoria Spivey.

➢ Dogs and Cats

* 66. "Salty Dog Blues," Paramount 12236. Papa Charlie Jackson (acoustic).
* 67. "Old Shep," Melotone 6-03-53. Red Foley.
* 68. "Aw, You Dog," Banner 332323. Cab Calloway.,
* 69. "Black Cat Blues," Okeh Helen Humes.
* 70. "Pussy Cat Blues," Columbia 14661-D. Bo Carter.

➢ Foods

* 71. "I've Got the Yes! We Have No Bananas Blues," Columbia A-3964. Eddie Cantor.

* 72. "Hold Tight, Hold Tight, Seafood Mama," Bluebird B-10116. Fats Waller.
* 73. "Bread and Gravy," Bluebird B-10415. Ethel Waters.
* 74. "Mama Don't Want No Peas, an' Rice or Coconut Oil," Decca 512. Cleo Brown.
* 75. "One Meat Ball," Ash 348-2B. Josh White.

➢ Alcohol

* 76. "And Her Tears Flowed Like Wine," Capital 145. Anita O'Day, Stan Kenton Orch.
* 77. "Rum and Coca Cola," Decca 18636. Andrews Sisters.
* 78. "The Drunkard Song-There Is a Tavern in Town," Victor 24721. Rudy Vallee.
* 79. "Beer Barrel Polka," Decca 2462. Andrews Sisters.
* 80. "Rye Whisky," Conquer 8144. Tex Ritter.

➢ Drugs

* 81. "Dope Head Blues," Okeh 8631. Victoria Spivey.
* 82. "Reefer Man," Banner 32944. Cab Calloway.
* 83. "You're Getting to Be a Habit with Me," Brunswick 6472. Bing Crosby.
* 84. "Cocaine Blues," Coast 262. Roy Hogsed and The Rainbow Riders.
* 85. "I Get a Kick Out of You," Brunswick 7342. Ethel Merman.

➢ Gambling and Fortune

* 86. "Those Gambler's Blues," Victor 22554. Jimmie Rodgers.
* 87. "You Lose," Okeh 41205. Emmett Miller.
* 88. "Fortune Telling Man," Variety 3865. Midge Williams.
* 89. "Hoodo Woman," Vocalion 3222. Memphis Minnie.
* 90. "Jack O'Diamond's Blues," Okeh 8328. Sippie Wallace.

➢ Designated Occupations

* 91. "Coal Man Blues," Paramount 12461. Papa Charlie Jackson (acoustic).
* 92. "Mill Man Blues," Vocalion. Big Bill.
* 93. "Ice Man, Come on Up," Vocalion 3222. Memphis Minnie.
* 94. "Oh Doctor the Blues," Okeh 8391. Lonnie Johnson.
* 95. "Mr. Conductor Man," Champion 16426. Big Bill Johnson (Broonzy).

➢ More Interesting Designated Occupations

* 96. "Bootlegger's Blues," Okeh 8843. Mississippi Sheiks.
* 97. "Mind Reader Blues," Vocalion 02652. Bertha Lee.
* 98. "Pot Licker Blues," Victor 20951. El Watson.
* 99. "Vigilante Man," Victor 26624. Woody Guthrie.
* 100. "Candy Man Blues," Okeh 8654. Mississippi John Hurt.

- The Color Black

  - * 101. "Black Woman's Blues," Columbia 14223-D. Clara Smith.
  - * 102. "Black Spatch Blues," Paramount 12230. Ethel Waters (acoustic).
  - * 103. "Black Moonlight," Brunswick 6643. Bing Crosby.
  - * 104. "Black Is the Color," Ash 345-2B. Burl Ives.

- The Color Blue

  - * 105. "Blue Orchids," Bluebird B-10397. Dick Todd.
  - * 106. "Blue Room," Victor 20-3329. Perry Como.
  - * 107. "Blue Skies," Decca 23646. Bing Crosby.
  - * 108. "Blue Shadows on the Trail," Victor 20-2780. Roy Rogers.
  - * 109. "Blue Tail Fly," Ash 345-3A. Burl Ives.

- Some Blues—The Mood

  - * 110. "Blues on My Mind," Okeh 6735. Roy Acuff and his Smoky Mountain Boys.
  - * 111. "Am I Blue?" Columbia 1837-D. Ethel Waters.
  - * 112. "I Get the Blues When It Rains," Velvet Tone 1910-V. Annette Hanshaw.
  - * 113. "Shaking the Blues Away," Columbia 1113-D. Ruth Etting.
  - * 114. "Blue Prelude," Brunswick 6601. Bing Crosby

- Suicide and Death

  - * 115. "Gloomy Sunday," Okeh 6451. Billie Holiday.
  - * 116. "Drivin' Nails in My Coffin," Decca 46019. Ernest Tubb
  - * 117. "She's Making Woopie in Hell," Okeh 8768. Lonnie Johnson.
  - * 118. "The Death of Mother Jones," Banner 32133. Gene Autry.
  - * 119. "St. James Infirmary," Victor 22299. Gene Austin.

- States. USA

  - * 120. "Moonlight in Vermont," Capital 182. Margaret Whiting, Billy Butterfield Orch.
  - * 121. "Arkansas Blues," Okeh 4446. Mamie Smith (acoustic).
  - * 122. "Georgia Blues," Black Swan 14120. Ethel Waters and her Jazz Masters.
  - * 123. "Texas Moaner Blues," Columbia 14034-D. Clara Smith (acoustic).
  - * 124. "Kentucky Miner's Wife," Columbia 15731-D. Aunt Molly Johnson.

- Cities. USA

  - * 125. "St. Louis Blues," Columbia 14064-D. Bessie Smith (acoustic).
  - * 126. "Blue-Eyed Baby from Memphis," Brunswick 6560. Harlan Lattimore, Don Redman Orch.
  - * 127. "Sweet Home Chicago," Vocalion 03601. Robert Johnson.
  - * 128. "Kansas City Blues," Okeh 8537. Lonnie Johnson.
  - * 129. "Dallas Blues," Okeh 8774. Louis Armstrong.

- Designated Regions. USA

  - * 130. "Southern Blues," Bluebird B-5998. Big Bill.
  - * 131. "Just a Little South of North Carolina," Okeh 6130. Anita O'Day vocal, Gene, Krupa Orch.
  - * 132. "Oklahoma Hills," Capital 201. Jack Guthrie.
  - * 133. "Mississippi Valley Blues," Conquer 7908.
    Gene Autry and Jimmy Long.
  - * 134. "When the Cactus Is in Bloom," Victor 23636. Jimmie Rodgers.

- About Rivers

  - * 135. "Mississippi River Blues," Victor 23535. Jimmie Rodgers.
  - * 136. "Blue River," Brunswick 7319. Al Jolson.
  - * 137. "River, Stay 'Way from My Door," Columbia 2511-D. Ethel Waters.
  - * 138. "Roll On, Mississippi, Roll On," Brunswick 6109. Boswell Sisters.
  - * 139. "The River's Taking Care of Me," Brunswick 6603. Connie Boswell.

- Streets, Avenue, Highway

  - * 140. "Beale Street Blues," Victor 20771. Alberta Hunter.
  - * 141. "Between 18th and 19th on Chestnut Street," Decca 2948. B. Crosby and Connie Boswell.
  - * 142. "Get Your Kicks on Route 66," Capital 224. Nat Cole Trio.
  - * 143. "Blue Sky Avenue," Victor 24725. Gene Austin.
  - * 144. "Highway No. 61," Vocalion 13531. Will Batts.

- Outside of the USA

  - * 145. "Loch Lomond," Vocalion 3654. Maxine Sullivan,
    Claude Thornhill Orch.
  - * 146. "Cuban Love Song," Columbia 2580-D. Ruth Etting.
  - * 147. "Haitian Blues," Emerson 10613.
    Lizzie Miles and Her Creole Jazz Hounds.
  - * 148. "Mexico Joe," Exclusive 3113. Ivie Anderson
  - * 149. "The Last Time I Saw Paris," Columbia 35802. Kate Smith.

- Motor Vehicles (Except Trains)

  - * 150. "Terraplane Blues," Vocalion 03416. Robert Johnson.
  - * 151. "Henry's Made a Lady Out of Lizzie," Victor 21174.
    Ernest Hare and Billy Jones.
  - * 152. "Airplane Blues," Decca 7354. Sleepy John Estes.
  - * 153. "Black Hearst Blues," Okeh 8500. Sarah Martin.
  - * 154. "Street Car Blues," Victor V38614. John Estes.

- Train related

  - * 155. "Night Train to Memphis," Okeh 06693. Roy Acuff.
  - * 156. "Freight Train Boogie," Decca 46035. Red Foley.

* 157. "On the Atchison, Topeka and the Santa Fee," Decca 23436. Judy Garland and the Merry Macs.
* 158. "Wabash Cannonball," Victor 23731. Carter Family.
* 159. "Waiting for a Train," Victor 40014. Jimmie Rodgers.

➢ Prison or Prisoner related

* 160. "The Prisoner's Song," Victor 19427. Vernon Dalhart (acoustic).
* 161. "Blind Lemon's Penitentiary Blues," Paramount 12666. Blind Lemon Jefferson.
* 162. "Chain Gang Blues," Paramount 12338. Ma Rainey.
* 163. "Got the Blues for Murder Only," Okeh 8846. Lonnie Johnson.
* 164. "John Hardy," Musicraft-311. Leadbelly.

➢ Popular Dance Titles, with Vocal

* 165. "It Don't Mean a Thing If It Ain't Got That Swing," Brunswick 6265. Ivie Anderson (unaccredited) Duke Ellington Orch.
* 166. "Black Bottom," Pathe 32207. Annette Hanshaw.
* 167. "Doing the Raccoon," Velvet Tone 1759-D. Rudy Vallee.
* 168. "Sing Me a Swing Song and Let Me Dance," Decca 830. Ella Fitzgerald, Chick Webb Orch.
* 169. "Jitter Bug," Victor 24592. Cab Calloway.
* 170. "A Little Rhumba Numba," Decca 23243. Hildegarde.
* 172. "Boogie Woogie," Decca 1252. Jimmy Rushing, Count Basie Orchestra.
* 173. "I'm Gonna Dance With The Guy Wot Brung Me" Victor-20822 Aileen Stanley & Billy Murray
* 174. "The Hucklebuck," Columbia 38486. Frank Sinatra
* 175. "Tennessee Waltz," Mercury 5534. Patti Page.

➢ Social Significance (Domestic)

* 176. "Strange Fruit," Commodore 526. Billie Holiday.
* 177. "Black and Blue," Columbia 2184-D. Ethel Waters.
* 178. "The House I Live In," Columbia 36886. Frank Sinatra
* 179. "Talking Dust Bowl Blues," Victor 26619. Woody Guthrie.
* 180. "Brother, Can You Spare a Dime?" Brunswick 6414. Bing Crosby.

➢ World War II Directly Related, During the War

* 181. "There's a Star-Spangled Banner Waving Somewhere," Bluebird B-9000. Elton Britt. Elton had previously been a member of a 1930s group "The Beverly Hillbillies." (Yes, before the popular 1960s TV entity!)
* 182, 183. "Praise the Lord and Pass the Ammunition," Columbia 36640. Glee Club vocals, Kay Keyser's Orch., Merry Macs, Decca 18498, vocal group.
* 184. "Smoke on the Water," Decca 6102. Red Foley.
* 185. "Boogie Woogie Bugle Boy," Decca 3598. Andrews Sisters.
* 186, 187. "White Cliffs of Dover," Decca F-8110; Vera Lynn / Bluebird B-11406. Dick Todd.

- * 188. "Soldier's Last Letter," Decca 6098. Ernest Tubb.
- * 189. "Remember Pearl Harbor," Victor 27738. Sammy Kaye Orch., Allen Foster, vocal.
- * 190. "Der Fuehrer's Face," Bluebird B-11586. Carl Grayson vocal, Spike Jones Orch.
- * 191,192. "GI Jive," Louis Jordan, Decca 8654. Johnny Mercer, Capital 141.
- * 193. "A Slip of the Lip," Victor 20-1528. Ray Nance vocal, Duke Ellington Orch.
- * 194. "A Hot Time in the Town of Berlin," Decca 23350. Bing Crosby and Andrews Sisters.
- * 195. "Uncle Sammy, Here I Come," Bluebird B-11368. Eva Taylor.
- * 196. "We Did It Before and We'll Do It Again," Decca 4117. Dick Robertson and American Four.
- * 197, 198, 199, 200. "Coming in on a Wing and a Prayer," Bluebird B-0815. / Four Vagabonds, Decca 18553, / Song Spinners. Hit 7046, Willie Kelly Orch. Okeh 6713 / Golden Gate Quartet.
- * 201. "Seventh Air Force," Bing Crosby. Decca Master. Bootleg. Air force over Japan.
- * 202, 203, 204. "When the Lights Go On Again All Over the World," Victor 27945. Vaughn Monroe Orch., Vaughn's own vocal. Dick Todd, Bluebird B-11577. Vera Lynn, Decca F-8241.

➢ 20 Titles: Most Outrageous, Risqué, or Expletive titles, Including Bootlegged Material

- * 205. "Shave 'Em Dry" (bootleg of Banner 34475). Lucille Bogan alias Bessie Jackson perhaps produced, in 1935, the most x-rated version of the earlier, tamer, Ma Rainey-penned ditty. Moreover, even by latter-century standards, in true retrospective, this crude vocal, with even cruder added lyrics, is tough! Rough stuff?

Does latter-century rap count? Is this the most x-rated product ever?

- * 206. "Please Warm My Weiner," Bluebird B-6058. Bo Chatmon alias Bo Carter tells like it is, on this legit release.
- * 207. "Get 'Em from the Peanut Man" (Hot Nuts). Champion 50002. Lil Johnson.
- * 208. "Tom Cat and Pussy Blues," Victor 23763. Jimmie Davis.
- * 209. "Tramp," Hot Shots Master. Cleo Brown's (1936?) articulate vocal leaves no room for misunderstanding.
- * 210. "My Pencil Won't Write No More," Okeh 8912. Bo Carter again scores, or does he?
- * 211. "I'm Gonna Give It to Mary with Love," ARC Master (1936?). This boot of Cliff Edwards, before he made cartoon voices, was quite a fellow.
- * 212. "I'm a Bear in Lady's Boudoir," ARC Master (1936?) Another boot of Cliff Edwards.
- * 213. "A Guy Who Takes His Time," Brunswick 6495. Mae West.
- * 214. "Let Me Play with You, Poodle," Bluebird B-34-0700. Tampa Red.
- * 215. "Pussy Pussy Pussy," Vocalion 04560. Light Crust Dough Boys.

- * 216. "Where My Woman Usta Lay," Blind Boy Fuller. Decca 7903.
- * 217, 218. "Big Long Slidin' Thing," Mercury 70214. Dinah Washington (same as Ethel Waters acoustic title "Oh Joe, Play the Trombone" on Black Swan 14128).
- * 219. "He Had It Up Till Yesterday," Columbia 5064. Sophie Tucker (British release).
- * 220. "Snatch and Grab It," Capital 40028. Julia Lee.
- * 221. "Nasty Man," Alice Faye. Brunswick B-099. A crude bit of mischief for highbrows in 1934 ? Or was Alice just a hot, young showgirl with a clever tong? It's not exactly phone sex, but is it nasty? Listen!
- * 222. "You Can't Tell the Difference After Dark," ARC Master. Alberta Hunter. This 1935 rendering is full of smut, as its title implies! It more so implements race, which is why it was bootlegged.
- * 223. "Atomic Power," Decca 46014. Red Foley. This ditty is more than a patriotic war entity. Just how it is justifiable and religious to explain the bombing of Hiroshima and Nagasaki (Japan), in August 1945, is more than bizarre. Indeed, the heart-wrenching decision of President Truman definitely saved the lives of perhaps millions of Allied lives is reasonable, yet, in true retrospective, is it more than bad taste to celebrate it with this song ditty? Listen and decide!
- * 224. "Suicide Blues," Vocalion Master. This unusual Leroy Carr ditty was recorded in 1934, more so close to his own death. Creepy?
- * 225. "I'm My Own Grandpa," Victor 20-2563. Lonzo and Oscar. Not full of smut, just dumb! How dumb? Just listen!

➢ Above

o A recording of note by a recording artist, not featured in detail, within this book.

THE ALL TIME RUBBISH LIST OF RECORDED VOCALS (1926-1950+)

- There's so bad, they're bad—they reek! They suck! Listen and cringe, for various reasons! Did popular tastes lie?

    * Considerations about the limitations of acoustic recordings were considered, so are films that appear in the separate film section of this book

The search for the many recordings within this book found the author looking everywhere, including in piles of discarded garbage and rubbish. While some records did turn out to be gems, for the most part, after being played, the reasons for most of the records becoming discarded, besides scratches or of un-playable condition, are indeed found to be justifiable! While many readers of this book may find many of my own picks suspect, and belonging in the following list, the matter of tastes and times should be considered. The following commercial recordings, not usually considering poor sound acoustics, ethnic bashing, musical films, or operatic utterances, indeed suck, with consideration given to higher expectations.

➢ The "Top 10." Each merit subjective and particular attention.

1. "Sonny Boy," Brunswick 4033. The arrival of talking films found this ditty claimed by Buddy De Sylvia, Lew Brown, Ray Henderson, and Al Jolson introduced by Al in his second film in 1928 *The Singing Fool.* Somehow, this sentimental bit of slop became a huge contemporary best-selling record and even more popular than the film. While smatlz is used a lot within this book, it's also, in true retrospective, only fair to claim that the millions who heard and purchased this ditty were wrong! This agonizing piece of crap finds Jolson's vocal (typically) hamming it up but more than over the top—the top of the toilet tank!
2. "Making Whoopee," Victor 21831. The personable and talented Eddie Cantor made this Broadway entity penned by Walter Donaldson and Gus Kahn a huge (1929) film success as well. Sadly, these lyrics do not translate well nor survive as good novelty on record. This juvenile attempt at humor or dated attempt at camp reeks of stupidity, while other clumsy ditties, found as picks within this book, while usually less known, do not compel listeners to leave the room.

(Frank Sinatra, later in 1956, on Capital W-653, marginally succeeds—somehow!)

3. "Marta, Rambling Rose of the Wildwood," Brunswick 6216. Penned by L. Wolf Gilbert and Mois'es Simons, this awful song ditty is rendered even more horridly by Arthur Tracy. Also known as the "street singer," Tracy was (somehow) a huge radio entity! Moreover, his huge popularity on 1932 radio led to his inclusion into the contemporary 1932 film *The Big Broadcast*. Along with the vocals of Bing Crosby, the Boswell Sisters, Cab Calloway, Donald Novis and Kate Smith, Tracy and his terrible vocals and accordion playing are both seen and heard in this title as well. Somehow, despite him, he did not spoil the film.

(Was Arthur Tracy an inspiration for a young, contemporary aspiring bandleader Lawrence Welk?)

4. "I've Got the Girl," Columbia 824-D. The 1926 release of the Don Clark Biltmore Hotel Orchestra, in true retrospective, found its vocal refrain identified as Bing Crosby and Al Rinker, before they were part of Paul Whiteman's "Rhythm Boys." It had more so been a contemporary Gene Austin release and Don Clark's jazzy band arrangement, using a rhythmic vocal, and should have ushered in Bing and Al very well!

This initial release was unfortunately recorded at the wrong speed, with the peppy vocals sounding much like chipmunks, not meaning to insult the better-sounding 1950s recording entity "the Chipmunks." After Crosby's death, after playing with recorded speeds, this recording was independently remastered and bootlegged into a pleasant-sounding recording. While this is all well and good, those who do find this original recording will find it, as it was originally, a flawed piece of garbage! (Get the boot!)

5. "Minnie the Moocher," Brunswick 01217. This (1931) rendering by Adelaide Hall in England hardly matches the excellence of the contemporary Cab Calloway hit on Brunswick 6074. The highbrow and equally high-voiced Hall can always be suspect, as she is always inconsistent, even as a featured artist within this book. What more so makes this record really suck is Adelaide's own stiffness. "Minnie" was hot, and Adelaide, on this one, is not!
6. "Sweet Leilani," Decca 1175. This (1937) film entity penned by Harry Owens was introduced by Bing Crosby in the film *Waikiki Wedding*, which ain't a bad flick, considering its obvious, lighthearted entertainment. Moreover, as introduced within the film *Sweet Leilani*, it is at least OK. What does whack the ears is this recording, which perhaps defines smaltz as something mild, as in a laxative!

This ditty moreover became a huge Crosby best seller, perhaps outselling all his previous single, up to that time! While it's a wonder that the tastes of the public may be suspect as well as fickle, in true retrospective, the eventual million sales of this recording did indeed occur!

7. "I Want to Be a Cowboy's Sweetheart," Vocalion 03010. This combination of country yodel and perhaps (European) polka was a self-penned and best-selling entity for Patsy Montana in 1935. While the author of this book has endured and sometimes endorsed some of the yodels from the likes of Jimmie Rodgers and Gene Autry, this

ditty is perhaps best heard at the far end of a cow! What is more amazing is that this ditty was a huge contemporary success and gained for Patsy everlasting recognition as a hillbilly or country entity. Sorry, Patsy, without the yodeling, you may have had something!

8. "King Joe, Pt 1. and 2.," Okeh 6475. The likes of Paul Robeson's vocals are always operatic, and, although a featured artist within this book, he is always prone to hinder good listening. This attempt at jazz also included Count Basie, who was indeed someone who had already contributed to the idiom as well as the fine development of great voices such as Helen Humes and Jimmy Rushing. This ditty is more so a tribute to the contemporary American boxing champion Joe Louis, who, along with Robeson's already acquired worldwide fame, was especially a hero to many Afro-Americans, most of them living within a segregated and racist society. Even in hindsight, it should have been something special. What is totally wrong is Robeson's operatic vocal, which Basie, to his likely dismay, fails to capture. The un-hip Robson just did not get it. While noble attempts to save vocals are noted elsewhere within this book, this resulting recording fails badly, and perhaps even Joe Louis himself, after hearing it, just may have been embarrassed? (A two-sided stinker and a rare loss for Joe!)
9. "Temptation," Capital 412. Penned by Nacio Herb Brown and Arthur Freed, this ditty had been introduced by Bing Crosby in this 1933 film *Going Hollywood.* It's a stiff song, but Crosby's crooning job in the film and on his contemporary recording on Brunswick 6695 succeeds. Some years later in 1945, Perry Como revived it, attempting a crooning job, much like Crosby on Victor 20-1658.

In 1947, a novelty version by "Red Ingle and the Natural Seven" with a vocal by "Cinderella G. Stump" was issued. As more than likely, the vocals heard strongly indicated the vocal of Jo Stafford and the Paul Weston Orchestra. The takeoff on the serious "Temptation" was perhaps a good idea, yet its take upon the then emerging "country and western" genre is as obvious as it is weak. The resulting best seller, perhaps outselling both previous (straight) versions by Crosby and Como, is, in true retrospective, something forced to become funny! It is likely the "temptation" to give this ditty a hearing may be great! What will result is something indeed annoying as well as stupefying. So is the hard fact that this record, like many on this list, was a popular best seller! Taste?

10. "Gems from George White's Scandals, Pt. 1 and Part 2.," Brunswick 20102. This 12-inch release of 1932 was a well-thought-out Brunswick Records concept to capture the contemporary George White Broadway entity, along with its song ditties. The melody of songs are all by Lew Brown and Roy Henderson and are given a vocal by the following contemporary Brunswick recording artists:

* "This Is the Missus." The Boswell Sisters
* "The Thrill Is Gone." Bing Crosby
* "My Song." Frank Munn.
* "That's Love." The Boswell Sisters
* "That's Why Darkies Were Born." Frank Munn.
* "Life Is Just a Bowl of Cherries." The Mills Brothers, (solo) Connie Boswell, and Bing Crosby, the Boswell Sisters.

  * The Brunswick Orchestra is conducted by Victor Young, with trombone passage of "Thomas Dorsey," Jimmy's brother.

This record is full of some fine vocal performances and more so by some of the best of the era. The jazzy Boswell Sisters and Mills Brothers are well heard as well as the crooning and (even) hip, Bing Crosby. How can it fail? Sadly, in true retrospective, the whole thing is flawed by the tenor vocals of Frank Munn on "My Song" and "That's Why Darkies Are Born." Moreover, while the likes of "That's Why Darkies Are Born" is hardly a coon song, it contains a well-meaning, yet racist lyric, as its very title indicates. Even more sad is the fact that these titles of Crosby, the Boswell Sisters, and the Mills Brothers were not to be re-recorded as Brunswick entities, thus forcing their audiences of listeners to also hear and dread Frank Munn! Interesting? Yes! It started well, but it all sounds as if Frank Munn spoiled it. Start off with pleasure and end up cringing! Yup.

➢ The shit list continues with less comment, in no particular order.

- "How Lovely Cooks the Meat," Columbia 39693. Frankie Laine and Doris Day. This title is stupid, as are the clumsy vocals (1952).
- "Sugarbush," Columbia 39693. Doris Day and Frankie Laine. Another dumb duet! The original flip side of "How Lovely Cooks the Meat" doubles the dumbness! Un-clever and un-sexy implied lyrics or silly sex? (1952)
- "I Still Suits Me," Decca 24100. Bing Crosby and Lee Wiley. A major disappointment! This arrangement as well as vocals are all wrong (1946).
- "I Want to Yodel," Odeon 49180. This yodel recorded in France by Josephine Baker in 1926 hurt many French ears when played. More so, if played again, it will have the same affect on any listener, in France or elsewhere!
- "My Cousin Louella," Columbia 38045. Frank Sinatra. A stupid relative? (1948).
- "Chlo-E". As also known as "Song Of The Swamp", this 1927 (Gus Kahn & Neil Moret) penned ditty is at least an interesting and morbid tale about a girl being pursued stuck in a swamp. Sadly, contemporary versions of this ditty are dull, especially noting a Franklyn Baur release on (Victor-21149) and a more elaborate 1928 Paul Whiteman 12 inch release, on (Victor-35921), featuring a so-so Austin Young vocal. (Maybe Whiteman should have used Bing Crosby, who was part of his organization at this time? A better sung vocal by Eva Taylor was also attempted on (Okeh-8585), that was unfortunately sleep inducing, and NAP. Jazzy and sweet Valaida Snow's 1937 (British) release seemingly clinched it? Later, with a fuller sound with backing by Paul Lavel, Dinah Shore's 1941 soft and careful rendering (Victor-27625) noted (in text) offered perhaps a more intimate vocal? (A still later and more well known popular 1945 (parody) Spike Jones release on (Victor-20-1654), featuring a novel Red Ingle vocal release had a bit of fun with Chlo-e and became a huge best seller, although this tale of a girl named Chlo-E perhaps deserved better?
- "Yodelin' Jive," Decca 2800. Bing Crosby and the Andrews Sisters. It sucks! (1939)
- "A Wonderful Guy," Columbia 38460. Dinah Shore. A guy and no sex? (1949).
- "Smile," Columbia 12229-D. Ethel Waters. This boring arrangement does not produce a smile, but it yawns. Wake up when it's over! (1927).
- "Dennis the Menace," Columbia 39988. Rosemary Clooney. This tale about a young lad is not even mischievous. Let the kid play and break this recording, if found! (1953).

- "Rhapsody in Love," Brunswick 01217. Adelaide Hall. Adelaide just cannot control her (vocal) self! (1931).
- "Mockin Bird Hill". Mercury-5595. Patti Page's huge 1951 best seller success just had to have been purchased by the considerable nerd population of the world!
- "Stay as Sweet as You Are," Brunswick 7318. Lanny Ross. Don't be sweet, just stay away from this boring vocal (1934).
- "Feudin' and Fightin'," Columbia 37189. Dorothy Shay, the "Park Avenue Hillbilly." Real rednecks are even offended! (1947).
- "Let's Take an Old-Fashioned Walk," Columbia 38513. Frank Sinatra and Doris Day. Don't walk, run away from the record player! Or just break it?! (1949)
- "The One Rose," Decca 1201. Bing Crosby. A dull croon on a song that others did better! (1937).
- "The One I Love Belongs to Somebody Else," Brunswick 2671 Al Jolson and as on Okeh 40054 by Sophie Tucker. While this author always tries to put poor acoustic era ditties into different listening modes, this (1924) entity sucks. Luckily, Frank Sinatra and Sarah Vaughn would produce better results in the 1940s.
- "Gypsy Love Song," Decca 1678. This duet with Bing Crosby and Frances Langford fails because of its arrangement. Or does it just suck?
- "Oh My Pa Pa," Victor 20-5552. If your father is alive, do you want to drive him out of the house? Just play it for him! A huge best seller for Eddie Fisher in 1953.
- Any Nate King Cole recording with the 'singing Pussycats !
- "Open Up the Doghouse," Capital 2985. A duet with Nat King Cole and Dean Martin—that's a dog of a song. The dog ain't dumb, nor the dog a hound! (1953).
- "I Wanna Get Married". Decca-23382. As penned by (Dan Shapiro, Milton Pascal & Phil Charig,), this ditty finds Gertrude Niesen perhaps subbing the word 'slayed' for something more obvious? While a best seller in 1944, in true retrospective, earlier recorded fodder by (Adamson & McHugh) in 1937's "Where Are You", on Brunswick-7837 had found Gertrude better served? So would 1946's (Mercer & Arlen) penned "Legalize My Name", on Decca-23499. Or call it one miss and two hits? Or one Miss with two big (bleeps)?
- Bing Crosby's (1950) best seller "I Cross My Fingers", (NAP) when compared to Dinah Washington's contemporary version. More so reveals a tired formula (Crosby) vocal, that did not need a finger. Or a sigh for him to liven things up a bit?
- "Jim". Okeh-6369. Not even Billie Holiday's mellow & (almost) sweet 1941 vocal can save this (Caesar Petrillo, Ed Ross & Nelson Shaw) penned ditty about a careless and boring guy! Who wants to fall asleep listening to this tale about this idiot? While not all guys named 'Jim" are bad, Billie should have indeed left this one, and this recording about him!
- "Them There Eyes" Decca-27145. Billie Holiday's (1949) 2nd recording, when compared to her earlier 1st, on (Vocalion-5021), 10 years earlier is garbage, although a 3rd "live" rendering, as noted in text, makes up for it.

- Gene Austin's weak croon on "Jeannie I Dream Of Lilac Time" on Victor-21564 at least found Eva Taylor's better contemporary (also muddy) vocal at least interested, as sleep is inducing without turning any lights out.
- The (Gershwin Brothers) penned Broadway ditty "My Cousin In Milwaukee", as by Hildegarde on (Decca-23246), despite a pleasant vocal, cannot overcome it's silly title.
- While Hildegarde's "Lady In The Dark" Broadway entity "My Ship", found the (Kurt Weil and Ira Gershwin) tale a worthy voyage to fall asleep on (as a pick), the nonsense of "A Sage Of Jenny PT 1 & 2", on (Decca-23206), finds the storytelling about an adventurous girl's experiences a bit thin after PT 1, and leaves its listener waiting for her life to be over? Guess you had to be there? Or hear and see Ginger Rogers perform it very well in the subsequent 1944 film? Indeed, as with many ditties penned for the stage, the visual image is everything! Sorry Hildegarde. Thank you Ginger!
- "Medley Of Gus Edwards Song Hits", Decca-2700. The acoustic age of vaudevillian Gus Edwards and "School Days"(1910), "Sunbonnet Sue"(1907)," Jimmy Valentine" (1911) and "If I Was A Millionaire" (1910), was (even) a long time for Bing Crosby in 1939. As part of his contemporary film "The Star Maker", a bio about Edwards, it sounds like the (uninterested) and stiff Bing got stuck recording these ditties. (For fun, listen for Bing's wit and sarcasm, on his (interested) outtake (boot) of "Jimmy Valentine")? Look out?
- The death of George Gershwin in 1937 at about 38 years of age, found the contemporary music business saddened, as well as cashing in on the popular Broadway composer, usually assisted by his surviving brother, Ira.
  This brought a 1938 (Victor) attempt to produce a contrived 'songbook', as was already done for 'classical music' masters of Italian, German and Russian on it's popular 'red seal' label, usually on (extended) 12 inch discs. As released on Victor-12333, 13334, 12335, the likes of musician and orchestra leader Nathaniel Shilkrat (who had produced high brow Helen Morgan recordings very well), and vocals by Felix Knight, Sonny Schuyler, and especially Jane Froman, this 'tribute' seemingly had it all? Instead, the overblown Froman voice (hardly as controlled as previous Helen Morgan renderings) found melodies and song ditties like "Who Cares", "So Am I", "I Got Rhythm", "Maybe", "Do Do Do", "Clap Yo Hands", and "Some One To Watch Over Me" as a bunch of over the top mushy vocal utterances, not to induce sleep, but finger scratch the walls when heard. Indeed,—Jane had done better, and more so would do better. Sorry Jane.
- Bing Bashing Again. While (as noted in text), Leo Reisman's control over Fred Astaire's weak voice had produced a well done original vocal on "Night And Day", it was later versions as by Maxine Sullivan and Frank Sinatra that would define this Cole Porter penned ditty as a recording. A subsequent Bing Crosby version on (Decca-18887) is surprisingly awful. The same may be noted on another Crosby release on (Decca-18898), "Begin The Beguine", although this time the (Cole Porter) song ditty was perhaps a silly bit of contrived music for highbrows? Luckily, as noted in text, Frank Sinatra's well produced version, along with an excellent flowing vocal does indeed improve upon the song ditty itself, and indeed defines this song with a stupid title! Thank you—Frank. Bing's not awful but flatly sung, huge 1944 best selling (Decca-18595) recording of Cole Porter's Broadway ditty from "Mexican

Hayride"—"I Love You", found Jo Stafford's mellow contemporary version on (Capital-153), in true retrospective, defining.

- Any vocals as associated with Irving Mills are horrid. Perhaps the only reason the otherwise brilliant songwriter and bandleader did do vocals was because he had the big bucks?
- "The Song Is You".—The Song Is NOT you, Frank. As with many ditties laying around, the Tommy Dorsey excuse for 'swing' and fox-trot dance records would perhaps label (most) of his music as 'sweet band' music. While (even) in latter century re-issue CD product, the (Jerome Kern and Oscar Hammerstein II) penned ditty from the 1932 Broadway entity "Music In The Air" became associated with the Tommy Dorsey organization.Indeed Dorsey did a lot for Frank. In true retrospective, it was still lucky that Frank Sinatra had been his vocalist for his 1942 (Bluebird-B-11515) release. For the most part, Tommy Dorsey later became more associated with Frank Sinatra. While not being associated with a major name, the previous Paul Small croon, had done little to promote this ditty. The author's ears are more so not convinced that (even) Frank lifts this stupidly named ditty into something more. It is certainly NOT a Sinatra pick. After a long search to please the ears, the (noted in text) Doris Day version finally clinched this ditty. Sorry Frank!
- The 1929 Al Jolson best seller "Liza All the Clouds Roll Away" on Brunswick 4402, from the Gershwins Broadway entity *Show Girl* is not a pick and perhaps a sentimental bit of mush that somehow made it. Listen! It (still) sucks? While this *Jolson* verdict still stands, a lesser-known version by the Ipana Troubadors (a contemporary 1920s jazz group, owing its name to a product sold on the radio), featuring a vocal by Smith Ballew on Columbia 1903-D scores!

ACKNOWLEDGEMENTS

- The author had originally thought that original records containing record label releases and matrix numbers would be enough. While it is obvious that the scope of this book has relied upon much more, it has become more of a time-consuming issue, as this book has taken over ten years to complete.
- Along the way, in the search of differing vocal styles and actual histories, the advice of an older crowd, to be seen and heard in flea markets, record shows, and collectors, has led the author into more investigation as well as many dead ends. The followers of any generation of entertainers always have their favors as well as taste. While most of the reviews contained within this book were indeed discoveries, the obvious appreciation, or unsatisfied consumption of a heard product, still relies upon opinion and personal taste.
- It is imperative for all listeners to always consider the advancement of new technology and the (original) attempts to (even) hear an early recording, especially those noted as acoustic. What latter-century and new-century music listeners now take for granted took a while. It took a toll upon the recording artists themselves. A world without music videos? Television?
- Another consideration should include current events and the daily life of America. The effects of World War I, the Roaring Twenties, the Great Depression, World War II, and the postwar boom are important events and include many generations. In addition to racism, which much of the music itself indeed assisted to bring down, it is not that hard to figure that entertainment was more so a sideline, for a public that, for the most part, had to put food on the table.

- The author would especially like to personally acknowledge: my (late) mother, the (late) Richard Wagner, the (late) Estelle Swartzburger, (the late) William Hargrave of England, Al Barbaro, and Steve Batinich, Joe Cavilier (the authority on sheet music), Jim Di Orio, Robert Hammond, Bob Koster, (the Jazz Record Mart) Jim Klein, Nick Nardella, Mitch Taxy, Jon Oye, Hank Paul (Bandleader-Park Avenue), Phil Pospychala, Pete Sckenic, Ed Senczyson, Raffe Simonian, Tom Smith (Toledo, Ohio) Hank Shurba, (Remember When), Chuck Thiese, (the late) John Waldorf Sr. whose jazz collection made it easier, Mike Walstein, (collector and expert) (the late) Rick Whiting who collected and knew almost everything, the late Sid Witt-part time musician who claimed he worked with Frank Sinatra, Mark Witt. All contributed, some more than most, to assemble facts as well as music.

- The fine assistance of the Itasca Community (especially Jenny), the Elk Grove Library, the Schaumburg Library, the Chicago Public Library.
- The separate booklist is perhaps incomplete but served the author well.
- Information contained on record sleeves and more current CD issue product was also helpful.

APPENDIX—
LATE NOTES AND ADDITIONS

- More Gene—Gene Autry, known as 'Sam Hill', also produced a crude self penned ditty "Why Dont You Come Back To Me", on Van Dyke-5119, in 1929. Still later in 1941, and still delightfully crude in the same vein finds "Ill Never Let You Go Little Darlin", as penned by Gene and Fred Rose, as a standard 'Gene Autry' release on Okeh-06360. As both added picks for Gene, the latter song ditty later became better known as a 1954 "Sun" recording for Elvis Presley, (sung in part) just as crudly as Gene, and released on the groundbreaking 1956 (Victor) LP "Elvis Presley".
- Jackie Taylor's 1930 sweet dance band found a limited but useful vocal refrain for the Boswell Sisters on Victor 22500. In true retrospective, the ditty penned by Al Dubin and Joe Burke "We're on the Highway to Heaven" is indeed a huge plus. Another pick for the sisters!
- Ben Bernie was a very popular bandleader in the 1920s, especially noting his claimed penning of the standard "Sweet Georgia Brown" as well as his instrumental best seller of the same ditty. His 1929 recording of "Singin' in the Bathtub" on Brunswick 4610, penned by Magidson, Washington, and Cleary, from the contemporary film *Show of Shows*, is perhaps better noted by its (un-credited) vocal refrain.
- While the film has yet to be found by the author of this book, this silly novelty of a ditty works, although not as well as another and noted watery and contemporary film title *Singing in the Rain.* Maybe all it needed was Cliff Edwards. Speculation more ever has it that (stiff) Dick Robertson had been part of the 'vocal refrain'? If so, it's the best thing he was associated with?
- Ben Bernie was to remain a popular radio entity of the 1930s, featuring newer; swing era' acts of the latter 1930s. Perhaps his most popular 'find' was the Bailey Sisters, who's subsequent novelty recording 'No Mama No' on (Vocalion) just had to be influenced by the (contemporary) success of the Andrews Sisters.
- "Where Are You?"—indeed missing in the Connie Boswell review—This added 'pick', "Where Are You," penned by (Harold Adamson and Jimmy HcHugh), is a serious bit of business, released on (Decca-1160), as backed by the Ben Pollock Orchestra. A contemporary 1937 (Brunswick-7837) release by Gertrude Niesen, as backed by an orchestra by Cy Feuer is just as good, but a bit more gloomy. Connie or Gertrude?
- An Ernest Tubb honky tonk tune? Add a pick for Chick Bullock's earlier 1933 crooning job of "Have You Ever Been Lonely?" on Melotone M-12680 still later, Patsy Cline, on Decca-25718, would re-define it?
- 479.—Bing Crosby's second family with Katherine Grant became a seasonal T.V Christmas event for many baby boomers from the 1960s to 1977. In true retrospective, the last, *A Merry Ole Christmas,* filmed in Britain became the most documented. Along with (rocker) David Bowie the old but committed voice render (Peace on Earth), and penned by Buz Kohan, Larry Grossman and Ian Fraser, along with the standard (Little Drummer Boy), less than a month before his death in October, 1977.
- Another Musical Film Pick: The 1934 (British) film, based upon the earlier London entity *Evergreen* by the same name, found (British) Jessie Mathews defining the Harry

Woods, (Rogers and Hart) scored film, especially noting the ditty "Dancing on the Ceiling." As well as dancing up a storm, Jessie indeed does very well at exhibiting her great legs and body, while noting an obvious nude statue—to be gleefully seen and heard in the film. As credited to Afro-American Buddy Bradley, Buddy's witnessed choreography rivals any contemporary Hollywood entity—although American Hollywood's own racism kept Bradley from any employment. More so, his fellow and non-black Americans working on the film, Harry Woods, Richard Rodgers, and Lorenz Hart, all had or found jobs quit a bit easier! (Frank Sinatra's brilliant and later 1955 recording, "Dancing on the Ceiling," a noted pick, more so defined this ditty—totally differing from Mathews.)

- Another Jessie Mathews musical film pick from *Evergreen* is "When It's Springtime in Your Heart." As performed more than once in the film, her dated and shrill music hall vocal style somehow (still) delivers! (Al Bowlly more so produced a contemporary recording as a Roy Noble dance band release.)
- Yet another *Evergreen* musical film entity is far less pleasant. As by Jessie Mathews, the horrid song title "Daddy Wouldn't Buy Me a Bow Wow" lives up to its expectation—it sucks! Or perhaps, really bites? (Indeed, this title almost wrecked watching the flick.) A real dog? The song ditty title, penned by Joseph Tabrar, had actually been introduced by British music hall favorite Vista Victoria around 1892, who more ever found Jessie emulating, in turn of the century costume in the film.
- Still another *Evergreen* film entity performed by Sonnie Hale "Tinkle, Tinkle" is so bad that it turns into camp—it's a stupidly amusing bit of a song-and-dance performance that indeed produces more than chuckle or two! Watch and become amused? Or sickened? Watch and learn?
- As a musical film pick, the 1933 Walt Disney cartoon film *The Three Little Pigs* found Irving Berlin's publishing, penned by Frank Churchill association with "Who's Afraid of the Big Bad Wolf," something to really be concerned about. The silly symphony does entertain! The Great Depression could have easily become something worse, as millions where unemployed. Who was afraid? These were indeed hard times for many. While Germany and others turned to dictatorships, America turned to Franklin Roosevelt. No one knew what would happen, but as it would turn out, the US government did prevail. The legal right to strike, Social Security, and *The Three Little Pigs*? They all did indeed happen after 1933. All cultural events!
- As a popular song title, this ditty found much-recorded emulation, with noted contemporary best sellers for the Don Bestor Orchestra, with vocals by Florence Case, Charles Yontz, and Frank Sherry on Victor 24410 and Victor Young's Orchestra on Brunswick 6651, among others. As a further contemporary filmed event, it just well may be that Clark Gable, an unlikely crooner, fed the same wolf line to Claudette Colbert in the 1934 film *It Happened One Night*. Gable obviously had other ideas! While Disney did not invent the folklore, it is also obvious that the rest of the century was founded upon the Disney short. Is the (later) Barbara Streisand (1963) version on LP Columbia CL-2007 novel enough? Does the new century find a chosen name of a 2006 recording entity "Big Bad Wolf"? Yes!
- 1935s Disney film short *Who Killed Cock Robin*? was somewhat of a parody of the old English folktale. Seemingly, did Disney use the contemporary mimicked likes of Mae West, Harpo Marx, Stepin Fetchit, and a crooning Crosby? Somewhat of a musical pick? A year later, Alfred Hitchcock used some in his film *Sabotage*, which was about gruesome child-killing terrorists.

- While the *"Easter Parade"* film scores well, because of Judy Garland and Fred Astaire, the musical sequence of (tenor) Richard Beaver's singing of "The Girl In The Magazine Cover" just may be a good time for a bathroom or sleep break? Or do the great legs of Ann Miller, hidden mostly by red feathers, save it? Or perhaps the original Irving Berlin (1916) version that was part of Broadway's *"Stop, Look, and Listen"* was even worse? As released on (Victor 17945), Harry Mac Donough's was stiff enough, although it's fair to note that this acoustic age recording was very popular, indeed a huge best seller.
- "I Love A Piano", had also been re-introduced by Judy Garland in *"Easter Parade"*. This ditty had oddly been the 1916 'flip' side of Harry Mac Donough's "The Girl In The Magazine Cover", with a contemporary Billy Murray vocal—as a double sided best seller featuring two different voices!
- Yet another re-vamped title from Judy Garland and Fred Astaire from *"Easter Parade"* was the (long) Irving Berlin penned title "When The Midnight Choo Choo Leaves For Alabam". As released in (1913), this ditty had been a huge acoustic success for Collins and Harlan released on (cylinder) on Edison-Amberol 1719 and on disc on Columbia 1246. Hard to hear? What?
- The Andrews Sisters version of the Harry Woods-penned "We Just Couldn't Say Good-bye" on Decca 24406 sounds just like the earlier (and noted) Boswell Sisters version.
- Add a pick for Louis Armstrong's spirited 1928 recording "Squeeze Me" penned by Fats Waller and Clarence Williams on Okeh 8641. Squeezing who? A jazz classic at best! Is it just all those piano keys for squeezing?
- Add another pick for the 1932 Louis Armstrong recording of "Keeping Out of Mischief" released on Okeh 41560. Penned by the (black) team of Andy Razaf and Fats Waller, the rousing novelty, full of Louis's usual and familiar usage Afro-American slang, does indeed, have all the aspects of Armstrong's identity. Light years later, a 1963 LP version by Barbara Streisand, on Columbia CL-2007, found her version owing nothing to Louis and more so to the likes of Fannie Brice and perhaps Judy Garland, noting that these ladies did not produce a contemporary recording. An extended stretch of style? Listen and compare!
- Note: The Louis Armstrong pick "Sweethearts on Parade" perhaps does have an answer to the pop aspirations of Louis. Indeed, Louis himself had backed up a Little Delk Christian recording released on Okeh 8650 in 1928, which achieved noted (black) competition for the popular Carmen Lombardo vocal, already noted in the text. Did Louis do it better? Yes!
- Gene Austin's mushy 1929 best seller, "A Garden In The Rain" as penned by Carrol Gibbons and James Dyrenforth had been perhaps inspired by Lynn Kurland's novel of the same name? After WW II, the ditty again attracted attention by many, including a defining 1946 version by Jane Froman, on Majestic-1086. Still later in 1952, the song became a huge best seller by the Four Aces on Decca-27860. As Jane Froman was (then) enjoying some renewed interest, her original (Majestic) recording was re issued on Royale-350, perhaps finding a bit more recognition?
- Brother Bob: Bing's Brother Bob Crosby, had a fine crooning vocal style. While not as defining as his brother, he did well as a band singer with the Dorsey Brothers, as well as a few with his own bands, as already noted in text. As (not) previously noted was his 1934 (Dorsey Brothers release) best seller vocal of the (Pete Wendling, Sam M. Lewis and George W. Meyer) penned ditty "I Believe In Miracles". While in

true retrospective, the contemporary (British) recording from the melodious voice of Hildegarde is better, it was hardly known outside of Britain.

- Relatively obscure band singer and song bird Eugenie Baird's vocal on "My Shining Hour", penned by Harold Arlen and Johnny Mercer for the contemporary 1943 film *"The Sky's The Limit"* was considered by many as a clever propaganda ploy based upon Winston Churchill's stirring 1940 speech, subsequently released on (HMV) for the defence of the British isles. Modern ears mayeasily dismiss this speculation but might catch a bit of dubbing on actress Joan Leslie's vocal of the song ditty? Was it the voice of Sally Sweetland?
- Tony Bennett's (2011) huge success as an album seller on Billboard's listing found him with duets of (most) people *not* living in 1950! Not bad for an eighty-five-year-old! They would include the likes of Mariah Carey, Sheryl Crow, Lady Gaga, Faith Hill, Queen Latifah, Carrie Underwood, and among others, Amy Whinehouse, who has since passed away. As this latter-day product all sounds well enough, it is its video twin, unheard-of in 1950, noting Bennett's own turned-on charisma, that makes it all relevant. It surely makes an addition to his already legit claims upon American popular music and more so (for him) into another century.
- A popular (1932) "Crosby, Columbo And Vallee". 1932 Merrie Melodies cartoon also featured on (uncredited vocal chorus), of the (Dubin & Burke) penned parody of Bing Crosby, Russ Columbo and Rudy Vallee. This silly flick works, and perhaps used the same uncredited chorus on a subsequent recording, as backed by Victor Young, on (Brunswick-6239). A later (1944) Looney Tunes cartoon flick "Swooner Crooner", better produced, found a parody of (swooner) Frank Sinatra and (crooner) Bing Crosby perhaps demonstrating ways to entertain female audiences, with Dick Haymes thrown in?
- Lillian Glinn's 1927 bit of slang "Doggin Me Blues" on Columbia 14775-D find Blind Blake's "Doggin Me Mama" berhaps better said?
- Despite better contemporary vocals from the Boswell Sisters and Edythe Wright, the silly Mike Riley and Eddie Farley best selling (Decca) recording of their self penned ditty "The Music Goes Round And Round" somehow still works? Just listen.
- Fannie Brice's 1920s recordings found much adaptation, especially noting the later years of Barbara Streisand. More so, Barbara's own latter-day 1965 45 rpm single "Second Hand Rose" on Columbia 43469, in comparison, proves it. Style? It's a winner!
- As this author has been unsuccessful in finding a contemporary 1931 Fannie Brice recording of "I Found A Million Dollar Baby In A Five And Ten Cent Store", she had indeed re-introduced the ditty as a Broadway entity in the production *"Crazy Quilts"*. While a popular 1926 version by the Radio Franks had been well known, it's also hard to figure between many others recorded in 1931, especially noting releases by Bing Crosby and the Boswell Sisters. It's also interesting to note that while contemporary bank robbers Clyde Barrow and Bonnie Parker were indeed producing headlines robbing banks (without a 'theme') until finally exploited (light years away) in the 1967 film; *"Bonnie And Clyde"*, subsequently inspired the 1968 best selling recording "Bonnie And Clyde", on Epic 10283, another husband and wife (bank robbing) team actually did. Speculation has it that Lester Gillis, alias 'Baby Face" Nelson, had met his (future) wife behind the counter in a five and dime store, more so humming the tune "I Found A Million Dollar Baby At A Five And Ten Cent Store"? It's interesting to also speculate just which version the Gillis family liked best, before Lester was gunned down by the FBI, in 1934.
- Doris Day's early 1940s Panoram of *"My Lost Horizon,"* with Les Brown's Orchestra (an additional pick for Doris, also an additional musical film picks).

- A. P. Carter's cultural contributions were substantial, as were the likes of the original Carter Family. As noted in pick no. 9 "Will the Circle Be Unbroken?" the secular of the southern United States was a huge part of the culture. While it's also possible that A. P. could have heard the (previous) 1928 J. C. Burnett recording "Will the Circle Be Unbroken?" on Columbia 143-85-D, it's more likely that he did not. Consider that the Reverend Burnett and his Quartet were black. A.P. did not rip him off. Yet, it is, indeed, less of a stretch that both men got it from the same shared culture, despite a crudely segregated society.
- Another musical film pick: Sexy and black Dorothy Dandridge's dance and vocal in the filmed Panoram *"Jungle Jive,"* with Cee Pee Johnson overcomes its 1940s racial overtones. It proves that the hot and limb Dandridge could sing solo, which disputes the later overdubbing in films she would have to live with. She would not officially become a solo recording artist until 1958, indeed late for purposes of this book.
- Clyde Mc Phatter's novel and rocking "Hot Ziggity" penned by Winfield Scott was perhaps the inspiration for Perry Como's "Hot Ziggity Boom" contemporary slang!
- Vaughn De Leath's acoustic version of "Lovin' Sam (The Sheik of Alabam)" on Bell P-182 is just as hot and jazzy as the noted Mamie Smith version, ditto for the (later) and noted electric version by the playful vocal by Emmett Miller.
- While Thomas A. Dorsey is not a featured artist within this book, this bluesman is noted as a backup (piano) player as well as a vocalist and songwriter, known as Georgia Tom, for featured artists Ma Rainey and Frankie "Half Pint" Jaxon. As Dorsey, he just may have converted an old spiritual "We Shall Walk Through the Valley of Peace," into "Peace in the Valley." It is more so very certain that the former "Georgia Tom" called this music "gospel," with even white country acts recording it. Later, in 1957, to the delight of many young baby boomers, Elvis Presley performed it live on the *Ed Sullivan TV Show* and later that year recorded the ditty. More so, it produced a best-selling entity on 45 rpm Extended Play-Victor (EPA 4054).
- While the young and hotter Marlene Dietrich of her 1930's's *Blue Angel* film is already noted in the text, a few more musical film picks are due to her. Her exceptional 1939 rendering of "The Boys in the Backroom" as penned by Fred Hollander and Frank Loesser, in the film *Destry Rides Again*, still stirs up some heat. Still another and later film, a 1949 Alfred Hitchcock film *Stage Fright*, found the older Marlene as poignant and wicked as ever, introducing (Cole Porter's) "The Laziest Gal in Town" to the screen. What a gal!
- Doris Day's 1955 film bio *"Love Me Or Leave Me"* of Ruth Etting used her vocal gifts to the fullest on many Etting introduced songs, although hardly in the (older) style of the 'flapper' era. It seems that the (still) alive Ruth became upset about viewing herself as an alledged drinker while viewing the film. Ruth sued. Like all bios, fact and fictionbecome a blur. It's a matter of record that Doris Day had already become a major film entity, far exceeding anything that (pioneer) Ruth Etting had achieved. Speculation had it that in retrospective, the film did find actor James Cagney mean enough to be Moe Snyder, Ruth's first husband, as some former associates and contemporaries of Ruth had observed. It's also interesting to note that Doris Day also had problems with ex-husbands, especially noting second husband, Marty Melcher. Melcher, previously married to Patty Andrews of the Andrews Sisters, was alledged to have been exploiting his wife's income, soon afer his death in 1968. Subsequent lawsuits against her former husband's associates by Doris more ever lasted until 1974. Baby boomers may also be more familiar with Doris's talented son Terry, who became associated with the newer rock age acts Byrds and Beach Boys.

- The noted Cliff Edwards pick "Love Is Just Around The Corner" may also have found the back up vocals of the "Eton Boys"—Charles Day, Jack Day, Art Gentry, Earle Smith, Ford Smith and (pianist?) Roy Bloch. As popular radio entities of the 1930s, they were also better heard in *"Betty Boop"* cartoons. (Roy Bloch was to be later associated with comic Jackie Gleason's: *"Honeymooners"* popular television theme).
- Jane Froman's earliest (1930) Victor recordings (1 side each of 2 releases)""June Kisses" (penned by John Roberts &Jack Clifford) and "Sharing" (penned by Benny Davis & J. Fred Coots) found her vocal controlled well by 'sweet' bandleader—Henry Thies. Indeed, a pleasing light mellow croon on both ditties. Many later recordings found Jane trying to show-boat semi-operatic tendencies, betraying a need for bandleaders like Thies, who knew best on how to keep her vocal from straying off.
- More Jane Froman. #12. Jane's 1946? version of "For You, For Me Evermore" of a Gershwin Brothers penned ditty—then considered "lost and found", may be considered defining.
- Speculation had it that Lee Morse's problems with alcohol led her to be dropped from the 1930 Broadway entity *"Simple Simon"* in which (replacement) Ruth Etting introduced the racy "Ten Cents A Dance". Subsequently, Barbara Stanwick, in a non-singing role, would star in a fine film of the same name a year later, with a vocal of the song used only in credits. Too bad Ruth was not hired to sing it?
- Adelaide Hall had introduced "Old-Fashioned Love" in the all-black 1923 Broadway review entity *Running Wild*, which did not produce a contemporary recording as Alberta Hunter did. A later (electric) mid-1940s Lena Horne version perhaps defined it. As Alberta's later recording, recorded light years away is also noted, a later Adelaide Hall version, recorded light years away in 1970, does indeed exist on the LP Monmouth Evergreen 7080. Adelaide's LP? As good as *Alberta*? No! *Lena*—definitely not!
- Another *Adelaide Hall* introduced ditty "Ill Wind" from the Cotton Club Review in 1934, also found a contemporary recording by her lacking. While it's already noted that a later 1941 Lena Horne recording (who was also in the show backing up Hall) defined it, as well as a later Frank Sinatra version, re-defining it. This title also shows up her later (1970) Monmouth Evergreen LP. As good as Lena or Frank? No!
- Yet another song ditty that Adelaide Hall may have introduced but did not record as a contemporary recording is "Diga Diga Do" from *Blackbirds of 1928*. It should be noted, however, that the excellent contemporary recording by Elisabeth Welch also found Welch in the same show. Both ladies could have performed it, with Hall the headliner. Another contemporary recording with vocals by Ozzie Ware and Irving Mills is an already loser-noted by the horrible vocal of *Irving Mills*. A later recording by the Mills Brothers is a fine group effort, and a still (later) film visual performance by Lena Horne and Cab Calloway is a winning visual. Hall's later (1970) LP version? Call it OK?
- Annette Hanshaw's "Lazy Lou'siana Moon" (penned by Walter Donaldson), on Velvet Tone 2121, was officially a "Frank Ferera" Hawaiian Trio is an added pick for her. It also beats out the Chick Bullock version, already noted.
- Annette Hanshaw's "Pale Blue Waters," penned by Van Smith, is also a Frank Ferera's Trio release, the original flip side of "Lazy Lou'siana Moon," is more so an added pick for her.
- Grace Hayes, not a featured artist within this book, did produce some fine 1920s popular recordings. While not as good as Adelaide Hall's "I Must Have That Man," her contemporary 1928 recording on Victor 21571 notes a softer and polished vocal style that indeed works. Listen and compare. Grace, who also made films, would later open her own Los Angeles area nightclub as "Grace Hayes Lodge," a popular entity in the 1940s. Still later in the 1950s, she would own another, of the same name, in Las Vegas.

- Billie Holiday's 1937 smoky and jazzy version of "My Man" on Brunswick 8008 is an added pick. As previously identified with Broadway in the 1920s, along with styles of Fannie Brice and Ruth Etting, Billie's version, with the expert assistance of Teddy Wilson's small studio group, Billie, as she usually did with any material, redefined it for herself. Light years later, in 1965, Barbara Streisand rediscovered it and released it on 45 rpm Columbia 3322. Although Barbara's version was more influenced by Fannie and Ruth than Billie, listen to all!

Hutton Sisters—who 1. Ina Ray Hutton was a highly regarded performer who could sing and (especially) dance in the 1930s. While this author has not been able to secure any recordings with her (own) vocals, it's still easy to find her sexy 'platinum blond'image, as backed by her 'Melodears'—an all woman orchestra, in film shorts like *"Accent On Girls"* 1935 and *"Swing Hutton Swing"* 1937, introducing song ditties "Truckin" and "Doing The Suzy Q". Not bad for an (Afro-American) lady with bleached hair!

Hutton Sisters—who 2. June Hutton, half sister of Ina Ray Hutton, was also know as Elaine Merrit, became a well known band singer as part of the Pied Piepers, with Tommy Dorsey, gigs at Capital Records with Johnny Mercer and Paul Weston, as well as a solo career in the early 1950s. She later married recording producer, Axel Stordahl, who had been very much involved as mentor for Frank Sinatra.

Hutton Sisters Again—Betty Hutton, the vocalist and actress was the sister of Marion Hutton, who was perhaps most identified as a band singer with Glenn Miller.

- Sisters & Brothers—& Others. The Mills Brothers section should have included "OK America", sharing well done vocal harmonies with the Boswell Sisters and (musician). Fran Frey—although reviewed in text with Boswell Sisters—"The Old Man Of The Mountain". (A single release of this title, minus the sister act, is reviewed). The Mills Brothers also shared vocals with Bing Crosby and the Boswell Sisters in "Life Is Just A Bowl Of Cherries", also noted in text with the Boswell Sisters & Bing Crosby—"Gems From George White's Scandals", and should have been in the Mills Brother section. (The author cannot find a separate Mills Brothers release of "Life Is Just A Bowl Of Cherries").
- Four Brothers & a missing Carpenter 'pick'. Before The Four Amory Brothers-Joe, Gene, Vic and Ed, became known as the Ames Brothers, they (vocally) backed up Thelma Carpenter on the 1946 "American Lullaby" (Majestic-7254), penned by (Gladys Rich). While this title is sleep inducing, the pleasing and pleasant vocals found on it betray Thelma's strong yet mellow vocal as good showboating, and the brothers in perfect back up harmony. (Later, in the early 50s, Royale Records re-issued this ditty, as the Ames Brothers became a very popular 'adult' alternative to the new r&b and rock & roll trends.
- A fine and differing vocal of the Ink Spot's release of "I Dont Want To Set The World On Fire" by contemporary Amy Arnell, as a Tommy Tucker Orchestra (Okeh) release is worth hearing. So was Ann Shelton's contemporary British release, linking this title to the 1940 fires of the London Blitz.
- Irving Kaufman, also known as Frank Harris, produced many 1920s era recording, which betray a stiff and dated vocal style, very much better suited to the acoustic era. Oddly his 1917 (Columbia) recording of an Irving Berlin penned ditty "Mr. Jazz Himself" is perhaps his best vocal?

- Harlan Lattimore, a. k. a. the "black Crosby," seemingly dropped out of recording in the mid-1930s? A postwar release on King 4359, "I Love You I Do," while not as good as earlier, is interesting enough! This Lattimore one side, backed by Henry Glover Orchestra, also contains a written on record label tribute to Harlan by Billy Eckstine, then a hot entity, Harlan seemingly apes Billy, or did Billy sound like Harlan? Listen and compare.
- While Lulu Belle and Scotty are not featured artists, the Scott Weisman-penned "Time Will Tell," a country duet, ain't bad. It was more so a picture disc on Vogue R-720.
- While most baby boomers know Fred Mac Murray from latter-day television, his earlier attempts at crooning were realized with the George Olson Orchestra. Indeed, his fine version of the ditty penned by Leslie and Donaldson, "After a Million Dreams" on Victor 22248, clinches it (not a featured artist).
- Al Jolson's smaltzy 1921 acoustic recording of "April Showers" had been more ever introduced by him in the contemporary Broadway entity "Bombo", penned by Buddy De Sylvia and Louis Silvers. In retrospective, this ditty became part of his (then) already huge legacy that in retrospective, would be less appreciated. Jolson would later re-record the ditty as a better heard 'electric' recording on (Brunswick) and (Decca) with great success, although the 1932 Brunswick recording perhaps finds all this 'smaltz' sounding best.
- The emotional edge of Frankie Laine is very much appreciated in his 1947 recording of "Two Loves Have I" on Mercury 5064. Penned by Geo Koger, H. Varna, J. P. Murray, Barry Trivers, and Vincent Scotto, this ditty of French origins perhaps also defined smaltz but so what! It also defined Laine's popular style. Moreover, add another pick for Frankie Laine? Yes!
- The Frankie Laine pick as number 20."Cool Water" as noted in text on (Columbia) was even more popular in England when issued in 1955. This ditty had been a popular "Sons Of The Pioneers" entity, with vocal led by Dick Nolan, the (real) Canadian cowboy who had also penned it and recorded it on (Decca-5939) and (Victor-20-1724). While its possible, the author can not hear former Sons Of The Pioneers member Roy Rogers on it? By the time Laine recorded this tale about a man & his horse (or mule) named "Dan" stuck in a hot desert dealing with devilish heat, it's obvious that heat stroke could not overlook a well written song ditty-nor for Frankie Laine to define it with (his) own sweltering vocal style
- Snookied? Snooky Larson was a well known radio and recording entity of the latter 1940s. As a stiff voiced bandsinger with Roy Noble his recordings of "I Wonder Who's Kissing Her Now" and "By The Light Of The Silvery Moon", along with (fellow) bandsinger Larry Stewart's "Sweet Dreams Sweetheart" somehow found success despite the the trends of 'rhythm and blues' and 'country and western'.
- Snooky Larson was to later find more recognition on the 1950s television off shoot of radio's *"Your Hit Parade"*. Along with the (mostly) snooty 'pop' vocals of Gesele Mac Kenzie, Dorothy Collins, June Vallee and Eileen Wilson, Larson could not compete well with the change to rock and roll. In retrospective, the 'adult' producers could have hired younger 'rock' inspired performers, but stuck to Snooky.
- Snookied again—The old Irving Berlin penned "Snooky Ookums", that had been stupidly added to the the 1948 "Easter Parade" film, at least had Judy Garland to somehow saved it. The 1913 penned ditty had been a huge acoustic entity, especially noting apopular best selling cylinder release on Indestructable 3296 by Arthur Collins and Byron Harlan.

- Harold "Scrappy" Lambert, as noted in text was known by many other names, include as Burt Lorin. When signed to 'exclusive contracts, a good way to avoid problems was to change your name! While in retrospective, the vocals of this artist may considered at least well done, he may have just changed his name for the fun of it? As an early radio entity with Billy Hillpot they became well known in 1925 on the *"Smith Brothers nCough Drop Program"* on WEAF-NBC. This led to many recording opportunities, including a recording with the popular contemporary Ben Bernie Orchestra of "Ain't She Sweet'. As Scrappy Lambert he was to record many mid-1920s era classics, including "SWonderful" (with the Ipana Troubadours) and "How Am I To Know", with the Arden and Ohman Orchestra. As Burt Lorin he recorded 'Should I" with Arden and Ohman. He also recorded "Bashful Baby", a contemporary (Cliff Friend and Abner Silver) 'flapper' song ditty with the Ben Pollack Orchestra. Aroun the same time (1928-1930), Lambert was known as Charles Roberts. Using this name he recorded the novel (Kalmar and Ruby) penned ditty "Keep Your Undershirt On", with the Ben Pollack Orchestra, released on Victor-22267. While it's a stretch that contemporary vocalist Smith Ballew was any better a vocalist than Lambert, a fine version of the (Elisu and Meyers) penned "From Now On" was identified as a Ben Pollack release with a Charles Roberts vocal, and later identified (by some) as a vocal by Smith Ballew. A mis-printed label on the Ben Pollock release on Victor 21997? A still later 1930 Don Voorhees release of the (Fields and Mc Hugh) penned ditty "Go Home And Tell Your Mother" on (HOW) has been only identified as a vocal by Lambert by some, as one of his many names, is not shown on the original record release. Who care? Or some one does?
- Dean's List—more detail The following 'picks' found on Dean's subsequent LP "Everybody Loves Somebody"—Reprise-RS-6130, noting the title track has been reviewed as a 'single' release. a. "Your Other Love". This (Mort Schuman & Doc Pomus) penned ditty had been a R&B "Flamingos release, featuring a slick vocal and perhaps a mock take on a Spanish style tango, oddly in rock and roll mode. While Dean does not rock, Jimmy Bowen's bright arraingement in mid-tempo is a great fit for Dean's croon. b. Dean takes on Bobby Darin's self penned 1962 "Things" (Atco-6229), almost as well as Darin's original. c. As penned by (Scott Turner & Audie Murphy), Dean's vocal of "Shutters And Boards" could be better that the C&W Jerry Wallace original, as released on (Challenge-9171), a few years before? d. His well done but tamed vocal on the old (noted in text) Joe Turner associated ditty "Corrine Corrine", aint bad. e. Nor is his (almost rocking vocal on the (Ben Raleigh & Jeff Barry) penned ditty; "Siesta Fiesta". Its also interesting to note that more than a few of these titles are 'rock' era originals. Dean's vocals are brilliant! While Dean and his Reprise Records boss (Frank Sinatra) would remain "adult" alternatives to "rock" music, a welcomed change in attitude, material and arraingements were developed, as well as profits—that had started with (former rocker) producer, Jimmy Bowen. Ernie Freeman & Bill Justis. ADDED—. Dean's solo vocal "rat pack" entity from the 1964 film "Robin And The Seven Hoods", (Reprise-RS-2021) an original penned by (Jimmy Van Heusen & Sammy Cahn), "Any Man Who Loves His Mother", while meant to be silly, somehow works. When this author first viewed this film people cringed and laughed when Dean introduced it. More so, this author still does!
- Irving Mills, also known as Joe Primrose or Goody Goodwin, was a music publisher, record producer, promoter, writer, manager (of Duke Ellington), as well as a violinist. While his attempts as a vocalist are horrid, he did lead an informal jazz band. As his "Hotsy Totsy Boys" or "Hotsy Totsy Gang", Mills found the likes of such free

wheeling musicians as Tommy and Jimmy Dorsey, Bix Beiderbecke, Benny Goodman, Eddie Lang and Hoagy Carmichael, amoung others. Subsequent recordings included a fine Elisabeth Welch session (noted in text) and a vocal with Ozie Ware of "Diga Diga Do" that almost ruins the recording due to his added vocal.

- The mid-1930s success of Billie Holiday found many clones. The Sue Mitchell (Variety) release of "Get It Southern Style" and it's flip side "If Youre Ever In My Arms Again" more ever notes an excellent jazzy performance.
- While it's already noted that Emmet Miller was the inspiration for Hank William's rendering of "Lovesick Blues," it's easy to find that Emmett's grit defined the vaudeville entity into something better, both acoustically and electronically, and hugely differing from than the earlier (acoustic) 1922 Elsie Clark version on Okeh 4589.
- Helen Morgan's first recordings were made in England in 1927 and not all subsequently released in the United States. One of these, a typically semi-operatic entity, "When I Discover My Man" penned by "Kern"—Jerome Kern? is a personable bit of torch that indeed precedes her later (American) and even later (American) Brunswick masters. As released on (British) Brunswick 104,—added pick for Helen.
- Helen Morgan's English recordings were a mixed lot, starting with the already noted in the text picks "Me and My Shadow" (Brunswick 104) and "A Tree in the Park," (Brunswick 111). Some of them found her attempting to apply her operatic tendencies toward mid-tempo jazz, rarely something that she would find later, as on her later (American) recording of the already noted Victor master of "Mean to Me." On "Lazy Weather" Brunswick 113, along with an unknown jazzy backup, possibly including (black) pianist Leslie A. "Hutch" Henderson, Helen proves she is no slouch—a fine added pick.
- As a further note, for Helen's credited ditty penned by Jo Trent and Peter De Rose, the later and noted Ted Weems Orchestra release, featuring a well-done and differing crooning job by Perry Como, also credits Trent and De Rose but with differing lyric. To add to the confusion, a contemporary and noted Harlan Lattimore version used the same lyrics as Como does, but with differing (writer) credits, Kahal and Levant. More so, the crooning vocal styles of Harlan and Perry are very close, while Helen's style differs greatly. Listen and compare!
- Another mid-tempo (British) release of Helen Morgan's "Nothing But," is on Brunswick 122. Penned by Henry Busse, Ferde Grofe, and Sam Ward, this ditty especially notes Helen's ability to keep up with a hot and especially jazzy arrangement and is indeed something very well done! it's a pick! Maybe the best of her English recordings?
- Yet another faster paced arrangement for Helen Morgan turns up on her vocal for the (Gershwin Brothers) penned ditty "Do Do Do" on Brunswick 129. As already noted, Gertrude Lawrence had introduced the ditty in the stage entity *Oh, Kay*, in both England and the United States. Her subsequent record on Victor 20331 is typical highbrow, stuff, something that Helen's vocal does indeed emulate. While noting the similar style, Helen's recording is a bit brighter, along with her excellent and jazzy backing. As a further note, it's worth noting the (already) noted contemporary version by perky Annette Hanshaw. Annette's version, with only piano backing, is hotter!
- Many baby boomers, as kids in front of black and white TV remember fondly the antic and nose of former vaudevillian Jimmy Durante. This can all be seen and heard, in a limited but effective fashion in a 1930 black and white film, which Jimmy made with Helen Morgan. As a limited musical film pick the film also featured Jimmy's contemporary vaudeville buddies Lou Clayton and Eddie Jackson, and more

importantly, Jimmy own jazz band orchestra. While noting a horrid cut up of a fine musical performance, featuring Helen Morgan singing "I Can't Go on Like This" backed by Durante's Orchestra, it's (still) well worth seeing and hearing. Too bad Helen and Jimmy did not produce a contemporary recording and skip the film!

- Anita O'Day's very hip and hot swing version of "Massachusetts," with the Gene Krupa Orchestra, on Okeh 6695, blows out the still fine (and noted) version by the Andrews Sisters (add a pick for Anita).
- Irish tenor Dan Quinn's 1905 acoustic (Victor) rendering of "Football", at least took notice of the then American college game that would later become more popular, more so with out his hard to hear recording. It's also interesting that, another acoustic rendering, about a (then) more popular sport baseball, 'Take Me Out To The Ballgame", by rival Irish tenor Billy Murray, became better known and acccepted, although the song itself became better remembered than Billy Murray himself.
- Tex Ritter's 1945 recording of "Green Grow the Lilac" was late for Tex, a film entity by this time. He had introduced this ditty on Broadway in 1931, by the same name. "A Riding Old Paint," the contemporary 1931 recording, was also an already noted pick from the same show.
- The Ginger Rogers noted pick no. 12, "Eeny Meeny Miny Mo," should also be noted as a vocal duet with Johnny Mercer as well as an added pick for him. While a British release is indicated Decca F-6822, it was also released in the United States on Decca 638 in 1935.
- While the already noted 1933 Bing Crosby recording of "Did You Ever See a Dream Walking?" on Brunswick 6724 did define this ditty, a Crosby pick, it was Ginger Rogers and (stiff) Art Jarret, who introduced it first in a film entity *Sitting Pretty*. Yet another musical pick for Ginger? Yes!
- In 1930, Lilian Roth was considered a major new voice, especially in new talking film musicals. While it did not turn out this way, her duet with Jack Oakie "This Must Be Illegal" in the contemporary film *Sea Legs* is indeed well done. More so is "Sing You Sinners", in the contemporary film "Honey", of the same year. As her (later) 1954 bio tells it, the influences of excess and alcohol affected her behavior, and sadly limited her career and her excellent vocal abilities. A later 1956 film bio, found Susan Hayward portraying Roth in the film *"I'll Cry Tomorrow"*. Speculation has it that Heyward used her own voice on vocals, which is odd because she had been dubbed previously on an earlier 1952 film bio, when she had portrayed Jane Froman in *"With A Song In My Heart"*.
- Jimmy Rushing's comical, effective rendering of "Take Me Back, Baby," finds the big man in a dream sequence very much believed, along the excellent Count Basie, in a filmed Panoram (an additional pick for Jimmy Rushing and an additional musical film pick).
- Phil Spitalny's noted backing of Eddie Cantor on 'Ballyhoo' is noted in text. Speculation also has it that he was involved with the famed contemporary Arthur Murray dance instructor, when planning band events. His later radio work, forming an 'all girl' orchestra was perhaps a better sideline. His 1934 'Hour Of Charm" radio program, as on CBS and later NBC, subsequently found 'Evelyn and her Magic Violin" a long lasting favorite of radio fans, including some added film work. Had Phil been aware of Thelma Terry's successful 1920s (Chicago) band? Or Thelma's more famous (black) contemporary Blanche Calloway who had led all the men (in the band) around? Yet he just had to be aware of Ina Ray Hutton's all girl Melodears? All this 'girl' activity was seemingly not lost on Lawrence Clifton Jones, who operated a 1937 orphanage in Piney Woods, Mississippi. As led by Eddie Durham, and with greater success by Jesse Stone, with Ann Mae Winburn, amoung others, the "International

Sweethearts Of Rhythm' would find huge recognition, on radio and especially on many military bases duringWWII.

- Snowed Again? Yes.Another V.S. pick! Valaida Snow's jazzy (British) recording of "Chlo-E Song Of The Swamp" Parlophone-F-1048, should not be forgotten, despite the fact that it was hardly known at all in America, in 1937. Valaida's (always) beautiful and sweeter vocal (with here own trumpet solo to boot) about the weird swamp girl is well done and differs in style with Dinah Shore's smoother but not sweeter 1941 jazzy attempt to define it. Indeed, both of these ladies do much to lift this dreary song! Snow or Shore?
- Kay Starr's filmed (1941?) Panoram of *"Stop Dancing Up There"* is fun. It also features one Jimmy Dodd, later to find recognition with young baby boomers on TV, as in the Mickey Mouse Club, later in the mid-1950s (another pick for Kay, also an additional Musical film pick).
- Maxine Sullivan's "A Brown Bird Singing" penned by Barris and Wood is finely sung. As well as a typical soft Claude Thornhill arrangement, released on Vocalion 4068, it's another pick for her!
- Shirley Temple's 1936 film performance of the Irving Ceasarand Gerald Marks penned "That's What I Want For Christmas" in *"Stowaway"* in front of a Christmas Tree with Alice Faye and Robert Young (later known an the TV sitcom *'Father Knows Best"*, remains a classic. (This ditty should not be confused with the (later) Earl Lawrence penned ditty that jazzy Nancy Wilson had introduced in 1963 on Capital 5084.
- A TV Note: Experimental American TV had found the likes of Kate Smith, Ruth Etting, the Ink Spots and Hildegarde before 1939, among others. The advent of American commercial television at the 1939 NYC World's Fair found the likes of Scottish-born Broadway entity Ella Logan broadcasted live from NYC's "Le Ruban Blue" Club as well as the black sightings of Ethel Waters and Alberta Hunter from Broadway's *Mamba's Daughter*. While this venture founded by RCA and NBC was largely put off until the end of World War II in 1946, this book should note that this was a "catch up" to BBC (British) interests, who had a commercial lead on the USA since 1929. Among those broadcasts by the Brits were such American-born likes of Josephine Baker and Elisabeth Welch, since 1929, not limited by contemporary American racism but indeed by the economic reality of under nineteen thousand TV sets by 1939.
- While it may be noted that when commercial TV broadcasting did indeed take off after the war, the interests of radio live programs featuring vocalists did nothing to replace the playing of disks over the radio airwaves (finally legal) after 1942. As noted elsewhere, the advent of TV became more evident after 1950, more so leaving the focus of this book, although some, including Tony Bennett, Dean Martin, Rosemary Clooney, Nat King Cole, Perry Como, Sammy Davis Jr., Vic Damone, Dinah Shore, Frank Sinatra, and Kate Smith (again), (all featured artists within this book), did establish and reintroduce themselves as successful American recording artists with a continued visual image. While racism did hamper Cole and Davis, the demand for the likes of young Elvis Presley's visual image of shaking hips and dynamic style, fuelled by his (1956) personal appearances and the playing of his recordings on radio, could not be ignored. Considered something very unique, as well as dangerous, for many of the performers who proceeded him, a new era emerged, with the unlikely help of hosts (previous radio entities) like bandleaders Tommy and Jimmy Dorsey, comic Milton Berle, and columnist Ed Sullivan, who did indeed ban Presley's hips for a show! (Enough for TV!)
- Sophie Tucker's already noted acoustic (1923) novelty release of "Old King Tut," penned by Jerome and von Tilzer more so originally noted the contemporary event of

the modern discovery of Tutankhamen's tomb discovery the year before 1922. Call her "mummy"? It's still a jump to the 1931 Boris Karloff film *The Mummy* as well as the leap to the later novelty of comic Steve Martin's vocal "King Tut," novelty release of 1978 on Warner 8677 on 45 rpm. Gee, both speeds are basically obsolete!

- Sophie Tucker's (already noted*)* defining acoustic and (later) electric rendering's of "Some of These Days," also noted, found some creative twists from the likes many contemporaries. Those most noteworthy were the electric recordings as by the blues of Bessie Smith, and a still later spunky and jazzy version by Bing Crosby. A later rock era version by "Little" Brenda Lee, on Decca 30885, is found to be full of depth, with a raunchy vocal style worthy of both Sophie and Bessie. Listen and compare.
- As noted in text, Joe Turner's early association with Pete Johnson founded his association with early 'rhythm and blues' trends, and had (more) real claims upon the coming 'rock' era. As myth has it, Pete Johnson's instrumental of "Rocket 88 Boogie" and Jimmy Liggin's vocal on "Cadillac Boogie" had inspitred Ike Turner's "Rocket 88", as fronting Jackie Brenstson's vocal with his Delta Cats on Chess 113, that could be considered the first 'rock and roll' recording. While a (Chess) release, owned by Chicago pioneers Phil and Leonard, the song ditty was actual recording was produced in Memphis, Tennessee, at the Sun Recording Service, owned by Sam Phillips.
- Sarah Vaughan's 1948 version of "Love Me or Leave Me," penned by Donaldson and Kahn on Musicraft 539, was the original flip side of the already noted ditty penned by Hurwitt and Lewine. "Gentleman Friend" is an added pick for her. While it's a wide range between the differing styles of the earlier 1930 Ruth Etting and later 1955 Doris Day versions of "Love Me or Leave Me," it's all the more interesting to judge and compare. Listen! Why not?
- It IS so-Rudy Vallee's original 'flip' side title of Columbia-2714-D of "Three's A Crowd" (noted elsewhere in text) "Say It Isn't So", is a missing 'pick' in Rudy's section review.
- The flamboyant prohibition era New York City mayor, Jimmy (James or as "Beau James") Walker who had previously been a New York state legislater, had also been a 'tin pan alley' songwriter (with Ernest Ball), resulting in a (1906) poor sounding Harry Macdonough & Hayden Quartet acoustic vocal on (Victor-4575) as titled "Will You Love Me In December As You Did In May". As a poigient political statement (in any era), political popularity in May can be crushing (after November elections—if loosing) in December. As a ressurrected 1927 'electric' recording, as a popular George Hall Orchestra release on (Cameo-1242), the song ditty again became popular (with Walker as mayor), despite a prissy "vocal refrain", which had been identified by (some), as by Harold Scrappy Lambert? Hardly a winning vocal but interesting enough?
- Dinah Washington's smokey update of a 1930 standard 'Bye Bye Blues", penned by (Hann, Bennett and Gray), as a Bert Lown release, had found a soft vocal group known as 'the Biltmore Rhythm Boys", who may have included Frank Luthur and Elmer Feldkamp? Thank you Dinah!
- Great-looking Helen Ward may also be seen and heard in a (1934) Vitaphone film short. In it she is featured with Will Osborne's Orchestra, performing "Midnight—the Stars and You." Another musical film pick? Yes! Check her out!
- Ethel's missing bottom? While already noted in text elsewhere, but not in the Ethel Waters section—her crude and silly 1927 (Columbia) rendering of "Take Your Black Bottom Outside", found Ethel lifting a contrived title (interesting because of it's reference to the contemporary dance craze as well as the body part)—an added 'pick' for her.Rapping in the 'roaring twenties'?

- The noted 1946 Ethel Waters recording of "Blues In My Heart" owes nothing to the earlier 1931 Brunswick release of Chick Webb, with an un credited vocal identified by many as by Webb's band member Louis Bacon. Is Bacon close? No! The title had more ever been defined by Greta Keller's 1931 (London) recording, a well done soft and intiment vocal, in true retrospective—hardly known anywhere else than in Britain. Was Ethel's more poigient approach better? Ethel or Greta?
- Williams Sisters. While it's already noted in text that "Sam The Old Accordian Man" was a 'hot' flapper era entity by the sisters Hannah and Dorothy, their recording of "He's The Last Word", with the Ben Pollack Orchestra, released on Victor 20425 provides interesting vocal comparisons with Annette Hanshaw and Josephine Baker, who both provide a clash of 'style' on the same song ditty. (These sisters later went on to radio, Broadway and film success. They should more ever not to be confused with the three Williams Sisters, Alice, Ethelyn and Laura of the Woodbury Radio program with Bing Crosby.
- While is generally known that Margaret Whiting's father was the famous composer and writer Richard Whiting, it's less known that her aunt was 'flapper' era vocalist Margaret Young.
- Dooley Wilson's 1942 filmed rendering of the older 1931 recording of "As Time Goes By' in *'Casablanca'*, greatly overshadowed other song ditties he performed in the film. This would include an original song ditty, penned by M.K. Jerome and Jack Scholl," Knock On Wood". While hardly as good as "As Time Goes By", the rhythmic number would later become recorded by Dooley, as a flip side. Good speculation also has it that while he was not dubbed singing, his piano playing in the film was?
- The already noted Lee Wiley pick "Sweet and Low-Down" had found its origins within the Ira Gershwin Broadway entity *Tiptoes* in 1925. While a contemporary rendering by the Singing Sophomores on Columbia 568-D is a group rendering and indeed done well enough, Lee's later sultry but soft rendering surely best defined it.
- Lee Wiley's (Gala) recording of "A Little Birdie Told Me So' differes so greatly in style with the later and better selling (Decca) Evelyn Knight ditty "A Little Bird Told Me So", and the earlier Johnny Marvin version that vocal plus backing differences just have to be noted.
- Still another noted pick by Lee Wiley, "My One and Only," found its origins in the 1927 Gershwin Broadway entity *Funny Face*. A contemporary 1928 recording by the Clicquot Club Eskimos, on Columbia 1213-D, betters anything from the show. The Clicquot Club Eskimos were a jazzy group of the 1920s, usually led vocally by a Tom Stacks, who owed their name, as radio entities to a commodity. Nevertheless, it's Lee's (later) 1939 sensual vocal that's most emotional and full of cool fire. Defined? Bet on it!
- Gender Designations: Blanche Calloway, Ruth Etting and Ethel Waters respective and (noted) early 1930s recordings of "Without That Gal" did change "gal" to "man", although, as record releases, the ditty was titled "Without That Gal". While breaking the rule, the Ethel Waters release of "My Kind Of Man", was changed from the performance in the (1930) film *"Floridora Girl"*, when Lawrence Gray sang it to Marion Davies as "My Kind Of A Girl".
- Sarah Vaughan's late 1940s style found "Youre Blasé", from the 1932 London stage production of *"Bow Bells"*, vastly differing from Binnie Hale's orginal. Did Binnie's somewhat raspy style sound much like her (1932) contemporary, Josephine Baker?
- British Crooner Al Bowlly was also a talented jazz guitarist. Add another 'pick" for him while he plays some 'Hawaiian' guitar strings and sings a bit to young Ella Logan, who lightly finishes up crooning the (Percy Wenrich) penned song ditty, "By The Old Oak Tree", on Decca-F-2206, in 1930.

- Racism in Britain? While Adelaide Hall, and Elisabeth Welch found it MUCH better to perform and reside there, the "N" word was indeed common there—even in the 1930s. This would include the likes of a popular 1930 Al Bowlly recording "Nigger Blues", released on Decca-F-2560. While meanings and interpetitations do become clowdy after time, and Al Bowlly was known to have had great respect forblack musicians, this recording does indeed qualify for an addition to my rubbish pile list. Or shit list!
- While Sarah Vaughan's rich vocal abilities had lost much of their luster by 1974, her rendition of (Stephen Sondheim's) "Send In The Clowns", on LP album (Mainstream-MLR-412) is poignant enough!
- Does Kay Starr's noted pick "You've Got To Buy Buy For Baby, penned by Walter Kent and Walter Farrar, link up with the previous Ben Pollack 1928 title "Buy Buy Buy For Baby", penned by Irving Caesar and Joseph Meyer, on (Victor-21743) featuring a vocal by Belle Mann?
- Ruth Etting's noted "I'll Be Blue Just Thinking Of You", penned by George Wandling and Richard Whiting also found a contemporary 1930 crooning job by Frank Sylvano, as an Isham Jones release, well done. Ruth or Frank? It's original 'flip side, on Columbia 2307-D; the mushy yet a bit provotitive "Just A little Closer", penned by Joseph Meyer and Howard Johnson for the contemporary film "Remote Control", is a film this author just could not find?
- More for Lee Morse: The great depression era just has to figure in Lee's 1931 title, penned by Washington, Monaco and Leslie, "I'm An Unemployed Sweetheart Looking For Someone To Love, on Columbia 2497-D.". Is Lee's low vocal enough to conceal laughter or contempt? Or did contemporary Chick Bullock answer her with his (already noted pick)" "Are You Making Any Money"?
- Lee Morse's silly 1926 recording of (Bolshevik) released an (perfect—4722) did not give her any political trouble. While Lee's politics were limited, her younger brother's politics were not. After sometime as a 1930's (singing cowboys) Glen Taylor ran for Idaho senate office in 1945. In congress he would become known as the "singing senator" providing protest songs on capital hill. He also got himself arrested in Alabama protesting segregation, and more so known as being less than a skeptic about the 1948 contemporary events concerning UFO's in Roswell, New Mexico.

- S. H. Dudley was a name used by at least two entertainers of the Victorian age.

  (a). Sherman Houston Dudley was a successful (black) vaudevillian.

  (b). Samuel H. Dudley, or Samuel Rous was a (white) baritone vocalist who was originally identified with the Hayden Quartette, (leader known as the Hayden Quartette) in the 1890's. As a vocal group conceived by Thomas Edison's primitive acoustic cylinder recording company to improve sound for its listener. The Hayden Quartette became a huge success. When the group moved to Emil Berliner's disk company, the group became even better known, with Dudley also producing recordings as a single entity, (also noted in text). A subsequent move to Victor records also found Dudley (or as Samuel Rous) successful although he probably left the group before 1910?

Similar founding groups appeared such as The American Quartette, The Peerless Quartette, and (even) the Afro American entities known as The Tusketee Institute and the Dinwiddie Colored Quartette. This (group) concepts continued with huge success, at least until the advent of the jazz age around 1920. Later—while the origins of the (rhythm and blues group) started with the Mills Brothers in 1931, they also brought back the old style, in a newer (electric) form, in many recordings—especially noting their 1943 million selling recording of (Paper Doll), (also noted in text). Still later young baby boomer's were exposed to this old style, despite rock and roll, in the early 1960's t.v. sitcom (Mitch Miller's *Sing a Long with Mitch*).

- Hildegarde, or Hildegarde Loretta Sell, was an American from Adell, Wisconsin, of German Immigrants. As a young theater and vaudvillian pianist, she became involved with Marion Harris, and a 1933 tour in London. In the same year she began working for the BBC. A subsequent recording, (I Was In The Mood), as penned by Eddie Pola and Michael Carr, revealed a vocal style of a young 1920s flapper, and sounding like nobody. By 1935, she had adapted her speaking voice with an English accent, very much like her fellow 1930s American in resident contemporaries—Elisabeth Welch and Adelaide Hall. Like them also, she became very well known as a BBC radio entity, as well as a cabaret club performer on the continent. Her soft, polished and sophisticated vocal style on European recordings, as noted in text, became very popular, which led to a brief trip back to the States to record (Pennies From Heaven), NYC night club work, and an early (American) experimental television broadcast, in 1936.

  After attracting attention from high brows and royalty, she more so caught the attention of the American magazine *Life*, who put her on the cover—a big deal in 1939. This led the way for a return to the United States that same year—this time with more publicity! She then became a huge American radio success, along with recordings and night club work. More ever, her slim, sexy image, wearing long gloves, without film success, became recognized as part of Americana. (note: She should not become confused with the German born vocalist and actress Hildegarde Neff).

- More Hildegarde—pick #29. (Lilli Marlene). Decca—23348. This tale of a soldier's love had been a product of the earlier WW I era, and had been claimed by Hans Lip, Norbert Schultz and Tommy Connor. It had been more famously recorded in 1939 by German national Lale Anderson and released on Electrola—6993 as The Girl Under the Lantern. This WW II released found itself steep with in Nazi propaganda and the excellent radio vocals of Lale Anderson for axis troops was indeed a lift. While in true retrospective, the only decent thing about German broadcast was perhaps the voice of Lale, the competing BBC broadcast featuring Vera Lynn, as Under the Latern, Ann Shelton's British recording, OSS broadcast—featuring anti-Nazi German born actress-singer Marlene Dietrich, and the fine 1944 recording by Hildegarde, amongst others that made it another win for the Allies!
- Another pick—Hildegarde's melodious 1936 British release of "There's A Small Hotel" on Columbia-FB-1598 competes with anyone, including contemporaries like Durelle Alexander, (faster paced) Helen Ward and later likes of Bing Crosby (on V-Disc), and Frank Sinatra. Check this hotel out with Hildegarde! Yes! Glad I caught the verse!
- More D.T. pick 27. A Nightingale Sang in Berkley Square. While the sweet voice of Vera Lynn had already defined this Erik Maschwitz and Manning Sherwin penned ditty in Britain, it's Dick Todd's American release that challenged it, despite better known contemporary 1940 stiff band singer versions by Ray Eberle (Glenn Miller) and Tommy Ryan (Sammy Kaye). Vera or Dick?

- International cabaret entity, Rosita Serrano, the "Clilean Nightingale', after escaping Nazi German in 1943, still managed to record a bit, although not so much in German. Perhaps her Decca (British?) recording of the (Afro-Cuban) ditty "Babalu" in her natural Spanish suites her better? While hardly as famous as the (baby boomer TV) favorite Desi Arnez version of the (Margarita Lecuona) penned song as heard on ("I Love Lucy"), Rosita's own (natural) Spanish makes it all sound better.
- Touring American radio entity Midge Williams's (Japanese) 1934 success led to some recordings on (Nippon Columbia), as backed by the Tommy Missman Orchestra-Columbia Jazz Band. As a pick, her (Japanese) version of the contemporary (Hoagy Carmicael and Johnny Mercer) penned "Lazybones"is crystal clear, and pre-dates her noted (American) recordings. A later (American broadcast on Ray Block's "Make Believe Ballroom" in (1938) featuring "Lazy Bones" and the already old (Ethel Waters standard)"Dinah" in Japanese, also provided her some unwanted (protest) publicity-being accused of supporting the imperial goals of Chinese occupation, indeed well before the (1941) attack on Pearl Harbor. It's also sad to note that the US government did not make good use of (loyal) American Midge Williams in AFRN and OSS broadcasts using her knowledge of Japanese during the war?
- Frankie Trumbauer's late 1920s jazz age recordings, noted in text with Bing Crosby, also found Trumbauer successfully moving along with changing times into the 'swing era' of the latter 1930s and early 1940s. His raved up version of an (already) old Ethel Waters ditty, (as noted in text as "Maybe Not At All"), is well done as "Not On The First Night Baby" with his 'canary' band vocalist, Fredda Gibson, sounding just as good and sultry as Ethel had in 1925. A contemporary (1940) Cole Porter penned ditty "The Laziest Gal In Town", later popularized in film by Marlene Deitrich also found Fredda's vocal up to the chore. Fredda, especially influenced vocally by the likes of Ethel Waters, Lee Wiley and Mildred Bailey, as a later 1940s radio entity, later changed her name to "Georgia Gibbs". She more so became a best selling entity in the early 1950s. While her 1952 best seller "Kiss Of Fire", (penned by Lester Allen & Robert Hill) was indeed a "pop" entity, later best sellers like "Tweedle Dee', (penned by Winfield Scott) was to become very much critisized as a watered down version of the real thing, as by R & B performer, Lavern Baker. The same can be said for her version of Etta James's self penned, (with P. Otis or Johnny Otis) 'answer' record to the contemporary Hank Ballard "Midnighters' ditty "Work With Me Annie', known as 'The Wall Flower, or "Work With Me Annie'. Indeed, the Georgia Gibbs version as "Dance With Me Henry' de-frocked the original sexual expression, making it more acceptable to the mores of the times, and in direct opposition to the newer musical tastes of a younger generation drifting into rock and roll. Oddly, as "Fredda", this band singer was 'hot', and as 'Georgia'. was not! While not in the same league as (white) contemporary Ella Mae Morse, the (musical) result, in true retrospective, was that the 'rock and roll' craze did not die, as the band singers had. Sorry Georgia!
- Another pick—Jo Stafford's 1944 original flip side of "Far Away Ago Long Ago, on Capital-153 (noted in text) had found her softly defining Cole Porter's "I Love You".
- a. The "Sunshine Boys" were a latter 1920s vocal duet who where also musicians Joe and Dan Mooney, inspired by vaudvillians Van and Schenck, and the contemporary success of Carleton Coon & Joe Sanders, the Rhythm Boys, Nick Lucas and Rudy Vallee. Perhaps their best recordings on (Columbia) are the (Benny Davis & J. Fred Coots) penned ditty "I'm Crooning A Tune About June" and the (Jimmy Monoco and Edgar Leslie) penned "My Troubles Are Over" in 1929? Whether actual contemporary George Burns (light years later-1975) in Neal Simon's film 'The

Sunshine Boys') could have known them as a vaudville act is huge speculation? b. Yet another same named act, led by 'hillbilly' entity identified as Slim Harbert, is perhaps best known for his 1941 (Okeh) recording of a true honky-tonk entity "Don't Cry In My Beer".

- More Beatles—Frank & Beatles—Frank Sinatra's 1969 recording of "Yesterday", on his LP release "My Way" on (Reprise-FS-1029), had preceded his recording of the already reviewed (Beatles release "Something". Indeed another 'win' for the new rock era, as well as for the old guy, with the older pre-rock vocal style!
- Breaking the rules for Ella & Frank. As this author had not planned to use non-commercial (V-disc) recordings, the rule had already been broken for Bing Crosby's "There's A Small Hotel". While sorting a lot of this material, Ella Fitzgerald's scatting job on "Blue Skies" (V-775) cannot be left out. A more curious 'pick' begins with a Sinatra non-pick, released on Columbia-36679) of his well done version of the (contemporary) original Crosby hit "Sunday, Monday and Always". Like other non-picks, while this author's search through recorded material is always subjective, good enough vocals may still be dull, of creatures of their time. Or style? What is very interesting about this ditty is Frank's (better & more fun) 1944 parody of it as "Dick Haymes, Dick Todd And Como". While recorded as a (V-disc), it would seemingly not become officially released (as a CD product) in 1994-50 years)! More ever-while the author has not run across a contemporary 1944 'live' rendering of this re-named ditty, good speculation has it that Frank had indeed introduced this ditty as "Dick Haymes, Russell, and Como"? Indeed Frank just had to be keenly aware of his (mid-1940s) contemporary rivals—Dick Haymes, Andy Russell, and Perry Como.
- "As Time Goes By" Ambigious Bing—The following 4 Bing Crosby recordings just have to be added (late) picks:

  Actor and song writer Charles King found his facination with Hawaiian island music, (adapted into American culture since perhaps stealing the isles) producing actual Hawaiian language in his 1926 ditty 'Ke Kaii Nei', also known as 'Waiting For Thee'. A subsequent 1928 recording, as by a (real) Hawaiian—Helen Desha Beamer and Sam Kapu on (Columbia-1583-D), was more so pleasing enough. A still later (1951) Bing Crosby (with Betty Mullin) rendering of 'Here Comes The Rainbow Ive Found My Dream', on (Decca-27595), while not the same lyrics, is the same tune! Later at the end of the decade (1959), 'pop' singer Andy Williams, (as noted in text who had sang with Bing as a child), recorded the same tune, (credited to Charles King, Al Hoffman and Dick Manning) as "Hawaiian Wedding Song" on (Cadance-1358). The ditty became a huge best seller for Andy, with an uncredited female vocal (later identified by some as by Anita Wood, also a contemporary girlfriend of Elvis Presley. The ditty subsequently was ressurrected by Elvis himself in his 1961 film "Blue Hawaii", also noting the new film title "Blue Hawaii", already noted in text as had been previously introduced by Bing in film and recording in 1937. While it's doesent hurt anyone, it is easy to speculate that Bing's interested (1951) vocal would have been given more notice and interest in (1937)—when his crooning power was more evident!

- Beatle Bing—Bing's dislike of rock and roll did not stop his 1969 LP release "Hey Jude Hey Bing" (Amos-AAS-7001), produced by Jimmy Bowen. The at least interested enough old groaner's so-so vocal attempt and clumsy improvisation of the contemporary Beatles "Hey Jude" (Apple-2276) and (Beatle) Paul Mc Cartney's produced Mary Hopkin's "Those Where The Days", released on (Apple-2) is interesting enough? Yes! Bing is a bit better in the updated (old) Russian folk entity (penned by Gene Raskin and Boris Fomin) "Those Were The Days".

- Despite the advanced efforts of the recording technics of Ken Barnes and Pete Moore, Bing Crosby's (late) 1976 recording of "As Time Goes By", released on London LP PS-679 expose a time and vocal very much lost. When compared to his (noted in text) radio rendering in 1931, it's sadly obvious that Crosby's attention to to this ditty came too late, and the time did indeed fly!

INDEX

Persons and Caricature

B

C

D

F

H

K

M

Q

R

S

T

U

V

W

Y

Z

Film and Stage Productions

C

D

E

F

G

H

I

Y

Z

Edwards Brothers Malloy
Thorofare, NJ USA
October 28, 2014